Contents

Preface

This, the sixteenth edition of *The Chicago Manual of Style*, marks the first edition to be prepared and published simultaneously in print and online. As opportunities for publishing have grown dramatically in an era of electronic publication and distribution, the guiding principles for this edition have been twofold: to recognize the continuing evolution in the way authors, editors, and publishers do their work, on the one hand, and to maintain a focus on those aspects of the process that are independent of the medium of publication, on the other.

In service of the former principle, this edition assumes that all publishers might benefit from an extended discussion of the organizational and proofreading requirements of electronic publications (chapters 1 and 2). More attention has also been given to the role of software for manuscript editors—for example, with the addition of a manuscript cleanup checklist intended to benefit authors and editors alike. Complementing chapters 1 and 2 is an overview (in appendix A) of production technologies and in particular the role of electronic markup in a publishing workflow. Coverage of copyright and permissions (chapter 4) includes new information on fair use and electronic rights, including a discussion of the NIH Public Access Policy for journal articles, and the treatment of bias-free language in chapter 5 has been significantly expanded. The chapters on documentation (14 and 15) offer updated information on citing electronic sources, including many more examples, and an updated glossary (appendix B) includes more terms related to electronic publishing.

Also new to this edition is an introduction to Unicode (in chapter 11), a widely adopted computing standard that defines many of the letters and symbols required by the world's writing systems. Unicode identifiers and descriptions are included alongside special characters in the chapters on foreign languages and math and elsewhere to aid authors, editors, and publishers in the positive identification and proper implementation of these characters. More generally, an effort has been made to acknowledge organizations that publish their standards and guidelines online—in an era when this has become routine. For example, we defer not only to the website of the Unicode Consortium for more information on the tens of thousands of characters defined by that organization thus far but also to the romanization tables published online by the Library of Congress for guidelines on transliteration. And, though we continue to present guidance on abbreviating country names in general contexts—including our new preference for US over U.S.—we also direct readers to the International Organization for Standardization (ISO) for the latest two- and three-letter country codes for the 250-odd areas of the world for which these have been defined.

With an eye to facilitating navigation and streamlining our recommendations, a few organizational changes have been made. Part titles organize the body of the manual into three sections: on the *process* of writing, editing, and publishing; on matters of *style and usage*; and on *documentation* (including indexing). Titles of individual paragraphs have been expanded to become more meaningful, and many smaller paragraphs that treated different aspects of the same issue have been combined. To facilitate finding related discussions and for faster navigation online, more cross-references have been added. To recognize the overlapping roles of authors, editors, and proofreaders, the discussion of manuscript preparation and editing has been combined with that of proofreading into a single chapter, as have the discussions on illustrations and tables, which are typically prepared and edited separately from the text. In response to overwhelming reader input, our hyphenation guidelines (chapter 7) are now presented as a four-part table. And, in a significant departure from previous editions, Chicago now recommends a uniform stylistic treatment for the main elements of a citation—authors' names, titles of works, and so forth—in both its systems of documentation. The differences between the notes and bibliography system (chapter 14) and the author-date system (chapter 15) are now a simple matter of arrangement of elements, eliminating the need for repetitive examples.

Though most of the fundamental principles of the manual remain in place, a few changes were once again in order. In response mainly to comments from our readers (on our Q&A page and on e-mail lists for editors), this edition has moved toward recommending a single rule for a given stylistic matter rather than presenting multiple options. We now recommend, for example, a single approach to ellipses—a three- or four-dot method (chapter 13, where we also explain the European preference for bracketed ellipses). And we have eliminated most of the exceptions to the rules for forming the possessive of proper names (chapter 7) as well as those for implementing headline-style capitalization (chapter 8). We have come to understand that even in the case of somewhat arbitrary rules, writers and editors tend to look to this manual for the most efficient, logical, and defensible solution to a given editorial problem. On the other hand, none of our recommendations are meant to foreclose breaking or bending rules to fit a particular case, something we continue to do ourselves. Once again, we have looked to what has become a maxim (from the first edition of the manual in 1906): "Rules and regulations such as these, in the nature of the case, cannot be endowed with the fixity of rock-ribbed law. They are meant for the average case, and must be applied with a certain degree of elasticity."

This edition marks an evolution of more than forty years, starting with the landmark twelfth edition, published in 1969. As part of this evolution, and as with the fifteenth edition, Chicago consulted a broad range of scholars and professionals in the fields of publishing and academics throughout the revision process. We also continued to benefit from the many helpful comments and suggestions sent to us by our readers, many of whom come from fields outside of scholarly publishing. Their input, in particular, helped us to keep in mind those principles of writing and editing that remain true regardless of the medium or field of publication.

On behalf of the University of Chicago Press
Russell David Harper
Spring 2010

Acknowledgments

An undertaking such as the publication of *The Chicago Manual of Style*, which strives to codify the best practices of an institution and an industry, must be an effort of many hands and many voices if it is to succeed. This edition has benefited from the carefully crafted recommendations— some broad, some minute, all essential—of a legion of publishing professionals. At the same time, it was equally essential that those recommendations be compared, vetted, and applied in a consistent manner and with a clear vision, a challenging task performed in exemplary fashion by this edition's principal reviser, Russell David Harper.

A preliminary outline as well as the entire penultimate draft of the manuscript was read and commented on by an advisory board representing various communities of readers:

David Bevington, Department of English, University of Chicago
William Germano, The Cooper Union for the Advancement of Science and Art
John Hevelin, Publications Consultant
Alex Holzman, Temple University Press
Beth Luey, Editorial Consultant
Evan Owens, Portico
Margaret Perkins, *New England Journal of Medicine*
Nancy Perry, Bedford/St. Martin's
Oona Schmid, American Anthropological Association
Sem Sutter, University of Chicago Library
Robert Wald, Department of Physics, University of Chicago

We would like to thank the many experts who contributed to our coverage of languages: T. David Brent, Erik Carlson, Wendy Doniger, Teresa Fagan, Ariela Finkelstein, Victor Friedman, Kathleen Hansell, Wadad Kadi, Elsi Kaiser, Kathryn Krug, John Lipski, Line Mikkelsen, Carol Neidle, Christina von Nolcken, Eizaburo Okuizumi, David Pharies, Thomas Shannon, Malynne Sternstein, Anna Szabolcsi, Ivey Pittle Wallace, and Yuan Zhou. We are indebted to Brian Albrecht, Dean Blobaum, Michael Brehm, Deborah Bruner, Anthony Crouch, Keir Graff, Rich Hendel, Todd Pollak, and Deb Wong for their formative input on coverage of production for both print and electronic publications; to Diana Gillooly, Michael Koplow, Diane Lang, and Sharon Jennings for their advice on mathematics; and to Leslie Keros and Carol Anne Meyer for their guidance on documentation. We are also grateful to Perry Cartwright and Lolly Gasaway for their review of copyright and permissions material; to Molly Balikov, Michael Brondoli, Jean Eckenfels, Fred Kameny, Randy Petilos, and Angela Yokoe for their insights on a variety of particular style matters; and to others, too many to name individually, who responded to queries and informal polls about specific sections of the manual. We also owe a particular debt to Bryan A. Garner and William S. Strong for their authorship of whole chapters.

Within the University of Chicago Press, special thanks go to Mary E. Laur and David Morrow, who oversaw the revision process, reviewed the many incarnations of the manuscript, and kept the print and online editions on track for simultaneous publication; to Susan Allan, Carol Kasper, Sylvia Mendoza, John Muenning, Carol Fisher Saller, Anita Samen, and Jill Shimabukuro for their essential role in shaping the manuscript; to Rossen Angelov, Eric Gamazon, Ellen Gibson, Debra D. Hebda, and Courtney Turlington for their leadership in developing the online edition; to Paul Schellinger, who sponsored the project; and to Garrett Kiely, who fostered the environment of collegiality and professionalism within which this effort took place. Many other staff members contributed their knowledge and skills at various stages of the process: Laura Andersen, Matt Avery, Kira Bennett, Erik Carlson, Lindsay Dawson, Erin C. DeWitt, Katherine M. Frentzel, Mary Gehl, Ruth Goring, Sandra Hazel, David Jiambalvo, Dustin Kilgore, Kailee R. Kremer, Ryan Li, Renaldo Migaldi, David O'Connor, Patricia O'Shea, Mark Reschke, Christopher Rhodes, Maia Rigas, Christina Samuell, Joel Score, Ed Scott, Rhonda Smith, Isaac Tobin, Maia Wright, and Aiping Zhang. On behalf of the press, Christine Gever proofread the book, and Margie Towery prepared the index.

On a final note, this edition is in many ways most indebted to Catharine Seybold (1915–2008) and Bruce Young (1917–2004), who compiled the landmark twelfth edition of this manual as well as the thirteenth, to John Grossman, who compiled the fourteenth edition, and to Margaret Mahan, who was responsible for the fifteenth. It is to their high standard for what has come to be known as "Chicago style" that we have looked in preparing this, the sixteenth edition of the manual.

The University of Chicago Press Staff
Spring 2010

Part One: The Publishing Process

1 Books and Journals

Overview

1.1   *Books and journals as the core of scholarly publishing.* Printed-and-bound books and journals and their electronic counterparts constitute the core of scholarly publishing. Book-length works in particular—in their breadth and variety, not to mention their long history—provide an overview of the anatomy of a scholarly work that, in conjunction with the discussion of journals (see 1.72–110), can be usefully applied to other types of published works.

1.2   *Electronic publishing.* Electronic publication of scholarly books and journals in various formats is increasingly common. Most journals at Chicago have implemented a simultaneous print and electronic publishing model (see 1.72)—a model that has become the industry standard. For books, if print has remained the most common format, publishers are increasingly gravitating toward a simultaneous print and electronic model. In general, electronic books tend to emulate the organization and structure of their printed-and-bound counterparts, whether they are offered as page images or in an e-book format, proprietary or not—and whether or not they incorporate hyperlinks, search engines, and other features that are unique to the electronic environment. In fact, the industry-wide goal for e-book versions of printed monographs has been one of approximating on-screen the experience of reading the printed book. The discussion on the parts of a book—though it assumes electronic publication is an option for any scholarly book—therefore includes special considerations for electronic book formats only where these might differ from those for print. But see 1.111–17.

The Parts of a Book

Introduction

1.3   *Rectos and versos.* Publishers refer to the trimmed sheets of paper that you turn in a printed-and-bound book as leaves, and a page is one side of a leaf. The front of the leaf, the side that lies to the right in an open book, is called the recto. The back of the leaf, the side that lies to the left when the leaf is turned, is the verso. Rectos are always odd-numbered, versos always even-numbered. In an electronic book, the distinction between rectos and versos can be represented or simulated but need not be.

1.4   *Outline of divisions and parts of a book.* Books are traditionally organized into three major divisions: the front matter (also called preliminary matter, or prelims), the text, and the back matter (or end matter). The front matter presents information about a book's title, publisher, and copyright; it acknowledges debts to the work of others; it provides a way to navigate the structure of the book; and it introduces the book and sets its tone. The text proper comprises the narrative—including arguments, data, illustrations, and so forth—often divided into chapters and other meaningful sections. The back matter presents sources or source notes, appendixes, and other types of documentation supporting the text but outside its central focus or narrative. This section discusses the parts of a book according to a standard outline of these divisions and their components, starting with the list below. Few books contain all these elements, and some books have components not on the list. Books published electronically may depart especially from the order or presentation of elements. The list that follows presents the traditional arrangement, using lowercase roman numerals for pages in the front matter and arabic numerals for all the rest, including the back matter. Indications of recto (right-hand page) or verso (left-hand page) may be applicable only to printed-and-bound books; starting pages that cannot be assigned at manuscript stage are simply indicated as recto, the right-hand page being the traditional choice. Every page is counted in the page sequence, even those on which no number actually appears, such as the title and half-title pages, copyright page, and blank pages (see 1.5–8).

FRONT MATTER

Book half title	i
Series title, frontispiece, or blank	ii
Title page	iii
Copyright page	iv
Dedication	v
Epigraph	v or vi
(Table of) Contents	v or vii
(List of) Illustrations	recto or verso
(List of) Tables	recto or verso
Foreword	recto
Preface	recto
Acknowledgments (if not part of preface)	recto
Introduction (if not part of text)	recto
Abbreviations (if not in back matter)	recto or verso
Chronology (if not in back matter)	recto

TEXT

First text page (introduction or chapter 1)	1
or	
Second half title or first part title	1
Blank	2
First text page	3

BACK MATTER

Acknowledgments (if not in front matter)	recto
Appendix (or first, if more than one)	recto
Second and subsequent appendixes	recto or verso
Chronology (if not in front matter)	recto
Abbreviations (if not in front matter)	recto
Notes	recto
Glossary	recto
Bibliography or References	recto
(List of) Contributors	recto
Illustration Credits (if not in captions or elsewhere)	recto
Index(es)	recto

Page Numbers

1.5   *Pages and folios.* Modern books are paginated consecutively, and all pages except endpapers (see 1.68) are counted in the pagination whether or not the numbers appear. The page number, or folio, is most commonly found at the top of the page, flush left verso, flush right recto. The folio may also be printed at the bottom of the page, and in that location it is called a drop folio. Drop folios usually appear either centered on each page or flush left verso and flush right recto. A page number that does not appear is sometimes referred to as a blind folio. *Not* paginated are pages that are inserted into printed books after pages have been made up—for example, color illustrations or photo galleries printed on a different type of paper (see 1.38).

1.6   *Roman numerals for front matter.* The front matter of a book is paginated with lowercase roman numerals (see 1.4). This traditional practice prevents renumbering the remainder of a book when, for example, a dedication page or additional acknowledgments are added at the last moment. By convention, no folio appears on blank pages or on "display" pages (i.e., such stand-alone pages as those for the half title, title, copyright, dedication, and epigraph), and a drop folio (or no folio) is used on the opening page of each succeeding section of the front matter (e.g., table of contents, foreword, preface).

1.7   *Arabic numbers for text and back matter.* The text, or the central part of a book, begins with arabic page 1. If the text is introduced by a second half title or opens with a part title, the half title or part title counts as page 1, its verso counts as page 2, and the first arabic number to appear is the drop folio 3 on the first page of text (see 1.45, 1.48). (Some publishers ignore the second half title in paginating their books, counting the first page of text as p. 1.) Page numbers generally do not appear on part titles, but if text appears on a part-title page (see 1.47), a drop folio may be used. Arabic numbering continues for the back matter. As in the front matter, the opening page of each chapter in the text and each section in the back matter carries either a drop folio or no page number. On pages containing only illustrations or tables, page numbers are usually omitted, except in the case of a long sequence of figures or tables.

1.8   *Separate versus consecutive pagination across more than one volume.* Publishers weighing pagination schemes for works that run to more than one volume should consider the index and the projected number of volumes. If an index to two volumes is to appear at the end of volume 2, consecutive pagination saves index entries from having to refer to volume as well as page number. In rare cases where back matter, such as an index, must be added to volume 1 later in the production process, lowercase roman folios may be used; these should continue the sequence from the front matter in that volume (including a final blank page)—if, for example, the last page of the front matter is xii, the back matter would start with page xiii. Multivolume works that run into the thousands of pages are usually paginated separately to avoid unwieldy page numbers. Index entries and other references to such works must include volume as well as page number. In either scenario—consecutive or separate pagination across volumes—the front matter in each volume begins anew with page i.

Running Heads

1.9   *Running heads defined.* Running heads—the headings at the tops of pages—function, like page numbers, as signposts. Especially useful in scholarly books and textbooks, they are sometimes omitted for practical or aesthetic reasons—in a novel or a book of poems, for example. Running heads are sometimes placed at the bottom of the page, where they are referred to as running feet, or, more rarely, in the left- and right-hand margins. In endnotes and other places where the information conveyed by these signposts is essential to readers, placement at the tops of pages is preferred. In this manual, *running head* is used for this element wherever it appears. For preparation of running-head copy, see 2.73.

1.10   *Running heads for front matter.* Running heads are never used on display pages (half title, title, copyright, dedication, epigraph) or on the first page of the table of contents, preface, and so forth (see also 1.15). Any element that runs more than one page usually carries running heads. Each element in the front matter normally carries the same running head on verso and recto pages.

VERSO	RECTO
Contents	Contents
Preface	Preface

1.11   *Running heads for text.* Chapter openings and other display pages carry no running heads (see also 1.15). The choice of running heads for other text pages is governed chiefly by the structure and nature of the book. Among acceptable arrangements are the following:

VERSO	RECTO
Part title	Chapter title
Chapter number	Chapter title
Chapter title	Subhead
Chapter title	Chapter subtitle
Chapter title	Chapter title
Subhead	Subhead
Chapter author	Chapter title

See also 2.73. Chicago generally advises against putting the book title on the verso (partly to minimize complications from a last-minute change to a title)—though the practice of doing so has persisted, especially for works of fiction. In electronic books, verso and recto running heads, when they are not the same, are sometimes combined and separated by a colon or a slash or other device.

1.12   *Subheads as running heads.* When subheads in the text are used as running heads on recto pages and more than one subhead falls on a single page, the *last* one on the page is used as the running head. When subheads are used as running heads on versos, however, the *first* subhead on the page is used as the running head. (The principle is the same as for dictionary running heads.)

1.13   *Running heads for back matter.* Running heads for back matter follow the same pattern as those for front matter and text (but see 1.14). If there is an appendix, Appendix (or Appendix 1 or Appendix A, etc.) appears verso, the appendix title recto. If there is more than one index, it is essential that the running heads so indicate (Index of Names, Index of Subjects, etc.).

1.14   *Running heads for endnotes.* The running heads for a section of notes in the back of the book should give the inclusive page numbers or (much less useful for readers but more expedient for the publisher) the chapter where the relevant note references are found in the text. If chapter numbers are used, it is essential that the verso running heads in the text also give chapter numbers. Thus, two facing running heads might read:

VERSO	RECTO
Notes to Pages 2–10	Notes to Pages 11–25
or	
Notes to Chapter One	Notes to Chapter Two

For a fuller explanation, see 14.42.

1.15   *Omission of running heads.* Besides display pages in the front matter (see 1.10), running heads are omitted on part titles, chapter openings, and any page containing only an illustration or a table. (For the omission of page numbers, see 1.7.) Pages that include lines of text in addition to an illustration or table should include running heads. Running heads may also be included in long sequences of illustrations or tables to keep readers oriented.

Front Matter

TITLE PAGES

1.16   *Half title.* The half title (p. i in a printed book, no folio) normally consists only of the main title (less any subtitle) and is usually counted as the very first page in a printed-and-bound book. All other information—including author name, publisher, and edition—is omitted.

1.17　*Series title or frontispiece.* The verso following the half-title page (p. ii in a printed book) is usually blank. But if the book is part of a series, it may include the title and volume number of the series, the name of the general editor of the series, and sometimes the titles of previously published books in the series. (A series title may appear on the title page instead.) If the book is the published proceedings of a symposium, the title of the symposium and the date it was held and other relevant details may appear on page ii. Some publishers list an author's previous publications on page ii; Chicago generally lists these on the copyright page and on the jacket or cover (see 1.20). Alternatively, page ii might carry an illustration, called a frontispiece. If the frontispiece is printed on a different stock from the text, and thus is inserted separately, it will not constitute page ii, though it will still appear opposite the title page, which is normally page iii (see 1.18). Page ii might also be used for a title page across pages ii and iii.

1.18　*Title page.* The title page (p. iii or sometimes pp. ii and iii) presents the full title of the book; the subtitle, if any; the name of the author, editor, or translator; and the name and location of the publisher. If the type size or style of the subtitle differs from that of the main title, no colon or other mark of punctuation is needed to separate them. In a new edition of a work previously published, the number of the edition (e.g., Third Edition) should also appear on the title page, usually following the title (see also 1.25, 1.26). The author's name, or authors' names (see also 1.62), may appear below or above the title. Given first names should not be shortened to initials unless the author's name is widely known in such a form (e.g., P. D. James, J. M. Coetzee), or unless the author prefers initials (see 14.73). Chicago does not print academic degrees or affiliations after an author's name on the title page (though exceptions have been made for MD in medical publications). Editors or translators should be listed in the form "Edited by" or "Translated by." The publisher's full name (imprint) should be given on the title page and is usually followed by the name of the city (or cities) where the principal offices are located. The publisher's logo may also appear there. The year of publication is best omitted from the title page, particularly if it conflicts with copyright information on page iv (see 1.22).

COPYRIGHT PAGE

1.19　*Components of a copyright page.* The Copyright Act of 1989 does not require that published works carry a copyright notice in order to secure copyright protection; nevertheless, most publishers continue to carry the notice to discourage infringement. The copyright notice is just one of several items typically included on the copyright page (p. iv). The University of Chicago Press includes the following:

- Biographical note on author
- Publisher's address
- Copyright notice—including, if applicable, copyright dates of previous editions and indication of copyright renewal or other changes, and followed by the statement "All rights reserved"
- Publication date, including publishing history
- Country of printing
- Impression line, indicating number and year of current printing
- International Standard Book Number (ISBN)
- International Standard Serial Number (ISSN), if applicable
- For translations, indication of original-language title, publisher, and copyright
- Acknowledgments, permissions, and other credits, including acknowledgment of grants, if applicable and space permitting
- Cataloging-in-Publication (CIP) data
- Paper durability statement

For an example, see figure 1.1. These items are discussed in more detail in the paragraphs that follow.

1.20   *Biographical note.* A brief note on the author or authors (including any editors, compilers, and translators) lists previous publications and, if relevant, academic affiliation. The details, if not the wording, must be consistent with any related information on the jacket or cover. Though such a note typically appears at the top of the copyright page, it may appear instead on a separate page, either in the front matter or the back matter, according to the publisher's preference.

1.21   *Publisher's address.* The address of the publisher—and sometimes the addresses of overseas agents—is typically, though not always, given on the copyright page. An address may be abbreviated, consisting, for example, only of a city and perhaps a postal code. A publisher's URL (uniform resource locator) may also be included.

1.22   *Copyright notice.* The usual notice consists of three parts: the symbol ©, the first year the book is published, and the name of the copyright owner (see fig. 1.1). This may be followed by the phrase "All rights reserved" and a statement of publication date or publishing history (see 4.40, 1.25). The year of publication should correspond to the copyright date. If a book is physically available near the end of a year but not formally published until the beginning of the next, the later date is preferred as both copy-

Gloria Ferrari is professor emerita of classical archaeology
and art at Harvard University. She is the author of *Materiali
del Museo Archeologico di Tarquina XI: I vasi attici a figure rosse
del periodo arcaico* and *Figures of Speech: Men and Maidens in
Ancient Greece*, the latter published by the University of Chicago
Press and the 2002 recipient of the James R. Wiseman Book
Award from the Archaeological Institute of America. Her articles
have been published in a range of scholarly journals, including
Opuscula Romana, *Metis*, and *Classical Philology*.

The University of Chicago Press, Chicago 60637
The University of Chicago Press, Ltd., London
© 2008 by The University of Chicago
All rights reserved. Published 2008.
Printed in the United States of America
17 16 15 14 13 12 11 10 09 08   1 2 3 4 5
ISBN-13: 978-0-226-66867-3 (cloth)
ISBN-10: 0-226-66867-3 (cloth)

The University of Chicago Press gratefully acknowledges the generous
support of Harvard University's Loeb Fund of the Department of the
Classics toward the publication of this book.

Library of Congress Cataloging-in-Publication Data
Ferrari, Gloria, 1941–
    Alcman and the cosmos of Sparta / Gloria Ferrari.
        p. cm.
    Includes bibliographical references and index.
    ISBN-13: 978-0-226-66867-3 (hardcover : alk. paper)
    ISBN-10: 0-226-66867-3 (hardcover : alk. paper)
        1. Alcman—Criticism and interpretation. 2. Cosmology, Ancient.
    3. Theater—Greece—Sparta—History—To 500. I. Title.
    PA3862.A5 F47 2008
    884'.01—dc22

                                            2007041681

    ∞ This paper meets the requirements of
ANSI/NISO Z39.48-1992 (Permanence of Paper).

FIGURE 1.1.   A typical copyright page, including biographical note, copyright notice, impression date and number (denoting 2008 for the first impression), International Standard Book Number (ISBN), publisher's acknowledgment of a subvention, Library of Congress Cataloging-in-Publication (CIP) data, and paper durability statement. See 1.19.

The University of Chicago Press, Chicago 60637
The University of Chicago Press, Ltd., London

© 2001, 2007 by The University of Chicago
All rights reserved. First edition 2001.
Second edition 2007

Printed in the United States of America
16 15 14 13 12 11 10   3 4 5

FIGURE 1.2. Copyright notice of a second edition (2007), with impression line indicating that this edition was reprinted for the third time in 2010. See 1.23.

right and publication date. Books published by the University of Chicago Press are usually copyrighted in the name of the university ("© 2010 by The University of Chicago"). Some authors, however, prefer to copyright their works in their own names ("© 2006 by Alison A. Author"), a preference discussed in 4.41. For information on copyright notices for journals, see 1.97; for a full discussion, see 4.38–45.

1.23 *Copyright dates of previous editions.* Each new edition of a book (as distinct from a new impression, or reprinting, but including an electronic edition of a printed book) is copyrighted, and the copyright dates of at least the most recent previous editions should appear in the copyright notice (see fig. 1.2). If the new edition is so extensive a revision that it virtually constitutes a new publication, previous copyright dates may be omitted. See also 1.25, 4.40.

1.24 *Copyright renewal or other changes.* The date of copyright renewal or a change in the name of the copyright owner is sometimes reflected in the copyright notice if the work is reprinted. Copyright renewal is shown in the following manner (note the second period; see 1.25):

© 1943 by Miriam Obermerker. © renewed 1971 by Miriam Obermerker.

To indicate a change in copyright ownership (e.g., if copyright is assigned to the author or someone else after the initial copyright has been registered and printed in the first impression), the name of the new copyright owner is substituted for that of the previous owner. The copyright date remains the same unless the copyright has been renewed. Copyrights remain legally valid even if renewal or reassignment information cannot, for some reason, appear in a new edition or printing (see also 4.30–32).

1.25 *Publishing history.* The publishing history of a book, which usually follows the copyright notice, begins with the date (year) of original publication, followed by the number and date of any new edition. In books with a long publishing history, it is acceptable to present only the original edition and the latest edition in the publishing history. (A previous publisher's name need not be given unless the licensing agreement requires that it appear in the new edition.) Items in the publishing history may appear on separate lines; periods separate multiple items on the same line. In a departure from former usage, Chicago now recommends a final period at the end of a line with two or more items separated by periods.

First edition published 1906. Sixteenth edition 2010.

Revised edition originally published 1985
University of Chicago Press edition 2002

If a book is reprinted, the number and date of the current impression may be indicated in the publishing history (e.g., Fifth Printing, 2010), but Chicago usually indicates these separately, in an impression line (see 1.28).

1.26 *What constitutes a new edition? Edition* (as opposed to *impression*, or *printing*) is used in at least two senses. (1) A new edition may be defined as one in which a substantial change has been made in one or more of the essential elements of the work (e.g., text, notes, appendixes, or illustrations). As a general rule, at least 20 percent of a new edition should consist of new or revised material. A work that is republished with a new preface or afterword but is otherwise unchanged except for corrections of typographical errors is better described as a new impression or a reissue; the title page may include such words as "With a New Preface." (2) *Edition* may be used to designate a reissue in a different format—for example, a paperback, deluxe, or illustrated version, or an electronic edition of a printed work—or under the imprint of a different publisher. A new edition is best designated on the title page: Second Edition, Third Edition, and so forth. Such phrases as "revised and expanded" are redundant on the title page, since the nature and extent of the revision are normally described in the prefatory material or on the cover.

1.27 *Country of printing.* The country in which a book is printed is traditionally identified inside the work. In addition, if a book is printed in a country other than the country of publication, the jacket or cover must so state: for example, "Printed in China."

1.28   *Impression number.* Each new printing of a book, or impression, may be identified by a line of numerals running below the publishing history (see fig. 1.1). The first group of numerals, reading from right to left, represents the last two digits of succeeding years starting with the date of original publication (see 1.22). The second set, following at least an em space (see A.22) and reading from left to right, represents the numbers of possible new impressions. The lowest number in each group indicates the present impression and date. In figure 1.1, therefore, the impression is identified as the first, and the year of printing as 2008; in figure 1.2, the numbers indicate a third printing in 2010. This method is expedient for printed books, as printers need only delete the lowest number(s) rather than generate new text. Impression lines work to the advantage of readers and publishers both—a new impression not only reflects the sales record of a book but also signals that corrections may have been made. (Note that impression lines for print-on-demand titles are typically changed not with each new order but only to signal that corrections have been made.)

1.29   *Indication of original-language edition for translations.* If a book is a translation from another language, the original title, publisher, and copyright information should be recorded on the copyright page (see fig. 1.3).

1.30   *Acknowledgments, permissions, and other credits.* The copyright page, if space permits, may include acknowledgments of previously published parts of a book, illustration credits, and permission to quote from copyrighted material (fig. 1.4), unless such acknowledgments appear elsewhere in the book—as in an acknowledgments section (see 1.40–41) or in source notes (see 2.43, 14.49).

The illustration on the title page is a detail from a photograph of Nietzsche in Basel, ca. 1876. Photo Stiftung Weimarer Klassik. GSA 101/17.

For more on illustration credits, see 3.28–36. For a full discussion of permissions, see chapter 4.

1.31   *Acknowledgment of grants.* Publishers should acknowledge grants of financial assistance toward publication on the copyright page. Acknowledgments requiring more space or greater prominence may appear elsewhere, in a separate section in the front or back matter. Wording should be as requested (or at least approved) by the grantors (see fig. 1.1). Finan-

Georges Didi-Huberman is professor at l'École des haute études en
sciences sociales in Paris. He is the author of more than thirty books on
the history and theory of images, including *Fra Angelico: Dissemblance
and Figuration*, also published by the University of Chicago Press.

Shane B. Lillis recently received his PhD in French literature from
the University of California, Berkeley.

The University of Chicago Press, Chicago 60637
The University of Chicago Press, Ltd., London
© 2008 by The University of Chicago
All rights reserved. Published 2008.
Printed in the United States of America

Originally published as *Images malgré tout*
© Les Éditions de Minuit, 2003

17 16 15 14 13 12 11 10 09 08   1 2 3 4 5

ISBN-13: 978-0-226-14816-8 (cloth)
ISBN-10: 0-226-14816-5 (cloth)

Library of Congress Cataloging-in-Publication Data

Didi-Huberman, Georges.
     [Images malgré tout. English]
     Images in spite of all : four photographs from Auschwitz /
Georges Didi-Huberman ; translated by Shane B. Lillis.
          p.   cm.
     Includes index.
       ISBN-13: 978-0-226-14816-8 (cloth : alk. paper)
       ISBN-10: 0-226-14816-5 (cloth : alk. paper)
       1. Holocaust, Jewish (1939–1945)—Historiography. 2. World War,
1939–1945—Photography. 3. Historiography and photography. I. Title.
       D804.348.D5313 2008
       940.53'18072—dc22
                                                              2008018328

♾ This paper meets the requirements of ANSI/NISO Z39.48-1992
(Permanence of Paper).

FIGURE 1.3.   The copyright page of a translation, including title and copyright of the original edition (as required by contract with the original publisher), and biographical notes
on both author (Georges Didi-Huberman) and translator (Shane B. Lillis). See 1.29.

RAMIE TARGOFF is associate professor of English at Brandeis University and the author of *Common Prayer*, published by the University of Chicago Press.

The University of Chicago Press, Chicago 60637
The University of Chicago Press, Ltd., London
© 2008 by The University of Chicago
All rights reserved. Published 2008.
Printed in the United States of America

17 16 15 14 13 12 11 10 09 08   1 2 3 4 5

ISBN-13: 978-0-226-78963-7 (cloth)
ISBN-10: 0-226-78963-2 (cloth)

An earlier version of chapter 3 was published as "Traducing the Soul: Donne's *Second Anniversarie*," in *Publications of the Modern Language Association (PMLA)* 121, no. 5 (October 2006): 1493–1508, and is reprinted with permission. Parts of chapter 6 were included in "Facing Death," in *The Cambridge Companion to John Donne*, ed. Achsah Guibbory (Cambridge: Cambridge University Press, 2006), 217–32, and are also reprinted with permission.

Library of Congress Cataloging-in-Publication Data

Targoff, Ramie.
  John Donne, body and soul / Ramie Targoff.
     p. cm.
  Includes bibliographical references and index.
  ISBN-13: 978-0-226-78963-7 (alk. paper)
  ISBN-10: 0-226-78963-2 (alk. paper)
     1. Donne, John, 1572–1631—Criticism and interpretation. 2. Donne, John, 1572–1631—Religion. 3. Donne, John, 1572–1631—Philosophy. 4. Body and soul in literature. 5. Christianity and literature—England—History—16th century. 6. Christianity and literature—England—History—17th century. I. Title.
  PR2248 .T37 2008
  821'.3—dc22

                                                          2007024574

♾ This paper meets the requirements of ANSI/NISO Z39.48-1992 (Permanence of Paper).

FIGURE 1.4.   A copyright page acknowledging earlier publication of certain chapters. See 1.30.

cial assistance made to authors is usually mentioned as part of the author's acknowledgments (see 1.40, 1.41).

1.32   *International Standard Book Number (ISBN).* An ISBN is assigned to each book by its publisher under a system set up in the late 1960s by the R. R. Bowker Company and the International Organization for Standardization (ISO). The ISBN uniquely identifies the book, thus facilitating order fulfillment and inventory tracking. In addition to appearing on the copyright page (see fig. 1.1), the ISBN should also be printed on the book jacket or cover (see 1.71). Each format or binding must have a separate ISBN (i.e., for hardcover, paperbound, CD-ROM, e-book format, etc.). Electronic publications should include the ISBN on the screen that displays the title or its equivalent, or on the first display. Additional information about the assignment and use of ISBNs may be obtained from the US ISBN Agency, R. R. Bowker, or from the International ISBN Agency. Some books that are part of a monograph series may be assigned an ISSN (International Standard Serial Number) in addition to an ISBN; for more information, contact the Library of Congress. (For the use of ISSNs in journal copyright statements, see 1.97.)

1.33 *Cataloging-in-Publication (CIP) data.* Since 1971 most publishers have printed the Library of Congress Cataloging-in-Publication (CIP) data on the copyright pages of their books. An example of CIP data may be found in figure 1.1. To apply for CIP data, and for up-to-date information about the program, consult the Library of Congress's online resources for publishers.

1.34 *Paper durability statement.* Durability standards for paper have been established by the American National Standards Institute (ANSI), which since 1984 has issued statements to be included in books meeting these standards. In 1992 the standards were revised by the National Information Standards Organization (NISO) to extend to coated paper. Under this revision, coated and uncoated papers that meet the standards for alkalinity, folding and tearing, and paper stock are authorized to carry the following notice (or any reasonable variation thereof), which should include the circled infinity symbol:

♾ This paper meets the requirements of ANSI/NISO Z39.48-1992 (Permanence of Paper).

DEDICATION AND EPIGRAPH

1.35 *Dedication.* Choice of dedication—including whether to include one or not—is up to the author. It may be suggested, however, that the word *dedicated* is superfluous. Editors of contributed volumes do not customarily include a dedication unless it is jointly offered by all contributors. Nor do translators generally offer their own dedication unless it is made clear that the dedication is not that of the original author. The dedication usually appears by itself, preferably on page v.

1.36   *Epigraph and epigraph source.* An author may wish to include an epigraph—a quotation that is pertinent but not integral to the text—at the beginning of the book. If there is no dedication, the epigraph may be placed on page v (see 1.4); otherwise, it is usually placed on page vi, opposite the table of contents. Epigraphs are also occasionally used at chapter openings and, more rarely, at the beginnings of sections within chapters. The source of an epigraph is usually given on a line following the quotation, sometimes preceded by a dash (see 13.34). Only the author's name (in the case of a well-known author, only the last name) and, usually, the title of the work need appear; beyond this, it is customary not to annotate book epigraphs. If a footnote or an endnote to a chapter epigraph is required, the reference number should follow the source, or, to avoid the intrusion of a number, the supplementary documentation may be given in an unnumbered note (see 14.47).

TABLE OF CONTENTS AND
LIST OF ILLUSTRATIONS OR TABLES

1.37   *Table of contents.* The table of contents for a printed work usually begins on page v or, if page v carries a dedication or an epigraph, page vii. It should include all preliminary material that follows it but exclude anything that precedes it. It should list the title and beginning page number of each section of the book: front matter, text divisions, and back matter, including the index (see fig. 1.5). If the book is divided into parts as well as chapters, the part titles appear in the contents, but their page numbers are omitted, unless the parts include separate introductions. Subheads within chapters are usually omitted from the table of contents, but if they provide valuable signposts for readers, they may be included. In a volume consisting of chapters by different authors, the name of each author should be given in the table of contents with the title of the chapter:

The Supreme Court as Republican Schoolmaster
Ralph Lerner 127
or
Self-Incrimination and the New Privacy, *Robert B. McKay* 193

In a book containing illustrations that are printed together in a gallery or galleries (see 3.6), it is seldom necessary to list them separately in a list of illustrations. Their location may be noted at the end of the table of contents; for example, "Illustrations follow pages 130 and 288."

1.38   *List of illustrations or tables.* In a book with very few illustrations or tables or one with very many, all tied closely to the text, it is not essential to list

Contents

Plates follow page 370.

FIGURE 1.5.   Table of contents showing front matter, introduction, parts, chapters, back matter, and location of photo gallery. See 1.37.

ILLUSTRATIONS

FIGURE 1.6. Partial list of illustrations, with subheads. If the book contained no tables, the subhead "Figures" would be omitted. If it contained many tables, these would probably be listed on a new page under the heading "Tables." How best to list illustrations of various sorts depends as much on space as on logic. See 1.38.

them in the front matter. Multiauthor books, proceedings of symposia, and the like commonly do not carry lists of illustrations or tables. Where a list is appropriate (see 3.37), the list of illustrations (usually titled Illustrations but entered in the table of contents as List of Illustrations to avoid ambiguity) should match the table of contents in type size and general style. In books containing various kinds of illustrations, the list may be divided into sections headed, for example, Figures, Tables (see fig. 1.6), or Plates, Drawings, Maps. Page numbers are given for all illus-

Illustrations

Following page 46

1. Josaphat's first outing
2. Portrait of Marco Polo
3. Gold-digging ant from Sebastian Münster's *Cosmographei*, 1531
4. An Indian "Odota" from Sebastian Münster's *Cosmographei*, 1531

. . . .

Following page 520

84. *Doctrina Christam* printed at Quilon
85. First book printed at Macao by Europeans, 1585
86. First book printed in China on a European press, 1588
87. Title page of *Doctrina Christiana* printed at Manila, 1593, in Tagalog and Spanish
88. Final page of above
89. Title page of *Doctrina Christiana* printed at Manila, 1593, in Spanish and Chinese

FIGURE 1.7.   Partial list of illustrations showing numbers, titles, and placement of unpaginated plates. (Compare fig. 1.5.) See 1.38.

trations printed with the text and counted in the pagination, even when the numbers do not actually appear on the text page. When pages of illustrations are printed on different stock and not counted in the pagination, their location is indicated by "Facing page 000" or "Following page 000" in the list of illustrations (see fig. 1.7) or, more commonly, in the table of contents (fig. 1.5). A frontispiece, because of its prominent position at the front of the book, is not assigned a page number; its location is simply given as frontispiece. Titles given in lists of illustrations and tables may be shortened or otherwise adjusted (see 3.39). For treatment of titles, see 8.155–65.

FOREWORD, PREFACE AND ACKNOWLEDGMENTS, AND INTRODUCTION

1.39   *Foreword.* The term *foreword* should be reserved for prefatory remarks by someone other than the author—including those of an editor or compiler, especially if a work already includes an author's preface (see 1.40).

The publisher may choose to mention the foreword on the title page (e.g., "With a Foreword by Conor Cruise O'Brien"). A foreword, which is set in the same size and style of type as the text, normally runs only a few pages, and its author's name usually appears at the end, often flush right, with a line space (or less) between it and the text. The title or affiliation of the author of a foreword may appear under the name, often in smaller type. If a place and date are included, these are sometimes set across from the author's name, flush left. If a foreword runs to a substantial length, with or without a title of its own, its author's name may be given at the beginning instead of at the end. See also 1.42.

1.40   *Preface and acknowledgments.* The author's own statement about a work is usually called a preface. It is set in the same size and style of type as the text and includes reasons for undertaking the work, method of research (if this has some bearing on readers' understanding of the text), brief acknowledgments (but see 1.41), and sometimes permissions granted for the use of previously published material. A preface need not be signed; if there might be some doubt about who wrote it, however, or if an author wishes to sign the preface (sometimes just with initials), the signature normally appears at the end (see 1.39). When a new preface is written for a new edition or for a reprinting of a book long out of print, it should precede the original preface. The original preface is then usually retitled Preface to the First Edition, and the new preface may be titled Preface to the Second Edition, Preface to the Paperback Edition, Preface 2010, or whatever fits. In a book containing both an editor's preface and an author's preface, the editor's preface, which may be titled as such or retitled Editor's Foreword, comes first and should bear the editor's name at its conclusion.

1.41   *Separate acknowledgments.* If the author's acknowledgments are long, they may be put in a separate section following the preface; if a preface consists only of acknowledgments, its title should be changed to Acknowledgments. Acknowledgments are occasionally put at the back of a book, preceding the other back matter. Acknowledgments that apply to all volumes of a multivolume work may be presented only in the first. See also 4.98–99.

1.42   *Introduction belonging to front matter.* Most introductions belong not in the front matter but at the beginning of the text, paginated with arabic numerals (see 1.46). Material about the book—its origins, for example—rather than about the subject matter should be included in the preface or in the acknowledgments (see 1.40). A substantial introduction by someone other than the author is usually included in the front matter, following the acknowledgments, but if it is not more than three to five pages, it may more appropriately be called a foreword (see 1.39) and placed before the preface.

OTHER FRONT MATTER

1.43   *List of abbreviations.* Not every work that includes abbreviations needs a separate list of abbreviations with the terms or names they stand for. If many are used, or if a few are used frequently, a list is useful (see fig. 1.8); its location should always be given in the table of contents. If abbreviations are used in the text or footnotes, the list may appear in the front matter. If they are used only in the back matter, the list should appear before the first element in which abbreviations are used, whether the appendixes, the endnotes, or the bibliography. A list of abbreviations is generally not a substitute for using the full form of a term at its first occurrence in the text (see 10.3). In the list, alphabetize terms by the abbreviation, not by the spelled-out form. See also 14.55.

1.44   *Publisher's, translator's, and editor's notes.* Notes on the text are usually treated typographically in the same way as a preface or foreword. A publisher's note—used rarely and only to state something that cannot be included elsewhere—should either precede or immediately follow the table of contents. A translator's note, like a foreword, should precede any element, such as a preface, that is by the original author. An explanation of an editor's method or a discussion of variant texts, often necessary in scholarly editions, may appear either in the front matter (usually as the last item there) or in the back matter (as an appendix or in place of one). Brief remarks about editorial method, however—such as noting that spelling and capitalization have been modernized—are often better incorporated into an editor's preface, if there is one.

Text

1.45   *Determining page 1.* The first page of the first chapter or the introduction (see 1.46) is usually counted as arabic page 1. Where the front matter is extensive, however, a second half title, identical to the one on page i, may be added before the text. The second half title should be counted as page 1, the first of the pages to be counted with an arabic page number (though the page number does not appear). The page following the second half title (its verso) is usually blank, though it may contain an illustration or an epigraph. A second half title is also useful when the book design specifies a double-page spread for chapter openings; in such a

Abbreviations

abl.	ablative	Lat.	Latin
ac.	accusative	Leon.	Leonese
act.	active	lit.	literally
adj.	adjective	m.	masculine
And.	Andalusian	Med.	Medieval
Ar.	Arabic	Mod.	Modern
Cast.	Castilian	Moz.	Mozarabic
Cat.	Catalan	n.	neuter
cf.	*confer* (compare)	nom.	nominative
conj.	conjugation	Occ.	Occitan
Cub.	Cuban	p.	person
dat.	dative	pas.	passive
decl.	declension	pl.	plural
Dom. Repub.	Dominican Republic	Port.	Portuguese
Eng.	English	sg.	singular
Equat. Guin.	Equatorial Guinea	Sp.	Spanish
ex.	example	var.	variant
f.	feminine	viz.	*videlicet* (namely)
Fr.	French	voc.	vocative
gen.	genitive		
Gr.	Greek		
irreg.	irregular		
It.	Italian		

FIGURE 1.8. A list of abbreviations. See 1.43.

case, chapter 1 starts on page 2. If a book begins with a part title, the part title page is treated as arabic page 1 in the same manner as a second half title. See also 1.3, 1.5.

TEXT DIVISIONS

1.46 *Introduction belonging to main text.* Unlike the kind of introduction that may be included in the front matter (see 1.42), a text introduction is integral to the subject matter of the book and should not include acknowledgments, an outline of the contents ("In the first two chapters I discuss . . ."), or other material that belongs in the front or back matter. (This rule may not apply in the case of a reprint or facsimile edition, where the front matter is furnished by a volume editor.) A text introduction carries arabic page numbers. A new introduction to a classic work may be considered a text introduction even if it includes biographical or other material about the original author. If titled simply Introduction, it does not normally carry a chapter number and is usually considerably shorter than a chapter. An author who has titled chapter 1 Introduction should be encouraged to give the chapter a more evocative title.

1.47 *Division into parts.* Some books are divided into parts (see fig. 1.5). Each part usually carries a number and a title and should contain at least two chapters (an exception may be made for a part that includes only an introductory or concluding chapter). Chapters are numbered consecutively throughout the book; they do not begin with 1 in each part. Parts are sometimes called sections, though *section* is more commonly used for a subdivision within a chapter. Part titles that do not include introductions usually begin recto, followed by a blank verso and a recto chapter opening. If a part includes an introduction—usually short, titled or untitled—it may begin on a new recto following the part title, or on the verso of the part title, or on the part title itself. A text introduction to a book that is divided into parts precedes the part title to part 1 and needs no part title of its own. Also, no part title need precede the back matter of a book divided into parts, though one may be useful before a series of appendixes or a notes section.

1.48 *Division into chapters.* Most nonfiction prose works are divided into numbered chapters of a more or less consistent length. Authors should aim for short, descriptive titles, which tend to give readers a better overview of a book's contents than longer, more whimsical titles. Each chapter normally starts on a new page, verso or recto, and its opening page should carry a drop folio (see 1.3, 1.5)—or sometimes no folio—and no running head (see 1.9–15). (Recto openers may facilitate the production of individual chapter offprints.) The first chapter ordinarily begins on a recto (but see 1.45). Chapter openers usually consist of the chapter number (*chapter* is often omitted), the chapter title, and the chapter subtitle, if any; together, these are referred to as the chapter display. Footnote reference numbers or symbols should not appear anywhere in the chapter display. A note that refers to the chapter as a whole should be unnumbered and should precede the numbered notes, whether it appears on the first page of the chapter or in the endnotes (see 14.47). A chapter epigraph, sometimes considered part of the chapter display, may include a note reference, though traditionalists will prefer an unnumbered note.

1.49   *Division into chapters by multiple authors.* In multiauthor books, the chapter author's name is usually given at the head of the chapter. An affiliation or other identification is put in an unnumbered footnote on the first page of the chapter (see 14.50) or in a list of contributors (1.62). An unnumbered footnote is also used to disclose the source of a chapter or other contribution that is being reprinted from an earlier publication. When both the author's affiliation and the source of the contribution are given in the note, it is customary, but not essential, that the affiliation come first.

1.50   *Divisions for poetry.* In a book of previously unpublished poetry, each poem usually begins on a new page. Any part titles provided by the poet should appear on separate pages (rectos) preceding the poems grouped under them. In a collection of previously published poems, more than one poem, or the end of one and the beginning of another, may appear on the same page.

1.51   *Divisions for letters and diaries.* Letters and diaries are usually presented in chronological order, so they are seldom amenable to division into chapters or parts. For diary entries, dates may be used as headings, and in published correspondence the names of senders or recipients of letters (or both) may serve as headings. The date of a letter may be included in the heading if it does not appear in the letter itself. Such headings in diaries and correspondence do not usually begin a new page.

1.52   *Concluding elements.* Epilogues and afterwords are relatively brief sections that sometimes end a text. They bear no chapter numbers. Conclusions tend to be more extensive and may assume the significance and proportions of final chapters, with or without a chapter number. In such concluding sections, the author may make some final statement about the subject presented, the implications of the study, or questions inviting further investigation. Epilogues, afterwords, and conclusions may begin either recto or verso unless the book is divided into parts, in which case they must begin recto so that they do not appear to belong to the final part only. Typographically they are usually treated like forewords or prefaces.

TEXT SUBDIVISIONS

1.53   *Subheads—general principles.* Subheads within a chapter should be short and meaningful and, like chapter titles, parallel in structure and tone. It is rarely imperative that a subhead begin a new page. The first sentence of text following a subhead should not refer syntactically to the subhead; words should be repeated where necessary. For example:

SECONDARY SPONGIOSA
The secondary spongiosa, a vaulted structure . . .
not
SECONDARY SPONGIOSA
This vaulted structure . . .

1.54   *Subhead levels and placement.* Many works require only one level of subhead throughout the text. Some, particularly scientific or technical works, require further subdivision. Where more than one level is used, the subheads are sometimes referred to as the A-level subhead (the first-level heading after the chapter title), B-level, C-level, and so on (or A-head, B-head, C-head, etc.). Only the most complicated works need more than three levels. The number of subhead levels required may vary from chapter to chapter. A lower-level subhead may follow an upper-level subhead with no intervening text, but when a section of text is subdivided, there should ordinarily be at least two subsections. A single subhead in a chapter or a single B-level subhead under an A-level subhead may be viewed as illogical and asymmetrical. (There are cases, however, when a single subdivision is needed—e.g., for a notes section at the end of a chapter.) Subheads are generally set on a line separate from the following text, the levels differentiated by type style and placement. The lowest level, however, may be run in at the beginning of a paragraph, usually set in italics and followed by a period. It is then referred to as a run-in subhead (or run-in sidehead). Run-in heads are usually capitalized sentence-style (see 8.156).

1.55   *Numbered subheads.* Unless sections in a chapter are cited in cross-references elsewhere in the text, numbers are usually unnecessary with subheads. In general, subheads are more useful to a reader than section numbers alone. In scientific and technical works, however, the numbering of sections, subsections, and sometimes sub-subsections provides easy reference. There are various ways to number sections. The most common is double numeration or multiple numeration. In this system, sections are numbered within chapters, subsections within sections, and subsubsections within subsections. The number of each division is preceded by the numbers of all higher divisions, and all division numbers are separated by periods, colons, or hyphens. Thus, for example, the numbers 4.8 and 4.12 signify, respectively, the eighth section and the twelfth section of chapter 4.[1] The series 4.12.3 signifies the third subsection in the twelfth section of chapter 4, and so on. The system employed by this manual is chapter number followed by paragraph number for easy cross-referencing. The multiple-numeration system may also be used for illustrations, tables, and mathematical equations (see, respectively, 3.11, 3.51, and 12.24–25).

1.56   *Ornamental or typographic breaks in text.* Where a break stronger than a paragraph but not as strong as a subhead is required, a set of asterisks or a type ornament, or simply a blank line, may be inserted between paragraphs. Using a blank line has the disadvantage that it may be missed if the break falls at the bottom of a page. This quandary can be solved by differentiating the first few words of each paragraph that follows a break—for example, by using small capitals.

Back Matter

1.57   *Appendixes.* An appendix may include explanations and elaborations that are not essential parts of the text but are helpful to a reader seeking further clarification, texts of documents, long lists, survey questionnaires, or sometimes even charts or tables. The appendix should not, however, be a repository for odds and ends that the author could not work into the text. Relevant information that is too unwieldy or expensive to produce in print may be suitable for presentation on the publisher's website and under its aegis (a practice more common with online journals, including some University of Chicago Press journals). Appendixes usually follow the last book chapter, though an appendix may be included at the end of a chapter (introduced by an A-level subhead) if what it contains is essential to understanding the chapter. In multiauthor books and in books from which offprints of individual chapters will be required, any appendix must follow the chapter it pertains to. When two or more appendixes are required, they should be designated by either numbers

---

1. Multiple numeration using periods should not be confused with decimal fractions. Paragraph or section 4.9 may be followed by 4.10—quite unlike the decimal fraction system.

MADISON CHRONOLOGY
1787

27 May– 17 September	JM attends Federal Convention at Philadelphia; takes notes on the debates
29 May	Virginia Plan presented
6 June	JM makes first major speech, containing analysis of factions and theory of extended republic
8 June	Defends "negative" (veto) on state laws
19 June	Delivers critique of New Jersey Plan
27 June–16 July	In debate on representation, JM advocates proportional representation for both branches of legislature
16 July	Compromise on representation adopted
26 July	Convention submits resolutions to Committee of Detail as basis for preparing draft constitution
6 August	Report of Committee of Detail delivered
7 August	JM advocates freehold suffrage
7 August– 10 September	Convention debates, then amends, report of 6 August
31 August	JM appointed to Committee on Postponed Matters
8 September	Appointed to Committee of Style
17 September	Signs engrossed Constitution; Convention adjourns
ca. 21 September	Leaves Philadelphia for New York
24 September	Arrives in New York to attend Congress
26 September	Awarded Doctor of Laws degree in absentia by College of New Jersey

FIGURE 1.9.   Opening page of a chronology. See 1.58. For date style, see 6.45.

(Appendix 1, Appendix 2, etc.) or letters (Appendix A, Appendix B, etc.), and each should be given a title as well. Appendixes may be set either in the same type size as the text proper or in smaller type.

1.58   *Chronology.* A chronological list of events may be useful in certain works. It may appear in the back matter under its own heading, but if it is essential to readers, it is better placed in the front matter, immediately before the text. For an example, see figure 1.9.

1.59   *Endnotes.* Endnotes, simply headed Notes, follow any appendix material and precede the bibliography or reference list (if there is one). The notes to each chapter are introduced by a subhead indicating the chapter number and sometimes the chapter title. The running heads to the endnotes should identify the text pages the notes apply to (see 1.14). Endnotes are normally set smaller than the text but larger than footnotes. Notes may have to be placed at the ends of chapters in multiauthor books (see 14.38). For unnumbered notes and notes keyed to line or page numbers, see 14.47, 14.48. For endnotes versus footnotes, see 14.38–43.

1.60   *Glossary.* A glossary is a useful tool in a book containing many foreign words or unfamiliar terms. Words to be defined should be arranged in alphabetical order, each on a separate line and followed by its definition (see, for example, the list of key terms in appendix B). A glossary usually precedes a bibliography or reference list.

1.61   *Bibliography or reference list.* Bibliographies (except for bibliographical essays) and reference lists are normally set smaller than the text and in flush-and-hang style. For a discussion of the various kinds of bibliographies, see 14.59; for reference lists, see 15.10. For a full discussion and examples, see chapters 14 and 15.

1.62   *List of contributors.* A list of contributors may be appropriate for a work by many authors in which only the volume editor's name appears on the title page. The list (usually headed Contributors) may appear in the front matter of a printed book, but the preferred location is in the back matter, immediately before the index. Names are arranged alphabetically by last name but not inverted ("Koren D. Writer," not "Writer, Koren D."). Brief biographical notes and academic affiliations may accompany the names. See figure 1.10. A work by only a handful of authors whose names appear on the title page does not require a list of contributors if biographical data can be included on the copyright page or elsewhere in the book (see 1.20, 1.49, 14.49).

1.63   *Index.* The index, or the first of several indexes, begins on a recto; subsequent indexes begin verso or recto. In a book with both name and subject indexes, the name index should precede the subject index. Indexes in printed books are normally set two columns to a page and in smaller type than the text. For a full discussion of indexes and indexing, see chapter 16.

1.64   *Colophon.* The last page of a specially designed and produced book occasionally contains a colophon—an inscription including the facts of production. For an example, see the last page of the print edition of this manual. For another meaning of colophon, see 1.66.

CONTRIBUTORS

MARK ANTLIFF is associate professor of art history at Duke University. He is the author of *Inventing Bergson: Cultural Politics and the Parisian Avant-Garde* (1993); coeditor, with Matthew Affron, of *Fascist Visions: Art and Ideology in France and Italy* (1997); and coauthor, with Patricia Leighten, of *Cubism and Culture* (2001). He is currently completing two books: a coedited collection of primary documents titled *A Cubism Reader, 1906–1914* (with Patricia Leighten) and *The Advent of Fascism: Art, Myth, and Ideology in France.*

NINA ATHANASSOGLOU-KALLMYER is professor of modern European art at the University of Delaware and the author of *French Images from the Greek War of Independence, 1821–1830: Art and Politics under the Restoration* and *Eugène Delacroix: Prints, Politics, and Satire.* She edited the special issue of the *Art Journal* on Romanticism and has published articles on nineteenth-century French art and culture. Her most recent book, *Cézanne and Provence: The Painter in His Culture,* is forthcoming from the University of Chicago Press. She is currently working on a project involving Victor Hugo and his circle.

STEPHEN BANN is professor of history of art at the University of Bristol, England. His most recent books are *Paul Delaroche: History Painted* and *Parallel Lines: Printmakers, Painters, and Photographers in Nineteenth-Century France.*

HOMI K. BHABHA is the Anne F. Rothenberg Professor of English and American Literature at Harvard University and visiting professor in the humanities at University College, London. He is the author of *The Location of Culture* and is a regular contributor and columnist of *Art Forum.* He is currently at work on *A Measure of Dwelling,* forthcoming from Harvard University Press, and *The Right to Narrate,* forthcoming from Columbia University Press.

SUZANNE PRESTON BLIER is the Allen Whitehill Clowes Professor of Fine Arts and professor of Afro-American studies at Harvard University. She is the author most recently of *African Vodun: Art, Psychology, and Power*; *The Anatomy of Architecture: Ontology and Metaphor in Batammaliba Architectural Expression*; *The Royal Arts of Africa: The Majesty of Form*; and *Imaging African Amazons: The Art of Dahomey Women Warriors* (forthcoming). She is also completing a book on art, conflict, and diplomacy in ancient Ife (Nigeria).

FIGURE 1.10. Partial list of contributors to an edited collection. See 1.62.

1.65   *Errata.* An errata sheet should never be supplied to correct simple typographical errors (which may be corrected in a later printing, if there is one) or to insert additions to, or revisions of, the printed text (which should wait for a subsequent edition of the book). It should be used only in extreme cases where errors severe enough to cause misunderstanding are detected too late to correct in the normal way but before the finished book is distributed. If the corrected material can be pasted over the incorrect material, it should be printed on adhesive paper. A bound-in errata page may be justified when all or part of a book is photographically reproduced from an earlier publication. It may be placed either at the end of the front matter or at the end of the book and should be listed in the table of contents. Publishers may also choose to post significant errata online; for electronic projects, links to and from any documentation of corrections should be provided. The following form may be adapted to suit the particulars:

Errata

PAGE	FOR	READ
37, line 5	Peter W. Smith	John Q. Jones
182, line 15	is subject to	is not subject to
195, line 8	figure 3	figure 15
23, 214	Transpose captions of plates 2 and 51.	

Covers and Jackets

1.66   *Clothbound covers.* The traditional clothbound hardcover book—so-called for the integument of cloth stretched over a laminated cardboard cover—may include a paper dust jacket (see 1.69). Underneath the jacket, on the cloth itself, the spine is generally imprinted with the author's (or editor's) full name, or the last name only if space is tight; the title of the book (and any edition number); and the publisher's name. The subtitle is usually omitted. The publisher's name is often shortened or replaced by an emblem or device known as a colophon or logo. (For another meaning of colophon, see 1.64.) Considering a book as it stands upright on a shelf, spine copy on American publications is most commonly printed vertically (and read from the top down), but when space allows (as with longer books with wider spines), it may be printed horizontally (for easier reading on the shelf). The front cover may be blank, but it sometimes bears stamped or printed material, such as the title and author's name or the publisher's colophon or some other decoration. The back cover is usually blank, though a product code may be necessary for books with no jacket (see 1.71). For credit lines, see 1.70, 3.28–36.

1.67   *Paperback covers.* The spine of paperback covers (and other flexible covers) usually carries the author's or editor's name, the publisher's name or colophon or both, and the title. The front cover carries the author's or editor's name, the title and (usually) the subtitle, and sometimes the name of a translator, a contributor of a foreword, an edition number, or the like. The back cover usually carries promotional copy, such as a description of the book or quotations from reviews or signed blurbs, a brief biographical statement about the author, the series title if the book is part of a series, and, sometimes, information about the publisher. (Some paperbacks include gatefolds, also called French flaps—extensions to the front and back covers that are folded into the book just like the dust jacket to a hardcover book; see 1.69.)

1.68   *Endpapers.* An endpaper is one of two folded sheets of paper appearing at the beginning and end of a hardcover book (or, more rarely, a book with a sturdy paperback or other flexible binding). Half of each sheet is glued against the inside of the cover, one to the front and one to the back; the base of each is then glued, at the fold (near the spine), to the first and last page of the book. Endpapers help secure a book within its covers. The free half of each sheet is called a flyleaf. Endpapers, sometimes colored, are usually of a heavier stock than the book pages, and they sometimes feature printed text or illustrations.

1.69   *Dust jackets.* Hardcover books are often protected by a coated paper jacket (or dust jacket). In addition to the three parts to be found on the book cover itself, the jacket also has flaps that tuck inside the front and back covers. The front and spine carry the same kind of material as the front and spine of paperback covers (see 1.67). The material included on the back of a paperback cover is begun on the front flap of the hardcover jacket and completed on the back flap. The back panel is sometimes used to promote other books by the publisher.

1.70   *Credit lines for cover art.* If a credit line is required for artwork included on a jacket or cover, it normally appears on the back flap of the jacket or the back cover of a paperback or other book without a jacket. Credit for artwork on a paperback cover or on the actual cover (as opposed to the jacket) of a hardcover book may also appear inside the book, usually on the copyright page, since the cover is a permanent part of the bound book. See 3.28–36 for styling of credit lines.

1.71   *ISBN and bar codes on covers.* In addition to the International Standard Book Number (ISBN; see 1.32), book covers need to include product and price codes (bar codes). These should appear at the foot of the back cover or dust jacket or any other protective case or wrapper. A detailed overview of the process and related resources can be found at the website of the US ISBN Agency, R. R. Bowker, or the International ISBN Agency.

The Parts of a Journal

Introduction

1.72   *Print and electronic formats for journals.* The majority of scholarly journals are produced either in print and electronic versions or as electronic-only journals, though many print-only journals persist, mainly in nonscientific fields. Electronically published journals usually contain all the material included in any printed counterpart except, in some cases, advertising. Electronic journals typically present the material in one of two ways (and often both): (1) as searchable page images suitable for printing by the end user and corresponding to the pages of the journal's print issues (i.e., as a PDF); or (2) as full-text HTML versions suitable for viewing in a web browser and containing features and supplementary materials not available in the print edition. (For definitions of *PDF*, *HTML*, and related terms, see appendix B.)

1.73   *Noting differences between print and electronic versions.* Although a printed article should include all elements that are essential to understanding, interpreting, and documenting the text, many journals publish special materials electronically that are not available in the print version. These features may include very large tables, supplemental reading lists, audiovisual components, large data sets that can be exported to third-party software for analysis, or color versions of figures published in black and white in the printed journal; some of this material may constitute the basis of an online-only appendix. In addition, some journals release unedited "in press" versions of manuscripts that have been accepted for publication (see 1.106). With the exception of these "preprints," electronic-only articles, appendixes, and other features must be listed in the print version (either in the table of contents or on the first page of the applicable article), and differences between the print and electronic versions must be made apparent in the latter. See also 3.26.

1.74 *Unique identifiers for electronic journals.* Print journals are usually identified by volume and date. Electronic journals and their components must be further identified by means of stable and unique identifiers. Articles in Chicago's electronic journals are identified in three ways: (1) by page ranges for their published articles, either print pages or e-pages; (2) by the inclusion of numbers that can be found in the Copyright Clearance Center code, which includes the ISSN and other information, including an article number (see 1.97; electronic journals are also assigned an eISSN, distinct from any counterpart for print); and (3) by Digital Object Identifiers (DOIs). The DOI is a unique, persistent identification string assigned to journals and their components—including articles, images, and other "objects"—and can be used as the basis of a persistent URL. See also 14.6.

Page Numbers and Running Heads

1.75 *Volume as organizing principle.* A volume of a journal usually comprises the issues published in a calendar year, though some journals (such as *Modern Philology*) prefer the academic year beginning in the autumn. For a journal published quarterly, a volume has four issues; for one published monthly, twelve issues. Some journals, however, publish two or more volumes in one year, depending on the frequency and length of issues.

1.76 *Page numbers for journals.* Page numbers in a printed journal usually start with 1 in the volume's first issue and run continuously to the end of the volume. An issue always begins on a right-hand page (recto) and ends on a left-hand page (verso); thus the last page of an issue is an even number and the first page an odd one. If issue 1 ends with page 264, then issue 2 starts on page 265. Electronic versions of printed journals should use the printed pagination scheme, indicating page ranges for full-text versions of articles that are not presented as page images. (Articles published electronically ahead of print may need to employ "dummy folios"—e.g., 000–000—until the print issue has been paginated.) For articles that are published only in electronic form but can be printed as pages formatted to look like those in the print journal, a separate page-numbering system is used (such as E1, E2, etc.), again running continuously to the end of the volume.

1.77 *Running heads or running feet in journals.* Running heads or feet bear the name of the journal (either spelled out or in abbreviated form); the author's surname or, for more than one author, a shortened version of the author list (such as Aldrich et al.); the title of the article, usually shortened, or the name of the journal section (such as Brief Reports). Arrangement of these pieces of information across rectos and versos varies among journals. Full-text, scrollable electronic articles will not have running heads per se; printable page images, however, generally reproduce the format of articles in a printed-and-bound journal.

Covers and Home Pages

1.78   *Covers for printed journals.* A printed journal is usually bound in soft covers, like a paperback, and each issue generally uses the same overall design and color scheme. A journal's spine contains the name of the journal, the volume and issue numbers, and the date, month, or season and year of publication. It may also note the beginning and ending page numbers of that issue. Each of the remaining four sides of the cover also contains important information, as follows:

- *Cover 1*, the front cover, displays the name of the journal; the volume and issue numbers; the date, month, or season and the year of the issue; the publisher's name; and sometimes the table of contents or an illustration. The title of a special issue, along with the name(s) of the editor(s) of the special issue, appears on cover 1. The front cover may be offered as an image on the home page of the online version for each issue.

- *Cover 2*, the inside front cover, usually contains the masthead with the names of the editor(s) and staff, the editorial board, the journal's International Standard Serial Number (ISSN), its dates or frequency of publication, subscription information, addresses for business and editorial correspondence, and the copyright line for the entire issue (see also 1.97). Cover 2 may also include information about postage; a statement about paper durability; a statement about copying beyond fair use; information about obtaining microfilm copies of back issues; mention of a submission fee, if that is part of the journal's practice; information about indexing of the journal's articles; a statement about advertising policy; and a caption for any illustration that appears on cover 1. It may also list the URL of the electronic version. If the journal is sponsored by a scholarly society or other organization, cover 2 may supply the name and address of the society and the names of officers. Occasionally on cover 2 but more often in the front or back matter of each issue (see 1.81–86), there may be a statement of editorial policy for the journal indicating what kind of articles the journal publishes as well as information for contributors about how and in what form to submit a manuscript.

- *Cover 3*, the inside back cover, is often given over to advertising, or it may be used for information for contributors. If the table of contents begins on the back cover, it may be completed on cover 3.

- *Cover 4*, the back cover, carries the bar code for the journal issue in the lower right-hand corner. It may also carry the table of contents or titles of articles scheduled to appear in a forthcoming issue, or advertising. (If there is advertising on cover 4, the bar code may be put on cover 2 or cover 3.) If the table of contents begins on cover 1, it may be completed on cover 4.

1.79   *Home pages for electronic journals.* The home page for an electronic journal—in addition to identifying such essential information as the volume number and date of the current issue—generally features a table of contents for navigating the articles in that issue and navigational aids for getting to other issues and to information about the journal. Chicago also includes links to full citation information with each article, which consists of author name(s), article title, page range, volume and issue number, and the DOI for the article. Links to information typically included on the covers of printed journals—such as a statement of copyright, frequency of publication, and ISSN—should also be provided on the front page of each issue and with each full-text presentation of individual articles (see also 1.81–86).

1.80   *Maintaining the context of electronic articles.* Information may be lost when articles are uncoupled from the electronic issues of a journal. Editors of electronic journals should seek to preserve the historical context by maintaining, in connection with each article, information that might affect interpretation of its contents or its selection for publication. Information such as the names of the editors and editorial board, any sponsors or advertisers in the journal, and the information for contributors—as they existed at the time of the article's publication—are as relevant as the date of publication in assessing the import of a work.

Front Matter

1.81   *Front matter in printed journals.* Many of the elements discussed in 1.78 can equally occur in the front matter, or preliminary ("prelim") pages. Some journals, because they have a large staff and a large number of editors on their advisory board, have space on cover 2 only for the masthead and advisory board editors; the other items then appear in the front matter.

1.82   *Front matter and home pages for electronic journals.* Most journal home pages include hypertext links to all materials typically found in the front matter of a printed journal. Journal home pages may also provide (or provide links to) some or all of the following resources:

- A fuller description of the journal and its policies
- Information about the history of the journal and, if applicable, the sponsoring society
- More extensive information about preparation and submission of electronic text, tables, math, art, and other files (e.g., video files or large data sets)
- Links to other home pages (e.g., the publisher's home page, the sponsoring society's home page, other relevant societies' home pages, and databases or other online resources associated with the journal or the field)
- Individual and institutional subscription forms
- Lists of institutional subscribers
- Site license agreement and registration forms
- Links to tables of contents for all issues of the journal or for those currently available online
- Lists of articles scheduled for upcoming issues, or links to articles published electronically ahead of upcoming issues
- A link to a journal-specific or broader search engine
- Society meeting abstracts and information about upcoming meetings
- Society membership information and application forms
- Information about special services for subscribers (e.g., tables of contents distributed by e-mail before publication in print)
- Mail-to links for questions about manuscript submission and review, subscriptions, back issues, advertising, copyright and permissions, books and new media for review, passwords and other technical issues, and other topics

These resources typically are not associated with a particular issue of the journal but are simply updated as needed.

1.83   *Journal table of contents.* The table of contents, usually headed Contents, appears in the front matter or on the cover(s) of the print issue (see 1.78) and is typically the main feature of a journal's home page. The table of contents should include the title of the journal (or, for a special issue, the title of a special issue and the names of its editors); the date, month, or season and the year of publication; the volume and issue numbers; and the titles of the articles in the issue along with the authors' names and, for the print issue, the page number on which each article begins. It may contain section titles, such as Reviews, or subheads for specific content areas. Additional items listed may include review articles, book reviews, book notes, commentaries, editorials, or other substantive items, and should include a list of articles published in electronic form only (e-articles) or direct readers to the journal's website for a list of those articles. See figure 1.11. The electronic table of contents, in addition to providing links to each format of each item in the list, will include links to any abstracts, which can usually be viewed without a subscription. Some journals

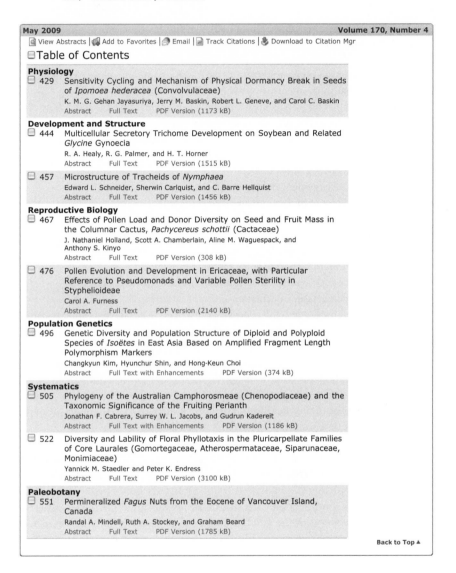

FIGURE 1.11. Table of contents for an issue of an online scholarly journal. Note that the page numbers, as in most scholarly journals, are sequential throughout a volume. See 1.83.

also include options for downloading and customizing citations to individual articles for use in citation management software (see also 14.13).

1.84   *Information for contributors.* Information for potential contributors can vary in length from a sentence to several pages. Some journals also include a statement of editorial policy. These components—when they do not appear on cover 2 or cover 3 in a printed journal (see 1.78)—may appear in an issue's front or back matter. In many cases, the print journal will contain a brief version of these components and point the potential author to the electronic version for more details.

1.85   *Acknowledgments, announcements, and calls for papers.* Acknowledgments of reviewers, announcements of awards or conferences, and calls for papers are published periodically, and may appear in the preliminary pages or at the end of a journal issue. If the issue is a supplement or special issue on a single topic, perhaps representing the proceedings of a conference or symposium, the print issue may begin with a title page that contains the title of the supplement, the name(s) of any guest editor(s), information about the source of the articles (perhaps a conference or symposium), and sponsorship information, if any.

1.86   *Journals errata.* Journals periodically publish errata, which, in print issues, may appear in the front or the back matter. Electronic journals should provide two-way links from errata to the articles that contain the errors; in other words, the articles themselves should be updated to link to or otherwise indicate the relevant errata. The entries in the issue table of contents for the original articles should also contain links to the errata. Small errors in online articles that are corrected after the original publication date (e.g., broken images and typographical errors) are best accompanied by a note indicating the nature of the changes and when they were made. See also 1.105.

Articles and Other Components

1.87   *Majors and minors.* Items published in a journal are often described as being majors or minors. The majors, principally the articles, are so named because these items have been traditionally set in the major (or regular) type size and style of the printed journal. Special kinds of articles—such as review essays, survey articles, or articles grouped as a symposium—are typically treated as majors. Minors, often set in smaller type, are items such as brief reports, letters to the editor, book reviews, book notes, announcements, calls for papers, errata, and notes on contributors.

1.88   *Article title, authorship, and other first-page information.* An article should include—on the first page or, in the full-text version, at or near the top of the article—the title of the article, the author's or authors' name(s), and the copyright line for the particular article (see 1.97). Depending on the journal or on the needs of a given article, the first page may also include the affiliation of each author (and any relevant financial interests or potential conflicts of interest), an address for correspondence and reprints, dates of submission and acceptance of the article (most commonly in scientific journals), an abstract, an acknowledgment note, and sometimes an editor's note. Of course, the first page will also include any footnotes that are referenced on that page and, depending on the length of the other information, the beginning of the text. A general section heading such as Articles, Review Essay, or Symposium or a specific heading such as Medical Microbiology may appear above the article title.

1.89 *Hyperlinks within electronic articles.* Full-text electronic journal articles typically contain links to other elements within the document (perhaps illustrations, tables, and the reference list, notes, or bibliography) and often to outside resources such as field-specific indexes or databases. Articles are also typically accompanied by other linked items, including an article-specific list (or menu) that allows readers to move directly to other sections or elements of the article and a standard menu that allows them to move to the issue's table of contents, to the previous or next article in the issue, to the journal's home page, to a search page, or elsewhere. The display may also include thumbnail versions of the article's tables and illustrations (see 1.99–100).

1.90 *Article abstracts.* Many journals—particularly in the sciences but also in the social sciences—include abstracts. These summaries, sometimes as much as a few hundred words but usually somewhat shorter, appear at the beginning of an article and are generally offered without cost to subscribers and nonsubscribers alike by online journals and third-party hosts and search engines. (Some abstracts are supplemented by targeted keywords intended to increase visibility to search engines.) The content of an abstract is extremely important because it can influence decisions made by researchers and other potential readers. Some journals have strict guidelines for what an abstract must include and how it should be structured—especially those that publish the results of original research. Abstracts are not typically required for letters, reviews, and other minors.

1.91 *Article subheads.* An article, like a chapter in a book, may be divided into sections and subsections headed by subheads, sub-subheads, and so on (see 1.53–56). The number of subhead levels required may vary from article to article.

1.92 *Book review and book notes sections.* Many journals include a book review section. Such sections, usually headed Reviews or Book Reviews, vary greatly in length from journal to journal. Within a section, each review carries a heading that lists information about the book being reviewed. The heading includes the author's name, the title of the book, place and date of publication, publisher's name, number of pages (including front matter), and price. If the book is part of a series, the series name may be given. Some journals include reviews of other journals and of other media. The name of the reviewer usually appears at the end of the review but occasionally follows the heading. Book notes use the same form of headings as book reviews, but the text is much shorter and reviewers may be listed by their initials. Some journals also publish a list of books or other materials received for review from publishers.

1.93   *Journal announcements.* Announcements include such items as notices of future conferences and symposia; calls for papers, award nominations, or research subjects; and employment opportunities.

1.94   *Journal contributors.* Some journals have a special section with information about the contributors to the issue, such as their affiliations and publications or fields of study. The names must be checked against the authors' names on the first page of every article and in the table of contents to be sure they are spelled correctly (see also 2.29–31).

1.95   *Letters to the editor.* Letters to the editor are usually treated as a minor. In some scientific journals, on the other hand, letters appear as a regular, prominent feature, often with replies, and may contain equations, tables, and figures.

1.96   *Journal editorials.* An editorial is not a regular feature in most academic journals but appears on a particular occasion. When there is a change of some sort—a new editor, modifications in editorial policy or style, features added or dropped, or graphic redesign of the journal (see 1.110)—an editorial announces and explains the change. A journal may provide an annual editorial summing up the year's activity. Some journals publish invited editorials, written by someone who is neither the journal's editor in chief nor a member of its editorial board, that comment on a particular article or group of articles. A special issue usually includes an introduction by the special issue's editor(s). The heading Editorial or Introduction is used, and the editor's name appears at the end of the piece.

1.97   *Journal copyright lines.* In addition to the copyright line that appears on cover 2, each substantive article or element in the journal normally carries its own copyright line. This usually appears at the bottom of the first page of the article, below any footnotes on that page, or, for electronic articles, at the head of the article or some other prominent location. It contains three basic parts: (1) information on the current issue, including the name of the journal, the volume number, the date, month, or season and year of publication, and the inclusive page numbers of the article; (2) the actual copyright notice, containing the copyright symbol, the year, and the name of the copyright owner (usually either the publisher or the sponsoring society); and (3) a series of numbers (the Copyright Clearance Center code) containing the journal's unique identification number (its International Standard Serial Number, or ISSN), the year, the volume and issue numbers, the article number (assigned by the publisher), and the per copy fee for photocopying, payable through the Copyright Clearance Center (CCC; see below). Chicago also includes a fourth element—the article's DOI (see 14.6).

The Journal of Modern History 78 (March 2006): 1–36
© 2006 by The University of Chicago. All rights reserved.
0022-2801/2006/7801-0001$10.00
doi:10.1086/499793

Most but not all US journals use the CCC, which provides systems through which copyright owners can license the reproduction and distribution of materials in both print and electronic form. Its relations with equivalent agencies in other countries enable the CCC to collect fees for uses in those countries. Note that fees apply only to copyrighted material and not to articles in the public domain. See also 4.55–58, 4.91.

1.98 *Publication history for electronic-first articles.* For all articles that are published electronically before they are published in print, the date of electronic publication should appear as part of the article's history, in both the print and the electronic versions, on the first page or otherwise near the head of the article. This date is also part of the context for interpretation of the article; in the sciences, especially, what is known—or at least what has been reported—can change rapidly.

Tables and Illustrations

1.99 *Tables in journal articles.* Tables in electronic articles can be presented in multiple formats—for example, as an image of the typeset table, as a searchable hypertext version with links, or as a machine-readable version that allows readers to download the data and either repeat the analyses used in the article or use the data, perhaps in combination with data from other sources, for their own analyses. Table footnote citations can be linked to the table footnotes themselves; this is especially useful for navigation in very large tables. Links also allow readers to move freely from text to tables and back again, as well as from one table to another. Very large tables may be published in electronic form only; if there is also a print version of the article, both versions should make this difference explicit (see 1.73). For a full discussion of tables, see 3.46–85. See also A.33.

1.100　*Illustrations in journal articles.* An electronic article might display the same illustrations available in the print version of the article, though they may be presented in the text as thumbnail versions linked to larger, higher-resolution images. These images may contain additional navigational aids like the ones described for tables (see 1.99). Moreover, a greater range of illustrations can be offered in electronic journals, which can include more illustrations than would be practical in print. Color can be used freely, without the costs associated with color printing (although color accuracy can vary considerably between display devices). High-resolution images can allow readers to see more detail, and electronic illustrations may include an audio component. Videos and animations can go beyond conventional illustrations to allow readers to view movement and understand processes. For a full discussion of illustrations, see 3.3–45; see also A.32.

Documentation

1.101　*Notes or author-date citations in journals.* One of the fundamental identifying marks of a journal is its documentation style—either notes (sometimes accompanied by a bibliography) or author-date citations. Notes still prevail in many humanities journals. Author-date citations—used mostly by journals in science and the social sciences—consist of parenthetical text citations keyed to a reference list, which appears at the end of the article. Notes may be footnotes or endnotes; if the latter, they appear at the end of the article, with the heading Notes. For a discussion of different styles of documentation, see chapters 14 and 15.

1.102　*Links to citations and to outside resources.* In full-text electronic articles, text citations typically link to references, notes, or items in a bibliography, as the case may be, allowing readers to move from the text citation to the cited item and back to the text. Reference lists and bibliographies may also contain links to resources outside the article—for example, to cited articles or to an outside index or database (see 1.104).

Index

1.103   *Indexes to printed volumes.* At the end of a volume, most journals publish an index to the articles and other pieces published in that volume. The index appears in the volume's last issue. Names of authors, titles of articles, and titles and authors of books reviewed are indexed. In the sciences, subject indexes are sometimes included (but see 1.104).

1.104   *Electronic indexes and indexed searches.* Some electronic journals, especially in the sciences, have dispensed with subject indexes; in some fields, journal subject indexes have been almost completely superseded by large online databases (such as the National Library of Medicine's bibliographic database of journal articles, PubMed) that allow readers to search an entire field of indexed journals, perhaps using terms from a standard list of keywords, rather than searching individually at each journal's or each journal publisher's website. In some fields, more readers may reach an article by this means than by subscribing to the journal (though they will typically need to have a subscription to gain access to the full article). A subject index may nonetheless appear as part of a larger collection in something like PubMed, or journals may offer it individually.

Version Control and Material Not Available in Print

1.105   *Corrections to journal articles.* For many of its journals, Chicago considers the electronic version of an article to be the version of record; the print version, which should contain all elements that are essential to the article, may nevertheless include only a subset of the material available electronically. Whenever the electronic version is considered the version of record, it is extremely important not to make undocumented changes to the file after the electronic publication date. Note that release of electronic articles before they are published in print means that errors may turn up well before the print issue has been assembled; consequently, a print issue may include an erratum that concerns an article in the same issue. In this case, the erratum should state that the article is in the current issue and should specify the date of electronic publication. See also 1.86. For more information on best practices related to version control for journal articles, consult *Journal Article Versions (JAV): Recommendations of the NISO/ALPSP JAV Technical Working Group*, published by the National Information Standards Organization and available from its website (bibliog. 2.7).

1.106   *Preprints.* Manuscripts are sometimes released before publication: authors themselves may circulate drafts within a research community, or they may circulate versions submitted to a journal. They may post drafts on a preprint server—as is standard practice in the physics community—or on their own web pages. Some journals post accepted but not yet edited articles on their websites. Preprints are not to be confused with final, edited electronic articles published in advance of the print issue (see 1.105). See also 1.73, 4.64.

1.107   *Material not available in print.* In addition to preprints (see 1.106), electronic journals often publish material not available in print or not applicable to print (e.g., audiovisual components, large data sets). It is essential that publishers provide this content in a way that ensures its ongoing availability and accessibility; any electronic-only material published under the imprimatur of a journal is every bit as much a part of the scholarly record as a printed-and-bound volume. To this end, the role of publishers and third-party archival services is crucial because, unlike the case with printed journals, libraries may not physically own a copy of the material or the journals it supplements. By implementing standard practices for document structure and markup and for the inclusion and identification of supplemental media such as video and audio files, publishers can help to ensure the permanence and accessibility of their material in libraries and other archives even as software evolves and archives grow and migrate. Publishers should remain abreast of the latest standards for archival practices by consulting such groups as the International Organization for Standardization and the Digital Library Federation.

Design and Style

1.108   *Journal design.* A journal's design features—physical, visual, and editorial—are determined when the journal is founded. At that time, a designer creates a design for the cover and the overall look of a journal and specifications for all of its regular features. Because the designer designs not for a specific text but for categories of text—article title, author's name, text, heads, subheads, and such—the design of a journal should be simple and flexible as well as being visually pleasing and easy to read. It is then the job of the manuscript editor and production personnel to fit the items for a particular issue into the overall design.

1.109   *Editorial style.* A journal's editorial style (see 2.46) governs such things as when to use numerals or percent signs, how to treat abbreviations or special terms, and how tables are typically organized. Consistency of design and style contributes to a journal's identity; readers know what to expect, and the substantive contribution of each article stands out more sharply when typographical distractions are at a minimum.

1.110   *Redesign.* A long-running journal may occasionally be redesigned typographically. More rarely in print but commonly in electronic journals—where the pace of software development will drive new possibilities or require adjustments to formats—the editors may introduce minor alterations in style to accommodate changing needs. Once established, however, a new design or style must be adhered to as carefully as the one it replaces.

Considerations for Web-Based Publications

1.111   *Suitability for the web.* A web-based publication is any publication designed to be consulted online through a web browser or similar application. Any book or journal article may be published on the web, and many scholarly journals, in particular, offer full-text HTML versions of their articles (see 1.72). Because of their relative brevity and because they are often consulted without reference to a particular issue, journal articles have adapted well to this model. Reference works such as manuals, encyclopedias, and dictionaries are, to an even greater degree, designed in any medium to be consulted in a piecemeal fashion, making them particularly suitable for publishing on the web. This section highlights some basic organizational differences between print and web-based publications.

1.112   *Functional features.* As even a casual user of the Internet knows, web-based publications involve much more than content. Any discussion of the parts of a web-based publication must also consider the functional features it will have—search engines, note-taking capability, user-controlled display options, and so forth. The process of determining, designing, and implementing such features, while driven largely by technical expertise, must also be guided by editorial sensibilities. This type of work represents a significant departure from traditional editorial duties, but it is nonetheless essential that functional features be developed with a clear understanding of the content and how the user will interact with that content. Editors involved in any work being developed as a web-based publication may therefore reasonably be asked to play a role in the development of the publication's functional features.

1.113   *Navigation as the primary organizing principle for web-based publications.* A web-based reference work must take into account the fact that readers will typically consult smaller pieces of content and will expect to be able to click through many parts of a work in a very short period of time. Books and journals designed for the web also need to take this reality into account. Nonetheless, not every publication needs to be modeled on the perfect online dictionary—in which any term within a definition is hyperlinked to the entry for that term and so on, providing endless pathways through a significant subset of a single written language. Some readers will want the option merely to browse. At the very least, cross-references, by being hyperlinked, will become more useful in any online publication, and most web publications will need to augment or even replace standard tables of contents with a search engine—one that may need to accommodate complex queries. Furthermore, any web-based work that allows full-text searching will benefit from context-sensitive keyword indexing (see 16.8). Readers will also want to know where they've been and perhaps where other readers have been (or where the majority have chosen to land). They may want to take notes that they can return to later— through a search or other means. They may want to send comments to the author or publisher, and they may want to read and comment on the comments of others. Finally, readers of web publications may expect links to related resources. All these items will need to be made accessible through a clear and consistent navigational hierarchy.

1.114   *Hyperlinks.* In a web-based publication, cross-references become one of the primary ways in which a reader can expect to move quickly from one part of a work to another. There is no cost to following a hyperlink, provided there is a means of stepping or linking back and forth between the hyperlink and the item it points to. But if there are too many links, or if they do not tend to lead to strongly related content—or, worse, if they fail—a publication risks irritating its readers. Beyond cross-references and hyperlinked tables of contents and indexes or other navigational items, a link can of course be made to point to almost anything. Words might be linked to their definitions—either in a glossary or through a third-party dictionary. Authors' names might contain mail-to links or lead to their networking pages or to lists of their other works. URLs or other identifiers can be embedded in any piece of content. All of these must be maintained and updated, however, often at significant cost. Internal cross-references are the most stable type of hyperlink because they need only be tested against and updated along with the work itself—a process that can be at least partly automated. Most other types of text-based links need to be weighed for their utility and persistence. On the other hand, some links can be generated programmatically—for example, links to related titles or related subjects generated by matching author, title, or subject metadata against an evolving database each time a user calls up a specific piece of content (see also A.10).

1.115 *"Front matter" for web-based publications.* Readers of web-based publications will want to be able to navigate primarily to the core content of the publication (and the content that it generates) rather than to ancillary elements such as prefaces, copyright information, or information about the publication or its authors. Online, these elements can be demoted from their usual position in the front of a printed-and-bound book and made accessible through a link at the edge of the screen or the base of a document, from which they can be consulted if need be. Copyright information, however, should usually be included with each subdocument, and help and related documentation should also be available from any part of a publication. Much of the usual taxonomy for printed works—from copyright page to table of contents to preface, foreword, and introduction—will benefit from a different set of categories (e.g., "about us" links, site maps, help menus and other tools, search engines, and the other elements mentioned in 1.113). The table of contents, however, especially in works that can be read in larger chunks—such as an online journal or this manual—may be a significant driver in the top-level navigation of a web-based publication.

1.116 *Folios, running heads, and other "print" elements.* One of the primary advantages of a traditional printed-and-bound book or journal is the presence of page numbers. Page numbers allow students and researchers to make precise citations to the works they consult, allowing readers in turn to retrace their steps. Web-based publications should keep this in mind when designing and organizing content. Dictionaries and encyclopedias have a de facto organizing principle: readers cite material *sub verbo*—or "under the word"—that is, by entry or entry title (14.247). But other types of publications broken into scrollable sections or articles (including encyclopedias with longer articles)—though they may be designed for convenient navigation online—do not necessarily include page numbers to which readers can refer when documenting a specific quotation or idea. Publishers are encouraged to incorporate stable page numbers—as in PDF versions of a journal article—or to otherwise number the elements in their web-based publications (e.g., through paragraph or section numbers) whenever possible. Running heads, on the other hand, almost always have an analogous presence in the basic navigational elements of a web-based publication. Readers require clear indications not only of "where" they are within a publication at any moment (not to mention an indication of the size and scope of each of its elements) but also where they have been and where they might go—for example, to a related portion of the alphabet in a dictionary or, in any type of work, to a section with related content (or, for that matter, to another publication with related content).

1.117   *Indexes, notes, and other "back matter."* Any web-based project can benefit from keyword-enhanced searches, cross-references to related content, and other navigational cues. Web-based works that have a printed counterpart complete with index, on the other hand, should take advantage of the intellectual labor that went into choosing and arranging the index entries and marry it to the linking capabilities of an electronic work. An index prepared with human input—whether it is "embedded" and shows up only in the results of keyword searches (see 16.7) or is prepared as a separate list according to the guidelines in chapter 16—is an asset in any electronic work, whether or not it has a printed counterpart. Note references are hyperlinked to the text in electronic works, solving the problem of footnotes versus endnotes that arises in printed books (see 14.38–43). Other traditional back matter—such as appendixes and bibliographies—may benefit in web-based works from electronic enhancements (e.g., downloadable data sets) or links out to other resources (e.g., through a database such as CrossRef; see 14.6).

2 *Manuscript Preparation, Manuscript Editing, and Proofreading*

Overview and Process Outline

2.1   *Overview — authors, manuscript editors, and proofreaders.* This chapter is divided into three parts. The first part (2.3–44) is addressed primarily to authors, conceived broadly to include compilers, translators, volume editors, editors of journals, and contributors to journals or books. It provides guidelines for preparing manuscripts that have been accepted for publication. As in the discussion of parts in chapter 1, the book-length work is used as the primary model, though considerations for journals are included where applicable. Scholarly journals and periodicals tend to have very specific requirements for manuscript preparation; those writing for such publications will need to consult the specific publication's instructions for authors. The second part of the chapter (2.45–96) gives a detailed look at what happens to a manuscript once it has been submitted to a publisher. Specifically, the role of manuscript editors (also called copyeditors) is discussed. The third part (2.97–136) deals with proofreading — essentially, the steps authors and publishers must take to ensure that their publications are ready to be presented to the public.

2.2   *Process outline — from approved manuscript to published work.* The following outline highlights the basic steps of the publication process from approved manuscript to published work. These steps are broadly modeled on a typical manuscript editing and proofreading schedule for a book-length work; the procedures for journals will vary. For a more detailed look at manuscript preparation, editing, and proofreading, see the discussions in the remainder of this chapter. For sample timetables for producing a book and a journal, see figures 2.1 and 2.2. For an overview of production procedures, including design, see appendix A.

1. **Manuscript submission.** In addition to the final, unedited manuscript, the author submits to the publisher all artwork and any necessary permissions to reproduce illustrations or previously published material or to cite unpublished data or personal communications. See 2.3–6.

2. **Manuscript editing.** The manuscript editor makes changes to the manuscript (and, where necessary, queries the author) and demarcates or checks the order and structure of the elements (e.g., illustrations, headings, text extracts). See 2.54–64, 2.66.

3. **Author review.** The author reviews the edited manuscript and answers any queries. All remaining changes and adjustments to the manuscript need to be indicated by the author at this stage. See 2.85.

4. **Final manuscript.** The manuscript editor produces a final manuscript, incorporating the results of the author's review of the edited manuscript and,

	BUSINESS DAYS	DATES	
Transmittal	n/a	06/24/10	
Contract OK	n/a	06/24/10	
Begin MS edit	5	07/01/10	
MS to author	45	09/02/10	*In editing*
MS design in	15	09/23/10	*three months*
MS from author	5	09/30/10	
MS design OK	5	10/07/10	
Final MS to production	5	10/14/10	
Sample pages in	10	10/28/10	
Sample pages OK	3	11/02/10	*In production*
Pages in/to author	9	11/15/10	*six months*
Pages and index MS from author	20	12/13/10	
Pages and index MS to design	5	12/20/10	
Pages to production	5	12/27/10	
Pages to typesetter	1	12/28/10	
Index MS to typesetter		12/28/10	
Revised pages in	9	01/10/11	
Index pages in		01/10/11	
Mfg quotes requested		01/10/11	
Mfg quotes received	5	01/17/11	
Revised pages to typesetter		01/17/11	
Index pages to typesetter		01/17/11	
Estimate and release routing	2	01/19/11	
Page revisions completed	8	01/31/11	
Final lasers requested	5	02/07/11	
Final lasers in	5	02/14/11	
Final lasers OK	10	02/28/11	
Estimate and release approved		01/21/11	
Cover/dust jacket copy in/OK		12/21/10	
Cover/dust jacket design in		01/17/11	
Cover/dust jacket design OK		01/21/11	
Cover mechanical in		02/11/11	
Cover mechanical OK		02/16/11	
Order date text/cover/dust jacket		02/16/11	
Blues in	17	03/11/11	
Blues OK	1	03/14/11	
Advances in	19	04/08/11	
Books in warehouse		04/08/11	

FIGURE 2.1. Sample design and production schedule for a printed book.

	BUSINESS DAYS	JAN ISSUE	APR ISSUE	JUL ISSUE	OCT ISSUE
MSS at Press		08/02	11/01	01/31	05/02
MS files converted / to Press editorial	7	08/13	11/12	02/11	05/13
MSS edited / typeset / proofed	21	09/11	12/11	03/12	06/11
Proofs to authors	1	09/12	12/12	03/13	06/12
Proofs from authors to journal office / journal office check / back to Press editorial	21	10/11	01/10	04/11	07/11
Revised proofs generated / checked	10	10/25	01/24	04/25	07/25
Revised proofs to journal office	1	10/26	01/25	04/26	07/26
Revised proofs back from journal office to Press editorial	10	11/09	02/08	05/10	08/09
Final proofs (generated by Press editorial) to production	3	11/14	02/13	05/15	08/14
Production paginates issue	5	11/21	02/20	05/22	08/21
Final check (1 day Press editorial, 1 day journal office)	2	11/23	02/22	05/24	08/23
PDF file to printer	3	11/28	02/27	05/29	08/28
Post electronic issue	3	12/03	03/04	06/03	09/02
Mail print edition	24	12/19	03/20	06/19	09/18

FIGURE 2.2. Sample production schedule for a quarterly journal published in both print and electronic forms.

among other things, double-checking each element in the manuscript against a design template for completeness, consistency, and proper markup. See 2.70–74.

5. **Proofreading and indexing.** Once the final manuscript has been converted to its final form—for example, typeset and paginated book or journal pages (*page proofs* or *proof*) or the full text of an electronic publication—it will need to be checked by the author and any additional proofreaders for errors and inconsistencies. See 2.97–136. It is also at this stage that an index may be prepared and subsequently edited (see chapter 16; for journal indexes, see 1.103–4).

6. **Final revisions.** As the publisher makes sure all necessary corrections have been made, the index, if there is one, is proofread in its final format and corrected as needed (see 2.103). Book pages, especially, may go through several rounds of revision, though publishers usually set firm limits on changes beyond the first round of revisions. See 2.102.

7. **Prepress or final review.** For a printed-and-bound book, publishers usually review the typesetter's final files—either as an inexpensive printout or on-screen—before ink is committed to paper. Once the job is on the press, an

initial set of folded and gathered sheets may be sent from the printer to the publisher for review before the job is finished (see 2.104). For electronic publications, a final version must be reviewed before it is posted or otherwise made available to the public (see 2.133–36).

8. **Publication.** In the stages leading up to publication it is critically important to make all possible efforts to eliminate any errors or inconsistencies (typographical or otherwise) or other problems. The occasional error in a published work is inevitable, but even minor errors reflect badly on publishers and authors alike.

Manuscript Preparation Guidelines for Authors

Basic Submission Requirements

2.3 *Elements to be furnished.* Before manuscript editing begins (see 2.45–96), an author should plan to provide the publisher with any of the elements in the list that follows that are to be included in the work. This list is modeled on the parts of a book (see 1.3–71). An author contributing to a journal should consult the journal's specific submission requirements.

- Title page
- Dedication
- Epigraph
- Table of contents
- List of illustrations
- List of tables
- Preface
- Acknowledgments
- Any other front matter
- All text matter, including introduction and part titles
- Notes
- Appendixes
- Glossary
- Bibliography or reference list
- Any other back matter
- All illustrations and all tables
- Illustration captions
- A list of special characters used in the manuscript
- An abstract (required for some books)

- All permissions, in writing, that may be required to reproduce illustrations or previously published material or to cite unpublished data or personal communications (see chapter 4)

All elements should be final and up to date—including any URLs cited in the work (see 14.4–13). The publisher usually furnishes the half-title page (see 1.16), the copyright page (see 1.19–34), and copy for the running heads (see 1.9–15, 2.73).

2.4 *Submitting electronic manuscripts.* Publishers usually require the latest version of the electronic file(s) for the work, and authors are advised to make a secure backup of this final manuscript and to avoid making any further changes to it. Many publishers also require hard copy as a safeguard against any glitches in the electronic files—especially for book-length works. (Some publishers will want a PDF version—the electronic equivalent of hard copy—instead.) To ensure that the hard copy is identical to the electronic files, any last-minute changes made to the electronic files must be reflected in the hard copy—either by means of a new printout or marked by hand (see also 2.5). Authors are advised to include a cover letter specifying the author's name, the title of the work, the electronic file names, and the software used. Any material (such as artwork) that cannot be included in electronic form must be noted and described. Conversely, any material that cannot be printed out (such as videos, animations, or large data files that might be included in an electronic journal or web-based publication) must also be noted and described; for all such material, the software used, the number of items, their type(s), and the individual file names must be specified. For any additional instructions, authors should check with their publishers. For advice on manuscript formatting, see 2.7–22. For advice on preparing index manuscripts, see chapter 16. For paper-only manuscripts, see 2.6. For manuscripts consisting largely of previously published material, see 2.40.

2.5 *Later changes—version control.* Once an author has submitted a final manuscript to the publisher, the publisher is responsible for maintaining the version of record. An author who needs to make further changes after submitting the files must therefore alert the publisher immediately. Minor changes can usually be indicated later, on the edited document that the manuscript editor will send to the author for review (see 2.85). For major changes, the author may need to send a revised manuscript to the publisher *before* editing begins. For journals, major changes are rarely permitted after an article has been accepted; schedules do not allow for them. Peer-reviewed articles that require major changes may also require additional review.

2.6   *Submitting paper-only manuscripts.* In the increasingly rare case of the type-written manuscript, authors are typically required to submit two paper copies of the manuscript; they should keep a third copy for themselves. All copy must be vertically double-spaced (double line spacing) to leave sufficient room for pencil-editing marks. It is essential, moreover, that everything in a paper-only manuscript be legible. Anything added in handwriting before the manuscript is submitted to the publisher must be clearly written, in upper- and lowercase letters, directly above the line or in the margin. Avoid writing on the backs of pages in case the publisher photocopies the manuscript. Any correction longer than a short phrase should be provided as a separate document and inserted in the manuscript following the page to which it pertains—clearly labeled in both places to show where it should be inserted. Finally, to facilitate photocopying, use good-quality paper in a standard size—8½ × 11 inches or A4 (210 × 297 mm). See also 2.40.

Formatting

2.7   *Publishers' manuscript-preparation guidelines.* Many publishers have specific requirements or preferences regarding choice of software and typeface, as well as formats for submitting illustrations and tables along with your manuscript. These should be followed to the letter. Consistency and simplicity in all matters is essential: authors should know that their manuscripts will almost always be converted into another software environment for publication and that, therefore, the consistency and accuracy of the content (i.e., the words themselves) are more important than the style of presentation. A simple presentation is always preferable to an elaborately formatted manuscript. Authors who want a more explicit idea of what publishers look for in the format and structure of a manuscript would do well to consider the steps in a manuscript editor's typical cleanup routine (see 2.77).

2.8   *Line spacing.* Though authors may prefer to use minimal line spacing on the screen, publishers have customarily required that any printout be double-spaced—including all extracts, notes, bibliography, and other material. The extra line spacing is crucial for manuscripts edited with pencil on paper, and some publishers will choose to edit the paper copy and update the electronic files based on this edited copy. (Authors concerned about saving paper are encouraged to consult with their publishers about line-spacing requirements.) Avoid extra space or blank lines between paragraphs. If such a break is intended to appear in the printed version, indicate this explicitly with three asterisks set on a line by themselves (see also 1.56).

2.9 *Word spacing—one space or two?* Like most publishers, Chicago advises leaving a single character space, not two spaces, between sentences and after colons used within a sentence (but see 14.121), and this recommendation applies to both the manuscript and the published work.

2.10 *Justification and margins.* To avoid the appearance of inconsistent spacing between words and sentences, all text in a manuscript should be presented flush left (ragged right)—that is, lines should not be "justified" to the right margin. To leave enough room for handwritten queries, margins of at least one inch should appear on all four sides of the hard copy.

2.11 *Spaces, tabs, and hard returns within paragraphs.* A well-structured electronic document will never include more than one consecutive character space. To indent the first line of a paragraph or items in a vertical list, use the Tab key or your software's paragraph indention features rather than the space bar. (Also eliminate any extra character space or tab after the final punctuation at the end of a paragraph; the hard return should follow the punctuation immediately.) To achieve hanging indention for runover lines (as in a bibliography or index), use your software's indent features—not hard returns and tabs or spaces (see 2.22). A tab or a hard return (i.e., a paragraph break, generally made with the Enter key) should never appear within a paragraph. For prose extracts, see 2.18; for poetry, see 2.19.

2.12 *Hyphenation.* The hyphenation function on your word processor should be turned off. The only hyphens that should appear in the manuscript are hyphens that would appear regardless of where they appeared on the page (e.g., in compound forms). Do not worry if such hyphens happen to fall at the end of a line or if the right-hand margin is extremely ragged. By the same token, do not attempt to manually break excessively long words (e.g., long URLs) with a hyphen. See also 2.93.

2.13 *Dashes.* For an em dash—one that indicates a break in a sentence like this—either use the em dash character on your word processor or type two hyphens (leave no space on either side). For the long dash (three-em dash) in bibliographies, use three consecutive em dashes or six unspaced hyphens. (For more on the em dash, see 6.82–89, 6.90–91.) Ensuring proper use of the en dash—a shorter dash that has special significance in certain types of compounds and in number ranges—is usually considered the manuscript editor's responsibility; authors can generally avoid the en dash and use hyphens instead. (For more on the en dash, see 6.78–81.)

2.14   *Italics, underline, and boldface.* Though underlining will generally be construed by publishers to mean italics, italics should be used instead wherever italics are intended. (In an electronically redlined manuscript, underlining may denote editorial changes; see 2.81 and fig. 2.4.) An author who in fact intends underlining rather than italics to appear in certain instances in the published work must make these instances clear in a letter to the publisher (or a note to the manuscript editor). Use boldface only for words that must appear thus in the published version.

2.15   *Special characters.* As far as your software allows, use the character that you intend rather than any keyboard substitute. For example, if you want a prime symbol, use the prime symbol from your word processor's list of special characters rather than an apostrophe. Since the advent of the Unicode standard for character encoding (see 11.2), many software environments include a wide array of special characters without the need for special fonts or other add-ons. Nonetheless, if you run up against a character that is not available to you, enclose a descriptive shorthand in angle brackets; for example, <bhook>aci might indicate that the publisher should render the Hausa word ɓaci. In either case, include a list of special characters used in your manuscript. See tables 11.1 and 11.2, which list some special characters and their names. If you plan to use a special font that may not support Unicode, consult your publisher first. For some caveats related to quotation marks and apostrophes, see 6.112, 6.114.

2.16   *Chapter and other titles.* Titles for chapters and other parts of a manuscript usually begin on a new page. Use upper- and lowercase letters rather than full capitals. The titles should match the entries in the table of contents. "Chapter 1," "Chapter 2," and so on should appear above the titles to numbered chapters.

2.17   *Subheads.* Set subheads on a new line, flush left. Each level of subhead must be distinguished by type size and style, such as larger boldface for first-level subheads versus smaller italics for second-level heads. (A word processor's style palette can be useful in managing subhead levels.) Use upper- and lowercase letters rather than full capitals (see 8.157). Except for run-in heads, which are usually italicized and given initial capitals for the first word and proper names only (sentence style; see 8.156), subheads are almost never followed by a period. See also 1.54.

2.18   *Prose extracts.* Prose extracts (also known as block quotations) should have double line spacing and be indented from the left margin using your word processor's indent feature. The first line should not have an additional paragraph indent. If there is more than one paragraph within the extract, new paragraphs should have an additional first-line paragraph indent, which can be created using the Tab key or your software's paragraph indention feature. Use hard returns (i.e., the Enter key) only at the end of the extract and after any paragraphs within the extract. See also 13.20–22. For ellipses, see 13.48–56.

2.19   *Poetry extracts.* Poetry extracts should be double-spaced and indented, *not* centered (even if they are to appear centered in the printed version). Let runover lines wrap to the next line normally; do not use the Tab key to indent them. Use a hard return only at the end of each full line of poetry. Only if certain new lines of a poem are to receive deeper indention than others should you use the Tab key, at the beginning of the indented line. You must clearly distinguish between runover lines and indented lines of poetry. If there are either runover or double-indented lines, or if there is any unusual spacing or indention in your hard copy, append a photocopy of the original printed poem. For ellipses, see 13.55. Indicate a stanza break with an extra hard return. The source, if given after the extract, should appear in parentheses on a separate line, aligned vertically with the beginning of the first line of the poem. (In the printed version, the source may appear flush right.) See also 13.23–27.

2.20   *Footnotes and endnotes.* To take advantage of automatic renumbering, create notes that are linked to the text by using the footnote or endnote function on your word processor. For the printout, they must be double-spaced throughout. Unless your publisher requests otherwise, in the manuscript they may appear either as footnotes or as chapter or book endnotes (starting over at 1 for each chapter), regardless of how they are to appear in the published version. Avoid appending note references to chapter titles (see 1.48). Notes to tables should be numbered separately (see 2.28). For note form, see 14.19–55. For some caveats regarding source citation software, see 14.13.

2.21   *Glossaries and lists of abbreviations.* Each entry in a glossary or list of abbreviations should begin on a new line, capitalized only if the term is capitalized in the text. Separate each term from the definition that follows with a period, a colon, or an em dash. In a glossary, begin the definition with a capital letter, as if it were a new sentence; in a list of abbreviations, the expanded term should be capitalized or lowercased as it would be in text. Glossary entries need closing punctuation unless all definitions consist of incomplete sentences. Any term or abbreviation that is consistently italicized in the text (not just on first use) should also be italicized in the glossary or list of abbreviations. (Abbreviations of consistently italicized terms should generally themselves be italicized; see also

14.55.) Entries should be double-spaced and may be formatted in flush-and-hang style (see 2.22) or with ordinary first-line paragraph indents. Avoid multiple columns. (For an example of a glossary, see appendix B.) See also 1.43 and 1.60.

2.22   *Bibliographies and reference lists.* Although a bibliography or reference list will often appear in flush-and-hang (or hanging-indention) style in the published version (like the bibliography in this manual), you may either use the hanging-indention function on your word processor or format each entry like a normal paragraph with a first-line indent. Never use the Tab key to indent runover lines. As with all parts of your manuscript, use double line spacing. For capitalization, use of italics, and other matters of bibliographic style, see chapter 14. For some caveats regarding source citation software, see 14.13.

Illustrations and Tables

2.23   *Separate files for illustrations, captions, and tables.* Publishers usually prefer separate files for illustrations. Many publishers also prefer tables in separate files, but those created in the same application as the rest of your manuscript may not need to be; consult your publisher. The approximate placement of illustrations or tables submitted as separate files should be called out in the text, keeping in mind that the exact locations of figures in a manuscript will be determined during typesetting (see 2.27). Captions for all illustrations (as distinct from a list of illustrations following the table of contents; see 1.38) should be furnished in a separate file. For manuscripts of journal articles, consult the specific journal's instructions for authors. For a more detailed overview of illustrations and tables, see chapter 3.

2.24   *Prints of artwork versus scans.* Text figures that are to be reproduced by scanning a hard-copy original—such as paintings, maps, and photographic prints—should be furnished in whatever form the publisher requests. Publishers often prefer to do their own scans. Glossy prints must be clearly labeled, usually on the back of the print or on a self-sticking label, in a manner that does not impair their quality (see 3.16). For further discussion, see 3.15–20.

2.25   *Numbering illustrations.* Illustrations may be consecutively numbered, or, in scientific and technical books, heavily illustrated books, and books with chapters by different authors, double numeration may be used. In double numeration, provide the chapter number, followed by a period, followed by the figure number (e.g., fig. 1.1, 1.2, 1.3, . . . , 2.1, 2.2, 2.3, . . . , etc.). In the event a figure is dropped or added, double numeration will help simplify the work needed to renumber not just the illustrations but any applicable cross-references, especially in a heavily illustrated book. Illustrations are enumerated separately from tables. Plates to be grouped in a gallery are numbered separately from figures interspersed in the text (see 3.14). Even if numbers are not to appear with the illustrations in the published version, working numbers should be assigned for identification and should accompany the captions (see 3.13). For more details, see 3.8–14.

2.26   *Numbering tables.* Tables may be numbered consecutively throughout a book or, in a book with many tables or with chapters by different authors, double numeration may be used (e.g., table 1.1, 1.2, 1.3, . . . , 2.1, 2.2, 2.3, . . . , etc.). In a book with many tables, double numeration can simplify the task of renumbering in the event a table is dropped or added. Tables are enumerated separately from illustrations. Very simple tabular material (e.g., a two-column list) may be presented, unnumbered, along with the text. See also 3.51.

2.27   *Text references and callouts to tables and illustrations.* A *text reference* is addressed to the reader ("see table 5," or "fig. 3.2") and will appear in the published version. A *callout* is an instruction, which will not appear in the published work, telling where a table or an illustration is to appear. In the manuscript, a callout should be enclosed in angle brackets or some other delimiter and placed on a separate line following the paragraph in which the table or illustration is first referred to ("<table 5 here>"; "<fig. 3.2 here>") or, if a later location is preferable, where the table or illustration is to appear. Tables and such illustrations as graphs and diagrams require both a text reference and a placement callout, unless they are to be grouped in a section separate from the regular text. Photographs and maps—at least in printed books—do not always need to be referred to in the text but do need a placement callout if they are to appear with the text (see 3.8–14).

2.28   *Table notes and source notes.* Source notes appear at the foot of the table before any other notes. They are preceded by the word "Source" followed by a colon. Other notes to the table as a whole follow any source note and may be preceded by the word "Note" followed by a colon. Specific notes follow any other notes and must carry their own numbering (preferably letters; see 3.77), keyed to parts of the table. They must never be numbered along with the notes to the text. For a fuller discussion of notes to tables, see 3.74–78.

Cross-Checking

2.29   *Items to cross-check.* Before submitting a manuscript for publication, an author must cross-check all of its parts to avoid discrepancies. The following list includes major items to check:

- All titles and subtitles (introduction, parts, chapters, etc.) against table of contents
- Subheads against table of contents (if subheads are included there; see 1.37)
- Illustrations against their captions, text references, and callouts
- Illustration captions against list of illustrations
- Tables against their text references and callouts
- Table titles against list of tables
- All cross-references (see also 2.32)
- In an electronic work, all hyperlinks
- Notes against their text references
- Notes against bibliography
- Parenthetical text citations against reference list
- Abbreviations against list of abbreviations
- In a multiauthor work, authors' names in table of contents against chapter headings and list of contributors

2.30   *Checking quotations.* All quoted matter should be checked against the original source, for both content and citation, before a manuscript is submitted for publication. This authorial task is crucial because manuscript editors will not have access to all the sources that the author has used.

2.31   *Checking URLs.* Any URLs cited in a manuscript—including any mentioned in the text—need to be checked before a manuscript is submitted for publication. Those that no longer point to the intended source should be updated. By a similar token, authors should consider not including any URLs that seem potentially unstable or subject to change. See also 14.4–13.

2.32   *Checking cross-references.* All cross-references, whether to a chapter, a section, an appendix, or even a sentence of text, should be verified before a manuscript is submitted for publication. A chapter number or title may have been changed, or a passage deleted, after the original reference to it. Cross-references are best made to chapter or section numbers, which can be entered at the manuscript stage. (Keep in mind that references to whole chapters are often gratuitous and unhelpful; it's best to avoid peppering a manuscript with "see chapter 2 above" and "see chapter 4 below.") References to page numbers are generally discouraged because the pagination of a published work will not correspond to that of the manuscript, and the correct number will have to be supplied later in the process (usually by the author). Where absolutely necessary, use three bullets (e.g., "see p. • • •") to signal the need to supply the final page number.

Naming and Saving the Electronic Files

2.33   *Creating separate files.* For book-length projects, publishers may prefer to get separate electronic files for each of the various elements—front matter through table of contents, preface, chapters, appendixes, and so on (some of which will include embedded notes). It is recognized, however, that some authors will prefer to work in one file. Nonetheless, appropriately named separate files—especially for complex works—can help publishers get a sense of a book's component parts. Illustrations, which publishers handle separately from the text, should always be in separate files; tables created in an author's word-processing software may not need to be; see 2.23. Many journals specify that all elements of an article manuscript, including tables but excluding other illustrations, should be stored in a single file. Always consult your publisher's manuscript preparation guidelines before submitting a final manuscript.

2.34   *Naming files.* For books with more than a few parts, it may be helpful to choose file names that will line up in book order in an alphanumerically sorted directory. The names "chapter 01, Code as Consciousness," "chapter 02, Unmediated Scripts," and "chapter 03, Electricity as Messenger" will not only stay ordered together in a directory sorted alphanumerically by name (some operating systems will require the zeros to properly order more than nine numbered elements) but will also indicate the name or subject of each chapter—an additional organizational cue. File names should correspond more or less to the parts of the manuscript as listed in the table of contents. A complete list of all submitted files, including lists of illustrations or tables and any electronic-only elements, should accompany the manuscript. (In the hard copy the various divisions should be arranged in the order specified in the table of contents, which is not necessarily the order of the electronic directory.) Files for color illustrations may include the word *color* in their names, especially if black-and-white prints have also been submitted.

2.35   *Numbering manuscript pages.* Each page of a manuscript, whether electronic or hard copy, must be numbered. Manuscripts submitted as multiple files need not be numbered consecutively from page 1 through to the end of the book. Instead, to ensure that no two pages in the manuscript are numbered the same, descriptive page headers can be added next to the page numbers in each file (e.g., "Introduction: 1," "Introduction: 2," etc.; "chapter 1: 1," "chapter 1: 2," etc.). Arabic numerals may be used for the front matter even though these pages may take on roman numerals in the published work. The manuscript editor will indicate the appropriate roman numerals for the book designer (see 2.72). Manuscripts submitted as one file, on the other hand, can be numbered consecutively across the book starting with page 1. In a paper-only manuscript, pages added after the initial numbering may be numbered with *a* or *b* (e.g., 55, 55a, 55b).

2.36   *Embedded comments and revision marks.* Authors should delete any comments embedded in their electronic manuscripts *before* submitting them for publication. This includes any text formatted as "hidden" and any comments generated using the commenting feature in a word processor. Any outstanding queries should be addressed in a cover letter. Moreover, it is crucial that any revision marks (or "tracked changes") be removed before the manuscript is submitted—and that the final manuscript represent the very latest version. (Manuscript editors should always check for hidden text, comments, and revision marks and alert the author or publisher about any potential problems.)

2.37   *Backing up the final manuscript.* In addition to saving a separate electronic copy of each crucial stage of work on their manuscripts, authors are advised to save a backup copy of the version sent to the publisher for editing and publication. Prudence dictates keeping at least two copies for yourself (e.g., on a computer hard drive and on a disk or portable hard drive) and, if practical, uploading another copy to a trusted Internet storage vendor.

Preparing a Manuscript for a Multiauthor Book or Journal

2.38   *Volume editor's manuscript preparation responsibilities.* The specific responsibilities of the volume editor, contributors, and publisher (including manuscript editor) must be determined before a multiauthor manuscript is submitted. If there is more than one volume editor, the responsibilities of each must be spelled out. After ensuring that the contributors furnish their papers in a uniform style agreed to by all parties, the volume editor is usually responsible for the following:

- Getting manuscripts, including illustrations, from all contributors in a form acceptable to the publisher well before the date for submitting the volume

- Getting written permission from copyright owners to reproduce material in copyrighted works published elsewhere, illustrations taken from another work, and the like (see chapter 4)
- Editing each contribution for sense and checking references and other documentation for uniformity of style, then sending edited manuscripts to the contributors for their approval before the volume is submitted to the publisher (an activity distinct from the manuscript editing that will be done later by the publisher)
- Providing a list of contributors with their affiliations and brief biographical notes to be included in the volume
- Providing a title page, table of contents, and any necessary prefatory material
- Sending the complete manuscript to the publisher in a form acceptable for publication (having first made sure that the manuscript includes only the latest version of each contributor's chapter)
- Adhering to the publisher's schedule, ensuring that contributors do likewise, keeping track of the contributors' whereabouts at all stages of publication, and assuming the responsibilities of any contributor who cannot fulfill them

Most if not all of these responsibilities also apply to journal editors.

2.39 *Additional responsibilities of the volume editor.* Depending on the arrangement with the publisher, the volume editor may also be responsible for the following:

- Sending a publishing agreement (provided by the publisher) to each contributor and returning the agreements, fully executed, to the publisher (see 4.53)
- Checking the edited manuscript and responding to all queries, or distributing the edited manuscript to the contributors and checking it after their review to ensure that all queries have been answered
- Proofreading the final version of the volume or delegating proofreading to the contributors and then checking their corrections
- Preparing the index

Compiling a Manuscript from Previously Published Material

2.40 *Preparing previously published material.* Manuscripts for an anthology or other work comprising previously published material are said to have been *compiled*. If the compiler retypes or scans the original source (i.e., using character-recognition software), the resulting text should be incorporated into a manuscript that follows the formatting requirements outlined in paragraphs 2.7–22. Such manuscripts must be proofread word for word against the original material *before* the final manuscript is submitted to the publisher for editing; in addition, publishers may request copies of the originals. If the original material is submitted on paper only, make sure the material is entirely legible (publishers may prefer legible single-sided photocopies to pages from the original source). Unless there is ample space to insert corrections above the printed lines, any corrections should be written in the margins (see 2.116–29). See also 4.101.

2.41 *Permissible changes to published material.* The compiler of previously published material may make the following changes to the published material without editorial comment: notes may be renumbered; cross-references to parts of the original work that are no longer relevant may be deleted; obvious typographical errors and inadvertent grammatical slips may be silently corrected. See also 13.7–8. If wholesale changes have been made—for example, in spelling or capitalization conventions or notes style—the compiler should note such changes in a preface or elsewhere. For deletions indicated by ellipsis points, see 13.48–56.

2.42 *Footnotes or endnotes in previously published material.* Footnotes that appear as such in the original pages may be presented as footnotes or endnotes in the published version. If a compiler's or volume editor's notes are being added along with the original footnotes or endnotes, the new notes should be intermingled with but distinguished from the original notes (see 14.46); if the original material is being submitted to the publisher on paper only, it may be preferable to produce a separate electronic document for the notes.

2.43 *Source notes for previously published material.* Each selection of previously published material should be accompanied by either a headnote (a brief introduction preceding the selection) or, more commonly, an unnumbered footnote on the first page of text, giving the source (see 14.49), the name of the copyright owner if the selection is in copyright (see chapter 4, esp. 4.2–49), and the original title if it has been changed. If a selection has previously appeared in various places and different versions, the source note need not give the entire publishing history but must state which version is being reprinted.

2.44 *Reproducing previously published illustrations.* Compilers should contact their publisher about how to obtain illustrations from previously published material in a format suitable for printing. Photocopies of illustrations are not acceptable for reproduction. The compiler should procure glossy prints or the original publisher's scans. If these are unavailable, it may be possible to reproduce an illustration from the original publication; consult your publisher.

Manuscript Editing

Principles of Manuscript Editing

2.45 *Manuscript editing as opposed to developmental editing.* Manuscript editing, also called copyediting or line editing, requires attention to every word and mark of punctuation in a manuscript, a thorough knowledge of the style to be followed, and the ability to make quick, logical, and defensible decisions. It is undertaken by the publisher when a manuscript has been accepted for publication. It may include both mechanical editing (see 2.46) and substantive editing (see 2.47). It is distinct from developmental editing (not discussed in this manual), which more directly shapes the content of a work, the way material should be presented, the need for more or less documentation and how it should be handled, and so on. Since editing of this kind may involve total rewriting or reorganization of a work, it should be done—if needed—*before* manuscript editing begins. For more on developmental editing, consult Scott Norton's *Developmental Editing: A Handbook for Freelancers, Authors, and Publishers* (bibliog. 2.1).

2.46 *Mechanical editing.* Mechanical editing involves the consistent application of a particular style to a written work—including text and documentation and any tables and illustrations. The central focus of part 2 in this manual, *style* is used here to refer to rules related to capitalization, spelling, hyphenation, and abbreviations; punctuation, including ellipsis points, parentheses, and quotation marks; and the way numbers are treated. Mechanical editing also includes attention to grammar, syntax, and usage. The rules set forth in a style manual like this one may be supplemented by a publisher's house style or the style of a particular discipline. Journal editors in particular follow a journal's established style, augmented by additional resources specific to the subject area. Books in a series or multivolume works should all follow one style consistently, as should separately authored chapters in a multiauthor book. The style of any work, as well as occasional deviations from it, must be determined by author, editor, and publisher before editing begins. For substantive editing, see 2.47, 2.48. See also 2.52.

2.47 *Substantive editing.* Substantive editing deals with the organization and presentation of content. It involves rewriting to improve style or to eliminate ambiguity, reorganizing or tightening, recasting tables, and other remedial activities. (It should not be confused with developmental editing, a more drastic process; see 2.45.) In general, no substantive editing should be undertaken without agreement between publisher and editor, especially for book-length works; if major substantive work is needed, the author should be consulted and perhaps invited to approve a sample before the editing proceeds. A journal's manuscript editors, however, working on rigid schedules, may need to do substantive editing without prior consultation with authors if problems of organization, presentation, and verbal expression have not been addressed at earlier stages.

2.48   *Discretion in substantive editing.* A light editorial hand is nearly always more effective than a heavy one. An experienced editor will recognize and not tamper with unusual figures of speech or idiomatic usage and will know when to make an editorial change and when simply to suggest it, whether to delete a repetition or an unnecessary recapitulation or simply to point it out to the author, and how to suggest tactfully that an expression may be inappropriate. An author's own style should be respected, whether flamboyant or pedestrian. All manuscript editors should be aware of any requirements of house style that are essential to the publisher—for example, those covering bias-free language (see 5.221–30). For communicating with the author and querying, see 2.65–69.

2.49   *Estimating editing time.* Estimates for how long the job of manuscript editing should take—a figure generally determined by the publisher and agreed to by the manuscript editor—usually start with the length of the manuscript. Because of inevitable variations in typefaces and margins and other formatting characteristics from one manuscript to another, the length is best determined by a word count rather than a page count (though a word count can be derived from a page count for paper-only manuscripts). A 100,000-word book manuscript, edited by an experienced editor, might take seventy-five to one hundred hours of work before being sent to the author, plus ten to twenty additional hours after the author's review. This rough estimate may need to be adjusted to take into account any complexities in the text or documentation, the presence and characteristics of any tables and illustrations, and the degree of electronic formatting and markup that an editor will need to remove or impose (see 2.77). If in doubt, edit a small sample to serve as the basis of an estimate. An additional factor is of course the publication schedule, which will determine how many days are available for the editing stage. Also pertinent is information about the author's availability to review the edited manuscript, amenability to being edited, propensity to revise, and so forth.

2.50   *Stages of editing.* Editors usually go through a manuscript three times—once to do the initial editing, easily the longest stage; a second time to review, refine, and sometimes correct the editing; and a third time after the author's review (see 2.69). Editors working on electronic manuscripts may also be required to perform an initial, systematic cleanup (see 2.77)—though a publisher's manuscript editing or production department may perform such a cleanup before turning a manuscript over to an editor. Careful editors begin the initial editing stage—sometimes in conjunction with the electronic cleanup—by looking through the entire document to assess the nature and scope of the work that will be required, to identify any matters that should be clarified with the author before editing begins, and to reduce the number of surprises that could cause delays if discovered later in the process. Some edit each element in a work (text, notes, tables, bibliography, etc.) separately to help attain consistency; others edit the apparatus, or a part of it, along with the text. Whatever the procedure, all elements must be compared to ensure that the notes match their text references and correspond in turn to the entries in the bibliography or reference list, the tables correspond to any discussion of them in the text, and so on.

2.51 *Choosing a dictionary and other reference works.* A good dictionary is essential. Chicago recommends *Webster's Third New International Dictionary* and the latest edition of its chief abridgment, *Merriam-Webster's Collegiate Dictionary*; both are available in print and online (see bibliog. 3.1). Editors also need reference works that furnish reliable spellings and identifications of persons, places, historical events, technical terminology, and the like. If a system of documentation other than Chicago is to be used, the applicable style manual should be at hand (see bibliog. 1.1). For some basic reference works, see section 4 of the bibliography. For a complete discussion of names and terms, see chapter 8.

2.52 *Keeping a style sheet.* To ensure consistency, for each manuscript the editor must keep an alphabetical list of words or terms to be capitalized, italicized, hyphenated, spelled, or otherwise treated in any way unique to the manuscript. Changes that are made simply for consistency with house style need not be noted on the style sheet. It is enough to note, for example, "In all other respects, Chicago style is followed." (For paper-only manuscripts it is useful to add the page number of the first occurrence of each item.) Special punctuation, unusual diacritics, and other items should also be noted on the style sheet. Not only the author but also the publisher may need to refer to the style sheet at various stages of editing and production. See figure 2.3.

2.53 *Fact-checking.* In book publishing, the author is finally responsible for the accuracy of a work; most book publishers do not perform fact-checking in any systematic way or expect it of their manuscript editors unless spe-

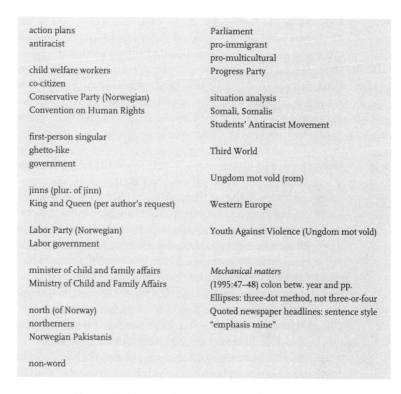

action plans	Parliament
antiracist	pro-immigrant
	pro-multicultural
child welfare workers	Progress Party
co-citizen	
Conservative Party (Norwegian)	situation analysis
Convention on Human Rights	Somali, Somalis
	Students' Antiracist Movement
first-person singular	
ghetto-like	Third World
government	
	Ungdom mot vold (rom)
jinns (plur. of jinn)	
King and Queen (per author's request)	Western Europe
Labor Party (Norwegian)	Youth Against Violence (Ungdom mot vold)
Labor government	
minister of child and family affairs	*Mechanical matters*
Ministry of Child and Family Affairs	(1995:47–48) colon betw. year and pp.
	Ellipses: three-dot method, not three-or-four
north (of Norway)	Quoted newspaper headlines: sentence style
northerners	"emphasis mine"
Norwegian Pakistanis	
non-word	

FIGURE 2.3. Manuscript editor's style sheet. When prepared for a pencil-edited manuscript, the style sheet usually indicates the page number for the first appearance of each item.

cifically agreed upon up front. Nonetheless, obvious errors, including errors in mathematical calculations, should always be pointed out to the author, and questionable proper names, bibliographic references, and the like should be checked and any apparent irregularities queried. Editors need to be systematic about what they fact-check to avoid being distracted from the work at hand. It will sometimes be efficient to point out and correct obvious errors of fact that can be easily double-checked against reliable sources. For anything beyond that, however, fact-checking should be limited to what is needed to form an effective and judicious query to the author (see 2.66).

Editing Specific Parts of a Manuscript

2.54   *Editing front matter.* An editor should check any half title, title page, table of contents, and list of illustrations against the text and captions and against any applicable documentation included with the manuscript; discrepancies should be queried. If subheads are to be dropped from the table of contents, the author should be consulted (see 1.37). The editor should insert comments on the manuscript pages to indicate where particular elements are to begin (e.g., "dedication, p. v") and which pages are to remain blank (e.g., "page ii blank"). For the sequence and form of front matter for books, see 1.16–44; for items always or sometimes required on the copyright page, see 1.19–34.

2.55 *Editing part titles and chapter or article titles.* The editor of a book manuscript should ensure that part and chapter titles, and their subtitles if any, are consistent with the text in spelling, hyphenation, and italics. Part and chapter titles must be checked against the table of contents, and any discrepancy must be queried. Chicago recommends that all titles be in headline style unless a work is part of a series or journal that follows some other capitalization style (see 8.157). All elements should be tagged or otherwise identified according to the publisher's requirements (for electronic manuscripts, see 2.78–80; for paper manuscripts, see 2.96).

2.56 *Editing subheads.* Subheads should be checked for consistency with the text in spelling, hyphenation, and italics, and for parallel structure and tone. If there is more than one level of subhead, the hierarchy needs to be checked for sense and each level clearly tagged or otherwise labeled (for electronic manuscripts, see 2.78–80; for paper manuscripts, see 2.96). If there are more than three levels of subhead, determine whether the lowest level can be eliminated. For electronic manuscripts, it may be wise to tag the different subhead levels based on the author's typographic distinctions at the outset, lest these distinctions be eliminated by any cleanup routine (see 2.77). If subheads are to appear in the table of contents, they must be cross-checked for consistency. Chicago recommends that all subheads be in headline style unless a work is part of a series or journal that follows some other capitalization style (see 8.157). But if an author has consistently used sentence style for subheads (see 8.156), that style should not be altered without consultation with the author and publisher, since it may be more appropriate in a particular work. Where subheads consist of full sentences, sentence-style capitalization is preferable.

2.57 *Editing cross-references.* All references to tables, figures, appendixes, bibliographies, or other parts of a work should be checked by the manuscript editor. If the author, for example, mentions a statistic for 2008 and refers readers to table 4, which gives statistics only through 2007, the editor must point out the discrepancy. Place-names on a map that illustrate the text must be spelled as in the text. Cross-references to specific pages—

the numbering of which is subject to change in the published version—
should be minimized or eliminated. See also 2.32.

2.58   *Editing quotations and previously published material.* Aside from adjusting
quotation marks and ellipsis points to conform to house style (see 13.7–8),
the editor must do nothing to quoted material unless the author is trans-
lating it from another language (or modernizing it), in which case it may
be lightly edited (see 13.78). Misspelled words and apparent transcription
errors should be queried. An author who appears to have been careless
in transcribing should be asked to check all quotations for accuracy, including punctuation. The editor should ensure that sources are given for
all quoted material, whether following the quotation or in a note. In editing previously published material, especially if it has been abridged, the
editor should read for sense to ensure that nothing is out of order or has
been inadvertently omitted. Discrepancies should be queried. If the previously published material has been provided on paper only, any ambiguous end-of-line hyphens should be clarified (see 2.93). For field notes,
see 13.47. See also 2.40.

2.59   *Editing notes.* Each note must be checked against the text to ensure that
its text reference is correct and in the right place and that any terms used
in the note are treated the same way as in the text. When notes are to be
printed as footnotes, the author may be asked to shorten an excessively
long note or to incorporate some of the note into the text. Lists, tables,
and figures should be placed not in footnotes but in the text or in an appendix. Manuscript editors may sometimes request an additional note
to accommodate a needed source or citation. More frequently, in consultation with the author, they will combine notes or delete unneeded
ones. See 14.51–55. An editor working on paper must take special care in
renumbering notes. Editors working on-screen may need to make sure
that citations in the notes are free of any underlying codes generated by
the author in creating or organizing them (see 14.13).

2.60   *Editing note citations, bibliographies, and reference lists.* Citations in notes,
bibliographies, and reference lists must be carefully checked for documentation style (chapters 14 and 15; but see 2.61). Further, every subsequent reference to a work previously cited in the text or in a note must
be given in the same form as the first reference or in the same shortened form (see 14.24–31). In a work containing a bibliography as well as
notes, each citation in the notes should be checked against the bibliography and any discrepancy resolved or, if necessary, queried in both contexts so that the author can easily compare them (see 2.66). A bibliography need not include every work cited in the notes and may properly

include some entries that are not cited. If a reference list is used, the editor will have checked all text citations against the list while editing the text and will have queried or resolved discrepancies. Bibliographies and reference lists should be checked for alphabetical order and, where applicable, for chronological order. For bibliographies, see 14.56–67; for reference lists and text citations, see 15.10–30. Many editors find it helpful to edit the bibliography or reference list before the text and notes. Editors working on-screen may need to make sure that the source citations and related text are free of any underlying codes generated by the author in creating or organizing them (see 14.13).

2.61   *Flexibility in citation style.* Imposing house style on notes prepared in another style can be immensely time-consuming and, if the existing form is consistent and clear to the reader, is often unnecessary. This is especially true of books, many of which are intended to stand alone. Before making sweeping changes, the manuscript editor should consult with the author or the publisher or both. In journal editing, on the other hand, such flexibility is generally not acceptable. This has become more true in the era of electronic publication; because citations may be linked to an outside database, absolute consistency of format is essential.

2.62   *Editing tables.* Tables are usually best edited together, as a group, to ensure consistent style and presentation. Tables should also be checked for consistent numbering and correspondence with the text—including text references and placement callouts (see 2.27). For specific guidelines on editing tables, see 3.79–85.

2.63   *Checking illustrations and their placement and editing captions.* Wording on a diagram or chart should conform to the spelling and capitalization used in the caption or the text. (If the wording on the illustration cannot be changed, it is sometimes acceptable to adjust the spelling in the caption or text.) Captions must conform to the style of the text. Source information should be edited in consultation with the publisher and in conformance with any letters of permission. (If permissions are outstanding, the publisher, not the editor, should take up the matter with the author.) Illustrations may be added, dropped, or renumbered during editing; therefore, it is essential to make a final check of all illustrations against their text references and callouts and against the captions and list of illustrations to be sure that they match and that the illustrations show what they say they do. For details on preparing illustrations and captions, see 3.3–45. For checking credits, see 3.28–36.

2.64   *Editing indexes.* The schedule for editing an index—which, if it depends on page number locators rather than paragraph numbers, is almost never prepared before book or journal pages have been composed—must usually correspond to the schedule for reviewing corrections to proofs. For a more detailed discussion, including an index-editing checklist, see 16.132–34.

Communicating with Authors

2.65   *Establishing early contact with authors.* Editors of book-length works are urged to contact their authors early on, after an initial review of the manuscript. This is especially important if an editor has questions or plans to make significant changes that, in the event the author proves not to be amenable, might take time and effort to undo. Likewise, to expedite production, a journal's manuscript editors may notify authors of systematic changes early in the game. Most authors are content to submit to a house style; those who are not may be willing to compromise. Unless usage is determined by journal or series style, the author's wishes should generally be respected. For a manuscript that requires extensive changes, it may be wise, if the schedule allows, to send a sample of the editing for the author's approval before proceeding (see 2.47).

2.66   *Writing author comments and queries.* Editors may generally impose a consistent style and correct errors without further comment—assuming these changes are apparent on the edited manuscript. Corrections to less obvious problems may warrant a comment. Comments should be concise, and they should avoid sounding casual, pedantic, condescending, or indignant; often, a simple "OK?" is enough. Comments that are not answerable by a yes or a no may be more specific: "Do you mean X or Y?" Examples of instances in which an editor might comment or query include the following:

- To note, on an electronic manuscript, that a particular global change has been corrected silently after the first instance
- To point out a discrepancy, as between two spellings in a name, or between a source cited differently in the notes than in the bibliography
- To point out an apparent omission, such as a missing quotation mark or a missing source citation
- To point out a possible error in a quotation
- To point out repetition (e.g., "Repetition intentional?" or "Rephrased to avoid repetition; OK?")

- To ask for verification, as of a name or term whose spelling cannot be easily verified
- To ask for clarification where the text is ambiguous or garbled
- To point to the sources an editor has consulted in correcting errors of fact (but see 2.53)

For the mechanics of entering queries on a manuscript, see 2.83 (for electronic manuscripts) and 2.89 (for paper manuscripts).

2.67   *Writing a cover letter to the author.* The letter sent to the author with the edited manuscript, or sometimes separately, should include some or all of the following items (unless already communicated):

- An explanation of the nature and scope of the editing—for example, adjustment of spelling and punctuation to conform to house style, occasional rephrasing for clarity or to eliminate inadvertent repetition, and so forth
- If the editing has been shown, an indication of how this has been done—that is, with change-tracking (redlining) software (see 2.81) or with pencil and paper—and brief instructions for interpreting the marks
- Instructions as to how the author should respond to queries, veto any unwanted editing, and make any further adjustments to the edited manuscript (see 2.84, 2.88)
- A warning that the author's review of the edited manuscript constitutes the last opportunity to make any substantive changes, additions, or deletions and that quoted matter and citations should be checked if necessary
- A reminder to review the editing carefully, since even editors are fallible, and the correction of any errors missed in editing and not caught until proofs may be deemed "author's alterations" and charged to the author (see 2.132)
- A reminder to retain a copy of the reviewed and corrected manuscript (to refer to at the proofreading stage)
- The deadline for return of the edited copy
- A brief discussion about the index, if any—whether the author is to prepare it, whether instructions are needed (see chapter 16), or whether a freelance indexer is to be engaged at the author's expense
- A request for confirmation of the author's contact information for the rest of the publishing process

2.68   *Sending the edited manuscript to the author.* An electronically edited book manuscript—because of its length and, often, its complexity—may be sent to the author as hard copy (or, alternatively, as a PDF that the author is asked to print out). The author reads and marks this printout as necessary, then returns it to the editor, who incorporates the author's marks into the electronic manuscript. The author may instead review the electronic manuscript (using the same software that the editor has used)—a procedure that saves printing and shipping costs. An editor working with an author in this manner needs to have procedures in place for making sure the author does not make any undocumented changes—inadvertently or otherwise. A pencil-edited manuscript should be photocopied before being sent to the author; likewise, authors are advised to photocopy paper manuscripts with their handwritten comments before sending them back to the editor. Any manuscript that has been pencil edited—as well as electronically edited printouts that have been marked up by hand—is one of a kind; if lost, the work must be done over.

2.69   *Checking the author's final changes.* When the manuscript comes back from the author, the editor goes through it once again to see what the author has done, checking that all queries have been answered and editing any new material. Except for style adjustments, the author's version should prevail; if that version is unacceptable for any reason, a compromise should be sought. As a part of this process, the editor updates the electronic files or, if a manuscript is to be updated or typeset from a pencil-edited paper copy, clarifies or retypes the new material and crosses out the queries.

Preparing a Final Manuscript for Production

2.70   *Ensuring correct markup.* From the standpoint of production, a manuscript consists of two levels of information: content and structure. The content generally includes all the text and any figures that are to appear in the published book or article. The structure describes the manuscript's component parts—such as heads and subheads, text, extracts, footnote reference numbers and footnotes, illustrations and tables, and so forth. These parts are identified on the manuscript by electronic or handwritten codes or instructions (for electronic manuscripts, see 2.78–80; for paper manuscripts, see 2.96). When a manuscript is typeset—that is, when book or article pages or full-text HTML is produced from the manuscript— each identified element is formatted or displayed according to specifications in a design template (which are often encoded into an electronic style sheet). The design specifies the typeface, type size, color, and line spacing for each element in the text and any tables, as well as sizing and placement parameters for figures. Final manuscripts must therefore be reviewed to make sure markup has been consistently and correctly applied and that it corresponds to the elements in the design template. For a fuller discussion of markup and design, see appendix A.

2.71 *Type specifications and hand markup.* In the rare event that no designer's layout or list of specifications is available, an editor may need to mark up the hard copy with appropriate type specifications at the first occurrence of the element they apply to. For example, in the margin next to the first block of regular text, "text: 10/12 Times Roman × 26" (meaning 10-point type with 12-point leading, each line 26 picas wide); and next to the first extract, "extract: 9/11 Times Roman; indent 2 pi from left." As long as all extracts have been coded "ext," all first-level subheads "A," and so forth, markup can be kept to a minimum. For more on hand markup, see 2.87–96.

2.72 *Ensuring correct pagination.* Editors should indicate on the manuscript where roman page numbers end and arabic numbers begin—whether or not the number will actually appear (i.e., whether the folio is to be "expressed" or "blind"; see 1.45). Furthermore, if there is a part title and the first chapter begins on page 3, "arabic p. 3" should be specified at the chapter opening. The editor should also specify whether subsequent elements are to begin on a recto or on a verso (see 1.4). Repagination of typeset, printed books is expensive; the editor should check that all elements—in the front matter, the text, and the back matter—are in their correct order and that the order is reflected in the table of contents. For journals, see 1.76.

2.73 *Preparing running heads.* The editor usually provides a list of copy for running heads (or feet) (see 1.9–15). The list must clearly indicate which heads are to appear on versos (left-hand pages) and which on rectos (right-hand pages). To fit on a single line, usually containing the page number as well, a chapter or article title may have to be shortened for a running head but must include the key terms in the title. (In some cases, the keywords will be in the chapter subtitle.) The author's approval may be needed; if possible, the editor should send the running-head copy to the author along with the edited manuscript. In shortened foreign-language titles, no word may be omitted that governs the case ending of another word in the running head. Running-head copy normally accompanies the manuscript to the typesetter and should be included with the other electronic files. If the running heads are to reflect the content of particular pages (rather than chapters or sections), the exact copy must be determined after (or as) the pages are typeset. For example, running heads to notes that include page ranges can be determined only from the typeset pages (see 1.14). These are typically indicated by the publisher on the first proofreading copy.

2.74 *A production checklist.* Manuscripts that are ready to be typeset are usually accompanied by a checklist of vital statistics that includes information about the project and how it is to be produced. Such a checklist, especially necessary for one-of-a-kind book-length works, might consist of the following information:

- Name of author(s) and title of work
- A list of component parts of the project: electronic files, printout, illustrations, and so forth
- An indication of the software used to prepare the final manuscript and a list of file names
- An indication of how the electronic files have been coded for typesetting, a list of codes, and any special instructions, including a list of any special characters or fonts
- A list of any material that is still to come
- An indication of how notes are to be set—for example, as footnotes or chapter endnotes or endnotes to the book
- A list of elements to be included in the front matter, the text, and the end matter, and an indication of which elements must start recto (see 1.4)
- For book-length manuscripts, an indication of how many paper sets of proofs should be produced, if any

The Mechanics of Electronic Editing

2.75 *Making backup copies.* It is best to back up a manuscript in stages by saving separate copies of each significant version. The author's original, unedited copy should be archived (i.e., saved without further changes), as should every significant stage of the editing process. Some editors make daily backups and weekly sequential backups—so that an earlier stage of the editing can be consulted if necessary. Each major stage should be saved with a different name (e.g., by appending A, B, C, etc., or something more descriptive, to the file names) and in a different directory (or folder), and care should be taken to avoid saving over—or inadvertently working on—an earlier version of a file. During editing, open documents should be saved frequently. Finally, it may be wise, as an extra precaution, to send backup copies to an offsite server.

2.76 *Preparing to make a clean, unedited copy.* Some publishers provide manuscript editors with a cleaned-up version of the author's electronic file(s)—converted (if necessary), formatted (including, in some cases, electronic markup), and ready to edit, usually in a specific word-processing program or specialized text-editing environment. (Publishers may instead give editors hard copy only, updating the electronic files from the pencil-edited copy as part of the production process; for paper editing, see 2.87–96.) Many editors, however, are required to clean up and format the author's electronic files themselves. All editors working on electronic files should have more than a passing familiarity with the software they are required to use. Even standard, "out of the box" word-processing programs have become powerful text editors; at the very least, it is important to learn about macros (short for *macroinstructions*) and to become thoroughly versed in search-and-replace options (including the use of pattern matching or "wildcards"), which, used properly and with care, can save many steps. A good place to begin is with a software's "help" documentation. More advanced users will customize their software—sometimes with the help of sets of macros written especially for editors by third-party companies.

2.77   *Cleaning up electronic files.* Before editing the manuscript, the editor must be certain that the files represent the author's latest version (the presence of embedded revision marks may be a sign that this is not the case; see 2.36). The next step is to get the electronic files ready to edit—if the publisher has not done this already. The following checklist suggests a set of steps that can be adapted as necessary to become part of an editor's detailed electronic manuscript cleanup routine. Not all manuscripts will require each step, and the suggested order need not be adhered to. Moreover, though many editors will want to automate at least some of these steps and perform them up front, most of the checklist can also be accomplished manually—that is, considered case by case, as part of the first read-through (see 2.50). Indeed, some of these steps will not lend themselves to wholesale transformation without first weighing the exceptions. (The value of performing this checklist up front is that any exceptions not considered can be fixed later, in the first read-through. Nonetheless, beware of unintended consequences, and always review—and be prepared to undo—any global change before saving a permanent version of a file.) Finally, this checklist should be modified as needed to accord not only with the requirements of a specific manuscript but also with those of the publisher. In general, automatic redlining should be turned *off* during these steps (see 2.81).

1. Convert files for use in the editing software required by the publisher, if necessary.
2. If necessary, change the language settings of the manuscript and any subdocuments (e.g., from British English to American English, or vice versa). This will ensure, among other things, that the main dictionary gives appropriate suggestions.
3. For book-length works, which may arrive as a directory (or folder) of separate

files for each chapter and other components, assembling the text into a single electronic file can save a significant amount of time. (Care must be taken to produce a complete manuscript, in the proper order and with no inadvertent deletions; always double-check the beginning and ending of each component and any notes thereto both when combining multiple files and when breaking a single file into smaller components.) Another option is to use macros that work across multiple files in a single directory.

4. Scroll through the whole manuscript (with the editing software set to display formatting and any markup—including marks for such "invisible" elements as spaces and hard returns), looking for and fixing any obvious conversion errors (e.g., with special characters) and formatting problems (e.g., hard returns in the middle of a paragraph), with reference to the original manuscript as necessary.

5. Identify any graphic elements and tables and handle appropriately—for example, moving figures or tables to separate files (see 2.23, 2.27).

6. Apply tags or other codes, as required, to any elements that are easy to identify at the outset (such as chapter titles, subheads, epigraphs, text extracts, poetry and stanza breaks, intentional instances of extra line space that may require an ornament or other device, etc.) but whose visual cues may be lost as the text is formatted. See also 2.78–80.

7. Delete or fix extraneous spaces and tabs, including instances of two or more consecutive spaces (between sentences or anywhere else) or spaces or tabs at the ends of paragraphs. Multiple spaces used to create first-line paragraph and other indents should be replaced either with tabs or with software-defined indents (be consistent).

8. Change instances of multiple hard returns to single hard returns.

9. Change underlining to italics. Some underlining, however, may be intended to represent true underscore—in, for example, a collection that transcribes handwritten letters; this should be preserved, with a note to the publisher explaining the exception. See also 6.2.

10. Fix quotation marks and apostrophes; make sure that apostrophes at the beginning of words are correct (e.g., 'em *not* 'em for "them"). But first determine, as applicable, that left and right single quotation marks have not been used by the author to stand in for breathing marks or other orthographic devices in transliterated languages (see chapter 11). See also 6.112, 6.114.

11. Fix commas and periods relative to quotation marks (see table 6.1).

12. Regularize em dashes and ellipses. For proper use of em dashes, see 6.82–89. For ellipses, see 13.48–56.

13. Replace hyphens between numerals with en dashes as appropriate. If you are using a macro to do this, it may be more efficient to let the macro run and to fix or add any exceptions during the first editing pass. For proper use of en dashes, see 6.78–81.

14. Convert footnotes to endnotes, or vice versa.

15. Delete any optional or conditional hyphens (i.e., software-dependent hyphens that allow words to break across the end of a line whether or not the hyphenation feature is turned on). Most word processors will allow you to search for these.

16. Find any lowercase els used as ones and any ohs (capital or lowercase) used as zeros—or vice versa—and fix. This can be done by using pattern matching to search for two-character combinations containing either an el or an oh next to an expression that will find any numeral.

17. Fix any other global inconsistencies that might be amenable to pattern-matching strategies. For example, in a bibliography in which two- or three-letter initials in names have been closed up, you can search for and evaluate capital letter combinations and replace as necessary with the same combination plus a space (e.g., changing E.B. White to E. B. White).

18. Adjust line spacing, font, and margins as desired.

As a final step—assuming these steps have been applied before editing—save a backup copy of the resulting clean, unedited manuscript.

2.78 *Generic markup for electronic manuscripts.* Each element of a manuscript—chapter display, subheads, text, prose extracts, poetry, notes, captions, and so forth—must be identified using consistent markup. A common way of doing this is with generic codes modeled on the descriptive identifiers used on pencil-edited manuscripts (see 2.96). Generic codes should be enclosed in angle brackets (< >), curly brackets ({ }), or some other delimiters such that they can be systematically identified and replaced for publication by formal typesetting codes. (This generic application of delimiters must not be mistaken for the tags used in formal markup languages such as XML.) Except for codes meant to be replaced with a character or string of characters, they are usually applied at the beginning and end of each element to which they apply. Publishers differ not only in what codes they recommend but also in what elements they code. Some require that every element be coded, including body text; others regard body text as a default. Most do not require codes for character-level formatting (e.g., italics, small capitals, boldface) because a word-processing software's built-in formatting codes can be manipulated as necessary. Editors may need to invent codes for unusual elements. Consistency and accuracy are crucial. Moreover, editors must supply a complete list of codes with the manuscript. Some sample codes are as follows:

<cn> . . . </cn>	chapter number
<ct> . . . </ct>	chapter title
<a> . . . </a>	first-level subhead (A-head)
<b> . . . </b>	second-level subhead (B-head)

`<ext> . . . </ext>`	block quotation (prose extract)
`<po> . . . </po>`	poetry extract
`<note-a> . . . </note-a>`	first-level subhead in endnotes section
`<tdotb>`	t with dot below (i.e., when the Unicode character for ṭ is not available in the font being used to prepare the manuscript; see 11.2)
`<! . . . !>`	instruction to the typesetter—for example, to consult hard copy or page image for proper alignment or other formatting

The end tags—those that include a forward slash (/) and that indicate the end of a coded element—may be unnecessary for elements that consist of an entire paragraph. Consult the publisher's or typesetter's requirements. (For using a word processor's built-in styles, see 2.79; for formal markup languages such as XML, see 2.80.)

2.79 *Software-generated styles.* Many word-processing programs allow users to apply named styles to the elements in a manuscript instead of, or in addition to, generic codes. Each style carries a unique name (included with the software or defined by the user) and is applied either at the paragraph level or at the character level, usually from a menu. (A "paragraph" is any string of text that follows a hard return and ends with a hard return.) Each paragraph style should have a descriptive name (e.g., "Chapter number," "Chapter title," "First-level subhead," "Second-level subhead," "Body text," "Extract"). On the other hand, it is usually unnecessary to define styles at the character level: a word processor's built-in formatting options for italics, boldface, and so forth can be used instead. Type size, line spacing, and other formatting options can be defined for each paragraph style as desired; it is helpful to be able to distinguish visually, for example, between different levels of subheads. On the other hand, accuracy and consistency in applying styles is more important than any formatting because the styles will eventually be mapped to a design template for the published work. If there are any text elements that do not lend themselves easily to styles, it may be necessary to combine styles and generic codes with instructions or messages to the typesetter. A list of styles and any generic codes should always accompany the manuscript.

2.80 *Formal markup languages.* Some manuscripts, especially those that will be published in electronic as well as printed form, may be written or edited in or converted to a formal markup language such as XML (extensible markup language). In this type of markup, each element, including the document as a whole, is identified by a pair of opening and closing tags according to the rules of the particular markup language. Tags are "nested"; for example, the body of the document, enclosed between an opening and a closing "body" tag, will include all sections and subsections of the document, with each of those parts also enclosed between an opening and a closing tag that identify the element and its place in the hierarchy. The names of larger elements are typically used to indicate what the elements are rather than how they are to be presented; this practice streamlines subsequent presentation of the document in various forms. Smaller portions of text may be marked according to how they are to be presented (e.g., in italic type), though it is often better to mark such text instead according to the intent of the presentation (e.g., emphasis). If editing takes place after conversion to a formal markup language, the editor can help to ensure that the tags have been applied correctly, usually with the help of tools designed to identify certain types of errors. For an extended discussion of formal markup languages, including XML, see appendix A.

2.81   *Tracking and showing changes (redlining).* To show their work and thus facilitate the author's review, many editors use the change-tracking feature available in some word processors and in some more specialized text-editing environments to produce what is sometimes referred to as a redlined version (a name that invokes, in another medium, the editor's red pencil). Depending on the software and a user's or publisher's preferences, material that has been changed—added, deleted, moved, reformatted—may appear in a variety of ways (see fig. 2.4). Added material, for example, may appear in red, underlined or double-underlined, shaded, or boldface—or some consistent combination thereof. Deleted material may appear in a different color and be struck through, singly or doubly. (Care must be taken, however, that all editing marks remain legible on a black-and-white printout.) The editor may use a word processor's commenting function to make queries to the author (see 2.83). Whether all the editing, mechanical as well as substantive, is shown depends on a number of factors, including the editor's and publisher's preferences. Some editors, for example, will prefer to alert the author to global changes (such as capitalization of a certain term) the first time each such change is made and to show only changes the author must approve individually. Certain adjustments should almost never be shown—for example, changes to margins or global changes to directional or "smart" quotation marks. In general, most of the things listed on the cleanup checklist (see 2.77) may be done silently. If an element such as a bibliography has been heavily edited, the editor may send a clean version of that element for the author to approve, as well as a version showing the edits for reference. If changes are not shown, the editor must let the author know what has been done to the manuscript (see 2.67).

<ct>How an Editor ~~m~~Marks a~~n Electronic~~ Manuscript</ct>

Editing an electronic manuscript is a more straightforward process than editing on paper. One could say it's ~~a~~ binary ~~process~~; most ~~markup~~ "redlining" is a matter of indicating one of two things: delete or add. The trick is showing an author what you've done ~~to an author~~ and communicating stylistic instructions to the compositor.

<a>~~Specific Marks~~Showing Your Work</a>

An electronic manuscript should first be cleaned up to get rid of extra spaces, errant hard returns, and superfluous formatting. This may be done "silently." Subsequent changes can be shown using the features built in to most word-processing programs. Deleted text is most often struck through~~, like this~~; added text is usually underlined or double-underlined, like this. A vertical line may appear in the margin next to a line that has been altered. Make sure your presentation is legible. For the most part, what you see is what you get. *Italics*, ~~boldface~~**boldface**, SMALL CAPITALS—not to mention tens of thousands of special characters—may be displayed rather than specially coded. If you need to query the author, there are a number of options for inserting "marginal" comments ~~to authors~~ in a manuscript. Built-in ~~comment~~ annotation functions or embedded footnotes,[A] being easiest to remove ~~from a manuscript before publication~~, are often preferred to bracketed comments inserted in the text. Be consistent: an editor should be able to remove redlining and comments to produce a final manuscript in just a few steps.

<a>Markup</a>

Another aspect of electronic editing involves markup. A document might be tagged using a standard markup language like XML. Or it might use a generic form of markup, usually applied in one of two ways. The elements of a manuscript can be defined using a word processor's "style palette," which assigns discrete names to chapter titles, subheads, prose extracts, and the like. Or such elements may be delimited with generic codes (e.g., "<ct>" and "</ct>" for a chapter title, "<a>" and "</a>" for a first-level subhead, and "<ext>" and "</ext>" for an extract). Generic markup will be imported into a page-layout application or converted to a standard markup system, so it is important to be consistent. Include a list of styles or codes with the edited manuscript.

[A]This is a sample of a footnoted comment or query to an author.

FIGURE 2.4. A manuscript page illustrating the principles of on-screen revision marks (redlining) and author queries. See 2.81.

2.82   *Document comparison software.* Document comparison software can highlight the differences between two versions of a document. Best results are had with shorter documents in which the latest version is compared against an earlier version that has already been cleaned up and formatted (see 2.77). Comparing an edited document against the author's original manuscript may result in too many changes being reported or, worse, may result in an unintelligible document. Editors should use document comparison software only occasionally—for example, to make sure they are working on the latest version of a document. For communicating changes to the author, which requires a more predictable presentation in which every change is spelled out as clearly as possible, editors should instead track their changes as they edit (see 2.81).

2.83   *Inserting author queries on electronic manuscripts.* Queries in electronic manuscripts may take one of several forms. Most word processors and specialized text editors include some sort of comment mechanism or syntax. Some editors instead use the footnote function to enter their queries (see fig. 2.4). Alternatively, queries may be run in to the text in an easily searchable form that will not be confused by humans or computers for any other element in the text (e.g., enclosed in brackets or other delimiters and appearing in boldface or some font not used elsewhere in the text). This latter method, especially, must be used with care to ensure that such comments are deleted from the final manuscript; moreover, inserting more than a few in-text queries risks cluttering the run of text and making the author's review arduous.

2.84   *Retaining the version of record.* Many authors will prefer to review a printout of their edited manuscript, pencil in hand. Time and shipping can be saved by e-mailing a PDF of the edited manuscript for the author to print out—if the publisher and author are amenable to this. One advantage of having the author review hard copy is that the editor—whose job it is to produce the final manuscript—retains the version of record. In some cases, however, the author might instead be asked to review and return the editor's electronic files. Authors who do this must highlight their changes in such a way that they are distinct from the editor's changes, and editors will want to consider password-protecting the edited manuscript from silent alteration. See also 2.68.

2.85   *The author's review of the edited manuscript.* Authors should mark their changes (or, if necessary, stets; see 2.127) in a bright color, fully legible, in upper- and lowercase. If the author adds more than a sentence or two, the new material may be furnished either as a printout or in electronic form with a hard copy, but the printout or file must contain only the new material; it must never be a revised form of the chapter or article, which could require a total reediting. (If a recalcitrant author were to do such a thing, an electronic comparison of the author's revised version against the author's original final manuscript might save an editor from having to do a total reedit; see 2.82.) The editor should make this procedure clear to the author when sending the edited manuscript. Moreover, the editor should remind the author that a careful review at this stage will reduce the number of errors later, during proofreading.

2.86   *Preparing a final electronic manuscript.* Editors should double-check that all changes have been made and all queries resolved; that any markup has been consistently applied; and that a final spelling check has been performed (including a check for mistakes that might fall outside the purview of a spelling checker—e.g., *it's* for *its*, *led* for *lead*, *breath* for *breathe*). In addition, all changes tracked in the document must be re-solved—either accepted or rejected—in the final electronic manuscript. Before sending the final manuscript to be typeset, editors should archive at least one electronic copy. For proofreading purposes, publishers may also require a printout matching the final electronic manuscript. (Authors will sometimes be asked to proofread against the copy of the redlined, edited manuscript that they reviewed earlier to ensure that their revisions made it into the typeset copy.)

The Mechanics of Editing on Paper

2.87   *Keeping a clean copy of paper manuscripts.* An editor working on paper should always keep a clean copy of the unedited manuscript to refer to—or as a backup in case any reediting is necessary. If the paper copy is a printout of an electronic manuscript, it is enough to archive a copy of the latter.

2.88   *Marking manuscripts on paper.* Editing a manuscript on paper—whether it is to be typeset from scratch or used to update the author's electronic manuscript—requires a technique that is similar to that of marking corrections on proofs (see 2.116–29). To allow for the more extensive changes typical of the editing stage, however, paper manuscripts are usually double-spaced so that editing can appear above the word or words it pertains to, rather than in the margin. (Manuscripts that consist of photocopies of tightly spaced previously published material are edited in the manner of page proofs.) All editorial changes should be made in a color that will reproduce clearly if the edited manuscript is photocopied or faxed, and the author should be asked to respond to the editing in a

(CT) How and Editor marks a Manuscript

PAPER MANUSCRIPTS are edited using marks that are not all that different than those used to correct proofs. A correction or an operational sign are, however, inserted in a line of type not in the margin as in proof reading. Editing marks are usually more expensive from those for proofreading, so any editoral change must be in it's proper place and written clearly - even if the edited manuscript will only be used to update the electronic files.

(A) Specific Marks
A caret shows where additional material is to be inserted. three lines under a lowercase letter tell the typesetter to make it a capital; 2 lines mean a small capital (A.D.); one line means italic; a wavy line means boldface; and a stroke through a capital letter means lowercase. Unwanted underlining is removed thus. A small circle around a comma indicates a period A straight line between parts of a closed compound, or between two words accidentally run together, will request space between the two words to be doubly sure, add a spacemark as well two short parallel lines mean a hyphen is to be added between two words as in two-thirds of a welldone fish.

(run in) A circle around an abbrev. or numeral instructs the typesetter to spell it out abbreviations ambiguous or not likely to be recognized by a typesetter should be spelled out by the editor (Biol. Biology or Biological; gen. gender, genitive, or (Equals signs) genus) as should figures that might be spelled out more than one way (2500 twenty-five hundred or two thousand five hundred). Dots (Equals signs) under a crossed-out word or passage mean stet (let it stand). Hyphens apearing when dashes should be used—except double hyphens representing an em dash--should always be marked; otherwise a hyphen may be used between continuing numbers like 15-18 or may confusingly be used to set off parenthetical matter. Whenever it is ambiguous or likely to confuse the typesetter an end-of-line hyphen should be underlined or crossed out so that the typesetter will know whether to retain the hyphen in the line or close up the word.

FIGURE 2.5. An example of a hand-marked manuscript page.

color distinct from that used by the editor. For marking queries, see 2.89. For a sample of a correctly marked manuscript, see figure 2.5.

2.89 *Marking author queries on paper manuscripts.* In manuscripts edited on paper, queries are best written in the margin. When the author has responded, they can simply be crossed out. Chicago discourages the use of gummed slips for queries: they cannot be easily photocopied, and they may have to be detached in the process of updating the electronic files or (for paper-only manuscripts) typesetting the final pages (and thus may no longer be in place when the pencil-edited manuscript is sent back to the author with the proofs). For more extensive queries that require more space than the margin affords, a separate sheet, keyed by letter or symbol to a specific place in the manuscript, may be prepared.

2.90   *Three uses for circling.* Circling has three meanings on a manuscript. (1) Circling a number or an abbreviation in the text means that the element is to be spelled out. If a number can be spelled out in different ways, or if an abbreviation could possibly be misconstrued, the editor should write out the form required. (2) Circling a comma or a colon means that a period is to replace the comma or colon; when a period is inserted by hand, it should be circled so it will not be missed by whoever is updating or typesetting the manuscript. (3) Circling a marginal comment shows that the comment is not to be set in type (or incorporated into the manuscript) but is either a query to the author or an instruction for typesetting or updating the manuscript.

2.91   *Inserting, deleting, and substituting.* A regular caret (∧), used to indicate an insertion point for added text but also used to indicate subscripts (and, similarly, to indicate an added comma), should be carefully distinguished from an inverted caret (∨), used to mark superscripts, apostrophes, and the like. But, in general, do not use a caret to indicate added text that is being substituted for deleted text; simply cross out the deleted text and write the text to be substituted above it. See fig. 2.5.

2.92   *Adding, deleting, or transposing punctuation.* Special attention should be paid to punctuation when words are transposed or deleted; the new position of commas, periods, and the like must be clearly shown. Likewise, any punctuation at the beginning or end of text marked for transposition must be clearly marked for deletion or inclusion, as the case may be. More generally, any added or changed punctuation should be clearly marked—for example, by circling an added period, placing a caret over an added comma, or placing an inverted caret under added quotation marks. If necessary, write (and circle) "colon," "exclamation point," or whatever applies, either in the margin or close to the punctuation change.

2.93   *Marking dashes and hyphens.* Two hyphens with no space between or on either side clearly signal em dashes and need not be marked on a paper-only manuscript. Actual em dashes, which may be mistaken for en dashes in some typefaces, should be marked. Two- or three-em dashes, even if consistently typed, should also be marked, as should en dashes, which might be mistaken for hyphens. Alternatively, a global instruction may be issued—for example, "all hyphens between inclusive numbers are to be set as en dashes." End-of-line hyphens should be marked to distinguish between soft (i.e., conditional, or "optional") and hard hyphens. Soft hyphens are those hyphens that are invoked only to break a word at the end of a line; hard hyphens are permanent (such as those in *cul-de-sac*) and must remain no matter where the hyphenated word or term appears. See also 2.12.

2.94 *Capitalizing, lowercasing, and marking for italics or boldface.* To indicate that a lowercase letter should be capitalized, triple underline it; to make it a small capital, double underline it. To lowercase a capital letter, run a slanted line through it. To mark for italics, underscore the word(s) to be italicized with a straight line; for boldface, make the underscoring wavy. For manuscripts that are to be typeset from scratch, there is usually no need to underline words that appear in italics in the manuscript, as long as the typesetter is instructed to italicize them. (Italics in some fonts are difficult to distinguish at a glance; underlining may reduce the incidence of missed italics.) If an author has used both underlining and italics, special instructions are needed (see 2.14). For mathematical copy, see 12.61–67.

2.95 *Marking paragraph indention, flush left or right, and vertical spacing.* Use a three-sided rectangular mark to indicate that text or other elements should be moved to the left (⊏) or to the right (⊐). A line may be drawn from the open side of the mark to the element to be moved (see fig. 2.5). To indicate paragraph indention, use the symbol ¶. To mark vertical space, use a rectangular mark that "points" up (∩) or down (⊔); adjust the width to accommodate the element. To indicate a blank line, write "one-line #" and circle it. (In typographic usage the sign # means space, not number.)

2.96 *Marking, or coding, elements on a paper manuscript.* Indications of elements on a paper manuscript—chapter number and title, subheads, prose extracts, poetry, and so forth—are circled and placed at the beginning of the element or in the margin next to it. For example, a circled "A" may be used to indicate a first-level subhead (see fig. 2.5). For these and other elements that need coding, and for examples of codes, see 2.78. See also 2.90.

Proofreading

Introduction

2.97   *What is proofreading?* Proofreading is the process of reading a text and scrutinizing all its components to find errors and mark them for correction. Each major stage of a manuscript intended for publication—especially the final version the author submits to the publisher and, later, the copyedited version of the same—is generally proofread. Proofreading here, however, applies to the review of the manuscript *after* it has been converted to its final form—for example, the typeset and (usually) paginated pages of a printed book or journal article (referred to as proofs or proof), or the full-text format of an electronic book or journal article—but *before* publication. Also subject to a proofreading stage are covers and jackets or other packaging and electronic components such as navigational aids that frame an electronic publication. For an illustration of how the stages described in this chapter fit into the overall publishing process for books and journals, see the outline at 2.2. For proofreading electronic publications, see 2.133–36.

2.98   *Who should proofread?* For the majority of publications, authors are considered the primary proofreaders, and it is they who bear final responsibility for any errors in the published work. To help mitigate this responsibility, a professional proofreader may be hired by either the author or the publisher. Moreover, the manuscript editor and book designer and other publishing personnel generally ensure that the author's corrections (and those of any other proofreader) are successfully incorporated into the work before it gets published and that all related materials (promotional copy, website apparatus, etc.) are free of errors and inconsistencies.

2.99   *Proofreading schedule.* Since many people are involved in the production of a book, a few days' delay in returning proofs to the publisher or typesetter can cause a major delay in publication. When the time scheduled for proofreading appears to conflict with the demands of accuracy, or if any other problem arises that might affect the schedule, the proofreader should immediately confer with the publisher. For journals, where there is little room for delays of any kind, proofreading deadlines are generally nonnegotiable. See also 2.2.

Stages of Proof

2.100 *Keeping a record of each proofreading stage.* A record must be kept by the publisher of when each stage of proof has been corrected and by whom. For printed books, the best record for the first proofreading stage is a master set—usually the laser printout read and marked for corrections by the author and marked with additional corrections by the publisher and any others who have read or reviewed the master set or copies thereof. (Some publishers send a duplicate set of page proofs to the author and then transfer the author's corrections to the master set.) At the next stage, revised proofs are usually reviewed by the publisher, who retains the master set and a record of each additional round of corrections until the work has been published. For electronic publications, the author and other proofreaders should each be required to sign off before a corrected version is delivered for further review. Likewise, for covers and jackets or other packaging, each person assigned to proofread should be required to sign off on the proofreading copy before a corrected version is routed for further review.

2.101 *First proofs and "galley" proofs.* The author and sometimes a designated proofreader read the first proofreading copy (*first proofs* or *first pages*), usually against the edited manuscript (see 2.107). For books, an index may be prepared from this first set of page proofs, either by the author or by a professional indexer (see chapter 16). For some complex book-length works, first proofs are issued in the form of "galleys." Strictly speaking, the term *galley proofs* is an anachronism, dating from the era when printers would arrange type into "galleys" from which long, narrow prints were prepared to proofread or edit type before the arduous task of composing it, by hand, into the form of book pages. Today, if a complex project presents a danger of extensive corrections at the page-proof stage, a publisher might request galley proofs (loosely paginated and with or without such elements as illustrations in place), since corrections to galleys will not entail having to redo page references in an index. These galleys are generated from the same electronic files as first proofs would be. (As an alternative to the galley stage, publishers might choose to undertake a proofreading of the final electronic manuscript.) The index is prepared not from the galleys, since pagination is not final, but from the "first" proofs that are issued at the next stage.

2.102 *Revised proofs.* After corrections to the first proofs have been made, the revisions must be checked to be sure all corrections have been made accurately. For print publications, this usually involves comparing a set of *revised proofs* for all pages against the first set (now known as "foul" proofs).

These revised proofs should also be checked for any other differences between them and the first proofs and to make sure hyphenation errors or other page makeup problems have not been introduced. If the typesetter has circled or bracketed or otherwise indicated any changes to page makeup resulting from the corrections, the proofreader can check revised proofs more efficiently. Any corrections that have resulted in repagination may require adjustment to page references in the index. To maintain a proper record, nothing must be marked on the foul proofs at this stage; any further corrections must be marked only on the revised set. Any additional rounds of revision should be kept to a minimum.

2.103   *Index proofs.* Most indexes are prepared from the paginated first set of proofs (unless they reference paragraph numbers rather than page numbers, in which case they can be prepared from the final manuscript). Indexes must be proofread quickly, in the same time that the revisions to the first proofs are being checked. For the sake of efficiency, editors rather than authors usually proofread indexes. For a full discussion of indexes, see chapter 16.

2.104   *Prepress and press proofs.* For works that will be printed and bound, publishers usually review prepress proofs. Prepress proofs present an inexpensive image of what will come off the printing press—generated either from negative film or, more commonly, from electronic files. (The final typesetter's files—usually PDF—can generally be considered equivalent to prepress proofs.) These proofs—a "now or never" opportunity to look at what will be published, *before* ink is committed to paper—are normally checked for completeness of contents; page sequence; margins; location, sizing, position, and cropping (if any) of illustrations; and, for contact proofs made from film, any spots or smudges. For reasons of press schedule and expense, publishers will generally allow only the correction of grave errors at this stage, such as an incorrect title or a misspelled author's name. One additional look—at actual press sheets, folded and gathered into the proper page sequence (and called F&Gs)—is sometimes also granted book and journal publishers. (Press sheets that include full-color illustrations are occasionally sent to the publisher to approve before the entire work is printed.) By the time the publisher sees a complete set of F&Gs, copies of the work are off the press and may be in the bindery. Since any correction at this stage would involve reprinting an entire signature, the publisher may prefer to turn a blind eye. See also 1.65.

2.105   *Book cover and jacket proofs.* Jackets and covers are the most viewed part of any printed book. Whereas most publishers (and authors) will live, if not happily, with the inevitable typo inside a book, an error on the cover is liable to halt the presses. Proofs of die copy—author's name, title, publisher's imprint, and any other matter to be stamped on the spine or cover of a hardbound book—should therefore be checked with extreme care. Likewise, proofs of jacket copy and paperback cover copy should be read and checked word for word (if not letter by letter), with special attention paid as follows:

- Anything on the cover should be consistent with the interior of the work in content and style. For example, the author's name and the title of the work—everywhere they appear, including cover, spine, and jacket flaps—must match those on the title page of the book (though the subtitle may be omitted from the cover or jacket). An author's full name is sometimes shortened in the running text of flap copy.
- Biographical material on the author should be checked against any biographical material inside the book, though the wording need not be identical.
- If the work is part of a series or a multivolume set, the series title or volume number must match its counterpart inside the book.
- The price (if it is to appear), the ISBN, and any necessary credit line for a photograph of the author or for artwork used on the cover or jacket must be verified.

Jacket and cover proofs and each stage of revisions thereto should be reviewed by everyone involved in the production of the book—including authors, editors, designers, and marketing personnel.

2.106   *Journal cover proofs.* Although the elements that appear on the covers of academic journals vary considerably, the following suggestions should apply to most journals. The front cover (called cover 1) must be checked carefully to ensure that elements that change with each issue, such as the volume and issue numbers and the month, date, or season of publication, are accurate and up to date. The spine must be similarly checked. If the contents of the issue are listed on cover 1, they must be checked against the interior to be sure that authors' names and article titles match exactly and, for journals that publish various types of articles, that articles have been listed in the correct section of the journal. If inclusive page numbers appear on the spine, these must be verified. The inside of the front cover (cover 2) often includes subscription prices and information on how to subscribe, names of editors and members of the editorial board, or copyright information; all such information must be checked. Covers 3 (inside of back cover) and 4 (back cover) may contain advertisements, instructions to authors on submitting articles, or a list of articles to appear in future issues. They all must be verified by the proofreader.

How to Proofread and What to Look For

2.107 *Proofreading against copy.* In proofreading parlance, *copy* refers to the edited manuscript. Proofs should be checked against the version of the manuscript that contains the author's final changes and responses to queries (see 2.69). In the event that the page proofs were typeset from a paper-only manuscript, the proofreader must read word for word against the edited manuscript, noting all punctuation, paragraphing, capitalization, italics, and so forth and ensuring that any handwritten editing has been correctly interpreted by the typesetter. Likewise, any element in an otherwise electronic manuscript that has been set from edited hard copy (e.g., math or tables) should be proofread carefully against the hard copy. Whether type has been set from electronic files or from paper, the proofreader must mark only the proofs, never the manuscript, which is now known as "dead" (or "foul") copy. To assign responsibility for error correctly (see 2.131), the manuscript as earlier approved by the author must be kept intact. For checking revised proofs, see 2.102.

2.108 *Proofreading for spelling errors.* The proofreader should remain alert for the kind of errors that are typically missed by computerized systems for checking spelling—from common typos such as *it's* where *its* is meant or *out* where *our* is meant, to more subtle errors like *lead* for *led* or *breath* for *breathe*—as well as other misspellings. (See also 2.86.) The manuscript editor's style sheet (see 2.52) may be a useful reference. Note that a change to the spelling of a particular term should never be indicated globally; instead, each change must be marked throughout the manuscript.

2.109 *Checking word breaks.* End-of-line hyphenation should be checked, especially in proper names and foreign terms. The first set of proofs is usually the first time that words have been divided, conditionally, at the ends of lines. Chicago recommends the word breaks given in *Merriam-Webster's Collegiate Dictionary* (see bibliog. 3.1). (There are electronic dictionaries, including *Webster's*, that can be used in conjunction with automated typesetting systems.) For words or names not listed in a dictionary, a liberal approach is advisable, since formal usage varies widely and any change requested may entail further breaks or create tight or loose lines (lines with too little or too much space between words). Such problems may be avoided if a list of nondictionary words and their preferred hyphenation (or an editor's style sheet if it includes this information) is submitted to the typesetter along with the manuscript. When it is a question of an intelligible but nonstandard word break for a line that would otherwise be too loose or too tight, the nonstandard break (such as the hyphenation of an already hyphenated term) may be preferred. No more than three succeeding lines should end in a hyphen (see 7.43). See also 2.12, 7.31–43. For dividing URLs at the ends of lines, see 7.42.

2.110   *Checking typeface and font.* Each element in proofs—for example, chapter numbers and titles, subheads, text, extracts, figure captions—should be checked to ensure that it is presented in a consistent typeface and style in accordance with the design for the publication. Heads and subheads, in particular, should be checked for the typographic style assigned to their level (see 2.17, 2.56), and all set-off material (excerpts, poetry, equations, etc.) should be checked for font, size, and indention. All material in italics, boldface, small capitals, or any font different from that of the surrounding text should be looked at to be sure the new font starts and stops as intended. Note that the conversion of electronic manuscript files into typeset pages or full-text electronic presentations can result in unexpected errors, such as the dropping or transmutation of a special character throughout the work or the inadvertent incorporation of a comment or other "invisible" electronic material into the text. For a systematic error, it may be preferable to indicate a single, or "global," instruction for making the change—to avoid cluttering the proofs with corrections of each instance. When a systemic problem is identified—especially one on proofs for a printed work that will affect pagination across more than a few pages and therefore the index—the publisher should be alerted immediately in case new first proofs are needed.

2.111   *Checking and proofreading page numbers and running heads.* Page numbers and running heads must be checked to ensure that they are present where they are supposed to be and absent where they are not (see 1.5–8, 1.9–15, 2.73), that the correct page number appears following a blank page, and that the typesetter has followed instructions as to what should appear on a recto, a verso, or a double-page spread. Running heads must be both proofread and checked for placement. For running heads to endnotes, the page numbers may need to be verified or supplied by checking the text pages the notes pertain to (see 1.14).

2.112   *Checking and proofreading illustrations and tables.* The proofreader must verify that all illustrations appear in the right location in the text, in the right size, right side up, not "flopped" (turned over left to right, resulting in a mirror image) or distorted, and with their own captions. Captions should be read as carefully as the text. Tables must be proofread both for content and for alignment. Where an illustration or a table occupies a full page, no running head or page number should appear; but if several full pages of illustrations or tables appear in sequence, the proof-reader may request that page numbers, and sometimes running heads as well, be added to better orient readers (see 1.15). For a table presented as a two-page broadside, the proofreader should make sure it falls on facing pages (i.e., verso and recto; see also 3.85). If there are lists of illustrations and tables, all captions and titles should be checked against the lists, and page numbers must be verified or added.

2.113   *Checking overall appearance.* For printed works, each page or, better, each pair of facing pages should be checked for length (see 2.114), vertical spacing, position of running heads and page numbers, and so forth. Conformity to the design specifications must be verified. Such apparent impairments as fuzzy type, incomplete letters, and blocks of type that appear lighter or darker than the surrounding text may be due to poor photocopying or a faulty printout. If in doubt, the proofreader may query "Type OK?" or "Too dark?" Four or more consecutive lines that end with a hyphen or the same word should be pointed out and, if possible, appropriate adjustments indicated. A page should not begin with the last line of a paragraph unless it is full measure. (A page can, however, end with the first line of a new paragraph.) Nor should the last word in any paragraph be broken—that is, hyphenated, with the last part of the word beginning a new line. To correct any of these occurrences, page length may be adjusted. (A short last line of a paragraph carried over to the top of a page is sometimes referred to as a "widow"; when the first line of a paragraph appears at the bottom of a page, it is sometimes called an "orphan.")

2.114   *Checking facing pages for text alignment.* Although facing pages of text must align, it is usually acceptable for both pages to run a line long or short to avoid widows (see 2.113) or to accommodate corrections. For example, if a correction on page 68 requires an added line, the typesetter may be asked to add space above a subhead on page 69 so that the two pages wind up the same length. Type can sometimes be rerun more loosely or more tightly to add (*save*) or eliminate (*lose*) a line.

2.115   *Proofreading for sense.* The proofreader must query—or correct, if possible—illogical, garbled, repeated, or missing text. Any rewriting, however, must be limited to the correction of fact or of gross syntactical error, since all source checking and substantive and stylistic changes should have been done at the editing stage. Changes that would alter page makeup across more than a couple of pages in printed works should be avoided, since repagination not only is expensive but, for books, can affect the index.

How to Mark Proofs

2.116 *Proofreaders' marks.* The marks explained in the following paragraphs and illustrated in figures 2.6 and 2.7 are commonly understood by typesetters and other publishing and printing personnel working in English. Moreover, these marks and conventions form the basis of online proofreading tools (though paper remains the gold standard for proofreading—especially for book-length works). Other instructions provided by printers and publishers are unlikely to differ substantially from what is given here. Note that all verbal instructions to the typesetter are best circled (see 2.118).

2.117 *Where to mark proofs.* Corrections to proofs must always be written in the margin, left or right, next to the line concerned. A mark must also be placed in the text—a caret for an addition, a line through a letter or word to be deleted or replaced—to indicate where a correction is to be made. Never should a correction be written between the lines, where it could be missed. If a line requires two or more corrections, these should be marked in the margin in the order in which they occur, separated by vertical lines (see fig. 2.7). A guideline or an arrow should be used only when a correction cannot be written next to the line in which it occurs.

2.118 *Circling comments and instructions.* As with queries and instructions handwritten on a paper manuscript (see 2.90), verbal instructions written on proofs—such as "see attached typescript" or "ital" or "rom"—should be circled. Such circling indicates that these are instructions and that the words and abbreviations themselves should not be incorporated into the actual work.

2.119 *Communicating extensive changes.* Wherever the marks required to fix a line or two threaten to become byzantine, cross out the whole passage and rewrite it correctly in the margin. If there is not enough room in the margin, make a separate document and include it with the proofs; the insertion point should be indicated in both places. To avoid repagination of print works, every effort must be made to match the word count of new material to that of the old. For material to be transposed from one page to another, circle or otherwise mark the passage and make a note in the margin; clearly mark the new location and make a note in that margin as well. Most types of global changes should be marked individually to ensure that each change is made correctly (see also 2.110).

2.120 *Making marks legible.* All corrections must be written clearly (such that they can be spotted at a glance) in upper- and lowercase letters. Red proof

Proofreaders' Marks

OPERATIONAL SIGNS

⤳	Delete
◡	Close up; delete space
⤳◡	Delete and close up (use only when deleting letters *within* a word)
(stet)	Let it stand
#	Insert space
(eq #)	Make space between words equal; make space between lines equal
(hr #)	Insert hair space
(ls)	Letterspace
¶	Begin new paragraph
☐	Indent type one em from left or right
]	Move right
[	Move left
][	Center
⊓	Move up
⊔	Move down
(fl)	Flush left
(fr)	Flush right
═	Straighten type; align horizontally
‖	Align vertically
(tr)	Transpose
(sp)	Spell out

TYPOGRAPHICAL SIGNS

(ital)	Set in italic type
(rom)	Set in roman type
(bf)	Set in boldface type
(lc)	Set in lowercase
(caps)	Set in capital letters
(sc)	Set in small capitals
(wf)	Wrong font; set in correct type
✕	Check type image; remove blemish
⋁	Insert here *or* make superscript
⋀	Insert here *or* make subscript

PUNCTUATION MARKS

⌃	Insert comma
ˏ ˏ	Insert apostrophe *or* single quotation mark
ˮ ˮ	Insert quotation marks
⊙	Insert period
(set) ?	Insert question mark
;	Insert semicolon
⌃ or :	Insert colon
═	Insert hyphen
M̲	Insert em dash
N̲	Insert en dash
{│} or (│)	Insert parentheses

FIGURE 2.6. Proofreaders' marks.

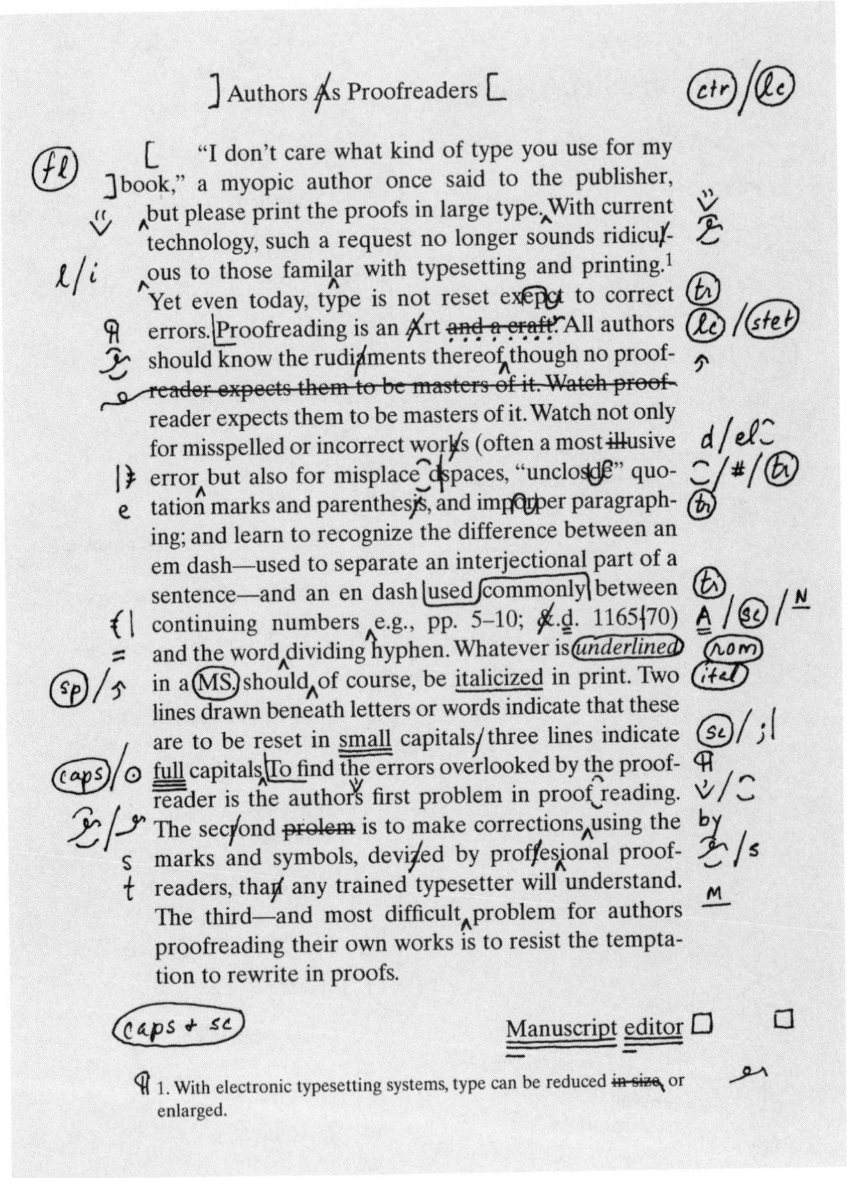

["I don't care what kind of type you use for my] book," a myopic author once said to the publisher, but please print the proofs in large type. With current technology, such a request no longer sounds ridicul- ous to those familar with typesetting and printing.[1] Yet even today, type is not reset except to correct errors. Proofreading is an Art and a craft. All authors should know the rudiments thereof though no proof- reader expects them to be masters of it. Watch proof- reader expects them to be masters of it. Watch not only for misspelled or incorrect works (often a most illusive error but also for misplace dspaces, "unclosde" quo- tation marks and parenthesjs, and improper paragraph- ing; and learn to recognize the difference between an em dash—used to separate an interjectional part of a sentence—and an en dash used commonly between continuing numbers e.g., pp. 5–10; q.d. 1165–70) and the word dividing hyphen. Whatever is underlined in a MS should, of course, be italicized in print. Two lines drawn beneath letters or words indicate that these are to be reset in small capitals/three lines indicate full capitals To find the errors overlooked by the proof- reader is the authors first problem in proof reading. The second prolem is to make corrections using the marks and symbols, devized by proffesional proof- readers, thay any trained typesetter will understand. The third—and most difficult problem for authors proofreading their own works is to resist the tempta- tion to rewrite in proofs.

Manuscript editor

1. With electronic typesetting systems, type can be reduced in size, or enlarged.

FIGURE 2.7. Marked proofs.

markings are often preferred for visibility, but any color will do as long as the proofreader's corrections are distinct from any made by the publisher or typesetter. Either a pen or a pencil may be used; in either case, the proofreader must be prepared to eradicate unwanted marks. Messy corrections may lead to further errors; indistinct corrections may be overlooked. If a small number of late-stage, hand-marked corrections to proofs must be transmitted to the typesetter electronically, the marks must be dark enough to scan or fax clearly, and they must not extend to the edges of the paper lest they be incomplete on the recipient's copy.

2.121 *Marking copy for deletion.* To remove a letter, a word, or more, draw a diagonal line through a letter or a straight line through a word or phrase and write the delete mark (see fig. 2.6) in the margin. No part of the text should be obliterated, and a punctuation mark that is to be removed should be circled rather than crossed through, so that it is still visible. The form of the delete mark in the margin need not be exactly as shown in figure 2.6, but it should be made in such a way as not to be confused with a *d*, an *e*, or an *l*. The mark for "delete and close up" should be used when a letter or a hyphen is deleted from within a word, or, in the case of longer deletions, when the material that remains is to be joined with no intervening space. The delete mark is used only when something is to be removed. When something is to be substituted for the deleted matter, only the substitution is written in the margin next to the line or lines that have been struck through (see fig. 2.7).

2.122 *Adding or deleting space between letters or words.* All words in the same line should be separated by the same amount of space, though the spacing will vary from line to line in justified setting. When word spaces within a line are unequal, insert carets in the problem areas of the text and write the equal-space mark (eq #) in the margin. To delete space between letters or words, use the close-up mark (see fig. 2.6) in the text as well as in the margin. To call for more space between words or letters, insert a vertical line in the text where the space is to be inserted and make a space mark (#) in the margin. The space mark is also used to show where more vertical space (or *leading*, a term derived from the lead that was used in hot-metal typesetting) is needed between lines. See also 2.95.

2.123 *Indicating changes to paragraphing or indention.* To indicate a new paragraph, insert an L-shaped mark in the text to the left and partly under the word that is to begin a new paragraph and write the paragraph mark (¶) in the margin. To run two paragraphs together, draw a line in the text from the end of one paragraph to the beginning of the next and write "run in" in the margin. To indent a line one em space (see A.22) from the left or right margin, draw a small square (☐) to the left of the material to be indented and repeat the square in the margin. To indent two or more ems, draw a rectangle divided into two or more squares. To repeat the indention for more than one consecutive line, draw a line down from the square to the level of the baseline of the last affected line.

2.124   *Indicating adjustments to position or alignment (justification).* If a line of type, a title, an item in a table, or any other text appears too far to the left or right, use the marks for moving type right (⊐) or left (⊏). If text that is supposed to be centered appears not to be, use both marks (⊐⊏)—one on each side—to indicate centering. Use the marks for moving type up (⊓) or down (⊔) when something appears vertically out of place. All these marks must be inserted in the text as well as in the margin. To indicate that an indented line of type should start flush left (at the left-hand margin), insert a move-left (⊏) mark at the left of the first word in that line and write "fl" (flush left) in the margin, circled (see fig. 2.7). To indicate that an element should appear flush right—or that a line of type should be justified at the right margin—do the same thing but with the move-right (⊐) mark and marginal "fr" (flush right) or "justify." Finally, to indicate inaccurate alignment in tabular matter, use the mark for vertical alignment (‖) or horizontal alignment (=), as the case may be. To apply any of these marks to more than one consecutive line, make the mark long enough to encompass each affected line.

2.125   *Marking items to be transposed.* To move letters, words, or phrases from one place to another, circumscribe them in a way that precisely demarcates the items (including any punctuation) to be interchanged and write and circle "tr" (transpose) in the margin (see fig. 2.7). For transposition of larger chunks of text or other elements, it may be best to draw a bracket or other mark around each item and include a circled instruction in the margin.

2.126   *Marking items to be spelled out.* When an abbreviation or numeral is to be spelled out, circle the item and write the spell-out mark (circled "sp") in the margin. If there is any ambiguity about the spelling, write the full word in the margin. See also 2.90.

2.127   *Using "stet" to revert corrections or deletions.* To undelete or restore something that has earlier been marked for deletion or correction, place a row of dots in the text under the material that is to remain, cross out the marginal mark or correction, and write "stet" ("let it stand")—or to avoid any ambiguity, "stet as set"—in the margin, circled.

2.128 *Marking changes to capitalization and font.* Mark changes to capitalization and font as follows, and remember to circle all marginal instructions (see 2.118 and figs. 2.6 and 2.7):

- To lowercase a capital letter, draw a slash through the letter and write "lc" in the margin.
- To capitalize a lowercase letter, draw three lines under it and write "cap" in the margin.
- For small capital letters, draw two lines under the letters or words and write "sc" in the margin.
- For italics, draw a single line under the letter or words and write "ital" in the margin.
- To remove italics, circle the italicized letter or words and write "rom" in the margin.
- For boldface, draw a wavy line under the letter or words and write "bf" in the margin.
- To remove boldface, circle the boldface letter or words and write "not bf" in the margin.

2.129 *Indicating changes to punctuation and accents.* To change a punctuation mark, circle it and write the correct mark in the margin. To add a mark, insert a caret and write the mark in the margin. Lest they be missed or misinterpreted, all punctuation marks in the margin should be clarified thus: a comma should have a caret over it; an apostrophe or a quotation mark should have an inverted caret under it; a parenthesis should have two short horizontal lines through it; a period should be circled; semicolons and colons should be followed by a short vertical line; question marks and exclamation points should be accompanied by the circled word "set"; and hyphens, en dashes, and em dashes should be differentiated by their appropriate symbols (see fig. 2.6). If an accent or a diacritical mark is missing or incorrect, the entire letter should be crossed out in the text and written in the margin with its correct accent; never must the accent alone appear in the margin. For clarity, the name of any unusual accent or diacritical mark (e.g., "breve") should also be written and circled in the margin (see 11.2).

Double-Checking and Assigning Responsibility for Errors

2.130 *Double-checking proofs.* In addition to the tasks outlined in 2.107–15, the proofreader must perform the following checks, according to the needs of the particular work:

- Check article or chapter titles and, if necessary, subheads or other heads against the table of contents to ensure consistent wording, and verify or add beginning page numbers in the table of contents. Query—or delete, if necessary—any item listed in the table of contents that does not appear in the work.
- If footnotes are used, ensure that each footnote appears, or at least begins, on the page that includes its superscript reference number or symbol.
- Complete any cross-references (see 2.32).
- For a book, check the half title and the title page to be sure the title is correct and the author's or volume editor's name is spelled right; verify that the information on the copyright page is accurate and complete.
- For a journal, check the covers, spine, and any front or back matter copy that is unique to the particular journal; with the previous year's volume at hand, check the elements that change with each issue, such as volume and issue numbers and date, month, or season of publication; ensure that the inclusive page numbers that appear on the spine are accurate; check front and back matter for any elements that may have changed, such as subscription prices or names of editors and members of the editorial board; ensure that copyright lines are included and accurate on all individual articles or other elements of the journal that carry them.

For additional checking required for electronic works, see 2.133–36.

2.131   *Assigning responsibility for errors on proofs.* The proofreader may be asked to distinguish between errors introduced by the typesetting process and errors that were left uncorrected in the manuscript or those that were introduced during editorial cleanup after the author has reviewed the editing. In such cases, corrections should be accompanied by abbreviations determined by the publisher or typesetter, such as PE (printer's error—the customary term for what is generally a typesetter's error), AA (author's alteration), EA (editor's alteration), and DA (designer's alteration). All such indications should be circled to prevent their being incorporated into the corrected proofs.

2.132   *Author's alterations (AAs) versus editor's alterations (EAs).* For books, a publisher's contract may allow an author to make, without penalty, alterations in proofs in terms of a percentage of the initial cost of the typesetting. Since the cost of corrections is far higher relative to the cost of the original typesetting, an AA allowance of (for example) 5 percent does not mean that 5 percent of the proofs may be altered. An author may be asked to pay the cost of AAs beyond the AA allowance stipulated in the contract. Page numbers added to cross-references in proofs are usually considered AAs. Corrections of errors uncaught or even introduced in editing are considered AAs if the author reviewed and approved the edited manuscript. Correction of an error introduced into the manuscript by the publisher after the author's review—made by the manuscript editor, for example, in entering the author's final adjustments—is an EA and not chargeable to the author. Supplying page numbers in lists of tables and illustrations and in running heads to notes constitutes an EA. For articles, consult the journal publisher.

Proofing and Testing Electronic Publications

2.133 *Checklist for proofing electronic publications.* Every element in an electronic publication must be proofread, checked, and tested in its final form—*before* it gets published. No element should be overlooked. In addition to many of the tasks outlined in 2.107–15 and 2.130, a thorough check will include some or all of the following steps:

1. Look carefully at the layout to make sure that no elements are missing, that all elements are presented as intended, and that no markup added for another purpose (e.g., for a print version) adversely affects the electronic version.
2. Confirm that all special characters have been converted correctly (see 2.110; see also 11.2). Characters that have been treated as bitmapped images must be checked for correctness, legibility, and proper appearance (see also A.34).
3. Verify that all hypertext links and other clickable features work—including links and features within the work and those that lead to other sites or resources. For web publications, a site map (i.e., a list or chart of all navigable pages) may facilitate this process.
4. Make sure that any illustrations or other nontext features of the work are present and function and appear as desired.
5. For a work that will be published in print and online, make sure that the forms either match exactly—if that is the intent—or vary as intended, and that such variation is noted explicitly in both versions (see 1.73).
6. Proofread any recent changes for spelling and sense.

Although initial checking and testing will have been done during the editing stage, the person (or persons) responsible for proofreading electronic copy must look at every element of the publication systematically—preferably according to a larger checklist that will have been created during the development stages of the project.

2.134 *Testing web-based publications.* In addition to comprising well-edited, accurate, error-free information, a web-based publication (see 1.111) must function as intended—usually across a variety of platforms. This functionality must be tested at several stages in the development of a project—not just at the end and not only by a team of editors or proofreaders. By the time the content for a web-based publication has been finalized, the interface will usually have gone through several stages of editorial review to scrutinize basic design elements and navigational structure and to edit ancillary items such as error messages, label text (as on buttons), and metadata (see A.10). Some publications will also benefit from a beta test stage in which potential users are invited to report errors and suggest changes before the official release date. More specific testing routines should adhere to use-case documents (see 2.135). Testing after the release date will include editorial oversight of any new content generated by the publication such as readers' comments. At all stages, procedures should be in place for regression testing—that is, testing that safeguards against unforeseen errors caused by the correction of other errors or by the introduction of new features or content or other changes. For online journals and other periodical publications, it is not necessary to repeat all of these testing stages on the recurring design elements and features every time new content is added, but the new content itself should be checked before publication as described in 2.133.

2.135   *Documentation for testing.* Thorough testing of a web-based publication should involve checking it against various documents that describe its intended functionality, behavior, and navigation. Several types of documents are typically created as part of a publication's development process. *Feature definition documents*, for example, provide detailed descriptions of how the various features of the website will function. Feature definition for a search engine would specify how search results are ordered and displayed on the page, how users are able to limit the search to certain kinds of results, how terms with diacritics are handled, and so forth. *Use-case documents* provide a more complete description of a feature's behavior, specifying exactly how the feature will respond to the user's every mouse click and keystroke. *Wire frames* or *design mockups* provide visual representations of the page's design and layout, and *user interface specifications* may provide additional guidelines. Finally, *test-case documents* provide step-by-step instructions on exactly how a given feature or page will be tested.

2.136   *Communicating changes to web-based publications.* Just as manuscript editors redline changes and keep a style sheet for a book manuscript and proofreaders use a specific set of marks to communicate changes, those involved in producing a web-based publication will need to follow a system for tracking and implementing changes and stylistic decisions. Whereas such matters for a printed book are traditionally recorded on a series of printouts, a web-based project generally benefits from the use of a centralized database. Procedures for using such a system should be developed (and fully documented) with the input of the web developers, designers, editors, proofreaders, and testers who will use it. In any single project, the entries in such a database—in conjunction with the documentation for testing described in 2.135—can serve as a contract between editors and the production team to ensure that changes get implemented properly and elements function as they should. Responsibility, revision dates, and other information should be complemented by checklists for testers that follow the same guidelines. Editorial oversight of the project database is crucial, and to allow for this oversight, every change, no matter how trivial, must be documented. Finally, changes made after the initial development stage should generally be subject not only to editorial oversight but also to authorization.

3 Illustrations and Tables

Overview

3.1   *Illustrations defined.* Illustrations, also called figures, consist of artwork—which is to say, anything that is represented by means of an image rather than by the letters and other orthographic symbols that make up the text of a book or an article. Illustrations, then, include paintings, photographs, line drawings, maps, charts, and examples from musical scores. This list is sometimes extended to include audio and video files presented as enhancements to electronic publications. For a full discussion of illustrations—including guidelines on preparation, placement, numbering, and captioning, with examples drawn from University of Chicago Press publications—see 3.3–45.

3.2   *Tables defined.* A table is a more or less complex list presented as an array of vertical columns and horizontal rows. Like illustrations, tables are presented separately from the run of text. Tables are also related to illustrations in that both can be said to constitute a visual representation of data. Because they consist of alphanumeric text, however, tables are usually typeset along with the text rather than produced separately as artwork (but see A.33). For a full discussion of tables—including guidelines on preparation, placement, numbering, and editing, with examples drawn from University of Chicago Press publications—see 3.46–85.

Illustrations

Types of Illustrations and Their Parts

3.3   *Continuous tone versus halftone.* Continuous-tone art is any image such as a painting or a photograph that contains gradations of shading from light to dark—in black and white (grayscale) or color (see fig. 3.1). In order to duplicate continuous-tone images in offset printing, which uses one ink color (black) for black and white and four for color (cyan, magenta, yellow, and black—abbreviated CMYK), a halftone reproduction must be produced (see fig. 3.2). (Color images intended for the screen are rendered in RGB—red, green, and blue—mode.) A halftone breaks the image into an equally spaced array of dots that vary in size to create the illusion of continuous tone from dark to light. For black-and-white halftone reproduction, authors should submit glossy prints of original art. For illustrations to be reproduced in color, which involves a four-color process, color transparencies are usually preferred. Authors submitting digital photo-

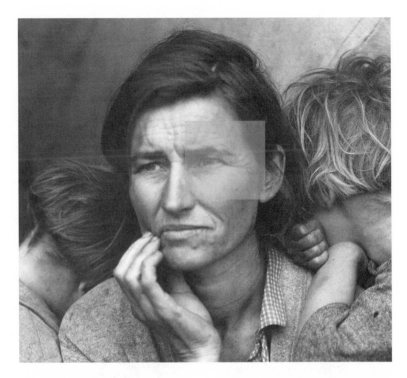

Migrant Mother, by Dorothea Lange, 1936.

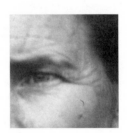

FIGURE 3.1.
Above, a halftone image of an original photo.

FIGURE 3.2.
Right, detail of figure 3.1 showing the
halftone dot pattern. See 3.3.

graphs or scans should consult their publisher's guidelines for preparing electronic artwork. (Chicago offers such guidelines on its books and journals websites.)

3.4   **Line art.** Artwork containing only black on a white background, with no gray screens (i.e., shading)—such as a pen-and-ink drawing—is traditionally known as line art (or, less commonly, line copy). See figures 3.3 and 3.4. Line art may be published in black and white or in color. For the

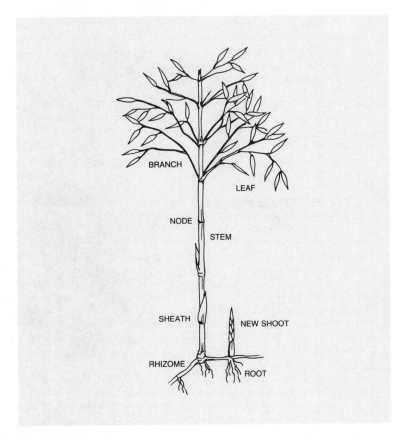

FIGURE 3.3. A line drawing with descriptive labels (see 3.4, 3.7). The surrounding text of the work from which this unnumbered and uncaptioned figure was drawn identifies the plant as a *Sinarundinaria* stem.

purpose of reproduction or presentation in both printed and electronic works, charts may also be treated as line art, though strictly speaking they are often typeset using specialized software applications, even if the result is output as an image. (For more on charts, see 3.40–45.) Musical examples may be treated as line art and scanned if they are not typeset from scratch for publication—generally by specialists. See figure 3.5. Publishers can often reproduce computer-generated line art without having to remake it as long as it has been properly prepared; authors should obtain guidelines from the publisher. For the use of shading in line art, see 3.19. For more on the conventions related to musical notation, see 7.66–71.

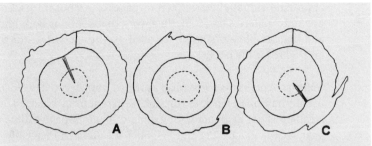

FIG. 3 Outline drawings of serial sections of parental root axis of *Carpinus caroliniana*. The vertical line at the top of each drawing represents the incision mentioned in "Materials and Methods." The outermost outline marks the surface of the axis, the next line inward marks the location of the vascular cambium, and the dotted line represents the terminus of the first season of growth. A and C are from sections that were 4 mm apart, each immediately adjacent to a branch root trace, with diminished secondary xylem accumulation toward the side with the branch root (cf. fig. 1B to understand the position of these sections relative to PBR). B represents a section between A and C, showing secondary xylem that is uniform in thickness around the parental axis.

FIGURE 3.4. A line drawing, including figure number and caption (see 3.4, 3.8–14, 3.21–27). The drawing's three parts, labeled with capital letters, are discussed in the caption (see 3.7).

EXAMPLE 7.6 *Daliso e Delmita*, act 2, "Nel lasciarti, oh Dio! mi sento," mm. 86–97

FIGURE 3.5. Musical examples carry their captions above the illustration rather than below. Such examples can be reproduced photographically (e.g., from a published score) or typeset by specialists (see 3.4).

3.5   *Text figures and plates.* Illustrations—whether halftones or line art—that are interspersed in the text are referred to as text figures. (Occasionally, a special type of illustration, such as a map or a musical example, will be referred to in a work by type rather than by the generic term *figure*. See fig. 3.5.) The term *plate*, strictly speaking, refers to a full-page illustration that is printed separately, typically on coated paper; plates can appear individually between certain pages of text but are more often gathered into galleries (see 3.6). (In a work that contains both photographs and line art, *plate* is sometimes used—a little loosely—for the former and *figure* for the latter.)

3.6   *Galleries.* A gallery is a section of a printed work devoted to illustrations—usually halftones. If printed on stock different from that used for the text, a gallery is not paginated; for example, an eight-page gallery could appear between pages 134 and 135. Such a gallery will typically consist of four, eight, twelve, or more pages (for purposes of printing and binding, it is always a number that can be divided by four). If the gallery is printed along with the text, on the same paper, its pages may be included in the numbering, even if the numbers do not actually appear (see 1.38). A gallery always begins on a recto (a right-hand page) and must fall between signatures (see A.49).

3.7   *Captions, legends, keys, and labels.* The terms *caption* and *legend* are sometimes used interchangeably for the explanatory text that appears with an illustration—usually immediately below but sometimes above or to the side. (In a distinction rarely made today, the term *caption* once referred strictly to a phrasal title or a headline, whereas *legend* referred to the full-sentence explanation immediately following the caption. This manual uses *caption* to refer to both.) A *key* (also sometimes called a legend) appears within the illustration itself and not as part of the caption; it identifies the symbols used in a map or a chart. For more on captions, see 3.21–27. *Labels* are any descriptive terms that appear within an illustration. They may also be symbols (often letters) used to indicate an illustration's parts. See figures 3.3, 3.4, 3.6. See also 3.12, 3.43.

Placement and Numbering of Illustrations

3.8   *Placement of illustrations relative to text.* Unless illustrations are presented separately (as in a gallery; see 3.6, 3.14), each should appear as soon as possible after the first text reference to it. In an electronic work, a captioned thumbnail image linked to its larger counterpart(s) may appear after the paragraph in which the image is first referenced. In printed works, to accommodate page makeup, the image may precede the reference only if it appears on the same page or same two-page spread as the reference or if the text is too short to permit placing all figures and tables after their references. If illustrations or thumbnail images are interspersed in the text, the author or (if the author has not done so) the editor must provide callouts that indicate in the manuscript the preferred

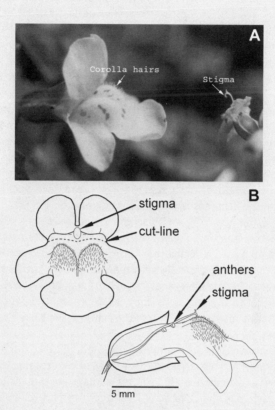

Fig. 1 Flower of *Mimulus guttatus*. *A*, Side-view photograph of two flowers illustrating the corolla hairs and stigma. The corolla and anthers have been pulled back to reveal the stigma and style on the left-hand flower. *B*, Line drawings of a front view and a side view. The cut line used in the phenotypic manipulation is illustrated in the front view. For the side view, the upper portion of the corolla has been removed to reveal the positions of the reproductive parts relative to the corolla hairs.

FIGURE 3.6. A figure consisting of a photograph and a line drawing, each with descriptive labels and identified by the letters *A* and *B*, respectively (see 3.12, 3.7).

location for each (see 2.27). Note that a callout (e.g., "fig. 5 about here") is an instruction for typesetting or production and will not appear in the published work (compare text references, which are addressed to readers; see 3.9). In a printed work, most illustrations will appear at either the top or the bottom of a page. No callouts are needed for illustrations that are to appear together in a printed gallery. In a work published online, callouts may be obviated or superseded by the electronic markup for text references and their associated figures and captions.

3.9 *Text references to numbered illustrations.* If there are more than a handful of illustrations in a work, they normally bear numbers (but see 3.13), and all text references to them should be by the numbers: "as figure 1 shows . . . ," "compare figures 4 and 5." If an online version of a work contains figures not available in a printed counterpart, the text references in the print version may refer readers to the figures in the online version (thereby avoiding separate numbering for illustrations in each version; see 1.73). An illustration should never be referred to in the text as "the photograph opposite" or "the graph on this page," for such placement may not be possible in the final version (but see 3.24). In text, the word *figure* is typically set roman, lowercased, and spelled out except in parenthetical references ("fig. 10"). *Plate,* however, should not be abbreviated to *pl.* In captions, these terms are sometimes distinguished typographically from the rest of the caption (see 3.23).

3.10 *Continuous versus separate numbering of illustrations.* All types of illustrations may be numbered together in one continuous sequence throughout a work. In book-length works, maps are sometimes numbered separately (e.g., map 1, map 2, . . .) as a convenience to readers; illustrations in a different medium are always numbered separately (e.g., video 1, video 2, . . .). In a work published in both print and electronic versions, illustrations that appear only in the electronic version sometimes necessitate separate enumeration in the two versions (but see 3.9). For double numeration, see 3.11. For illustrations in a gallery, see 3.6, 3.14.

3.11 *Double numeration of illustrations.* In scientific and technical books, heavily illustrated books, and books with chapters by different authors, double numeration may be employed. Each illustration carries the number of the chapter followed by the illustration number, usually separated by a period. Thus, for example, figure 9.6 is the sixth figure in chapter 9. Should a chapter contain only one illustration, a double number would still be used (e.g., figure 10.1). Appendix figures may be numbered A.1, A.2, and so on, or, if there are several appendixes and each bears a letter, A.1, A.2, B.1, B.2, and so on. At the editing stage, double numeration makes it easier to handle multiple illustrations and, should any be added or removed, involves far less renumbering. It also makes it easier for readers to find a particular illustration. This manual uses double numeration for illustrations and tables as well as for text paragraphs. See also 1.55.

3.12 *Identifying the parts of an illustration.* Chicago recommends the use of arabic numerals for illustrations of all kinds: "figure 12," "fig. 10.7." Where a figure consists of several parts, the parts may carry letters (*A, B, C,* etc.); a single caption, keying the letters to the parts, suffices (see figs. 3.4, 3.6). Text references may then refer, for example, to "fig. 10.7*C*" (note that the letters are usually italicized—with the number and when referred to alone). Parts may also be described according to their relative positions on a printed page (see fig. 3.7; see also 3.24); the relative positions must be maintained in an electronic version if the same description is to be used. (In the rare and undesirable event that a figure has to be added at a late stage to a work destined for print, when it is no longer feasible to renumber all the other figures, "fig. 10.7*A*" might refer to a figure inserted between figures 10.7 and 10.8.)

3.13 *Working numbers for unnumbered illustrations.* In some works, where illustrations are neither integral to the text nor specifically referred to, numbers are unnecessary. In the editing and production stages, however, all illustrations should carry working numbers, as should their captions, to ensure that they are correctly placed. As a further measure of insurance for printed books, after page proofs have been approved, copies of scans and prints might also be labeled with page numbers or other relevant information (e.g., "fig. 1, page 47, top" or "plate 3, gallery").

3.14 *Numbering illustrations in a gallery.* When illustrations are gathered together in a gallery, they need not be numbered unless referred to in the text, although in the editing and production stages they should carry working numbers to ensure the correct order (see 3.13). If numbers are required and the work also contains illustrations interspersed in the text, two number sequences must be adopted. For example, text illustrations may be referred to as "figure 1" and so on and gallery illustrations as "plate 1" and so on.

Preparation of Artwork

3.15 *Submitting artwork to the publisher.* Authors preparing illustrations electronically must consult their publishers before submitting the files. Most publishers require hard copies along with artwork submitted in elec-

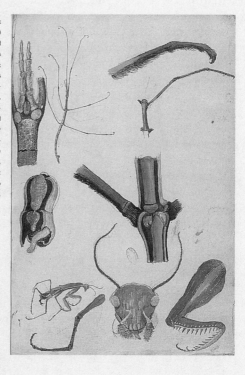

Fig. 8.34. *Above,* stick insect (fam. *Phasmatidae*) with details of head and legs; *center,* further details of parts of a stick insect; *below,* praying mantis (fam. *Mantidae*) with details of head and of legs, including, *right below,* details of tarsus, femur, and elongate coxa (trocaster not shown). Paris, Bibliothèque de l'Institut de France, MS 974, fol. between 112 and 113. © Photo RMN—Gérard Blot.

FIGURE 3.7.   The relative position of each part in this composite figure is identified in the caption (see 3.24).

tronic form. (A still image may be required for an audiovisual file submitted as an enhancement to an electronic work.) A list of the software programs used to create the digital artwork should also be furnished, and the publisher should be made aware of any special fonts used in the construction of drawings, diagrams, maps, and so forth; the publisher may need the author to supply these fonts. See also 2.4, 2.33. Any author-supplied scans must be made in accordance with the publisher's guidelines, preferably by a professional graphic arts service; Chicago offers such guidelines on its books and journals websites. (Publishers usually prefer to scan illustrations themselves, to ensure consistent quality and to facilitate subsequent stages in the publication process.) For color art intended for print, transparencies are usually preferred. (Authors should check their contracts to ensure that color illustrations are permitted.)

Images obtained from the Internet—barring the unlikely scenario that they have been optimized for print—are usually not acceptable.

3.16   *Identifying artwork for the publisher.* Artwork submitted in electronic form should be saved in separate files with descriptive names that accurately identify each file; these names should be included on the corresponding hard copies along with the numbers that correspond to the figure call-outs in the manuscript. Original artwork submitted as hard copy (e.g., photographic prints) must be clearly identified by the author or, failing that, by the publisher, in a manner that does not harm the original. Each item should be numbered on the back in pencil, very gently, making sure no mark is visible on the other side. If the paper does not accept lead pencil, a self-sticking label should be used. To be avoided are ballpoint pens, grease pencils, felt-tip markers, staples, or paper clips. For numbering, see 3.8–14; for captions, see 3.21–27.

3.17   *Author's inventory of artwork.* Along with artwork, the author should supply a complete list of illustrations, noting any that are to appear in color, any duplicates or extras, and any that are still to come. (Note, however, that for both books and journals, it is always expected and often mandatory that all illustrations be supplied at the time a manuscript is submitted; see 2.3.) If the work is to be published in print and electronic versions that will vary in the number of illustrations or in the use of color, that information must be noted in the inventory.

3.18   *Publisher's inventory of artwork.* As soon as the illustrations arrive from the author, publishers should check each one against the author's inventory (see 3.17). If an illustration is damaged or otherwise may not be reproducible, a better copy will need to be requested. (Missing illustrations will also need to be tracked down.) Each illustration should also be checked to be sure that it is properly numbered and labeled and that it corresponds correctly to each caption. (Authors should supply captions as a separate file; see 2.23.) If the author has not already done so, a photocopy should be made of each illustration furnished as a print, including all numbering and other information. (Publishers should beware, however, of using such photocopies to prepare or check caption or credit information unless the copies reproduce the original with total clarity. For these purposes, originals or high-resolution digital prints are best.) Finally, publishers should check for any necessary permissions (see 4.69–91, 4.92–101).

3.19   *Cropping and scaling and shading.* To make suggestions for reframing, or cropping, an image—that is, cutting it down to remove extraneous parts—authors should mark a printout or photocopy, or on an original print, use a tissue overlay to avoid damaging it. For images that need to be scaled, finished dimensions must be computed from the dimensions of the original. Authors need to be aware of this especially when preparing line art that contains labels or a key. The relations between font size, line weight (thickness, measured in points), and final printed size should be considered when drawings are created to ensure legibility. By scaling the image to its intended size and printing it out (or by using a photocopying machine), it is possible to get an idea of what the printed version will look like. Avoid hairline rules, which may disappear when printed. Likewise, avoid shading, which may print out poorly when reduced; use stripes, spots, and other black-and-white fill patterns in charts to distinguish areas from plain black or white. Many publishers, however, allow shading within line art submitted electronically in specific formats; consult your publisher's manuscript submission guidelines before preparing final art. See also 3.40–45.

3.20 *Artwork to be redrawn by the publisher.* Authors submitting line art (e.g., a line drawing or a chart) that the publisher has agreed to redraw should clearly mark any labels (words or symbols) to be altered or added on a photocopy or, if there are more than a few, in a separate document, keyed to the illustration. Where possible, wording, abbreviations, and symbols should be consistent with those used in the text. By a similar token, capitalization should be reserved for those terms that would be capitalized in running text. All names on a map that is to be redrawn should be prepared as a separate list, in which countries, provinces, cities, rivers, and so forth are divided into separate groups, each group arranged alphabetically.

Captions

3.21 *Syntax, punctuation, and capitalization.* A caption—the explanatory material that appears outside (usually below) an illustration—is distinct from a key and from a label, which appear within an illustration (see 3.7; see also 3.43). A caption may consist of a word or two, an incomplete or a complete sentence, several sentences, or a combination. No punctuation is needed after a caption consisting solely of an incomplete sentence. If one or more full sentences follow it, each (including the opening phrase) has closing punctuation. In a work in which most captions consist of full sentences, incomplete ones may be followed by a period for consistency. Captions should be capitalized in sentence style (see 8.156), but formal titles of works included in captions should be capitalized in headline style (see 3.22).

Wartime visit to Australia, winter 1940

The White Garden, reduced to its bare bones in early spring. The box hedges, which are still cut by hand, have to be carefully kept in scale with the small and complex garden as well as in keeping with the plants inside the "boxes."

3.22   *Formal titles in captions.* Titles of works should be presented according to the rules set forth in chapter 8 (see 8.154–95), whether standing alone or incorporated into a caption. Accordingly, most titles in English will appear in headline style (see 8.157), and many titles—including those for paintings, drawings, photographs, statues, and books—will be italicized; others will appear in roman type, enclosed in quotation marks (see 8.161). For foreign titles, see 11.3–8. Generic titles, however (as in the last example below), are not usually capitalized.

Frontispiece of *Christian Prayers and Meditations* (London: John Daye, 1569), showing Queen Elizabeth at prayer in her private chapel. Reproduced by permission of the Archbishop of Canterbury and the Trustees of the Lambeth Palace Library.

The head of Venus—a detail from Botticelli's *Birth of Venus.*

Francis Bedford, *Stratford on Avon Church from the Avon,* 1860s. Albumen print of collodion negative, 18.8 × 28.0 cm. Rochester, International Museum of Photography at George Eastman House.

Friedrich Overbeck and Peter Cornelius, double portrait, pencil drawing, 1812. Formerly in the Collection Lehnsen, Scarsdale, New York.

3.23   *Separating illustration numbers from captions.* Illustration numbers should be distinct from the captions they introduce. A period after the number usually suffices. If the number is distinguished typographically—for example, by boldface—the period may not be necessary. Extra space may be added between the number and the caption to ensure legibility, as in the second example. Whether *figure* is spelled out or abbreviated as *fig.* may be specified by journal style or, for books, may be up to the designer or editor or both.

Figure 3. Detailed stratigraphy and geochronology of the Dubawnt Supergroup.

PLATE 5   Palace of the Governors, Santa Fe, New Mexico. Undated photograph, circa 1900.

The word *figure* or *plate* is occasionally omitted—for example, in a book whose illustrations consist of a long series of continuously numbered photographs.

3.24 *Using locators in captions.* Italicize such terms as *top, bottom, left, right, above, below, left to right, clockwise from left,* or *inset* to identify elements within a single illustration or parts of a composite or, in print publications, an illustration that does not appear on the same page as the caption. If the term precedes the element it identifies, it should be followed by a comma or, if a list follows, a colon. When it appears in midsentence or follows the element, it may appear in parentheses. See figure 3.7.

Fig. 4. *Above left*, William Livingston; *above right*, Henry Brockholst Livingston; *below left*, John Jay; *below right*, Sarah Livingston Jay

Left to right: Madeleine K. Albright, Dennis Ross, Ehud Barak, and Yasir Arafat

Overleaf: The tall trees of the valley, planted by Russell Page, are reflected among the water lilies, *Nymphaea*, and pickerelweed, *Pontederia cordata*.

Figure 2. Schematic block diagram showing upper plate (*top*) and lower plate (*bottom*) of the Battle Lake thrust-tear fault system.

If the various parts of a figure have been assigned letters, these are used in a similar way, usually italicized (see also 3.12). Likewise, descriptive terms used to identify parts of a figure are usually italicized.

Figure 3. DNA sequence from a small region within the PC gene, showing the G→T transition at nucleotide 2229. The partial sequence of intron 13 is also shown. *A*, wild-type sequence; *B*, sequence from a PC-deficient Micmac homozygous for the mutation.

Figure 2. Duration of hospital stay for 22 patients colonized or infected with extended-spectrum β-lactamase-producing *Escherichia coli* isolates belonging to clonally related groups A (*gray bars*) and B (*white bars*). The black point represents the date when the microorganism was isolated, and the asterisk indicates stay in the geriatric care hospital.

In the last example, the letters identify the study groups and not parts of the figure and are therefore not italicized.

3.25 *Identifying symbols or patterns used in figures.* When symbols or patterns are used in a map or chart, they must be identified either in a key within the figure or in the caption. See figures 3.8, 3.9.

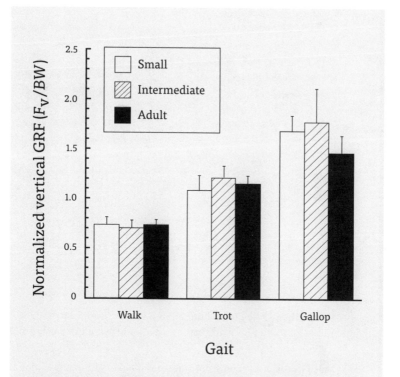

Figure 4. Normalized peak vertical forelimb GRFs versus gait. Normalized peak vertical forelimb GRFs for different gaits in the small, intermediate, and adult groups. Peak vertical forces (F_V) were normalized by dividing the forces by the body weight (BW) of the goat. Error bars represent ±1 sd.

FIGURE 3.8. A bar chart (also called a bar graph) with a key to the three types of bars (see 3.25). The caption includes the standard deviation (sd) for the T-shaped error bars. See also 3.40–45.

Fig. 9.4. Photosynthetic light response. Data are presented from shade-grown (■) and open-grown (□) culms of the current year.

or

Fig. 9.4. Photosynthetic light response. Data are presented from shade-grown (*solid squares*) and open-grown (*open squares*) culms of the current year.

3.26 *Identifying electronic enhancements in captions.* The caption to an illustration published both in print and online should add in the print version an indication of any electronic enhancement—such as color or video— available in the online version.

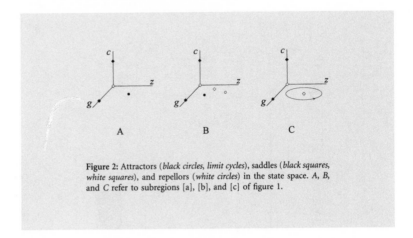

Figure 2: Attractors (*black circles, limit cycles*), saddles (*black squares, white squares*), and repellors (*white circles*) in the state space. *A, B,* and *C* refer to subregions [a], [b], and [c] of figure 1.

FIGURE 3.9. The symbols in this graph are identified in the caption. Compare figure 3.8 and the examples in 3.25. See also 3.40–45.

Fig. 3. Highlighting orbital lines in the Virtual Solar System (Gazit et al. 2005; Yair et al. 2001). This figure appears in color in the online version of this article.

Video 1. Still photograph from a video (available in the online edition of the *American Naturalist*) depicting a juvenile gorilla sniffing, tasting, and discarding *Nauclea* fruits. Apes are often very choosy about the fruits they eat, which can result in many discarded food items at "magnet" resources that have been handled or tested by previous visitors. Video by Thomas Breuer (Max Planck Institute and Wildlife Conservation Society).

The online version should generally specify which features are available only online—for example, in a list of an online journal article's contents, under a subheading "Enhancements" or "Online-Only Supplements." See also 1.73.

3.27 *Including original dimensions in captions.* When a caption provides the dimensions of an original work of art, these follow the work's medium and are listed in order of height, width, and (if applicable) depth. This information need appear only if relevant to the text, unless the rights holder requests that it be included (see 3.31).

Oil on canvas, 45 × 38 cm   Bronze, 49 × 22 × 16 in.

See also the example in 3.22. Photomicrographs, in scientific publications, may include in their captions information about the degree of magnification (e.g., original magnification, ×400; *bar*, 100 μm).

Credit Lines

3.28   *Sources and permissions.* A brief statement of the source of an illustration, known as a credit line, is usually appropriate and sometimes required by the owner of the illustration. Illustrative material under copyright, whether published or unpublished, usually requires permission from the copyright owner before it can be reproduced. You cannot simply snap a photo of your favorite Picasso and use it to illustrate your history of cubism; before attempting to reproduce the painting, you must write to obtain written permission, as well as a print of the work, from the museum, or person, that owns it. Nor may you use a photograph or other portrayal of an identifiable human subject without the consent of that person or someone acting on his or her behalf. Although it is the author's responsibility, not the publisher's, to obtain permissions, the publisher should be consulted about what needs permission and the best way to obtain it. For a fuller discussion of permissions, see 4.83, 4.92–101. For a work that will be published in electronic as well as printed form, see 4.60.

3.29   *Placement of credit lines.* A credit line usually appears at the end of a caption, sometimes in parentheses or in different type (or both). A photographer's name occasionally appears in small type parallel to the bottom or side of a photograph.

Fig. 37. The myth that all children love dinosaurs is contradicted by this nineteenth-century scene of a visit to the monsters at Crystal Palace. (Cartoon by John Leech. "Punch's Almanac for 1855," *Punch* 28 [1855]: 8. Photo courtesy of the Newberry Library, Chicago.)

If most or all of the illustrations in a work are from a single source, that fact may be stated in a note or, in the case of a book, in the preface or acknowledgments or on the copyright page. In a heavily illustrated book, all credits are sometimes listed together in the back matter (see 1.4) or, more rarely, in the front matter—sometimes as part of a list of illustrations (see 3.37). Note, however, that some permissions grantors stipulate placement of the credit with the illustration itself; others may charge a higher fee if the credit appears elsewhere.

3.30   *Crediting author as source of illustration.* Although illustrations created by the author do not need credit lines, such wording as "Photo by author" may be appropriate if other illustrations in the same work require credit. In works with more than one author, such wording may include the name of a particular author.

3.31   *Crediting material that requires permission.* Unless fair use applies (see 4.77–87), an illustration reproduced from a published work under copyright always requires formal permission. In addition to author, title, publication details, and (occasionally) copyright date, the credit line should include any page or figure number. If the work being credited is listed in the bibliography or reference list, only a shortened form need appear in the credit line (see third example). For material acquired from a commercial agency, see 3.35. For proper citation style, see chapters 14 and 15.

Reproduced by permission from Mark Girouard, *Life in the English Country House: A Social and Architectural History* (New Haven, CT: Yale University Press, 1978), 162.

Reproduced by permission from George B. Schaller et al., *The Giant Pandas of Wolong* (Chicago: University of Chicago Press, 1985), 52. © 1985 by the University of Chicago.

Reprinted by permission from Duncan (1999, fig. 2).

Some permissions grantors request specific language in the credit line. In a work with many illustrations, such language in one or two credit lines may conflict with consistent usage in the rest. Editorial discretion should then be exercised; in giving full credit to the source, an editor may follow the spirit rather than the letter. (Where the grantor is intractable, it may be simpler to use the language requested.)

3.32   *Crediting commissioned material.* Work commissioned by the author—such as maps, photographs, drawings, or charts—is usually produced under a "work made for hire" contract (see 4.9–12). Even if no credit is required under such an arrangement, professional courtesy dictates mentioning the creator (unless the illustration is legibly signed and the signature reproduced).

Map by Kevin Hand   Photograph by Ted Lacey   Drawing by Barbara Smith

3.33   *Crediting material obtained free of charge.* For material that the author has obtained free and without restrictions on its use, the credit line may use the word *courtesy.*

Photograph courtesy of Ford Motor Company

Mies at the groundbreaking ceremony of the National Gallery, September 1965. Courtesy of Reinhard Friedrich.

3.34   *Crediting material in the public domain.* Illustrations from works in the public domain (see 4.19–32) may be reproduced without permission. For readers' information, however, a credit line is appropriate.

Illustration by Joseph Pennell for Henry James, *English Hours* (Boston, 1905), facing p. 82.

Reprinted from John D. Shortridge, *Italian Harpsichord-Building in the 16th and 17th Centuries*, US National Museum Bulletin 225 (Washington, DC, 1960).

3.35   *Crediting agency material.* Photographs of prints, drawings, paintings, and the like obtained from a commercial agency usually require a credit line.

Woodcut from Historical Pictures Service, Chicago
Photograph from Wide World Photos

3.36   *Crediting adapted material.* An author creating an illustration adjusted from, or using data from, another source should credit that source for reasons of professional courtesy and readers' information.

Figure 1.2. Weight increase of captive pandas during the first years of life. (Data from New York Zoological Park; National Zoological Park; Giron 1980.)

Adapted from Pauly (2001, fig. 5.5).

Lists of Illustrations

3.37   *When to include a list of illustrations.* For book-length printed works, the criterion for when to include a list of illustrations is whether the illustrations are of intrinsic interest apart from the text they illustrate. A book on Roman architecture, illustrated by photographs of ancient buildings, would benefit from a list. Electronic works as a matter of course, on the other hand, will often include a list as an aid to navigation. In a printed work, a list of illustrations, if included, usually follows the table of contents. A list of illustrations may occasionally double as a list of credits if these do not appear with the illustrations themselves (see 3.29). For guidelines and examples, see 1.38 and figures 1.6, 1.7.

3.38   *Listing illustrations from a gallery.* Illustrations that are to appear in printed galleries are not always listed separately. For example, in a book containing interspersed line art and two photo galleries, a line reading "Photographs follow pages 228 and 332" might be inserted after the detailed list of figures. If all the illustrations were in galleries, that line could appear at the end of the table of contents (see fig. 1.5). (All illustrations, including those in galleries, should be listed if integral to the text.)

3.39   *Shortening captions for a list of illustrations.* In the list of illustrations, long captions should be shortened to a single line (or two at the most). The number at the end of each of the two entry examples indicates the page on which the illustration would be found.

[*Caption*] Fig. 18. The White Garden, reduced to its bare bones in early spring. The box hedges, which are still cut by hand, have to be carefully kept in scale with the small and complex garden as well as in keeping with the plants inside the "boxes."

[*Entry in list*] 18. The White Garden in early spring   43

[*Caption*] Plate 21. The tall trees of the valley, planted by Russell Page, are reflected among the water lilies, *Nymphaea*, and pickerelweed, *Pontederia cordata*.

[*Entry in list*] 21. Page's tall trees reflected among water lilies   75

Charts

3.40   *What is a chart?* A chart, also called a graph, is a device that presents data in a simple, comprehensible form—often along a set of x and y axes. A chart is considered line art and should be numbered and labeled as a figure (fig. 1, fig. 2, etc.). It should be used only if it summarizes the data more effectively than mere words can. While integral to the text, it should, like a table, make sense on its own terms. For guidance in chart design, consult Edward R. Tufte, *The Visual Display of Quantitative Information* (bibliog. 2.2). Charts intended for black-and-white reproduction should not be produced in color. For an example of a typical chart, see figure 3.8. Figure 3.9—essentially a three-part graph—is a less typical example.

3.41   *Consistency among charts.* Where two or more charts are used within a work, especially if they deal with comparable material, they should follow a consistent style in graphics and typography. Whatever graphic device is used, elements of the same kind must always be represented in the same way. Different visual effects should be used only to distinguish one element from another, never just for variety.

3.42   *Axes and curves in graphs.* Both the x (horizontal) and the y (vertical) axes should be labeled (as in fig. 3.8); the axes serve a function similar to that of column heads and stubs in a table (see 3.49). The label on the y axis is read from the bottom up. Curves are usually presented in graphically distinct forms—for example, one may be a continuous line, another a broken line. The elements in a bar chart or a pie chart that correspond to curves—the bars or the wedges—are also usually distinct. Black-and-white fill elements should be used rather than shading unless the publisher allows shading in specially prepared electronic files (see 3.19). All such elements should be labeled or else identified in a key or in the caption (see 3.7, 3.25).

3.43   *Chart titles and labels.* The title of a chart appears as part of the caption, immediately following the figure number, and is capitalized sentence-style (see 8.156). See 3.7; compare 3.52. Labels, the descriptive items within a chart, are normally lowercased (with the exception of proper nouns or other terms that would be capitalized in running text); if phrases, they may be capitalized sentence-style. Labels may be explained or discussed in a caption as needed (as in fig. 3.9).

3.44   *Abbreviations in labels.* Abbreviations and symbols may be used in labels as long as they are easily recognizable or explained in a key or in the caption. A form such as "US\$millions" may be more appropriate for nonspecialized (or non-English-speaking) readers than "US\$M," but the shorter form is acceptable if readers will find it clear and it is used consistently. Numbers and abbreviations are covered in chapters 9 and 10.

3.45   *Genealogical and pedigree charts.* Some charts show relationships between elements in a way that cannot be conveniently arranged along axes or into rows and columns. Charts that show family or genetic structure, in particular, may require a different visual arrangement that highlights multiple relationships. A genealogical chart (often called a table and treated as such in previous editions of this manual), for example, attempts to show important relationships within a family or several families by means of branching and connecting lines. Figure 3.10, for instance, illustrates the complicated connection of Constantine the Great to Hilderic, King of the Vandals. These charts require careful planning to illustrate relationships with minimal crossing of lines or extraneous data and, for a printed work, to remain within a reproducible shape and size. Similar to the genealogi-

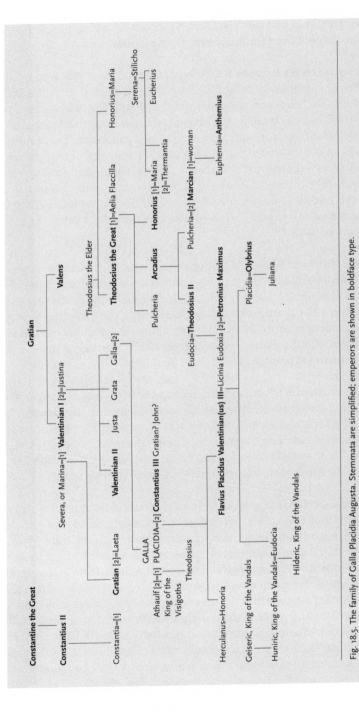

FIGURE 3.10. A genealogical chart (see 3.45).

cal chart is the pedigree chart, used mainly in genealogical works. These fan-shaped diagrams illustrate the ancestry of a given person, typically detailing the two parents, four grandparents, eight great-grandparents, and sixteen great-great-grandparents. They may also show several generations of offspring from a single pair of ancestors and can be used to trace the inheritance of a trait or disorder. These special types of charts should be checked carefully for sense, consistency, and correlation to the surrounding text.

Tables

Introduction

3.46 *Table preparation.* This section describes and illustrates the basic elements of a table and accepted ways of editing, arranging, and typesetting these elements. No one table in this chapter should be taken as a prototype; all merely illustrate workable patterns and may be adapted according to the data and the potential users of the tables. Though most tables can be created using the table editor in a word processor, they are nonetheless expensive (i.e., time-consuming) both to typeset and to correct in proofs and should therefore be designed and constructed with care. It is wise to consult the publisher on the appropriate number, size, and physical form of any tables to be included in a work. A table should be as simple as the material allows and understandable on its own; even a reader unfamiliar with the material presented should be able to make general sense of a table. The text may highlight the main points in a table and summarize its message but should not duplicate the details. For excellent advice on table preparation, consult the *Publication Manual of the American Psychological Association* (bibliog. 1.1). For specific instructions on preparing electronic table files, consult your publisher. Chicago offers instructions for table preparation on its journals website.

3.47 *Use of tables.* A table offers an excellent means of presenting a large number of individual, similar facts so that they are easy to scan and compare. A simple table can give information that would require several paragraphs to present textually, and it can do so more clearly. An electronic table allows presentation of even more data, well beyond what may be practical in print. Tables are most appropriate for scientific, statistical, financial, and other technical material. In certain contexts—if, for example, exact values are not essential to an author's argument—a graph or a bar chart (see 3.40), or plain text, may more effectively present the data.

3.48 *Consistency among tables.* Because a prime virtue of tables is easy comparison, consistency in style is indispensable both within one table and among several. A consistent style for titles, column heads, abbreviations, and the like should be selected and followed for all tables in a single work. Similarly, choices related to line spacing, indention, fonts, rules, and other distinguishing features must be made uniformly for all tables in a work. Certain tables, however, may require rules or other devices not needed in other tables in the same work.

The Parts of a Table

3.49 *Table structure and use.* A table normally consists of rows and columns, which are analogous to the horizontal (x) and vertical (y) axes of a graph, respectively. The data in most tables include two sets of variables. One set of variables is defined in the top row of a table, in the column headings (see 3.54); the other set is defined along the far left-hand column of the table by the stub entries (see 3.57). If the data consist of dependent and independent variables, the independent variables are usually presented in the stub column, though this choice is sometimes limited by the physical dimensions of the table (see 3.84). The intersection between a row defined by a stub entry and a column defined by a column head is a cell (sometimes called a data cell). See figure 3.11.

3.50 *Horizontal and vertical rules.* To produce a clear, professional-looking table, rules should be used sparingly. Many tables will require just three rules, all of them horizontal—one at the very top of the table, below the title and above the column heads; one just below the column heads; and one at the bottom of the table, along the bottom of the last row, above any notes to the table. Additional horizontal rules may be required to separate spanner heads from column heads (see 3.55) or to enclose cut-in heads (see 3.56). A rule above a row of totals is traditional but not essential (unless required by a journal or series style). See also 3.61. The double rule traditionally used between title and column heads, still used by some journals, is seen less than it once was. Vertical rules should be used sparingly—for example, when a table is doubled up (see 3.84) or as an aid to comprehension in an especially long or complex table (such as the ten-page hyphenation guide at the end of chapter 7 of this manual; see 7.85).

TABLE 1. Fraction of movers by desertion status

	State mover	Within-state county mover	County stayer
Nondeserter	.440	.331	.229
Returned deserter	.422	.353	.225
Deserter	.636	.242	.122

Note: State mover is an individual who moved across states; within-state county mover is an individual who moved within a state but across a county; and county stayer is an individual who remained in the same county between enlistment and 1880.

FIGURE 3.11. A four-column table with three column headings (*top row*), three stub entries (*far left-hand column*), and nine data cells (see 3.49).

3.51 *Numbering tables.* Tables should be numbered separately from any illustrations (table 1, table 2, etc.). In a book with many tables, or with chapters by different authors, double numeration by chapter is often used, as it is for illustrations (table 1.1, table 1.2, . . . , table 2.2, table 2.3, . . . , etc.; see 3.11). For table titles, see 3.52. Every table should be cited in the text by the number, either directly or parenthetically.

The first column of table 2 displays the results of a model predicting the age trajectory of health, controlling for differences by cohort and excluding all other predictors.

Ethnographic observation brought to light four analytically distinct but empirically interrelated types of worker response to the new regimes (see table 5.3).

Note that the word *table* is lowercased in text references. Table numbers follow the order in which the tables are to appear in the text, and first mentions should follow that order as well. (But where context demands a reference to a table in a subsequent chapter of a book, such wording as "A different set of variables is presented in chapter 5, table 10" may be appropriate.) Each table, even in a closely related set, should be given its own number (tables 14, 15, and 16, *rather than* tables 14A–C). A simple list or other tabular matter that requires only two columns can usually be presented in the run of text and left unnumbered and untitled (see, e.g., the two-column list at 1.4 in this manual).

3.52 *Table titles.* Titles should be as succinct as possible and should not suggest any interpretation of the data. For example, a title such as "Recidivism among reform school parolees" is preferable to "High degree of recidivism among reform school parolees." Titles should be in noun form, and participles are preferred to relative clauses: for example, "Families subscribing to weekly news magazines," not "Families that subscribe to weekly news magazines." Table titles may be capitalized in sentence style (see 8.156), as in the examples in this chapter, or in the more traditional headline style (see 8.157) as long as one style prevails throughout the work. The title, which appears above the table, usually follows the number on the same line, separated by punctuation or by space and typographic distinction. (Less commonly, the number appears on a line by itself, the title starting a new line.) The number is always preceded by the word *table*.

Table 6. Ratios of parental income coefficients to SAT score coefficients

Table 12 Fertilizer treatment effects on *Lythrum salicaria* and *Penthorum sedoides*

3.53 *Parenthetical information in table titles.* Important explanatory or statistical information is often included in parentheses in a title. Such material should be set in sentence style even if the main title is in headline style. More detailed information should go in a note to the table (see 3.76, 3.77).

Federal employees in the Progressive Era (total plus selected agencies)
Scan statistics S_L of varying lengths L for sib-pair data (broad diagnosis)
Gender as a factor in successful business transactions (N = 4,400)

For the significance of N used in statistical tables, see 3.83.

3.54 *Column heads.* Space being at a premium, column heads should be as brief as possible and are best capitalized sentence-style (as in all examples in this chapter). As long as their meaning is clear to readers, abbreviations may be used as needed. The first column (the stub) does not always require a head (see 3.57). In a work that includes a number of tables, column heads should be treated consistently. Like table titles, a column head may require an indication of the unit of measurement used or some other clarification of the data in the column. Such material, which may consist of a symbol or an abbreviation ($, %, km, n, and so on), should follow the column head in parentheses. See figure 3.12. Parentheses may also be used in column heads when some of the data in the cells are in parentheses. For example, a column head might read "Children with positive results, % (no. positive/no. tested)" and a cell under this head could contain "27.3 (6/22)." If columns must be numbered for text reference, use arabic numerals in parentheses, centered immediately below the column head, above the rule separating the head from the column (see also 3.84).

TABLE 2. Real-world magnitudes of the relationship between tort reform and death rates

Tort reform	Annual death rates (%)	Number of deaths in 2000	Deaths across all years
Cap on noneconomic damages	−3.54	−333	−5,242
Higher evidence standard for punitive damages	−2.57	−982	−11,798
Product liability reform	−3.83	−1,267	−16,841
Prejudgment interest reform	−4.88	−647	−9,060
Collateral source reform			
Offset awards	+4.71	+938	+14,160
Admit evidence	+2.43	+294	+4,468
Net effect		−1,998	−24,314

Note: Values presented are average changes. These computations are based on the coefficients from the primary regression (table 3) and the average annual populations and average annual death rates in the states that had each reform. The sums of the individual reforms differ by one from the net effects owing to rounding.

FIGURE 3.12. A four-column table with two levels of stub entries (*first column*). Note the parenthetical indication in the second column head, specifying percentages for the values in that column (see 3.54).

3.55   *Spanner heads.* When a table demands column heads of two or more levels—when related columns require both a collective head and individual heads—spanner heads, or spanners (sometimes called decked heads), are used. A horizontal rule, called a spanner rule (or straddle), appears between the spanner and the column heads to show which columns the spanner applies to (see fig. 3.13). For ease of reading, spanner heads should seldom exceed two levels.

3.56   *Cut-in heads.* Cut-in heads, spanning all columns but the first, may be used as subheads within a table. They usually appear between horizontal rules (see fig. 3.14), though extra vertical space above each head may be used instead. An exceptionally long table with one or more cut-in heads may be a candidate for division into two or more tables.

3.57   *Stub entries.* The left-hand column of a table, known as the stub, is usually a vertical listing of categories about which information is given in the following columns. If all the entries are of like kind, the stub usually carries a column head (e.g., "Tort reform" in fig. 3.12); even a general head such as "Characteristic" or "Variable" or "Year" aids readers. If the entries are self-explanatory (as in figs. 3.11 and 3.14), a head may be

TABLE 3. Survey responses from patients who received intravenous (IV) prostanoids at center 1 in 2006

Question type and characteristic	No. (%) of patients, by prostanoid received		P
	Epoprostenol ($n = 48$)	Treprostinil ($n = 24$)	
IV catheter–related question			
Person responsible for care of IV catheter			
Patient	22 (47)	10 (43)	
Adult caregiver	23 (49)	13 (57)	
Both	2 (4)	0 (0)	.82
Catheter type			
Groshong	23 (50)	12 (50)	
Broviac	23 (50)	12 (50)	1.0
Catheter-dressing type			
Occlusive	27 (57)	15 (63)	
Nonocclusive	20 (43)	9 (38)	.68
Allowed >2 days between changes of dressing	14 (29)	7 (29)	1.00
Used sterile gloves when changing dressings	38 (79)	17 (71)	.43
Used mask when changing dressings	28 (58)	13 (54)	.74
Always washed hands before changing dressings	46 (96)	22 (92)	.60
Medication-related question			
Person responsible for medication preparation			
Patient	21 (45)	12 (52)	
Adult caregiver	24 (51)	10 (43)	
Both	2 (4)	1 (4)	.82
Used needleless device to access vial of medication or diluent[a]	4 (8)	5 (21)	.15
Cleaned top of vial of medication or diluent[a] with alcohol before use	45 (94)	24 (100)	.55
Always washed hands before medication preparation	46 (96)	22 (92)	.60
Miscellaneous question			
Used a swimming pool or hot tub	3 (6)	4 (17)	.18

[a]Refers to the treprostinil vial for patients who received treprostinil and to the diluent vial for patients who received epoprostenol.

FIGURE 3.13. A four-column table with a spanner head across the second and third columns, separated from the column heads by a horizontal rule (see 3.55). Note the three levels of stub entries (see 3.58). Note also that the spanner head specifies two units for each column—number and, in parentheses, percentage (see 3.54).

TABLE 4. Distribution of estimated school quality

	All schools	Rural	Urban
	OLS estimates[a]		
Mean	−.120	−.178	−.063
Minimum	−.72	−.72	−.30
Maximum	.33	.33	.18
	MLE estimates[b]		
Mean	−.063	−.101	−.025
Minimum	−.43	−.43	−.26
Maximum	.40	.40	.17

Note: School quality is measured as proportional deviations from Taha Hussein School.
[a]School-quality estimates from col. 1, table 1.
[b]School-quality estimates from col. 3, table 1.

FIGURE 3.14. A four-column table with two cut-in heads ("OLS estimates" and "MLE estimates") across three columns, separated by horizontal rules (see 3.56); a general note (see 3.76); and two lettered footnotes (see 3.77).

omitted from the stub; a head may also be omitted if the entries are too unlike (as in fig. 3.16). If the stub entries are words, they are capitalized sentence-style. Unless they are questions, they carry no end punctuation. They should be consistent in syntax: Authors, Publishers, Printers (*not* Authors, Publishing concerns, Operates printshop).

3.58 *Stub entries with subheads.* Items in the stub may form a straight sequential list (e.g., all the states in the Union listed alphabetically) or a classified list (e.g., the states listed by geographic region, with a subhead above each region). The first word in a subentry as well as in a main entry is capitalized, to avoid confusion with runover lines. Subentries are further distinguished from main entries by being indented (as in fig. 3.12), or italics may be used for the main entries and roman for the subentries. A combination of italics and indention may also be used, especially if subsubentries are required. There is generally no need for colons following main entries, but a particular journal style may require them. See also 3.59.

3.59 *Runover lines in stub columns.* If there are no subentries, runover lines in stub entries should be indented (typically by one em in typeset copy). Only if there is extra space between rows should runovers be set flush left. If there are indented subentries, any runover lines must be more deeply indented than the lowest level of subentry (see fig. 3.12). Runovers from main entries and subentries carry the same indention from the left margin (in typeset copy, typically one em farther to the right than the indent for the lowest level of subentry).

3.60   *Abbreviations in stub columns.* As in column heads (see 3.54), where space is at a premium, symbols or abbreviations ($, %, km, *n*, and so on) are acceptable in the stub. Ditto marks (" ") to indicate information that repeats from one row to the next are not, however, since they save no space and make work for readers. Any nonstandard abbreviations must be defined in a table footnote (see 3.77).

3.61   *Totals.* When the word *Total* appears at the foot of the stub, it is often indented more deeply than the greatest indention above (see fig. 3.21) or distinguished typographically (see fig. 3.15). See also 3.72, 3.73.

3.62   *Using leaders with stub entries.* Leaders—several spaced periods following a stub entry—are sometimes used in a table where the connection between the stub entries and the rows they apply to would otherwise be unclear. Some journals routinely use leaders in stubs (see fig. 3.16); books use them more rarely. Another practice—used routinely by some journals—is to apply shading to every other row.

3.63   *Table body and cells.* Strictly speaking, the table body includes all rows, columns, and heads. Nonetheless, it is often convenient to consider the body of a table as consisting of the points of intersection between the stub entries and the column headings—the real substance of the table. These intersections are called cells (or data cells). The fifth cell in the fourth column of the table in figure 3.12, for example, contains the datum "+14,160." Though cells are usually occupied by data, they may be empty (see 3.65).

3.64   *Column data.* Whenever possible, columns should carry the same kinds of information. For instance, amounts of money should appear in one column, percentages in another, and information expressed in words in another (though two types of data can share the same column, as in the table in fig. 3.13; see 3.67). No column should contain identical information in all the cells; such information is better handled in a footnote.

3.65   *Empty cells.* If a column head does not apply to one of the entries in the stub, the cell should either be left blank or, better, filled in by an em dash

TABLE 5. State expansion in the Progressive Era: Number of federal employees (total plus selected agencies)

Selected agencies	1909	1917	Increase (%)
Dept. of Agriculture	11,279	20,269	79.7
Interstate Commerce Commission	560	2,370	323.2
Dept. of Justice	3,198	4,512	41.1
Dept. of Commerce and Labor[a]	11,999	14,993	25.0
Dept. of the Navy[b]	3,390	6,420	89.4
Dept. of War[c]	22,292	30,870	38.5
Dept. of the Interior[d]	17,900	22,478	25.6
Federal Reserve Board	...	75	
Civil Service Commission	193	276	43.0
Federal Trade Commission	...	244	
Shipping Board	...	22	
Total			
DC and non-DC	342,159	497,867[e]	45.5
Excluding Post Office	136,799	198,199	44.9

Sources: Reports of the United States Civil Service Commission (Washington, DC: GPO): 1910, table 19; 1917, tables 9–10; 1919, p. vi; U.S. Department of Commerce, Bureau of the Census, *Statistical Abstract of the United States, 1917* (Washington, DC: GPO, 1918), table 392.

[a]The Departments of Commerce and Labor were combined until 1913. The Civil Service Commission continued to combine their employees in its subsequent reports through 1917. Separate employment figures for the Labor Department, taken from *The Anvil and the Plow: A History of the Department of Labor* (Washington, DC: GPO, 1963), appendix, table 6, show an essentially stable personnel level (2,000 in 1913, 2,037 in 1917). The bulk of employees (1,740) were attached to the Bureau of Immigration and Naturalization in 1917. The Bureau of Labor Statistics was second in importance, with 104. The Children's Bureau had 103, an increase of 88 from 1913; and the Conciliation Service had only 12, taken from the secretary's personal allotment. In the next two years of wartime, given new labor-market and conciliation functions, the departments' personnel would almost triple; however, the number fell back sharply in 1920.

[b]Exclusive of trade and labor employees.

[c]Excludes "ordinance and miscellaneous" categories.

[d]Includes Land, Pension, Indian, and Reclamation Services.

[e]Excludes Panama Canal workforce.

FIGURE 3.15. Four-column table with *Total* appearing in italics, to distinguish it from the stub entries above and below. Compare figure 3.21. See also 3.61. Also note the use of ellipsis dots for cells with no data; cells for which data is not applicable are blank. See 3.65.

or three unspaced ellipsis dots. If a distinction is needed between "not applicable" and "no data available," a blank cell may be used for the former and an em dash or ellipsis dots for "no data" (see fig. 3.15). If this distinction is not clear from the text, a note may be added to the table. (Alternatively, the abbreviations *n/a* and *n.d.* may be used, with definitions given in a note.) A zero means literally that the quantity in a cell is zero (see figs. 3.13, 3.16).

TABLE 6. Decisions on submitted manuscripts

	2006	2005	Less than 1 month		1-2 months		2-3 months		More than 3 months	
			2006	2005	2006	2005	2006	2005	2006	2005
Accepted										
Original manuscript accepted as submitted or with minor revisions	0	2	0	0	0	0	0	1	0	1
Conditional acceptance of original manuscript; revised version accepted	0	0	0	0	0	0	0	0	0	0
Acceptance of resubmission of revised manuscript	16	14	2	1	1	0	4	2	9	9
Rejected										
Original manuscript rejected with suggestion of resubmission	34	26	5	3	6	4	3	2	20	17
Original manuscript rejected without suggestion of resubmission	249	260	165	161	34	34	16	18	34	47
Rejection of resubmission of revised manuscript	22	26	2	0	1	0	2	1	14	26
Total new submissions received	283	288								
Total resubmissions received	38	41								
Manuscripts withdrawn	0	3								
Total submissions received	321	332	174	165	42	38	25	26	77	100
Percentage of total	100	100	54	50	13	11	8	8	24	30

Time from receipt to decision (spanning Less than 1 month, 1-2 months, 2-3 months, More than 3 months columns)

FIGURE 3.16. An eleven-column table with three levels of column heads, separated by spanner rules (see 3.55), and with leader dots from stub entries (see 3.62). Note also the two rows of totals; the rule above these rows is common but by no means required (see 3.61).

TABLE 7. Innovations in measures of Amgen operating performance and stock market returns: Correlation matrix for the variables

	Revenue	Net income	Operating cash flow	Free cash flow	S&P 500 return	CRSP return
Revenue	1.00					
Net income	.03	1.00				
Operating cash flow	−.07	.91	1.00			
Free cash flow	.09	.12	.04	1.00		
S&P 500 return	.05	.04	.22	.16	1.00	
CRSP return	.08	.00	.19	.16	.99	1.00

Note: For revenue, the innovation is defined as the log-first difference. For all the other operating variables, it is the arithmetic-first difference.

FIGURE 3.17. A seven-column matrix, in which the six column heads are identical to the six stub entries. Those cells that repeat order-independent relationships from other cells are left blank. See 3.66.

TABLE 8. Average Euclidean distances between populations, calculated from morphological data

Population	Chunliao	Lona	Yunshanchau	Tunchiu	Tenchu	Hohuanshan	Tatachia
Chunliao	...						
Lona	.57	...					
Yunshanchau	.75	1.25	...				
Tunchiu	.71	1.03	.78	...			
Tenchu	1.15	1.10	1.59	.97	...		
Hohuanshan	1.51	1.43	2.00	1.65	1.16	...	
Tatachia	1.85	2.03	2.17	1.69	1.24	1.55	...

FIGURE 3.18. An eight-column matrix. The intersections of like columns and stub entries are marked with ellipsis dots. See 3.66.

3.66   *Matrixes.* A matrix is a tabular structure designed to show reciprocal relationships within a group of individuals, concepts, or whatever. In a matrix, the stub entries are identical to the column heads; therefore, the cells present two identical sets of intersections. The cells that would contain repeated data may be left blank if the relational order is not significant (see fig. 3.17); in some matrixes, the intersection of matching heads may be left blank or marked with an em dash or ellipsis dots (as in fig. 3.18).

3.67   *Presenting multiple values in a single cell.* To allow for fewer columns, a single cell may contain two values, with one appearing in parentheses (see fig. 3.13). Such cases should be clarified in the column heading (see 3.54) or in a note.

Cell Alignment and Formatting

3.68 *Alignment of rows.* Each cell in a row aligns with the stub entry it applies to. If the stub entry occupies more than one line, the cell entry is normally aligned on the last line of the stub entry (see fig. 3.13). But if both the stub and one or more cells contain more than one line, the first lines are aligned throughout the body of the table. First lines are also aligned in a table where the content of each column is of the same sort—in other words, where the first column is not a stub as described in 3.57 (see fig. 3.19). See also 3.69.

TABLE 9. Role-style differentiae in the Lewin, Lippitt, and White "group atmosphere" studies

Authoritarian	Democratic	Laissez-faire
All determination of policy by leader	All policies a matter of group discussion and decision, encouraged and assisted by the leader	Complete freedom for group or individual decision, with a minimum of leader participation
Techniques and activity steps dictated by the authority, one at a time, so that future steps were uncertain to a large degree	Activity perspective gained during discussion period. General steps to group goal sketched; when advice was needed, the leader suggested two or more alternative procedures from which choice could be made	Various materials supplied by leader, who made clear a willingness to supply technical information when asked. He took no other part in work discussion
Leader usually dictated the task and companion of each member	Members were free to work with whomever they chose, and division of tasks was left to the group	Complete nonparticipation of the leader
Leader tended to be "personal" in praise and criticism of each member's work; remained aloof from active group participation except when demonstrating	Leader was "objective" in praise and criticism and tried to be a regular group member in spirit without doing too much work	Leader did not comment on member activities unless questioned, did not attempt to appraise or regulate the course of events

FIGURE 3.19. Three-column table with no stub entries (see 3.57, 3.68).

3.69 *Alignment of column heads.* Column heads that share a row align on the baseline; if any head occupies more than one line, all the heads in that row align on the last (lowest) line. Each column head except in the stub column is normally centered on the longest (i.e., widest) cell entry. If the latter is unusually long, adjustment may be necessary to give an appearance of balance. If centering does not work, align column heads and cells on the left. The stub head and entries are always aligned on the left.

3.70 *Alignment of numbers within columns.* Within a column, numbers without decimal points are usually aligned on the last digit, "ranged right" (see fig. 3.16). If the numbers include decimal points, they are typically aligned on the decimal point (see fig. 3.13). For quantities less than 1.0, zeros do not need to be added before the decimal in a table unless prescribed by a journal or series style (though they would usually be required in running text). See also 9.19. Where spaces rather than commas are used to separate groups of digits (see 9.20), alignment is made on the implicit comma. In all these arrangements, the column of numerals as a whole is usually centered within the column on the longest (i.e., widest) numeral. A column including different kinds of numbers is best aligned on the ones that occur most frequently (as in the table in fig. 3.20, in which most of the values are aligned on the decimal point, but the values for *N* are centered; see also 3.83). Ellipses and em dashes are centered (see fig. 3.15).

3.71 *Alignment of columns consisting of words.* When a column consists of words, phrases, or sentences, appearance governs left-right alignment. If no runover lines are required, entries may be centered. Longer entries usually look better if they begin flush left. Runover lines may be indented or, if enough space is left between entries, aligned flush left with the first line (as in fig. 3.19).

3.72 *Format for totals, averages, and means.* Extra vertical space or short rules sometimes appear above totals at the foot of columns but may equally well be omitted. No rules, however, should appear above averages or means. Consistency must be maintained and, where applicable, journal or series style followed. The word *Total* in the stub is often indented. Subtotals are similarly treated. See figure 3.21. See also 3.61, 3.73.

3.73 *When to use totals.* Totals and subtotals may be included or not, according to how useful they are to the presentation. When the percentages in a column are based on different *n*'s, a final percentage based on the total *N* may be informative and, if so, should be included (see 3.83). Note that rounding often causes a percentage total to be slightly more or less than

TABLE 10. Descriptive statistics

Variable	Mean	Standard deviation
Cohort dummy		
1946	.128	.33
1947	.140	.35
1948	.145	.35
1949	.148	.35
1950	.145	.35
1951	.145	.35
1952	.148	.35
Education dummy		
Less than *baccalauréat*	.718	.45
Baccalauréat only	.096	.29
University diploma (*bac* + 2)	.074	.26
University degree	.111	.31
Years of higher education	1.440	2.47
Wage (log)	9.170	.49
Middle-class family background	.246	.43
N	26,371	26,371

Source: Labor Force Survey 1990, 1993, 1996, and 1999.

Note: Sample is male wage earners born between 1946 and 1952.

FIGURE 3.20. Three-column table in which values are aligned on the decimal point except for *N* values (*last row*); see 3.70.

100. In such cases the actual value (e.g., 99% or 101%) should be given—if it is given at all—and a footnote should explain the apparent discrepancy. See also 3.61, 3.72.

Notes to Tables

3.74 *Order and placement of notes to tables.* Footnotes to a table are of four general kinds and, where two or more kinds are needed, should appear in this order: (1) source notes, (2) other notes applying to the whole table, (3) notes applying to specific parts of the table, and (4) notes on significance levels. Table footnotes always appear immediately below the table they belong to and must be numbered separately from the text notes. But if a multipage table contains no general notes and any specific notes pertain only to a single page, these notes may appear at the foot of the printed pages they apply to. In an electronic version that includes hypertext links, all footnotes are usually grouped at the bottom of the table.

TABLE 11. Samples sizes across language versions, role groups, and years

Language/year	Undergraduates	Postgraduates	Faculty	Subtotal
		Role/group		
American				
2004	38,026	18,330	13,138	69,494
2005	53,954	17,015	12,669	83,638
2006	44,132	18,375	12,169	74,676
Subtotal	136,112	53,720	37,976	227,808
British				
2004	12,853	4,263	2,054	19,170
2005	26,140	7,774	1,900	35,814
2006	9,902	3,357	1,107	14,366
Subtotal	48,895	5,394	5,061	69,350
Total				297,158

FIGURE 3.21. Five-column table with subtotals and total (see 3.61, 3.72).

3.75 *Acknowledging data in source notes to tables.* If data for a table are not the author's own but are taken from another source or other sources, professional courtesy requires that full acknowledgment be made in an unnumbered footnote. The note is introduced by *Source* or *Sources*, in italics and followed by a colon (see fig. 3.20), though other treatments are acceptable if consistently followed.

Sources: Data from Richard H. Adams Jr., "Remittances, Investment, and Rural Asset Accumulation in Pakistan," *Economic Development and Cultural Change* 47, no. 1 (1998): 155–73; David Bevan, Paul Collier, and Jan Gunning, *Peasants and Government: An Economic Analysis* (Oxford: Clarendon Press, 1989), 125–28.

If the sources are listed in the bibliography or reference list, a shortened form may be used:

Sources: Data from Adams (1998); Bevan, Collier, and Gunning (1989).

Unless fair use applies (see 4.77–87), a table reproduced without change from a published work under copyright requires formal permission. Credit should be given in a source note. See 3.31 for more information about styling credit lines, including examples. For more on source citations, see chapters 14 and 15.

3.76   *Notes applying to the whole table.* A note applying to the table as a whole follows any source note, is also unnumbered, and is introduced by the word *Note*, in italics and followed by a colon, though other treatments are acceptable if consistently followed. See figures 3.11, 3.12, 3.14, 3.17, 3.20. If the substance of a general note can be expressed as a brief phrase, it may be added parenthetically to the title (for examples, see 3.53).

3.77   *Notes to specific parts of a table.* For notes that apply to specific parts of a table, superior (superscript) letters, numbers, or symbols may be used; one system should be used consistently across all tables. Though superior letters are generally preferred, the choice may depend on context. Numerals may be preferred for tables whose data consist mainly of words or letters (e.g., tables 11.3, 11.4, and 11.5 in this manual), whereas symbols may be preferred for tables that include mathematical or chemical equations, where superior letters or numerals might be mistaken for exponents. Each table should have its own series of notes—beginning with a, 1, or *—separate from the text notes and the notes to other tables. The sequence runs from left to right, top to bottom, as in text. Unlike note reference numbers in text, however, the same letter, number, or symbol is used on two or more elements if the corresponding note applies to them. (A footnote reference attached to a column head is assumed to apply to the items in the column below it; a reference attached to a stub entry applies to that row.) The superior letter, number, or symbol is repeated at the foot of the table at the beginning of the corresponding note and is followed neither by a period nor, usually, by a space. See figures 3.13, 3.14, 3.24. Where symbols are used, the sequence is as follows:

1.   * (asterisk; but do not use if p values occur in the table; see 3.78)
2.   † (dagger)
3.   ‡ (double dagger)
4.   § (section mark)
5.   ‖ (parallels)
6.   # (number sign, or pound)

When more symbols are needed, these may be doubled and tripled in the same sequence:

*, †, ‡, etc., **, ††, ‡‡, etc., ***, †††, ‡‡‡, and so on.

3.78   *Notes on significance levels.* If a table contains notes on significance levels (also called probability notes), asterisks may be used as reference marks. If two or three standard significance levels are noted, a single asterisk is

TABLE 12. Determinants of vote for McClellan in 1864

	Coefficient	SE	Odds ratio
Church seats held by			
Pietist sects (%)	−.454**	.117	.635
Liturgical sects (%)	.356*	.183	1.428
Labor force in manufacturing (%)	−.700**	.269	.497
Dummy = 1 if county above county mean for			
Personal property wealth	−.024	.040	.976
Real estate wealth	−.082*	.039	.921
Free population who are slave owners (%)	.159**	.025	1.172
Free population born in			
Ireland (%)	.009*	.004	1.010
Britain (%)	−.025**	.006	.975
Germany (%)	.013**	.003	1.013
Other foreign country (%)	−.011**	.004	.989
Logarithm of county population	−.053*	.026	.948
Dummy = 1 if region is			
Middle Atlantic	.506**	.062	1.659
East north central	.304**	.074	1.355
West north central	−.199**	.097	.820
Border	.115	.133	1.122
West	.110	.126	1.116
Constant	.374	.269	

Note: Results are from a weighted generalized least squares regression in which the dependent variable is $\log[M_i/(100 - M_i)]$, where M_i is the percentage of the vote cast for McClellan. County characteristics are county characteristics in 1860. $N = 941$ observations. Adjusted $R^2 = .223$. Our electoral data come from Clubb, Flanigan, and Zingale (2006). Our county characteristics are from Inter-university Consortium for Political and Social Research (2004), with the exception of the percentage born in a particular country, which we estimated from the 1860 census sample of Ruggles et al. (2004).

*$p < .05$

**$p < .01$

FIGURE 3.22. Four-column table with notes on significance, or probability, levels (*p*), following a general note (see 3.78).

used for the least significant level, two for the next higher, and three for the third. If values other than these three are given, however, footnote letters are preferable to asterisks, to avoid misleading the reader. In the note, the letter *p* (probability) is usually lowercase and in italics. Zeros are generally omitted before the decimal point. Probability notes follow all other notes (see fig. 3.22).

*$p < .05$

**$p < .01$

***$p < .001$

These short notes may be set on the same line; if they are spaced, no intervening punctuation is needed, but if they are run together, they should be separated by semicolons. For more on *p* values, consult the *Publication Manual of the American Psychological Association* (bibliog. 1.1). Some journals capitalize *p*, and some give probability values in regular table footnotes.

Editing Tables

3.79 *Editing table content.* Tables should be edited for style—with special attention to matters of capitalization, spelling, punctuation, abbreviations, numbers, and use of symbols. They should be checked for internal consistency, consistency across multiple tables (e.g., to ensure uniform treatment of column heads and stub entries), and consistency with the style of the surrounding text. Any totals should be checked and discrepancies referred to the author for resolution. As in the text, footnote references must be checked against the footnotes, and the correct sequence of letters or symbols must be verified (see 3.77). Tables should be checked for relevance vis-à-vis the text, and they should be checked alongside each other for redundancy. A lay reader or a nontechnical editor should be able to make logical sense of a table, even if the material is highly technical.

3.80 *"Percent" versus "percentage."* Despite changing usage, Chicago continues to regard *percent* as an adverb ("per, or out of, each hundred," as in *10 percent of the class*)—or, less commonly, an adjective (*a 10 percent raise*)—and to use *percentage* as the noun form (*a significant percentage of her income*). The symbol %, however, may stand for either word. See also 3.82.

3.81 *Number ranges.* Anyone preparing or editing a table must ensure that number ranges do not overlap, that there are no gaps between them, and that they are as precise as the data require. It must be clear whether "up to" or "up to and including" is meant. Dollar amounts, for example, might be given as "less than $5, $5–$9, $10–$14, and $15–$19" (not "$1–$5, $5–$10," etc.). If greater precision is needed, they might be given as "$1.00–$4.99, $5.00–$9.99," and so forth. The symbols < and > must be used only to mean less than and more than. In a table including age ranges, >60 means "more than 60 years old" (*not* "60 and up," which would be represented by ≥60).

3.82 *Signs and symbols in tables.* In a column consisting exclusively of, for example, dollar amounts or percentages, the signs should be omitted from the cells and included in the column head (see 3.54 and figs. 3.12, 3.13) or, occasionally, in the stub entry (see fig. 3.22). Mathematical operational signs preceding quantities in a column of numbers are not necessarily aligned with other such signs but should appear immediately to the left of the numbers they belong to (see fig. 3.12).

3.83   *"N" versus "n."* An italic capital *N* is used in many statistical tables to stand for the total number of a group from which data are drawn (see fig. 3.20). An italic lowercase *n* stands for a portion of the total group (see fig. 3.13). For example, if *N* refers to the total number of subjects (of both sexes) in a study, a lowercase *n* might be used when specifying the number of males and the number of females in the study.

3.84   *Adjusting and checking tables.* When preparing a table for publication, editors and compositors may need to adjust or check its format according to the following general guidelines:

1.   *Adjusting long tables and wide tables.* Tables that are long and narrow with few columns but many rows, on the one hand, and very wide tables with many columns but few rows, on the other, may not work well—if at all—especially in print. The remedy for a long, skinny table is to double it up, running the table in two halves, side by side, with the column heads repeated over the second half. This approach can also allow a narrow but not necessarily long table to run the width of a page (see fig. 3.23). For a wide, shallow table, the remedy is to turn it around, making column heads of the stub items and stub items of the column heads; if the table turns out to be too narrow that way, it can then be doubled up. Some tables may need to be presented broadside (rotated 90 degrees counterclockwise and read left to right from the bottom to the top of a page); see figure 3.16. See also 3.49. For long tables, the editor may need

TABLE 13. Relative contents of odd isotopes for heavy elements

Element	Z	γ	Element	Z	γ
Sm	62	1.480	W	74	0.505
Gd	64	0.691	Os	76	0.811
Dy	66	0.930	Pt	78	1.160
Eb	68	0.759	Hg	80	0.500
Yb	70	0.601	Pb	82	0.550
Hf	72	0.440			

FIGURE 3.23.   Three-column table doubled into two columns (see 3.84).

TABLE 14. Timing of socialist entry into elections and of suffrage reforms

Country	(1)	(2)	(3)	(4)	(5)	(6)	(7)
Austria	1889	1897	1907	—	1919	—	—
Belgium	1885[a]	1894	1894	45.7	1948	38.4	22.2
Denmark	1878[a]	1884	1849	28.1[b]	1915	24.6	23.9
Finland	1899	1907	1906	22.0	1906	—	22.0
France	1879	1893	1876	36.5[c]	1946	33.9	24.9
Germany	1867	1871	1871	25.5	1919	34.2[d]	34.0[d]
Italy	1892[a]	—	1913	—	1945	—	—
Netherlands	1878	1888	1917	—	1917	—	—
Norway	1887	1903	1898	34.1	1913	27.7	28.8
Spain	1879	1910	1907	—	1933	—	—
Sweden	1889	1896	1907	28.9	1921	35.0	37.0
Switzerland	1887	1897	1848	—	—	—	—
United Kingdom	1893[a]	1892[e]	1918	—	1928	—	—

Note: Column headings are as follows: (1) Socialist Party formed; (2) first candidates elected to Parliament; (3) universal male suffrage; (4) workers as a proportion of the electorate in the first elections after universal male suffrage; (5) universal suffrage; (6) workers as a proportion of the electorate in the last election before extension of franchise to women; and (7) workers as a proportion of the electorate in the first election after the extension.

[a] Major socialist or workers' parties existed earlier and dissolved or were repressed.

[b] In 1884, approximate.

[c] In 1902.

[d] Under different borders.

[e] Keir Hardie elected.

FIGURE 3.24. Eight-column table with numbers replacing column heads to reduce width. The heads are defined in a general note to the table. Notes to specific parts of the table are indicated by superior (superscript) letters. See 3.84, 3.77.

to specify whether and where "continued" lines and repeated column heads are allowed (see 3.85) and where footnotes should appear (see 3.77).

2. *Adjusting oversize tables—other options.* If an oversize table cannot be accommodated in a printed work by the remedies suggested above, further editorial or typographic adjustments will be needed. Wording may be shortened or abbreviations used. Omitting the running head when a table takes a full page (see 1.15) allows more space for the table itself. A wide table may extend a little into the left margin if on a verso or the right margin if on a recto or, if it looks better, equally on both sides. For a particularly large table, the publisher may decide to reduce the type size or to publish the table in electronic form only, if that is an option. To reduce excessive width, two other measures (neither very convenient for readers) are worth considering: (1) numbers are used for column heads, and the text of the heads is relegated to footnotes, as

TABLE 15. Type of private capital flow (millions of US dollars)

	1992	1993	1994	1995	1996
			Asia		
China					
GDP	469,003	598,765	546,610	711,315	834,311
Current account	6,401	−11,609	6,908	1,618	7,243
Capital inflows	−250	23,474	32,645	38,674	39,966
Equity	7,922	24,266	34,208	36,185	39,981
Bank credits	4,008	2,146	3,786	8,405	10,625
Indonesia					
GDP	139,116	158,007	176,892	202,131	227,370
Current account	−2,780	−2,106	−2,792	−6,431	−7,663
Capital inflows	6,129	5,632	3,839	10,259	10,847
Equity	1,947	2,692	2,573	4,285	5,195
Bank credits	663	1,573	2,030	8,021	12,602
			Latin America		
Argentina					
GDP	228,990	257,842	281,925	279,613	297,460
Current account	−5,462	−7,672	−10,117	−2,768	−3,787
Capital inflows	7,373	9,827	9,279	574	7,033
Equity	4,630	4,038	3,954	4,589	7,375
Bank credits	1,152	9,945	1,139	2,587	959

· · · · · · · · · ·

TABLE 15 (*continued*)

	1992	1993	1994	1995	1996
			Latin America		
Brazil					
GDP	446,580	438,300	546,230	704,167	774,868
Current account	6,089	20	−1,153	−18,136	−23,602
Capital inflows	5,889	7,604	8,020	29,306	33,984
Equity	3,147	4,062	5,333	8,169	15,788
Bank credits	11,077	4,375	9,162	11,443	14,462
Chile					
GDP	41,882	44,474	50,920	65,215	69,218
Current account	−958	−2,554	−1,585	−1,398	−3,744
Capital inflows	3,134	2,996	5,294	2,488	6,781
Equity	876	1,326	2,580	1,959	4,090
Bank credits	2,192	804	1,108	1,100	1,808

· · · · · · · · · ·

FIGURE 3.25. Six-column table with repeated column heads and "continued" indication following a page break (see 3.85).

illustrated in figure 3.24; or (2) column heads are turned on their sides so that they read up the printed page rather than across.

3. *Checking rules.* The editor should ensure that rules appear as needed and that spanner rules are the right length and are distinct from underlining (so that a rule and not italicized text appears in the typeset version). See 3.50, 3.55.

4. *Checking alignment of numbers and text.* Alignment of rows and columns must be clearly specified in the manuscript. Editors should check to make sure that numbers have been aligned properly (e.g., by decimal point) and that stub entries are aligned with and correspond to the rows to which they apply. See 3.68–73. Old-style numbers (like this: 1938), though elegant as page numbers or in text that contains few numerals, should be avoided in tabular matter because they do not align as well as (and can be harder to read than) regular "lining" numbers (like this: 1938).

5. *Checking running heads on full-page tables.* The editor should be sure that running heads are omitted on full-page and multipage tables (but see 1.15, 2.112).

6. *Checking typefaces and markup.* In a book that is not part of a series, the designer will set the typographic style for tables, as for the text and other elements. Journals follow their own established style for presentation and markup. Editors should make sure tables are edited in accord with the design, and formatting and markup for electronically prepared tables should be checked to make sure they have been consistently and correctly applied. For a useful discussion of table design, see Richard Eckersley et al., *Glossary of Typesetting Terms* (bibliog. 2.7).

3.85 *Indicating "continued" and specifying repeating column heads.* For a vertical table of more than one page, the column heads are repeated on each page. For a two-page broadside table—which should be presented on facing pages if at all possible—column heads need not be repeated; for broadside tables that run beyond two pages, column heads are repeated only on each new verso (see also 2.112). Where column heads are repeated, the table number and "continued" should also appear. See figure 3.25. For any table that is likely to run to more than one page, the editor should specify whether "continued" lines and repeated column heads will be needed and where footnotes should appear (usually at the end of the table as a whole; but see 3.74). The editor should also be sure that running heads are omitted on full-page and multipage tables (see 1.15).

4 Rights, Permissions, and Copyright Administration

WILLIAM S. STRONG

Overview

4.1 *The scope of this chapter.* The foundation on which the entire publishing industry rests is the law of copyright, and a basic knowledge of it is essential for both authors and editors. This chapter gives readers that basic knowledge: how copyright is acquired, how it is owned, what it protects, what rights it comprises, how long it lasts, how it is transferred from one person to another. Once that foundation is laid, the key elements of publishing contracts are discussed, as well as the licensing of rights (what publishers call the "rights and permissions" function). The treatment of rights and permissions includes some guidelines for "fair use." While every effort is made here to be accurate, copyright law is both wide and intricate, and this chapter makes no claim to be exhaustive. Also, this chapter should not be considered legal advice or substitute for a consultation with a knowledgeable attorney in any particular circumstance. (For more detailed treatment of specific issues, see the works listed in sec. 2.3 of the bibliography.)

Copyright Law and the Licensing of Rights

4.2 *Relevant law.* For most publishing purposes the relevant law is the Copyright Act of 1976 (Public Law 94-553), which took effect on January 1, 1978, and the various amendments enacted since then. The 1976 act was a sweeping revision, superseding previous federal law and eliminating (though not retroactively) the body of state law known as common-law copyright. It did not, however, make old learning obsolete. Because prior law continues to govern most pre-1978 works in one way or another, anyone involved with publishing should understand both the old and the new regimes. Both will affect publishing for decades to come. Note that the law discussed in this chapter is that of the United States. The United States and most other countries are members of the Berne Convention, the oldest international copyright treaty. While the Berne Convention and certain other treaties have fostered significant uniformity around the world, anyone dealing with foreign copyrights should bear in mind that, conventions aside, the laws of other countries may contain significant differences from US law.

4.3 *How copyright comes into being.* Whenever a book or article, poem or lecture, database or drama comes into the world, it is automatically covered by copyright so long as it is "fixed" in some "tangible" form and embodies original expression. The term *tangible* applies to more than paper and traditional media; it includes things such as electronic memory. A copyrightable work is "fixed" as long as it is stored in some manner that is not purely transitory. Thus an e-mail message that is stored in the sender's computer is fixed and copyrightable, but an extemporaneous lecture that is broadcast without being recorded is not.

4.4 **Registration and notice not required.** Although it is advisable to register works with the United States Copyright Office, registration is not a prerequisite to legal protection. The practical reasons for registering are discussed in 4.49. Copyright notice is no longer required but is recommended.

4.5 **Original expression.** Copyright protects the original expression contained in a work. The term *expression* means the words, sounds, or images that an author uses to express an idea or convey information. Copyright protects the expression but not the underlying conceptual or factual material. *Originality* for copyright purposes has a very low threshold. Only a modicum of creativity is required; the law protects such minimal intellectual effort as the selection and arrangement of entries in a guide to prices of used automobiles. What counts is not quality or novelty but only that the work be original with the author and not copied, consciously or unconsciously, from some other source. When a work includes material that is not original, only the original material is protected. Thus, copyright in a new, annotated edition of an eighteenth-century book will cover only the annotations.

4.6 **Author the original owner.** Whoever is the author (a term not synonymous with *creator*, as will be seen) controls copyright at the outset and automatically possesses certain rights in the work. How these rights are owned, transferred, and administered is the focus of this chapter.

Varieties of Authorship

4.7 **Individual and joint authors.** In popular (or "trade") publishing and in the humanities, the typical author is likely to be an individual. In scientific, technical, and medical publishing, especially in the realm of journals, a work will more likely than not involve the efforts of more than one author. Such works are typically joint works. As defined by the statute, a joint work is "a work prepared by two or more authors with the intention that their contributions be merged into inseparable or interdependent parts of a unitary whole."

4.8   *Collective works.* Works in which the independent contributions of two or more authors are combined are considered collective rather than joint works. Copyright in a collective work as such, which covers the selection and arrangement of materials, belongs to the compiler or editor and is separate from the copyright in each of the various components. Typical examples of collective works are newspapers, anthologies, journal issues, and the proceedings of academic conferences (see 4.59).

WORKS MADE FOR HIRE

4.9   *Employer as author.* Another type of authorship is work made for hire. The law regards the employer or other controlling party as the "author" of any such work and hence as the initial owner of the copyright. Some works are considered made for hire by definition; some can be treated as such by agreement.

4.10   *The three categories of work made for hire.* Present law defines much more stringently than pre-1978 law the conditions that must be met for a work to be considered made for hire. First, the work may be prepared within the scope of a person's employment. Common examples of this type of work made for hire include the editorial column in a scholarly journal, a story in a newspaper or weekly magazine, or the entry for "aardvark" written by a person on an encyclopedia's paid staff. Second, someone *not* on the payroll will in certain instances be treated as an "employee" in determining authorship if that person is acting as the agent of another party. Determining agency is a difficult and somewhat ad hoc task, and involves considerations such as the control of one party over the other party's hours, assignments, and tools used in creating the work. The third type of work made for hire is the specially ordered or commissioned work that both hiring party and creator agree *in writing* to treat as such. This sort of arrangement is available for only a few narrowly defined types of work:

- contributions to collective works, such as a book review commissioned for a journal
- contributions to motion pictures or sound recordings
- translations
- instructional texts
- tests
- atlases
- compilations of existing materials such as anthologies
- "supplementary works" such as forewords, bibliographies, indexes, appendixes, textual notes, illustrations, and answer material for tests

A work that qualifies for such treatment will not be considered made for hire unless the written agreement between the commissioning party and the creative party expressly says so. The written agreement can be signed retroactively, although the safer practice is to obtain the parties' signatures before the work is created.

4.11   *Ineligible works.* It bears emphasizing that many kinds of works that could conceivably be commissioned do not qualify as works made for hire no matter what agreement may be made between writer and publisher. Monographs and novels, for example, are not eligible because they are not in any of the specific categories listed above. Thus, copyright in such a work remains with the writer unless expressly assigned. Although for most purposes an assignment of copyright from the author is indistinguishable in practical effect from a work-for-hire agreement, they have different implications for copyright duration (see 4.23) and termination (see 4.37).

4.12   *Joint authorship.* Although the law is not entirely clear on this point, it appears that any work that is partially made for hire will be treated as made for hire for copyright duration (see 4.22–24) and certain other purposes, even though a joint coauthor might be independent and not writing "for hire."

Rights of the Copyright Owner

4.13   *Rights of reproduction, distribution, and display.* The author of a work possesses, at the beginning, a bundle of rights that collectively make up copyright. They belong originally to the author, who can sell, rent, give away, will, or transfer them in some other way, individually or as a package, to whomever the author wishes. When a work is to be published, the author normally transfers some or all of these rights to the publisher, by formal agreement. Two of these rights are basic from the publisher's point of view: the right to make copies of the work (traditionally by printing and now often by digital reproduction) and the right to distribute such copies to the public—in sum, to publish the work. In the case of online publishing, reproduction and distribution blend into the act of transmitting the work on demand to the reader's computer. A third right—the right of public display—applies to online exploitation of works. A work is publicly displayed when made viewable online; if the user downloads or prints out the material concerned, a distribution of a copy also occurs.

4.14   *Derivative work and performance rights.* A fourth and very important right is the right to make what the law terms derivative works—that is, works based on or derived from the original work, such as translations, abridgments, dramatizations, or other adaptations. A revised edition of a published work is generally noticeably different enough from the prior edition to qualify as a derivative work with a separate copyright (see 4.27). The fifth basic copyright right, the right of public performance, has only limited relevance for literary works as such; it applies, for example, when a poet gives a public reading of a poem. However, it has great significance for other works, such as motion pictures, that may spring from literary works.

4.15   *Moral rights—integrity of copyright management information.* In addition to the foregoing rights, the law gives the creators of certain works of fine art a so-called moral right against mutilation and misattribution. A dozen or more states have enacted legislation to roughly the same effect as the federal law but generally broader. This moral right, however, whether federal or state, has little effect on publishers (except perhaps while in possession of original artwork) and will not be dealt with further here. Authors may also be able under common law to prevent the attribution to them of things that they did not write. In addition, federal law protects the integrity of "copyright management information." This information, for publications, consists of the following:

- the title and other information identifying the work, including the content of the copyright notice
- the name of, and other identifying information about, the author
- the name of, and other identifying information about, the copyright owner, including the content of the copyright notice
- terms and conditions for use of the work
- identifying numbers or symbols referring to such information or links to such information

Specifically, the law prevents intentional removal or alteration of copyright management information, or intentional use of false copyright management information, if done with intent to induce, enable, facilitate, or conceal infringement. This prohibition has seen little exercise in the courts and is likely to be of less use to publishers than to industries that deal frequently with counterfeit goods.

4.16   *Trademark protection of titles and other elements.* Copying only the title of a work likely would not be considered a copyright infringement. But a title may be entitled to trademark protection under federal or state law or both. Book titles are harder to protect as trademarks than journal or lecture titles, because of judicial and administrative reluctance to give trademark protection to names that are used on only one specific product. Nevertheless, it is fair to say that some book titles are clearly protectable; *Gone with the Wind* and *Winnie-the-Pooh* are titles that cannot be used without permission, at least so long as the books remain under copyright. And active franchising such as has occurred with both of those books will enable the trademark to survive long after that, although not in such a way as to prevent reproduction of the book itself, title and all. The same principles would apply to the names of characters or imaginary locales used in a work.

4.17   *Basic versus subsidiary rights.* Whoever controls the copyright in a work, whether author or publisher, may not only exercise those rights directly but also empower or authorize others to exercise them. If, for example, the author of a book has transferred the whole bundle of rights to a publishing house, the publishing house will itself exercise the basic rights of reproducing and distributing (i.e., publishing) the book. It will also be responsible for administering subsidiary rights. These rights (discussed in 4.60) usually involve exploiting markets in which the publishing house is not active. For example, foreign-language, book-club, and motion-picture rights involve specialized markets and require special expertise. For this reason, subsidiary rights are likely to be exercised by third parties under license from the publisher, although, if the publisher is part of a large media conglomerate, licensing is often intramural. Part of the publisher's responsibility to the author should be to see that subsidiary rights are exploited as effectively as possible. Licensing subsidiary rights also includes granting what the publishing industry calls permissions, a term that refers to such things as the licensing of photocopying for classroom use and allowing others to quote or reproduce small portions of the book in a new work.

4.18   *Author retention of subsidiary rights.* Authors of "trade" books—fiction, biography, cookbooks, and other books for the general reader—are more likely than scholarly authors to be represented by agents and more likely to retain some or all subsidiary rights. In such cases, subsidiary rights are licensed directly by the author (through his or her agent) to foreign publishers, motion-picture producers, and the like. Typically, however, permissions are still handled by the publisher rather than the agent or author.

Copyright and the Public Domain

4.19   *Copyright duration before 1978.* Until January 1, 1978, a dual system of copyright existed in the United States. Common-law copyright, created by the individual states, protected works from the time of their creation until publication, however long that might be. A personal letter written in the eighteenth century but never published was protected as effectively as a 1977 doctoral thesis in the making. In neither case could the document be copied and distributed (that is, published) without the express permission of either the creator of the work or the creator's legal heirs. Statutory, or federal, copyright protected works at the moment of publication and for twenty-eight years thereafter, provided that a proper copyright notice appeared in the published work. Thereafter, copyright in the work could be renewed for another twenty-eight years if the original copyright claim had been registered with the United States Copyright Office (a division of the Library of Congress) and if a renewal claim was filed by the appropriate person(s) during the final year of the first term of copyright. Thus in the normal course of things federal copyright in a work was intended to last for a total of fifty-six years from the date of publication, after which time the work went into the public domain—that is, it became public property and could be reproduced freely. See 4.20–21, 4.45. Works created by employees of the US government in the course of their official duties are in the public domain.

4.20   *Lengthening of copyright duration in 1978.* To enter the public domain is of course the ultimate fate of all copyrighted works. However, the elaborate system described in 4.19 was replaced as of 1978 by a unitary federal copyright of substantially greater length. Subsequent amendments have lengthened the term yet further and eliminated a number of formalities that used to be required. All these changes have made entering the public domain almost theoretical for works currently being created. As will be discussed below, other changes to the law have given many older works, particularly those of foreign origin, an unexpected reprieve (see 4.28).

4.21   *Uses of public-domain works.* Once in the public domain, a work is free for all to use. The use may be direct and simple; for example, Mark Twain's novels have now lost their copyrights and may be republished free of royalty. Or the public-domain works may be the compost from which new works, adaptations or other derivative works, spring in due course. Such new works are entitled to copyright, but their copyright is limited to the new material they contain. Determining whether a work is in the public domain requires attention to complex rules. These are discussed at 4.25–29 and 4.38–45. The rules are also set out in tabular form at the website of the University of Chicago Press.

DURATION OF COPYRIGHT FOR WORKS CREATED AFTER 1977

4.22   *"Life plus seventy."* Enacted in 1976 and effective on January 1, 1978, the present copyright law did away with the dual system of federal/common-law copyright. Present law is both simpler and more complex regarding copyright duration. It is simpler in that now one unified, federal system protects all works fixed in tangible form from the moment so fixed. It is more complex in that terms of protection differ depending on authorship, and in that works existing before 1978 are subject to a variety of special rules. The paradigmatic copyright term, under the new law, is "life plus seventy"—that is, life of the author plus seventy years. (In the case of joint authors, the seventy years are added to the life of the last author to die.) As will be seen below, however, there are many exceptions to this rule.

4.23   *Works made for hire.* Since the owner of the copyright in a work made for hire is not the actual creator of the work (often, indeed, the copyright owner is a corporate entity), the law specifies a fixed term of years for the duration of copyright. This term is 95 years from the date of publication or 120 years from the date of creation, whichever is the shorter.

4.24   *Anonymous and pseudonymous works.* The regular rule for duration of copyright cannot be applied if an author publishes anonymously or under a pseudonym. The law prescribes the same fixed term of copyright for these works as for works made for hire—95 years from the date of publication or 120 years from creation, whichever is the shorter. If after publication, however, such an author's name is revealed and recorded in the documents of the Copyright Office, the regular "life plus seventy" rule takes over, unless, of course, the work is made for hire.

DURATION OF COPYRIGHT FOR WORKS CREATED BEFORE 1978

4.25   *Pre-1978 unpublished works.* For unpublished works that were still under common-law copyright when the new law went into effect, there is a transitional rule. Such works are given the same copyright terms as post-1977 works, but in recognition of the fact that their authors might have died so long ago as to make life-plus-seventy meaningless, Congress added two provisos. First, such works were granted protection at least until December 31, 2002. Second, any such work that was ultimately published before December 31, 2002, is protected at least until December 31, 2047. Thus, these late-published works have a copyright term of not less than seventy years from the date the new law went into effect.

4.26   *Pre-1978 published US works.* Works published before January 1, 1923, are now in the public domain. Works published during the years 1923 through 1963 are still under copyright if their copyrights were properly renewed in the twenty-eighth year after first publication. (The safest way to determine this is to commission a search of the Copyright Office records through a copyright attorney or a reputable search firm.) The renewal term for such works is now sixty-seven years rather than twenty-eight. Works published from 1964 through 1977 will be protected without fail for ninety-five years from first publication, because renewal for such works is automatic. All the above assumes that these works were at all times published with proper copyright notice. For a discussion of copyright notice, see 4.38–45.

4.27   *New copyright for new editions.* When deciding whether a work may be republished without permission, bear in mind that each time a work is materially revised a new copyright comes into being, covering the new or revised material. Thus a seminal treatise published in 1920 is now in the public domain, but the author's revision published in 1934 may not be. One is free to republish the 1920 version, but that may be an empty privilege.

4.28   *Pre-1978 published foreign works.* The rules just described do not apply to foreign works. Such works are generally protected in their own countries for the life of the author plus fifty or seventy years, depending on the country concerned. In the United States, a pre-1978 foreign work automatically receives the same term of copyright as a pre-1978 US work, but without regard to whether proper copyright notice ever appeared on it or whether copyright was renewed in the twenty-eighth year after publication. This is so because, effective January 1, 1996, Congress restored to copyright all foreign works that had forfeited copyright as a result of noncompliance with US notice and renewal requirements but that were still protected in their home country. Copyrights restored in this manner are subject to certain protections given to those who produced copies or derivative works before December 8, 1994, relying on the apparent forfeiture of copyright. Two points should be noted here, however. First, an anomalous decision in the Ninth Circuit Court of Appeals has held that foreign works published abroad prior to 1923 may still be eligible for copyright protection in the United States, if no effort was made at the time to comply with US copyright law. This is out of sync with the rest of US copyright jurisprudence, but it remains the law in California and other states in the Ninth Circuit. Second, it should be noted that the US copyright term for foreign works, even after restoration, does not synchronize with the protection of those works outside the United States. If a French author of a work published in 1922 lived until 1970, the work would now be in the public domain in the United States but would remain under copyright in France until 2040. If the same author had published another work in 1923, that work would retain copyright in the United States until 2018, still twenty-two years less than in France. Publishers who wish to reissue or otherwise make use of foreign public-domain works need to be aware that foreign markets may be foreclosed to them.

4.29   *Definition of "foreign."* For purposes of the special restoration rules discussed in 4.28, a work is a foreign work if it was first published outside the United States. The only substantial exception is for works published in the United States within thirty days after foreign publication, as used to be done by some US publishers to get Berne Convention treatment "by the back door" before the United States became a member of Berne. Such works are not eligible for copyright restoration.

RENEWING COPYRIGHT IN PRE-1978 WORKS

4.30   *Benefits of renewal.* Although renewal is now automatic, the law gives certain benefits to those who take the trouble to file actively for renewal. Filing for renewal fixes the ownership of the second-term copyright on the date of filing; automatic renewal fixes ownership in whoever could have renewed on the *last day* of the first term. A renewal that has been actively obtained constitutes prima facie evidence of copyright and its ownership; the evidentiary value of an automatically renewed copyright is discretionary with the courts. Finally, and most important, if the renewal is allowed to happen automatically, existing derivative works can continue to be exploited for the second term of copyright, whereas active renewal gives the renewal-term owner—unless he or she signed a derivative work license explicitly covering the renewal term—the right to relicense derivative-work rights.

4.31   *Renewal by the author.* The author, if living, is the person entitled to file for renewal. Publishers who have obtained renewal-term rights from authors should continue to file for renewal on the author's behalf as they have traditionally done.

4.32   *Renewal if the author is deceased.* Whether renewal occurs by filing or automatically, if the author is not alive the law allocates the copyright to his or her surviving spouse, children, or other heirs according to complex rules that will not be parsed here.

Assigning or Licensing Copyright

4.33   *Subdividing a copyright.* Copyright is often referred to as a "bundle" of rights. The basic components, as noted above, are the right to reproduce the work, the right to distribute copies of a work to the public, the right to make derivative works, and the rights to perform and display a work publicly. Each of these rights may be separately licensed or assigned. Furthermore, each of them may be carved up into smaller rights along lines of geography, time, or medium. Thus, for example, the right to publish a treatise may be carved up so that Publisher A gets North American rights while Publisher B gets United Kingdom rights. A French translation license may be given to Librairie C for a ten-year fixed term. Or Publisher A may receive print rights while D-DISC gets CD-ROM rights and E-NET gets online publication rights. There is theoretically no end to the ways of subdividing a copyright, other than the limits of human ingenuity and the marketplace.

4.34   *Exclusive versus nonexclusive licenses.* Licenses may be exclusive or nonexclusive. Typically, anyone making a substantial investment will insist on exclusive rights, whereas persons making ephemeral use at low marginal cost—a typical case being classroom photocopying—need no more than nonexclusive rights. An exclusive licensee is treated in general like an owner of copyright and has standing to sue any infringer of that right. A nonexclusive licensee is more like the holder of a personal privilege than the holder of a property interest, and cannot sue infringers or even, without the permission of the licensor, transfer the license to someone else. While most authorities believe that, by contrast, an exclusive licensee has the power to assign and sublicense the right concerned, a federal court opinion in mid-2002 cast doubt on that presumption. As a precaution, anyone drafting an exclusive license should expressly state that the license may be assigned and sublicensed at the discretion of the licensee.

4.35   *Goals of the parties to a license.* Many issues in license negotiation are common to all contracts: payment terms, duration, allocation of risk, remedies for default, and so on. But in drafting a copyright license the parties need to be very careful to define clearly the scope of the license, taking into account possible evolution of technologies and markets. The goal of a licensor is to define the licensed right narrowly so as to preserve flexibility for future licensing. The licensee also wants flexibility and so seeks to define the licensed right broadly. Both sides, though, have a common interest in seeing that the license is clear and understandable. Drafting a license demands and deserves care and skill, as well as good communication between lawyers and their clients.

4.36   *Payment.* A license and the obligation to pay for that license are usually treated as reciprocal obligations, not mutually dependent ones. Thus the failure of a licensee to pay royalties does not automatically terminate the license and turn the licensee into an infringer. It gives the licensor a claim for contract damages, not a copyright infringement claim. Shrewd licensors will whenever possible reverse this presumption in their contracts, and shrewd licensees will usually resist.

4.37   *Termination of transfers.* Apart from contractual rights, the statute itself gives individual authors the right to terminate licenses and assignments of copyright under certain conditions. The law specifically grants authors the right to terminate any post-1977 copyright arrangement after thirty-five years, and a roughly comparable termination right applies to licenses signed before 1978. The mechanics of termination, including the determination of who has the right to terminate, are extraordinarily complicated and are of importance to only the most lucrative of copyrights, so no more will be said here. The termination right does not apply to agreements stipulating that a work is made for hire. See 4.10.

Copyright Notice

4.38   *Changes to the rules.* No aspect of copyright has caused more grief than the rules of copyright notice. These rules have been responsible for most forfeitures of copyright. Largely a trap for the unwary, they were softened somewhat in 1978 and removed almost entirely in 1989. They were not without purpose or utility, but the rules prevented the United States from joining the Berne Convention, and in the end this and other disadvantages outweighed their utility.

4.39   *Three different regimes.* Congress could not easily dispense with the rules retroactively, however, and the resulting 1989 legislation means that we now operate simultaneously under three doctrines: (1) for works first published on or after March 1, 1989, no copyright notice is required; (2) for works first published in the United States between January 1, 1978, and February 28, 1989, copyright notice must have been used on all copies published before March 1, 1989, with the proviso that certain steps could be taken to redeem deficient notice (see 4.45); and (3) for US works first published before January 1, 1978, the copyright was almost certainly forfeited if the notice was not affixed to all copies; few excuses were or are available. (As noted above, foreign works have been retroactively exempted from these rules.) Notwithstanding the liberality of the new law, continued use of notice is strongly advised to deprive infringers of any possible defense of ignorance. The rules in 4.40–45 should therefore still be followed.

CONTENT OF NOTICE

4.40   *Three elements of the notice.* Under present law, as under the old law, the notice consists of three parts: (1) either the symbol © (preferred because it also suits the requirements of the Universal Copyright Convention), or the word *copyright*, or the abbreviation *copr.*; (2) the year of first publication; and (3) the name of the copyright owner. Many publishers also add the phrase "all rights reserved," and there is no harm in doing so, but the putative advantages of it (which were limited to Latin America) have all but vanished. The year of first publication is not needed for greeting cards, postcards, stationery, and certain other works not germane to the publishing industry. Where a work is in its renewal term of copyright, it is customary, but not required, to include the year of renewal as well as the year of first publication. See also 1.19–34.

4.41   *Name used in the notice.* The name used in the notice should be the name of the author unless the author has assigned all rights to the publisher. However, it is not uncommon to see the publisher's name in the notice even when it does not own all rights. Conversely, authors sometimes insist on notice in their names even when they have assigned all rights— and publishers often acquiesce, thereby giving up something that has no value except to the ego of the author. Such vagaries are regrettable but harmless, except where they mislead those seeking permission to use the copyrighted material.

4.42   *Placement of notice.* The copyright notice should be placed so as to give reasonable notice to the consumer. The old law was very specific about its location: for books, on either the title page or the page immediately following, and for journals and magazines, on the title page, the first page of text, or the front cover. Present law simply states that the notice should be so placed as "to give reasonable notice of the claim of copyright," but most publishers continue to place it in the traditional locations required by the old law. See also 1.78, 1.88, 1.97.

4.43   *United States government materials.* When a work consists "preponderantly" of materials created by the federal government, this must be stated in the notice. This may be done either positively (e.g., "Copyright is claimed only in the introduction, notes, appendixes, and index of the present work") or negatively (e.g., "Copyright is not claimed in 'Forest Management,' a publication of the United States government reprinted in the present volume"). Works produced by state or local governments or by foreign governments are not per se in the public domain and are not subject to this notice provision.

4.44   *Notice on derivative works.* The new copyright in a derivative work entitles its publisher to use a new copyright notice with the current year date, and nothing requires that such notice delineate what is and is not covered by the copyright. This sometimes has the unfortunate by-product (not always unintended, let it be said) of making users think that the scope of copyright extends to the public-domain material. However, the better practice, at least where the derivative work is a revised edition, is to include the publication years of various editions. See 1.23.

4.45   *Correcting mistakes.* Under pre-1978 law, no mechanism was available to cure the effects of a defective notice: copyright was forfeited and that was that, unless the omission of notice was accidental and occurred in a very small number of copies. For publication between January 1, 1978, and March 1, 1989 (when the notice requirement was finally dropped altogether), a more lenient regime prevailed. A mistake in the owner's name, or a mistake by no more than a year in the date element of the notice, was largely excused. Any more serious mistake was treated as an omission of notice. Any omission of one or more of the necessary three elements would be excused if the omission was from a "relatively small" number of copies. If more extensive omission occurred, the copyright owner could still save the copyright from forfeiture by registering it (see 4.46–49) within five years after the defective publication and making a "reasonable effort" to add the notice to all copies distributed to the public after the omission was discovered. Very few cases have discussed what a "reasonable effort" is, and their explanations, being somewhat ad hoc, give limited guidance to anyone trying to determine whether a work in this category is still protected by copyright.

Deposit and Registration

4.46   *Deposit requirements.* The law requires copyright owners to send copies of their published works to the Copyright Office for deposit and use in the

Library of Congress. The copies must be sent within three months of publication. Although failure to make the required deposit does not forfeit the copyright, the copyright owner is subject to a fine for noncompliance if a specific request from the Library of Congress is ignored. For printed works, the deposit of two copies of the "best edition" is required. If, for example, clothbound and paperback editions of a book are published simultaneously, the publisher should submit two copies of the cloth edition. If the work is a very expensive or limited edition, one may apply to the Library of Congress for permission to submit only one copy. Databases published only online are exempt. When sending deposit copies to the Copyright Office, publishers usually have the copyright registered as well. In the case of printed materials, the deposit copies also serve the requirements for registration. In the case of electronic publications, the submission of certain "identifying material" will suffice.

4.47   *Registration forms and fees.* To register a work the author or other claimant must fill out the appropriate application, either in paper form or online. The Copyright Office offers online registration through its eCO service, using an interactive application form. For paper registration there are several forms, tailored to different types of works. Form TX is used for books and other works in the broad category called literary works, other than periodicals. For all periodicals, including but not limited to newspapers, magazines, newsletters, journals, and even annuals, use form SE. As an alternative, one may use form CO for any type of work; this form can be filled out electronically, printed out, and submitted by mail. The Copyright Office offers all these forms and intelligible explanations of its registration rules, including its complex deposit requirements, on its website. The fees for registration vary depending on which process one uses, but by far the least expensive is online registration. For a group of works, one fee covers the entire group. Group registration is available for multiple photographs or multiple contributions to periodicals by a single author, and for certain serial publications. Publishers with large lists tend to keep funds on deposit at the Copyright Office and to charge their registration fees against their deposit accounts.

4.48   *Need for accuracy and candor.* It is important to answer all questions on the application accurately. Copyright owners have been sanctioned by courts for misleading the Copyright Office by (for example) failing to disclose that a work is based on preexisting materials. Statements on the application do not need to be exhaustive, but they must be correct and not evasive. However, in contrast to patent applications, there is no requirement for disclosure of adverse claims or any other information not specifically called for on the form.

4.49 *Benefits of registration.* Registration is not necessary to *obtain* a copyright (which exists in the work from the moment it is fixed in tangible form; see 4.3) or to ensure its validity. However, the prudent course is to register copyright because of the added protection registration affords. In cases of infringement, registration is a prerequisite to bringing suit unless the work was written by a non-US author and first published abroad. Registering at the time of publication avoids a scramble to register later if infringement is discovered. Moreover, if registration has been made within three months of publication, or before an infringement begins, the copyright owner, instead of going through the difficulties of proving actual damages, can sue for "statutory damages" (in effect, an award of damages based on equity rather than on proof of loss) and, most significantly, is eligible to be reimbursed for attorney's fees. Publishers fearing prepublication piracy of books in development should also consider the "preregistration" procedure at the website of the United States Copyright Office.

The Publishing Agreement

4.50 *Basic rights.* No publishing house may legally publish a copyrighted work unless it first acquires the basic rights to copy the work and distribute it to the public. Although in theory a publisher could proceed with no more than a nonexclusive license of these rights—and this is done in rare circumstances—for obvious reasons publishers generally insist on exclusive rights. In most instances these rights are acquired from the author by means of a contract called the publishing agreement.

New Books

4.51 *Basic book-contract provisions.* In book publishing the publisher typically draws up the contract for a new book, to be signed by both the publisher and the author or, in the case of a joint work, by all authors. In this contract the publisher and author agree to certain things. The publisher undertakes to publish the book after acceptance of the manuscript and to pay the author for the rights conveyed. Usually, publishers pay book authors a stipulated royalty out of the proceeds, but in some cases a publisher will instead pay a lump-sum fee. The author, in addition to granting rights to the publisher, typically guarantees that the work is original and has never before been published and that it does not violate copyright or libel anyone or otherwise expose the publisher to legal liability.

The author usually agrees to correct and return proofs and to cooperate in future revisions of the work. Book-publishing agreements are generally fairly lengthy and detailed documents and include many other points of agreement. Among the common areas of negotiation are royalty schedules; royalty advances and (for certain types of books, such as textbooks) expense allowances; the standards for acceptance of the manuscript; the period following acceptance within which the publisher must issue the work; what rights, beyond North American print rights, are granted to the publisher; what share of royalties the author receives for revised editions to which he or she does not contribute; how rights revert to the author if the book goes out of print; and on what terms the author may audit the publisher's financial records to ensure full payment of royalties due. Typically, publishing agreements prohibit the author from publishing works that compete with the work under contract.

4.52   *Option clauses.* In former years publishing agreements often contained legally binding options on the author's next book. These are almost a thing of the past. Some publishers insist on a right of first refusal or a right to match outstanding offers on the author's next book, but such provisions are becoming rare.

4.53   *Edited works.* The agreement just described is intended for books with one or a few authors. Another type of book, common in scholarly but not in trade publishing, is one in which the chapters are contributed by various authors, chosen and guided by an editor who is an authority in the relevant field. The editor, by selecting and arranging the contributions included in the work, adds another layer of authorship. As author of the collective work, the book as a whole, he or she should sign an agreement similar to the standard author agreement described above. In dealing with the chapter contributors, a publisher may in some circumstances use an agreement of the same type, especially if the contributors are to receive royalty shares. All such agreements, though, need to be modified to reflect the particular allocation of responsibilities between editor and contributors. Alternatively, in appropriate circumstances, publishers can use simpler forms (such as that in fig. 4.1), closer in style to journal author forms (see fig. 4.2). Finally, it is possible to use work-made-for-hire agreements for all these persons, although that is the least common solution. For symposia, see 4.59.

4.54   *Other contracts.* In scholarly publishing, in addition to contracts with the authors of new books, several other types of agreement are in use for special kinds of works. Two of the common ones cover contributions to scholarly journals (see 4.55–58 and fig. 4.2) and to symposia (see 4.59 and fig. 4.1).

Journal Articles

4.55   *Transfers of rights.* Contributors to a journal possess at the beginning exactly the same rights in their work as authors of books. Consequently, when an article has been accepted for publication in a scholarly journal, the publisher usually asks the author to sign a formal transfer of rights in the contribution. In the absence of a written copyright transfer agreement, all that the publisher acquires is the privilege of printing the contribution in the context of that journal. Contributors frequently do not know this and do not understand that without broad rights the publisher cannot license anthology, database, classroom photocopying, or other uses that spread the author's message. Explaining this will often overcome the author's reluctance to sign the transfer. In the agreement currently in use at the University of Chicago Press, the publisher returns to the contributor the right to reprint the article in other scholarly works (see fig. 4.2). Such a provision is fair to both sides and is to be encouraged.

4.56   *Less than full rights.* Some journal publishers, when an author refuses to transfer copyright in toto, ask instead for a license more closely tailored to their specific needs. Care must be taken in such cases to ensure that the contract covers all the subsidiary rights that the publisher may want to exercise or sublicense and that the publisher's rights are exclusive where they need to be. This is especially important for electronic database rights. The right to publish an article in a journal does not carry with it ipso facto the right to include that article in an electronic database. Journal publishers who wish to put their publications up on their own websites, or license them to database publishers, need to ensure that their contracts give them that right. In general, the trend toward narrowing or customization of licenses from journal authors to their publishers imposes on publishers a need to keep careful records of what rights they have obtained in each article, so they do not grant subsidiary rights that they do not in fact control.

4.57   *New alternative licensing arrangements.* Quite early in the evolution of the software industry a movement emerged of people anxious to eliminate copyright control over software and replace it with a system geared toward sharing and free distribution. More recently this ethos, combined with antipathy to the publishing industry in some circles, has led to efforts to restrict the licenses given to publishers of scholarly journals (see

[Date]

Books Division

[Name and Address]

Dear _____ :

The University of Chicago, acting through its Press (the "Press"), is pleased to undertake the publication of your essay or chapter _____ (the "Contribution") to be included in the volume now entitled _____ written/edited by _____ (the "Work").

Accordingly, the following terms of publication are submitted for your consideration:

APPROVAL AND ACCEPTANCE: We mutually agree that publication of the Contribution is contingent upon its acceptance for publication by the Press volume/acquisition editor and upon its meeting Press editorial standards. Publication is additionally contingent upon the formal and final assessment of the Contribution and the Work by the Board of University Publications, without whose approval publication by the Press may not take place.

COPYRIGHT ASSIGNMENT: Whereas the Press will undertake to publish the Contribution as above, and whereas you desire to have the Contribution so published, now, therefore, you grant and assign to The University of Chicago all right, title, and interest in and to the Contribution. This grant includes, but is not limited to, the right to publish the Contribution in all languages and in all media throughout the world, and the continuing right to reprint (and to license third parties to reprint) the Contribution in any format or medium, including electronic media. We will secure copyright for the Contribution in the name of the University of Chicago.

However, you may include or adapt the Contribution for publication in any book of which you are the sole author without your being required to seek our formal permission. If you include or adapt the Contribution in such a book, we require that you provide routine credit and acknowledgment to our Work and to the Press as the original publisher. The acknowledgment with this subsequent use should also include the identical copyright notice as it appears in our publication.

WARRANTY: You warrant that the Contribution is original with you; that it contains no matter which is libelous or is otherwise unlawful or which invades individual privacy or infringes any proprietary right or any statutory copyright; and you agree to indemnify and hold the Press harmless against any claim or judgment to the contrary. Further, you warrant that you have the right to assign the copyright to The University of Chicago, and that no right protected by copyright to the Contribution has been previously assigned. It is understood that the copyright to the Contribution has not been registered with the United States Copyright Office, but in the event

THE UNIVERSITY OF CHICAGO PRESS

1427 EAST 60TH STREET, CHICAGO, ILLINOIS 60637   www.press.uchicago.edu

FIGURE 4.1. Agreement, or consent, for publication of an article or a chapter commissioned as a contribution to a collective work, such as a symposium. Different forms of agreement are required for "works made for hire," such as translations, forewords, or indexes.

that such registration has taken place, you will promptly transfer the copyright to The University of Chicago.

PREVIOUS PUBLICATION AND PERMISSION: You warrant that the Contribution has not been published elsewhere in whole or in part (except as may be set out in a rider annexed hereto and signed by a representative of the Press) and that no agreement to publish the Contribution or any part or version thereof is outstanding. Should the Contribution contain any material which requires written permission for inclusion as part of the Contribution, such permission shall be obtained by you and at your own expense from the copyright proprietor and submitted for review by the Press at the time you submit the manuscript copy of the Contribution.

PROOF HANDLING: You will be given an opportunity to read and correct proofs, but if you fail to return them by the date separately agreed, production and publication may proceed without your participation.

COMPENSATION: As total compensation for your preparation of the Contribution and the above grant and assignment of rights, the Press will publish the Contribution and you will receive, upon publication, _____ free copies of the hardcover edition of the Work and _____ free copies of the paperbound edition when published by the Press. You may purchase additional copies of the Work for your own use at 40% discount from the then-prevailing list price. Following publication you may request the Press to provide you with an electronic copy of the print-ready file for your own personal use, including posting to your own or your employer's website, provided that there are no fees for access and the posting is not being made in conjunction with an effort to distribute copies of the Contribution in competition with the Press's publication.

If the foregoing terms are satisfactory, please sign and date this Agreement; return the Press's copy to _____ immediately, retaining a copy for your files.

ACCEPTED AND APPROVED: FOR THE UNIVERSITY OF CHICAGO:

_____   _____
[Name]   Garrett P. Kiely, Director
_____   The University of Chicago Press
Date

_____
Federal Tax ID (Social Security) Number

_____
Citizenship

_____
Permanent Address

FIGURE 4.1. (*continued*)

PUBLICATION AGREEMENT
Journal Name

From: Firstname Lastname, Editor, *Journal Name*   **To:**

Contribution:

The University of Chicago, on behalf of The University of Chicago Press ("the Press"), is pleased to consider for publication your contribution identified above ("the Contribution"), in its journal ("the Journal") *Journal Name*.

In consideration of the publication of your Contribution, we ask you to assign the copyright to the Press, thus granting us all rights in the Contribution. The Press, in turn, grants to you as author several rights described herein and in the Guidelines for Journal Authors' Rights After Acceptance, available on the website of the Press (the "Guidelines"). The Press may amend the Guidelines at any time with or without notice to you, and your rights in the Contribution shall be governed by this agreement and the Guidelines in effect at the time of your proposed use. You will receive no monetary compensation from the Press for the assignment of copyright and publication of the Contribution. By signing below, you and the Press agree as follows:

Copyright Assignment:

The Press undertakes to publish the Contribution, subject to approval by the editor(s), in its Journal named above. In consideration of such publication, you hereby grant and assign to the Press the entire copyright in the Contribution, including any and all rights of whatever kind or nature now or hereafter protected by the copyright laws of the United States and of all foreign countries, in all languages and forms of communication. It is understood that the copyright to the Contribution has not been registered with the Library of Congress, but that in the event such registration has taken place you will promptly transfer the copyright registration to the Press. If the Contribution is deemed unacceptable for Publication, you will be notified and all rights will revert to you.

Grant of Rights to Author

The University grants to you the following nonexclusive rights, subject to your giving proper credit to the original publication of the Contribution in the Journal, including reproducing the exact copyright notice as it appears in the Journal:

(i)   to reprint the Contribution, in whole or in part, in any book, article, or other scholarly work of which you are the author or editor,

(ii) to use the Contribution for teaching purposes in your classes, including making multiple copies for all students, either as individual copies or as part of a printed course pack, provided that these are to be used solely for classes you teach,

(iii) to post a copy of the Contribution on your personal or institutional web server, provided that the server is noncommercial and there are no charges for access, and

(iv) to deposit a copy of the Contribution in a noncommercial data repository maintained by an institution of which you are a member, after the embargo period identified in the Guidelines and provided all relevant conditions described in the Guidelines have been met.

The rights granted in clauses (i) and (ii) above are intended to benefit the original creators of the Contribution only. Accordingly, if you claim ownership of or rights in the Contribution because it was created by your employee or as a work made for hire, as defined in the Copyright Act, the rights granted in clauses (i) and (ii) above shall not apply to you, and you must contact the Press for permission to make these uses.

Warranties and Indemnifications

You warrant to the Press as follows:

(i)   that the Contribution is your original work;

(ii) that it contains no matter which is defamatory or is otherwise unlawful or which invades rights of privacy or publicity or infringes any proprietary right (including copyright);

(iii) that you have the right to assign the copyright to the Press and that no portion of the copyright to the Contribution has been assigned previously; and

(iv) that the Contribution has not been published elsewhere in whole or in part (except as may be set out in a rider annexed hereto and signed by the Press) and that no agreement to publish is outstanding other than this agreement.

You agree to indemnify and hold the Press harmless against any claim arising from or related to the breach or inaccuracy of any of the warranties listed above.

Requirements for Publication

You agree to prepare and revise the Contribution according to the instructions of the editor(s) and to meet all other requirements for publication communicated to you by the editor(s) or the Press. It is your responsibility to determine whether the Contribution includes material that requires written permission for publication in the Journal, including any material that is supplementary or ancillary to the Contribution; to obtain such permission, at your own expense, from the copyright owner; and to submit that permission to the editor(s) with the manuscript.

Please complete, sign, and date this agreement, and return it to the editor(s) by mail, fax, or e-mail, retaining a copy for your files. An electronic signature may be used. You agree that an electronic signature shall be valid and binding for all purposes, and hereby waive any objection to use of an electronic version of this agreement as a substitute for the original for any legally recognized purpose. *All joint authors must sign, each on a separate form if necessary.*

AUTHOR SIGNATURE: **FOR THE UNIVERSITY OF CHICAGO:**

_____

Name: _____ Date: _____   Garrett Kiely
(Please print or type)   Director, The University of Chicago Press

Address: _____   Please return to the following address:

_____   *Journal Name*
_____   Address1
_____   Address 2
                                                  City, ST 00000 USA
Telephone: _____ Fax: _____   Fax: (###) ###-####
E-mail: _____   E-mail: xxx@xxx.xxx

For internal use only: MSID _____   10.01.2007

FIGURE 4.2. Agreement for publication of a journal article, currently in use by the University of Chicago Press. Here the author transfers all copyright rights to the publisher of the journal, and the publisher transfers back to the author the right to reprint the article in other scholarly contexts.

PUBLICATION AGREEMENT—ALTERNATE SIGNATURE FORM

Use this form only if you belong to one of the categories below. All other authors should sign the Publication Agreement. Return the completed form with the Publication Agreement by mail, fax, or e-mail, retaining a copy for your files.

Contribution: _____

US Government employees: Your signature below indicates that you were an employee of the United States Government at the time the Contribution was prepared and its preparation was undertaken as part of your official duties. Accordingly, you agree to the terms of the attached Publication Agreement with the exception of the section entitled Copyright Assignment, which does not apply to you.

Institution or Agency: _____
(Please print or type)

Signature of author or agency representative: _____

Name: _____ Date: _____
(Please print or type)

Please note that in the case of a Contribution jointly authored by government employees and nongovernment employees, only the government employees should sign this form; all nongovernment authors should sign the Publication Agreement.

Work made for hire: Your signature below indicates that the Contribution was prepared as a "work made for hire" on your behalf and you are thereby entitled to grant and assign copyright as requested in the Publication Agreement. You understand that the rights granted in clause (i) and (ii) of the Grant of Rights to Author do not apply to you.

Employer: _____
(Please print or type)

Signature of employer representative: _____

Name: _____ Date: _____
(Please print or type)

Title: _____
(Please print or type)

Author signing on behalf of joint author(s): Your signature below indicates that you have assigned copyright in the Contribution on behalf of the joint author(s) named below. You warrant that you have been granted by each such joint author the authority to act as his or her agent in this behalf and indemnify the Journal, its sponsor (if applicable), and the University of Chicago Press from any claim arising from the breach or inaccuracy of this warranty. It is your responsibility to communicate the terms of publication to each author named below.

Name(s) of joint author(s): _____
(Please print or type)

Your signature: _____

Your name: _____ Date: _____
(Please print or type)

For internal use only: MSID _____

10.01.2007

FIGURE 4.2. *(continued)*

4.63, 4.64), and to the development of an "open source" model for other types of copyrighted works. The latter, called Creative Commons, offers a number of alternatives to standard copyright distribution. While authors (particularly of journal articles) may show enthusiasm for this model, publishers should approach it with caution. The basic Creative Commons license throws any work subject to it open to public use of all kinds. It allows any member of the public to carry out unlimited free redistribution of copies of a work and to alter and otherwise create derivatives of works. The only requirement it imposes on the licensee is that he or she give the most elementary sort of credit to the author/copyright owner of the original work. However, Creative Commons also offers variants of the basic model that allow the publisher to prohibit both commercial uses and the creation of derivative works. (All these license forms may be found at the Creative Commons website.) Thus, if an author of a journal article presses for the article to be subjected to a Creative Commons license, the publisher in turn may wish to insist that the license include a "noncommercial" clause so that the article may not be published by commercial competitors. In licensing entire journal issues under a Creative Commons license, the publisher will normally also wish to include a "no derivatives" clause; otherwise it will have no control over how others rearrange and otherwise alter the collective work. And as with any license, the publisher should be certain the author has the necessary clearances for any third-party material included in the work. A photographer, for example, may be willing to license electronic distribution of a photograph in the context of a particular journal in online form but balk at inclusion in an electronic version subject to a Creative Commons license. If a work is going to be distributed under a Creative Commons license, that should be disclosed to any licensor of material included in the work.

4.58   *Journal editors.* The role of the journal editor must not be forgotten. Unless he or she is an employee or agent of the company or society that owns the journal, the editor has a separate copyright in each issue as a collective work. Journal publishers should make sure that ownership of that separate copyright is clearly agreed on.

Contributions to Symposia

4.59   *Symposium proceedings.* Symposium proceedings, made up of papers by different authors, are sometimes published as special issues of journals and sometimes as stand-alone books. The editor of the proceedings, in either case, has a separate status as author because the proceedings, as a whole, are a collective work. If the proceedings are being published as a journal issue, the publisher needs to make clear who owns copyright in the editor's work and to secure from every contributor a contract more or less identical to that used for authors of articles published in regular issues of the journal concerned. If the proceedings are being published as a book, the editor should sign a standard book author agreement, modified as appropriate, and the contributors should sign separate forms covering their own papers (see fig. 4.1). Either the volume editor or the publisher will send these forms to all contributors. When these have been signed, they are returned to the publisher and filed with the contract for the volume. See also 4.53.

Subsidiary Rights and Permissions

Handling Subsidiary Rights

4.60   **Categories.** Subsidiary rights are usually thought of as including the following categories, some applicable to all types of published works and others to books only:

Foreign rights, whereby a foreign publisher may be licensed to sell the book in its original version in that publisher's own territory. Where the license is for the English-language version, the licensor should be careful to limit the license to the print medium, because electronic distribution cannot easily, if at all, be limited geographically. (And a work that the original publisher makes available online will be of less appeal to foreign print distributors.)

Translation rights, whereby a foreign publisher may be licensed to translate the work into another language and to have standard publisher's rights in the translation (other than live-stage rights, motion-picture rights, and perhaps electronic rights).

Serial rights, whereby a magazine or newspaper publisher may be licensed to publish the book or excerpts from it in a series of daily, weekly, or monthly installments. *First serial rights* refers to publication before the work has come out in book form, *second serial rights* to publication afterward.

Paperback rights, whereby a publisher is licensed to produce and sell a paperback version of the book. So-called quality, or trade, paperbacks are normally sold in bookstores, like clothbound books. Mass-market paperbacks are typically marketed through newsstands and supermarkets, although many now find their way into bookstores. Where the publisher of the paperback is the original publisher, paperback rights are not subsidiary but primary, usually with their own royalty scale. Some books are published only in paper, with no previously published clothbound version; these are called original paperbacks.

Book-club rights, whereby a book club is given the right to distribute the book to its members for less than the regular trade price. Copies generally are sold to the book club in bulk at a steep discount.

Reprint rights, whereby another publisher is licensed to reprint the work, in whole or in part, in an anthology or some other collection or (usually if the work has gone out of print in English) in a cheap reprint edition. This category also includes licensing document-delivery companies to reproduce chapters of works on demand.

Live-stage rights, whereby a theatrical producer is given the right to produce a play or musical based on the work.

Motion-picture rights, whereby a movie producer or studio is given the right to make a motion picture based on the work. This applies primarily to works of fiction, but motion-picture producers will often license rights to biographies and other nonfiction works so as to avoid possible infringement claims.

Audio rights, whereby the work is licensed for recording on compact disc, for audio delivery over the Internet, or the like.

Electronic rights, whereby the work, or portions of it, is licensed for distribution online, in CD-ROM format, or via other electronic means. However, if the publisher itself intends to issue the work in e-book or other electronic form, electronic rights should be considered not subsidiary rights but part of the publisher's basic publication right and subject to a primary royalty. Publishers should normally assign new ISBNs for the electronic versions of their works, just as they have always done when (for example) issuing a hardcover work in paperback form (see 1.32). Publishers should bear in mind that electronic versions may sometimes be considered derivative works rather than mere copies of the print version. The addition of substantial hyperlinks, video data, and the like may create a derivative work. If the publisher is for any reason not acquiring general derivative work rights in the contract, it should make sure to obtain the right to enhance the electronic version of the work with such features. The publisher should also be sure to obtain the right to license electronic educational use (see 4.61, 4.90).

Rights for scholarly use, whereby the publisher grants others permission to quote text or copy charts and other illustrations from the original.

Rights for educational use, whereby teachers are permitted to make copies of the work for their classes or to include excerpts from the work in course-specific anthologies ("course packs"). Until recently, photocopying was the standard medium for classroom use, but electronic reproduction is becoming more common and blurring some of the boundaries of subsidiary rights. Educational use may also include such things as inclusion in electronic reserves in libraries or distribution over campus intranets.

Subsidiary rights in the context of journals also include microform (including microfilm and microfiche) and the right to make summaries of articles in so-called abstract form. Reproduction by document-delivery houses and licensing of electronic database rights are particularly relevant to journals.

4.61   *Electronic-rights licensing.* The term *electronic rights* covers a wide range of possibilities, and the number is constantly growing. Among the users of electronic rights are aggregators, who make available online a large number of publications in a given field or fields; research services, both current and archival, that permit access to databases of publications, often by subscription; and services that allow users to purchase or "borrow" electronic copies of works. The decision whether to license some or all of such uses is both an economic and a strategic one. For the most part, electronic delivery services are too new for publishers to predict with any certainty what income may flow from them. Rather, the economic issue is whether the availability of a work through these services may "cannibalize" the publisher's projected print sales. The strategic issue is even harder to quantify, involving the need to be on the cutting edge of publishing or, at least, not to be seen as a laggard in such matters. In entering into electronic-rights licenses, the publisher should satisfy itself that the delivery mechanism of the particular licensee has safeguards against excessive downloading—or that such downloading is something the publisher can tolerate. The publisher should also ensure that no electronic license lasts more than a few years, for the pace of change is such that all these issues need to be revisited frequently.

4.62 *Authors' electronic use of their own works.* Where books are concerned, the author seldom retains any right of electronic publication. In scholarly journals, on the other hand, the right of authors to make electronic use of their own works has become contentious. For example, publishers that have traditionally allowed their authors to make unlimited photocopies for their own students now face an analogous demand: that authors be permitted to post their works on campus websites. If the website is accessible only by password and only to members of the university, the risk of lost revenue is probably modest and probably less important than retaining the goodwill of the author. More problematic is the demand, increasingly frequent, that the author be permitted to post the article on his or her personal website, or on an open-access university website or other "institutional repository." While such dissemination may not necessarily affect sales of the journal as such, it is likely to diminish licensing revenues. The fact that licensing revenue helps support the publication of important scholarly work seems to have escaped general notice.

4.63 *University licenses.* Several universities have adopted policies under which they presumptively receive nonexclusive licenses of journal articles written by their faculty, with the right to post those articles on the Internet and to make and license "noncommercial" uses. (Commonly, faculty are permitted but not encouraged to opt out of this arrangement on a case-by-case basis.) Where this arrangement applies, a faculty author is supposed to present his or her publisher with an addendum to the publisher's standard contract, listing rights granted to the university. There are various forms of addenda in circulation; all are problematic. One, for example, contains the following provision:

> Notwithstanding any terms in the Publication Agreement to the contrary, AUTHOR and PUBLISHER agree that in addition to any rights under copyright retained by Author in the Publication Agreement, Author retains: (i) the rights to reproduce, to distribute, to publicly perform, and to publicly display the Article in any medium for noncommercial purposes; (ii) the right to prepare derivative works from the Article; and (iii) the right to authorize others to make any noncommercial use of the Article so long as Author receives credit as author and the journal in which the Article has been published is cited as the source of first publication of the Article. For example, Author may make and distribute copies in the course of teaching and research and may post the Article on personal or institutional websites and in other open-access digital repositories.

Among its faults, this language (i) does not make clear what the author can, and cannot, do with derivative works that he or she creates; (ii) does not make clear whether what the author can distribute, display, and otherwise use is the author's own manuscript or the finished, published work; and (iii) does not prevent the author from licensing the article to a competing journal, if the latter is "noncommercial" (a word that has no commonly accepted legal meaning). Another problem is that only the publisher as copyright owner has the ability to police compliance with whatever "noncommercial" licenses the author or university may give—yet the publisher has no control over the licensing activity. Publishers would be well advised to develop their own addenda to use when presented with author requests for nonexclusive rights. Such addenda might give the author and his or her employer unlimited rights to use the article internally, the right to post manuscript versions of the article on the author's website, and the right to post a PDF or similar file of the final published version on the author's website after a decent interval of time.

4.64   *The NIH Public Access Policy.* In a similar vein to the university policies addressed in the previous paragraph, a "Public Access Policy" has been adopted by the National Institutes of Health pursuant to congressional mandate. This policy requires submission, for posting on the National Library of Medicine's PubMed Central, of the final manuscripts of all peer-reviewed articles derived from NIH-funded research. Manuscripts are to be submitted upon final acceptance for publication—that is, after the entire peer review and editorial process is complete and the article is ready for publication. This policy, unlike the university policies discussed above, is not subject to any opt-out and cannot be altered by any addendum. (Publishers may, however, choose to substitute their own published versions of articles for such manuscripts.) Authors' contracts with their publishers must stipulate a time, no later than twelve months after the official date of publication, when their articles will be posted for public access. If publishers believe that licensing revenue will be directly affected once an article is available at no cost from PubMed Central, they will wish to push for the maximum delay (i.e., twelve months) on public posting.

4.65   *Economic considerations.* The list above by no means exhausts the various forms of subsidiary rights the publisher may handle, but it includes the major ones. Depending on the administrative structure of the publishing house and the importance and marketability of the work involved, various persons or departments may handle different aspects of subsidiary rights work—a special rights and permissions department, the sales or marketing department, the acquiring editor, or even the chief executive officer. When the publisher sells or licenses rights to others, money is paid, either in a lump sum or as a royalty, and these proceeds are normally split between the publisher and the author according to whatever terms are specified in the publishing contract. In a typical book-publishing agreement the author receives at least 50 percent of such income. Some publishers have tried to avoid paying the author so much by licensing at an artificially low royalty to a sister company or other affiliate, but such "sweetheart" arrangements are suspect and of doubtful legality. In general, licenses between related companies should be handled in the same way as those between unrelated companies unless the author agrees otherwise in advance.

Granting Permission

4.66   *Handling permission requests.* A publisher with a relatively large backlist of books and journals, such as the University of Chicago Press, may receive dozens of communications every day from people seeking to license material from its list. Some requests are for standard subsidiary rights licenses, as described above. Others are for permission to reproduce snippets of prose or verse, or an illustration or two, from a book or journal. Most publishers have a "rights and permissions" staff to handle these requests. Rights and permissions can be a major source of income but also a major item of expense. Strategies for streamlining the permissions function are discussed later in this chapter.

4.67   *The rights file.* One prerequisite to an efficient and legally safe rights and permissions program is a complete and accurate record of what rights the publisher has. This is especially sensitive where third-party materials such as illustrations are embedded in the material to be licensed. The publisher's rights file should also record any other conditions that might restrict the publisher's ability to license, such as a requirement that the author's approval be obtained.

The Author's Responsibilities

4.68   *Author's warranties.* In signing a contract with a publisher an author warrants (guarantees) that the work is original, that the author owns it, that no part of it has been previously published, and that no other agreement to publish it or part of it is outstanding. The author should also warrant that the work does not libel anyone or infringe any person's right of privacy. If the work contains scientific formulas or practical advice, the author should also be asked to warrant that no instructions in the work will, if accurately followed, cause injury to anyone. Some publishers ask for a further warranty that any statement of fact in the work is indeed accurate.

Obtaining Permissions

4.69   *General principles.* Budget permitting, an author may wish to commission illustrations on a work-made-for-hire basis, using forms supplied by the publisher. With this exception, an author must obtain permission to use any copyrighted material created by others, unless the intended use is a "fair use" (see 4.77–87). Technically, permission need not be in writing, but it would be most unwise to rely on oral permission. No permission is required to quote from works of the United States government or works for which copyright has expired. See 4.25–29 for guidelines to determine whether copyright for old material has expired. Bear in mind that although the original text of a classic reprinted in a modern edition may be in the public domain, recent translations and abridgments, as well as editorial introductions, notes, and other apparatus, are protected by copyright. But whether permission is needed or not, the author should always, as a matter of good practice (and to avoid any possible charge of plagiarism), credit any sources used. See 4.98.

4.70   *Author's role in obtaining permissions.* Publishing agreements place on the author the responsibility to request any permission needed for the use of material owned by others. In the course of writing a book or article, the author should keep a record of all copyright owners whose permission may be necessary before the work is published. For a book containing many illustrations, long prose passages, or poetry, obtaining permissions may take weeks, even months. For example, the author may find that an American publisher holds rights only for distribution in the United States and that European and British Commonwealth rights are held by a British publisher. The author, wishing worldwide distribution for the book (world rights), must then write to the British publisher requesting permission to reprint, mentioning (if true) that permission has already been obtained from the US publisher. If the author of copyrighted material has died, or if the copyright owner has gone out of business, a voluminous correspondence may ensue before anyone authorized to grant permission can be found (see 4.75). The author should therefore begin requesting permissions as soon as a manuscript is accepted for publication. Most publishers wisely decline to start setting type for a book until all the author's permissions are in hand.[1]

4.71   *Author's own work.* The author should remember that permission is sometimes needed to reuse or even to revise his or her own work. If the author has already allowed a chapter or other significant part to appear in print elsewhere—as a journal article, for example—then written permission to reprint it, or to update or revise it, will need to be secured from the copyright owner of the other publication, unless the author secured the right of reuse in the contract with that earlier publisher. The law does not require that the prior publication be credited in the new publication, but it is a common courtesy to give credit on the copyright page of the book, in a footnote on the first page of the reprinted material, or in a special list of acknowledgments. And if the first publisher owns copyright in the material, it may make credit a condition of permission to reprint. Also, if the first publisher owns copyright, the new publisher will need to flag its files so that subsequent permissions requests for that material are referred to the original copyright owner.

4.72   *Fees and record keeping.* Most publishing agreements stipulate that any fees to be paid will be the author's responsibility. (Textbooks are a rare exception; see 4.100.) When all permissions have been received, the author should send them, or copies of them, to the publisher, who will note and comply with any special provisions they contain. The publisher will file all permissions with the publishing contract, where they may be consulted in the event of future editions or of requests for permission to reprint from the work. The copyeditor will check the permissions against the manuscript to be sure all necessary credits have been given. See 1.30, 2.43, 4.98, 14.49.

4.73   *Permissions beyond the immediate use.* Many publishers, when giving permission to reprint material they control, will withhold the right to sublicense that material. In such a case the publisher of the later work will not be able to give third parties free and clear permission to use material in which content from the earlier work is embedded; they will have to go back to the original source. Some publishers will also limit their licenses to a single edition, sometimes even with a maximum print run

---

1. It is possible to engage professional help in obtaining permissions for a large project. Specialists in this work are listed under "Consultants" in the annual publication *LMP* (*Literary Market Place*; see bibliog. 2.8). Note also that the allocation of responsibility described here may not apply in some cases, such as large-market college textbooks, for which the publisher may take on the permissions paperwork. See 4.100.

stipulated, or to a specific time period such as five or seven years. Where this is so, the publisher receiving the permission will have to go back to the source for new permission, usually for an additional fee, for any new edition, paperback reprint, serialization, or whatever. Alternatively, the publisher granting permission can stipulate up front what fees are to be paid for further uses and permit the new publisher to secure such permission automatically on payment of the agreed-on fee.

4.74   *Unpublished works.* Getting permission for unpublished material presents an entirely different problem. Instead of a publishing corporation or licensing agent, one must deal with the author or author's heirs, who may not be easily identified or found. If the writer is dead, it may be especially difficult to determine who controls the copyrights.

4.75   *The missing copyright owner.* The problem presented by unpublished works whose authors are dead is, in a larger sense, just an example of the problem of the missing copyright owner. Another typical example is the publisher that has gone out of business or at least is no longer doing business under a given imprint. This problem has come to be known as the "orphan works" problem and has been the subject of proposed legislation. The draft bills suggest practices that a publisher would do well to follow in dealing with an orphan work. The most important thing is to conduct a reasonable (and well-documented) effort to locate the copyright owner. The elements of a bona fide search will vary with the circumstances but would probably include a search of the Copyright Office records, an Internet search, and queries to both private and public databases that might reasonably be expected to contain information as to the owner of the copyright. If such efforts yield no results, there is still some risk in going forward. Technically, use of the work might still be ruled an infringement of copyright should a copyright owner surface, but it is unlikely that any court would do more than require the payment of a reasonable permissions fee. Anyone proceeding with publication under these conditions should certainly be prepared to offer and pay a reasonable fee on receiving any objection from the rediscovered owner.

4.76   *Noncopyright restrictions on archives.* Authors who wish to include unpublished material in their works should be aware that private restrictions, unrelated to copyright, may limit its use. The keeper of a collection, usually a librarian or an archivist, is the best source of such information, including what permissions must be sought and from whom. Bear in mind that copyright in a manuscript is different from ownership of the actual paper. Most often a library or collector will own the physical object itself but not the right to reproduce it. Thus there may be two permissions required: one for access to the material and one for the right to copy. It is important not to mistake one for the other.

FAIR USE: QUOTING WITHOUT PERMISSION

4.77 *Overview of the legal doctrine.* The doctrine of fair use was originally developed by courts as an equitable limit on the absolute rights of copyright. Although incorporated into the new copyright law, the doctrine still does not attempt to define the exact limits of the fair use of copyrighted work. It does state, however, that in determining whether the use made of a work in any particular case is fair, the factors to be considered must include the following:

1. The purpose and character of the use, including whether such use is of a commercial nature or is for nonprofit educational purposes
2. The nature of the copyrighted work
3. The amount and substantiality of the portion used in relation to the copyrighted work as a whole
4. The effect of the use on the potential market for, or value of, the copyrighted work

Essentially, the doctrine excuses copying that would otherwise be infringement. For example, it allows authors to quote from other authors' work or to reproduce small amounts of graphic or pictorial material for purposes of review or criticism or to illustrate or buttress their own points. Authors invoking fair use should transcribe accurately and give credit to their sources. They should not quote out of context, making the author of the quoted passage seem to be saying something opposite to, or different from, what was intended.

4.78 *Validity of "rules of thumb."* Although the law lays out no boundaries or ironclad formulas for fair use, some publishers have their own rules of thumb. Such rules, of course, have no legal force: courts, not publishers, adjudicate fair use. The rules exist in part to give an overworked permissions department, which often cannot tell whether a proposed use of a quotation is actually fair, something to use as a yardstick. See also 4.87.

4.79 *A few general rules.* Fair use is use that is fair—simply that. Uses that are tangential in purpose to the original, and uses that transform the copied material by changing its context or the way it is perceived, will always be judged more leniently than those that merely parallel or parrot the original. For example, substantial quotation of the original is acceptable in the context of a critique but may well not be acceptable if one is simply using the first author's words to reiterate the same argument or embellish one's own prose. Use of any literary work in its entirety—a poem, an essay, a chapter of a book—is hardly ever acceptable. Use of less than the whole will be judged by whether the second author appears to be taking a free ride on the first author's labor. As a general rule, one should never quote more than a few contiguous paragraphs of prose or lines of poetry at a time or let the quotations, even if scattered, begin to overshadow the quoter's own material. Quotations or graphic reproductions should not be so substantial that they substitute for, or diminish the value of, the copyright owner's own publication. Proportion is more important than the absolute length of a quotation: quoting five hundred words from an essay of five thousand is likely to be riskier than quoting that amount from a work of fifty thousand. But an even smaller percentage can be an infringement if it constitutes the heart of the work being quoted.

4.80   *Epigraphs and interior monologues.* Quotation in the form of an epigraph does not fit neatly into any of the usual fair-use categories but is probably fair use by virtue of scholarly and artistic tradition. The same can be said of limited quotation of song lyrics, poetry, and the like in the context of an interior monologue or fictional narrative. Of course, this would not excuse the publication of a collection of epigraphs or lyrics without permission of the various authors being quoted.

4.81   *Unpublished works.* Where the work to be quoted has never been published, the same considerations apply. But if the author or the author's spouse or children are still living, some consideration should be given to their interest in controlling when the work is disclosed to the public.

4.82   *Paraphrasing.* Bear in mind that although fair use will protect verbatim copying, unfair use will not be excused by paraphrasing. Traditional copyright doctrine treats extensive paraphrase as merely disguised copying. Thus, fair-use analysis will be the same for both. Paraphrase of small quantities of material, on the other hand, may not constitute copying at all, so that fair-use analysis would never come into play.

4.83   *Pictorial and graphic materials.* With respect to pictorial and graphic materials, there is little legal precedent to navigate by. At the level of intuition, it seems that a monograph on Picasso should be free to reproduce details from his paintings in order, for example, to illustrate the critic's discussion of Picasso's brushwork. Reproducing the entire image in black and white may also be reasonably necessary to illustrate the author's analysis of Picasso's techniques of composition. Reproducing "thumbnail sketches" of images has been held to be a fair use since they are so small and of such poor resolution that they cannot reduce the commercial value of the original. However, justification wears thin when a painting is reproduced in vivid color occupying a full page; the result begins to compete with large-scale reproductions of artwork that have no scholarly purpose. Likewise, reproduction on the cover would in almost all cases count as commercial rather than scholarly use and therefore be unjustified. As for photographs, using them merely as illustrations would require permission, but use as described above in a scholarly treatment of photography might not.

4.84   *Charts, tables, and graphs.* Reproduction of charts, tables, and graphs presents a difficult judgment call. An aggressive approach would justify copying a single item on the ground that one chart is the pictorial equivalent of a few sentences. A more conservative approach would argue that a graph is a picture worth a thousand words and that reproducing it without permission is taking a free ride on the first author's work. This latter approach has the flaw of being too absolute in practice, for it is difficult under this rationale to imagine *any* fair use of such an image. Where the item in question represents a small portion of the original work and a small portion of the second work, the harm seems minimal, outweighed by the benefits of open communication. Certainly, reproduction of a single graph, table, or chart that simply presents data in a straightforward relationship, in contrast to reproduction of a graph or chart embellished with pictorial elements, should ordinarily be considered fair use. Indeed, some graphs that merely present facts with little or no expressive input—the equivalent, in two dimensions, of a mere list—may even be beyond the protection of copyright.

4.85   *Importance of attribution.* With all reuse of others' materials, it is important to identify the original as the source. This not only bolsters the claim of fair use but also helps avoid any accusation of plagiarism. Nothing elaborate is required; a standard footnote will suffice, or (in the case of a graph or table, for example) a simple legend that says "Source: [author, title, and date of earlier work]." Note that such a legend is not always clear: Does it mean that the data are taken from the original but reformatted by the second author or that the graph or table has itself been copied? If the latter, it is preferable to say "Reprinted from [author, title, and date of earlier work]" rather than merely "Source." See also 3.28–36, 3.75, 14.49.

4.86   *Unnecessary permissions.* Given the ad hoc nature of fair use and the absence of rules and guidelines, many publishers tend to seek permission if they have the slightest doubt whether a particular use is fair. This is unfortunate. The right of fair use is valuable to scholarship, and it should not be allowed to decay because scholars fail to employ it boldly. Furthermore, excessive permissions processing tends to slow down the gestation of worthwhile writings. Even if permission is sought and denied, that should not necessarily be treated as the end of the matter. The US Supreme Court has held that requesting permission should not be regarded as an admission that permission is needed. In other words, where permission is denied, or granted but for an unreasonable price, there is an opportunity for a second look.

4.87   *Chicago's fair-use guidelines.* To reduce the expense of responding to permissions requests, and to reduce the friction in scholarly publishing that permissions handling can create, the University of Chicago Press posts guidelines on its website for what it considers to be fair use of excerpts from its own publications. These guidelines are intended to be generous and fair to all parties. They are beginning to be adopted by other publishers.

LIBRARY AND EDUCATIONAL COPYING AS FAIR USE

4.88   *The Copyright Act.* Fair use has been much in dispute as applied to photocopying for classroom and library use. The Copyright Act contains specific guidelines for library photocopying, and the legislative history of the act includes specific, though not official, guidelines for classroom photocopying.

4.89   *Library photocopying.* The new law does attempt to define minimum fair-use limitations on machine copying by libraries, in a long section with many exemptions and caveats too complex to discuss here. In general, it allows libraries to make single copies of copyrighted works, provided each copy bears the original copyright notice and provided the copies are made for one of the purposes specifically defined in the statute, including the following:

1. If the copy is made for a library's own use because the library's own copy of the work is damaged or missing and a replacement cannot be obtained at a fair price
2. If the copy is made for a patron's use and is limited to an article or a small part of a larger work—or the whole of a larger work if a printed copy cannot be obtained at a fair price—and only if the copy is intended for use by the patron in "private study, scholarship, or research"

The law specifically forbids "systematic" copying by libraries. Presumably this includes but is not limited to (1) making copies of books or periodicals as a substitute for buying them and (2) making copies for patrons indiscriminately without regard to the patrons' identities or intended use of the material.

4.90   *Educational photocopying.* The Copyright Act does not include similar guidelines for educational photocopying. But a congressional report published at the time the law was being written includes privately negotiated guidelines, implicitly approved by Congress, for fair use of copyrighted material. These guidelines are available at the website of the United States Copyright Office. "Brevity" and "spontaneity" are the guiding principles; the latter reflects the premise that photocopying for classroom use should be done only when there is too little time to obtain permission. Multiple copies should not exceed the number of students in the class. They should not substitute for anthologies or regular school purchases. The same items should not be copied from year to year or semester to semester, but once only and at the instance of a particular teacher for immediate use in the classroom. Workbooks and other consumable materials should not be copied, and the students should not be charged more than the actual copying cost. Any copy must include the copyright notice used in the original. As for the widespread practice of making customized anthologies ("course packs") for individual teachers' classes, cases subsequent to the guidelines make clear that this is an infringement if express permission is not received from the copyright owners of the materials included in them. More recently, the legality of posting digital copies of published materials on campus intranets for so-called e-reserve purposes has been the subject of hotly contested litigation.

4.91   *Digitizing and automating the permissions process.* The technologies of photocopying and electronic reproduction present a major institutional challenge to publishers. The volume of license requests under these headings exceeds the ability of traditional techniques to process them. Publishers have customarily processed such requests by hand, case by case, evaluating each request on its own merits and often tailoring a fee to the specific circumstances. Whether this approach can or should survive is an open question. The Internet—the very electronic technology that publishers have often regarded as a threat—provides a powerful tool for handling requests rapidly and with little or no staff involvement. A properly designed website, coupled with the adoption of standard, publicly quoted fees, can create a highly efficient marketplace for copying, to the benefit of both the publisher and its customers. Authors seeking permission for use of other authors' work can obtain that permission immediately and can realistically budget for permissions fees in advance. The marketplace can be even more efficient when a royalty-rights organization such as the

Copyright Clearance Center (see 1.97) enables users to obtain online permissions from multiple publishers through a single website. Whether these services become the standard, or inspire publishers to move their own rights and permissions work to the web, remains to be seen.

Requesting Permission

4.92   *Information required.* Would-be users can help reduce delay and miscommunication by submitting their requests for permission in the best possible form. All requests for permission to reprint should be sent to the copyright holder in writing and in duplicate. The request should contain the following explicit information:

1. The title of the original work and exact identification, with page numbers, of what is to be reprinted. Identification should include, in the case of a table or figure, its number and the page it appears on (e.g., fig. 6 on p. 43); in the case of a poem, the title and the page on which the poem appears; in the case of a prose passage, the opening and closing phrases in addition to the page numbers (e.g., "from 'The military genius of Frederick the Great' on p. 110 through 'until the onset of World War I' on p. 112"). The requester should be sure to cite the original source of the material, not any subsequent reprinting of it.
2. Information about the publication in which the author wishes to reproduce the material: title, approximate number of printed pages, form of publication (clothbound book, paperback book, journal, electronic journal), publisher, probable date of publication, approximate print run, and list price (if available).
3. The kind of rights requested. The most limited rights a user ought to accept are "nonexclusive world rights in the English language, for one edition." The best opening gambit would be "nonexclusive world rights in all languages and for all editions in print and other media, including the right to grant customary permissions requests but only where the licensed material is incorporated in [the requester's work]." The request for "the rights to grant customary permissions" would, if granted, greatly simplify the downstream licensing of the new work. Unfortunately, such a right is not implicit in any nonexclusive license (see 4.34) and is seldom granted, and licensees of works in which earlier material is used end up needing to get multiple layers of permission.

Submitting a request in this form does not guarantee that the copyright owner will sign and return it—the owner may well have its own standard form that it returns to the requester—but it at least helps both parties by clearly defining what is under discussion. It is up to the copyright owner to state clearly what fee is demanded for the proposed use and what special conditions apply to the grant. When agreement on all terms is reached, the requester and the copyright owner should both retain copies of the final agreement, and a third copy (with original signature, if the process has been done on paper rather than electronically) should go to the publisher.

4.93   *Sample permissions letters.* The University of Chicago Press supplies authors or editors of books requiring many permissions with a model request letter (fig. 4.3) but suggests that they write on their own personal or (when appropriate) institutional letterhead. Every publisher would be well advised to adopt some variation of this practice, for authors typically are rudderless at sea without it.

ILLUSTRATIONS

4.94   *Rights holders.* Permission to reproduce pictorial works—as opposed to charts, graphs, or the like, which are usually created by the same author(s) as the text—will sometimes, but not reliably, be available from the publisher. A publisher who has used the pictorial work to illustrate text that someone is seeking to reprint may very well not have the right to sublicense use of the illustration. Even a publisher of, say, a collection of the artist's work may not have rights to the individual images. In such a case the permission seeker must deal with the owner of the object or the artist or both. Copyright ownership of artworks sold before 1978 is not always easy to determine, because before 1978 the law generally, but not always, assumed that so long as an original artwork remained unpublished, its copyright passed from hand to hand with ownership of the object itself. For post-1977 works, copyright belongs to the artist unless the artist has explicitly assigned it to someone else. But even for such works, the person seeking permission to reproduce the artwork in a book or journal may, as a practical matter, need to deal with a museum that expects a fee for the privilege of allowing reproduction. Where the museum can deny permission to photograph the object, such a fee is the tariff one pays for physical access if nothing else. Where the museum is licensing its own reproduction or photograph of the work, it has less justification, for the law denies copyright to photographs that merely reproduce another two-dimensional image. Be that as it may, authors and publishers are generally loath to antagonize museums by challenging their positions.

4.95   *Stock agencies and image archives.* The only kind of pictorial work for which permissions are easily granted is photographs, at least where one is dealing with a stock agency or other commercial image archive.

To:

Reference:

Date:

Contracts &
Subsidiary Rights

Books Division

I am writing to request permission to print the following material:

Author/Title/Date of publication:

Pages as they appear in your publication:

Other identifying information and remarks:

This material is to appear as originally published (any changes or deletions are noted on the reverse side of this letter) in the following work which the University of Chicago Press is presently preparing for publication:

Author (Editor)/Title:

Proposed date of publication:

Remarks:

I request nonexclusive world rights, including electronic rights, but only as part of my volume, in all languages, for all editions, and in all media. In addition, I ask permission for the Univ. of Chicago Press to include the illustrations in connection with advertising and promoting the book.

If you are the copyright holder, may I have your permission to reprint the above material in my book? If you do not indicate otherwise, I will use the usual scholarly form of acknowledgment, including publisher, author, title, etc.

If you are not the copyright holder, or if additional permission is needed for world rights from another source, please indicate so.

Thank you for your consideration of this request. A duplicate copy of this form is enclosed for your convenience.

Sincerely yours,

_____

The above request is hereby approved on the conditions specified below, and on the understanding that full credit will be given to the source.

Date: _____ Approved by: _____

THE UNIVERSITY OF CHICAGO PRESS _____

1427 EAST 60TH STREET, CHICAGO, ILLINOIS 60637   TEL: 773.702.7700   FAX: 773.702.2706

FIGURE 4.3. Suggestions for a letter seeking permission to reprint material in a scholarly book. Some of the information about the proposed book may be lacking when the author begins to request permissions, but as much information as possible should be supplied. Note that spaces are left so that the person addressed can use the letter itself for granting or denying the request or for referring the author elsewhere.

Such agencies have vast inventories of images and published, easy-to-understand fee structures. There are also websites that act as clearing-houses for photographic permissions.

4.96 *Information required.* A permission request for an illustration should be sent to the picture agency, museum, artist, or private individual controlling reproduction rights. Again, the request should be as specific as possible regarding the identity of what is to be reproduced, the form of publication in which it will appear, and the kind of rights requested. If the author making the request knows that the illustration will also be used elsewhere than in the text proper (such as on the jacket or in advertising), this fact should be noted.

4.97 *Fees.* Fees paid for reproducing material, especially illustrations procured from a stock-photo agency, usually cover one-time use only—in, say, the first edition of a book. If an illustration is also to be used on the jacket or in advertising, a higher fee is customary. And if a book is reprinted as a paperback or goes into a second edition, another fee is usually charged. Ideally such a fee should be agreed upon in advance, at the time of the initial permission. Whether the publisher or the author should pay whatever additional fee is charged for cover use is a matter for negotiation.

ACKNOWLEDGING SOURCES

4.98 *Credit lines.* Whether or not the use of others' material requires permission, an author should give the exact source of such material: in a note or internal reference in the text, in a source note to a table, or in a credit line under an illustration. Where formal permission has been granted, the author should, within reason, follow any special wording stipulated by the grantor. For a text passage complete in itself, such as a poem, or for a table, the full citation to the source may be followed by this simple acknowledgment:

Reprinted by permission of the publisher.

A credit line below an illustration may read, for example, as follows:

Courtesy of the Newberry Library, Chicago, Illinois.

For examples of various kinds of credit lines, see 3.28–36, 3.75, 14.49.

4.99 *Acknowledgments sections.* In a work that needs many permissions, acknowledgments are often grouped in a special acknowledgments section at the front or back of the work (see 1.41). Some citation of the source should still, however, be made on the page containing the relevant material.

FEES

4.100   *Responsibility for payment.* As noted above, publishing agreements generally make the author responsible for any fees charged for use of others' material. A publisher may agree to pay the fees and to deduct them from the author's royalties or—in rare instances—to split the fees with the author. If it appears that a book would be enhanced by illustrations not provided by the author, many publishing agreements enable the publisher to find the illustrations and (with the author's consent) charge any fees involved to the author's royalty account. One exception to these generalizations is school and college textbooks, where it is common for the publisher to provide a certain amount of its own funds to pay for illustrations.

4.101   *Anthologies.* A book made up entirely of other authors' copyrighted materials—stories, essays, poems, documents, selections from larger works—depends for its existence on permissions from the various copyright owners. The compiler of such a volume therefore should begin seeking permissions as soon as a contract for publication of the volume has been executed or a letter of intent has been received from the prospective publisher. Informal inquiries to copyright owners may be initiated before that time, but no sensible publisher of material to be anthologized is likely to grant permission for its use or to set fees without knowing the details of eventual publication. Once those details are known, the compiler must act quickly. Permission for a selection may be refused, or the fee charged may be so high that the compiler is forced to drop that selection and substitute another. And until all permissions have been received and all fees agreed on, the table of contents cannot be considered final.

Part Two: Style and Usage

5 *Grammar and Usage*

BRYAN A. GARNER

Grammar 5.1

Grammar

Introduction

5.1   *Grammar defined.* Grammar consists of the rules governing how words are put together into sentences. These rules, which native speakers of a language learn largely by osmosis, govern most constructions in a given language. The small minority of constructions that lie outside these rules fall mostly into the category of idiom and usage.

5.2   *Schools of grammatical thought.* There are many schools of grammatical thought—and differing vocabularies for describing grammar. Grammatical theories have been in great flux in recent years. And the more we learn the less we seem to know: "An entirely adequate description of English grammar is still a distant target and at present seemingly an unreachable one, the complications being what they are."[1] In fact, the more detailed the grammar (it can run to many large volumes), the less likely it is to be of any use to most writers and speakers.

5.3   *Parts of speech.* As traditionally understood, grammar is both a science and an art. Often it has focused—as it does here—on parts of speech and their syntax. Each part of speech performs a particular function in a sentence or phrase. Traditional grammar has held that there are eight parts of speech: nouns, pronouns, adjectives, verbs, adverbs, prepositions, conjunctions, and interjections.[2] Somewhat surprisingly, modern grammarians cannot agree on precisely how many parts of speech there are in English. At least one grammarian says there are as few as three.[3] Another insists that there are "about fifteen," noting that "the precise number is still being debated."[4] This section deals with the traditional eight; each part of speech is treated below. The purpose here is to sketch some of the main lines of English grammar using traditional grammatical terms.

---

1. Robert W. Burchfield, *Unlocking the English Language* (New York: Hill and Wang, 1991), 22.
2. See Robert L. Allen, *English Grammars and English Grammar* (New York: Scribner, 1972), 7.
3. Ernest W. Gray, *A Brief Grammar of Modern Written English* (Cleveland: World, 1967), 70.
4. R. L. Trask, *Language: The Basics* (London: Routledge, 1995), 37.

Nouns

DEFINITIONS

5.4 *Nouns generally.* A noun is a word that names something, whether abstract (intangible) or concrete (tangible). It may be a common noun (the name of a generic class or type of person, place, thing, process, activity, or condition) or a proper noun (the formal name of a specific person, place, or thing).

5.5 *Common nouns.* A common noun is the generic name of one item in a class or group {a chemical} {a river} {a pineapple}.[5] It is not capitalized unless it begins a sentence or appears in a title. Common nouns are often broken down into three subcategories: concrete nouns, abstract nouns, and collective nouns. A concrete noun denotes something solid or real, something perceptible to the physical senses {a building} {the wind} {honey}. An abstract noun denotes something you cannot see, feel, taste, hear, or smell {joy} {expectation} {neurosis}. A collective noun—which can be viewed as a concrete noun but is often separately categorized—refers to a group or collection of people or things {a crowd of people} {a flock of birds} {a committee}.

5.6 *Proper nouns.* A proper noun is the specific name of a person, place, or thing {John Doe} {Moscow} {the Hope Diamond}, or the title of a work {*Citizen Kane*}. A proper noun is always capitalized, regardless of how it is used. A common noun may become a proper noun {Old Hickory} {the Big Easy}, and sometimes a proper noun may be used figuratively and informally, as if it were a common noun {like Moriarty, he is a Napoleon of crime} (*Napoleon* here connoting an ingenious mastermind who is ambitious beyond limits). Proper nouns may be compounded when used as a unit to name something {the Waldorf-Astoria Hotel} {*Saturday Evening Post*}. Over time, some proper nouns (called eponyms) have developed common-noun counterparts, such as *sandwich* (from the Earl of Sandwich) and *china* (from China, where fine porcelain was produced).

5.7 *Count nouns.* A count noun has singular and plural forms and expresses enumerable things {dictionary-dictionaries} {hoof-hooves} {newspaper-newspapers}. As the subject of a sentence, a singular count noun takes a singular verb {the jar is full}; a plural count noun takes a plural verb {the jars are full}.

---

5. The examples in this chapter are presented in curly brackets to save space.

5.8   *Mass nouns.* A mass noun (sometimes called a noncount noun) is one that denotes something uncountable, either because it is abstract {cowardice} {evidence} or because it refers to an indeterminate aggregation of people or things {the faculty} {the bourgeoisie}; the latter type is also called a collective noun. As the subject of a sentence, a mass noun usually takes a singular verb {the litigation is varied}. But in a collective sense, it may take either a singular or a plural verb form {the ruling majority is unlikely to share power} {the majority are nonmembers}. A singular verb emphasizes the group; a plural verb emphasizes the individual members.

5.9   *Mass noun followed by a prepositional phrase.* Mass nouns are sometimes followed by a prepositional phrase, such as *number of* plus a plural noun. The article that precedes the mass noun signals whether the mass noun or the number of the noun in the prepositional phrase controls the number of the verb. If a definite article (*the*) precedes, the mass noun controls, and typically a singular verb is used {the quantity of pizzas ordered this year has increased}. If an indefinite article (*a* or *an*) precedes, then the number of the noun in the prepositional phrase controls {a small percentage of the test takers have failed the exam}.

5.10   *Noun-equivalents and substantives.* A noun-equivalent is a phrase or clause that serves the function of a noun in a sentence {*To serve your country* is honorable} {Bring *whomever you like*}. Nouns and noun-equivalents collectively are called substantives.

PROPERTIES OF NOUNS

5.11   *Noun properties.* Nouns have properties of case and number. Some grammarians also consider gender and person properties of nouns.

5.12   *Noun case.* In English, only nouns and pronouns have case. Case denotes the relationship between a noun (or pronoun) and other words in a sentence. Grammarians disagree about the number of cases English nouns possess. Those who consider inflection (word form) the defining characteristic tend to say that there are two: common, which is the uninflected form, and genitive (or possessive), which is formed by adding 's or just an apostrophe. But others argue that it's useful to distinguish how the common-case noun is being used in the sentence, whether it is playing a nominative role {the doctor is in} or an objective role {go see the doctor}. Except with personal pronouns (*who/whom, she/her*, etc.), this distinction makes no practical difference in word use. See also 5.16–20.

5.13   *Noun number.* Number shows whether one object or more than one object is referred to, as with *clock* (singular) and *clocks* (plural). For a discussion of plurals, see 7.5–14.

5.14   *Noun gender.* English nouns have no true gender as that property is understood in many other languages. For example, whether a noun refers to a masculine or feminine person or thing does not determine the form of the accompanying article as it does in French, German, Spanish, and other languages. Still, some English words—almost exclusively nouns denoting a person or an animal—are inherently masculine {uncle} {rooster} {lad} or feminine {aunt} {hen} {lass} and take the gender-appropriate pronouns. But by far, most English nouns are common in gender and may refer to either sex {relative} {chicken} {child}. Many words that once were considered strictly masculine—especially words associated with jobs and professions—have been accepted as common in gender over time {author} {executor} {proprietor}. Similarly, many forms made feminine by the addition of a suffix {aviatrix} have been abandoned. See 5.221–30.

5.15   *Noun person.* A few grammarians attribute the property of person to nouns, distinguishing first person {I, Dan Walls, do swear that . . .}, second person {you, the professor, are key}, and third person {she, the arbiter, decides}. While those examples all use nouns in apposition to pronouns, that fact is not closely relevant to the question whether nouns have the property of person in the traditional grammatical sense.

CASE

5.16   *Function of case.* Case denotes the relationship between a noun or pronoun and other words in a sentence.

5.17   *Common case, nominative function.* The nominative (sometimes called the "subjective") function denotes the person, place, or thing about which an assertion is made in a clause, as in *the governor delivered a speech* (*governor* being the subject) or *the shops are crowded because the holiday season has begun* (*shops* and *season* being the subjects of their respective clauses). A noun in a nominative function controls the verb and usually precedes it {the troops retreated in winter} (*troops* is the subject), but it can appear anywhere in the sentence {high up in the tree sat a leopard} (*leopard* is the subject). A noun or pronoun that follows a *be*-verb and refers to the same thing as the subject is called a predicate nominative {my show dogs are Australian shepherds} (*Australian shepherds* is a predicate nominative). Generally, a sentence's predicate is the part that contains a verb and makes an assertion about the subject.

5.18   *Common case, objective function.* The objective (sometimes called the "accusative") function denotes either (1) the person or thing acted on by a transitive verb in the active voice {the balloon carried a pilot and a passenger} (*pilot* and *passenger* are objective) or (2) the person or thing related to another element by a connective, such as a preposition {place the slide under the microscope} (*under* is a preposition, *microscope* is objective). A noun in an objective function usually follows the verb {the queen consulted the prime minister} (*queen* is nominative and *prime minister* is objective). But with an inverted construction, the objective can appear elsewhere in the sentence {everything else was returned; the medicine the villain withheld} (*medicine* is objective and *villain* is nominative). A noun in the objective case is never the subject of the following verb and usually does not control the number of the verb (but see 5.9).

5.19   *Genitive case.* The genitive case denotes (1) ownership, possession, or occupancy {the architect's drawing board} {Arnie's room}; (2) a relationship {the philanthropist's secretary}; (3) agency {the company's representative}; (4) description {a summer's day}; (5) the role of a subject {the boy's application} (the boy applied); (6) the role of an object {the prisoner's release} (someone released the prisoner); or (7) an idiomatic shorthand form of an *of*-phrase (e.g., *one hour's delay* is equal to *a delay of one hour*). The genitive case is also called the possessive case, but *possessive* is a misleadingly narrow term, given the seven different functions of this case. The genitive is formed in different ways, depending on the noun or nouns and their usage in a sentence. The genitive of a singular noun is formed by adding *'s* {driver's seat} {engineer's opinion}. The genitive of a plural noun that ends in *-s* or *-es* is formed by adding an apostrophe {parents' house} {foxes' den}. The genitive of an irregular plural noun is formed by adding *'s* {women's rights} {mice's cage}. The genitive of a compound noun is formed by adding the appropriate ending to the last word in the compound {parents-in-law's message}. See also 7.15–28.

5.20   *The "of"-genitive.* The preposition *of* may precede a noun or proper name to express relationship, agency, or possession. The choice between a genitive ending and an *of* construction depends mostly on style. Compare *the perils of Penelope* with *the saucer of the chef.* Some nouns can readily take either the genitive form or the *of*-genitive {the theater's name} {the name of the theater}, but others sound right only in the *of*-genitive. Compare *everything's end* with *the end of everything.* The *of*-genitive is also useful when a double genitive is called for {an idea of Hill's} {an employee of my grandfather's business}.

APPOSITIVES

5.21   *Appositives defined; use.* An appositive noun or noun phrase is one that immediately follows another noun or noun phrase in order to define or further identify it {George Washington, our first president, was born in Virginia} (*our first president* is an appositive of the proper noun *George Washington*). Commas frame an appositive noun or noun phrase unless it is restrictive—for example, compare *Robert Burns, the poet, wrote many songs about women named Mary* (*poet* is a nonrestrictive appositive noun) with *the poet Robert Burns wrote many songs about women named Mary* (*Robert Burns* restricts *poet* by precisely identifying which poet). A restrictive appositive cannot be removed from a sentence without obscuring the identity of the word or phrase that the appositive relates to. See also 6.22.

FUNCTIONAL VARIATION

5.22   *Nouns as adjectives.* Words that are ordinarily nouns sometimes function as other parts of speech, such as adjectives or verbs. A noun-to-adjective shift takes place when a noun modifies another noun {the morning newspaper} {a state legislature} {a varsity sport} (*morning*, *state*, and *varsity* function as adjectives). These are also termed *attributive nouns*. Occasionally the use of a noun as an adjective can produce an ambiguity. For example, the phrase *fast results* can be read as meaning either "rapid results" or (less probably but possibly) "the outcome of a fast." Sometimes the noun and its adjectival form can be used interchangeably—for example, *prostate cancer* and *prostatic cancer* both refer to cancer of the prostate gland. But sometimes the use of the noun instead of the adjective may alter the meaning—for instance, *a study group* is not necessarily *a studious group*. A preposition may be needed to indicate a noun's relationship to other sentence elements. But if the noun functions as an adjective, the preposition must be omitted; at times this can result in a vague phrase—for example, *voter awareness* (awareness *of* voters or *by* them?). Context might suggest what preposition is implied, but a reader may have to deduce the writer's meaning.

5.23   *Nouns as verbs.* It is (and always has been) fairly common in English for nouns to pass into use as verbs. For example, in 1220 the noun *husband* meant one who tilled and cultivated the earth {the husband has worked hard to produce this crop}. It became a verb meaning to till, cultivate, and tend crops around 1420 {you must husband your land thoughtfully}. New noun-to-verb transitions often occur in dialect or jargon. For example, the noun *mainstream* is used as a verb in clauses such as *more school districts are mainstreaming pupils with special needs.* In formal prose, such recently transformed words should be used cautiously if at all.

5.24 *Adverbial functions.* Words that are ordinarily nouns occasionally function as adverbs {we rode single file} {Sam walked home}. This shift usually happens when a preposition is omitted {we rode in a single file} {Sam walked to his home}.

5.25 *Other functional shifts.* Words that ordinarily function as other parts of speech, as well as various types of phrases, may function as nouns. Aside from the obvious instance of pronouns (see 5.26), these include adjectives such as *poor* {the poor are always with us} (see 5.92), adverbs such as *here* and *now* {we cannot avoid the here and now}, participles (gerunds) such as *swimming* {swimming in that lake can be dangerous} (see 5.110), infinitives such as *to discover* {to discover the truth is our goal} (see 5.105), phrases indicating monetary amounts {six million dollars went toward restoring the arena}, and clauses such as *what the people want* {what the people want is justice}. Such functional shifts are normal and acceptable.

Pronouns

DEFINITION AND USES

5.26 *Pronouns defined.* A pronoun is a word used as a substitute for a noun or, sometimes, another pronoun. It is used in one of two ways: (1) A pronoun may substitute for an expressed noun or pronoun, especially to avoid needless repetition. For example, most of the nouns in the sentence *The father told the father's daughter that the father wanted the father's daughter to do some chores* can be replaced with pronouns: *The father told his daughter that he wanted her to do some chores.* (2) A pronoun may also stand in the place of an understood noun. For example, if the person addressed has been identified elsewhere, the question *Susan, are you bringing your boots?* can be more simply stated as *Are you bringing your boots?* And in the sentence *It is too hot,* the indefinite *it* is understood to mean the temperature (of something).

5.27 *Antecedents of pronouns.* A pronoun typically refers to an antecedent—that is, an earlier noun, pronoun, phrase, or clause in the same sentence or, if the reference is unambiguous, in a previous sentence. An antecedent may be explicit or implicit, but it must be clear. Miscues and ambiguity commonly arise from (1) a missing antecedent (as in *the clown's act with his dog made it a pleasure to watch,* where *it* is intended to refer to the circus, not explicitly mentioned in context); (2) multiple possible antecedents (as in *Scott visited Eric after his discharge from the army,* where it is unclear who was discharged—Eric or Scott); and (3) multiple pronouns and antecedents in the same sentence (e.g., *when the bottle is empty or the baby stops drinking, it must be sterilized with hot water because if it drinks from a dirty bottle it could become ill*—where one hopes that the hot-water sterilization is for the bottle).

5.28 *Pronouns without antecedents.* Some pronouns do not require antecedents. The first-person pronoun *I* stands for the speaker, so it almost never has an antecedent. Similarly, the second-person pronoun *you* usually needs no antecedent {Are you leaving?}, although one is sometimes supplied in direct address {Katrina, do you need something?}. Expletives (some of which are pronouns) have no antecedents {it's time to go} {this is a fine mess}. And the relative pronoun *what* and the interrogative pronouns *who, which,* and *what* never take an antecedent {Who cares what I think?}. In colloquial usage, *they* often appears without an antecedent {they say that she's a good golfer}, but vigilant listeners and readers often demand to know who "they" are.

5.29 *Adjective as antecedent.* A pronoun normally requires a noun or another pronoun as its antecedent. And because possessives function as adjectives, some writers have argued that possessives should not serve as antecedents of pronouns used in the nominative or objective case. But compare *Mr. Blain's background qualified him for the job* with *Mr. Blain had a background that qualified him for the job.* Not only is the identity of "him" perfectly clear in either construction, but the possessive in the first—a usage blessed by respected authorities—makes for a more economical sentence.

PROPERTIES OF PRONOUNS

5.30 *Four properties of pronouns.* A pronoun has four properties: number, person, gender, and case. (See 5.11–15.) A pronoun must agree with its antecedent in number, person, and gender. A few special uses of pronouns should be noted.

5.31 *Pronoun number and antecedent.* A pronoun's number is guided by that of its antecedent noun or nouns {a book and its cover} {the dogs and their owner}. A collective noun takes a singular pronoun if the members are treated as a unit {the audience showed its appreciation} but a plural if they act individually {the audience rushed back to their seats}. A singular noun that is modified by two or more adjectives to denote different varieties, uses, or aspects of the object may take a plural pronoun {British and American writing differ in more ways than just their spelling} (where *writing* may be thought of as an understood noun after *British*). Two or more singular nouns or pronouns that are joined by *and* are taken jointly and referred to by a plural pronoun {the boy and girl left their bicycles outside}.

5.32   *Exceptions regarding pronoun number.* There are several refinements to the rules stated just above: (1) When two or more singular antecedents denote the same thing and are connected by *and*, the pronoun referring to the antecedents is singular {a lawyer and role model received her richly deserved recognition today}. (2) When two or more singular antecedents are connected by *and* and modified by *each, every,* or *no,* the pronoun referring to the antecedents is singular {every college and every university encourages its students to succeed}. (3) When two or more singular antecedents are connected by *or, nor, either–or,* or *neither–nor,* they are treated separately and referred to by a singular pronoun {neither the orange nor the peach smells as sweet as it should}. (4) When two or more antecedents of different numbers are connected by *or* or *nor,* the pronoun's number agrees with that of the nearest (usually the last) antecedent; if possible, cast the sentence so that the plural antecedent comes last {neither the singer nor the dancers have asked for their paychecks}. (5) When two or more antecedents of different numbers are connected by *and,* they are usually referred to by a plural pronoun regardless of the nouns' order {the horses and the mule kicked over their water trough}.

5.33   *Pronoun with multiple antecedents.* When a pronoun's antecedents differ from the pronoun in person, and the antecedents are connected by *and, or,* or *nor,* the pronoun must take the person of only one antecedent. The first person is preferred to the second, and the second person to the third. For example, in *you or I should get to work on our experiment* the antecedents are in the second and first person. The following pronoun *our* is in the first person, as is the antecedent *I.* In *you and she can settle your dispute,* the antecedents are in the second and third person, so the following pronoun *your* takes the second person. If the pronoun refers to only one of the connected nouns or pronouns, it takes the person of that noun {you and Marian have discussed her trip report}.

5.34   *Antecedents of different genders.* If the antecedents are of different genders and are joined by *and,* a plural pronoun is normally used to refer to them {the sister and brother are visiting their aunt}. But if a pronoun refers to only one of the antecedent nouns connected by *and*, the pronoun's gender is that of the noun referred to {the uncle and niece rode in his car}. A special problem arises when the antecedent nouns are singular, are of different genders or an indeterminate gender, and are joined by *or* or *nor*. Using *he, his,* and *him* as a common-sex pronoun is now widely considered sexist, and picking the gender of the nearest antecedent may be misleading (e.g., *some boy or girl left her lunch box on the bus*). A good writer can usually recast the sentence to eliminate the need for any personal pronoun at all {some child left a lunch box on the bus}. See 5.41, 5.221–30.

5.35   *Pronoun case.* A pronoun that is the subject of a finite verb is in the nominative case {they went to town}. A personal pronoun in the genitive case is governed by the gender of the possessor {President George W. Bush invited his advisers to Crawford}. A pronoun that functions as the object of a verb or preposition is in the objective case {they gave her a farewell party} {they gave it to him}. A pronoun put after an intransitive verb or participle agrees in case with the preceding noun or pronoun referring to the same thing {it is I} (see 5.43, 5.44).

5.36   *Nominative case misused for objective.* The objective case governs personal pronouns used as direct objects of verbs {call me tomorrow}, indirect objects of verbs {write me a letter}, or objects of prepositions {makes sense to me}. One of the most persistent slips in English is to misuse the nominative case of a personal pronoun in a compound object:

WRONG: The test would be simple for you and I.
RIGHT: The test would be simple for you and me.
WRONG: Read this and tell Laura or I what you think.
RIGHT: Read this and tell Laura or me what you think.

The error arises in compounds so exclusively that the foolproof way to check for it is to read the sentence with the personal pronoun alone: no one would mistake "The test would be simple for I" or "Read this and tell I what you think" for correct grammar.

CLASSES OF PRONOUNS

5.37   *Six classes of pronouns.* There are six classes of pronouns:

personal—*I, you, he, she, it, we,* and *they*
demonstrative—*that, this*
interrogative—*what, which,* and *who*

relative—*that, what, which,* and *who*
indefinite—for example, *another, any, each, either,* and *none*
adjective—for example, *any, each, that, this, what,* and *which*

Many pronouns, except personal pronouns, may function as more than one type—for instance, *that* may be a demonstrative, relative, or adjective pronoun—depending on its use in a particular sentence.

PERSONAL PRONOUNS

5.38 *Form of personal pronoun.* A personal pronoun shows by its form whether it is referring to the speaker, the person or thing spoken to, or the person or thing spoken of. It also displays number, gender, and case by form. As with nouns, the first person is the speaker or speakers {I need some tea} {we heard the news}. The first-person singular pronoun *I* is always capitalized no matter where it appears in the sentence {if possible, I will send you an answer today}. All other pronouns are capitalized only at the beginning of a sentence, unless they are part of an honorific title {Her Majesty, the Queen of England}. The second person shows who is spoken to {you should write that essay tonight}. And the third person shows who or what is spoken of {she is at work} {it is in the glove compartment}.

5.39 *Changes in form.* Personal pronouns change form ("decline") according to person, number, and case. Apart from the second person, all personal pronouns show number by taking a singular or plural form. Although the second-person pronoun *you* is both singular and plural, it always takes a plural verb, even if only a single person or thing is addressed.

SINGULAR PRONOUNS

	Nominative	Objective	Genitive
First Person	I	me	my, mine
Second Person	you	you	your, yours
Third Person	he, she, it	him, her, it	his, her, hers, its

PLURAL PRONOUNS

	Nominative	Objective	Genitive
First Person	we	us	our, ours
Second Person	you	you	your, yours
Third Person	they	them	their, theirs

5.40 *Agreement of pronoun with noun.* A personal pronoun agrees with the noun for which it stands in both gender and number {John writes, and he will soon write well} {Sheila was there, but she couldn't hear what was said}.

5.41   *Pronoun and gender.* Only the third-person singular pronouns directly express gender. In the nominative and objective cases, the pronoun takes the antecedent noun's gender {the president is not in her office today; she's at a seminar}. In the genitive case, the pronoun always takes the gender of the possessor, not of the person or thing possessed {the woman loves her husband} {Thomas is visiting his sister} {the kitten disobeyed its mother}. Some nouns may acquire gender through personification, a figure of speech that refers to a nonliving thing as if it were a person. Pronouns enhance personification when a feminine or masculine pronoun is used as if the antecedent represented a female or male person (as was traditionally done, for example, when a ship or other vessel was referred to with the pronoun *she* or *her*).

5.42   *Personal pronoun case.* Some special rules apply to personal pronouns. (1) If a pronoun is the subject of a clause, it must be in the nominative case {she owns a tan briefcase} {Delia would like to travel, but she can't afford to}. (2) If a pronoun is the object of a verb or of a preposition, it must be in the objective case {the rustic setting soothed him} {that's a matter between him and her}. (3) If a prepositional phrase contains more than one personal-pronoun object, then all the objects must be in the objective case {Will you send an invitation to him and me?}. (4) If a pronoun is the subject of an infinitive, it must be in the objective case {Does Tina want me to leave?}.

5.43   *Pronoun case after linking verb.* Strictly speaking, a pronoun serving as the complement of a *be*-verb or other linking verb should be in the nominative case {it was she who asked for a meeting}. In formal writing, some fastidious readers will consider the objective case to be incorrect in every instance. But in many sentences, the nominative pronoun sounds pedantic or eccentric to the modern ear {Was that he on the phone?}.

5.44   *Pronoun case after "than" or "as . . . as."* The case of a pronoun following this kind of comparative structure, typically at the end of a sentence, depends on who or what is being compared. In *my sister looks more like our father than I* [or *me*], for example, if the point is whether the sister or the speaker looks more like their father, the pronoun should be nominative because it is the subject of an understood verb: *my sister looks more like our father than I do.* But if the point is whether the sister looks more like the father or the speaker, the pronoun should be objective because it is the object of a preposition in an understood sentence: *my sister looks more like our father than she looks like me.* Whatever the writer's intent, the reader can't be certain about the meaning. It would be better to reword the sentence and avoid the elliptical construction.

5.45   *Special uses of personal pronouns.* Some personal pronouns have special uses. (1) *He, him,* and *his* have traditionally been used as pronouns of indeterminate gender equally applicable to a male or female person {if the finder returns my watch, he will receive a reward}. Because these pronouns are also masculine-specific, they have long been regarded as sexist when used generically, and their indeterminate-gender use is declining. (See 5.34, 5.221–30.) (2) *It* eliminates gender even if the noun's sex could be identified. Using *it* does not mean that the noun has no sex—only that the sex is unknown or unimportant {the baby is smiling at its mother} {the mockingbird is building its nest}. (3) *We, you,* and *they* can be used indefinitely—that is, without antecedents—in the sense of "persons," "one," or "people in general." *We* is sometimes used by an individual who is speaking for a group {the magazine's editor wrote, "In our last issue, we covered the archaeological survey of Peru"}. This latter use is called the editorial *we. You* can apply indefinitely to any person or all persons {if you read this book, you will learn how to influence people} (*you* is indefinite—anyone who reads the book will learn). The same is true of *they* {they say that Stonehenge may have been a primitive calendar} (*they* are unidentified and, perhaps, unimportant). This use of *they,* however, is objectionable in scholarly writing: it unjustifiably avoids specificity. (4) *It* also has several uses as an indefinite pronoun: (a) *it* may refer to a phrase, clause, sentence, or implied thought {he said that the website is down, but I don't believe it} (without the pronoun *it,* the clause might be rewritten *I don't believe what he said*); (b) *it* can be the subject of a verb (usually a *be*-verb) without an antecedent noun {it was too far}, or an introductory word or expletive for a phrase or clause that follows the verb {it is possible that Dody is on vacation}; (c) *it* can be the grammatical subject in an expression about time, weather, or distance and the like {it is almost midnight} {it is beginning to snow}; and (d) *it* may be an expletive that anticipates the true grammatical subject or object {I find it hard to accept this situation}.

5.46   *The singular "they."* A singular antecedent requires a singular referent pronoun. Because *he* is no longer accepted as a generic pronoun referring to a person of either sex, it has become common in speech and in informal writing to substitute the third-person plural pronouns *they, them, their,* and *themselves,* and the nonstandard singular *themself.* While this usage is accepted in casual contexts, it is still considered ungrammatical in formal writing. Avoiding the plural form by alternating masculine and feminine pronouns is awkward and only emphasizes the inherent problem of not having a generic third-person pronoun. Employing an artificial form such as *s/he* is distracting at best, and most readers find it ridiculous. There are several better ways to avoid the problem. For example, use the traditional, formal *he or she, him or her, his or her, himself or herself*. Stylistically, this device is usually awkward or even stilted, but if used sparingly it can be functional. For other techniques, see 5.225.

POSSESSIVE PRONOUNS

5.47 *Possessive pronouns.* The possessive pronouns, *my, our, your, his, her, its,* and *their*, are used as limiting adjectives to qualify nouns {my dictionary} {your cabin} {his diploma}. Each has a corresponding absolute (also called independent) form that can stand alone without a noun: *mine, ours, yours, his, hers, its,* and *theirs*. The independent form does not require an explicit object: the thing possessed may be either an antecedent or something understood {this dictionary is mine} {this cabin of yours} {Where is hers?}. An independent possessive pronoun can also stand alone and be treated as a noun: it can be the subject or object of a verb {hers is on the table} {pass me yours} or the object of a preposition {put your coat with theirs}. When it is used with the preposition *of*, a double possessive is produced: *that letter of Sheila's* becomes *that letter of hers*. Such a construction is unobjectionable. Note that none of the possessive personal pronouns are spelled with an apostrophe.

5.48 *Compound personal pronouns; -self forms.* Several personal pronouns form compounds by taking the suffix *-self* or *-selves*. These are *my–myself; our–ourselves; your–yourself; your–yourselves; him–himself; her–herself; it–itself;* and *them–themselves*. The indefinite pronoun *one* forms the compound pronoun *oneself*. All these compound personal pronouns are the same in both the nominative and the objective case. They have no possessive forms. They are used for two purposes: (1) for emphasis (in which case they are termed intensive pronouns) {I saw Queen Beatrice herself} {I'll do it myself} and (2) to refer to the subject of the verb (in which case they are termed reflexive pronouns) {he saved himself the trouble of asking} {we support ourselves}.

5.49 *Reflexive and intensive pronouns.* Both reflexive and intensive personal pronouns are *-self* forms, but the distinction between them is useful and important. A reflexive pronoun reflects the action described by the verb by renaming the subject as either an object or an indirect object {she gave herself a pat on the back}. It is similar in appearance to an intensive pronoun but differs in function. An intensive pronoun is used in apposition to its referent to add emphasis {I myself have won several writing awards}. Intensive pronouns lend force to a sentence. And unlike reflexive pronouns, they are in the nominative case. Compare the intensive pronoun in *I burned the papers myself* (in which the object of *burned* is *papers*) with the reflexive pronoun in *I burned myself* (in which the object of *burned* is *myself*). Constructions in which the *-self* form does not serve either of those functions are common but nonstandard, whether it is serving as subject or as object:

WRONG: The staff and myself thank you for your contribution.
RIGHT: The staff and I thank you for your contribution.
WRONG: Deliver the equipment to my partner or myself.
RIGHT: Deliver the equipment to my partner or me.

5.50   *Possessive pronouns versus contractions.* The possessive forms of personal pronouns are *my, mine, our, ours, your, yours, his, her, hers, its, their, theirs*. None of them takes an apostrophe. Nor does the possessive form of *who* (*whose*). These exceptions aside, the apostrophe is a universal signal of the possessive in English, so it is a natural tendency (and a common error) to insert an apostrophe in the forms that end in *-s* (or the sibilant *-se*). Aggravating that tendency is the fact that some possessive personal pronouns have homophones that are contractions—forms that are also signaled by apostrophes. The pronouns that don't sound like legitimate contractions seldom present problems, even if they do end in *-s* (*hers, yours, ours*). But several do require special attention, specifically *its* (the possessive of *it*) and *it's* ("it is"); *your* (the possessive of *you*) and *you're* ("you are"); *whose* (the possessive of *who*) and *who's* ("who is"); and the three homophones *their* (the possessive of *they*), *there* ("in that place" or "in that way"), and *they're* ("they are").

DEMONSTRATIVE PRONOUNS

5.51   *Demonstrative pronouns defined.* A demonstrative pronoun (or, as it is sometimes called, a deictic pronoun) is one that points directly to its antecedent: *this* and *that* for singular antecedents {this is your desk} {that is my office}, and *these* and *those* for plural antecedents {these have just arrived} {those need to be answered}. *This* and *these* point to objects that are close by in space, time, or thought, while *that* and *those* point to objects that are comparatively remote in space, time, or thought. The antecedent of a demonstrative pronoun can be a noun, phrase, clause, sentence, or implied thought, as long as the antecedent is clear. *Kind* and *sort*, each referring to "one class," are often used with an adjectival *this* or *that* {this kind of magazine} {that sort of school}. The plural forms *kinds* and *sorts* should be used with the plural demonstratives {these kinds of magazines} {those sorts of schools}.

INTERROGATIVE PRONOUNS

5.52 *Interrogative pronouns defined.* An interrogative pronoun asks a question. The three interrogatives are *who, what,* and *which.* Only one, *who,* declines: *who* (nominative), *whom* (objective), *whose* (possessive) {Who starred in *Casablanca*?} {To whom am I speaking?} {Whose cologne smells so strong?}. In the nominative case, *who* is used in two ways: (1) as the subject of a verb {Who washed the dishes today?} and (2) as a predicate nominative after a linking verb {It was who?}. In the objective case, *whom* is used two ways: (1) as the object of a verb {Whom did you see?} and (2) as the object of a preposition {For whom is this building named?}.

5.53 *Referent of interrogative pronouns.* To refer to a person, either *who* or *which* can be used. But they are not interchangeable. *Who* is universal or general: it asks for any one or more persons among all persons. The answer may potentially include any person, living or dead, present or absent {Who wants to see that movie?} {Who were your greatest inspirations?}. *Who* also asks for a particular person's identity {Who is that person standing near the samovar?}. *Which* is usually selective or limited; it asks for a particular member of a group, and the answer is limited to the group addressed or referred to {Which explorers visited China in the sixteenth century?}. To refer to a person, animal, or thing, either *which* or *what* may be used {Which one of you did this?} {What kind of bird is that?}. When applied to a person, animal, or thing, *what* asks about character, occupation, qualities, and the like {What do you think of our governor?}. When applied to a thing, *what* often asks for one or more items in a category {What is your quest?} {What is your favorite color?}.

RELATIVE PRONOUNS

5.54 *Relative pronouns defined.* A relative pronoun is one that introduces a dependent (or relative) clause and relates it to the independent clause. Relative pronouns in common use are *who, which, what,* and *that. Who* is the only relative pronoun that declines: *who* (nominative), *whom* (objective), *whose* (possessive) {the woman who presented the award} {a source whom he declined to name} {the writer whose book was a best seller}. *Who,* which normally refers to a person, can be used in the first, second, or third person. *Which* normally refers to an animal or a thing. *What* generally refers to a nonliving thing. *Which* and *what* are used only in the second and third persons. *That* refers to a person, animal, or thing, and can be used in the first, second, or third person. See also 5.61.

5.55 *Case with relative pronouns.* A personal pronoun does not govern the case of a relative pronoun. Hence, an objective pronoun such as *me* may be the antecedent of the nominative pronoun *who*, although a construction formed in this way sounds increasingly archaic or (to the nonliterary) incorrect {she was referring to me, who never graduated from college}. When a construction is technically correct but sounds awkward or artificial {I, who am wronged, have a grievance}, the best course may be to use "preventive grammar" and find a different construction {I have a grievance, for I have been wronged} {having been wronged, I have a grievance}.

5.56 *Positional nuances with relative pronouns.* A relative pronoun is in the nominative case when no subject comes between it and the verb {the professor who lectured was brilliant}. When a subject comes between the relative pronoun and the verb, the relative is governed by the following verb or by some other word in its own clause {he whom I called is no longer there} {she, whom I believed to be very bright, failed her exams} {it was John who they thought was in the bleachers}.

5.57 *Antecedent of relative pronoun.* Usually a relative pronoun's antecedent is a noun or pronoun in the independent clause on which the relative clause depends. For clarity it should immediately precede the pronoun {the diadem that I told you about is in this gallery}. The antecedent may also be a noun phrase or a clause, but the result can sometimes be ambiguous: in *the bedroom of the villa, which was painted pink*, does *which* refer to the bedroom or to the villa?

5.58 *Omitted antecedent of relative pronoun.* If no antecedent noun is expressed, *what* can be used to mean *that which* {Is this what you were looking for?}. But if there is an antecedent, use a different relative pronoun: *who* {Where is the man who spoke?}, *that* (if the relative clause is restrictive, i.e., essential to the sentence's basic meaning) {Where are the hunters that Jones told us about?}, or *which* (if the relative clause is nonrestrictive, i.e., could be deleted without affecting the sentence's basic meaning) {the sun, which is shining brightly, feels warm on my face}. See also 6.22.

5.59 *Relative pronoun after "one."* A relative pronoun takes its number from its antecedent. That's easy enough when the antecedent is simply *one* {this is one that everybody likes}. But if *one* is part of a noun phrase with a plural noun such as *one of the few* or *one of those*, the relative pronoun's antecedent is usually not *one* but the noun in the genitive construction {one of the few countries that cultivate farm-raised fish as a staple} {she is one of those people who are famous just for being famous}. Always read carefully, though; in some constructions like these the antecedent is still *one* {he is the one among them who is trustworthy}.

5.60   *Possessive forms of relative pronouns.* The forms *of whom* and *of which* are possessives {the child, the mother of whom we talked about, is in kindergarten} {this foal, the sire of which Belle owns, will be trained as a hunter-jumper}. (These forms have an old-fashioned sound and can often be rephrased more naturally {the child whose mother we talked about is in kindergarten}.)

5.61   *"Whose" and "of which."* The relatives *who* and *which* can both take *whose* as a possessive form (*whose* substitutes for *of which*) {a movie the conclusion of which is unforgettable} {a movie whose conclusion is unforgettable}. Some writers object to using *whose* as a replacement for *of which*, especially when the subject is not human, but the usage is centuries old and widely accepted as preventing unnecessary awkwardness. Compare *the company whose stock rose faster* with *the company the stock of which rose faster.* Either form is acceptable, but the possessive *whose* lends greater smoothness.

5.62   *Compound relative pronouns.* *Who, whom, what,* and *which* form compound relative pronouns by adding the suffix *-ever.* The compound relatives *whoever, whomever, whichever,* and *whatever* apply universally to any or all persons or things {whatever you do, let me know} {whoever needs to write a report about this book may borrow it}.

5.63   *"Who" versus "whom."* *Who* and *whoever* are the nominative forms, used as subjects {Whoever said that?} or predicate nominatives {It was who?}. *Whom* and *whomever* are the objective forms, used as the object of a verb {You called whom?} or a preposition {To whom are you referring?}. Three problems arise with determining the correct case. First, because the words are so often found in the inverted syntax of an interrogative sentence, their true function in the sentence can be hard to see unless one sorts the words into standard subject–verb–object syntax. In this example, sorting the syntax into "I should say who is calling" makes the case easier to determine:

WRONG: Whom should I say is calling?
RIGHT: Who should I say is calling?

Second, determining the proper case can be confusing when the pronoun serves a function (say, nominative) in a clause that itself serves a different function (say, objective) in the main sentence. It is the pronoun's function in its clause that determines its case. In the first example below, the entire clause *whoever will listen* is the object of the preposition *to*. But in the clause itself, *whoever* serves as the subject, and that function determines its case. Similarly, in the second sentence *whomever* is the object of *choose* in the clause, so it must be in the objective case even though the clause itself serves as the subject of the sentence.

WRONG: I'll talk to whomever will listen.
RIGHT: I'll talk to whoever will listen.
WRONG: Whoever you choose will suit me.
RIGHT: Whomever you choose will suit me.

As the second example above shows, a further distraction can arise when the *who* clause contains a nested clause, typically of attribution or identification (here, *you choose*).

OTHER TYPES OF PRONOUNS

5.64 *Indefinite pronouns.* An indefinite pronoun is one that generally or indefinitely represents an object, usually one that has already been identified or doesn't need specific identification. The most common are *another, any, both, each, either, neither, none, one, other, some,* and *such*. There are also compound indefinite pronouns, such as *anybody, anything, anyone, everybody, everyone, everything, nobody, no one, oneself, somebody,* and *someone*. *Each, either,* and *neither* are also called distributive pronouns because they separate the objects referred to from others referred to nearby. Indefinite pronouns have number. When an indefinite pronoun is the subject of a verb, it is usually singular {everyone is enjoying the dinner} {everybody takes notes during the first week}. But sometimes an indefinite pronoun carries a plural sense {nobody could describe the music; they hadn't been listening to it} {everyone understood the risk, but they were lured by promises of big returns}. The forms of indefinite pronouns are not affected by gender or person, and the nominative and objective forms are the same. To form the possessive, the indefinite pronoun may take *'s* {that is no one's fault} {Is this anyone's jacket?} or the adverb *else* plus *'s* {don't interfere with anybody else's business} {no one else's cups were broken}.

5.65 *Adjective pronouns.* An adjective pronoun (also called a pronominal adjective) functions as a noun modifier. It must agree in number with the noun to which it belongs {all people} {these sorts of favors} {those kinds of indulgences}. All pronouns other than nonpossessive personal pronouns, *who,* and *none* may serve as adjectives {those windows} {some coyotes}. The adjective *no* is used instead of *none* {no one astronaut} {no other paradise}.

Adjectives

DEFINITIONS

5.66 *Adjectives defined.* An adjective is a word that modifies a noun or pronoun; it is often called a "describing word." An adjective tells you what sort, how many, how large or small, whose, and so on. An adjective may add a new idea to a noun or pronoun by describing it more definitely or fully {red wagon} {human error}. Or it may be limiting {three pigs} {this time}. Most adjectives derive from nouns, as *plentiful* derives from *plenty* or as *stylish* derives from *style*; some derive from verbs, roots, or other adjectives. Usually a suffix creates the adjective. Among the suffixes that often distinguish adjectives are *-able* {manageable}, *-al* {mystical}, *-ary* {elementary}, *-ed* {hammered}, *-en* {wooden}, *-esque* {statuesque}, *-ful* {harmful}, *-ible* {inaccessible}, *-ic* {artistic}, *-ish* {foolish}, *-ive* {demonstrative}, *-less* {helpless}, *-like* {childlike}, *-ly* {ghostly}, *-ous* {perilous}, *-some* {lonesome}, and *-y* {sunny}. But many adjectives do not have distinctive endings and are recognizable only by their function {old} {tall} {brilliant}.

5.67 *Proper adjectives.* A proper adjective is one that, being or deriving from a proper name, always begins with a capital letter {a New York minute} {a Cuban cigar} {a Canadian dollar}. (But see 8.60.) The proper name used attributively is still capitalized, but it does not cause the noun it modifies to be capitalized. A place-name containing a comma—such as *Toronto, Ontario,* or *New Delhi, India*—should generally not be used as an adjective because a second comma may be deemed obligatory {we met in a Toronto, Ontario, restaurant} (the comma after *Ontario* being somewhat awkward). Compare the readability of *a New Delhi, India, marketplace* with that of *a New Delhi marketplace* or *a marketplace in New Delhi, India* (substituting a prepositional phrase for the proper adjective).

ARTICLES AS LIMITING ADJECTIVES

5.68 *Articles defined.* An article is a limiting adjective that precedes a noun or noun phrase and determines the noun or phrase's use to indicate something definite (*the*) or indefinite (*a* or *an*). An article might stand alone or be used with other adjectives {a road} {a brick road} {the yellow brick road}.

5.69 *Definite article.* A definite article points to a definite object that (1) is so well understood that it does not need description (e.g., *the package is here* is a shortened form of *the package that you expected is here*); (2) is a thing that is about to be described {the sights of Chicago}; or (3) is important {the grand prize}. The definite article belongs to nouns in the singular {the star} or the plural number {the stars}.

5.70 *Indefinite article.* An indefinite article points to nonspecific objects, things, or persons that are not distinguished from the other members of a class. The thing may be singular {a student at Princeton}, or uncountable {a multitude}, or generalized {an idea inspired by Milton's *Paradise Lost*}.

5.71 *Indefinite article in specific reference.* In a few usages, the indefinite article provides a specific reference {I saw a great movie last night} and the definite article a generic reference {the Scots are talking about independence} (generalizing by nationality).

5.72 *Choosing "a" or "an."* With the indefinite article, the choice of *a* or *an* depends on the sound of the word it precedes. *A* comes before words with a consonant sound, including /y/, /h/, and /w/, no matter how the word is spelled {a eulogy} {a historic occasion} {a Ouachita tribe member}. *An* comes before words with a vowel sound {an LSAT exam room} {an *X-Files* episode} {an hour ago}. See 5.220, under *a; an*. See also 7.44, 10.9.

5.73 *Articles with coordinate nouns.* With a series of coordinate nouns, an article may appear before each noun but is not necessary {the rose bush and hedge need trimming}. If the things named make up a single idea, an article need not be repeated {in the highest degree of dressage, the horse and rider appear to be one entity}. And if the named things are covered by one plural noun, the definite article should not be repeated {in the first and second years of college}.

5.74 *Effect of article on meaning.* Because articles have a demonstrative value, the meaning of a phrase may shift depending on the article used. For example, *an officer and gentleman escorted Princess Plum to her car* suggests (though ambiguously) that the escort was one man with two descriptive characteristics. But *an officer and a friend escorted Princess Plum to her car* suggests that two people acted as escorts. Similarly, *Do you like the red and blue cloth?* suggests that the cloth contains both red and blue threads. But *Do you like the red and the blue cloth?* suggests that two different fabrics are being discussed. The clearest way to express the idea that the cloth contains both red and blue is to hyphenate the phrase as a compound modifier: *red-and-blue cloth*; and with two kinds of cloth, clarity requires either repeating the word *cloth* (*the red cloth and the blue cloth*) or using *cloth* with the first adjective rather than the second (*the red cloth and the blue*).

5.75 *Zero article.* Some usages call for a zero article, an article implicitly present, usually before a mass or plural noun {although both new and washed bottles are stacked nearby, cider is poured into new bottles only} (*the* is implicit before *new bottles*). The zero article usually occurs in idiomatic references to time, illness, transportation, personal routines, and meals {by sunset} {has cancer} {travel by train} {go to bed} {make breakfast}.

5.76 *Omitted article.* The absence of an article may alter a sentence's meaning—for example, the meaning of *the news brought us little comfort* (we weren't comforted) changes if *a* is inserted before *little*: *the news brought us a little comfort* (we felt somewhat comforted).

5.77 *Article as pronoun substitute.* An article may sometimes substitute for a pronoun. For example, the blanks in *a patient who develops the described rash on ___ hands should inform ___ doctor* may be filled in with the pronoun phrase *his or her* or the article *the*.

POSITION OF ADJECTIVES

5.78 *Basic rules.* An adjective that modifies a noun, noun phrase, or pronoun usually precedes it {perfect storm} {spectacular view} {a good bowl of soup}. An adjective may follow the noun if (1) special emphasis is needed {reasons innumerable} {captains courageous}; (2) it occurs in this position in standard usage {court-martial} {notary public}; (3) it is a predicate adjective following a linking verb {I am ready}; or (4) the pronoun is of a type usually followed by the adjective {anything good} {everything yellow} {nothing important} {something wicked}. Some adjectives are always in the predicate and never appear before what they modify {the city is asleep} {the door was ajar}. Others appear uniformly before the nouns they modify {utter nonsense} {a mere child}. Phrasal adjectives may precede or follow what they modify. See 5.91.

5.79 *After possessive pronoun.* When a noun phrase includes a possessive noun, as in *children's shoes* or *the company's president*, the adjective follows the possessive {children's athletic shoes} {the company's former president} (unless they're athletic children or it's a former company).

5.80 *Adjective modifying pronoun.* When modifying a pronoun, an adjective usually follows the pronoun {the searchers found him unconscious} {some like it hot}, sometimes as a predicate adjective {it was insensitive} {Who was so jealous?}.

5.81   *Predicate adjective.* A predicate adjective is an adjective that follows a linking verb (see 5.99) but modifies the subject {the child is afraid} {the night became colder} {this tastes delicious} {I feel bad}. If an adjective in the predicate modifies a noun or pronoun in the predicate, it is not a predicate adjective. For example, in *the train will be late* the adjective *late* modifies the subject *train*. But in *the train will be here at a late hour* the adjective *late* modifies the noun *hour*, not the subject *train*. So even though it occurs in the predicate, it is not known as a *predicate adjective*, which by definition follows a linking verb.

5.82   *Dates as adjectives.* Dates are often used as descriptive adjectives, more often today than in years past. If a month-year or month-day date is used as an adjective, no hyphen or comma is needed {October 31 festivities} {December 2003 financial statement}. If a full month-day-year date is used, then a comma is considered necessary both before and after the year {the May 18, 2002, commencement ceremonies}. But this construction is awkward because the adjective (which is forward looking) contains two commas (which are backward looking); the construction is therefore best avoided {commencement ceremonies on May 18, 2002}.

DEGREES OF ADJECTIVES

5.83   *Three adjectival degrees.* An adjective has three degrees: the positive or absolute {hard}, the comparative {harder}, and the superlative {hardest}. A positive adjective simply expresses an object's quality without reference to any other thing {a big balloon} {bad news}.

5.84   *Comparative adjectives.* A comparative adjective expresses the relationship between a specified quality shared by two things, often specifying which has more of that quality {a cheaper ticket} {a happier ending}. The suffix *-er* usually signals the comparative form of a common adjective having one or two syllables {light-lighter} {merry-merrier}. An adjective with three or more syllables takes *more* instead of a suffix to form the comparative {intelligent-more intelligent} {purposeful-more purposeful}. Some adjectives with two syllables take the *-er* suffix {lazy-lazier} {narrow-narrower}, but most two-syllable adjectives take *more* {more hostile} {more careless}. Two-syllable adjectives ending in *-er*, *-le*, *-ow*, *-ure*, or *-y* can typically use either the *-er* suffix or *more*.

5.85   *Superlative adjectives.* A superlative adjective expresses the relationship between at least three things and denotes an extreme of intensity or amount in a particular shared quality {the biggest house on the block} {the bitterest pill of all}. The suffix -*est* usually signals the superlative form of a common adjective having one or two syllables {lighter-lightest}. An adjective with three or more syllables takes *most* instead of a suffix to form the superlative {quarrelsome-most quarrelsome} {humorous-most humorous}. Some adjectives with two syllables take the -*est* suffix {holy-holiest} {noble-noblest}, but most two-syllable adjectives take *most* {most fruitful} {most reckless}.

5.86   *Forming comparatives and superlatives.* There are a few rules for forming a short regular adjective's comparative and superlative forms. (1) If the adjective is a monosyllable ending in a single vowel followed by a single consonant, the final consonant is doubled before the suffix is attached {red-redder-reddest}. (2) If the adjective ends in a silent -*e*, the -*e* is dropped before the suffix is added {polite-politer-politest}. (3) Participles used as adjectives require *more* or *most* before the participle; no suffix is added to form the comparative or the superlative {this teleplay is more boring than the first one} {I am most tired on Fridays}. (4) A few one-syllable adjectives—such as *real, right,* and *wrong*—can take only *more* and *most.* Even then, these combinations occur only in informal speech. (5) *Eager, proper,* and *somber,* unlike many two-syllable adjectives, also take only *more* and *most*; none can take a suffix. (6) Two-syllable adjectives to which the negative prefix *un-* has been added can usually either take a suffix or take *more* or *most,* even if the total number of syllables is three {unhappiest} {most unhappy}. (7) Many adjectives are irregular—there is no rule that guides their comparative and superlative forms {good-better-best} {less-lesser-least}. A good dictionary will show the forms of an irregular adjective.

5.87   *Equal and unequal comparisons.* A higher degree of comparison is signaled by a suffix (-*er* or -*est*), or by *more* or *most.* (See 5.84, 5.85.) A lower degree is shown by *less* (comparative) or *least* (superlative) {cold-less cold} {less cold-least cold}. Equivalence is shown by the use of the *as . . . as* construction {this is as old as that} and sometimes by *so* {that test was not so hard as the last one}.

5.88   *Uncomparable adjectives.* An adjective that, by definition, describes an absolute state or condition—such as *entire, impossible, pregnant, unique*—is called uncomparable. It cannot take a comparative suffix and cannot be coupled with the comparative terms *more, most, less,* or *least.* Nor can it be intensified by words like *very, largely,* or *quite.* But on the rare occasion when a particular emphasis is needed, a good writer may depart from this rule and use a phrase like *more perfect,* as the framers of the United

States Constitution did in composing its preamble {We the People of the United States, in order to form a more perfect Union . . .}.

SPECIAL TYPES OF ADJECTIVES

5.89   *Participial adjectives.* A participial adjective is simply a verb's participle that modifies a noun or pronoun. It can be a present participle (verb ending in -*ing*) {the dining room} {a walking stick} {a rising star} or a past participle (usually a verb ending in -*ed*) {an endangered species} {a completed assignment} {a proven need}. Some past-participial forms have only this adjectival function, the past-participial verb having taken a different form {a shaven face} {a graven image}. A past participle functioning as an adjective may be modified with an adverb such as *quite* {quite surprised}, *barely* {barely concealed}, or *little* {little known}, or an adverbial phrase such as *very much* {very much distrusted}. If the past participle has gained a strong adjectival quality, *very* will do the job alone without the quantitative *much* {very tired} {very drunk}. But if the participial form seems more like a verb, *very* needs *much* to help do the job {very much appreciated} {very much delayed}. A few past participles (such as *bored, interested, pleased, satisfied*) are in the middle of the spectrum between those having mostly adjectival qualities and those having mostly verbal qualities. With these few, the quantitative *much* is normally omitted. See also 5.108, 5.139.

5.90   *Coordinate adjectives.* A coordinate adjective is one that appears in a sequence with one or more related adjectives to modify the same noun. Coordinate adjectives should be separated by commas or by *and* {skilled, experienced chess player} {nurturing and loving parent}. But if one adjective modifies the noun and another adjective modifies the idea expressed by the combination of the first adjective and the noun, the adjectives are not considered coordinate and should not be separated by a comma. For example, *a lethargic soccer player* describes a soccer player who is lethargic. Likewise, phrases such as *red brick house* and *wrinkled canvas jacket* are unpunctuated because the adjectives are not coordinate: they have no logical connection in sense (a red house could be made of many different materials; so could a wrinkled jacket). The most useful test is this: if *and* would fit between the two adjectives, a comma is necessary.

5.91   *Phrasal adjectives.* A phrasal adjective (also called a compound modifier) is a phrase that functions as a unit to modify a noun. A phrasal adjective follows these basic rules: (1) Generally, if it is placed before a noun, you should hyphenate the phrase to avoid misdirecting the reader {dog-eat-dog competition}. There may be a considerable difference between the hyphenated and the unhyphenated forms. For example, compare *small animal hospital* with *small-animal hospital*. (2) If a compound noun is an element of a phrasal adjective, the entire compound noun must be hyphenated to clarify the relationship among the words {time-clock-punching employees}. (3) If more than one phrasal adjective modifies a single noun, hyphenation becomes especially important {nineteenth-century song-and-dance numbers} {state-inspected assisted-living facility}. (4) If two phrasal adjectives end in a common element, the ending element should appear only with the second phrase, and a suspension hyphen should follow the unattached words to show that they are related to the ending element {middle- and upper-class operagoers}. But if two phrasal adjectives *begin* with a common element, a hyphen is usually inappropriate, and the element should be repeated {left-handed and left-brained executives}. (5) If the phrasal adjective denotes an amount or a duration, plurals should be dropped. For instance, *pregnancy lasts nine months* but is *a nine-month pregnancy*, and a shop *open twenty-four hours a day* requires *a twenty-four-hour-a-day schedule*. The plural is retained only for fractions {a two-thirds majority}. (6) If a phrasal adjective becomes awkward, the sentence should probably be recast. For example, *The news about the lower-than-expected third-quarter earnings disappointed investors* could become *The news about the third-quarter earnings, which were lower than expected, disappointed investors*. Or perhaps this: *Investors were disappointed by the third-quarter earnings, which were lower than expected*. There are exceptions for hyphenating phrasal adjectives: (1) If the phrasal adjective follows a verb, it is usually unhyphenated—for example, compare *a well-trained athlete* with *an athlete who is well trained*. (2) When a proper name begins a phrasal adjective, the name is not hyphenated {the Monty Python school of comedy}. (3) A two-word phrasal adjective that begins with an adverb ending in *-ly* is not hyphenated {a sharply worded reprimand} (but *a not-so-sharply-worded reprimand*). For a full discussion of hyphenation—including treatment of compound noun forms and other parts of speech—see 7.77–85.

FUNCTIONAL VARIATION

5.92   *Adjectives as nouns.* Adjective-to-noun transitions are relatively common in English. Some adjectives are well established as nouns and are perfectly suitable for most contexts. For example, *a postmortem examination* is often called *a postmortem*; *collectible objects* are *collectibles*; and *French people* are *the French*. Any but the most established of these, however, should be used only after careful consideration. If there's an alternative, it will almost certainly be better. For example, there is probably no good reason to use the adjective *collaborative* as a noun (i.e., a shortened form of *collaborative enterprise*) when the perfectly good *collaboration* is available. See also 5.22–25.

5.93 *Adjectives as verbs.* Adjective-to-verb transitions occur in English only once in a while, usually as jargon or slang {the cargo tanks were *inerted* by introducing carbon dioxide into them} {it would be silly to *low-key* the credit for this achievement}. They are not acceptable in formal prose.

5.94 *Other parts of speech functioning as adjectives.* Words that ordinarily function as other parts of speech, but sometimes as adjectives, include nouns (see 5.22), pronouns (see 5.47), and verbs (see 5.105).

Verbs

DEFINITIONS

5.95 *Verbs generally.* A verb denotes the performance or occurrence of an action or the existence of a condition or a state of being, such as an emotion. Action verbs include *walk, shout, taste,* and *fly.* Nonaction verbs include *imagine, exist,* and *dread.* The verb is the most essential part of speech— the only one that can express a thought by itself (with the subject understood) {Run!} {Enjoy!} {Think!}.

5.96 *Transitive and intransitive verbs.* Depending on its relationship with objects, a verb is classified as transitive or intransitive. A transitive verb requires an object to express a complete thought; the verb indicates what action the subject exerts on the object. For example, *the cyclist hit a curb* states what the subject *cyclist* did to the object *curb.* An intransitive verb does not require an object to express a complete thought {the rescuer jumped}, although it may be followed by a prepositional phrase serving an adverbial function {the rescuer jumped to the ground}. Many verbs may be either transitive or intransitive, the different usages often distinguishable by their meanings. For example, when used transitively, as in *the king's heir will succeed him, succeed* means "to follow and take the place of"; when used intransitively, as in *the chemist will succeed in identifying the toxin,* it means "to accomplish a task." With other verbs, no such distinction is possible. For example, in *I will walk; you ride, ride* is intransitive. In *I will walk; you ride your bike, ride* is transitive, but its meaning is unchanged. A verb that is normally used transitively may sometimes be used intransitively to emphasize the verb and leave the object undefined or unknown {the patient is eating poorly} (*how well* the patient eats is more important than *what* the patient eats).

5.97   *Ergative verbs.* Some verbs, called ergative verbs, can be used transitively or intransitively with a noun that becomes the object when the verb's use is transitive and the subject when the verb's use is intransitive. For example, with the noun *door* and the verb *open*, one can say *I opened the door* (transitive) or *the door opened* (intransitive). Many words undergo ergative shifts. For example, the verb *ship* was once exclusively transitive {the company shipped the books on January 16}, but in commercial usage it is now often intransitive {the books shipped on January 16}. Likewise, *grow* (generally an intransitive verb) was transitive only in horticultural contexts {the family grew several types of crops}, but commercial usage now makes it transitive in many other contexts {how to grow your business}. Careful writers and editors employ such usages cautiously if at all, preferring well-established idioms.

5.98   *Regular and irregular verbs.* The past-tense and past-participle forms of most English words are formed by appending *-ed* to the basic form {draft-drafted-drafted}. If the verb ends in *-e*, only a *-d* is appended, and sometimes a final consonant is doubled. These verbs are classified as regular, or weak (the latter is a term used in philology to classify forms of conjugation). But a few common verbs have maintained forms derived mostly from Old English roots {begin-began-begun} {bet-bet-bet} {bind-bound-bound} {bite-bit-bitten}. These verbs are called irregular, or strong. The various inflections of strong verbs defy simple classifications, but many past-tense and past-participle forms (1) change by changing the vowel sound of the base verb (as *begin*); (2) keep the same form as the base verb (as *bet*); (3) share an irregular form (as *bind*); or (4) change endings (as *bite*). The verb *be* is highly irregular, with eight forms {*be, am, are, is, was, were, been, being*}. Because no system of useful classification is possible for irregular verbs, a reliable memory and a general dictionary are essential tools for using the correct forms consistently. Further complicating the spelling of irregular verbs is the fact that the form may vary according to the sense of the word. When used to mean "to offer a price," for example, *bid* keeps the same form in the past tense and past participle, but when it means "to offer a greeting" it forms *bade* and *bidden*. The form may also depend on whether the verb is being used literally {wove a rug} or figuratively {weaved in traffic}. Finally, a few verbs that are considered regular have an alternative past tense and past participle that is formed by adding *-t* to the simple verb form {dream-dreamed} {dream-dreamt}. When these alternatives are available, American English tends to prefer the forms in *-ed* (e.g., *dreamed, learned, spelled*), while British English tends to prefer the forms in *-t* (*dreamt, learnt, spelt*).

5.99 *Linking verbs.* A linking verb (also called a copula or connecting verb) is one that links the subject to an equivalent word in the sentence—a predicate pronoun, predicate noun, or predicate adjective. The linking verb itself does not take an object. There are two kinds of linking verbs: *be*-verbs and intransitive verbs that are used in a weakened sense, such as *seem, smell, appear, feel,* and *look.* When used as a link, the weakened intransitive verb often has a figurative sense akin to that of *became,* as in *he fell heir to a large fortune* (he didn't physically fall on or into anything) or *the river ran dry* (a waterless river doesn't run—it just dries up). See 5.167.

5.100 *Phrasal verbs.* A phrasal verb is usually a verb plus a preposition (or particle) {settle down} {get up}. A phrasal verb is not hyphenated, even though its equivalent noun or phrasal adjective might be—compare *to flare up* with *a flare-up,* and compare *to step up the pace* with *a stepped-up pace.* Three rules apply: (1) if the phrasal verb has a sense distinct from the component words, use the entire phrase—for example, *hold up* means "to rob" or "to delay," and *get rid of* and *do away with* mean "to eliminate"; (2) avoid the phrasal verb if the verb alone conveys essentially the same meaning—for example, *rest up* is essentially equivalent to *rest*; and (3) don't compress the phrase into a one-word verb, especially if it has a corresponding one-word noun form—for example, one *burns out* and suffers *burnout.*

5.101 *Principal and auxiliary verbs.* Depending on its uses, a verb is classified as principal or auxiliary (also termed modal). A principal verb is one that can stand alone to express an act or state {he jogs} {I dreamed about Xanadu}. If combined with another verb, it expresses the combination's leading thought {a tiger may roar}. An auxiliary verb is used with a principal verb to form a verb phrase that indicates mood, tense, or voice {You must study for the exam!} {I will go to the store} {the show was interrupted}. The most commonly used auxiliaries are *be, can, do, have, may, must, ought, shall,* and *will.* For more on auxiliary verbs, see 5.142–50.

5.102 *Verb phrases.* The combination of an auxiliary verb with a principal verb is a verb phrase, such as *could happen, must go,* or *will be leaving.* When a verb phrase is modified by an adverb, the modifier typically goes directly after the first auxiliary verb, as in *could certainly happen, must always go,* and *will soon be leaving.* The idea that verb phrases should not be "split" in this way is quite mistaken (see 5.168). A verb phrase is negated by placing the negative adverb *not* after the first auxiliary {we have not called him}. In an interrogative sentence, the first auxiliary begins the sentence and is followed by the subject {Must I repeat that?} {Do you want more?}.

An interrogative can be negated by placing *not* after the subject {Do you not want more?}; contractions are often more natural but may paradoxically serve as positive intensifiers {Don't you want more?} {Isn't the sunset beautiful?}. Most negative forms can be contracted {we do not-we don't} {I will not-I won't} {he has not-he hasn't} {she does not-she doesn't}, but *I am not* is contracted to *I'm not* (never *I amn't*). The corresponding interrogative form is *Aren't I?* Sometimes the negative is emphasized if the auxiliary is contracted with the pronoun and the negative is left standing alone {he is not-he isn't-he's not} {we are not-we aren't-we're not} {they have not-they haven't-they've not}.

5.103   *Contractions.* Most types of writing benefit from the use of contractions. If used thoughtfully, contractions in prose sound natural and relaxed and make reading more enjoyable. *Be*-verbs and most of the auxiliary verbs are contracted when followed by *not: are-aren't; was-wasn't; cannot-can't; could not-couldn't; do not-don't*; and so on. A few, such as *ought not-oughtn't*, look or sound awkward and are best avoided. Pronouns can be contracted with auxiliaries, forms of *have*, and some *be*-verbs. Think before using one of the less common contractions, which often don't work well in prose, except perhaps in dialogue or quotations. Some examples are *I'd've* (I would have), *she'd've* (she would have), *it'd* (it would), *should've* (should have), *there're* (there are), *who're* (who are), and *would've* (would have). Also, some contracted forms can have more than one meaning. For instance, *there's* may be *there is* or *there has*, and *I'd* may be *I had* or *I would*. The particular meaning may not always be clear from the context.

INFINITIVES

5.104   *Infinitives defined.* An infinitive verb, also called the verb's root or stem, is a verb that in its principal uninflected form may be preceded by *to* {to dance} {to dive}. In the active voice, *to* is generally dropped when the infinitive follows an auxiliary verb {you must flee} and can be dropped after several principal verbs, such as *bid, dare, feel, hear, help, let, make, need,* and *see* {You dare say that to me!}. But when the infinitive follows one of these verbs in the passive voice, *to* should be retained {he cannot be heard to deny it} {they cannot be made to listen}. The *to* should also be retained after *ought* (see 5.148).

5.105   *Uses of the infinitive.* The infinitive has great versatility. It is sometimes called a verbal noun because it can function as a verb or a noun. The infinitive also has limited uses as an adjective or an adverb. As a verb, it can take (1) a subject {we wanted the lesson to end}; (2) an object {to throw the javelin}; (3) a predicate complement {to race home}; or (4) an adverbial modifier {to think quickly}. As a noun, the infinitive can perform as (1) the subject of a finite verb {to fly is a lofty goal} or (2) the object of a transitive verb or participle {I want to hire a new assistant}. An infinitive may be governed by a verb {cease to do evil}, noun {we all have a talent to be improved}, adjective {she is eager to learn}, or pronoun {give it to them to do}.

5.106   *Split infinitive.* Although from about 1850 to 1925 many grammarians stated otherwise, it is now widely acknowledged that adverbs sometimes justifiably separate an infinitive's *to* from its principal verb {they expect to more than double their income next year}. See also 5.168.

5.107   *Dangling infinitive.* An infinitive phrase can be used, often loosely, to modify a verb—in which case there must be an express or implied logical subject in the sentence. If there is none, then the sentence may be confusing. For example, in *to repair your car properly, it must be sent to a mechanic,* the infinitive *repair* does not have a logical subject; the infinitive phrase *to repair your car* is left dangling. But if the sentence is rewritten as *to repair your car properly, you must take it to a mechanic,* the logical subject is *you.*

PARTICIPLES AND GERUNDS

5.108   *Forming participles.* A participle is a nonfinite verb that is not limited by person, number, or mood, but does have tense. Two participles are formed from the verb stem: the present participle invariably ends in *-ing,* and the past participle usually ends in *-ed.* The present participle denotes the verb's action as in progress or incomplete at the time expressed by the sentence's principal verb {watching intently for a mouse, the cat settled in to wait} {hearing his name, Jon turned to answer}. The past participle denotes the verb's action as completed {planted in the spring} {written last year}.

5.109   *Participial phrases.* A participial phrase is made up of a participle plus any closely associated word or words, such as modifiers or complements. It can be used (1) as an adjective to modify a noun or pronoun {nailed to the roof, the slate stopped the leaks} or (2) as an adverb to modify the predicate, or any adverb or adjective in the predicate {she succeeded, persevering despite discouragement}. For more on participial adjectives, see 5.89, 5.112.

5.110   *Gerunds.* A gerund is a present participle used as a noun. It is not limited by person, number, or mood, but does have tense. Being a noun, the gerund can be used as (1) the subject of a verb {complaining about it won't help}; (2) the object of a verb {I don't like your cooking}; (3) a predicate nominative or complement {his favorite hobby is sleeping}; or (4) the object of a preposition {reduce erosion by terracing the fields}. In some sentences, a gerund may substitute for an infinitive. Compare the infinitive *to lie* used as a noun in *to lie is wrong* with the gerund *lying* in *lying is wrong.*

5.111   *Distinguishing between participles and gerunds.* Because participles and gerunds are both derived from verbs, the difference between them depends on their function. A participle is used as a modifier {the running water} or as part of a verb phrase {the meter is running}. A gerund is used as a noun {running is great exercise}.

5.112   *Dangling participles.* Both participles and gerunds are subject to dangling. A participle that has no syntactical relationship with the nearest subject is called a *dangling participle* or a *dangler.* Often, the sentence is illogical, ambiguous, or even incoherent {frequently used in early America, experts suggest that shaming is an effective punishment} (*used* does not modify the closest noun, *experts*; it modifies *shaming*); {being a thoughtful mother, I believe Meg gives her children good advice} (the writer at first seems to be attesting to his or her own thoughtfulness rather than Meg's). Recasting the sentence so that the misplaced modifier is associated with the correct noun is a serviceable cure {experts suggest that shaming, often used in early America, is an effective punishment}. But rewording to avoid the participle or gerund may be preferable {I believe that because Meg is a thoughtful mother, she gives her children good advice}. A careful writer will likewise avoid using *it* or *there* as the subject of the independent clause after a participial phrase, for this produces a dangler without a logical subject {reviewing the suggestions, it is clear that no consensus exists} (a possible revision: *our review of the suggestions shows that no consensus exists*). See also 5.171.

5.113   *Dangling gerunds.* When the participle in a dangling gerund is the object of a preposition, it functions as a noun rather than as a modifier. For example, *after finishing the research, the screenplay was easy to write* (who did the research and who wrote the screenplay?). The best way to correct a dangling gerund is to give the sentence its proper subject. The example above could be revised as *after finishing the research, Pooks found the screenplay easy to write.* Dangling gerunds can result in improbable statements. Consider *while driving to San Antonio, my map was lost.* The map was not the driver. Clarifying the subject makes the sentence work {while driving to San Antonio, I lost my map}. Of course a gerund phrase as object of a preposition can function perfectly well, without dangling, in a sentence whose sense allows it {after dining with royalty, the next item on my to-do list is picnicking on the Eiffel Tower}.

PROPERTIES OF VERBS

5.114   *Five properties of verbs.* A verb has five properties: voice, mood, tense, person, and number.

5.115   *Active and passive voice.* Voice shows whether the subject acts (active voice) or is acted on (passive voice)—that is, whether the subject performs or receives the action of the verb. Only transitive verbs are said to have voice. The clause *the judge levied a $50 fine* is in the active voice because the subject *judge* is acting. But *the tree's branch was broken by the storm* is in the passive voice because the subject *branch* does not break itself—it is acted on by the object *storm*. The passive voice is always formed by joining an inflected form of *be* (or, in colloquial usage, *get*) with the verb's past participle. Compare *the ox pulls the cart* (active voice) with *the cart is pulled by the ox* (passive voice). A passive-voice verb in a modifying phrase often has an implied *be*-verb: in *the advice given by the novelist*, the implied (or understood) words *that was* come before *given*; so the passive construction is *was given*. Although the *be*-verb is sometimes implied, the past participle must always be expressed. Sometimes the agent isn't named {his tires were slashed}. As a matter of style, passive voice {the matter will be given careful consideration} is typically, though not always, inferior to active voice {we will consider the matter carefully}. The choice between active and passive voice may depend on which point of view is desired. For instance, *the mouse was caught by the cat* describes the mouse's experience, whereas *the cat caught the mouse* describes the cat's.

5.116   *Progressive conjugation and voice.* If an inflected form of *be* is joined with another verb's present participle, a progressive conjugation is produced {the ox is pulling the cart}. The progressive conjugation is in the active voice because the subject is performing the action, not being acted on.

5.117   *Mood.* Mood (or mode) indicates the manner in which the verb expresses an action or state of being. The three moods are indicative, imperative, and subjunctive.

5.118   *Indicative mood.* The indicative mood is the most common in English. It is used to express facts and opinions and to ask questions {amethysts cost very little} {the botanist lives in a garden cottage} {Does that bush produce yellow roses?}.

5.119   *Imperative mood.* The imperative mood expresses commands {Go away!}, direct requests {bring the tray in here}, and, sometimes, permission {Come in!}. The subject of the verb, *you*, is understood although the sentence might include a direct address {give me the magazine} {Cindy, take good care of yourself} (*Cindy* is a direct address, not the subject). Use the imperative mood cautiously: in some contexts it could be too blunt or unintentionally rude. You can soften the imperative by using words such as *please* {please stop at the store}. If that isn't satisfactory, recast the sentence in the indicative {Will you stop at the store please?}.

5.120   *Subjunctive mood.* Although the subjunctive mood is not often used in American English, it is useful when you want to express an action or state not as a reality but as a mental conception. Typically the subjunctive expresses an action or state as doubtful, imagined, desired, conditional, hypothetical, or otherwise contrary to fact. In addition to the hypothetical {if I were you}, the subjunctive mood can be used to signal wishes {if I were a rich man}, conjectures {oh, were it so}, demands {the landlord insists that the dog go}, and suggestions {I recommend that she take a vacation}. And despite its decline, the subjunctive mood persists in stock expressions such as *perish the thought, heaven help us,* or *be that as it may.*

5.121   *Indicative instead of subjunctive.* Although the subjunctive mood is often signaled by *if,* not every *if* takes a subjunctive verb. When the action or state might be true but the writer does not know, the indicative is called for instead of the subjunctive {if I am right about this, please call} {if Napoleon was in fact poisoned with arsenic, historians will need to reevaluate his associates}.

5.122   *Tenses generally.* Tense shows the time in which an act, state, or condition occurs or occurred. The three major divisions of time are present, past, and future. (Some modern grammarians hold that English has no future tense; see 5.125.) Each division of time includes a perfect tense that indicates a comparatively more remote time: present perfect, past perfect, and future perfect.

5.123   *Present tense.* The present tense is the infinitive verb's stem, also called the present indicative {walk} {drink}. It primarily denotes acts, conditions, or states that occur in the present {the dog howls} {the air is cold} {the water runs}. It is also used (1) to express a habitual action or general truth {cats prowl nightly} {polluted water is a health threat}; (2) to refer to timeless facts, such as memorable persons and to works of the past that are still extant or enduring {Julius Caesar describes his strategies in *The Gallic War*} {the Pompeiian mosaics are exquisite}; and (3) to narrate a fictional work's plot {the scene takes place aboard the *Titanic*}. This third point is important for those who write about literature. Characters in books, plays, and films *do* things—not *did* them. If you want to distinguish between present action and past action in literature, the present perfect tense is helpful {Hamlet, who has spoken with his father's ghost, reveals what he has learned to no one but Horatio}. See 5.126.

5.124 *Past tense.* The past tense is formed by inflection (see 5.98); the basic inflected form is called the past indicative {walked} {drank}. It denotes an act, state, or condition that occurred or existed at some explicit or implicit point in the past {the auction ended yesterday} {we returned the shawl}.

5.125 *Future tense.* The future tense is formed by using *will* with the verb's stem form {will walk} {will drink}. It refers to an expected act, state, or condition {the artist will design a wall mural} {the restaurant will open soon}. *Shall* may be used instead of *will*, but in American English it typically appears only in first-person questions involving choice {Shall we go?} and in legal commands {the debtor shall pay within 30 days}. In most contexts, *will* is preferred. Incidentally, most linguists are now convinced that, technically speaking, English has no future tense at all—that *will* is simply a modal verb that should be treated with all the others.[6] Yet the future tense remains a part of traditional grammar and is discussed here in the familiar way.

5.126 *Present perfect tense.* The present perfect tense is formed by using *have* or *has* with the principal verb's past participle {have walked} {has drunk}. It denotes an act, state, or condition that is now completed or continues up to the present {I have put away the clothes} {it has been a long day}. The present perfect is distinguished from the past tense because it refers to (1) a time in the indefinite past {I have played golf there before} or (2) a past action that comes up to and touches the present {I have played cards for the last eighteen hours}. The past tense, by contrast, indicates a more specific or a more remote time in the past.

5.127 *Past perfect tense.* The past perfect (or pluperfect) tense is formed by using *had* with the principal verb's past participle {had walked} {had drunk}. It refers to an act, state, or condition that was completed before another specified or implicit past time or past action {the engineer had driven the train to the roundhouse before we arrived} {by the time we stopped to check the map, the rain had begun falling} {the movie had ended already}.

5.128 *Future perfect tense.* The future perfect tense is formed by using *will have* with the verb's past participle {will have walked} {will have drunk}. It refers to an act, state, or condition that is expected to be completed before

---

6. Trask, *Language*, 60.

some other future act or time {the entomologist will have collected sixty more specimens before the semester ends} {the court will have adjourned by five o'clock}. *Shall* can also form the future perfect, but usually only for the first person, and it is not preferred {I shall have finished by tomorrow} {we shall have written before we embark}.

5.129   *Person.* A verb's person shows whether the act, state, or condition is that of (1) the person speaking (first person, *I* or *we*); (2) the person spoken to (second person, *you*); or (3) the person spoken of (third person, *he*, *she*, *it*, or *they*).

5.130   *Number.* The number of a verb must agree with the number of the noun or pronoun used with it. In other words, the verb must be singular or plural. Only the third-person present-indicative singular changes form to indicate number and person {you sketch, they sketch, *but* she sketches}. The second-person verb is always plural in form, whether one person or more than one person is spoken to {you are a wonderful person} {you are wonderful people}.

5.131   *Agreement in person and number.* A finite verb agrees with its subject in person and number. When a verb has two or more subjects connected by *and*, it agrees with them jointly and is plural {Socrates and Plato were wise}. When a verb has two or more singular subjects connected by *or* or *nor*, it is singular {Jill or Jan is prepared to speak} {neither Bob nor John has learned his lesson}. When the subject is a collective noun conveying the idea of unity or multitude, the verb is singular {the nation is powerful}. When the subject is a collective noun conveying the idea of plurality, the verb is plural {the faculty were divided in their sentiments}.

5.132   *False attraction to predicate nominative.* A plural predicate nominative after a singular subject may mislead a writer by suggesting a plural verb. When this occurs, the simple correction of changing the number of the verb may make the sentence awkward, and the better approach then is to rework the sentence:

WRONG: My downfall are sweets.
RIGHT: My downfall is sweets.
BETTER: Sweets are my downfall.

5.133   *Misleading connectives: "as well as," "along with," "together with," and so forth.* Adding to a singular subject by using phrasal connectives such as *along with, as well as, in addition to, together with*, and the like does not make the subject plural. This type of distraction can be doubly misleading because the intervening material seems to create a compound subject, and the modifying prepositional phrase may itself contain one or more plural objects. If the singular verb sounds awkward in such a sentence, it may be better to use the conjunction *and* instead:

WRONG: The bride as well as her bridesmaids were dressed in mauve.
RIGHT: The bride as well as her bridesmaids was dressed in mauve.
BETTER: The bride and her bridesmaids were dressed in mauve.

CONJUGATION OF VERBS

5.134 *Conjugation defined.* Conjugation means changing (inflecting) a verb's form to reflect voice, mood, tense, person, and number. A verb has seven conjugated parts: the present indicative, the present participle, the present subjunctive, the past indicative, the past participle, the past subjunctive, and the imperative. The rules for conjugation of all verbs except auxiliaries are explained in the following sections.

5.135 *Verb stem (present indicative).* The present indicative is the verb stem for all persons, singular and plural, in the present tense—except for the third-person singular, which adds an *-s* to the stem {takes} {strolls} {says}. If the verb ends in *-o*, an *-es* is added {goes} {does}. If the verb ends in a consonant followed by *-y*, the *-y* is changed to *-i* and then an *-es* is added {identify–identifies} {carry–carries}.

5.136 *Forming present participles.* The present participle is formed by adding *-ing* to the stem of the verb {reaping} {wandering}. If the stem ends in *-ie*, the *-ie* usually changes to *-y* before the *-ing* is added {die–dying} {tie–tying}. If the stem ends in a silent *-e*, that *-e* is usually dropped before the *-ing* is added {giving} {leaving}. There are two exceptions to this rule. The silent *-e* is retained when (a) the word ends with *-oe* {toe–toeing} {hoe–hoeing} {shoe–shoeing} or (b) the verb has a participle that would resemble another word but for the distinguishing *-e* (e.g., *dyeing* means something different from *dying*, and *singeing* means something different from *singing*). Regular and irregular verbs both form the present participle in the same way. The present participle is the same for all persons and numbers.

5.137 *Present subjunctive.* Apart from a few set phrases (e.g., *so be it, be they, she need not*), in present-day English the present subjunctive typically appears in the form *if I [he, she, it] were* {if I were king} {if she were any different}. That is, the present subjunctive ordinarily uses a past-tense verb (e.g., *were*) to connote uncertainty, impossibility, or unreality. Compare *if I am threatened, I will quit* (indicative) with *if I were threatened, I would* *quit* (subjunctive), or *if the canary sings, I smile* (indicative) with *if the canary sang* [or *should sing*, or *were to sing*], *I would smile* (subjunctive). See also 5.120.

5.138 *Past indicative.* The past indicative of a regular verb is formed by adding *-ed* to its base form {like-liked} {spill-spilled}. In words of more than one syllable, the final consonant is doubled if it is part of the syllable that is stressed both before and after the inflection {prefer-preferred} but not otherwise {travel-traveled}. In British English there is no such distinction: all such consonants are doubled. Irregular verbs form the past tense in various ways {give-gave} {stride-strode} {read-read}. A good dictionary will show an irregular verb's past indicative form.

5.139 *Forming past participles.* With regular verbs, the past participle is formed in the same way as the past indicative—that is, the past-indicative and past-participial forms are always identical {stated-stated} {pulled-pulled}. For irregular verbs, the forms are sometimes the same {paid-paid} {sat-sat} and sometimes different {forsook-forsaken} {shrank-shrunk}. A good dictionary will show the past participles.

5.140 *Past subjunctive.* The past subjunctive typically appears in the form *if I* [*he, she, it*] *had been* {if I had gone} {if he had been there}. That is, the past subjunctive ordinarily uses a past-perfect verb (e.g., *had been*) to connote uncertainty or impossibility. Compare *if it arrived, it was not properly filed* (indicative) with *if it had arrived, it could have changed the course of history* (subjunctive).

5.141 *Imperative.* The imperative is the verb's stem used to make a command, a request, an exclamation, or the like {Come here!} {Give me a clue.} {Help!}.

AUXILIARY VERBS

5.142 *Auxiliary verbs defined.* An auxiliary verb (sometimes termed a modal or helping verb) is a highly irregular verb that is used with other verbs to form voice, tense, and mood. The main ones are explained in the following sections. See also 5.101.

5.143 *"Can."* This verb uses only its stem form in the present indicative {I can} {it can} {they can}. In the past indicative, *can* becomes *could* for all persons {he could see better with glasses}. *Can* does not have an infinitive form (*to be able to* is substituted) or a present or past participle. When it denotes ability, capacity, or permission, *can* is always followed by an explicit or implicit principal verb {you can carry this trunk}. When used in the sense of permission, *can* is colloquial for *may* {Can I go to the movies?}. *Can* also connotes an actual possibility {spring storms can be severe} {days can pass before a decision is announced}.

5.144 *"Do."* This verb has two forms in the present indicative: *does* for the third-person singular and *do* for all other persons. In the past indicative, the only form for all persons is *did*. The past participle is *done*. As an auxiliary verb, *do* is used only in the present and past indicative {Did you speak?} {we do plan some charity work}. When the verb in an imperative statement is coupled with *not*, *do* also appears {Do not touch!} {Don't be an idiot!}. When denoting performance, *do* can also act as a principal verb {he does well in school} {they do good work}. *Do* can sometimes substitute for another verb as a means of avoiding repetition {Marion dances well, and so do you} {he caught fewer mistakes than you did}.

5.145 *"Have."* This verb has two forms in the present indicative: *has* for the third-person singular and *have* for all other persons. In the past indicative, the only form for all persons is *had*; the past participle is also *had*. When the present or past indicative of the auxiliary *have* precedes the past participle of any verb, that verb's present-perfect or past-perfect indicative mood is formed {I have looked everywhere} {he had looked for a better rate}. When denoting possession, *have* can also be a sentence's principal verb {she has a car and a boat} {you have a mosquito on your neck}. When *have got* precedes *to* plus an infinitive, it means *must* {I have got to pass this test!}. *Had* plus *to* and an infinitive expresses the past form of *must* {I had to leave yesterday afternoon}.

5.146 *"May" and "might."* *May* denotes permission {you may go to the movies}. In its negative form, *may not* is sometimes displaced by the more intensive *must not*. Compare *you may not climb that tree* with *you must not climb that tree*. *May* sometimes connotes an uncertain possibility {you may find that assignment too difficult} and often becomes *might* {you might find that assignment too difficult}. This verb has only its stem form in the present indicative {I may} {it may} {they may}. In the past indicative, *may* often becomes *might*, especially to connote uncertainty {the jeweler might have forgotten to call}. *May* does not have an infinitive form, or a present or past participle. As an auxiliary, *may*, denoting wishfulness or purpose, forms a subjunctive equivalent {may you always be happy} {give so that others may live}.

5.147 *"Must."* *Must* denotes a necessity that arises from someone's will {we must obey the rules} or from circumstances {you must ask what the next step is}. *Must* also connotes a logical conclusion {that must be the right answer} {that must be the house we're looking for} {it must have been Donna who phoned}. This verb does not vary its form in either the present or past indicative. It does not have an infinitive form (*to have to* is substituted) or a present or past participle. Denoting obligation, necessity, or inference, *must* is always used with an express or implied infinitive {we must finish this design} {everyone must eat} {the movie must be over by now}.

5.148   *"Ought."* *Ought* denotes what is reasonably expected of a person or circumstances {they ought to fix the fence} {they left at dawn, so they ought to be here soon}. It is more emphatic than *should*. This verb does not vary its form in either the present or past indicative. It has no infinitive form, or present or past participle. Denoting a duty or obligation, *ought* is always used with an infinitive, even in the negative {we ought to invite some friends} {the driver ought not to have ignored the signal}. *To* is occasionally omitted after *not* {you ought not worry}, but the better usage is to include it {you ought not to worry}. See also 5.104.

5.149   *"Shall" and "should."* *Shall* uses only its stem form in the present indicative. It is a relatively rare word in present-day American English, except in first-person jocular uses {Shall we dance?} {Shall I fetch you some coffee?}. The past indicative form, *should*, is used for all persons and always with a principal verb {they should be at home} {Should you read that newspaper?} (note that these verbs do not actually function as past indicatives). *Should* does not have an infinitive form, or a present or past participle. *Should* often carries a sense of duty, compulsion, or expectation {I should review those financial-planning tips} {you should clean the garage today} {it should be ready by now}; sometimes it carries a sense of inference {the package should have been delivered today}; and sometimes it conveys the speaker's attitude {How should I know?} {you shouldn't have to deal with that}.

5.150   *"Will" and "would."* In its auxiliary uses, *will* has several senses. This verb uses only its stem form in the present indicative {she will} {they will}. In the past indicative, the only form for all persons is *would* {we would go fishing on Saturdays} {She would say that!}. *Would* sometimes expresses a condition {I would slide down the hill if you lent me your sled}. *Will* often carries a sense of the future {she will be at her desk tomorrow} or, in the past form *would*, expresses a conditional statement {I would recognize the house if I saw it again}.

"BE"-VERBS

5.151   *Forms of "be"-verbs.* The verb *be* has eight forms (*be, is, are, was, were, been, being,* and *am*) and has several special uses. First, it is sometimes a sentence's principal verb meaning "exist" {I think, therefore I am}. Second, it is more often used as an auxiliary verb {I was born in Lubbock}. When joined with a verb's present participle, it denotes continuing or progressive action {the train is coming} {the passenger was waiting}. When joined with a past participle, the verb becomes passive {a signal was given} {an earring was dropped} (see 5.115). Often this type of construction can be advantageously changed to active voice {he gave the signal} {she dropped her earring}. Third, *be* is the most common linking verb that connects the subject with something affirmed of the subject {truth is beauty} {we are the champions}. Occasionally a *be*-verb is used as part of an adjective {a rock star wannabe [want to be]} {a would-be hero} or noun {a has-been}.

5.152   *Conjugation of "be"-verbs.* *Be* is conjugated differently from other verbs. (1) The stem is not used in the present indicative form. Instead, *be* has three forms: for the first-person singular, *am*; for the third-person singular, *is*; and for all other persons, *are*. (2) The present participle is formed by adding *-ing* to the root *be* {being}. It is the same for all persons, but the present perfect requires also using *am, is,* or *are* {I am being} {it is being} {you are being}. (3) The past indicative has two forms: the first- and third-person singular use *was*; all other persons use *were* {she was} {we were}. (4) The past participle for all persons is *been* {I have been} {they have been}. (5) The imperative is the verb's stem {Be yourself!}.

Adverbs

DEFINITION AND FORMATION

5.153   *Adverbs defined.* An adverb is a word that qualifies, limits, describes, or modifies a verb, an adjective, or another adverb {she studied constantly} (*constantly* qualifies the verb *studied*); {the juggler's act was really unusual} (*really* qualifies the adjective *unusual*); {the cyclist pedaled very swiftly} (*very* qualifies the adverb *swiftly*). An adverb may also qualify a preposition, a conjunction, or a clause {the birds flew right over the lake} (*right* qualifies the preposition *over*); {this is exactly where I found it} (*exactly* qualifies the conjunction *where*); {apparently you forgot to check your references} (*apparently* qualifies the rest of the clause). Finally, grammarians have traditionally used the term *adverb* as a catch-all category to sweep in words that aren't readily put into categories (such as the infinitival *to* [see 5.104] and the particle in a phrasal verb [see 5.100]).

5.154   *Adverbs with suffixes.* Many adjectives have corresponding adverbs distinguished by the suffix *-ly* or, after most words ending in *-ic, -ally* {slow-

slowly} {careful–carefully} {public–publicly} {pedantic–pedantically}. Most adjectives ending in -y preceded by a consonant change the -y to -i when the suffix is added, but some do not {happy–happily} {shy–shyly}. A few adjectives ending in -e drop the vowel {true–truly} {whole–wholly}. If an adjective ends in -le and it is sounded as part of a syllable, it is replaced with -ly {terrible–terribly} {simple–simply}. An adjective that ends in a double -l takes only a -y suffix {dull–dully}. Many adjectives ending in -le or -ly do not make appealing adverbs {juvenile–juvenilely} {silly–sillily}. If an -ly adverb looks clumsy (e.g., ghastlily or uglily), either rephrase the sentence or use a phrase (e.g., in a ghastly manner or in an ugly way). Adverbial suffixes are sometimes added to phrases {replied matter-of-factly}. Some terms are compounded with nouns to form adverbs {he rides cowboy-style}; a few nouns form adverbs by taking the ending -ways {side–sideways}, -ward {sky–skyward}, or -wise {clock–clockwise}.

5.155 *Adverbs without suffixes.* Many adverbs do not have an identifying suffix (e.g., almost, never, here, now, just, seldom, late, near, too). And not every word ending in -ly is an adverb—some are adjectives (e.g., lovely, curly).

5.156 *Adverbs distinguished from adjectives.* Unlike an adjective, an adverb doesn't modify a noun or pronoun {we made an early start and arrived at the airport early} (the first early is an adjective modifying the noun start; the second is an adverb modifying arrived). Some adverbs are identical to prepositions (e.g., up or off) but are distinguishable because they are not attached to a following noun {he ran up a large bill} {let's cast off}. These prepositional adverbs (sometimes called particles or particle adverbs) are typically parts of phrasal verbs. See 5.100.

SIMPLE VERSUS COMPOUND ADVERBS

5.157 *Simple and flat adverbs.* A simple adverb is a single word that qualifies a single part of speech {hardly} {now} {deep}. A flat or bare adverb is one that has an -ly form but whose adjectival form may work equally well or even better, especially when used with an imperative in an informal context {drive slow} {hold on tight} {tell me quick}. Some flat adverbs are always used in their adjectival form {work fast} because the -ly has become obsolete (although it may linger in other words—e.g., steadfast and steadfastly). And the flat adverb may have a different meaning from the -ly adverb. Compare I am working hard with I am hardly working.

5.158 *Phrasal and compound adverbs.* A phrasal adverb consists of two or more words that function together as an adverb {in the meantime} {for a while} {here and there}. A compound adverb appears to be a single word but is a compound of several words {notwithstanding} {heretofore} {thereupon}. Compound adverbs should be used cautiously and sparingly because they make the tone stuffy.

5.159 *Three adverbial degrees.* Like adjectives (see 5.83), adverbs have three degrees: the positive, the comparative, and the superlative. A positive adverb simply expresses a quality without reference to any other thing {the nurse spoke softly} {the choir sang merrily}.

5.160 *Comparative forms.* Most one-syllable adverbs that do not end in *-ly* form the comparative by taking the suffix *-er* {sooner} {harder}. Multisyllable adverbs usually form the comparative with *more* or *less* {the Shakespearean villain fenced more ineptly than the hero} {the patient is walking less painfully today}. But there are exceptions for adverbs that end in *-ly* if the *-ly* is not a suffix {early-earlier}. A comparative adverb compares the quality of a specified action or condition shared by two things {Bitey worked longer than Arachne} {Rachel studied more industriously than Edith}.

5.161 *Superlative forms.* Most one-syllable adverbs that do not end in *-ly* form the superlative by taking the suffix *-est* {soonest} {hardest}. Multisyllable adverbs usually form the superlative with *most* or *least* {everyone's eyesight was acute, but I could see most acutely} {of all the people making choices, he chose least wisely}. But there are exceptions for adverbs that end in *-ly* if the *-ly* is not a suffix {early-earliest}. A superlative adverb compares the quality of a specified action or condition shared by at least three things {Sullie bowled fastest of all the cricketers} {of the three doctoral candidates, Rebecca defended her dissertation the most adamantly}. In a loose sense, the superlative is sometimes used for emphasis rather than comparison {the pianist played most skillfully}.

5.162 *Irregular adverbs.* A few adverbs have irregular comparative and superlative forms {badly-worse-worst} {little-less-least}. A good dictionary is the best resource for finding an irregular adverb's forms of comparison.

5.163 *Uncomparable adverbs.* Many adverbs are uncomparable. Some, by definition, are absolute and cannot be compared {eternally} {never} {singly} {uniquely} {universally}. Most adverbs indicating time {now} {then}, position {on}, number {first} {finally}, or place {here} are also uncomparable.

5.164 *Intensifiers.* An adverb can be intensified with words like *very* and *quite* {the very fashionably dressed actor} {everyone ate quite heartily}.

POSITION OF ADVERBS

5.165 *Placement of adverbs.* The adverb should generally be placed as near as possible to the word it is intended to modify. For example, in *the marathoners submitted their applications to compete immediately,* what does *immediately* modify—*compete* or *submitted*? Placing the adverb with the word it modifies makes the meaning clear—for instance, *the marathoners immediately submitted their applications to compete.* A misplaced adverb can completely change a sentence's meaning. For example, *we nearly lost all our camping equipment* states that the equipment was saved; *we lost nearly all our camping equipment* states that almost everything was lost.

5.166 *Adverbs modifying intransitive verbs.* If the adverb qualifies an intransitive verb, it should immediately follow the verb {the students sighed gloomily when homework was assigned} {the owl perched precariously on a thin branch}. Some exceptions are *always, never, often, generally, rarely,* and *seldom,* which may precede the verb {mountaineers seldom succeed in climbing K2}.

5.167 *Adverbs and linking verbs.* Adverbs do not generally modify linking verbs (see 5.99), such as *be*-verbs, *appear, seem, become, look, smell, taste, hear,* and *feel.* These verbs connect a descriptive word with the clause's subject; the descriptive word applies to the subject, not the verb {he seems modest}. To determine whether a verb is a linking verb, the writer must consider whether the descriptive word describes the action or condition, or the subject. For example, *the sculptor feels badly* literally describes the act of feeling or touching as not done well. But *the sculptor feels bad* describes the sculptor as unwell or perhaps experiencing guilt.

5.168 *Adverb within a verb phrase.* When an adverb qualifies a verb phrase, the natural place for the adverb is between the auxiliary verb and the principal verb {the administration has consistently repudiated this view} {the reports will soon generate controversy} {public opinion is sharply divided}. (See 5.102.) Some adverbs may follow the principal verb {you must go quietly} {Are you asking rhetorically?}. There is no rule against adverbial modifiers between the parts of a verb phrase. In fact, it's typically preferable to put them there {the heckler was abruptly expelled} {the bus had been seriously damaged in the crash}. And sometimes it is perfectly appropriate to split an infinitive verb with an adverb to add emphasis or to produce a natural sound. (See 5.106.) A verb's infinitive or *to* form is split when an intervening word immediately follows *to* {to bravely assert}. If the adverb bears the emphasis in a phrase {to boldly go} {to strongly favor}, then leave the split infinitive alone. But if moving the adverb to the end of the phrase doesn't suggest a different meaning or impair the sound, then it's an acceptable way to avoid splitting the verb. Recasting a sentence just to eliminate a split infinitive or avoid splitting the infinitive can alter its nuance or meaning—for instance, *it's best to always get up early* (*always* modifies *get up*) is not quite the same as *it's always best to get up early* (*always* modifies *best*). Moreover, sometimes "fixing" a split infinitive makes the sentence sound unnatural, as in *it's best to get up early always.*

Prepositions

DEFINITION AND TYPES

5.169 *Prepositions defined.* A preposition is a word or phrase that links an object and an antecedent to show the relationship between them. A preposition's object is usually a noun, or else a pronoun in the objective case {between me and them}, but an adjective, adverb, verb, or phrase may follow instead. Usually a preposition comes before its object, but there are exceptions. For example, the preposition can end a clause, especially a relative clause, or sentence {this isn't the pen that Steve writes with}. And a preposition used with the relative pronoun *that* (or with *that* understood) always follows the object {this is the moment [that] I've been waiting for}. It also frequently, but not always, follows the relative pronouns *which* {Which alternative is your decision based on?} {this is the alternative on which my decision is based} and *whom* {there is a banker [whom] I must speak with} {I can't tell you to whom you should apply}.

5.170 *Simple and compound prepositions.* Many prepositions are relatively straightforward. A simple preposition consists of a single monosyllabic word—for example, *as, at, by, down, for, from, in, like, of, off, on, plus, since, through, to, toward, up,* and *with.* A compound preposition has two or more syllables; it may be made up of two or more words {into} {outside} {upon}. Some examples are *about, above, across, after, against, alongside, around, before, below, beneath, between, despite, except, inside, onto, opposite, throughout, underneath, until,* and *without.*

5.171 *Participial prepositions.* A participial preposition is a participial form that functions as a preposition (or sometimes as a subordinating conjunction). Examples include *assuming, barring, concerning, considering, during, notwithstanding, owing to, provided, regarding, respecting,* and *speaking.*

Unlike other participles, these words do not create danglers when they have no subject {considering the road conditions, the trip went quickly} {regarding Watergate, he had nothing to say}. See 5.112.

5.172 *Phrasal prepositions.* A phrasal preposition (sometimes called a complex preposition) is two or more separate words used as a prepositional unit. These include *according to, because of, by means of, by reason of, by way of, contrary to, for the sake of, in accordance with, in addition to, in apposition with, in case of, in consideration of, in front of, in regard to, in respect to, in spite of, instead of, on account of, out of, with reference to, with regard to,* and *with respect to.* Many of these phrasal prepositions are symptoms of officialese, bureaucratese, or other types of verbose style. If a one-word preposition will do in context, use it. For example, if *about* will serve as well as *with regard to* or *in connection with,* a judicious editor will inevitably prefer to use the simpler expression.

PREPOSITIONAL PHRASES

5.173 *Prepositional phrases defined.* A prepositional phrase consists of a preposition, its object, and any words that modify the object. A prepositional phrase can be used as a noun {for James to change his mind would be a miracle}, an adverb (also called an adverbial phrase) {we strolled through the glade}, or an adjective (also called an adjectival phrase) {the cathedrals of Paris}.

5.174 *Prepositional function.* Prepositions signal many kinds of relationships. For example, a preposition may express a spatial relationship {to} {from} {out of} {into}, time {at} {for} {throughout} {until}, cause {because of} {on account of}, means {like} {with} {by}, possession {without} {of}, exceptions {but for} {besides} {except}, support {with} {for}, opposition {against}, or concession {despite} {for all} {notwithstanding}.

5.175 *Placement of prepositional phrases.* A prepositional phrase with an adverbial or adjectival function should be as close as possible to the word it modifies to avoid awkwardness, ambiguity, or unintended meanings {Is a person with blond hair named Sandy here?} {the woman with the Popular Front circulates petitions}. If a prepositional phrase equally modifies all the elements of a compound construction, the phrase follows the last element in the compound {the date, the place, and the budget for the wedding have been decided}. Note that if a prepositional phrase with plural objects follows the singular subject of a sentence, the predicate must still be singular—compare the predicate in *the man and two daughters have* *arrived* with that in *the man with two daughters has arrived* and in *the man has arrived with his two daughters.*

5.176   *Ending a sentence with a preposition.* The traditional caveat of yesteryear against ending sentences with prepositions is, for most writers, an unnecessary and pedantic restriction. As Winston Churchill famously said, "That is the type of arrant pedantry up with which I shall not put." A sentence that ends in a preposition may sound more natural than a sentence carefully constructed to avoid a final preposition. Compare, for example, *this is the case I told you about* with *this is the case about which I told you.* The "rule" prohibiting terminal prepositions was an ill-founded superstition. Today many grammarians use the dismissive term *pied-piping* for this phenomenon.

5.177   *Clashing prepositions.* If a phrasal verb {give in} precedes a prepositional phrase using the same term {in every argument}, the adverb will clash with the preposition {he gives in in every argument}. Recast the sentence when possible to avoid such repetition—for example, *rather than continue arguing, he always gives in,* or *in every argument, he gives in* (see also 6.44). For more on phrasal verbs, see 5.100.

5.178   *Elliptical prepositional phrases.* Sometimes a prepositional phrase is elliptical—that is, an independent expression without an antecedent. Often such a phrase starts a clause and can be detached from the statement without affecting the meaning. Elliptical prepositional phrases include *for example, for instance, in a word, in any event, in the last analysis,* and *in the long run* {in any event, call me when you arrive}.

5.179   *Effect of prepositional phrase on pronoun.* A pronoun that appears in a prepositional phrase is usually in the objective case (see 5.18). There are exceptions. *Than* may function either as a conjunction {he's taller than I [am]} or as a preposition {he's taller than me}. Traditional grammarians prefer the nominative *than I [am]* over the objective *than me,* even though the latter represents common usage. In formal prose, treat *than* as a conjunction requiring a nominative pronoun {she is a more careful researcher than he}.

OTHER PREPOSITIONAL ISSUES

5.180   *Prepositions and functional variation.* Some words that function as prepositions may also function as other parts of speech. The distinguishing feature of a preposition is that it always has an object. A word such as *above, behind, below, by, down, in, off, on,* or *up* can be used as either an adverb or a preposition. When used as a preposition, it takes an object {let's slide down the hill}. When used as an adverb, it does not {we sat down}. (Sometimes such a term may appear to have an object {I looked up his biography}. To test, detach the apparent prepositional phrase and see if it makes sense; *up his biography* does not and therefore *up* is an adverb here.) Likewise, some conjunctions may serve as prepositions (e.g., *than* and *but*). Such a conjunction points to an explicit or implied separate action. Compare the prepositional *but* in *everyone but Fuzzy traveled abroad last summer* (*but* is used to mean "except") with the conjunctive *but* in *I like the cut but not the color* (*but* joins a clause containing an implied separate action: *I don't like the color*).

5.181   *Use and misuse of "like." Like* is probably the least understood preposition. Its traditional function is adjectival, not adverbial, so that *like* is governed by a noun or a noun phrase {teens often see themselves as star-crossed lovers like Romeo and Juliet}. As a preposition, *like* is followed by a noun or pronoun in the objective case {the person in that old portrait looks like me}. Increasingly (but loosely) today in ordinary speech, *like* displaces *as* or *as if* as a conjunction to connect clauses. For example, in *it happened just like I said it would happen, like* should read *as*; and in *you're looking around like you've misplaced something, like* should read *as if*. Because *as* and *as if* are conjunctions, they are followed by nouns in the nominative case {Do you work too hard, as I do?}. Although *like* as a conjunction has been considered nonstandard since the seventeenth century, today it is common in dialectal and colloquial usage {he ran like he was really scared}. Consider context and tone when deciding whether to impose standard English, as in the examples above.

5.182   *Use and misuse of "only." Only* functions as an adjective, an adverb, and a conjunction, and it can modify any part of speech. It is probably poorly placed in sentences more often than any other word. *Only* emphasizes the word or phrase that immediately follows it. When *only* appears too early in the sentence, it has a deemphasizing effect; it can also alter the meaning of the sentence or produce ambiguity. Compare *I bought only tomatoes at the market* (I bought nothing else) with *I bought tomatoes only at the market* (I bought nothing other than tomatoes or I didn't buy tomatoes from any other place?). In idiomatic spoken English, *only* is placed before the verb, regardless of what it modifies: *I only bought tomatoes at the market.* This may be acceptable in speech because the speaker can use intonation to make the meaning clear. But since in writing there is no guidance from intonation, rigorous placement of *only* is preferable to aid the reader's comprehension.

LIMITING PREPOSITIONAL PHRASES

5.183 *Avoiding overuse of prepositions.* Prepositions can easily be overused. Stylistically, a good ratio to strive for is one preposition for every ten to fifteen words. There are five editorial methods that can reduce the number of prepositions in a sentence.

5.184 *Cutting prepositional phrases.* If the surrounding prose's context permits, a prepositional phrase can be eliminated—for instance, within a passage focused on a particular recipe, *the most important ingredient in this recipe* could be reduced to *the most important ingredient.*

5.185 *Cutting unnecessary prepositions.* Many nouns ending in *-ance, -ence, -ity, -ment, -sion,* or *-tion* are formed from a verb {qualification-qualify} {performance-perform}. Such nouns are sometimes called nominalizations or buried verbs, and they often require additional words, especially prepositions (that is, *during her performance of the concerto* is essentially equivalent to *while she performed the concerto,* but it is somewhat more abstract and requires the preposition *of*). Using the noun's verb form may eliminate one or two prepositions. For example, *our efforts toward maximization of profits failed* might be edited down to *our efforts to maximize profits failed.*

5.186 *Replacing prepositional phrases with adverbs.* A strong adverb may replace a weaker prepositional phrase. For example, *the cyclist pedaled with fury* is weak compared with *the cyclist pedaled furiously.*

5.187 *Replacing prepositional phrases with genitives.* A genitive may replace a prepositional phrase, especially an *of*-genitive. For example, *I was dismayed by the complexity of the street map* essentially equals *the street map's complexity dismayed me.* See 5.19.

5.188 *Using active voice to eliminate prepositions.* Changing from passive voice to active almost always eliminates a preposition—that is, whenever the actor appears in a *by*-phrase. For example, *the ship was sailed by an experienced crew* equals *an experienced crew sailed the ship.*

PREPOSITIONAL IDIOMS

5.189 *Idiomatic uses of prepositions.* Among the most persistent word-choice issues are those concerning prepositions. Which prepositions go with which words? You *fill* A *with* B but *instill* B *into* A; you *replace* A *with* B but *substitute* B *for* A; you *prefix* A *to* B but *preface* B *with* A; you *force* A *into* B but *enforce* B *on* A; finally, A *implies* B, so you *infer* B *from* A. And that's only the beginning of it.

5.190   *Shifts in prepositional idiom.* Prepositional idioms often give nonnative speakers of English nightmares, and even native speakers of English need to double-check them at times. The language occasionally shifts. There may be a difference between traditional literary usage (*oblivious of*) and prevailing contemporary usage (*oblivious to*). Sometimes the writer may choose one or the other preposition for reasons of euphony. (Is it better, in a given context, to *ruminate on, about,* or *over* a specified problem?) Sometimes, too, the denotative and connotative differences can be striking: it's one thing to be *smitten with* another and quite a different thing to be *smitten by* another.

5.191   *List of words and the prepositions construed with them.* The list below contains the words that most often give writers trouble. Note that some of the words included here—such as verbs that can be used transitively {the tire abutted the curb} or words that can be used without further qualification {she refused to acquiesce} {his words were considered blasphemy}—do not always take prepositions.

abide (vb.): with ("stay"); by ("obey"); *none* (transitive)

abound (vb.): in, with [resources]

absolve (vb.): from [guilt]; of [obligation]

abut (vb.): on, against [land]; *none* (transitive)

accompanied (adj.): by (not *with*) [something *or* someone else]

accord (vb.): in *or* with [an opinion]; to [a person]

acquiesce (vb.): in [a decision]; to [pressure]

acquit (vb.): of (not *from*) [a charge]; *none* (transitive)

adept (adj.): at [an activity]; in [an art]

admit (vb.) ("acknowledge"): *none* (not *to*) (transitive)

admit (vb.) ("let in"): to, into

admit (vb.) ("allow"): of

anxious (adj.): about, over (preferably not *to*) [a concern]

badger (vb.): into [doing something]; about [a situation]

ban (vb.): from [a place]

ban (n.): on [a thing; an activity]; from [a place]

based (adj.): on (preferably not *upon*) [a premise]; in [a place; a field of study]; at [a place]

becoming (adj.): on, to [a person]; of [an office or position]

bestow (vb.): on (preferably not *upon*) [an honoree]

binding (adj.): on (preferably not *upon*) [a person]

blasphemy (n.): against [a religious tenet]

center (vb.): on, upon (not *around*) [a primary issue]

chafe (vb.): at [doing something]; under [an irritating authority]

coerce (vb.): into [doing something]

cohesion (n.): between [things; groups]

collude (vb.): with [a person to defraud another]

commiserate (vb.): with [a person]

compare (vb.): with (literal comparison); to (poetic or metaphorical comparison)

comply (vb.): with (not *to*) [a rule; an order]

confide (vb.): to, in [a person]

congruence (n.): with [a standard]

connive (vb.): at [a bad act]; with [another person]

consider (vb.): *none* (transitive); as [one of several possible aspects (*not* as a substitute for "to be")]; for [a position]

consist (vb.): of [components (said of concrete things)]; in [qualities (said of abstract things)]

contemporary (adj.): with [another event]

contemporary (n.): of [another person]

contiguous (adj.): with, to [another place]

contingent (adj.): on (preferably not *upon*)

contrast (vb.): to, with [a person or thing]

conversant (adj.): with, in [a field of study]

convict (vb.): of, for (not *in*)

depend (vb.): on (preferably not *upon*)

differ (vb.): from [a thing or quality]; with [a person]; about, over, on [an issue]

different (adj.): from (but when a dependent clause follows *different*, the conjunction *than* is a defensible substitute for *from what*: "movies today are different than they were in the fifties")

dissent (n. & vb.): from, against (preferably not *to* or *with*)

dissimilar (adj.): to (not *from*)

dissociate (vb.): from

enamored (adj.): of (not *with*)

equivalent (adj.): to, in (preferably not *with*)

excerpt (n.): from (not *of*)

forbid (vb.): to (formal); from (informal)

foreclose (vb.): on [mortgaged property]

hale (vb.): to, into [a place]; before [a magistrate]

hegemony (n.): over [rivals]; in [a region]

identical (adj.): with (preferred by purists), to [something else]

impatience (n.): with [a person]; with, at, about [a situation]

impose (vb.): on (preferably not *upon*) [a person]

inaugurate (vb.): as [an officer]; into [an office]

inculcate (vb.): into, in [a person]

independent (adj.): of (not *from*) [something else]

infringe (vb.): *none* (transitive); on (preferably not *upon*) [a right]
inhere (vb.): in (not *within*) [a person; a thing]
inquire (vb.): into [situations]; of [people]; after [people]
instill (vb.): in, into (not *with*) [a person]
juxtapose (vb.): to (not *with*)
mastery (n.): of [a skill or knowledge]; over [people]
militate (vb.): against [a harsher outcome]
mitigate (vb.): *none* (transitive)
oblivious (adj.): of (preferred), to [a danger; an opportunity]
off (prep. & adv.): *none* (not *of*)
predilection (n.): for [a preferred thing]
predominate (vb.) (not transitive): in, on, over [a field; rivals]
preferable (adj.): to (not *than*); over [an alternative]
pretext (n.): for [a true intention]
reconcile (vb.): with [a person]; to [a situation]
reticent (adj.): about [speaking; a topic]
sanction (n.): for [misbehavior]; of [a sponsoring body]; to [a person; an event]
shiver (vb.): from [cold]; at [something frightening]
stigmatize (vb.): *none* (transitive); as [dishonorable]
subscribe (vb.): to [a periodical or an opinion]; for [stock]
trade (vb.): for ("swap"); in ("sell"); with ("do business with"); at ("patronize"); in [certain goods]; on ("buy and sell at")
trust (n.): in [faith]; for ("beneficial trust")
undaunted (adj.): in [a task]; by [obstacles]
unequal (adj.): to [a challenge]; in [attributes]
used (adj.): to ("accustomed"); for ("applied to")
vexed (adj.): with [someone]; about, at [something]

Conjunctions

5.192   *Conjunctions defined.* A conjunction connects sentences, clauses, or words within a clause {My daughter graduated from college in December. And my son will graduate from high school in May.} (*and* connects two sentences); {I said hello, but no one answered} (*but* connects two clauses); {we're making progress slowly but surely} (*but* joins two adverbs within an adverbial clause). Conjunctions connect pronouns in the same case {he and she are colleagues} {the teacher encouraged her and me}.

5.193   *Simple versus compound conjunctions.* A conjunction may be simple, a single word such as *and, but, if, or,* or *though.* Most are derived from prepositions. Compound conjunctions are single words formed by combining two or more words. Most are relatively modern formations and include words such as *although, because, nevertheless, notwithstanding,* and *unless.* Phrasal conjunctions are connectives made up of two or more separate words. Examples include *as though, inasmuch as, in case, provided that, so that,* and *supposing that.*

5.194 *Coordinating conjunctions.* The two main classes of conjunctions are *coordinating* and *subordinating.* Coordinating conjunctions join words or groups of words of equal grammatical rank, such as two nouns, two verbs, two phrases, or two clauses {Are you speaking to him or to me?} {the results are disappointing but not discouraging}. Coordinating conjunctions are further broken down into *copulative, adversative, disjunctive,* and *final.* A coordinating conjunction may be either a single word or a correlative conjunction. For subordinating conjunctions, see 5.200, 5.201.

5.195 *Correlative conjunctions.* Correlative conjunctions are conjunctions used in pairs, often to join successive clauses that depend on each other to form a complete thought. Some examples of correlative conjunctions are *as–as; if–then; either–or, neither–nor; both–and; where–there; so–as;* and *not only–but also.* Correlative conjunctions must frame structurally identical or matching sentence parts {an attempt both to win the gold medal and to set a new record}; in other words, each member of the pair should immediately precede the same part of speech {they not only read the book but also saw the movie} {if the first claim is true, then the second claim must be false}.

5.196 *Copulative conjunctions.* Copulative or additive coordinating conjunctions denote addition. The second element states an additional fact that is related to the first element. The conjunctions include *and, also, moreover,* and *no less than* {one associate received a raise, and the other was promoted} {the jockeys' postrace party was no less exciting than the race itself}.

5.197 *Adversative conjunctions.* Adversative or contrasting coordinating conjunctions denote contrasts or comparisons. The second element usually qualifies the first element in some way. The conjunctions include *but, still, yet,* and *nevertheless* {the message is sad but inspiring} {she's earned her doctorate, yet she's still not satisfied with herself}.

5.198 *Disjunctive conjunctions.* Disjunctive or separative coordinating conjunctions denote separation or alternatives. Only one of the statements joined by the conjunction may be true; both may be false. The conjunctions include *either, or, else, but, nor, neither, otherwise,* and *other* {that bird is either a heron or a crane} {you can wear the blue coat or the green one}.

5.199 *Final conjunctions.* Final or illative coordinating conjunctions denote inferences or consequences. The second element gives a reason for the first element's statement, or it shows what has been or ought to be done in view of the first element's content. The conjunctions include *consequently, for, hence, so, thus, therefore, as a consequence, as a result, so that,* and *so then* {he had betrayed the king; therefore he was banished} {it's time to leave, so let's go}.

5.200 *Subordinating conjunctions.* A subordinating conjunction connects clauses of unequal grammatical rank. The conjunction introduces a clause that is dependent on the independent clause {follow this road until you reach the highway} {that squirrel is friendly because people feed it} {Marcus promised that he would help}. A pure subordinating conjunction has no antecedent and is not a pronoun or an adverb {take a message if someone calls}.

5.201 *Special uses of subordinating conjunctions.* Subordinating conjunctions or conjunctive phrases often denote the following relationships: (1) Comparison or degree—for example, *than* (if it follows comparative adverbs or adjectives, or if it follows *else, rather, other,* or *otherwise*), *as, else, otherwise, rather, as much as, as far as,* and *as well as* {Is a raven less clever than a magpie?} {these amateur musicians play as well as professionals} {it's not true as far as I can discover}. (2) Time—for instance, *since, until, as long as, before, after, when, as,* and *while* {while we waited, it began to snow} {the tire went flat as we were turning the corner} {we'll start the game as soon as everyone understands the rules} {the audience returned to the auditorium after the concert's resumption was announced}. (3) Condition or assumption—for example, *if, though, unless, except, without,* and *once* {once we agree on a design, we can begin remodeling the house} {your thesis must be presented next week unless you have a good reason to postpone it} {I'll go on this business trip if I can fly first class}. (4) Reason or concession—for example, *as, inasmuch as, why, because, for, since, though, although,* and *albeit* {since you won't share the information, I can't help you} {Sir John decided to purchase the painting although it was very expensive} {she deserves credit because it was her idea}. (5) Purpose or result—for instance, *that, so that, in order that,* and *such that* {we dug up the yard so that a new water garden could be laid out} {he sang so loudly that he became hoarse}. (6) Place—such as *where* {I found a great restaurant where I didn't expect one to be}. (7) Manner—for example, *as if* and *as though* {he swaggers around the office as if he were an executive}. (8) Appositions—for instance, *and, or, what,* and *that* {the buffalo, or American bison, was once nearly extinct}. (9) Indirect questions—for instance, *whether, why,* and *when* {he could not say whether we were going the right way}.

5.202 *Adverbs as conjunctions.* Many adverbs are used as conjunctions to connect a dependent clause to an independent clause {Robin arrived after we had eaten dinner}. Such an adverb may appear to modify the verb in the clause it introduces, but its primary function is to connect the two clauses. Adverbs functioning as conjunctions typically denote time {Jay returned before we could find the vitamin E} or place {I know the river where the largest trout can be caught}.

5.203 *Relative pronouns as conjunctions.* In addition to its pronoun function, a relative pronoun serves a conjunctive function. In fact, relative pronouns may be treated as a special class of subordinating conjunctions when they join sentences. A conjunctive relative pronoun is one that has an antecedent in the independent clause {bring me the suitcase that is upstairs} (*that* refers to *suitcase*).

5.204 *Expletive conjunctions.* An expletive conjunction is a conjunction that connects two thoughts that are not expressed in the same sentence. The conjunction refers back to a preceding sentence and often, but not always, begins the sentence {but then the professor pointed out the flaws in their reasoning} {survival is thus the most important motivation}.

5.205 *Disguised conjunctions.* So-called disguised conjunctions are participles that have long been used as subordinating conjunctions; examples are *barring, considering, regarding, speaking, supposing,* and *provided.* Unlike a verb, a disguised conjunction does not have a subject {we traveled swiftly, considering the poor road conditions} (*considering* as a disguised conjunction), {the committee is considering a budget increase} (*considering* as a verb).

5.206 *Beginning a sentence with a conjunction.* There is a widespread belief—one with no historical or grammatical foundation—that it is an error to begin a sentence with a conjunction such as *and, but,* or *so.* In fact, a substantial percentage (often as many as 10 percent) of the sentences in first-rate writing begin with conjunctions. It has been so for centuries, and even the most conservative grammarians have followed this practice. Charles Allen Lloyd's 1938 words fairly sum up the situation as it stands even today:

> Next to the groundless notion that it is incorrect to end an English sentence with a preposition, perhaps the most wide-spread of the many false beliefs about the use of our language is the equally groundless notion that it is incorrect to begin one with "but" or "and." As in the case of the superstition about the prepositional

ending, no textbook supports it, but apparently about half of our teachers of English go out of their way to handicap their pupils by inculcating it. One cannot help wondering whether those who teach such a monstrous doctrine ever read any English themselves.[7]

Still, *but* as an adversative conjunction can occasionally be unclear at the beginning of a sentence. Evaluate the contrasting force of the *but* in question, and see whether the needed word is really *and*; if *and* can be substituted, then *but* is almost certainly the wrong word. Consider this example: *He went to school this morning. But he left his lunch box on the kitchen table.* Between those sentences is an elliptical idea, since the two actions are in no way contradictory. What is implied is something like this: *He went to school, intending to have lunch there, but he left his lunch behind.* Because *and* would have made sense in the passage as originally stated, *but* is not the right word—the idea for the contrastive *but* should be explicit. To sum up, then, *but* is a perfectly proper word to open a sentence, but only if the idea it introduces truly contrasts with what precedes. For that matter, *but* is often an effective word for introducing a paragraph that develops an idea contrary to the one preceding it.

5.207   *Beginning a sentence with "however."* *However* has been used as a conjunction since the fourteenth century. Like other conjunctions, it can be used at the beginning of a sentence. But *however* is more ponderous and has less impact than the simple *but*. *However* is more effectively used as an adverb within a sentence to emphasize the word or phrase that precedes it {The job seemed exciting at first. Soon, however, it turned out to be exceedingly dull.}.

Interjections

5.208   *Interjections defined.* An interjection or exclamation is a word, phrase, or clause that denotes strong feeling {Never again!} {You don't say!}. An interjection has little or no grammatical function in a sentence; it is used absolutely {Really, I can't understand why you put up with the situation.} {Oh no, how am I going to fix the damage?} {Hey, it's my turn next!}. It is frequently allowed to stand as a sentence by itself: {Oh! I've lost my wallet!} {Ouch! I think my ankle is sprained!} {Get out!} {Whoa!}. Introductory words like *well* and *why* may also act as interjections when they are meaningless utterances {Well, I tried my best.} {Why, I would never do that!}. The punc-

---

7. Charles Allen Lloyd, *We Who Speak English: And Our Ignorance of Our Mother Tongue* (New York: Thomas Y. Crowell, 1938), 19.

tuation offsetting the interjections distinguishes them (see 6.39, 6.37). Compare the different meanings of *Well, I didn't know him* with *I didn't know him well,* and *Why, here you are!* with *I have no idea why you are here* and *Why? I have no idea.*

5.209   *Interjections as informal and colloquial.* Interjections are natural in speech {your order should be shipped, oh, in eight to ten days} and frequently used in poetry and dialogue. But an interjection may impede the flow of some types of prose when an informal and colloquial tone is inappropriate {because our business case was, ahem, poorly presented, our budget will not be increased this year}.

5.210   *Interjections and functional variation.* Because interjections are usually grammatically independent of the rest of the sentence, most parts of speech may be used as interjections. A word that is classified as some other part of speech but used with the force of an interjection is called an exclamatory noun, exclamatory adjective, and so forth. Some examples are *Good!* (adjective); *Idiot!* (noun); *Help!* (verb); *Indeed!* (adverb); *Dear me!* (pronoun); *If only!* (conjunction); *How wonderful!* (adverb).

5.211   *Words that are exclusively interjections.* Some interjections are used only as such. Words like *ouch, whew, ugh, psst,* and *oops* are not used as any other parts of speech.

Parallel Structure

5.212   *Parallel structure generally.* Parallel constructions—series of like sentence elements—are common in good writing. Compound structures may link words {win, lose, or draw}, **phrases** {government of the people, by the people, for the people}, **dependent clauses** {that all men are created equal; that they are endowed by their creator with certain inalienable rights; that among these are life, liberty, and the pursuit of happiness}, **or sentences** {I came; I saw; I conquered}. Every element of a parallel series must be a functional match of the others (word, phrase, clause, sentence) and serve the same grammatical function in the sentence (e.g., noun, verb, adjective, adverb). When linked items are not like items, the syntax of the sentence breaks down:

> WRONG: She did volunteer work in the community kitchen, the homeless shelter, and taught free ESL classes offered by her church.
> RIGHT: She did volunteer work in the community kitchen and the homeless shelter, and taught free ESL classes offered by her church.

WRONG: The candidate is a former county judge, state senator, and served two terms as attorney general.
RIGHT: The candidate is a former county judge, state senator, and two-term attorney general.

The examples illustrate how the syntax breaks down when a series is not parallel. In the second one, for example, the subject, verb, and modifier (*The candidate is a former*) fit with the noun phrases *county judge* and *state senator*, but the third item in the series renders nonsense: "The candidate is a former served two terms as attorney general." The first two elements in the series are nouns, while the third is a separate predicate. The corrected version makes each item in the series a noun phrase.

5.213 *Prepositions and parallel structure.* In a parallel series of prepositional phrases, repeat the preposition with every element unless they all use the same preposition. A common error occurs when a writer lets two or more of the phrases share a single preposition but inserts a different one with another element:

WRONG: I looked for my lost keys in the sock drawer, the laundry hamper, the restroom, and under the bed.
RIGHT: I looked for my lost keys in the sock drawer, in the laundry hamper, in the restroom, and under the bed.

If the series had not included *under the bed*, the preposition could have been used once to apply to all the objects:

RIGHT: I looked for my lost keys in the sock drawer, the laundry hamper, and the restroom.

5.214 *Paired joining terms and parallel structure.* Correlative conjunctions such as *either–or*, *neither–nor*, *both–and*, and *not only–but also* and some adverb pairs such as *where–there*, *as–so*, and *if–then* must join grammatically parallel sentence elements. It is a common error to put the first correlative term in the wrong position.

WRONG: I'd like to either go into business for myself or else to write freelance travel articles.
RIGHT: I'd like either to go into business for myself or else to write freelance travel articles.
WRONG: Our guests not only ate all the turkey and dressing but both pumpkin pies, too.

RIGHT: Our guests ate not only all the turkey and dressing but both pumpkin pies, too.

The verb *ate*, when placed after the first correlative, grammatically attaches to *all the turkey* but not to *both pies, too*. When moved outside the two phrases containing its direct objects, it attaches to both.

5.215   *Auxiliary verbs and parallel structure.* If an auxiliary verb appears before a series of verb phrases, it must apply to all of them. A common error is to include one phrase that takes a different auxiliary verb:

WRONG: The proposed procedure would streamline the application process, speed up admission decisions, and has proved to save money when implemented by other schools.

RIGHT: The proposed procedure would streamline the application process, speed up admission decisions, and save money.

RIGHT: The proposed procedure would streamline the application process and speed up admission decisions. It has proved to save money when implemented by other schools.

The auxiliary verb *would* in that example renders the nonsensical *would has proved* when parsed with the third element of the predicate series. The first solution resolves that grammatical conflict, while the second breaks out the third element into a separate sentence—which also avoids shifting from future tense to past tense in midsentence.

Word Usage

Introduction

5.216   *Grammar versus usage.* The great mass of linguistic issues that writers and editors wrestle with don't really concern grammar at all—they concern usage: the collective habits of a language's native speakers. It is an arbitrary fact, but ultimately an important one, that *corollary* means one thing and *correlation* something else. And it seems to be an irresistible law of language that two words so similar in sound will inevitably be confounded by otherwise literate users of language. Some confusions, such as the one just cited, are relatively new. Others, such as *lay* versus *lie* and *infer* versus *imply*, are much older.

5.217 *Standard Written English.* In any age, careful users of language will make distinctions; careless users of language will blur them. The words someone uses and the way they go together tell us something about the education and background of that person. We know whether people speak educated English and write what is commonly referred to as Standard Written English.

5.218 *Dialect.* Of course, some writers and speakers prefer to use dialect, and use it to good effect. Will Rogers is a good example. He had power as a speaker of dialect, as when he said: "Liberty don't work near as good in practice as it does in speeches." And fiction writers often use dialect in dialogue. They may even decide to put the narrator's voice in dialect. Such decisions fall outside the scope of this manual.

5.219 *Focus on tradition.* In the short space of this section, only the basics of Standard Written English can be covered. Because no language stands still—because the standards of good usage change, however slowly—no guide could ever be written to the satisfaction of all professional editors. What is intended here is a guide that steers writers and editors toward the unimpeachable uses of language—hence it takes a fairly traditional view of usage. For the writer or editor of most prose intended for a general audience, the goal is to stay within the mainstream of literate language as it stands today.

Glossary of Problematic Words and Phrases

5.220 *Good usage versus common usage.* Although Chicago recommends *Merriam-Webster's Collegiate Dictionary*, there are several other first-rate American desktop dictionaries on the market. The best dictionary makers are signaled by the imprints Merriam-Webster, Webster's New World, American Heritage, Oxford University Press, and Random House. But one must use care and judgment in consulting *any* dictionary. The mere presence of a word in the dictionary's pages does not mean that the word is in all respects fit for print. The dictionary merely describes how speakers of English use the language; despite occasional usage notes, lexicographers generally disclaim any intent to guide writers and editors on the thorny points of English usage—apart from collecting evidence of what others do. So *infer* is recorded as meaning, in one of its senses, *imply; irregardless* may mean *regardless; restauranteur* may mean *restaurateur;* and on and on. That is why, in the publishing world, it is generally necessary to consult a style or usage guide in addition to a dictionary. While common usage can excuse many slipshod expressions, the standards of good usage make demands on writers and editors. Even so, good usage should make only *reasonable* demands without setting outlandishly high standards. The purpose of the following glossary is to set out the reasonable demands of good usage as it stands today.

a; an. Use the indefinite article *a* before any word beginning with a consonant sound {a utopian dream}. Use *an* before any word beginning with a vowel sound {an officer} {an honorary degree}. The word *historical* and its variations cause missteps, but since the h in these words is pronounced, it takes an *a* {an hour-long talk at a historical society}. Likewise, an initialism (whose letters are sounded out) may be paired with one article while an acronym (which is pronounced as a word) beginning with the same letter is paired with the other {an HTML website for a HUD program}. See 5.72.

ability; capability; capacity. *Ability* refers to a person's physical or mental skill or power to achieve something {the ability to ride a bicycle}. *Capability* refers more generally to power or ability {she has the capability to play soccer professionally} or to the quality of being able to use or be used in a certain way {a jet with long-distance-flight capability}. *Capacity* refers especially to a vessel's ability to hold or contain something {a high-capacity fuel tank}. Used figuratively, *capacity* refers to a person's physical or mental power to learn {an astounding capacity for mathematics}.

abjure; adjure. To *abjure* is to deny or renounce under oath {the defendant abjured the charge of murder} or to declare one's permanent abandonment of a place {abjure the realm}. To *adjure* is to require someone to do something as if under oath {I adjure you to keep this secret} or to urge earnestly {the executive committee adjured all the members to approve the plan}.

about; approximately. When idiomatically possible, use the adverb *about* instead of *approximately*. In the sciences, however, *approximately* is preferred {approximately thirty coding-sequence differences were identified}. Avoid coupling either word with other words of approximation, such as *guess* or *estimate*.

abstruse. See **obtuse**.

access, vb. The use of nouns as verbs has long been one of the most common ways that word-usage changes happen in English. Today, few people quibble with using *contact*, *debut*, and *host*, for example, as verbs. *Access* can be safely used as a verb when referring to computing {access a computer} {access the Internet} {access a database}. Outside the digital world, though, it is still best avoided.

accord; accordance. The first word means "agreement" {we are in accord on the treaty's meaning}; the second word means "conformity" {the book was printed in accordance with modern industry standards}.

accuse; charge. A person is *accused of* or *charged with* a misdeed. *Accused* is less formal than *charged* (which suggests official action). Compare *Jill accused Jack of eating her chocolate bar* with *Maynard was charged with theft*.

actual fact, in. Redundant. Try *actually* instead, or simply omit.

addicted; dependent. One is physically *addicted* to something but psychologically *dependent* on something.

adduce; deduce; induce. To *adduce* is to give as a reason, offer as a proof, or cite as an example {as evidence of reliability, she adduced her four years of steady volunteer work as a nurse's aide}. *Deduce* and *induce* are opposite processes. To *deduce* is to reason from general principles to specific conclusions, or to draw a specific conclusion from general bases {from these clues about who committed the crime, one deduces that the butler did it}. To *induce* is to form a general principle based on specific observations {after years of studying ravens, the researchers induced a few of their social habits}.

adequate; sufficient; enough. *Adequate* refers to the suitability of something in a particular circumstance {an adequate explanation}. *Sufficient* refers to an amount that is enough to meet a need (always with an abstract concept, a mass noun, or a plural) {sufficient water} {sufficient information} {sufficient cause} {sufficient resources}. *Enough*, the best word for everyday purposes, modifies both count nouns {enough people} and mass nouns {enough oil}.

adherence; adhesion. With a few exceptions, the first term is figurative, the second literal. Your *adherence* to the transportation code requires the *adhesion* of an inspection sticker to your windshield.

adjure. See **abjure**.

administrator. See **executor**.

admission; admittance. *Admission* is figurative, suggesting particularly the rights and privileges granted upon entry {the student won admission to a first-rate university}. *Admittance* is purely physical {no admittance beyond this point}.

adverse; averse. *Adverse* means either "strongly opposed" or "unfortunate" and typically refers to things, not people {adverse relations between nations} {an adverse wind blew the ship off course}. *Averse* means "feeling negatively about" and refers to people {averse to asking for directions}.

affect; effect. *Affect*, almost always a verb, means "to influence, have an effect on" {the adverse publicity affected the election}. (The noun *affect* has a specialized meaning in psychology: manifestation of emotion or mood. Consult your dictionary.) *Effect*, usually a noun, means "outcome, result" {the candidate's attempted explanations had no effect}. But it may also be a verb meaning "to make happen, produce" {the goal had been to effect a major change in campus politics}.

affirmative, in the; in the negative. These are slightly pompous ways of saying *yes* and *no*. They result in part because people are unsure how to punctuate *yes* and *no*. The ordinary way is this: *he said yes* (without quotation marks around *yes*, and without a capital); *she said no* (ditto).

afflict. See **inflict**.

affront. See **effrontery**.

after having [+ past participle]. Though common, this phrasing is redundant. Try instead *after* [+ present participle]: change *after having passed the audition, she*

... to *after passing the audition, she* ... Or this: *having passed the audition, she* ... See 5.108.

afterward, adv.; afterword, n. The first means "later"; the second means "an epilogue." On *afterward(s)*, see **toward**.

aged (four) years old. Redundant. Write *aged four years, four years old*, or *four years of age*.

aggravate. Traditionally, *aggravate* means "to intensify (something bad)" {aggravate an injury} {an aggravated crime}. If the sense is "to bother," use *annoy* or *irritate*.

aid; aide. *Aid* can be a verb (= to help) or a noun (= assistance or a means of assistance) {audiovisual aids}. *Aide* is a noun (= helper), as in "teacher's aide," and always denotes a person, not an object.

alibi. Avoid this as a synonym for *excuse*. The traditional sense is "the defense of having been elsewhere when a crime was committed."

all (of). Delete the *of* whenever possible {all the houses} {all my children}. The only common exceptions occur when *all of* precedes a nonpossessive pronoun {all of us} and when it precedes a genitive {all of North Carolina's players}.

alleged. Traditional usage applies this participial adjective to things, especially acts {alleged burglary}, not to the actors accused of doing them {alleged burglar}. That distinction is still observed by some publications, but it has largely been abandoned. Although *allegedly* /e-LEJ-ed-lee/ has four syllables, *alleged* has only two: /e-LEJD/.

all ready. See **already**.

all right. Two words. Avoid *alright*.

all together. See **altogether**.

allude; elude; illude. To *allude* is to refer to something indirectly {allude to a problem}. It's often loosely used where *refer* or *quote* would be better—that is, where there is a direct mention or quotation. To *elude* is to avoid capture {elude the hunters}. To *illude* (quite rare) is to deceive {your imagination might illude you}.

allusion; reference. An *allusion* is an indirect or casual mention or suggestion of something {the cockroach in this story is an allusion to Kafka}. A *reference* is a direct or formal mention {the references in this scholarly article have been meticulously documented}.

alongside. This term, meaning "at the side of," should not be followed by *of*.

a lot. Two words, not one.

already; all ready. The first refers to time {the movie has already started}; the second refers to degree of preparation {Are the actors all ready?}.

alright. See **all right**.

altar, n.; alter, vb. An *altar* is a table or similar object used for sacramental purposes. To *alter* is to change.

alternate, adj. & n.; alternative, adj. & n. *Alternate* implies (1) substitute for another {we took the alternate route} or (2) taking turns with another {her alternate chaired the meeting}. *Alternative* implies a choice between two or more things {I prefer the second alternative}.

altogether; all together. *Altogether* means "wholly" or "entirely" {that story is altogether false}. *All together* refers to a unity of time or place {the family will be all together at Thanksgiving}.

amend; emend. The first is the general term, meaning "to change or add to" {the city amended its charter to abolish at-large council districts}. The second means "to correct [text]" {for the second printing, the author emended several typos}. The noun corresponding to *amend* is *amendment*; the one corresponding to *emend* is *emendation*.

amiable; amicable. Both mean "friendly," but *amiable* refers to people {an amiable waiter} and *amicable* to relationships {an amicable divorce}.

amid. See **between.**

among. See **between.**

amount; number. *Amount* is used with mass nouns {a decrease in the amount of pollution}, *number* with count nouns {a growing number of dissidents}.

an. See *a.*

and. Popular belief to the contrary, this conjunction usefully begins sentences, typically outperforming *moreover, additionally, in addition, further,* and *furthermore.* See 5.206.

and/or. Avoid this Janus-faced term. It can often be replaced by *and* or *or* with no loss in meaning. Where it seems needed {take a sleeping pill and/or a warm drink}, try *or . . . or both* {take a sleeping pill or a warm drink or both}. But think of other possibilities {take a sleeping pill with a warm drink}.[8]

anecdotal. This adjective corresponds to *anecdote,* but in one sense the words have opposite connotations. An anecdote is a story that is thought (but not known) to be true. But *anecdotal evidence* is suspect because it has not been objectively verified.

anticipate. Avoid this word as a loose synonym for *expect.* Strictly, it means "to foresee, take care of in advance, or forestall."

anxious. Avoid it as a synonym for *eager.* The standard sense is "worried, distressed."

anyone; any one. The one-word *anyone* is a singular indefinite pronoun {anyone would know that}. The two-word phrase *any one* is a more emphatic form of *any,* referring to a single person or thing in a group {Do you recognize any one of those boys?} {I don't know any one of those stories}.

anyplace. See **anywhere.**

anywhere; any place. The first is preferred for an indefinite location {my keys could be anywhere}. But *any place* (two words) is narrower when you mean "any location" {they couldn't find any place to sit down and rest}. Avoid the one-word *anyplace.*

appertain. See **pertain.**

---

8. See Bryan A. Garner, *Legal Writing in Plain English* (Chicago: University of Chicago Press, 2001), 112–13.

appraise; apprise. To *appraise* is to put a value on something {the jeweler appraised the necklace}. To *apprise* is to inform or notify someone {keep me apprised of any developments}.

appreciate. Three senses: (1) to understand fully; (2) to increase in value; (3) to be grateful for (something). Sense 3 often results in verbose constructions; instead of *I would appreciate it if you would let me know*, use *I would appreciate your letting me know* or, more simply, *please let me know*.

apprise. See **appraise**.

approve; endorse. *Approve* implies positive thought or a positive attitude rather than action apart from consent. *Endorse* implies both a positive attitude and active support.

approve (of). *Approve* alone connotes official sanction {the finance committee approved the proposed budget}. *Approve of* suggests favor {she approved of her sister's new hairstyle}.

approximately. See **about**.

apt; likely. Both mean "fit, suitable," but *apt* is used for general tendencies or habits {the quarterback is apt to drop the football}. *Likely* expresses probability {because he didn't study, it's likely that he'll do poorly on the exam}. Although *likely* is traditional as a synonym of *probable*, many writers and editors object to its use as a synonym of *probably*.

area. Often a nearly meaningless filler word, as in *the area of partnering skills*. Try deleting *the area of*. In the sciences, however, its more literal meaning is often important and should be retained.

as far as. Avoid the nonstandard substitution of *as far as* for *as for*—that is, avoid using *as far as* without the completing verb *is concerned* or *goes*. Even with the verb, though, this is usually a wordy construction. Compare *as far as change is concerned, it's welcome* with *as for change, it's welcome*.

as is. In reference to an acquisition, *as is* is framed in quotation marks and refers to the acceptance of something without guarantees or representations of quality {purchased "as is"}. The phrase *on an "as is" basis* is verbose.

as of yet. See **as yet**.

as per. This phrase, though common in the commercial world, has long been considered nonstandard. Instead of *as per your request*, write *as you requested* or (less good) *per your request*.

assault; battery. These are popularly given the same meaning. But in law *assault* refers to a threat that causes someone to reasonably fear physical violence, and *battery* refers to a violent or repugnant intentional physical contact with another person. An assault doesn't involve touching; a battery does.

assemblage; assembly. An *assemblage* is an informal collection of people or things. An *assembly* is a group of people organized for a purpose.

assent; consent. The meanings are similar, but *assent* connotes enthusiasm, while *consent* connotes mere allowance.

as such. This pronominal phrase is now often loosely used as a synonym for *therefore*, but in well-honed writing the *such* always requires an antecedent {diamond-studded water bottles are a luxury and, as such, have a limited market}.

assumption; presumption. An *assumption* is not drawn from evidence; typically, it is a hypothesis {your assumption can be tested by looking at the public records}. A *presumption* implies a basis in evidence; if uncontradicted, a *presumption* may support a decision {the legal presumption of innocence}.

assure. See *ensure*.

as to. This two-word preposition is best used only to begin a sentence that could begin with *on the question of* or *with regard to* {as to those checks, she didn't know where they came from}. Otherwise, use *about* or some other preposition.

as yet; as of yet. Stilted and redundant. Use *yet*, *still*, *so far*, or some other equivalent.

attain; obtain. To *attain* something is to accomplish it through effort (e.g., a goal) or endurance (e.g., an age); to *obtain* something is to gain possession of it. So in best usage you *attain* a degree and *obtain* a diploma. It can be a fine distinction, and in common usage the words are often treated as synonyms.

at the present time; at this time; at present. These are turgid substitutes for *now*, *today*, *currently*, or even *nowadays* (a word of perfectly good literary standing). Of the phrasal versions, *at present* is least suggestive of bureaucratese.

at the time that; at the time when. Use the plain and simple *when* instead.

auger; augur. The spellings of these words can be tricky because they are pronounced the same (/AW-ger/). The tool for boring is an *auger*. *Augur* means "a seer" (noun) or "to foretell" (verb).

avenge, vb.; revenge, vb. & n. *Avenge* connotes an exaction for a wrong {historically, family grudges were privately avenged}. The corresponding noun is *vengeance*. *Revenge* connotes the infliction of harm on another out of anger or resentment {the team is determined to revenge its humiliating loss in last year's championship game}. *Revenge* is much more commonly a noun {they didn't want justice—they wanted revenge}.

averse. See *adverse*.

avocation; vocation. An *avocation* is a hobby {stamp collecting is my weekend avocation}. A *vocation* is one's profession or, especially in a religious sense, one's calling {she had a true vocation and became a nun}.

awhile; a while. The one-word version is adverbial {let's stop here awhile}. The two-word version is a noun phrase that follows the preposition *for* or *in* {she worked for a while before beginning graduate studies}.

backward(s). See *toward*.

bale; bail. *Bale*, a noun or verb, means "a bundle" or "to form into a bundle," as of hay or cotton. *Bail* is most often a verb (= to drain by scooping, as in getting water out of a boat using a pail); it is also a noun or verb meaning "security" or "to post security" (to get out of jail pending further proceedings). *Bail* is used informally as well to mean "to leave quickly" or "to escape" {the couple bailed from the party}.

based on. This phrase has two legitimate and two illegitimate uses. It may unimpeachably have verbal force (*base* being a transitive verb, as in *they based their position on military precedent*) or, in a passive sense, adjectival force (*based* being read as a past-participial adjective, as in *a sophisticated thriller based on a John le Carré novel*). Two uses, however, are traditionally considered slipshod. *Based on* should not have adverbial force {rates are adjusted annually, based on the 91-day Treasury bill} or prepositional force (as a dangling participle) {based on this information, we decided to stay}. Try other constructions {rates are adjusted annually on the basis of the 91-day Treasury bill} {with this information, we decided to stay}.

basis. Much overworked, this word most properly means "foundation." It often appears in the phrase *on a . . . basis* or some similar construction. When possible, substitute adverbs (*personally*, not *on a personal basis*) or simply state the time (*daily*, not *on a daily basis*). The plural is *bases* {the legislative bases are complicated}.

battery. See **assault**.

begging the question. This phrase denotes a logical fallacy of assuming as true what has yet to be proved—or adducing as proof for some proposition something that's every bit as much in need of proof as the first proposition. For example, someone might try to "prove" the validity of a certain religion by quoting from that religion's holy text. But the phrase gets misused in many ways—as (erroneously) meaning "raising a question," "inviting an obvious question," "evading a question," and "ignoring a question."

behalf. *In behalf of* means "in the interest or for the benefit of" {the decision is in behalf of the patient}. *On behalf of* means "acting as agent or representative of" {on behalf of Mr. Scott, I would like to express heartfelt thanks}.

bemused. This word means "bewildered" or "distracted." It is not a synonym of "amused."

beneficence; benevolence. *Beneficence* is the attribute of being disposed to do or capable of doing good {the priest's beneficence was plainly evident}. It applies most often to people. *Benevolence* is the act of performing a good deed {the villagers thanked him for his benevolence}. The first term denotes a quality, the second conduct.

between; among; amid. *Between* indicates one-to-one relationships {between you and me}. *Among* indicates undefined or collective relationships {honor among thieves}. *Between* has long been recognized as being perfectly appropriate for more than two objects if multiple one-to-one relationships are understood from the context {trade between members of the European Union}. *Amid* is used with mass nouns {amid talk of war}, *among* with plurals of count nouns {among the children}. Avoid *amidst* and *amongst*.

bi-; semi-. Generally, *bi-* means "two" (*biweekly* means "every two weeks"), while *semi-* means "half" (*semiweekly* means "twice a week"). Because these prefixes are often confounded, writers should be explicit about the meaning.

biannual; semiannual; biennial. *Biannual* and *semiannual* both mean "twice a year" {these roses bloom biannually}. But *biennial* means "once every two years" or "every other year" {the state legislature meets biennially}. To avoid confusion, write *semiannual* instead of *biannual*, and consider writing *once every two years* instead of *biennial*.

billion; trillion. The meanings vary in different countries. In the United States, a *billion* is 1,000,000,000 (a thousand millions). A *trillion* is a thousand times that (a million millions). In French-speaking Canada, Germany, and many other non-English-speaking regions—according to a system that was also until recently preferred by Great Britain—a *billion* is a million millions; by extension, a *trillion* is a million million millions. Writers encountering these terms need to be aware of the historical and geographic distinctions. See also 9.8.

blatant; flagrant. An act that is *blatant* is plain for all to see {a blatant error}. One that is *flagrant* is done brazenly as well as openly {a flagrant insult}.

bombastic. A *bombastic* person is pompous in speech or writing. The word has nothing to do with temper.

born; borne. *Born* is used only as an adjective {a born ruler} or in the fixed passive-voice verb *to be born* {the child was born into poverty}. *Borne* is the past participle of *bear* {this donkey has borne many heavy loads} {she has borne three children}. It is also used to form compound terms in the sciences {foodborne} {vector-borne}.

breach, n. & vb.; breech, n. A *breach* is a gap in or violation of something {a breach of contract}. To *breach* is to break, break open, or break through {breach the castle walls}. *Breech* refers to the lower or back part of something, especially the buttocks {a breech birth} or a firearm {the rifle's breech}.

bring; take. The distinction may seem obvious, but the error is common. The simple question is, where is the action directed? If it's toward you, use *bring* {bring home the bacon}. If it's away from you, use *take* {take out the trash}. You *take* (not *bring*) your car to the mechanic.

but. Popular belief to the contrary, this conjunction usefully begins contrasting sentences, typically better than *however*. See 5.206.

by means of. Often verbose. Use *by* or *with* if either one suffices.

by reason of. Use *because* or *because of* unless *by reason of* is part of an established phrase {by reason of insanity}.

can; could. *Can* means "to be able to" and expresses certainty {I can be there in five minutes}. *Could* is better for a sense of uncertainty or a conditional statement {Could you stop at the cleaners today?} {if you send a deposit, we could hold your reservation}. See 5.143.

can; may. *Can* most traditionally applies to physical or mental ability {she can do calculations in her head} {the dog can leap over a six-foot fence}. In colloquial English, *can* also expresses a request for permission {Can I go to the movies?}, but this usage is not recommended in formal writing. *May* suggests possibility {the class may have a pop quiz tomorrow} or permission {you may borrow my car}. A denial of permission is properly phrased formally with *may not* {you may not borrow my credit card} or with *cannot* or *can't* {you can't use the computer tonight}. See 5.143, 5.146.

capability. See **ability**.

capacity. See **ability**.

capital; capitol. A *capital* is a seat of government (usually a city) {Austin is the capital of Texas}. A *capitol* is a building in which a legislature meets {the legislature opened its new session in the capitol today}.

carat; karat; caret. *Carat* measures the weight of a gemstone; *karat* measures the purity of gold. To remember the difference, think of "24K." *Caret* is a mark on a manuscript indicating where matter is to be inserted.

career; careen. The word *career*'s career as a verb meaning "to go full speed" may be about over. Its duties have been assumed by *careen* ("to tip to one side while moving"), even though nothing in that verb's definition denotes high speed. Still, careful writers recognize the distinction.

caret. See **carat**.

case. In its abstract sense, this word is often a sign of verbal inflation. For example, *in case* means *if*; *in most cases* means *usually*; *in every case* means *always*. The word is justifiably used in law (in which a *case* is a lawsuit or judicial opinion) and in medicine (in which the word refers to an instance of a disease or disorder).

cause célèbre. This word most strictly denotes a legal case, especially a prosecution, that draws great public interest. By extension it refers to a notorious person or event. It does not properly denote a person's pet cause.

censer; censor, n.; sensor. The correct spellings can be elusive. A *censer* is either a person who carries a container of burning incense or the container itself. A *censor* is a person who suppresses objectionable subject matter. A *sensor* is a mechanical or electronic detector.

censor, vb.; censure, vb. To *censor* is to review and cut out objectionable material—that is, to suppress {soldiers' letters are often censored in wartime}. To *censure* is to criticize strongly or disapprove, or to officially reprimand {the House of Representatives censured the president for the invasion} {In some countries the government *censors* the press. In the United States the press often *censures* the government.}.

center around. Although this illogical phrasing does have apologists, careful writers tend to use either *center on* or *revolve around*.

certainty; certitude. If you are absolutely sure about something, you display both *certainty* (firm conviction) and *certitude* (assurance of being certain). That fact you are sure about, however, is a *certainty* but not a *certitude*—the latter is a trait applied to people only.

chair; chairman; chairwoman; chairperson. *Chair* is widely regarded as the best gender-neutral choice. Since the mid-seventeenth century, *chair* has referred to an office of authority. See 5.221–30.

charge. See **accuse**.

childish; childlike. *Childlike* is used positively to connote innocence, mildness, and freshness {a childlike smile}. *Childish* is pejorative; it connotes immaturity and unreasonableness {childish ranting}.

circumstances. Both *in the circumstances* and *under the circumstances* are acceptable, but *under* is now much more common.

cite, n.; site. As a noun, *cite* is colloquial for *citation*, which refers to a source of information {a cite to *Encyclopaedia Britannica*}. A *site* is a place or location {building site} {grave site} {website}. Cf. **sight; site.**

citizen; subject. In a governmental sense, these are near-synonyms that should be distinguished. A *citizen* owes allegiance to a nation whose sovereignty is a collective function of the people {a citizen of Germany}. A *subject* owes allegiance to an individual sovereign {a subject of the queen}.

class. This word denotes a category or group of things {the class of woodwind instruments}, never one type {an oboe is a type of woodwind} or one kind of thing {a snare drum is one kind of percussion instrument}.

classic; classical. *Classic* means "important, authoritative" {*The Naked Night* is one of Bergman's classic films}. *Classical* applies to the traditional "classics" of literature, music, and such (and sometimes to specific periods and movements) {classical Greek} {a classical composer} or to the definitive or earliest-characterized form {classical EEC syndrome}.

clean; cleanse. Although various cleaning agents are called *cleansers*, *clean* displaced *cleanse* long ago in most of the word's literal senses. *Cleanse* retains the Old English root meaning "purify": its use today usually refers to spiritual purification.

cleave. This verb was originally two different words, and that difference is reflected in the opposite meanings that *cleave* has: (1) to cut apart {to cleave meat} and (2) to cling together {standing in the rain, his clothes cleaving to his body}. The conjugations are (1) *cleave, cleft* (or *clove*), *cloven*, and (2) *cleave, cleaved, cleaved*.

clench; clinch. *Clench* connotes a physical action {he clenched his hand into a fist}. *Clinch* generally has figurative uses {she clinched the victory with her final putt}.

climactic; climatic. *Climactic* is the adjective corresponding to *climax* {during the movie's climactic scene, the projector broke}. *Climatic* corresponds to *climate* {the climatic conditions of northern New Mexico}.

clinch. See **clench**.

close proximity, in. Redundant. Write either *close* or *in proximity*.

cohabit; cohabitate. *Cohabit* is the traditional verb. *Cohabitate*, a back-formation from *cohabitation*, is best avoided.

collaborate; corroborate. To *collaborate* means to cooperate on some undertaking; the participants are *collaborators*. To *corroborate* something means to back up its reliability with proof or evidence.

collegial; collegiate. *Collegial* answers to *colleague*; *collegiate* answers to *college*.

commendable; commendatory. What is done for a worthy cause is *commendable* {commendable dedication to helping the poor}. What expresses praise is *commendatory* {commendatory plaque}.

common; mutual. What is *common* is shared by two or more people {borne by different mothers but having a common father}. What is *mutual* is reciprocal or directly exchanged by and toward each other {mutual obligations}. Strictly, *friend in common* is better than *mutual friend* in reference to a third person who is a friend of two others.

commonweal; commonwealth. The *commonweal* is the public welfare. Traditionally, a commonwealth was a state established by public compact or by the consent of the people to promote the general good ("commonweal"), and where the people reserved supreme authority. In the United States, the word is synonymous with *state*, four of which are still called commonwealths: Kentucky, Massachusetts, Pennsylvania, and Virginia.

compare. To *compare with* is to discern both similarities and differences between things. To *compare to* is to note primarily similarities between things.

compelled; impelled. If you are *compelled* to do something, you have no choice in the matter {Nixon was compelled by the unanimous Supreme Court decision to turn over the tapes}. If you are *impelled* to do something, you may not like it, but you are convinced that it must be done {the voter disliked some candidates but was impelled by the income-tax issue to vote a straight party ticket}.

compendious; voluminous. These are not synonyms, as many apparently believe. *Compendious* means "concise, abridged." *Voluminous*, literally "occupying many volumes," most commonly means "vast" or "extremely lengthy."

complacent; complaisant; compliant. To be *complacent* is to be content with oneself and one's life—with the suggestion that one may be smug and unprepared for future trouble. To be *complaisant* is to be easygoing and eager to please. To be *compliant* is to be amenable to orders or to a regimen.

compliment; complement. A *compliment* is a flattering or praising remark {a compliment on your skill}. A *complement* is something that completes or brings to perfection {the lace tablecloth was a complement to the antique silver}. The words are also verbs: to *compliment* is to praise, while to *complement* is to supplement adequately or to complete.

comprise; compose. Use these with care. To *comprise* is "to be made up of, to include" {the whole comprises the parts}. To *compose* is "to make up, to form the substance of something" {the parts compose the whole}. The phrase *comprised of*, though increasingly common, is poor usage. Instead, use *composed of*, *consisting of*, or *made up of*.

concept; conception. Both words may refer to an abstract thought, but *conception* also means "the act of forming an abstract thought." Avoid using either word as a high-sounding equivalent of *idea*, *design*, *thought*, or *program*.

condole, vb.; console, vb. These are closely related but not identical. To *condole with* is to express sympathy to {community leaders condoled with the victims' families}. The corresponding noun is *condolence* {they expressed their condolences at the funeral}. To *console* is to comfort {the players consoled their humiliated coach}. The corresponding noun is *consolation* {their kind words were little consolation}.

confidant; confidante; confident. A *confidant* is a close companion, someone (male or female) you confide in. *Confidante* is a fading alternative spelling of *confidant* (used only in reference to a female confidant). *Confident* is the adjective meaning "having faith, being certain."

congruous; congruent. Both terms mean "in harmony, in agreement." The first is seen most often in its negative form, *incongruous*. The second is used in math to describe triangles that are identical in their angles as well as in the length of their sides; in psychology it refers to the consistency and appropriateness of a person's words and behavior.

connote; denote. To *connote* (in reference to language) is to convey an additional meaning, especially an emotive nuance {the new gerund *parenting* and all that it connotes}. To *denote* (again in reference to language) is to specify the literal meaning of something {the phrase "freezing point" denotes 32 degrees Fahrenheit or 0 degrees Celsius}. Both words have figurative uses {all the joy that parenthood connotes} {a smile may not denote happiness}.

consent. See *assent*.

consequent; subsequent. The first denotes causation; the second does not. A *consequent* event always happens after the event that caused it, as does a *subsequent* event. But a *subsequent* event is not necessarily a consequence of the first event.

consider. Add *as* only when you mean "to examine or discuss for [a particular purpose]" {handshaking considered as a means of spreading disease}. Otherwise, omit *as* {we consider him qualified}.

consist. There are two distinct phrases: *consist of* and *consist in*. The first applies to the physical components that make up a tangible thing {the computer-system package consists of software, the CPU, the monitor, and a printer}. The second refers to the essence of a thing, especially in abstract terms {moral government consists in rewarding the righteous and punishing the wicked}.

console. See *condole*.

contact, vb. If you mean *write* or *call* or *e-mail*, say so. But *contact* is undeniably a brief way of referring to communication without specifying the means.

contagious; infectious. A *contagious* disease spreads by direct contact with an infected person or animal {rabies is a contagious disease}. An *infectious* disease is spread by germs on a contaminated object or element, such as earth or water {tetanus is infectious but not contagious}. In nonliteral usage the terms are synonymous {his pessimism is contagious} {her smile is infectious}.

contemporary; contemporaneous. Both express coinciding time, but *contemporary* usually applies to people, and *contemporaneous* applies to things or actions. Because *contemporary* has the additional sense "modern," it is unsuitable for contexts involving multiple times. That is, a reference to *Roman, Byzantine, and contemporary belief systems* is ambiguous; change *contemporary* to *modern*.

contemptuous; contemptible. If you are *contemptuous* you are feeling contempt for someone or something. If you are *contemptible*, others will have that attitude toward you.

content; contents. *Content* applies to the information or ideas contained in a written or oral presentation {the lecture's content was offensive to some who were present}. *Contents* usually denotes physical ingredients {the package's contents were difficult to discern by x-ray}. If the usage suggests many items, material or nonmaterial, *contents* is correct {table of contents} {the investigative report's contents}.

continual; continuous. What is *continual* is intermittent or frequently repeated. What is *continuous* never stops—it remains constant or uninterrupted.

contravene; controvert. To *contravene* is to conflict with or violate {the higher speed limit contravenes our policy of encouraging fuel conservation}. To *controvert* is to challenge or contradict {the testimony controverts the witness's prior statement}.

convince. See **persuade**.

copyright, vb. The verb is conjugated *copyright–copyrighted–copyrighted*. Note the spelling, which has nothing to do with *write*. (*Copywriting* is a term used in marketing.)

corollary; correlation. A *corollary* is either (1) a subsidiary proposition that follows from a proven mathematical proposition, often without requiring additional evidence to support it, or (2) a natural or incidental result of some action or occurrence. A *correlation* is a positive connection between things or phenomena. If used in the context of physics or statistics, it denotes the degree to which the observed interactions and variances are not attributable to chance alone.

corporal; corporeal. What is *corporal* relates in some way to the body {corporal punishment}; what is *corporeal* has a body {not our spiritual but our corporeal existence}.

corps; core. A *corps* is a body of like workers {Marine Corps} {press corps} but is often misspelled like its homonym, *core*.

correlation. See **corollary**.

could. See **can**.

couldn't care less. This is the standard phrasing. Avoid the illogical form *could care less*.

councillor; counselor. A *councillor* is one who sits on a council {city councillor}. A *counselor* is a person who gives advice {personal counselor}.

couple of. Using *couple* as an adjective is poor phrasing. Add *of* {we watched a couple of movies}.

court-martial. This is two words joined by a hyphen, whether the phrase functions as a noun or as a verb. Because *martial* acts as an adjective meaning "military," the plural of the noun is *courts-martial*.

credible; credulous. *Credible* means "believable"; *credulous* means "gullible." The most common error involving cognate forms of these words is in the malapropism "strains credulity." If that cliché must be used, it should read "strains credibility."

crevice; crevasse. Size matters. A crack in the sidewalk is a *crevice* (accent on the first syllable); a fissure in a glacier or a dam is a *crevasse* (accent on the second syllable).

criminal. See **unlawful**.

criteria. This is the plural form of *criterion* ("a standard for judging"): one *criterion*, two *criteria*.

damp, vb.; dampen. Both words convey the sense "to moisten." *Damp* also means "to reduce with moisture" {damp the fire} or "to diminish vibration or oscillation of [a wire or voltage]" {damp the voltage}. In a figurative sense, *dampen* means "to depress, curtail" {dampen one's hopes}.

data. Though originally this word was a plural of *datum*, it is now commonly treated as a mass noun and coupled with a singular verb. In formal writing (and always in the sciences), use *data* as a plural.

deadly; deathly. *Deadly* means "capable of causing death" {deadly snake venom}. *Deathly* means "deathlike" {deathly silence}.

decide whether; decide if. See **determine whether**.

decimate. This word literally means "to kill every tenth person," a means of repression that goes back to Roman times. But the word has come to mean "to inflict heavy damage," and that use is accepted. Avoid *decimate* when (1) you are referring to complete destruction or (2) a percentage other than 10 percent is specified. That is, don't say that a city was "completely decimated," and don't say that some natural disaster "decimated 23 percent of the city's population."

deduce. See **adduce**.

defamation; libel; slander. *Defamation* is the communication of a falsehood that damages someone's reputation. If it is recorded, especially in writing, it is *libel*; otherwise it is *slander*.

definite; definitive. *Definite* means "clear, exact" {a definite yes}. *Definitive* means "conclusive, final, most authoritative" {a definitive treatise}.

delegate. See **relegate**.

deliberate; deliberative. As an adjective, *deliberate* means either "carefully thought out" {a deliberate response} or "slow and steady" {deliberate progress}. *Deliberative* means "of or characterized by debate"; the word most often applies to an assembly {deliberative body} or a process.

denote. See **connote**.

denounce; renounce. To *denounce* is either to criticize harshly or to accuse. To *renounce* is either to relinquish or to reject.

dependent. See **addicted**.

deprecate. In general, to *deprecate* is to disapprove. But in the phrase *self-deprecating*—which began as a mistaken form of *self-depreciating* but is now standard—the sense of *deprecate* is "to belittle." In the computer-software world, *deprecate* serves as a warning: a *deprecated* feature or function is one that will be phased out of future release of software, so users should quickly begin looking for alternatives.

derisive; derisory. What is *derisive* ridicules {derisive laughter}. What is *derisory* invites or deserves ridicule {that derisory "banana" hat}.

deserts; desserts. The first are deserved {your just deserts}, the second eaten {the many desserts on the menu}.

despite; in spite of. For brevity, prefer *despite*.

determine whether; determine if. The first phrasing is irreproachable style; the second is acceptable as a colloquialism. The same is true of *decide whether* versus *decide if*. See also **if; whether**.

different. The phrasing *different from* is generally preferable to *different than* {this company is different from that one}, but sometimes the adverbial phrase *differently than* is all but required {she described the scene differently than he did}.

differ from; differ with. *Differ from* is the usual construction denoting a contrast {the two species differ from each other in subtle ways}. *Differ with* regards differences of opinion {the state's senators differ with each other on many issues}.

disburse; disperse. To *disburse* is to distribute money. To *disperse* can be (1) to distribute other things or (2) to break up, as an unruly crowd.

disc. See **disk**.

discomfort; discomfit. *Discomfort* is a noun meaning "ill at ease." It can also be used as a verb meaning "to put ill at ease." But doing so often invites confusion with *discomfit*, which originally meant "to defeat utterly." Today it means "to thwart or confuse" {the ploy discomfited the opponent}. The distinction has become a fine one, since a *discomfited* person is also uncomfortable. *Discomfiture* is the corresponding noun.

discreet; discrete. *Discreet* means "circumspect, judicious" {a discreet silence}. *Discrete* means "separate, distinct, unconnected" {six discrete parts}.

discriminating, adj.; discriminatory. The word *discrimination* can be used in either a negative or a positive sense, and these adjectives reflect that ambivalence. *Discriminatory* means "reflecting a biased treatment" {discriminatory employment policy}. *Discriminating* means "analytical, discerning, tasteful" {a discriminating palate}.

disinterested. This word should be reserved for the sense "not having a financial personal interest at stake, impartial." Avoid it as a replacement for *uninterested* (which means "unconcerned, bored").

disk; disc. *Disk* is the usual spelling {floppy disk}. But *disc* is preferred in a few specialized applications {compact disc} {disc brakes} {disc harrow}.

disorganized; unorganized. Both mean "not organized," but *disorganized* suggests a group in disarray, either thrown into confusion or inherently unable to work together {the disorganized 1968 Democratic National Convention in Chicago}.

disperse. See **disburse**.

distinctive; distinguished; distinguishable. A *distinctive* feature is something that makes a person (or place or thing) easy to distinguish (pick out) from others. But it does not necessarily make that person *distinguished* (exalted) {the distinguished professor wears a distinctive red bow tie}. It does, however, make the person *distinguishable*, a term that does not carry the positive connotation of *distinguished*.

dive, vb. The preferred conjugation is *dive–dived–dived*. The form *dove*, though common in certain regions and possibly on the rise, has not traditionally been considered good form.

doctrinal; doctrinaire. *Doctrinal* means "of, relating to, or constituting a doctrine"; it is neutral in connotation {doctrinal differences}. *Doctrinaire* shares the pejorative sense of *dogmatic*, suggesting that the person described is stubborn and narrow-minded {a doctrinaire ideologue}.

doubtless, adv. Use this form—not *doubtlessly*.

doubt that; doubt whether; doubt if. *Doubt that* conveys a negative sense of skepticism or questioning {I doubt that you'll ever get your money back}. *Doubt whether* also conveys a sense of skepticism {the official says that he doubts whether the company could survive}. *Doubt if* is a casual phrasing for *doubt that*.

drag. Conjugated *drag–dragged–dragged*. The past form *drug* is dialectal.

dream. Either *dreamed* (more typical in American English) or *dreamt* (more typical in British English) is acceptable for the past-tense and past-participial forms.

drink, vb. Correctly conjugated *drink–drank–drunk* {they had not drunk any fruit juice that day}.

drown, vb. Conjugated *drown–drowned–drowned*.

drunk, adj.; drunken. *Drunk* describes a current state of intoxication {drunk driver}. (By contrast, a *drunk*—like a *drunkard*—is someone who is habitually intoxicated.) *Drunken* describes either a trait of habitual intoxication {drunken sot} or intoxicated people's behavior {a drunken brawl}.

due to. In strict traditional usage, *due to* should be interchangeable with *attributable to* {the erratic driving was due to some prescription drugs that the driver had taken}. When used adverbially, *due to* is often considered inferior to *because of* or *owing to*. So in the sentence *due to the parents' negligence, the entire family suffered*, the better phrasing would be *because of* [or *owing to*] *the parents' negligence, the entire family suffered*.

due to the fact that. Use *because* instead.

dumb. This word means either "stupid" or "unable to speak." In the second sense, *mute* is clearer for most modern readers.

dying; dyeing. *Dying* is the present participle of *die* ("to cease living"); *dyeing* is the present participle of *dye* ("to color with a liquid").

each other; one another. Traditionalists use *each other* when two things or people are involved, *one another* when more than two are involved.

eatable. See **edible**.

economic; economical. *Economic* means "of or relating to large-scale finances" {federal economic policy}. *Economical* means "thrifty; financially efficient" {an economical purchase}.

edible; eatable. What is *edible* is fit for human consumption {edible flowers}. What is *eatable* is at least minimally palatable {the cake is slightly burned but still eatable}.

effect. See **affect**.

effete. Traditionally, it has meant "decadent, worn out, sterile." Today it is often used to mean either "snobbish" or "effeminate." Because of its ambiguity, the word is best avoided altogether.

effrontery; affront. *Effrontery* is an act of shameless impudence or audacity. An *affront* is a deliberate insult.

e.g. See **i.e.**

elemental; elementary. Something that is *elemental* is an essential constituent {elemental ingredients} or a power of nature {elemental force}. Something that is *elementary* is basic, introductory, or easy {an elementary math problem}.

elicit; illicit. *Elicit* ("to draw out [an answer, information, etc.]") is a verb {to elicit responses}; *illicit* ("illegal") is an adjective {an illicit scheme}. Writers often mistakenly use *illicit* when they mean *elicit*.

elude. See **allude**.

emend. See **amend**.

emigrate. See **immigrate**.

empathy; sympathy. *Empathy* is putting oneself in someone else's shoes to understand that person's situation. *Sympathy* is compassion and sorrow one feels for another.

endemic. See **epidemic**.

endorse. See **approve**.

enervate; innervate. These words are antonyms. To *enervate* is to weaken or drain of energy. To *innervate* is to stimulate or provide with energy.

enormity; enormousness. *Enormity* means "monstrousness, moral outrageousness, atrociousness" {the enormity of the Khmer Rouge's killings}. *Enormousness* means "abnormally great size" {the enormousness of Alaska}.

enough. See **adequate**.

ensure; insure; assure. *Ensure* is the general term meaning to make sure something will (or won't) happen. In best usage, *insure* is reserved for underwriting financial risk. So we *ensure* that we can get time off for a vacation and *insure* our car against an accident on the trip. We *ensure* events and *insure* things. But we *assure* people that their concerns are being addressed.

enthused, adj. Use *enthusiastic* instead.

enumerable; innumerable. What's *enumerable* is countable. What's *innumerable* can't be counted, at least not practically {innumerable stars in the sky}.

envy. See **jealousy**.

epidemic; endemic; pandemic. An *epidemic* disease breaks out, spreads through a limited area (such as a state), and then subsides {an epidemic outbreak of measles}. (The word is frequently used as a noun {a measles epidemic}.) An *endemic* disease is perennially present within a region or population {malaria is endemic in parts of Africa}. (Note that *endemic* describes a disease and not a region: it is incorrect to say *this region is endemic for* [a disease].) A *pandemic* disease is prevalent over a large area, such as a nation or continent, or the entire world {the 1918-19 flu pandemic}.

equally as. This is typically faulty phrasing. Delete *as*.

et al. This is the abbreviated form of *et alii* ("and others")—the *others* being people, not things. Since *al.* is an abbreviation, the period is required. Cf. **etc.**

etc. This is the abbreviated form of *et cetera* ("and other things"); it should never be used in reference to people. *Etc.* implies that a list of things is too extensive to recite (and indeed it should be used only after at least two items, never just one). But often writers seem to run out of thoughts and tack on *etc.* for no real purpose. Also, two redundancies often appear with this abbreviation: (1) *and etc.*, which is poor style because *et* means "and," and (2) *etc.* at the end of a list that begins with *e.g.*, which properly introduces a short list of examples. Cf. **et al.**; see also 6.20.

event. The phrase *in the event that* is a long and formal way of saying *if*.

eventuality. This term often needlessly displaces more specific everyday words such as *event, result,* and *possibility*.

every day, adv.; everyday, adj. The first is adverbial, the second adjectival. One may wear one's *everyday* clothes *every day*.

every one; everyone. The two-word version is an emphatic way of saying "each" {every one of them was there}; the second is a pronoun equivalent to *everybody* {everyone was there}.

evoke; invoke. To *evoke* something is to bring it out {evoke laughter} or bring to mind {evoke childhood memories}. *Invoke* has a number of senses, including to assert (something) as authority {invoke martial law}, to appeal (to someone or a higher power) for help {invoke an ally to intervene}, or to conjure up {invoke spirits of the past}.

exceptional; exceptionable. What is *exceptional* is uncommon, superior, rare, or extraordinary {an exceptional talent}. What is *exceptionable* is objectionable or offensive {an exceptionable slur}.

executor; administrator. In a will, a person designates an *executor* to distribute the estate after death. When a person dies without a will or without specifying an executor, the court will appoint an *administrator* to do the same. The feminine forms *administratrix* and *executrix* are unnecessary and should be avoided.

explicit; implicit. If something is *explicit* it is deliberately spelled out, as in the writing of a contract or the text of a statute. If it is *implicit* it is not specifically stated but either is suggested in the wording or is necessary to effectuate the purpose. Avoid *implicit* to mean "complete, unmitigated."

fact that, the. This much-maligned phrase is not always avoidable. But hunt for a substitute before deciding to use it. Sometimes *that* alone suffices.

farther; further. The traditional distinction is to use *farther* for a physical distance {we drove farther north to see the autumn foliage} and *further* for a figurative distance {let's examine this further} {look no further}.

fax, n. & vb. Derived from *facsimile transmission*, the foreshortened *fax* is almost universally preferred for convenience. The plural is *faxes*. Note that the word is governed by the same rules of capitalization as other common nouns. FAX is incorrect: the word is not an acronym.

faze; phase, vb. To *faze* is to disturb or disconcert {Jones isn't fazed by insults}. To *phase* (usually *phase in* or *phase out*) is to schedule or perform a plan, task, or the like in stages {phase in new procedures} {phase out the product lines that don't sell}.

feel. This verb is weak when used as a substitute for *think* or *believe*.

feel bad. Invariably, the needed phrase is *feel bad* (not *badly*). See 5.167.

fewer. See **less**.

fictional; fictitious; fictive. *Fictional* (from *fiction* as a literary genre) means "of, relating to, or characteristic of imagination" {a fictional story}. *Fictitious* means "imaginary; counterfeit; false" {a fictitious name}. *Fictive* means "possessing the talent for imaginative creation" {fictive gift}; it can also be a synonym for *fictional* but in that sense is a needless variant. Also, anthropologists apply *fictive* to relationships in which people are treated as family members despite having no bond of blood or marriage {fictive kin}.

finalize. Meaning "to make final or bring to an end," this word has often been associated with inflated jargon. Although its compactness may recommend it in some contexts, use *finish* when possible.

first. In enumerations, use *first, second, third,* and so on. Avoid the *-ly* forms.

fit. This verb is undergoing a shift. It has traditionally been conjugated *fit–fitted–fitted*, but today *fit–fit–fit* is prevalent in American English {when she tried on the dress, it fit quite well}. In the passive voice, however, *fitted* is still normal {the horse was fitted with a new harness}.

flair. See **flare**.

flammable; inflammable. *Flammable* was invented as an alternative to the synonymous word *inflammable*, which some people misunderstood—dangerously—as meaning "not combustible." Today *flammable* is the standard term.

flare; flair. A *flare* is an unsteady and glaring light {an emergency flare} or a sudden outburst {a flare-up of fighting}. A *flair* is an outstanding talent {a flair for mathematics} or originality and stylishness {performed with flair}.

flaunt; flout. *Flaunt,* meaning "to show off ostentatiously" {they flaunted their wealth}, should not be confused with *flout,* meaning "to treat with disdain or contempt" {flouting the rules}.

flounder; founder. Keep the figurative meanings of these terms straight by remembering their literal meanings. To *flounder* is to struggle awkwardly, as though walking through deep mud {the professor glared while the unprepared student floundered around for an answer}. To *founder* is to sink or fall to the ground {without any editorial expertise, the publisher soon foundered}.

following. Avoid this word as an equivalent of *after.* Consider: *Following the presentation, there was a question-and-answer session. After* is both simpler and clearer. But *following* is unobjectionable in meaning "next" {the following example illustrates the point}.

forbear, vb.; forebear, n. The terms are unrelated, but the spellings are frequently confused. To *forbear* is to refrain {he wanted to speak but decided to forbear}. (The conjugation is *forbear–forbore–forborne.*) A *forebear* is an ancestor {the house was built by Murray's distant forebears}.

forego; forgo. To *forego* is to go before {the foregoing paragraph}. (The word appears most commonly in the phrase *foregone conclusion.*) To *forgo,* by contrast, is to do without or renounce {they decided to forgo that opportunity}.

foreword; preface. A *foreword* (not *forward*) is a brief essay of endorsement that is written by someone other than the book's author. An introductory essay about the book written by the book's author is called a *preface* and is usually shorter and more personal than the book's introduction, which gives an overview of the book's content. See 1.39, 1.40, 1.42, 1.46.

forgo. See *forego*.

former; latter. In the best usage, these words apply only to pairs. The *former* is the first of two, the *latter* the second of two.

fortuitous; fortunate. *Fortuitous* means "by chance," whether the fortune is good or bad {the rotten tree could have fallen at any time; it was just fortuitous that the victims drove by when they did}. *Fortunate* means "by good fortune" {we were fortunate to win the raffle}.

forward(s). See *toward*.

founder. See *flounder*.

fulsome, adj. This word does not preferably mean "very full" but "too much, excessive to the point of being repulsive." Its slipshod use arises most often in the phrase *fulsome praise,* which suggests the opposite of what the writer probably intends.

further. See *farther*.

future, in the near. Use *soon* or *shortly* instead.

gantlet; gauntlet. See **run the gantlet**.

gentleman. This word is a vulgarism when used as a synonym for *man* {two gentlemen were in the car} (better to use *men* there). When used in reference to a cultured, refined man, it is susceptible to some of the same objections as those leveled against *lady*. Use it cautiously. Cf. **lady**.

get. Though shunned by many writers as too casual, *get* often sounds more natural than *obtain* or *procure* {get a job}. It can also substitute for a stuffy *be-*

come {get hurt}. The verb is conjugated *get–got–gotten* in American English, *get–got–got* in British English.

gibe, n.; jibe, vb. A *gibe* is a biting insult or taunt; *gibes* are figuratively thrown at their target {the angry crowd hurled gibes as the suspect was led into the court-house}. *Jibe* means to fit, usually with negation {the verdict didn't jibe with the judge's own view of the facts}.

gild. See **guild**.

go. This verb is conjugated *go–went–gone*. *Went* appears as a past participle only in dialect.

gourmet; gourmand. Both are aficionados of good food and drink. But a *gourmet* knows and appreciates the fine points of food and drink, whereas a *gourmand* is a glutton.

grateful; gratified. To be *grateful* is to be thankful or appreciative. To be *gratified* is to be pleased, satisfied, or indulged.

grisly; grizzly. What is *grisly* is gruesome or horrible {grisly details}. What is *grizzly* is grayish {grizzly hair} or bearish {the North American grizzly bear}.

guild, n.; gild, vb. A *guild* is an organization of persons with a common interest or profession {a guild of fine carpenters}. To *gild* is to put a thin layer of gold on something {gild a picture frame}.

half (of). Delete the *of* whenever possible {half the furniture}.

handful. If *handful* applies to a mass noun, use a singular verb {a handful of trouble is ahead}. But if *handful* applies to a plural count noun, use a plural verb {there are only a handful of walnut trees lining Main Street}.

hangar; hanger. One finds *hangars* at an airport {airplane hangars}. Everywhere else, one finds *hangers* {clothes hangers} {picture hangers}.

hanged; hung. *Hanged* is used as the past participle of *hang* only in its transitive form when referring to the killing (just or unjust) of a human being by suspending the person by the neck {criminals were hanged at Tyburn Hill}. But if death is not intended or likely, or if the person is suspended by a body part other than the neck, *hung* is correct {he was hung upside down as a cruel prank}. In most senses, of course, *hung* is the past form of *hang* {Mark hung up his clothes}. All inanimate objects, such as pictures and Christmas stockings, are hung.

hanger. See **hangar**.

harass; embarrass. The first word has one *-r-*; the second has two. The pronunciation of *harass* also causes confusion. The dominant American pronunciation stresses the second syllable, while British English stresses the first.

harebrained. So spelled (after the timid, easily startled animal)—not *hairbrained*.

healthy; healthful. Traditionally, a living thing that is *healthy* enjoys good health; something that is *healthful* promotes health {a healthful diet will keep you healthy}. But gradually *healthy* is taking over both senses.

help (to). Omit the *to* when possible {talking will help resolve the problem}.

he or she. To avoid sexist language, many writers use this alternative phrasing (in place of the generic *he*). Use it sparingly—preferably after exhausting all the less obtrusive methods of achieving gender neutrality. In any event, *he or she* is much preferable to *he/she*, *s/he*, *(s)he*, and the like. See also 5.46.

historic; historical. The shorter word refers to what is momentous in history {January 16, 1991, was a historic day in Kuwait}. *Historical*, meanwhile, refers simply to anything that pertains to or occurred in history.

hoard; horde. A *hoard* is a supply, usually secret and often valuable. *Hoard* is also a verb meaning "to amass" such a cache. A *horde* was originally a tribe of Asian nomads; today a *horde* is a large crowd.

hoi polloi. The *hoi polloi* are the common people, not the elite. This term is a plural. Although *hoi* is Greek for "the," the phrase is commonly rendered "the hoi polloi" and has been at least since it was used by John Dryden in 1668.

holocaust. When capitalized, this word refers to the Nazi genocide of European Jews in World War II. When not capitalized, it refers (literally or figuratively) to extensive devastation caused by fire, or to the systematic and malicious killings of human beings on a vast scale.

home in. This phrase is frequently misrendered *hone in*. (*Hone* means "to sharpen.") *Home in* refers to what homing pigeons do; the meaning is "to come closer and closer to a target."

homicide. See **murder**.

hopefully. The old meaning of the word ("in a hopeful manner") seems unsustainable; the newer meaning ("I hope" or "it is to be hoped") seems here to stay. But many careful writers deplore the new meaning.

horde. See **hoard**.

hung. See **hanged**.

I; me. When you need the first-person singular, use it. It's not immodest to use it; it's superstitious not to.

idyllic. An *idyll* is a short pastoral poem, and by extension *idyllic* means charming or picturesque. It is not synonymous with *ideal* (perfect).

i.e.; e.g. The first is the abbreviation for *id est* ("that is"); the second is the abbreviation for *exempli gratia* ("for example"). The English equivalents are preferable in formal prose; Chicago style is to use these two-character abbreviations only within parentheses or in notes. Always put a comma after either of them.

if; whether. While *if* is conditional, *whether* introduces an alternative, often in the context of an indirect question. Use *whether* in two circumstances: (1) to introduce a noun clause {he asked whether his tie was straight} (the answer is either *yes* or *no*), and (2) when using *if* would produce ambiguity. In the sentence *He asked if his tie was straight*, the literal meaning is "whenever his tie was straight, he asked"; the popular meaning "he wanted someone to tell him whether his tie needed straightening" may not be understood by all readers. More tellingly, *call me to let me know if you can come* means that you should call only if you're coming; *call to let me know whether you can come* means that you should call regardless of your answer. Avoid substituting *if* for *whether* unless your tone is intentionally informal or you are quoting someone. See also *determine whether*.

illegal. See **unlawful**.

illegible; unreadable. Handwriting or printing that is *illegible* is not clear enough to be read {illegible scrawls}. Writing that is *unreadable* is so poorly composed as to be either incomprehensible or intolerably dull.

illicit. See **elicit**; **unlawful**.

illude. See **allude**.

immigrate; emigrate. To *immigrate* is to enter a country to live, leaving a past home. To *emigrate* is to leave one country to live in another one. The cognate forms also demand attention. Someone who moves from Ireland to the United States is an *immigrant* here and an *emigrant* there. An *emigré* is also an *emigrant*, but especially one in political exile.

impact. Resist using this word as a verb. Try *affect* or *influence* instead. Besides being hyperbolic, *impact* used as a verb is widely considered a solecism (though it is gaining ground).

impeachment. *Impeachment* is the legislative equivalent of an indictment, not a conviction. In the US federal system, the House of Representatives votes on impeachment and the Senate votes on removal from office.

impelled. See **compelled**.

implicit. See **explicit**.

imply; infer. The writer or speaker *implies* (hints, suggests); the reader or listener *infers* (deduces). Writers and speakers often use *infer* as if it were synonymous with *imply*, but careful writers always distinguish between the two words.

in actual fact. See **actual fact, in**.

inasmuch as. *Because* or *since* is almost always a better choice.

in behalf of. See **behalf**.

in connection with. This is a vague, fuzzy phrase {she explained the financial consequences in connection with the transaction} {a liking for everything in connection with golf} {Phipson was compensated in connection with its report}. Try replacing the phrase with *of*, *related to*, or *associated with* {she explained the financial consequences of the transaction}, *about* {a liking for everything about golf}, or *for* {Phipson was compensated for its report}.

incredible; incredulous. *Incredible* properly means "unbelievable." Colloquially, it is used to mean "astonishing (in a good way)" {it was an incredible trip}. *Incredulous* means "disbelieving, skeptical" {people are incredulous about the rising gas costs}.

inculcate; indoctrinate. One *inculcates* values *into* a child but *indoctrinates* the child *with* values. That is, *inculcate* always takes the preposition *into* and a value or values as its object {inculcate courage into soldiers}. *Indoctrinate* takes a person as its object {indoctrinate children with the habit of telling the truth}.

indicate. Often vague. When possible, use a more direct verb such as *state*, *comment*, *show*, *suggest*, or *say*.

individual. Use this word to distinguish a single person from a group. When possible, use *person* or a more specific term such as *adult, child, man,* or *woman*.

indoctrinate. See **inculcate**.

induce. See **adduce**.

in excess of. Try replacing this verbose phrase with *more than* or *over*.

infectious. See **contagious**.

infer. See **imply**.

inference. Use the verb *draw*, not *make*, with *inference* {they drew the wrong inferences}. Otherwise, readers may confuse *inference* with *implication*.

inflammable. See **flammable**.

inflict; afflict. Events, illnesses, punishments, and the like are *inflicted on* living things or entities {an abuser inflicts cruelty}. The sufferers are *afflicted with* or *by* disease or troubles {agricultural communities afflicted with drought}.

ingenious; ingenuous. These words are similar in form but not in meaning. *Ingenious* describes what is intelligent, clever, and original {an ingenious invention}. *Ingenuous* describes what is candid, naive, and without dissimulation {a hurtful but ingenuous observation}.

innate; inherent. An *innate* characteristic is one that a living thing has from birth; it should be distinguished, then, from a talent or disposition that one acquires from training or experience. An *inherent* characteristic is also part of a thing's nature, but life is not implied; a rock, for example, has an inherent hardness.

innervate. See **enervate**.

innocent; not guilty. If you are *innocent*, you are without blame. If you are *not guilty*, you have been exonerated by a jury. Newspapers avoid the "not guilty" phrase, though, because the consequences of accidentally leaving off the "not" could be serious.

innumerable. See **enumerable**.

in order to; in order for. Often these expressions can be reduced to *to* and *for*. When that is so, and rhythm and euphony are preserved or even heightened, use *to* or *for*.

in proximity. See **close proximity, in**.

in regard to. This is the phrase, not *in regards to*. Try a single-word substitute instead: *about, regarding, concerning*.

insidious; invidious. What is *insidious* involves deceit and treachery {an insidious conspiracy}; what is *invidious* involves malice but not necessarily deceit {invidious discrimination}.

in spite of. See **despite**.

insure. See **ensure**.

intense; intensive. *Intense* is preferred in reference to colors, emotions, and personal efforts. *Intensive* describes concentration of attention and resources and is more often used to refer to work or study methods {labor-intensive} {intensive care}.

interpretive; interpretative. Although *interpretative* was considered the preferred form through the mid-twentieth century, it has largely fallen into disuse. To-day *interpretive* is the standard term.

in the affirmative. See **affirmative, in the**.

in the event that. See **event**.

in the near future. See **future**.

in the negative. See **affirmative, in the**.

inveigh; inveigle. To *inveigh* is to protest, usually against something {picketers inveighed against annexation}. To *inveigle* is to cajole or ensnare {inveigle into attending the party}.

invidious. See **insidious**.

irregardless. An error. Use *regardless* (or possibly *irrespective*).

it is I; it is me. Both are correct and acceptable. The first phrase is strictly grammatical (and stuffy); the second is idiomatic (and relaxed), and it is often contracted to *it's me*. In the third-person constructions, however, a greater stringency holds sway in good English {this is he} {it isn't she who has caused such misery}.

its; it's. *Its* is the possessive form of *it; it's* is the contraction for *it is* {it's a sad dog that scratches its fleas}.

jealousy; envy. *Jealousy* connotes feelings of resentment toward another, particularly in matters relating to an intimate relationship. *Envy* refers to covetousness of another's advantages, possessions, or abilities.

jibe. See **gibe**.

karat. See **carat**.

lady. When used as a synonym for *woman*—indeed when used anywhere but in the phrase *ladies and gentlemen*—this word will be considered objectionable by some readers who think that it refers to a patronizing stereotype. This is especially true when it is used for unprestigious jobs {cleaning lady} or as an adjective {lady lawyer}. Some will insist on using it to describe a refined woman. If they've consulted this entry, they've been forewarned. Cf. **gentleman**.

latter. See **former**.

laudable; laudatory. *Laudable* means "praiseworthy" {a laudable effort}. *Laudatory* means "expressing praise" {laudatory phone calls}.

lay; lie. *Lay* is a transitive verb—that is, it demands a direct object {lay your pencils down}. It is inflected *lay–laid–laid* {I laid the book there yesterday} {these rumors have been laid to rest}. (The children's prayer *Now I lay me down to sleep* is a good mnemonic device for the transitive *lay*.) *Lie* is an intransitive verb—that is, it never takes a direct object {lie down and rest}. It is inflected *lie–lay–lain* {she lay down and rested} {he hasn't yet lain down}.

leach; leech. To *leach* is to percolate or to separate out solids in solution by percolation. A *leech* is a bloodsucker (both literal and figurative).

lease; let. Many Americans seem to think that *let* is colloquial and of modern origin. In fact, the word is three hundred years older than *lease* and just as proper. One distinction between the two words is that either the owner or the tenant can be said to *lease* property, but only the owner can be said to *let* it.

led. This is the correct spelling of the past tense and past participle of the verb *lead*. It is often misspelled *lead*, maybe in part because of the pronunciation of the noun *lead* (the metal) or the past tense and past participle *read*, which rhyme with *led*.

lend, vb.; loan, vb. & n. *Lend* is the correct term for letting someone use something with the understanding that it (or its equivalent) will be returned. The verb *loan* is standard only when money is the subject of the transaction. *Loan* is the noun corresponding to both *lend* and *loan*, vb. The past-tense and past-participial form of *lend* is *lent*.

less; fewer. Reserve *less* for amounts or mass nouns—for example, *less salt*, *dirt*, *water*. Reserve *fewer* for countable things—for example, *fewer people*, *calories*, *suggestions*. One easy guideline is to use *less* with singular nouns {less money} and *fewer* with plural nouns {fewer dollars}.

let. See **lease**.

libel. See **defamation**.

lie. See **lay**.

life-and-death; life-or-death. The problem of logic aside (life and death being mutually exclusive), the first phrase is the standard idiom {a life-and-death decision}.

like; as. The use of *like* as a conjunction (as in the old jingle "like a cigarette should") has long been a contentious issue. Purists insist that *as* must introduce a clause and *like* must always be a preposition coupled with a noun {cool like springwater}. The fall of that old rule has been predicted for five decades, but today *like* as a conjunction is still not standard. See also 5.181.

likely. See **apt**.

literally. This word means "actually; without exaggeration." It should not be used loosely as an intensifier, as in *they were literally glued to their seats* (unless glue had in fact been applied).

loan. See **lend**.

loathe, vb.; loath, adj. To *loathe* something is to detest it or to regard it with disgust {I loathe tabloid television}. Someone who is *loath* is reluctant {Tracy seems loath to admit mistakes}.

lose; loose, vb.; loosen. To *lose* something is to be deprived of it. To *loose* something is to release it from fastenings or restraints. To *loosen* is to make less tight or to ease a restraint. *Loose* conveys the idea of complete release, whereas *loosen* refers to only a partial release.

luxuriant; luxurious. The two terms are fairly often confused. What is *luxuriant* is lush and grows abundantly {a luxuriant head of hair}. What is *luxurious* is lavish and extravagant {a luxurious resort}.

malevolent; maleficent. *Malevolent* means "evil in mind" {with malevolent intent}. *Maleficent* means "evil in deed" {a maleficent bully}.

malodorous. See **odious**.

maltreatment. See **mistreatment**.

manslaughter. See **murder**.

mantle; mantel. A *mantle* is a long, loose garment like a cloak. A *mantel* is a wood or stone structure around a fireplace.

masterful; masterly. *Masterful* describes a person who is dominating and imperious. *Masterly* describes a person who has mastered a craft, trade, or profession; the word often means "authoritative" {a masterly analysis}. Because *masterly* does not readily make an adverb (*masterlily* being extremely awkward [see 5.154]), try *in a masterly way.*

may; can. See *can.*

may; might. *May* expresses what is possible, is factual, or could be factual {I may have turned off the stove, but I can't recall doing it}. *Might* suggests something that is uncertain, hypothetical, or contrary to fact {I might have won the marathon if I had entered}. See 5.146.

me. See *I.*

media; mediums. In scientific contexts and in reference to mass communications, the plural of *medium* is *media* {some bacteria flourish in several types of media} {the media are now issuing reports}. But if *medium* refers to a spiritualist, the plural is *mediums* {several mediums have held séances here}.

memoranda; memorandums. Although both plural forms are correct, *memoranda* is more common. *Memoranda* is sometimes misused as if it were singular.

minuscule. Something that is minuscule is "very small." Probably because of the spelling of the modern word *mini* (and the prefix of the same spelling, which is recorded only from 1936), it is often misspelled *miniscule* (which is treated as a variant in some dictionaries). In printing, *minuscules* and *majuscules* are lowercase and capital letters, respectively.

mistreatment; maltreatment. *Mistreatment* is the more general term. *Maltreatment* denotes a harsh form of *mistreatment*, involving abuse by rough or cruel handling.

mitigate; militate. *Mitigate*, like its synonym *extenuate*, means "to lessen or soften"; so *mitigating circumstances* lessen the seriousness of a crime. *Militate*, by contrast, means "to have a marked effect on" and is usually followed by *against* {his nearsightedness militated against his ambition to become a commercial pilot}.

moot; mute. *Mute* means silent {he remained mute}. *Moot* traditionally meant debatable, so that a *moot point* was an arguable one, but today a *moot point*, in American English, is one that has no practical significance because it is hypothetical. The shift in meaning resulted from American legal usage.

much; very. *Much* generally intensifies past-participial adjectives {much obliged} {much encouraged} and some comparatives {much more} {much worse} {much too soon}. *Very* intensifies adverbs and most adjectives {very carefully} {very bad}, including past-participial adjectives that have more adjectival than verbal force {very bored}. See 5.89.

murder; manslaughter; homicide. All three words denote the killing of one person by another. *Murder* and *manslaughter* are both unlawful killings, but *murder* is done maliciously and intentionally. *Homicide* includes killings that are not unlawful, such as by a police officer acting properly in the line of duty. *Homicide* also refers to a person who kills another.

mutual. See *common*.

myself. Avoid using *myself* as a pronoun in place of *I* or *me*. Use it reflexively {I did myself a favor} or emphatically {I myself have tried to get through that tome!}. See also 5.48.

naturalist; naturist. *Naturalist* most often denotes a person who studies natural history, especially a field biologist or an amateur who observes and photographs, sketches, or writes about nature. *Naturist* denotes a nature worshiper or a nudist.

nauseous; nauseated. Whatever is *nauseous* induces a feeling of nausea—it makes us feel sick to our stomachs. To feel sick is to be *nauseated*. The use of *nauseous* to mean *nauseated* may be too common to be called error anymore, but strictly speaking it is poor usage. Because of the ambiguity in *nauseous*, the wisest course may be to stick to the participial adjectives *nauseated* and *nauseating*.

necessary; necessitous. *Necessary* means "required under the circumstances" {the necessary arrangements}. *Necessitous* means "impoverished" {living in necessitous circumstances}.

no. See *affirmative, in the*.

noisome. This word has nothing to do with *noise*. It means noxious, offensive, foul-smelling {a noisome factory}.

none. This word may take either a singular or a plural verb. A guideline: if it is followed by a singular noun, treat it as a singular {none of the building was painted}; if by a plural noun, treat it as a plural {none of the guests were here when I arrived}. But for special emphasis, it is quite proper (though possibly stilted) to use a singular verb when a plural noun follows {none of the edits was accepted}.

notable; noticeable; noteworthy. *Notable* ("readily noticed") applies both to physical things and to qualities {notable sense of humor}. *Noticeable* means "detectable with the physical senses" {a noticeable limp}. *Noteworthy* means "remarkable" {a noteworthy act of kindness}.

notwithstanding. One word. Less formal alternatives include *despite*, *although*, and *in spite of*. The word *notwithstanding* may precede or follow a noun {notwithstanding her bad health, she decided to run for office} {her bad health notwithstanding, she decided to run for office}.

number. See *amount*.

numerous. This is typically a bloated word for *many*.

observance; observation. *Observance* means "obedience to a rule or custom" {the family's observance of Passover}. *Observation* means either "a study of something" or "a remark based on such a study" {a keen observation about the defense strategy}. Each term is sometimes used when the other would be the better word.

obtain. See *attain*.

obtuse; abstruse. *Obtuse* describes a person who can't understand; *abstruse* describes an idea that is hard to understand. A person who is *obtuse* is dull and, by extension, dull-witted. What is *abstruse* is incomprehensible or nearly so.

odious; odorous; odoriferous; malodorous. *Odious* means hateful {odious Jim Crow laws}. It is not related to the other terms, but it is sometimes misused as if it were. *Odorous* means detectable by smell, for better or worse. *Odoriferous* means essentially the same thing, although it has meant "fragrant" as often as it has meant "foul." *Malodorous* means smelling quite bad. The mistaken form *odiferous* is often used as a jocular equivalent of *smelly*—but most dictionaries don't record it.

odoriferous. See **odious**.

off. Never put *of* after this word {we got off the bus}.

officious. A person who is *officious* is aggressively nosy and meddlesome. The word has nothing to do with an *officer* and should not be confused with *official*.

on; upon. Prefer *on* to *upon* unless introducing an event or condition {put that on the shelf, please} {upon the job's completion, you'll get paid}. For more about *on*, see **onto**.

on behalf of. See **behalf**.

one another. See **each other**.

oneself. One word—not *one's self*.

onto; on to; on. When is *on* a preposition and when is it an adverb? The sense of the sentence should tell, but the distinction can be subtle. *Onto* implies a movement, so it has an adverbial flavor even though it is a preposition {the gymnast jumped *onto* the bars}. When *on* is part of the verbal phrase, it is an adverb and *to* is the preposition {the gymnast held *on to* the bars}. One trick is to mentally say "up" before *on*: if the sentence still makes sense, then *onto* is probably the right choice. Alone, *on* does not imply motion {the gymnast is good *on* the parallel bars}.

oppress; repress. *Oppress*, meaning "to persecute or tyrannize," is more negative than *repress*, meaning "to restrain or subordinate."

oral. See **verbal**.

oration. See **peroration**.

ordinance; ordnance. An *ordinance* is a municipal regulation or an authoritative decree. *Ordnance* is military armament, especially artillery but also weapons and ammunition generally.

orient; orientate. To *orient* is to get one's bearings or point another in the right direction (literally to find east) {it took the new employee a few days to get oriented to the firm's suite}. Unless used in the sense "to face or turn to the east," *orientate* is a poor variation to be avoided. It is a back-formation from the noun *orientation*, analogous to the illegitimate *interpretate* for *interpret*.

ought; should. Both express a sense of duty, but *ought* is stronger. Unlike *should*, *ought* requires a fully expressed infinitive, even in the negative {you ought not to see the movie}. See 5.148, 5.149.

outside. In spatial references, no *of* is necessary—or desirable—after this word unless it is used as a noun {outside the shop} {the outside of the building}. But *outside of* is acceptable as a colloquialism meaning "except for" or "aside from."

over. As an equivalent of *more than*, this word is perfectly good idiomatic English.

overly. Avoid this word, which is widely considered poor usage. Try *over-* as a prefix or *unduly*.

pair. This is a singular form, despite the inherent sense of twoness. The plural is *pairs* {three pairs of shoes}.

pandemic. See **epidemic**.

parameters. Though it may sound elegant or scientific, this word is usually just pretentious when it is used in nontechnical contexts. Stick to *boundaries, limits, guidelines, grounds, elements,* or some other word.

partake in; partake of. To *partake in* is to participate in {the new student refused to partake in class discussions}. To *partake of* is either to get a part of {partake of the banquet} or to have a quality, at least to some extent {this assault partakes of revenge}.

partly; partially. Both words convey the sense "to some extent; in part" {partly disposed of}. *Partly* is preferred in that sense. But *partially* has the additional senses of "incompletely" {partially cooked} and "unfairly; in a way that shows bias toward one side" {he treats his friends partially}.

pastime. This word combines *pass* (not *past*) and *time*, and is spelled with a single t.

peaceable; peaceful. A *peaceable* person or nation is inclined to avoid strife {peaceable kingdom}. A *peaceful* person, place, or event is serene, tranquil, and calm {a peaceful day free from demands}.

peak; peek; pique. These three sometimes get switched through writerly blunders. A *peak* is an apex, a *peek* is a quick or illicit glance, and a fit of *pique* is an episode of peevishness and wounded vanity. To *pique* is to annoy or arouse: an article *piques* (not *peaks*) one's interest.

pendant, n.; pendent, adj. A *pendant* is an item of dangling jewelry, especially one worn around the neck. What is *pendent* is hanging or suspended.

penultimate. This word means "the next to last." Many people have started misusing it as a fancy equivalent of *ultimate*.

people; persons. The traditional view is that *persons* is used for smaller numbers {three persons} and *people* with larger ones {millions of people}. But today most people use *people* even for small groups {only three people were there}.

period of time; time period. Avoid these phrases. Try *period* or *time* instead.

peroration; oration. A *peroration*, strictly speaking, is the conclusion of an *oration* (speech). Careful writers avoid using *peroration* to refer to a rousing speech or text.

perpetuate; perpetrate. To *perpetuate* something is to sustain it or prolong it indefinitely {perpetuate the species}. To *perpetrate* is to commit or perform (an act) {perpetrate a crime}.

personally. Three points. First, use this word only when an actor does something that would normally be done through an agent {the president personally signed this invitation} or to limit other considerations {Jean was affected by the decision but was not personally involved in it}. Second, *personally* is redundant when combined with an activity that requires the actor's presence (*personally shook hands* should be simply *shook hands*). Third, *personally* shouldn't appear with *I* when stating an opinion; it weakens the statement and doesn't reduce the speaker's liability for the opinion. The only exception arises if a person is required to advance someone else's view but holds a different personal opinion {in the chamber I voted to lower taxes because of the constituencies I represented; but I personally believed that taxes should have been increased}.

persons. See **people**.

persuade; convince. *Persuade* is associated with actions {persuade him to buy a suit}. *Convince* is associated with beliefs or understandings {she convinced the auditor of her honesty}. The phrase *persuade to* [*do*] has traditionally been considered better than *convince to* [*do*]. But either verb will take a *that*-clause {the committee was persuaded that an all-night session was necessary} {my three-year-old is convinced that Santa Claus exists}.

pertain; appertain. *Pertain to*, the more common term, means "to relate to" {the clause pertains to assignment of risk}. *Appertain to* means "to belong to by right" {Fifth Amendment rights appertaining to the defendant}.

phase. See **faze**.

phenomenon. This is a singular form. The plural is *phenomena*.

pique. See **peak**.

pitiable; pitiful. To be *pitiable* is to be worthy of pity. To be *pitiful* is to be contemptible.

pleaded; pled. The first is the standard past-tense and past-participial form {he pleaded guilty} {they have pleaded with their families}. Avoid *pled*.

pore. To *pore over* something written is to read it intently. Some writers mistakenly substitute *pour*.

practicable; possible; practical. These terms differ in shading. What is *practicable* is capable of being done; it's feasible. What is *possible* might be capable of happening or being done, but there is some doubt. What is *practical* is fit for actual use.

precipitate, *adj.*; precipitous. What is *precipitate* occurs suddenly or rashly; the term describes demands, actions, or movements. What is *precipitous* is dangerously steep; this term describes cliffs and inclines.

precondition. Try *condition* or *prerequisite* instead.

predominant; predominate. Like *dominant*, *predominant* is an adjective {a predominant point of view}. Like *dominate*, *predominate* is a verb {a point of view that predominates throughout the state}. Using *predominate* as an adjective is common but loose usage—and the adverb *predominately* (for the correct *predominantly*) is likely to make the literary person's teeth hurt.

preface. See **foreword**.

prejudice, *vb.* Although *prejudice* is a perfectly normal English noun to denote an all-too-common trait, the verb is a legalism. For a plain-English equivalent, use *harm* or *hurt*.

preliminary to. Make it *before, in preparing for,* or some other natural phrasing.

prescribe. See **proscribe**.

presently. This word is ambiguous. Write *now* or *soon,* whichever you really mean.

presumption. See **assumption**.

preventive. Although the corrupt form *preventative* (with the superfluous syllable in the middle) is fairly common, the strictly correct form is *preventive.*

previous to. Make it *before.*

principle; principal. A *principle* is a natural, moral, or legal rule {the principle of free speech}. The corresponding adjective is *principled* {a principled decision}. A *principal* is a person of high authority or prominence {a school principal} or a loan amount requiring repayment {principal and interest}. A *principal* role is a primary one.

prior to. Make it *before* or *until.*

process of, in the. You can almost always delete this phrase without affecting the meaning.

propaganda. This is a singular noun {propaganda was everywhere}. The plural is *propagandas.*

prophesy; prophecy. *Prophesy* is the verb {the doomsayers prophesied widespread blackouts for Y2K}. *Prophecy* is the noun {their prophecies did not materialize}. *Prophesize* is an erroneous form sometimes encountered.

proscribe; prescribe. To *proscribe* something is to prohibit it {legislation that pro-scribes drinking while driving}. To *prescribe* is to appoint or dictate (a rule or course of action) {Henry VIII prescribed the order of succession to include three of his children} or to specify a medical remedy {the doctor prescribed anti-inflammatory pills and certain exercises}.

protuberance. So spelled. Perhaps because *protrude* means "to stick out," writers want to spell *protuberance* (something that bulges out) with an extra *r* (after the *t*). But the words are from different roots.

proved; proven. *Proved* is the preferred past-participial form of *prove* {it was proved to be true}. Use *proven* as an adjective {a proven success}.

proximity. See **close proximity, in**.

purposely; purposefully. What is done *purposely* is done intentionally, or "on pur-pose." What is done *purposefully* is done with a certain goal in mind. An ac-tion may be done *purposely* without any particular interest in a specific re-sult—that is, not *purposefully.*

question whether; question of whether; question as to whether. The first phrasing is the best, the second is next best, and the third is to be avoided. See **as to**.

quick(ly). *Quickly* is the general adverb. But *quick* is properly used as an adverb in the idiomatic phrases *get rich quick* and *come quick.* See 5.157.

quote; quotation. Traditionally a verb, *quote* is often used as an equivalent of *quo-tation* in speech and informal writing. Also, there is a tendency for writers (especially journalists) to think of *quotes* as contemporary remarks usable in their writing and of *quotations* as being wisdom of the ages expressed pithily.

rack. See **wrack**.

reason why. Although some object to the supposed redundancy of this phrase, it is centuries old and perfectly acceptable English. And *reason that* is not always an adequate substitute.

reek. See **wreak**.

refrain; restrain. To *refrain* is to restrain yourself (to *refrain from* or stop doing something); it is typically an act of self-discipline. Other people *restrain* you {if you don't refrain from the disorderly conduct, the police will restrain you}.

regrettable; regretful. What is *regrettable* is unfortunate or deplorable. A person who is *regretful* feels regret or sorrow for something done or lost. The adverb *regrettably*, not *regretfully*, is the synonym of *unfortunately*.

rein; reign. A *rein* (usu. plural) controls a horse; it is the right word in idioms such as "take the reins," "give free rein," and, as a verb, "rein in." A *reign* is a state of or term of dominion, especially that of a monarch but by extension dominance in some field. This is the right word in idioms such as "reign of terror" and, as a verb, "reign supreme."

relegate; delegate. To *relegate* is to assign a lesser position {the officer was relegated to desk duty pending an investigation} or to hand over for decision or execution {the application was relegated to the human services committee}. To *delegate* is to authorize another to act on one's behalf {Congress delegated environmental regulation to the EPA}.

renounce. See **denounce**.

repellent; repulsive. *Repellent* and *repulsive* both denote the character of driving others away. But *repulsive* has strong negative connotations of being truly disgusting.

repetitive; repetitious. Both mean "occurring over and over." But whereas *repetitive* is fairly neutral in connotation, *repetitious* has taken on the nuance of tediousness.

repulsive. See **repellent**.

restive; restful. *Restive* has two senses: (1) "impatient, stubborn" and (2) "restless, agitated." *Restful* means "conducive to rest."

restrain. See **refrain**.

reticent. This word should not be used as a synonym for *reluctant*. It means "inclined to be silent; reserved; taciturn" {when asked about the incident, the congressional representative became uncharacteristically reticent}.

revenge. See **avenge**.

rob; steal. Both verbs mean "to wrongfully take [something from another person]." But *rob* also includes a threat or act of harming, usually but not always to the person being robbed.

run the gantlet; throw down the gauntlet. These are the traditional idioms, a *gantlet* being a path between two lines of tormentors and a *gauntlet* being a knight's glove. The first idiom refers to a means of punishment, the second to a dare (which the challenger accepts by picking up the gauntlet). Purists object to the frequently seen *run the gauntlet*.

sacrilegious. This is the correct spelling, though there is a tendency by some to switch the *i* and *e* on either side of the *l*. In fact, the word is related to *sacrilege*, not *religion* and *religious*.

seasonal; seasonable. *Seasonal* means either "dependent on a season" {snow skiing is a seasonal hobby} or "relating to the seasons or a season" {the seasonal aisle stays stocked most of the year, starting with Valentine's Day gifts in January}. *Seasonable* means "timely" {seasonable motions for continuance} or "fitting the season" {it was unseasonably cold for July}.

self-deprecating. See **deprecate**.

semi-. See **bi-**.

semiannual. See **biannual**.

sensor. See **censor**.

sensual; sensuous. What is *sensual* involves indulgence of the senses—especially sexual gratification. What is *sensuous* usually applies to aesthetic enjoyment; only hack writers imbue the word with salacious connotations.

sewer; sewage; sewerage. *Sewer* denotes wastewater pipes; *sewage* denotes the matter carried through those pipes. *Sewerage* is the better term for the sewer system as a whole, including treatment plants and other facilities, and for the function of the disposal of sewage and wastewater in general.

shine. When this verb is intransitive, it means "to give or make light"; the past tense is *shone* {the stars shone dimly}. When it is transitive, it means "to cause to shine"; the past tense is *shined* {the caterer shined the silver}.

sight; site. A *sight* may be something worth seeing {the sights of London} or a device to aid the eye {the sight of a gun}, among other things. A *site* is a place, whether physical {a mall will be built on this site} or electronic {website}. The figurative expression meaning "to focus on a goal" is *to set one's sights*. Cf. **cite**.

since. This word may relate either to time {since last winter} or to causation {since I'm a golfer, I know what "double bogey" means}. Some writers erroneously believe that the word relates exclusively to time. But the causal *since* was a part of the English language before Chaucer wrote in the fourteenth century, and it is useful as a slightly milder way of expressing causation than *because*. But where there is any possibility of confusion with the temporal sense, use *because*.

site. See **cite**; **sight**.

slander. See **defamation**.

slew; slough; slue. *Slew* is an informal word equivalent to *many* or *lots* {you have a slew of cattle}. It is sometimes misspelled *slough* (a legitimate noun meaning "a grimy swamp" and pronounced to rhyme with *now*) or *slue* (a legitimate verb meaning "to swing around"). The phrase *slough of despond* (from Bunyan's *Pilgrim's Progress* [1678]) means a state of depression. This is etymologically different from *slough* (/sləf/), meaning "to discard" {slough off dry skin}.

slow. This word, like *slowly*, may be an adverb. Generally, prefer *slowly* {go slowly}. But when used after the verb in a pithy statement, especially an injunction, *slow* often appears in colloquial usage {Go slow!} {take it slow}. See 5.157.

slue. See **slew**.

sneak. This verb is conjugated *sneak–sneaked–sneaked*. Reserve *snuck* for dialect and tongue-in-cheek usages.

spit. If used to mean "to expectorate," the verb is inflected *spit–spat–spat* {he spat a curse}. But if used to mean "to skewer," it's *spit–spitted–spitted* {the hens have been spitted for broiling}.

stanch. See **staunch**.

stationary; stationery. *Stationary* describes a state of immobility or of staying in one place {if it's stationary, paint it}. *Stationery* denotes writing materials {love letters written on perfumed stationery}. To remember the two, try associating the *-er* in *stationery* with the *-er* in *paper*; or remember that a *stationer* is someone who sells the stuff.

staunch; stanch. *Staunch* is an adjective meaning "ardent and faithful" {a staunch Red Sox supporter}. *Stanch* is a verb meaning "to stop the flow"; it is almost always used in regard to bleeding, literally or metaphorically {after New Hampshire the campaign was hemorrhaging; only a big win in South Carolina could stanch the bleeding}.

steal. See **rob**.

strait; straight. A *strait* (often pl.) is (1) literally, a narrow channel between two large bodies of water {Strait of Magellan} or (2) figuratively, a difficult position {dire straits} {straitened circumstances}. This is the word used in compound terms with the sense of constriction {straitlaced} {straitjacket}. *Straight* is most often an adjective meaning unbent, steady, sober, candid, honest, or heterosexual.

strategy; tactics. A *strategy* is a long-term plan for achieving a goal. *Tactics* are shorter-term plans for achieving an immediate but limited success. A strategy might involve several tactics.

subsequent. See **consequent**.

subsequently. Try *later*.

subsequent to. Make it *after*.

such. This word, when used to replace *this* or *that*—as in "such building was later condemned"—is symptomatic of legalese. *Such* is actually no more precise than *the, this, that, these,* or *those*. It is perfectly acceptable, however, to use *such* with a mass noun or plural noun when the meaning is "of that type" or "of this kind" {such impudence galled the rest of the family} {such vitriolic exchanges became commonplace in the following years}.

sufficient. See **adequate**.

supersede. This word derives from *sedeo*, the Latin word for "to sit, to be established," not *cedo*, meaning "to yield." Hence the spelling variation from words such as *concede, recede,* and *secede*.

sympathy. See **empathy**.

systematic; systemic. *Systematic* means "according to a plan or system, methodical, or arranged in a system." *Systemic* is limited in use to physiological systems {a systemic disease affecting several organs} or, by extension, other systems that may be likened to the body {systemic problems within the corporate hierarchy}.

tactics. See **strategy**.

take. See **bring**.

tantalizing; titillating. A *tantalizing* thing torments us because we want it badly and it is always just out of reach. A *titillating* thing tickles us pleasantly, literally or figuratively.

thankfully. This word traditionally means "appreciatively; gratefully." It is not in good use as a substitute for *thank goodness* or *fortunately*. Cf. **hopefully**.

that; which. These are both relative pronouns (see 5.54–63). In polished American prose, *that* is used restrictively to narrow a category or identify a particular item being talked about {any building that is taller must be outside the state}; *which* is used nonrestrictively—not to narrow a class or identify a particular item but to add something about an item already identified {alongside the officer trotted a toy poodle, which is hardly a typical police dog}. *Which* should be used restrictively only when it is preceded by a preposition {the situation in which we find ourselves}. Otherwise, it is almost always preceded by a comma, a parenthesis, or a dash. In British English, writers and editors seldom observe the distinction between the two words. See also 6.22.

there; their; they're. *There* denotes a place or direction {stay there}. *Their* is the possessive pronoun {all their good wishes}. *They're* is a contraction of *they are* {they're calling now}.

therefore; therefor. The words have different senses. *Therefore*, the common word, means "as a consequence; for that reason" {the evidence of guilt was slight; therefore, the jury acquitted the defendant}. *Therefor*, a legalism, means "in return for" or "for it" {he brought the unworn shirt back to the store and received a refund therefor}.

thus. This is the adverb—not *thusly*.

till. This is a perfectly good preposition and conjunction {open till 10 p.m.}. It is not a contraction of *until* and should not be written *'til*.

timbre; timber. *Timbre* is a musical term meaning tonal quality. *Timber* is the correct spelling in all other uses.

time period. See **period of time**.

titillating. See **tantalizing**.

tolerance; toleration. *Tolerance* is the habitual quality of being *tolerant*; *toleration* is a particular instance of being *tolerant*.

torpid. See **turbid**.

tortious; tortuous; torturous. What is *tortious* relates to torts (civil wrongs) or to acts that give rise to legal claims for torts {tortious interference with a contract}. What is *tortuous* is full of twists and turns {a tortuous path through the woods}. What is *torturous* involves torture or severe discomfort {a torturous exam}.

toward; towards. The preferred form is without the *-s* in American English, with it in British English. The same is true for other directional words, such as *upward*, *downward*, *forward*, and *backward*, as well as *afterward*. The use of *afterwards* and *backwards* as adverbs is neither rare nor incorrect. But for the sake of consistency, it is better to stay with the simpler form.

transcript; transcription. A *transcript* is a written record, as of a trial or a radio program. *Transcription* is the act or process of creating a transcript.

trillion. See **billion**.

triumphal; triumphant. Things are *triumphal* {a triumphal arch}, but only people feel *triumphant* {a triumphant Caesar returned to Rome}.

turbid; turgid; torpid. *Turbid* water is thick and opaque from churned-up mud {a turbid pond}; by extension *turbid* means "unclear, confused, or disturbed" {a turbid argument}. *Turgid* means "swollen," and by extension "pompous and bombastic" {turgid prose}. *Torpid* means "idle and lazy" {a torpid economy}.

unique. Reserve this word for the sense "one of a kind." Avoid it in the sense "special, unusual." Phrases such as *very unique*, *more unique*, *somewhat unique*, and so on—in which a degree is attributed to *unique*—are poor usage. See also 5.88.

unlawful; illegal; illicit; criminal. This list is in ascending order of negative connotation. An *unlawful* act may even be morally innocent (for example, letting a parking meter expire). But an *illegal* act is something society formally condemns, and an *illicit* act calls to mind moral degeneracy {illicit drug use}. Unlike *criminal*, the first three terms can apply to civil wrongs.

unorganized. See **disorganized**.

unreadable. See **illegible**.

upon. See **on**.

use; usage; utilize. *Use* is usually the best choice for simplicity. *Usage* refers to a customary practice. *Utilize* is usually an overblown alternative of *use*, but it is occasionally the better choice when the distinct sense is "to use to best effect."

venal; venial. A person who is *venal* is mercenary or open to bribery {a venal government official}; a thing that is *venal* is purchasable {venal livestock}. What is *venial* is pardonable or excusable {a venial offense} {a venial error}.

verbal; oral. If something is put into words, it is *verbal*. Technically, *verbal* covers both written and spoken utterance. But if you wish to specify that something was conveyed through speech, use *oral*.

very. See **much**.

vocation. See **avocation**.

voluminous. See **compendious**.

whether. Generally, use *whether* alone—not with the words *or not* tacked on {they didn't know whether to go}. The *or not* is necessary only when you mean to convey the idea of "regardless of whether" {we'll finish on time whether or not it rains}. See also **if; whether**.

which. See **that**.

while. *While* may substitute for *although* or *whereas*, especially if a conversational tone is desired {while many readers may disagree, the scientific community has overwhelmingly adopted the conclusions here presented}. Yet because *while* can denote either time or contrast, the word is occasionally ambiguous; when a real ambiguity exists, *although* or *whereas* is the better choice.

who; whom. Here are the traditional rules. *Who* is a nominative pronoun used as (1) the subject of a finite verb {it was Jim who bought the coffee today} or (2) a predicate nominative when it follows a linking verb {that's who}. *Whom* is an objective pronoun that may appear as (1) the object of a verb {I learned nothing about the man whom I saw} or (2) the object of a preposition {the woman to whom I owe my life}. Today there are two countervailing trends: first, there's a decided tendency to use *who* colloquially in most contexts; second, among those insecure about their grammar, there's a tendency to overcorrect oneself and use *whom* when *who* would be correct. Writers and editors of formal prose often resist the first of these; everyone should resist the second. See also 5.63.

whoever; whomever. Avoid the second unless you are certain of your grammar {give this book to whoever wants it} {I cook for whomever I love}. If you are uncertain why these examples are correct, use *anyone who* or (as in the second example) *anyone*.

who's; whose. The first is a contraction {Who's on first?}, the second a possessive {Whose life is it, anyway?}. Unlike *who* and *whom*, *whose* may refer to things as well as people {the Commerce Department, whose bailiwick includes intellectual property}. See 5.61.

whosever; whoever's. The first is correct (though increasingly rare) in formal writing {whosever bag that is, it needs to be moved out of the way}; the second is acceptable in casual usage {whoever's dog got into our garbage can, he or she should clean up the mess}.

wrack; rack. To *wrack* is to severely damage or completely destroy {a storm-wracked ship}. (*Wrack* is also a noun denoting wreckage {the storm's wrack}.) To *rack* is to torture by means of stretching with an instrument {rack the prisoner until he confesses} or to stretch beyond capacity {to rack one's brain}.

wreak; reek. *Wreak* means "to force (something) on" in the sense of causing damage or revenge; the past tense is *wreaked*, not *wrought*. (The latter is an archaic form of the past tense and past participle of *work*.) *Reek* can be a verb meaning "to stink" or a noun meaning "stench."

wrong; wrongful. These terms are not interchangeable. *Wrong* has two senses: (1) "immoral, unlawful" {it's wrong to bully smaller children} and (2) "improper, incorrect, unsatisfactory" {the math answers are wrong}. *Wrongful* likewise has two senses: (1) "unjust, unfair" {wrongful conduct} and (2) "unsanctioned by law; having no legal right" {it was a wrongful demand on the estate}.

yes. See *affirmative, in the*.

your; you're. *Your* is the possessive form of *you*. *You're* is the contraction for *you are*.

Bias-Free Language

5.221   *Maintaining credibility.* Discussions of bias-free language—language that is neither sexist nor suggestive of other conscious or subconscious prejudices—have a way of descending quickly into politics. But there is a way to avoid the political quagmire: if we focus solely on maintaining credibility with a wide readership, the argument for eliminating bias from published works becomes much simpler. Biased language that is not central to the meaning of a work distracts readers, and in their eyes the work is less credible. Few texts warrant the deliberate display of linguistic biases. Nor is it ideal, however, to call attention to the supposed absence of linguistic biases, since this will also distract readers and weaken credibility.

5.222   *Gender bias.* Consider the issue of gender-neutral language. On the one hand, it is unacceptable to a great many reasonable readers to use the generic masculine pronoun (*he* in reference to no one in particular). On the other hand, it is unacceptable to a great many readers (often different readers) either to resort to nontraditional gimmicks to avoid the generic masculine (by using *he/she* or *s/he*, for example) or to use *they* as a kind of singular pronoun. Either way, credibility is lost with some readers.

5.223   *Other biases.* The same is true of other types of biases, such as slighting allusions or stereotypes based on characteristics such as race, ethnicity, disability, religion, sexual orientation, or birth or family status. Careful writers avoid language that reasonable readers might find offensive or distracting—unless the biased language is central to the meaning of the writing.

5.224   *Bias and the editor's responsibility.* A careful editor points out to authors any biased terms or approaches in the work (knowing, of course, that the bias may have been unintentional), suggests alternatives, and ensures that any biased language that is retained is retained by choice. Although some publishers prefer to avoid certain terms or specific usages in all cases, Chicago's editors do not maintain a list of words or usages considered unacceptable. Rather, they adhere to the reasoning presented here and apply it to individual cases. They consult guides to avoiding bias in writing (see bibliography) and work with authors to use the most appropriate language. What you should strive for—if you want readers to focus on your ideas and not on the political subtext—is a style that doesn't even hint at the issue. So unless you're involved in a debate about, for example, sexism, you'll probably want a style, on the one hand, that no reasonable person could call sexist and, on the other hand, that never suggests you're contorting your language to be nonsexist.

5.225   *Nine techniques for achieving gender neutrality.* There are many ways to achieve gender-neutral language, but it takes some thought and often some hard work. Nine methods are suggested below because no single method will work for every writer. And one method won't neatly resolve every gender-bias problem. Some of them—for example, repeating the noun or using "he or she"—will irritate readers if overused. All of them risk changing the intended meaning: though slight changes in meaning are inevitable, additional rewording may be necessary.

1.   Omit the pronoun: *the programmer should update the records when data is transferred to her by the head office* becomes *the programmer should update the records when data is transferred by the head office.*

2.   Repeat the noun: *a writer should be careful not to needlessly antagonize readers, because her credibility will suffer* becomes *a writer should be careful not to needlessly antagonize readers, because the writer's credibility will suffer.*

3.   Use a plural antecedent: *a contestant must conduct himself with dignity at all times* becomes *contestants must conduct themselves with dignity at all times.*

4.   Use an article instead of a personal pronoun: *a student accused of cheating must actively waive his right to have his guidance counselor present* becomes *a student accused of cheating must actively waive the right to have a guidance counselor present.*

5.   Use the neutral singular pronoun *one*: *an actor in New York is likely to earn more than he is in Paducah* becomes *an actor in New York is likely to earn more than one in Paducah.*

6.   Use the relative pronoun *who* (works best when it replaces a personal pronoun that follows *if*): *employers presume that if an applicant can't write well, he won't be a good employee* becomes *employers presume that an applicant who can't write well won't be a good employee.*

7.   Use the imperative mood: *a lifeguard must keep a close watch over children while he is monitoring the pool* becomes *keep a close watch over children while monitoring the pool.*

8.   Use *he or she* (sparingly): *if a complainant is not satisfied with the board's decision, then he can ask for a rehearing* becomes *if a complainant is not satisfied with the board's decision, then he or she can ask for a rehearing.*

9.   Revise the clause: *a person who decides not to admit he lied will be considered honest until someone exposes his lie* becomes *a person who denies lying will be considered honest until the lie is exposed.*

5.226   *Sex-specific labels as adjectives.* When gender is relevant, it's acceptable to use the noun *woman* as a modifier {woman judge}. In recent decades, *woman* has been rapidly replacing *lady* in such constructions. The adjective *female* is also often used unobjectionably. In isolated contexts it may strike some readers as being dismissive or derogatory (perhaps because it's a biological term used for animals as well as humans), but when parallel references to both sexes are required, the adjectives *male* and *female* are typically the most serviceable choices {the police force has 834 male and 635 female officers}.

5.227   *Gender-neutral singular pronouns.* The only gender-neutral third-person singular personal pronoun in English is *it*, which doesn't refer to humans (with very limited exceptions). Clumsy artifices such as *s/he* and *(wo)man* or artificial genderless pronouns have been tried—for many years—with no success. They won't succeed. And those who use them invite credibility problems. Indefinite pronouns such as *anybody* and *someone* don't always satisfy the need for a gender-neutral alternative because they are traditionally regarded as singular antecedents that call for a third-person singular pronoun. Many people substitute the plural *they* and *their* for the singular *he* or *she*. Although *they* and *their* have become common in informal usage, neither is considered acceptable in formal writing, so unless you are given guidelines to the contrary, do not use them in a singular sense.

5.228   *Problematic suffixes.* The trend in American English is toward eliminating sex-specific suffixes. Words with feminine suffixes such as *-ess* and *-ette* are easily replaced with the suffix-free forms, which are increasingly accepted as applying to both men and women. For example, *author* and *testator* are preferable to *authoress* and *testatrix*. Compounds with *-man* are more problematic. The word *person* rarely functions well in such a compound; *chairperson* and *anchorperson* sound more pompous and wooden than the simpler (and correct) *chair* or *anchor*. Unless a word is established (such as *salesperson*, which dates from 1901), don't automatically substitute *-person* for *-man*. English has many alternatives that are not necessarily newly coined, including *police officer* (first recorded in 1797), *firefighter* (1903), and *mail carrier* (1788).

5.229   *Necessary gender-specific language.* It isn't always necessary or desirable to use gender-neutral terms and phrasings. If you're writing about something that clearly concerns only one sex (e.g., *women's studies*; *men's golf championship*) or an inherently single-sex institution (e.g., a sorority; a Masonic lodge), trying to use gender-neutral language may lead to absurd prose {be solicitous of a pregnant friend's comfort; he or she will need your support}.

5.230 *Avoiding other biased language.* Comments that betray a writer's conscious or unconscious biases or ignorance may cause readers to lose respect for the writer and interpret the writer's words in ways that were never intended. In general, emphasize the person, not a characteristic. A characteristic is a label. It should preferably be used as an adjective, not as a noun. Instead of referring to someone as, for instance, *a Catholic* or *a deaf-mute*, put the person first by writing *a Catholic man* or *he is Catholic*, and *a deaf-and-mute child* or *the child is deaf and mute*. Avoid irrelevant references to personal characteristics such as sex, race, ethnicity, disability, age, religion, sexual orientation, or social standing. Such pointless references may affect a reader's perception of you or the person you are writing about or both. They may also invoke a reader's biases and cloud your meaning. When it is important to mention a characteristic because it will help the reader develop a picture of the person you are writing about, use care. For instance, in the sentence *Shirley Chisholm was probably the finest African American woman member of the House of Representatives that New York has ever had*, the phrase *African American woman* may imply to some readers that Chisholm was a great representative "for a woman" but may be surpassed by many or all men, that she stands out only among African American members of Congress, or that it is unusual for a woman or an African American to hold high office. But in *Shirley Chisholm was the first African American woman to be elected to Congress and one of New York's all-time best representatives*, the purpose of the phrase *African American woman* is not likely to be misunderstood.

6   *Punctuation*

Overview

6.1   *The role of punctuation and the scope of this chapter.* Punctuation should be governed by its function, which in ordinary text is to promote ease of reading by clarifying relationships within and between sentences. This function, although it allows for a degree of subjectivity, should in turn be governed by the consistent application of some basic principles lest the subjective element obscure meaning. The principles set forth in this chapter are based on a logical application of traditional American practice. For the special punctuation requirements of mathematics, foreign languages, source citations, bibliographies, indexes, and so on, see the appropriate chapters in this manual and consult the index.

Punctuation in Relation to Surrounding Text

6.2   *Punctuation and italics.* All punctuation marks should appear in the same font—roman or italic—as the main or surrounding text, except for punctuation that belongs to a title in a different font (usually italics). So, for example, the word *and*, which in this sentence is in italics, is followed by a comma in roman type; the comma, strictly speaking, does not belong to *and*, which is italicized because it is a word used as a word (see 7.58). Of course, it may be difficult to tell whether a comma is in italics or not (to say nothing of periods); for other marks it will be more evident. Readers of the online edition of this manual can look at the underlying source coding, and all those who prepare manuscripts in electronic environments will need to pay attention to this level of detail (see 2.77). In the first four examples that follow, the punctuation marks next to italic text belong with the surrounding sentence and are therefore presented in roman. In the last two examples, the two punctuation marks that belong with the italic titles—the exclamation mark following "Help" and the comma following "Eats"—are in italics (the comma following "Leaves" is in roman).

For light amusement he turns to the *Principia Mathematica*!
How can they be sure that the temperature was in fact *rising*?
The letters *a*, *b*, and *c* are often invoked as being fundamental.
I had yet to consider the central thesis of Malthus's *Essay*: the imperfectibility of
    humankind.
but
The Beatles' *Help!* was released long before the heyday of the music video.

I love *Eats, Shoots & Leaves*, but I would have preferred to see "and" in the title rather than the ampersand—which would allow for a serial comma after "Shoots."

For parentheses and brackets, see 6.5; for quotation marks, see 6.6. For a different approach, see 6.4.

6.3   *Punctuation and boldface or color.* The choice of boldface (or, by extension, type in a different color), unlike that of italics (see 6.2), is more often an aesthetic than a purely logical decision. Punctuation marks following boldface or color should be dealt with case by case, depending on how the boldface is used. In the first example, the period following "line spacing" belongs with the boldface glossary term and is therefore set in bold; the period following "leading" is part of the surrounding sentence and is therefore *not* set in bold. In the middle two examples, the punctuation next to the boldface terms belongs with them, like the first period in the first example. In the final example, the question mark belongs to the surrounding sentence and not to the boldface word.

line spacing. See **leading**.
Figure 6. Title page from an apocryphal *Second Poetics*.
For sale: three ten-year-old CPUs and five refurbished monitors.
Will the installation remain stalled until I choose **I accept**?

6.4   *Punctuation and font—aesthetic considerations.* According to a more traditional system, periods, commas, colons, and semicolons should appear in the same font as the word, letter, character, or symbol immediately preceding them if different from that of the main or surrounding text. In the third and fourth examples in 6.2, the commas following *a* and *b* and the colon following the Malthus title would be italic, as would the comma following the book title (*Eats, Shoots & Leaves*) in the last example. A question mark or exclamation point, however, would appear in the same font as the immediately preceding word only if it belonged to that word, as in the title *Help!* in 6.2. This system, once preferred by Chicago and still preferred by some as more aesthetically pleasing, should be reserved—if it must be used—for publications destined for print only. In electronic publications, where typeface may be determined by content as well as appearance (e.g., a book title might be tagged as such, separate from any surrounding punctuation), the more logical system described in 6.2 should be preferred.

6.5   *Parentheses and brackets in relation to surrounding text.* Parentheses and brackets should appear in the same font—roman or italic—as the surrounding text, not in that of the material they enclose. This system, though it may occasionally cause typefitting problems when a slanting italic letter touches a nonslanting roman parenthesis or bracket, has two main virtues: it is easy to use, and it has long been practiced. For printed works, a thin space or hair space may need to be added between overlapping characters. For electronic works, where type display will vary depending on hardware and software, no such adjustments should normally be made.

> The Asian long-horned beetle (*Anoplophora glabripennis*) attacks maples.
> The letter stated that my check had been "recieved [*sic*] with thanks."

When a phrase in parentheses or brackets appears on a line by itself, however, the parentheses or brackets are usually in the same font as the phrase.

6.6 *Quotation marks in relation to surrounding text.* Like parentheses and brackets (see 6.5), quotation marks should appear in the same font—roman or italic—as the surrounding text, which may or may not match that of the material they enclose. In the second example, the quotation marks, as part of the italicized title, are in italics.

> The approach to the runway was, they reported, *"extremely dangerous"* (italics in original).
> I just finished reading *Sennacherib's "Palace without Rival" at Nineveh*, by John Malcolm Russell.

As with parentheses and brackets, when a sentence or phrase in quotation marks appears on a line by itself, the quotation marks are usually in the same font as the sentence or phrase. See also 13.60.

6.7 *Punctuation and space—one space or two?* In typeset matter, one space, not two, should be used between two sentences—whether the first ends in a period, a question mark, an exclamation point, or a closing quotation mark or parenthesis. By the same token, one space, not two, should follow a colon. When a particular design layout calls for more space between two elements—for example, between a figure number and a caption—the design should specify the exact amount of space (e.g., em space).

6.8 *Punctuation with URLs and e-mail addresses.* Sentences that include an e-mail address or a uniform resource identifier such as a URL should be punctuated normally. Though angle brackets or other "wrappers" are standard in some applications, these are generally unnecessary in nor-

TABLE 6.1. Punctuation relative to closing quotation marks and parentheses or brackets

Closing mark	Double or single quotation marks*	Parentheses or brackets†
Period	Inside	Inside or outside; see 6.13
Comma	Inside	Outside
Semicolon	Outside	Outside
Colon	Outside	Outside
Question mark or exclamation point	Inside or outside; see 6.10	Inside or outside; see 6.70, 6.74
Em dash	Inside or outside; see 6.84	Outside

*See also 6.9, 6.70, 6.74.   †See also 6.53, 6.96, 6.99, 6.101.

mal prose (see 6.102). Readers of print sources should assume that any punctuation at the end of an e-mail address or URL belongs to the sentence. URLs as hypertext should point to the URL, ignoring the surrounding punctuation (some applications do this automatically). For dividing e-mail addresses and URLs at the end of a line, see 7.42.

Chicago's Q&A forum, which can be found at http://www.chicagomanualofstyle .org, has attracted much constructive comment.
Write to me at grammar88@parsed-out.edu.

Punctuation in Relation to Closing Quotation Marks

6.9   *Periods and commas in relation to closing quotation marks.* Periods and commas precede closing quotation marks, whether double or single. (An apostrophe at the end of a word should never be confused with a closing single quotation mark; see 6.115.) This is a traditional style, in use well before the first edition of this manual (1906). For an exception, see 7.75. See also table 6.1.

Growing up, we always preferred to "bear those ills we have."
"Thus conscience does make cowards of us all," she replied.

In an alternative system, sometimes called British style (as described in *The Oxford Style Manual*; see bibliog. 1.1), single quotation marks are used, and only those punctuation points that appeared in the original material should be included within the quotation marks; all others follow the closing quotation marks. (Exceptions to the rule are widespread: periods, for example, are routinely placed inside any quotation that begins with a capital letter and forms a grammatically complete sentence.) Double quotation marks are reserved for quotations within quotations. This system or a variation may be appropriate in some works of textual criticism. See also 7.50, 7.55, 13.7–8, 13.28–29.

6.10   *Other punctuation in relation to closing quotation marks.* Colons and semicolons—unlike periods and commas—follow closing quotation marks; question marks and exclamation points follow closing quotation marks unless they belong within the quoted matter. (This rule applies the logic that is often absent from the US style described in 6.9.) See also table 6.1.

Take, for example, the first line of "To a Skylark": "Hail to thee, blithe spirit!"
I was invited to recite the lyrics to "Sympathy for the Devil"; instead I read from the Op-Ed page of the *New York Times*.
Which of Shakespeare's characters said, "All the world's a stage"?
but
"Timber!"
"What's the rush?" she wondered.

6.11   *Single quotation marks next to double quotation marks.* When single quotation marks nested within double quotation marks appear next to each other, no space need be added between the two except as a typographical nicety subject to the publisher's requirements. For example, most typesetters will use a thin space between the two marks to enhance readability (as in the print edition of this manual). In online works, a nonbreaking space should be used (as in the online edition of this manual). See also 13.28. In the example that follows, note that the period precedes the single quotation mark (see also 6.9).

"Admit it," she said. "You haven't read 'The Simple Art of Murder.'"

Periods

6.12   *Use of the period.* A period marks the end of a declarative or an imperative sentence. Between sentences, it is followed by a single space (see 2.9, 6.7). A period may also follow a word or phrase standing alone, as in the third example. For the many other uses of the period, consult the index.

The two faced each other in silence.
Wait here.
My answer? Never.

6.13 *Periods in relation to parentheses and brackets.* When an entire independent sentence is enclosed in parentheses or square brackets, the period belongs inside the closing parenthesis or bracket. When matter in parentheses or brackets, even a grammatically complete sentence, is included within another sentence, the period belongs outside (but see also 6.96). Avoid enclosing more than one complete sentence within another sentence. For the location of a period with quotation marks, see 6.9.

> Fiorelli insisted on rewriting the paragraph. (His newfound ability to type was both a blessing and a curse.)
> Farnsworth had left an angry message for Isadora on the mantel (she noticed it while glancing in the mirror).
> "All the evidence pointed to the second location [the Lászlós' studio]."

6.14 *When to omit a period.* No period should follow display lines (chapter titles, subheads, and similar headings), running heads, column heads in tables, phrases used as captions (but see 3.21), datelines in correspondence, signatures, or addresses. (Likewise, a comma is sometimes omitted for aesthetic reasons at the ends of lines set in large display type; see 8.163.) A run-in subhead at the beginning of a paragraph, however, is followed by a period (see 1.54). When an expression that ends in a period (e.g., an abbreviation) falls at the end of a sentence, no additional period follows (see 6.117). For use or omission of the period in outline style, see 6.121–26. For punctuation with URLs and e-mail addresses, see 6.8.

6.15 *Periods in ellipses and suspension points.* For the use of an ellipsis (a series of periods) to indicate an omission in quoted material, see 13.48–56. For the use of suspension points to indicate interruptions or breaks in thought in foreign-language material, see 11.10, 11.35, 11.54, 11.81, 11.122.

Commas

6.16 *Use of the comma.* The comma, aside from its technical uses in mathematical, bibliographical, and other contexts, indicates the smallest break in sentence structure. Especially in spoken contexts, it usually denotes a slight pause. In formal prose, however, logical considerations come first. Effective use of the comma involves good judgment, with ease of reading the end in view.

6.17 *Commas in pairs.* Whenever a comma is used to set off an element (such as "1928" or "Minnesota" in the first two examples below), a second comma is required if the phrase or sentence continues beyond the element being set off. This principle applies to many of the uses for commas described in this section. An exception is made for commas within the title of a work (third example).

June 5, 1928, lives on in the memories of only a handful of us.
Sledding in Duluth, Minnesota, is facilitated by that city's hills and frigid winters.
but
Look Homeward, Angel was not the working title of the manuscript.

Series and the Serial Comma

6.18 **Serial commas.** Items in a series are normally separated by commas (but see 6.58). When a conjunction joins the last two elements in a series of three or more, a comma—known as the serial or series comma or the Oxford comma—should appear before the conjunction. Chicago strongly recommends this widely practiced usage, blessed by Fowler and other authorities (see bibliog. 1.2), since it prevents ambiguity. If the last element consists of a pair joined by *and*, the pair should still be preceded by a serial comma and the first *and* (see the last two examples below).

She took a photograph of her parents, the president, and the vice president.
Before heading out the door, she took note of the typical outlines of sweet gum, ginkgo, and elm leaves.
I want no ifs, ands, or buts.
Paul put the kettle on, Don fetched the teapot, and I made tea.
Their wartime rations included cabbage, turnips, and bread and butter.
John was singing, Jean was playing guitar, and Alan was running errands and furnishing food.

Note that the phrase *as well as* is not equivalent to *and*.

The team fielded one Mazda, two Corvettes, and three Bugattis, as well as a battered Plymouth Belvedere.
not
The team fielded one Mazda, two Corvettes, three Bugattis, as well as a battered Plymouth Belvedere.

In a series whose elements are all joined by conjunctions, no commas are needed unless the elements are long and delimiters would be helpful.

Would you prefer Mendelssohn or Schumann or Liszt?
You can turn left at the second fountain and right when you reach the temple, or turn left at the third fountain and left again at the statue of Venus, or just ask a local person how to get there.

6.19 *Using semicolons instead of commas in a series.* When elements in a series include internal punctuation, or when they are very long and complex, they may need to be separated by semicolons rather than by commas (see 6.58). For a simple list, however—even if it is introduced with a colon— commas are preferred.

6.20 *Commas with "etc." and "et al."* Traditional use dictates that the abbreviation *etc.* (*et cetera*, literally "and others of the same kind") is preceded and (unless it ends a sentence) followed by a comma when it is the final item in a series. Such equivalents as *and so forth* and *and the like* are usually treated the same way. (In formal prose, *etc.* should be avoided, though it is usually acceptable in lists and tables, in notes, and within parentheses.) See also 5.220 under *etc.*

Proper technique (with attention paid to posture, wrist position, distance from the keyboard, etc., in the later performances) is not in and of itself sufficient to explain Rubinstein's endurance.
The philosopher's population studies, classic textbooks, stray notes, and so forth, were found in the attic.

The abbreviation *et al.* (*et alia* [neut.], *et alii* [masc.], or *et aliae* [fem.], literally "and others"), whether used in regular text or (more often) in bibliographical references, should be treated like *etc.* If *et al.* follows a single item, however (e.g., "Jones et al."), it requires no preceding or following comma. Note that neither *etc.* nor *et al.* is italicized in normal prose (see the first example above).

6.21 *Omitting serial commas before ampersands.* When an ampersand is used instead of the word *and* (as in company names), the serial comma is omitted.

Winken, Blinken & Nod is a purveyor of nightwear.

Commas with Relative Clauses

6.22 *Restrictive and nonrestrictive clauses—"which" versus "that."* A relative clause is said to be restrictive if it provides information that is essential to the meaning of the sentence. Restrictive relative clauses are usually introduced by *that* (or *who/whom/whose*) and are never set off by commas from the rest of the sentence. The pronoun *that* may occasionally be omitted (but need not be) if the sentence is just as clear without it, as in the second example (before "I").

> The version of the manuscript that the editors submitted to the publisher was well formatted.
> The book I have just finished is due back tomorrow; the others can wait.
> I prefer to share the road with drivers who focus on the road rather than on what they happen to be reading.

A relative clause is said to be nonrestrictive if it could be omitted without obscuring the identity of the noun to which it refers or otherwise changing the meaning of the rest of the sentence. Nonrestrictive relative clauses are usually introduced by *which* (or *who/whom/whose*) and are set off from the rest of the sentence by commas.

> The final manuscript, which was well formatted, was submitted to the publisher on time.
> *Ulysses*, which I finished early this morning, is due back on June 16.
> I prefer to share the road with illiterate drivers, who are unlikely to read books while driving.

Although *which* can be substituted for *that* in a restrictive clause (a common practice in British English), many writers preserve the distinction between restrictive *that* (with no commas) and nonrestrictive *which* (with commas). See also 5.220 under *that; which*.

Commas with Appositives

6.23   *Restrictive and nonrestrictive appositives.* A word, abbreviation, phrase, or clause that is in apposition to a noun (i.e., provides an explanatory equivalent) is normally set off by commas if it is nonrestrictive—that is, if it can be omitted without obscuring the identity of the noun to which it refers.

> K. Lester's only collection of poems, *An Apocryphal Miscellany*, first appeared as a series of mimeographs.
> This year's poet laureate, K. Lester, spoke first.
> Ursula's husband, Jan, is also a writer.

Ursula's son, Clifford, had been a student of Norman Maclean's. (Ursula has only one son.)

If, however, the word or phrase is restrictive—that is, provides essential information about the noun (or nouns) to which it refers—no commas should appear.

O'Neill's play *The Hairy Ape* was being revived. (O'Neill wrote a number of plays.)
The renowned poet and historian K. Lester scheduled a six-city tour for April.
Caligula's sister Drusilla has been the subject of much speculation. (Caligula had more than one sister.)

See also 5.21.

Commas with Parenthetical and Descriptive Phrases

6.24 *Commas with parenthetical elements.* If only a slight break is intended, commas should be used to set off a parenthetical element inserted into a sentence as an explanation or comment. If a stronger break is needed or if there are commas within the parenthetical element, em dashes (6.82) or parentheses (6.92) should be used.

All the test participants, in spite of our initial fears, recovered.
The Hooligan Report was, to say the least, a bombshell.
The most provocative, if not the most important, part of the statement came last.
Most children fail to consider the history behind new technologies, if they think of it at all.

6.25 *Commas with "however," "therefore," "indeed," and so forth.* Commas—sometimes paired with semicolons (see 6.55)—are traditionally used to set off adverbs such as *however, therefore,* and *indeed.* When the adverb is essential to the meaning of the clause, or if no pause is intended or desired, commas are not needed (as in the last two examples).

A truly efficient gasoline-powered engine remains, however, a pipe dream.
Indeed, not one test subject accurately predicted the amount of soup in the bowl.
but
If you cheat and are therefore disqualified, you may also risk losing your scholarship.
That was indeed the outcome of the study.

6.26   *Commas with restrictive and nonrestrictive phrases.* A phrase that is restrictive—that is, essential to the meaning (and often the identity) of the noun it belongs to—should not be set off by commas. A nonrestrictive phrase, however, should be enclosed in commas (or, if at the end of a sentence, preceded by a comma). See also 6.22.

> The woman with the guitar over her shoulder is my sister.
> *but*
> My sister, with her guitar over her shoulder, turned to the drummer and gave the
> signal to begin.

6.27   *Commas with "such as" and "including."* The principles delineated in 6.26 apply also to phrases introduced by *such as* or *including*. Phrases introduced by these terms are set off by commas when they are used nonrestrictively (as in the first two examples below) but not when they are used restrictively (as in the last example).

> The entire band, including the matutinal lead singer, overslept the noon rehearsal.
> Some words, such as *matutinal* and *onomatopoetic*, are best avoided in everyday
> speech.
> *but*
> Words such as *matutinal* and *onomatopoetic* are best avoided in everyday speech.

Commas with Independent Clauses

6.28   *Commas with independent clauses joined by conjunctions.* When independent clauses are joined by *and*, *but*, *or*, *so*, *yet*, or any other conjunction, a comma usually precedes the conjunction. If the clauses are very short and closely connected, the comma may be omitted unless the clauses are part of a series. These recommendations apply equally to imperative sentences, in which the subject (*you*) is omitted but understood (as in the fifth and last examples). (For the use of a semicolon between independent clauses, see 6.54.)

> We activated the alarm, but the intruder was already inside.
> All watches display the time, and some of them do so accurately.
> Do we want to foster creativity, or are we interested only in our intellectual prop-
> erty?
> The bus never came, so we took a taxi.
> Wait for me at the bottom of the hill on Buffalo Street, or walk up to Eddy Street
> and meet me next to the yield sign.

Donald cooked, Sally trimmed the tree, and Maddie and Cammie offered hors d'oeuvres.
but
Electra played the guitar and Tambora sang.
Raise your right hand and repeat after me.

6.29   *Commas with compound predicates.* A comma is not normally used between the parts of a compound predicate—that is, two or more verbs having the same subject, as distinct from two independent clauses (see 6.28). A comma may occasionally be needed, however, to prevent a misreading (as in the last example).

He printed out a week's worth of crossword puzzles and arranged them on his clipboard.
Kelleher tried to contact the mayor but was informed that she had stopped accepting unsolicited calls.
but
She recognized the man who entered the room, and gasped.

Commas with Dependent Clauses

6.30   *Comma preceding main clause.* A dependent clause that precedes a main clause should be followed by a comma.

If you accept our conditions, we shall agree to the proposal.

6.31   *Comma following main clause.* A dependent clause that follows a main clause should *not* be preceded by a comma if it is restrictive, that is, essential to the meaning of the main clause. For instance, in the first example below, it is *not* necessarily true that "we will agree to the proposal"; it is, however, true that "we will agree" to it "if you accept our conditions."

We will agree to the proposal if you accept our conditions.
Paul was astonished when he heard the terms.
He wasn't running because he was afraid; he was running because he was late.

If the dependent clause is merely supplementary or parenthetical, it should be preceded by a comma. Such distinctions are occasionally tenuous. In fact, as the third example below makes clear, the meaning in such cases can depend entirely on the presence or absence of a comma (compare with the third example above). If in doubt, rephrase.

I'd like the *tom yum*, if you don't mind.
At last she arrived, when the food was cold.
He didn't run, because he was afraid to move.
or
Because he was afraid to move, he didn't run.

6.32 **"And if," "that if," and the like.** When two conjunctions appear next to each other (e.g., *and if, but if*), they need not be separated by a comma. See also 6.30, 6.31.

Burton examined the documents for over an hour, and if Smedley had not intervened, the forgery would have been revealed.
They decided that if it rained, they would reschedule the game.

Commas with Two or More Adjectives Preceding a Noun

6.33 *Commas with coordinate adjectives.* As a general rule, when a noun is preceded by two or more adjectives that could, without affecting the meaning, be joined by *and*, the adjectives are normally separated by commas. Such adjectives, which are called coordinate adjectives, can also usually be reversed in order and still make sense. If, on the other hand, the adjectives are not coordinate—that is, if one or more of the adjectives is essential to (i.e., forms a unit with) the noun being modified—no commas are used.

Shelly had proved a faithful, sincere friend. (Shelly's friendship has proved faithful *and* sincere.)
It is going to be a long, hot, exhausting summer. (The summer is going to be long *and* hot *and* exhausting.)
She has a young, good-looking friend. (Her friend is young *and* good-looking.)
but
She has many young friends.
He has rejected traditional religious affiliations.
She opted for an inexpensive quartz watch.

6.34 *Commas with repeated adjectives.* When an adjective is repeated before a noun, a comma normally appears between the pair.

Many, many people have enjoyed the book.

Commas with Introductory Words and Phrases

6.35   *Commas with introductory participial phrases.* An introductory participial phrase should be set off by a comma unless the sentence is inverted and the phrase immediately precedes the verb.

> Exhilarated by the morning's work, she skipped lunch and headed for the ocean.
> Failing in their quest, the team resolved to train harder in the off-season.
> *but*
> Running along behind the wagon was the archduke himself!

6.36   *Commas with introductory adverbial phrases.* An introductory adverbial phrase is often set off by a comma but need not be unless misreading is likely. Shorter adverbial phrases are less likely to merit a comma than longer ones.

> After reading the note, Henrietta turned pale.
> On the other hand, his vices could be considered virtues.
> After 1956 such complaints about poor fidelity became far less common.
> *but*
> Before eating, the members of the committee met in the assembly room.
> To Anthony, Blake remained an enigma.

A comma should *not* be used if the introductory adverbial phrase immediately precedes the verb it modifies.

> Before the footlights stood one of the most notorious rakes of the twenty-first century.

6.37   *Commas with "oh" and "ah."* A comma usually follows an exclamatory *oh* or *ah* unless it is followed by an exclamation mark or forms part of a phrase (e.g., "oh boy," "ah yes"). No comma follows vocative *oh* or (mainly poetic and largely archaic) *O*. See also 7.45.

> Oh, you're right!   Oh mighty king!
> Ah, here we are at last!   "O wild West Wind . . ."
> Oh no! Ah yes! Oh yeah?

6.38   *Commas with direct address.* A comma is used to set off names or words used in direct address and informal correspondence (in formal correspondence, a colon usually follows the name).

Ms. Jones, please come in.
James, your order is ready.
I am not here, my friends, to discuss personalities.
Hello, Ms. Philips.
Dear Judy, . . .

6.39 *"Yes," "no," and the like.* A comma should follow an introductory *yes*, *no*, *well*, and the like, except in certain instances more likely to be encountered in informal prose or dialogue.

Yes, it is true that 78 percent of the subjects ate 50 percent more than they reported.
No, neither scenario improved the subjects' accuracy.
Well then, we shall have to take a vote.
but
No you will not!

Other Uses of the Comma

6.40 *Commas with "not" phrases.* When a phrase beginning with *not* is interjected in order to clarify a particular noun, commas should be used to set off the phrase. See also 6.41.

We hoped the mayor herself, not her assistant, would attend the meeting.
It's you they want, not him.

6.41 *Commas with "not . . . but," "not only . . . but," and the like.* With an interjected phrase of the type *not . . . but* or *not only . . . but*, commas are usually unnecessary.

They marched to Washington not only armed with petitions and determined to get their senators' attention but also hoping to demonstrate their solidarity with one another.
Being almost perfectly ambidextrous, she wore not one watch but two.

If, however, such a phrase seems to require special emphasis or clarification (usually a matter of editorial judgment), commas may be used to set off the *not* phrase. Alternatively, a dash may be used in place of the first comma.

She was in the habit of placing her orders months ahead of the competition—
not only as a matter of personal pride, but also to bolster her credibility as an
early adopter.

6.42 *Commas with "the more," "the less," and so on.* A comma is customarily used
between clauses of the *more . . . the more* type. Shorter phrases of that type,
however, rarely merit commas.

The more I discover about the workings of mechanical movements, the less I seem
to care about the holy grail of perfectly accurate timekeeping.
but
The more the merrier.

6.43 *Commas with "that is," "namely," "for example," and similar expressions.* Expressions of the type *that is* are traditionally followed by a comma. They
may be preceded by an em dash or a semicolon, or the entire phrase they
introduce may be enclosed in parentheses or em dashes.

There are simple alternatives to the stigmatized plastic shopping bag—namely,
reusable cloth bags and foldable carts.
The committee (that is, its more influential members) wanted to drop the matter.
Keesler managed to change the subject; that is, he introduced a tangential issue.
Bones from various small animals—for example, a squirrel, a cat, a pigeon, and
a muskrat—were found in the doctor's cabinet.

When *or* is used in a sense analogous to *that is* (to mean "in other words"),
the phrase it introduces is usually set off by commas.

The compass stand, or binnacle, must be situated within the helmsman's field
of vision.

The abbreviations *i.e.* ("that is") and *e.g.* ("for example"), if used in formal writing, should be confined to parentheses or notes and followed
by a comma.

The most noticeable difference between male and female ginkgo trees (i.e., the
presence of berries in the latter) is also the species' most controversial feature.

6.44 *Commas between homonyms.* For ease of reading and subject to editorial
discretion, two words that are spelled alike but have different functions
may be separated by a comma if such clarification seems desirable.

Let us march in, in twos.
Whatever is, is good.
but
"It depends on what *means* means."

6.45 **Commas with dates.** In the month-day-year style of dates, commas must be used to set off the year. In the day-month-year system—useful in material that requires many full dates (and standard in British English)—no commas are needed. Where month and year only are given, or a specific day (such as a holiday) with a year, neither system uses a comma. For dates used adjectivally, see 5.82. See also 9.30–37. For the year-month-day (ISO) date style, see 9.37.

The performance took place on February 2, 2006, at the State Theatre in Ithaca.
Bradford gradually came to accept the verdict. (See his journal entries of 6 October 1999 and 4 January 2000.)
In March 2008 she turned seventy-five.
On Thanksgiving Day 1998 they celebrated their seventy-fifth anniversary.

6.46 **Commas with addresses and place-names in text.** Commas are used to set off the individual elements in addresses or place-names that are run in to the text. In a mailing address, commas should be used as sparsely as possible (e.g., no comma appears between a street name and an abbreviation such as SW or before a postal code; see first example); if in doubt, consult the applicable postal service. For place-names used adjectivally, see 5.67.

Proofs were sent to the author at 743 Olga Drive NE, Ashtabula, OH 44044, on May 2.
Waukegan, Illinois, is not far from the Wisconsin border.
The plane landed in Kampala, Uganda, that evening.

Some institutional names include place-names set off by commas. When such a name appears in the middle of a clause, a second comma is required to set off the place-name. See also 6.81.

California State University, Northridge, has an enrollment of . . .
but
The University of Wisconsin–Madison has an enrollment of . . .

6.47 **"Jr.," "Sr.," and the like.** Commas are not required around *Jr.* and *Sr.*, and they are never used to set off II, III, and the like when these are used as part of a name. In an inverted name, however (as in an index; see 16.41), a comma is required before such an element, which comes last.

John Doe Sr. continues to cast a shadow over his son.
Jason Deer III has turned over stewardship of the family business to his cousin.
but
Doe, John, Sr.
Stag, Jason, III

If commas must be used with *Jr.* or *Sr.*, rephrase as needed to avoid the possessive.

6.48 **"Inc.," "Ltd.," and the like.** Commas are not required around *Inc.*, *Ltd.*, and such as part of a company's name. A particular company may use such commas in its corporate documentation; articles and books about such companies, however, should generally opt for a consistent style rather than make exceptions for particular cases.

QuartzMove Inc. was just one such company named in the suit.

6.49 *Commas to indicate elision.* A comma is often used to indicate the omission of a word or words readily understood from the context.

In Illinois there are seventeen such schools; in Ohio, twenty; in Indiana, thirteen.
Thousands rushed to serve him in victory; in defeat, none.

The comma may be omitted if the elliptical construction is clear without it.

One student excels at composition, another at mathematics, and the third at sports.
Jasper missed her and she him.

6.50 *Commas with quotations.* Material quoted in the form of dialogue or from text is traditionally introduced with a comma (but see 6.63, 13.17). If a quotation is introduced by *that*, *whether*, or a similar conjunction, no comma is needed.

It was Thoreau who wrote, "One generation abandons the enterprises of another like stranded vessels."
She replied, "I hope you aren't referring to us."
Was it Stevenson who said that "the cruelest lies are often told in silence"?
He is now wondering whether "to hold, as 'twere, the mirror up to nature."

For the location of a comma in relation to closing quotation marks, see 6.9. For quoted maxims and proverbs, see 6.51. For detailed discussion and illustration of the use or omission of commas before and after quoted material, including dialogue, see 13.18, 13.48–56, and the examples throughout chapter 13.

6.51 *Commas with maxims and proverbs.* With maxims, proverbs, mottoes, and other familiar expressions, commas are used or omitted in the same way as with appositives (6.23), unless an expression is being attributed directly to a speaker or writer (in which case the rules in 6.50 and 13.18 apply). Whether such expressions are enclosed in quotation marks depends largely on the syntax of the sentence in which they appear. See also 8.197.

The motto "All for one and one for all" appears over the door.
Tom's favorite proverb, "A rolling stone gathers no moss," proved wrong.
It is untrue that a rolling stone gathers no moss.

6.52 *Commas with questions.* A question is sometimes included within another sentence either directly or indirectly—not as a quotation but as part of the sentence as a whole. A direct question (unless it comes at the beginning of a sentence) is usually introduced by a comma. A direct question may take an initial capital letter if it is relatively long or has internal punctuation.

Suddenly he asked himself, where am I headed?
The question on everyone's mind was, how are we going to tell her?
Legislators had to be asking themselves, Can the fund be used for the current emergency, or must it remain dedicated to its original purpose?

If the result seems awkward, rephrase as an indirect question. An indirect question does not require a question mark, nor does it need to be set off with a comma. Indirect questions are never capitalized (except at the beginning of a sentence). See also 6.66–70.

Suddenly he asked himself where he was headed.
The question of how to tell her was on everyone's mind.
Ursula wondered why her watch had stopped ticking.
Where to find a reliable clock is the question of the hour.

6.53 *Commas relative to parentheses and brackets.* When the context calls for a comma at the end of material in parentheses or brackets, the comma should follow the closing parenthesis or bracket. A comma never precedes a closing parenthesis. (For its rare appearance before an opening parenthesis, see the examples in 6.123.) Rarely, a comma may appear inside and immediately before a closing bracket as part of an editorial interpolation (as in the last example; see also 13.57).

> After several drummers had tried out for the part (the last having destroyed the kit), the band decided that a drum machine was their steadiest option.
> Her delivery, especially when she would turn to address the audience (almost as if to spot a long-lost friend), was universally praised.
> "Conrad told his assistant [Martin], who was clearly exhausted, to rest."
> "The contents of the vault included fennel seeds, tweezers, [straight-edged razors,] and empty Coca-Cola cans."

Semicolons

6.54   *Use of the semicolon.* In regular prose, a semicolon is most commonly used between two independent clauses not joined by a conjunction to signal a closer connection between them than a period would.

> She spent much of her free time immersed in the ocean; no mere water-*resistant* watch would do.
> Though a gifted writer, Miqueas has never bothered to master the semicolon; he insists that half a colon is no colon at all.

For the use of the semicolon in index entries, see 16.96, 16.17. For its use in parenthetical text citations, see 15.29. For its use with a second subtitle of a work, see 14.98.

6.55   *Semicolons with "however," "therefore," "indeed," and the like.* Certain adverbs, when they are used to join two independent clauses, should be preceded by a semicolon rather than a comma. These transitional adverbs include *however, thus, hence, indeed, accordingly, besides, therefore,* and sometimes *then* (see also 6.56). A comma usually follows the adverb but may be omitted if the sentence seems just as effective without it (see also 6.36).

> The accuracy of Jesse's watch was never in question; besides, he was an expert at intuiting the time of day from the position of the sun and stars.
> Kallista was determined not to miss anything on her voyage; accordingly, she made an appointment with her ophthalmologist.

The trumpet player developed a painful cold sore; therefore plans for a third show were scrapped.

6.56   *Semicolons with "that is," "for example," "namely," and the like.* A semicolon may be used before expressions such as *that is, for example,* or *namely* when they introduce an independent clause. For an example, see 6.43. See also 6.55.

6.57   *Semicolons before a conjunction.* Normally, an independent clause introduced by a conjunction is preceded by a comma (see 6.28). In formal prose, a semicolon may be used instead—either to effect a stronger, more dramatic separation between clauses or when the second independent clause has internal punctuation.

Frobisher had always assured his grandson that the house would be his; yet there was no provision for this bequest in his will.

Garrett had insisted on remixing the track; but the engineer's demands for overtime pay, together with the band's reluctance, persuaded him to accept the original mix.

6.58   *Semicolons in a complex series.* When items in a series themselves contain internal punctuation, separating the items with semicolons can aid clarity. If ambiguity seems unlikely, commas may be used instead (see 6.18). See also 6.123.

The membership of the international commission was as follows: France, 4; Germany, 5; Great Britain, 1; Italy, 3; United States, 7.

The defendant, in an attempt to mitigate his sentence, pleaded that he had recently, on doctor's orders, gone off his medications; that his car—which, incidentally, he had won in the late 1970s on *Let's Make a Deal*—had spontaneously caught on fire; and that he had not eaten for several days.

but

She decided to buy three watches—an atomic watch for travel within the United States, a solar-powered, water-resistant quartz for international travel, and an expensive self-winding model for special occasions.

Colons

6.59   *Use of the colon.* A colon introduces an element or a series of elements illustrating or amplifying what has preceded the colon. Between independent clauses it functions much like a semicolon, and in some cases either mark may work as well as the other; use a colon sparingly, however, and *only* to emphasize that the second clause illustrates or amplifies the first. (The colon should generally convey the sense of "as follows.") The colon may sometimes be used instead of a period to introduce a series of related sentences (as in the third example below).

> The watch came with a choice of three bands: stainless steel, plastic, or leather.
> They even relied on a chronological analogy: just as the Year II had overshadowed 1789, so the October Revolution had eclipsed that of February.
> Yolanda faced a conundrum: She could finish the soup, pretending not to care that what she had thought until a moment ago was a vegetable broth was in fact made from chicken. She could feign satiety and thank the host for a good meal. Or she could use this opportunity to assert her preference for a vegan diet.

For use of the em dash instead of a colon, see 6.82. For the use of colons with subtitles, see 14.97. For the use of colons in indexes, see 16.95. For other uses of the colon—in source citations, URLs, mathematical expressions, and other settings—consult the index or search the online edition of this manual.

6.60   *Space after colon.* In typeset matter, no more than one space should follow a colon. Further, in some settings—as in a source citation between a volume and page number with no intervening date or issue number (see 14.186), a biblical citation, or a ratio—*no* space should follow a colon. See also 6.7.

6.61   *Lowercase or capital letter after a colon.* When a colon is used within a sentence, as in the first two examples in 6.59, the first word following the colon is lowercased unless it is a proper name. When a colon introduces two or more sentences (as in the third example in 6.59), when it introduces a speech in dialogue or an extract (as in the examples in 6.63), or when it introduces a direct question, the first word following it is capitalized.

6.62   *Colons with "as follows" and other introductory phrases.* A colon is normally used after *as follows,* *the following,* and similar expressions. (For lists, see 6.121–26.)

> The steps are as follows: first, make grooves for the seeds; second, sprinkle the seeds; third, push the earth back over the grooves; fourth, water generously.
> Kenzie's results yield the following hypotheses: First, . . . Second, . . . Third, . . .

6.63   *Colons to introduce speech or quotations.* A colon is often used to introduce speech in dialogue.

> Michael: The incident has already been reported.
> Timothy: Then, sir, all is lost!

A colon may also be used instead of a comma to introduce a quotation, either where the syntax of the introduction requires it or to more formally introduce the quotation. For the use of the comma with quotations, see 6.50. See also 13.17.

> Julian Duguid, author of *Green Hell* (1931), starts his book boldly: "When a man yields to the urge of Ishmael . . ."

6.64   *Colons with formal direct address.* At the beginning of a speech or a formal communication, a colon usually follows the identification of those addressed. For use of a comma, see 6.38.

> Ladies and Gentlemen: Dear Credit and Collections Manager:
> To Whom It May Concern:

6.65   *Some common misuses of colons.* Many writers assume—wrongly—that a colon is always needed before a series or a list. In fact, if a colon intervenes in what would otherwise constitute a grammatical sentence—even if the introduction appears on a separate line, as in a list (see 6.121–26)—it is probably being used inappropriately. A colon, for example, should *not* be used before a series that serves as the object of a verb. When in doubt, apply this test: to merit a colon, the words that introduce a series or list must themselves constitute a grammatically complete sentence.

> The menagerie included cats, pigeons, newts, and deer ticks.
> *not*
> The menagerie included: cats, pigeons, newts, and deer ticks.

Nor should a colon normally be used after *namely, for example,* and similar expressions (see 6.43).

Question Marks

6.66   *Use of the question mark.* The question mark, as its name suggests, is used to indicate a direct question. It may also be used to indicate editorial doubt (e.g., regarding a date or facts of publication; see 14.138) or (occasionally) at the end of a declarative or imperative sentence in order to express surprise, disbelief, or uncertainty. See also 6.72, 6.116, 6.118.

Who will represent the poor?
Thomas Kraftig (1610?–66) was the subject of the final essay.
This is your reply?

6.67 *Question mark within a sentence.* A question mark is used to mark the end of a direct question within a sentence. If the question does not begin the sentence, it need not start with a capital letter (but see 6.52).

Is it worth the risk? he wondered.

For the omission of a comma following a question mark, see 6.119.

6.68 *Indirect questions.* An indirect question never takes a question mark. See also 6.52.

He wondered whether it was worth the risk.
How the two could be reconciled was the question on everyone's mind.

When a question within a sentence consists of a single word, such as *who*, *when*, *how*, or *why*, a question mark may be omitted, and the word is sometimes italicized.

She asked herself why.
The question was no longer *how* but *when*.

6.69 *Requests as questions.* A request disguised as a question does not require a question mark. Such formulations can usually be reduced to the imperative.

Would you kindly respond by March 1.
or
Please respond by March 1.

6.70 *Question marks in relation to surrounding text and punctuation.* A question mark should be placed inside quotation marks, parentheses, or brackets only when it is part of (i.e., applies to) the quoted or parenthetical matter. See also 6.10, 6.120.

The ambassador asked, "Has the Marine Corps been alerted?"
Why was Farragut trembling when he said, "I'm here to open an inquiry"?

Emily (had we met before?) winked at me.

Why did she tell him only on the morning of his departure (March 18)?

"What do you suppose he had in mind," inquired Newman, "when he said, 'You are all greater fools than I thought'?"

Exclamation Points

6.71   *Use of the exclamation point.* An exclamation point (which should be used sparingly to be effective) marks an outcry or an emphatic or ironic comment. See also 6.116, 6.118.

Heads up!

The procedure resulted in a 3 percent increase—a far cry from the 50 percent predicted by the doomsayers!

6.72   *Exclamation rather than question.* A sentence in the form of a direct question can often be styled as an exclamation simply by using an exclamation point rather than a question mark.

How could you possibly believe that!

When will I ever learn!

6.73   *Exclamation point as editorial protest or amusement.* Writers and editors should be aware that an exclamation point added in brackets to quoted matter to indicate editorial protest or amusement is likely to be interpreted as contemptuous; unless such a sentiment is intended, this device should be avoided. The Latin expression *sic* ("thus") should be reserved to indicate an error in the source that might be taken as an error of transcription. See 13.59.

6.74   *Exclamation points with quotation marks, parentheses, or brackets.* An exclamation point should be placed inside quotation marks, parentheses, or brackets only when it is part of the quoted or parenthetical matter.

The performer walked off the stage amidst cries of "Brava!"

She actually wants me to believe the manufacturer's claim that her watch is "water resistant to 300 meters"!

Alex Ramirez (I could have had a stroke!) repeated the whole story.

Hyphens and Dashes

6.75   *Hyphens and dashes compared.* Hyphens and the various dashes all have
their specific appearance (shown below) and uses (discussed in the following paragraphs). The hyphen, the en dash, and the em dash are the
most commonly used. Though many readers may not notice the difference—especially between an en dash and a hyphen—correct use of the
different types is a sign of editorial precision and care. These characters
are easy enough to create with modern software, but publications must
be proofread carefully for any conversion errors along the way from manuscript to published work. See also 2.12, 2.13, 2.93.

hyphen -   en dash –   em dash —   2-em dash ——   3-em dash ———

Hyphens

6.76   *Hyphens in compound words.* The use of the hyphen in compound words
and names and in word division is discussed in 5.91 and in chapter 7, especially 7.31–43 and 7.77–85. See also 6.80.

6.77   *Hyphens as separators.* A hyphen is used to separate numbers that are not
inclusive, such as telephone numbers, social security numbers, and
ISBNs. (For hyphens with dates, see 9.37.) It is also used to separate letters when a word is spelled out letter by letter, in dialogue, in reference
to American Sign Language (see 11.144–54), and elsewhere.

1-800-621-2376 *or* (1-800) 621-2376
0-226-10389-7
"My name is Phyllis; that's p-h-y-l-l-i-s."
A proficient signer can fingerspell c-o-l-o-r-a-d-o in less than two seconds.

Hyphens can also appear in URLs and e-mail addresses. A hyphen must
not be added to such a string when it breaks at the end of a line (see 2.12,
7.42).

En Dashes

6.78   *En dash as "to."* The principal use of the en dash is to connect numbers
and, less often, words. With continuing numbers—such as dates, times,

and page numbers—it signifies *up to and including* (or *through*). For the sake of parallel construction, the word *to*, never the en dash, should be used if the word *from* precedes the first element in such a pair; similarly, *and*, never the en dash, should be used if *between* precedes the first element.

The years 1993–2000 were heady ones for the computer literate.
For documentation and indexing, see chapters 14–16.
In Genesis 6:13–21 we find God's instructions to Noah.
Join us on Thursday, 11:30 a.m.–4:00 p.m., to celebrate the New Year.
I have blocked out December 2009–March 2010 to complete my manuscript.
Her articles appeared in *Postwar Journal* (3 November 1945–4 February 1946).
but
She was in college from 1998 to 2002 (*not* from 1998–2002).

In other contexts, such as with scores and directions, the en dash signifies, more simply, *to*.

The London–Paris train leaves at two o'clock.
On November 20, 1966, Green Bay defeated Chicago, 13–6.
The legislature voted 101–13 to adopt the resolution.

For more on dates and times, see 9.30–37, 9.38–41. For more on number ranges, see 9.60. For the slash, see 6.105.

6.79   *En dash with an unfinished number range.* An en dash may be used to indicate a number range that is ongoing—for example, to indicate the dates of a serial publication or to give the birth date of a living person. No space intervenes between the en dash and the mark of punctuation that follows.

The Chicago translation of *The Mahābhārata* (1973–) is projected to run to ten volumes.
Jack Stag (1950–) *or* Jack Stag (b. 1950)

6.80   *En dashes with compound adjectives.* The en dash can be used in place of a hyphen in a compound adjective when one of its elements consists of an open compound or when both elements consist of hyphenated compounds (see 7.78). This editorial nicety may go unnoticed by the majority of readers; nonetheless, it is intended to signal a more comprehensive link than a hyphen would. It should be used sparingly, and only when a more elegant solution is unavailable. As the first two examples illustrate, the distinction is most helpful with proper compounds, whose limits are established within the larger context by capitalization. The relationship in the third example, though clear enough, depends to some small degree on an en dash that many readers will perceive as a hyphen connecting *music* and *influenced*. The relationships in the fourth example, though also clear enough, are less awkwardly conveyed with a comma.

the post–World War II years
Chuck Berry–style lyrics
country music–influenced lyrics (*or* lyrics influenced by country music)
a quasi-public–quasi-judicial body (*or, better,* a quasi-public, quasi-judicial body)

A single word or prefix should be joined to a hyphenated compound by another hyphen rather than an en dash; if the result is awkward, reword.

non-English-speaking peoples
a two-thirds-full cup (*or, better,* a cup that is two-thirds full)

An abbreviated compound is treated as a single word, so a hyphen, not an en dash, is used in such phrases as "US-Canadian relations" (Chicago's sense of the en dash does not extend to *between*).

6.81   *Other uses for the en dash.* The en dash is sometimes used as a minus sign, but minus signs and en dashes are distinct characters (defined by the Unicode standard as U+2212 and U+2013, respectively; see 11.2, 12.9). Both the characters themselves and the spacing around them may differ; moreover, substituting any character for another may hinder searches in electronic publications. Thus it is best to use the correct character, especially in mathematical copy. In certain scientific disciplines, the en dash may sometimes be used where one would normally expect a hyphen (see *Scientific Style and Format*; bibliog. 1.1). Some universities that have more than one campus use the en dash to link the campus location to the name of the university.

the University of Wisconsin–Madison
the University of Wisconsin–Milwaukee

Em Dashes

6.82   *Em dashes instead of commas, parentheses, or colons.* The em dash, often simply called the dash, is the most commonly used and most versatile of the dashes. Em dashes are used to set off an amplifying or explanatory element and in that sense can function as an alternative to parentheses (second and third examples), commas (fourth and fifth examples), or a colon (first example)—especially when an abrupt break in thought is called for.

It was a revival of the most potent image in modern democracy—the revolutionary idea.

The influence of three impressionists—Monet, Sisley, and Degas—is obvious in her work.

The chancellor—he had been awake half the night—came down in an angry mood.

She outlined the strategy—a strategy that would, she hoped, secure the peace.

My friends—that is, my former friends—ganged up on me.

To avoid confusion, the em dash should never be used within or immediately following another element set off by an em dash (or pair of em dashes). Use parentheses or commas instead.

The Whipplesworth conference—which had already been interrupted by three demonstrations (the last bordering on violence)—was adjourned promptly.

or

The Whipplesworth conference—which had already been interrupted by three demonstrations, the last bordering on violence—was adjourned promptly.

6.83   *Em dash between noun and pronoun.* An em dash is occasionally used to set off an introductory noun, or a series of nouns, from a pronoun that introduces the main clause.

Consensus—that was the will-o'-the-wisp he doggedly pursued.

Broken promises, petty rivalries, and false rumors—such were the obstacles he encountered.

Darkness, thunder, a sudden scream—nothing alarmed the child.

Kingston, who first conceived the idea; Barber, who organized the fundraising campaign; and West, who conducted the investigation—those were the women most responsible for the movement's early success.

6.84   *Em dashes to indicate sudden breaks.* An em dash or a pair of em dashes may indicate a sudden break in thought or sentence structure or an interruption in dialogue. (Where a faltering rather than sudden break is intended, suspension points may be used; see 13.39.)

"Will he—can he—obtain the necessary signatures?" asked Mill.

"Well, I don't know," I began tentatively. "I thought I might—"

"Might what?" she demanded.

If the break belongs to the surrounding sentence rather than to the quoted material, the em dashes must appear outside the quotation marks.

"Someday he's going to hit one of those long shots, and"—his voice turned huffy—
"I won't be there to see it."

6.85   *Em dashes with "that is," "namely," "for example," and similar expressions.*
An em dash may be used before expressions such as *that is* or *namely.*
For examples, see 6.43; see also 6.56.

6.86   *Em dashes in place of commas.* In modern usage, if the context calls for an
em dash where a comma would ordinarily separate a dependent clause
from an independent clause, the comma is omitted. Likewise, if an em
dash is used at the end of quoted material to indicate an interruption, the
comma can be safely omitted before the words that identify the speaker.

Because the data had not been fully analyzed—let alone collated—the publication of the report was delayed.
"I assure you, we shall never—" Sylvia began, but Mark cut her short.

6.87   *Em dashes with other punctuation.* In modern usage, a question mark or
an exclamation point—but never a comma, a colon, or a semicolon, and
rarely a period (see 14.46)—may precede an em dash.

Without further warning—but what could we have done to stop her?—she left
the plant, determined to stop the union in its tracks.
Only if—heaven forbid!—you lose your passport should you call home.

6.88   *Em dashes in lieu of quotation marks.* Em dashes are occasionally used instead of quotation marks to set off dialogue (à la writers in some European languages). Each speech starts a new paragraph. No space follows
the dash.

—Will he obtain the necessary signatures?
—Of course he will!

6.89   *Em dashes in indexes.* For the use of em dashes in an index, see 16.27.

2-Em and 3-Em Dashes

6.90   *2-em dash.* A 2-em dash represents a missing word or part of a word, either omitted to disguise a name (or occasionally an expletive) or else

missing from or illegible in quoted or reprinted material. When a whole word is missing, space appears on both sides of the dash. When only part of a word is missing, no space appears between the dash and the existing part (or parts) of the word; when the dash represents the end of a word, a space follows it (unless a period or other punctuation immediately follows). See also 7.62, 13.57.

"The region gives its —— to the language spoken there."
Admiral N—— and Lady R—— were among the guests.
David H——h [Hirsch?] voted aye.

Although a 2-em dash sometimes represents material to be supplied, it should not be confused with a blank line to be filled in; a blank in a form should appear as an underscore (e.g., ____).

6.91   *3-em dash.* In a bibliography, a 3-em dash followed by a period represents the same author or editor named in the preceding entry (see 14.63–67, 15.17–19).

McCloskey, Deirdre N. *The Bourgeois Virtues*. Chicago: University of Chicago Press, 2006.
———. *Crossing: A Memoir*. Chicago: University of Chicago Press, 1999.

Parentheses

6.92   *Use of parentheses.* Parentheses—stronger than a comma and similar to the dash—are used to set off material from the surrounding text. Like dashes but unlike commas, parentheses can set off text that has no grammatical relationship to the rest of the sentence.

He suspected that the noble gases (helium, neon, etc.) could produce a similar effect.
Intelligence tests (e.g., the Stanford-Binet) are no longer widely used.
Our final sample (collected under difficult conditions) contained an impurity.
Wexford's analysis (see chapter 3) is more to the point.
Dichtung und Wahrheit (also known as *Wahrheit und Dichtung*) has been translated as *Poetry and Truth*.
The disagreement between Johns and Evans (its origins have been discussed elsewhere) ultimately destroyed the organization.

For parenthetical references to a list of works cited, see 15.20–30. For parenthetical references following quoted material, see 13.62–70. For parentheses in notes and bibliographies, see chapter 14. For parentheses in mathematics, see chapter 12, especially 12.26–35. For roman versus italic type, see 6.5.

6.93   *Parentheses for glosses or translations.* Parentheses are used to enclose glosses of unfamiliar terms or translations of foreign terms—or, if the term is given in English, to enclose the original word. In quoted matter, brackets should be used (see 6.97). See also 7.50, 11.6.

> A drop folio (a page number printed at the foot of a page) is useful on the opening page of a chapter.
> The term you should use for 1,000,000,000 is *mil millones* (billion), not *billón* (trillion).
> German has two terms for eating—one for the way humans eat (*essen*) and another for the way animals eat (*fressen*).

6.94   *Parentheses to enclose numbers or letters.* Parentheses are used to enclose numerals or letters marking divisions in lists that are run in to the text (see 6.123) or to mark certain sublevels in an outline (see 6.126).

6.95   *Parentheses within parentheses.* Although the use of parentheses within parentheses (usually for bibliographic purposes) is permitted in some publications—especially in law—Chicago prefers brackets within parentheses (see 6.99). (British style is to use parentheses within parentheses.) For parentheses in mathematics, see 12.26.

6.96   *Parentheses with other punctuation.* An opening parenthesis should be preceded by a comma or a semicolon only in an enumeration (see 6.123); a closing parenthesis should never be preceded by a comma, a semicolon, or a colon. A question mark, an exclamation point, and closing quotation marks precede a closing parenthesis if they belong to the parenthetical matter; they follow it if they belong to the surrounding sentence. A period precedes the closing parenthesis if the entire sentence is in parentheses; otherwise it follows. (Avoid enclosing more than one sentence within another sentence; see 6.13.) Parentheses may appear back to back (with a space in between) if they enclose entirely unrelated material; sometimes, however, such material can be enclosed in a single set of parentheses, usually separated by a semicolon. See also table 6.1. For parentheses in documentation, see chapters 14 and 15.

Having entered (on tiptoe), we sat down on the nearest seats we could find.

Come on in (quietly, please!) and take a seat.

On display were the watchmakers' five latest creations (all of which Shellahan coveted).

Five new watches were on display. (Shellahan coveted the battery-powered quartz model.)

Strabo is probably referring to instruction (διδασκαλία) (Jones et al. 2008).

Brackets and Braces

6.97 *Use of square brackets.* Square brackets (in the United States usually just called brackets) are used in scholarly prose mainly to enclose material—usually added by someone other than the original writer—that does not form a part of the surrounding text. Specifically, in quoted matter, reprints, anthologies, and other nonoriginal material, square brackets enclose editorial interpolations, explanations, translations of foreign terms, or corrections. Sometimes the bracketed material replaces rather than amplifies the original word or words. For brackets in mathematical copy, see 12.26. See also 13.57–61.

"They [the free-silver Democrats] asserted that the ratio could be maintained."

"Many CF [cystic fibrosis] patients have been helped by the new therapy."

Satire, Jebb tells us, "is the only [form] that has a continuous development."

[This was written before the discovery of the Driscoll manuscript.—Ed.]

If quoted matter already includes brackets of its own, the editor should so state in the source citation (e.g., "brackets in the original"); see 13.60 for an analogous situation with italics.

6.98 *Square brackets in translated text.* In a translated work, square brackets are sometimes used to enclose a word or phrase in the original language to avoid ambiguity. (Translators should use this device sparingly.)

The differences between society [*Gesellschaft*] and community [*Gemeinschaft*] will now be analyzed.

6.99 *Square brackets for parentheses within parentheses.* Chicago prefers square brackets as parentheses within parentheses, usually for bibliographic purposes. For mathematical groupings, see 12.26.

(For further discussion see Richardson's excellent analysis [1999] and Danneberger's survey [2000].)

6.100   *Square brackets in phonetics.* Square brackets may be used to enclose a phonetic transcription.

> The verb *entretenir* [ātrətnir], like *keep*, is used in many idioms.

6.101   *Square brackets with other punctuation.* For brackets with other punctuation, most of the same principles apply as for parentheses (see 6.96). For their use in enclosing editorial interpolations, however, the appearance of other punctuation and its position relative to the brackets will depend on the source.

> The original letter, the transcription of which was incomplete, probably read as follows: "[Dear Jacob,] It's been seventy years since I last set eyes on you [. . .]"

6.102   *Angle brackets and braces.* The term *angle brackets* is used here to denote the mathematical symbols for less than (<) and greater than (>) paired to work as delimiters (<. . .>). (True mathematical angle brackets, ⟨ and ⟩, not readily available from most keyboards, are reserved for mathematical notation; see, for example, 12.55.) Angle brackets are most often used to enclose tags in certain markup languages (e.g., XML). By extension, some manuscript editors opt for angle brackets—unlikely to appear elsewhere in a typical word-processed manuscript—to enclose generic instructions for typesetting (see 2.78). Although angle brackets are sometimes used to set off URLs and e-mail addresses (e.g., in message headers in e-mail applications), Chicago discourages this practice for regular prose. Angle brackets are also occasionally used instead of brackets in textual studies to indicate missing or illegible material (see 6.97). Braces, {}, often called curly brackets, provide yet another option for enclosing data and are used in various ways in certain programming languages. They are also used in mathematical and other specialized writing (see, e.g., 12.28). They are not interchangeable with parentheses or brackets. See the example phrases throughout chapter 5 for one possible use of braces.

Slashes

6.103   *Other names for the slash.* The slash (/)—also known as virgule, solidus, slant, or forward slash, to distinguish it from a backward slash, or backslash (\)—has various distinct uses. For a discussion of the niceties associated with the various terms, see Richard Eckersley et al., *Glossary of Typesetting Terms* (bibliog. 2.7).

6.104 *Slashes to signify alternatives.* A slash most commonly signifies alternatives. In certain contexts it is a convenient (if somewhat informal) shorthand for *or*. It is also used for alternative spellings or names. Where one or more of the terms separated by slashes is an open compound, a space before and after the slash can be helpful.

he/she	Hercules/Heracles
his/her	Margaret/Meg/Maggie
and/or	World War I / First World War

Occasionally a slash can signify *and*—though still usually conveying a sense of alternatives.

an insertion/deletion mutation
an MD/PhD program
a Jekyll/Hyde personality

6.105 *Slashes with two-year spans.* A slash is sometimes used in dates instead of an en dash (see 6.78), or even in combination with an en dash, to indicate the last part of one year and the first part of the next. See also 9.63.

The winter of 1966/67 was especially severe.
Enrollment has increased between 1998/99 and 2001/2.
The fiscal years 2005/6–2009/10 were encouraging in several respects.

6.106 *Slashes with dates.* Slashes (or periods or hyphens) are used informally in all-numeral dates (e.g., 3/10/02), but this device should be avoided in formal publications to prevent ambiguity: Americans usually put the month first, but other countries do not (e.g., Canadians and Europeans put the day first). If an all-numeral format must be used, use the ISO standard date format (year, month, date, in the form YYYY-MM-DD; see 9.37).

6.107 *Slashes in abbreviations.* A slash may stand as shorthand for *per*, as in "110 km/sec," "$450/week," or, in certain abbreviations, in lieu of periods, as in "c/o" (in care of).

6.108 *Slashes as fraction bars.* A slash can be used to mean "divided by" when a fraction bar is inappropriate or impractical. When available, single-glyph fractions may be used (e.g., ½ *rather than* 1/2). See also 12.45.

6.109   *Slashes to show line breaks in quoted poetry.* When two or more lines of poetry are quoted in regular text, slashes with space on each side are used to show line breaks. See also 13.27.

> "Thou hast not missed one thought that could be fit, / And all that was improper dost omit."

6.110   *Slashes in URLs and other paths.* Slashes are used in URLs and other paths to separate directories and file names. Spaces are never used in such contexts. In typeset paths, line breaks may occur before a slash but not between two slashes (see 7.42). Some operating systems use backward slashes (or backslashes, \) or colons rather than, or in addition to, slashes. See also 14.11.

> http://www.loc.gov/index.html

Quotation Marks

6.111   *Quotation marks relative to other punctuation and text.* For the location of closing quotation marks in relation to other punctuation, see 6.9–11. For the use of quotation marks with a comma, see 6.50; with a colon, 6.63; with a question mark, 6.70; with an exclamation point, 6.74. For a full discussion of quotation marks with dialogue and quoted matter, see 13.9–10, 13.17–19, 13.28–47. For the use of quotation marks with single words or phrases to signal some special usage, see 7.55, 7.57, 7.58. For quotation marks in French, see 11.32, 11.33; in German, 11.44; in Italian, 11.52; in Spanish, 11.79. For quotation marks with titles of certain types of works, see the examples in chapter 8.

6.112   *Typographer's or "smart" quotation marks.* Published works should use directional (or "smart") quotation marks, sometimes called typographer's or "curly" quotation marks. These marks, which are available in any modern word processor, generally match the surrounding typeface. For a variety of reasons, including the limitations of typewriter-based keyboards and of certain software programs, these marks are often rendered incorrectly. Care must be taken that the proper mark—left or right, as the case may be—has been used in each instance. All software also includes a "default" mark ("); in published prose this unidirectional mark, far more portable than typographer's marks, nonetheless signals a lack of typographical sophistication. Proper directional characters should also be used for single quotation marks (''). The Unicode numbers are as follows: left double quotation mark ("), U+201C; right double quotation mark ("), U+201D; left single quotation mark ('), U+2018; right single quotation mark or apostrophe ('), U+2019 (see 11.2). See also 6.114.

Apostrophes

6.113   *Use of the apostrophe.* The apostrophe has three main uses: to indicate the possessive case, to stand in for missing letters or numerals, and—more rarely—to form the plural of certain expressions. For more on the possessive case, see 7.15–28, 5.19. For contractions, see 7.29. For plurals, see 7.5–14—especially 7.14.

6.114   *"Smart" apostrophes.* Published works should use directional (or "smart") apostrophes. In most typefaces, this mark will appear as a raised (but not inverted) comma. The apostrophe is the same character as the right single quotation mark (defined for Unicode as U+2019; see 6.112). Thanks to the limitations of conventional keyboards and many software programs, the apostrophe has been one of the most abused marks in punctuation—especially in the last generation or so. There are two common pitfalls: using the "default" unidirectional mark ('), on the one hand, and using the left single quotation mark, on the other. The latter usage in particular should always be construed as an error. Some software programs automatically turn a typed apostrophe at the beginning of a word into a left single quotation mark; authors and editors need to be vigilant in overriding such automation and producing the correct mark, and typesetters need to take care not to introduce errors of their own. (If necessary, consult your software's help documentation or special characters menu.)

We spent the '90s (*not* '90s) in thrall to our gadgets.
Where'd you get 'em (*not* 'em)?

6.115   *Apostrophes relative to other punctuation.* An apostrophe (') is considered part of the word (or number) in which it appears. An apostrophe should not be confused with a single closing quotation mark; when a word ends in an apostrophe, no period or comma should intervene between the word and the apostrophe.

The last car in the lot was the Smiths'.

Multiple Punctuation Marks

6.116 *Likely combinations.* The use of more than one mark of punctuation at the same location usually involves quotation marks, em dashes, parentheses, or brackets in combination with periods, commas, colons, semicolons, question marks, or exclamation points. For quotation marks see 6.9–11, 6.50, 6.63, 6.70, 6.74. For em dashes see 6.86, 6.91. For parentheses and brackets see 6.82, 6.95, 6.96, 6.99, 6.101, 6.123. See also table 6.1.

6.117 *Abbreviation-ending periods with other punctuation.* When an expression (such as an abbreviation) that takes a period ends a sentence, no additional period follows (see 6.14). Of course, when any other mark of punctuation is needed immediately after the period, both the period and the additional mark appear.

The study was funded by Mulvehill & Co.
Johnson et al., in *How to Survive,* describe such an ordeal.

6.118 *Periods with question marks or exclamation points.* A period (aside from an abbreviating period; see 6.117) never accompanies a question mark or an exclamation point. The latter two marks, being stronger, take precedence over the period. This principle continues to apply when the question mark or exclamation point is part of the title of a work, as in the final example (cf. 6.119).

Their first question was a hard one: "Who is willing to trade oil for water?"
What did she mean when she said, "The foot now wears a different shoe"?
She owned two copies of *Will You Please Be Quiet, Please?*

6.119 *Commas with question marks or exclamation points.* When a question mark or exclamation point appears at the end of a quotation where a comma would normally appear, the comma is omitted (as in the first example below; see also 6.52). When, however, the title of a work ends in a question mark or exclamation point, a comma should also appear if the grammar of the sentence would normally call for one. This departure from previous editions of the manual overrides aesthetic considerations to recognize not only the syntactic independence of titles but also the potential for clearer sentence structure—especially apparent in the final example, where the comma after *Help!* separates it from the following title. (The occasional awkward result may require rewording.) Compare 6.118. See also 14.105, 14.178.

"Are you a doctor?" asked Mahmoud.

but

"Are You a Doctor?," the fifth story in *Will You Please Be Quiet, Please?*, treats modern love.

All the band's soundtracks—*A Hard Day's Night*, *Help!*, *Yellow Submarine*, and *Magical Mystery Tour*—were popular.

6.120   **Question mark with exclamation point.** In the rare case of a question or exclamation ending with a title or quotation that ends in a question mark or exclamation point, include both marks only if they are different and the sentence punctuation seems essential. See also 6.72.

Have you seen *Help!*?

Who shouted, "Long live the king!"?

I just love *Who's Afraid of Virginia Woolf*?!

but

Who starred opposite Richard Burton in *Who's Afraid of Virginia Woolf*?

Who wrote "Are You a Doctor?"

Where were you when you asked, "Why so blue?"

Lists and Outline Style

6.121   *Lists and outlines—general principles.* All items in a list should be constructed of parallel elements. Unless introductory numerals or letters serve a purpose—to indicate the order in which tasks should be done, to suggest chronology or relative importance among the items, to facilitate text references, or, in a run-in list, to clearly separate the items—they may be omitted. Where similar lists are fairly close together, consistent treatment is essential.

6.122   *Run-in versus vertical lists.* Lists may be either run in to the text or set vertically (outline style). Short, simple lists are usually better run in, especially if the introduction and the items form a complete grammatical sentence (see 6.123). Lists that require typographic prominence, that are relatively long, or that contain items of several levels (see 6.126) should be set vertically.

6.123   *Run-in lists.* If numerals or letters are used to mark the divisions in a run-in list, enclose them in parentheses. If letters are used, they are sometimes italicized (within roman parentheses; see 6.5). If the introductory material forms a grammatically complete sentence, a colon should precede the first parenthesis (see also 6.59, 6.62, 6.65). The items are separated by commas unless any of the items requires internal commas, in which case all the items will usually need to be separated by semicolons (see 6.58). When each item in a list consists of a complete sentence or several sentences, the list is best set vertically (see 6.124).

The qualifications are as follows: a doctorate in physics, five years' experience in a national laboratory, and an ability to communicate technical matter to a lay audience.

Compose three sentences to illustrate analogous uses of (1) commas, (2) em dashes, and (3) parentheses.

For the duration of the experiment, the dieters were instructed to avoid (a) meat, (b) bottled drinks, (c) packaged foods, and (d) nicotine.

Data are available on three groups of counsel: (1) the public defender of Cook County, (2) the member attorneys of the Chicago Bar Association's Defense of Prisoners Committee, and (3) all other attorneys.

You are advised to pack the following items: (a) warm, sturdy outer clothing and enough underwear to last ten days; (b) two pairs of boots, two pairs of sneakers, and plenty of socks; and (c) three durable paperback novels.

6.124 *Vertical lists—punctuation and format.* A vertical list is best introduced by a complete grammatical sentence, followed by a colon (but see 6.125). Items carry no closing punctuation unless they consist of complete sentences. If the items are numbered, a period follows the numeral and each item begins with a capital letter. (When items in a numbered list consist of very long sentences, or of several sentences, and the list does not require typographic prominence, the items may be set in regular text style as numbered paragraphs, with only the first line indented, punctuated as normal prose.) To avoid long, skinny lists, short items may be arranged in two or more columns. If items run over a line, the second and subsequent lines are usually indented (flush-and-hang style, also called hanging indention, as used in bibliographies and indexes). In a numbered or bulleted list, runover lines are aligned with the first word following the numeral or bullet. An alternative to indenting runover lines is to insert extra space between the items.

Your application must include the following documents:

a full résumé
three letters of recommendation
all your diplomas, from high school to graduate school

a brief essay indicating why you want the position and why you consider yourself qualified for it
two forms of identification

. . . . .

An administrative facility can be judged by eight measures:

image   quality
security   functional organization
access   design efficiency
flexibility environmental systems

Each of these measures is discussed below.

. . . . .

Compose three sentences:
1. To illustrate the use of commas in dates
2. To distinguish the use of semicolons from the use of periods
3. To illustrate the use of parentheses within dashes

. . . . .

To change the date display from "31" to "1" on the day following the last day of a
thirty-day month, the following steps are recommended:
1. Pull the stem out to the time-setting position (i.e., past the date-setting posi-
    tion).
2. Make a mental note of the exact minute (but see step 4).
3. Turn the stem repeatedly in a clockwise direction through twenty-four hours.
4. If you are able to consult the correct time, adjust the minute hand accordingly,
    and press the stem all the way in on the exact second. If you are not able to
    consult the correct time, settle on a minute or so past the time noted in step 2.

. . . . .

Use the control panel on your printer to manage basic settings:
•   Control toner usage by turning EconoMode on or off.
•   Adjust print quality by changing the Resolution Enhancement technology
    and Print Density settings.
•   Manage printer memory by changing the Image Adapt and Page Protect set-
    tings.

6.125   *Vertical lists punctuated as a sentence.* In a numbered vertical list that completes a sentence begun in an introductory element and that consists of phrases or sentences with internal punctuation, semicolons may be used between the items, and a period should follow the final item. Each item begins with a lowercase letter. A conjunction (*and* or *or*) before the final item is optional. Such lists, often better run in to the text, should be set vertically only if the context demands that they be highlighted.

> Reporting for the Development Committee, Jobson reported that
> 1.   a fundraising campaign director was being sought;
> 2.   the salary for this director, about $50,000 a year, would be paid out of campaign funds; and
> 3.   the fundraising campaign would be launched in the spring of 2005.

If bullets were used instead of numbers in the example above, the punctuation and capitalization would remain the same.

6.126   *Vertical lists with subdivided items (outlines).* Where items in a numbered list are subdivided, both numerals and letters may be used. Any runover lines should be aligned with the first word following the numeral.

> Applicants will be tested for their skills in the following areas:
> 1. Punctuation
>   a. Using commas appropriately
>   b. Deleting unnecessary quotation marks
>   c. Distinguishing colons from semicolons
> 2. Spelling
>   a. Using a dictionary appropriately
>   b. Recognizing homonyms
>   c. Hyphenating correctly
> 3. Syntax
>   a. Matching verb to subject
>   b. Recognizing and eliminating misplaced modifiers
>   c. Distinguishing phrases from clauses while singing the "Conjunction Junction" song

In the following example, note that the numerals and letters denoting the top three levels are set off by periods and those for the lower four by single or double parentheses, thus distinguishing all seven levels by punctuation as well as indention. Note also that numerals are aligned vertically on the last digit.

I. Historical introduction
II. Dentition in various groups of vertebrates
    A. Reptilia
        1. Histology and development of reptilian teeth
        2. Survey of forms
    B. Mammalia
        1. Histology and development of mammalian teeth
        2. Survey of forms
            a) Primates
                (1) Lemuroidea
                (2) Anthropoidea
                    (a) Platyrrhini
                    (b) Catarrhini
                        i) Cercopithecidae
                        ii) Pongidae
            b) Carnivora
                (1) Creodonta
                (2) Fissipedia
                    (a) Ailuroidea
                    (b) Arctoidea
                (3) Pinnipedia
            c) Etc. . . .

In a list with fewer levels, one might dispense with capital roman numerals and capital letters and instead begin with arabic numerals. What is important is that readers see at a glance the level to which each item belongs. Note that each division and subdivision should normally contain at least two items.

7 *Spelling, Distinctive Treatment of Words, and Compounds*

Overview

7.1   *Recommended dictionaries.* For general matters of spelling, Chicago recommends using *Webster's Third New International Dictionary* and the latest edition of its chief abridgment, *Merriam-Webster's Collegiate Dictionary* (referred to below as *Webster's*). If more than one spelling is given, or more than one form of the plural (see 7.6), Chicago normally opts for the first form listed (even for equal variants), thus aiding consistency. If, as occasionally happens, the *Collegiate* disagrees with the *Third International*, the *Collegiate* should be followed, since it represents the latest lexical research. For further definitions or alternative spellings, refer to a standard dictionary such as the *American Heritage Dictionary of the English Language* or *Random House Webster's College Dictionary*. At least for spelling, one source should be used consistently throughout a single work. (For full bibliographic information on these and other English dictionaries, see bibliog. 3.1.)

7.2   *Spellings peculiar to particular disciplines.* Where a variant spelling carries a special connotation within a discipline, the author's preference should be respected. For example, "archeology," though it is listed as an equal variant of "archaeology" in *Webster's*, is the spelling insisted on by certain specialists. In the absence of such a preference, Chicago prefers the first-listed "archaeology." (*Webster's* separates equal variants by *or*; secondary variants are preceded by *also*.)

7.3   *Non-US spelling.* In English-language works by non-US authors that are edited and produced in the United States, editors at Chicago generally change spelling used in other English-speaking countries to American spelling (e.g., *colour* to *color*, *analyse* to *analyze*). Since consistency is more easily maintained by this practice, few authors object. In quoted material, however, spelling is left unchanged (see 13.7).

7.4   *Supplementing the dictionary.* Much of this chapter is devoted to matters not easily found in most dictionaries: how to form the plural and possessive forms of certain nouns and compounds; how to break words at the end of a printed line, especially those that are not listed in the dictionary; when to use capitals, italics, or quotation marks for distinctive treatment of words and phrases; and, perhaps most important but placed at the end of the chapter for easy reference (7.85), when to use hyphens with compound words, prefixes, and suffixes.

Plurals

7.5	*Standard plural forms.* Most nouns form their plural by adding *s* or—if they end in *ch, j, s, sh, x,* or *z*—by adding *es*. Most English speakers will not need help with such plural forms as *thumbs, churches, fixes,* or *boys,* and these are not listed in standard dictionary entries, including those in *Webster's Collegiate.* (All inflected forms are listed in *Webster's Third New International*; moreover, the online versions of most dictionaries accommodate the correct plural forms in their search engines.) Most dictionaries do, however, give plural forms for words ending in *y* that change to *ies* (*baby,* etc.); for words ending in *o* (*ratio, potato,* etc.); for certain words of Latin or Greek origin such as *crocus, datum,* or *alumna*; and for all words with irregular plurals (*child, leaf,* etc.).

7.6	*Alternative plural forms.* Where *Webster's* gives two forms of the plural— whether as primary and secondary variants, like *zeros* and *zeroes,* or as equal variants, like *millennia* and *millenniums*—Chicago normally opts for the first. In some cases, however, different forms of the plural are used for different purposes. A book may have two *indexes* and a mathematical expression two *indices,* as indicated in the *Webster's* entry for *index.*

7.7	*Plurals of compound nouns.* *Webster's* gives the plural form of most compounds that are tricky (*fathers-in-law, coups d'état, courts-martial, chefs d'oeuvre,* etc.). For those not listed, common sense can usually provide the answer.

bachelors of science	masters of arts	spheres of influence	child laborers

7.8	*Plurals of proper nouns.* Names of persons and other capitalized nouns normally form the plural by adding *s* or *es*. Rare exceptions, including the last example, are generally listed in *Webster's.*

Tom, Dick, and Harry; *pl.* Toms, Dicks, and Harrys
the Jones family, *pl.* the Joneses
the Martinez family, *pl.* the Martinezes
the Bruno family, *pl.* the Brunos
Sunday, *pl.* Sundays
Germany, *pl.* Germanys
Pakistani, *pl.* Pakistanis
but
Romany, *pl.* Romanies

An apostrophe is never used to form the plural of a family name: "The Jeffersons live here" (*not* "Jefferson's"). For the apostrophe in the possessive form of proper nouns, see 7.16.

7.9 *Plural form for Native American group names.* According to current preference, names of Native American groups usually form their plural by adding *s*. In earlier writings the *s* was often omitted (indeed, *Webster's* has continued to present both forms as equal variants).

the Hopis of northeastern Arizona (*not* Hopi)
the language spoken by Cherokees
but
the languages of the Iroquois

7.10 *Singular form used for the plural.* Names ending in an unpronounced *s* or *x* are best left in the singular form.

the seventeen Louis of France
the two Dumas, father and son
two Charlevoix (*or, better,* two towns called Charlevoix)

7.11 *Plural form of italicized words.* If italicized terms—names of newspapers, titles of books, and the like—are used in the plural, the *s* is normally set in roman. A title already in plural form, however, may be left unchanged. In case of doubt, avoid the plural by rephrasing.

two *Chicago Tribune*s and three *Milwaukee Journal Sentinel*s
several *Madame Bovary*s
too many *sic*s
but
four *New York Times*

The plural endings to italicized foreign words should also be set in italics.

Blume, Blumen   *cheval, chevaux*   *señor, señores*

7.12 *Plural form for words in quotation marks.* The plural of a word or phrase in quotation marks may be formed in the usual way (without an apostrophe—a departure from Chicago's former preference). If the result is awkward, reword. Chicago discourages a plural ending following a closing quotation mark.

How many more "To be continueds" (*not* "To be continued"s) can we expect?

or, better,

How many more times can we expect to see "To be continued"?

7.13 *Plurals of noun coinages.* Words and hyphenated phrases that are not nouns but are used as nouns usually form the plural by adding *s* or *es*. (If in doubt, consult an unabridged dictionary like *Webster's Third New International*, which indicates the preferred inflected forms for most nouns, including all of the examples below.)

ifs and buts	thank-yous
dos and don'ts	maybes
threes and fours	yeses and nos

7.14 *Plurals for letters, abbreviations, and numerals.* Capital letters used as words, numerals used as nouns, and abbreviations usually form the plural by adding *s*. To aid comprehension, lowercase letters form the plural with an apostrophe and an *s*. For some exceptions beyond those listed in the last three examples, see 10.43; see also 10.55 (for the International System). For the omission of periods in abbreviations like "BS," "MA," and "PhD," see 10.4. See also 7.58–65.

the three Rs	vols.
x's and *y*'s	eds.
the 1990s	*but*
IRAs	p. (page), pp. (pages)
URLs	n. (note), nn. (notes)
BSs, MAs, PhDs	MS (manuscript), MSS (manuscripts)

Possessives

The General Rule

7.15 *Possessive form of most nouns.* The possessive of most *singular* nouns is formed by adding an apostrophe and an *s*. The possessive of *plural* nouns (except for a few irregular plurals, like *children*, that do not end in *s*) is formed by adding an apostrophe only. For the few exceptions to these principles, see 7.19–21. See also 5.19.

the horse's mouth   a bass's stripes   puppies' paws   children's literature
a herd of sheep's mysterious disappearance

7.16 *Possessive of proper nouns, letters, and numbers.* The general rule extends to proper nouns, including names ending in s, x, or z, in both their singular and plural forms, as well as letters and numbers.

SINGULAR FORMS

Kansas's legislature   Tacitus's *Histories*
Chicago's lakefront   Borges's library
Marx's theories   Dickens's novels
Jesus's adherents   Malraux's masterpiece
Berlioz's works   Josquin des Prez's motets

PLURAL FORMS

the Lincolns' marriage
the Williamses' new house
the Martinezes' daughter
dinner at the Browns' (*that is, at the Browns' place*)

LETTERS AND NUMBERS

FDR's legacy   1999's heaviest snowstorm

7.17 *Possessive of words and names ending in unpronounced "s."* In a return to Chicago's earlier practice, words and names ending in an unpronounced s form the possessive in the usual way (with the addition of an apostrophe and an s). This practice not only recognizes that the additional s is often pronounced but adds to the appearance of consistency with the possessive forms of other types of proper nouns.

Descartes's three dreams
the marquis's mother
François's efforts to learn English
Vaucouleurs's assistance to Joan of Arc
Albert Camus's novels

7.18 *Possessive of names like "Euripides."* In a departure from earlier practice, Chicago no longer recommends the traditional exception for proper classical names of two or more syllables that end in an *eez* sound. Such names form the possessive in the usual way (though when these forms are spoken, the additional s is generally not pronounced).

Euripides's tragedies
the Ganges's source
Xerxes's armies

Exceptions to the General Rule

7.19 *Possessive of nouns plural in form, singular in meaning.* When the singular form of a noun ending in s is the same as the plural (i.e., the plural is un-inflected), the possessives of both are formed by the addition of an apostrophe only. If ambiguity threatens, use *of* to avoid the possessive.

politics' true meaning
economics' forerunners
this species' first record (*or, better,* the first record of this species)

The same rule applies when the name of a place or an organization or a publication (or the last element in the name) is a plural form ending in s, such as *the United States*, even though the entity is singular.

the United States' role in international law
Highland Hills' late mayor
Callaway Gardens' former curator
the National Academy of Sciences' new policy

7.20 *"For . . . sake" expressions.* For the sake of euphony, a few *for . . . sake* ex-pressions used with a singular noun that ends in an s end in an apostro-phe alone, omitting the additional s.

for goodness' sake
for righteousness' sake

Aside from these traditional formulations, however, the possessive in *for . . . sake* expressions may be formed in the normal way.

for expedience's sake
for appearance's sake (*or* for appearances' sake [plural possessive] *or* for the sake of appearance)
for Jesus's sake

7.21 *An alternative practice for words ending in "s."* Some writers and publish-ers prefer the system, formerly more common, of simply omitting the possessive s on all words ending in s—hence "Dylan Thomas' poetry," "Etta James' singing," and "that business' main concern." Though easy to apply and economical, such usage disregards pronunciation in the ma-jority of cases and is therefore not recommended by Chicago.

Particularities of the Possessive

7.22 *Joint versus separate possession.* Closely linked nouns are considered a single unit in forming the possessive when the thing being "possessed" is the same for both; only the second element takes the possessive form.

> my aunt and uncle's house
> Gilbert and Sullivan's *Iolanthe*
> Minneapolis and Saint Paul's transportation system

When the things possessed are discrete, both nouns take the possessive form.

> my aunt's and uncle's medical profiles
> Dylan's and Jagger's hairlines
> New York's and Chicago's transportation systems
> Gilbert's or Sullivan's mustache

7.23 *Compound possessives.* In compound nouns and noun phrases the final element usually takes the possessive form, even in the plural.

> student assistants' time cards
> my daughter-in-law's address
> my sons-in-law's addresses

7.24 *Possessive with genitive.* Analogous to possessives, and formed like them, are certain expressions based on the old genitive case. The genitive here implies *of*.

> in three days' time
> an hour's delay (*or* a one-hour delay)
> six months' leave of absence (*or* a six-month leave of absence)

7.25 *Possessive versus attributive forms.* The line between a possessive or genitive form (see 7.24) and a noun used attributively—to modify another noun—is sometimes fuzzy, especially in the plural. Although terms such as *employees' cafeteria* sometimes appear without an apostrophe, Chicago dispenses with the apostrophe only in proper names (often corporate names) that do not use one or where there is clearly no possessive meaning.

> children's rights
> farmers' market

women's soccer team
boys' clubs
taxpayers' associations (*or* taxpayer associations)
consumers' group (*or* consumer group)
but
Publishers Weekly
Diners Club
Department of Veterans Affairs

7.26   **Possessive with gerund.** A noun followed by a gerund (see 5.110) may take the possessive form in some contexts. This practice, usually limited to proper names and personal nouns or pronouns, should be used with caution. For an excellent discussion, see "Possessive with Gerund," in *Fowler's Modern English Usage* (bibliog. 1.2). The possessive is most commonly used when the gerund rather than the noun that precedes it can be considered to be the subject of a clause, as in the first four examples below. In the fifth example, *Fathers* is clearly the subject of the sentence and *assuming* is a participle (verb form) rather than a gerund (noun form); the possessive would therefore be incorrect.

> Fathers' assuming the care of children has changed the traditional household economy.
> We all agreed that Jerod's running away from the tigers had been the right thing to do.
> Our finding a solution depends on the nature of the problem.
> Eleanor's revealing her secret (*or* Eleanor's revelation) resulted in a lawsuit.
> *but*
> Fathers assuming the care of children often need to consult mothers for advice.

When the noun or pronoun follows a preposition, the possessive is usually optional.

> She was worried about her daughter (*or* daughter's) going there alone.
> I won't put up with him (*or* his) being denigrated.
> The problem of authors (*or* authors') finding the right publisher can be solved.

7.27   **Possessive with "of."** The possessive form may be preceded by *of* where *one of several* is implied. "A friend of Dick's" and "a friend of his" are equally acceptable. See also 5.20.

7.28   **Possessive with italicized or quoted terms.** As with plurals, when an italicized term appears in roman text, the possessive *s* should be set in roman. When the last element is plural in form, add only an apostrophe (see 7.19). Chicago discourages, however, attempting to form the possessive of a term enclosed in quotation marks (a practice that is seen in some periodical publications where most titles are quoted rather than italicized).

the *Atlantic Monthly*'s editor
the *New York Times*' new fashion editor
Gone with the Wind's admirers
but
admirers of "Ode on a Grecian Urn"

Contractions and Interjections

7.29 *Contractions.* In contractions, an apostrophe normally replaces omitted letters. Some contractions, such as *won't* or *ain't*, are formed irregularly. Colloquialisms such as *gonna* or *wanna* take no apostrophe (there being no obvious place for one). *Webster's* lists many common contractions, along with alternative spellings and, where appropriate, plurals. Note that an apostrophe—the equivalent of a right single quotation mark (' not ')—is always used to form a contraction (see 6.114).

singin'   gov't   'tis (*not* 'tis)   dos and don'ts   rock 'n' roll

7.30 *Interjections.* As with contractions, *Webster's* lists such interjections as *ugh, er, um,* and *sh*. For those not found in the dictionary—or where a different emphasis is required—plausible spellings should be sought in literature or invented.

atchoo!   shhh!

Word Division

7.31 *Dictionary word division.* For end-of-line word breaks, as for spelling and plural forms, Chicago turns to *Webster's* as its primary guide. The dots between syllables in *Webster's* indicate where breaks may be made; in words of three or more syllables, there is usually a choice of breaks. The paragraphs in this section are intended merely to supplement, not to replace, the dictionary's system of word division—for example, by suggesting preferred breaks where more than one might be possible. For

division of foreign words (other than those given in an English dictionary), see chapter 11. The advice in this section applies only to published
works, especially print works; word breaks should not be applied at the
manuscript stage (see 2.12).

7.32 *Words that should not be divided.* Single-syllable words, including verb
forms such as *aimed* and *helped*, are never divided. Since one-letter divisions are not permissible, such words as *again*, *enough*, and *unite* cannot
be divided. Words that may be misread if divided, such as *water*, *women*,
and *prayer*, should be divided only with reluctance.

7.33 *Dividing according to pronunciation.* In the usage preferred by Chicago and
reflected in *Webster's*, most words are divided according to pronunciation rather than derivation.

knowl-edge (*not* know-ledge)
democ-racy *or* de-mocracy (*not* demo-cracy)

Special attention should be paid to breaks in certain words with multiple
meanings and pronunciations, such as *proj-ect* (noun) and *pro-ject* (verb).

7.34 *Dividing after a vowel.* Unless a resulting break affects pronunciation,
words are best divided after a vowel. When a vowel forms a syllable in
the middle of a word, it should run in to the first line if possible. Diphthongs are treated as single vowels (e.g., the *eu* in *aneurysm*).

criti-cism (*rather than* crit-icism)
liga-ture (*rather than* lig-ature)
an-tipodes *or* antipo-des (*rather than* antip-odes)
aneu-rysm (*rather than* an-eurysm)

7.35 *Dividing compounds, prefixes, and suffixes.* Hyphenated or closed compounds and words with prefixes or suffixes are best divided at the natural breaks.

poverty- / stricken (*rather than* pov- / erty-stricken)
thanks-giving (*rather than* thanksgiv-ing)
dis-pleasure (*rather than* displea-sure)
re-inforce (*rather than* rein-force)

7.36 *Dividing words ending in "ing."* Most gerunds and present participles may
be divided before the *ing*. When the final consonant before the *ing* is

doubled, however, the break occurs between the consonants. For words ending in *ling*, check the dictionary.

certify-ing run-ning
giv-ing fiz-zling
dab-bing bris-tling

7.37   *Two-letter word endings.* Two-letter word endings are best *not* carried over to a second line.

losses (*rather than* loss-es)
sur-prises (*rather than* surpris-es)

It is, however, not only permissible but customary to carry over certain two-letter word endings in some foreign languages.

7.38   *Dividing proper nouns and personal names.* Proper nouns of more than one element, especially personal names, should be broken, if possible, between the elements rather than within any of the elements. If a break within a name is needed, consult the dictionary. Many proper nouns appear, with suggested divisions, in the listings of biographical and geographical names in *Webster's Collegiate*. For fuller treatment, consult *Merriam-Webster's Biographical Dictionary* (bibliog. 4.1) and *Merriam-Webster's Geographical Dictionary* (bibliog. 4.2). Those that cannot be found in a dictionary should be broken (or left unbroken) according to the guidelines elsewhere in this section. If pronunciation is not known or easily guessed, the break should usually follow a vowel.

Alek-sis   Heitor Villa- / Lobos (*or, better,* Heitor / Villa-Lobos)   Ana-stasia

A personal name that includes initials should be broken after the initials. A break before a number or *Jr.* or *Sr.* should be avoided.

Frederick L. / Anderson
M. F. K. / Fisher
Elizabeth II (*or, if necessary,* Eliza- / beth II)

7.39   *Dividing numerals.* Large numbers expressed as numerals are best left intact. To avoid a break, reword the sentence. If a break must be made, however, it should come only after a comma and never after a single digit. See also 12.23.

1,365,- / 000,000 *or* 1,365,000,- / 000

7.40   *Dividing numerals with abbreviated units of measure.* A numeral used with an abbreviated unit of measure is best left intact; either the numeral should be carried over to the next line or the abbreviation should be moved up. (Numerals used with spelled-out units of measure, which tend to form longer expressions, may be broken across a line as needed.)

345 m   24 kg   55 BCE   6:35 p.m.

7.41   *Division in run-in lists.* A number or letter, such as (3) or (c), used in a run-in list (see 6.123) should not be separated from the beginning of what follows it. If it occurs at the end of a line, it should be carried over to the next line.

7.42   *Dividing URLs and e-mail addresses.* In printed works, it is often necessary to break an e-mail address or a uniform resource identifier such as a URL at the end of a line. Such a break should be made between elements if at all possible: *after* a colon or a double slash; *before or after* an equals sign or an ampersand; or *before* a single slash, a period, or any other punctuation or symbols. To avoid confusion, an address that contains a hyphen should never be broken at the hyphen; nor should a hyphen be added to break an e-mail address or URL. If a particularly long element must be broken to avoid a seriously loose line, it should be broken between syllables according to the guidelines offered above. See also 6.8, 14.12. (Authors should not break URLs in their manuscripts; see 2.12.)

http://
www.chicagomanualofstyle.org/
or
http://www
.chicagomanualofstyle.org/
or
http://www.chicago
manualofstyle.org/

7.43   *Hyphenation and appearance.* For aesthetic reasons, no more than three succeeding lines should be allowed to end in hyphens. (Such hyphens are sometimes referred to as a hyphen stack.) And though hyphens are necessary far more often in justified text, word breaks may be needed in material with a ragged right-hand margin to avoid exceedingly uneven lines. (In manuscript preparation, however, word breaks should always be avoided; see 2.12, 2.109.) End-of-line hyphenation is rarely necessary in online publications, except those modeled on or otherwise representing the printed page.

A and An, O and Oh

7.44 *"A" and "an."* The indefinite article *a*, not *an*, is used in American English before words beginning with a pronounced *h*. See also 5.72.

a hotel   a historical study
but
an honor   an heir

Before an abbreviation, a numeral, or a symbol, the use of *a* or *an* depends on (or, conversely, determines) how the term is pronounced. In the first example below, MS would be pronounced *em ess*; in the second, it would be pronounced *manuscript*. In the last two examples, *007* would be pronounced *oh oh seven* and *double oh seven*, respectively.

an MS treatment (a treatment for multiple sclerosis)
a MS in the National Library
an NBC anchor
a CBS anchor
a URL
an @ sign
an 800 number
an 007 field (in a library catalog)
a 007-style agent

7.45 *"O" and "oh."* The vocative *O* (largely obsolete) is always capitalized, whereas the interjection *oh* is capitalized only when beginning a sentence or standing alone. See also 6.37.

"Thine arm, O Lord, in days of old . . ."
Where, oh where, have you been?
Oh! It's you!

Ligatures

7.46 *When to use ligatures.* The ligatures æ (*a* + *e*) and œ (*o* + *e*) should not be used in Latin or transliterated Greek words. Nor should they be used in words adopted into English from Latin, Greek, or French (and thus to be found in English dictionaries).

aesthetics
Encyclopaedia Britannica (contrary to corporate usage)
oedipal
a trompe l'oeil mural
a tray of hors d'oeuvres
Emily Dickinson's oeuvre

The ligature æ (along with other special characters) is, however, needed for spelling Old English words in an Old English context. And the ligature œ is needed for spelling French words in a French context. (See also 11.12.)

Ælfric   es hæl   le nœud gordien   *Œuvres complètes*

Italics, Capitals, and Quotation Marks

Emphasis

7.47   *Italics for emphasis.* Use italics for emphasis only as an occasional adjunct to efficient sentence structure. Overused, italics quickly lose their force. Seldom should as much as a sentence be italicized for emphasis, and never a whole passage. In the first example below, the last three words, though clearly emphatic, do not require italics because of their dramatic position at the end of the sentence.

> The damaging evidence was offered not by the arresting officer, not by the injured plaintiff, but by the boy's own mother.

On the other hand, the emphasis in the following example depends on the italics:

> It *was* Leo!

7.48   *Capitals for emphasis.* Initial capitals, once used to lend importance to certain words, are now used only ironically (but see 8.93).

> "OK, so I'm a Bad Mother," admitted Mary cheerfully.

Capitalizing an entire word or phrase for emphasis is rarely appropriate. If capitals are wanted—in dialogue or in representing newspaper headlines, for example—small caps rather than full capitals look more graceful. Note that "capitalizing" a word means setting only the initial letter as a capital. Capitalizing a whole word, LIKE THIS, is known as "setting in full caps." Setting a word in small capitals—or "small caps"—results in THIS STYLE. (For the use of small capitals in representing terms in American Sign Language, see 11.144–54.) See also 10.8.

"Be careful—WATCH OUT!" she yelled.
We could not believe the headline: POLAR ICE CAP RETURNS.

Foreign Words

7.49   *Italics for unfamiliar foreign words and phrases.* Italics are used for isolated words and phrases in a foreign language if they are likely to be unfamiliar to readers (but see 7.52). If a foreign word becomes familiar through repeated use throughout a work, it need be italicized only on its first occurrence. If it appears only rarely, however, italics may be retained.

The *grève du zèle* is not a true strike but a nitpicking obeying of work rules.
Honi soit qui mal y pense is the motto of the Order of the Garter.

An entire sentence or a passage of two or more sentences in a foreign language is usually set in roman and enclosed in quotation marks (see 13.71).

7.50   *Parentheses and quotation marks for foreign words and phrases.* A translation following a foreign word, phrase, or title is enclosed in parentheses or quotation marks. See also 6.93, 11.6, 14.109.

The word she wanted was *pécher* (to sin), not *pêcher* (to fish).
The Prakrit word *majjao*, "the tomcat," may be a dialect version of either of two Sanskrit words: *madjaro*, "my lover," or *marjaro*, "the cat" (from the verb *mrij*, "to wash," because the cat constantly washes itself).
Leonardo Fioravanti's *Compendio de i secreti rationali* (Compendium of rational secrets) became a best seller.

In linguistic and phonetic studies a definition is often enclosed in single quotation marks with no intervening punctuation; any following punctuation is placed *after* the closing quotation mark. (For a similar usage in horticultural writing, see 8.129.)

The gap is narrow between *mead* 'a beverage' and *mead* 'a meadow'.

7.51   *Proper nouns.* Foreign proper nouns are not italicized in an English context.

> A history of the Comédie-Française has just appeared.
> Mexico City's Ángel de la Independencia is known familiarly as "El Ángel."
> Leghorn—in Italian, Livorno—is a port in Tuscany.

7.52   *Roman for familiar foreign words.* Foreign words and phrases familiar to most readers and listed in *Webster's* should appear in roman (*not* italics) if used in an English context; they should be spelled as in *Webster's*. German nouns, if in *Webster's*, are lowercased. (See also 7.53.)

> pasha   in vitro   recherché   de novo
> weltanschauung   a priori   the kaiser   eros and agape
> *but*
> He never missed a chance to *épater les bourgeois.*

If a familiar foreign term, such as *mise en scène*, should occur in the same context as a less familiar one, such as *mise en bouteille* (not listed in *Webster's*), either both or neither should be italicized, so as to maintain internal consistency.

7.53   *Roman for Latin words and abbreviations.* Commonly used Latin words and abbreviations should not be italicized.

> ibid.   et al.   ca.   passim

Because of its peculiar use in quoted matter, *sic* is best italicized.

> "mindful of what has been done here by we [*sic*] as agents of principle"

Highlighting Key Terms and Expressions

7.54   *Italics for key terms.* Key terms in a particular context are often italicized on their first occurrence. Thereafter they are best set in roman.

> The two chief tactics of this group, *obstructionism* and *misinformation*, require careful analysis.

7.55   *"Scare quotes."* Quotation marks are often used to alert readers that a term is used in a nonstandard (or slang), ironic, or other special sense. Nicknamed *scare quotes*, they imply, "This is not my term" or "This is not how the term is usually applied." Like any such device, scare quotes lose their force and irritate readers if overused. See also 7.56, 7.57.

> On a digital music player, a "track" is really just a separately encoded file in a directory.
> "Child protection" sometimes fails to protect.

In works of philosophy, single quotation marks are sometimes used for similar purposes, but Chicago discourages that practice unless it is essential to the author's argument and not confusing to readers.

7.56 *"So-called."* A word or phrase preceded by *so-called* need not be enclosed in quotation marks. The expression itself indicates irony or doubt. If, however, it is necessary to call attention to only one part of a phrase, quotation marks may be helpful.

> So-called child protection sometimes fails to protect.
> Her so-called mentor induced her to embezzle from the company.
> *but*
> These days, so-called "running" shoes are more likely to be seen on the feet of walkers.

7.57 *Common expressions and figures of speech.* Quotation marks are rarely needed for common expressions or figures of speech (including slang). Reserve them, if at all, for phrases borrowed verbatim from another context or terms used ironically (see 7.55).

> Myths of paradise lost are common in folklore.
> I grew up in a one-horse town.
> Only techies will appreciate this joke.
> *but*
> Though she was a lifetime subscriber to the *Journal of Infectious Diseases*, she was not one to ask "for whom the bell tolls."

Words and Letters Used as Words

7.58 *Words and phrases used as words.* When a word or term is not used functionally but is referred to as the word or term itself, it is either italicized or enclosed in quotation marks. Proper nouns used as words, on the other hand, are usually set in roman.

The term *critical mass* is more often used metaphorically than literally.

What is meant by *neurobotics*?

The *i* in the name iPod is supposed to invoke the Internet.

Although italics are the traditional choice, quotation marks may be more appropriate in certain contexts. (And in some electronic environments, quotation marks may be more portable or otherwise practical than italics.) In the first example below, italics set off the foreign term, and quotation marks are used for the English. In the second example, quotation marks help to convey the idea of speech.

The Spanish verbs *ser* and *estar* are both rendered by "to be."

Many people say "I" even when "me" would be more correct.

7.59   *Letters as letters.* Individual letters and combinations of letters of the Latin alphabet are usually italicized.

the letter *q*

a lowercase *n*

a capital *W*

The plural is usually formed in English by adding *s* or *es*.

He signed the document with an *X*.

I need a word with two *e*'s and three *s*'s.

Roman type, however, is traditionally used in two common expressions (see also 7.14).

Mind your p's and q's!   dotting the i's and crossing the t's

Roman type is always used for phonetic symbols. For details, consult Geoffrey K. Pullum and William A. Ladusaw, *Phonetic Symbol Guide* (bibliog. 5).

7.60   *Scholastic grades.* Letters used to denote grades are usually capitalized and set in roman type. No apostrophe is required in the plural (see also 7.14).

She finished with three As, one B, and two Cs.

7.61   *Plurals of letters.* As an aid to legibility (compare "two *as* in *llama*" with "two *a*'s in *llama*"), the plural of single lowercase letters is formed by adding an apostrophe before the *s*. The *s* is roman even when the letter is italic. Capital letters, however, do not normally require an apostrophe in the plural. To prevent misreading, avoid beginning a sentence with the plural of "A" or "I." See also 7.14.

There really are two *x*'s in Foxx.   the three Rs

7.62 *Letters standing for names.* A letter used in place of a name is usually capitalized and set in roman type. If it bears no relation to an actual name, it is not followed by a period.

Let us assume that A sues B for breach of contract . . .

If a single initial is used to abbreviate an actual name, it is usually followed by a period; if used to conceal a name, it may be followed by a 2-em dash and no period (see 6.90). If no punctuation follows the dash, it must be followed by a space.

Professor D. will be making his entrance shortly.
Senator K—— and Representative L—— were in attendance.

If two or more initials are used as an abbreviation for an entire name, no periods are needed. See also 8.4, 10.12.

Kennedy and Johnson soon became known as JFK and LBJ.

7.63 *Letters as shapes.* Letters that are used to represent shapes are capitalized and set in roman type (an S curve, an L-shaped room). (Using a sans serif font in a serif context, as is sometimes done, does not necessarily aid comprehension and, unless the sans serif perfectly complements the serif, tends to look clumsy.)

7.64 *Names of letters.* When legibility cannot be counted on, editors and proofreaders occasionally need to name letters ("a cue, not a gee"). The name of a letter, as distinct from the letter itself, is usually set in roman type, without quotation marks. The following standard spellings are drawn from *Webster's Collegiate.* With vowels, which are not named in standard dictionaries, it may be best to give an example ("*a* as in *apple*"). (For the names of special characters, see chapter 11, esp. tables 11.1 and 11.2.)

b	bee	*g*	gee	*l*	el	*q*	cue	*v*	vee	*z*	zee
c	cee	*h*	aitch	*m*	em	*r*	ar	*w*	double-u		
d	dee	*j*	jay	*n*	en	*s*	ess	*x*	ex		
f	ef	*k*	kay	*p*	pee	*t*	tee	*y*	wye		

7.65 *Rhyme schemes.* Lowercase italic letters, with no space between, are used to indicate rhyme schemes or similar patterns.

The Shakespearean sonnet's rhyme scheme is *abab, cdcd, efef, gg.*

Music: Some Typographic Conventions

7.66 *Suggested reference for music publishing.* Music publishing is too specialized to be more than touched on here. Authors and editors requiring detailed guidelines may refer to D. Kern Holoman, *Writing about Music* (bibliog. 1.1). For an illustration of typeset music, see figure 3.5. For styling the titles of musical works, see 8.188–92. For a more general reference work, consult *The New Grove Dictionary of Music and Musicians* and the other Grove musical dictionaries, available from Oxford Music Online (bibliog. 5).

7.67 *Musical pitches.* Letters standing for musical pitches (which in turn are used to identify keys, chords, and so on) are usually set as roman capitals. The terms *sharp, flat,* and *natural,* if spelled out, are set in roman type and preceded by a hyphen. Editors unfamiliar with musicological conventions should proceed with caution. In the context of harmony, for example, some authors may regard a hyphenated "C-major triad" as being based on the note rather than the key of C. See also 7.70.

middle C
the key of G major
the D-major triad *or* D major triad
an F augmented triad (an augmented triad on the note F)
G-sharp *or* G♯
the key of B-flat minor *or* B♭ minor
Beethoven's E-flat Major Symphony (the *Eroica*)
an E string

A series of pitches are joined by en dashes.

The initial F–G–F–B♭

7.68 *Octaves.* In technical works, various systems are used to designate octave register. Those systems that group pitches by octaves begin each ascending octave on C. In one widely used system, pitches in the octave below middle C are designated by lowercase letters: c, c♯, d, . . . , a♯, b. Octaves from middle C up are designated with lowercase letters bearing superscript numbers or primes: c^1, c^2, and so on, or c', c'', and so on. Lower octaves are designated, in descending order, by capital letters and capital letters with subscript numbers: C, C_1, C_2. Because of the many systems and their variants in current use, readers should be alerted to the system employed (e.g., by an indication early in the text of the symbol used for middle C). Technical works on the modern piano usually designate all pitches with capital letters and subscripts, from A_1 at the bottom of the keyboard to C_{88} at the top. Scientific works on music usually designate octaves by capital letters and subscripts beginning with C_0 (middle C = C_4). When pitches are otherwise specified, none of these systems is necessary.

middle C   A 440   the soprano's high C

To indicate simultaneously sounding pitches (as in chords), the pitches are listed from lowest to highest and are sometimes joined by plus signs.

C + E + G

7.69   *Chords.* In the analysis of harmony, chords are designated by roman numerals indicating what degree of the scale the chord is based on.

V (a chord based on the fifth, or dominant, degree of the scale)
V^7 (dominant seventh chord)
iii (a chord based on the third, or mediant, degree of the scale)

Harmonic progressions are indicated by capital roman numerals separated by en dashes: IV–I–V–I. While roman numerals for all chords suffice for basic descriptions of chordal movement, in more technical writing, minor chords are distinguished by lowercase roman numerals, and other distinctions in chord quality and content are shown by additional symbols and arabic numerals.

7.70   *"Major" and "minor."* In some works on musical subjects where many keys are mentioned, capital letters are used for major keys and lowercase for minor. If this practice is followed, the words *major* and *minor* are usually omitted.

7.71   *Dynamics.* Terms indicating dynamics are usually given in lowercase, often italicized: *piano*, *mezzo forte*, and so on. Where space allows, the spelled-out form is preferred in both text and musical examples. Symbols for these terms are rendered in lowercase boldface italics with no periods: **p**, **mf**, and so on. "Editorial" dynamics—those added to a composer's original by an editor—are sometimes distinguished by another font or by parentheses or brackets.

Computer Terms

7.72   *Application-specific variations.* In the realm of computer hardware and software—where nomenclature and function are closely related—typographic conventions for expressing the names of particular keys, commands, and other computer terms vary across systems and applications. The paragraphs in this section offer a few common patterns. It is important not only to practice consistency in using a particular style or font to refer to a particular element but also to consider the usage followed within a specific system or application.

7.73   *Capitalization for keys and menu items.* The basic alphabet keys as well as all named keys are capitalized even if they are lowercased on a particular keyboard. Menu items and icon names are usually spelled and capitalized as in a particular application. Acronyms for file formats are rendered in full capitals.

> The function key F2 has no connection with the keys F and 2.
> The Option key on a Mac is similar to the Alt key on a typical PC.
> Choosing Cut from the Edit menu is an alternative to pressing Ctrl+X.
> Save the file as a PNG or a GIF, not as a JPEG.

7.74   *Keyboard combinations and shortcuts.* To indicate that different keys are to be pressed simultaneously (as in a keyboard shortcut), use the plus sign or the hyphen—according to the practice of the particular operating system or application in question—without a space on either side. Spell out *Shift*, *Hyphen*, and *Space*—and anything else that might otherwise be ambiguous. (The capital *S* in the first two examples below does not indicate that the Shift key should be pressed as part of the combination.)

> To save, press Ctrl+S.
> To save, press Command-S.
> If the screen freezes, press Ctrl+Alt+Delete.
> To empty the trash without a prompt, press Option-Shift-Command-Delete.

7.75   *Distinguishing words to be typed and other elements.* When a greater prominence than capitalization is called for, boldface, italics, color, or some other scheme may be used to distinguish elements. A single treatment may be applied across different types of elements. In general, avoid quotation marks lest they be interpreted as part of the element they enclose. If quotation marks must be used, any punctuation that is not part of the quoted expression should appear outside the quotation marks (as in the second example; see also 6.9).

> To insert a thorn, choose **Symbol** from the **Insert** tab, then enter **00FE** in the character code field.
> Click on **Save As**; name your file "appendix A, v. 10".

Directory paths, file names, variables, and other computer-related syntax are sometimes distinguished by a monospaced font such as Courier.

> Use $OLDPWD to indicate your previous working directory.

For related matters in computer writing, see Eric S. Raymond, "Hacker Writing Style," in *The New Hacker's Dictionary* (bibliog. 5).

7.76   *Terms like "web" and "Internet."* In keeping with Chicago's recommendations elsewhere (see 8.67), generic terms that are capitalized as part of the official name of a system or an organization may be lowercased when used alone or in combination. (In a departure, Chicago now considers *web* to be generic when used alone or in combination with other generic terms.) Abbreviations for file formats are normally presented in full capitals (see also 10.52). For treatment of the names of keys and menu items, see 7.73. For terms such as *e-mail*, see 7.85.

> Macintosh; PC; personal computer
> hypertext transfer protocol (HTTP); a transfer protocol; hypertext
> Internet protocol (IP); the Internet; the net; an intranet
> the Open Source Initiative (the corporation); open-source platforms
> the World Wide Web Consortium; the World Wide Web; the web; a website; a web page

Compounds and Hyphenation

7.77   *To hyphenate or not to hyphenate.* Far and away the most common spelling questions for writers and editors concern compound terms—whether to spell as two words, hyphenate, or close up as a single word. Prefixes (and occasionally suffixes) can be troublesome also. The first place to look for answers is the dictionary. This section, including the hyphenation guide in 7.85, offers guidelines for spelling compounds not necessarily found in the dictionary (though some of the examples are drawn from *Webster's*) and for treatment of compounds according to their grammatical function (as nouns, adjectives, or adverbs) and their position in a sentence. See also 5.91.

7.78   *Some definitions.* An open compound is spelled as two or more words (*high school, lowest common denominator*). A hyphenated compound is spelled with one or more hyphens (*mass-produced, kilowatt-hour, non-English-speaking*). A closed (or solid) compound is spelled as a single word (*birthrate, notebook*). A permanent compound is one that has been accepted into the general vocabulary and can be found in the dictionary (like all but one of the examples in this paragraph thus far). A temporary compound is a new combination created for some specific, often one-time purpose (*dictionary-wielding, impeachment hound*); such compounds, though some eventually become permanent, are not normally found in the dictionary. Not strictly compounds but often discussed with them are words formed with prefixes (*antigrammarian, postmodern*); these are dealt with in section 4 of 7.85. (For examples of combining forms—a type of prefix in which a word like *electric* is modified to form a combination like *electromagnetic*—see section 2 of 7.85, under *combining forms*.)

7.79   *The trend toward closed compounds.* With frequent use, open or hyphenated compounds tend to become closed (*on line* to *on-line* to *online*). Chicago's general adherence to *Webster's* does not preclude occasional exceptions when the closed spellings have become widely preferred by writers (e.g., *website*) and pronunciation and readability are not at stake.

7.80   *Hyphens and readability.* A hyphen can make for easier reading by showing structure and, often, pronunciation. Words that might otherwise be misread, such as *re-creation* or *co-op*, should be hyphenated. Hyphens can also eliminate ambiguity. For example, the hyphen in *much-needed clothing* shows that the clothing is greatly needed rather than abundant and needed. Where no ambiguity could result, as in *public welfare administration* or *graduate student housing*, hyphenation is unnecessary.

7.81   *Compound modifiers before or after a noun.* When compound modifiers (also called phrasal adjectives) such as *open-mouthed* or *full-length* precede a noun, hyphenation usually lends clarity. With the exception of proper nouns (such as *United States*) and compounds formed by an adverb ending in *ly* plus an adjective (see 7.82), it is never incorrect to hyphenate adjectival compounds before a noun. When such compounds *follow* the noun they modify, hyphenation is usually unnecessary, even for adjectival compounds that are hyphenated in *Webster's* (such as *well-read* or *ill-humored*).

7.82   *Adverbs ending in "ly."* Compounds formed by an adverb ending in *ly* plus an adjective or participle (such as *largely irrelevant* or *smartly dressed*) are not hyphenated either before or after a noun, since ambiguity is virtually impossible. (The *ly* ending with adverbs signals to the reader that the next word will be another modifier, not a noun.)

7.83   *Multiple hyphens.* Multiple hyphens are usually appropriate for such phrases as *an over-the-counter drug* or *a winner-take-all contest*. If, however, the compound modifier consists of an adjective that itself modifies a compound, additional hyphens may not be necessary. The expressions *late nineteenth-century literature* and *early twentieth-century growth* are clear without a second hyphen. (Similar expressions formed with *mid*—which Chicago classifies as a prefix—do not follow this pattern; see 7.85, section 4, under *mid*.) See also 7.85, section 3, under *century*.

7.84   *Omission of part of a hyphenated expression.* When the second part of a hyphenated expression is omitted, the hyphen is retained, followed by a space.

fifteen- and twenty-year mortgages
Chicago- or Milwaukee-bound passengers
but
a five-by-eight-foot rug (a single entity)

Omission of the second part of a solid compound follows the same pattern.

both over- and underfed cats
but
overfed and overworked mules (*not* overfed and -worked mules)

7.85   *Hyphenation guide for compounds and words formed with prefixes.* When using this guide (a return to the tabular format of earlier editions of this manual), consult the preceding paragraphs in this section (7.77–84)—especially if a relevant example cannot be found. In general, Chicago prefers a spare hyphenation style: if no suitable example or analogy can be found either in this section or in the dictionary, hyphenate only if doing so will aid readability. Each of the four sections of the following table is arranged alphabetically (by first column). The first section deals with compounds according to category; the second section, with compounds according to parts of speech. The third section lists examples for words commonly used as elements in compounds. The fourth section lists common prefixes, most of which join to another word to form one unhyphenated word; note especially the hyphenated exceptions, not all of which agree with *Webster's*. (Compounds formed with suffixes—e.g., *nationhood*, *penniless*—are almost always closed.)

Category/specific term	Examples	Summary of rule
1. COMPOUNDS ACCORDING TO CATEGORY		
age terms	a *three-year-old* a *five-year-old* child a *fifty-five-year-old* woman a group of *eight-* to *ten-year-olds* but *seven years old* *eighteen years of age*	Hyphenated in both noun and adjective forms (except as in the last two examples); note the space after the first hyphen in the fourth example (see 7.84). The examples apply equally to ages expressed as numerals.
chemical terms	*sodium chloride* *sodium chloride* solution	Open in both noun and adjective forms.
colors	*emerald-green* tie *reddish-brown* flagstone *blue-green* algae *snow-white* dress *black-and-white* print but his tie is *emerald green* the stone is *reddish brown* the water is *blue green* the clouds are *snow white* the truth isn't *black and white*	Hyphenated before but not after a noun. This departure from Chicago's former usage serves both simplicity and logic.
compass points and directions	*northeast* *southwest* *east-northeast* a *north–south* street the street runs *north–south*	Closed in noun, adjective, and adverb forms unless three directions are combined, in which case a hyphen is used after the first. When *from . . . to* is implied, an en dash is used (see 6.78).
ethnic terms. See **proper nouns and adjectives relating to geography or nationality** in section 2.		
foreign phrases	an *a priori* argument a *Sturm und Drang* drama *in vitro* fertilization a *tête-à-tête* approach	Open unless hyphens appear in the original language.

Category/specific term	Examples	Summary of rule
1. COMPOUNDS ACCORDING TO CATEGORY (continued)		
fractions, compounds formed with	a *half hour* a *half-hour* session a *quarter mile* a *quarter-mile* run an *eighth note*	Noun form open; adjective form hyphenated. See also **numbers** in this section and **half** in section 3.
fractions, simple	*one-half* *two-thirds* *three-quarters* *one twenty-fifth* *one and three-quarters* a *two-thirds* majority *three-quarters* done a *one twenty-fifth* share	Hyphenated in noun, adjective, and adverb forms, except when second element is already hyphenated. See also **number + noun** and 9.14.
number + abbreviation	the *33 m* distance a *2 kg* weight a *3 ft.* high wall	Always open. See also **number + noun**.
number + noun	a *hundred-meter* race a *250-page* book a *fifty-year* project a *three-inch-high* statuette it's *three inches high* a *one-and-a-half-inch* hem *one and a half inches* a *five-foot-ten* quarterback *five feet ten* [inches tall] *five-* or *ten-minute* intervals	Hyphenated before a noun, otherwise open. Note the space after the first number in the last example. See also **number + abbreviation**. See also 9.13.
number + percentage	*50 percent* a *10 percent* raise	Both noun and adjective forms always open.
number, ordinal, + noun	on the *third floor* *third-floor* apartment *103rd-floor* view *fifth-place* contestant *twenty-first-row* seats	Adjective form hyphenated before a noun, otherwise open. See also **century** in section 3.
number, ordinal, + superlative	a *second-best* decision *third-largest* town *fourth-to-last* contestant he arrived *fourth to last*	Hyphenated before a noun, otherwise open.
numbers, spelled out	*twenty-eight* *three hundred* *nineteen forty-five* *five hundred fifty-two*	Twenty-one through ninety-nine hyphenated; others open. See also **fractions, simple**.
relationships. See **foster, grand, in-law,** and **step** in section 3.		

Category/specific term	Examples	Summary of rule
1. COMPOUNDS ACCORDING TO CATEGORY (continued)		
time	at *three thirty* the *three-thirty* train a *four o'clock* train the *5:00 p.m.* news	Usually open; forms such as "three thirty," "four twenty," etc., are hyphenated before the noun.
2. COMPOUNDS ACCORDING TO PARTS OF SPEECH		
adjective + noun	*small-state* senators a *high-quality* alkylate a *middle-class* neighborhood the neighborhood is *middle class*	Hyphenated before but not after a noun.
adjective + participle	*tight-lipped* person *high-jumping* grasshoppers *open-ended* question the question was *open ended*	Hyphenated before but not after a noun.
adverb ending in ly + participle or adjective	a *highly paid* ragpicker a *fully open* society he was *mildly amusing*	Open whether before or after a noun.
adverb not ending in ly + participle or adjective	a *much-needed* addition it was *much needed* a very *well-read* child *little-understood* rules a *too-easy* answer the *best-known* author the *highest-ranking* officer the *worst-paid* job a *lesser-paid* colleague the *most efficient* method a *less prolific* artist a *more thorough* exam the *most skilled* workers (most in number) but the *most-skilled* workers (most in skill) a very much *needed* addition	Hyphenated before but not after a noun; compounds with *more, most, less, least,* and *very* usually open unless ambiguity threatens. When the adverb rather than the compound as a whole is modified by another adverb, the entire expression is open.
combining forms	*electrocardiogram* *socioeconomic* *politico-scientific* studies the *practico-inert*	Usually closed if permanent, hyphenated if temporary. See 7.78.
gerund + noun	*running shoes* *cooking class* *running-shoe* store	Noun form open; adjective form hyphenated. See also **noun + gerund**.
noun + adjective	*computer-literate* accountants *HIV-positive* men the stadium is *fan friendly* she is *HIV positive*	Hyphenated before a noun; usually open after a noun.

Category/specific term	Examples	Summary of rule
2. COMPOUNDS ACCORDING TO PARTS OF SPEECH (continued)		
noun + gerund	*decision making* a *decision-making* body *mountain climbing* *time-clock-punching* employees a *Nobel Prize–winning* chemist (see 6.80) *bookkeeping* *caregiving* *copyediting*	Noun form usually open; adjective form hyphenated before a noun. Some permanent compounds closed (see 7.78).
noun + noun, single function (first noun modifies second noun)	*student nurse* *restaurant owner* *directory path* *tenure track* *tenure-track* position *home-rule* governance *shipbuilder* *gunrunner* *copyeditor*	Noun form open; adjective form hyphenated before a noun. Some permanent compounds closed (see 7.78).
noun + noun, two functions (both nouns equal)	*writer-director* *philosopher-king* *city-state* *city-state* governance	Both noun and adjective forms always hyphenated.
noun + numeral or enumerator	*type A* a *type A* executive *type 2* diabetes *size 12* slacks a *page 1* headline	Both noun and adjective forms always open.
noun + participle	a *Wagner-burdened* repertoire *flower-filled* garden a *clothes-buying* grandmother a day of *clothes buying*	Hyphenated before a noun, otherwise open.
participle + noun	*chopped-liver* pâté *cutting-edge* methods their approach was *cutting edge*	Adjective form hyphenated before but not after a noun.
participle + up, out, and similar adverbs	*dressed-up* children *burned-out* buildings *ironed-on* decal we were *dressed up* that decal is *ironed on*	Adjective form hyphenated before but not after a noun. Verb form always open.
phrases, adjectival	an *over-the-counter* drug a *matter-of-fact* reply an *up-to-date* solution sold *over the counter* her tone was *matter of fact* his equipment was *up to date*	Hyphenated before a noun; usually open after a noun.

Category/specific term	Examples	Summary of rule
2. COMPOUNDS ACCORDING TO PARTS OF SPEECH (continued)		
phrases, noun	*stick-in-the-mud* *jack-of-all-trades* a *flash in the pan*	Hyphenated or open as listed in *Webster's*. If not in the dictionary, open.
proper nouns and adjectives relating to geography or nationality	*African Americans* *African American* president a *Chinese American* *French Canadians* *South Asian Americans* the *Scotch Irish* the *North Central* region *Middle Eastern* countries but *Sino-Tibetan* languages the *Franco-Prussian* War the *US-Canada* border *Anglo-American* cooperation *Anglo-Americans*	Open in both noun and adjective forms, unless the first term is a prefix or unless *between* is implied. See also 8.38.
3. COMPOUNDS FORMED WITH SPECIFIC TERMS		
ache	*toothache* *stomachache*	Always closed.
all	*all out* *all along* *all over* an *all-out* effort an *all-American* player the book is *all-encompassing* but we were *all in* [tired]	Adverbial phrases open; adjectival phrases usually hyphenated both before and after a noun.
book	*reference book* *coupon book* *checkbook* *cookbook*	Closed or open as listed in *Webster's*. If not in the dictionary, open.
borne	*waterborne* *food-borne* *e-mail-borne* *mosquito-borne*	Closed if listed as such in *Webster's*. If not in *Webster's*, hyphenated; compounds retain the hyphen both before and after a noun.
century	the *twenty-first century* *fourteenth-century* monastery *twenty-first-century* history a *mid-eighteenth-century* poet *late nineteenth-century* politicians her style was *nineteenth century*	Noun forms always open; adjectival compounds hyphenated before but not after a noun. See also **old** (below), **mid** (in section 4), and 7.83.

Category/specific term	Examples	Summary of rule
3. COMPOUNDS FORMED WITH SPECIFIC TERMS (continued)		
cross	a *cross section* a *cross-reference* *cross-referenced* *cross-grained* *cross-country* *crossbow* *crossover*	Many compounds formed with *cross* are in *Webster's* (as those listed here). If not in *Webster's*, noun, adjective, adverb, and verb forms should be open.
e	*e-mail* *e-book* *eBay*	Hyphenated except with proper nouns. See also 8.153.
elect	*president-elect* *vice president elect* *mayor-elect* *county assessor elect*	Hyphenated unless the name of the office consists of an open compound.
ever	*ever-ready* help *ever-recurring* problem *everlasting* he was *ever eager*	Usually hyphenated before but not after a noun; some permanent compounds closed.
ex	*ex-partner* *ex-marine* *ex–corporate executive*	Hyphenated, but use en dash if *ex-* precedes an open compound.
foster	*foster mother* *foster parents* a *foster-family* background	Noun forms open; adjective forms hyphenated.
free	*toll-free* number *accident-free* driver the number is *toll-free* the driver is *accident-free*	Compounds formed with *free* as second element are hyphenated both before and after a noun.
full	*full-length* mirror the mirror is *full length* three *bags full* a *suitcase full*	Hyphenated before a noun, otherwise open. Use *ful* only in such permanent compounds as *cupful, handful.*
general	*attorney general* *postmaster general* *lieutenants general*	Always open; in plural forms, *general* remains singular.
grand, great-grand	*grandfather* *granddaughter* *great-grandmother* *great-great-grandson*	*Grand* compounds closed; *great* compounds hyphenated.

Category/specific term	Examples	Summary of rule
3. COMPOUNDS FORMED WITH SPECIFIC TERMS (continued)		
half	*half-asleep* *half-finished* a *half* sister a *half* hour a *half-hour* session *halfway* *halfhearted*	Adjective forms hyphenated before and after the noun; noun forms open. Some permanent compounds closed, whether nouns, adjectives, or adverbs. Check *Webster's*. See also **fractions** in section 1.
house	*schoolhouse* *courthouse* *safe house* *rest house*	Closed or open as listed in *Webster's*. If not in the dictionary, open.
in-law	*sister-in-law* *parents-in-law*	All compounds hyphenated; only the first element takes a plural form.
like	*catlike* *childlike* *Christlike* *bell-like* a *penitentiary-like* institution	Closed if listed as such in *Webster's*. If not in *Webster's*, hyphenated; compounds retain the hyphen both before and after a noun.
mid. See section 4.		
near	in the *near* term a *near* accident a *near-term* proposal a *near-dead* language	Noun forms open; adjective forms hyphenated.
odd	a *hundred-odd* manuscripts *350-odd* books	Always hyphenated.
old	a *three-year-old* a *105-year-old* woman a *decade-old* union a *centuries-old* debate a child who is *three years old* the debate is *centuries old*	Noun forms hyphenated. Adjective forms hyphenated before a noun, open after. See also **age terms** in section 1.
on	*online* *onstage* *ongoing* *on-screen* *on-site*	Sometimes closed, sometimes hyphenated. Check *Webster's* and hyphenate if term is not listed. See also 7.79.
percent	*5 percent* a *10 percent* increase	Both noun and adjective forms always open.

Category/specific term	Examples	Summary of rule
3. COMPOUNDS FORMED WITH SPECIFIC TERMS (continued)		
pseudo. See section 4.		
quasi	a *quasi corporation* a *quasi-public* corporation *quasi-judicial* *quasiperiodic* *quasicrystal*	Noun form usually open; adjective form usually hyphenated. A handful of permanent compounds are listed in *Webster's*.
self	*self-restraint* *self-realization* *self-sustaining* *self-conscious* the behavior is *self-destructive* *selfless* *unselfconscious*	Both noun and adjective forms hyphenated, except where *self* is followed by a suffix or preceded by *un*. Note that *unselfconscious*, Chicago's preference, is contrary to *Webster's*.
step	*stepbrother* *stepparent* *step-granddaughter* *step-great-granddaughter*	Always closed except with *grand* and *great*.
style	dined *family-style* *1920s-style* dancing danced *1920s-style* *Chicago-style* hyphenation according to *Chicago style* *headline-style* capitalization use *headline style*	Adjective and adverb forms hyphenated; noun form usually open.
vice	*vice-consul* *vice-chancellor* *vice president* *vice presidential* duties *vice admiral* *viceroy*	Sometimes hyphenated, sometimes open, occasionally closed. Check *Webster's* and hyphenate if term is not listed.
web	a *website* a *web page* *web-related* matters	Noun form open or closed, as shown; if term is not in any dictionary, opt for open. Adjective form hyphenated. See also 7.76.
wide	*worldwide* *citywide* *Chicago-wide* the canvass was *university-wide*	Closed if listed as such in *Webster's*. If not in *Webster's*, hyphenated; compounds retain the hyphen both before and after a noun.

4. WORDS FORMED WITH PREFIXES

Compounds formed with prefixes are normally closed, whether they are nouns, verbs, adjectives, or adverbs. A hyphen should appear, however, (1) before a capitalized word or a numeral, such as *sub-Saharan*, *pre-1950*; (2) before a compound term, such as *non-self-sustaining*, *pre–Vietnam War* (before an open compound, an en dash is used; see 6.80); (3) to separate two *i*'s, two *a*'s, and other combinations of letters or syllables that might cause misreading, such as *anti-intellectual*, *extra-alkaline*, *pro-life*; (4) to separate the repeated terms in a double prefix, such as *sub-subentry*; (5) when a prefix or combining form stands alone, such as *over-* and *underused*, *macro-* and *microeconomics*. The spellings shown below conform largely to *Merriam-Webster's Collegiate Dictionary*. Compounds formed with combining forms not listed here, such as *auto*, *tri*, and *para*, follow the same pattern.

ante	antebellum, antenatal, antediluvian
anti	antihypertensive, antihero, *but* anti-inflammatory, anti-Hitlerian
bi	binomial, bivalent, bisexual
bio	bioecology, biophysical, biosociology
co	coequal, coauthor, coeditor, coordinate, cooperation, coworker, *but* co-op, co-opt
counter	counterclockwise, counterrevolution
cyber	cyberspace, cyberstore
extra	extramural, extrafine, *but* extra-administrative
hyper	hypertension, hyperactive, hypertext
infra	infrasonic, infrastructure
inter	interorganizational, interfaith
intra	intrazonal, intramural, *but* intra-arterial
macro	macroeconomics, macromolecular
mega	megavitamin, megamall, *but* mega-annoyance
meta	metalanguage, metaethical, *but* meta-analysis (not the same as *metanalysis*)
micro	microeconomics, micromethodical
mid	midthirties, a midcareer event, midcentury, *but* mid-July, the mid-1990s, the mid-twentieth century, mid-twentieth-century history
mini	minivan, minimarket
multi	multiauthor, multiconductor, *but* multi-institutional
neo	neonate, neoorthodox, Neoplatonism, neo-Nazi (*neo* lowercase or capital and hyphenated as in dictionary; lowercase and hyphenate if not in dictionary)
non	nonviolent, nonevent, nonnegotiable, *but* non-beer-drinking
over	overmagnified, overshoes, overconscientious
post	postdoctoral, postmodernism, posttraumatic, *but* post-Vietnam, post–World War II (see 6.80)
pre	premodern, preregistration, prewar, preempt, *but* pre-Columbian, Pre-Raphaelite (*pre* lowercase or capital as in dictionary; lowercase if term is not in dictionary)
pro	proindustrial, promarket, *but* pro-life, pro-Canadian

4. WORDS FORMED WITH PREFIXES (continued)	
proto	protolanguage, protogalaxy, protomartyr
pseudo	pseudotechnocrat, pseudomodern, *but* pseudo-Tudor
re	reedit, reunify, reproposition, *but* re-cover, re-creation (as distinct from *recover, recreation*)
semi	semiopaque, semiconductor, *but* semi-invalid
sub	subbasement, subzero, subcutaneous
super	superannuated, supervirtuoso, superpowerful
supra	supranational, suprarenal, supraorbital, *but* supra-American
trans	transsocietal, transmembrane, transcontinental, transatlantic, *but* trans-American
ultra	ultrasophisticated, ultraorganized, ultraevangelical
un	unfunded, unneutered, *but* un-English, un-unionized
under	underemployed, underrate, undercount

8 *Names and Terms*

Overview

8.1   *Chicago's preference for the "down" style.* Proper nouns are usually capitalized, as are some of the terms derived from or associated with proper nouns. For the latter, Chicago's preference is for sparing use of capitals—what is sometimes referred to as a "down" style. Although *Brussels* (the Belgian city) is capitalized, Chicago prefers *brussels sprouts*—which are not necessarily from Brussels (see 8.60). Likewise, *President Obama* is capitalized, but *the president* is not (see 8.18–32). (In certain nonacademic contexts—e.g., a press release—such terms as *president* may be capitalized.)

8.2   *Italics and quotation marks.* Chicago prefers italics to set off the titles of major or freestanding works such as books, journals, movies, and paintings. This practice extends to cover the names of ships and other craft, species names, and legal cases. Quotation marks are usually reserved for the titles of subsections of larger works—including chapter and article titles and the titles of poems in a collection. Some titles—for example, of a book series or a website, under which any number of works or documents may be collected—are neither italicized nor placed in quotation marks. For more on the titles of works, including matters of capitalization and punctuation, see 8.154–95.

Personal Names

General Principles

8.3   *Personal names—additional resources.* For names of well-known deceased persons, Chicago generally prefers the spellings in *Merriam-Webster's Biographical Dictionary* or the biographical section of *Merriam-Webster's Collegiate Dictionary* (referred to below as *Webster's*). For living persons, consult *Who's Who* or *Who's Who in America*, among other sources. (See bibliog. 4.1 for these and other useful reference works.) Where different spellings appear in different sources (e.g., W. E. B. DuBois *versus* W. E. B. Du Bois), the writer or editor must make a choice and stick with it. The names of known and lesser-known persons not in the standard references can usually be checked and cross-checked at any number of officially sponsored online resources (e.g., for authors' names, online library catalogs or booksellers). The name of a living person should, wherever possible, correspond to that person's own usage.

8.4   *Capitalization of personal names.* Names and initials of persons, real or fictitious, are capitalized. A space should be used between any initials, except when initials are used alone. See also 7.62, 10.12.

Jane Doe	P. D. James	Malcolm X
George S. McGovern	M. F. K. Fisher	LBJ

Unconventional spellings strongly preferred by the bearer of the name or pen name (e.g., bell hooks) should usually be respected in appropriate contexts (library catalogs generally capitalize all such names). E. E. Cummings can be safely capitalized; it was one of his publishers, not he himself, who lowercased his name. Most editors will draw the line at beginning a sentence with a lowercased name and choose either to rewrite or to capitalize the first letter for the occasion.

8.5   *Names with particles.* Many names include particles such as *de, d', de la, von, van,* and *ten.* Practice with regard to capitalizing and spacing the particles varies widely, and confirmation should be sought in a biographical dictionary or other authoritative source. When the surname is used alone, the particle is usually retained, capitalized or lowercased and spaced as in the full name (though always capitalized when beginning a sentence). *Le, La,* and *L'* are always capitalized when not preceded by *de; the,* which sometimes appears with the English form of a Native American name, is always lowercased. See also 8.7, 8.8, 8.9, 8.10, 8.11, 8.14, 8.33.

Alfonse D'Amato; D'Amato	John Le Carré; Le Carré
Diana DeGette; DeGette	Pierre-Charles L'Enfant; L'Enfant
Walter de la Mare; de la Mare	Anwar el-Sadat; Sadat
Paul de Man; de Man	Abraham Ten Broeck; Ten Broeck
Thomas De Quincey; De Quincey	the Prophet (Tenskwatawa)
Page duBois; duBois	Robert van Gulik; van Gulik
W. E. B. DuBois; DuBois (but see 8.3)	Stephen Van Rensselaer; Van Rensselaer
Daphne du Maurier; du Maurier	Wernher von Braun; von Braun
Robert M. La Follette Sr.; La Follette	

8.6   *Hyphenated and extended names.* A hyphenated last name or a last name that consists of two or more elements should never be shorn of one of its elements. For names of prominent or historical figures, *Webster's* and other reliable alphabetical listings usually indicate where the last name begins.

Victoria Sackville-West; Sackville-West
Ralph Vaughan Williams; Vaughan Williams (*not* Williams)

Ludwig Mies van der Rohe; Mies van der Rohe (*not* van der Rohe); Mies
but
John Hope Franklin; Franklin
Charlotte Perkins Gilman; Gilman

For unhyphenated compound names of lesser-known persons for whom proper usage cannot be determined, use only the last element (including any particle[s]; see 8.5). But see 8.11.

Non-English Names in an English Context

8.7   *French names.* The particles *de* and *d'* are lowercased (except at the beginning of a sentence). When the last name is used alone, *de* (but not *d'*) is often dropped. Its occasional retention, in *de Gaulle*, for example, is suggested by tradition rather than logic. (When a name begins with closed-up *de*, such as *Debussy*, the *d* is always capitalized.)

Jean d'Alembert; d'Alembert
Alfred de Musset; Musset
Alexis de Tocqueville; Tocqueville
but
Charles de Gaulle; de Gaulle

When *de la* precedes a name, *la* is usually capitalized and is always retained when the last name is used alone. The contraction *du* is usually lowercased in a full name but is retained and capitalized when the last name is used alone. (When a name begins with closed-up *Du*, such as *Dupont*, the *d* is always capitalized.)

Jean de La Fontaine; La Fontaine
René-Robert Cavelier de La Salle; La Salle
Philippe du Puy de Clinchamps; Du Puy de Clinchamps

When the article *le* accompanies a name, it is capitalized with or without the first name.

Gustave Le Bon; Le Bon

Initials standing for a hyphenated given name should also be hyphenated.

Jean-Paul Sartre; J.-P. Sartre; Sartre

Since there is considerable variation in French usage, the guidelines and examples above merely represent the most common forms.

8.8 *German and Portuguese names.* In the original languages, particles in German and Portuguese names are lowercased and are usually dropped when the last name is used alone. But in English contexts, if another form is widely known, it may be used instead.

Alexander von Humboldt; Humboldt
Maximilian von Spee; Spee
Heinrich Friedrich Karl vom und zum Stein; Stein
Ludwig van Beethoven; Beethoven
Agostinho da Silva; Silva
but
Vasco da Gama; da Gama

8.9 *Italian names.* Particles in Italian names are most often uppercased and retained when the last name is used alone.

Gabriele D'Annunzio; D'Annunzio
Lorenzo Da Ponte; Da Ponte
Luca Della Robbia; Della Robbia

In many older aristocratic names, however, the particle is traditionally lowercased and dropped when the last name is used alone.

Beatrice d'Este; Este   Lorenzo de' Medici; Medici

8.10 *Dutch names.* In English usage, the particles *van*, *van den*, *ter*, and the like are lowercased when full names are given but usually capitalized when only the last name is used.

Joannes van Keulen; Van Keulen
Pieter van den Keere; Van den Keere
Vincent van Gogh; Van Gogh
Gerard ter Borch; Ter Borch

8.11 *Spanish names.* Many Spanish names are composed of both the father's and the mother's family names, usually in that order, sometimes joined by *y* (and). When the given name is omitted, persons with such names are usually referred to by both family names but sometimes by only one (usually, but not always, the first of the two family names), according to their own preference. It is never incorrect to use both.

José Ortega y Gasset; Ortega y Gasset *or* Ortega
Pascual Ortiz Rubio; Ortiz Rubio *or* Ortiz
Federico García Lorca; García Lorca (known among speakers of English, how-
ever, as Lorca)

Spanish family names that include an article, a preposition, or both are
treated in the same way as analogous French names.

Tomás de Torquemada; Torquemada
Manuel de Falla; Falla
Bartolomé de Las Casas; Las Casas
Gonzalo Fernández de Oviedo; Fernández de Oviedo

Traditionally, a married woman replaced her mother's family name with
her husband's (first) family name, sometimes preceded by *de*. If, for example, María Carmen Mendoza Salinas married Juan Alberto Peña Montalvo, she could change her legal name to María Carmen Mendoza (de)
Peña or, if the husband was well known by both family names, to María
Carmen Mendoza (de) Peña Montalvo. Many modern women in Spanish-
speaking countries, however, no longer take their husband's family name.
For alphabetizing, see 16.84.

8.12   *Russian names.* Russian family names, as well as patronymics (the name
preceding the family name and derived from the name of the father),
sometimes take different endings for male and female members of the
family. For example, Lenin's real name was Vladimir Ilyich Ulyanov (given
name, patronymic, family name); his sister Maria was Maria Ilyinichna
Ulyanova. In Russian sources (and, by extension, their English translations), often only the given name and patronymic are used; in such instances the patronymic should not be confused either for a middle name
or for the family name.

8.13   *Hungarian names.* In Hungarian practice the family name precedes the
given name—for example, Molnár Ferenc, Kodály Zoltán. In English contexts, however, such names are usually inverted—Ferenc Molnár, Zoltán
Kodály. In some cases, the family name includes an initial—for example,
É. Kiss Katalin. When such a name is inverted for English contexts (i.e.,
to become Katalin É. Kiss), the initial should not be confused for a middle
initial. When such a name is inverted, as for an index, it is properly listed
under the initial (see 16.79).

8.14   *Arabic names.* Surnames of Arabic origin (which are strictly surnames
rather than family names) are often prefixed by such elements as *Abu*,

Abd, Ibn, al, or *el.* Since these are integral parts of a name, just as *Mc* or *Fitz* are parts of certain names, they should not be dropped when the surname is used alone. Capitalization of such elements varies widely, but terms joined with a hyphen may usually be lowercased. See also 11.99, 11.100, 16.76.

Syed Abu Zafar Nadvi; Abu Zafar Nadvi
Abdul Aziz Ibn Saud; Ibn Saud
Tawfiq al-Hakim; al-Hakim

Names of rulers of older times, however, are often shortened to the first part of the name rather than the second.

Harun al-Rashid; Harun (al-Rashid, "Rightly Guided," was Harun's *laqab*, a descriptive name he took on his accession to the caliphate)

8.15   *Chinese names.* In Chinese practice, the family name comes before the given name. (This practice should be followed in English contexts with names of Chinese persons but not with those of persons of Chinese origin whose names have been anglicized.) For use of the Pinyin and Wade-Giles systems of transliteration, see 11.102–10.

Chiang Kai-shek; Chiang (Wade-Giles)
Mao Tse-tung; Mao (Wade-Giles)
Li Bai; Li (Pinyin)
Du Fu; Du (Pinyin)
but
Anthony Yu; Yu
Tang Tsou; Tsou

8.16   *Japanese names.* In Japanese usage the family name precedes the given name. Japanese names are sometimes westernized, however, by authors writing in English or persons of Japanese origin living in the West.

Tajima Yumiko; Tajima
Yoshida Shigeru; Yoshida
but
Noriaki Kurosawa; Kurosawa

8.17   *Other Asian names.* In some Asian countries, people are usually known by their given name rather than by a surname or family name. The Indonesian writer Pramoedya Ananta Toer, for example, is referred to in short form as Pramoedya (not as Toer). For further examples, see 16.77, 16.81, 16.85, 16.86. If in doubt, use the full form of a name in all references or consult an expert or consult the usage in a reputable source that discusses the person in question.

Titles and Offices

8.18   *Titles and offices—the general rule.* Civil, military, religious, and professional titles are capitalized when they immediately precede a personal name and are thus used as part of the name (typically replacing the title holder's first name). In formal prose and other generic text (as opposed to promotional or ceremonial contexts or a heading), titles are normally lowercased when following a name or used in place of a name (but see 8.19). For abbreviated forms, see 10.11–27.

President Lincoln; the president
General Bradley; the general
Cardinal Newman; the cardinal
Governors Quinn and Paterson; the governors

Although both first and second names may be used after a capitalized title (President Abraham Lincoln; but see 8.20)—and though it is perfectly correct to do so—Chicago prefers to avoid such usage in formal prose, especially with civil, corporate, and academic titles (see 8.21, 8.26, 8.27). Note also that once a title has been given, it need not be repeated each time a person's name is mentioned.

John F. Kerry, senator from Massachusetts; Senator Kerry; Kerry

8.19   *Exceptions to the general rule.* In promotional or ceremonial contexts such as a displayed list of donors in the front matter of a book or a list of corporate officers in an annual report, titles are usually capitalized even when following a personal name. Exceptions may also be called for in other contexts for reasons of courtesy or diplomacy.

Maria Martinez, Director of International Sales

A title used alone, in place of a personal name, is capitalized only in such contexts as a toast or a formal introduction, or when used in direct address.

Ladies and Gentlemen, the Prime Minister.
I would have done it, Captain, but the ship was sinking.
Thank you, Mr. President.

8.20 *Titles used in apposition.* When a title is used in apposition before a personal name—that is, not alone and as part of the name but as an equivalent to it, usually preceded by *the* or by a modifier—it is considered not a title but rather a descriptive phrase and is therefore lowercased.

the empress Elizabeth of Austria (*but* Empress Elizabeth of Austria)
German chancellor Angela Merkel (*but* Chancellor Merkel)
the German-born pope Benedict XVI
former president Carter
former presidents Reagan and Ford
the then secretary of state Colin Powell

8.21 *Civil titles.* Much of the usage below is contradicted by the official literature typically generated by political offices, where capitalization of a title in any position is the norm (see 8.19). In formal academic prose, however, civil titles are capitalized only when used as part of the name (except as noted). See also 10.13.

the president; George Washington, first president of the United States; President Washington; the presidency; presidential; the Washington administration; Washington; Gloria Macapagal Arroyo, president of the Philippines; President Arroyo; Arroyo
the vice president; John Adams, vice president of the United States; Vice President Adams; vice presidential duties
the secretary of state; Hillary Clinton, secretary of state; Secretary of State Clinton *or* Secretary Clinton
the senator; the senator from New York; New York senator Kirsten E. Gillibrand (see 8.20); Senator Gillibrand; Senators Gillibrand and Schumer; Senator Mikulski, Democrat from Maryland (*or* D-MD)
the representative; the congressman; the congresswoman; Jesse Jackson Jr., representative from Illinois *or* congressman from Illinois; Congressman Jackson *or* Rep. Jesse Jackson Jr. (D-IL); Kay Granger, representative from Texas; Congresswoman Granger; the congresswoman *or* the representative; Representatives Jackson and Granger
the Speaker; Nancy Pelosi, Speaker of the House of Representatives; Speaker Pelosi (*Speaker* is best capitalized in all contexts to avoid conflation with generic speakers)
the chief justice; John G. Roberts Jr., chief justice of the United States; Chief Justice Roberts (see also 8.63)

the associate justice; Ruth Bader Ginsburg, associate justice; Justice Ginsburg; Justices Ginsburg and Stevens

the chief judge; Timothy C. Evans, chief judge; Judge Evans

the ambassador; Robert Holmes Tuttle, ambassador to the Court of St. James's *or* ambassador to the United Kingdom; Ambassador Tuttle

the governor; Joe Manchin, governor of the state of West Virginia; Governor Manchin

the mayor; Richard M. Daley, mayor of Chicago; Mayor Daley

the state senator; Teresa Fedor, Ohio state senator; the Honorable Teresa Fedor

the state representative (same pattern as state senator)

the governor general of Canada; the Right Honourable Michaëlle Jean

the finance minister; Pranab Kumar Mukherjee, finance minister of India; Mukherjee

the prime minister; the Right Honourable Pierre Elliott Trudeau, former prime minister of Canada; Gordon Brown, the British prime minister

the premier (of a Canadian province); the Honourable Brad Wall

the member of Parliament (UK and Canada); Jane Doe, member of Parliament, *or, more commonly,* Jane Doe, MP; Jane Doe, the member for West Hamage

the chief whip; Nathi Mthethwa, chief whip of the African National Congress; Mthethwa

the foreign secretary (UK); the foreign minister (other nations); the British foreign secretary; the German foreign minister (not used as a title preceding the name)

the chancellor; Angela Merkel, chancellor of Germany; Chancellor Merkel

the chancellor of the exchequer (UK); Alistair Darling; Chancellor Darling

the Lord Privy Seal (UK; always capitalized)

For use of *the Honorable* and similar terms of respect, see 8.32, 10.18.

8.22   *Titles of sovereigns and other rulers.* Most titles of sovereigns and other rulers are lowercased when used alone. See also 8.31.

King Abdullah II; the king of Jordan

Queen Elizabeth; Elizabeth II; the queen (in a British Commonwealth context, the Queen)

the Holy Roman emperor

Nero, emperor of Rome; the Roman emperor

Hamad ibn Isa al-Khalifah, king of Bahrain; King Hamad

the shah of Iran

the sharif of Mecca

the paramount chief of Basutoland

Wilhelm II, emperor of Germany; Kaiser Wilhelm II; the kaiser

the führer (Adolf Hitler)

Il Duce (used only of Benito Mussolini; both *i* and *d* capitalized)

8.23 *Military titles.* As is the case with civil titles, military titles are routinely capitalized in the literature of the organization or government with which they are associated. Nonetheless, in formal academic prose, most such titles are capitalized only when used as part of a person's name. Occasional exceptions may be made if ambiguity threatens. See also 10.13.

> the general; General Ulysses S. Grant, commander in chief of the Union army; General Grant; the commander in chief
> the general of the army; Omar N. Bradley, general of the army; General Bradley
> the admiral; Chester W. Nimitz, fleet admiral; Admiral Nimitz, commander in chief of the Pacific Fleet
> the chairman; Michael G. Mullen, chairman of the Joint Chiefs of Staff; Admiral Mullen
> the captain; Captain Frances LeClaire, company commander
> the sergeant; Sergeant Carleton C. Singer; a noncommissioned officer (NCO)
> the warrant officer; Warrant Officer John Carmichael
> the chief petty officer; Chief Petty Officer Tannenbaum
> the private; Private T. C. Alhambra
> the British general; General Sir Guy Carleton, British commander in New York City; General Carleton

For abbreviations, often used when a title precedes a name and appropriate in material in which many military titles appear, see 10.15.

8.24 *Quasi-military titles.* Titles and ranks used in organizations such as the police, the merchant marine, or the Salvation Army are treated the same way as military titles.

> the chief of police; Frederick Day, Parkdale chief of police; Chief Day
> the warden; Jane Simmons, warden of the state penitentiary; Warden Simmons

8.25 *Religious titles.* Religious titles are treated much like civil and military titles (see 8.21, 8.23).

> the rabbi; Rabbi Avraham Yitzhak ha-Kohen Kuk; the rabbinate
> the cantor *or* hazzan; Deborah Bard, cantor; Cantor Bard
> the sheikh; Sheikh Ibrahim el-Zak Zaky
> the imam; Imam Shamil
> the ayatollah; Ayatollah Khomeini
> the Dalai Lama (traditionally capitalized); *but* previous dalai lamas
> the sadhu; the guru; the shaman
> the pope; Pope Benedict XVI; the papacy; papal

the cardinal; Francis Cardinal George *or, less formally,* Cardinal George; the sacred college of cardinals

the patriarch; Cyrillus Lucaris, patriarch of Constantinople; the patriarchate

the archbishop; the archbishop of Canterbury; Archbishop Williams (*or, in this case,* Dr. Williams)

the bishop; the bishop of Toledo; Bishop Donnelly; bishopric; diocese

the minister; the Reverend Shirley Stoops

the rector; the Reverend James Williams (see also 10.18, 8.32)

8.26   *Corporate and organizational titles.* Titles of persons holding offices such as those listed below are rarely used as part of a name. If a short form is required, either the generic term or simply a personal name suffices.

the chief executive officer; Pat Beldos, chief executive officer of Caterham Industries; the CEO

the director; Gabriel Dotto, director of the Michigan State University Press

the school superintendent; Janice Bayder, superintendent of Coriander Township High School District

the secretary-treasurer; Georgina Fido, secretary-treasurer of the Kenilworth Kennel Society

8.27   *Academic titles.* Academic titles generally follow the pattern for civil titles (see 8.21).

the professor; Françoise Meltzer, professor of comparative literature; Professor Meltzer

the chair; Jonathan M. Hall, chair of the Department of Classics; Professor Hall (but see 8.29)

the provost; Thomas F. Rosenbaum, provost of the University of Chicago; Rosenbaum

the president; Robert J. Zimmer, president of the University of Chicago; Zimmer *or* President Zimmer

the dean; John W. Boyer, dean of the College at the University of Chicago (*the College* is an official division of the University of Chicago); Dean Boyer

named professorships; Wendy Doniger, Mircea Eliade Distinguished Service Professor of the History of Religions in the Divinity School; Professor Doniger; Anthony Grafton, Dodge Professor of History, Princeton University; Professor Grafton

the professor emeritus (masc.); the professor emerita (fem.); professors emeriti (masc. or masc. and fem.); professors emeritae (fem.); Professor Emerita Neugarten (note that *emeritus* and *emerita* are honorary designations and do not simply mean "retired")

8.28   *Other academic designations.* Terms denoting student status are lower-cased.

freshman *or* first-year student   sophomore   junior   senior

Names of degrees, fellowships, and the like are lowercased when referred to generically. See also 10.20.

a master's degree; a doctorate; a fellowship; master of business administration (MBA)

8.29   *Descriptive titles.* When preceding a name, generic titles that describe a person's role or occupation—such as *philosopher* or *historian*—should be lowercased and treated as if in apposition (see 8.20). Compare 8.27.

the historian William McNeill (*not* Historian McNeill)

8.30   *Civic and academic honors.* Titles denoting civic or academic honors are capitalized when following a personal name. For awards, see 8.82; for abbreviations, see 10.21.

Laurence L. Bongie, Fellow of the Royal Society of Canada; the fellows

8.31   *Titles of nobility.* Unlike most of the titles mentioned in the previous paragraphs, titles of nobility do not denote offices (such as that of a president or an admiral). Whether inherited or conferred, they form an integral and, with rare exceptions, permanent part of a person's name and are therefore usually capitalized. The generic element in a title, however (duke, earl, etc.), is lowercased when used alone as a short form of the name. (In British usage, the generic term used alone remains capitalized in the case of royal dukes but not in the case of nonroyal dukes; in North American usage such niceties may be disregarded.) For further advice consult *The Times Style and Usage Guide* (bibliog. 1.1), and for a comprehensive listing consult the latest edition of *Burke's Peerage, Baronetage, and Knightage* (bibliog. 4.1). See also 8.22.

the prince; Prince Charles; the Prince of Wales
the duke; the duchess; the Duke and Duchess of Windsor
the marquess; the Marquess of Bath; Lord Bath
the marchioness; the Marchioness of Bath; Lady Bath
the earl; the Earl of Shaftesbury; Lord Shaftesbury; Anthony Ashley Cooper, 7th
    (*or* seventh) Earl of Shaftesbury; previous earls of Shaftesbury
the countess (wife of an earl); the Countess of Shaftesbury; Lady Shaftesbury

the viscount; Viscount Eccles; Lord Eccles
Baroness Thatcher; Lady Thatcher (a conferred title)
Dame Judi Dench; Dame Judi (a conferred title)
the baron; Lord Rutland
the baronet; the knight; Sir Paul McCartney; Sir Paul (*not* Sir McCartney)
Lady So-and-So [husband's last name] (wife of a marquess, earl, baron, or baronet)
Lady Olivia So-and-So (daughter of a duke, marquess, or earl); Lady Olivia
the Honourable Jessica So-and-So (daughter of a baron)
the duc de Guise (lowercased in accordance with French usage); François de Lor-
    raine, duc de Guise
the count; Count Helmuth von Moltke *or* Graf Helmuth von Moltke; the Count of
    Toulouse *or* the comte de Toulouse

Note that marquesses, earls, viscounts, barons, and baronesses are addressed, and referred to after first mention, as Lord or Lady So-and-So,
at least in British usage. The following entry, drawn from *Burke's Peerage,
Baronetage, and Knightage*, illustrates the complexities of British noble
nomenclature:

The 5th Marquess of Salisbury (Sir Robert Arthur James Gascoyne-Cecil, K.G.,
    P.C.), Earl of Salisbury, Wilts; Viscount Cranborne, Dorset, and Baron Cecil of
    Essendon, Rutland; co-heir to the Barony of Ogle

8.32   *Honorifics.* Honorific titles and respectful forms of address are capitalized in any context. For the use of many such terms in formal correspondence, see "Forms of Address," a comprehensive listing at the back of the
print edition of *Merriam-Webster's Collegiate Dictionary*. For abbreviations,
see 10.18. See also 8.25.

the Honorable Olympia J. Snowe (US senator, member of Congress, etc.)
the Right Honourable Stephen Harper (Canadian prime minister)
the First Gentleman; the First Lady
the Queen Mother
Pandit Nehru
Mahatma Gandhi
Her (His, Your) Majesty; His (Her, Your) Royal Highness
the Most Reverend William S. Skylstad (Roman Catholic bishop)
Your (Her, His) Excellency
Mr. President; Mrs. President; Ms. President
Madam Speaker
Your Honor
but
sir, ma'am   my lord, my lady

Epithets, Kinship Names, and Personifications

8.33 *Epithets (or nicknames) and bynames.* A descriptive or characterizing word or phrase used as part of, or instead of, a person's name is capitalized. A *the* used as part of such a name is not capitalized (except, e.g., at the beginning of a sentence).

the Great Emancipator (Abraham Lincoln)
the Sun King (Louis XIV)
the Wizard of Menlo Park (Thomas Edison)
Stonewall Jackson
Old Hickory (Andrew Jackson)
the Young Pretender (Charles Edward Stuart)
the Great Commoner (William Jennings Bryan)
Catherine the Great
Babe Ruth
the Swedish Nightingale (Jenny Lind)
Ivan the Terrible

When used in addition to a name, an epithet is enclosed in quotation marks and placed either within or after the name. Parentheses are unnecessary.

George Herman "Babe" Ruth
Jenny Lind, "the Swedish Nightingale"
Ivan IV, "the Terrible"

8.34 *Epithets as names of characters.* In references to works of drama or fiction, epithets or generic titles used in place of names are normally capitalized.

John Barrymore performed brilliantly as Chief Executioner.
Alice encounters the Red Queen and the Mad Hatter.

8.35 *Kinship names.* Kinship names are lowercased unless they immediately precede a personal name or are used alone, in place of a personal name. Used in apposition, however, such names are lowercased (see 8.20).

my father and mother
the Brontë sisters
Let's write to Aunt Maud.
I believe Grandmother's middle name was Marie.

Please, Dad, let's go.
but
She adores her aunt Maud.

Kinship terms used in connection with religious offices or callings are treated similarly.

The note referred to a certain Brother Thomas, one of the brothers from the Franciscan monastery, . . .

8.36 *Personifications.* The poetic device of giving abstractions the attributes of persons, and hence capitalizing them, is rare in today's writing. The use of capitals for such a purpose is best confined to quoted material.

"The Night is Mother of the Day, / The Winter of the Spring, / And ever upon old Decay / The greenest mosses cling." (John Greenleaf Whittier)
but
In springtime, nature is at its best.
It was a battle between head and heart; reason finally won.

Ethnic, Socioeconomic, and Other Groups

8.37 *Ethnic and national groups and associated adjectives.* Names of ethnic and national groups are capitalized. Adjectives associated with these names are also capitalized. For hyphenation or its absence, see 8.38.

Aborigines; an Aborigine; Aboriginal art
African Americans; African American culture (see also 8.39)
American Indians; an American Indian (see text below)
Arabs; Arabian
Asians; Asian influence in the West; an Asian American
the British; a British person *or, colloquially,* a Britisher, a Brit
Caucasians; a Caucasian (see also 8.39)
Chicanos; a Chicano; a Chicana
European Americans
the French; a Frenchman; a Frenchwoman
French Canadians
Hispanics; a Hispanic
Hopis; a Hopi; Hopi customs
Inuit; Inuit sculpture
Italian Americans; an Italian American neighborhood

Jews; a Jew; Jewish ethnicity (see also 8.95)
Latinos; a Latino; a Latina; Latino immigration
Native Americans; Native American poetry (see text below)
New Zealanders; New Zealand immigration
Pygmies; a Pygmy; Pygmy peoples
Romanies; a Romany; the Romany people

Many among those who trace their roots to the aboriginal peoples of the Americas prefer *American Indians* to *Native Americans*, and in certain historical works *Indians* may be more appropriate. Canadians often speak of *First Peoples* (and of *First Nations*). See also 7.9.

8.38   *Compound nationalities.* Whether terms such as *African American*, *Italian American*, *Chinese American*, and the like should be spelled open or hyphenated has been the subject of considerable controversy, the hyphen being regarded by some as suggestive of bias. Chicago doubts that hyphenation represents bias, but since the hyphen does not aid comprehension in such terms as those mentioned above, it may be omitted unless a particular publisher requires it. See also the table at 7.85, section 2, under *proper nouns and adjectives relating to geography or nationality.*

8.39   *Color.* Common designations of ethnic groups by color are usually lowercased unless a particular publisher or author prefers otherwise. See also 8.37.

black people; blacks; people of color   white people; whites

8.40   *Class.* Terms denoting socioeconomic classes or groups are lowercased.

the middle class; a middle-class neighborhood
the upper-middle class; an upper-middle-class family
blue-collar workers
the aristocracy
the proletariat
homeless people

8.41   *Generation.* Terms denoting generations are best lowercased.

the me generation   generation X; generation Y; generation Z
baby boomer(s); baby busters   the MTV generation

8.42   *Physical characteristics.* Terms describing groups or individuals according to a physical characteristic or a disability are usually lowercased.

wheelchair users   blind persons   deaf children

Some writers capitalize *deaf* when referring to people who identify themselves as members of the distinct linguistic and cultural group whose primary language is ASL—the Deaf community—and lowercase it when
referring to people who have a hearing loss or to those deaf people who
prefer oral methods of communication. See also 11.144.

Names of Places

8.43   *Names of places—additional resources.* For the spelling of names of places,
consult *Merriam-Webster's Geographical Dictionary* (bibliog. 4.2). Since
names of countries and cities often change, however, even the most recent edition of such a reference work cannot be current in every detail.
Moreover, not all writers will be in agreement on the proper form of every place-name (e.g., some will insist on Burma rather than Myanmar).
For country names, the US Central Intelligence Agency's *World Factbook*—
continually updated—is a good place to start (bibliog. 4.2). For historical works, writers and editors should attempt to use the form of names
appropriate to the period under discussion.

Parts of the World

8.44   *Continents, countries, cities, oceans, and such.* Entities that appear on maps
are always capitalized, as are adjectives and nouns derived from them.
An initial *the* as part of a name is lowercased in running text, except in
the rare case of an initial *the* in the name of a city.

Asia; Asian   South China Sea
Ireland; Irish   the North Pole
California; Californian   the Netherlands; Dutch
Chicago; Chicagoan   *but*
Atlantic Ocean; Atlantic   The Hague

8.45   *Points of the compass.* Compass points and terms derived from them are
lowercased if they simply indicate direction or location. But see 8.46.

pointing toward the north; a north wind; a northern climate
to fly east; an eastward move; in the southwest of France; southwesterly

8.46 *Regions of the world and national regions.* Terms that denote regions of the world or of a particular country are often capitalized, as are a few of the adjectives and nouns derived from such terms. The following examples illustrate not only the principles sketched in 8.1 but also variations based on context and usage. For terms not included here or for which no suitable analogy can be made, consult *Webster's* or an encyclopedia: if an otherwise generic term is not listed there (either capitalized or, for dictionary entries, with the indication *capitalized* next to the applicable subentry), opt for lowercase. Note that exceptions based on specific regional, political, or historical contexts are inevitable and that an author's strong preference should usually be respected. See also 8.45.

the Swiss Alps; the Australian Alps; the Alps; an Alpine village (if in the European or Australian Alps); Alpine skiing; *but* alpine pastures in the Rockies (see also 8.52)

Antarctica; the Antarctic Circle; the Antarctic Continent

the Arctic; the Arctic Circle; Arctic waters; a mass of Arctic air (*but* lowercased when used metaphorically, as in "an arctic stare"; see 8.60)

Central America, Central American countries; central Asia; central Illinois; central France; central Europe (*but* Central Europe when referring to the political division of World War I)

the continental United States; the continent of Europe; *but* on the Continent (used to denote mainland Europe); Continental cuisine; *but* continental breakfast

the East, eastern, an easterner (referring to the eastern part of the United States or other country); the Eastern Seaboard (or Atlantic Seaboard), East Coast (referring to the eastern United States); the East, the Far East, Eastern (referring to the Orient and Asian culture); the Middle East (*or*, formerly more common, the Near East), Middle Eastern (referring to Iran, Iraq, etc.); the Eastern Hemisphere; eastern Europe (*but* Eastern Europe when referring to the post–World War II division of Europe); east, eastern, eastward, to the east (directions)

the equator; equatorial climate; the Equatorial Current; Equatorial Guinea (formerly Spanish Guinea)

the Great Plains; the northern plains; the plains (*but* Plains Indians)

the Midwest, midwestern, a midwesterner (as of the United States)

the North, northern, a northerner (of a country); the North, Northern, Northerner (in American Civil War contexts); Northern California; North Africa, North African countries, in northern Africa; North America, North American, the North American continent; the North Atlantic, a northern Atlantic route; the Northern Hemisphere; the Far North; north, northern, northward, to the north (directions)

the Northeast, the Northwest, northwestern, northeastern, a northwesterner, a northeasterner (as of the United States); the Pacific Northwest; the Northwest Passage

the poles; the North Pole; the North Polar ice cap; the South Pole; polar regions (*see also* Antarctica; the Arctic)

the South, southern, a southerner (of a country); the South, Southern, a Southerner (in American Civil War contexts); the Deep South; Southern California; the South of France (region); Southeast Asia; South Africa, South African (referring to the Republic of South Africa); southern Africa (referring to the southern part of the continent); south, southern, southward, to the south (directions)

the Southeast, the Southwest, southeastern, southwestern, a southeasterner, a southwesterner (as of the United States)

the tropics, tropical; the Tropic of Cancer; the Neotropics, Neotropical (of the New World biogeographical region); the subtropics, subtropical

the Upper Peninsula (of Michigan); the upper reaches of the Thames

the West, western, a westerner (of a country); the West Coast; the West, Western (referring to the culture of the Occident, or Europe and the Western Hemisphere); west, western, westward, to the west (directions)

8.47 *Popular place-names or epithets.* Popular names of places, or epithets, are usually capitalized. Quotation marks are not needed. Some of the following examples may be used of more than one place. None should be used in contexts where they will not be readily understood. See also 8.33.

Back Bay	the Gaza Strip	Skid Row
the Badger State	the Gulf	the South Seas
the Badlands	the Holy City	the South Side
the Bay Area	the Jewish Quarter	the Sun Belt
the Beltway	the Lake District	the Twin Cities
the Bible Belt	the Left Bank	the Upper West Side
the Cape	the Loop (Chicago)	the Village
the Delta	the Old World	(Greenwich Village)
the East End	the Panhandle	the West End
the Eastern Shore	the Promised Land	the Wild West
the Eternal City	the Rust Belt	the Windy City
the Fertile Crescent	Silicon Valley	

Certain terms considered political rather than geographical need not be capitalized. Some editorial discretion is advisable, however. In reference to Soviet-era global politics, for example, the following terms might be suitably capitalized:

the iron curtain *or* Iron Curtain   the third world *or* Third World

8.48 *Urban areas.* Generic terms used for parts of urban areas are not capitalized.

the business district   the inner city

But when *greater* is used with the name of a city to denote a whole metropolitan area, it is capitalized.

Greater Chicago (*but* the greater Chicago metropolitan area)
Greater London

8.49   *Real versus metaphorical names.* Mecca is capitalized when referring to the Islamic holy city, as is *Utopia* when referring to Thomas More's imaginary country. Both are lowercased when used metaphorically. See also 8.60.

Stratford-upon-Avon is a mecca for Shakespeare enthusiasts.
She is trying to create a utopia for her children.

Political Divisions

8.50   *Political divisions—capitalization.* Words denoting political divisions—from *empire, republic,* and *state* down to *ward* and *precinct*—are capitalized when they follow a name and are used as an accepted part of the name. When preceding the name, such terms are usually capitalized in names of countries but lowercased in entities below the national level (but see 8.51). Used alone, they are usually lowercased.

the Ottoman Empire; the empire
the British Commonwealth; Commonwealth nations; the Commonwealth (*but* a
    commonwealth)
the United States; the Republic; the Union
the United Kingdom; Great Britain; Britain (*not* the kingdom)
the Russian Federation (formerly the Union of Soviet Socialist Republics; the So-
    viet Union); Russia; the federation
the Republic of South Africa (formerly the Union of South Africa); South Africa;
    the republic
the Fifth Republic (France)
the Republic of Indonesia; the republic
the Republic of Lithuania; the republic
the Federal Democratic Republic of Ethiopia; the republic; the State of the Gam-
    bella Peoples; the state
the Commonwealth of Australia; the commonwealth; the state of New South
    Wales; the Australian Capital Territory

the Commonwealth of Puerto Rico
Washington State; the state of Washington
the New England states
the province of Ontario
Jiangxi Province
Massachusetts Bay Colony; the colony at Massachusetts Bay
the British colonies; the thirteen colonies
the Indiana Territory; the territory of Indiana
the Northwest Territory; the Old Northwest
the Western Reserve
Lake County; the county of Lake; the county; county Kildare (Irish usage)
New York City; the city of New York
the City (the old city of London, now the financial district, always capitalized)
Shields Township; the township
the Eleventh Congressional District; the congressional district
the Fifth Ward; the ward
the Sixth Precinct; the precinct

8.51   *Governmental entities.* In contexts where a specific governmental body rather than the place is meant, the words *state, city,* and the like are usually capitalized when used as part of the full name of the body. See also 8.50.

She works for the Village of Forest Park.
That is a City of Chicago ordinance.
but
Residents of the village of Forest Park enjoy easy access to the city of Chicago.

Topographical Divisions

8.52   *Mountains, rivers, and the like.* Names of mountains, rivers, oceans, islands, and so forth are capitalized. The generic term (*mountain,* etc.) is also capitalized when used as part of the name. In the plural, it is capitalized when it is part of a single name (Hawaiian Islands) and when it is used of two or more names, whether beginning with the generic term (Mounts Washington and Rainier) or—in a return to earlier editions of this manual—when the generic term comes second and applies to two or more names (e.g., the Illinois and the Chicago Rivers). Such capitalization signals unambiguously that the generic term forms part of each proper noun. See also 8.55.

Walden Pond
Silver Lake
Lake Michigan; Lakes Michigan and Erie; the Great Lakes
the Illinois River; the Illinois and the Chicago Rivers
the Nile River valley; the Nile valley; the Nile delta; the Mississippi River valley;
    the Mississippi delta (where *river* forms part of the proper names but *valley*
    and *delta* do not)
the Bering Strait
the Mediterranean Sea; the Mediterranean
the Pacific Ocean; the Pacific and the Atlantic Oceans
the Great Barrier Reef
the Hawaiian Islands; Hawaii; *but* the island of Hawaii
the Windward Islands; the Windwards
the Iberian Peninsula
Cape Verde
the Black Forest
Stone Mountain
Mount Washington; Mount Rainier; Mounts Washington and Rainier
the Rocky Mountains; the Rockies (see also 8.46)
Death Valley; the Valley of Kings
the Continental Divide
the Horn of Africa
the Indian subcontinent (a descriptive rather than proper geographical name)

8.53   *Generic terms for geographic entities.* When a generic term is used descriptively (or in apposition; see 8.20) rather than as part of a name, or when used alone, it is lowercased.

the Amazon basin
along the Pacific coast (*but* the West Coast; see 8.46)
the California desert
the river Thames
the Hudson River valley

8.54   *Foreign terms for geographic entities.* When a foreign generic term forms part of a geographic name, the equivalent English term should not be included.

the Rio Grande (*not* the Rio Grande River)
Fujiyama (*not* Mount Fujiyama)
Mauna Loa (*not* Mount Mauna Loa)
the Sierra Nevada (*not* the Sierra Nevada Mountains)

Public Places and Major Structures

8.55   *Thoroughfares and the like.* The names of streets, avenues, squares, parks, and so forth are capitalized. The generic term is lowercased when used alone but—in a return to earlier editions of this manual—capitalized when used as part of a plural name (see also 8.52).

> Broadway
> Fifty-Fifth Street; Fifty-Seventh and Fifty-Fifth Streets
> Hyde Park Boulevard; the boulevard
> Interstate 80; I-80; an interstate highway
> the Ishtar Gate; the gate
> Jackson Park; the park
> London Bridge; the bridge
> the Mall (in London)
> Park Lane
> Pennsylvania Avenue; Carnegie and Euclid Avenues
> Piccadilly Circus
> the Spanish Steps; the steps
> Tiananmen Square; the square
> US Route 66; Routes 1 and 2; a state route

See also 9.51–53.

8.56   *Buildings and monuments.* The names of buildings and monuments are generally capitalized. The generic term is usually lowercased when used alone but capitalized when used as part of a plural name (as in the fifth example; see also 8.52, 8.55).

> the Babri Mosque; the mosque
> the Berlin Wall; the wall
> Buckingham Fountain; the fountain
> the Capitol (where the US Congress meets, *as distinct from* the capital city)
> the Chrysler Building; the building; the Empire State and Chrysler Buildings
> the Houses of Parliament
> the Jefferson Memorial; the memorial
> the Leaning Tower of Pisa
> the Pyramids (*but* the Egyptian pyramids)
> Shedd Aquarium; the aquarium
> the Stone of Scone
> Symphony Center; the center
> Tribune Tower; the tower

the Washington Monument; the monument
Westminster Abbey; the abbey
the White House

Though major works of art are generally italicized, some massive works of sculpture are regarded primarily as monuments and therefore not italicized (see 8.193).

the Statue of Liberty; the statue
Mount Rushmore National Memorial; Mount Rushmore
the Colossus of Rhodes; the colossus

8.57 *Rooms, offices, and such.* Official names of rooms, offices, and the like are capitalized.

the Empire Room (*but* room 421)
the Amelia Earhart Suite (*but* suite 219)
the Lincoln Bedroom
the Oval Office
the West Wing of the White House

8.58 *Foreign names for places and structures.* Foreign names of thoroughfares and buildings are not italicized and may be preceded by English *the* if the definite article would appear in the original language.

the Champs-Elysées	Unter den Linden (never preceded by *the*)
the Bibliothèque nationale	the Marktstrasse
the Bois de Boulogne	the Piazza delle Terme

Words Derived from Proper Names

8.59 *When to capitalize.* Adjectives derived from personal names are normally capitalized. Those in common use may be found in *Webster's*, sometimes in the biographical names section (e.g., *Aristotelian, Jamesian, Machiavellian, Shakespearean*). If not in the dictionary, adjectives can sometimes be coined by adding *ian* (to a name ending in a consonant) or *an* (to a name ending in *e* or *i*)—or, failing these, *esque*. As with Foucault and Shaw, the final consonant sometimes undergoes a transformation as an aid to pronunciation. If a name does not seem to lend itself to any such coinage, it is best avoided. See also 8.60, 8.78.

Baudelaire; Baudelairean
Bayes; Bayesian
Dickens; Dickensian
Foucault; Foucauldian
Jordan; Jordanesque (à la Michael Jordan)
Kafka; Kafkaesque
Marx; Marxist
Mendel; Mendelian
Rabelais; Rabelaisian
Sartre; Sartrean
Shaw; Shavian

8.60   *When not to capitalize.* Personal, national, or geographical names, and words derived from such names, are often lowercased when used with a *nonliteral* meaning. For example, the cheese known as "gruyère" takes its name from a district in Switzerland but is not necessarily from there; "swiss cheese" (lowercase *s*) is a cheese that resembles Swiss emmentaler (which derives its name from the Emme River valley). Although some of the terms in this paragraph and the examples that follow are capitalized in *Webster's*, Chicago prefers to lowercase them in their nonliteral use. See also 8.78.

anglicize	italic type
arabic numerals	italicize
arctics (boots)	jeremiad
bohemian	lombardy poplar
brie	manila envelope
brussels sprouts	morocco leather
cheddar	pasteurize
delphic	pharisaic
diesel engine	philistine, philistinism
dutch oven	platonic (but see 8.78)
epicure	quixotic
frankfurter	roman numerals
french dressing	roman type
french fries	scotch whisky; scotch
french windows	stilton
gruyère	swiss cheese (not made in Switzerland)
herculean	venetian blinds
homeric	vulcanize
india ink	wiener

Names of Organizations

Governmental Bodies

8.61   *Legislative and deliberative bodies.* The full names of legislative and deliberative bodies, departments, bureaus, and offices are capitalized (but see 8.64). Adjectives derived from them are usually lowercased, as are many of the generic names for such bodies when used alone (as on subsequent mentions). For generic names used alone but not listed here, opt for lowercase. For administrative bodies, see 8.62; for judicial bodies, see 8.63. See also 11.8.

the United Nations General Assembly; the UN General Assembly; the assembly
the League of Nations; the league
the United Nations Security Council; the Security Council; the council
the United States Congress; the US Congress; the Ninety-Seventh Congress; Congress; 97th Cong.; congressional
the United States Senate; the Senate; senatorial; the upper house of Congress
the House of Representatives; the House; the lower house of Congress
the Electoral College
the Committee on Foreign Affairs; the Foreign Affairs Committee; the committee
the Illinois General Assembly; the assembly; the Illinois legislature; the state senate
the Chicago City Council; the city council
the British Parliament (or UK Parliament); Parliament; an early parliament; parliamentary; the House of Commons; the Commons; the House of Lords; the Lords
the Crown (the British monarchy); Crown lands
the Privy Council (*but* a Privy Counsellor)
the Parliament of Canada; Parliament; the Senate (upper house); the House of Commons (lower house)
the Legislative Assembly of British Columbia; the National Assembly of Quebec *or* Assemblée nationale du Québec
the Dáil Éireann (lower house of the Irish parliament)
the Assemblée nationale *or* the National Assembly (present-day France); the (French) Senate; the parliamentary system; the Parlement de Paris (historical)
the States General *or* Estates General (France and Netherlands, historical)
the Cortes (Spain; a plural form in Spanish but used as a singular in English)
the Cámara de Diputados (the lower house of Mexico's congress)
the Bundestag (German parliament); the Bundesrat (German upper house); the Reichstag (imperial Germany)
the House of People's Representatives; the House of Federation; the Council of Ministers (Ethiopia)

the Dewan Perwakilan Rakyat *or* House of Representatives; the Majelis Permusya-
   waratan Rakyat *or* People's Consultative Assembly (Indonesia)
the European Parliament; the Parliament

8.62   *Administrative bodies.* The full names of administrative bodies are capital-
        ized. Adjectives derived from them are usually lowercased, as are many
        of the generic names for such bodies when used alone. See also 8.61.

the Bureau of the Census; census forms; the census of 2000
the Centers for Disease Control and Prevention; the CDC (abbreviation did not
   change when "and Prevention" was added to name)
the Department of the Interior; the Interior
the Department of State; the State Department; the department; departmental
the Department of the Treasury; the Treasury
the Federal Bureau of Investigation; the bureau; the FBI
the Federal Reserve System; the Federal Reserve Board; the Federal Reserve
the National Institutes of Health; the NIH; the National Institute of Mental Health;
   the NIMH
the Occupational Safety and Health Administration; OSHA
the Office of Human Resources; Human Resources
the Peace Corps
the United States Postal Service; the Postal Service; the post office
the Illinois State Board of Education; the board of education
the Ithaca City School District; the school district; the district

8.63   *Judicial bodies.* The full name of a court, often including a place-name, is
        capitalized. Subsequent references to a court (or district court, supreme
        court, etc.) are lowercased, except for the phrase "Supreme Court" at the
        national level.

the United States (*or* US) Supreme Court; the Supreme Court; *but* the court
the United States Court of Appeals for the Seventh Circuit; the court of appeals
the Arizona Supreme Court; the supreme court; the supreme courts of Arizona
   and New Mexico
the District Court for the Southern District of New York; the district court
the Court of Common Pleas (Ohio); the court
the Circuit Court of Lake County, Family Division (Illinois); family court
the Supreme Court of Canada; the Supreme Court; the court
the Birmingham Crown Court; Dawlish Magistrates' Court (England)
the Federal Supreme Court (Ethiopia)

States, counties, and cities vary in the way they name their courts. For
example, *court of appeals* in New York State and Maryland is equivalent

to *supreme court* in other states; and such terms as *district court, circuit court, superior court,* and *court of common pleas* are used for similar court systems in different states. Generic names should therefore be used only after the full name or jurisdiction has been stated.

8.64   *Government entities that are lowercased.* Certain generic terms associated with governmental bodies are lowercased. Compare 8.50.

> administration; the Carter administration
> brain trust
> cabinet (*but* the Kitchen Cabinet in the Jackson administration)
> city hall (the municipal government and the building)
> civil service
> court (a royal court)
> executive, legislative, or judicial branch
> federal; the federal government; federal agencies
> government
> monarchy
> parlement (French; *but* the Parlement of Paris)
> parliament, parliamentary (*but* Parliament, usually not preceded by *the,* in the United Kingdom)
> state; church and state; state powers

Political and Economic Organizations and Movements

8.65   *Organizations, parties, alliances, and so forth.* Official names of national and international organizations, alliances, and political movements and parties are capitalized (e.g., "the Labor Party in Israel"). Words like *party, union,* and *movement* are capitalized when they are part of the name of an organization. Terms identifying formal members of or adherents to such groups are also usually capitalized (e.g., "a Socialist"; "a Republican"). Names of the systems of thought and references to the adherents to such systems, however, are often lowercased (e.g., "an eighteenth-century precursor of socialism"; "a communist at heart"). Nonliteral or metaphorical references are also lowercased (e.g., "fascist parenting techniques"; "nazi tendencies"). For consistency, however—as in a work about communism in which the philosophy, its adherents, the political party, and party members are discussed—capitalizing the philosophy, together with the organization and its adherents, in both noun and adjective forms, will prevent editorial headaches.

the African National Congress party (*party* is not part of the official name); the ANC

Arab Socialist Ba'th Party; the Ba'th Party; the party; Ba'thists

Bahujan Samaj Party; the BSP

Bolshevik(s); the Bolshevik (*or* Bolshevist) movement; bolshevism *or* Bolshevism
(see text above)

Chartist; Chartism

the Communist Party (*but* Communist parties); the party; Communist(s); Communist countries; communism *or* Communism (see text above)

the Democratic Party; the party; Democrat(s) (party members or adherents); democracy; democratic nations

the Entente Cordiale (signed 1904); the Entente; *but* an entente cordiale

the Ethiopian Somali Democratic League; the league; the party

the European Union; the EU; the Common Market

the Fascist Party; Fascist(s); fascism *or* Fascism (see text above)

the Federalist Party; Federalist(s) (US history); federalism *or* Federalism (see text above)

the Free-Soil Party; Free-Soiler(s)

the General Agreement on Tariffs and Trade; GATT

the Green Party; the party; Green(s); the Green movement

the Hanseatic League; Hansa; a Hanseatic city

the Holy Alliance

the Know-Nothing Party; Know-Nothing(s)

the Labour Party; Labourite(s) (members of the British party)

the League of Arab States; the Arab League; the league

the Libertarian Party; Libertarian(s); libertarianism *or* Libertarianism (see text above)

Loyalist(s) (American Revolution; Spanish Civil War)

Marxism-Leninism; Marxist-Leninist(s)

the National Socialist Party; National Socialism; the Nazi Party; Nazi(s); Nazism

the North American Free Trade Agreement; NAFTA (see 10.6)

the North Atlantic Treaty Organization; NATO

the Organisation for Economic Co-operation and Development; the OECD; the organization

the Popular Front; the Front; *but* a popular front

the Populist Party; Populist(s); populism *or* Populism (see text above)

the Progressive Party; Progressive movement; Progressive(s); progressivism *or* Progressivism (see text above)

the Quadruple Alliance; the alliance

the Rashtriya Janata Dal; the RJD (National People's Party)

the Republican Party; the party; the GOP (Grand Old Party); Republican(s) (party members or adherents); republicanism; a republican form of government

the Social Democratic Party; the party; Social Democrat(s)

the Socialist Party (*but* Socialist parties); the party; Socialist(s) (party members or
    adherents); socialism *or* Socialism (see text above)
the United Democratic Movement; the movement
the World Health Organization; WHO

8.66   *Adherents of unofficial political groups and movements.* Names for adherents of political groups or movements other than recognized parties are usually lowercased.

anarchist(s)
centrist(s)
independent(s)
moderate(s)
mugwump(s)
opposition (*but* the Opposition, in British and Canadian contexts, referring to the
    party out of power)
but
the Left; members of the left wing; left-winger(s); on the left
the Right; members of the right wing; right-winger(s); on the right
the Far Left
the Far Right
the radical Right

Institutions and Companies

8.67   *Institutions and companies—capitalization.* The full names of institutions, groups, and companies and the names of their departments, and often the shortened forms of such names (e.g., the Art Institute), are capitalized. A *the* preceding a name, even when part of the official title, is lowercased in running text. Such generic terms as *company* and *university* are usually lowercased when used alone (though they are routinely capitalized in promotional materials, business documents, and the like).

the University of Chicago; the university; the University of Chicago and Harvard
    University; Northwestern and Princeton Universities; the University of Wisconsin–Madison
the Department of History; the department; the Law School
the University of Chicago Press; the press
the Board of Trustees of the University of Chicago; the board of trustees; the board
the Art Institute of Chicago; the Art Institute
the Beach Boys; the Beatles; the Grateful Dead, the Dead; the Who (*but* Tha East-
    sidaz)

Captain Beefheart and His Magic Band; the band
the Cleveland Orchestra; the orchestra
the General Foods Corporation; General Foods; the corporation
the Green Bay Packers; the Packers
the Hudson's Bay Company; the company
the Illinois Central Railroad; the Illinois Central; the railroad
the Library of Congress; the library
the Manuscripts Division of the library
the Museum of Modern Art; MOMA; the museum
the New York Stock Exchange; the stock exchange
Skidmore, Owings & Merrill; SOM; the architectural firm
the Smithsonian Institution; the Smithsonian
Miguel Juarez Middle School; the middle school

8.68   *Names with unusual capitalization.* Parts of names given in full capitals on the letterhead or in the promotional materials of particular organizations may be given in upper- and lowercase when referred to in other contexts (e.g., "the Rand Corporation" rather than "the RAND Corporation"). Company names that are spelled in lowercase letters in promotional materials may be capitalized (e.g., DrKoop.net rather than drkoop.net). Names like eBay and iPod, should they appear at the beginning of a sentence or heading, need not take an initial capital in addition to the capitalized second letter. See also 8.153.

Associations

8.69   *Associations, unions, and the like.* The full names of associations, societies, unions, meetings, and conferences, and often the shortened forms of such names, are capitalized. A *the* preceding a name, even when part of the official title, is lowercased in running text. Such generic terms as *society* and *union* are usually lowercased when used alone.

the Congress of Industrial Organizations; CIO; the union
the Fifty-Seventh Annual Meeting of the American Historical Association; the annual meeting of the association
Girl Scouts of the United States of America; a Girl Scout; a Scout
the Independent Order of Odd Fellows; IOOF; an Odd Fellow
Industrial Workers of the World; IWW; the Wobblies
the International Olympic Committee; the IOC; the committee
the League of Women Voters; the league
the National Conference for Community and Justice; the conference
the National Organization for Women; NOW; the organization

the New-York Historical Society (the hyphen is part of the official name of the society); the society
the Quadrangle Club; the club
the Textile Workers Union of America; the union

On the other hand, a substantive title given to a single meeting, conference, speech, or discussion is enclosed in quotation marks. For lecture
series, see 8.86.

"Making Things Better with XML," a panel discussion presented at the AAUP Annual Meeting on June 27, 2008

Historical and Cultural Terms

Periods

8.70   *Numerical designations for periods.* A numerical designation of a period is
lowercased unless it is considered part of a proper name. For the use of
numerals, see 9.34.

the twenty-first century	the second millennium BCE
the nineteen hundreds	*but*
the nineties	the Eighteenth Dynasty (Egypt)
the quattrocento	the Fifth Republic

8.71   *Descriptive designations for periods.* A descriptive designation of a period
is usually lowercased, except for proper names. For traditionally capitalized forms, see 8.72.

ancient Greece
the antebellum period
antiquity
the baroque period
the colonial period
a golden age
the Hellenistic period
imperial Rome
modern history
the romantic period (see also 8.78)
the Shang dynasty (considered an era rather than a political division; see 8.50)
the Victorian era

8.72   *Traditional period names.* Some names of periods are capitalized, either by tradition or to avoid ambiguity. See also 8.74.

the Augustan Age
the Common Era
the Counter-Reformation
the Dark Ages
the Enlightenment
the Gay Nineties
the Gilded Age
the Grand Siècle
the High Middle Ages (*but* the early Middle Ages, the late Middle Ages)
the High Renaissance
the Jazz Age
the Mauve Decade
the Middle Ages (*but* the medieval era)
the Old Kingdom (ancient Egypt)
the Old Regime (*but* the ancien régime)
the Progressive Era
the Reformation
the Renaissance
the Restoration
the Roaring Twenties

8.73   *Cultural periods.* Names of prehistoric cultural periods are capitalized. For geological periods, see 8.133–35.

the Bronze Age	the Iron Age
the Ice Age	the Stone Age

Similar terms for modern periods are often lowercased (but see 8.72).

the age of reason	the information age
the age of steam	the nuclear age

Events

8.74   *Historical events and programs.* Names of many major historical events and programs are conventionally capitalized. Others, more recent or known by their generic descriptions, are usually lowercased. If in doubt, do not capitalize. For wars and battles, see 8.112–13; for religious events, 8.107; for acts and treaties, 8.79.

the Boston Tea Party
the Cold War (*but* a cold war, used generically)
the Cultural Revolution
the Great Chicago Fire; the Chicago fire; the fire of 1871
the Great Depression; the Depression
the Great Fire of London; the Great Fire
the Great Plague; the Plague (*but* plague [the disease])
(President Johnson's) Great Society
the Industrial Revolution
the New Deal
Prohibition
Reconstruction
the Reign of Terror; the Terror
the South Sea Bubble
the War on Poverty
but
the baby boom
the civil rights movement
the crash of 1929
the Dreyfus affair
the gold rush

8.75　*Speeches.* A very few speeches have attained the status of titles and are thus traditionally capitalized. Others are usually lowercased.

Washington's Farewell Address
the Gettysburg Address
the annual State of the Union address
Franklin Roosevelt's second inaugural address
the Checkers speech
Martin Luther King Jr.'s "I Have a Dream" speech

8.76　*Meteorological and other natural phenomena.* Named hurricanes and other tropical cyclones are capitalized, as are many other named meteorological phenomena. If in doubt, consult a dictionary or encyclopedia. Natural phenomena identified generically by a place-name or a year are usually lowercased.

Cyclone Becky; the 2007 cyclone
Hurricane Katrina; the 2005 hurricane
El Niño
the Northridge earthquake of 1994

Use the pronoun *it*, not *he* or *she*, when referring to named storms, hurricanes, and the like (notwithstanding the practice of using male and female proper names to refer to such events).

8.77 *Sporting events.* The full names of major sporting events are capitalized.

the Kentucky Derby; the derby
the NBA Finals; the finals
the Olympic Games; the Olympics; the Winter Olympics
the World Cup

Cultural Movements and Styles

8.78 *Movements and styles—capitalization.* Nouns and adjectives designating cultural styles, movements, and schools—artistic, architectural, musical, and so forth—and their adherents are capitalized if derived from proper nouns. (The word *school* remains lowercased.) Others may be lowercased, though a few (e.g., Cynic, Scholastic, New Criticism) are capitalized to distinguish them from the generic words used in everyday speech. Some of the terms lowercased below may appropriately be capitalized in certain works if done consistently—especially those that include the designation "often capitalized" in *Webster's*. (But if, for example, *impressionism* is capitalized in a work about art, other art movements must also be capitalized—which could result in an undesirable profusion of capitals.) For religious movements, see 8.96. See also 8.59.

abstract expressionism	Dadaism; Dada
Aristotelian	deconstruction
art deco	Doric
art nouveau	Epicurean (see text below)
baroque	existentialism
Beaux-Arts (derived from École des	fauvism
Beaux-Arts)	formalism
camp	Gothic (*but* gothic fiction)
Cartesian	Gregorian chant
Chicago school (of architecture, of	Hellenism
economics, of literary criticism)	Hudson River school
classicism, classical	humanism
conceptualism	idealism
cubism	imagism
Cynicism; Cynic	impressionism

Keynesianism	Pre-Raphaelite
mannerism	Reaganomics
miracle play	realism
modernism	rococo
mysticism; mystic	Romanesque
naturalism	romanticism; romantic
neoclassicism; neoclassical	Scholasticism; Scholastic; Schoolmen
Neoplatonism	scientific rationalism
New Criticism	Sophist (see text below)
nominalism	Stoicism; Stoic (see text below)
op art	structuralism
Peripatetic (see text below)	Sturm und Drang (*but* storm and stress)
philosophe (French)	surrealism
Platonism	symbolism
pop art	theater of the absurd
postimpressionism	transcendentalism
postmodernism	

Some words capitalized when used in reference to a school of thought are lowercased when used metaphorically.

epicurean tastes	she's a sophist, not a logician
peripatetic families	a stoic attitude

Acts, Treaties, and Government Programs

8.79 *Formal names of acts, treaties, and so forth.* Formal or accepted titles of pacts, plans, policies, treaties, acts, programs, and similar documents or agreements are capitalized. Incomplete or generic forms are usually lowercased. For citing the published text of a bill or law, see 14.294, 14.295.

the Fifteenth Amendment (to the US Constitution); the Smith Amendment; the amendment
the Articles of Confederation
the Bill of Rights
the Brady law
the Constitution of the United States; the United States (*or* US) Constitution; the Constitution (usually capitalized in reference to the US Constitution); Article VI; the article (see also 9.29)
the Illinois Constitution; the constitution
the Constitution Act, 1982 (Canada)

the Corn Laws (Great Britain)
the Declaration of Independence
the due process clause
the Equal Rights Amendment (usually capitalized though not ratified); ERA; *but*
  an equal rights amendment
the Family and Medical Leave Act of 1993; FMLA; the 1993 act
the Food Stamp Act of 1964; food stamps
the Hawley-Smoot (*or* Smoot-Hawley) Tariff Act; the tariff act
Head Start
impeachment; the first and second articles of impeachment
the Marshall Plan
the Mayflower Compact; the compact
Medicare (lowercase in Canada); Medicaid
the Monroe Doctrine; the doctrine
the Munich agreement (1938); Munich
the New Economic Policy; NEP (Soviet Union)
the Open Door policy
the Peace of Utrecht
the Reform Bills; the Reform Bill of 1832 (Great Britain)
the Social Security Act; Social Security (*or, generically,* social security)
Temporary Assistance for Needy Families; TANF
Title VII *or* Title 7
Treaty for the Renunciation of War, *known as* the Pact of Paris *or* the Kellogg-
  Briand Pact; the pact
the Treaty of Versailles; the treaty
the Treaty on European Union (official name); the Maastricht treaty (informal
  name)
the Wilmot Proviso

8.80   *Generic terms for pending legislation.* Informal, purely descriptive references to pending legislation are lowercased.

The anti-injunction bill was introduced on Tuesday.

Legal Cases

8.81   *Legal cases mentioned in text.* The names of legal cases are italicized when
mentioned in text. The abbreviation *v.* (versus) occasionally appears in
roman, but Chicago recommends italics. In footnotes, legal dictionaries,
and contexts where numerous legal cases appear, they are sometimes set
in roman. For legal citation style, see 14.281–317.

Bloomfield Village Drain Dist. v. Keefe   *Miranda v. Arizona*

In discussion, a case name may be shortened.

the *Miranda* case (or simply *Miranda*)

Awards

8.82 **Capitalization for names of awards and prizes.** Names of awards and prizes are capitalized, but some generic terms used with the names are lowercased. For military awards, see 8.114.

> the 2010 Nobel Prize in Physiology or Medicine; a Nobel Prize winner; a Nobel Prize–winning physiologist (see 6.80); a Nobel Peace Prize; the Nobel Prize in Literature
> the 2010 Pulitzer Prize for Commentary; a Pulitzer in journalism
> an Academy Award; an Oscar
> an Emmy Award; she has three Emmys
> the Presidential Medal of Freedom
> a Guggenheim Fellowship (*but* a Guggenheim grant)
> an International Music Scholarship
> National Merit Scholarship awards; Merit Scholarships; Merit Scholar

Oaths and Pledges

8.83 **Lowercase for oaths and pledges.** Formal oaths and pledges are usually lowercased.

> the oath of citizenship   marriage vows
> the Hippocratic oath   *but*
> the presidential oath of office the Pledge of Allegiance

Academic Subjects, Courses of Study, and Lecture Series

8.84 **Academic subjects.** Academic subjects are not capitalized unless they form part of a department name or an official course name or are themselves proper nouns (e.g., English, Latin).

> She has published widely in the history of religions.
> They have introduced a course in gender studies.

He is majoring in comparative literature.
She is pursuing graduate studies in philosophy of science.
but
Jones is chair of the Committee on Comparative Literature.

8.85   *Courses of study.* Official names of courses of study are capitalized.

I am signing up for Archaeology 101.
A popular course at the Graham School of General Studies is Basic Manuscript
    Editing.
but
His ballroom dancing classes have failed to civilize him.

8.86   *Lectures.* Names of lecture series are capitalized. Individual lectures are
capitalized and usually enclosed in quotation marks. See also 8.69.

This year's Robinson Memorial Lectures were devoted to the nursing profession.
The first lecture, "How Nightingale Got Her Way," was a sellout.

Calendar and Time Designations

8.87   *Days of the week, months, and seasons.* Names of days and months are capitalized. The four seasons are lowercased (except when used to denote an
issue of a journal; see 14.180). For centuries and decades, see 8.70.

Tuesday	spring	the vernal (*or* spring) equinox
November	fall	the winter solstice

8.88   *Holidays.* The names of secular and religious holidays or officially designated days or seasons are capitalized.

All Fools' Day	Inauguration Day
Christmas Day	Independence Day
Earth Day	Kwanzaa
Election Day	Labor Day
Father's Day	Lent
the Fourth of July, the Fourth	Lincoln's Birthday
Good Friday	Martin Luther King Jr. Day
Halloween	Memorial Day
Hanukkah	Mother's Day
Holy Week	National Poetry Month

New Year's Day	Saint Patrick's Day
New Year's Eve	Thanksgiving Day
Passover	Yom Kippur
Presidents' Day	Yuletide
Ramadan	*but*
Remembrance Day (Canada)	D-day
Rosh Hashanah	a bank holiday

8.89 **Time and time zones.** When spelled out, designations of time and time zones are lowercased (except for proper nouns). Abbreviations are capitalized. See also 9.38–41.

eastern standard time; EST	Pacific daylight time; PDT
central daylight time; CDT	Greenwich mean time; GMT
mountain standard time; MST	daylight saving time; DST

Religious Names and Terms

Deities and Revered Persons

8.90 **Deities.** Names of deities, whether in monotheistic or polytheistic religions, are capitalized.

Allah	Jehovah
Astarte	Mithra
Freyja	Satan (*but* the devil)
God	Serapis
Itzamna	Yahweh

Some writers follow a pious convention of not fully spelling out the name of a deity (e.g., *G-d*). This convention should be respected when it is practical to do so.

8.91 **Alternative names.** Alternative or descriptive names for God as supreme being are capitalized. See also 8.92.

Adonai
the Almighty
the Deity
the Holy Ghost *or* the Holy Spirit *or* the Paraclete
the Lord

Providence
the Supreme Being
the Trinity

8.92 *Prophets and the like.* Designations of prophets, apostles, saints, and other revered persons are often capitalized.

the Buddha
the prophet Isaiah
Jesus; Christ; the Good Shepherd; the Son (*or* son) of man
John the Baptist
the Messiah
Muhammad; the Prophet
Saint John; the Beloved Apostle
the Virgin Mary; the Blessed Virgin; Mother of God
but
the apostles
the patriarchs
the psalmist

8.93 *Platonic ideas.* Words for transcendent ideas in the Platonic sense, especially when used in a religious context, are often capitalized. See also 7.48.

Good; Beauty; Truth; the One

8.94 *Pronouns referring to religious figures.* Pronouns referring to God or Jesus are not capitalized. (Note that they are lowercased in most English translations of the Bible.)

They prayed to God that he would deliver them.
Jesus and his disciples

Religious Groups

8.95 *Major religions.* Names of major religions are capitalized, as are their adherents and adjectives derived from them.

Buddhism; Buddhist
Christianity; Christian; Christendom (see also 8.97)
Confucianism; Confucian
Hinduism; Hindu

Islam; Islamic; Muslim
Judaism; Jew; Jewry; Jewish
Shinto; Shintoism; Shintoist
Taoism; Taoist; Taoistic
but
atheism
agnosticism

8.96 *Denominations, sects, orders, and religious movements.* Like the names of major religions, names of denominations, communions, sects, orders, and religious movements are capitalized, as are their adherents and adjectives derived from them. See also 8.98.

the Amish; Amish communities
Anglicanism; the Anglican Communion (*see also* Episcopal Church)
Baptists; a Baptist church; the Baptist General Convention; the Southern Baptist Convention
Catholicism (*see* Roman Catholicism)
Christian Science; Church of Christ, Scientist; Christian Scientist
the Church of England (*but* an Anglican church)
the Church of Ireland
Conservative Judaism; a Conservative Jew
Dissenter (lowercased when used in a nonsectarian context)
Druidism; Druid (sometimes lowercased)
Eastern Orthodox churches; the Eastern Church (*but* an Eastern Orthodox church)
the Episcopal Church; an Episcopal church; an Episcopalian
the Episcopal Church of Scotland
Essenes; an Essene
Gnosticism; Gnostic
Hasidism; Hasid (singular); Hasidim (plural); Hasidic
Jehovah's Witnesses
Jesuit(s); the Society of Jesus; Jesuitic(al) (lowercased when used pejoratively)
Methodism; the United Methodist Church (*but* a United Methodist church); Wesleyan
Mormonism; Mormon; the Church of Jesus Christ of Latter-day Saints (Utah); Community of Christ (Missouri)
Nonconformism; Nonconformist (lowercased when used in a nonsectarian context)
Old Catholics; an Old Catholic church
the Order of Preachers; the Dominican order; a Dominican
Orthodox Judaism; an Orthodox Jew
Orthodoxy; the (Greek, Serbian, etc.) Orthodox Church (*but* a Greek Orthodox church)

Protestantism; Protestant (lowercased when used in a nonsectarian context)
Puritanism; Puritan (lowercased when used in a nonsectarian context)
Quakerism; Quaker; the Religious Society of Friends; a Friend
Reform Judaism; a Reform Jew
Roman Catholicism; the Roman Catholic Church (*but* a Roman Catholic church)
Satanism; Satanist
Seventh-day Adventist; Adventist; Adventism
Shiism; Shia; Shiite
Sufism; Sufi
Sunnism; Sunni; Sunnite
Theosophy; Theosophist; the Theosophical Society
Vedanta
Wicca; Wiccan
Zen; Zen Buddhism

8.97 *"Church" as institution.* When used to refer to the institution of religion or of a particular religion, *church* is usually lowercased.

church and state
the early church
the church in the twenty-first century
the church fathers

Church is capitalized when part of the formal name of a denomination (e.g., the United Methodist Church; see other examples in 8.96) or congregation (e.g., the Church of St. Thomas the Apostle).

8.98 *Generic versus religious terms.* Many terms that are lowercased when used generically, such as *animism, fundamentalism,* or *spiritualism,* may be capitalized when used as the name of a specific religion or a sect.

a popular medium in turn-of-the-century Spiritualist circles
but
liberal versus fundamentalist Christians

8.99 *Religious jurisdictions.* The names of official divisions within organized religions are capitalized. The generic terms used alone are lowercased.

the Archdiocese of Chicago; the archdiocese
the Eastern Diocese of the Armenian Church
the Fifty-Seventh Street Meeting; the (Quaker) meeting
the Holy See
the Missouri Synod; the synod

8.100   *Buildings.* The names of the buildings in which religious congregations meet are capitalized. The generic terms used alone are lowercased.

Babri Mosque; the mosque
Bethany Evangelical Lutheran Church; the church
Temple Emanuel; the temple; the synagogue
Nichiren Buddhist Temple; the temple

8.101   *Councils, synods, and the like.* The accepted names of historic councils and the official names of modern counterparts are capitalized.

the Council of Chalcedon (*or* the Fourth Ecumenical Council)
the General Convention (Episcopal)
the Second Vatican Council; Vatican II
the Synod of Whitby

Religious Writings

8.102   *Scriptures.* Names of scriptures and other highly revered works are capitalized but not usually italicized (except when used in the title of a published work).

the Bhagavad Gita (*or* Bhagavad Gītā)
the Bible (*but* biblical)
the Book of Common Prayer
the Dead Sea Scrolls
the Hebrew Bible
Koran; Koranic (*or, less commonly,* Qur'an; Qur'anic)
the Mahabharata (*or* Mahābhārata)
Mishnah; Mishnaic
Sunna
Talmud; Talmudic
Tripitaka
the Upanishads
the Vedas; Vedic
but
sutra(s)

8.103   *Other names and versions for bibles.* Other names and versions of the Hebrew and Christian bibles are usually capitalized but not italicized.

the Authorized Version *or* the King James Version
the Breeches (*or* Geneva) Bible

Codex Sinaiticus
Complutensian Polyglot Bible
the Douay (*or* Rheims-Douay) Version
the Holy Bible
Holy Writ (sometimes used figuratively)
the New English Bible
the New Jerusalem Bible
the New Revised Standard Version
Peshitta
the Psalter (*but* a psalter)
the Septuagint
the Vulgate
but
scripture(s); scriptural

8.104   *Books of the Bible.* The names of books of the Bible are capitalized but never italicized. The word *book* is usually lowercased, and the words *gospel* and *epistle* are usually capitalized. But in a work in which all three terms are used with some frequency, they may all be treated alike, either lowercased or capitalized. See also 9.27, 10.45–51.

Genesis; the book of Genesis
Job; the book of Job
2 Chronicles; Second Chronicles; the second book of the Chronicles
Psalms (*but* a psalm)
John; the Gospel according to John
Acts; the Acts of the Apostles
1 Corinthians; the First Epistle to the Corinthians

8.105   *Sections of the Bible.* Names of sections of the Bible are usually capitalized but not italicized.

the Hebrew scriptures *or* the Old Testament
the Christian scriptures *or* the New Testament
the Apocrypha; Apocryphal (*or, generically,* apocryphal)
the Epistles; the pastoral Epistles
the Gospels; the synoptic Gospels
the Pentateuch *or* the Torah; Pentateuchal
Hagiographa *or* Ketuvim; hagiographic

8.106   *Prayers, creeds, and such.* Named prayers, canticles, creeds, and such, as well as scriptural terms of special importance, are usually capitalized. Parables and miracles are usually lowercased.

the Decalogue; the Ten Commandments; the first commandment
Kaddish; to say Kaddish
the Lord's Prayer; the Our Father
Luther's Ninety-Five Theses
the Nicene Creed; the creed
Salat al-Fajr
the Sermon on the Mount
the Shema
but
the doxology
the parable of the prodigal son
the miracle of the loaves and fishes
the star of Bethlehem

Religious Events, Concepts, Services, and Objects

8.107 *Religious events and concepts.* Religious events and concepts of major theological importance are often capitalized. Used generically, such terms are lowercased.

the Creation
the Crucifixion
the Diaspora
the Exodus
the Fall
the Hegira
the Second Coming
but
Most religions have creation myths.
For the Romans, crucifixion was a common form of execution.

Doctrines and principles are usually lowercased.

atonement
dharma
original sin
resurrection

8.108 *Heaven, hell, and so on.* Terms for divine dwelling places, ideal states, places of divine punishment, and the like are usually lowercased (though they are often capitalized in a purely religious context). See also 8.49.

heaven	purgatory
hell	*but*
limbo	Eden
nirvana	Elysium
outer darkness	Hades
paradise	Olympus
the pearly gates	

8.109 *Services and rites.* Names of services and rites are usually lowercased (though they may be capitalized in strictly religious contexts; if in doubt, consult *Webster's*).

baptism	morning prayer; matins
bar mitzvah	the seder
bat mitzvah	the sun dance
confirmation	vespers

Terms denoting the Eucharistic sacrament, however, are traditionally capitalized, though they may be lowercased in nonreligious contexts.

the Eucharist
Holy Communion
Mass; to attend Mass; High Mass; Low Mass; *but* three masses are offered daily

8.110 *Objects.* Objects of religious use or significance are usually lowercased, especially in nonreligious contexts.

altar	mandala	sacred pipe
ark	mezuzah	sanctuary
chalice and paten	rosary	stations of the cross

Military Terms

Forces and Troops

8.111 *Armies, battalions, and such.* Titles of armies, navies, air forces, fleets, regiments, battalions, companies, corps, and so forth are capitalized. Unofficial but well-known names, such as Green Berets, are also capitalized. Words such as *army* and *navy* are lowercased when standing alone, when used collectively in the plural, or when not part of an official title. Note that many of the lowercased terms below are routinely capitalized in official or promotional contexts (see also 8.18).

the Allies (World Wars I and II); the Allied forces
American Expeditionary Force; the AEF
Army Corps of Engineers; the corps
Army of Northern Virginia; the army
Army of the Potomac
Army Special Forces
the Axis powers (World War II)
Canadian Forces (unified in 1968)
the Central powers (World War I)
Combined Chiefs of Staff (World War II)
Confederate army (American Civil War)
Continental navy (American Revolution)
Eighth Air Force; the air force
Fifth Army; the army
First Battalion, 178th Infantry; the battalion; the 178th
French Foreign Legion
Green Berets
Joint Chiefs of Staff
the Luftwaffe; the German air force
National Guard
Pacific Fleet (US, World War II)
Red Army (Russian, World War II); Russian army
the Resistance; the French Resistance; a resistance movement
Rough Riders
Royal Air Force; RAF; British air force
Royal Canadian Air Force (until 1968; *see* Canadian Forces)
Royal Canadian Mounted Police; the Mounties; a Mountie
Royal Canadian Navy (until 1968; *see* Canadian Forces)
Royal Navy; the British navy
Royal Scots Fusiliers; the fusiliers
Seventh Fleet; the fleet
Thirty-Third Infantry Division; the Thirty-Third Division; the division
Union army (American Civil War)
United States (*or* US) Army; the army
United States Coast Guard; the Coast Guard *or* the coast guard
United States Marine Corps; the Marine Corps *or* the marine corps; the US Marines; a marine
United States Navy; the navy
United States Army Signal Corps; the Signal Corps *or* the signal corps

Wars, Revolutions, Battles, and Campaigns

8.112 *Wars and revolutions.* Names of most major wars and revolutions are capitalized. The generic terms are usually lowercased when used alone.

American Civil War; the War between the States
American Revolution; American War of Independence; the revolution (sometimes
 capitalized); the Revolutionary War
Crusades; the Sixth Crusade; a crusader
French Revolution; the Revolution of 1789; the Revolution (usually capitalized
 to distinguish the Revolution of 1789 from the revolutions in 1830 and 1848);
 revolutionary France
Great Sioux War; the Sioux war
Gulf War
Korean War; the war
Mexican Revolution; the revolution
Napoleonic Wars
Norman Conquest; the conquest of England
the revolution(s) of 1848
Russian Revolution; the revolution
Seven Years' War
Shays's Rebellion
Six-Day War
Spanish-American War
Spanish Civil War
Vietnam War
War of 1812
Whiskey Rebellion
World War I; the First World War; the Great War; the war
World War II; the Second World War; World Wars I and II; the First and Second
 World Wars; the two world wars

8.113 *Battles and campaigns.* Some of the names of major battles and campaigns
that have entered the general lexicon are capitalized. In other, more generic descriptions, only proper names are capitalized. For names not included here, consult an encyclopedia.

Battle of Britain
Battle of the Bulge (*or* Battle of the Ardennes)
Battle of Bunker Hill; Bunker Hill; the battle
battle of Vimy Ridge
the Blitz

European theater of operations; ETO
Mexican border campaign
Operation Devil Siphon
third battle of Ypres
Vicksburg Campaign
western front (World War I)

Military Awards

8.114   *Medals and awards.* Specific names of medals and awards are capitalized. For civil awards, see 8.82.

Medal of Honor (US congressional award); the medal
Croix de Guerre (sometimes lowercased)
Distinguished Flying Cross; DFC
Distinguished Service Order; DSO
Purple Heart
Silver Star
Victoria Cross; VC

Names of Ships and Other Vehicles

8.115   *Ships and other named vessels.* Names of specific ships and other vessels are both capitalized and italicized. Note that when such abbreviations as USS (United States ship) or HMS (Her [or His] Majesty's ship) precede a name, the word *ship* or other vessel type should not be used. The abbreviations themselves are not italicized. For much useful information, consult Eric Wertheim, *The Naval Institute Guide to Combat Fleets of the World* (bibliog. 5).

Mars global surveyor; Mars polar lander; *Phoenix* Mars lander; *Phoenix*
the space shuttle *Discovery*
the *Spirit of St. Louis*
HMS *Frolic*; the British ship *Frolic*
SS *United States*; the *United States*
USS *SC-530*; the US ship *SC-530*

Every US Navy ship is assigned a hull number (according to a system formally implemented in 1920), consisting of a combination of letters (indicating the type of ship) and a serial number. Where necessary to avoid confusion between vessels of the same name—in a work on naval history, for example—the numbers should be included at first mention. Smaller ships such as landing craft and submarine chasers are individually numbered but not named.

USS *Enterprise* (CVN-65) was already on its way to the Red Sea.

8.116   *Other vehicle names.* Names of makes and classes of aircraft, models of automobiles and other vehicles, names of trains or train runs, and names of space programs are capitalized but not italicized.

Acela Express	Concorde	Project Apollo
Boeing 747	Metroliner	Toyota Prius

8.117   *Pronouns referring to vessels.* When a pronoun is used to refer to a vessel, the neuter *it* or *its* (rather than *she* or *her*) is preferred. See also 5.41, 8.76.

Scientific Terminology

Scientific Names of Plants and Animals

8.118   *Scientific style—additional resources.* The following paragraphs offer only general guidelines. Writers or editors requiring detailed guidance should consult *Scientific Style and Format* (bibliog. 1.1). The ultimate authorities are the *International Code of Botanical Nomenclature* (*ICBN*), whose guidelines are followed in the botanical examples below, and the *International Code of Zoological Nomenclature* (*ICZN*) (see bibliog. 5). Note that some fields, such as virology, have slightly different rules. Writers and editors should try to follow the standards established within those fields.

8.119   *Genus and specific epithet.* Whether in lists or in running text, the Latin names of species of plants and animals are italicized. Each *binomial* contains a genus name (or *generic name*), which is capitalized, and a species name (also called *specific name* or *specific epithet*), which is lowercased (even if it is a proper adjective). Do not confuse these names with phyla, orders, and such, which are not italicized; see 8.125.

The Pleistocene saber-toothed cats all belonged to the genus *Smilodon*.
Many species names, such as *Rosa caroliniana* and *Styrax californica*, reflect the locale of the first specimens described.
The pike, *Esox lucius*, is valued for food as well as sport.

For the grass snake *Natrix natrix*, longevity in captivity is ten years.

Certain lizard taxa such as *Basiliscus* and *Crotaphytus* are bipedal specialists.

8.120   ***Abbreviation of genus name.*** After the first use the genus name may be abbreviated to a single capital letter. If two or more species of the same genus are listed together, the abbreviation may be doubled (to indicate the plural) before the first species, though repeating the abbreviation with each species is more common. But if species of different genera beginning with the same letter are discussed in the same context, abbreviations may not be appropriate.

> Two methods allow us to estimate the maximum speeds obtained by *Callisaurus draconoides* in the field. Irschick and Jayne (1998) found that stride durations of both *C. draconoides* and *Uma scoparia* do not change dramatically after the fifth stride during accelerations from a standstill.
>
> The "quaking" of the aspen, *Populus tremuloides*, is due to the construction of the petiole; an analogous phenomenon has been noted in the cottonwood, *P. deltoides*.
>
> Among popular species of the genus *Cyclamen* are *CC. coum, hederifolium,* and *persicum* . . . [or, more commonly, *C. coum, C. hederifolium,* and *C. persicum* . . .]
>
> Studies of *Corylus avellana* and *Corokia cotoneaster* . . . ; in further studies it was noted that *Corylus avellana* and *Corokia cotoneaster* . . .

8.121   ***Subspecies and varieties.*** A subspecific zoological name or epithet, when used, follows the binomial species name and is also italicized. If the two names are the same, the first one may be abbreviated.

> *Noctilio labialis labialis* (or *Noctilio l. labialis*)   *Trogon collaris puella*

In horticultural usage, the abbreviations "subsp." (or "ssp."), "var.," and "f." (none of them italicized) are inserted before the subspecific epithet or variety or form name. See also 8.122.

> *Buxus microphylla* var. *japonica*
> *Hydrangea anomala* subsp. *petiolaris*
> *Rhododendron arboreum* f. *album*

8.122   ***Unspecified species and varieties.*** The abbreviations "sp." and "var.," when used without a following element, indicate that the species or variety is unknown or unspecified. The plural "spp." is used to refer to a group of species. The abbreviations are *not* italicized.

> *Rhododendron* spp.   *Rosa rugosa* var.   *Viola* sp.

8.123 *Author names.* The name of the person who proposed a specific epithet is sometimes added, often abbreviated, and never italicized. A capital *L.* stands for Linnaeus.

Diaemus youngi cypselinus Thomas   *Molossus coibensis* J. A. Allen
Euchistenes hartii (Thomas)   *Quercus alba* L.
Felis leo Scop.

The parentheses in the second example mean that Thomas described the species *E. hartii* but referred it to a different genus.

8.124 *Plant hybrids.* The crossing of two species is indicated by a multiplication sign (×; *not* the letter *x*) between the two species names, with space on each side. Many older primary plant hybrids are indicated by a multiplication sign immediately before the specific epithet of the hybrid, with space only before it.

Magnolia denudata × *M. liliiflora* (crossing of species)
Magnolia ×*soulangeana* (hybrid name)

8.125 *Higher divisions.* Divisions higher than genus—phylum, class, order, and family—are capitalized but *not* italicized. (The terms *order*, *family*, and so on are not capitalized.) Intermediate groupings are treated similarly.

Chordata (phylum)
Chondrichthyes (class)
Monotremata (order)
Ruminantia (suborder)
Hominidae (family)
Felinae (subfamily)
Selachii (term used of various groups of cartilaginous fishes)
The new species *Gleichenia glauca* provides further details about the history of Gleicheniaceae.

8.126 *English derivatives.* English words derived from the taxonomic system are lowercased and treated as English words.

carnivore(s) (from the order Carnivora)
hominid(s) (from the family Hominidae)
irid(s) (from the family Iridaceae)
feline(s) (from subfamily Felinae)
astilbe(s) (from the genus *Astilbe*)
mastodon(s) (from the genus *Mastodon*)

Vernacular Names of Plants and Animals

8.127 *Plants and animals—additional resources.* For the correct capitalization and spelling of common names of plants and animals, consult a dictionary or the authoritative guides to nomenclature, the *ICBN* and the *ICZN*, mentioned in 8.118. In general, Chicago recommends capitalizing only proper nouns and adjectives, as in the following examples, which conform to *Merriam-Webster's Collegiate Dictionary*:

Dutchman's-breeches	Cooper's hawk
jack-in-the-pulpit	rhesus monkey
mayapple	Rocky Mountain sheep

8.128 *Domestic animals and horticultural categories.* Either a dictionary or the guides to nomenclature *ICZN* and *ICBN* should be consulted for the proper spelling of breeds of domestic animals and broad horticultural categories.

German shorthaired pointer	Rhode Island Red
Hereford	boysenberry
Maine coon *or* coon cat	rambler rose
Thoroughbred horse (*but* purebred dog)	

8.129 *Horticultural cultivars.* Many horticultural cultivars (cultivated varieties) have fanciful names that must be respected since they may be registered trademarks.

the Peace rose	a Queen of the Market aster

In some horticultural publications, such names are enclosed in single quotation marks; any following punctuation is placed *after* the closing quotation mark. If the English name follows the Latin name, there is no intervening punctuation. For examples of this usage, consult any issue of the magazine *Horticulture* (bibliog. 5).

> The hybrid *Agastache* 'Apricot Sunrise', best grown in zone 6, mingles with sheaves of cape fuchsia (*Phygelius* 'Salmon Leap').

Genetic Terms

8.130 *Genetic nomenclature—additional resources.* Only the most basic guidelines can be offered here. Writers or editors working in the field of genetics should consult the *AMA Manual of Style* or *Scientific Style and Format* (both in bibliog. 1.1) and online databases including the HUGO Gene Nomenclature Database and the Mouse Genome Database (both in bibliog. 5).

8.131   *Genes.* Names of genes, or gene symbols, including any arabic numerals that form a part of such symbols, are usually italicized. (Italicization helps differentiate genes from entities with similar names.) Symbols for genes contain no Greek characters or roman numerals. Human gene symbols are set in full capitals, as are the gene symbols for other primates. Mouse and rat gene symbols are usually spelled with an initial capital. Gene nomenclature systems for other organisms (yeast, fruit flies, nematodes, plants, fish) vary. Symbols for proteins, also called gene products and often derived from the symbols of the corresponding genes, are set in roman.

HUMAN GENES
BRCA1
GPC3
IGH@ (the symbol @ indicates a family or cluster)
SNRPN

MOUSE GENES
Cmv1
Fgf12
Rom1
Wnt1
NLP3 (gene symbol); NLP3p (encoded protein; note p suffix)
GIF (gene symbol); GIF (gastric intrinsic factor)

Only a very few gene symbols contain hyphens.

HLA-DRB1, for human leukocyte antigen D-related β chain 1

8.132   *Enzymes.* Enzyme names consist of a string of italic and roman characters. The first three letters, which represent the name of the organism (usually a bacterium) from which the enzyme has been isolated, are italicized. The roman numeral that follows represents the series number. Sometimes an upper- or lowercase roman letter or an arabic numeral (or both), representing the strain of bacterium, intervenes between the name and series number.

*Ava*I   *Bam*HI   *Cla*I   *Eco*R   *Hind*III   *Sau*3AI

Geological Terms

8.133 *Geological terms—additional resources.* The following paragraphs offer only the most general guidelines. Writers or editors working in geological studies should consult US Geological Survey, *Suggestions to Authors of the Reports of the United States Geological Survey*, and *Scientific Style and Format* (both listed in bibliog. 1.1).

8.134 *Formal versus generic geological terms.* Formal geological terms are capitalized in both noun and adjective forms; terms used generically are not. The generic terms *eon*, *era*, and the like are lowercased or omitted immediately following a formal name. Eons are divided into eras, eras into periods, periods into epochs, and epochs into stages. The term *ice age* is best lowercased in scientific contexts because of the uncertainty surrounding any formal use of the term (cf. *Little Ice Age*); but see 8.73.

the Archean (eon)
the Mesoproterozoic (era)
the Tertiary period of the Cenozoic (era)
the Paleocene (epoch)
Pleistocene-Holocene transition
the second interglacial stage *or* II interglacial
Illinoian glaciation

The modifiers *early*, *middle*, or *late* are capitalized when used formally but lowercased when used informally.

Early Archean	*but*
Middle Cambrian	early Middle Cambrian
Late Quaternary	in late Pleistocene times

8.135 *Stratigraphy.* Formal stratigraphic names are capitalized. For prehistoric cultural terms, see 8.73.

Fleur de Lys Supergroup	Niobrara Member
Ramey Ridge Complex	Morrison Formation

Astronomical Terms

8.136 *Astronomical terms—additional resources.* The following paragraphs offer only the most general guidelines. Writers or editors working in astronomy or astrophysics should consult *Scientific Style and Format* (bibliog. 1.1) and the website of the International Astronomical Union.

8.137   *Celestial bodies.* The names of galaxies, constellations, stars, planets, and such are capitalized. For *earth, sun,* and *moon,* see 8.139, 8.140.

Aldebaran
Alpha Centauri *or* α Centauri
the Big Dipper *or* Ursa Major *or* the Great Bear
Cassiopeia's Chair
the Crab Nebula
the Magellanic Clouds
the Milky Way
the North Star *or* Polaris, polestar
85 Pegasi
Saturn
but
Halley's comet
the solar system

8.138   *Catalog names for celestial objects.* Celestial objects listed in well-known catalogs are designated by the catalog name, often abbreviated, and a number.

Bond 619   Lalande 5761   Lynds 1251 *or* L1251   NGC 6165

8.139   **"Earth."** In nontechnical contexts the word *earth,* in the sense of our planet, is usually lowercased when preceded by *the* or in such idioms as "down to earth" or "move heaven and earth." When used as the proper name of our planet, especially in context with other planets, it is capitalized, and *the* is usually omitted.

Some still believe the earth is flat.
The gender accorded to the moon, the sun, and the earth varies in different mythologies.
Where on earth have you been?
The astronauts have returned successfully to Earth.
Does Mars, like Earth, have an atmosphere?

8.140   **"Sun" and "moon."** The words *sun* and *moon* are usually lowercased in nontechnical contexts and always lowercased in the plural.

The moon circles the earth, as the earth circles the sun.
Some planets have several moons.

Some publications in the fields of astronomy and related sciences, however, routinely capitalize these words when used as proper nouns. (See also 8.137.)

8.141   *Descriptive terms.* Merely descriptive terms applied to celestial objects or phenomena are not capitalized.

aurora borealis *or* northern lights
gegenschein
interstellar dust
the rings of Saturn

Medical Terms

8.142   *Medical terms—additional resources.* The following paragraphs offer only the most general guidelines. Medical writers or editors should consult the *AMA Manual of Style* or *Scientific Style and Format* (both in bibliog. 1.1).

8.143   *Diseases, procedures, and such.* Names of diseases, syndromes, diagnostic procedures, anatomical parts, and the like are lowercased, except for proper names forming part of the term. Acronyms and initialisms are capitalized.

acquired immunodeficiency syndrome *or* AIDS
Alzheimer disease (see below)
computed tomography *or* CT
Down syndrome (see below)
finger-nose test
islets of Langerhans
non-Hodgkin lymphoma (see below)
ultrasound; ultrasonography

The possessive forms *Alzheimer's*, *Down's*, *Hodgkin's*, and the like, though less common in medical literature, may be preferred in a general context. For x-rays and radiation, see 8.150.

8.144   *Infections.* Names of infectious organisms are treated like other specific names (see 8.118–26). Names of conditions based on such names are neither italicized nor capitalized.

Microorganisms of the genus *Streptococcus* are present in the blood of persons
with streptococcal infection.

The larvae of *Trichinella spiralis* are responsible for the disease trichinosis.

8.145   *Drugs.* Generic names of drugs, which should be used wherever possible
in preference to brand names, are lowercased. Brand names must be capitalized; they are often enclosed in parentheses after the first use of the
generic name. For guidance, consult the *AMA Manual of Style* and *Scientific Style and Format* (bibliog. 1.1) and *USP Dictionary of USAN and International Drug Names* (bibliog. 5). For brand names and trademarks, see 8.152.

The patient takes weekly injections of interferon beta-1a (Avonex) to control his
multiple sclerosis.

Physical and Chemical Terms

8.146   *Physical and chemical terms—additional resources.* The following paragraphs offer only the most general guidelines for nontechnical editors.
Writers or editors working in physics should consult *The AIP Style Manual* (bibliog. 1.1) or, among other journals, *Physical Review Letters*; those
working in chemistry should consult *The ACS Style Guide* (bibliog. 1.1).

8.147   *Laws and theories.* Though usage varies widely, Chicago recommends that
names of laws, theories, and the like be lowercased, except for proper
names attached to them.

Avogadro's hypothesis (*or* Avogadro's law)
the big bang theory
Boyle's law
(Einstein's) general theory of relativity
Newton's first law

8.148   *Chemical names and symbols.* Names of chemical elements and compounds
are lowercased when written out. Symbols, however, are capitalized and
set without periods; the number of atoms in a molecule appears as a subscript. For a list of symbols for the elements, including atomic numbers,
see 10.66.

ozone; O_3
sodium chloride; NaCl
sulfuric acid; H_2SO_4
tungsten carbide; WC

8.149 *Mass number.* In formal chemical literature, the mass number appears as a superscript to the left of the symbol. In work intended for a general audience, however, it may follow the symbol, after a hyphen, in full size.

^{14}C (formal style); C-14 *or* carbon-14 (informal style)
^{238}U (formal style); U-238 *or* uranium-238 (informal style)

8.150 *Radiations.* Terms for electromagnetic radiations may be spelled as follows:

β-ray (noun or adjective) *or* beta ray (in nonscientific contexts, noun or adjective)
γ-ray (noun or adjective) *or* gamma ray (in nonscientific contexts, noun or adjective)
x-ray (noun, verb, or adjective)
cosmic ray (noun); cosmic-ray (adjective)
ultraviolet ray (noun); ultraviolet-ray (adjective)

Note that the verb *to x-ray*, though acceptable in a general context, is not normally used in scholarly medical literature, where writers would more likely speak of obtaining an x-ray film, or a radiograph, of something, or of subjecting something to x-ray analysis.

8.151 *Metric units.* Although the spellings *meter, liter,* and so on are widely used in the United States, some American business, government, or professional organizations have adopted the European spellings (*metre, litre,* etc.). Chicago's publications show a preference for the traditional American spellings. For abbreviations used in the International System of Units, see 10.54–62.

Brand Names and Trademarks

8.152 *Trademarks.* Brand names that are trademarks—often so indicated in dictionaries—should be capitalized if they must be used. A better choice is to substitute a generic term when available. Although the symbols ® and ™ (for registered and unregistered trademarks, respectively) often accompany trademark names on product packaging and in promotional material, there is no legal requirement to use these symbols, and they should be omitted wherever possible. (If one of these symbols must be used at the end of a product name, it should appear before any period, comma, or other mark of punctuation.) Note also that some companies encourage the use of both the proper and the generic term in reference to their products ("Kleenex facial tissue," not just "Kleenex") and discourage turning product names into verbs, but these restrictions, while they may be followed in corporate documentation, are not legally binding. (In fact, *Webster's* includes entries for lowercase verbs *google* and *xerox*.) For computer-related names and terms, see 7.76.

Bufferin; buffered aspirin	Ping-Pong; table tennis
Coca-Cola; cola	Pyrex; heat-resistant glassware
Google; search engine; search	Scrabble
Jacuzzi; whirlpool bath	Vaseline; petroleum jelly
Kleenex; (facial) tissue	Xerox; photocopier; copy
Levi's; jeans	

More information about registered trademarks can be found on the websites of the US Patent and Trademark Office and the International Trademark Association.

8.153 *Names like eBay and iPod.* Brand names or names of companies that are spelled with a lowercase initial letter followed by a capital letter (eBay, iPod, iPhone, etc.) need not be capitalized at the beginning of a sentence or heading, though some editors may prefer to reword. This departure from Chicago's former usage recognizes not only the preferred usage of the owners of most such names but also the fact that such spellings are already capitalized (if only on the second letter). Company or product names with additional, internal capitals (sometimes called "midcaps") should likewise be left unchanged (GlaxoSmithKline, HarperCollins, LexisNexis). See also 8.4.

eBay posted strong earnings.
User interfaces varied. iTunes and its chief rival, Amazon.com, . . .

In text that is set in all capitals, such distinctions are usually overridden (e.g., EBAY, IPOD, HARPERCOLLINS); with a mix of capitals and small capitals, they are preserved (e.g., eBAY).

Titles of Works

8.154 *Treatment of titles in text and notes—overview.* The following guidelines apply primarily to titles as they are mentioned or cited in text or notes. They apply to titles of books, journals, newspapers, and websites as well as to shorter works (stories, poems, articles, etc.), divisions of longer works (parts, chapters, sections), unpublished works (lectures, etc.), plays and films, radio and television programs, musical works, and artworks. For details on citing titles in bibliographies and reference lists, see chapters 14 and 15.

Capitalization, Punctuation, and Italics

8.155   *Capitalization of titles of works—general principles.* Titles mentioned or cited in text or notes are usually capitalized headline-style (see 8.157). For aesthetic purposes, titles appearing on the cover or title page or at the head of an article or chapter may deviate from Chicago's rules for the capitalization of titles. For capitalization of foreign titles, see 11.3.

8.156   *Principles and examples of sentence-style capitalization.* In sentence-style capitalization only the first word in a title, the first word in a subtitle, and any proper names are capitalized. This style or some variant of it is commonly used in library catalogs and in the reference lists of some journals (see 15.13) and is the style recommended for most foreign titles (see 11.3). It is also useful for some types of subheads (see 2.17), including those that include terms (such as species names) that require their own internal capitalization (but note that the specific epithet remains lowercase in headline style; see 8.157, rule 7). See also 8.160.

> The house of Rothschild: The world's banker, 1849–1999
> Crossing *Magnolia denudata* with *M. liliiflora* to create a new hybrid: A success story

8.157   *Principles of headline-style capitalization.* The conventions of headline style are governed mainly by emphasis and grammar. The following rules, though occasionally arbitrary, are intended primarily to facilitate the consistent styling of titles mentioned or cited in text and notes:

1.   Capitalize the first and last words in titles and subtitles (but see rule 7), and capitalize all other major words (nouns, pronouns, verbs, adjectives, adverbs, and some conjunctions—but see rule 4).
2.   Lowercase the articles *the*, *a*, and *an*.
3.   Lowercase prepositions, regardless of length, except when they are used adverbially or adjectivally (*up* in *Look Up*, *down* in *Turn Down*, *on* in *The On Button*, *to* in *Come To*, etc.) or when they compose part of a Latin expression used adjectivally or adverbially (*De Facto*, *In Vitro*, etc.).
4.   Lowercase the conjunctions *and*, *but*, *for*, *or*, and *nor*.

5. Lowercase *to* not only as a preposition (rule 3) but also as part of an infinitive (*to Run, to Hide,* etc.), and lowercase *as* in any grammatical function.

6. Lowercase the part of a proper name that would be lowercased in text, such as *de* or *von.*

7. Lowercase the second part of a species name, such as *fulvescens* in *Acipenser fulvescens,* even if it is the last word in a title or subtitle.

For examples, see 8.158. For hyphenated compounds in titles, see 8.159.

8.158 *Examples of headline-style capitalization.* The following examples illustrate the numbered rules in 8.157. All of them illustrate the first rule; the numbers in parentheses refer to rules 2–7.

Mnemonics That Work Are Better Than Rules That Do Not
Singing While You Work
A Little Learning Is a Dangerous Thing (2)
Four Theories concerning the Gospel according to Matthew (2, 3)
Taking Down Names, Spelling Them Out, and Typing Them Up (3, 4)
Tired but Happy (4)
The Editor as Anonymous Assistant (5)
From *Homo erectus* to *Homo sapiens*: A Brief History (3, 7)
Defenders of da Vinci Fail the Test: The Name Is Leonardo (2, 3, 6)
Sitting on the Floor in an Empty Room (2, 3), *but* Turn On, Tune In, and Enjoy (3, 4)
Ten Hectares per Capita, *but* Landownership and Per Capita Income (3)
Progress in In Vitro Fertilization (3)

8.159 *Hyphenated compounds in headline-style titles.* The following rules apply to hyphenated terms appearing in a title capitalized in headline style. For reasons of consistency and editorial efficiency, Chicago no longer advises making exceptions to these rules for the rare awkward-looking result (though such niceties may occasionally be observed in display settings, as on the cover of a book). For rules of hyphenation, see 7.77–85.

1. Always capitalize the first element.

2. Capitalize any subsequent elements unless they are articles, prepositions, coordinating conjunctions (*and, but, for, or, nor*), or such modifiers as *flat* or *sharp* following musical key symbols.

3. If the first element is merely a prefix or combining form that could not stand by itself as a word (*anti, pre,* etc.), do not capitalize the second element unless it is a proper noun or proper adjective.

4. Capitalize the second element in a hyphenated spelled-out number (*twenty-one* or *twenty-first,* etc.) or hyphenated simple fraction (*two-thirds* in *two-thirds*

majority). This departure from previous Chicago recommendations recognizes the functional equality of the numbers before and after the hyphen.

The examples that follow demonstrate the numbered rules (all the examples demonstrate the first rule; the numbers in parentheses refer to rules 2–4).

Under-the-Counter Transactions and Out-of-Fashion Initiatives (2)
Bed-and-Breakfast Options in Upstate New York (2)
Record-Breaking Borrowings from Medium-Sized Libraries (2)
Cross-Stitching for Beginners (2)
A History of the Chicago Lying-In Hospital (2; "In" functions as an adverb, not a preposition)
The E-flat Concerto (2)
Self-Sustaining Reactions (2)
Anti-intellectual Pursuits (3)
Does E-mail Alter Thinking Patterns? (3)
A Two-Thirds Majority of Non-English-Speaking Representatives (3, 4)
Ninety-Fifth Avenue Blues (4)
Atari's Twenty-First-Century Adherents (4)

Under another, simplified practice that is not recommended by Chicago, only the first element and any subsequent element that is a proper noun or adjective are capitalized.

8.160 *Titles containing quotations.* When a direct quotation of a sentence or an independent clause is used as a title, headline-style capitalization may be imposed, even for longer quotations. This departure from Chicago's earlier practice aids identification of titles. See also 14.104.

"We All Live More like Brutes Than like Humans": Labor and Capital in the Gold Rush

8.161 *Italics versus quotation marks for titles.* The choice of italics or quotation marks for a title of a work cited in text or notes is determined by the type of work. Titles of books and periodicals are italicized (see 8.166); titles of articles, chapters, and other shorter works are set in roman and enclosed in quotation marks (see 8.175).

Many editors use *The Chicago Manual of Style*.
Refer to the article titled "A Comparison of MLA and APA Style."

For treatment of book series and editions, see 8.174; for poems and plays, see 8.179–82; for unpublished works, see 8.184; for movies, television, and radio, see 8.185; for websites and blogs, see 8.186–87; for musical works, see 8.188–92; for works of art and exhibitions, see 8.193–95. For foreign titles, see 11.3–8.

8.162   *Subtitle capitalization.* A subtitle, whether in sentence-style or headline-style capitalization, always begins with a capital letter. Although on a title page or in a chapter heading a subtitle is often distinguished from a title by a different typeface, when referred to it is separated from the title by a colon. When an em dash rather than a colon is used, what follows the em dash is not normally considered to be a subtitle, and the first word is not necessarily capitalized. See also 14.98.

"Manuals of Style: Guidelines, Not Strangleholds" (headline style)
Tapetum character states: Analytical keys (sentence style)
but
Chicago—a Metropolitan Smorgasbord

8.163   *Permissible changes to titles.* When a title is referred to in text or notes or listed in a bibliography or reference list, its original spelling (including non-Latin letters such as π or γ) and hyphenation should be preserved, regardless of the style used in the surrounding text. Capitalization may be changed to headline style (8.157) or sentence style (8.156), as applicable. As a matter of editorial discretion, an ampersand (&) may be changed to *and*, or, more rarely, a numeral may be spelled out (see 14.96). On title pages, commas are sometimes omitted from the ends of lines for aesthetic reasons. When such a title is referred to, such commas should be added, including any comma omitted before a date that appears on a line by itself at the end of a title or subtitle. (Serial commas need be added only if it is clear that they are used in the work itself; see 6.18.) If title and subtitle on a title page are distinguished by typeface alone, a colon must be added when referring to the full title. A dash in the original should be retained; however, a semicolon between title and subtitle may usually be changed to a colon. (For two subtitles in the original, see 14.98. For older titles, see 14.106.) The following examples illustrate the way titles and subtitles are normally punctuated and capitalized in running text, notes, and bibliographies using headline capitalization. The first three are books, the fourth an article.

Disease, Pain, and Sacrifice: Toward a Psychology of Suffering
Melodrama Unveiled: American Theater and Culture, 1800–1850

Browning's Roman Murder Story: A Reading of "The Ring and the Book"
"Milton Friedman's *Capitalism and Freedom*—a Best-Seller for Chicago"

For titles within titles (as in the third and fourth examples above), see 8.171, 8.175.

8.164   *Titles in relation to surrounding text.* A title, which is considered to be a singular noun, always takes a singular verb. Moreover, any punctuation that is part of the title should not affect the punctuation of the surrounding text (with the exception of a sentence-ending period, which should be omitted after a title ending in a question mark or exclamation point; see 6.118). See also 6.23, 6.119, 8.172.

The Waves is not a typical novel. (singular verb in spite of plural in title)
Her role in *Play It Again, Sam* confirmed her stature. (no comma after *Sam*)
Three stories she never mentioned were "Are You a Doctor?," "The Library of Babel," and "Diamond as Big as the Ritz." (comma after first title in spite of the question mark)

8.165   *Double titles connected by "or."* Old-fashioned double titles (or titles and subtitles) connected by *or* are traditionally referred to as in the first example, less traditionally but more simply as in the second. Chicago prefers the first form, but either form is acceptable if used consistently.

England's Monitor; or, The History of the Separation
England's Monitor, or The History of the Separation

Books and Periodicals

8.166   *Treatment of book and periodical titles.* When mentioned in text, notes, or bibliography, the titles and subtitles of books and periodicals are italicized and capitalized headline-style (see 8.157), though some publications may require sentence style for reference lists (see 8.156, 15.13). A book title cited in full in the notes or bibliography may be shortened in text (e.g., a subtitle may be omitted). For short titles in notes, see 14.25.

8.167   *An initial "a," "an," or "the" in book titles.* An initial *a, an,* or *the* in running text may be dropped from a book title if it does not fit the surrounding syntax. When in doubt, or if the article seems indispensable, it should be retained.

Fielding, in his introduction to *The History of Tom Jones, a Foundling*, announces
  himself as a professional author.
Fielding's *History of Tom Jones* . . .
That dreadful *Old Curiosity Shop* character, Quilp . . .
but
In *The Old Curiosity Shop*, Dickens . . .
In L'Amour's *The Quick and the Dead* . . .

8.168   *An initial "the" in periodical titles.* When newspapers and periodicals are
mentioned in text, an initial *the*, even if part of the official title, is lowercased (unless it begins a sentence) and not italicized. Foreign-language
titles, however, retain the article in the original language—but only if it
is an official part of the title. (In citation form, an initial *the* is dropped
from periodical titles, but foreign-language articles are retained; see
14.210, 14.211.)

She reads the *Chicago Tribune* on the train.
We read *Le Monde* and *Die Zeit* while traveling in Europe.
Did you see the review in the *Frankfurter Allgemeine*?

8.169   *"Magazine" and other descriptive terms.* A word like *magazine, journal,* or
review should be italicized only when it forms part of the official name
of a particular periodical. When such a word functions as an added descriptive term, it is treated as part of the surrounding text.

She used to subscribe to *Newsweek* and the *Partisan Review*; now she gets all her
  information from blogs.
I read it both in *Time* magazine and in the *Wall Street Journal*.
but
His article was reprinted in the *New York Times Magazine*.

8.170   *Periodical titles in awards, buildings, and so forth.* When the name of a newspaper or periodical is part of the name of a building, organization, prize,
or the like, it is not italicized.

Los Angeles Times Book Prize   Chicago Defender Charities   Tribune Tower

8.171   *Italicized terms and titles within titles.* Any term within an italicized title
that would itself be italicized in running text—such as a foreign word, a
genus name, or the name of a ship—should be set in roman type (*reverse
italics*). A title of a work within a title, however, should remain in italics
and be enclosed in quotation marks. See also 8.163, 8.115, 8.119, 14.103.

From Tyrannosaurus rex *to King Kong: Large Creatures in Fact and Fiction*
The Big E: The Story of the USS Enterprise
A Key to Whitehead's "Process and Reality"

8.172 *Title not interchangeable with subject.* The title of a work should not be used to stand for the subject of a work.

> Dostoevsky wrote a book about crime and punishment (*not* . . . about *Crime and Punishment*).
> Edward Wasiolek's book on Dostoevsky's *Crime and Punishment* is titled *"Crime and Punishment" and the Critics.*
> In their book *The Craft of Translation*, Biguenet and Schulte . . . (*not* In discussing *The Craft of Translation*, Biguenet and Schulte . . .)

8.173 *Multivolume works.* Titles of multivolume books are treated in the same manner as titles of single-volume works, as are named titles of individual volumes. The word *volume* may be abbreviated in parentheses and notes; it is capitalized (and never abbreviated) only if part of the title. For treatment of multivolume works in bibliographies and reference lists, see 14.121–27. See also 8.174.

> *The Day of the Scorpion*, volume 2 of *The Raj Quartet*
> *Art in an Age of Counterrevolution, 1815–1848* (vol. 3, *A Social History of Modern Art*)
> the fourth volume of *Encyclopaedia Britannica*

8.174 *Series and editions.* Titles of book series and editions are capitalized but not italicized. The words *series* and *edition* are capitalized only if part of the title. See also 14.128–32.

> the Loeb Classical Library
> a Modern Library edition
> Late Editions: Cultural Studies for the End of the Century
> the Crime and Justice series
> a book in the Heritage of Sociology Series

Articles in Periodicals and Parts of a Book

8.175 *Articles, stories, chapters, and so on.* Titles of articles and features in periodicals and newspapers, chapter and part titles, titles of short stories or essays, and individual selections in books are set in roman type and enclosed in quotation marks. (If there are quotation marks in the original title, single quotation marks must be used, as in the fourth example.)

John S. Ellis's article "Reconciling the Celt" appeared in the *Journal of British Studies*.

In chapter 3 of *The Footnote*, "How the Historian Found His Muse," Anthony Grafton . . .

"Tom Outland's Story," by Willa Cather, . . .

The article "Schiller's 'Ode to Joy' in Beethoven's Ninth Symphony" received unexpected attention.

Titles of regular departments or columns in periodicals, however, are set in roman (see also 14.202, 14.205).

In this week's Talk of the Town, Lizzie Widdicombe features . . .

8.176   *Collected works.* When two or more works, originally published as separate books, are included in a single volume, often as part of an author's collected works, they are best italicized rather than placed in quotation marks.

The introduction to the *Critique of Pure Reason* in Kant's *Collected Works* . . .

8.177   *Terms like "foreword," "preface," and so on.* Such generic terms as *foreword, preface, acknowledgments, introduction, appendix, bibliography, glossary,* and *index,* whether used in cross-references or in reference to another work, are lowercased and set in roman type.

The author states in her preface that . . .

For further documentation, see the appendix.

Full details are given in the bibliography.

The book contains a glossary, a subject index, and an index of names.

8.178   *Numbered chapters, parts, and so on.* The words *chapter, part, appendix, table, figure,* and the like are lowercased and spelled out in text (though sometimes abbreviated in parenthetical references). Numbers are given in arabic numerals, regardless of how they appear in the original. If letters are used, they may be upper- or lowercase (following the original) and are sometimes put in parentheses. See also 9.27–29.

This matter is discussed in chapters 4 and 5.

The Latin text appears in appendix B.

The range is presented numerically in table 4.2 and diagrammed in figure 4.1.
These connections are illustrated in table A3.
Turn to section 5(a) for further examples.

Poems and Plays

8.179 *Titles of poems.* Titles of most poems are set in roman type and enclosed in quotation marks. A very long poetic work, especially one constituting a book, is italicized and not enclosed in quotation marks.

Robert Frost's poem "The Housekeeper" in his collection *North of Boston*
Dante's *Inferno*

In a stand-alone literary study where many poems, short and long, are mentioned, it may be better to set all their titles in italics.

8.180 *Poems referred to by first line.* Poems referred to by first line rather than by title are capitalized sentence-style, even if the first word is lowercased in the original, but any words capitalized in the original should remain capitalized. See also 8.156, 16.145.

E. E. Cummings, in "My father moved through dooms of love," . . . ("my" is lowercased in the original)
"Shall I compare thee to a Summer's day?"

8.181 *Titles of plays.* Titles of plays, regardless of the length of the play, are italicized.

Shaw's *Arms and the Man*, in volume 2 of his *Plays: Pleasant and Unpleasant*

8.182 *Divisions of plays or poems.* Words denoting parts of long poems or acts and scenes of plays are usually lowercased, neither italicized nor enclosed in quotation marks. Numbers are arabic, regardless of the original.

canto 2   stanza 5   act 3, scene 2

Pamphlets and Reports

8.183 *Titles of freestanding publications.* Titles of pamphlets, reports, and similar freestanding publications are treated much like books (see 8.166, 14.249)—italicized when mentioned or cited in text or notes.

Common Sense, first published anonymously . . .
The CDC's *Third National Report on Human Exposure to Environmental Chemicals*,
    available online . . .

Unpublished Works

8.184   *Titles of unpublished works.* Titles of unpublished works—theses, dissertations, manuscripts in collections, unpublished transcripts of speeches,
and so on—are set in roman type, capitalized as titles, and enclosed in
quotation marks. Names of manuscript collections take no quotation
marks. The title of a not-yet-published book that is under contract may
be italicized, but the word *forthcoming* (or *in press* or some other equivalent term), in parentheses, must follow the title. For speeches, see 8.75.
See also 15.42.

In a master's thesis, "Charles Valentin Alkan and His Pianoforte Works," . . .
"A Canal Boat Journey, 1857," an anonymous manuscript in the Library of Con-
    gress Manuscripts Division, describes . . .
Letters and other material may be found in the Collis P. Huntington Papers at the
    George Arents Library of Syracuse University.
Gianfranco's *Fourth Millennium* (forthcoming) continues this line of research.

Movies, Television, and Radio

8.185   *Titles of movies and television and radio programs and series.* Titles of movies and of television and radio programs and series are italicized. A single
episode in a television or radio series is set in roman and enclosed in quotation marks.

Gone with the Wind
The Godfather, Part II (see also 9.44)
PBS's *Sesame Street*
The Ten O'Clock News, WGBH's long-running program
WFMT's *From the Recording Horn*
"Casualties," an episode in *The Fortunes of War*, a *Masterpiece Theatre* series
but
the ten o'clock news

The names of broadcast networks, channels, and the like are set in roman.

Voice of America	the Discovery Channel
Sirius Satellite Radio	the Sundance and Disney channels

Electronic Publications

8.186 *Websites and web pages.* General titles of websites mentioned or cited in text or notes are normally set in roman, headline-style, without quotation marks. An initial *the* in such titles should be lowercased in midsentence. Titled sections, pages, or special features on a website should be placed in quotation marks. Titles of the types of works discussed elsewhere in this chapter (i.e., books, journals, etc.) should usually be treated the same whether they are published in print or online. Some websites share the name of a printed counterpart, and others (such as *Wikipedia*) are analogous to one of the types of works discussed elsewhere in this chapter; these titles should be styled accordingly. See also 14.243–46.

> Project Gutenberg; Jane Austen's *Emma*, available as an audiobook from Project Gutenberg
> the Internet Movie Database; IMDb (note lowercase *b*); IMDb's page for *Live and Let Die*; "Roger Moore (I)"; the page for well-known Bond portrayer Roger Moore
> Google; Google Maps; the "Google Maps Help Center"
> Facebook, MySpace, and other social-networking sites
> *The Chicago Manual of Style Online*; the online edition of *The Chicago Manual of Style*; "Chicago Style Q&A"; "New Questions and Answers"
> *Encyclopaedia Britannica Online*; the online version of *Encyclopaedia Britannica*
> *Wikipedia*; *Wikipedia*'s "Let It Be" entry; *Wikipedia*'s entry on the Beatles' album *Let It Be*
> the *Oxford English Dictionary Online*; the *OED Online*; the online version of the *Oxford English Dictionary*

Many websites either do not have a formal title or do not have a title that distinguishes it as a website. These can usually be identified according to the entity responsible for the site along with a description of the site and, in some cases, a short form of the URL (e.g., http://www.apple.com/ might be referred to in running text as Apple.com).

> The website for Apple Inc.; Apple.com
> Microsoft's website; Microsoft.com
> the website for the University of Chicago Press, Books Division

8.187 *Blogs and blog entries.* Titles of named blogs, like the titles of journals and other periodicals (see 8.161), should be italicized. An initial "the" should be treated as part of the title (compare 8.168). Titles of blog entries should be placed in quotation marks (untitled entries should be referred to by date). For citing blogs (and comments to blogs) in notes and bibliographies, see 14.243–46.

The Pour; "A Beaujolais Maker's Pain," in *The Pour*, a blog by Eric Asimov in the
   New York Times
Wasted Food; "Friday Buffet," in *Wasted Food*, a blog by Jonathan Bloom

The titles of named podcasts, video blogs, and similar electronic formats
mentioned or cited in text or notes can generally be styled according to
an analogy to blogs. The name of a regular, ongoing feature or publication should be italicized; individually titled pieces should be placed in
quotation marks. For more examples, see 14.221, 14.280.

"Visiting Priest Shows Family How Grace Is Done," on *Onion Radio News* (podcast)

Musical Works

8.188   *Musical works—additional resources.* The following paragraphs are intended only as general guidance for citing musical works. Writers or editors working with highly musicological material should consult D. Kern
Holoman, *Writing about Music* (bibliog. 1.1). For a more general reference work, consult *The New Grove Dictionary of Music and Musicians* and
the other Grove musical dictionaries, available from Oxford Music Online (bibliog. 5). For typographic conventions used in musicology, see
7.66–71.

8.189   *Operas, songs, and the like.* Titles of operas, oratorios, tone poems, and other
long musical compositions are italicized and given standard title capitalization. Titles of songs and other shorter musical compositions are set
in roman and enclosed in quotation marks, capitalized in the same way
as poems (see 8.179, 8.180).

"La vendetta, oh, la vendetta" from *The Marriage of Figaro*
the "Anvil Chorus" from Verdi's *Il Trovatore*
Handel's *Messiah*
Rhapsody in Blue
Finlandia
"All You Need Is Love" (a song by the Beatles)
"So What" (a composition by Miles Davis)
"The Star-Spangled Banner"
"Oh, What a Beautiful Mornin' " from *Oklahoma!*
"Wohin?" from *Die schöne Müllerin*

8.190   *Instrumental works.* Many instrumental works are known by their generic
names—*symphony, quartet, nocturne,* and so on—and often a number or

key or both. Such names are capitalized but not italicized. A descriptive title, however, is usually italicized if referring to a full work, set in roman and in quotation marks if referring to a section of a work. The abbreviation *no.* (number; plural *nos.*) is set in roman and usually lowercased. (For letters indicating keys, see 7.67.)

B-flat Nocturne; Chopin's nocturnes
the Menuetto from the First Symphony; the third movement
Concerto no. 2 for Piano and Orchestra; the second movement, Allegro appassion-
    ato, from Brahms's Second Piano Concerto; two piano concertos
Bartók's Concerto for Orchestra (or *Concerto for Orchestra*)
Bach's Mass in B Minor
Hungarian Rhapsody no. 12; the Twelfth Hungarian Rhapsody
Charles Ives's Piano Sonata no. 2 (Concord, Mass., 1840–60); the *Concord* Sonata
Symphony no. 6 in F Major; the Sixth Symphony; the *Pastoral* Symphony
Air with Variations ("The Harmonious Blacksmith") from Handel's Suite no. 5 in E
Elliott Carter's String Quartet no. 5 and his *Figment* for cello
Augusta Read Thomas's Triple Concerto (*Night's Midsummer Blaze*)

8.191   *Opus numbers.* The abbreviation *op.* (opus; plural *opp.* or *opera*) is set in roman and usually lowercased. An abbreviation designating a catalog of a particular composer's works is always capitalized (e.g., BWV [Bach-Werke-Verzeichnis]; D. [Deutsch] for Schubert; K. [Köchel] for Mozart; WoO [Werke ohne Opuszahl], assigned by scholars to certain unnumbered works). When *op.* or a catalog number is used restrictively (see 6.26), no comma precedes it.

Sonata in E-flat, op. 31, no. 3; Sonata op. 31
Fantasy in C Minor, K. 475; Fantasy K. 475

8.192   *Recordings.* The official title of an album (and sometimes a title under which it has come to be known) is italicized; that of the performer or ensemble is set in roman. Individual items on the album—songs, movements, and the like—are treated as illustrated in the paragraphs above. See also 14.276–77.

On *The Art of the Trumpet*, the New York Trumpet Ensemble plays . . .
The single "Revolution" should not be confused with "Revolution 1," an earlier
    take of the song that appeared on *The Beatles* (a.k.a. *The White Album*).
Miles Davis's *Kind of Blue* is one of the most influential jazz records ever made.
His Majestie's Clerkes' *Hear My Prayer: Choral Music of the English Romantics* in-
    cludes Vaughan Williams's Mass in G Minor.

Works of Art and Exhibitions

8.193 *Paintings, statues, and such.* Titles of paintings, drawings, photographs, statues, and other works of art are italicized, whether the titles are original, added by someone other than the artist, or translated. The names of works of antiquity (whose creators are often unknown) are usually set in roman.

> Rothko's *Orange Yellow Orange*
> Leonardo da Vinci's *Mona Lisa* and *The Last Supper*
> *North Dome*, one of Ansel Adams's photographs of Kings River Canyon
> Hogarth's series of drawings *The Rake's Progress*
> Michelangelo's *David*
> the Winged Victory
> the Venus de Milo

8.194 *Cartoons.* Titles of regularly appearing cartoons or comic strips are italicized.

> *The Far Side*   *Doonesbury*   *Rudy Park*   *Dilbert*

8.195 *Exhibitions and such.* Titles of world's fairs and other large-scale exhibitions and fairs are capitalized but not italicized. Smaller exhibitions (e.g., at museums) and the titles of exhibition catalogs (often one and the same) are italicized.

> the Great Exhibition of the Works of All Nations; the Great Exhibition of 1851;
>   London's Crystal Palace Exhibition; the exhibition
> the World's Columbian Exposition
> the Century-of-Progress Expositions (included more than one fair)
> the New York World's Fair
> *but*
> A remarkable exhibition, *Motor Cycles*, was mounted at the Guggenheim Museum.
> We saw the exhibition *Ansel Adams at 100* when visiting the Museum of Modern Art.
> We decided to buy the catalog *Ansel Adams at 100*, by John Szarkowski.

Signs and Mottoes

8.196 *Signs and notices.* Specific wording of common short signs or notices is capitalized headline-style in running text. A longer notice is better treated as a quotation.

The door was marked Authorized Personnel Only.

She encountered the usual Thank You for Not Smoking signs.

We were disturbed by the notice "Shoes and shirt required of patrons but not of personnel."

8.197 *Mottoes.* Mottoes may be treated the same way as signs. If the wording is in another language, it is usually italicized and only the first word capitalized. See also 6.51.

The flag bore the motto Don't Tread on Me.

My old college has the motto *Souvent me souviens*.

The motto "All for one and one for all" appears over the door.

9 Numbers

Overview

9.1 *Overview and additional resources.* This chapter summarizes some of the conventions Chicago observes in handling numbers, especially in making the choice between spelling them out and using numerals. Such a choice should be governed by a number of factors, including whether the number is large or small, whether it is an approximation or an exact quantity, what kind of entity it stands for, and what context it appears in. Sometimes the goal of consistency must give way to readability (e.g., at the beginning of a sentence; see 9.5). The guidelines in this chapter apply mainly to general works and to scholarly works in the humanities and social sciences, where numeric quantities are relatively infrequent. But even in scientific and other technical contexts, numerals can never totally replace spelled-out numbers. For more detailed treatment of numbers in technical contexts, consult *Scientific Style and Format* (bibliog. 1.1). See also 9.13–17.

Numerals versus Words

General Principles

9.2 *Chicago's general rule—zero through one hundred.* In nontechnical contexts, Chicago advises spelling out whole numbers from zero through one hundred and certain round multiples of those numbers. Most of the rest of this chapter deals with the exceptions to this rule and special cases. For hyphens used with spelled-out numbers, see 7.85, section 1. For some additional considerations, consult the index, under *numbers*. For numerals in direct discourse, see 13.42. For an alternative rule, see 9.3.

> Thirty-two children from eleven families were packed into eight vintage Beetles.
> Many people think that seventy is too young to retire.
> The property is held on a ninety-nine-year lease.
> According to a recent appraisal, my house is 103 years old.
> The three new parking lots will provide space for 540 more cars.
> The population of our village now stands at 5,893.

9.3 *An alternative rule—zero through nine.* Many publications, including those in scientific or journalistic contexts, follow the simple rule of spelling out only single-digit numbers and using numerals for all others (but see

9.7). Most of the exceptions to the general rule (9.2) also apply to this alternative rule.

9.4 *Hundreds, thousands, and hundred thousands.* Any of the whole numbers mentioned in 9.2 followed by *hundred, thousand,* or *hundred thousand* are usually spelled out (except in the sciences)—whether used exactly or as approximations. See also 9.8.

> Most provincial theaters were designed to accommodate large audiences—from about seven hundred spectators in a small city like Lorient to as many as two thousand in Lyon and Marseille.
> A millennium is a period of one thousand years.
> The population of our city is more than two hundred thousand.
> Some forty-seven thousand persons attended the fair.
> *but*
> The official attendance at this year's fair was 47,122.

9.5 *Number beginning a sentence.* When a number begins a sentence, it is always spelled out. To avoid awkwardness, a sentence can often be recast. In the first example, some writers prefer the form *one hundred and ten*; Chicago's preference is to omit the *and*.

> One hundred ten candidates were accepted.
> *or*
> In all, 110 candidates were accepted.

If a year must begin a sentence, spell it out; it is usually preferable, however, to reword. Avoid *and* in such expressions as *two thousand one, two thousand ten, two thousand fifty,* and the like (see also 9.30).

> Nineteen thirty-seven was marked, among other things, by the watershed eleventh edition of Bartlett's *Familiar Quotations.*
> *or, better,*
> The year 1937 . . .

If a number beginning a sentence is followed by another number of the same category, spell out only the first or reword.

> One hundred eighty of the 214 candidates had law degrees; the remaining 34 were doctoral candidates in fish immunology.
> *or, better,*
> Of the 214 candidates, 180 had law degrees; the remaining 34 were doctoral candidates in fish immunology.

9.6 *Ordinals.* The general rule applies to ordinal as well as cardinal numbers. Note that Chicago prefers, for example, *122nd* and *123rd* (with an *n* and an *r*) over *122d* and *123d*. The latter, however, are common especially in legal style (see 14.281–317). The letters in ordinal numbers should *not* appear as superscripts (e.g., 122nd *not* 122nd).

> Gwen stole second base in the top half of the first inning.
> The restaurant on the forty-fifth floor has a splendid view of the city.
> She found herself in 125th position out of 360.
> The 122nd and 123rd days of the strike were marked by a rash of defections.
> The ten thousandth child to be born at Mercy Hospital was named Mercy.

In the expression "*n*th degree," Chicago style is to italicize the *n* (see also 7.59).

9.7 *Consistency and flexibility.* Where many numbers occur within a paragraph or a series of paragraphs, maintain consistency in the immediate context. If according to rule you must use numerals for one of the numbers in a given category, use them for all in that category. In the same sentence or paragraph, however, items in one category may be given as numerals and items in another spelled out. In the first example, the numerals 50, 3, and 4 would normally be spelled out (see 9.2); in the second and third examples, 30,000 and 2,000, respectively, would normally be spelled out (see 9.4; see also 9.8). For numerals in direct discourse, see 13.42.

> A mixture of buildings—one of 103 stories, five of more than 50, and a dozen of only 3 or 4—has been suggested for the area.
> In the second half of the nineteenth century, Chicago's population exploded, from just under 30,000 in 1850 to nearly 1.7 million by 1900.
> Between 1,950 and 2,000 people attended the concert.

To avoid a thickly clustered group of spelled-out numbers, numerals may be used instead in exception to the general rule.

Large Numbers

9.8 *Millions, billions, and so forth.* Whole numbers used in combination with *million*, *billion*, and so forth usually follow the general rule (see 9.2). See also 9.4. For monetary amounts, see 9.21–26; for the use of superscripts in scientific contexts, see 9.9.

The city had grown from three million in 1960 to fourteen million in 1990.
The survey was administered to more than half of the city's 220 million inhabitants.
The population of the United States recently surpassed three hundred million.

To express fractional quantities in the millions or more, a mixture of numerals and spelled-out numbers is used. In the second example below, the number fourteen is expressed as a numeral for the sake of consistency (see 9.7).

By the end of the fourteenth century, the population of Britain had probably reached 2.3 million.
According to some scientists, the universe is between 13.5 and 14 billion years old.

Note that *billion* in some countries (including, until recently, Great Britain) means a million million (a trillion in American usage), not, as in American usage, a thousand million; in this alternate system, the prefix *bi-* indicates twelve zeros (rather than the American nine), or twice the number of zeros in one million. Likewise, *trillion* indicates eighteen zeros (rather than the American twelve), *quadrillion* twenty-four (rather than the American fifteen), and so on. Editors working with material by British or other European writers may need to query the use of these terms. See 5.220 under *billion; trillion*.

9.9   **Powers of ten.** Large round numbers may be expressed in powers of ten, especially in scientific writing. This system is known as scientific notation. For further examples, consult *Scientific Style and Format* (bibliog. 1.1).

$10^2 = 100$ $10^9 = 1,000,000,000$
$10^3 = 1,000$ $10^{12} = 1,000,000,000,000,000$
$10^6 = 1,000,000$ $5.34 \times 10^8 = 534,000,000$

Inversely, very small numbers may be expressed in negative powers of ten.

$10^{-2} = 0.01$ $10^{-9} = 0.000000001$
$10^{-3} = 0.001$ $10^{-12} = 0.000000000001$
$10^{-6} = 0.000001$ $5.34 \times 10^{-8} = 0.0000000534$

9.10   **"Mega-," "giga-," "tera-," and so forth.** According to the International System of Units (*Système international d'unités*, abbreviated internationally as SI), very large quantities may also be indicated in some contexts by the use of the prefixes *mega-* (million), *giga-* (billion), *tera-* (trillion), and so on, as part of the unit of measure. Inversely, very small numbers may be expressed by *milli-* (thousandth), *micro-* (millionth), *nano-* (billionth), and so on. These expressions are often formed with symbols (e.g., *M*, for *mega-*, as in MB, *megabytes*). In astrophysical contexts, the abbreviations *Myr* and *Gyr*, standing for megayear (one million years) and gigayear (one billion years), are sometimes used. See also 9.9. For a complete list of SI prefixes, see 10.57. See also 9.11.

3 terahertz = 3×10^{12} hertz   7 Gyr = 7×10^9 years

9.11   *Binary systems.* Bases other than ten are common especially in computing, where numbers are usually expressed with bases that are powers of two (e.g., binary, octal, or hexadecimal). When such numbers are used, the base if other than ten should be indicated. Abbreviations *b* (binary), *o* (octal), and *h* (hexadecimal) may precede the number with no intervening space. Alternatively, the base can be expressed as a subscript. In the following example, the four-digit base-ten number is expressed without a comma, following SI usage:

b11110010001 = 1937   *or* $11110010001_2 = 1937_{10}$

Note that terms such as *megabyte*, when used as binary multiples, are approximations—a megabyte was originally equal to 1,048,576 bytes. Current SI usage dictates that such prefixes refer to positive powers of ten (where a megabyte is equal to 1,000,000 bytes). If binary multiples must be referred to, the first two letters of the prefix plus *bi* should be used (*kibibyte*, *mebibyte*, *gibibyte*, etc.).

9.12   *Use of "dex."* The term *dex* is sometimes used in scientific notation as shorthand for *decimal exponent*.

Errors of 3 dex (i.e., 10^3) can lead to dangerous misconceptions.

Physical Quantities

9.13   *Physical quantities in general contexts.* In nontechnical material, physical quantities such as distances, lengths, areas, and so on are usually treated according to the general rule (see 9.2). See also 9.15.

Within fifteen minutes the temperature dropped twenty degrees.
The train approached at seventy-five miles an hour.

Some students live more than fifteen kilometers from the school.
Three-by-five-inch index cards are now seldom used in index preparation.
She is five feet nine (*or, more colloquially,* five foot nine *or* five nine).

It is occasionally acceptable to depart from the general rule for certain types of quantities that are commonly (or more conveniently) expressed as numerals; such a departure, subject to editorial discretion, must be consistently applied for like quantities across a work. See also 9.7. For the absence of the hyphen in the second example below, see 7.85, section 2, under *noun + numeral or enumerator.*

a 40-watt bulb
a size 14 dress
a 32-inch inseam
a fuel efficiency of 80 miles per gallon (or 3 liters per 100 kilometers)

9.14   *Simple fractions.* Simple fractions are spelled out. For the sake of readability and to lend an appearance of consistency, they are hyphenated in noun, adjective, and adverb forms. In the rare event that individual parts of a quantity are emphasized, however, as in the last example, the fraction is spelled open. See also 7.85, section 1, under *fractions, simple.* For decimal fractions, see 9.19.

She has read three-fourths of the book.
Four-fifths of the students are boycotting the class.
I do not want all of your material; two-thirds is quite enough.
A two-thirds majority is required.
but
We divided the cake into four quarters; I took three quarters, and my brother one.

9.15   *Whole numbers plus fractions.* Quantities consisting of whole numbers and simple fractions may be spelled out if short but are often better expressed in numerals (especially if a symbol for the fraction is available, as in the examples here). For decimal fractions, see 9.19. For fractions in mathematical text, see 12.45. See also 9.17, 10.69.

We walked for three and one-quarter miles.
I need 6⅞ yards of the silk fabric.
Lester is exactly 3 feet 5¼ inches tall.
Letters are usually printed on 8½″ × 11″ paper.

9.16   *Abbreviations and symbols.* If an abbreviation or a symbol is used for the unit of measure, the quantity is always expressed by a numeral. Such usage is standard in mathematical, statistical, technical, or scientific text, where physical quantities and units of time are expressed in numerals, whether whole numbers or fractions, and almost always followed by an abbreviated form of the unit (see also 10.52–71). Any writer or editor working with highly technical material should consult *Scientific Style and Format* or the *AMA Manual of Style* (bibliog. 1.1). Note that hyphens are never used between the numeral and the abbreviation or symbol, even when they are in adjectival form (see 7.85, section 1, under *number + abbreviation*). In the last example, note the use of symbols for prime and double prime, which are *not* equivalent to the apostrophe and quotation mark.

50 km (kilometers); a 50 km race	240 V (volts)
21 ha (hectares)	10°C, 10.5°C
4.5 L (liters)	3'6"
85 g (grams)	

A unit of measurement used *without* a numeral should always be spelled out, even in scientific contexts.

We took the measurements in kilojoules (*not* kJ).

9.17 *Units for repeated quantities.* For expressions including two or more quantities, the abbreviation or symbol is repeated if it is closed up to the number but not if it is separated. See also 10.52. For the use of spaces with SI units and abbreviations or symbols, see 10.61.

35%–50%	3°C–7°C	6⅝" × 9"	2 × 5 cm

Percentages and Decimal Fractions

9.18 *Percentages.* Except at the beginning of a sentence, percentages are usually expressed in numerals. In nontechnical contexts, the word *percent* is generally used; in scientific and statistical copy, the symbol % is more common.

Fewer than 3 percent of the employees used public transportation.
With 90–95 percent of the work complete, we can relax.
A 75 percent likelihood of winning is worth the effort.
Her five-year certificate of deposit carries an interest rate of 5.9 percent.
Only 20% of the ants were observed to react to the stimulus.
The treatment resulted in a 20%–25% increase in reports of night blindness.

Note that *percent*, an adverb, is not interchangeable with the noun *percentage* (1 percent is a very small percentage). Note also that no space appears between the numeral and the symbol %.

9.19 *Decimal fractions and use of the zero.* Large or complex fractions are expressed as numeric decimal fractions (compare 9.14). When a quantity equals less than 1.00, a zero normally appears before the decimal point as an aid to readability, particularly in scientific contexts and especially if quantities greater than 1.00 appear in the same context. (Note that a unit of measure with a quantity of less than one is generally pronounced as if it were plural; see 10.68.)

a mean of 0.73
the ratio 0.85
The average number of children born to college graduates dropped from 2.3 to
    0.95 per couple.

In contexts where decimal quantities must be 1.00 or less, as in probabilities, correlation coefficients, and the like, a zero is typically omitted before the decimal point. For zeros with decimal points in tables, see 3.70.

$p < .05$ $R = .10$

By a similar token, the zero is routinely omitted in baseball batting averages and firearm calibers.

Ty Cobb's average was .367.
They found and confiscated a .38 police special and a .22-caliber single-shot rifle.

9.20 *Decimal places—European practice.* In European countries, except for Great Britain, the decimal point is represented by a comma. A thin, fixed space, not a comma, separates groups of three digits, whether to the left or to the right of the decimal point. (In electronic publications, a nonbreaking space may be used.) This practice reflects European-style SI usage (see 9.56). Canadians increasingly follow SI usage, retaining the decimal point (or, in French-language contexts, the comma) but using a thin space to separate groups of three digits. In US publications, US style should be followed, except in direct quotations. See also 10.61.

36 333,333 (European style)
36 333.333 (Canadian style)
36,333.333 (US and British style)

Money

9.21 ***Words versus monetary symbols and numerals.*** Isolated references to amounts of money are spelled out for whole numbers of one hundred or less, in accordance with the general principle presented in 9.2. See also 9.3.

seventy-five cents = 75¢   fifteen dollars = $15   seventy-five pounds = £75

Whole amounts expressed numerically should include zeros and a decimal point only when they appear in the same context with fractional amounts (see also 9.19). Note the singular verb in the second example.

Children can ride for seventy-five cents.
The eighty-three dollars was quickly spent.
The instructor charged €125 per lesson.
Prices ranged from $0.95 up to $10.00.

For larger amounts, see 9.25.

9.22 ***Non-US currencies using the dollar symbol.*** In contexts where the symbol $ may refer to non-US currencies, these currencies should be clearly identified.

three hundred Canadian dollars = C$300 *or* Can$300
$749 in New Zealand dollars = NZ$749
If you subtract A$15.69 from US$25, . . .
ninety-eight Mexican pesos = Mex$98

In more formal usage, the International Organization for Standardization's three-letter currency codes (e.g., USD for United States dollars, CAD for Canadian dollars, NZD for New Zealand dollars, and AUD for Australian dollars) may be more appropriate. See also 9.24. For a complete list, consult the ISO website. Also consult *Scientific Style and Format* or the *United States Government Printing Office Style Manual* (bibliog. 1.1). Where the context makes clear what currency is meant, the dollar sign alone is enough.

9.23 ***British currency.*** The basic unit of British currency is the pound, or pound sterling, for which the symbol is £. One-hundredth of a pound is a penny (plural *pence*), abbreviated as *p* (no period).

fifteen pounds = £15   fifty pence = 50p   £4.75, £5.00, and £5.25

Until the decimalization of British currency in 1971, the pound was divided into shillings (s.) and pence (d.).

Ten pounds, fifteen shillings, and sixpence = £10 15s. 6d.
twopence halfpenny = 2½d.

9.24   *Other currencies.* Most other currencies are handled the same way as US currency, with a decimal point between the main unit and subunits (e.g., EUR 10.75). When letters rather than symbols are used, a space separates the letter(s) from the numeral.

forty euros (*or, in European Union documents,* 40 euro) = EUR 40 (*or* €40)
95 (euro) cents (*or, in European Union documents,* 95 cent)
725 yen = ¥725
65.50 Swiss francs = SF 65.50

Before adoption of the euro, monetary symbols included *F* (French franc), *DM* (deutsche mark), and *Lit* (Italian lira), among others. The International Organization for Standardization defines three-letter codes (including EUR) for most countries. See also 9.22.

9.25   *Large monetary amounts.* Sums of money of more than one hundred dollars are normally expressed by numerals or, for numbers of a million or more, by a mixture of numerals and spelled-out numbers, even for whole numbers (compare 9.4, 9.8).

An offer of $1,000 once seemed low; we eventually agreed to pay more than fifteen times that amount.
Most of the homes that went into foreclosure were valued at more than $95,000.
She signed a ten-year, $250 million contract.
The military requested an additional $7.3 billion.
The marquess sold his ancestral home for £25 million.

In certain financial contexts, thousands are sometimes represented by *K*.

Three-bedroom condominiums are priced at $350K.

9.26   *Currency with dates.* In contexts where the value of a currency in any particular year is relevant to the discussion, the date may be inserted in parentheses, without intervening space, after the currency symbol. When letters alone are used, spaces intervene before and after the parentheses (see also 9.22, 9.24).

US$(1992)2.47
£(2002)15,050
but
USD (1992) 2.47

Numbered Divisions in Publications and Other Documents

9.27 *Page numbers, chapter numbers, and so forth.* Numbers referring to pages, chapters, parts, volumes, and other divisions of a book, as well as numbers referring to illustrations or tables, are set as numerals. Pages of the front matter are usually in lowercase roman numerals; those for the rest of the book are in arabic numerals (see 1.5–8). For the use of en dashes with number ranges, see 6.78. For documentation style, see chapters 14 and 15. See also 8.178.

The preface will be found on pages vii–xiv and the introduction on pages 1–35.
See part 3, especially chapters 9 and 10, for further discussion; see also volume 2, table 15 and figures 7–9.
Upon completion of step 3, on page 37, the reader is asked to consult appendix B, table 7.

Biblical references are given in numerals only; chapter and verse are separated by a colon with no space following it. For abbreviations, see 10.45–51.

Acts 27:1	2 Corinthians 11:29–30
Exodus 20:3–17	Gen. 47:12
Psalm 121; Psalms 146–50	

9.28 *Volume, issue, and page numbers for periodicals.* References to volumes, issues, and pages of a journal are usually made, in that order, with arabic numerals; the words *volume* and *page* are usually omitted. See also 14.170–217.

Their article appeared in *Current Anthropology* 49, no. 1 (2008): 87–114.

9.29 *Numbered divisions in legal instruments.* Arabic or roman numerals are sometimes used to distinguish divisions within legal instruments and other documents. When in doubt about a reference to a legal document, use arabic numerals or, if possible, consult the document itself for guidance. A mixture of arabic and roman numerals sometimes distinguishes smaller from larger divisions. For legal style in source citations, see 14.281–317.

> They have filed for Chapter 11 protection from creditors.
> Proposition 20 will be voted on next week.
> A search of Title IX (of the Education Amendments of 1972) turns up no mention of athletics.
> Do you have a 401(k)?
> In paragraph 14(vi) of the bylaws, . . .
> According to the Constitution of the United States, article 2, section 4 (*or* Article II, Section 4), . . .
> *but*
> the Fifth Amendment (*or* Amendment V)

Dates

9.30   *The year alone.* Years are expressed in numerals unless they stand at the beginning of a sentence (see 9.5), in which case rewording may be a better option. For eras, see 9.35.

> We all know what happened in 1776.
> Records for solar eclipses go back at least as far as 3000 BCE.
> Twenty twenty (*or* Two thousand twenty) should be a good year for clairvoyants.
> *or, better,*
> The year 2020 should be a good year for clairvoyants.

9.31   *The year abbreviated.* In informal contexts, the first two digits of a particular year are often replaced by an apostrophe (not an opening single quotation mark).

> the spirit of '76 (*not* '76)   the class of '06

9.32   *Month and day.* When specific dates are expressed, cardinal numbers are used, although these may be pronounced as ordinals. For the month-day-year date form versus the day-month-year form, see 6.45.

> May 26, 2008, was a sad day for film buffs.
> The *Watchmaker's Digest* (11 November 2011) praised the new model's precision.

When a day is mentioned without the month or year, the number is usually spelled out in ordinal form.

> On November 5, McManus declared victory. By the twenty-fifth, most of his supporters had deserted him.

9.33   *Centuries.* Particular centuries are spelled out and lowercased. See also 9.35.

> the twenty-first century
> the eighth and ninth centuries
> from the ninth to the eleventh century
> the eighteen hundreds (the nineteenth century)

9.34   *Decades.* Decades are either spelled out (as long as the century is clear) and lowercased or expressed in numerals. Chicago calls for no apostrophe to appear between the year and the *s*.

> the nineties   the 1980s and 1990s (*or, less formally,* the 1980s and '90s)

Note that the first decade of any century cannot be treated in the same way as other decades. "The 1900s," for example, could easily be taken to refer to the whole of the twentieth century. To refer to the second decade (i.e., without writing "second decade"), an expression like "the 1910s" might be used if absolutely necessary, but "the teens" should be avoided. Note also that some consider the first decade of, for example, the twenty-first century to consist of the years 2001–10; the second, 2011–20; and so on. Chicago defers to the preference of its authors in this matter. See also 8.70, 9.63.

> the first decade of the twenty-first century (*or* the years 2000–2009)
> the second decade of the twenty-first century (*or* the years 2010–19)

9.35   *Eras.* Era designations, at least in the Western world, are usually expressed in one of two ways: either CE ("of the Common Era") and BCE ("before the Common Era"), or AD (*anno Domini*, "in the year of the Lord") and BC ("before Christ"). Other forms include AH (*anno Hegirae*, "in the year of [Muhammad's] Hegira," or *anno Hebraico*, "in the Hebrew year"); AUC (*ab urbe condita*, "from the founding of the city [Rome]"); and—for archaeological purposes—BP ("before the present"). Note that the Latin abbreviations AD and AH precede the year number, whereas the others follow it. Choice of the era designation depends on tradition, academic discipline, or personal preference. These abbreviations often appear in small capitals, sometimes with periods following each letter. For consistency with the guidelines in chapter 10, Chicago recommends full capitals and no periods; see also 10.39.

> Herod Antipas (21 BCE–39 CE) was tetrarch of Galilee from 4 BCE until his death.
> Britain was invaded successfully in 55 BC and AD 1066.
> The First Dynasty appears to have lasted from 4400 BP to 4250 BP in radiocarbon years.
> Mubarak published his survey at Cairo in 1886 (AH 1306).
> The campsite seems to have been in use by about 13,500 BP.
> Rome, from its founding in the eighth century BCE, . . .

Note that the second half of a pair of inclusive dates used with BCE or BC, where the higher number comes first, should be given in full to avoid confusion (e.g., "350–345 BCE"). See also 9.63.

9.36   *All-numeral dates and other brief forms.* For practical reasons, all-numeral styles of writing dates (5/10/99, etc.) should not be used in formal writing (except with certain dates that may be known that way: e.g., 9/11, for September 11, 2001). Whereas in American usage the first numeral refers to the month and the second to the day, in the usage of other English-speaking countries and of most European languages it is the other way around. When quoting letters or other material dated, say, 5/10/03, a writer must first ascertain and then make it clear to readers whether May 10 or October 5 is meant (not to mention 1903 or 2003). In text, therefore, the full date should always be spelled out (see 9.32). In documentation and in tables, if numerous dates occur, months may be abbreviated, and the day-month-year form, requiring no punctuation, may be neater (e.g., 5 Oct 2003). See also 10.40. For ISO style, see 9.37.

9.37   *ISO style for dates.* The International Organization for Standardization (ISO) recommends an all-numeral style consisting of year-month-day (i.e., from largest component to smallest), hyphenated. The year is given in full, and the month or day, if one digit only, is preceded by a zero. Thus January 19, 2010, appears as 2010-01-19. Among other advantages, this style allows dates to be sorted correctly in an electronic spreadsheet and other applications.

Time of Day

9.38   *Numerals versus words for time of day.* Times of day in even, half, and quarter hours are usually spelled out in text. With *o'clock*, the number is always spelled out. In the third example, the *a* before *quarter* is optional.

Her day begins at five o'clock in the morning.
The meeting continued until half past three.
He left the office at a quarter of four (*or* a quarter to four).
We will resume at ten thirty.
Cinderella almost forgot that she should leave the ball before midnight. (See also 9.39.)

Numerals are used (with zeros for even hours) when exact times are emphasized. Chicago recommends lowercase a.m. (*ante meridiem*) and p.m. (*post meridiem*), though these sometimes appear in small capitals, with or without periods.

The first train leaves at 5:22 a.m. and the last at 11:00 p.m.
She caught the 6:20 p.m. flight.
Please attend a meeting in Grand Rapids, Michigan, on December 5 at 10:30 a.m. (EST).

For more on time zones, see 10.42.

9.39   *Noon and midnight.* Except in the twenty-four-hour system (see 9.40), numbers should never be used to express noon or midnight (except, informally, in an expression like *twelve o'clock at night*). Although noon can be expressed as 12:00 m. (m. = *meridies*), very few use that form. And the term 12:00 p.m. is ambiguous, if not illogical. In the second example below, note the double date for clarity.

The meeting began at 9:45 a.m. and was adjourned by noon.
Rodriguez was born at midnight, August 21–22.

9.40   *The twenty-four-hour system.* In the twenty-four-hour system of expressing time (used in Europe and in the military), four digits always appear, often with no punctuation between hours and minutes.

1200 = noon
2400 *or* 0000 = midnight
0001 = 12:01 a.m.
1438 = 2:38 p.m.
At 1500 hours (*or* 1500h) we started off on our mission.
General quarters sounded at 0415.

9.41   *Seconds and dates included.* A variation of the twenty-four-hour system shows hours, minutes, and seconds separated by colons; it also shows fractions of a second following a period. This format may be preceded by an ISO-style date (see 9.37).

09:27:08.6 = 27 minutes, 8.6 seconds after 9:00 a.m.
2010-01-19 16:09:41.3 = January 19, 2010, at 9 minutes, 41.3 seconds after 4:00 p.m.

For further details, consult *Scientific Style and Format* (bibliog. 1.1).

Numbers with Proper Names and Titles

9.42   *Numerals for monarchs, popes, and so forth.* Sovereigns, emperors, popes, and Orthodox patriarchs with the same name are differentiated by numerals, traditionally roman.

Elizabeth II   Benedict XVI

In continental European practice, the numeral is sometimes followed by a period (e.g., Wilhelm II.) or a superscript (e.g., François Ier) indicating that the number is an ordinal. In an English context, the roman numeral alone should appear. See also 11.30.

9.43   *Numerals with personal names.* Some personal names are followed by a roman numeral or an arabic ordinal numeral. No punctuation precedes the numeral unless the name is inverted (as in an index entry). For *Jr.*, see 6.47.

Adlai E. Stevenson III
Michael F. Johnson 2nd
but
Stevenson, Adlai E., III

9.44   *Numbers for sequels.* Numerals are often used to designate the sequel to a novel or a movie or to differentiate two chapter titles dealing with the same subject matter. When quoting such titles, follow the usage—roman or arabic (or spelled out)—reflected in the source itself.

The Godfather; The Godfather, Part II; The Godfather, Part III
Jaws; Jaws 2; Jaws 3-D
chapter 9, "Alligator Studies in the Everglades—I"
chapter 10, "Alligator Studies in the Everglades—II"

9.45   *Vehicle and vessel numbers.* Boats and the like differentiated by a number usually take a roman numeral, spacecraft an arabic numeral. See also 8.115–16.

Bluebird III   *Mariner 9*

9.46   *Successive governments.* Ordinal numbers designating successive dynasties, governments, and other governing bodies are spelled out if one hundred or less.

Eighteenth Dynasty   Second International
Fifth Republic   Ninety-Seventh United States Congress
Second Continental Congress   111th Congress

9.47   *Numbered political and judicial divisions.* Ordinal numbers designating political or judicial divisions are spelled out if one hundred or less.

Fifth Ward   Twelfth Congressional District   Tenth Circuit   101st Precinct

9.48   *Numbered military units.* Ordinal numbers designating military units are spelled out if one hundred or less.

Fifth Army   First Corps Support Command
Fourth Infantry Division   101st Airborne Division

9.49   *Numbered places of worship.* Ordinal numbers that are part of the names of places of worship are spelled out.

Fourth Presbyterian Church   Twenty-First Church of Christ, Scientist

9.50   *Unions and lodges.* Numbers designating local branches of labor unions and fraternal lodges are usually expressed in arabic numerals after the name. Commas are generally omitted.

Chicago Typographical Union No. 16   United Auto Workers Local 890
American Legion Post 21

Addresses and Thoroughfares

9.51   *Numbered highways.* State, federal, and interstate highways are designated by arabic numerals. Names for state routes vary from state to state. See also 8.55.

US Route 41 (*or* US 41)   Illinois Route 50 (*or* Illinois 50; IL 50); Route 50
Interstate 90 (*or* I-90)   M6 motorway (England)

9.52 *Numbered streets.* Names of numbered streets, avenues, and so forth are usually spelled out if one hundred or less. For the use of *N, E, SW,* and the like, see 10.35. See also 8.55.

First Avenue   Ninety-Fifth Street   122nd Street

9.53 *Building and apartment numbers.* Building numbers, in arabic numerals, precede the street name. For readability, text usage may differ slightly from an address on an envelope. For preferred forms of addresses in the United States, consult the website of the US Postal Service.

They lived in Oak Park, at 1155 South Euclid Avenue, for almost ten years.
She now lives in unit 114A, 150 Ninth Avenue, with an unrivaled view of the city.
Our office is at 1427 East Sixtieth Street, Chicago, Illinois.
Please mail a copy of the German-language edition to 1427 E. 60th St., Chicago,
   IL 60637.

When a building is referred to in running text by its address, the number is often spelled out.

One Thousand Lake Shore Drive   One IBM Plaza

Plurals and Punctuation of Numbers

9.54 *Plural numbers.* Spelled-out numbers form their plurals as other nouns do (see 7.5).

The contestants were in their twenties and thirties.
The family was at sixes and sevens.

Numerals form their plurals by adding *s.* No apostrophe is needed.

Among the scores were two 240s and three 238s.
Jazz forms that were developed in the 1920s became popular in the 1930s.

9.55 *Comma between digits.* In most numerals of one thousand or more, commas are used between groups of three digits, counting from the right. (In scientific writing, commas are often omitted from four-digit numbers.) See also 9.56.

1,512   32,987   4,000,500

No commas are used in page numbers, line numbers (e.g., in poetry and plays), addresses, and years (though years of five digits or more do include the comma). See also 9.35.

Punctuation conventions can be found on page 1535 of the tenth edition.
Our business office is at 11030 South Langley Avenue.
Human artifacts dating from between 35,000 BP and 5000 BP have been found there.

9.56   *Space between digits.* In the International System of Units (SI units), thin, fixed spaces rather than commas are used to mark off groups of three digits, both to the left and to the right of the decimal point (represented by a comma in many non-English settings). (In electronic publications, a nonbreaking space may be used.) In numbers of only four digits either to the left or the right of the decimal point, no space is used (except in table columns that also include numbers having five or more digits). This system is far more common in Europe than in the United States. See also 9.20, 9.55.

3 426 869
0.000 007
2501.4865 (no space is used with four-digit sequences)

For more on SI units, see Ambler Thompson and Barry N. Taylor, *Guide for the Use of the International System of Units (SI)*, and *The International System of Units*, a brochure published in English and French by the Bureau International des Poids et Mesures and available online (see bibliog. 2.4).

9.57   *Numbered lists and outline style.* For the use of numerals (arabic and roman) and letters to distinguish items in lists, see 6.121–26.

Inclusive Numbers

9.58   *When to use the en dash.* An en dash used between two numbers implies *up to and including*, or *through*. For more on the use of the en dash, see 6.78–81.

Please refer to pages 75–110.
Here are the figures for 2001–10.
Campers were divided into age groups 5–7, 8–10, 11–13, and 14–16.

9.59   *When not to use the en dash.* If *from* or *between* is used before the first of a pair of numbers, the en dash should not be used; instead, *from* should be followed by *to* or *through*, *between* should be followed by *and*.

from 75 to 110 (*not* from 75–110)
from 1898 to 1903
from January 1, 1898, through December 31, 1903
between about 150 and 200

Inclusive spelled-out numbers should be joined by *to*, not by an en dash.

women aged forty-five to forty-nine years   sixty- to seventy-year-olds

9.60   *Abbreviating, or condensing, inclusive numbers.* Inclusive numbers are abbreviated according to the principles illustrated below (examples are page or serial numbers, which do not require commas). This system, used by Chicago in essentially this form since the first edition of this manual, is efficient and unambiguous. See also 9.61, 6.78.

FIRST NUMBER	SECOND NUMBER	EXAMPLES
Less than 100	Use all digits	3–10
		71–72
		96–117
100 or multiples of 100	Use all digits	100–104
		1100–1113
101 through 109, 201 through 209, etc.	Use changed part only	101–8
		808–33
		1103–4
110 through 199, 210 through 299, etc.	Use two digits unless more are needed to include all changed parts	321–28
		498–532
		1087–89
		1496–500
		11564–615
		12991–3001

To avoid ambiguity, inclusive roman numerals are always given in full.

xxv–xxviii   cvi–cix

9.61   *Alternative systems for inclusive numbers.* A foolproof system is to give the full form of numbers everywhere (e.g., 234–235, 25039–25041). Another practice, more economical, is to include in the second number only the changed part of the first (e.g., 234–5, 25000–1). Chicago, however, prefers the system presented in 9.60.

9.62   *Inclusive numbers with commas.* When inclusive numbers with commas are abbreviated, and only numbers in the hundreds place and below change, the rules described in 9.60 should apply. If a change extends to the thousands place or beyond, it is best to repeat all digits.

6,000–6,018   12,473–79   1,247,689–710   1,247,689–1,248,125

9.63   *Inclusive years.* Inclusive years may be abbreviated following the pattern illustrated in 9.60. When the century changes, however, or when the sequence is BCE, BC, or BP (diminishing numbers), all digits must be presented. See also 9.35.

1897–1901
the war of 1914–18
fiscal year 1997–98 (*or* 1997/98; see 6.105); FY 1997–98
the winter of 2000–2001
in 1504–5
327–321 BCE (seven years, inclusively)
327–21 BCE (307 years, inclusively)
115 BC–AD 10
15,000–14,000 BP

In book titles it is customary but not obligatory to repeat all digits; when mentioning or citing a title, the form of the original should be respected.

Roman Numerals

9.64   *Roman numerals—general principles.* Table 9.1 shows the formation of roman numerals with their arabic equivalents. The general principle is that a smaller letter before a larger one subtracts from its value, and a smaller letter after a larger one adds to it; a bar over a letter multiplies its value by one thousand. Roman numerals may also be written in lowercase letters (i, ii, iii, iv, etc.). In older sources, a final *i* was often made like a *j* (vij, viij); citations to roman numeral page numbers in older works should follow the original usage.

TABLE 9.1 Roman and arabic numerals

Arabic	Roman	Arabic	Roman	Arabic	Roman
1	I	17	XVII	200	CC
2	II	18	XVIII	300	CCC
3	III	19	XIX	400	CD
4	IV	20	XX	500	D
5	V	21	XXI	600	DC
6	VI	22	XXII	700	DCC
7	VII	23	XXIII	800	DCCC
8	VIII	24	XXIV	900	CM
9	IX	30	XXX	1,000	M
10	X	40	XL	2,000	MM
11	XI	50	L	3,000	MMM
12	XII	60	LX	4,000	$M\overline{V}$
13	XIII	70	LXX	5,000	$\overline{V}$
14	XIV	80	LXXX	10,000	$\overline{X}$
15	XV	90	XC	100,000	$\overline{C}$
16	XVI	100	C	1,000,000	$\overline{M}$

9.65 *The advent of subtrahends (back counters).* The use of subtrahends (back counters) was introduced during the Renaissance. Note that IIII, not IV, still appears on some clock faces. The Romans would have expressed the year 1999, for example, as MDCCCCLXXXXVIIII. A more modern form, approved by the US government and accepted (if reluctantly) by classical scholars, is MCMXCIX (*not* MIM, considered a barbarism).

9.66 *Chicago's preference for arabic rather than roman numerals.* Chicago uses arabic numerals in many situations where roman numerals were formerly common, as in references to volume numbers of books and journals or chapters of books (see 9.28). Most of the exceptions are treated elsewhere, as follows: for the use of roman numerals in the front matter of books, see 1.4, 1.6, 9.27; in legal instruments, 9.29; with the names of monarchs, prelates, and such, 9.42; with personal names, 9.43; in titles of sequels, 9.44; with names of certain vessels, 9.45; and in outline style, 6.126.

10 *Abbreviations*

Overview

10.1   *Abbreviations—additional resources.* This chapter provides guidance for using abbreviations and symbols in general and scholarly writing. It also offers some guidance in technical work, especially for the generalist editor confronted with unfamiliar terms. For abbreviations not listed here, Chicago recommends *Merriam-Webster's Collegiate Dictionary* (bibliog. 3.1); Dean Stahl and Karen Kerchelich, *Abbreviations Dictionary* (bibliog. 4.7); and the multivolume *Acronyms, Initialisms, and Abbreviations Dictionary* (bibliog. 4.7). Authors and editors of technical material will need to refer to more specialized manuals, starting with *Scientific Style and Format* (bibliog. 1.1).

10.2   *Acronyms, initialisms, contractions.* The word *acronym* refers to terms based on the initial letters of their various elements and read as single words (AIDS, laser, NASA, scuba); *initialism* refers to terms read as a series of letters (AOL, NBA, XML); and *contraction* refers to abbreviations that include the first and last letters of the full word (Mr., amt.). (For the type of contractions normally formed with apostrophes, see 7.29.) The definitions are not perfect. For example, sometimes a letter in an initialism is formed not, as the term might imply, from an initial letter but rather from an initial sound (as the *X* in XML, for extensible markup language), or from the application of a number (W3C, for World Wide Web Consortium). Furthermore, an acronym and initialism are occasionally combined (JPEG), and the line between initialism and acronym is not always clear (FAQ, which can be pronounced either as a word or as a series of letters). In this chapter the umbrella term *abbreviation* will be used for all three, as well as for shortened (i.e., abbreviated) forms (ibid., vol., prof., etc.), except where greater specificity is required. (Occasionally, a *symbol* abbreviates a term, as in © for *copyright*. On the other hand, abbreviations for units are often referred to as symbols in SI usage; see 10.54–62.)

10.3   *When to use abbreviations.* Outside the area of science and technology, abbreviations and symbols are most appropriate in tabular matter, notes, bibliographies, and parenthetical references. Even in regular prose, a number of expressions are almost always abbreviated and may be used without first spelling them out. Many of these will be listed as main entries with pronunciation (rather than as abbreviations) in the latest edition of *Webster's* (e.g., DNA, GPS, HMO, HTML, IQ, JPEG, laser, Ms., NASA). Others, though in more or less common use (CGI, FDA, HVAC,

MLA), should generally be spelled out at first occurrence—at least in formal text—as a courtesy to those readers who might not easily recognize them. The use of less familiar abbreviations should be limited to those terms that occur frequently enough to warrant abbreviation—roughly five times or more within an article or chapter—and the terms must be spelled out on their first occurrence. (The abbreviation usually follows immediately, in parentheses, but it may be introduced in other ways; see examples. Such an abbreviation should not be offered only once, never to be used again.) Writers and editors should monitor the number of different abbreviations used in a document; readers trying to keep track of a large number of abbreviations, especially unfamiliar ones, will benefit from a list of abbreviations (see 1.43, 2.21). For rules concerning the plural form of various abbreviations, see 7.14. For abbreviations preceded by *a, an,* or *the,* see 7.44, 10.9.

Among recent recommendations of the Federal Aviation Administration (FAA) are . . .

According to the weak law of large numbers (WLLN) . . .

The National Aeronautics and Space Administration was founded in 1958. Since its inception, NASA has . . .

The benefits of ERISA (Employee Retirement Income Security Act) are familiar to many.

10.4   *Periods with abbreviations.* In using periods with abbreviations, Chicago recommends the following general guidelines in nontechnical settings. For the use of space between elements, see 10.5.

1. Use periods with abbreviations that end in a lowercase letter: p. (page), vol., e.g., i.e., etc., a.k.a., a.m., p.m., Ms., Dr., et al. (*et* is not an abbreviation; *al.* is). An exception may be made for the few academic degrees that end in a lowercase letter (e.g., DLitt, DMin); see 10.20 and rule 3.

2. Use periods for initials standing for given names: E. B. White; do not use periods for an entire name replaced by initials: JFK.

3. Use no periods with abbreviations that appear in full capitals, whether two letters or more and even if lowercase letters appear within the abbreviation: VP, CEO, MA, MD, PhD, UK, US, NY, IL (*but see rule 4*).

4. In publications using traditional state abbreviations, use periods to abbreviate *United States* and its states and territories: U.S., N.Y., Ill. Note, however, that Chicago recommends using the two-letter postal codes (and therefore *US*) wherever abbreviations are used; see 10.28. For Canadian provinces and territories, see 10.29. See also 14.286.

Note that the British and the French (among others) omit periods from contractions (Dr, assn, Mme). Note also that a slash is occasionally used instead of periods (as in *c/o* or *n/a*) but more often denotes *per* (see 6.107). Units of measure in nontechnical settings are usually spelled out. In scientific usage, periods are generally omitted for abbreviated units of measure and other technical terms: see 10.52–71.

10.5 *Space or no space between elements.* No space is left between the letters of initialisms and acronyms, whether lowercase or in capitals. Space is usually left between abbreviated words, unless an abbreviated word is used in combination with a single-letter abbreviation. For personal names, see 10.12.

RN	Gov. Gen.	*but*
C-SPAN	Mng. Ed.	S.Dak. (but see 10.28)
YMCA	Dist. Atty.	S.Sgt.

10.6 *Capitals versus lowercase for acronyms and initialisms.* Initialisms tend to appear in all capital letters, even when they are not derived from proper nouns (HIV, VP, LCD). With frequent use, however, acronyms—especially those of five or more letters—will sometimes become lowercase (scuba); those that are derived from proper nouns retain an initial capital. Chicago generally prefers the all-capital form, unless the term is listed otherwise in *Webster's*.

NAFTA (*not* Nafta)

On the other hand, if the words in a spelled-out version of an acronym or initialism are not derived from proper nouns or do not themselves constitute a proper noun (as in the official name of an organization), they should generally be lowercased, even when they appear alongside the abbreviated form.

transmission-control protocol/Internet protocol (TCP/IP)

10.7 *Italic versus roman type for abbreviations.* Chicago italicizes abbreviations only if they stand for a term that would be italicized if spelled out—the title of a book or periodical, for example. Common Latin abbreviations are set in roman (see also 7.53).

OED (*Oxford English Dictionary*)
JAMA (*Journal of the American Medical Association*)
ibid.   etc.   e.g.   i.e.

10.8   *Small versus full-size capitals for acronyms and initialisms.* Some book designs call for small capitals rather than full-size capitals for acronyms and initialisms (e.g., NASA rather than NASA). Though such usage may be considered desirable for a book that includes many acronyms and initialisms, Chicago does not generally recommend it. If small capitals must be used, the decision of what to mark should be made by the editor, who should apply small capitals on the final manuscript (e.g., using a word processor's small capitals feature). In general, small capitals should be limited to acronyms or initialisms mentioned in running text. Avoid applying small capitals to such items as two-letter postal codes in notes or bibliographies or to roman numerals (e.g., following a personal name). Editors and typesetters should be aware that small capitals are not treated in the same way across all software and coding platforms: some applications use lowercase letters presented (or "styled") as small capitals, whereas in other systems small capitals are based on uppercase letters. See also 10.39, 10.42. For the use of small capitals for emphasis, see 7.48.

10.9   *"A," "an," or "the" preceding an abbreviation.* When an abbreviation follows an indefinite article, the choice of *a* or *an* is determined by the way the abbreviation would be read aloud. Acronyms are read as words and are rarely preceded by *a, an,* or *the* ("member nations of NATO"), except when used adjectivally ("a NATO initiative"). Initialisms are read as a series of letters and are often preceded by an article ("member nations of the EU"). See 10.2; see also 7.44.

an HMO
a UFO
a NATO member
a LOOM parade
an AA meeting
a AA battery (pronounced "double A")
an NAACP convention
an NBA coach
an HIV test
an MS symptom (a symptom of multiple sclerosis)
but
a MS by . . . (would be read as "a manuscript by . . .")

10.10   *Ampersands.* No space is left on either side of an ampersand used within an initialism.

R&D   Texas A&M

Names and Titles

Personal Names and Titles

10.11 *Personal names.* Normally, abbreviations should not be used for given names. A signature, however, should be transcribed as the person wrote it.

Benj. Franklin   Geo. D. Fuller   Ch. Virolleaud

10.12 *Initials in personal names.* Initials standing for given names are followed by a period and a space. A period is normally used even if the middle initial does not stand for a name (as in Harry S. Truman).

Roger W. Shugg   P. D. James   M. F. K. Fisher

If an entire name is abbreviated, spaces and periods are usually omitted.

FDR (Franklin Delano Roosevelt)
MJ (Michael Jordan)
but
H.D. (pen name for Hilda Doolittle, with periods but no space between initials)

10.13 *Abbreviating titles before names.* Many civil or military titles preceding a full name may be abbreviated. Preceding a surname alone, however, they should be spelled out. See also 8.18.

Rep. Dan Lipinski; Representative Lipinski
Sen. Kirsten E. Gillibrand; Senator Gillibrand
Rear Adm. Carol M. Pottenger; Rear Admiral Pottenger

10.14 *Civil titles.* The following abbreviations, among others, may precede a full name where space is tight:

Ald.	Atty. Gen.	Insp. Gen.	Prof.
Assoc. Prof.	Fr. (father)	Judge Adv. Gen.	Sr. (sister)
Asst. Prof.	Gov.	Pres.	Supt.

10.15 *US military titles.* The US military omits periods in the official abbreviated forms of its ranks. The abbreviations for a given title may vary across branches. The army, for example, uses *SSG* for *staff sergeant*; the air force and marines prefer *SSgt*. (In the examples below, such variants are not presented.) In general contexts, however, including military history, traditional abbreviations—which tend not to vary across the armed forces—are preferred. The following very selective list merely illustrates the difference between military usage and traditional forms. Where no traditional abbreviation is appropriate before a name, use the full form.

ADM	Adm.	2LT	2nd Lt.
A1C	Airman First Class	LG	Lt. Gen.
BG	Brig. Gen.	LTC	Lt. Col.
CDR	Cdr.	MAJ	Maj.
COL	Col.	MG	Maj. Gen.
CPT	Capt.	MSG	M.Sgt. (master sergeant)
CWO	Chief Warrant Officer	PO	Petty Officer
GEN	Gen.	SGT	Sgt.
LT	Lt.	SSG	S.Sgt. (staff sergeant)
1LT	1st Lt.	WO	Warrant Officer

For the latest official forms of rank insignia, consult the website of the US Department of Defense. In addition, there are many reference books containing more detailed lists of abbreviations and terms, some of which are published regularly. See, for example, Timothy Zurick, *Army Dictionary and Desk Reference* (bibliog. 5).

10.16   *Social titles.* Social titles are always abbreviated, whether preceding the full name or the surname only. (The spelled-out forms *Mister* or *Doctor* might be used without a name—as in direct address.)

Ms.	Mr.	*but*
Mrs.	Dr. Jekyll	Thank you, Doctor.
Messrs.		

Social titles are routinely omitted in most prose, though a few periodicals in particular persist in using them. When an academic degree or professional designation follows a name, such titles are always omitted.

Jennifer James, MD (*not* Dr. Jennifer James, MD)

Similarly, the now somewhat archaic abbreviation *Esq.* (Esquire) is used only after a full name and never when *Mr., Dr.,* or the like precedes the name.

10.17   *French social titles.* Note the presence or absence of periods after the following French forms used with either a full name or a surname only. (*Mme* and *Mlle* are considered contractions; in French usage, periods are often omitted for all four titles.)

M.   MM.   Mme   Mlle

When *Monsieur, Messieurs, Madame,* or *Mademoiselle* is used without a name, in direct address, it is spelled out (and, in French usage, generally lowercased).

10.18   *"Reverend" and "Honorable."* The abbreviations *Rev.* and *Hon.* are traditionally used before a full name when *the* does not precede the title. With *the,* such titles should be spelled out.

Rev. Sam Portaro; the Reverend Sam Portaro
Hon. Henry M. Brown; the Honorable Henry M. Brown

With a last name only, such titles are normally omitted. The construction "Reverend So-and-So," however, is common, especially in informal prose or speech.

Rev. Jane Schaefer; Schaefer (*or* Reverend Schaefer)
the Honorable Patricia Birkholz; Birkholz

10.19   *"Jr.," "Sr.," and the like.* The abbreviations *Jr.* and *Sr.,* as well as roman or arabic numerals such as III or 3rd, after a person's name are part of the name and so are retained in connection with any titles or honorifics. Note that these abbreviations are used only with the full name, never with the surname only. See also 6.47, 9.43.

Jordan Balfence Jr. spoke first. After Mr. Balfence relinquished the podium, . . .
Zayd Zephyr III, MBA, spoke last. In closing, Mr. Zephyr reiterated . . .

10.20   *Academic degrees.* Chicago recommends omitting periods in abbreviations of academic degrees (BA, DDS, etc.) unless they are required for reasons of tradition or consistency with, for example, a journal's established style. In the following list of some of the more common degrees, periods are shown only where uncertainty might arise as to their placement. Spelled-out terms, often capitalized in institutional settings (and on business cards and other promotional items), should be lowercased in normal prose. See also 8.28.

AB   artium baccalaureus (bachelor of arts)
AM   artium magister (master of arts)

BA	bachelor of arts
BD	bachelor of divinity
BFA	bachelor of fine arts
BM	bachelor of music
BS	bachelor of science
DB	divinitatis baccalaureus (bachelor of divinity)
DD	divinitatis doctor (doctor of divinity)
DDS	doctor of dental surgery
DLitt *or* DLit	doctor litterarum (doctor of letters; doctor of literature)
DMD	dentariae medicinae doctor (doctor of dental medicine)
DMin	doctor of ministry
DO	doctor of osteopathy *or* osteopathic physician
DVM	doctor of veterinary medicine
EdM	educationis magister (master of education)
JD	juris doctor (doctor of law)
LHD	litterarum humaniorum doctor (doctor of humanities)
LittD	litterarum doctor (doctor of letters)
LLB (LL.B.)	legum baccalaureus (bachelor of laws)
LLD (LL.D.)	legum doctor (doctor of laws)
LLM (LL.M.)	legum magister (master of laws)
MA	master of arts
MBA	master of business administration
MD	medicinae doctor (doctor of medicine)
MDiv	master of divinity
MFA	master of fine arts
MS	master of science
MSN	master of science in nursing
MSW	master of social welfare *or* master of social work
PhB	philosophiae baccalaureus (bachelor of philosophy)
PhD	philosophiae doctor (doctor of philosophy)
PhG	graduate in pharmacy
SB	scientiae baccalaureus (bachelor of science)
SM	scientiae magister (master of science)
STB	sacrae theologiae baccalaureus (bachelor of sacred theology)

These designations are set off by commas when they follow a personal name.

David H. Pauker, JD, attended Northwestern University Law School.

10.21 *Professional, religious, and other designations.* Abbreviations for many other designations, professional and otherwise, follow the pattern of academic degrees, for which Chicago recommends dispensing with periods.

Spelled-out terms, often capitalized in institutional settings, are lower-case unless they designate the proper name of an organization. (See 10.20.)

CNM certified nurse midwife
FAIA fellow of the American Institute of Architects
FRS fellow of the Royal Society
JP justice of the peace
LPN licensed practical nurse
MP member of Parliament
OFM Order of Friars Minor
OP Ordo Praedicatorum (Order of Preachers)
RN registered nurse
SJ Society of Jesus

These designations, like academic degrees, are set off by commas when they follow a personal name.

Joan Hotimlanska, LPN, will be working on the second floor.

Firms and Companies

10.22   *Some commonly used generic abbreviations.* All of the abbreviations in the following list may be found in *Webster's* and other standard dictionaries. Use periods, or not, according to the recommendations in 10.4. See also 10.72.

Assoc.	LP (limited partnership)
Bros.	Ltd.
Co.	Mfg.
Corp.	PLC (public limited company)
Inc.	RR (railroad)
LLC (limited liability company)	Rwy. *or* Ry. (railway)
LLP (limited liability partnership)	

Abbreviations of foreign-language terms omit the period if they are contractions (see 10.2).

Cia (Sp. *compañia*)   Cie (Fr. *compagnie*)

10.23   *Company names.* Abbreviations and ampersands are appropriate in notes, bibliographies, tabular matter, and the like. See also 14.141.

Ginn & Co.   JPMorgan Chase & Co.   Moss Bros.   Rand Corp.

In running text, company names are best given in their full forms. It should be noted, however, that some full forms include ampersands and abbreviations. If in doubt, especially with reference to contemporary firms, look up the company name at a corporate website or other authoritative source. Such elements as *Inc.*, *& Co.*, and *LLC* may be omitted unless relevant to the context.

Brooks Brothers was purchased and later resold by Marks & Spencer.
JPMorgan Chase operates in more than sixty countries.
AT&T Corporation was once known as the American Telephone and Telegraph Company.

Agencies and Organizations

10.24 *Associations and the like.* Both in running text (preferably after being spelled out on first occurrence) and in tabular matter, notes, and so forth, the names of many agencies and organizations, governmental and fraternal, are commonly abbreviated. Whether acronyms or initialisms (see 10.2), such abbreviations appear in full capitals and without periods. For *a*, *an*, or *the*, with abbreviations, see 10.9.

AAUP   EU (European Union)   WHO
AFL-CIO   HMO (*pl.* HMOs)   WTO (*formerly* GATT)
EPA

10.25 *Broadcasting companies.* Call letters, often derived from the name of a broadcasting company, are always capitalized but do not take periods.

ABC   CBS   HBO   KFTV   MTV   NBC   TBS   WFMT   WTTW

Saints and Personal Names with "Saint" or "St."

10.26 *Names of saints.* The word *Saint* is often abbreviated (*St.*, pl. *SS.*) before the name of a Christian saint; it should normally be spelled out in formal prose but need not be if space is at a premium. (But see 10.27.) The choice for one or the other should be implemented consistently.

Saint (*or* St.) Teresa
Saints (*or* SS.) Francis of Paola and Francis of Sales

10.27   *Personal names with "Saint" or "St."* When *Saint* or *St.* forms part of a personal name, the bearer's usage is followed. See also 10.31.

Augustus Saint-Gaudens   Muriel St. Clare Byrne

Geographical Terms

10.28   *US states and territories.* In running text, the names of states, territories, and possessions of the United States should always be spelled out when standing alone and preferably (except for DC) when following the name of a city: for example, "Lake Bluff, Illinois, was incorporated in 1895." In bibliographies, tabular matter, lists, and mailing addresses, they are usually abbreviated. In all such contexts, Chicago prefers the two-letter postal codes to the conventional abbreviations. Note that if traditional abbreviations must be used, some terms may not be subject to abbreviation. See also 10.4.

AK	Alaska *or* Alas.	MA	Mass.
AL	Ala.	MD	Md.
AR	Ark.	ME	Maine
AS	American Samoa	MH	Marshall Islands
AZ	Ariz.	MI	Mich.
CA	Calif.	MN	Minn.
CO	Colo.	MO	Mo.
CT	Conn.	MP	Northern Mariana Islands
DC	D.C.	MS	Miss.
DE	Del.	MT	Mont.
FL	Fla.	NC	N.C.
FM	Federated States of	ND	N.Dak.
	Micronesia	NE	Neb. *or* Nebr.
GA	Ga.	NH	N.H.
GU	Guam	NJ	N.J.
HI	Hawaii	NM	N.Mex.
IA	Iowa	NV	Nev.
ID	Idaho	NY	N.Y.
IL	Ill.	OH	Ohio
IN	Ind.	OK	Okla.
KS	Kans.	OR	Ore. *or* Oreg.
KY	Ky.	PA	Pa.
LA	La.	PR	P.R. *or* Puerto Rico

PW	Palau	VA	Va.
RI	R.I.	VI	V.I. *or* Virgin Islands
SC	S.C.	VT	Vt.
SD	S.Dak.	WA	Wash.
TN	Tenn.	WI	Wis. *or* Wisc.
TX	Tex.	WV	W.Va.
UT	Utah	WY	Wyo.

10.29   ***Canadian provinces and territories.*** Canadian provinces and territories are normally spelled out in text (e.g., "Kingston, Ontario, is worth a visit") but may be abbreviated in bibliographies and the like—using the two-letter postal abbreviations, which have the advantage of applying to both the English and French forms.

AB	Alberta
BC	British Columbia *or* Colombie-Britannique
MB	Manitoba
NB	New Brunswick *or* Nouveau-Brunswick
NL	Newfoundland and Labrador *or* Terre-Neuve-et-Labrador
NS	Nova Scotia *or* Nouvelle-Écosse
NT	Northwest Territories *or* Territoires du Nord-Ouest
NU	Nunavut
ON	Ontario
PE	Prince Edward Island *or* Île-du-Prince-Édouard
QC	Quebec *or* Québec
SK	Saskatchewan
YT	Yukon

10.30   ***Comma with city plus state.*** When following the name of a city, the names of states, provinces, and territories are enclosed in commas, whether they are spelled out (as in running text) or abbreviated (as in tabular matter or lists). In an exception to the rule, no comma appears between the postal code and a zip code. See also 6.46, 6.17.

Bedford, PA, and Jamestown, NY
but
Send the package to J. Sprocket, 3359 Fob Dr., Quartz, IL 60000.

10.31   ***Place-names with "Fort," "Mount," "Saint," and the like.*** Generic terms as elements of geographic names should be abbreviated only where space is at a premium. *San* and *Santa* (e.g., San Diego, Santa Barbara) are never abbreviated. For French place-names with *Saint*, see 11.29.

Fort (Ft.) Myers	Mount (Mt.) Airy	Port (Pt.) Arthur
Saint (St.) Louis	Saint (St.) Paul	

Names of Countries

10.32 *When to abbreviate country names.* Names of countries are spelled out in text but may be abbreviated in tabular matter, lists, and the like. Use discretion in forming the abbreviations and make sure they are defined below the table (or in some fashion) if there is any possibility of confusion (see 3.74–78). The examples below reflect entries in standard dictionaries (all are listed in *Webster's*, with the exception of *Swed.*, which is listed in *American Heritage*). In certain technical applications, it may be advisable to use either the two-letter or three-letter standard abbreviations based on the English names of countries as defined by the International Organization for Standardization (ISO 3166-1, alpha-2 and alpha-3, respectively). For these lists, consult the ISO website. For *US*, see 10.33.

Fr.	Ger.	Isr.	It.	Neth.	Russ.	Sp.	Swed.
UAE (United Arab Emirates)			UK				

Note that before reunification (in 1990) East Germany was generally known as the GDR (German Democratic Republic) or DDR (Deutsche Demokratische Republik), and West Germany as the FRG (Federal Republic of Germany) or BRD (Bundesrepublik Deutschland). The former Soviet Union was abbreviated USSR (Union of Soviet Socialist Republics).

10.33 *"US" versus United States.* In running text, spell out *United States* as a noun; reserve *US* for the adjective form only (in which position the abbreviation is generally preferred). See also 10.4.

US dollars	*but*
US involvement in China	China's involvement in the United States

Addresses

10.34 *Mailing addresses—postal versus standard abbreviations.* Standard abbreviations preferred by the US Postal Service (first column) are in all caps and do not use periods; these forms are most appropriate for mailing addresses. In tabular matter and the like, Chicago prefers the form of abbreviations presented in the second column. For those not listed here, consult a dictionary. For a complete list of abbreviations preferred by the

USPS, consult their website. In running text, spell out rather than abbreviate. See also 10.35.

AVE	Ave.	PO Box	PO Box
BLDG	Bldg.	RD	Rd.
CT	Ct.	RM	Rm.
DR	Dr.	RTE	Rte.
EXPY	Expy.	SQ	Sq.
HWY	Hwy.	ST	St.
LN	Ln.	STE	Ste. (*or* Suite)
PKWY	Pkwy.	TER	Ter. (*or* Terr.)
PL	Pl.		

10.35   *Compass points in mailing addresses.* Single-letter compass points accompanying a street name are normally followed by a period; two-letter ones are not. (The US Postal Service does not use periods for either; see 10.34; see also 10.4.) Note that when used in an address, the abbreviations *NE*, *NW*, *SE*, and *SW* remain abbreviated even in running text (there is no comma before them when they follow a street name). The *N* in the third example is a street name and not a compass point.

> 1060 E. Prospect Ave.
> 456 NW Lane St.
> I stayed in a building on N Street SW, close to the city center.

A compass point that is the name (or part of the name) of a street or a place-name must never be abbreviated (e.g., South Ave., Northwest Hwy., South Shore Dr., West Bend, East Orange). For the use of numerals in addresses, see 9.52, 9.53.

Compass Points, Latitude, and Longitude

10.36   *Compass points.* Points of the compass may be abbreviated as follows, without periods (but see 10.35). In formal, nontechnical text, however, these terms are usually spelled out.

> N, E, S, W, NE, SE, SW, NW, NNE, ENE, ESE, etc.
> N by NE, NE by N, NE by E, etc.

10.37   *"Latitude" and "longitude."* In nontechnical contexts, the words *latitude* and *longitude* are never abbreviated in running text or when standing alone.

longitude 90° west   the polar latitudes

Global positioning coordinates are expressed in a variety of ways (though latitude is always given first). Some systems use a minus sign (or hyphen) to indicate south or west. Others use decimal minutes. The following three coordinates are equivalent. The comma is often omitted.

36 25.217, −44 23.017   N 36°25′13″, W 44°23′01″   N 36 25.217, W 44 23.017

In technical work, the abbreviations *lat* and *long*, usually without periods, may be used when part of a coordinate. They can sometimes be dropped, since the compass point identifies the coordinate.

lat 42°15′09″ N, long 89°17′45″ W
lat 45°16′17″ S, long 116°40′18″ E
The chart showed shoal water at 19°29′59″ N, 107°45′36″ W.

Note that primes (′) and double primes (″), *not* quotation marks, are used. For greater detail, consult *Scientific Style and Format* (bibliog. 1.1).

Designations of Time

10.38   *Other discussions.* For units of time (seconds, minutes, etc.), see 10.71. For numerical designations of dates and times of day, see 9.31, 9.34, 9.36, 9.38–41.

10.39   *Systems of chronology.* The following abbreviations are used in running text and elsewhere. Although these have traditionally appeared in small capitals (with or without periods), Chicago recommends full capitals without periods, in keeping with the general guidelines in this chapter (see 10.4; see also 10.8). The first four precede the year number; the others follow it. See also 9.35.

AD   anno Domini (in the year of [our] Lord)
AH   anno Hegirae (in the year of the Hegira); anno Hebraico (in the Hebrew year)
AM   anno mundi (in the year of the world) (not to be confused with ante meridiem; see 10.42)
AS   anno salutis (in the year of salvation)
AUC   ab urbe condita (from the founding of the city [Rome, in 753 BCE])

BC   before Christ
BCE   before the Common Era
BP   before the present
CE   Common Era
MYA   million years ago
YBP   years before the present

10.40   *Months.* Where space restrictions require that the names of months be abbreviated, one of the following systems is often used. The second and third, which take no periods, are used respectively in computer systems and indexes of periodical literature. In formal prose, Chicago prefers the first.

Jan.	*or*	Jan	*or*	Ja	July	*or*	Jul	*or*	Jl
Feb.	*or*	Feb	*or*	F	Aug.	*or*	Aug	*or*	Ag
Mar.	*or*	Mar	*or*	Mr	Sept.	*or*	Sep	*or*	S
Apr.	*or*	Apr	*or*	Ap	Oct.	*or*	Oct	*or*	O
May		May	*or*	My	Nov.	*or*	Nov	*or*	N
June	*or*	Jun	*or*	Je	Dec.	*or*	Dec	*or*	D

10.41   *Days of the week.* Where space restrictions require that days of the week be abbreviated, one of the following systems is often used. The second (common in computer code) and third use no periods. In formal prose, Chicago recommends the first.

Sun.	*or*	Sun	*or*	Su	Thurs.	*or*	Thu	*or*	Th
Mon.	*or*	Mon	*or*	M	Fri.	*or*	Fri	*or*	F
Tues.	*or*	Tue	*or*	Tu	Sat.	*or*	Sat	*or*	Sa
Wed.	*or*	Wed	*or*	W					

10.42   *Time of day.* The following abbreviations are used in text and elsewhere. Though these sometimes appear in small capitals (with or without periods), Chicago prefers the lowercase form, with periods, as being the most immediately intelligible. For further explanation and examples, see 9.38, 9.40. See also 10.4.

a.m.   *ante meridiem* (before noon)
m.   *meridies* (noon [rarely used])
p.m.   *post meridiem* (after noon)

The abbreviations *a.m.* and *p.m.* should not be used with *morning, afternoon, evening, night,* or *o'clock*. (See also 7.85, section 1, under *time*.)

10:30 a.m. *or* ten thirty in the morning
11:00 p.m. *or* eleven o'clock at night

Time zones, where needed, are usually given in parentheses—for example, 4:45 p.m. (CST).

GMT	Greenwich mean time		MST	mountain standard time
EST	eastern standard time		MDT	mountain daylight time
EDT	eastern daylight time		PST	Pacific standard time
CST	central standard time		PDT	Pacific daylight time
CDT	central daylight time			

Scholarly Abbreviations

10.43   *Scholarly abbreviations.* Scholarly abbreviations and symbols such as those listed in this section are normally confined to bibliographic references, glossaries, and other scholarly apparatus. If used in running text, they should be confined to parentheses or notes. Some can stand for several terms; only the terms likely to be encountered in scholarly works (mainly in the humanities) and serious nonfiction are included here. The choice between different abbreviations for one term (e.g., *L.* and *Lat.* for *Latin*) depends on the writer's preference, context, readership, and other factors; if in doubt, choose the longer form. Note that Latin abbreviations are normally set in roman. Note also that *ab, ad, et,* and other Latin terms that are complete words take no periods. See also 10.4, 7.53. For terms used more commonly in science and technology, see 10.52.

abbr.	abbreviated, -ion
ab init.	*ab initio,* from the beginning
abl.	ablative
abr.	abridged, abridgment
acc.	accusative
act.	active
add.	addendum
ad inf.	*ad infinitum*
ad init.	*ad initium,* at the beginning
ad int.	*ad interim,* in the intervening time
adj.	adjective
ad lib.	*ad libitum,* at will (often used without a period)
ad loc.	*ad locum,* at the place
adv.	adverb

aet. *or* aetat.	*aetatis*, aged
AFr.	Anglo-French
AN	Anglo-Norman
anon.	anonymous (see 14.79, 14.80)
app.	appendix
arch.	archaic
art.	article
AS	Anglo-Saxon
b.	born; brother
Bd.	*Band* (Ger.), volume
bib.	Bible, biblical
bibl.	*bibliotheca*, library
bibliog.	bibliography, -er, -ical
biog.	biography, -er, -ical
biol.	biology, -ist, -ical
bk.	book
c.	century; chapter (in law citations)
c. *or* cop.	copyright (see 10.44)
ca. *or* c.	*circa*, about, approximately (*ca.* preferred for greater clarity)
Cantab.	*Cantabrigiensis*, of Cambridge
cet. par.	*ceteris paribus*, other things being equal
cf.	*confer*, compare ("see, by way of comparison"; should not be used when *see* alone is meant)
chap. *or* ch.	chapter
col.	color (best spelled out); column
colloq.	colloquial, -ly, -ism
comp.	compiler (*pl.* comps.), compiled by
compar.	comparative
con.	*contra*, against
conj.	conjunction; conjugation
cons.	consonant
constr.	construction
cont.	continued
contr.	contraction
corr.	corrected
cp.	compare (rarely used; *cf.* is far more common)
d.	died; daughter
Dan.	Danish
dat.	dative
def.	definite; definition
dept.	department
deriv.	derivative
d.h.	*das heisst*, namely (used only in German text)

d.i.	*das ist*, that is (used only in German text)
dial.	dialect
dict.	dictionary
dim.	diminutive
dist.	district
div.	division; divorced
do.	ditto
dram. pers.	*dramatis personae*
Dr. u. Vrl.	*Druck und Verlag*, printer and publisher
DV	*Deo volente*, God willing; Douay Version (see 10.51)
ea.	each
ed.	editor (*pl.* eds.), edition, edited by (never add *by* after *ed.*: either "ed. Jane Doe" or "edited by Jane Doe"; use *eds.* only after, never before, the names of two or more editors; see examples throughout chapter 14)
EE	Early English
e.g.	*exempli gratia*, for example (not to be confused with *i.e.*)
ellipt.	elliptical, -ly
ency. *or* encyc.	encyclopedia
eng.	engineer, -ing
Eng.	English
engr.	engraved, -ing
enl.	enlarged
eq.	equation (*pl.* eqq. *or* eqs.; see also 10.44)
esp.	especially
et al.	*et alii* (or *et alia*), and others (normally used of persons; no period after *et*)
etc.	*et cetera*, and so forth (normally used of things)
et seq.	*et sequentes*, and the following
ex.	example (*pl.* exx. *or* exs.)
f. *or* fem.	feminine; female
f.	*für* (Ger.), for
fasc.	fascicle
ff.	and following (see 14.156)
fig.	figure
fl.	*floruit*, flourished (used with a date to indicate the productive years of a historical figure whose birth and death dates are unknown)
fol.	folio
Fr.	French
fr.	from
fut.	future
f.v.	*folio verso*, on the back of the page

Gael.	Gaelic
gen.	genitive; genus
geog.	geography, -er, -ical
geol.	geology, -er, -ical
geom.	geometry, -ical
ger.	gerund
Ger. *or* G.	German
Gk.	Greek
hist.	history, -ian, -ical
HQ	headquarters
ibid.	*ibidem*, in the same place (see 14.29)
id.	*idem*, the same (see 14.30)
i.e.	*id est*, that is (not to be confused with *e.g.*)
IE	Indo-European
ill.	illustrated, -ion, -or
imp. *or* imper.	imperative
incl.	including
indef.	indefinite
indic.	indicative
inf.	*infra*, below (best spelled out)
infin.	infinitive
in pr.	*in principio*, in the beginning
inst.	instant (this month); institute, -ion
instr.	instrumental
interj.	interjection
intrans.	intransitive
introd. *or* intro.	introduction
irreg.	irregular
It.	Italian
L.	Latin; left (in stage directions)
l.	left; line (*pl.* ll., but best spelled out to avoid confusion with numerals 1 and 11)
lang.	language
Lat. *or* L.	Latin
lit.	literally
loc.	locative
loc. cit.	*loco citato*, in the place cited (best avoided; see 14.31)
loq.	*loquitur*, he or she speaks
m.	male; married; measure (*pl.* mm.)
m. *or* masc.	masculine
marg.	margin, -al
math.	mathematics, -ical
MHG	Middle High German

mimeo.	mimeograph, -ed
misc.	miscellaneous
MM	Maelzel's metronome
m.m.	*mutatis mutandis*, necessary changes being made
Mod.E.	Modern English
MS (*pl.* MSS)	*manuscriptum* (pl. *manuscripta*), manuscript
mus.	museum; music, -al
n.	*natus*, born; note, footnote (*pl.* nn.); noun
nat.	national; natural
NB, n.b.	*nota bene*, take careful note (capitals are illogical but often used for emphasis)
n.d.	no date; not determined
neg.	negative
neut.	neuter
no. (*pl.* nos.)	number
nom.	nominative
non obs.	*non obstante*, notwithstanding
non seq.	*non sequitur*, it does not follow
n.p.	no place; no publisher; no page
n.s.	new series
NS	New Style (dates)
ob.	*obiit*, died
obs.	obsolete
occas.	occasional, -ly
OE	Old English
OFr.	Old French
OHG	Old High German
ON	Old Norse
op. cit.	*opere citato*, in the work cited (best avoided; see 14.31)
o.s.	old series
OS	Old Style (dates)
Oxon.	*Oxoniensis*, of Oxford
p.	page (*pl.* pp.); past (*also* pa.)
para. *or* par.	paragraph (see 10.44)
pass.	passive
pa. t.	past tense
path.	pathology, -ist, -ical
perf.	perfect
perh.	perhaps
pers.	person, -al
pers. comm.	personal communication
pl.	plate (best avoided; see 3.9); plural

p.p.	past participle
ppl.	participle
PPS	*post postscriptum*, a later postscript
prep.	preposition
pres.	present
pron.	pronoun
pro tem.	*pro tempore*, for the time being (often used without a period)
prox.	*proximo*, next month
PS	*postscriptum*, postscript
pt.	part
pub.	publication, publisher, published by
QED	*quod erat demonstrandum*, which was to be demonstrated
quar. *or* quart.	quarter, -ly
q.v.	*quod vide*, which see (used only in a cross-reference *after* the term referred to; cf. *s.v.*)
R.	*rex*, king; *regina*, queen; right (in stage directions)
r.	right; recto; reigned
refl.	reflexive
repr.	reprint, -ed
rev.	review; revised, revised by, revision (never add *by* after *rev.*: either "rev. Jane Doe" or "revised by Jane Doe")
RIP	*requiescat in pace*, may he or she rest in peace
s.	son; substantive, -ival
s.a.	*sine anno*, without year; *sub anno*, under the year
sc.	scene; *scilicet*, namely; *sculpsit*, carved by
Sc. *or* Scot.	Scottish
s.d.	*sine die*, without setting a day for reconvening; stage direction
sd.	sound
sec.	section (see 10.44); *secundum*, according to
ser.	series
s.h.	speech heading
sing. *or* sg.	singular
s.l.	*sine loco*, without place (of publication)
s.n.	*sine nomine*, without name (of publisher)
sociol.	sociology, -ist, -ical
Sp.	Spanish
s.p.	speech prefix
st.	stanza
subj.	subject, -ive; subjunctive
subst. *or* s.	substantive, -al
sup.	*supra*, above
superl.	superlative

supp. *or* suppl.	supplement
s.v. (*pl.* s.vv.)	*sub verbo*, *sub voce*, under the word (used in a cross-reference *before* the term referred to; cf. *q.v.*)
syn.	synonym, -ous
t.	*tome* (Fr.), *tomo* (Sp.), volume
techn.	technical, -ly
theol.	theology, -ian, -ical
t.p.	title page
trans.	translated by, translator(s) (never add *by* after *trans.*: either "trans. Jane Doe" or "translated by Jane Doe"); transitive
treas.	treasurer
TS	typescript
ult.	*ultimatus*, ultimate, last; *ultimo*, last month
univ.	university
usw.	*und so weiter*, and so forth (equivalent to *etc.*; used only in German text)
ut sup.	*ut supra*, as above
v.	verse (*pl.* vv.); verso; versus; *vide*, see
v. *or* vb.	verb
v.i.	*verbum intransitivum*, intransitive verb; *vide infra*, see below
viz.	*videlicet*, namely
voc.	vocative
vol.	volume
vs. *or* v.	versus (in legal contexts use *v.*)
v.t.	*verbum transitivum*, transitive verb
yr.	year; your

10.44   *A few scholarly symbols.* The symbols below often appear in bibliographies and other scholarly apparatus rather than their equivalent abbreviations (see 10.43).

©	copyright
=	equals, the same as (for examples, see 10.49)
¶ (*pl.* ¶¶)	paragraph
§ (*pl.* §§)	section

Biblical Abbreviations

10.45   *Biblical abbreviations—additional resources.* For authoritative guidance in many biblical areas not covered here, consult *The SBL Handbook of Style* (bibliog. 1.1). For citing scriptural references in notes and bibliographies, see 14.252–55.

10.46 *Books of the Bible in text and notes.* In running text, books of the Bible are generally spelled out. See also 9.27.

> The opening chapters of Ephesians constitute a sermon on love.
> Jeremiah, chapters 42–44, records the flight of the Jews to Egypt.
> According to Genesis 1:27, God created man in his own image.

In parenthetical citations or in notes, or where many such references appear in the text, abbreviations are appropriate.

> My concordance lists five instances of the word *nourish*: Gen. 47:12, Ruth 4:15, Isa. 44:14, Acts 7:21, and 1 Tim. 4:6.

10.47 *Biblical abbreviations and short forms—an overview.* For traditional abbreviations and commonly used shorter forms for books of the Bible, see 10.48, 10.49, 10.50. (Note that the shorter forms have no periods.) The listing is alphabetical, both for easier reference and because the order varies slightly in the Jewish, Protestant, and Roman Catholic versions of the Bible. Alternative names for the same books are indicated by an equals sign (see 10.44).

10.48 *The Old Testament.* See also 10.47.

Amos *or* Am	Amos
1 Chron. *or* 1 Chr	1 Chronicles
2 Chron. *or* 2 Chr	2 Chronicles
Dan. *or* Dn	Daniel
Deut. *or* Dt	Deuteronomy
Eccles. *or* Eccl	Ecclesiastes
Esther *or* Est	Esther
Exod. *or* Ex	Exodus
Ezek. *or* Ez	Ezekiel
Ezra *or* Ezr	Ezra
Gen. *or* Gn	Genesis
Hab. *or* Hb	Habakkuk
Hag. *or* Hg	Haggai
Hosea *or* Hos	Hosea
Isa. *or* Is	Isaiah
Jer. *or* Jer	Jeremiah
Job *or* Jb	Job

Joel *or* Jl	Joel
Jon. *or* Jon	Jonah
Josh. *or* Jo	Joshua
Judg. *or* Jgs	Judges
1 Kings *or* 1 Kgs	1 Kings
2 Kings *or* 2 Kgs	2 Kings
Lam. *or* Lam	Lamentations
Lev. *or* Lv	Leviticus
Mal. *or* Mal	Malachi
Mic. *or* Mi	Micah
Nah. *or* Na	Nahum
Neh. *or* Neh	Nehemiah
Num. *or* Nm	Numbers
Obad. *or* Ob	Obadiah
Prov. *or* Prv	Proverbs
Ps. (*pl.* Pss.) *or* Ps (*pl.* Pss)	Psalms
Ruth *or* Ru	Ruth
1 Sam. *or* 1 Sm	1 Samuel
2 Sam. *or* 2 Sm	2 Samuel
Song of Sol. *or* Sg	Song of Solomon (= Song of Songs)
Zech. *or* Zec	Zechariah
Zeph. *or* Zep	Zephaniah

10.49   *The Apocrypha.* The books of the Apocrypha are accepted in Roman Catholic versions of the Bible, though not in Jewish and Protestant versions. Some are not complete in themselves but are continuations of books listed in 10.48. Where no abbreviation is given, the full form should be used. See also 10.47.

Bar. *or* Bar	Baruch
Ecclus.	Ecclesiasticus (= Sirach)
1 Esd.	1 Esdras
2 Esd.	2 Esdras
Jth. *or* Jdt	Judith
1 Macc. *or* 1 Mc	1 Maccabees
2 Macc. *or* 2 Mc	2 Maccabees
Pr. of Man.	Prayer of Manasses (= Manasseh)
Sir. *or* Sir	Sirach (= Ecclesiasticus)
Sus.	Susanna
Tob. *or* Tb	Tobit
Ws	Wisdom (= Wisdom of Solomon)
Wisd. of Sol.	Wisdom of Solomon (= Wisdom)

10.50   *The New Testament.* See also 10.47.

Acts	Acts of the Apostles
Apoc.	Apocalypse (= Revelation)
Col. *or* Col	Colossians
1 Cor. *or* 1 Cor	1 Corinthians
2 Cor. *or* 2 Cor	2 Corinthians
Eph. *or* Eph	Ephesians
Gal. *or* Gal	Galatians
Heb. *or* Heb	Hebrews
James *or* Jas	James
John *or* Jn	John (Gospel)
1 John *or* 1 Jn	1 John (Epistle)
2 John *or* 2 Jn	2 John (Epistle)
3 John *or* 3 Jn	3 John (Epistle)
Jude	Jude
Luke *or* Lk	Luke
Mark *or* Mk	Mark
Matt. *or* Mt	Matthew
1 Pet. *or* 1 Pt	1 Peter
2 Pet. *or* 2 Pt	2 Peter
Phil. *or* Phil	Philippians
Philem. *or* Phlm	Philemon
Rev. *or* Rv	Revelation (= Apocalypse)
Rom. *or* Rom	Romans
1 Thess. *or* 1 Thes	1 Thessalonians
2 Thess. *or* 2 Thes	2 Thessalonians
1 Tim. *or* 1 Tm	1 Timothy
2 Tim. *or* 2 Tm	2 Timothy
Titus *or* Ti	Titus

10.51   *Versions and sections of the Bible.* Versions and sections of the Bible are usually abbreviated in the form of initialisms, especially when they consist of more than one word.

Apoc.	Apocrypha
ARV	American Revised Version
ASV	American Standard Version
AT	American Translation
AV	Authorized (King James) Version
CEV	Contemporary English Version
DV	Douay Version

ERV	English Revised Version
EV	English version(s)
HB	Hebrew Bible
JB	Jerusalem Bible
LXX	Septuagint
MT	Masoretic Text
NAB	New American Bible
NEB	New English Bible
NJB	New Jerusalem Bible
NRSV	New Revised Standard Version
NT	New Testament
OT	Old Testament
RSV	Revised Standard Version
RV	Revised Version
Syr.	Syriac
Vulg.	Vulgate
WEB	World English Bible

Technology and Science

10.52 *Miscellaneous technical abbreviations.* The following list, which cannot aim to be comprehensive, includes some abbreviations used in various branches of the physical and biological sciences and in technical writing. Some, such as *PC* and *DVD*, are also in wide general use. Abbreviations used in highly specialized areas have generally been omitted, as have most adjectival forms. Many of the abbreviations for units are identical to or compatible with those used in the International System of Units, or SI (see 10.54–62). Periods are omitted in any context (compare 10.4). The capitalization given below, based largely on current usage, sometimes departs from that used in *Merriam-Webster's Collegiate Dictionary* (see bibliog. 3.1). The first letter of abbreviations derived from proper names (e.g., A [ampere], V, Wb, and the C in °C) are usually capitalized (though the spelled-out term is lowercased—unless it follows the word "degree," as in "degree[s] Celsius"), as are the prefix letters for *mega-* (M), *giga-* (G), *tera-* (T), and so on (see 10.57). Plurals do not add an *s* (10 A, 5 ha). With few exceptions (mainly abbreviations with degree symbols), a space usually appears between a numeral and an abbreviation (22 m *but* 36°C); see also 10.61. For units with repeated quantities, see 9.17. For statistical abbreviations, see 10.53. For traditional US units of measure, see 10.67–71. See also 9.16.

A	ampere; adenine (in genetic code)
Å	angstrom
ac	alternating current
AF	audio frequency
Ah	ampere-hour
AM	amplitude modulation
ASCII	American Standard Code for Information Interchange
atm	atmosphere, -ic
av *or* avdp	avoirdupois
bar	bar (no abbreviation)
Bé *or* °Bé	degree Baumé
bhp	brake horsepower
BMI	body mass index
bp	boiling point; base pair
bps	bits per second
Bps	bytes per second
Bq	becquerel
Btu	British thermal unit
C	coulomb; cytosine (in genetic code)
°C	degree Celsius
cal	calorie
Cal	kilocalorie (in nonscientific contexts; *see also* kcal)
cc	cubic centimeter (in clinical contexts; *see also* cm^3)
cd	candela
CD	compact disc
cgs	centimeter-gram-second system (SI)
Ci	curie
cm	centimeter
cM	centimorgan
cm^3	cubic centimeter (in scientific contexts; *see also* cc)
cp	candlepower
CP	chemically pure
cps *or* c/s	cycles per second
CPU	central processing unit
cu	cubic
d	day; deuteron
Da	dalton
dB	decibel
dc	direct current
DNS	domain name system
DOI	Digital Object Identifier (a registered trademark)
DOS	disk operating system
dpi	dots per inch

DVD	digital versatile (*or* video) disc
dyn	dyne
emf	electromotive force
erg	erg (no abbreviation)
eV	electron volt
F	farad
°F	degree Fahrenheit
FM	frequency modulation
fp	freezing point
FTP	file transfer protocol
g	gram; gas
G	guanine (in genetic code)
Gb	gigabit
GB	gigabyte
Gbps	gigabits per second
GeV	10^9 electron volts
GIF	graphic interchange format
GIS	geographic information system
GPS	global positioning system
Gy	gigayear; gray (joule per kilogram)
H	henry (*pl.* henries)
h	hour; helion
ha	hectare
hp	horsepower
HTML	hypertext markup language
HTTP	hypertext transfer protocol
Hz	hertz
IP	Internet protocol
IR	infrared
IU	international unit
J	joule
JPEG	*from* Joint Photographic Experts Group (file format)
K	kelvin (no degree symbol used); kilobyte (in commercial contexts)
kat	katal
kb	kilobar (DNA); kilobase (RNA)
kb *or* kbit	kilobit
KB *or* K	kilobyte
Kbps	kilobits per second
kc	kilocycle
kcal	kilocalorie (in scientific contexts; *see also* Cal)
KE	kinetic energy
kg	kilogram

kHz	kilohertz
kJ	kilojoule
km	kilometer
kmh *or* kmph	kilometers per hour
kn	knot (nautical mph)
kW	kilowatt
kWh	kilowatt-hour
L	liter (capitalized to avoid confusion with numeral 1)
lm	lumen
lx	lux
m	meter
M	molar; metal
Mb	megabase; megabit
MB	megabyte
Mbps	megabits per second
Mc	megacycle
mCi	millicurie
MeV	million electron volts
mg	milligram
MIDI	musical instrument digital interface
mks	meter-kilogram-second system (SI)
mL	milliliter
mol	mole
mp	melting point
MPEG	*from* Moving Pictures Experts Group (file format)
mpg	miles per gallon
mph	miles per hour
MP3	*from* MPEG-1 Audio Layer 3 (file format)
MP4	*from* MPEG-4 Part 14 (file format)
N	newton; number (often italic; see also 10.53)
neg	negative
nm	nanometer; nautical mile
Ω	ohm
OCR	optical character recognition
OS	operating system
Pa	pascal
pc	parsec
PC	personal computer
PDF	portable document format
PE	potential energy
pF	picofarad
pH	negative log of hydrogen ion concentration (measure of acidity)
PNG	*from* portable network graphics (file format)

pos	positive
ppb	parts per billion
ppm	parts per million
ppt	parts per trillion; precipitate
R	electrical resistance
°R	degree Réaumur
rad	radian
RAM	random-access memory
RF	radio frequency
ROM	read-only memory
rpm *or* r/min	revolutions per minute
s	second
S	siemens
SGML	standard generalized markup language
soln	solution
sp gr	specific gravity
sq	square
sr	steradian
std	standard
STP	standard temperature and pressure
Sv	sievert
t	metric ton (10^3 kg); triton (nucleus of tritium)
T	tesla; thymine (in genetic code)
Tb	terabit
TB	terabyte
Tbps	terabits per second
TCP/IP	transmission-control protocol/Internet protocol
temp	temperature
U	uracil (in genetic code)
UCS	universal character set
URI	uniform resource identifier
URL	uniform resource locator
USB	universal serial bus
UV	ultraviolet
V	volt
W	watt
Wb	weber
wt	weight
w/v	weight per volume
w/w	weight per weight
XML	extensible markup language
y	year
Z	atomic number (often italic)

10.53   *Statistics.* The following abbreviations are used in statistical material, especially in tables. They are often italicized. See also 12.57, 12.58, and table 12.3.

ANCOVA	analysis of covariance
ANOVA	analysis of variance
CI	confidence interval
CL	confidence limit
CLT	central limit theorem
df, DF, *or* dof	degrees of freedom
GLIM	generalized linear model
IQR	interquartile range
LS	least squares
MLE	maximum likelihood estimate
MS	mean square
N	number (of population)
n	number (of sample)
ns	not (statistically) significant
OLS	ordinary least squares
OR	odds ratio
p	probability
r	bivariate correlation coefficient
R	multivariate correlation coefficient
R^2	coefficient of determination
RMS	root mean square
sd *or* SD	standard deviation
se *or* SE	standard error
sem *or* SEM	standard error of the mean
SS	sum of squares
SSE	error sum of squares
SST	total sum of squares
WLLN	weak law of large numbers
$\bar{x}$ *or* $\bar{X}$	mean value
χ^2	chi-square distribution

The International System of Units

10.54   *SI units.* The International System of Units (*Système international d'unités*, abbreviated internationally as SI) is an expanded version of the metric system. It is in general use among the world's scientists and in many other areas. The following paragraphs discuss only the basics. For the latest official guidelines, consult *The International System of Units*, a brochure published in English and French by the Bureau International des Poids et Mesures and available online. For further guidance, see Ambler Thompson and Barry N. Taylor, *Guide for the Use of the International System of Units* (bibliog. 2.4); and *Scientific Style and Format* (bibliog. 1.1).

10.55 *SI units—form.* No periods are used after any of the SI symbols for units, and the same symbols are used for both the singular and the plural. Most symbols are lowercased; exceptions are those that stand for units derived from proper names (e.g., A, for *ampere*) and those that must be distinguished from similar lowercased forms. All units are lowercased in their spelled-out form except for degree Celsius (°C).

10.56 *Base SI units.* There are seven fundamental, or base, SI units. Note that although *weight* and *mass* are usually measured in the same units, they are not interchangeable. Weight is a force due to gravity that depends on an object's mass. Note also that no degree sign is used with the symbol K.

QUANTITY	UNIT	SYMBOL
length	meter	m
mass	kilogram	kg
time	second	s
electric current	ampere	A
thermodynamic temperature	kelvin	K
amount of substance	mole	mol
luminous intensity	candela	cd

Not to be confused with the symbols for base *units* are the corresponding symbols for base *quantities*. These symbols, which represent variable quantities, appear in italic type (e.g., l, length; m, mass; t, time).

10.57 *SI prefixes.* Prefixes, representing a power of ten, are added to the name of a base unit to allow notation of very large or very small numerical values. The units so formed are called multiples and submultiples of SI units. For example, a kilometer, or km, is equal to a thousand meters (or 10^3 m), and a millisecond, or ms, is equal to one-thousandth of a second (or 10^{-3} s). The following prefixes, with their symbols, are used in the international system. Note that in three cases the final vowel of an SI prefix is omitted: kΩ, kilohm (*not* kiloohm); MΩ, megohm (*not* megaohm); ha, hectare (*not* hectoare).

FACTOR	PREFIX	SYMBOL	FACTOR	PREFIX	SYMBOL
10^{24}	yotta	Y	10^{-1}	deci	d
10^{21}	zetta	Z	10^{-2}	centi	c
10^{18}	exa	E	10^{-3}	milli	m
10^{15}	peta	P	10^{-6}	micro	μ
10^{12}	tera	T	10^{-9}	nano	n
10^9	giga	G	10^{-12}	pico	p
10^6	mega	M	10^{-15}	femto	f
10^3	kilo	k	10^{-18}	atto	a
10^2	hecto	h	10^{-21}	zepto	z
10^1	deka	da	10^{-24}	yocto	y

These prefixes should not be used to indicate powers of two (as in the field of electrical technology, or computing). If binary multiples must be used, the first two letters of the SI prefixes must be followed by *bi*, to form *kibi-* (Ki), *mebi-* (Mi), *gibi-* (Gi), *tebi-* (Ti), *pebi-* (Pi), and *exbi-* (Ei). See also 9.11.

10.58 **Grams.** Although for historical reasons the kilogram rather than the gram was chosen as the base unit, prefixes are applied to the term *gram*—megagram (Mg), milligram (mg), nanogram (ng), and so forth.

10.59 **Derived units expressed algebraically.** Derived units are expressed algebraically in terms of base units or other derived units (see also 10.60).

DERIVED UNIT	IN TERMS OF SI BASE UNITS
square meter	m^2
cubic meter	m^3
meter per second	m/s
meter per second squared	m/s^2
kilogram per cubic meter	kg/m^3

10.60 **Derived units with special names.** Certain derived units have special names and symbols. Several of the most common—hertz (Hz), volt (V), watt (W), and so forth—are listed in 10.52. These are used in algebraic expressions to denote further derived units. A few are listed below. Note the raised dot in the second expression.

DERIVED UNIT	SYMBOL	IN TERMS OF SI BASE UNITS
joule per kelvin	J/K	$m^2 \, kg \, s^{-2} \, K^{-1}$
newton meter	N · m	$m^2 \, kg \, s^{-2}$
newton per meter	N/m	$kg \, s^{-2}$

A derived unit can often be expressed in different ways. For example, the weber may be expressed either as Wb or, in another context, in terms of the volt second (V · s).

10.61 *SI units and abbreviations—spacing.* Only numbers between 0.1 and 1,000 should be used to express the quantity of any SI unit. Thus 12,000 meters is expressed as 12 km (not 12 000 m), and 0.003 cubic centimeters as 3 mm³ (not 0.003 cm³). (For the use of spaces rather than commas between groups of digits in SI units, see 9.56.) In SI usage as in general usage, a space usually appears between the numeral and any abbreviation or symbol; however, contrary to general usage, SI usage stipulates a space before a percentage sign (%) or before a degree symbol used with a C (compare the advice toward the end of 10.52). SI usage also stipulates a space between expressions of degrees, minutes, and seconds (compare 10.37). Many publications do not observe these exceptions, and Chicago does not require them in its publications.

22° 14′ 33″ but 22 °C   0.5 % (not 0.5%)

10.62 *Non-SI units accepted for use.* Certain widely used units such as liter (L, capitalized to avoid confusion with the numeral 1), metric ton (t), and hour (h) are not officially part of the international system but are accepted for use within the system.

Astronomy

10.63 *Astronomy—additional resources.* Astronomers and astrophysicists employ the international system of measure supplemented with special terminology and abbreviations. The paragraphs in this section offer a minimum of examples for the generalist. Additional guidelines may be found at the website of the International Astronomical Union.

10.64 *Celestial coordinates.* Right ascension, abbreviated RA or α, is given in hours, minutes, and seconds (abbreviations set as superscripts) of sidereal time. Declination, abbreviated δ, is given in degrees, minutes, and seconds (using the degree symbol, prime, and double prime) of arc north (marked + or left unmarked) or south (marked −) of the celestial equator. Note the abbreviations (set as superscripts) and symbols used.

$14^h6^m7^s$ $-49°8′22″$

Decimal fractions of the basic units are indicated as shown.

$14^h6^m7^s.2$ $+34°.26$

10.65   *Some other astronomical abbreviations.*

AU *or* ua	astronomical unit (mean earth–sun distance)
lt-yr	light-year (9.46×10^{12} km)
pc	parsec (parallax second: 3.084×10^{13} km)
kpc	10^3 pc
Mpc	10^6 pc
UT *or* UTC	universal time

Chemical Elements

10.66   *Naming conventions for chemical elements.* The International Union of Pure and Applied Chemistry (IUPAC) is the recognized body that formally approves element names. Each element bears a number (reflecting the number of protons in its nucleus) as well as a name—as in "element 106," also known as seaborgium. This number is an important identifier in cases where formal names are in dispute; between 1995 and 1997, for example, the American Chemical Society and IUPAC adopted different names for some of the same elements. The differences were reconciled, and the list that follows reflects names and symbols approved by IUPAC. Names for undiscovered or unconfirmed elements (as of publication, 111, roentgenium, was the last confirmed element) are provisionally assigned using Latin for the digits of their atomic number (e.g., *ununbium*, one-one-two, for element 112). The elements in the following list are arranged in alphabetical order by common name. If the symbol is based on a term other than the common name—for example, Sb (*stibium*) for antimony—the term is added in parentheses. Although the names of elements are always lowercased, the symbols all have an initial capital. No periods are used. In specialized works, the abbreviations commonly appear in text as well as in tables, notes, and so forth. See also 8.148, 8.149.

89	Ac	actinium	33	As	arsenic
13	Al	aluminum (US),	85	At	astatine
		aluminium (IUPAC)	56	Ba	barium
95	Am	americium	97	Bk	berkelium
51	Sb	antimony (*stibium*)	4	Be	beryllium
18	Ar	argon	83	Bi	bismuth

107	Bh	bohrium	12	Mg	magnesium
5	B	boron	25	Mn	manganese
35	Br	bromine	109	Mt	meitnerium
48	Cd	cadmium	101	Md	mendelevium
20	Ca	calcium	80	Hg	mercury (*hydrargy-*
98	Cf	californium			*rum*)
6	C	carbon	42	Mo	molybdenum
58	Ce	cerium	60	Nd	neodymium
55	Cs	cesium	10	Ne	neon
17	Cl	chlorine	93	Np	neptunium
24	Cr	chromium	28	Ni	nickel
27	Co	cobalt	41	Nb	niobium
29	Cu	copper	7	N	nitrogen
96	Cm	curium	102	No	nobelium
110	Ds	darmstadtium	76	Os	osmium
105	Db	dubnium	8	O	oxygen
66	Dy	dysprosium	46	Pd	palladium
99	Es	einsteinium	15	P	phosphorus
68	Er	erbium	78	Pt	platinum
63	Eu	europium	94	Pu	plutonium
100	Fm	fermium	84	Po	polonium
9	F	fluorine	19	K	potassium (*kalium*)
87	Fr	francium	59	Pr	praseodymium
64	Gd	gadolinium	61	Pm	promethium
31	Ga	gallium	91	Pa	protactinium
32	Ge	germanium	88	Ra	radium
79	Au	gold (*aurum*)	86	Rn	radon
72	Hf	hafnium	75	Re	rhenium
108	Hs	hassium	45	Rh	rhodium
2	He	helium	111	Rg	roentgenium
67	Ho	holmium	37	Rb	rubidium
1	H	hydrogen	44	Ru	ruthenium
49	In	indium	104	Rf	rutherfordium
53	I	iodine	62	Sm	samarium
77	Ir	iridium	21	Sc	scandium
26	Fe	iron (*ferrum*)	106	Sg	seaborgium
36	Kr	krypton	34	Se	selenium
57	La	lanthanum	14	Si	silicon
103	Lr	lawrencium	47	Ag	silver (*argentum*)
82	Pb	lead (*plumbum*)	11	Na	sodium (*natrium*)
3	Li	lithium	38	Sr	strontium
71	Lu	lutetium	16	S	sulfur

73	Ta	tantalum	118	Uuo	ununoctium
43	Tc	technetium	115	Uup	ununpentium
52	Te	tellurium	114	Uuq	ununquadium
65	Tb	terbium	117	Uus	ununseptium
81	Tl	thallium	113	Uut	ununtrium
90	Th	thorium	92	U	uranium
69	Tm	thulium	23	V	vanadium
50	Sn	tin (*stannum*)	54	Xe	xenon
22	Ti	titanium	70	Yb	ytterbium
74	W	tungsten (*wolfram*)	39	Y	yttrium
112	Uub	ununbium	30	Zn	zinc
116	Uuh	ununhexium	40	Zr	zirconium

US Measure

10.67 *Periods with abbreviations of US measure.* In the rare instances in which abbreviations for US units of measure are used in scientific copy, they are usually set without periods; in nonscientific contexts, periods are customary. See also 10.4.

10.68 *Plural forms for abbreviations of US measure.* Abbreviations of US units of measure, like their scientific counterparts, are identical in the singular and the plural. See also 10.71.

10 yd.   5 lb.   8 sq. mi.

Note that the unit of measure in such expressions as 0.5 yd. and 1.5 yd. is generally pronounced as if it were plural (i.e., point five yards; one point five yards).

10.69 *Length, area, and volume.* In the following examples, note that the proper symbols for foot and inch are prime (') and double prime ("), *not* the single (') and double (") quotation mark:

LENGTH		AREA		VOLUME	
in. *or* "	inch	sq. in.	square inch	cu. in.	cubic inch
ft. *or* '	foot	sq. ft.	square foot	cu. ft.	cubic foot
yd.	yard	sq. yd.	square yard	cu. yd.	cubic yard
rd.	rod	sq. rd.	square rod		
mi.	mile	sq. mi.	square mile		

There is no space in such expressions as the following (for *6 ft. 1 in.*):

6'1"

Exponents are sometimes used with abbreviations to designate area or volume, but only when no ambiguity can occur.

425 ft.^{2} (= 425 sq. ft. *not* 425 ft. by 425 ft.)   638 ft.^{3} (= 638 cu. ft.)

10.70 *Weight and capacity.* The US system comprises three systems of weight and mass: avoirdupois (the common system), troy (used mainly by jewelers), and apothecaries' measure. Although confusion is unlikely, an abbreviation can, if necessary, be referred to the appropriate system thus: lb. av., lb. t., lb. ap. Also, the systems of capacity measure used in the United States and the British Commonwealth differ (an American pint being more than three ounces smaller than a British pint, for example), but the same abbreviations are used.

WEIGHT OR MASS		LIQUID MEASURE	
gr.	grain	min. *or* ℳ	minim
s.	scruple	fl. Dr. or f. ʒ	fluid dram
dr.	dram	fl. oz. or f. ℥	fluid ounce
dwt.	pennyweight	gi.	gill
oz.	ounce	pt.	pint
lb. *or* #	pound	qt.	quart
cwt.	hundredweight	gal.	gallon
tn.	ton	bbl.	barrel

DRY MEASURE	
pt.	pint
qt.	quart
pk.	peck
bu.	bushel

As with length and so forth, abbreviations do not change in the plural.

12 gal.   3 pt.

10.71 *Time.* The following abbreviations, though not limited to the US system of measure, are used mainly in nontechnical contexts:

sec.	second	h. *or* hr.	hour	mo.	month
min.	minute	d. *or* day	day	yr.	year

In nontechnical writing, the plurals of these abbreviations, unlike those of length, area, weight, and the like, are often formed by adding an *s*.

5 secs.   12 hrs. *or* 12 h.   15 yrs.

Business and Commerce

10.72   *Commercial terms—some examples.* Like many other abbreviations in non-scientific contexts, periods for abbreviations of commercial terms are normally used in lowercased forms (see 10.4). See also 10.43–44, 10.67–71. For company names, see 10.22.

acct.	account, -ant
agt.	agent
a.k.a.	also known as
amt.	amount
AP	amounts payable
APR	annual percentage rate
AR	amounts receivable
ASAP	as soon as possible
att.	attached, -ment
attn.	attention
a.v. *or* AV	ad valorem
bal.	balance
bbl.	barrel(s)
bcc	blind carbon copy *or* blind copy, -ies
bdl. *or* bdle.	bundle
bl.	bale(s)
BS	bill of sale
bu.	bushel(s)
c. *or* ct.	cent
cc	carbon copy *or* copy, -ies
c.l. *or* CL	carload
c/o	in care of
COD	cash on delivery
COLA	cost-of-living adjustment
CPI	consumer price index
CPM	cost per thousand (*mille*)
cr.	credit, -or
ctn.	carton
cttee. *or* comm.	committee

d/b/a	doing business as
dis.	discount
dist.	district
distr.	distributor, -ion
DJIA	Dow Jones Industrial Average
doz.	dozen
dr.	debtor
dstn.	destination
ea.	each
EEO	equal employment opportunity
EOE	equal opportunity employer
EOM	end of month
exec.	executive
f.a.s. *or* FAS	free alongside ship
f.o.b. *or* FOB	free on board
FY	fiscal year
GAAP	generally accepted accounting principles
GL	general ledger
GM	general manager; genetically modified
gro.	gross
inst.	instant (this month)
inv.	invoice
IPO	initial public offering
JIT	just in time
LBO	leveraged buyout
LCL	less-than-carload lot
LIFO	last in, first out
M and A *or* M&A	mergers and acquisitions
mdse.	merchandise
mfg.	manufacturing
mfr.	manufacturer
mgmt.	management
mgr.	manager
MO	mail order; money order
msg.	message
mtg.	meeting
mtge.	mortgage
NA *or* n/a	not applicable; not available
NGO	nongovernmental organization
nt. wt.	net weight
OJT	on-the-job training
OS	operating system; out of stock
OTC	over the counter

P and H *or* P&H	postage and handling
pd.	paid
pkg.	package
POE	port of embarkation; port of entry
POP	point of purchase
POS	point of sale; point of service
PP	parcel post
ppd.	postpaid; prepaid
pr.	pair
QA	quality assurance
Q&A	question and answer
QC	quality control
qtr.	quarter
qty.	quantity
®	registered trademark (see 8.152)
recd. *or* rec'd	received
S and H *or* S&H	shipping and handling
SM	unregistered service mark
std.	standard
TBA	to be announced
TBD	to be determined
™	unregistered trademark (see 8.152)
treas.	treasurer, -y
ult.	ultimo (last month)
VAT	value-added tax
whsle.	wholesale

11   *Foreign Languages*

Overview

11.1   *Scope and organization.* This chapter provides guidelines for presenting foreign-language text in English-language publications. These guidelines are general: authors or editors working with languages in which they are not fluent should seek additional guidance from someone who is. More than two dozen languages are covered, with those languages that commonly appear and those that present complex problems being treated most fully. The chapter begins with some typographic matters—capitalization, italics, and so forth—that apply to most of the languages discussed (see 11.3–8). It then deals with languages using the Latin alphabet; transliterated (or romanized) languages; classical Greek; Old English and Middle English; and American Sign Language. Individual languages or groups of languages are presented in alphabetical order within their particular sections.

11.2   *Unicode.* Many of the letters and symbols required by the world's languages are included in a widely used standard for character encoding called Unicode. The Unicode standard (published as a book of the same name, by the Unicode Consortium; bibliog. 2.7), which is widely supported by modern operating systems and browsers and many other applications (including many word processors) and is required by such standards as XML, assigns a unique identifying hexadecimal number (or code point) and description to tens of thousands of characters. Even fonts with Unicode character mapping, however, typically support only a subset of the Unicode character set. For this reason, it is desirable to determine at the outset which characters will be needed for a publication. Table 11.1 lists special characters, with Unicode numbers and abbreviated descriptions, needed for each of the languages treated in this chapter that use the Latin alphabet. Table 11.2 lists special characters that may be needed for certain transliterated languages. For Russian (Cyrillic) and Greek characters, see tables 11.3, 11.4, and 11.5. Unicode numbers mentioned in text should be prefixed by U+ (e.g., U+00E0 for *à*).

Titles and Other Proper Names

11.3   *Capitalization of foreign titles.* For foreign titles of works, whether these appear in text, notes, or bibliographies, Chicago recommends a simple rule: capitalize only the words that would be capitalized in normal prose—first word of title and subtitle and all proper nouns. That is, use *sentence style* (see 8.156). This rule applies equally to titles using the Latin alphabet and to transliterated titles. For examples, see 14.107. For exceptions, see 14.193, 11.24, 11.42. For variations in French, see 11.30.

11.4   *Punctuation of foreign titles.* When a foreign title is included in an English-language context, the following changes are permissible: a period (or, more rarely, a semicolon) between title and subtitle may be changed to a colon (and the first word of the subtitle may be capitalized); guillemets (« »; see 11.32, 11.79) may be changed to standard quotation marks; and any space between a word and a mark of punctuation that follows may be eliminated. Commas should not be inserted (even in a series or before dates) or deleted, nor should any other mark of punctuation be added or deleted. See also 8.163.

11.5   *Italic versus roman type.* Titles of works in languages that use the Latin alphabet (including transliterated titles) are set in italic or roman type according to the principles set forth in 8.154–95—for example, books and periodicals italic; poems and other short works roman.

> Stendhal's *Le rouge et le noir* was required reading in my senior year.
> We picked up a copy of the *Neue Zürcher Zeitung* to read on the train.
> She published her article in the *Annales de démographie historique*.
> Strains of the German carol "Es ist ein' Ros' entsprungen" reached our ears.
> Miguel Hernández's poem "Casida del sediento" has been translated as "Lament of the Thirsting Man."

11.6   *Foreign titles with English translation.* When the title of a foreign work is mentioned in text, an English gloss often follows in parentheses (see 6.93). If the translation has not been published, the English should be capitalized sentence-style (as in the first example below; see 8.156) and should appear neither in italics nor within quotation marks. A published translation, however, is capitalized headline-style (as in the second example; see 8.157) and appears in italics or quotation marks depending on the type of work (see 8.154–95). For translations of foreign titles in notes and bibliographies, see 14.108. See also 11.7.

> Leonardo Fioravanti's *Compendio de i secreti rationali* (Compendium of rational secrets) became a best seller.
> Proust's *À la recherche du temps perdu* (*Remembrance of Things Past*) was the subject of her dissertation.

11.7   *Translated titles.* Whether to use the original title of a foreign work or the translated title when discussing a work in text depends on context and readership. In a general work, titles that are widely known in their English translation could be cited in English first, with the original following in parentheses; in some cases, the original might be omitted entirely. Some authors prefer to cite all foreign titles in an English form, whether or not they have appeared in English translation. As long as the documentation makes clear what has been published in English and what has not, translated titles standing in for the original may be capitalized headline-style and treated like other English-language titles (see 8.157, 8.161). See also 11.6.

> A Chinese textbook, *Elementary Learning* (*Xiao xue*), has gained a wide following. Molière's comedy *The Miser* may have drawn on an obscure, late-medieval French treatise, *The Evils of Greed*, recently discovered in an abandoned château.

11.8   *Foreign institutions.* If given in the original language, names of foreign institutions and businesses are presented in roman type and capitalized according to the usage of the country concerned. Such usage may be difficult to determine; if in doubt, opt for sentence-style capitalization (see 8.156). If translated, such names are capitalized according to English usage.

> He is a member of the Société d'entraide des membres de l'ordre national de la Légion d'honneur.
> He was comforted to learn of the Mutual Aid Society for Members of the National Order of the Legion of Honor.

Original (or transliterated) names of institutions presented as glosses should not be italicized.

> The number of cases adjudicated by the Supreme People's Court of the People's Republic of China (Zhonghua renmin gongheguo zuigao renmin fayuan) has increased sharply.

Languages Using the Latin Alphabet

11.9   *Capitalization—English versus other languages.* Capitalization is applied to more classes of words in English than in any other Western language (but see 8.1). The remarks under "Capitalization" in the sections that follow suggest some of the ways other languages differ from English in their use of capitals. Except where stated to the contrary, the language in question is assumed to lowercase all adjectives (except those used as proper nouns), all pronouns, months, and days of the week. In addition, capitals are used more sparingly than in English for names of offices, institutions, and so on. Translated terms, however, are subject to Chicago's recommendations for capitalization of names and terms (see chapter 8). For foreign personal names, see 8.7–17.

11.10 *Punctuation—original language versus English context.* The remarks in this chapter about punctuation point out the more obvious departures from what is familiar to English speakers. They apply to foreign-language contexts—books, articles, or lengthy quotations wholly in a foreign language (as in the examples in 11.34). In English-language contexts and translations of foreign-language works, English-style punctuation is generally used. For example, the tightly spaced suspension points (to indicate omissions or breaks in thought) common in French, Italian, and Spanish publications should be converted to spaced periods in English publications. (For ellipses, see 13.48–56.) English-style quotation marks will replace the guillemets or whatever is used in the original, and em dashes used to introduce dialogue need not be followed by a space. One exception is the punctuation at the beginning of Spanish questions and exclamations (see 11.78), which may be preserved if entire sentences are presented in Spanish (but omitted when the passage is translated).

11.11 *Word division.* Anyone who has ever read a book in English that was composed and printed in a non-English-speaking country knows how easy it is to err in word division when working with a language not one's own. The following general rules, however, apply to foreign languages as well as to English: (1) Single-syllable words should never be broken. (2) No words should be broken after one letter, nor should a single letter be carried over to another line (see also 7.37). (3) Hyphenated words and solid compounds should be broken at the hyphen or between elements, if at all possible. See also 7.32, 7.35; for proper nouns, see 7.38. Specific rules for some of the languages covered in this chapter appear in the relevant sections below.

11.12 *Special characters.* Foreign words, phrases, or titles that occur in an English-language work must include any special characters that appear in the original language. Those languages that use the Latin alphabet may include letters with accents (diacritical marks), ligatures, and, in some cases, alphabetical forms that do not normally occur in English. Table 11.1 lists the special characters that might be required for each language treated in this section. Many authors will have access to Unicode-compliant software (see 11.2) and will therefore be able to reproduce each of these characters without the addition of any specialized fonts. Authors

TABLE 11.1. Special characters (and Unicode numbers) for languages using the Latin alphabet

Character (and Unicode number)	Description	Languages that use it
„ (201E), " (201C)	double low-9 quotation mark, left double quotation mark	German
« (00AB), » (00BB)	double angle quotation marks (guillemets)	French, German (reversed), Italian, Spanish
À (00C0), à (00E0)	A/a with grave	French, Italian, Portuguese
Á (00C1), á (00E1)	A/a with acute	Czech, Hungarian, Portuguese, Spanish
Â (00C2), â (00E2)	A/a with circumflex	French, Moldavian, Portuguese, Romanian, Turkish
Ã (00C3), ã (00E3)	A/a with tilde	Portuguese
Ä (00C4), ä (00E4)	A/a with diaeresis	Finnish, German, Swedish
Å (00C5), å (00E5)	A/a with ring above	Danish, Norwegian, Swedish
Ā (0100), ā (0101)	A/a with macron	Latin
Ă (0102), ă (0103)	A/a with breve	Latin, Moldavian, Romanian
Ą (0104), ą (0105)	A/a with ogonek	Polish
Æ (00C6), æ (00E6)	ligature Æ/æ	Danish, Norwegian, Old English and Middle English
Ɓ (0181), ɓ (0253)	B/b with hook	Hausa
Ç (00C7), ç (00E7)	C/c with cedilla	Albanian, Azeri, French, Portuguese, Turkish
Ć (0106), ć (0107)	C/c with acute	Bosnian, Croatian, Montenegrin, Polish, Serbian
Č (010C), č (010D)	C/c with caron (haček)	Bosnian, Croatian, Czech, Montenegrin, Serbian
Ð (00D0), ð (00F0)	eth	Old English and Middle English
Ď (010E), ď (010F)	D/d with caron (haček)	Czech
Đ (0110), đ (0111)	D/d with stroke	Bosnian, Croatian, Montenegrin, Serbian
Ɗ (018A), ɗ (0257)	D/d with hook	Hausa
È (00C8), è (00E8)	E/e with grave	French, Italian, Portuguese
É (00C9), é (00E9)	E/e with acute	Czech, French, Hungarian, Italian, Portuguese, Spanish
Ê (00CA), ê (00EA)	E/e with circumflex	French, Portuguese
Ë (00CB), ë (00EB)	E/e with diaeresis	Albanian, French
Ē (0112), ē (0113)	E/e with macron	Latin
Ĕ (0114), ĕ (0115)	E/e with breve	Latin
Ę (0118), ę (0119)	E/e with ogonek	Polish
Ě (011A), ě (011B)	E/e with caron (haček)	Czech
Ȝ (021C), ȝ (021D)	yogh	Old English and Middle English
Ə (018F), ə (0259)	schwa	Azeri
Ğ (011E), ğ (011F)	G/g with breve	Azeri, Turkish
Ì (00CC), ì (00EC)	I/i with grave	Italian, Portuguese
Í (00CD), í (00ED)	I/i with acute	Czech, Hungarian, Portuguese, Spanish
Î (00CE), î (00EE)	I/i with circumflex	French, Moldavian, Romanian
Ï (00CF), ï (00EF)	I/i with diaeresis	French, Portuguese
Ī (012A), ī (012B)	I/i with macron	Latin

TABLE 11.1. *(continued)*

Character (and Unicode number)	Description	Languages that use it
Ĭ (012C), ĭ (012D)	I/i with breve	Latin
İ (0130)	I with dot above	Azeri, Turkish
ı (0131)	dotless i	Azeri, Turkish
Ƙ (0198), ƙ (0199)	K/k with hook	Hausa
Ł (0141), ł (0142)	L/l with stroke	Polish
Ñ (00D1), ñ (00F1)	N/n with tilde	Spanish
Ń (0143), ń (0144)	N/n with acute	Polish
Ň (0147), ň (0148)	N/n with caron (háček)	Czech
Ò (00D2), ò (00F2)	O/o with grave	Italian, Portuguese
Ó (00D3), ó (00F3)	O/o with acute	Czech, Hungarian, Polish, Portuguese, Spanish
Ô (00D4), ô (00F4)	O/o with circumflex	French, Portuguese
Õ (00D5), õ (00F5)	O/o with tilde	Portuguese
Ö (00D6), ö (00F6)	O/o with diaeresis	Azeri, Finnish, German, Hungarian, Swedish, Turkish
Ø (00D8), ø (00F8)	O/o with stroke	Danish, Norwegian
Ō (014C), ō (014D)	O/o with macron	Latin
Ŏ (014E), ŏ (014F)	O/o with breve	Latin
Ő (0150), ő (0151)	O/o with double acute	Hungarian
Œ (0152), œ (0153)	ligature Œ/œ	French
Ř (0158), ř (0159)	R/r with caron (háček)	Czech
Ś (015A), ś (015B)	S/s with acute	Polish
Ş (015E), ş (015F)	S/s with cedilla	Azeri, Turkish
Ș (0218), ș (0219)	S/s with comma below	Moldavian, Romanian
Š (0160), š (0161)	S/s with caron (háček)	Bosnian, Croatian, Czech, Montenegrin, Serbian
ß (00DF)	sharp S (eszett)	German
Ț (021A), ț (021B)	T/t with comma below	Moldavian, Romanian
Ť (0164), ť (0165)	T/t with caron (háček)	Czech
Þ (00DE), þ (00FE)	thorn	Old English and Middle English
Ù (00D9), ù (00F9)	U/u with grave	French, Italian, Portuguese
Ú (00DA), ú (00FA)	U/u with acute	Czech, Hungarian, Portuguese, Spanish
Û (00DB), û (00FB)	U/u with circumflex	French, Turkish
Ü (00DC), ü (00FC)	U/u with diaeresis	Azeri, French, German, Hungarian, Portuguese, Spanish, Turkish
Ů (016E), ů (016F)	U/u with ring above	Czech
Ū (016A), ū (016B)	U/u with macron	Latin
Ŭ (016C), ŭ (016D)	U/u with breve	Latin
Ű (0170), ű (0171)	U/u with double acute	Hungarian
Ý (00DD), ý (00FD)	Y/y with acute	Czech
Ƴ (01B3), ƴ (01B4)	Y/y with hook	Hausa
Ź (0179), ź (017A)	Z/z with acute	Polish
Ż (017B), ż (017C)	Z/z with dot above	Polish
Ž (017D), ž (017E)	Z/z with caron (háček)	Bosnian, Croatian, Czech, Montenegrin, Serbian

should nonetheless supply a list of special characters used within a manuscript (see 2.15) to ensure the correct conversion to a particular font required for publication or, for electronic projects, to ensure compliance across systems that may not support Unicode. If type is to be reproduced from an author's hard copy, marginal clarifications may be needed for handwritten accents or special characters. In either case, use table 11.1 to correctly identify the character by name and Unicode number (e.g., for Đ or đ, indicate "D with stroke [U+0110]" or "d with stroke [U+0111]"). Such positive identification of special characters from manuscript through final proofreading stage is crucial, as conversion problems are always possible and in some settings are inevitable. For diacritical marks used in transliteration, see 11.94.

11.13   *International Phonetic Alphabet (IPA).* Phonetic symbols using IPA notation are based on the Latin alphabet and are defined for Unicode (see 11.2). For the latest version of the IPA alphabet, consult the website of the International Phonetic Association. For additional information on the subject of phonetics, including treatment of other systems of notation, consult Geoffrey K. Pullum and William A. Ladusaw, *Phonetic Symbol Guide* (bibliog. 5).

African Languages

11.14   *African capitalization and punctuation.* Most African languages—with the exception, most notably, of Arabic (11.96–101)—use the Latin alphabet and follow English capitalization and punctuation. The most widespread of these is Swahili, spoken by many different ethnic groups in eastern and central Africa. Hausa, Fulfulde, Yoruba, Igbo, Wolof, and Bambara are also spoken by millions, largely in western Africa; the same is true for Kikongo (or Kongo) and Lingala in the Congo-Zaire region and of Amharic and Somali in the Horn of Africa region. Amharic and other Ethiopian Semitic languages such as Tigrinya use the Ge'ez alphabet, not covered here. Xhosa and other "click" languages spoken in southern Africa do not follow English capitalization. The names of African languages themselves vary widely from ethnic group to ethnic group and from region to region. It is now standard practice to capitalize the names of African languages in the traditional way—for example, Kiswahili rather than KiSwahili or KISwahili. Xhosa speakers refer to and spell their language "isiXhosa" but "Isixhosa" (sometimes "Isizhosa") is also found in English-language publications.

11.15 *African special characters.* Swahili uses no additional letters or diacritics. Among the more than two thousand other African languages, however, many rely on diacritics and phonetic symbols to stand for sounds that cannot be represented by letters or combinations of letters. Hausa, which is spoken by millions of people across western Africa, requires the following special characters (see also table 11.1):

Ɓɓ, Ɗɗ, Ƙƙ, Yƴ

In Nigeria, both the upper and the lowercase y with a "hook" are represented instead with an apostrophe ('Y 'y). Additional diacritics, too numerous to be listed here, may be needed in other African languages. Languages such as French, Portuguese, and Arabic that are used in Africa are dealt with in separate sections in this chapter.

Albanian

11.16 *Albanian capitalization.* See 11.3, 11.9.

11.17 *Albanian special characters.* Since 1972 a single, unified Albanian orthography has been in use. The following special characters are needed for Albanian:

Çç, Ëë

Croatian and Bosnian

11.18 *Croatian and Bosnian capitalization.* See 11.3, 11.9.

11.19 *Croatian and Bosnian special characters.* The former Serbo-Croatian language used both Latin and Cyrillic alphabets. The modern Bosnian and Croatian standard languages use only the Latin version of that same alphabet. The following special characters are needed for Bosnian and Croatian (see also 11.74–75):

Čč, Ćć, Đđ, Šš, Žž

Although the substitution of *dj* for *đ* is sometimes seen (e.g., in informal correspondence), standard orthographic practice in all the successor languages of Serbo-Croatian distinguishes these two consistently.

Czech

11.20   *Czech capitalization.* See 11.3, 11.9.

11.21   *Czech special characters.* Czech, a Slavic language written in the Latin alphabet, uses many diacritical marks to indicate sounds not represented by this alphabet.

Áá, Čč, Ďď, Éé, Ěě, Íí, Ňň, Óó, Řř, Šš, Ťť, Úú, Ůů, Ýý, Žž

Danish

11.22   *Danish capitalization.* See 11.3, 11.9. The polite personal pronouns *De, Dem*, and *Deres* (now used ever more rarely) and the familiar *I* are capitalized in Danish. Until the mid-twentieth century, common nouns were capitalized, as in German, but they no longer are.

11.23   *Danish special characters.* Danish has three additional alphabetic letters, which require special characters (see also table 11.1).

Åå, Ææ, Øø

Dutch

11.24   *Dutch capitalization.* See 11.3, 11.9. For the capitalization of particles with personal names, see 8.10. Proper adjectives (as well as nouns) are capitalized as in English. When a word beginning with the diphthong *ij* is capitalized, both letters are capitals: *IJsland*. When a single letter begins a sentence, it is lowercased, but the next word is capitalized: *'k Heb niet . . .*

11.25   *Dutch special characters.* Dutch requires no special characters.

Finnish

11.26   *Finnish capitalization.* See 11.3, 11.9.

11.27   *Finnish special characters.* Finnish requires two umlauted vowels (see also table 11.1).

Ää, Öö

Because Swedish is the second official language in Finland, the Finnish alphabet taught in schools and the standard keyboard used in Finland include the Swedish *a* with ring above (or overcircle).

Åå

French

11.28 *French—additional resources.* As is the case with many languages, there is considerable variation in French publications with respect to capitalization and punctuation. For excellent advice, with frequent reference to the Académie française and numerous examples from literature, consult the latest edition of *Le bon usage*, known to many by the name of its original editor, Maurice Grevisse (bibliog. 5). Further guidance may be had at the website of the Académie française itself.

11.29 *French capitalization.* See 11.3, 11.9. Generic words denoting roadways, squares, and the like are lowercased, whether used alone or with a specific name as part of an address. Only the proper name is capitalized.

le boulevard Saint-Germain   la place de l'Opéra   13, rue des Beaux-Arts

In most geographical names, the generic word is lowercased and the modifying word capitalized.

la mer Rouge   le pic du Midi

Names of buildings are usually capitalized.

l'Hôtel des Invalides   le Palais du Louvre

In names of organizations and institutions, only the first substantive and any preceding modifier are capitalized, but not the preceding article (except at the beginning of a sentence).

l'Académie française   la Légion d'honneur   le Grand Théâtre de Québec

In hyphenated names, both elements are capitalized.

la Comédie-Française   la Haute-Loire

Names of religious groups are usually lowercased.

un chrétien   des juifs

In names of saints, the word *saint* is lowercased. But when a saint's name is used as part of a place-name or the name of a church or other institution, *saint* is capitalized and hyphenated to the following element.

le supplice de saint Pierre   *but*   l'église de Saint-Pierre

Adjectives formed from proper nouns are usually lowercased.

une imagination baudelairienne

11.30   *Titles of French works.* French publications vary in the way they capitalize titles of works. Chicago recommends sentence-style capitalization (see 8.156), the rule followed by Grevisse, *Le bon usage* (see 11.3, 11.28). (An exception may be made for titles of journals and periodicals, which are often capitalized headline-style; see 14.193.) Note that a superscript ordinal letter should remain in the superior position, as in the last example (cf. 14.96).

L'Apollon de Bellac: Pièce en un acte   Les Rougon-Macquart
L'assommoir   Le père Goriot
L'exil et le royaume   Paris au XXe siècle

For another practice—in which the first substantive (noun or noun form) and any preceding article or modifier are capitalized—consult *French Review*, *PMLA*, or *Romanic Review* (bibliog. 5). For punctuation in titles, see 11.4.

11.31   *Spacing with French punctuation.* In French typeset material, fixed thin spaces generally occur before colons, semicolons, question marks, and exclamation marks; between guillemets (« ») and the text they enclose (see 11.32); and after an em dash used to introduce dialogue (see 11.34). In electronic documents, fixed (i.e., nonbreaking) spaces are used to avoid stranding a mark at the beginning of a line. In an English context, where the typographic conventions of the publication as a whole should be observed, such spacing need not be duplicated. (If for any reason French spacing is required, however, it must be followed consistently and according to French practice for all marks.) See also 11.10.

11.32   *French use of guillemets.* For quotation marks, the French use guillemets (« »), often with a fixed thin space (or, especially in electronic documents, a regular nonbreaking space) to separate the guillemets from the quoted matter (but see 11.10). In English-language publications, such spaces need not be used (see 11.31). Such tags as *écrit-il* or *dit-elle* are often inserted within the quoted matter without additional guillemets. Only punctuation belonging to the quoted matter is placed within the closing guillemets; other punctuation follows them.

«Mission accomplie?» a-t-il demandé.
En ce sens, «avec» signifie «au moyen de».
À vrai dire, Abélard n'avoue pas un tel rationalisme: «je ne veux pas être si philosophe, écrit-il, que je résiste à Paul, ni si aristotélicien que je me sépare du Christ».

As in English, when a quotation (other than a block quotation) continues for more than one paragraph, opening guillemets appear at the beginning of each additional paragraph. Closing guillemets appear only at the end of the last paragraph. See also 11.33.

11.33 *Quotation marks in French.* For quotations within quotations, double (or sometimes single) quotation marks are used. Formerly, additional guillemets were used, with opening guillemets repeated on each runover line. (Note that when guillemets are used, if the two quotations end simultaneously, only one set of closing guillemets appears.)

«Comment peux-tu dire, "Montre-nous le père"?»

It should perhaps be noted that regular quotation marks are seen increasingly in French contexts in lieu of guillemets—especially in e-mail correspondence and other electronic settings. This usage is considered informal.

11.34 *French dialogue.* In dialogue, guillemets are often replaced by em dashes. In French publications, the dash is usually followed by a thin space; in English publications, the space is not necessary (see 11.31). Such dashes are used before each successive speech but are not repeated at the end of a speech. To set off a quotation within a speech, guillemets may be used.

—Vous viendrez aussitôt que possible? a-t-il demandé.
—Tout de suite.
—Bien. Bonne chance!

—Tu connais sans doute la parole «De l'abondance du cœur la bouche parle».
—Non, je ne la connais pas.

11.35 *French suspension points and ellipses.* The French often use suspension points to indicate interruptions or breaks in thought. In French practice, these dots are generally unspaced; in English contexts, they may be spaced in the manner of English-style suspension points or ellipses (see 13.48–56). Suspension points are also used in lieu of *and so forth.* See also 11.10.

> «Ce n'est pas que je n'aime plus l'Algérie . . . mon Dieu! un ciel! des arbres! . . . et le reste! . . . Toutefois, sept ans de discipline . . .»

To indicate omissions, the French use unspaced dots enclosed in brackets, with thin spaces between the brackets and the dots. In English contexts, the dots may be spaced in the manner of English-style ellipses (see 13.56).

> «Oh, dit-elle avec un mépris écrasant, des changements intellectuels! [. . .]»
> Les deux amis se réunissaient souvent chez Luc [. . .].

11.36 *French word division—vowels.* In French, a word is divided after a vowel wherever possible. One-letter syllables at the ends or beginnings of lines should be avoided (see 11.11).

ache-ter (*not* a-cheter)   in-di-vi-si-bi-li-té   tri-age

Two or more vowels forming a single sound, or diphthong, are never broken.

écri-vain   fouet-ter   Gau-guin   éloi-gner   vieux

11.37 *French word division—consonants.* A division is normally made between two adjacent consonants, whether the same or different.

der-riè-re	Mal-raux	*but*
feuil-le-ter	ob-jet	qua-tre
ba-lan-cer	par-ler	ta-bleau

Groups of three adjacent consonants are normally divided after the first.

es-prit   res-plen-dir

11.38 *French words containing apostrophes.* Division should never be made immediately after an apostrophe.

jus-qu'au   au-jour-d'hui

11.39 *French words best left undivided.* Since there are as many syllables in French as there are vowels or diphthongs (even if some are unsounded except in poetry), the French break words that appear to English speakers to be of only one syllable (e.g., *fui-te, guer-re, sor-tent*). French practice also permits division after one letter (e.g., *é-tait*). In English-language publications, however, such breaks should be avoided, since they may confuse readers not fluent in French. Words of four or fewer letters should in any case be left undivided. See also 7.32.

11.40 *French special characters.* French employs the following special characters (see also table 11.1):

Àà, Ââ, Çç, Éé, Èè, Êê, Ëë, Îî, Ïï, Ôô, Œœ, Ùù, Ûû, Üü

Although French publishers often omit accents on capital letters (especially A) and may set the ligature Œ as two separate letters (*OE*), all the special characters needed for French—including capitalized forms—are available in most software and in most fonts, and they should appear where needed in English works. This practice, advocated by the Académie française, is helpful to readers who may not be familiar with French typographic usage.

German

11.41 *The new German orthography.* The new rules for German orthography (including spelling and capitalization) adopted in 1998 and made mandatory in 2005 have been controversial. Some publications have continued to follow traditional rules, or a combination of house style and traditional rules, whereas others have adopted the new rules. Some book publishers honor the preference of their authors and, by a similar token, do not update spelling when reprinting older works. Material quoted from German should therefore reflect the spelling in the source. For principles and details of the new orthography, consult the latest edition of *Duden: Die deutsche Rechtschreibung* (bibliog. 5). The recommendations and examples in this section reflect the new orthography.

11.42 *German capitalization.* In German, all nouns and words used as nouns are capitalized, whether in ordinary sentences or in titles of works (see 11.3).

ein Haus	Deutsch (the German language)
die Weltanschauung	eine Deutsche (a German woman)
das Sein	etwas Schönes

Adjectives derived from proper names are generally lowercased. Exceptions include invariable adjectives ending in *er* (often referring to a city or region) and adjectives that themselves are part of a proper name. For further exceptions, consult *Duden* (see 11.41).

die deutsche Literatur
nordamerikanische Sprachen
die platonischen Dialoge
but
eine berühmte Berliner Straße
der Nahe Osten
der Deutsch-Französische Krieg

The pronouns *Sie, Ihr,* and *Ihnen,* as polite second-person forms, are capitalized. As third-person pronouns they are lowercased. The familiar second-person forms *du, dich, dein, ihr, euch,* and so on—once routinely capitalized—are now lowercased.

11.43   *German apostrophes.* An apostrophe is used to denote the colloquial omission of *e.*

wie geht's   was gibt's   hab' ich

Although an apostrophe rarely appears before a genitive *s,* an apostrophe is used to denote the omission of the *s* after proper names ending in an *s* sound (*ce, s, ss, ß, tz, x,* or *z*) or in a silent *s, x,* or *z.*

Alice' Geburtstag   Cixous' Theaterstücke
Jaspers' Philosophie   Leibniz' Meinung

11.44   *German quotation marks.* In German, quotations usually take reversed guillemets (» «); split-level inverted quotation marks („ "); or, in Switzerland, regular guillemets (see 11.32). Other punctuation is placed outside the closing quotation marks unless it belongs to the quoted matter.

Eros bedeutet für sie primär »zusammen-sein mit« und nicht »anschauen«.
Denn: „An die Pferde", hieß es: „Aufgesessen!"

11.45   *German word division—vowels.* In German, division is made after a vowel wherever possible. See also 11.11.

Fa-brik   hü-ten   Bu-ße

Two vowels forming a single sound, or diphthong, are never broken.

Lau-ne   blei-ben

11.46   *German word division—consonants.* Two or more adjacent consonants, whether the same or different, are divided before the last one unless they belong to different parts of a compound (see also 11.11).

klir-ren   Meis-ter
Was-ser   *but*
Verwand-te   Morgen-stern

The consonant combinations *ch, ck, ph, sch,* and *th* are not divided unless they belong to separate syllables. (Until the 1998 spelling change, *st* was subject to this rule. The combination *ck,* on the other hand, used to be changed at the end of a line to *kk* and divided between the *k*'s.)

Mäd-chen   *but*
Zu-cker   Klapp-hut
Philo-so-phie   Häus-chen
rau-schen

11.47   *German word division—compounds.* Compound words should be divided between their component elements whenever possible (see also 11.11).

Meeres-ufer   Rasier-apparat
mit-einander   Tür-angel

11.48   *German special characters.* For setting German in roman type (the old Gothic or Fraktur type having long been out of use), the eszett, or sharp *s* (ß), and three umlauted vowels are needed (see also table 11.1).

Ää, Öö, ß, Üü

Although umlauted vowels are occasionally represented by omitting the accent and adding an *e* (*ae, Oe,* etc.), the availability of umlauted characters in text-editing software makes such a practice unnecessary. The eszett (ß), also widely available, must not be confused with, or replaced by, the Greek beta (β). In the new spelling it is replaced by *ss* in certain words. Consult a German dictionary published after 1998. In German-speaking areas of Switzerland, the eszett is rarely used.

Hungarian

11.49 *Hungarian capitalization.* See 11.3, 11.9.

11.50 *Hungarian special characters.* Hungarian requires several varieties of accented vowels (see also table 11.1).

Áá, Éé, Íí, Óó, Öö, Őő, Úú, Üü, Űű

Italian

11.51 *Italian capitalization.* See 11.3, 11.9. In Italian, a title preceding a proper name is normally lowercased.

il commendatore Ugo Emiliano   la signora Rossi

In commercial correspondence, the formal second-person pronouns are capitalized in both their nominative forms, *Lei* (singular) and *Voi* (plural), and their objective forms, *La* (accusative singular), *Le* (dative singular), and *Vi* (accusative and dative plural). The older singular and plural forms *Ella* (*Le, La*) and *Loro* (*Loro, Loro*) are handled the same way. These pronouns are capitalized even in combined forms.

Posso pregarLa di farmi una cortesia?
Vorrei darLe una spiegazione.

11.52 *Italian quotations and dialogue.* Italian uses guillemets (*virgolette a caporale*) to denote quoted matter, but usually without the space between guillemets and quoted text that appears in many French publications. Regular quotation marks are also frequently used in Italian—sometimes as scare quotes (see 7.55) in the same text in which guillemets are used for quotations. Note that the period is correctly placed *after* the closing *caporali*.

«Cosa pensi del fatto che io possa diventare "un qualcosa di imperial regio"?
    Questo non è proprio possibile».

In dialogue, em dashes are sometimes used, as in French. The dash is used before each successive speech. Unlike French, however, another dash is used at the end of the speech if other matter follows in the same paragraph. The spaces that typically surround the dashes in Italian texts need not be used in English contexts (see 11.10).

—Avremo la neve,—annunziò la vecchia.

—E domani?—chiese Alfredo, voltandosi di scatto dalla finestra.

11.53   *Italian apostrophes.* An apostrophe is used to indicate the omission of a letter. A space should appear after an apostrophe that follows a vowel; after an apostrophe that follows a consonant, however, *no* space should appear.

po' duro   de' malevoli   l'onda   all'aura

11.54   *Italian suspension points and ellipses.* Italian, like French, uses suspension points to indicate interruptions or breaks in thought. To indicate omitted material (i.e., an ellipsis), the dots are enclosed in brackets. Though Italian typography usually calls for unspaced dots, in English publications Chicago recommends spaced dots for suspension points and ellipses (see 13.48–56). See also 11.10.

Voglio . . . quattro milioni.   Davvero? [. . .] Non ci avevo pensato.

11.55   *Italian word division—vowels.* In Italian, division is made after a vowel wherever possible. One-letter syllables at the ends or beginnings of lines should be avoided (see 11.11).

acro-po-li (*not* a-cropoli)   mi-se-ra-bi-le   ta-vo-li-no

Consecutive vowels are rarely divided, and two vowels forming a single sound, or diphthong, are never divided.

miei   pia-ga   Gio-van-ni   Giu-sep-pe   pau-sa   gio-iel-lo

11.56   *Italian word division—consonants.* Certain consonant groups must never be broken: *ch, gh, gli, gn, qu, sc,* and *r* or *l* preceded by any consonant other than itself.

ac-qua-rio   na-sce   ri-flet-te-re
fi-glio   pa-dre   so-gna-re
la-ghi   rau-che

Three groups of consonants, however, may be divided: double consonants; the group *cqu;* and any group beginning with *l, m, n,* or *r.*

bab-bo   ac-qua   cam-po   den-tro
af-fre-schi   cal-do   com-pra   par-te

11.57   *Italian word division—words containing apostrophes.* Division should never be made immediately after an apostrophe (but see 11.53).

dal-l'accusa   del-l'or-ga-no   quel-l'uomo   un'ar-te   l'i-dea

11.58   *Italian special characters.* In Italian, the following special characters are required (see also table 11.1):

Àà, Èè, Éé, Ìì, Òò, Ùù

Although the grave accent on capitalized vowels is sometimes dropped, in stressed final syllables it must be retained to avoid confusion.

CANTÒ (he sang)   CANTO (I sing)   PAPÀ (daddy)   PAPA (pope)

If an accented capital is not available, an apostrophe may be used in place of the accent on stressed final (or single) vowels.

E' (it is)   E (and)   PAPA' (daddy)

Latin

11.59   *Latin capitalization—titles of works.* In English-speaking countries, titles of ancient and medieval Latin works are capitalized in sentence style— that is, only the first word in the title or subtitle, proper nouns, and proper adjectives are capitalized (see 8.156).

De bello Gallico   *De viris illustribus*   *Cur Deus homo?*

Renaissance and modern works or works in English with Latin titles are usually capitalized in the English fashion (i.e., headline style; see 8.157). (If there is any doubt about the era to which the title belongs, opt for sentence style.)

Novum Organum   *Religio Medici*

11.60   *Latin word division—syllables.* A Latin word has as many syllables as it has vowels or diphthongs (*ae, au, ei, eu, oe, ui,* and, in archaic Latin, *ai, oi, ou*) and should be divided between syllables (see also 11.11).

na-tu-ra   cae-li-co-la   in-no-cu-us

11.61 *Latin word division—single consonants.* When a single consonant occurs between two vowels, the word is divided before the consonant unless it is an *x*. Note that *i* and *u* sometimes act as consonants (and, when they do, are sometimes written as *j* and *v*).

Cae-sar   me-ri-di-es   in-iu-ri-or (*or* in-ju-ri-or)   *but*   lex-is

11.62 *Latin word division—multiple consonants.* When two or more consonants come together, the word is divided before the last consonant, except for the combinations in the examples below.

om-nis   cunc-tus

The combinations *ch, gu, ph, qu,* and *th* are treated as single consonants and thus never separated.

co-phi-nus   lin-gua   ae-qua-lis

The following consonant groups are never broken: *bl, br, chl, chr, cl, cr, dl, dr, gl, gr, phl, phr, pl, pr, thl, thr, tl,* and *tr.*

pan-chres-tus   li-bris   ex-em-pla   pa-tris

11.63 *Latin word division—compounds.* Compound words are first separated into their component elements; within each element the foregoing rules apply.

ab-rum-po   ad-est   red-eo   trans-igo

11.64 *Latin special characters.* Latin requires no special characters for setting ordinary copy. Elementary texts, however, usually mark the long vowels with a macron and, occasionally, the short vowels with a breve, as follows. (See also table 11.1.)

Āā, Ăă, Ēē, Ĕĕ, Īī, Ĭĭ, Ōō, Ŏŏ, Ūū, Ŭŭ

Norwegian

11.65 *Norwegian capitalization.* See 11.3, 11.9. The polite personal pronouns *De, Dem,* and *Deres* (now used ever more rarely) are capitalized in Norwegian.

Until the mid-twentieth century, common nouns were capitalized (as in German), but they no longer are.

11.66 *Norwegian special characters.* Norwegian requires the same special characters as Danish (see also table 11.1).

Åå, Ææ, Øø

Polish

11.67 *Polish capitalization.* See 11.3, 11.9. In formal address the second-person plural pronoun *Państwo* (you) is capitalized, as are related forms.

Czekam na Twój przyjazd. (I await your arrival.)
Pozdrawiam Cię! (Greetings to you!)

11.68 *Polish word division.* Division of Polish words is similar to that of transliterated Russian (see 11.118–28). Division normally follows syllabic structure.

kom-pli-ka-cja   sta-ro-pol-ski

Note that the conjunction *i* (and) should never appear at the end of a line but must be carried over to the beginning of the next—a print nicety that need not be maintained in electronic publications (e.g., by the use of a nonbreaking space after every instance of *i* to prevent a line break).

11.69 *Polish special characters.* Polish requires the following special characters (see also table 11.1):

Ąą, Ćć, Ęę, Łł, Ńń, Óó, Śś, Źź, Żż

Since *Ą*, *Ę*, and *Ń* never occur at the beginning of a word, these capitalized forms would be needed only if an entire word were capitalized.

Portuguese

11.70 *Portuguese capitalization.* See 11.3, 11.9. Titles and nouns or adjectives denoting nationality are capitalized as in Spanish (see 11.77).

11.71   *Portuguese special characters.* Portuguese requires the following special characters (except that European Portuguese does not use Ü or ü):

Àà, Áá, Ââ, Ãã, Çç, Èè, Éé, Êê, Ìì, Íí, Ïï, Òò, Óó, Ôô, Õõ, Ùù, Úú, Üü

Accented capitals, sometimes dropped in Portuguese running text, should always be used when Portuguese is presented in an English context.

Romanian and Moldavian

11.72   *Romanian and Moldavian capitalization.* See 11.3, 11.9.

11.73   *Romanian and Moldavian special characters.* Romanian and Moldavian are now both written using the same Latin orthography. The following special characters are needed for Romanian and Moldavian:

Ââ, Ăă, Îî, Şş, Ţţ

Note that Şş and Ţţ—Latin Ss and Tt with comma below—often appear instead with a cedilla, though the comma is correct. Ââ and Îî represent identical sounds but have different etymological origins. The use of Ââ has been restricted, eliminated, and reinstated in whole or in part during various orthographic reforms. Writers and editors, therefore, should take care to determine whether a spelling is conditioned by the specific time when it was used or whether it is preferable to follow the current norm.

Serbian and Montenegrin

11.74   *Serbian and Montenegrin capitalization.* See 11.3, 11.9.

11.75   *Serbian and Montenegrin special characters.* The former Serbo-Croatian language used both Latin and Cyrillic alphabets. In the modern Montenegrin standard language, both versions of that alphabet are official. In the modern Serbian standard language, the Cyrillic version of that same alphabet is official. The following special characters are needed when using the Latin version (see also 11.18–19):

Ćć, Čč, Đđ, Šš, Žž

Although the substitution of *dj* for *đ* is sometimes seen (e.g., in informal correspondence), standard orthographic practice in all the successor languages of Serbo-Croatian distinguishes these two consistently.

Spanish

11.76 **Spanish—additional resources.** There is considerable variation in Spanish publications throughout the world with respect to capitalization, punctuation, and other matters. For further guidance, consult María Moliner, *Diccionario de uso del español* (bibliog. 5). One may also consult the extensive resources at the website of the Real Academia Española.

11.77 **Spanish capitalization.** See 11.3, 11.9. In Spanish, a title preceding a proper name is normally lowercased. When abbreviated, however, titles are in uppercase.

el señor Jaime López   *but*
la señora Lucía Moyado de Barba   el Sr. López
doña Perfecta

Nouns as well as adjectives denoting membership in nations are lowercased, but names of countries are capitalized.

los mexicanos   la lengua española   Inglaterra

11.78 **Spanish question marks and exclamation points.** A question or an exclamation in Spanish is preceded by an inverted question mark or exclamation point and followed by a regular mark.

¿Qué pasa, amigo?   ¡Olvídalo en ese caso!

If a vocative or dependent construction precedes a question or exclamation, it is written as follows:

Amigo, ¿qué pasa?   En ese caso, ¡olvídalo!

Because the opening marks are so integral to Spanish punctuation, they should be retained even when Spanish is being quoted in an English context (see 11.10).

11.79 **Spanish guillemets and quotation marks.** For quotation marks, Spanish traditionally uses guillemets («»). Only punctuation belonging to the quoted matter is placed within the closing guillemets; other punctuation follows them. Within a quotation, em dashes may be used to set off words identifying the speaker. In Spanish publications, the opening dash is usually *preceded* by a space; the closing dash is then *followed* by a space unless immediately followed by punctuation. In English contexts, such spaces need not be used (see also 11.10).

> «Vino el negocio a tanto—comenta Suárez—, que ya andaban muchos tomados
>   por el diablo».

In lexical studies, single quotation marks are used for glosses (see 7.50). It should also be noted that English-style quotation marks rather than guillemets are increasingly encountered in Spanish publications, especially in electronic environments.

11.80   *Spanish dialogue.* In dialogue, an em dash (or, less frequently, a guillemet) introduces each successive speech. Any other matter that follows the quoted speech in the same paragraph should be preceded by a dash or a comma. See also 11.79.

> —Esto es el arca de Noé, afirmó el estanciero.
> —¿Por qué estas aquí todavía?—preguntó Juana alarmada.

11.81   *Spanish suspension points and ellipses.* In Spanish, as in French, suspension points are used to indicate interruptions or breaks in thought. In Spanish publications, these dots are generally unspaced; in English contexts, they may be spaced in the manner of English-style suspension points or ellipses (see 13.48–56). To indicate omitted material (that is, to serve as ellipses), the dots are enclosed in brackets. See also 11.10.

> Hemos comenzado la vida juntos . . . quizá la terminaremos juntos también . . .
> La personalidad más importante del siglo XIX es Domingo Faustino Sarmiento
>   [. . .], llamado el hombre representante del intelecto sudamericano. [. . .] El
>   gaucho [. . .] servía de tema para poemas, novelas, cuentos y dramas.

11.82   *Spanish word division—vowels.* In Spanish, division is made after a vowel whenever possible. See also 11.11.

ca-ra-co-les   mu-jer   re-cla-mo   se-ño-ri-ta

Two or more vowels that form a single syllable (a diphthong or a triphthong) may not be divided.

cam-bias   fue-go   miau   tie-ne   viu-da

If adjacent vowels belong to separate syllables, however, they are divided between syllables.

ba-úl   cre-er   pa-ís   te-a-tro

11.83 *Spanish word division—consonants.* If two adjacent consonants form a combination that would generally not occur at the beginning of a Spanish word, the break is made between them.

ac-cio-nis-ta   ad-ver-ten-cia   al-cal-de   an-cho   efec-to   is-leño

The consonant groups *bl, br, cl, cr, dr, fl, fr, gl, gr, pl, pr,* and *tr*—all pairs that can occur at the beginning of Spanish words—are inseparable (unless each belongs to a different element of a compound; see 11.84, 11.11).

ci-fra	li-bro	no-ble	re-gla
co-pla	ma-dre	pa-tria	se-cre-to
im-po-si-ble	ne-gro	re-fle-jo	te-cla
le-pra			

Groups of three consonants not ending with one of the inseparable pairs listed above always have an *s* in the middle. They are divided after the *s*.

cons-pi-rar   cons-ta   ins-tan-te   obs-cu-ro   obs-tan-te

Spanish *ch* and *ll* were long considered single characters, alphabetized as such, and never divided. The Spanish Royal Academy has now declared that these combinations are to be alphabetized as two-letter groups, and new publications have adopted this convention. Along with *rr,* however, they still cannot be divided, since they represent single sounds. For details, consult Real Academia Española, *Ortografía de la lengua española* (bibliog. 5).

ci-ga-rri-llo   mu-cha-cho

11.84 *Dividing Spanish compounds.* Compound words are often but not always divided between their component parts.

des-igual	trans-al-pi-no	sub-lu-nar	*but*
in-útil	semi-es-fe-ra	sub-ra-yar	no-so-tros
mal-es-tar	bien-aven-tu-ra-do		

11.85   *Spanish special characters.* Spanish employs the following special characters (see also table 11.1):

Áá, Éé, Íí, Ññ, Óó, Úú, Üü

Swedish

11.86   *Swedish capitalization.* See 11.3, 11.9. In Swedish the second-person pronouns *Ni* and *Er*, traditionally capitalized in correspondence, are now lowercased in all contexts.

11.87   *Swedish special characters.* Swedish requires the following special characters (see also table 11.1):

Ää, Åå, Öö

Turkish and Azeri

11.88   *Turkish spelling.* Modern Turkish has undergone a number of orthographic reforms since the original change to the Latin alphabet in 1928. Differences in the spellings of a name or word can therefore depend on the time period. Writers and editors should take care to determine whether a spelling is conditioned by the specific time when it was used or whether it is preferable to follow the current norm.

11.89   *Turkish and Azeri capitalization.* See 11.3, 11.9. In Turkish, as in English, the names of months and days of the week are capitalized. Azeri is similar to Turkish except for the differences noted in 11.90.

11.90   *Turkish and Azeri special characters.* Turkish requires the following special characters:

Ââ, Çç, Ğğ, İ, ı, Öö, Şş, Ûû, Üü

The Azeri (Azerbaijani) standard alphabet in use since 1992 is identical to Turkish except for the presence of *Qq* and *Xx* (lacking in Turkish), the absence of vowels with circumflex, and the addition of the schwa.

Çç, Əə, Ğğ, İ, ı, Öö, Şş, Üü

Note that there are dotted and undotted varieties of both the capital and the lowercase *i*. A dotted lowercase *i* retains its dot when capitalized.

Languages Usually Transliterated (or Romanized)

11.91 *Transliteration.* In nonspecialized works it is customary to transliterate—that is, convert to the Latin alphabet, or romanize—words or phrases from languages that do not use the Latin alphabet. These languages include Arabic, Chinese, Hebrew, Japanese, Russian, and other living languages as well as ancient languages such as Greek and Sanskrit. For discussion and illustration of scores of alphabets, see Peter T. Daniels and William Bright, eds., *The World's Writing Systems* (bibliog. 5). For alphabetic conversion, the most comprehensive resource is the Library of Congress publication *ALA-LC Romanization Tables* (bibliog. 5), available online. Do not attempt to transliterate from a language unfamiliar to you.

11.92 *Character sets for non-Latin alphabets.* Modern word-processing software readily allows users to key in words in several of the non-Latin alphabets used in the languages mentioned in the previous paragraph—for example, Cyrillic, Greek, and Hebrew. For a given alphabet, there may be a variety of character sets available in a variety of typefaces, but authors who want to include such copy should opt for the correct Unicode characters if at all possible (see 11.2), after consulting their publisher. See also 2.15.

11.93 *Proofreading copy in non-Latin alphabets—a warning.* Anyone unfamiliar with a language that uses a non-Latin alphabet should exercise extreme caution in proofreading even single words set in that alphabet. Grave errors can occur when similar characters are mistaken for each other. If in doubt, editors should query the author; when referring to a given character or diacritical mark, it may be advisable to consult the Unicode number and description (see 11.2).

11.94 *Diacritics—specialized versus general contexts.* Nearly all systems of transliteration require diacritics—including, in the languages discussed below, macrons, underdots, and overdots, to name just a few. Except in linguistic studies or other highly specialized works, a system using as few diacritics as are needed to aid pronunciation is easier on readers, publisher, and author. Most readers of a nonspecialized work on Hindu mythology, for example, will be more comfortable with Shiva than Śiva or with Vishnu than Viṣṇu, though many specialists would want to differentiate the *Sh* in Shiva from the *sh* in Vishnu as distinct Sanskrit letters. For nonspecialized works, the transliterated forms without diacritics that are listed in any of the latest editions of the Merriam-Webster dictionaries are usually preferred by readers and authors alike.

11.95   *Italics versus roman for transliterated terms.* Transliterated terms (other than proper names) that have not become part of the English language are italicized. If used throughout a work, a transliterated term may be italicized on first appearance and then set in roman. Words listed in the dictionary are usually set in roman. See also 7.49–53.

> The preacher pointed out the distinction between agape and eros.
>
> *but*
>
> Once the Greek words *erōs* and *agapē* had been absorbed into the English language, it became unnecessary to italicize them or to use the macrons.

Arabic

11.96   *Arabic transliteration.* There is no universally accepted form for transliterating Arabic. One very detailed system may be found in the *ALA-LC Romanization Tables* (bibliog. 5). Another system is followed by the *International Journal of Middle East Studies* (bibliog. 5). Having selected a system, an author should stick to it with as few exceptions as possible. In the following examples, only the hamza (') and the ʿayn (ʿ) are used (see 11.97). Letters with underdots and some of the other special characters used in transliteration from Arabic are included in table 11.2. (The Arabic alphabet may be found in the alphabet table in *Merriam-Webster's Collegiate Dictionary* [bibliog. 3.1], among other sources.)

11.97   *The hamza and the ʿayn.* The hamza (') and the ʿayn (ʿ) frequently appear in transliterated Arabic words and names. Writers using hamzas or ʿayns must on every occurrence make it clear, by coding or by careful instructions to the editor or typesetter, which of the two marks is intended. It should be noted that the Arabic characters are not the same as the ones used for transliteration; see table 11.2 for the preferred Unicode characters for hamza and ʿayn in transliteration. The hamza is sometimes represented—especially in nonspecialized works—by an apostrophe, as in Qur'an, and the ʿayn by a single opening quotation mark ('ayn). (Since an ʿayn often occurs at the beginning of a word, a quotation mark must be used with caution.) Most transliteration systems drop the hamza when it occurs at the beginning of a word (anzala *not* 'anzala).

TABLE 11.2. Special characters (and Unicode numbers) for transliterated Arabic, Hebrew, Japanese, and South Asian languages

Character (and Unicode number)	Description	Languages that use it
ʹ (02B9)	soft sign (modifier letter prime)	Arabic, Hebrew
ʿ (02BF)	ʿayn or ʿayin (represented by modifier letter left half ring)	Arabic, Hebrew
ʾ (02BE)	alif (hamza) or ʾalef (represented by modifier letter right half ring)	Arabic, Hebrew
Ā (0100), ā (0101)	A/a with macron	Arabic, Hebrew, Japanese, South Asian languages
Ǎ (01CD), ǎ (01CE)	A/a with caron (háček)	Hebrew
Á (00C1), á (00E1)	A/a with acute	Arabic
Æ (00C6), æ (00E6)	ligature Æ/æ	South Asian languages
Ǽ (01E2), ǽ (01E3)	Æ/æ with macron	South Asian languages
Ḍ (1E0C), ḍ (1E0D)	D/d with dot below	Arabic, South Asian languages
Ē (0112), ē (0113)	E/e with macron	Hebrew, Japanese, South Asian languages
Ě (011A), ě (011B)	E/e with caron (háček)	Hebrew
ə (0259)	small schwa	Hebrew
Ḥ (1E24), ḥ (1E25)	H/h with dot below	Arabic, Hebrew, South Asian languages
Ī (012A), ī (012B)	I/i with macron	Arabic, Hebrew, Japanese, South Asian languages
Ḳ (1E32), ḳ (1E33)	K/k with dot below	Arabic, Hebrew
Ḷ (1E36), ḷ (1E37)	L/l with dot below	South Asian languages
Ḹ (1E38), ḹ (1E39)	L/l with dot below and macron	South Asian languages
Ṃ (1E42), ṃ (1E43)	M/m with dot below	South Asian languages
Ṇ̄ (004E+0304), n̄ (006E+0304)	N/n with macron (combining character)	South Asian languages
Ṅ (1E44), ṅ (1E45)	N/n with dot above	South Asian languages
Ṇ (1E46), ṇ (1E47)	N/n with dot below	South Asian languages
Ō (014C), ō (014D)	O/o with macron	Hebrew, Japanese, South Asian languages
Ṛ (1E5A), ṛ (1E5B)	R/r with dot below	South Asian languages
Ṝ (1E5C), ṝ (1E5D)	R/r with dot below and macron	South Asian languages
Ś (015A), ś (015B)	S/s with acute	Hebrew, South Asian languages
Ṣ (1E62), ṣ (1E63)	S/s with dot below	Arabic, South Asian languages
Ṭ (1E6C), ṭ (1E6D)	T/t with dot below	Arabic, Hebrew, South Asian languages
Ū (016A), ū (016B)	U/u with macron	Arabic, Hebrew, Japanese, South Asian languages
Ṿ (1E7E), ṿ (1E7F)	V/v with dot below	Hebrew
Ẓ (1E92), ẓ (1E93)	Z/z with dot below	Arabic

11.98   *Arabic spelling.* Isolated references in text to well-known persons or places should employ the forms familiar to English-speaking readers.

> Avicenna (*not* Ibn Sina)   Damascus (*not* Dimashq)   Mecca (*not* Makkah)

11.99   *The Arabic definite article.* Though there is considerable variation across publications, Chicago recommends joining the Arabic definite article, *al*, to a noun with a hyphen.

> al-Islam   al-Nafud   Bahr al-Safi   al-Qaeda (*or* al-Qaida)

In speech the sound of the *l* in *al* is assimilated into the sounds *d, n, r, s, sh, t,* and *z.* Where rendering the *sound* of the Arabic is important (for example, when transliterating poetry), the assimilations are often shown, as in the examples below. In most other situations, the article-noun combination is written without indication of the elision, as above.

> an-Nafud   Bahr as-Safi

Some authors drop the *a* in *al* and replace it with an apostrophe when it occurs after a long syllable (Abū 'l-Muhallab). Some also drop the *a* when it occurs connected with a particle (wa 'l-layl).

11.100   *Arabic capitalization.* Since the Arabic alphabet does not distinguish between capital and lowercase letter forms, practice in capitalizing transliterated Arabic varies widely. Chicago recommends the practice outlined in 11.3: capitalize only the first word and any proper nouns. This practice applies to titles of works as well as to names of journals and organizations. Note that *al*, like *the*, is capitalized only at the beginning of a sentence or a title.

> ʿAbd al-Rahman al-Jabarti, *ʿAjaʾib al-athar fi al-tarajim wa al-akhbar* (The marvelous remains in biography and history)

For citing and alphabetizing Arabic personal names, see 8.14, 16.76.

11.101   *Arabic word division.* Breaking transliterated Arabic words or names at the ends of lines should be avoided wherever possible. If necessary, a break may be made after *al* or *Ibn.* A break may be made after two letters if the second has an underdot (e.g., *iṭ-baq*). Breaks must never be made between the digraphs *dh, gh, kh, sh,* or *th* unless both letters have underdots. Nor should breaks be made before or after a hamza. Aside from these niceties, the rules governing English word division may be followed (see 7.31–43).

Chinese and Japanese

11.102 *Chinese romanization.* The Hanyu Pinyin romanization system, introduced by the Chinese in the 1950s, has largely supplanted both the older Wade-Giles system and the place-name spellings of the *Postal Atlas of China* (last updated in the 1930s), making Pinyin the standard system for romanizing Chinese. Representing sounds of Chinese more explicitly, Pinyin has been widely accepted as the system for teaching Chinese as a second language. As of 2000, the Library of Congress issued new romanization guidelines reflecting the conversion of its entire online catalog records for the Chinese collection to comply with Pinyin. Although a few scholars, long familiar with Wade-Giles or other older systems, have not switched to Pinyin in their writings, Chicago joins librarians in urging that Pinyin now be used in all scholarly writing about China or the Chinese language. (In some contexts it may be helpful to the reader to add the Wade-Giles spelling of a name or term in parentheses following the first use of the Pinyin spelling.) The *ALA-LC Romanization Tables* (bibliog. 5) available online from the Library of Congress should be used with caution by anyone unfamiliar with Chinese.

11.103 *Exceptions to Pinyin.* Even where Pinyin is adopted, certain place-names, personal names, and other proper nouns long familiar in their older forms may be presented that way in English texts. Or, for greater consistency, the old spelling may be added in parentheses after the Pinyin version. If in doubt, consult the latest edition of *Merriam-Webster's Collegiate Dictionary*; names not listed there in older forms should be presented in Pinyin. Editors who wish to alter spellings should do so in consultation with the author.

11.104 *Apostrophes, hyphens, and tone marks in Chinese romanization.* Pinyin spellings often differ markedly from the older ones. Personal names are usually spelled without apostrophes or hyphens, but an apostrophe is sometimes used to avoid ambiguity when syllables are run together (as in Xi'an to distinguish it from Xian), except in contexts where tone marks are used. Note that the Pinyin romanization system of the Library of Congress does not include tone marks (the system of accents on certain vowels prescribed by the Hanyu Pinyin system of 1962).

11.105   *Some common Chinese names.* Some names frequently encountered are listed below.

Dynasties		Personal names	
WADE-GILES	*PINYIN*	*WADE-GILES*	*PINYIN*
Chou	Zhou	Fang Li-chih	Fang Lizhi
Ch'in	Qin	Hua Kuo-feng	Hua Guofeng
Ch'ing	Qing	Lin Piao	Lin Biao
Sung	Song	Lu Hsün	Lu Xun
T'ang	Tang	Mao Tse-tung	Mao Zedong
Yüan	Yuan	Teng Hsiao-p'ing	Deng Xiaoping

The names Sun Yat-sen and Chiang Kai-shek, among a few others, usually retain the old spellings.

Geographical names

WADE-GILES	*POSTAL ATLAS*	*PINYIN*
Kuang-tung	Kwangtung	Guangdong
Pei-ching (Pei-p'ing)	Peking (Peiping)	Beijing
Shang-hai	Shanghai	Shanghai
Su-chou	Soochow	Suzhou
Ta-lien	Dairen	Dalian

11.106   *Japanese romanization.* The Japanese language in its usual written form is a mixture of Chinese characters (called *kanji* in Japanese) and two *kana* syllabaries. (A syllabary is a series of written characters, each used to represent a syllable.) Since romanized Japanese, *rōmaji*, was introduced into Japan in the sixteenth century, a number of systems of romanization have been developed. The one in most common use since the early part of the Meiji period (1868–1912) is the modified Hepburn (or *hyōjun*) system. This system is used in *Kenkyūsha's New Japanese–English Dictionary* (bibliog. 3.2) and most other Japanese–English dictionaries (and is the basis of the Japanese romanization tables available online from the Library of Congress); outside Japan, it is also used almost exclusively, notably in Asian collections in libraries throughout the world.

11.107   *Modified Hepburn system.* In the modified Hepburn system (after James Curtis Hepburn, 1815–1911), an apostrophe is placed after a syllabic *n* that is followed by a vowel or *y*: *Gen'e*, *San'yo*. A macron is used over a long vowel in all Japanese words except well-known place-names (e.g., Tokyo, Hokkaido, Kobe) and words such as "shogun" and "daimyo" that have entered the English language and are thus not italicized. (When the pronunciation of such names or words is important to readers, however, macrons may be used: Tōkyō, Hokkaidō, Kōbe, shōgun, daimyō.) Hyphens should be used sparingly: *Meiji jidai-shi* (or *jidaishi*) *no shinkenkyū. Shinjuku-ku* (or *Shinjukuku*) *no meisho.*

11.108 *Chinese and Japanese—capitalization and italics.* Although capital letters do not exist in Japanese or Chinese, they are introduced in romanized versions of these languages where they would normally be used in English (see chapter 8). Personal names and place-names are capitalized. In hyphenated names, only the first element is capitalized in romanized Chinese, though both elements may be capitalized in Japanese. Common nouns and other words used in an English sentence are lowercased and italicized (see 7.49, 7.50). Names of institutions, schools of thought, religions, and so forth are capitalized if set in roman, lowercased if set in italics.

Donglin Academy; the Donglin movement
Buddhism, Taoism, feng shui [see 7.52], and other forms . . .
Under the Ming dynasty the postal service was administered by the Board of War (*bingbu*) through a central office in Beijing (*huitong guan*).
The heirs of the Seiyūkai and Minseitō are the Liberal and Progressive parties of Japan.
It was Genrō Saionji (the *genrō* were the elder statesmen of Japan) who said . . . (note that *genrō* is both singular and plural)

11.109 *Titles of Japanese and Chinese works.* As in English, titles of books and periodicals are italicized, and titles of articles are set in roman and enclosed in quotation marks (see 8.154–95). The first word of a romanized title is always capitalized, as are many proper nouns (especially in Japanese).

Chen Shiqi, *Mingdai guan shougongye de yanjiu* [Studies on government-operated handicrafts during the Ming dynasty], . . .
Hua Linfu, "Qingdai yilai Sanxia diqu shuihan zaihai de chubu yanjiu" [A preliminary study of floods and droughts in the Three Gorges region since the Qing dynasty], *Zhongguo shehui kexue* 1 (1999): 168–79.
Okamoto Yoshitomo, *Jūrokuseiki Nichi-Ō kōtsūshi no kenkyū* [Study of the intercourse between Japan and Europe during the sixteenth century], . . .
Akiyama Kenzō, "Goresu wa Ryūkyūjin de aru" [The Gores and the Ryūkyūans], *Shigaku-Zasshi* (or *Shigaku Zasshi*) . . .

11.110 *Inclusion of Chinese and Japanese characters.* Chinese and Japanese characters, immediately following the romanized version of the item they represent, are sometimes necessary to help readers identify references cited or terms used. They are largely confined to bibliographies and glossaries. Where needed in running text, they may be enclosed in parentheses. The advent of Unicode has made it easier for authors to include words in non-Latin alphabets in their manuscripts, but publishers need to be alerted of the need for special characters in case particular fonts are needed for publication (see 11.2).

Harootunian, Harry, and Sakai Naoki. "Nihon kenkyū to bunka kenkyū" 日本研究と文化研究. *Shisō* 思想 7 (July 1997): 4–53.

Hua Linfu 華林甫. "Qingdai yilai Sanxia diqu shuihan zaihai de chubu yanjiu" 清代以來三峽地區水旱災害的初步研究 [A preliminary study of floods and droughts in the Three Gorges region since the Qing dynasty]. *Zhongguo shehui kexue* 中國社會科學 1 (1999): 168–79.

That year the first assembly of the national Diet was held and the Imperial Rescript on Education (*kyōiku chokugo* 教育勅語) was issued.

Hebrew

11.111 *Hebrew transliteration systems.* There are several acceptable romanization systems for Hebrew, including the one in the *ALA-LC Romanization Tables* (see bibliog. 5). Any such system may be used, but it is the author's responsibility to use it consistently in a given work. (The Hebrew alphabet may be found in the alphabet table in *Merriam-Webster's Collegiate Dictionary* [bibliog. 3.1], among other sources.)

11.112 *Diacritics in transliterated Hebrew.* In transliterated Hebrew, the following accents and characters are sometimes needed: underdots (Ḥḥ, Ḳḳ, Ṭṭ, Ṿṿ); macrons (Āā, Ēē, Īī, Ōō, Ūū); acute accents (Śś); hačeks, or carons (Ǎǎ, Ěě); and superscript ə (ᵊ). The ʾalef and the ʿayin may be represented in the same way as the Arabic hamza and ʿayn (see 11.97 and table 11.2). In some systems, a prime (soft sign) may also be needed.

11.113 *Hebrew prefixes.* In Hebrew, several prepositions, conjunctions, and articles appear as prefixes. Some authors use apostrophes or hyphens after these prefixes in romanized text and some do not. (In Hebrew, no such marker is used.) Either approach is acceptable if used consistently.

11.114 *Hebrew capitalization and italics.* The Hebrew alphabet has no capital letters, and there is no universally used system for capitalizing romanized Hebrew. Writers may follow normal English usage—capitalizing proper names, book titles, and so forth (see 11.3, 11.9). Some writers eschew capitalization altogether. As always, the author must ensure internal consistency. For italics in romanized Hebrew, the normal English usage may also be followed (see 11.5).

11.115 *Hebrew word division.* For romanized Hebrew, or Hebrew words incorporated into English, the principles set forth in 7.31–43 may be followed. When a double consonant occurs at the point of division, one consonant goes with each division.

Rosh Ha-shana   Yom Kip-pur

11.116 *Unromanized Hebrew phrases.* Hebrew is read from right to left. In English sentences that contain an unromanized Hebrew phrase, the Hebrew order is maintained within the sentence. (Modern operating systems can often handle a mix of left-right and right-left input in the same context.)

The first phrase in Lamentations is איכה ישבה בדד (How she sits in solitude!).

If a line break occurs within a Hebrew phrase, the words must still be read right to left on each line. Thus, if the Hebrew phrase in the example above had to be broken, the Hebrew words would appear to be in a different order.

The first phrase in Lamentations is איכה ישבה
בדד (How she sits in solitude!).
or
The first phrase in Lamentations is איכה
ישבה בדד (How she sits in solitude!).

As a safeguard, the author should highlight all the words in Hebrew phrases and furnish detailed instructions on dealing with line breaks.

11.117 *A note on Hebrew vowels.* Most Hebrew vowels are not letters; they are marks attached to the letters, most of which are consonants. In Hebrew texts the vowel marks (as well as dots that modify the pronunciation of consonants) rarely appear. Among texts in which the marks do appear are prayer books, printed Bibles, and poetry.

Russian

11.118 *Russian transliteration.* Of the many systems for transliterating Russian, the most important are summarized in table 11.3. Journals of Slavic studies generally prefer a "linguistic" system that makes free use of diacritics and ligatures. In works intended for a general audience, however, diacritics and ligatures should be avoided. For general use, Chicago recommends the system of the United States Board on Geographic Names. Regardless of the system followed, the name spellings in *Merriam-Webster's Biographical Dictionary* (bibliog. 4.1) and *Merriam-Webster's Geographical Dictionary* (bibliog. 4.2) should prevail.

Catherine the Great	Moscow
Chekhov	Nizhniy (*or* Nizhni) Novgorod
Dnieper River	Tchaikovsky

11.119 *Russian capitalization.* Capitalization conventions in Cyrillic are much like those of French and should be preserved in transliteration. Pronouns, days of the week, months, and most proper adjectives are lowercased. Geographic designations are capitalized when they apply to formal institutions or political units but otherwise lowercased.

Tverskaya guberniya
tverskoye zemstvo
Moskovskiy universitet
russkiy kompozitor

11.120 *Titles of Russian works.* Only the first word and any proper nouns are capitalized in titles.

N. A. Kurakin, *Lenin i Trotskiy*
O. I. Skorokhodova, *Kak ya vosprinimayu i predstavlyayu okruzhayushchiy mir* [How I perceive and imagine the external world]

Note that in the original Cyrillic, titles are set in ordinary type; the Cyrillic *kursiv* is used more sparingly than our italic and never for book titles. In transliterations, however, italic should be used.

11.121 *Russian quotations and dialogue.* Russian generally resembles French in its use of guillemets (« ») for dialogue and quoted material and of dashes for dialogue (see 11.32, 11.34).

«Bozhe, bozhe, bozhe!» govorit Boris.

—S kem ya rabotayu?
—S tovarishchem.
—Kak my rabotayem?
—S interesom.

TABLE 11.3. Russian alphabet (and Unicode numbers) and romanization

Basic Russian (Cyrillic) alphabet (and Unicode numbers)		US Board on Geographic Names	Library of Congress	"Linguistic" system
Upright	Cursive[1]			
А (0410), а (0430)	*А, а*	a		
Б (0411), б (0431)	*Б, б*	b		
В (0412), в (0432)	*В, в*	v		
Г (0413), г (0433)	*Г, г*	g		
Д (0414), д (0434)	*Д, д*	d		
Е (0415), е (0435)	*Е, е*	ye,[2] e	e	e
Ё (0401), ё[3] (0451)	*Ё, ё*	yë,[2] ë (00EB)	ë	e, ë
Ж (0416), ж (0436)	*Ж, ж*	zh		ž
З (0417), з (0437)	*З, з*	z		
И (0418), и (0438)	*И, и*	i		
Й (0419), й (0439)	*Й, й*	y	ĭ (012D)	j
К (041A), к (043A)	*К, к*	k		
Л (041B), л (043B)	*Л, л*	l		
М (041C), м (043C)	*М, м*	m		
Н (041D), н (043D)	*Н, н*	n		
О (041E), о (043E)	*О, о*	o		
П (041F), п (043F)	*П, п*	p		
Р (0420), р (0440)	*Р, р*	r		
С (0421), с (0441)	*С, с*	s		
Т (0422), т (0442)	*Т, т*	t		
У (0423), у (0443)	*У, у*	u		
Ф (0424), ф (0444)	*Ф, ф*	f		
Х (0425), х (0445)	*Х, х*	kh		x
Ц (0426), ц (0446)	*Ц, ц*	ts	t͡s[4]	c
Ч (0427), ч (0447)	*Ч, ч*	ch		č
Ш (0428), ш (0448)	*Ш, ш*	sh		š
Щ (0429), щ (0449)	*Щ, щ*	shch		šč
Ъ (042A), ъ[5] (044A)	*Ъ, ъ*	″ (201D)[6]	″ (02BA)[7]	″ (02BA)[7]
Ы (042B), ы[5] (044B)	*Ы, ы*	y		
Ь (042C), ь[5] (044C)	*Ь, ь*	′ (2019)[8]	′ (02B9)[9]	′ (02B9)[9]
Э (042D), э (044D)	*Э, э*	e	ė (0117)	è (00E8)
Ю (042E), ю (044E)	*Ю, ю*	yu	i͡u[4]	ju
Я (042F), я (044F)	*Я, я*	ya	i͡a[4]	ja

NOTE: The Library of Congress and "linguistic" systems employ the same characters as the US Board system except where noted.

[1]The Unicode numbers are the same for the upright and cursive characters; the differences in appearance depend on the italic version of a given typeface.   [2]Initially and after a vowel or ъ or ь.

[3]Not considered a separate letter; usually represented in Russian by *e*.

[4]Character tie, sometimes omitted, may be produced by using the combining double inverted breve (U+0361).

[5]Does not occur initially.   [6]Right double quotation mark.   [7]Modifier letter double prime.

[8]Right single quotation mark.   [9]Modifier letter prime.

To set off a quotation within a speech, guillemets may be used, as in French. For an example, see 11.34.

11.122   *Russian suspension points.* Suspension points are used as in French (see 11.35) to indicate interruptions or breaks in thought.

Ya . . . vy . . . my tol'ko chto priyekhali.

In Russian, an exclamation point or a question mark often takes the place of one of the dots; this convention may be regularized to three dots in English publications.

Mitya! . . . Gde vy byli? . . .

11.123   *Russian uses of the dash.* A dash is sometimes inserted, with a space on either side, between subject and complement when the equivalent of *is* or *are* is omitted.

Moskva — stolitsa Rossii.

Similarly, a dash, preceded and followed by a word space, is used in place of a verb omitted because it would be identical to the preceding verb.

Ivan i Sonya poyedut v Moskvu poyezdom, Lev i Lyuba — avtobusom.

11.124   *Russian word division—general.* Transliterated Russian should be divided according to the rules governing word division in the Cyrillic original. The rules in this section are adapted from the transliteration system of the United States Board on Geographic Names.

11.125   *Combinations not to be divided in Cyrillic transliteration.* Combinations representing single Cyrillic letters—*ch, kh, sh, shch, ts, ya, ye, yë, yu, zh*—should never be divided, nor should combinations of a vowel plus short *i* (or *yod*, transliterated *y*): *ay, ey, yey,* and so on.

11.126   *Division between Russian consonants.* Words may be divided between single consonants or between a consonant and a consonant combination.

ubor-ku   chudes-nym   mol-cha   sred-stvo   mor-skoy

The following consonant combinations are not normally divided: *bl, br, dr, dv, fl, fr, gl, gr, kl, kr, ml, pl, pr, sk, skr, skv, st, str, stv, tr, tv, vl, vr, zhd.*

They may, however, be divided if they fall across the boundary of a prefix and a root or other such units (e.g., ob-lech', ras-kol).

11.127 *Division of Russian words after prefixes or between parts.* Words may be divided after a prefix, but generally the prefix itself should not be divided.

bes-poryadok   pere-stroyka   za-dat'   pred-lozhit'   pro-vesti   obo-gnat'

Compound words should be divided between parts.

radio-priyëmnik   gor-sovet   kino-teatr

11.128 *Division of Russian words after vowel or diphthong.* Words may be divided after a vowel or a diphthong before a single (Cyrillic) consonant.

Si-bir'   voy-na   Gorba-chev   da-zhe

Division after a vowel may also be made before a consonant combination.

puteshe-stvennik   khi-trit'   pro-stak   ru-brika

South Asian Languages

11.129 *South Asian special characters.* Transliteration of the principal South Asian languages requires some or all of the following special characters (see also table 11.2):

Āā, Ææ, Ǣǣ, Ḍḍ, Ēē, Ḥḥ, Īī, Ḷḷ, Ḹḹ, Ṃṃ, Ṇṇ, Ṅṅ, Ññ, Ōō, Ṛṛ, Ṝṝ, Ṣṣ, Śś, Ṭṭ, Ūū

Increasingly, however, writers using South Asian languages are employing a simplified style that does not use diacritics at all—for example, substituting *sh* for various *s*'s, ignoring subscript dots for dental consonants, and omitting macrons altogether.

Classical Greek

11.130 *Transliterating Greek.* Isolated Greek words and phrases in works not dealing with ancient Greece are usually transliterated. Table 11.4 shows the Greek alphabet (with Unicode numbers) and corresponding Latin-

TABLE 11.4. Greek alphabet (and Unicode numbers) and romanization

Name of letter	Greek alphabet (and Unicode numbers)	Transliteration
Alpha	A (0391), α (03B1)	a
Beta	B (0392), β (03B2)	b
Gamma	Γ (0393), γ¹ (03B3)	g
Delta	Δ (0394), δ² (03B4)	d
Epsilon	E (0395), ε (03B5)	e
Zeta	Z (0396), ζ (03B6)	z
Eta	H (0397), η (03B7)	ē (0113)
Theta	Θ (0398), θ³ (03B8)	th
Iota	I (0399), ι (03B9)	i
Kappa	K (039A), κ (03BA)	k
Lambda	Λ (039B), λ (03BB)	l
Mu	M (039C), μ (03BC)	m
Nu	N (039D), ν (03BD)	n
Xi	Ξ (039E), ξ (03BE)	x
Omicron	O (039F), o (03BF)	o
Pi	Π (03A0), π (03C0)	p
Rho	P (03A1), ρ (03C1)	r; *initially,* rh; *double,* rrh
Sigma	Σ (03A3), σ (03C3), ς⁴ (03C2)	s
Tau	T (03A4), τ (03C4)	t
Upsilon	Y (03A5), υ (03C5)	u; *often* y, *exc. after* a, e, ē, i
Phi	Φ (03A6), φ⁵ (03C6)	ph
Chi	X (03A7), χ (03C7)	kh, ch
Psi	Ψ (03A8), ψ (03C8)	ps
Omega	Ω (03A9), ω (03C9)	ō (014D)

¹Note that γγ becomes ng, and γκ becomes nk.

²Sometimes appears as ∂ (U+2202, partial differential), but mainly in mathematical contexts.

³Also ϑ (U+03D1). ⁴Final letter. ⁵Also ϕ (U+03D5).

alphabet letters. In transliteration, all Greek accents are omitted. The macron is used to distinguish the long vowels eta (ē) and omega (ō) from the short vowels epsilon (e) and omicron (o). The iota subscript is transliterated by an i on the line, following the vowel it is associated with (ἀνθρώπῳ, *anthrōpōi*). The rough breathing is transliterated by h, which precedes a vowel or diphthong and follows the letter *rho* (as in the English word *rhythm*). The smooth breathing is ignored, since it represents merely the absence of the h sound. If a diaeresis appears in the Greek, it also appears in transliteration. Transliterated Greek words or phrases are usually italicized unless the same words occur frequently, in which case they may be italicized at first mention and then set in roman.

11.131 *Typesetting Greek.* Authors who need to present Greek should use a Unicode-enabled font if at all possible (see 11.2). Publishers need to make sure that a Greek font is available for publication; Greek may need to be set in a slightly different size to make it visually match the surrounding type. Greek is normally not set in italics. Extra white space must occasionally be added where more than one diacritic appears over a vowel.

Breathings and Accents

11.132 *Greek breathing marks.* When Greek is set in the Greek alphabet, every initial vowel or diphthong or rho must be marked with a breathing, either rough (ʽ, dasia) or smooth (ʼ, psili). The breathing mark is placed over the initial lowercase vowel (or the second vowel of a diphthong). It is placed to the left of capital letters. Note that a single quotation mark cannot function as a breathing because it is the wrong size and does not sit close enough to the letter.

αὖτε ἕτεραι Ἕλλην ἥβη Ἶρις ὑπέχω ὠκύς ῥάδιος

11.133 *Greek accent marks.* There are three Greek accent marks: acute, or oxia (ʼ); circumflex, or perispomeni, either tilde-shaped or rounded (˜ or ˆ), depending on the typeface; and grave, or varia (ˋ). Accents in Greek occur only over vowels. The circumflex occurs only on the two final syllables of a word. The grave accent occurs only on the last syllable. Like breathings, accents are placed over lowercase vowels, over the second vowel of a diphthong, and to the left of capital vowels. A diaeresis is used to indicate that two successive vowels do not form a diphthong but are voiced separately (as in French *naïf*).

11.134 *Unaccented Greek words.* With two exceptions, all Greek words are marked with accents—usually one, occasionally two (see below). The first exception is a group of monosyllabic words called proclitics, which are closely connected with the words following them. The proclitics are the forms of the definite article ὁ, ἡ, οἱ, αἱ; the prepositions εἰς, ἐν, ἐκ (ἐξ); the conjunctions εἰ, ὡς; and the adverb οὐ (οὐκ, οὐχ). The second exception is a group called enclitics, short words pronounced as if part of the word preceding them. Enclitics usually lose their accents (Ἀρταξερξής τε), and in certain circumstances the word preceding them gains a second accent (φοβεῖταί τις).

11.135 *Greek vowels.* Vowels complete with breathing marks and accents, in all combinations, are an integral part of every Greek font used in publishing. Each font, for example, should be able to provide, for lowercase eta, η, ή, ῆ, ἤ, ἢ, ἥ, ἦ, ἧ, ἥ, ἢ, ἦ, ἧ, and, for uppercase eta, Η, Ἡ, Ἠ, ῝Η, ῍Η, ῝Η, ῏Η, ῝Η, ῍Η. Additional symbols are needed for scholarly works dealing with ancient manuscripts or papyri. Consult the latest Unicode character charts for Greek alphabets.

Punctuation and Numbers

11.136   *Greek punctuation.* In Greek the period and comma are the same as in English; the colon and semicolon are both represented by a midlevel dot (·); the question mark is represented by a semicolon. The apostrophe (which looks almost like a smooth breathing mark) is used as an elision mark when the final vowel of one word is elided before a second word beginning with a vowel. In English texts, quoted words or passages in the Greek alphabet, of whatever length, should not be enclosed in quotation marks.

11.137   *Greek numbers.* Numbers, when not written out, are represented in ordinary Greek text by the letters of the alphabet, supplemented by three additional, obsolete Greek letters—stigma, koppa, and sampi: ϛ′ = 6, ϟ′ = 90, ϡ′ = 900. The diacritical mark resembling a prime (and defined for Unicode as the Greek numeral sign, U+0374) distinguishes the letters as numerals and is added to a sign standing alone or to the last sign in a series. For example, ρια′ means 111. For thousands, the foregoing signs are used with a different diacritical mark (the Greek lower numeral sign, U+0375): ͵α = 1,000, ͵αρια′ = 1,111, ͵βσκβ′ = 2,222. See table 11.5.

TABLE 11.5. Greek numerals

1	α′	13	ιγ′	30	λ′	600	χ′
2	β′	14	ιδ′	40	μ′	700	ψ′
3	γ′	15	ιε′	50	ν′	800	ω′
4	δ′	16	ιϛ′	60	ξ′	900	ϡ′[3]
5	ε′	17	ιζ′	70	ο′	1,000	͵α
6	ϛ′[1]	18	ιη′	80	π′	2,000	͵β
7	ζ′	19	ιθ′	90	ϟ′[2]	3,000	͵γ
8	η′	20	κ′	100	ρ′	4,000	͵δ
9	θ′	21	κα′	200	σ′	10,000	͵ι
10	ι′	22	κβ′	300	τ′	100,000	͵ρ
11	ια′	23	κγ′	400	υ′		
12	ιβ′	24	κδ′	500	φ′		

[1]Stigma (U+03DB); also represented with digamma (U+03DD): ϝ′.

[2]Archaic koppa (U+03D9); also represented with koppa (U+03DF): ϟ′.

[3]Sampi (U+03E1); formerly disigma (double sigma).

Word Division

11.138 *Greek word division—consecutive vowels.* Diphthongs (αι, αυ, ει, ευ, ηυ, οι, ου, υι, ωυ) are never divided. But two consecutive vowels that do not form a diphthong are divided.

θε-ά-ο-μαι   υἱ-ός   παύ-ε-τε   νε-ώς

11.139 *Greek word division—single consonants.* When a single consonant occurs between two vowels, the word is divided before the consonant.

φω-νή   κε-φα-λίς   μέ-γα   δέ-δω-κεν   μή-τηρ

11.140 *Greek word division—two or more consonants.* If a consonant is doubled, or if a mute is followed by its corresponding aspirate (πφ, βφ, κχ, γχ, τθ, δθ), the word is divided after the first consonant.

θά-λασ-σα   συγ-χαί-ρω

If the combination of two or more consonants begins with a liquid (λ, ρ) or a nasal (μ, ν), division is made after the liquid or nasal.

ἔμ-προ-σθεν   (*but before* μν: μέ-μνημαι)

All other combinations of two or more consonants *follow* the division.

πρᾶ-γμα	τέ-χνη	βα-θμός	αἰ-σχρός
βι-βλί-ον	δά-κτυ-λος	σκῆ-πτρον	βά-κτρον

11.141 *Greek word division—compound words.* Compound words are divided between parts; within each part the above rules apply. The commonest type of compound word begins with a preposition or a prefix.

ἀμφ-	ἀφ-	ὑπ-	ἐξ-έβαλον
ἀν-	ἐφ-	ὑφ-	καθ-ίστημι
ἀπ-	κατ-		δύσ-μορφος

Old English and Middle English

11.142 *Special characters in Old and Middle English.* Several Old English or Middle English letters not used in modern English occur in both lowercase and capital forms (see also table 11.1).

Ðð   Edh or eth   Þþ   Thorn

Both edh and thorn represent voiced or unvoiced *th*, as in *them* or *three*.

ȝȝ   Yogh; occurs in Old English representing *g* as in *good*, *y* as in *year*, or *gh* as in
      light and *thought*. Yogh sometimes occurs in Middle English representing *y*
      as in *year* and *gh* as in *light* and *thought*, but normally not *g* as in *good*.
Æ æ   Ligature; should *not* be printed as two letters in Old English names and text
      (Ælfric).

Authors should use the correct Unicode characters for the ligature and for
edh, thorn, and yogh, and should provide their publisher with a list of
these and any other special characters (see 11.2). For the Latin small esh
(ʃ), see 13.7.

11.143   *Ampersand and wynn.* In Old English and Middle English texts a sort of
stylized seven (the Tironian *et*) may be found for *and*, but the modern ampersand may be substituted for this. In Old English texts Ƿ or ƿ (wynn) is
found for *w*; the modern *w* is often substituted for this.

American Sign Language

11.144   *Signed languages.* The visual-gestural languages used by deaf people in
different parts of the world are called signed languages. Signed languages
are quite different from spoken languages (although there may be regional effects of language contact), and a particular signed language may
or may not share the same national or geographic boundaries as spoken
languages in the same locations. The individual elements of these languages are known as signs.

11.145   *Components of signs.* Signs have five major articulatory components—
handshape, location, orientation, movement, and (in some cases) distinctive nonmanual signals.

11.146   *Writing ASL.* Many formal systems for writing signed languages exist;
however, none has been adopted for use by large numbers of deaf sign-
ers. This section offers an overview of some of the most frequently employed conventions for written transcription of signing. For additional
resources, see Charlotte Baker-Shenk and Dennis Cokely, *American Sign
Language: A Teacher's Resource Text on Grammar and Culture*; and Clayton

Valli, Ceil Lucas, and Kristin J. Mulrooney, *Linguistics of American Sign Language: An Introduction* (bibliog. 5).

11.147 *Glosses in ASL.* The written-language transcription of a sign is called a *gloss.* Glosses are words from the spoken language written in small capital letters: WOMAN, SCHOOL, CAT. (Alternatively, regular capital letters may be used.) When two or more written words are used to gloss a single sign, the glosses are separated by hyphens. The translation is enclosed in double quotation marks.

The sign for "a car drove by" is written as VEHICLE-DRIVE-BY.

One obvious limitation of the use of glosses from the spoken/written language to represent signs is that there is no one-to-one correspondence between the words or signs in any two languages.

11.148 *Compound signs.* Some combinations of signs have taken on a meaning separate from the meaning of the individual signs. Various typographical conventions are used to indicate these compounds, including a "close-up" mark or a plus sign. Depending on the transcription system, the sign for "parents" might be glossed as follows:

MOTHER^FATHER   *or*   MOTHER+FATHER

11.149 *Fingerspelling.* For proper nouns and other words borrowed from the spoken language, the signer may fingerspell the word, using the handshapes from a manual alphabet. (There are numerous fingerspelling alphabets used by different signed languages, among them the American Manual Alphabet.) Fingerspelled words may be transcribed in any of the following ways:

fs-JOHN   *or*   J-O-H-N   *or*   j-o-h-n

11.150 *Lexicalized signs.* Over time, some fingerspelled words have taken on the quality of distinct signs, either by omission of some of the individual letter signs or by a change in the orientation or movement of the letter signs. These lexicalized signs are represented by the "pound" symbol (#): #WHAT, #BACK, #DO.

11.151 *Handshapes.* Most of the handshapes of American Sign Language are described by the corresponding alphabetic or numerical handshape or a variation thereof. For example, APPLE is made with an X handshape; CRE-ATE is made with a 4 handshape; ANY is made with an Open A handshape; YELL is made with a Bent 5 handshape. Handshapes without a clear relative in the fingerspelling or number system are labeled idiosyncratically according to the transcription system in use. For example, SARCASTIC is made with the HORNS handshape; AIRPLANE is made with the ILY handshape. Handshapes for signed languages that do not use the American Manual Alphabet are often described in relation to the ASL handshapes.

11.152 *Transcriptions of signed sentences.* Signed sentences are written as a sequence of glosses, often with the spoken/written-language translation underneath in italics or quotation marks or both. (For examples, see 11.153, 11.154.) Punctuation is generally omitted from sentence transcriptions (though not from the translations). Some writers, however, add question marks and exclamation points, and a comma may be used to indicate a short pause in the sentence.

11.153 *Pronouns, possessives, and reference.* Pronouns are commonly transcribed either as IX (since these are frequently produced with the "index" finger) or as PRO. Either of these is followed by indication of person and sometimes number. A similar convention is used with the possessive marker, sometimes glossed as POSS. There are varying conventions about how to indicate person and number. Thus, a third-person singular pronoun in ASL (equivalent to English "he," "she," or "it") might be glossed as IX_{3p}, IX-3p, or PRO.3. A second-person plural pronoun could be glossed as IX_{2p-pl}. Subscript indices are often used to show signs articulated in the same location or to indicate coreferential noun phrases. The following example indicates that *he* and *his* refer back to the same person:

IX_{3pi} LOSE $POSS_{3pi}$ HOUSE
He lost his house.

11.154 *Nonmanual signals.* Nonmanual gestures may be labeled based on anatomical behavior or grammatical interpretive function. These gestures, indicated by various abbreviations and terms, are typeset in a smaller font followed by a half-point rule above the ASL sentence. For example, the label *whq* is commonly used to refer to the facial expression that marks questions involving "who," "what," "when," "where," "how," or "why." This expression consists of a cluster of features that include furrowed brows and slightly squinted eyes. In the example below, *whq* occurs over the entire question (i.e., the expression is articulated simultaneously with all of the manual signs over which the line extends). In the same example, the label *rap hs* indicates a rapid headshake that occurs simultaneously with the sign WHO. Correct alignment is critical to an accurate transcription.

$$\overline{ \overset{whq}{\underset{\overline{\textit{rap hs}}}{}}}$$

fs-JOHN SEE YESTERDAY WHO
Whom did John see yesterday?

12 Mathematics in Type

Overview

12.1 *Additional resources.* This chapter is mainly intended to provide guidance to authors and editors working in the sciences who have occasional need to compose or edit mathematical expressions. Those who work exclusively with mathematics should consult Ellen Swanson's *Mathematics into Type* and Donald Knuth's *TeXbook*, among the other sources listed in bibliog. 2.4.

12.2 *Tools.* Many authors in mathematics and related quantitative fields prepare their manuscripts in LaTeX, a freely available, device-independent document markup and preparation system developed in the 1980s. In LaTeX, which is designed to work with the TeX typesetting system developed by Donald Knuth, a properly coded manuscript will generate equation numbers, cross-references, and many other elements automatically. Manuscript editors working with LaTeX documents (generally on paper) should have some understanding of how the markup works to avoid, for example, marking unnecessary changes or instructions and to know when a particular change can be indicated globally. A good place to start for more information is the LaTeX website. Manuscripts that include only the occasional in-line or displayed equation, on the other hand, are usually prepared using a word processor's equation editor. For marking mathematical copy on paper manuscripts, see 12.60–67.

Style of Mathematical Expressions

General Usage

12.3 *Standards for mathematical copy.* The author and editor should give careful attention to matters of style, usage, sense, meaning, clarity, accuracy, and consistency. Authors should use correct terminology and notation and should carefully follow the conventions of their special fields, and editors should query any apparent typographical or grammatical violations. As a general rule, mathematical copy, including displayed equations, should "read" as clearly and grammatically as any other kind of copy. The signs for simple mathematical operations and relations have direct verbal translations: $a < b$ reads "a is less than b"; $a > b$ reads "a is greater than b"; $a + b = c$ reads "a plus b equals c." The translation is not always straightforward, however, as is the case with $df(x)/dx$, which means "the derivative of the function f of x with respect to x" and is not the quotient of two numbers $df(x)$ and dx. Moreover, mathematical notation is often abbreviated: the pair of inequalities $a < b$ and $b < c$ is usually written $a < b < c$. In mathematics it is also standard to read terms with indices, such as x_i ("x sub i"), as plural or singular depending on the context (e.g., "for a unique x_i" and "for all the x_i" are both grammatically correct). Use this convention wherever possible to avoid ugly mixtures of italic mathematics and roman "s" in forming a plural.

12.4   *Consistency of notation.* Notation should be consistent and unambiguous: the same symbol should denote the same thing whenever it occurs and not be used for more than one thing. Typographical distinctions should also be made consistently; for example, if uppercase italic letters A, B, and C are used to denote sets and lowercase italic letters x, y, and z to denote the elements of sets, then a, b, and c should not be used for sets at another place without good reason.

12.5   *Words versus symbols in text.* In general, mathematical symbols may be used in text in lieu of words, and such statements as "$x \geq 0$" should not be rewritten as "x is greater than or equal to zero." Nonetheless, symbols should not be used as a shorthand for words if the result is awkward or ungrammatical. In the phrase

the vectors $r_1, \dots, r_n, \neq 0,$

the condition "$\neq 0$" is better expressed in words:

the nonzero vectors $r_1, \dots, r_n$

or

the vectors $r_1, \dots, r_n$, all nonzero,

depending on the emphasis desired. Moreover, logical symbols should generally not appear in text:

$\exists$ a minimum value of the function f on the interval $[a, b]$

should be replaced by

there exists a minimum value of the function f on the interval $[a, b]$

or

the function f has a minimum value on the interval $[a, b]$.

See also 12.7.

12.6   *Concise expression.* Mathematical symbols should not be used superfluously. For example, in the first statement the symbol n is extraneous, as are the parentheses in the second statement:

There is no integer n between 0 and 1.
This quantity is bounded above by the sum $(a + b)$.

As a general rule, no letter standing for a mathematical object should be used only once. Symbols that appear to be redundant may be qualified later in the same discussion, however, and editors should never delete a symbol without explicit instruction from the author.

12.7   *Sentence beginning with a mathematical symbol.* Mathematical symbols should not begin a sentence, especially if the preceding sentence ended with a symbol, since it may be difficult to tell where one sentence ends and another begins. For example, it is difficult to read

Assume that $x \in S$. S is countable.

If a sentence starting with a symbol cannot easily be rephrased, the appropriate term for the symbol can be inserted in apposition at the beginning of the sentence:

Assume that $x \in S$. The set S is countable.

If the sentences are closely related, a semicolon may be used to connect them:

A function f is even if $f(-x) = f(x)$; f is odd if $f(-x) = -f(x)$.

12.8   *Adjacent mathematical symbols.* Mathematical symbols in adjacent mathematical expressions should be separated by words or punctuation (or both), for the reasons discussed in 12.7:

Suppose that $a = bq + r$, where $0 \le r < b$.

Signs and Symbols

12.9   *Mathematical characters.* The smallest units of mathematical writing are mathematical signs and symbols, which include letters and numbers. Table 12.1 lists some of the standard mathematical characters and their verbal translations. Unicode numbers are included, where applicable (see also 11.2), as are the LaTeX commands for producing each character. (It should be noted that old-style figures [like this: 1938] should be avoided in mathematical contexts; lining figures [like this: 1938] should be used instead. See also 3.84, item 4.)

12.10   *Letters and diacritical marks.* Ordinary italic letters are used to represent various kinds of mathematical objects. The set of letters can be greatly extended by the use of diacritics (including accents), such as $\hat{a}$, $\tilde{a}$, $\bar{a}$, $\breve{a}$, $\dot{a}$, $\ddot{a}$, $\check{a}$, and $\vec{a}$. All such diacritics and additional characters are considered to be separate from the letters they modify, rather than forming a single glyph. (Note that when an i or a j appears with a diacritical mark—e.g., with an overbar or a circumflex—the dotless i or j should be used.) Double diacritics may also be used; for example, $\bar{\bar{a}}$, and $\dot{\bar{a}}$. These can, however, be difficult to center over a letter and, in combination with capital letters, may interfere with descenders from the line above, so they should be avoided if possible. Marks over or beneath several letters or groups of letters—for example, overlines, underlines, overbraces, and underbraces—are frequently encountered in mathematics, as are other types of stacked expressions.

12.11   *Italic letters and kerning.* Although italic letters are used to denote mathematical objects, mathematical expressions require special treatment in typesetting. In particular, contiguous italic letters must never be kerned. To this end—and as a general aid to readability—fonts intended for mathematics are typically designed so that italic letters are less slanted than they might otherwise be (and, therefore, unlikely to crowd or overlap other typeset elements). Contiguous letters that form an abbreviation—e.g., "Aut" for "automorphism group"—should be set roman; see also 12.17.

12.12   *Letters and fonts.* The number of symbols can be extended by using letters from other alphabets, most often the Greek alphabet, and by representing letters from the Latin alphabet in other fonts and typefaces. Examples of characters from four fonts and typefaces commonly used in mathematics are

GREEK	SCRIPT	BOLDFACE ITALIC	BOLDFACE GREEK
ΑΒΓΔαβγδ	$\mathcal{ABCD}abcd$	**ABCDabcd**	**ΑΒΓΔαβγδ**

TABLE 12.1 Common mathematical signs and symbols (with Unicode numbers and LaTeX commands)

Sign/ symbol	Name	Unicode	LaTeX
OPERATIONS			
+	Plus sign	002B	+
−	Minus sign	2212	-
×	Multiplication sign	00D7	\times
·	Middle dot (multiplication)	00B7	\cdot
÷	Division sign	00F7	\div
/	Division slash	2215[a]	/[b]
∘	Ring operator (composition)	2218	\circ
∪	Union	222A	\cup
∩	Intersection	2229	\cap
±	Plus or minus	00B1	\pm
∓	Minus or plus	2213	\mp
∗	Asterisk operator (convolution)	2217[c]	\ast
⊛	Circled asterisk operator (convolution)	229B	\circledast
⊕	Circled plus (direct sum, various)	2295	\oplus
⊖	Circled minus (various)	2296	\ominus
⊗	Circled times (various)	2297	\otimes
⊙	Circled dot operator (various)	2299	\odot
:	Ratio	2236[d]	\colon
⨿	Coproduct or amalgamation	2210	\amalg
RELATIONS			
=	Equals sign	003D	=
≠	Not equal to	2260	\neq
≈	Almost equal to, asymptotic to	2248	\approx
≅	Approximately equal to, isomorphic to	2245	\approxeq
<	Less than	003C	<
≪	Much less than	226A	\ll
>	Greater than	003E	>
≫	Much greater than	226B	\gg
≤	Less than or equal to	2264	\leq
≥	Greater than or equal to	2265	\geq
≡	Identical to, congruent to	2261	\equiv
≢	Not identical to, not congruent to	2262	\nequiv
∣	Divides, divisible by	2223[e]	\divides
∼	Tilde operator (similar to, asymptotically equal to)	223C[f]	\sim
≔	Colon equals (assignment)	2254	\coloneqq
∈	Element of	2208	\in
∉	Not an element of	2209	\notin
⊂	Subset of	2282	\subset
⊆	Subset of or equal to	2286	\subseteq
⊃	Superset of	2283	\supset

TABLE 12.1 (*continued*)

Sign/ symbol	Name	Unicode	LaTeX
RELATIONS (*continued*)			
⊇	Superset of or equal to	2287	\supseteq
∝	Proportional to	221D[g]	\propto
≐	Approaches the limit, definition	2250	\doteq
→	Tends to, maps to	2192	\rightarrow
←	Maps from	2190	\leftarrow
↦	Maps to	21A6	\mapsto
↪	Maps into	21AA	\hookrightarrow
↩	Maps into	21A9	\hookleftarrow
OPERATORS			
∑	Summation	2211[h]	\sum
∏	Product	220F[i]	\prod
∫	Integral	222B[j]	\int
∮	Contour integral	222E	\oint
LOGIC			
∧	And, conjunction	2227	\wedge
∨	Or, disjunction	2228	\vee
¬	Not sign (negation)	00AC	\neg
⇒	Implies	21D2	\Rightarrow
→	Implies	2192	\rightarrow
⇔	If and only if	21D4	\Leftrightarrow
↔	If and only if	2194	\leftrightarrow
∃	There exists (existential quantifier)	2203	\exists
∀	For all (universal quantifier)	2200	\forall
⊢	Assertion	22A6	\vdash
∴	Hence, therefore	2234	\therefore
∵	Because	2235	\because
RADIAL UNITS			
′	Minute (prime)	2032	\prime
″	Second (double prime)	2033	\second
°	Degree	00B0	\degree
CONSTANTS			
π	Pi (≈3.14159265)	03C0	\pi
e	Base of natural logarithms (≈2.71828183)	0065[k]	e
GEOMETRY			
⊥	Perpendicular to (up tack)	22A5	\perp
∥	Parallel to	2225[l]	\parallel
∦	Not parallel to	2226	\nparallel
∠	Angle	2220	\angle
∢	Spherical angle	2222	\sphericalangle
⩦	Equiangular to	225A	\veedoublebar

TABLE 12.1 (*continued*)

Sign/ symbol	Name	Unicode	LaTeX
MISCELLANEOUS			
i	Square root of −1	0069[m]	i
′	Prime	2032	\prime
″	Double prime	2033	\second
‴	Triple prime	2034	\third
√	Square root, radical	221A	\sqrt
∛	Cube root	221B	\sqrt[3]
!	Factorial	0021	!
‼	Double factorial	203C	!!
∅	Empty set, null set	2205[n]	\varnothing[o]
∞	Infinity	221E	\infty
∂	Partial differential	2202	\partial
Δ	Increment, Laplace operator	2206	\triangle
∇	Nabla, del; also Laplace operator (with superscript 2)	2207	\nabla
□	d'Alembert operator (white square)	25A1	\square

NOTE: Where an alternate symbol is given in a note, the symbol listed in the table is preferred.

[a]Also fraction slash (2044) or solidus (002F).

[b]LaTeX also defines \slash, which permits a line break after the slash.

[c]Also asterisk (002A).   [d]Also colon (003A).

[e]Also vertical line (007C) or Latin letter dental click (01C0).   [f]Also tilde (007E).

[g]Also α (Greek small letter alpha, 03B1).   [h]Also Σ (Greek capital letter sigma, 03A3).

[i]Also Π (Greek capital letter pi, 03A0).   [j]Also ʃ (Latin small letter esh, 0283).   [k]Italic "e."

[l]Also Latin letter lateral click (01C1) or double vertical line (2018).   [m]Italic "i."

[n]Also Latin capital letter O with stroke (00D8).   [o]Also \emptyset.

Lowercase script characters are often not available, though they have been defined for the mathematical alphabets in Unicode (see also 11.2). See also 12.64 for marking fonts on paper manuscripts.

12.13   *List of unusual characters.* Before editing begins, it may be advisable, depending on the typesetter and the publisher's knowledge of the typesetter's resources, to prepare a list of unusual mathematical signs, symbols, and special characters used in the manuscript. This is preferably done by the author but may be done by the editor. In preparing an electronic manuscript, the author should make a list of any special, nonstandard fonts. A copy should be given to the publisher, who will check with the typesetter to make sure the necessary characters are available. If some are not, the author may be asked to use more accessible forms; if that is impossible, the typesetter must be asked to obtain or generate the characters needed.

12.14 *Special mathematical symbols.* Many mathematical symbols have a reserved meaning: π stands for the number $3.14159265\ldots$, e for the number $2.71828182\ldots$, and i for the square root of -1. The symbols $\forall$, $\exists$, $\in$, $\subset$, and $\varnothing$ are used in all mathematical disciplines. Double-struck (blackboard) symbols are reserved for familiar systems of numbers: $\mathbb{N}$ for the natural numbers, $\mathbb{Z}$ for the integers ($\mathbb{Z}^+$ is the same as $\mathbb{N}$), $\mathbb{Q}$ for the rational numbers, $\mathbb{R}$ for the real numbers, and $\mathbb{C}$ for the complex numbers.

12.15 *Signs for binary operations and relations.* *Binary operations* act as conjunctions to combine two mathematical expressions. Examples of binary operation signs are $+$ (plus sign), $-$ (minus sign), $\cdot$ (multiplication dot), $\times$ (multiplication cross), $\div$ (division sign), $/$ (solidus or slash), and $\circ$ (composition sign). *Binary relations* act as verbs and express a relationship between two mathematical expressions. Examples of relation signs are $=$ (equals), $\neq$ (does not equal), $>$ (is greater than), and $<$ (is less than).

12.16 *Basic spacing in mathematics.* Mathematics isn't simply read left to right in a machine-like manner, and one should be able to see the parts of an equation if it is properly set. Good mathematical spacing helps to indicate grouping: things that are more closely related should be set more tightly than things that are less closely related. Such spacing will vary according to the elements being set. In simple expressions, however, absolute spacing may be called for. Signs for binary operations (i.e., conjunctions); symbols of integration, summation, or union; and signs for binary relations (i.e., verbs) are preceded and followed by medium spaces:

$$x^n + y^n = z^n, \qquad X \cup \varnothing = X, \qquad (a \circ b) \circ c = a \circ (b \circ c).$$

No space follows a binary operation or relation sign when it is modifying a symbol (i.e., used as an adjective):

$$-1, \qquad +\infty, \qquad \times 5, \qquad > 7.$$

In subscripts and superscripts, no space precedes or follows operation or relation signs:

$$x^{a+b}, \qquad y^{c-2}.$$

Commas used between coordinate points or in lists should be followed by a medium space (see 12.19). See also A.22.

12.17 *Functions.* For a list of abbreviated functions, see table 12.2. These abbreviations are followed by a thin space unless the argument is enclosed in delimiters, or fences (see 12.26), in which case they are usually closed up to the opening delimiter:

$$\ln 2\pi, \quad \sin(x+y), \quad \min(x_1, x_2).$$

Limits are set as subscripts to the right of the abbreviation in text and below the abbreviation in display:

$$\lim_{x\to a} f(x), \quad \lim_{x\to a} f(x),$$

$$\max_{a_i \in S}(a_i), \quad \max_{a_i \in S}(a_i).$$

TABLE 12.2. Standard abbreviated notations in mathematical copy

sin	Sine	sn	Elliptic function, sn
cos	Cosine	cn	Elliptic function, cn
		dn	Elliptic function, dn
tan	Tangent	tg	Tangent[a]
cot	Cotangent	ctg	Cotangent[a]
sec	Secant	csc	Cosecant
sinh	Hyperbolic sine	cosh	Hyperbolic cosine
tanh	Hyperbolic tangent	coth	Hyperbolic cotangent
$\sin^{-1}$	Inverse sine	arcsin	Inverse sine
log	Common logarithm ($\log_{10}$)	ln	Natural logarithm
lg	Binary logarithm ($\log_2$)	$\log_e$	Natural logarithm, alternate form
sgn	Sign	arg	Argument
det or Det	Determinant	Tr	Trace (also Sp, or *spur*)
Re, $\Re$	Real part	Im, $\Im$	Imaginary part
curl	Curl; vector operator, same as $\nabla \times$	div	Divergence; vector operator, same as $\nabla \cdot$
prob or Pr	Probability	mod	Modulo (as in $a \bmod b$)
inf	Infimum; greatest lower bound	sup	Supremum; least upper bound
isom	Isomorphism	Hom	Homeomorphism
min	Minimum	max	Maximum
gcd	Greatest common divisor	lcm	Least common multiple
dex	Decimal exponent; from $10^{-1.5}$ to 10^{-3} is 1.5 dex	norm	Norm; norm $(a) = \|a\|$
dim or Dim	Dimension	ker	Kernel
wrt	With respect to[b]	iff	If and only if[b]
Var or var	Variance	Cov or cov	Covariance

[a] Frequently used by non–North American authors.

[b] Used in informal notation.

Punctuation

12.18   *Mathematical expressions and punctuation.* Mathematical equations, whether run in with the text or displayed on a separate line, are grammatically part of the text in which they appear. Thus, equations must be edited not only for the correct presentation of the mathematical characters but also for correct grammar in the sentence. Punctuation of mathematical expressions requires special attention. For example, if several expressions (i.e., a "list" of expressions) appear in a single display, they should be separated by commas or semicolons. For example,

$$x_1 + x_2 + x_3 = 3,$$
$$x_1 x_2 + x_2 x_3 + x_3 x_1 = 6,$$
$$x_1 x_2 x_3 = -1.$$

Consecutive lines of a single multiline expression, however, should not be punctuated:

$$(|a + b|)^2 = (a + b)^2 = a^2 + 2ab + b^2$$
$$\leq a^2 + 2|a||b| + b^2$$
$$= |a|^2 + 2|a||b| + |b|^2$$
$$= (|a| + |b|)^2.$$

Equations must carry ending punctuation if they end a sentence. All ending punctuation and the commas and semicolons separating expressions should be aligned horizontally on the baseline, even when preceded by constructs such as subscripts, superscripts, or fractions.

12.19   *Elided lists.* In elided lists, commas should come after each term in the list and after the ellipsis points if the list has a final term. For example,

$$y = 0, 1, 2, \ldots \quad \text{not} \quad y = 0, 1, 2\ldots;$$
$$x_1, x_2, \ldots, x_n \quad \text{not} \quad x_1, x_2, \ldots x_n.$$

The ellipsis points should be on the baseline when the terms of the list are separated by commas. Use a medium space after each comma.

12.20   *Elided operations and relations.* In elided sums or elided relations, the ellipsis points should be vertically centered between the operation or relation signs. For example,

$$x_1 + x_2 + \cdots + x_n \quad \text{not} \quad x_1 + x_2 + \ldots + x_n;$$

$$a_1 < a_2 < \cdots < a_n \quad \text{not} \quad a_1 < a_2 < \ldots < a_n.$$

Multiplication is often signified by the juxtaposition of the factors without a multiplication sign between them. That is,

$$abc \quad \text{means} \quad a \cdot b \cdot c.$$

When the multiplication sign is not explicit, the elided product may be denoted with ellipsis points either on the baseline or vertically centered:

$$a_1 a_2 \ldots a_n \quad \text{or} \quad a_1 a_2 \cdots a_n.$$

The second alternative is commonly used in displays with built-up factors:

$$\phi(n) = n\left(1 - \frac{1}{p_1}\right)\left(1 - \frac{1}{p_2}\right)\cdots\left(1 - \frac{1}{p_k}\right).$$

If the multiplication dot is present, then ellipsis points should be on the baseline and not centered. For example,

$$a_1 \cdot a_2 \cdot \ldots \cdot a_n \quad \text{not} \quad a_1 \cdot a_2 \cdots \cdots a_n.$$

If the multiplication cross is present, then ellipsis points should be centered. For example,

$$a_1 \times a_2 \times \cdots \times a_n.$$

Multiplication signs are always used when the factors need to be separated:

$$1 \times 2 \times \cdots \times 10.$$

In some contexts (such as for numbers) the use of the multiplication cross rather than the dot is merely a matter of preference, but in many other contexts (such as for vectors) multiplication dots and crosses have completely different meanings and cannot be used interchangeably.

Mathematical Expressions in Display

12.21   *Displaying mathematical expressions.* Mathematical expressions should be *displayed*—that is, set on a separate line clear of text—if they are important to the exposition, if they are referenced, or if they are difficult to read or typeset in the body of the text. If different mathematical expressions are displayed on the same line, the expressions should be separated by spacing, together with words or punctuation:

If $a = b$, then for all real numbers x,

$$a + x = b + x, \qquad ax = bx, \qquad -a = -b.$$

If different mathematical expressions are displayed on separate consecutive lines, regardless of whether there is an intervening word between two of the equations, each expression can usually be centered:

If $a = b$, then for all real numbers x,

$$a + x = b + x,$$

$$ax = bx,$$

$$-a = -b.$$

It should be noted that equals signs or other relation signs will not necessarily line up:

$$-\mu m_i^S - M_{iH} - M_{iL} + \frac{m_i^R}{r_i} = -I,$$

$$-\mu m_{iL}^M - \frac{m_{iL}^M}{T} + M_{iL} = 0,$$

$$-\mu m_{iH}^M - \frac{m_{iH}^M}{T} + M_{iH} = 0,$$

$$-\mu m_i^R - \frac{m_i^R}{r_i} + \frac{m_i^M}{T} = 0.$$

Some groups of displayed expressions, however, will be easier to read if they are lined up along an equals sign or other relational sign—for example, if only one of the lines includes an expression to the left of the equals sign or if all the expressions to the left of the equals sign are of the same length. For an example, see the three-line displayed expression in the next paragraph (12.22).

12.22   *Qualifying clauses for displayed expressions.* Qualifying clauses may be presented in several ways. If the main expression is displayed, the qualifying clause may also be displayed (separated from the expression by an em space or more):

> If f is a constant function, then
>
> $$f'(a) = 0 \quad \text{for all } a \in \mathbb{R}.$$

The qualifying clause may appear in the text, following the displayed main expression:

> Suppose that the prime factorization of the integer a is given by
>
> $$a = p_1^{k_1} \cdots p_r^{k_r},$$
>
> where the p_i are distinct prime numbers and $k_i > 0$.

The qualifying clause may appear in the text, preceding the displayed main expression:

> For all real numbers a and b,
>
> $$|a + b| \le |a| + |b|.$$

And qualifying clauses may themselves include displayed expressions:

> Suppose that assumptions 1 and 2 hold. Then a competitive equilibrium satisfies the following three differential equations:
>
> $$\frac{\dot{c}(t)}{c(t)} = \frac{1}{\theta}[(1-\alpha_1)\gamma\eta(t)^{1/e}\lambda(t)^{\alpha_1}\kappa(t)^{-\alpha_1}\chi(t)^{-\alpha_1} - \delta - \rho] - \frac{m_1}{\alpha_1},$$
>
> $$\frac{\dot{\chi}(t)}{\chi(t)} = \lambda(t)^{\alpha_1}\kappa(t)^{1-\alpha_1}\chi(t)^{-\alpha_1}\eta(t) - \chi(t)^{-1}c(t) - \delta - n - \frac{m_1}{\alpha_1},$$
>
> $$\frac{\dot{\kappa}(t)}{\kappa(t)} = \frac{[1 - \kappa(t)]\{\Delta[\dot{\chi}(t)/\chi(t)] + m_2 - (\alpha_2/\alpha_1)m_1\}}{(1-\varepsilon)^{-1} + \Delta[\kappa(t) - \lambda(t)]},$$

where

$$\eta(t) \equiv \gamma^{\varepsilon/(\varepsilon-1)} \left\{ 1 + \left(\frac{1-\alpha_1}{1-\alpha_2} \right) \left[\frac{1-\kappa(t)}{\kappa(t)} \right] \right\}^{\varepsilon/(\varepsilon-1)},$$

with initial conditions $\chi(0)$ and $\kappa(0)$, and also satisfies the transversality condition

$$\lim_{t\to\infty} \exp\left\{ -\left[\rho - \frac{(1-\theta)m_1}{\alpha_1} - n \right]t \right\} \chi(t) = 0.$$

12.23 *Breaking displayed expressions.* Long mathematical expressions may break badly at the end of a line and thus may need to be displayed. Even in displayed form, however, some long expressions may not fit on one line. In such cases, displayed expressions may be broken before a relation or operation sign. Examples of such signs are

Operation signs (conjunctions): $+ - \times \div \pm \cup \cap$
Relation signs (verbs): $= \neq > < \geq \leq \to \supset \subset \in \simeq \equiv$

See table 12.1 for a more complete list. In displayed expressions, runover lines are aligned on the relation signs, which should be followed by thick spaces:

$$h(x) = (x-\alpha)(x-\beta)(x-\gamma)$$
$$= x^3 - (\alpha+\beta+\gamma)x^2 + (\alpha\beta+\alpha\gamma+\beta\gamma)x - \alpha\beta\gamma.$$

If a runover line begins with an operation sign, the operation sign should be lined up with the first character to the right of the relation sign in the line above it, followed by a medium space:

$$\frac{\pi}{4} = \frac{1}{2} - \frac{1}{3\times 2^3} + \frac{1}{5\times 2^5} - \frac{1}{7\times 2^7} + \frac{1}{9\times 2^9} - \frac{1}{11\times 2^{11}} + \cdots$$
$$+ \frac{1}{3} - \frac{1}{3\times 3^3} + \frac{1}{5\times 3^5} - \frac{1}{7\times 3^7} + \frac{1}{9\times 3^9} - \cdots$$
$$+ \frac{1}{4} - \frac{1}{3\times 4^3} + \frac{1}{5\times 4^5} - \frac{1}{7\times 4^7} + \cdots.$$

For additional rules on breaking expressions, consult Ellen Swanson, *Mathematics into Type* (bibliog. 2.4).

Numeration

12.24   *Numbering displayed mathematical expressions.* Mathematical expressions that are referred to later in the text should be numbered or otherwise labeled. Displayed mathematical expressions that present important results are often numbered or labeled, as are important steps in a calculation or proof. All numbered mathematical expressions must be displayed. Displayed equations are usually centered on the line (without regard to the equation number or label). The number or label, enclosed in parentheses to prevent misreading, is usually put at the right margin, but it may be placed at the left margin.

Hence it is apparent that

$$1^3 + 2^3 + \cdots + n^3 = (1 + 2 + \cdots + n)^2. \tag{1.1}$$

In cross-references, display numbers or labels are enclosed in parentheses to match the marginal enumerations:

Recalling equation (1.1), we may conclude that . . .
or
Recalling (1.1), we may conclude that . . .

A range of equations is referred to by giving the first and last equation numbers, joined by an en dash:

From equations (2)–(5) we obtain . . .

12.25   *Methods of numeration.* Displayed mathematical expressions may be numbered or labeled, as may definitions, theorems, lemmas, and other formal parts of the exposition. A simple numbering system offers a convenient and space-saving method of cross-reference. In texts with many displayed equations, double or triple numeration is usually preferred. In this system, the displayed expressions in each chapter are labeled with the chapter number first, followed by the section number (if any), followed by the statement number, starting with number 1 (1.1.1, 1.1.2, . . . , 1.2.1, 1.2.2, . . . , etc.). If, on the other hand, single numeration is used (e.g., in a text with relatively few displayed equations), the displays are still usually numbered starting over with 1 in each chapter. It should be noted that definitions, theorems, lemmas, and so forth are usually numbered together, in a single sequence, and apart from displayed equations (e.g., definition 4.1, lemma 4.2, lemma 4.3, proposition 4.4, corollary 4.5).

Delimiters

12.26 *Common delimiters.* Three sorts of symbols are commonly used to group mathematical expressions: parentheses (), brackets [], and braces {}. They are used in pairs, and their normal order is {[()]}. When necessary, the sequence of delimiters can be extended by large parentheses, brackets, and braces as follows:

$$\{[(\{[(\quad)]\})]\}$$

In text, the braces are sometimes omitted from this sequence. Angle brackets, vertical bars, and double vertical bars carry special mathematical significance and should not be used to supplement the sequence of common delimiters.

12.27 *Functional notation.* In functional notation, nested pairs of parentheses are used instead of brackets or braces to indicate grouping:

$$(f \circ g \circ h)(x) = f(g(h(x))).$$

12.28 *Set notation.* Braces are used to delimit the elements of a set, and other delimiters should not be substituted. For example,

$$\{a_1, a_2, \ldots, a_n\}$$

denotes the set consisting of n objects $a_1, a_2, \ldots, a_n$, and

$$\{x : x \in D\}$$

denotes the set of all elements x in a set D. In the second example (called "set-builder" notation), the condition that defines the set follows the colon. A vertical bar is sometimes used instead of the colon to delimit the condition.

12.29 *Ordered set notation.* In ordered set notation, parentheses are used as delimiters. For example,

$$(a, b)$$

denotes the ordered pair of objects a and b, where a is the first element in the pair and b is the second element. More generally,

$$(a_1, a_2, \ldots, a_n)$$

denotes the ordered n-tuple of objects $a_1, a_2, \ldots, a_n$. This notation is standard, and other delimiters should not be substituted.

12.30   *Intervals.* In interval notation, parentheses are used to delimit an open interval, that is, one that does not include its endpoints; for example, (a, b) denotes the set of all real numbers between a and b, not including either a or b. Brackets are used to delimit a closed interval, that is, an interval that includes its endpoints. The notation $(a, b]$ signifies the interval not including a but including b, while $[a, b)$ denotes the interval including a but not including b. Parentheses and brackets in interval notation should not be replaced with other delimiters. (According to an alternative convention, $]a, b[$ denotes an open interval, $[a, b[$ an interval that includes a but not b, etc. This should not be changed if the author has used it consistently.)

12.31   *Delimiters denoting inner product.* Parentheses are sometimes used to denote the inner product of two vectors: $(\mathbf{u}, \mathbf{w})$. Angle brackets are also used as notation for the inner product: $\langle \mathbf{u}, \mathbf{w} \rangle$. See also 12.52–54.

12.32   *Binomial coefficients.* The notation $\binom{n}{k}$, "n choose k," is called the binomial coefficient and stands for the number of ways k objects can be chosen from among a collection of n objects. It is defined by

$$\binom{n}{k} = \frac{n!}{k!(n-k)!},$$

where n and k are positive integers and the notation $!$ stands for the factorial function,

$$n! = n \times (n-1) \times \cdots \times 1.$$

12.33   *Vertical bars.* Vertical bars serve several special purposes. The modulus or absolute value of x is denoted $|x|$. The notation $|\mathbf{u}|$ is used for the "length" of a vector $\mathbf{u}$ in a Euclidean vector space; this is sometimes called the norm of $\mathbf{u}$ and written with a double vertical bar, $\|\mathbf{u}\|$. Vertical bars are used to denote the cardinal number of a set. The notation $|A|$ can signify the determinant of a matrix A, which is also denoted det A.

12.34   *Single vertical bar.* A single vertical bar with limits is used to denote the evaluation of a formula at a particular value of one of its variables. For example,

$$\int_0^{\pi/2} \sin x \, dx = -\cos x \Big|_{x=0}^{x=\pi/2} = -\cos \pi/2 - (-\cos 0) = 1.$$

12.35   **Cases.** Displayed mathematical expressions that present a choice between alternatives may be grouped using a single brace and are punctuated as follows:

$$|a| = \begin{cases} a, & a \geq 0; \\ -a, & a < 0. \end{cases}$$

Another acceptable style is

$$f(x) = \begin{cases} 1 & \text{if } x \geq 0, \\ 0 & \text{otherwise.} \end{cases}$$

As a general rule, each alternative is equivalent to a clause in ordinary language and should be punctuated as such. If the alternatives are very long, they may be stated as separate equations:

$$I(t) = Ae^{\Gamma_1(t-t_p)}\{1 + \varepsilon_1 \cos[2\pi f(t - t_p)]\}$$
$$+ B\{1 + \varepsilon_2 \cos[2\pi f(t - t_p)]\}, \quad t \leq t_p, \tag{1a}$$

$$I(t) = Ae^{-\Gamma_2(t-t_p)}\{1 + \varepsilon_1 \cos[2\pi f(t - t_p)]\}$$
$$+ B\{1 + \varepsilon_2 \cos[2\pi f(t - t_p)]\}, \quad t > t_p. \tag{1b}$$

Subscripts and Superscripts

12.36   *Simple subscripts and superscripts.* Inferior and superior indices, exponents, and other subscript and superscript symbols occur very frequently in mathematical copy and are indispensable for concise expression in mathematics. Examples are

$$x_1, \quad x^2, \quad 2^x, \quad x', \quad x_{ij}y_{jk}, \quad x^{ab}, \quad a^x b^y, \quad x''_{12}.$$

Multiple indices are written without commas between them unless there is a possibility of confusion: x_{ij} instead of $x_{i,j}$, but $x_{1,2}$ if there is a possibility of confusing the subscripts "1,2" and "12." Abbreviations or words that serve as labels in subscripts or superscripts are usually set in roman type:

$$x_{\min}, \quad u_{\text{av}}.$$

12.37   *Complex subscripts and superscripts.* Subscripts and superscripts may themselves have subscripts and superscripts. For example,

$$x_{a_k}, \quad x_{a_k^2}, \quad 2^{x^2}, \quad 2^{x_i^2}.$$

Mathematical expressions may occur as subformulas in the superior or inferior positions. For example,

$$x^{a+b}, \quad a^{-x}b^{(y-z)^2}, \quad a_{2n}^{x'y'}, \quad 2^{\sqrt{n}}.$$

12.38   *Alignment of subscripts and superscripts.* Subscripts and superscripts may be stacked

$$x_i^n, \quad x_{ij}^{mn}$$

or staggered

$$X^{ab}{}_{cd}, \quad X_{ij}{}^{kl}.$$

Because there are standard conventions for raising and lowering indices in some branches of mathematics, most especially in tensor calculus, the relative position between superior and inferior indices must be respected. For example,

$$T^i{}_j$$

(the tensor arising from T^{ij} by lowering its second index) and

$$T_i{}^j$$

(the tensor arising from T^{ij} by lowering its first index) are different and must be clearly distinguished. Neither should be written T^i_j. Ordinary punctuation marks carrying special meaning may occur in subscript or superscript expressions. For instance,

$$T^i{}_{,j} \quad \text{and} \quad T^i{}_{;j}$$

have precise mathematical meanings and should not be changed. In tensor expressions, the symbol $R_{[i,j]}$ is not the same as $R_{(i,j)}$, and they should not be interchanged. See also 12.54.

Summations and Integrals

12.39   *Summation sign.* The summation sign Σ is used to stand for a sum, finite or infinite, of terms. For example, the sums

$$a_1 + a_2 + \cdots + a_n \quad \text{and} \quad a_1 + a_2 + \cdots$$

may be written

$$\sum_{i=1}^{n} a_i \quad \text{and} \quad \sum_{i=1}^{\infty} a_i,$$

respectively. The variable i in the expressions above is called the index of summation. The subformulas below and above the summation sign are called the limits of summation and indicate where the summation begins and, if it is finite, ends. Summation limits are sometimes omitted if it is clear from the context what the limits are; for example, if all vectors are stated to be of size n and all matrices are of size $n \times n$, it is acceptable to write

$$y_i = \sum_{j} a_{ij} x_j.$$

When a summation sign occurs in text, its limits are placed to the right of the summation sign to avoid spreading the lines of text: $\sum_{i=1}^{n} a_i$.

12.40   *Product sign.* Product notation follows similar conventions. The products

$$a_1 \cdot a_2 \cdot \ldots \cdot a_n \quad \text{and} \quad a_1 \cdot a_2 \cdot \ldots$$

may be written

$$\prod_{i=1}^{n} a_i \quad \text{and} \quad \prod_{i=1}^{\infty} a_i,$$

respectively, and in text the limits are placed to the right of the product symbol to avoid spreading lines: $\prod_{i=1}^{n} a_i$.

12.41   *Integral sign.* The integral sign $\int$ is used to denote two sorts of integrals, called definite and indefinite. The definite integral is the integral of a function f on an interval $[a, b]$. This integral is denoted

$$\int_a^b f(x)\, dx.$$

The numbers a and b are called the lower and upper limits of integration, and dx is called the element of integration or the differential. The limits of integration are often placed to the right of the integral sign in both text and display. The indefinite integral is denoted

$$\int f \quad \text{or} \quad \int f(x)\,dx,$$

without limits of integration. In more advanced texts the definite integral is written

$$\int_D f(x)\,dx,$$

where D is the set of integration. For a function of two variables, it is common to denote an integral over both variables by a double integral sign:

$$\int_a^b\int_c^d f(x, y)\,dx\,dy.$$

Triple integrals may be used if the integration is performed in three variables.

12.42 *Spacing around differentials.* Thin spaces are placed before and after differentials:

$$dV = r^2 \sin\theta\,dr\,d\theta\,d\phi.$$

Differential expressions appearing in derivatives must be closed up to the slash:

$$dx/dt.$$

Radicals

12.43 *Radical signs.* The radical sign $\sqrt{\ }$ is used to denote the square root. A horizontal bar extends from the top of the radical sign to the end of the radicand:

$$\sqrt{2}, \quad \sqrt{\sin^2 x + \cos^2 x}.$$

In display, the radical sign extends vertically to accommodate a built-up radicand:

$$\sqrt{\frac{\ln n}{n}}.$$

The radical sign may be used to denote cube and higher-order roots. For these roots, a superscript-sized number or letter is nested within the radical sign:

$$\sqrt[3]{5}, \quad \sqrt[n]{n!}.$$

12.44 *Radical signs in text.* Radical signs can be used in text if the radicand is a simple expression: $a = m + n\sqrt{3}$. If the radicand is more complex or if the text design uses tight leading, radical signs can give the page a crowded look or interfere with descending letters in the line above. One remedy is to substitute the appropriate exponent, using delimiters to indicate the extent of the radicand. For example,

$$\sqrt{a^2 + b^2}$$

may be replaced by

$$(a^2 + b^2)^{1/2}.$$

Fractions

12.45 *Fractions in text.* Fractions are set in text with a slash to separate the numerator and denominator:

$$1/2, \quad 2/3, \quad 1/10, \quad 97/100, \quad \pi/2, \quad 11/5, \quad a/b.$$

Some common numerical fractions may be set as case fractions (text-sized fractions with a horizontal bar):

$$\tfrac{1}{2}, \quad \tfrac{2}{3}, \quad \tfrac{1}{10}.$$

Fractions should be enclosed in parentheses if they are followed by a mathematical symbol or expression:

$$(a/b)x.$$

For simple algebraic fractions in text, the slash should be used rather than the horizontal fraction bar. For example,

$$(ax + b)/(cx + d) \quad \text{not} \quad \frac{ax+b}{cx+d}.$$

The slash connects only the two groups of symbols immediately adjacent to it. Thus, $a + b/c$ means

$$a + \frac{b}{c} \quad \text{not} \quad \frac{a+b}{c},$$

which should be written $(a + b)/c$.

12.46 *Fractions in display.* In displayed mathematical expressions, all fractions should be built up unless they are part of a numerator or denominator or in a subscript or superscript:

$$\left| x^2 \sin \frac{1}{x} \right| < \frac{1}{10} \quad \text{not} \quad |x^2 \sin \frac{1}{x}| < \frac{1}{10}.$$

Fractions that include summation, product, or integral signs should always be displayed. For example:

$$\frac{\int_0^{\pi/2} \sin^{2n} x \, dx}{\int_0^{\pi/2} \sin^{2n+1} x \, dx}.$$

If there are no built-up fractions in the display, common numerical fractions may be set as case fractions:

$$|a - b| < \tfrac{1}{10}.$$

12.47 *Fractions in subscripts and superscripts.* Fractions in subscripts and superscripts should always use the slash, both in text and in display:

$$x^{a/b}, \quad y_{3/2}.$$

12.48 *Multiple and multilevel fractions.* If a mathematical expression contains more than one fraction, it should be displayed, and the horizontal bar should be used for the principal fraction sign:

$$\frac{ax + b}{cx + d} = \frac{px + q}{rx + s}.$$

Fractions should preferably be limited to two levels:

$$\frac{a/b+c}{p/q+r} \quad \text{not} \quad \frac{\frac{a}{b}+c}{\frac{p}{q}+r}.$$

Continued fractions, that is, expressions of the form $a_1 + 1/b_1$, where $b_1 = a_2 + 1/b_2$, $b_2 = a_3 + 1/b_3$, and so on, are displayed:

$$a_1 + \cfrac{1}{a_2 + \cfrac{1}{a_3 + \cfrac{1}{a_4 + \cdots}}}.$$

12.49   *Rewriting fractions using exponents.* There are times when it is desirable to represent the denominator of a fraction without using a fraction rule or a slash. This may be done by using delimiters followed by the exponent −1:

$$ab(cd)^{-1} \quad \text{instead of} \quad \frac{ab}{cd}.$$

If there is already an exponent in the denominator, it can be changed to its negative:

$$ab(cd)^{-2} \quad \text{instead of} \quad \frac{ab}{(cd)^2}.$$

If an exponential expression, particularly in text, is very complex, it may be rewritten in a simpler form. An exponential term such as

$$e^{(2\pi i \Sigma n_j)/\sqrt{x^2+y^2}}$$

can be rewritten using the abbreviation *exp*:

$$\exp\left[\left(2\pi i \sum n_j\right)/(x^2 + y^2)^{1/2}\right].$$

Matrices and Determinants

12.50   *Matrices.* Matrices are arrays of terms displayed in rectangular arrangements of rows and columns and enclosed on the left and right by either large brackets or parentheses:

$$\begin{bmatrix} a_{11} & a_{12} & \cdots & a_{1n} \\ a_{21} & a_{22} & \cdots & a_{2n} \\ \vdots & \vdots & & \vdots \\ a_{m1} & a_{m2} & \cdots & a_{mn} \end{bmatrix} \quad \text{or} \quad \begin{pmatrix} a_{11} & a_{12} & \cdots & a_{1n} \\ a_{21} & a_{22} & \cdots & a_{2n} \\ \vdots & \vdots & & \vdots \\ a_{m1} & a_{m2} & \cdots & a_{mn} \end{pmatrix}.$$

The notation should be consistent. The horizontal lists of entries are called the rows of the matrix, and the vertical lists the columns. A matrix with m rows and n columns is called an $m \times n$ matrix. A matrix consisting of a single row is called a row matrix or a row vector; a matrix consisting of a single column is a column matrix or a column vector. For example,

$$[a \quad b \quad c] \quad \text{and} \quad \begin{bmatrix} a \\ b \\ c \end{bmatrix}$$

are row and column matrices, respectively. The transpose of a matrix A, denoted A^T, is the matrix obtained by interchanging the rows and columns of A. For example,

$$\begin{pmatrix} a_{11} & a_{21} & \cdots & a_{m1} \\ a_{12} & a_{22} & \cdots & a_{m2} \\ \vdots & \vdots & & \vdots \\ a_{1n} & a_{2n} & \cdots & a_{mn} \end{pmatrix}$$

is the transpose of the $m \times n$ matrix given above. Column matrices such as

$$\begin{bmatrix} a \\ b \\ c \end{bmatrix}$$

may be represented in text as $(a, b, c)^T$, col. (a, b, c), or the column vector (a, b, c), and a $2 \times n$ (for small n) matrix may be set, for example, as $\left(\begin{smallmatrix} a & c & e \\ b & d & f \end{smallmatrix}\right)$. Most matrices and determinants are displayed, however. In-line matrices cannot be broken on the line, and display matrices cannot be broken across the column or page.

12.51   *Determinants.* If A is a square matrix, the determinant of A, denoted $|A|$ or det A, is a function that assigns a specific number to the matrix A. If A is an $n \times n$ matrix, the determinant of A is represented by

$$\begin{vmatrix} a_{11} & a_{12} & \cdots & a_{1n} \\ a_{21} & a_{22} & \cdots & a_{2n} \\ \vdots & \vdots & & \vdots \\ a_{n1} & a_{2n} & \cdots & a_{nn} \end{vmatrix}.$$

Vertical bars are used to distinguish the determinant of A from the matrix A. The Jacobian matrix has a reserved notation:

$$J = \frac{\partial(f_1, f_2, \ldots, f_n)}{\partial(x_1, x_2, \ldots, x_n)}.$$

Its determinant (usually referred to as the Jacobian) is denoted as

$$\left| \frac{\partial(f_1, f_2, \ldots, f_n)}{\partial(x_1, x_2, \ldots, x_n)} \right|.$$

Scalars, Vectors, and Tensors

12.52   *Scalars, vectors, and tensors defined.* Three basic quantities often encountered in scientific mathematical material are scalars, vectors, and tensors. Scalars, usually denoted by lowercase italic or Greek letters, are ordinary numbers and are treated as such. Vectors are quantities that have direction as well as magnitude, and they are often denoted by boldface letters or by an arrow diacritic to distinguish them from scalars:

$\boldsymbol{r}$ or $\vec{r}$.

Because authors do not always follow these conventions, editors should be prepared to query. A vector may be written as the sum of its components:

$$\boldsymbol{r} = \sum_i r_i \hat{\boldsymbol{e}}^i.$$

The circumflex over the $\boldsymbol{e}$ is used to denote a vector of length 1, called a unit vector. Tensors are multidimensional quantities that extend the vector concept. A scalar is a tensor of rank 0, and a vector is a tensor of rank 1.

12.53   *Vector and tensor multiplication.* Vector and tensor multiplication employs a special notation that is relatively easy to identify in text. The inner or dot product of two vectors **u** and **w** is denoted **u · w**; the dot product is signified by the boldface multiplication dot. The vector or cross product of two vectors **u** and **w** is denoted **u × w**; the cross product is signified by the boldface multiplication cross. The multiplication dot and multiplication cross are not interchangeable for vectors as they are for ordinary multiplication. The standard notation for the tensor product of tensors T and S is $T \otimes S$. Index notation for vectors and tensors usually takes the following form:

$$S = S_{jk}\boldsymbol{e}^j\boldsymbol{e}^k,$$

$$T^{i\cdots m}_{k\cdots l} = A^{i\cdots m}_{k\cdots n}B^n_l,$$

$$b^i = a^i_j c^j.$$

Note the correspondence of the indices in these expressions (see 12.38 for discussion of index positioning). The Einstein convention has been used here, which implies summation over the repeated index. Thus

$$c_k = \sum_j a^j b_{jk} \quad \text{is the same as} \quad c_k = a^j b_{jk}$$

unless otherwise stated.

12.54   *Additional tensor notation.* Two additional special notations are used to differentiate tensors. One is $A^i{}_{,j}$, where the subscript comma indicates a coordinate (or "ordinary") derivative. The other is $A^i{}_{;j}$, where the subscript semicolon indicates the covariant derivative. See also 12.38.

12.55   *Dirac notation.* A special form of the inner product, used especially in physics, is the Dirac bracket notation,

$$\langle a|b \rangle,$$

which can also be used in combination with operators, as in $\langle a|\mathbf{T}|b \rangle$ (which is not the same as $\langle a\mathbf{T}b \rangle$) or $\langle \mathbf{T}a|b \rangle$. The combinations $\langle a|$ and $|b \rangle$ are also used to denote dual vectors and vectors, respectively.

Definitions, Theorems, and Other Formal Statements

12.56   *Formal statements in text.* For definitions, theorems, propositions, corollaries, lemmas, axioms, and rules, it is common practice to set the head in caps and small caps and the text (including symbolic expressions but not including numerals, which are always set in roman) in italics, sometimes indented from the left margin. Numbers for these statements, unlike those for equations, are not enclosed in parentheses, and in cross-references the numbers are also not enclosed.

DEFINITION. *A permutation is a one-to-one transformation of a finite set into itself.*

(In a definition, the term being defined is set in roman type in order to distinguish it from the rest of the text; alternatively, the term can be set in italics and the text in roman.)

THEOREM 1. *The order of a finite subgroup is a multiple of the order of every one of its subgroups.*

COROLLARY. *If p and q are distinct prime numbers and a is an integer not divisible by either p or q, then*

$$a^{(p-1)(q-1)} \equiv 1 \pmod{pq}.$$

LEMMA 2. *The product of any two primitive polynomials is itself primitive.*

AXIOM. *Every set of nonnegative integers that contains at least one element contains a smallest element.*

RULE 4.4. *The length of a vertical segment joining two points is given by the difference of the ordinates of the upper and the lower points.*

The text of proofs, examples, remarks, demonstrations, and solutions is usually set in roman, with only variables and other such letters in italics. The heads, however, are set in caps and small caps.

PROOF. Let $A = B$. Hence $C = D$.
SOLUTION. If $y = 0$, then $x = 5$.

Proofs of theorems often end with the abbreviation QED or a special symbol, □ or ■.

Probability and Statistics

12.57 *Probability.* The notation $\Pr(A)$ or $P(A)$ is used to denote the probability of an event A. The sample space, that is, the set of all possible outcomes of a given experiment, is usually denoted Ω. An event A is a subset of the sample space: $A \subseteq \Omega$. The elements of the sample space are usually denoted ω. The conditional probability of event A relative to event B—that is, the probability that event A occurs given that event B has occurred—is written

$$\mathrm{Pr}(A|B) \quad \text{or} \quad P(A|B).$$

Variance is denoted $\mathrm{Var}(X)$ and covariance is denoted $\mathrm{Cov}(X, Y)$. Both the variance and the covariance functions may be expressed with lowercase letters.

12.58   *Means and standard deviations.* The population mean is often given a special symbol in statistics, $\mu(X)$. The sample mean is denoted by $\bar{x}$. In evaluating an expression, be careful not to substitute angle brackets, $\langle X \rangle$, for an overbar, $\bar{x}$. They can mean very different things. The population standard deviation (the most common measure of dispersion) is denoted by σ (Greek lowercase sigma), and the sample standard deviation is more commonly denoted by s; sd or SD may be used to distinguish it from se or SE, for standard error. The arithmetic mean is most frequently written in physical sciences literature as $\langle A \rangle$ or $\bar{A}$ and the cumulant as $\langle\langle A \rangle\rangle$. Several abbreviations are used in stochastic theory and probability theory without special definition: a.e., almost everywhere; a.c., almost certainly; a.s., almost surely. See table 12.3 for statistical notation.

12.59   *Uncertainties.* Uncertainties in quantities are usually written with a plus or minus sign ($\pm$): 2.501 ± 0.002 or, if there is an exponent, $(6.157 \pm 0.07) \times 10^5$ or $10^{4.3 \pm 0.3}$. However, there are cases in which the bounds rather than the range are given, and these may be unequal; hence,

$$\ldots \text{where } D/H = 1.65^{+0.11}_{-0.08} \times 10^{-5}.\ldots$$

Uncertainties may also be specified as se for standard error, 1σ (or a larger multiple) or sd for standard deviation. Finally, separation into random and systematic uncertainties is written as

$$71.0 \pm 5.0 \text{ (random)} \pm 2.5 \text{ (sys)}$$

or $71.0^{+5.0}_{-4.8}$ (random) $^{+2.1}_{-1.8}$ (sys) for asymmetric bounds. When such expressions occur in an exponent, it is preferable to write a separate expression for the exponent (see 12.49).

TABLE 12.3. Statistical notation

GREEK ALPHABET

α	Probability of rejecting a true null hypothesis (type I error)	$\mu(X)$	Mean of the population
		Σ	Sum of
β	Probability of accepting a false null hypothesis (type II error)	σ	Population standard deviation
		σ^2	Population variance
κ	Cumulant; also kappa statistic	χ^2	Value for the chi-squared distribution

LATIN ALPHABET

df, DF, dof	Degrees of freedom	se, SE	Standard error
F	F-ratio	sem, SEM	Standard error of the mean
H	Value from the Kruskal-Wallis test		
H_0	Null hypothesis	t	Value from Student's t-test
ln	Natural logarithm	T	Value from the Wilcoxon matched-pairs signed-rank test
log	Logarithm to base 10		
mse, MSE	Mean squared error		
p, P, Pr	Probability	U	Value from the Mann-Whitney test
r_P	Pearson correlation coefficient	W_s	Value from the Wilcoxon rank sum test
r_S	Value from the Spearman rank-order test	z	Value from the normal distribution
s, sd, SD	Sample standard deviation		

Preparation and Editing of Paper Manuscripts

12.60   *Format of paper manuscripts.* Manuscripts for mathematical articles and books should be printed out one-sided and double-spaced, on 8½ × 11–inch white paper, with 1¼-inch margins for text and 2-inch margins for display work. The print quality should be 300 dots per inch or better. If handwritten equations or symbols are to be inserted in the printout, allow generous space for them. Since the editor will need to provide instructions to the typesetter, there should be ample margins.

12.61   *Setting from the author's hard copy.* In the event that the publisher cannot use the electronic files prepared by the author, and to the extent that a manuscript shows all the necessary characters, symbols, and signs as they should appear, the typesetter may simply be instructed to follow the author's hard copy. Any unusual characters not achieved in the manuscript must be marked or identified. Authors should supply the highest-quality printout possible.

12.62   *Marking italic type.* The editor of a mathematical text should either underline all copy that is to be set in italics or give general instructions to the typesetter to set all single-letter mathematical objects in italics unless they are marked otherwise. The general instructions to the typesetter should also specify italic type for letters used in subscripts or superscripts. If italics have been used in the manuscript, the editor can instruct the typesetter to follow the copy.

12.63   *Common abbreviations.* Abbreviations for common functions, geometric points, units of measurement, and chemical elements, which are set in roman type, should be marked as roman by the editor only where ambiguity could occur. For a list of some frequently used abbreviations, see table 12.2.

12.64   *Marking single letters in other type styles.* Special marking must be used when single letters representing mathematical objects are to be set in any typeface other than italics. A mathematical text may require the use of some roman letters, usually to indicate properties different from those expressed by the same letters in italics. Underlining is the standard method of indicating italics, but it can be used instead, with instructions to the typesetter, to indicate letters that are to be in roman. If, however, the editor does not use general instructions but underlines all letters to be set italic, then letters not underlined will be set, as implied, in roman type. Double underlining is used to indicate small capitals. Wavy underlining is used for boldface. Color codes are often used to indicate other typefaces. For example, red underlining or circling can be used for Fraktur, blue for script, green for sans serif, and so forth. The general instructions to the typesetter must clearly explain the marking and coding system used. If a photocopy must be made of the edited manuscript for estimating by the typesetter or for querying the author, avoid color coding.

12.65   *Mathematics fonts.* Boldface, script, Fraktur, and sans serif are frequently used in mathematical expressions.

BOLDFACE	SCRIPT	FRAKTUR	SANS SERIF
ABCD	*𝒜ℬ𝒞𝒟*	𝔄𝔅ℭ𝔇	ABCD

Double-struck, or blackboard, characters are often used for special mathematical symbols—for example, $\mathbb{N}, \mathbb{Z}, \mathbb{Q}, \mathbb{R}, \mathbb{C}$ (see 12.14).

12.66 *Marking subscripts and superscripts.* As long as inferior and superior characters have been marked in a few places by the symbols $\vee$ and $\wedge$ (see examples below), and new characters or symbols are identified when they first appear, a typesetter should have no difficulty interpreting the manuscript. If the spatial relationship of terms is not clearly shown in a typed or handwritten expression, the terms should be marked to avoid ambiguity. For example, given the copy

$$X^k_{t1},$$

it may not be clear from the manuscript whether this means

$$X^k_{t1} \quad \text{or} \quad X^k_{t^1} \quad \text{or} \quad X^k_{t_1}.$$

The expression should therefore be marked in one of the following ways for complete clarity:

$$X^k_{t1} \quad \text{or} \quad X^k_{t1} \quad \text{or} \quad X^k_{t_1}.$$

The examples above show the subscripts and superscripts aligned, or stacked. See 12.38 for discussion and examples of staggered subscripts and superscripts.

12.67 *Examples of marked copy.* Figure 12.1 shows a page of a paper manuscript as marked initially by the author and then by the editor before being sent to the typesetter. The author's marks merely identify ambiguous symbols. Figure 12.2 shows that same page set in type. Figure 12.3 shows the LaTeX source code that would generate the first part of figure 12.2. Signs and symbols that could be misread by the typesetter should be clearly identified on a paper manuscript by marginal notations or in a separate list. For lists of symbols and special characters commonly used in mathematics, see table 12.1. Illegible handwriting and unidentifiable signs and symbols can reduce composition speed and result in time-consuming and costly corrections. Certain letters, numbers, and symbols can easily be misread, especially when Greek, Fraktur, script, and sans serif letters are handwritten rather than typed. Some of the characters that cause the most difficulty are shown in table 12.4.

Opr.: Letter symbols in ital. unless marked

Therefore $F_x^n \subset G \cap B_n$ and $F_x^n \cap B_m = \emptyset$ for $n \neq m$, since $b \in G$.

null set   *"element of"*

The temperature function is

$$u(x,\ t) = \frac{2}{L} \sum_1^\infty \exp\left(-\frac{u^2\pi^2kt}{L^2}\right) \sin\frac{n\pi x}{L} \int_0^L f(x')\ \sin\frac{n\pi x'}{L}\ dx'. \quad (3.1)$$

An $m \times n$ matrix $\underset{\sim}{A}$ over a field F is a rectangular array of mn elements a_j^i in F, arranged in m rows and n columns:

$$\underset{\sim}{A} = \begin{bmatrix} a_1^1 & a_2^1 & \cdots & a_n^1 \\ a_1^2 & a_2^2 & \cdots & a_n^2 \\ \cdot & \cdot & \cdots & \cdot \\ a_1^m & a_2^m & \cdots & a_n^m \end{bmatrix}.$$

The modulus of the correlation coefficient of X_1 and X_2 is

"greater than"

(rho) $\rho = |\langle x_1,\ x_2 \rangle| / \|x_1\|\ \|x_2\|$ for $\|x_1\| > 0$, $1 = 1, 2$.

angle brackets   *all*   *all*

Hence

$$\frac{\partial F}{\partial x} = \lim_{\Delta x \to 0} \frac{\Delta F}{\Delta x} = \lim_{\Delta x \to 0} \frac{1}{\Delta x}\left\{\int_{a,b}^{x+\Delta x, y} P\ dx + Q\ dy\right.$$

$$\left. -\int_{a,b}^{x,y} P\ dx + Q\ dy\right\} + P + Q.$$

From equation (2.4), where $M = [(a + b - 1)/(k + 1)]$, we obtain

alpha

$$\alpha_\nu(a+b) = (-1)^\nu \sum' \frac{(i_1 + \cdots + i_M)!}{i_1! \cdots i_M!} \prod_{h=1}^M (-1)^h \binom{a + b - kh - 1}{h},$$

lc Gr. nu

the sum being extended over all sets $(i_1, \cdots, i_M)$.

To summarize our findings:

lc Gr. eta

$$v^*(z,\ t_n) \geqslant H_{\delta_1} [v(x) + o(1)] - 2\eta \geqslant v(z) + o(1) + \eta^{1/2}o(1).$$

lc oh   *lc oh*   *cap oh*

FIGURE 12.1. An example of typewritten and hand-marked mathematical copy. (Note that this page is not intended to make mathematical sense but is merely meant to illustrate some of the issues that may arise in preparing mathematical copy.)

Therefore $F_x{}^n \subset G \cap B_n$ and $F_x{}^n \cap B_m = \emptyset$ for $n \neq m$, since $b \in G$. The temperature function is

$$u(x,t) = \frac{2}{L} \sum_{1}^{\infty} \exp\left(-\frac{u^2 \pi^2 kt}{L^2}\right) \sin \frac{n\pi x}{L}$$

$$\times \int_0^L f(x') \sin \frac{n\pi x'}{L} dx'. \quad (3.1)$$

An $m \times n$ matrix $\mathbf{A}$ over a field F is a rectangular array of mn elements $a_j{}^i$ in F, arranged in m rows and n columns:

$$\mathbf{A} = \begin{bmatrix} a_1{}^1 & a_2{}^1 & \cdots & a_n{}^1 \\ a_1{}^2 & a_2{}^2 & \cdots & a_n{}^2 \\ \cdot & & \cdots & \cdot \\ \cdot & & \cdots & \cdot \\ a_1{}^m & a_2{}^m & \cdots & a_n{}^m \end{bmatrix}.$$

The modulus of the correlation coefficient of X_1 and X_2 is

$$\rho = |\langle X_1, X_2 \rangle| / \|X_1\| \, \|X_2\| \quad \text{for} \quad \|X_l\| > 0, \, l = 1, 2.$$

Hence

$$\frac{\partial F}{\partial x} = \lim_{\Delta x \to 0} \frac{\Delta F}{\Delta x} = \lim_{\Delta x \to 0} \frac{1}{\Delta x} \left\{ \int_{a,b}^{x+\Delta x, y} P\, dx + Q\, dy \right.$$

$$\left. - \int_{a,b}^{x,y} P\, dx + Q\, dy \right\} + P + Q.$$

From equation (2.4), where $M = [(a + b - 1)/(k + 1)]$, we obtain

$$a_v(a + b) = (-1)^v \sum{}' \frac{(i_1 + \cdots + i_M)!}{i_1! \cdots i_M!}$$

$$\times \prod_{h=1}^{M} (-1)^{i_h} \left(\frac{a + b - kh - 1}{h}\right)^{i_h},$$

the sum being extended over all sets $(i_1, \ldots, i_M)$. To summarize our findings:

$$v^*(z, t_n) \geq H_{\delta_1}[v(x) + o(1)] - 2\eta \geq v(z) + o(1) + \eta^{1/2} O(1).$$

FIGURE 12.2. The page of manuscript shown in figure 12.1 set in type.

```
\noindent Therefore $F_{x}{}^n\subset G\cap B_n$
and $F_{x}{}^n\cap B_m=\O$ for $n\ne m$,
since $b\in G$. The temperature function is
\begin{multline}
u(x,t)=\frac{2}{L}\sum_1^\infty \exp
\left(-\frac{u^2\pi^2 kt}{L^2}\right)\sin
\frac{n\pi x}{L}\\
\times \int\nolimits_0^L f(x')\sin
\frac{n\pi x'}{L}dx'.
\end{multline}
An $m\times n$ matrix {\bf A} over a field $F$
is a rectangular array of $mn$~ele\-ments~$a_{j}{}^i$ in $F$,
arranged  in $m$ rows and $n$ columns:
\begin{align*}
{\bf A}=\left[
{\arraycolsep5pt\begin{array}{@{}cccc@{}}
a_{1}{}^1 &a_{2}{}^1 &\ldots &a_{n}{}^1\\[4pt]
a_{1}{}^2 &a_{2}{}^2 &\ldots &a_{n}{}^2\\[4pt]
.&.&\ldots  &.\\[4pt]
a_{1}{}^m &a_{2}{}^m &\ldots &a_{n}{}^m\\
\end{array}}
\right].
\end{align*}
The modulus of the correlation coefficient of
$X_1$ and $X_2$ is
\begin{align*}
\rho=|\langle X_1,\ X_2\rangle|/\|X_1\|\ \|X_2\|
\quad{\rm for}\quad \|X_1\|>0,\ l=1,2.
\end{align*}
```

FIGURE 12.3. LaTeX source listing that would generate a portion of the mathematical copy shown in figure 12.2.

TABLE 12.4. Potentially ambiguous mathematical symbols

Symbols set in type[a]	Marginal notation to operator[b]	Remarks and suggestions for manuscript preparation
α	lc "aye"	
a	lc Gr. alpha	
$\propto$	proportional to	Leave medium space before and after $\propto$ and all
∞	infinity	binary operation signs (=, ≤, ∈, ∩, ⊂, etc.).
B	cap "bee"	
β	lc Gr. beta	
χ	lc Gr. chi	
X	cap "ex"	
x	lc "ex"	
$\times$	"times" or "mult"	Leave medium space before and after $\times$ and all other operation signs (+, −, ÷, etc.). Do not add space when such signs as −, +, or ± are used to modify symbols or expressions (−3, ±1, etc.). Do not add space when operations appear as subscripts or superscripts.
δ	lc Gr. delta	
∂	partial differential	Simpler to use printer's term "round dee."
d	lc "dee"	
ε	lc Gr. epsilon	
$\in$	"element of"	
η	lc Gr. eta	
n	lc "en"	
γ	lc Gr. gamma	
τ	lc Gr. tau	
r	lc "ar"	
t	lc "tee"	
ι	lc Gr. iota	Avoid using ι and i together because of similarity
i	lc "eye"	in print.
κ	lc Gr. kappa	
k	lc "kay"	
K	cap Gr. kappa	
K	cap "kay"	
l	lc "el"	In some fonts, l and 1 look identical; note "el" but
ℓ	script "el"	leave numeral unmarked; ℓ should not be used
1	numeral 1	if l is available.

TABLE 12.4 (*continued*)

Symbols set in type[a]	Marginal notation to operator[b]	Remarks and suggestions for manuscript preparation
ν	lc Gr. nu	Avoid using ν and v together because of similarity in print.
v	lc "vee"	
O	cap "oh"	Asymptotic upper bounds $O(x)$ and $o(x)$ may occur together.
o	lc "oh"	
0	zero	
O	cap Gr. omicron	
o	lc Gr. omicron	
°	degree sign	
Λ	cap Gr. lambda	
∧	wedge	
φ, φ	lc Gr. phi	
∅	empty or null set	
∏	product	
Π	cap Gr. pi	
π	lc Gr. pi	
ρ	lc Gr. rho	
p	lc "pee"	
Σ	summation	
Σ	cap Gr. sigma	
θ, ϑ	lc Gr. theta	Preference for form ϑ should be specified by author; θ more commonly used.
Θ	cap Gr. theta	
U	cap "you"	
U, ∪	union symbol	
υ	lc Gr. upsilon	
μ	lc Gr. mu	
ν	lc Gr. nu	
u	lc "you"	
ω	lc Gr. omega	
ϖ	round lc Gr. pi	
w	lc "double-u"	
Z	cap "zee"	
z	lc "zee"	
2	numeral 2	

TABLE 12.4 (*continued*)

Symbols set in type[a]	Marginal notation to operator[b]	Remarks and suggestions for manuscript preparation
′ 1	prime superscript 1	Use apostrophe for prime if no prime available. In handwritten formulas, take care to distinguish prime from superscript 1 and comma from subscript 1.
, 1	comma subscript 1	
—	em dash	Use two hyphens for em dash; no space on either side (except in LaTeX, where a double hyphen produces an en dash).
– –	minus sign en dash	To indicate subtraction, leave medium space on each side of sign; omit space after sign if negative quantity is represented.
·	multiplication dot	Use centered period for multiplication dot, allowing medium space on each side; do not show space around a center dot in a chemical formula ($CO_3 \cdot H_2$).

NOTE: Symbols and letters that are commonly mistaken for each other are arranged in groups.

[a] Letters in mathematical expressions will automatically be set in italics unless marked otherwise.

[b] Only if symbols, letters, or numbers are badly written or rendered in the manuscript is it necessary to identify them for the typesetter.

13 Quotations and Dialogue

Overview

13.1 *Scope of this chapter—and where else to look.* This chapter offers recommendations for incorporating words quoted from other sources—and, to a lesser degree, for presenting speech and other forms of dialogue—in text. For the use of quotation marks for purposes other than direct quotation, see the discussions throughout 7.47–76. For quotation marks with titles of works, see the discussions in 8.154–95. For citing the sources of quotations, discussed only peripherally here, see chapters 14 and 15. For formatting block quotations in a manuscript, see 2.18, 2.19; for the manuscript editor's responsibilities regarding quoted material, see 2.58. For quotation marks in relation to surrounding text and punctuation, see 6.6, 6.9–11.

13.2 *Quotations and modern scholarship.* Few ideas spring up on their own, and the act of assimilating the words of others is central to modern scholarship. In the words of Jacques Barzun and Henry F. Graff, "Quoting other writers and citing the places where their words are to be found are by now such common practices that it is pardonable to look upon the habit as natural, not to say instinctive. It is of course nothing of the kind, but a very sophisticated act, peculiar to a civilization that uses printed books, believes in evidence, and makes a point of assigning credit or blame in a detailed, verifiable way."[1] The observation holds true in a world where more and more ideas are created, published, shared, and archived electronically.

13.3 *Giving credit and seeking permission.* Whether quoting, paraphrasing, or using others' ideas to advance their own arguments, authors should give explicit credit to the source of those words or ideas. This credit often takes the form of a formal citation incorporated into a note or parenthetical reference. For a full discussion of documentation, see chapters 14 and 15. In addition, written permission may be needed, especially for direct quotations, as follows: for more than a line or two of a poem or a song lyric in copyright; for prose quotations of, say, more than three paragraphs or for many short passages from a work in copyright; or for any excerpt from certain unpublished materials (letters, e-mail messages, and so forth). For more information about permissions, consult chapter 4, especially 4.69–91.

---

1. *The Modern Researcher*, 5th ed. (Boston: Houghton Mifflin, 1992), 273.

13.4 *When to paraphrase rather than quote.* Authors drawing on the work of others to illustrate their arguments should first decide whether direct quotation or paraphrase will be more effective. Too many quotations with too little commentary can pose a distraction, and readers may choose to skip over long or frequent quotations. And in some cases, authors who notice an error in a passage they wish to quote should paraphrase the original, eliminating the error. For "silent correction," see 13.7 (item 5); for *sic*, see 13.59.

13.5 *When quotation and attribution is unnecessary.* Commonly known or readily verifiable facts, proverbs, and other familiar expressions can be stated without quotation or attribution unless the wording is taken directly from another source. Authors, of course, must be absolutely sure of such facts, and editors should flag anything that seems suspicious (see 13.6). No source need be cited for such statements as the following:

> On April 14, 1865, a few days after Lee's surrender, Lincoln was assassinated.
> No one can convince the young that practice makes perfect.
> If reading maketh a full man, Henry is half-empty.

See also 6.51.

13.6 *Ensuring accuracy of quotations.* It is impossible to overemphasize the importance of meticulous accuracy in quoting from the works of others. Authors should check every direct quotation against the original or, if the original is unavailable, against a careful transcription of the passage. This should be done *before* the manuscript is submitted to the publisher. Though manuscript editors will often query apparent errors of transcription, they typically will not have access to an author's sources. Moreover, it takes far less time for authors to accurately transcribe quotations during the writing stage than for authors or editors to go back to the original sources once a work is submitted for publication. See also 2.30, 2.132.

Permissible Changes to Quotations

13.7 *Permissible changes to punctuation, capitalization, and spelling.* Although in a direct quotation the wording should be reproduced exactly, the following changes are generally permissible to make a passage fit into the syntax and typography of the surrounding text. See also 13.8.

1. Single quotation marks may be changed to double, and double to single (see 13.28); punctuation relative to quotation marks should be adjusted accordingly (see 6.9). Guillemets and other types of quotation marks in a foreign language may be changed to regular single or double quotation marks (see 13.71).

2. The initial letter may be changed to a capital or a lowercase letter (see 13.13–16).

3. A final period may be omitted or changed to a comma as required, and punctuation may be omitted where ellipsis points are used (see 13.48–56).

4. Original note reference marks (and the notes to which they refer) may be omitted unless omission would affect the meaning of the quotation. If an original note is included, the quotation may best be set off as a block quotation (see 13.9), with the note in smaller type at the end, or the note may be summarized in the accompanying text. Authors may, on the other hand, add note references of their own within quotations.

5. Obvious typographic errors may be corrected silently (without comment or *sic*; see 13.59), unless the passage quoted is from an older work or a manuscript source where idiosyncrasies of spelling are generally preserved. If spelling and punctuation are modernized or altered for clarity, readers must be so informed in a note, in a preface, or elsewhere.

6. In quoting from early printed documents, the archaic Latin ſ (small letter esh, Unicode character U+0283, similar to the integral sign), used to represent a lowercase *s* at the beginning or in the middle but never at the end of a word ("Such goodneſs of your juſtice, that our ſoul . . ."), may be changed to a modern *s*. Similarly, *Vanitie and Vncertaintie* (a quoted title) may be changed to *Vanitie and Uncertaintie*, but writers or editors without a strong background in classical or Renaissance studies should generally be wary of changing *u* to *v*, *i* to *j*, or vice versa. See also 11.61, 11.142–43.

13.8   *Permissible changes to typography and layout.* The following elements of typography and layout may be changed to assimilate a quotation to the surrounding text:

1. The typeface or font should be changed to agree with the surrounding text.

2. Words in full capitals in the original may be set in small caps, if that is the preferred style for the surrounding text. (See also 10.8.)

3. In dialogue, names of speakers may be moved from a centered position to flush left.

4. Underlined words in a quoted manuscript may be printed as italics, unless the underlining itself is considered integral to the source or otherwise worthy of reproducing.

5. In quoting correspondence, such matters as paragraph indention and the position of the salutation and signature may be adjusted.

For paragraph indention in block quotations, see 13.20. For reproducing poetry extracts, see 13.23–27. For permissible changes to titles of books, articles, poems, and other works, see 8.163.

Quotations in Relation to Text

Run In or Set Off

13.9 *Run-in versus block quotations.* Quoted text may be either run in to the surrounding text and enclosed in quotation marks, "like this," or set off as a block quotation, or extract. Block quotations, which are not enclosed in quotation marks, always start a new line. They are further distinguished from the surrounding text by being indented (from the left and sometimes from the right) or set in smaller type or a different font from the text. These matters are normally decided by the publisher's designer or by journal style. Authors preparing block quotations should simply use the indention feature of their word processors (see 2.18). For poetry, see 13.23–27.

13.10 *Choosing between run-in and block quotations.* In deciding whether to run in or set off a quotation, length is usually the deciding factor. In general, a short quotation, especially one that is not a full sentence, should be run in. A hundred words or more (at least six to eight lines of text in a typical manuscript) can generally be set off as a block quotation. Other criteria apply, however. A quotation of two or more paragraphs is best set off (see 13.20–22), as are quoted correspondence (if salutations, signatures, and such are included), lists, and any material that requires special formatting. If many quotations of varying length occur close together, running them all in may make for easier reading. But where quotations are being compared or otherwise used as entities in themselves, it may be better to set them all as block quotations, however short. Poetry is set off far more often than prose (see 13.23–27).

Assimilation into the Surrounding Text

13.11 *Logical and grammatical assimilation.* In incorporating fragmentary quotations into a text, phrase the surrounding sentence in such a way that the quoted words fit into it logically and grammatically, quoting only as much of the original as is necessary.

The narrator's constant references to "malicious code and obsolete data" detract from a more fundamental issue—that we are dumping "the burden of human history" onto computer hard drives. It is this vision of the future that is most alarming: "If (when?) we run out of sources of electricity," she asks, "will we forget who we are?"

13.12 *Integrating tenses and pronouns.* In quoting verbatim, writers need to integrate tenses and pronouns into the new context.

[*Original*] Mr. Moll took particular pains to say to you, gentlemen, that these eleven people here are guilty of murder; he calls this a cold-blooded, deliberate and premeditated murder.

[*As quoted*] According to Darrow, Moll had told the jury that the eleven defendants were "guilty of murder" and had described the murder as "cold-blooded, deliberate and premeditated."

Occasional adjustments to the original may be bracketed. This device should be used sparingly, however.

Mr. Graham has resolutely ducked the issue, saying he won't play the game of rumormongering, even though he has "learned from [his] mistakes."

Initial Capital or Lowercase Letter

13.13 *Changing capitalization to suit syntax—an overview.* Aside from proper nouns and some of the words derived from them (see 8.1), words in English publications are normally lowercased unless they begin a sentence (or, often, a line of poetry). To suit this requirement, the first word in a quoted passage must often be adjusted to conform to the surrounding text. In most types of works, this adjustment may be done silently, as such capitalization does not normally affect the significance of the quoted matter, which is assumed to have been taken from another context. In some types of works, however, it may be obligatory to indicate the change by bracketing the initial quoted letter; for examples of this practice, appropriate to legal writing and some types of textual commentary, see 13.16.

13.14 *Initial capital or lowercase—run-in quotations.* When a quotation introduced midsentence forms a syntactical part of the sentence, it begins with a lowercase letter even if the original begins with a capital.

Benjamin Franklin admonishes us to "plough deep while sluggards sleep."

With another aphorism he reminded his readers that "experience keeps a dear school, but fools will learn in no other"—an observation as true today as then.

When the quotation has a more remote syntactic relation to the rest of the sentence, the initial letter remains capitalized.

As Franklin advised, "Plough deep while sluggards sleep."

His aphorism "Experience keeps a dear school, but fools will learn in no other" is a cogent warning to people of all ages.

On the other hand, if a quotation that is only a part of a sentence in the original forms a complete sentence as quoted, a lowercase letter may be changed to a capital if appropriate. In the example that follows, "those" begins midsentence in the original (see 13.15).

Aristotle put it this way: "Those who are eminent in virtue usually do not stir up insurrections, always a minority."
but
Aristotle believed that "those who are eminent in virtue usually do not stir up insurrections, always a minority."

13.15   *Initial capital or lowercase—block quotations.* The consideration of whether to lowercase a capital letter beginning a block quotation is exactly the same as it is for run-in quotations (see 13.14): the initial letter of a block quotation that is capitalized in the original may be lowercased if the syntax demands it. In the following example, the quotation from Aristotle in the Jowett translation (Modern Library) begins in the original with a capital letter and a paragraph indention. See also 13.20.

In discussing the reasons for political disturbances, Aristotle observes that

> revolutions also break out when opposite parties, e.g. the rich and the people, are equally balanced, and there is little or no middle class; for, if either party were manifestly superior, the other would not risk an attack upon them. And, for this reason, those who are eminent in virtue usually do not stir up insurrections, always a minority. Such are the beginnings and causes of the disturbances and revolutions to which every form of government is liable. (*Politics* 5.4)

On the other hand, the capital should be retained—or a lowercase letter should be changed to a capital—if the syntax requires it. See also 13.17.

In discussing the reasons for political disturbances, Aristotle makes the following observations:

> Revolutions also break out when opposite parties, e.g. the rich and the people, are equally balanced, and there is little or no middle class; . . .

13.16　*Brackets to indicate a change in capitalization.* In some legal writing, textual commentary, and other contexts, it is considered obligatory to indicate any change in capitalization by brackets. This practice, easy enough to apply in any context but unnecessary in most, must be practiced consistently throughout a work.

According to article 6, section 6, she is given the power "[t]o extend or renew any existing indebtedness."

"[R]eal estates may be conveyed by lease and release, or bargain and sale," according to section 2 of the Northwest Ordinance.

Let us compare Aristotle's contention that "[i]nferiors revolt in order that they may be equal, and equals that they may be superior" (*Politics* 5.2), with his later observation that "[r]evolutions also break out when opposite parties, e.g. the rich and the people, are equally balanced" (5.4).

Introductory Phrases and Punctuation

13.17　*Colon preceding a quotation.* A formal introductory phrase, such as *thus* or *as follows*, is usually followed by a colon.

The role of the author has been variously described. Henry Fielding, at the beginning of his *History of Tom Jones*, defines it thus: "An author ought to consider himself, not as a gentleman who gives a private or eleemosynary treat, but rather as one who keeps a public ordinary, at which all persons are welcome for their money."

13.18　*Comma preceding a quotation.* When it is simply a matter of identifying a speaker, a comma is used after *said, replied, asked*, and similar verbs; a colon, though never wrong in such instances, should be used sparingly (e.g., to introduce quotations that consist of more than one sentence).

Garrett replied, "I hope you are not referring to me."

Fish writes, "What [the students] did was move the words out of a context (the faculty club door) in which they had a literal and obvious meaning into another context (my classroom) in which the meaning was no less obvious and literal and yet was different."

13.19 *Period rather than colon preceding a quotation.* Unless introduced by *thus, as follows,* or other wording that requires a colon, a block quotation may be preceded by a period rather than a colon. Such usage should be applied consistently.

He then took a clearly hostile position toward Poland, having characterized it as a Fascist state that oppressed the Ukrainians, the Belorussians, and others.

> Under present conditions, suppression of that state will mean that there will be one less Fascist state. It will not be a bad thing if Poland suffers a defeat and thus enables us to include new territories and new populations in the socialist system.

Paragraphing

13.20 *Block quotations of more than one paragraph.* Quoted material of more than a paragraph, even if very brief, is best set off as a block quotation. (For a less desirable alternative, see 13.30.) A multiparagraph block quotation should generally reflect the paragraph breaks of the original. But if the first paragraph quoted includes the beginning of that paragraph, it need not start with a first-line paragraph indention. Subsequent paragraphs in the quotation should be indicated either by first-line paragraph indention or (less desirably) by extra line space between the paragraphs (see also 13.22). The following example, from Jane Austen's *Pride and Prejudice*, includes four full paragraphs:

> He began to wish to know more of her, and as a step towards conversing with her himself, attended to her conversation with others. His doing so drew her notice. It was at Sir William Lucas's, where a large party were assembled.
>
> "What does Mr. Darcy mean," said she to Charlotte, "by listening to my conversation with Colonel Forster?"
>
> "That is a question which Mr. Darcy only can answer."
>
> "But if he does it any more I shall certainly let him know that I see what he is about. He has a very satirical eye, and if I do not begin by being impertinent myself, I shall soon grow afraid of him."

If the first part of the opening paragraph were to be omitted, it would still begin flush left. For ellipsis points at the beginning of paragraphs, see 13.54.

13.21   *Block quotations beginning in text.* A long quotation may begin with a few words run in to the text. This device should be used only when text intervenes between the quoted matter in the text and its continuation.

"There is no safe trusting to dictionaries and definitions," observed Charles Lamb.

> We should more willingly fall in with this popular language, if we did not find *brutality* sometimes awkwardly coupled with *valour* in the same vocabulary. The comic writers . . . have contributed not a little to mislead us upon this point. To see a hectoring fellow exposed and beaten upon the stage, has something in it wonderfully diverting. ("Popular Fallacies," *Essays of Elia*, 277)

"In short," says Crane, summarizing Gordon's philosophy,

> there has been "almost a continual improvement" in all branches of human knowledge; . . .

A permissible alternative is to set off the entire quotation, enclosing the intervening words of text in brackets.

> There is no safe trusting to dictionaries and definitions [observed Charles Lamb]. We should more willingly . . .

13.22   *Text following a block quotation.* If the text following a block quotation is a continuation of the paragraph that introduces the quotation, it begins flush left. If the resuming text begins a new paragraph, it receives a paragraph indention. In works where all new paragraphs appear flush left, however, it may be necessary to impose extra line spacing before new paragraphs following block quotations.

Poetry

13.23   *Setting off poetry.* Two or more lines of verse are best set off as a block quotation (cf. 14.33). A poetry quotation, if isolated, is often visually centered on the page between the left and right margins (usually relative to the longest line), but if two or more stanzas of the same poem appear on the same page, a uniform indention from the left may work better (see 13.24).

A half line to a full line of space should appear between stanzas. Within each piece or stanza, the indention pattern of the original should be reproduced (but indention should be distinguished from runover lines; see 13.25). For placement of the source, see 13.69.

> Sure there was wine
> Before my sighs did drie it: there was corn
> Before my tears did drown it.
> Is the yeare onely lost to me?
> Have I no bayes to crown it?
> No flowers, no garlands gay? all blasted?
> All wasted?
> (George Herbert, "The Collar")

If the quotation does not begin with a full line, space approximating the omitted part should be left.

> there was corn
> Before my tears did drown it.

13.24   *Uniform indention for poetry.* Where all or most poetic quotations consist of blank verse (as in studies of Shakespeare) or are very long, uniform indention from the left margin usually works best (e.g., a left indention that matches the one, if any, used for prose extracts).

> I have full cause of weeping, but this heart
> Shall break into a hundred thousand flaws
> Or ere I'll weep. O Fool! I shall go mad.

13.25   *Long lines and runovers in poetry.* Runover lines (the remainder of lines too long to appear as a single line) are usually indented one em from the line above, as in the following quotation from Walt Whitman's "Song of Myself":

> My tongue, every atom of my blood, form'd from this
>   soil, this air,
> Born here of parents born here from parents the same,
>   and their parents the same,
> I, now thirty-seven years old in perfect health begin,
> Hoping to cease not till death.

Runover lines, although indented, should be distinct from new lines deliberately indented by the poet (as in the Herbert poem quoted in 13.23).

Generally, a unique and uniform indent for runovers will be enough to accomplish this.

13.26 *Quotation marks in poems.* In a departure from its former practice, Chicago no longer recommends "clearing" quotation marks at the start of a line of poetry—that is, placing them outside the alignment of the poem, with lines left-aligned as if the quotation marks were not there. Quotation marks at the start of a line should instead be aligned with the other lines in the excerpt.

> He holds him with his skinny hand.
> "There was a ship," quoth he.
> "Hold off! unhand me, grey-beard loon!"
> Eftsoons his hand dropt he.

13.27 *Run-in poetry quotations.* If space or context in the text or in a note requires that two or more lines be run in, the lines are separated by a slash, with one space on either side (in printed works, a thin space to an en space).

> Andrew Marvell's praise of John Milton, "Thou has not missed one thought that could be fit, / And all that was improper does omit" ("On *Paradise Lost*"), might well serve as our motto.

For running in more than one stanza (to be avoided if at all possible), see 13.32.

Quotation Marks

Double or Single

13.28 *Quotations and "quotes within quotes."* Quoted words, phrases, and sentences run into the text are enclosed in double quotation marks. Single quotation marks enclose quotations within quotations; double marks, quotations within these; and so on. (The practice in the United Kingdom and elsewhere is often the reverse: single marks are used first, then double, and so on.) When the material quoted consists entirely of a quotation within a quotation, only one set of quotation marks need be employed (usually double quotation marks). For permissible changes from single to double quotation marks and vice versa, see 13.7 (item 1); see also 13.61. For dialogue, see 13.37. For technical uses of single quotation marks, see 7.50, 8.129.

"Don't be absurd!" said Henry. "To say that 'I mean what I say' is the same as 'I say what I mean' is to be as confused as Alice at the Mad Hatter's tea party. You remember what the Hatter said to her: 'Not the same thing a bit! Why you might just as well say that "I see what I eat" is the same thing as "I eat what I see"!'"

Note carefully not only the placement of the single and double closing quotation marks but also that of the exclamation points in relation to those marks in the example above. Question marks and exclamation points are placed just within the set of quotation marks ending the element to which such terminal punctuation belongs. For the placement of other punctuation—commas, periods, question marks, and so on—in relation to closing quotation marks, see 6.9–11.

13.29   **Quotation marks in block quotations.** Although material set off as a block quotation is not enclosed in quotation marks, quoted matter *within* the block quotation is enclosed in double quotation marks—in other words, treated as it would be in text (see 13.28). An author or editor who changes a run-in quotation to a block quotation must delete the opening and closing quotation marks and change any internal ones. The following examples illustrate the same material first in run-in form and then as a block quotation:

The narrator then breaks in: "Imagine Bart's surprise, dear reader, when Emma turned to him and said, contemptuously, 'What "promise"?'"

The narrator then breaks in:

> Imagine Bart's surprise, dear reader, when Emma turned to him and said, contemptuously, "What 'promise'?"

Similarly, converting a block quotation to a run-in quotation requires adding and altering quotation marks. For interpolations that include quoted matter, see 13.61.

Run-In Quotations of More Than One Paragraph

13.30   **Quotation marks across paragraphs.** If quoted material of more than one paragraph cannot be set as a block quotation (which is normally much preferred; see 13.10), quotation marks are needed at the beginning of *each* paragraph but at the end of only the *final* paragraph. (Note that each successive paragraph must begin on a new line, as in the original.) The same practice is followed in dialogue when one speaker's remarks extend over more than one paragraph.

13.31 *Quotations within quotations across paragraphs.* If a run-in quoted passage contains an interior quotation that runs for more than one paragraph, a single quotation mark appears at the beginning and end of the interior quotation, and both double and single quotation marks appear before each new paragraph belonging to it. If the interior quotation concludes at the same point as the including one, the single closing quotation mark precedes the double one.

13.32 *Running in more than one stanza of poetry.* A quotation that spans more than one stanza should be presented as an extract if at all possible (see 13.23). If it must be run in to the text (set off by quotation marks), two slashes (//) should appear between stanzas. For the use of the slash between run-in lines of poetry, see 13.27.

13.33 *Running in letters.* A letter quoted in its entirety should be set off as a block quotation. In the undesirable event that it must be run in, it should carry opening quotation marks before the first line (including the salutation) and before each paragraph. Closing marks appear only after the last line (often the signature). See 13.30.

Quotation Marks Omitted

13.34 *Epigraphs.* Quotation marks are not used around epigraphs (quotations used as ornaments preceding a text rather than as illustration or documentation). Like block quotations, epigraphs receive a distinctive typographic treatment—often being set in a smaller typeface and indented from the right or left, and sometimes italicized. Treatment of sources, which are usually set on a separate line, also varies, though more than one epigraph used in the same work should receive consistent treatment. For more on sources, see 13.68–70. See also 1.36.

Oh, what a tangled web we weave,
When first we practice to deceive!
—Sir Walter Scott

It is a truth universally acknowledged, that a single man in possession of a good
fortune, must be in want of a wife.

    Jane Austen, *Pride and Prejudice*

13.35   *Decorative initials ("drop caps" and raised initials).* When the first word of
a chapter or section opens with a large raised or dropped initial letter,
and the first words of the chapter or section consist of a run-in quotation, the opening quotation mark is often omitted.

O F THE MAKING OF MANY BOOKS there is no end," declared
an ancient Hebrew sage, who had himself magnificently aggravated the situation he was decrying.

If the opening quotation mark is included, it should appear in the same
size and with the same vertical alignment as the regular text.

13.36   *Maxims, questions, and the like.* Maxims, mottoes, rules, and other familiar expressions, sometimes enclosed in quotation marks, are discussed
in 6.51 and 8.197. Questions that do not require quotation marks are discussed in 6.52 and 6.67.

Speech, Dialogue, and Conversation

13.37   *Direct discourse.* Direct discourse or dialogue is traditionally enclosed in
quotation marks. A change in speaker is usually indicated by a new paragraph, as in the following excerpt from *Huckleberry Finn*:

> "Ransomed? What's that?"
> "I don't know. But that's what they do. I've seen it in books; and so of course
> that's what we've got to do."
> "But how can we do it if we don't know what it is?"
> "Why, blame it all, we've *got* to do it. Don't I tell you it's in the books? Do you want
> to go to doing different from what's in the books, and get things all muddled up?"

If one speech (usually a particularly long one) occupies more than a paragraph, opening quotation marks are needed at the beginning of each new
paragraph, with a closing quotation mark placed at the end of only the
final paragraph (see also 13.30).

13.38   *Single-word speech.* Words such as *yes, no, where, how,* and *why,* when used
singly, are not enclosed in quotation marks except in direct discourse.
See also 6.68.

Ezra always answered yes; he could never say no to a friend.
Please stop asking why.
but
"Yes," he replied weakly.
Again she repeated, "Why?"

13.39   *Faltering or interrupted speech.* Suspension points—also used to indicate an ellipsis—may be used to suggest faltering or fragmented speech accompanied by confusion or insecurity. In the examples below, note the relative positions of the suspension points and other punctuation. (For the use of suspension points to indicate ellipses, see 13.48–56.)

"I . . . I . . . that is, we . . . yes, *we* have made an awful blunder!"
"The ship . . . oh my God! . . . it's sinking!" cried Henrietta.
"But . . . but . . . ," said Tom.

Interruptions or abrupt changes in thought are usually indicated by em dashes. See 6.84.

13.40   *Alternatives to quotation marks.* In some languages, em dashes are used to present dialogue; for examples, see 11.34, 11.52, 11.80, 11.121. For the use of guillemets (« »), see 11.32, 11.44, 11.52, 11.79, 11.121.

13.41   *Unspoken discourse.* Thought, imagined dialogue, and other interior discourse may be enclosed in quotation marks or not, according to the context or the writer's preference.

"I don't care if we have offended Morgenstern," thought Vera. "Besides," she told herself, "they're all fools."

Why, we wondered, did we choose this route?

The following passage from James Joyce's *Ulysses* illustrates interior monologue and stream of consciousness without need of quotation marks:

Reading two pages apiece of seven books every night, eh? I was young. You bowed to yourself in the mirror, stepping forward to applause earnestly, striking face. Hurray for the Goddamned idiot! Hray! No-one saw: tell no-one. Books you were going to write with letters for titles. Have you read his F?

13.42   *Numerals in direct discourse.* In quoting directly from spoken sources (e.g., interviews, speeches, or dialogue from a film or a play), or when writing direct discourse for a drama or a work of fiction, numbers that might otherwise be rendered as numerals can often be spelled out. This practice requires editorial discretion. Years can usually be rendered as numerals, as can trade names that include numerals. And for dialogue that includes more than a few large numbers, it may be more practical to use numerals. See also 9.2, 9.7.

Jarred's answer was a mix of rage and humiliation: "For the last time, I do not have seven hundred thirty-seven dollars and eleven cents! I don't even have a quarter for the parking meter, for that matter."

Like most proofreaders, she is a perfectionist. "I'm never happy with a mere ninety-nine and forty-four one-hundredths percent."
but
"Do you prefer shopping at 7-Eleven or Circle K?"

"I didn't get around to reading *Nineteen Eighty-Four* until 1985," he finally admitted.

13.43   *Indirect discourse.* Indirect discourse, which paraphrases dialogue, takes no quotation marks. See also 6.52.

Tom told Huck they had to do it that way because the books said so.
Very well, you say, but is there no choice?

Drama, Discussions and Interviews, and Field Notes

13.44   *Drama.* In plays, the speaker's name is usually set in a font distinct from the dialogue—caps and small caps, for example, or all small caps. The dialogue is not enclosed in quotation marks and is usually set in flush-and-hang style, or hanging indention (the style most often used in bibliographies and indexes and illustrated in the following examples).

R. ROISTER DOISTER. Except I have her to my wife, I shall run mad.
M. MERYGREEKE. Nay, "unwise" perhaps, but I warrant you for "mad."

Stage directions are usually italicized.

ALGERNON. That is quite a different matter. She is my aunt. (*Takes plate from below.*) Have some bread and butter. The bread and butter is for Gwendolen. Gwendolen is devoted to bread and butter.
JACK, *advancing to table and helping himself.* And very good bread and butter it is too.

13.45   *Shared lines and runover lines in verse drama.* In quoted excerpts, any indention used to indicate a single line of verse shared between two speakers in a play should be replicated (as in the example below, where the line begun by Barnardo is finished by Marcellus). Runover lines may be indicated as in poetry by an indention of one em or more from the line above (see also 13.25).

> BARNARDO.
>> It would be spoke to.
>
> MARCELLUS.   Speak to it, Horatio.
>
> HORATIO.
>> What art thou that usurp'st this time of night,
>> Together with that fair and warlike form
>> In which the majesty of buried Denmark
>> Did sometimes march? By heaven, I charge thee,
>>> speak.

13.46   *Discussions and interviews.* The transcription of a discussion or an interview is treated in much the same way as drama (see 13.44). Interjections such as "laughter" are italicized and enclosed in brackets (rather than parentheses). Paragraph indention is usually preferred to flush-and-hang style, though flush-and-hang, which allows easier identification of the speaker, may work better if several speakers' names appear and the comments are relatively brief. Though speakers' names are usually followed by a period, a colon may be used instead.

> INTERVIEWER. You weren't thinking that this technology would be something you could use to connect to the Office of Tibet in New York or to different Tibet support groups in Europe?
>
> RESPONDENT. No. Nobody seemed to have anything to do with GreenNet in the Tibet world at that time. That came much later. That's not really right. I specifically wasn't interested in connecting to the community of Tibet martyrs and fellow sufferers [*laughs*] and the emotional pathological there-but-for-the-grace-of-god-go-I people.

An author's previously unpublished transcriptions of interviews or discussions can usually be edited for such matters as capitalization, spelling, and minor grammatical slips or elisions. If an author has imposed more significant alterations, these should be explained in a note, a preface, or elsewhere. Previously published transcriptions should be quoted as they appear in the original source.

13.47   *Field notes.* An author's transcriptions of unpublished field notes (the author's own or those of a colleague or assistant) pose a special case. Unlike quotations from published sources or transcriptions of interviews, field notes need not be presented verbatim—whether they are presented as quotations or woven into the text. Rather, they should be edited for consistency—with other notes and with the surrounding text—in matters of spelling, capitalization, punctuation, treatment of numbers, and so forth. And even if the author is in possession of signed releases, any otherwise anonymous subjects or informants should generally be presented under pseudonyms; a note should be appended to the text to indicate that this is the case. Editors should query authors if it is not clear that appropriate provisions have been made.

Ellipses

13.48   *Ellipses defined.* An *ellipsis* is the omission of a word, phrase, line, paragraph, or more from a quoted passage. Such omissions are made of material that is considered irrelevant to the discussion at hand (or, occasionally, to adjust for the grammar of the surrounding text). Chicago style is to indicate such omissions by the use of three spaced periods (but see 13.51) rather than by another device such as asterisks. These points (or dots) are called ellipsis points when they indicate an ellipsis and suspension points when they indicate suspended or interrupted thought (see 13.39). They must always appear together on the same line (through the use of nonbreaking spaces, available in most software applications), along with any following punctuation; if an ellipsis appears at the beginning of a line, any preceding punctuation (including a period) will appear at the end of the line above. If they prefer, authors may prepare their manuscripts using the single-glyph three-dot ellipsis character on their word processors (Unicode 2026), usually with a space on either side; editors following Chicago style will replace these with spaced periods.

13.49   *Danger of skewing meaning.* Since quotations from another source have been separated from their original context, particular care needs to be exercised when eliding text to ensure that the sense of the original is not lost or misrepresented. A deletion must not result in a statement alien to the original material. And in general, ellipses should not be used to join two statements that are far apart in the original. Accuracy of sense and emphasis must accompany accuracy of transcription.

13.50 *When not to use ellipsis points.* Ellipsis points are normally *not* used (1) before the first word of a quotation, even if the beginning of the original sentence has been omitted; or (2) after the last word of a quotation, even if the end of the original sentence has been omitted, unless the sentence as quoted is deliberately incomplete (see 13.53).

13.51 *Ellipses with periods.* A period is added *before* an ellipsis to indicate the omission of the end of a sentence, unless the sentence is deliberately incomplete (see 13.53). Similarly, a period at the end of a sentence in the original is retained before an ellipsis indicating the omission of material immediately following the period. What precedes and, normally, what follows the four dots should be grammatically complete sentences as quoted, even if part of either sentence has been omitted. A complete passage from Emerson's essay "Politics" reads:

> The spirit of our American radicalism is destructive and aimless: it is not loving; it has no ulterior and divine ends; but is destructive only out of hatred and selfishness. On the other side, the conservative party, composed of the most moderate, able, and cultivated part of the population, is timid, and merely defensive of property. It vindicates no right, it aspires to no real good, it brands no crime, it proposes no generous policy, it does not build, nor write, nor cherish the arts, nor foster religion, nor establish schools, nor encourage science, nor emancipate the slave, nor befriend the poor, or the Indian, or the immigrant. From neither party, when in power, has the world any benefit to expect in science, art, or humanity, at all commensurate with the resources of the nation.

The passage might be shortened as follows:

> The spirit of our American radicalism is destructive and aimless. . . . On the other side, the conservative party . . . is timid, and merely defensive of property. . . . It does not build, nor write, nor cherish the arts, nor foster religion, nor establish schools.

Note that the first word after an ellipsis is capitalized if it begins a new grammatical sentence. Some types of works require that such changes to capitalization be bracketed; see 13.16. See also 13.56.

13.52 *Ellipses with other punctuation.* Other punctuation appearing in the original text—a comma, a colon, a semicolon, a question mark, or an exclamation point—may precede or follow three (but never four) ellipsis points. Whether to include the additional mark of punctuation depends on whether keeping it aids comprehension or is required for the grammar of the sentence. Placement of the other punctuation depends on whether the omission precedes or follows the mark; when the omission precedes it, a nonbreaking space should be used between the ellipsis and the mark of punctuation to prevent the mark from carrying over to the beginning of a new line (see 13.48). Note that this before-or-after distinction is usually *not* made with periods, where—without the aid of brackets (see 13.56)—it is likely to go unnoticed (see 13.51).

It does not build, . . . nor cherish the arts, nor foster religion.

As to *Endymion*, was it a poem . . . to be treated contemptuously by those who had celebrated, with various degrees of complacency and panegyric, *Paris*, and *Woman*, and *A Syrian Tale* . . . ? Are these the men who . . . presumed to draw a parallel between the Rev. Mr. Milman and Lord Byron?

When a species . . . increases inordinately in numbers in a small tract, epidemics . . . often ensue: and here we have a limiting check independent of the struggle for life. But even some of these so-called epidemics appear to be due to parasitic worms . . . : and here comes in a sort of struggle between the parasite and its prey.

13.53   *Deliberately incomplete sentence.* Three dots are used at the end of a quoted sentence that is deliberately left grammatically incomplete.

Everyone knows that the Declaration of Independence begins with the sentence "When, in the course of human events . . ." But how many people can recite more than the first few lines of the document?

Have you had a chance to look at the example beginning "The spirit of our American radicalism . . ."?

Note that no space intervenes between a final ellipsis point and a closing quotation mark.

13.54   *Whole or partial paragraphs omitted.* The omission of one or more paragraphs within a quotation is indicated by four ellipsis points at the end of the paragraph preceding the omitted part. (If that paragraph ends with an incomplete sentence, only three points are used; see 13.53.) If the first part of a paragraph is omitted within a quotation, a paragraph indention and three ellipsis points appear before the first quoted word. It is thus possible to use ellipsis points both at the end of one paragraph and at the beginning of the next, as illustrated in the following excerpt from Alexander Pope's "Letter to a Noble Lord":

I should be obliged indeed to lessen this respect, if all the nobility . . . are but so many hereditary fools, if the privilege of lords be to want brains, if noblemen can hardly write or read. . . .

Were it the mere excess of your Lordship's wit, that carried you thus triumphantly over all the bounds of decency, I might consider your Lordship on your Pegasus, as a sprightly hunter on a mettled horse. . . .

. . . Unrivalled as you are, in making a figure, and in making a speech, methinks, my Lord, you may well give up the poor talent of making a distich.

13.55 *Ellipsis points in poetry and verse drama.* Omission of the end of a line of verse is indicated by four ellipsis points if what precedes them is a complete grammatical sentence, otherwise by three. The omission of a full line or of several consecutive lines within a quoted poem or drama in verse is indicated by one line of widely spaced dots approximately the length of the line above (or of the missing line, if that is determinable). See also 13.23–27.

Type of the antique Rome! Rich reliquary
Of lofty contemplation . . .
   (Edgar Allan Poe, "The Coliseum")

She would dwell on such dead themes, not as one who remembers,
   But rather as one who sees.
. . . .
Past things retold were to her as things existent,
   Things present but as a tale.
   (Thomas Hardy, "One We Knew")

This royal throne of kings, this sceptred isle,
. . . .
This blessed plot, this earth, this realm, this England.
   (*Richard II*, 2.1.40–50)

13.56 *Bracketed ellipses.* Especially in languages that make liberal use of suspension points, it is a common practice to bracket ellipses (see, e.g., 11.35; see also 11.10). In an English context where both ellipses and suspension points are needed, the latter may be explained at each instance in a note (e.g., "suspension points in original"); for more than a few such instances, authors may choose instead to bracket ellipses, but only after explaining such a decision in a note, a preface, or elsewhere. The rules for placing bracketed ellipses are the same as the rules outlined in the rest of this section, with one exception—a period is placed before or after the ellipsis depending on its placement in the original. Compare the passage that follows to the passages in 13.51.

> The spirit of our American radicalism is destructive and aimless [. . .]. On the other side, the conservative party [. . .] is timid, and merely defensive of property. [. . .] It does not build, nor write, nor cherish the arts, nor foster religion, nor establish schools.

Note that a space appears before an opening bracket; a space appears after a closing bracket except when a period, comma, or other mark of punctuation follows. Within brackets, the sequence is bracket-period-space-period-space-period-bracket. Nonbreaking spaces are needed only for the two spaces between the periods within the brackets.

Interpolations and Clarifications

13.57   *Missing or illegible words.* In reproducing or quoting from a document in which certain words are missing or illegible, an author may use ellipsis points (see 13.48–56), a bracketed comment or guess (sometimes followed by a question mark), or both. If ellipsis points alone are used (useful for a passage with more than a few lacunae), their function as a stand-in for missing or illegible words must be explained in the text or in a note. If a bracketed gloss comes from a different source, the source must be cited in a note or elsewhere. See also 6.97.

> If you will assure me of your . . . [illegible], I shall dedicate my life to your endeavor.

> She marched out of the door, headed for the [president's?] office.

A 2-em dash (see 6.90), sometimes in combination with an interpolated guess, may also be used for missing material. As with ellipsis points, this device should be used consistently and should be explained (in prefatory material or a note).

> I have great marvel that ye will so soon incline to every man his device and [counsel and ——] specially in matters of small impor[tance ——] yea, and as [it is] reported [unto me——] causes as meseemeth th[a——] nothing to [——]ne gentlewomen.

13.58   *Bracketed clarifications.* Insertions may be made in quoted material to clarify an ambiguity, to provide a missing word or letters (see 13.57), to correct an error, or, in a translation, to give the original word or phrase where the English fails to convey the exact sense. Such interpolations, which should be kept to a minimum lest they irritate or distract readers, are enclosed in brackets (never in parentheses). See also 6.97, 13.12.

Marcellus, doubtless in anxious suspense, asks Barnardo, "What, has this thing [the ghost of Hamlet's father] appear'd again tonight?"

"Well," said she, "if Mr. L[owell] won't go, then neither will I."

Saha once remarked of Nehru that "his position in this country can be described by a phrase which Americans use with respect to Abraham Lincoln [read: George Washington], 'first in war, first in peace.'"

13.59 *"Sic."* Literally meaning "so," "thus," "in this manner," and traditionally set in italics, *sic* may be inserted in brackets following a word misspelled or wrongly used in the original. This device should be used only where it is relevant to call attention to such matters (and especially where readers might otherwise assume the mistake is in the transcription rather than the original) or where paraphrase or silent correction is inappropriate (see 13.4, 13.7 [item 5]).

In September 1862, J. W. Chaffin, president of the Miami Conference of Wesleyan Methodist Connection, urged Lincoln that "the confiscation law past [*sic*] at the last session of Congress should be faithfully executed" and that "to neglect this national righteousness" would prove "disastrous to the American people."

Sic should *not* be used merely to call attention to unconventional spellings, which should be explained (if at all) in a note or in prefatory material. Similarly, where material with many errors and variant spellings (such as a collection of informal letters) is reproduced as written, a prefatory comment or a note to that effect will make a succession of *sic*s unnecessary.

13.60 *"Italics added."* An author wishing to call particular attention to a word or phrase in quoted material may italicize it but must tell readers what has been done, by means of such formulas as "italics mine," "italics added," "emphasis added," or "emphasis mine." This information appears either in parentheses following the quotation or in a source note to the quotation. If there are italics in the original of the passage quoted, the information is best enclosed in brackets and placed directly after the added italics. Consistency in method throughout a work is essential.

You have watched the conduct of Ireland in the difficult circumstances of the last nine months, and that conduct I do not hesitate to risk saying on your behalf has evoked in every breast a responsive voice of sympathy, and an increased conviction that we may deal freely *and yet deal prudently* with our fellow-subjects beyond the Channel. Such is your conviction. (William Ewart Gladstone, October 1891; italics added)

In reality not one didactic poet has ever yet attempted to use any parts or processes of the particular art which he made his theme, unless in so far as they seemed susceptible of poetic treatment, and only *because* they seemed so. Look at the poem of *Cyder* by Philips, of the *Fleece* by Dyer, or (which is a still weightier example) at the *Georgics* of Virgil,—does any of these poets show the least anxiety for the *correctness of your principles* [my italics], or the delicacy of your manipulations, in the worshipful arts they affect to teach? (Thomas De Quincey, "Essay on Pope")

Occasionally it may be important to point out that italics in a quotation were indeed in the original. Here the usual phrase is "italics in the original" or, for example, "De Quincey's italics."

13.61   *Interpolations requiring quotation marks.* Occasionally a bracketed or parenthetical interpolation that includes quotation marks appears in material already enclosed in quotation marks. In such cases, the double/single rule (see 13.28) does not apply; the quotation marks within the brackets may remain double.

"Do you mean that a double-headed calf ["two-headed calf" in an earlier version] has greater value than two normal calves? That a freak of nature, even though it cannot survive, is to be more highly treasured for its rarity than run-of-the-mill creatures are for their potential use?"

Citing Sources in Text

13.62   *Use of parentheses with in-text citations.* If the source of a direct quotation is not given in a note, it is usually placed in the text in parentheses. Although the source normally follows a quotation, it may come earlier if it fits more smoothly into the introductory text (as in the second example in 13.63). The examples in this section focus on full and short forms of parenthetical citation that may be needed in shorter works with no notes or bibliography or to provide in-text citations to a frequently quoted work. The advice in this section on placement relative to surrounding text is applicable to both systems of citation recommended by Chicago: notes and bibliography (chapter 14) and author-date (chapter 15).

13.63 *Full in-text citation.* An entire source may be given in parentheses immediately following a quotation, or some of the data may be worked into the text, with details confined to parentheses. See also 6.99. For more on the proper form for full citations, see 14.18.

> "If an astronaut falls into a black hole, its mass will increase, but eventually the energy equivalent of that extra mass will be returned to the universe in the form of radiation. Thus, in a sense, the astronaut will be 'recycled'" (Stephen W. Hawking, *A Brief History of Time: From the Big Bang to Black Holes* [New York: Bantam Books, 1988], 112).

> In the preface to their revision of *The Complete Plain Words* by Sir Ernest Gowers (Penguin Books, 1986), Sidney Greenbaum and Janet Whitcut admit that "Gowers' frequent use of the first person pronoun 'I' presents a difficulty for revisers," since Fraser, having decided to retain the "I," tried "to distinguish the 'I' of Gowers from the 'I' of Fraser by listing in his preface the parts of the book that were wholly or mainly written by each of the authors."

13.64 *The use of "ibid." with subsequent in-text citations.* If a second passage from the same source is quoted close to the first and there is no intervening quotation from a different source, *ibid.* (set in roman) may be used in the second parenthetical reference (e.g., "ibid., 114"); *ibid.* alone may be used if the reference is to the same page. Avoid overusing *ibid.*: for more than the occasional repeated reference to the same source—as in an extended discussion of a work of fiction—only a parenthetical page number is necessary. If a quotation from another source has intervened, a shortened reference may be given (e.g., "Hawking, *Brief History of Time*, 114"). For more on shortened citations, see 14.24–31; for the use of *ibid.* in notes, see 14.29.

13.65 *Frequent reference to a single source cited in a note.* In a work containing notes, the full citation of a source may be given in a note at first mention, with subsequent citations made parenthetically in the text. This method is especially suited to literary studies that use frequent quotations from a single source. In a study of *Much Ado about Nothing*, for example, the note would list the edition and include wording such as "Text references are to act, scene, and line of this edition." A parenthetical reference to act 3, scene 4, lines 46–47, would then appear as in the example below. In references to a work of fiction, page numbers alone may be given.

"Ye light o' love with your heels! then, if your husband have stables enough, you'll see he shall lack no barns," says Beatrice (3.4.46–47).

Where a number of such sources (or different editions of a single source) are used in the same work, the title (or edition) may need to be indicated in the parenthetical references; it may be advisable to devise an abbreviation for each and to include a list of the abbreviations at the beginning or end of the work (see 14.54, 14.55). See also 14.260, 14.267, 14.43.

Sources Following Run-In Quotations

13.66   *Punctuation following source.* After a run-in quotation, the source is usually given after the closing quotation mark, followed by the rest of the surrounding sentence (including any comma, semicolon, colon, or dash; but see 13.67) or the final punctuation of that sentence.

With his "Nothing will come of nothing; speak again" (1.1.92), Lear tries to draw from his youngest daughter an expression of filial devotion.

It has been more than a century since Henry Adams said: "Fifty years ago, science took for granted that the rate of acceleration could not last. The world forgets quickly, but even today the habit remains of founding statistics on the faith that consumption will continue nearly stationary" (*Education*, 493).

Has it been more than a century since Henry Adams observed that "fifty years ago, science took for granted that the rate of acceleration could not last" (*Education*, 493)?

A parenthetical reference need not immediately follow the quotation as long as it is clear what it belongs to. For examples, see 13.63 (second example), 13.65. See also 15.25.

13.67   *Question mark or exclamation point preceding source.* When a quotation comes at the end of a sentence and is itself a question or an exclamation, that punctuation is retained within the quotation marks, and a period is still added after the closing parentheses. (Compare the third example in 13.66.)

And finally, in the frenzy of grief that kills him, Lear rails, "Why should a dog, a horse, a rat, have life, / And thou no breath at all?" (5.3.306–7).

Sources Following Block Quotations

13.68 *Punctuation preceding source.* The source of a block quotation is given in parentheses at the end of the quotation and in the same type size. The opening parenthesis appears *after* the final punctuation mark of the quoted material. No period either precedes or follows the closing parenthesis. See also 6.99, 15.25.

> If you happen to be fishing, and you get a strike, and whatever it is starts off with the preliminaries of a vigorous fight; and by and by, looking down over the side through the glassy water, you see a rosy golden gleam, the mere specter of a fish, shining below in the clear depths; and when you look again a sort of glory of golden light flashes and dazzles as it circles nearer beneath and around and under the boat; . . . and you land a slim and graceful and impossibly beautiful three-foot goldfish, whose fierce and vivid yellow is touched around the edges with a violent red—when all these things happen to you, fortunate but bewildered fisherman, then you may know you have been fishing in the Galapagos Islands and have taken a Golden Grouper. (Gifford Pinchot, *To the South Seas* [Philadelphia: John Winston, 1930], 123)

Shortened references are treated in the same way as full ones. If a qualifier such as *line, vol.,* or *p.* is required at the beginning of the shortened reference, it should be lowercased as with sources to run-in quotations.

> At last the fish came into sight—at first a mere gleam in the water, and then his full side. This was not even a distant cousin to the fish I thought I was fighting, but something else again entirely. (p. 142)

13.69 *Parenthetical citations with poetry extracts.* In order not to interfere with a poem's layout and overall presentation, parenthetical citations following poetry extracts are dropped to the line below the last line of the quotation. They may be centered on the last letter of the longest line of the quotation or set flush with the left margin of the poem; an additional line space may be added. Other positions are also possible (as in the examples in 13.23 and 13.70), as long as consistency and clarity are preserved.

> Now more than ever seems it rich to die,
> To cease upon the midnight with no pain,
> While thou art pouring forth thy soul abroad
>   In such an ecstasy!
> (Keats, "Ode to a Nightingale," stanza 6)

13.70 *Shortened references to poetry extracts.* Shortened references to poetry are treated the same way as full ones. A quotation from Edmund Spenser's *The Faerie Queene*, once the reader knows that reference is to book, canto, and stanza, might appear thus:

> Who will not mercie unto others shew,
> How can he mercy ever hope to have?
> (6.1.42)

Foreign-Language Quotations

13.71 *Typographic style of foreign quotations.* Quotations in a foreign language that are incorporated into an English text are normally treated like quotations in English, set in roman type and run in or set off as block quotations according to their length. They are punctuated as in the original except that quotation marks replace guillemets (or their equivalents), and spacing relative to punctuation is adjusted to conform to the surrounding text (see 11.10). For isolated words and phrases, see 7.49. For excerpts from the original language following an English translation, see 13.73.

> The narrator's "treinta o cuarenta molinos de viento" become Quixote's "treinta, o pocos más, desaforados gigantes"—a numerical correspondence that lets the reader trust, at the very least, the hero's basic grasp of reality.

If em dashes are used for dialogue in the original (see 11.34, 11.52, 11.80, 11.121), they should be retained in a block quotation but may be replaced by quotation marks if only a phrase or sentence is quoted.

13.72 *Whether translation is needed.* Whether to provide translations of quoted passages depends on the linguistic abilities of the likely readers. For example, in a work to be read by classicists, Latin or Greek sources may be quoted freely in the original. Or in a literary study of, say, Goethe, quotations from Goethe's work may be given in the original German only. For a wider readership, translations should be furnished.

13.73 *Where to place translations.* A translation may follow the original in parentheses—or, as in 13.74, the original may follow a translation. Quotation marks need not be repeated for the parenthetical translation (or parenthetical original, as the case may be); any internal quotation marks, however, should be included (as in the second example). See also 6.93,

7.50. If a long sentence or more than one sentence appears in parentheses or brackets, as in the second example, closing punctuation of both the original and the translation should remain distinct.

A line from Goethe, "Wer nie sein Brot mit Tränen aß" (Who never ate his bread with tears), comes to mind.

À vrai dire, Abélard n'avoue pas un tel rationalisme: "je ne veux pas être si philosophe, écrit-il, que je résiste à Paul, ni si aristotélicien que je me sépare du Christ." (As a matter of fact, Abelard admits no such rationalism. "I do not wish to be so much of a philosopher," he writes, "that I resist Paul, nor so much of an Aristotelian that I separate myself from Christ.")

13.74   *Source plus translation.* When both a source and a translation are required in text, the source may be placed in parentheses, with the original (or translation, as the case may be) following, separated by a semicolon. The following example quotes a thirteenth-century author writing in Middle Dutch. See also 13.66–67.

Hadewijch insists that the most perfect faith is "unfaith," which endlessly stokes desire and endlessly demands love from God. "Unfaith never allows desire to rest in any faith but always distrusts her, [feeling] that she is not loved enough" (letter 8:39; Ende ontrowe en laet gegherten niewers ghedueren in gheenre trowen, sine mestrout hare altoes, datse niet ghenoech ghemint en es).

If adding a translation or the original in text creates too much clutter, it may be placed in a note, in which case it is enclosed in quotation marks but not in parentheses or brackets (see 13.75).

13.75   *Including original-language version in note.* In many works, quotations from a foreign-language source need appear only in translation. Should the original be necessary, it can be placed in a note. If the parenthetical passage in the second example in 13.73 were to appear in text without the French, as either a run-in or a block quotation, a note could read as follows:

4. "À vrai dire, Abélard n'avoue pas un tel rationalisme: 'je ne veux pas être si philosophe, écrit-il, que je résiste à Paul, ni si aristotélicien que je me sépare du Christ.'"

See also 13.28.

13.76   *Crediting the translation.* When quoting a passage from a foreign language that requires a translation, authors should use a published English translation if one is available and give credit to the source of that translation, including the title of the translation, the translator's name, relevant bibliographic details, and page number (see 14.109). Authors providing their own translations should so state, in parentheses following the translation, in a note, or in the prefatory material—for example, "my translation" or "Unless otherwise noted, all translations are my own." See also 11.6, 11.7.

13.77   *Adjusting translations.* An author using a published translation may occasionally need to adjust a word or two. "Translation modified" or some such wording must then be added in parentheses or in a note (see also 13.60). In addition, it is recommended that such modifications be indicated by square brackets (see 13.57, 13.58). These devices should be used sparingly. If a published translation is unsuitable for the author's purpose, it should be abandoned and all quoted passages newly translated.

13.78   *Editing translations.* Quotations from published translations can be edited only with respect to the permissible changes described in 13.7. In new translations furnished by the author, however, capitalization, punctuation, spelling, and idiom may be adjusted for consistency with the surrounding text.

13.79   *The sin of retranslation.* Never should a passage from a work originally published in English (or any other language, for that matter) be retranslated from a foreign-language version. For example, an author quoting from a German study of Blackstone's *Commentaries* that quotes from Blackstone in German must track down the original Blackstone passages in English and reproduce them. If unable to locate the original, the author must resort to paraphrase.

Part Three: Documentation

14 · Documentation I: Notes and Bibliography

Source Citations: An Overview

14.1   *The purpose of source citations.* Ethics, copyright laws, and courtesy to readers require authors to identify the sources of direct quotations or paraphrases and of any facts or opinions not generally known or easily checked (see 13.1–6). Conventions for documentation vary according to scholarly discipline, the preferences of publishers and authors, and the needs of a particular work. Regardless of the convention being followed, the primary criterion of any source citation is sufficient information either to lead readers directly to the sources consulted or, for materials that may not be readily available, to positively identify the sources used, whether these are published or unpublished, in printed or electronic form.

14.2   *Chicago's two systems of source citation.* This chapter describes the first of Chicago's two systems of documentation, which uses a system of notes, whether footnotes or endnotes or both, and usually a bibliography. The notes allow space for unusual types of sources as well as for commentary on the sources cited, making this system extremely flexible. Because of this flexibility, the notes and bibliography system is preferred by many writers in literature, history, and the arts. Chicago's other system—which uses parenthetical author-date references and a corresponding reference list as described in chapter 15—is nearly identical in content but differs in form. The author-date system is preferred for many publications in the sciences and social sciences but may be adapted for any work, sometimes with the addition of footnotes or endnotes. For journals, the choice between systems is likely to have been made long ago; anyone writing for a journal should consult the specific journal's instructions to authors (and see 14.3).

14.3   *Other systems of source citation.* Among other well-known systems are those of the Modern Language Association and the American Psychological Association, both of which use variations of the author-date system (described in chapter 15), and that of the American Medical Association. The AMA uses a numbered list of references cited in the text by reference number; the text numbers appear as superior figures like note reference numbers. Guidelines and examples for these three systems are to be found in the manuals of those associations. *Scientific Style and Format,* published by the Council of Science Editors (CSE), also furnishes useful guidelines on both the author-date system and numbered references (see bibliog. 1.1 for these and other style manuals). Many journals and serials—including some of those published by the University of Chicago Press—either follow one of these styles or have their own styles, often based on or similar to the systems mentioned here and in 14.2. For legal and public documents, Chicago recommends *The Bluebook: A Uniform System of Citation*, published by the Harvard Law Review Association; see 14.281–317.

Considerations for Electronic Sources

14.4   *Electronic resource identifiers.* When citing electronic sources consulted online, Chicago recommends—as the final element in a citation that includes all the components described throughout this chapter and in chapter 15—the addition of a URL[1] or DOI.[2] Either of these elements has the potential to lead readers directly to the source cited, and authors are encouraged to record them as part of their source citations. Publishers, however, will have their own requirements, which may depend on the type of work and the uses to which it will be put. For example, publishers of electronic journals may provide hyperlinks to cited electronic sources as a matter of course—a process that authors facilitate when they provide resource identifiers with their source citations. Publishers of printed books, on the other hand, may require a URL or DOI only in citations of sources that may otherwise be difficult to locate. Authors are therefore advised to consult their publishers early in the publication process. The information in this section—together with the examples of URLs and DOIs throughout this chapter—is intended to provide guidance for those authors and publishers who wish to include them as part of their research or publications or both. For citing electronic sources on fixed media such as CD-ROMs, see 14.166, 14.168, 14.276, 14.279.

14.5   *Uniform resource locators (URLs).* A uniform resource locator, or URL—for example, http://www.chicagomanualofstyle.org/—is designed to lead a reader directly to an Internet source. For URL syntax, see 14.11 and 14.12. For examples of URLs in source citations, see 14.18 (under *Journal Article*), 14.167, 14.169, and throughout the discussions on periodicals (14.170–217), interviews and personal communications (14.218–23), websites and blogs (14.243–46), audiovisual materials (14.274–80), and elsewhere. Note that it is never sufficient simply to provide a URL (or other

---

1. For more information about URLs, consult the website of the World Wide Web Consortium. See also 14.5.
2. For more information about DOIs, consult the websites of the International DOI Foundation and CrossRef. See also 14.6.

resource locator); as far as they can be determined, the full facts of publication should always be recorded first. Although a URL has the potential to lead readers directly to the source cited, it is also the most vulnerable element in a citation; the source to which a URL points is apt to move to a different location on the web or to disappear altogether. Readers need to be able to judge the nature and authority of any source from the full facts of publication as detailed throughout this chapter and chapter 15.

14.6   *Digital Object Identifiers (DOIs).* One of a number of standards addressing the need for more reliable resource identifiers is that of the Digital Object Identifier (DOI). A DOI is a unique and permanent name assigned to a piece of intellectual property such as a journal article or book (or a component thereof), in any medium in which it is published. (The term "digital" refers to the identifier and not necessarily to the object.) A DOI consists of a prefix assigned by a DOI registration agency such as CrossRef and—following a forward slash—a name assigned by the publisher. For example, 10.1086/529076 identifies the article entitled "Before Democracy: The Production and Uses of Common Sense," by Sophia Rosenfeld, published in the March 2008 issue of the *Journal of Modern History*. At a minimum, typing or pasting the DOI into the DOI resolver available at the website of the International DOI Foundation or from CrossRef .org (or into a search engine that supports DOIs) will redirect you to a URL where the article may be found. (Alternatively, appending a DOI to http://dx.doi.org/ in the address bar of an Internet browser will lead to the source. For example, http://dx.doi.org/10.1086/529076 will resolve to the Rosenfeld article mentioned above.) Authors should include DOIs rather than URLs for sources that make them readily available. The examples included throughout the discussion on journals (14.175–98) may be applied to other types of sources as necessary, including books (see 14.167, 14.248).

14.7   *Access dates.* An access date—that is, the self-reported date on which an author consulted a source—is of limited value: previous versions will often be unavailable to readers; authors typically consult a source any number of times over the course of days or months; and the accuracy of such dates, once recorded, cannot readily be verified by editors or publishers. Chicago does not therefore require access dates in its published citations of electronic sources unless no date of publication or revision can be determined from the source (see 14.8). For such undated sources—or for any source that seems likely to change without notice—authors are encouraged, as an additional safeguard, to archive dated copies, either as hard copy or in electronic form. Because some publishers in some disciplines—in particular, research-intensive fields such as science and medicine—*do* require access dates, authors should check with their publishers early on, and it never hurts to record dates of access during research. (Students are typically required to include access dates for citations of online sources in their papers.) For examples, see 14.185, 14.245, and 14.248.

14.8   *"Last modified" and other revision dates.* Some electronic documents will include a date on each page or screen indicating the last time the document was modified or revised. There are no accepted standards for this practice, and for formally published material the date of publication is generally more important. A revision date should be included, however, if it is presented as the de facto date of publication or is otherwise the only available date. Such dates may be particularly useful for citing wikis and other continuously updated works. For an example, see 14.248.

14.9   *Authority and permanence.* Much as they do for printed publications, authors must weigh the authority of any electronic sources they choose to cite. Electronic content presented without formal ties to a publisher or sponsoring body has the authority equivalent to that of unpublished or self-published material in other media. Moreover, such content is far more likely to change without notice—or disappear altogether—than formally published materials. On the other hand, self-published material from an authority on a given subject—relatively inaccessible before the advent of blogs—may have a great deal of validity. Authors should note, moreover, that *anything* posted on the Internet is "published" in the sense of copyright and must be treated as such for the purposes of complete citation and clearance of permissions, if relevant (see 4.2, 4.60–65).

14.10   *Publications available in more than one medium.* In many cases the contents of the print and electronic forms of the same publication are intended to be identical. Moreover, publishers are encouraged to note explicitly any differences between the two (see 1.73). In practice, because there is always the potential for differences, intentional or otherwise, authors should cite the version consulted. Chicago recommends including a URL or DOI to indicate that a work was consulted online; for other nonprint items, the medium should be indicated (e.g., CD-ROM). Note, however, that alternate electronic formats offered by a single publisher from the same website—for example, PDF and HTML versions of the journal article mentioned in 14.6—do *not* constitute separate sources. The URL for each such version will generally differ, but the DOI will not. In fact, a DOI serves readers by pointing to each medium in which a work is published. (Though a print source may list a DOI, authors need not record it as part of their research unless their publisher or discipline requires it.)

14.11   *URLs and other such elements in relation to surrounding text.* URLs, DOIs, e-mail addresses, and the like are unique strings that contain no spaces. URLs should be presented in full, beginning with the protocol (usually *http,* for *hypertext transfer protocol,* or *ftp,* for *file transfer protocol*). Even if it follows a period, the first letter of the protocol (e.g., the *h* in *http*) is not capitalized; likewise, *doi* preceding a DOI in a source citation is never capitalized. (In running text, avoid beginning a sentence with a URL or DOI; see also 8.186.) The capitalization of the remaining components varies; because some resource identifiers are case sensitive, they should not be edited for style (but see 14.244). A "trailing slash" (/), the last character in a URL pointing to a directory, is part of the URL. Other punctuation marks that follow a URL or other such identifier will readily be perceived as belonging to the surrounding text. Citations that include such an element should therefore be punctuated normally. Though angle brackets or other "wrappers" are standard with e-mail addresses or URLs in some applications, these are unnecessary in the context of notes and bibliographies or in running text (see also 6.8).

14.12   *URLs or DOIs and line breaks.* In a printed work, if a URL or DOI has to be broken at the end of a line, the break should be made *after* a colon or a double slash (//); *before* a single slash (/), a tilde (~), a period, a comma, a hyphen, an underline (_), a question mark, a number sign, or a percent symbol; or *before or after* an equals sign or an ampersand. Such breaks help to signal that the URL or DOI has been carried over to the next line. A hyphen should never be added to a URL or DOI to denote a line break, nor should a hyphen that is part of a URL or DOI appear at the end of a line. It is usually unnecessary to break URLs or DOIs in electronic publications (except in PDFs and other formats modeled on the printed page), and authors should avoid forcing them to break (with hard returns or other devices) in their manuscripts (see 2.12). See also 7.42.

> http://press-pubs.uchicago
> .edu/founders/
> http://www.jstor.org/stable
> /2921689
> http://www.time.com/time/magazine/article/0,9171
> ,920400,00.html
> http://wardsix.blogspot.com/2008/07/two
> -atlantic-essays.html
> doi:10.1086
> /ahr.113.3.752

14.13   *Source citation software.* A number of software programs promise to automate the task of formatting source citations. The best of these programs can help authors save time transcribing and organizing citations. Moreover, a growing number of online documents include preformatted citations, sometimes designed to work in conjunction with source citation software. The variety of sources typically cited in a scholarly work, however, nearly always precludes an acceptable result from software alone. Authors are therefore strongly encouraged to review their citations for consistency, accuracy, and completeness according to the forms recommended in this chapter or chapter 15. Moreover, citations in manuscripts submitted to publishers should be presented as ordinary text, stripped of any of the underlying codes (e.g., fields or hyperlinks) used in creating or organizing them. (An author's review should generally occur *after* this conversion to ordinary text.) See also 2.20.

Notes and Bibliography: Basic Format, with Examples and Variations

14.14   *Notes and bibliography—an overview.* In the system favored by many writers in the humanities, bibliographic citations are provided in notes, preferably supplemented by a bibliography. The notes, whether footnotes or endnotes, are usually numbered and correspond to superscript note reference numbers in the text (but see 14.48); in electronic works, notes and note numbers are usually hyperlinked. If the bibliography includes all works cited in the notes, the notes need not duplicate the source information in full because readers can consult the bibliography for publication details and other information. In works with no bibliography or only a selected list, full details must be given in a note at first mention of any work cited; subsequent citations need only include a short form. For examples of the difference in format between note citations and bibliography entries, see 14.18. For a detailed discussion of notes, see 14.19–55. For shortened references, see 14.24–31. For a detailed discussion of bibliographies, see 14.56–67.

Full citation in a note:

1. Newton N. Minow and Craig L. LaMay, *Inside the Presidential Debates: Their Improbable Past and Promising Future* (Chicago: University of Chicago Press, 2008), 24–25.

Shortened citation in a note:

> 8. Minow and LaMay, *Presidential Debates*, 138.

Entry in a bibliography:

> Minow, Newton N., and Craig L. LaMay. *Inside the Presidential Debates: Their Improbable Past and Promising Future*. Chicago: University of Chicago Press, 2008.

Note citations are styled much like running text, with authors' names in normal order and the elements separated by commas or parentheses. In bibliographies, where entries are listed alphabetically, the name of the first author is inverted, and the main elements are separated by periods.

14.15   *Basic structure of a note.* A footnote or an endnote generally lists the author, title, and facts of publication, in that order. Elements are separated by commas; the facts of publication are enclosed in parentheses. Authors' names are presented in standard order (first name first). Titles are capitalized headline-style (see 8.157), unless they are in a foreign language (see 11.3). Titles of larger works (e.g., books and journals) are italicized; titles of smaller works (e.g., chapters, articles) or unpublished works are presented in roman and enclosed in quotation marks (see 8.161). Such terms as *editor/edited by*, *translator/translated by*, *volume*, and *edition* are abbreviated.

14.16   *Basic structure of a bibliography entry.* In a bibliography entry the elements are separated by periods rather than by commas; the facts of publication are not enclosed in parentheses; and the first-listed author's name, according to which the entry is alphabetized in the bibliography, is usually inverted (last name first). As in a note, titles are capitalized headline-style unless they are in a foreign language; titles of larger works (e.g., books and journals) are italicized; and titles of smaller works (e.g., chapters, articles) or unpublished works are presented in roman and enclosed in quotation marks. Noun forms such as *editor, translator, volume*, and *edition* are abbreviated, but verb forms such as *edited by* and *translated by*—abbreviated in a note—are spelled out in a bibliography. (Cf. 14.15.)

14.17   *Page numbers and other locators.* In notes, where reference is usually to a particular passage in a book or journal, only the page numbers (often a single page number) pertaining to that passage are given. In bibliographies, no page numbers are given for books; for easier location of journal

articles or chapters or other sections of a book, the beginning and ending page numbers of the entire article or chapter are given. Electronic
sources do not always include page numbers (and some that do include
them repaginate according to user-defined text size). For such unpaginated works, it may be appropriate in a note to include a chapter or paragraph number (if available), a section heading, or a descriptive phrase that
follows the organizational divisions of the work. In citations of shorter
electronic works presented as a single, searchable document, such locators may be unnecessary.

14.18   *Notes and bibliography—examples and variations.* The examples that follow are intended to provide an overview of the notes and bibliography
style, featuring books and journal articles as models. Each example includes a numbered note and a corresponding bibliography entry. Some
examples also include a shortened form of the note, suitable for subsequent citations of a source already cited in full. In practice, in works that
include a bibliography that lists in full all sources cited, it is acceptable
to use the shortened form in the notes even at first mention. For advice
on constructing short forms for notes, see 14.24–31. For many more examples, consult the sections dealing with specific types of works throughout this chapter.

BOOK WITH SINGLE AUTHOR OR EDITOR

For a book with a single author, invert the name in the bibliography but
not in the notes. Punctuate and capitalize as shown. Note the shortened
form in the second note. Note also that actual page numbers cited are
usually included in a note but not in a bibliography entry, unless the
entry is for a chapter, in which case the page range in which the item
appears is included (see "Chapter in an Edited Book," below; see also
9.58–63).

1. Michael Pollan, *The Omnivore's Dilemma: A Natural History of Four Meals* (New
York: Penguin, 2006), 99–100.
18. Pollan, *Omnivore's Dilemma*, 3.

Pollan, Michael. *The Omnivore's Dilemma: A Natural History of Four Meals.* New
York: Penguin, 2006.

A book with an editor in place of an author includes the abbreviation *ed.*
(*editor*; for more than one editor, use *eds.*). Note that the shortened form
does not include *ed.*

1. Joel Greenberg, ed., *Of Prairie, Woods, and Water: Two Centuries of Chicago Nature Writing* (Chicago: University of Chicago Press, 2008), 42.

33. Greenberg, *Prairie, Woods, and Water*, 326–27.

Greenberg, Joel, ed. *Of Prairie, Woods, and Water: Two Centuries of Chicago Nature Writing*. Chicago: University of Chicago Press, 2008.

BOOK WITH MULTIPLE AUTHORS

For a book with two authors, note that only the first-listed name is inverted in the bibliography entry.

2. Geoffrey C. Ward and Ken Burns, *The War: An Intimate History, 1941–1945* (New York: Knopf, 2007), 52.

Ward, Geoffrey C., and Ken Burns. *The War: An Intimate History, 1941–1945*. New York: Knopf, 2007.

For a book with three authors, adapt as follows:

15. Joyce Heatherton, James Fitzgilroy, and Jackson Hsu, *Meteors and Mudslides: A Trip through* . . .

Heatherton, Joyce, James Fitzgilroy, and Jackson Hsu. *Meteors and Mudslides: A Trip through* . . .

For a book with four or more authors, list all the authors in the bibliography entry. Word order and punctuation are the same as for two or three authors. In the note, however, cite only the name of the first-listed author, followed by *et al.* See also 14.76.

72. Dana Barnes et al., *Plastics: Essays on American Corporate Ascendance in the 1960s* . . .

101. Barnes et al., *Plastics* . . .

BOOK WITH AUTHOR PLUS EDITOR OR TRANSLATOR

In a book with an editor or translator in addition to the author, *ed.* or *trans.* in the note becomes *Edited by* or *Translated by* in the bibliography entry. See also 14.88.

1. Gabriel García Márquez, *Love in the Time of Cholera*, trans. Edith Grossman (London: Cape, 1988), 242–55.

18. García Márquez, *Cholera*, 33.

García Márquez, Gabriel. *Love in the Time of Cholera*. Translated by Edith Grossman. London: Cape, 1988.

CHAPTER IN AN EDITED BOOK

When citing a chapter or similar part of an edited book, include the chapter author; the chapter title, in quotation marks; and the editor. Precede the title of the book with *in*. Note the location of the page range for the chapter in the bibliography entry. See also 14.111–17.

1. Glenn Gould, "Streisand as Schwarzkopf," in *The Glenn Gould Reader*, ed. Tim Page (New York: Vintage, 1984), 310.

19. Gould, "Streisand as Schwarzkopf," 309.

Gould, Glenn. "Streisand as Schwarzkopf." In *The Glenn Gould Reader*, edited by Tim Page, 308–11. New York: Vintage, 1984.

JOURNAL ARTICLE

Citations of journals include the volume and issue number and date of publication. The volume number follows the italicized journal title in roman and with no intervening punctuation. A specific page reference is included in the notes; the page range for an article is included in the bibliography. In the full citation, page numbers are preceded by a colon. If a journal is paginated consecutively across a volume or if the month or season appears with the year, the issue number may be omitted (as in the second and third sets of examples below).

89. Walter Blair, "Americanized Comic Braggarts," *Critical Inquiry* 4, no. 2 (1977): 331–32.

111. Blair, "Americanized Comic Braggarts," 335.

Blair, Walter. "Americanized Comic Braggarts." *Critical Inquiry* 4, no. 2 (1977): 331–49.

The DOI in the following example indicates that the article was consulted online; it is preferred to a URL (see also 14.5, 14.6). Note that *DOI*, so capitalized when mentioned in running text, is lowercased and followed by a colon (with no space after) in source citations. Shortened citations for subsequent references to an online source follow the forms for printed books and journals.

> 1. William J. Novak, "The Myth of the 'Weak' American State," *American Historical Review* 113 (June 2008): 758, doi:10.1086/ahr.113.3.752.
> 3. Novak, "Myth," 770.

> Novak, William J. "The Myth of the 'Weak' American State." *American Historical Review* 113 (June 2008): 752–72. doi:10.1086/ahr.113.3.752.

For articles that have not been assigned a DOI (or if the DOI cannot be determined), include a URL. The URL in the following example—consulted through the academic journals archive JSTOR—was listed along with the article as a more stable (and shorter) alternative to the URL that appeared in the browser's address bar. For access dates (not shown here), see 14.185.

> 12. Wilfried Karmaus and John F. Riebow, "Storage of Serum in Plastic and Glass Containers May Alter the Serum Concentration of Polychlorinated Biphenyls," *Environmental Health Perspectives* 112 (May 2004): 645, http://www.jstor.org/stable/3435987.

> Karmaus, Wilfried, and John F. Riebow. "Storage of Serum in Plastic and Glass Containers May Alter the Serum Concentration of Polychlorinated Biphenyls." *Environmental Health Perspectives* 112 (May 2004): 643–47. http://www.jstor.org/stable/3435987.

Notes

Note Numbers

14.19 *Numbers in text versus numbers in notes.* Note reference numbers in text are set as superior (superscript) numbers. In the notes themselves, they are normally full size, not raised, and followed by a period. (In manuscripts, superscript numbers in both places—the typical default setting in the note-making feature of a word processor—are perfectly acceptable.)

"Nonrestrictive relative clauses are parenthetic, as are similar clauses introduced by conjunctions indicating time or place."[1]

1. William Strunk Jr. and E. B. White, *The Elements of Style*, 4th ed. (New York: Allyn and Bacon, 2000), 3.

14.20 *Sequencing of note numbers and symbols.* Notes, whether footnotes or endnotes, should be numbered consecutively, beginning with 1, throughout each article and for each new chapter—not throughout an entire book unless the text has no internal divisions. Where only a handful of footnotes appear in an entire book or, perhaps, just one in an article, symbols may be used instead of numbers. Usually an asterisk is enough, but if more than one note is needed on the same page, the sequence is * † ‡ §. For using a combination of numbers and symbols for two sets of notes, see 14.44–46. For notes to tables and other nontextual matter, which are usually handled independently of the notes to the text, see 3.74–78.

14.21 *Placement of note number.* A note number should generally be placed at the end of a sentence or at the end of a clause. The number normally follows a quotation (whether it is run in to the text or set as an extract). Relative to other punctuation, the number follows any punctuation mark except for the dash, which it precedes.

"This," wrote George Templeton Strong, "is what our tailors can do."[1]

The bias was apparent in the Shotwell series[3]—and it must be remembered that Shotwell was a student of Robinson's.

Though a note number normally follows a closing parenthesis, it may on rare occasion be more appropriate to place the number inside the closing parenthesis—if, for example, the note applies to a specific term within the parentheses.

(In an earlier book he had said quite the opposite.)[2]

Men and their unions, as they entered industrial work, negotiated two things: young women would be laid off once they married (the commonly acknowledged "marriage bar"[1]), and men would be paid a "family wage."

14.22 *Note numbers with chapter and article titles and subheads.* In books, a note number should never appear within or at the end of a chapter title. A note that applies to an entire chapter should be unnumbered and is preferably placed at the foot of the first page of the chapter, preceding any numbered notes (see 14.47–50). Some journals publishers, on the other hand, prefer to tie such notes more explicitly to a particular article title by placing a note reference number (or symbol) with the title and the corresponding note. In a departure from previous recommendations, Chicago no longer objects to this practice with journal article titles. Moreover, the occasional note reference appearing with a subhead within a book chapter or an article is now considered acceptable, though some editors will prefer to move it into the text that follows the subhead.

14.23 *Multiple citations and multiple references.* A note number cannot reappear out of sequence; the substance of a note that applies to more than one location must be repeated under a new note number. To avoid such repetition, especially for a longer discursive note, a cross-reference may be used—though these must be checked carefully before publication. (See also 14.24–31.)

> 18. See note 3 above.

Although more than one note reference should never appear at a single location (such as[5, 6]), a single note can contain more than one citation or comment (see 14.52). (A system of numbered references used by many medical publications, however, requires such multiple reference numbers; for more on this system, consult the *AMA Manual of Style* [bibliog. 1.1].)

Shortened Citations

14.24 *Purpose of shortened citations.* To reduce the bulk of documentation in scholarly works that use footnotes or endnotes, subsequent citations of sources already given in full should be shortened whenever possible. The short form, as distinct from an abbreviation, should include enough information to remind readers of the full title or to lead them to the appropriate entry in the bibliography. (Some short forms are not covered here: for citing different chapters in the same work, see 14.113; for letters, see 14.117; for legal citations, see 14.287. Other short forms may be patterned on the examples in this section.)

14.25 *Basic structure of the short form.* The most common short form consists of the last name of the author and the main title of the work cited, usually shortened if more than four words, as in examples 4–6 below. For more on authors' names, see 14.27. For more on short titles, see 14.28. For more on journal articles, see 14.196.

> 1. Samuel A. Morley, *Poverty and Inequality in Latin America: The Impact of Adjustment and Recovery* (Baltimore: Johns Hopkins University Press, 1995), 24–25.

2. Regina M. Schwartz, "Nationals and Nationalism: Adultery in the House of David," *Critical Inquiry* 19, no. 1 (1992): 131–32.

3. Ernest Kaiser, "The Literature of Harlem," in *Harlem: A Community in Transition*, ed. J. H. Clarke (New York: Citadel Press, 1964).

4. Morley, *Poverty and Inequality*, 43.

5. Schwartz, "Nationals and Nationalism," 138.

6. Kaiser, "Literature of Harlem," 189–90.

14.26   *Cross-reference to full citation.* When references to a particular source are far apart, readers encountering the short form may be helped by a cross-reference to the original note (especially in the absence of a full bibliography). Repeating the full details in each new chapter, formerly a common practice in scholarly works, is seldom necessary. These cross-references must be checked carefully before the work is published.

95. Miller, *Quest*, 81 (see chap. 1, n. 4).

14.27   *Short form for authors' names.* Only the last name of the author, or of the editor or translator if given first in the full reference, is needed in the short form. Full names or initials are included only when authors with the same last name must be distinguished from one another. Such abbreviations as *ed.* or *trans.* following a name in the full reference are omitted in subsequent references. If a work has two or three authors, give the last name of each; for more than three, the last name of the first author followed by *et al.*

1. Kathryn Petras and Ross Petras, eds., *Very Bad Poetry* . . .

2. Joseph A. Bellizzi, H. F. Kruckeberg, J. R. Hamilton, and W. S. Martin, "Consumer Perceptions of National, Private, and Generic Brands," . . .

3. Petras and Petras, *Very Bad Poetry* . . .

4. Bellizzi et al., "Consumer Perceptions," . . .

14.28   *Short form for titles.* The short title contains the key word or words from the main title. An initial *A* or *The* is usually omitted. The order of the words should not be changed (for example, *Daily Notes of a Trip around the World* should be shortened not to *World Trip* but to *Daily Notes* or *Around the World*). Titles of four words or fewer are seldom shortened. The short title is italicized or set in roman and quotation marks according to the way the full title appears.

The War Journal of Major Damon "Rocky" Gause
(Short title) *War Journal*

"A Brief Account of the Reconstruction of Aristotle's *Protrepticus*"
(Short title) "Aristotle's *Protrepticus*"

Kriegstagebuch des Oberkommandos der Wehrmacht, 1940–1945
(Short title) *Kriegstagebuch*

In short titles in languages other than English, no word should be omitted that governs the case ending of a word included in the short title. If in doubt, ask someone who knows the language.

14.29 "*Ibid.*" The abbreviation *ibid.* (from *ibidem*, "in the same place") usually refers to a single work cited in the note immediately preceding. It must never be used if the preceding note contains more than one citation. It takes the place of the name(s) of the author(s) or editor(s), the title of the work, and as much of the succeeding material as is identical. If the entire reference, including page numbers or other particulars, is identical, the word *ibid.* alone is used (as in note 7 below). The word *ibid.* (italicized in this paragraph only because it is a word used as a word—see 7.58) is capitalized at the beginning of a note and followed by a period. To avoid a succession of *ibid.* notes, the content of notes 6–8, 10, and 11 below might instead be placed parenthetically in the text in place of the note references (see 13.64).

> 5. Farmwinkle, *Humor of the Midwest*, 241.
> 6. Ibid., 258–59.
> 7. Ibid.
> 8. Ibid., 333–34.
> 9. Losh, *Diaries and Correspondence*, 1:150.
> 10. Ibid., 2:35–36.
> 11. Ibid., 2:37–40.

Ibid. may also be used within one note in successive references to the same work.

> 8. Morris Birkbeck, "The Illinois Prairies and Settlers," in *Prairie State: Impressions of Illinois, 1673–1967, by Travelers and Other Observers*, ed. Paul M. Angle (Chicago: University of Chicago Press, 1968), 62. "The soil of the Big-prairie, which is of no great extent notwithstanding its name, is a rich, cool sand; that is to say, one of the most desirable description" (ibid., 63).

14.30 "*Idem.*" When several works by the same person are cited successively in the same note, *idem* ("the same," sometimes abbreviated to *id.*) has sometimes been used in place of the author's name. Except in legal references, where the abbreviation *id.* is used in place of *ibid.*, the term is rarely used nowadays. Chicago discourages the use of *idem*, recommending instead that the author's last name be repeated.

14.31 *"Op. cit." and "loc. cit." Op. cit.* (*opere citato*, "in the work cited") and *loc. cit.* (*loco citato*, "in the place cited"), used with an author's last name and standing in place of a previously cited title, are rightly falling into disuse. Consider a reader's frustration on meeting, for example, "Wells, op. cit., 10" in note 95 and having to search back to note 2 for the full source or, worse still, finding that *two* works by Wells have been cited. Chicago disallows both *op. cit.* and *loc. cit.* and instead uses the short-title form described in 14.28.

Commentary and Quotations in Notes

14.32 *Citations plus commentary.* When a note contains not only the source of a fact or quotation in the text but related substantive material as well, the source comes first. A period usually separates the citation from the commentary. Such comments as "emphasis mine" are usually put in parentheses. See also 13.60.

> 11. Shakespeare, *Julius Caesar*, act 3, sc. 1. Caesar's claim of constancy should be taken with a grain of salt.
> 12. Little, "Norms of Collegiality," 330 (my italics).

14.33 *Quotation within a note.* When a note includes a quotation, the source normally follows the terminal punctuation of the quotation. The entire source need not be put in parentheses, which involves changing existing parentheses to brackets (see 6.99) and creating unnecessary clutter.

> 14. One estimate of the size of the reading public at this time was that of Sydney Smith: "Readers are fourfold in number compared with what they were before the beginning of the French war. . . . There are four or five hundred thousand readers more than there were thirty years ago, among the lower orders." *Letters*, ed. Nowell C. Smith (New York: Oxford University Press, 1953), 1:341, 343.

Long quotations should be set off as extracts in notes as they would be in text (see 13.10). In notes, more than three lines of poetry should be set off (but see 13.23; see also 13.27).

14.34 *Substantive notes.* Substantive, or discursive, notes may merely amplify the text and include no sources. Such notes may augment any system of documentation, including the author-date system (see chapter 15). When a source is needed, it is treated as in the example in 14.33 or, if brief and already cited in full, may appear parenthetically, as in the following example:

> 1. Ernst Cassirer takes important notice of this in *Language and Myth* (59–62) and offers a searching analysis of man's regard for things on which his power of inspirited action may crucially depend.

14.35 *Paragraphing within long notes.* To avoid page makeup problems, very long footnotes should be avoided (see 14.39). No such bar exists for endnotes, however, and very long endnotes should be broken into multiple paragraphs as an aid to reading. Authors and editors should first consider, however, whether such a note would be more effective if shortened or at least partially incorporated into the text. See also 14.40.

14.36 *Footnotes that break across pages in a printed work.* When a footnote begins on one page and continues on the next, the break should be made in mid-sentence lest readers miss the end of the note; a short rule appears above the continued part (see fig. 14.1). This advice applies only to the published form of a work (and is something that is generally imposed at the typesetting stage). At the manuscript stage, authors and editors should let the note-making feature in their word-processing software determine any such breaks.

14.37 *"See" and "cf."* Notes are often used to invite readers to consult further resources. When doing so, authors should keep in mind the distinction between *see* and *cf.*, using *cf.* only to mean "compare" or "see, by way of comparison." Neither term is italicized in notes (though *see* is italicized in indexes; see 16.22).

> 22. For further discussion of this problem, see Jones, *Conflict*, 49.
> 23. Others disagree with my position; cf. Fisher and Ury, *Getting to Yes*, 101–3.

Footnotes versus Endnotes

14.38 *Footnotes and endnotes—an overview.* As their name suggests, footnotes appear at the foot of a page. In a journal, endnotes appear at the end of an article; in a book, at the end of a chapter or, more commonly, at the back of the book. (In multiauthor books, where the notes may differ in kind and

the Advancement of Science in 1874 Stoney had already suggested that "[n]a-ture presents us in the phenomenon of electrolysis, with a single definite quantity of electricity which is independent of the particular bodies acted on."[2] In 1891 he proposed, "[I]t will be convenient to call [these elementary charges] *electrons*."[3] Stoney's electrons were permanently attached to atoms; that is, they could "not be removed from the atom," and each of them was "associated in the chemical atom with each bond." Furthermore, their oscil-lation within molecules gave rise to "electro-magnetic stresses in the sur-rounding aether."[4]

Even though Stoney coined the term "electron," the representation asso-ciated with that term had several ancestors.[5] Key aspects of that representa-tion, most notably the notion of the atomicity of charge, considerably pre-ceded his proposal. In the period between 1838 and 1851 a British natural philosopher, Richard Laming, conjectured "the existence of sub-atomic, unit-charged particles and pictured the atom as made up of a material core sur-rounded by an 'electrosphere' of concentric shells of electrical particles."[6] On the Continent several physicists had made similar suggestions. Those physi-cists attempted to explain electromagnetic phenomena by action-at-a-distance forces between electrical particles. As an example of the Continental approach to electrodynamics consider Wilhelm Weber's electrical theory of matter and ether.[7] Weber's theory originated in 1846 and continued to evolve till the time of his death (1891). According to the initial version of that theory, electricity consisted of two electrical fluids (positive and negative). The interactions of these fluids were governed by inverse square forces, which were functions of

---

the Electron (Dublin: Royal Dublin Society, 1993), 5–28. The introduction of a new term is an event that can be easily identified and, thus, provides a convenient starting point for a bio-graphical narrative whose subject is the corresponding representation. The appearance of a new term also signals the birth of a novel concept, whose identity has not yet solidified. Thus, it is not surprising that in its subsequent development the concept may merge with other re-lated concepts. As we will see below, this is what happened in the case of the electron.

2. Stoney's paper was first published in 1881. See G. J. Stoney, "On the Physical Units of Na-ture," *Scientific Proceedings of the Royal Dublin Society*, new series, 3 (1881–1883): 54.

3. Stoney, "On the Cause of Double Lines," 583.

4. Ibid.

5. Note that the biographical approach can also come to grips with the "prehistory" of the electron's representation.

6. Kragh, "Concept and Controversy: Jean Becquerel and the Positive Electron," *Centau-rus*, 32 (1989): 205.

7. For an extended discussion of Weber's program see M. N. Wise, "German Concepts of Force, Energy, and the Electromagnetic Ether, 1845–1880," in *Conceptions of Ether: Studies in the History of Ether Theories, 1740–1900*, G. N. Cantor and M. J. S. Hodge (eds.) (Cambridge: Cam-bridge Univ. Press, 1981), 269–307, esp. 276–83.

FIGURE 14.1. A page of text with footnotes; the first note is continued from the previous page (with a short rule above it). See 14.36.

length, and where chapters may be reprinted separately, they are usually placed at the end of the chapter to which they pertain.) At the manuscript stage, authors can work with whichever form seems most convenient, though notes should be created with a word processor's note function to facilitate renumbering when notes are added or deleted (see also 2.20). For footnotes to tables, see 2.28, 3.74–78. For notes in previously published material, see 2.42.

14.39   *Footnotes—pros and cons.* Readers of scholarly printed works usually prefer footnotes for ease of reference. This is especially true where the notes are closely integrated into the text and make interesting reading, or if immediate knowledge of the sources is essential to readers. The limiting factor in printed works is page makeup—it can be difficult or impossible to fit a close succession of long footnotes onto the pages they pertain to, especially in an illustrated work (a basic requirement for all footnotes is that they at least begin on the page on which they are referenced). There is also the matter of appearance; a page consisting almost exclusively of footnotes is daunting. For some remedies, see 14.51–55.

14.40   *Endnotes—pros and cons.* Endnotes, which pose no page makeup challenges beyond those of ordinary text, obviate many of the disadvantages of footnotes in printed works (see 14.39). Because of this flexibility, and because pages free of footnotes are less intimidating to many readers, publishers' marketing and sales staff may recommend endnotes in books directed to general as well as scholarly or professional readers. Nonetheless, because general readers may be disappointed to find a third or more of a book devoted to endnotes, authors still need to aim for a healthy balance between text and notes (i.e., by limiting the temptation to include an excessive number of discursive notes). The main problem with endnotes is that of finding a particular note. This difficulty (usually not encountered in electronic texts, where text and notes are linked) can be ameliorated by informative running heads (see 14.42).

14.41   *Endnote placement.* Endnotes to each chapter of a book are often best grouped in the end matter, following the text and any appendixes and preceding the bibliography if there is one (see 1.4). The main heading is simply "Notes," and the group of notes to each chapter is introduced by a subhead bearing the chapter number or title or both (see fig. 14.2). In a book that has a different author for each chapter, or whose chapters may be published separately, endnotes normally appear at the end of each chapter. In a journal, they appear at the end of each article. In the latter two cases, a subhead "Notes" usually appears between text and notes (see fig. 14.3).

general movement away from UN-led missions and the greater reliance on lead states, ad hoc coalitions, and regional bodies to lead military and civilian functions gave rise to a growing number of [war-oriented] NGOs and private military companies." Roland Paris, "International Machinery for Postwar Peace-Building: The Dilemmas of Coordination" (paper presented at PIPES Seminar, University of Chicago, May 2006).

24. See John W. Betlyon, "Afghan Archaeology on the Road to Recovery," *Daily Star*, October 12, 2004, 12.

25. Andrew Maykuth, "A Plea to Save Afghan Antiquities," *Philadelphia Inquirer*, May 3, 2006, http://www.philly.com/mld/philly/entertainment/14485199.htm.

26. Unwillingness to put one's life at risk was of course not limited to cultural heritage NGOs; according to Michael R. Gordon and Gen. Bernard E. Trainor, "The State Department disaster relief team did not want to venture into areas of Iraq that were still contested by Saddam's supporters." See Gordon and Trainor, *Cobra II: The Inside Story of the Invasion and Occupation of Iraq* (New York: Pantheon, 2006), 154.

27. For a discussion of the history of UNESCO's cultural heritage protection efforts, see Mounir Bouchenaki, "UNESCO and the Safeguarding of Cultural Heritage in Postconflict Situations," in *Antiquities under Siege*, ed. Rothfield, 207–18.

CHAPTER THREE

1. James Fallows, "Blind into Baghdad," *Atlantic Monthly*, January/February 2004, 58, http://www.theatlantic.com/doc/200401/fallows.

2. See Michael R. Gordon and Gen. Bernard E. Trainor, *Cobra II: The Inside Story of the Invasion and Occupation of Iraq* (New York: Pantheon, 2006), 106.

3. See ibid.

4. Ibid., 108.

5. Ibid., 107.

6. See Thomas E. Ricks, *Fiasco: The American Military Adventure in Iraq* (New York: Penguin, 2006), 79–80.

7. Gordon and Trainor, *Cobra II*, 205.

8. For more on the Civil Affairs mission, see http://www.armyreserve.army.mil/ARMYDRU/USACAPOC/Overview.htm.

9. Maj. Christopher Varhola (Civil Affairs officer), interviewed by the author, April 15, 2005.

10. McGuire Gibson, interviewed by the author, February 9, 2006.

11. Varhola interview.

12. Ibid.

13. George Packer, "War after the War," *New Yorker*, November 24, 2003, 62.

14. The humanitarian group was one of four set up by Rice following a contentious Senate Committee on Foreign Relations hearing in August, where

FIGURE 14.2. A page of endnotes, with a subhead introducing the notes to a new chapter and a running head showing the text pages on which the notes are referenced. See 14.41, 14.42.

equally valid appearances of a single absolute truth. Or, in more radical terms, is it possible for mutually contradictory truth claims to coexist? Such a question was not faced by the philosophers of the Enlightenment, who experienced a simple, Eurocentric, and monolithic reality in which religions no longer existed alongside one another but were ordered along the lines of advancement and retrogression, according to temporal or value-based terms.[58]

In the final analysis, Cassirer himself remains a philosopher of the Enlightenment. This explains the one-dimensional nature of his theories. However, the intuitions that led him back to medieval philosophy were correct, even if his attachment to historical stereotypes caused him to see this period as a precursor of the modern age—its precondition, as it were—an era to be addressed and learned from. In any case, his encounter with thinkers like Nicholas of Cusa eventually enabled him to develop an admirable model for resistance and opposition during one of the least enlightened periods of human history.

NOTES

1. Ernst Cassirer, *Die Philosophie der Aufklärung* (Tübingen: Mohr, 1932); *The Philosophy of the Enlightenment*, trans. Fritz C. A. Koelln and James P. Pettegrove (Boston: Beacon, 1951).

2. Ibid., 262: "The problem of history for the philosophy of the Enlightenment arises in the field of religious phenomena, and it is here that this problem first became urgent."

3. Ernst Cassirer, *The Philosophy of Symbolic Forms*, vol. 2, *Mythical Thought*, trans. Ralph Manheim (New Haven: Yale University Press, 1955), 238f; see also Cassirer, *An Essay on Man* (New Haven: Yale University Press, 1944), 87.

4. Cassirer, *Philosophy of Symbolic Forms*, 2:237.

5. Ibid., 2:239: "If we attempt to isolate and remove the basic mythical components from religious belief, we no longer have religion in its real, objectively historical manifestation; all that remains is a shadow of it, an empty abstraction."

6. Ibid., 2:239.

7. See below, n. 48.

8. About the specific places where Cassirer deals directly with Nicholas of Cusa, see esp. his *The Philosophy of the Enlightenment*, 166, and *Essay on Man*, 73.

9. Cassirer, *Essay on Man*, 95.

10. Ibid., 103.

11. "Odysseus oder Mythos und Aufklärung," in M. Horkheimer and T. Adorno, *Dialektik der Aufklärung* (1944; Frankfurt am Main: Fischer, 1990), 50–87.

12. Ernst Cassirer, *The Myth of the State* (1946; New York: Doubleday, 1955), 15.

FIGURE 14.3. Chapter endnotes (first page of notes only), prefaced by the subhead "Notes." See 14.41.

14.42   *Running heads for endnotes.* Where endnotes are gathered at the back of a printed book and occupy more than two or three pages, running heads (both verso and recto) carrying the page numbers to which the notes pertain are a boon to readers (see 1.14). To determine what text page numbers to use on a particular page of notes, find the numbers of the first and last notes beginning on that page (disregarding a runover from a previous page) and locate the references to these notes in the text. The numbers of the first and last pages on which these references appear in text are the numbers to use in the running head: for example, "Notes to Pages 123–125." The last number is *not* abbreviated; compare 9.60. (If, as occasionally happens, only one note appears on a page, use the singular: e.g., "Note to Page 23.") Since these running heads can be completed only when page proofs are available, the corrections are considered "alterations" (see 2.131), and the cost may be charged to the publisher. (Another option, less useful for readers but cheaper for the publisher, is to include running heads that simply read "Notes to Chapter One," "Notes to Chapter Two," and so on; since readers are often unaware of the number of the chapter they are reading, chapter numbers must also appear in the running heads of the text itself.) When notes appear at the ends of chapters, note-related running heads are rarely necessary.

14.43   *Special needs of endnotes.* Whereas footnote citations, because they appear so close to the text, can omit certain elements mentioned in the text, omitting them in endnotes risks irritating readers, who have to go back and forth. For example, an author or title mentioned in the text need not be repeated in the footnote citation, though it is often helpful to do so. In an endnote, however, the author (or at least the author's last name, unless it is obvious) and title should be repeated, since at least some readers may have forgotten whether the note number was 93 or 94 by the time they find it at the back of the work. It is particularly annoying to arrive at the right place in the endnotes only to find another "ibid." Such frustration can be further prevented by consolidating some of the endnote references, using the devices illustrated in the examples below.

> 34. This and the preceding four quotations are all from *Hamlet,* act 1, sc. 4.
>
> 87. Barbara Wallraff, *Word Court: Wherein Verbal Virtue Is Rewarded, Crimes against the Language Are Punished, and Poetic Justice Is Done* (New York: Harcourt, 2000), 34. Further citations of this work are given in the text.

The device in the second example should be used only if the source is clear from the text, without reference to the endnotes. See also 13.65.

Two Sets of Notes

14.44   *Endnotes plus footnotes.* In a heavily documented work it is occasionally helpful to separate substantive notes from source citations. In such a case, the citation notes should be numbered and appear as endnotes. The substantive notes, indicated by asterisks and other symbols, appear as footnotes. The first footnote on each printed page is referenced by an asterisk. If more than one footnote begins on a page, the sequence of symbols is * † ‡ §. Should more than four such notes appear on the same page, the symbols are doubled for the fifth to the eighth notes: ** †† ‡‡ §§. See also 3.77.

14.45   *Footnotes plus author-date citations.* The rather cumbersome practice described in 14.44 may be avoided by the use of author-date citations for sources (see 14.2 and chapter 15) and numbered footnotes or endnotes for the substantive comments. Moreover, the numbered notes can themselves contain parenthetical author-date citations when necessary, adding to the flexibility of such a system. See also 15.30.

14.46   *Editor's or translator's notes plus author's notes.* In an edited or translated work that includes notes by the original author, any additional notes furnished by the editor or translator must be distinguished from the others. Most commonly, the added notes are interspersed and consecutively numbered with the original notes but distinguished from them either by appending "—Ed." or "—Trans." (following a period) at the end of the note or by enclosing the entire note, except the number, in square brackets. (An editor's or translator's comment can also be added as needed in square brackets within an original note; see 6.97.)

> 14. Millicent Cliff was Norton Westermont's first cousin, although to the very last she denied it.—Ed.
> *or*
> 21. [The original reads *gesungen*; presumably *gesunken* is meant.]

Alternatively, if there are only a few added notes, these can be referenced by asterisks and other symbols and appear as footnotes; the original notes, numbered, then appear below them, as footnotes (see fig. 14.4), or are treated as endnotes (see 14.38, 14.20). See also 14.48.

Unnumbered Notes

14.47   *Unnumbered notes in relation to numbered notes.* Footnotes without numbers or symbols always precede any numbered notes on the same printed

Each county has a court of justice,[10] a sheriff to execute the decrees of tribunals, a prison to hold criminals.

There are needs that are felt in a nearly equal manner by all the townships of the county; it was natural that a central authority be charged with providing for them. In Massachusetts this authority resides in the hands of a certain number of magistrates whom the governor of the state designates with the advice[11] of his council.[12]

The administrators of the county have only a limited and exceptional power that applies only to a very few cases that are foreseen in advance. The state and the township suffice in the ordinary course of things. These administrators do nothing but prepare the budget of the county; the legislature votes it.[13] There is no assembly that directly or indirectly represents the county.

The county therefore has, to tell the truth, no political existence.

In most of the American constitutions one remarks a double tendency that brings legislators to divide executive power and concentrate legislative power. The New England township by itself has a principle of existence that they do not strip from it; but one would have to create that life fictitiously in the county, and the utility of doing so has not been felt: all the townships united have only one single representation, the state, center of all national* powers; outside township and national action one can say that there are only individual forces.

*Here "national" refers to the states.
10. See the law of February 14, 1821, *Laws of Massachusetts*, 1:551 [2:551–56].
11. See the law of February 20, 1819, *Laws of Massachusetts*, 2:494.
12. The governor's council is an elected body.
13. See the law of November 2, 1791 [November 2, 1781], *Laws of Massachusetts*, 1:61.

FIGURE 14.4. Translator's footnote referenced by an asterisk, followed by author's numbered notes. Notes referenced by symbols always precede numbered notes, regardless of the order in which the symbols and numbers appear in the text. See 14.46.

page. They most often appear on the opening page of a chapter or other main division of a work. In a work with endnotes in which an unnumbered footnote is not an option, an unnumbered endnote—to be used with caution because it is easily missed—should appear immediately before note 1 to the relevant chapter. An example of such a note would be a note applying to a book epigraph (see 1.36), which would precede the endnotes to the first chapter and appear under a heading "Epigraph." Notes to chapter epigraphs can be handled similarly. Source notes, biographical notes, and other unnumbered notes pertaining to an entire chapter or section—which appear as footnotes—are treated in 14.49 and 14.50.

14.48   *Notes keyed to text by line or page numbers.* In some works—translations and editions of the classics, for example, or books intended for a more general audience—it may be desirable to omit note numbers in the text. Any necessary notes may then be keyed to the text by line or page number, or both, usually followed by the word or phrase being annotated. (Line numbers are used as locators only if line numbers appear in the text.) Such notes may appear as footnotes or endnotes. The keywords may be distinguished from the annotation typographically (e.g., with italics or boldface) and separated from the annotation by a colon or the use of brackets or other devices. Quotation marks, if used at all, should be reserved for keywords that are themselves direct quotations in the text. See figures 14.5, 14.6.

14.49 *Unnumbered source notes.* In anthologies and other collections of previously published material, or in largely new publications that contain one or more previously published chapters, the source of each reprinted piece may be given in an unnumbered footnote on the first printed page of the chapter, preceding any numbered footnotes. If the other notes are endnotes, the source note should remain a footnote, and it must do so if it carries a copyright notice. For material still in copyright, the note should include the original title, publisher or journal, publication date, page numbers or other locators, and—very important—mention of permission from the copyright owner to reprint. It may also include a copyright notice if requested. Some permissions grantors demand particular language in the source note. For exercising discretion versus acceding literally to the grantor's request, see 3.31, which deals with illustrations but applies equally to text. In many cases, wording can be adjusted for consistency as long as proper credit is given. The following examples show various acceptable forms. See also 4.98.

Reprinted with permission from Steven Shapin, *The Scientific Revolution* (Chicago: University of Chicago Press, 1996), 15–64.

If an article or chapter is reprinted under a different title:

Originally published as "Manet in His Generation: The Face of Painting in the 1860s," *Critical Inquiry* 19, no. 1 (1992): 22–69, © 1992 by The University of Chicago. All rights reserved. Reprinted by permission.

If an article or chapter has been revised:

Originally published in a slightly different form in *The Metropolis in Modern Life*, ed. Robert Moore Fisher (New York: Doubleday, 1955), 125–48. Reprinted by permission of the author and the publisher.

If a work is in the public domain (such as government publications):

O sweete soule Phillis w'haue liu'd and lou'd for a great while,   45
(If that a man may keepe any mortal ioy for a great while)
Like louing Turtles and Turtledoues for a great while:
One loue, one liking, one sence, one soule for a great while,
Therfore one deaths wound, one graue, one funeral only
Should haue ioyned in one both loue and louer Amintas.   50
    O good God what a griefe is this that death to remember?
For such grace, gesture, face, feature, beautie, behauiour,
Neuer afore was seene, is neuer againe to be lookt for.
O frowning fortune, ô death and desteny dismal:
Thus be the poplar trees that spred their tops to the heauens,   55
Of their flouring leaues despoil'd in an houre, in a moment:
Thus be the sweete violets that gaue such grace to the garden,
Of their purpled roabe despoyld in an houre, in a moment.
    O how oft did I roare and crie with an horrible howling,
When for want of breath Phillis lay feintily gasping?   60
O how oft did I wish that Phœbus would fro my Phillis
Driue this feuer away: or send his sonne from Olympus,
Who, when lady Venus by a chaunce was prickt with a
    bramble,
Healed her hand with his oyles, and fine knacks kept for a
    purpose.
Or that I could perceiue Podalyrius order in healing,   65
Or that I could obtaine Medæas exquisite ointments,
And baths most precious, which old men freshly renewed.
Or that I were as wise, as was that craftie Prometheus,
Who made pictures liue with fire that he stole from Olympus.
Thus did I cal and crie, but no body came to Amintas,   70
Then did I raile and raue, but nought did I get by my railing,   [C₄ʳ]
Whilst that I cald and cry'd, and rag'd, and rau'd as a mad
    man,

45 for] *omit* C E	62 this] that D
49 Therfore] Thefore A	64 his] *omit* E purpose.] purpose:
58 roabe] roabes B C D E	C E; purpose? D
59 roare and crie] cry, and	70 Amintas,] Amintas. C E;
roare D	Amintas: D

FIGURE 14.5. Footnotes keyed to line numbers—a device best used with verse. (With prose, the notes cannot be numbered until the text has been typeset.) See 14.48.

Reprinted from Ambler Thompson and Barry N. Taylor, *Guide for the Use of the International System of Units (SI)* (Gaithersburg, MD: National Institute of Standards and Technology, 2008), 38–39.

14.50   *Unnumbered biographical notes and acknowledgments.* In journals or multi-author works, a brief biographical note on the author or authors may appear as an unnumbered note on the first page of each article or chap-

cusses Rilke's complex use of "Nacht" as a possible mediator between immanent and transcendent being.

166 *orthodox view of revelation*   Rilke suppresses two crucial details of Michelangelo's Cumaean Sibyl: her prominent breasts, which suggest the "celestial milk" that is "the future food of salvation" (Wind, "Michelangelo's Prophets and Sibyls," 68), and the massive book from which she is reading, which suggests the conversion of Sibylline leaves into Christian doctrine. Hence the poem deliberately empties the prophecy of its content. Rilke's early effort to make a Christ of his own may be studied in *Visions of Christ,* ed. Siegfried Mandel, trans. Aaron Kramer (Boulder: University of Colorado Press, 1967).

    sibyls and prophets   "Tenth Elegy," line 72.

167 *an ideal profession*   It may be worth noting that in the most authoritative study of the *Elegies,* Jacob Steiner, *Rilkes Duineser Elegien* (Bern: Francke, 1969), the index entry for "Frau" directs the reader to "Mutter, Mädchen, Liebende"—a fair commentary on Rilke's priorities.

    far more complex   The relations between the two artists are the subject of a full-length study by Heinrich Wigand Petzet, *Das Bildnis des Dichters* (Frankfurt am Main: Societäts-Verlag, 1957).

    self-justification   Paula Modersohn-Becker in Briefen und Tagebüchern, ed. Günter Busch and Liselotte von Reinken (Frankfurt am Main: S. Fischer, 1979), 307–11.

    to lay a ghost   Robert Hass discusses the raw and morbid emotions of the "Requiem" in his introduction to *The Selected Poetry of Rainer Maria Rilke,* trans. Stephen Mitchell (New York: Random House, 1982), xxvii–xxxiv.

168 *auf Besitz*   Rilke, *Sämtliche Werke* 1:653, 654.

    in mir   Ibid., 656.

169 *a countertruth*   "Paula Becker to Clara Westhoff" was reprinted in an epilogue to *The Letters and Journals of Paula Modersohn-Becker,* ed. J. Diane Radycki (Metuchen, NJ: Scarecrow Press, 1980), 328–30. The epilogue also contains a translation of Rilke's "Requiem" by Lilly Engler and Rich, 319–27.

    lonelier than solitude   Adrienne Rich, *The Dream of a Common Language* (New York: Norton, 1978), 43.

    her voice will go on   Ovid, *Metamorphoses* 14:129–53.

CHAPTER SIX

170 *dass ich wurde wie sie*   Duino Elegies, "First Elegy," lines 45–48.

    Rilke supplies some answers   In *Three Women Poets* (Lewisburg, PA: Bucknell University Press, 1987), which offers translations of poems by Stampa, Louise Labé, and Sor Juana Inés de la Cruz, Frank J. Warnke concludes that "Rilke has commented on what is truly in the text"—the transcendent divinity of the woman who loves (55).

171 *other lovers*   Duino Elegies, trans. C. F. MacIntyre (Berkeley: University of California Press, 1961), 7n.

FIGURE 14.6. Endnotes keyed to page numbers, with key phrases italicized. See 14.48.

ter. Alternatively, some publications put such notes at the end of the article or chapter. Such identifying notes are unnecessary when the work includes a list of contributors with their affiliations. (See also 1.62, 1.20.)

Alice Y. Kaplan teaches in the Department of Romance Studies at Duke University. She is the author of *Reproductions of Banality: Fascism, Literature, and French Intellectual Life* (1986); *Relevé des sources et citations dans "Bagatelles pour un massacre"* (1987); a memoir, *French Lessons* (1993); and *The Collaborator: The Trial and Execution of Robert Brasillach* (2000).

Similarly, special acknowledgments may be given in an unnumbered note, sometimes appended to the biographical information.

The authors gratefully acknowledge the assistance of Janni R. Blazer of the Chain and Fob Archive in the preparation of this chapter.

Michael Saler is assistant professor of history at the University of California, Davis. For their comments and assistance the author would like to thank T. W. Heyck, Norma Landau, D. L. LeMahieu, Fred Leventhal, Chun Li, Dianne Macleod, Peter Mandler, Paul Robinson, Peter Stansky, Meredith Veldman, Chris Waters, and the Mabel Macleod Lewis Memorial Foundation.

Remedies for Excessive Annotation

14.51   *Avoiding overlong notes.* Lengthy, discursive notes—especially footnotes—should be reduced or integrated into the text (see 14.39). Notes presented as endnotes can generally accommodate lengthier commentary, but this should be limited in a judicious manner (see 14.40). Complicated tabular material, lists, and other entities not part of the text should be put in an appendix rather than in the footnotes (see 1.57). A parenthetical note in the text might read, for example, "For a list of institutions involved, see appendix A."

14.52   *Several citations in one note.* The number of note references in a sentence or a paragraph can sometimes be reduced by grouping several citations in a single note. The citations are separated by semicolons and must appear in the same order as the text material (whether works, quotations, or whatever) to which they pertain. Take care to avoid any ambiguity as to what is documenting what.

Text:

Only when we gather the work of several scholars—Walter Sutton's explications of some of Whitman's shorter poems; Paul Fussell's careful study of structure in "Cradle"; S. K. Coffman's close readings of "Crossing Brooklyn Ferry" and "Passage to India"; and the attempts of Thomas I. Rountree and John Lovell, dealing with "Song of Myself" and "Passage to India," respectively, to elucidate the strategy in "indirection"—do we begin to get a sense of both the extent and the specificity of Whitman's forms.[1]

Note:

1. Sutton, "The Analysis of Free Verse Form, Illustrated by a Reading of Whitman," *Journal of Aesthetics and Art Criticism* 18 (December 1959): 241–54; Fussell, "Whitman's Curious Warble: Reminiscence and Reconciliation," in *The Presence of Walt Whitman*, ed. R. W. B. Lewis (New York: Columbia University Press, 1962), 28–51; Coffman, "'Crossing Brooklyn Ferry': A Note on the Catalog Technique in Whitman's Poetry," *Modern Philology* 51 (May 1954): 225–32; Coffman, "Form and Meaning in Whitman's 'Passage to India,'" *PMLA* 70 (June 1955): 337–49; Rountree, "Whitman's Indirect Expression and Its Application to 'Song of Myself,'" *PMLA* 73 (December 1958): 549–55; and Lovell, "Appreciating Whitman: 'Passage to India,'" *Modern Language Quarterly* 21 (June 1960): 131–41.

In the example above, authors' given names are omitted in the note because they appear in the text. For inclusion of names in endnotes versus footnotes, see 14.43.

14.53   *Parenthetical text references.* Another way to reduce the number of notes is to cite sources (usually in parentheses) in the text. A combination of *Ibid.* and page numbers for subsequent citations of the same source may be dealt with in the same way—that is, cited in the text rather than in notes (see 14.29). For discussion and examples, see 13.62–70.

14.54   *Abbreviations for frequently cited works.* A frequently mentioned work may be cited either parenthetically in text or in subsequent notes by means of an abbreviation, with full citation provided in a note at first mention. (This practice is more helpful with footnotes than with endnotes.) See also 13.65, 14.55, 14.24–31.

2. François Furet, *The Passing of an Illusion: The Idea of Communism in the Twentieth Century,* trans. Deborah Furet (Chicago: University of Chicago Press, 1999), 368 (hereafter cited in text as *PI*).

(Subsequent text references) "In this sense, the Second World War completed what the First had begun—the domination of the great political religions over European public opinion," Furet points out (*PI*, 360). But he goes on to argue . . .

An abbreviation differs from a short title (see 14.28) in that words may be abbreviated and the word order changed.

> 3. Nathaniel B. Shurtleff, ed., *Records of the Governor and Company of the Massachusetts Bay in New England (1628–86)*, 5 vols. (Boston, 1853–54), 1:126 (hereafter cited as *Mass. Records*).
> 4. *Mass. Records*, 2:330.

14.55   *List of abbreviations.* Where many abbreviations of titles, manuscript collections, personal names, or other entities are used in a work—say, ten or more—they are best listed alphabetically in a separate section. In a book, the list may appear in the front matter (if footnotes are used) or in the end matter preceding the endnotes (if these are used). It is usually headed "Abbreviations" and should be included in the table of contents (see 1.4, 1.43). Where only a few abbreviations are used, these are occasionally listed as the first section of the endnotes (see fig. 14.7) or at the head of the bibliography. Titles that are italicized in the notes or bibliography should be italicized in their abbreviated form in the list of abbreviations and elsewhere.

Bibliographies

Overview

14.56   *Relationship of bibliographies to notes.* Although not all annotated works require a bibliography, since full details can be given in the notes, an alphabetical bibliography serves a number of purposes. Specifically, a full bibliography that includes all the sources cited in the text, in addition to providing an overview of the sources and therefore an indication of the scope of an author's research, can serve as a convenient key to shortened forms of the notes (see 14.14, 14.24). In electronic publications, a full bibliography can significantly streamline the process of creating links to works cited and, in turn, can enable publishers of those cited works to identify and create "cited by" links.

14.57   *Format and placement of bibliography.* A bibliography arranged in a single alphabetical list is the most common and usually the most reader-friendly

Notes

In citing works in the notes, short titles have generally been used. Works frequently cited have been identified by the following abbreviations:

Ac. Sc.	Archives de l'Académie des sciences.
A.P.	*Archives parlementaires de 1787 à 1860, première série (1787 à 1799)*. Edited by M. J. Mavidal and M. E. Laurent. 2nd ed. 82 vols. Paris, 1879–1913.
Best.	Theodore Besterman, ed. *Voltaire's Correspondence.* 107 vols. Geneva, 1953–65.
B. Inst.	Bibliothèque de l'Institut de France.
B.N., nouv. acqu.	Bibliothèque nationale. Fonds français, nouvelles acquisitions.
Corresp. inéd.	Charles Henry, ed. *Correspondance inédite de Condorcet et de Turgot (1770–1779)*. Paris, 1883.
HMAS	*Histoire de l'Académie royale des sciences. Avec les mémoires de mathématique et de physique . . . tirés des registres de cette académie (1699–1790)*. 92 vols. Paris, 1702–97. Each volume comprises two separately paginated parts, referred to as *Hist.* and *Mém.*, respectively.
Inéd. Lespinasse	Charles Henry, ed. *Lettres inédites de Mlle de Lespinasse.* Paris, 1887.
O.C.	A. Condorcet-O'Connor and F. Arago, eds. *Oeuvres de Condorcet.* 12 vols. Paris, 1847–49.

Preface

1. Peter Gay. *The Enlightenment: An Interpretation,* 2 vols. (New York, 1966–69), 2:319. I have suggested some criticisms of Gay's treatment of this theme in a review of the second volume of his work, *American Historical Review* 85 (1970): 1410–14.

2. Georges Gusdorf, *Introduction aux sciences humaines: Essai critique sur leurs origines et leur développement* (Strasbourg, 1960), 105–331.

FIGURE 14.7. A short list of abbreviations preceding endnotes. See 14.55.

form for a work with or without notes to the text. All sources to be included—books, articles, dissertations, papers—are alphabetically arranged in a single list by the last names of the authors (or, if no author or editor is given, by the title or a keyword readers are most likely to seek). In a printed work, a bibliography is normally placed at the end, preceding the index. In a multiauthor book or a textbook, each chapter may be followed by a brief bibliography. For an illustration, see figure 14.8; for the arrangement of entries, see 14.60–62. For division into sections, see 14.58.

14.58 *Dividing a bibliography into sections.* A bibliography may occasionally be divided into sections—but only if doing so would make the reader's job significantly easier. Where readers need to refer frequently from notes

Bibliography

Abram, David. "The Consequences of Literacy: Reflections in the Shadow of Plato's *Phaedrus*." State University of New York at Stony Brook, 1986. Typescript.

———. "The Perceptual Implications of Gaia." *Ecologist* 15 (1985): 96–103.

Ariès, Philippe. *The Hour of Our Death*. Translated by Helen Weaver. New York: Alfred A. Knopf, 1981.

Aristotle. *The Basic Works of Aristotle*. Edited by Richard McKeon. New York: Random House, 1941.

———. "De Partibus Animalium." In *The Works of Aristotle*. Edited by J. A. Smith and W. D. Ross. London: Oxford University Press, 1912.

Augustine. *City of God*. Edited by David Knowles. Translated by Henry Bettenson. Harmondsworth: Penguin Books, 1972.

Bakan, David. *Disease, Pain and Sacrifice*. Boston: Beacon Press, 1971.

Barker, Francis. *The Tremulous Private Body*. London: Methuen, 1984.

Baron, Richard J. "An Introduction to Medical Phenomenology: I Can't Hear You While I'm Listening." *Annals of Internal Medicine* 103 (1985): 606–11.

Basmajian, John V., ed. *Biofeedback: Principles and Practice for Clinicians*. 3d ed. Baltimore: Williams and Wilkins, 1989.

Berg, J. H. van den. "The Human Body and the Significance of Human Movement." *Philosophy and Phenomenological Research* 13 (1952): 159–83.

———. *The Psychology of the Sickbed*. Pittsburgh: Duquesne University Press, 1966.

Berry, Donald L. *Mutuality: The Vision of Martin Buber*. Albany: State University of New York Press, 1985.

Blacking, John, ed. *The Anthropology of the Body*. New York: Academic Press, 1978.

Blom, John J. *Descartes: His Moral Philosophy and Psychology*. New York: New York University Press, 1978.

Bordo, Susan. "Anorexia Nervosa: Psychopathology as the Crystallization of Culture." *Philosophical Forum* 17 (1985–86): 73–104.

Borgmann, Albert. *Technology and the Character of Contemporary Life*. Chicago: University of Chicago Press, 1984.

Brener, Jasper. "Sensory and Perceptual Determinants of Voluntary Visceral Control." In *Biofeedback: Theory and Research*. Edited by Gary E. Schwartz and Jackson Beatty. New York: Academic Press, 1977.

Brentano, Franz. *Psychology from an Empirical Standpoint*. Edited by Oskar Kraus. Translated by Antos C. Rancurello, D. B. Terrell, and Linda L. McAlister. London: Routledge and Kegan Paul, 1973.

FIGURE 14.8. The first page of a bibliography for a book. See 14.57.

to bibliography, a continuous alphabetical list is far preferable, since in a subdivided bibliography the alphabetizing starts over with each section. Rarely should books be separated from articles, since a book and an article by the same author are best listed close together. It may be appropriate to subdivide a bibliography (1) when it includes manuscript sources, archival collections, or other materials that do not fit into a straight alphabetical list; (2) when readers need to see at a glance the distinction between different kinds of works—for example, in a study of one writer, between works by the writer and those about him or her; or (3) when the bibliography is intended primarily as a guide to further reading (as in this manual). When divisions are necessary, a headnote should appear at the beginning of the bibliography, and each section should be introduced by an explanatory subhead (see fig. 14.9). No source should be listed in more than one section. For alphabetizing, see 14.60–62.

14.59   *Kinds of bibliographies.* Though Chicago generally recommends a full bibliography for book-length works, any of the bibliography categories listed here may be suited to a particular type of work. (For reference lists, a form of bibliography adapted to the author-date system, see 15.10–16.)

1. **Full bibliography.** A full bibliography includes all works cited, whether in text or in notes, other than personal communications (see 14.222). Some particularly relevant works the author has consulted may also be listed, even if not mentioned in the text. The usual heading is Bibliography, though Works Cited or Literature Cited may be used if no additional works are included.

2. **Selected bibliography.** If, for whatever reason, the author does not wish to list all works cited, the title must so indicate: either Selected Bibliography or (less frequently) Select Bibliography may be used or, if the list is quite short, Suggested Readings or Further Readings. A headnote should explain the principles of selection. See figure 14.9.

3. **Annotated bibliography.** Generally more convenient for readers than a bibliographic essay (see next item) is an annotated bibliography. Annotations may simply follow the publication details (sometimes in brackets if only a few entries are annotated) or may start a new line, often with a paragraph indention. See figure 14.10.

4. **Bibliographic essay.** Less formal than an annotated bibliography is a bibliographic essay, in which the author treats the literature discursively. Since works are not alphabetized, subject divisions may freely be made (see 14.58). Such an essay may be particularly suited to certain types of archival sources that do not easily lend themselves to an alphabetical list. It may be included in addition to a bibliography, in which case it should come first. If works discussed in the essay are listed in the bibliography, they may be given in

SELECTED BIBLIOGRAPHY

I list here only the writings that have been of use in the making of this book. This bibliography is by no means a complete record of all the works and sources I have consulted. It indicates the substance and range of reading upon which I have formed my ideas, and I intend it to serve as a convenience for those who wish to pursue the study of humor, comic literature, the history of comic processes, the British novel, and the particular writers and fictions that are the subjects of this inquiry. (Unless there is a standard edition or only one widely available edition of the complete works of the novelists I study, I have not listed their complete works.)

1. THE THEORY, PSYCHOLOGY, AND HISTORY OF THE COMIC

Auden, W. H. "Notes on the Comic." In *Comedy: Meaning and Form,* edited by Robert Corrigan, 61–72. San Francisco: Chandler, 1965.

Bakhtin, Mikhail. *Rabelais and His World.* Translated from the Russian by Helene Iswolsky. Cambridge, MA: MIT Press, 1968.

. . . .

2. JANE AUSTEN AND *EMMA*

Austen, Jane. *The Novels of Jane Austen.* Edited by R. W. Chapman. 5 vols. 3rd ed. London: Oxford University Press, 1932–34.

———. *Jane Austen's Letters to Her Sister Cassandra and Others.* Edited by R. W. Chapman. 2nd ed. London: Oxford University Press, 1952.

———. *Minor Works.* Edited by R. W. Chapman. Vol. 6 of *The Novels of Jane Austen.* London: Oxford University Press, 1954.

———. *"Emma": An Authoritative Text, Backgrounds, Reviews, and Criticism.* Edited by Stephen M. Parrish. Includes commentary and criticism by Sir Walter Scott, George Henry Lewes, Richard Simpson, Henry James, A. C. Bradley, Reginald Ferrar, Virginia Woolf, E. M. Forster, Mary Lascelles, Arnold Kettle, Wayne Booth, G. Armour Craig, A. Walton Litz, W. A. Craik, and W. J. Harvey. New York: W. W. Norton, 1972.

FIGURE 14.9. The opening page of a bibliography divided into sections, with an author's note explaining the principle of selection. See 14.58, 14.59.

shortened form (as in notes). If there is no bibliography, the essay must include full facts of publication, whether or not the titles also appear in the notes. For an illustration, see figure 14.11.

5. **List of works by one author.** A list of works by one author, usually titled Published Works [of So-and-So] or Writings [of So-and-So], is most often arranged chronologically. If several titles are listed for each year, the dates may appear as subheads.

14

Annotated Bibliography of Further Reading

The following is a partial list of the anthologies of poetry and the handbooks, articles, and books about poetry and prosody that I have found useful in writing, teaching, and thinking about poetry. After each entry I have added a brief description of its most appealing features. You will notice a preference for the work of poets about poetry. Poets who are articulate about the craft of verse are among the best expositors.[1]

I. Anthologies

Allen, Donald M., ed. *The New American Poetry.* New York: Grove
  Press, 1960.
  Concentrates on the postwar period from 1945 to 1960 and presents
  the work of poets who identified themselves with antiformalist
  movements or waves, often associated with fugitive publications and
  little magazines (*Yugen, Neon, Kulchur, Big Table,* etc.): the most
  prominent groups were the Black Mountain school (Olson, Duncan)
  and the experimental city poets from New York (like Frank O'Hara,
  LeRoi Jones, and Gilbert Sorrentino) and San Francisco (the "Beats"
  Kerouac, Corso, Ginsberg). John Ashbery, James Schuyler, Denise
  Levertov, and Gary Snyder are also represented. An anthology that
  awakened many readers and would-be writers to another sort of pos-

1. W. H. Auden is exemplary, even in his eccentricity. (See my discussion of some
of the many volumes edited by him.) Another poet, F. T. Prince, has looked closely at
Milton's prosody in a way that sheds light on prosody in general; see *The Italian Element
in Milton's Verse* (1954). Poets John Frederick Nims and J. V. Cunningham are also acute
when they write about verse; and I have already mentioned Charles O. Hartman and
Timothy Steele in connection with meter and rhythm (see chapter 8 on accentual-
syllabic meter).

FIGURE 14.10. Part of the first section of an annotated bibliography. See 14.59.

1. The "Great Tradition" in the History of Science

Those setting out to acquaint themselves with the identity of the Scientific Revolution, and with its major actors, themes, problems, achievements, and conceptual resources, can draw on a distinguished body of what now is commonly called "traditional" scholarship. If indeed it *is* traditional, that is because this literature typically manifested robust confidence that there was a coherent and specifiable body of early modern culture rightly called revolutionary, that this culture marked a clear break between "old" and "new," that it had an "essence," and that this essence could be captured through accounts of the rise of mechanism and materialism, the mathematization of natural philosophy, the emergence of a full-blooded experimentalism, and for many, though not all, traditional writers, the identification of an effective "method" for producing authentic science.

Among the outstanding achievements of this type of scholarship are the early work of E. A. Burtt, *The Metaphysical Foundations of Modern Physical Science* (New York: Doubleday Anchor, 1954; orig. publ. 1924); A. C. Crombie, *Augustine to Galileo: The History of Science, A.D. 400–1650* (London: Falcon, 1952); A. Rupert Hall, *The Scientific Revolution, 1500–1800: The Formation of the Modern Scientific Attitude,* 2nd ed. (Boston: Beacon Press, 1966; orig. publ. 1954); Hall, *From Galileo to Newton, 1630–1720* (London: Collins, 1963); Marie Boas [Hall], *The Scientific Renaissance, 1450–1630*

FIGURE 14.11. Part of the first section of a bibliographic essay. See 14.59.

Arrangement of Entries

14.60 *Alphabetical order for bibliography entries.* The rules for alphabetizing index entries (see 16.56–93) apply also to a bibliography, with the modifications described in this section and in 14.63–67. As for index entries, Chicago recommends the letter-by-letter system unless your publisher prefers the word-by-word system. Under the letter-by-letter system, an entry for "Fernández, Angelines" would precede an entry for "Fernán Gómez, Fernando"; under the word-by-word system, the opposite order would prevail. Note that word processors, though they can provide a head start, are generally not capable of correctly sorting by either system. In addition to correcting any software-based errors and variations, authors may need to make adjustments for any entries beginning with a 3-em dash (see 14.63).

14.61 *Single author versus several authors.* A single-author entry precedes a multiauthor entry beginning with the same name. Only the name of the first author is inverted.

Kogan, Herman. *The First Century: The Chicago Bar Association, 1874–1974*. Chicago: Rand McNally, 1974.

Kogan, Herman, and Lloyd Wendt. *Chicago: A Pictorial History*. New York: Dutton, 1958.

14.62 *Author with different coauthors.* Successive entries by two or more authors in which only the first author's name is the same are alphabetized according to the coauthors' last names.

Brooks, Daniel R., and Deborah A. McLennan. *The Nature of Diversity: An Evolutionary Voyage of Discovery*. Chicago: University of Chicago Press, 2002.

Brooks, Daniel R., and E. O. Wiley. *Evolution as Entropy*. 2nd ed. Chicago: University of Chicago Press, 1986.

The 3-Em Dash for Repeated Names in a Bibliography

14.63 *The 3-em dash and sorting—advice to authors.* The advice in this section, which explains how to use the 3-em dash to stand in for repeated bibliography entries under the same name, applies only to the final stages of a book or article. Authors generally should not use the 3-em dash for repeated names until the final manuscript of the bibliography has been produced. Among other potential pitfalls, 3-em dashes do not work in computerized sorts (i.e., *all* entries with 3-em dashes will line up in one place). Moreover, an incorrectly applied dash may obscure an important detail—for example, the abbreviation *ed.* or *trans.* Often the best course is to leave this step up to the editor and concentrate on transcribing accurate, complete entries. See also 6.91.

14.64 *The 3-em dash for one repeated name.* For successive entries by the same author, editor, translator, or compiler, a 3-em dash (followed by a period or comma, depending on the presence of an abbreviation such as *ed.*) replaces the name after the first appearance. See also 14.67.

Judt, Tony. *A Grand Illusion? An Essay on Europe*. New York: Hill and Wang, 1996.

———. *Reappraisals: Reflections on the Forgotten Twentieth Century*. New York: Penguin Press, 2008.

———, ed. *Resistance and Revolution in Mediterranean Europe, 1939–1948*. New York: Routledge, 1989.

Squire, Larry R. "The Hippocampus and the Neuropsychology of Memory." In *Neurobiology of the Hippocampus*, edited by W. Seifert, 491–511. New York: Oxford University Press, 1983.

———. *Memory and Brain*. New York: Oxford University Press, 1987.

14.65 *The 3-em dash for more than one repeated name.* The 3-em dash can stand for the same two or more authors (or editors or translators, etc.) as in the previous entry, provided they are listed in the same order. Note that the second-listed work is *authored* by (rather than *edited* by) Marty and Appleby; abbreviations for editor, translator, and so forth cannot be replaced by the 3-em dash and must always be listed explicitly.

> Marty, Martin E., and R. Scott Appleby, eds. *Fundamentalisms Comprehended.* Chicago: University of Chicago Press, 1995.
> ———. *The Glory and the Power: The Fundamentalist Challenge to the Modern World.* Boston: Beacon Press, 1992.
> but
> Comaroff, Jean, and John Comaroff, eds. *Modernity and Its Malcontents: Ritual and Power in Postcolonial Africa.* Chicago: University of Chicago Press, 1993.
> Comaroff, John, and Jean Comaroff. *Of Revelation and Revolution.* 2 vols. Chicago: University of Chicago Press, 1991–97.

14.66 *The 3-em dash for an institutional name.* The 3-em dash may also be used for institutional or corporate authors. Note that identical titles must be repeated. See also 14.8.

> Unicode Consortium. *The Unicode Standard.* Version 5.0. Edited by Julie D. Allen et al. Upper Saddle River, NJ: Addison-Wesley, 2007.
> ———. *The Unicode Standard.* Version 5.1.0. Last updated December 16, 2008. http://www.unicode.org/versions/Unicode5.1.0/.

14.67 *Alphabetical order for titles by the same author.* In a bibliography (as opposed to a reference list; see 15.17), titles by the same author are normally listed alphabetically. An initial *the, a,* or *an* is ignored in the alphabetizing. Note that *all* works by the same person (or by the same persons in the same order)—whether that person is editor, author, translator, or compiler—appear together, regardless of the added abbreviation.

> Ginger, Ray. *The Bending Cross: A Biography of Eugene Victor Debs.* New Brunswick, NJ: Rutgers University Press, 1949.
> ———. *Six Days or Forever? Tennessee v. John Thomas Scopes.* Chicago: Quadrangle Books, 1969.
> Monmonier, Mark. *Coast Lines: How Mapmakers Frame the World and Chart Environmental Change.* Chicago: University of Chicago Press, 2008.
> ———. *From Squaw Tit to Whorehouse Meadow: How Maps Name, Claim, and Inflame.* Chicago: University of Chicago Press, 2006.
> Mulvany, Nancy C. "Copyright for Indexes, Revisited." *ASI Newsletter* 107 (November–December 1991): 11–13.

———, ed. *Indexing, Providing Access to Information—Looking Back, Looking Ahead: Proceedings of the 25th Annual Meeting of the American Society of Indexers.* Port Aransas, TX: American Society of Indexers, 1993.

———. "Software Tools for Indexing: What We Need." *Indexer* 17 (October 1990): 108–13.

A bibliography of works by a single author (Writings of So-and-So), however, is usually arranged chronologically. (For an example, see section 2 in fig. 14.9.) Two or more titles published in any one year are arranged alphabetically.

Books

14.68 *Books as a model for other sources.* Much of the advice in the section on books will pertain to other sources as well. Their long history as a formal publication ensures, in particular, that the variations in author names (14.72–92) and titles (14.93–110) will serve as a model for constructing documentary notes and bibliography entries for many other types of sources. Rather than repeat this information for each type of source, then, cross-references will be provided in those sections to the appropriate paragraph(s) in this section on books whenever applicable.

14.69 *Elements to include when citing a book.* A full reference must include enough information to enable an interested reader to locate the book. Most references contain at least some information not strictly needed for that purpose but potentially helpful nonetheless. The elements listed below are included, where applicable, in full documentary notes and bibliography entries. The order in which they appear will vary slightly according to type of book, and certain elements are sometimes omitted; such variation will be noted and illustrated in the course of this chapter.

1. Author: full name of author(s) or editor(s) or, if no author or editor is listed, name of institution standing in their place
2. Title: full title of the book, including subtitle if there is one
3. Editor, compiler, or translator, if any, if listed on title page in addition to author
4. Edition, if not the first
5. Volume: total number of volumes if multivolume work is referred to as a whole; individual number if single volume of multivolume work is cited, and title of individual volume if applicable
6. Series title if applicable, and volume number within series if series is numbered

7. Facts of publication: city, publisher, and date
8. Page number or numbers if applicable
9. For electronic books consulted online, a URL or DOI, or, for other types of electronic books, an indication of the medium consulted (e.g., DVD, CD-ROM); see 14.4–13

14.70 *Flexibility and consistency.* As long as a consistent style is maintained within any one work, logical and defensible variations on the style illustrated here are acceptable if agreed to by author and publisher. Such flexibility, however, is rarely possible in journal publication, which calls for adherence to the established style of the journal in question. See also 14.3.

14.71 *Foreign bibliographic terms and abbreviations.* When books in a language other than English are cited in an English-language work, terms used for volume, edition, and so on may be translated—but only if the author or editor has a firm grasp of bibliographic terms in the foreign language. It is often wiser to leave them in the original. "Ausgabe in einem Band," for example, may be rendered as "one-volume edition" or simply left untranslated. Moreover, abbreviations such as "Bd." and "t." (German and French/Spanish equivalents of *vol.*, respectively) that are likely to have been recorded that way in a library catalog may best be left in that form. If in doubt, check a major catalog such as that of the Library of Congress or WorldCat.

Author's Name

14.72 *Form of author's name.* Authors' names are normally given as they appear on the title pages of their books. Certain adjustments, however, may be made to assist correct identification (unless they conflict with the style of a particular journal or series). First names may be given in full in place of initials. If an author uses his or her given name in one cited book and initials in another (e.g., "Mary L. Jones" versus "M. L. Jones"), the same form, preferably the fuller one, should be used in all references to that author. To assist alphabetization, middle initials should be given wherever known. Degrees and affiliations following names on a title page are omitted.

14.73 *Authors preferring initials.* For authors who always use initials, full names should not be supplied—for example, T. S. Eliot, M. F. K. Fisher, O. Henry (pseud.), P. D. James, C. S. Lewis, J. D. Salinger, H. G. Wells. Note that space is added between initials. (Exceptions may be made for special cases like

H.D.—the pen name for Hilda Doolittle.) In some instances, a cross-reference may be appropriate (see 14.84). See also 10.12. Very rarely, a portion of an author's given name omitted on the title page is supplied in brackets in a bibliography entry. This practice should be limited to authors who may be known by both forms: for example, R. S. Crane may be listed as R[onald] S. Crane.

14.74 **Monarchs, saints, and the like.** Authors known only by their given names (i.e., and not by any surname) are listed and alphabetized by those names. Such titles as "King" or "Saint" are omitted.

> Augustine. *On Christian Doctrine.* Translated by D. W. Robertson Jr. Indianapolis: Bobbs-Merrill, 1958.
> Elizabeth I. *Collected Works.* Edited by Leah S. Marcus, Janel Mueller, and Mary Beth Rose. Chicago: University of Chicago Press, 2000.

14.75 **One author.** In a note, the author's name is given in the normal order. In a bibliography, where names are arranged alphabetically, it is inverted (last name first). See also 14.18.

> 1. David Shields, *The Thing about Life Is That One Day You'll Be Dead* (New York: Alfred A. Knopf, 2008).
> 2. Roger Martin du Gard, *Lieutenant-Colonel de Maumort,* trans. Luc Brébion and Timothy Crouse (New York: Alfred A. Knopf, 2000).

> Martin du Gard, Roger. *Lieutenant-Colonel de Maumort.* Translated by Luc Brébion and Timothy Crouse. New York: Alfred A. Knopf, 2000.
> Shields, David. *The Thing about Life Is That One Day You'll Be Dead.* New York: Alfred A. Knopf, 2008.

14.76 **Two or more authors (or editors).** Two or three authors (or editors) of the same work are listed in the order used on the title page. In a bibliography, only the first author's name is inverted, and a comma must appear both before and after the first author's given name or initials. Use the conjunction *and* (not an ampersand).

> 5. Sue-Ellen Jacobs, Wesley Thomas, and Sabine Lang, eds., *Two-Spirit People: Native American Gender Identity, Sexuality, and Spirituality* (Urbana: University of Illinois Press, 1997), 32.
> 6. Steven D. Levitt and Stephen J. Dubner, *Freakonomics: A Rogue Economist Explores the Hidden Side of Everything* (New York: William Morrow, 2005), 20–21.
> 7. Jacobs, Thomas, and Lang, *Two-Spirit People*, 65–71.

Jacobs, Sue-Ellen, Wesley Thomas, and Sabine Lang, eds. *Two-Spirit People: Native American Gender Identity, Sexuality, and Spirituality*. Urbana: University of Illinois Press, 1997.

Levitt, Steven D., and Stephen J. Dubner. *Freakonomics: A Rogue Economist Explores the Hidden Side of Everything*. New York: William Morrow, 2005.

For works by or edited by four to ten persons, all names are usually given in the bibliography. Word order and punctuation are the same as for two or three authors. In a note, only the name of the first author is included, followed by *et al.* with no intervening comma.

> 4. Jeri A. Sechzer et al., eds., *Women and Mental Health* (Baltimore: Johns Hopkins University Press, 1996), 243.
>
> 7. Sechzer et al., *Women and Mental Health*, 276.

For works with more than ten authors—more common in the natural sciences—Chicago recommends the policy followed by the *American Naturalist* (see bibliog. 5): only the first seven should be listed in the bibliography, followed by *et al.* (Where space is limited, the policy of the American Medical Association may be followed: up to six authors' names are listed; if there are more than six, only the first three are listed, followed by *et al.*)

14.77 **Two or more authors (or editors) with same family name.** When two or more authors (or editors) share the same family name, the name is repeated.

> 3. Christopher Kendris and Theodore Kendris, *501 Spanish Verbs*, 6th ed. (Hauppauge, NY: Barron's Educational Series, 2007), 88.
>
> 47. Kendris and Kendris, *501 Spanish Verbs*, 191–92.

14.78 **Author's name in title.** When the author's name appears in the title or subtitle of a cited work (such as an autobiography), the note citation may begin with the title. The bibliography entry, however, should begin with the author's name, even though it is repeated in the title. See also 14.87.

> 5. *Clapton: The Autobiography* (New York: Broadway Books, 2007), 212.
>
> 6. *The Letters of George Meredith*, ed. C. L. Cline, 3 vols. (Oxford: Clarendon Press, 1970), 1:125.
>
> 7. *Illumination and Night Glare: The Unfinished Autobiography of Carson McCullers*, ed. Carlos L. Dews (Madison: University of Wisconsin Press, 1999), 44–45.

Clapton, Eric. *Clapton: The Autobiography*. New York: Broadway Books, 2007.

McCullers, Carson. *Illumination and Night Glare: The Unfinished Autobiography of Carson McCullers*. Edited by Carlos L. Dews. Madison: University of Wisconsin Press, 1999.

Meredith, George. *The Letters of George Meredith*. Edited by C. L. Cline. 3 vols. Oxford: Clarendon Press, 1970.

14.79 *Anonymous works—unknown authorship.* If the author or editor is unknown, the note or bibliography entry should normally begin with the title. An initial article is ignored in alphabetizing.

> 8. *A True and Sincere Declaration of the Purpose and Ends of the Plantation Begun in Virginia, of the Degrees Which It Hath Received, and Means by Which It Hath Been Advanced* (London, 1610).
> 9. *Stanze in lode della donna brutta* (Florence, 1547).

> *Stanze in lode della donna brutta*. Florence, 1547.
> *A True and Sincere Declaration of the Purpose and Ends of the Plantation Begun in Virginia, of the Degrees Which It Hath Received, and Means by Which It Hath Been Advanced*. London, 1610.

Although the use of *Anonymous* is generally to be avoided, it may stand in place of the author's name in a bibliography in which several anonymous works need to be grouped. In such an instance, *Anonymous* or *Anon.* (set in roman) appears at the first entry, and 3-em dashes (see 14.64) are used thereafter. (The dashes do not necessarily imply the same anonymous author.)

> Anonymous. *Stanze in lode della donna brutta*. Florence, 1547.
> ———. *A True and Sincere Declaration of the Purpose and Ends of the Plantation Begun in Virginia, . . .* 1610.

14.80 *Anonymous works—known authorship.* If the authorship is known or guessed at but was omitted on the title page, the name is included in brackets.

> 10. [Samuel Horsley], *On the Prosodies of the Greek and Latin Languages* (London, 1796).
> 11. [Ebenezer Cook?], *Sotweed Redivivus; or, The Planter's Looking-Glass*, by "E. C. Gent" (Annapolis, 1730).

> [Cook, Ebenezer?]. *Sotweed Redivivus; or, The Planter's Looking-Glass*. By "E. C. Gent." Annapolis, 1730.
> [Horsley, Samuel]. *On the Prosodies of the Greek and Latin Languages*. London, 1796.

14.81 *Pseudonyms—unknown authorship.* If an author's real name is not known, *pseud.* (roman, in brackets) may follow the name. (In a text citation, *pseud.* is omitted.)

Centinel [pseud.]. Letters. In *The Complete Anti-Federalist*, edited by Herbert J. Storing. Chicago: University of Chicago Press, 1981.

14.82 *Pseudonyms—known authorship.* A widely used pseudonym is generally treated as if it were the author's real name.

Eliot, George. *Middlemarch*. Norton Critical Editions. New York: Norton, 1977.
Twain, Mark. *The Prince and the Pauper: A Tale for Young People of All Ages*. New York: Harper & Brothers, 1899.

The real name, if of interest to readers, may follow the pseudonym in brackets. See also 14.84.

Le Carré, John [David John Moore Cornwell]. *The Quest for Karla*. New York: Knopf, 1982.
Stendhal [Marie-Henri Beyle]. *The Charterhouse of Parma*. Trans. C. K. Scott-Moncrieff. New York: Boni and Liveright, 1925.

14.83 *Pseudonyms rarely used.* If the author's real name is better known than the pseudonym, the real name should be used. If needed, the pseudonym may be included in brackets, followed by *pseud.*

Brontë, Charlotte. *Jane Eyre*. London, 1847.
or
Brontë, Charlotte [Currer Bell, pseud.]. *Jane Eyre*. London, 1847.

14.84 *Cross-references for pseudonyms.* In some cases, a cross-reference from a real name to a pseudonym, or vice versa, may be desired. Italicize words like *See*.

Twain, Mark. *See* Clemens, Samuel.

If a bibliography includes two or more works published by the same author but under different pseudonyms, all may be listed under the real name followed by the appropriate pseudonym in brackets, with cross-references under the pseudonyms (see also 14.64). Alternatively, they may be listed under the pseudonyms, with a cross-reference at the real name to each pseudonym.

Ashe, Gordon. *See* Creasey, John.
Creasey, John [Gordon Ashe, pseud.]. *A Blast of Trumpets*. New York: Holt, Rinehart and Winston, 1976.
———— [Anthony Morton, pseud.]. *Hide the Baron*. New York: Walker, 1978.

———— [Jeremy York, pseud.]. *Death to My Killer*. New York: Macmillan, 1966.

Morton, Anthony. *See* Creasey, John.

York, Jeremy. *See* Creasey, John.

or

Ashe, Gordon [John Creasey]. *A Blast of Trumpets*. New York: Holt, Rinehart and Winston, 1976.

Creasey, John. *See* Ashe, Gordon; Morton, Anthony; York, Jeremy.

14.85 *Descriptive phrase as "author."* A descriptive phrase standing in place of the author is treated in much the same way as a pseudonym (see 14.81). An initial *The* or *A* may be omitted.

> 11. Cotton Manufacturer, *An Inquiry into the Causes of the Present Long-Continued Depression in the Cotton Trade, with Suggestions for Its Improvement* (Bury, UK, 1869), 4–5.

> Cotton Manufacturer. *An Inquiry* . . .

14.86 *Alternative real names.* When a writer has published under different forms of his or her name, the works should be listed under the name used on the title page—unless the difference is merely the use of initials versus full names (see 14.72). Cross-references are occasionally used.

> Doniger, Wendy. *The Bedtrick: Tales of Sex and Masquerade*. Chicago: University of Chicago Press, 2000.
> ————. *See also* O'Flaherty, Wendy Doniger.

If a person discussed in the text publishes under a name not used in the text, a cross-reference may be useful.

> Overstone, Lord. *See* Loyd, Samuel Jones.

14.87 *Editor in place of author.* When no author appears on the title page, a work is listed by the name(s) of the editor(s), compiler(s), or translator(s). In full note citations and in bibliographies, the abbreviation *ed.* or *eds.*, *comp.* or *comps.*, or *trans.* follows the name, preceded by a comma. In shortened note citations and text citations, the abbreviation is omitted.

> 3. Glenn Young, ed., *The Best American Short Plays, 2002–2003* (New York: Applause, 2007), 94.
> 4. Theodore Silverstein, trans., *Sir Gawain and the Green Knight* (Chicago: University of Chicago Press, 1974), 34.
> 5. Young, *Best American Short Plays*, 97–98; Silverstein, *Sir Gawain*, 38.

Silverstein, Theodore, trans. *Sir Gawain and the Green Knight*. Chicago: University of Chicago Press, 1974.

Young, Glenn, ed. *The Best American Short Plays, 2002–2003*. New York: Applause, 2007.

On the other hand, certain well-known reference works may be listed by title rather than by editor; for an example, see 14.247.

14.88   *Editor or translator in addition to author.* The edited, compiled, or translated work of one author is normally listed with the author's name appearing first and the name(s) of the editor(s), compiler(s), or translator(s) appearing after the title, preceded by *edited by* or *ed.*, *compiled by* or *comp.*, or *translated by* or *trans.* Note that the plural forms *eds.* and *comps.* are never used in this position. Note also that *edited by* and the like are usually spelled out in bibliographies but abbreviated in notes. If a translator as well as an editor is listed, the names should appear in the same order as on the title page of the original. When the title page carries such phrases as "Edited with an Introduction and Notes by" or "Translated with a Foreword by," the bibliographic or note reference can usually be simplified to "Edited by" or "Translated by." See also 14.78, 14.112, 14.109.

> 6. Yves Bonnefoy, *New and Selected Poems*, ed. John Naughton and Anthony Rudolf (Chicago: University of Chicago Press, 1995).
>
> 7. Rigoberta Menchú, *Crossing Borders*, trans. and ed. Ann Wright (New York: Verso, 1999).
>
> 8. *Four Farces by Georges Feydeau*, trans. Norman R. Shapiro (Chicago: University of Chicago Press, 1970).
>
> 10. Theodor W. Adorno and Walter Benjamin, *The Complete Correspondence, 1928–1940*, ed. Henri Lonitz, trans. Nicholas Walker (Cambridge, MA: Harvard University Press, 1999).

Adorno, Theodor W., and Walter Benjamin. *The Complete Correspondence, 1928–1940*. Edited by Henri Lonitz. Translated by Nicholas Walker. Cambridge, MA: Harvard University Press, 1999.

Bonnefoy, Yves. *New and Selected Poems*. Edited by John Naughton and Anthony Rudolf. Chicago: University of Chicago Press, 1995.

Feydeau, Georges. *Four Farces by Georges Feydeau*. Translated by Norman R. Shapiro. Chicago: University of Chicago Press, 1970.

Menchú, Rigoberta. *Crossing Borders*. Translated and edited by Ann Wright. New York: Verso, 1999.

14.89   *"With the assistance of" and the like.* The title page of some edited books carries information that must be dealt with ad hoc. The usual formats, phrases, and abbreviations may not work. If a title page lists, for example, one editor, followed in smaller type by "Associate Editor So-and-So" and "Assistant Editor So-and-So," the secondary names may be included with such wording as "With the assistance of So-and-So and So-and-So" (or simply omitted). For ghostwritten books, *with* is usually sufficient.

> *Chaucer Life-Records*. Edited by Martin M. Crow and Clair C. Olson from materials compiled by John M. Manly and Edith Rickert, with the assistance of Lilian J. Redstone et al. London: Oxford University Press, 1966.
>
> Cullen, John B. *Old Times in the Faulkner Country*. In collaboration with Floyd C. Watkins. Chapel Hill: University of North Carolina Press, 1961.
>
> Prather, Marla. *Alexander Calder, 1898–1976*. With contributions by Arnauld Pierre and Alexander S. C. Rower. New Haven, CT: Yale University Press, 1998.
>
> Rodman, Dennis. *Walk on the Wild Side*. With Michael Silver. New York: Delacorte Press, 1997.
>
> Schellinger, Paul, ed. *Encyclopedia of the Novel*. With the assistance of Christopher Hudson and Marijke Rijsberman. 2 vols. Chicago: Fitzroy Dearborn, 1998.
>
> Williams, Joseph M. *Style: Toward Clarity and Grace*. With two chapters coauthored by Gregory G. Colomb. Chicago: University of Chicago Press, 1995.

14.90 *Editor versus author.* Occasionally, when an editor or a translator is more important to a discussion than the original author, a book may be listed under the editor's name. (See also 14.88.)

> Eliot, T. S., ed. *Literary Essays*. By Ezra Pound. New York: New Directions, 1953.

14.91 *Authors of forewords and the like.* Authors of forewords or introductions to books by other authors are included in notes and bibliography entries only if the foreword or introduction is of major significance.

> Hayek, F. A. *The Road to Serfdom*. With a new introduction by Milton Friedman. Chicago: University of Chicago Press, 1994.

For specific citation of a foreword or an introduction, see 14.116.

14.92 *Organization as author.* If a publication issued by an organization, association, or corporation carries no personal author's name on the title page, the organization is listed as author in a bibliography, even if it is also given as publisher. (But cf. 14.79.)

> University of Chicago Press. *The Chicago Manual of Style*. 16th ed. Chicago: University of Chicago Press, 2010.
>
> World Health Organization. *WHO Editorial Style Manual*. Geneva: World Health Organization, 1993.

Title

14.93 *Additional discussion of titles.* The section "Titles of Works" in chapter 8 (8.154–95), though focusing on the way titles of books as well as other materials are treated when mentioned in running text, is obviously relevant to documentation and provides additional discussion and examples.

14.94 *Italics for book titles.* Book titles and subtitles are italicized. For titles within titles, see 14.102.

> Gilbert, Elizabeth. *Eat, Pray, Love: One Woman's Search for Everything across Italy, India, and Indonesia.* New York: Viking, 2006.

14.95 *Capitalization of book titles.* English-language book titles and subtitles are capitalized headline-style. In headline style, the first and last words of title and subtitle and all other major words are capitalized. For a more detailed definition and more examples, see 8.157. For hyphenated compounds in headline style, see 8.159. For headlines in newspapers, see 14.204.

> *The Fifth Miracle: The Search for the Origin and Meaning of Life*
> *How to Do It: Guides to Good Living for Renaissance Italians*

For foreign-language titles, which are usually capitalized sentence-style, see 14.107.

14.96 *Some permissible changes to titles.* The spelling, hyphenation, and punctuation in the original title should be preserved, with the following exceptions: words in full capitals on the original title page (except for initialisms or acronyms) should be set in upper- and lowercase; headline-style or sentence-style capitalization should be applied as applicable; and, subject to editorial discretion, an ampersand may be changed to *and*. Numbers should remain spelled out or given as numerals according to the original (*Twelfth Century* or *12th Century*) unless there is a good reason to make them consistent (but *12th* may be changed to *12th*). For more on permissible changes to titles, including the addition of colons and commas (including serial commas), see 8.163. For older titles, see 14.106. See also 14.97.

14.97 *Subtitles—the colon.* A colon, also italicized, is used to separate the main title from the subtitle. A space follows the colon. The subtitle, like the title, always begins with a capital letter. See also 8.162, 8.163.

Weiss, Andrea. *In the Shadow of the Magic Mountain: The Erika and Klaus Mann Story*. Chicago: University of Chicago Press, 2008.

Although in European bibliographic style a period often separates title from subtitle, English-language publications need not follow that convention for foreign titles. See also 14.107.

Fausts Himmelfahrt: Zur letzten Szene der Tragödie

14.98   Two subtitles. If, as occasionally happens, there are two subtitles in the original (an awkward contingency), a colon normally precedes the first and a semicolon the second. The second subtitle also begins with a capital.

Sereny, Gitta. *Cries Unheard: Why Children Kill; The Story of Mary Bell*. New York: Metropolitan Books / Henry Holt, 1999.

14.99   Use of "or" with double titles. Old-fashioned double titles (or titles and subtitles) connected by *or* are traditionally separated by a semicolon, with a comma following *or*, and less traditionally but more simply by a single comma preceding *or*. Chicago prefers the first form.

England's Monitor; or, The History of the Separation
or, less formally,
England's Monitor, or The History of the Separation

14.100   "And other stories" and such. Such tags as *and other stories* or *and other poems* are treated as part of the main title but usually separated from the title story, poem, essay, or whatever by a comma, even when such comma does not appear on the title page. The first part of the title is *not* enclosed in quotation marks.

34. Norman Maclean, *A River Runs through It, and Other Stories* (Chicago: University of Chicago Press, 1976), 104.

When the main title ends with a question mark or exclamation point, the comma is omitted. See also 14.105.

26. Herrlee Glessner Creel, *What Is Taoism? and Other Studies in Chinese Cultural History* (Chicago: University of Chicago Press, 1970), 34.

14.101   Dates in titles. When not introduced by a preposition (e.g., "from 1920 to 1945"), dates in a title or subtitle are set off by commas, even if differentiated only by type style on the title page. If a colon has been used in the original, however, it should be retained. (Note that commas should not be added to foreign titles before dates.)

Sundiata, Ibrahim. *Brothers and Strangers: Black Zion, Black Slavery, 1914–1940*. Durham, NC: Duke University Press, 2003.

14.102   *Titles within titles.* Titles of long or short works appearing within an italicized title are enclosed in quotation marks, regardless of how such titles would appear alone. For a title within an article or a chapter title, see 14.177.

22. Allen Forte, *The Harmonistic Organization of "The Rite of Spring"* (New Haven, CT: Yale University Press, 1978).
23. Roland McHugh, *Annotations to "Finnegans Wake"* (Baltimore: Johns Hopkins University Press, 1980).

Quotation marks within a book title do not, of course, always denote another title.

24. Henry Louis Gates Jr. and Kwame Anthony Appiah, eds., *"Race," Writing, and Difference* (Chicago: University of Chicago Press, 1986).

14.103   *Italicized terms within titles.* When terms normally italicized in running text, such as species names or names of ships or foreign words (but *not* titles of works; see 14.102), appear within an italicized title, they are set roman ("reverse italics"; see 8.171). When, however, such a term makes up the entire title, it should be italicized. For an italicized term within an article or a chapter title, see 14.177.

Stafford, Edward Peary. *The Big E: The Story of the USS* Enterprise. New York: Random House, 1962.
Van Wagenen, Gertrude, and Miriam E. Simpson. *Postnatal Development of the Ovary in* Homo sapiens *and* Macaca mulatta *and Induction of Ovulation in the Macaque*. New Haven, CT: Yale University Press, 1973.
Weigel, Detlef, and Jane Glazebrook. Arabidopsis: *A Laboratory Manual*. Cold Spring Harbor, NY: Cold Spring Harbor Laboratory Press, 2002.
but
Hume, Christine. *Musca domestica*. Boston: Beacon Press, 2000.

14.104   *Quotation marks in titles.* A quotation used as a book title should be enclosed in quotation marks only if it appears that way in the source (i.e., on the title page or its equivalent). Headline-style capitalization should be used. See also 8.160.

Bruccoli, Matthew J., ed. *"An Artist Is His Own Fault": John O'Hara on Writers and Writing*. Carbondale: Southern Illinois University Press, 1977.

14.105 *Question marks or exclamation points in book titles.* When a main title ends with a question mark or an exclamation point, no colon is added before any subtitle. When the question mark or exclamation point is within quotation marks, however, retain a colon before the subtitle (see third example below). Any punctuation other than a period required by the surrounding text, note, or bibliography entry should be retained (see fourth, fifth, and sixth examples). This slight departure from Chicago's former usage recognizes the syntactical independence of a title within a phrase or sentence (see 6.119).

1. Yogi Berra, *What Time Is It? You Mean Now? Advice for Life from the Zennest Master of Them All*, with Dave Kaplan (New York: Simon & Schuster, 2002), 63.
2. Alison Oram, *Her Husband Was a Woman! Women's Gender-Crossing and British Popular Culture* (London: Routledge, 2007), 183.
3. Edward Buscombe, *"Injuns!": Native Americans in the Movies* (London: Reaktion, 2006), 12.
14. Buscombe, *"Injuns!,"* 114–15.
44. Berra, *What Time Is It?*, 55–56.
66. Oram, *Her Husband Was a Woman!*, 184.

When a title ending with a question mark or an exclamation mark would normally be followed by a period, the period is omitted; see 6.118.

Hornby, Nick. *Vous descendez?* Translated by Nicolas Richard. Paris: Plon, 2005.

14.106 *Older titles and very long titles.* Titles of works published in the eighteenth century or earlier may retain their original punctuation, spelling, and capitalization (except for whole words in capital letters, which should be given an initial capital only). Very long titles may be shortened in a bibliography or a note, omissions being indicated by three ellipsis dots within a title and four at the end (see 13.51).

Escalante, Bernardino. *A Discourse of the Navigation which the Portugales doe make to the Realmes and Provinces of the East Partes of the Worlde. . . .* Translated by John Frampton. London, 1579.

Ray, John. *Observations Topographical, Moral, and Physiological: Made in a Journey Through part of the Low-Countries, Germany, Italy, and France: with A Catalogue of Plants not Native of England . . . Whereunto is added A Brief Account of Francis Willughby, Esq., his Voyage through a great part of Spain.* [London], 1673.

14.107 **Non-English titles.** Sentence-style capitalization is strongly recommended for non-English titles (see 11.3). Capitalize the first word of a title or subtitle and any word that would be capitalized in the original language (e.g., *Wahrheit, Sowjetunion,* and *Inquisición* in examples 2 and 3). Writers or editors unfamiliar with the usage of the language concerned, however, should not attempt to alter capitalization without expert help. For English forms of foreign cities, see 14.137.

> 1. Danielle Maisonneuve, Jean-François Lamarche, and Yves St-Amand, *Les relations publiques dans une société en mouvance* (Sainte-Foy, QC: Presses de l'Université du Québec, 1998).
>
> 2. Gabriele Krone-Schmalz, *In Wahrheit sind wir stärker: Frauenalltag in der Sowjetunion* (Frankfurt am Main: Fischer Taschenbuch Verlag, 1992).
>
> 3. Daniel Muñoz Sempere, *La Inquisición española como tema literario: Política, historia y ficción en la crisis del antiguo régimen* (Woodbridge, UK: Tamesis, 2008).
>
> 4. G. Martellotti et al., *La letteratura italiana: Storia e testi,* vol. 7 (Milan: Riccardo Ricciardi, 1955).
>
> 5. Ljiljana Piletić Stojanović, ed., *Gutfreund i češki kubizam* (Belgrade: Muzej savremene umetnosti, 1971).

14.108 **Translated title supplied by author or editor.** If an English translation of a title is needed, it follows the original title and is enclosed in brackets, without italics or quotation marks. It is capitalized sentence-style regardless of the bibliographic style followed. (In running text, parentheses are used instead of brackets; see 11.6.) See also 14.110.

> 7. Henryk Wereszycki, *Koniec sojuszu trzech cesarzy* [The end of the Three Emperors' League] (Warsaw: PWN, 1977); includes a summary in German.

Pirumova, Nataliia Mikhailovna. *Zemskoe liberal'noe dvizhenie: Sotsial'nye korni i evoliutsiia do nachala XX veka* [The zemstvo liberal movement: Its social roots and evolution to the beginning of the twentieth century]. Moscow: Izdatel'stvo "Nauka," 1977.

14.109 **Original plus published translation.** A published translation is normally treated as illustrated in 14.88. If, for some reason, both the original and the translation need to be cited, either of the following forms may be used, depending on whether the original or the translation is of greater interest to readers:

Furet, François. *Le passé d'une illusion*. Paris: Éditions Robert Laffont, 1995. Translated by Deborah Furet as *The Passing of an Illusion* (Chicago: University of Chicago Press, 1999).

or

Furet, François. *The Passing of an Illusion*. Translated by Deborah Furet. Chicago: University of Chicago Press, 1999. Originally published as *Le passé d'une illusion* (Paris: Éditions Robert Laffont, 1995).

14.110   *Unpublished translation of title standing in for original.* In those rare instances when a title is given only in translation and no published translation of the work is cited, the original language must be specified.

8. N. M. Pirumova, *The Zemstvo Liberal Movement: Its Social Roots and Evolution to the Beginning of the Twentieth Century* [in Russian] (Moscow: Izdatel'stvo "Nauka," 1977).

Chapters or Other Parts of a Book

14.111   *Chapter in a single-author book.* When a specific chapter (or other titled part of a book) is cited in the notes, the author's name is followed by the title of the chapter (or other part), followed by *in*, followed by the title of the book. The chapter title is enclosed in quotation marks. Either the inclusive page numbers (see 9.60) or the chapter or part number is usually given also. In the bibliography, either the chapter or the book may be listed first. For a multiauthor work, see 14.112. See also 14.160.

1. Brendan Phibbs, "Herrlisheim: Diary of a Battle," in *The Other Side of Time: A Combat Surgeon in World War II* (Boston: Little, Brown, 1987), 117–63.
8. John Samples, "The Origins of Modern Campaign Finance Law," chap. 7 in *The Fallacy of Campaign Finance Reform* (Chicago: University of Chicago Press, 2006).
33. Samples, "Campaign Finance Law," 30–31.

Phibbs, Brendan. "Herrlisheim: Diary of a Battle." In *The Other Side of Time: A Combat Surgeon in World War II*, 117–63. Boston: Little, Brown, 1987.
Samples, John. "The Origins of Modern Campaign Finance Law." Chap. 7 in *The Fallacy of Campaign Finance Reform*. Chicago: University of Chicago Press, 2006.
or
Samples, John. *The Fallacy of Campaign Finance Reform*. Chicago: University of Chicago Press, 2006. See esp. chap. 7, "The Origins of Modern Campaign Finance Law."

14.112 *Contribution to a multiauthor book.* When one contribution to a multiauthor book is cited, the contributor's name comes first, followed by the title of the contribution in roman, followed by *in* (also roman), followed by the title of the book in italics, followed by the name(s) of the editor(s). In a bibliography entry, the inclusive page numbers are usually given also (as in the second example below). In notes and bibliographies, the contribution title is enclosed in quotation marks. For several contributions to the same book, see 14.113.

> 3. Anne Carr and Douglas J. Schuurman, "Religion and Feminism: A Reformist Christian Analysis," in *Religion, Feminism, and the Family*, ed. Anne Carr and Mary Stewart Van Leeuwen (Louisville, KY: Westminster John Knox Press, 1996), 14.

> Ellet, Elizabeth F. L. "By Rail and Stage to Galena." In *Prairie State: Impressions of Illinois, 1673–1967, by Travelers and Other Observers*, edited by Paul M. Angle, 271–79. Chicago: University of Chicago Press, 1968.

14.113 *Several contributions to the same book.* If two or more contributions to the same multiauthor book are cited, the book itself, as well as the specific contributions, may be listed in the bibliography. The entries for the individual contributions may then cross-refer to the book's editor, thus avoiding clutter. In notes, details of the book may be given the first time it is mentioned, with subsequent references in shortened form (see also 14.26).

> 4. William H. Keating, "Fort Dearborn and Chicago," in *Prairie State: Impressions of Illinois, 1673–1967, by Travelers and Other Observers*, ed. Paul M. Angle (Chicago: University of Chicago Press, 1967), 84–87.
> 27. Sara Clarke Lippincott, "Chicago," in Angle, *Prairie State*, 362–70.

> Draper, Joan E. "Paris by the Lake: Sources of Burnham's Plan of Chicago." In Zukowsky, *Chicago Architecture*, 107–19.
> Harrington, Elaine. "International Influences on Henry Hobson Richardson's Glessner House." In Zukowsky, *Chicago Architecture*, 189–207.
> Zukowsky, John, ed. *Chicago Architecture, 1872–1922: Birth of a Metropolis*. Munich: Prestel-Verlag in association with the Art Institute of Chicago, 1987.

14.114 *Book-length work within a book.* If the cited part of a book would normally be italicized if published alone (see 8.161, 8.181), it too may be italicized.

> 3. Thomas Bernhard, *A Party for Boris*, in *Histrionics: Three Plays*, trans. Peter K. Jansen and Kenneth Northcott (Chicago: University of Chicago Press, 1990).

14.115 *Chapter originally published elsewhere.* When a chapter that was originally published as an article in a journal is cited, only the book version need be cited. If the original publication is of particular interest, details may be added to the entry in the bibliography after such wording as "originally published as" (see 14.190, first example).

14.116 *Introductions, prefaces, afterwords, and the like.* If the reference is to a generic title such as *introduction, preface,* or *afterword,* that term (lowercased unless following a period) is added before the title of the book. See also 8.177.

> 1. Valerie Polakow, afterword to *Lives on the Edge: Single Mothers and Their Children in the Other America* (Chicago: University of Chicago Press, 1993).

If the author of the introduction or other part is someone other than the main author of a book, that author comes first, and the author of the book follows the title. In a bibliography entry, include the page number range for the part cited, as shown in the second example below. See also 14.91.

> 6. Francine Prose, introduction to *Word Court: Wherein Verbal Virtue Is Rewarded, Crimes against the Language Are Punished, and Poetic Justice Is Done,* by Barbara Wallraff (New York: Harcourt, 2000).

> Mansfield, Harvey, and Delba Winthrop. Introduction to *Democracy in America,* by Alexis de Tocqueville, xvii–lxxxvi. Translated and edited by Harvey Mansfield and Delba Winthrop. Chicago: University of Chicago Press, 2000.

14.117 *Letters in published collections.* A reference to a letter (or memorandum or similar communication) in a published collection begins with the names of the sender and the recipient, in that order, followed by a date and sometimes the place where the communication was prepared. The word *letter* is unnecessary, but other forms, such as reports or memoranda, should be specified. The title of the collection is given in the usual form for a book. For date forms, see 6.45, 9.32. For unpublished communications, see 14.222.; see also 14.239.

> 1. Adams to Charles Milnes Gaskell, Baden, 22 September 1867, in *Letters of Henry Adams, 1858–1891,* ed. Worthington Chauncey Ford (Boston: Houghton Mifflin, 1930), 133–34.
> 2. EBW to Harold Ross, memorandum, 2 May 1946, in *Letters of E. B. White,* ed. Dorothy Lobrano Guth (New York: Harper & Row, 1976), 273.
> 3. Adams to Gaskell, London, 30 March 1868, 141.

Adams, Henry. *Letters of Henry Adams, 1858–1891*. Edited by Worthington Chauncey Ford. Boston: Houghton Mifflin, 1930.
White, E. B. *Letters of E. B. White*. Edited by Dorothy Lobrano Guth. New York: Harper & Row, 1976.

When it is necessary to include a single letter in a bibliography, it is listed under the writer's name only.

Jackson, Paulina. Paulina Jackson to John Pepys Junior, 3 October 1676. In *The Letters of Samuel Pepys and His Family Circle*, edited by Helen Truesdell Heath, no. 42. Oxford: Clarendon Press, 1955.

Edition

14.118 *Editions other than the first.* When an edition other than the first is used or cited, the number or description of the edition follows the title in the listing. An edition number usually appears on the title page and is repeated, along with the date of the edition, on the copyright page. Such wording as *Second Edition, Revised and Enlarged* is abbreviated in notes and bibliographies simply as *2nd ed.*; *Revised Edition* (with no number) is abbreviated as *rev. ed.* Other terms are similarly abbreviated. Any volume number mentioned follows the edition number. For the use of the word *edition* and Chicago's preferences, see 1.26. For inclusion of the original date of an older work cited in a modern edition, see 14.119.

1. Karen V. Harper-Dorton and Martin Herbert, *Working with Children, Adolescents, and Their Families*, 3rd ed. (Chicago: Lyceum Books, 2002), 43.
2. Florence Babb, *Between Field and Cooking Pot: The Political Economy of Marketwomen in Peru*, rev. ed. (Austin: University of Texas Press, 1989), 199.
3. Elizabeth Barrett Browning, *Aurora Leigh: Authoritative Text, Backgrounds and Contexts, Criticism*, ed. Margaret Reynolds, Norton Critical Editions (New York: Norton, 1996). All subsequent citations refer to this edition.

Strunk, William, Jr., and E. B. White. *The Elements of Style*. 4th ed. New York: Allyn and Bacon, 2000.

14.119 *Reprint editions and modern editions.* Books may be reissued in paperback by the original publisher or in paper or hardcover by another company. In bibliographic listings, if the original publication details—particularly the date—are relevant, include them. If page numbers are mentioned, give the date of the edition cited unless pagination is the same. The availability of a paperback or an electronic version (see 14.166), the addition of new material, or other such matters can be added as needed. Modern editions of Greek, Latin, and medieval classics are discussed in 14.256–66; modern editions of English classics in 14.267–68; online editions of books in 14.166–69.

22. Ernest Gowers, *The Complete Plain Words*, 3rd ed. (London: H.M. Stationery Office, 1986; Harmondsworth, UK: Penguin Books, 1987), 26. Citations refer to the Penguin edition.

23. Jacques Barzun, *Simple and Direct: A Rhetoric for Writers*, rev. ed. (1985; repr., Chicago: University of Chicago Press, 1994), 152–53.

Bernhardt, Peter. *The Rose's Kiss: A Natural History of Flowers*. Chicago: University of Chicago Press, 2002. First published 1999 by Island Press.

Emerson, Ralph Waldo. *Nature*. 1836. Facsimile of the first edition, with an introduction by Jaroslav Pelikan. Boston: Beacon, 1985.

Fitzgerald, F. Scott. *The Great Gatsby*. New York: Scribner, 1925. Reprinted with preface and notes by Matthew J. Bruccoli. New York: Collier Books, 1992. Page references are to the 1992 edition.

National Reconnaissance Office. *The KH-4B Camera System*. Washington, DC: National Photographic Interpretation Center, 1967. Now declassified and also available online, http://www.fas.org/irp/imint/docs/kh-4_camera_system .htm.

Schweitzer, Albert. *J. S. Bach*. Translated by Ernest Newman. 2 vols. 1911. Reprint, New York: Dover, 1966.

14.120   *Microform editions.* Works issued commercially in microform editions, including dissertations, are treated much like books. The form of publication, when needed, is given after the facts of publication. (In the first example below, the page number is to the printed text; the other numbers indicate the fiche and frame, and the letter indicates the row.)

5. Beatrice Farwell, *French Popular Lithographic Imagery, 1815–1870*, vol. 12, *Lithography in Art and Commerce* (Chicago: University of Chicago Press, 1997), text-fiche, p. 67, 3C12.

Tauber, Abraham. *Spelling Reform in the United States*. Ann Arbor, Mich.: University Microfilms, 1958.

Microform or other photographic processes used only to preserve printed material need not be mentioned in a citation. The source is treated as it would be in its published version.

Multivolume Works

14.121 *Volume numbers and page numbers.* In documentation, volume numbers are always given in arabic numerals, even if in the original work they appear in roman numerals or are spelled out. If the volume number is immediately followed by a page number, the abbreviation *vol.* is omitted and a colon separates the volume number from the page number with no intervening space. See the examples throughout this section.

14.122 *Citing a multivolume work as a whole.* When a multivolume work is cited as a whole, the total number of volumes is given after the title of the work (or, if an editor as well as an author is mentioned, after the editor's name). If the volumes have been published over several years, the dates of the first and last volumes are given, separated by an en dash (see 9.63). See also 14.78.

> Aristotle. *Complete Works of Aristotle: The Revised Oxford Translation.* Edited by J. Barnes. 2 vols. Bollingen Series. Princeton, NJ: Princeton University Press, 1983.
> Byrne, Muriel St. Clare, ed. *The Lisle Letters.* 6 vols. Chicago: University of Chicago Press, 1981.
> James, Henry. *The Complete Tales of Henry James.* Edited by Leon Edel. 12 vols. London: Rupert Hart-Davis, 1962–64.

14.123 *Citing a particular volume in a note.* If a particular volume of a multivolume work is cited, the volume number and the individual volume title, if there is one, are given in addition to the general title. If volumes have been published in different years, only the date of the cited volume is given.

> 36. Muriel St. Clare Byrne, ed., *The Lisle Letters* (Chicago: University of Chicago Press, 1981), 4:243.
> 37. *The Complete Tales of Henry James*, ed. Leon Edel, vol. 5, *1883–1884* (London: Rupert Hart-Davis, 1963), 32–33.

The different treatment of the volume numbers in the examples above is prescribed by logic: all six volumes of the Byrne work appeared in 1981 under the same title, whereas volume 5 of the James tales carries an additional title with a publication date not shared by all volumes in the set. See also 14.127.

14.124 *Citing a particular volume in a bibliography.* If only one volume of a multivolume work is of interest to readers, it may be listed alone in a bibliography in either of the following ways:

Pelikan, Jaroslav. *The Christian Tradition: A History of the Development of Doctrine.*
Vol. 1, *The Emergence of the Catholic Tradition (100–600).* Chicago: University
of Chicago Press, 1971.
or
Pelikan, Jaroslav. *The Emergence of the Catholic Tradition (100–600).* Vol. 1 of *The
Christian Tradition: A History of the Development of Doctrine.* Chicago: University of Chicago Press, 1971.

The publication date (or date range; see 14.122) should normally correspond to the last-mentioned title. See also 14.126, 14.151.

14.125 *Chapters and other parts of individual volumes.* Specific parts of individual
volumes of multivolume books are cited in the same way as parts of
single-volume books.

> 38. "Buddhist Mythology," in *Mythologies,* ed. Yves Bonnefoy (Chicago: Uni-
> versity of Chicago Press, 1991), 2:893–95.

For references to the entire chapter, a chapter number, if available, may
replace page numbers; for example, "vol. 2, chap. 6."

14.126 *One volume in two or more books.* Occasionally, if it is very long, a single
volume of a multivolume work may be published as two or more physical
books. The reference must then include book as well as volume number.

> 39. Donald Lach, *Asia in the Making of Europe,* vol. 2, bk. 3, *The Scholarly Disci-
> plines* (Chicago: University of Chicago Press, 1977), 351.

Harley, J. B., and David Woodward, eds. *The History of Cartography.* Vol. 2, bk. 2,
Cartography in the Traditional East and Southeast Asian Societies. Chicago: Uni-
versity of Chicago Press, 1994.
or
Harley, J. B., and David Woodward, eds. *Cartography in the Traditional East and
Southeast Asian Societies.* Vol. 2, bk. 2, of *The History of Cartography.* Chicago:
University of Chicago Press, 1987–.

14.127 *Authors and editors of multivolume works.* Some multivolume works have
both a general editor and individual editors or authors for each volume.
When individual volumes are cited, the editor's (or translator's) name
follows that part for which he or she is responsible.

> 40. Herbert Barrows, *Reading the Short Story,* vol. 1 of *An Introduction to Liter-
> ature,* ed. Gordon N. Ray (Boston: Houghton Mifflin, 1959).

41. *The Variorum Edition of the Poetry of John Donne*, ed. Gary A. Stringer, vol. 6, *The "Anniversaries" and the "Epicedes and Obsequies,"* ed. Gary A. Stringer and Ted-Larry Pebworth (Bloomington: Indiana University Press, 1995).

42. *Orestes*, trans. William Arrowsmith, in *Euripides IV* (unnumbered vol.), in *The Complete Greek Tragedies*, ed. David Grene and Richmond Lattimore (Chicago: University of Chicago Press, 1958), 185–288.

Note the different capitalization and punctuation of *edited by* in the following alternative versions, analogous to the treatment of a chapter in a multiauthor book (see 14.112). (Certain multivolume works may, for bibliographical purposes, more conveniently be treated as series; see 14.130.)

Donne, John. *The Variorum Edition of the Poetry of John Donne*. Edited by Gary A. Stringer. Vol. 6, *"The Anniversaries" and the "Epicedes and Obsequies,"* edited by Gary A. Stringer and Ted-Larry Pebworth. Bloomington: Indiana University Press, 1995.

or

Donne, John. *The "Anniversaries" and the "Epicedes and Obsequies."* Edited by Gary A. Stringer and Ted-Larry Pebworth. Vol. 6 of *The Variorum Edition of the Poetry of John Donne*, edited by Gary A. Stringer. Bloomington: Indiana University Press, 1995.

Ray, Gordon N., ed. *An Introduction to Literature*. Vol. 1, *Reading the Short Story*, by Herbert Barrows. Boston: Houghton Mifflin, 1959.

or

Barrows, Herbert. *Reading the Short Story*. Vol. 1 of *An Introduction to Literature*, edited by Gordon N. Ray. Boston: Houghton Mifflin, 1959.

Series

14.128 *Series titles, numbers, and editors.* Including a series title in a citation often helps readers decide whether to pursue a reference. But if books belonging to a series can be located without the series title, it may be omitted to save space (especially in a footnote). If the series title is included, it is capitalized headline-style, but it is neither italicized nor put in quotation marks or parentheses. The series editor is usually omitted, but see 14.129, 14.130. Some series are numbered; many are not. The number (if any) follows the series title with no intervening comma unless *vol.* or *no.* is used. These abbreviations may be omitted, however, unless both are needed in a single reference (see last example below), or unless a series editor or other notation intervenes (see 14.130, third example). For a foreign-language series, use sentence style (see 11.3 and third example below).

1. Gershon David Hundert, *The Jews in a Polish Private Town: The Case of Opatów in the Eighteenth Century*, Johns Hopkins Jewish Studies (Baltimore: Johns Hopkins University Press, 1992).

Fowler, Melvin L. *The Cahokia Atlas: A Historical Atlas of Cahokia Archaeology.* Studies in Illinois Archaeology 6. Springfield: Illinois Historic Preservation Agency, 1989.

Grenier, Roger. *Les larmes d'Ulysse.* Collection l'un et l'autre. Paris: Gallimard, 1998.

Wauchope, Robert. *A Tentative Sequence of Pre-Classic Ceramics in Middle America.* Middle American Research Records, vol. 1, no. 14. New Orleans, LA: Tulane University, 1950.

14.129 *Series editor.* The name of the series editor is usually omitted. When included, it follows the series title.

Howell, Martha C. *The Marriage Exchange: Property, Social Place, and Gender in Cities of the Low Countries, 1300–1550.* Women in Culture and Society, edited by Catharine R. Stimpson. Chicago: University of Chicago Press, 1998.

14.130 *Series or multivolume work?* Certain works may be treated bibliographically either as a multivolume work or as a series of volumes, depending on whether the emphasis is on the group of books as a whole (as in the first two examples) or on single volumes (as in the second two).

Boyer, John W., and Julius Kirshner, eds. *Readings in Western Civilization.* 9 vols. Chicago: University of Chicago Press, 1986–87.

Grene, David, and Richmond Lattimore, eds. *The Complete Greek Tragedies.* 9 vols. (unnumbered). Chicago: University of Chicago Press, 1942–58.

Cochrane, Eric W., Charles K. Gray, and Mark Kishlansky. *Early Modern Europe: Crisis of Authority.* Readings in Western Civilization, edited by John W. Boyer and Julius Kirshner, vol. 6. Chicago: University of Chicago Press, 1987.

Euripides. *Orestes.* Translated by William Arrowsmith. In *Euripides IV,* edited by David Grene and Richmond Lattimore. The Complete Greek Tragedies. Chicago: University of Chicago Press, 1958.

14.131 *Multivolume work within a series.* If a book within a series consists of more than one volume, the number of volumes or the volume number (if reference is to a particular volume) follows the book title.

Ferrer Benimeli, José Antonio. *Masonería, iglesia e ilustración*. Vol. 1, *Las bases de un conflicto (1700–1739)*. Vol. 2, *Inquisición: Procesos históricos (1739–1750)*. Publicaciones de la Fundación Universitaria Española, Monografías 17. Madrid, 1976.

14.132 *"Old series" and "new series."* Some numbered series have gone on so long that, as with certain long-lived journals, numbering has started over again, preceded by *n.s.* (new series), *2nd ser.* (second series), or some similar notation, usually enclosed in commas. (A change of publisher may also be the occasion for a change in series designation.) Books in the old series may be identified by *o.s.*, *1st ser.*, or whatever complements the notation for the new series.

> 3. Charles R. Boxer, ed. *South China in the Sixteenth Century*, Hakluyt Society Publications, 2nd ser., vol. 106 (London: Hakluyt, 1953).

Palmatary, Helen C. *The Pottery of Marajó Island, Brazil*. Transactions of the American Philosophical Society, n.s., 39, pt. 3. Philadelphia: American Philosophical Society, 1950.

Facts of Publication

14.133 *Place, publisher, and date.* Traditionally the facts of publication for books include the place (city), the publisher, and the date (year). These elements are put in parentheses in a note but not in a bibliography. A colon appears between place and publisher. In a note or a bibliography, the date follows the publisher, preceded by a comma. See also 14.18.

> 1. E. M. Forster, *Howards End* (London: Edward Arnold, 1910).

Smith, Zadie. *On Beauty*. New York: Penguin Press, 2005.

PLACE OF PUBLICATION

14.134 *Place and date only, for books published before 1900.* For books published before 1900, it is acceptable to omit publishers' names and to include only the place and date of publication. A comma, not a colon, follows the place. See also 14.138, 14.143.

> 2. Oliver Goldsmith, *The Vicar of Wakefield* (Salisbury, 1766).

Cervantes Saavedra, Miguel de. *El ingenioso hidalgo Don Quixote de la Mancha*. 2 vols. Madrid, 1605–15.

14.135 *Place—city.* The place to be included is the one that usually appears on the title page but sometimes on the copyright page of the book cited—the city where the publisher's main editorial offices are located. Where two or more cities are given ("Chicago and London," for example, appears on the title page of the print edition of this manual), only the first is normally included in the documentation.

> Berkeley: University of California Press
> Los Angeles: J. Paul Getty Trust Publications
> New York: Macmillan
> New York: Oxford University Press
> Oxford: Clarendon Press

14.136 *When to specify state, province, or country.* If the city of publication may be unknown to readers or may be confused with another city of the same name, the abbreviation of the state, province, or (sometimes) country is usually added. *Washington* is traditionally followed by *DC*, but other major cities, such as Los Angeles and Baltimore, need no state abbreviation. (For countries not easily abbreviated, spell out the name.) Chicago's preference is for the two-letter postal codes (IL, MA, etc.), but some publishers continue to prefer the conventional state abbreviations (Ill., Mass., etc.). See 10.4, 10.28. For Canadian provinces and territories, see 10.29.

> Cambridge, MA: Harvard University Press
> Cambridge, MA: MIT Press
> Cheshire, CT: Graphics Press
> Englewood Cliffs, NJ: Prentice Hall
> Harmondsworth, UK: Penguin Books
> Ithaca, NY: Cornell University Press
> New Haven, CT: Yale University Press
> Princeton, NJ: Princeton University Press
> Reading, MA: Perseus Books
> Washington, DC: Smithsonian Institution Press
> Waterloo, ON: Wilfrid Laurier University Press
> *but*
> Cambridge: Cambridge University Press

When the publisher's name includes the state name, the abbreviation is not needed.

> Chapel Hill: University of North Carolina Press

14.137 *Foreign city names.* Current, commonly used English names for foreign cities should be used whenever such forms exist.

Belgrade (*not* Beograd)	Prague (*not* Praha)
Cologne (*not* Köln)	Rome (*not* Roma)
Mexico City (*not* México)	The Hague (*not* den Haag)
Milan (*not* Milano)	Turin (*not* Torino)
Munich (*not* München)	Vienna (*not* Wien)

14.138 *"No place."* For older works, when the place of publication is not known, the abbreviation *n.p.* (or *N.p.* if following a period) may be used before the publisher's name. If the place can be surmised, it may be given with a question mark, in brackets. See also 14.134.

(n.p.: Windsor, 1910)   ([Lake Bluff, IL?]: Vliet & Edwards, 1890)

PUBLISHER'S NAME

14.139 *Preferred form of publisher's name.* The publisher's name may be given either in full (e.g., as printed on the title page of the book) or in a somewhat abbreviated form. The shorter forms are preferred in most bibliographies (see 14.140). The form should, however, reflect the publisher's name at the date of publication, not the current name if the name has changed. Most publishers' names at the time of publication can be double-checked through any number of reputable sources, including the catalogs of the Library of Congress, WorldCat, and the *Books in Print* resources available through R. R. Bowker (see bibliog. 4.5). For reprint and other editions, see 14.118–20.

14.140 *Abbreviations and omissible parts of a publisher's name.* In notes and bibliography, an initial *The* is omitted from a publisher's name, as are such abbreviations as *Inc., Ltd.,* or *S.A.* following a name. *Co., & Co., Publishing Co.,* and the like are also omitted. Such corporate features of a publisher's name—often subject to many changes over the years—are far less important in leading a reader to the source consulted than the publication date, and attempting to include them will invariably lead to inconsistencies. A given name or initials preceding a family name, however, may be retained, as may terms such as *Sons, Brothers,* and so forth. *Books* is usually retained (Basic Books, Riverhead Books). The word *Press* can sometimes be omitted (for example, Pergamon Press and Ecco Press can be abbreviated to Pergamon and Ecco, but Free Press and New Press—whose names might be confusing without *Press*—must be given in full). *Press* should not be omitted from the name of a university press because the university itself may issue publications independent of its press. The word *University* may be abbreviated to *Univ.* if done consistently.

Houghton Mifflin *not* Houghton Mifflin Co.
Little, Brown *not* Little, Brown & Co.
Macmillan *not* Macmillan Publishing Co.

Note that there is no comma in Houghton Mifflin, but there is one in Little, Brown. Likewise, Harcourt, Brace has a comma, but Harcourt Brace Jovanovich does not. If in doubt, consult one of the sources mentioned in 14.139.

14.141 *"And" or ampersand in publisher's name.* Either *and* or & may be used in a publisher's name, regardless of how it is rendered on the title page. It is advisable to stick to one or the other throughout a bibliography. Unless an ampersand is used in a foreign publisher's name, the foreign word for *and* must be used.

Duncker und Humblot *or* Duncker & Humblot
Harper and Row *or* Harper & Row

14.142 *Foreign publishers' names.* No part of a foreign publisher's name should be translated, even though the city has been given in its English form.

Mexico City: Fondo de Cultura Económica, 1981
Munich: Delphin Verlag, 1983
Paris: Presses Universitaires de France, 1982

Note that abbreviations corresponding to *Inc.* or *Ltd.* (German *GmbH,* for example) are omitted (see 14.140). Capitalization of a publisher's name should follow the original unless the name appears in full capitals there; in that case, it should be capitalized headline-style; if in doubt about the correct capitalization, consult one of the sources mentioned in 14.139.

14.143 *Publisher unknown or work privately published.* When the publisher is unknown, use just the place (if known) and date (see 14.134). Privately printed works should be cited with as much information as is known (e.g., Topeka, KS: privately printed, 1890 *or, if applicable,* Topeka, KS: printed by author, 1890).

14.144 *Parent companies, imprints, and such.* When a parent company's name appears on the title page in addition to the publisher's name or imprint, only the latter need be used in a bibliographical listing (but see 14.146).

For example, the title page of a 1995 edition of *Old New York: Four Novellas*, by Edith Wharton, bears the imprint "Scribner Paperback Fiction"; below that appears "Published by Simon & Schuster." (The cities listed are New York, London, Toronto, and Sydney.) The spine carries "Scribner Paperback Fiction" (but not Simon & Schuster). The copyright page gives an address for Simon & Schuster and further explains that (for the time being) Scribner Paperback Fiction is a trademark of Macmillan Library Reference USA. Such complex arrangements are common in book publishing. Cite the work as follows:

Wharton, Edith. *Old New York: Four Novellas*. New York: Scribner Paperback Fiction, 1995.

If it is not clear which name to list, check with one of the catalogs listed in 14.139 to see which publisher is listed there, being careful to find the entry in the catalog that matches the facts of publication for the item in question. If this is not possible, or if it remains unclear which name to list, include both, separated by a slash (/) with a space on either side.

14.145 *Joint imprint.* For books published jointly by a consortium and an individual member, the name of the consortium may be followed by that of the member, the two names separated by a slash (with space either side). (To save space, however, it is acceptable to list only the name of the consortium.)

MacDougall, Pauleena. *The Penobscot Dance of Resistance: Tradition in the History of a People*. Hanover, NH: University Press of New England / University of New Hampshire Press, 2004.

14.146 *Special academic imprint.* Some academic publishers issue certain books through a special publishing division or under a special imprint. In such instances the imprint may be given after the publisher's name, separated by a slash (with space on either side).

Gray, Jason. *Photographing Eden: Poems*. Athens: Ohio University Press / Swallow Press, 2008.

In some cases, however, the wording of such an imprint should conform to language specified by the publisher (on the title page or elsewhere).

Buell, Lawrence. *Emerson*. Cambridge, MA: Belknap Press of Harvard University Press, 2003.

14.147 *Copublication.* When books are published simultaneously (or almost so) by two publishers, usually in different countries, only one publisher need be listed—the one that is more relevant to the users of the citation. For example, if a book copublished by a British and an American publisher is listed in the bibliography of an American publication, only the American publication details need be given. If for some reason (e.g., as a matter of historical interest), information is included for both publishers, a semicolon should be used as a separator. (Occasionally, the dates of publication will be different; in such cases, record both.) For reprints, see 14.119.

> Lévi-Strauss, Claude. *The Savage Mind.* Chicago: University of Chicago Press; London: Weidenfeld and Nicolson, 1962.

14.148 *Distributed books.* For a book published by one company and distributed by another, the name on the title page should be used. Since distribution agreements are sometimes impermanent, the distributor's name is best omitted unless essential to users of a bibliography.

> Willke, Helmut. *Smart Governance: Governing the Global Knowledge Society.* Frankfurt am Main: Campus Verlag, 2007. Distributed by University of Chicago Press.

Wording on the title page such as "Published by arrangement with . . . ," if it is of particular interest, may be included in a similar manner.

DATE OF PUBLICATION

14.149 *Publication date—general.* For books, only the year, not the month or day, is included in the publication date. The date is found on the title page or, more commonly, on the copyright page. It is usually the same as the copyright date. If two or more copyright dates appear in a book, the first being those of earlier editions or versions, the most recent indicates the publication date. Chicago's books normally carry both copyright date and publication date on the copyright page. For any edition other than the first, both the edition and the date of that edition must be included in a listing (see 14.118–20).

> 14. *The Chicago Manual of Style,* 16th ed. (Chicago: University of Chicago Press, 2010), 7.85; cf. 15th ed. (2003), 7.90.

> Turabian, Kate L. *A Manual for Writers of Term Papers, Theses, and Dissertations.* 7th ed. Revised by Wayne C. Booth, Gregory G. Colomb, and Joseph M. Williams. Chicago: University of Chicago Press, 2007.

14.150   *New impressions and renewal of copyright.* The publication date must not be confused with the date of a subsequent printing or a renewal of copyright. Such statements on the copyright page as "53rd impression" or "Copyright renewed 1980" should be disregarded. For new editions as opposed to new impressions, see 1.26; for reprints, see 14.119.

14.151   *Multivolume works published over more than one year.* When an entire multivolume, multiyear work is cited, the range of dates is given (see 6.78). If the work has not yet been completed, the date of the first volume is followed by an en dash (with no space between the en dash and the punctuation that follows; see 6.79). See also 9.63. If a single volume is cited, only the date of that volume need appear. See also 14.121–27.

> 78. *The Collected Works of F. A. Hayek*, vol. 9, *Contra Keynes and Cambridge: Essays, Correspondence* (Chicago: University of Chicago Press, 1995), 44–45.

Hayek, F. A. *Contra Keynes and Cambridge: Essays, Correspondence.* Vol. 9 of *The Collected Works of F. A. Hayek.* Chicago: University of Chicago Press, 1988–.
Tillich, Paul. *Systematic Theology.* 3 vols. Chicago: University of Chicago Press, 1951–63.

14.152   *"No date."* When the publication date of a printed work cannot be ascertained, the abbreviation *n.d.* takes the place of the year in the publication details. A guessed-at date may either be substituted (in brackets) or added. See also 14.138.

Boston, n.d.
Edinburgh, [1750?] *or* Edinburgh, n.d., ca. 1750

A work for which no publisher, place, or date can be determined or reasonably guessed at should be included in a bibliography only if accompanied by the location where a copy can be found (e.g., "Two copies in the Special Collections Department of the University of Chicago Library").

14.153   *"Forthcoming."* When a book is under contract with a publisher and is already titled, but the date of publication is not yet known, *forthcoming* is used in place of the date. Although *in press* is sometimes used (strictly speaking for a printed work that has already been typeset and paginated), Chicago recommends the more inclusive term, which can also be used for nonprint media, for any work under contract. If page numbers are available, they should be given. Books not under contract are treated as unpublished manuscripts (see 14.224–46).

91. Jane Q. Author, *Book Title* (Place: Publisher, forthcoming).

92. John J. Writer, *Another Book Title* (Place: Publisher, forthcoming), 345–46.

Contributor, Anna. "Contribution." In *Edited Volume*, edited by Ellen Editor. Place: Publisher, forthcoming.

When a publication that cites a forthcoming title is reprinted, the citation need not be updated. For a revised edition, on the other hand, the citation can be updated to provide the final facts of publication, but only after direct quotations and other details have been checked for accuracy against the published source.

Page, Volume, and Other Locating Information

14.154   *Arabic versus roman numerals.* As the examples throughout this chapter (and chapter 15) suggest, arabic numerals should be used wherever possible in documentation—for volumes, chapters, and other divisions—regardless of the way the numerals appear in the works cited, with the notable exception of pages numbered with roman numerals in the original (usually lowercased, in the front matter of a book). Occasional exceptions are made, for example, in certain legal contexts (see 14.292).

21. See the article "Feathers," in *Johnson's Universal Cyclopaedia*, rev. ed. (New York: A. J. Johnson, 1886), vol. 3.

22. Jerome Kagan, "Introduction to the Tenth-Anniversary Edition," in *The Nature of the Child* (New York: Basic Books, 1994), xxii–xxiv.

14.155   *Ranges, or inclusive numbers.* For Chicago's preferred style in expressing a range of pages, paragraphs, or similar divisions, see 9.60. First and last numbers should be used rather than first number plus *ff.* (but see 14.156).

Chicago Manual of Style, 16th ed., 14.154–65.

14.156   *Using or avoiding "ff." and "passim."* Only when referring to a section for which no final number can usefully be given should *ff.* ("and the following pages, paragraphs, etc.") be resorted to. Instead of the singular *f.*, the subsequent number should be used (e.g., "140–41" not "140f."). Similarly, *passim* ("here and there") is to be discouraged unless it follows a stated range of pages within which there are more than three or four precise references ("324–32 passim"). When used, *ff.* has no space between it and the preceding number and is followed by a period; *passim*, being a complete word, takes no period. Neither is italicized. (For *passim* in indexes, see 16.13.)

14.157 *Abbreviations for "page," "volume," and so on.* In citations, the words *page*, *volume*, and the like are usually abbreviated and often simply omitted (see 14.158). The most commonly used abbreviations are *p.* (pl. *pp.*), *vol.*, *pt.*, *chap.*, *bk.*, *sec.*, *n.* (pl. *nn.*), *no.*, *app.*, and *fig.*; for these and others, see chapter 10, especially 10.43. Unless following a period, all are lowercased, and none is italicized unless an integral part of an italicized book title. All the abbreviations mentioned in this paragraph, except for *p.* and *n.*, form their plurals by adding *s*.

A Cry of Absence, chap. 6   A Dance to the Music of Time, 4 vols.

14.158 *When to omit "p." and "pp."* When a number or a range of numbers clearly denotes the pages in a book, *p.* or *pp.* may be omitted; the numbers alone, preceded by a comma, are sufficient. Where the presence of other numerals threatens ambiguity, *p.* or *pp.* may be added for clarity. (And if an author has used *p.* and *pp.* consistently throughout a work, there is no need to delete them.) See also 14.159.

Charlotte's Web, 75–76
but
Complete Poems of Michelangelo, p. 89, lines 135–36

14.159 *When to omit "vol."* When a volume number is followed immediately by a page number, neither *vol.* nor *p.* or *pp.* is needed. The numbers alone are used, separated by a colon. A comma usually precedes the volume number, except with periodicals (see 14.180; see also 14.181) and for certain types of classical references (see 14.256–66). For more on volume numbers, see 14.121–27. For citing a particular volume, with and without the abbreviation *vol.*, see 14.123.

The Complete Tales of Henry James, 10:122

14.160 *Page and chapter numbers.* Page numbers, needed for specific references in notes and parenthetical text citations, are usually unnecessary in bibliographies except when the piece cited is a part within a whole (see 14.111–17) or a journal article (see 14.183). If the chapter or other section number is given, page numbers may be omitted. The total page count of a book is not included in documentation. (Total page counts do, however, appear in headings to book reviews, catalog entries, and elsewhere. For book review headings, see 1.92.)

14. Claire Kehrwald Cook, "Mismanaged Numbers and References," in *Line by Line: How to Edit Your Own Writing* (Boston: Houghton Mifflin, 1985), 75–107.

15. Nuala O'Faolain, *Are You Somebody? The Accidental Memoir of a Dublin Woman* (New York: Holt, 1996), chap. 17.

14.161   *Signed signatures.* Some books printed before 1800 did not carry page numbers, but each signature (a group of consecutive pages) bore a letter, numeral, or other symbol (its "signature") to help the binder gather them in correct sequence. In citing pages in books of this kind, the signature symbol is given first, then the number of the leaf within the signature, and finally r (*recto*, the front of the leaf) or v (*verso*, the back of the leaf). Thus, for example, G6v identifies one page, G6r–7v a range of four pages.

14.162   *Folio editions.* In some early books the signatures consisted of folios—one large sheet folded once. Each folio thus had two sheets, or four pages. The sheets were numbered only on the front, or recto, side. Page citation therefore consists of sheet number plus r (*recto*) or v (*verso*)—for example, 176r, 231v, 232r–v; or, if entire folios are cited, fol. 49, fols. 50–53. See also 14.161, 14.236.

14.163   *Line numbers.* The abbreviations *l.* (line) and *ll.* (lines) can too easily be confused with the numerals 1 and 11 and so should be avoided. *Line* or *lines* should be used or, where it has been made clear that reference is to lines, simply omitted (see 13.65).

44. Ogden Nash, "Song for Ditherers," lines 1–4.

14.164   *Citing numbered notes.* Notes are cited with the abbreviation n or nn. The usage recommended here is also used for indexes (see 16.111, 16.112, 16.113). If the note cited is the only footnote on a particular page or is an unnumbered footnote, the page number is followed by n alone.

45. Anthony Grafton, *The Footnote: A Curious History* (Cambridge, MA: Harvard University Press, 1997), 72n, 80n.

If there are other notes on the same page as the note cited, a number must be added. In this case the page number is followed by n or (if two or more consecutive notes are cited) nn, followed by the note number (or numbers or, in rare cases, an asterisk or other symbol). No intervening space or punctuation is required.

46. Dwight Bolinger, *Language: The Loaded Weapon* (London: Longman, 1980), 192n23, 192n30, 199n14, 201nn16–17.
47. Richard Rorty, *Philosophical Papers* (New York: Cambridge University Press, 1991), 1:15n29.

14.165 *Citing illustrations and tables.* The abbreviation *fig.* may be used for *figure*, but *table, map, plate,* and other illustration forms are spelled out. The page number, if given, precedes the illustration number, with a comma between them.

50. Richard Sobel, ed., *Public Opinion in US Foreign Policy: The Controversy over Contra Aid* (Boston: Rowman and Littlefield, 1993), 87, table 5.3.

Electronic Books

14.166 *Books downloaded from a library or bookseller.* The majority of electronically published books offered for download from a library or bookseller will have a printed counterpart. Because of the potential for differences, however, authors must indicate that they have consulted a format other than print. This indication should be the *last* part of a full citation that follows the recommendations for citing printed books as detailed throughout this section. See also 14.4–13.

Austen, Jane. *Pride and Prejudice.* New York: Penguin Classics, 2007. Kindle edition.
Austen, Jane. *Pride and Prejudice.* New York: Penguin Classics, 2008. PDF e-book.
Austen, Jane. *Pride and Prejudice.* New York: Penguin Classics, 2008. Microsoft Reader e-book.
Austen, Jane. *Pride and Prejudice.* New York: Penguin Classics, 2008. Palm e-book.

The printed counterpart to the Penguin Classics e-book offerings would be cited as follows (note the different publication date):

Austen, Jane. *Pride and Prejudice.* New York: Penguin Classics, 2003.

Each of the Penguin Classics editions (as the books' documentation makes clear) is based on the 1813 edition published by T. Egerton. Though such information is optional, it may be included as follows (see 14.119):

Austen, Jane. *Pride and Prejudice*. London: T. Egerton, 1813. Reprint, New York: Penguin Classics, 2008. PDF e-book.

Note that electronic formats do not always carry stable page numbers (e.g., pagination may depend on text size), a factor that potentially limits their suitability as sources. In lieu of a page number, include an indication of chapter or section or other locator. See also 14.17.

> 1. Jane Austen, *Pride and Prejudice* (New York: Penguin Classics, 2008), Microsoft Reader e-book, chap. 23.
> 14. Austen, *Pride and Prejudice*, chap. 24.

14.167   *Books consulted online.* When citing the online version of a book, include the URL—or, if available, DOI—as part of the citation (see 14.5, 14.6). The URL or DOI should be the *last* part of a full citation based on the principles outlined throughout this section on citing books. Note the reference to section headings in lieu of page numbers in notes 2 and 4 (see 14.17).

> 1. Elliot Antokoletz, *Musical Symbolism in the Operas of Debussy and Bartók* (New York: Oxford University Press, 2008), doi:10.1093/acprof:oso/9780195365825 .001.0001.
> 2. Joseph Sirosh, Risto Miikkulainen, and James A. Bednar, "Self-Organization of Orientation Maps, Lateral Connections, and Dynamic Receptive Fields in the Primary Visual Cortex," in *Lateral Interactions in the Cortex: Structure and Function*, ed. Joseph Sirosh, Risto Miikkulainen, and Yoonsuck Choe (Austin, TX: UTCS Neural Networks Research Group, 1996), under "Dynamic Receptive Fields," http://nn.cs .utexas.edu/web-pubs/htmlbook96/.
> 3. Antokoletz, *Musical Symbolism*.
> 4. Sirosh, Miikkulainen, and Bednar, "Self-Organization of Orientation Maps," under "Conclusion."

Antokoletz, Elliot. *Musical Symbolism in the Operas of Debussy and Bartók*. New York: Oxford University Press, 2008. doi:10.1093/acprof:oso/9780195365825 .001.0001.

Sirosh, Joseph, Risto Miikkulainen, and James A. Bednar. "Self-Organization of Orientation Maps, Lateral Connections, and Dynamic Receptive Fields in the Primary Visual Cortex." In *Lateral Interactions in the Cortex: Structure and Function*, edited by Joseph Sirosh, Risto Miikkulainen, and Yoonsuck Choe. Austin, TX: UTCS Neural Networks Research Group, 1996. http://nn.cs.utexas.edu /web-pubs/htmlbook96/.

14.168   *Books on CD-ROM and other fixed media.* Citations of books on CD-ROM and other fixed media should carry an indication of the medium.

1. *The Chicago Manual of Style*, 15th ed. (Chicago: University of Chicago Press, 2003), CD-ROM, 1.4.

Hicks, Rodney J. *Nuclear Medicine: From the Center of Our Universe*. Victoria, Austral.: ICE T Multimedia, 1996. CD-ROM.

14.169 *Freely available electronic editions of older works.* Books and other documents that have fallen out of copyright are often freely available online. Such sources, while convenient, are not necessarily authoritative. It may not be possible to tell, for example, which edition was used to prepare the online text. When such information about a text is *not* available—and even when it is—consider consulting a printed edition. In the James example below, Project Gutenberg notes that their text is based on the 1909 New York edition of *The Ambassadors* (see 14.119). For the Whitman example, though electronic page images of the first edition (discoloration and all) were consulted—amounting, in a way, to having consulted the printed book without having handled it—it is still advisable to include a URL. See also 14.17.

1. Walt Whitman, *Leaves of Grass* (New York, 1855), 22, http://www.whitman archive.org/published/LG/1855/whole.html.
2. Henry James, *The Ambassadors* (1909; Project Gutenberg, 1996), bk. 6, chap. 1, ftp://ibiblio.org/pub/docs/books/gutenberg/etext96/ambas10.txt.

James, Henry. *The Ambassadors*. Reprint of the 1909 New York edition, Project Gutenberg, 1996. ftp://ibiblio.org/pub/docs/books/gutenberg/etext96 /ambas10.txt.
Whitman, Walt. *Leaves of Grass*. New York, 1855. http://www.whitmanarchive.org /published/LG/1855/whole.html.

Note that there is no place of publication in the James note example. Such information is less likely to accompany online works, and it may be dispensed with without the use of "n.p." (for "no place") when it cannot be readily determined.

Periodicals

14.170 *"Periodicals" defined.* The word *periodical* is used here to include scholarly and professional journals, popular magazines, and newspapers. Periodicals are far more likely than books to be consulted in electronic form. Except for the addition of a URL or DOI, the citation of an online periodical is the same as that recommended for printed periodicals. (Some publishers may also require access dates for sources consulted online.) See examples of such information, and special considerations, under specific types of periodicals. See also 14.4–13.

14.171   *Information to be included.* Citations of periodicals require some or all of the following data:

1. Full name(s) of author or authors
2. Title and subtitle of article or column
3. Title of periodical
4. Issue information (volume, issue number, date, etc.)
5. Page reference (where appropriate)
6. For online periodicals, a URL or, if available, a DOI (see 14.5, 14.6, 14.184)

Indispensable for newspapers and most magazines is the specific date (month, day, and year). For journals, the volume and year plus the month or issue number are usually cited. Additional data make location easier. See also 14.70.

14.172   *Journals versus magazines.* In this manual, *journal* is used for scholarly or professional periodicals available mainly by subscription (e.g., *Library Quarterly*, *Journal of the American Medical Association*). Journals are normally cited by volume and date (see 14.180). *Magazine* is used here for the kind of weekly or monthly periodical—professionally produced, sometimes specialized, but more accessible to general readers—that is available either by subscription or in individual issues at bookstores or newsstands or online (e.g., *Scientific American*, the *New Yorker*). Magazines are normally cited by date alone (see 14.199). If in doubt whether a particular periodical is better treated as a journal or as a magazine, use journal form if the volume number is easily located, magazine form if it is not.

14.173   *Punctuation in periodical citations.* In notes, commas appear between author; title of article; title of magazine, newspaper, or journal; and URL or DOI (for sources consulted online). In bibliographies, periods replace these commas. For more examples, see 14.18 and elsewhere in this chapter. Note that *in* is *not* used between the article title and the journal title. (*In* is used only with chapters or other parts of books; see 14.111, 14.112.)

1. Hope A. Olson, "Codes, Costs, and Critiques: The Organization of Information in *Library Quarterly*, 1931–2004," *Library Quarterly* 76, no. 1 (2006): 20, doi: 10.1086/504343.
34. Olson, "Codes, Costs, and Critiques," 22–23.

Olson, Hope A. "Codes, Costs, and Critiques: The Organization of Information in *Library Quarterly*, 1931–2004." *Library Quarterly* 76, no. 1 (2006): 19–35. doi:10.1086/504343.

14.174 *Page numbers in periodical citations.* In bibliography entries, the first and last pages of an article are given (for inclusive numbers, see 9.58, 9.60). In notes and text citations, only specific pages need be cited (unless the article as a whole is referred to). In some electronic formats, page numbers will be unavailable, in which case a section heading or other locator may be appropriate (see 14.17).

Journals

14.175 *Journal article—author's name.* Authors' names are normally given as they appear at the heads of their articles. Adjustments can be made, however, as indicated in 14.72. Most of the guidelines offered in 14.72–92 apply equally to authors of journal articles. For the treatment of two or more authors, see 14.76.

14.176 *Journal article—title.* Titles of articles are set in roman (except for words or phrases that require italics, such as species names or book titles; see 14.177); they are usually capitalized headline-style and put in quotation marks. As with a book, title and subtitle are separated by a colon. See also 8.154–95. For examples, see 14.18 and the paragraphs below. For shortened forms of article titles, see 14.196.

Menjívar, Cecilia. "Liminal Legality: Salvadoran and Guatemalan Immigrants' Lives in the United States." *American Journal of Sociology* 111, no. 4 (2006): 999–1037. doi:10.1086/499509.

14.177 *Italics and quotation marks within article titles.* Book titles and other normally italicized terms remain italicized within an article title. A term normally quoted is enclosed in single quotation marks (since it is already within double quotation marks). Retain both double and single quotation marks, if any, in short citations. See also 8.163, 8.175.

23. Judith Lewis, "'Tis a Misfortune to Be a Great Ladie': Maternal Mortality in the British Aristocracy, 1558–1959," *Journal of British Studies* 37, no. 1 (1998): 26–53, http://www.jstor.org/stable/176034.

44. Lewis, "'Tis a Misfortune to Be a Great Ladie,'" 32.

Loften, Peter. "Reverberations between Wordplay and Swordplay in *Hamlet.*" *Aeolian Studies* 2 (1989): 12–29.

14.178 *Question marks or exclamation points in article titles.* As with book titles (see 14.105), when a main title ends with a question mark or an exclamation point, no colon is added before any subtitle unless the question mark or exclamation point is followed by a closing quotation mark (as in the third example). Note the comma before the page number in the shortened citations (second and fourth examples). This departure from Chicago's former usage aids readability and consistency; see 6.119.

> 1. C. Daniel Batson, "How Social Is the Animal? The Human Capacity for Caring," *American Psychologist* 45 (March 1990): 336.
> 2. Batson, "How Social Is the Animal?," 337.
> 3. Daniel Bertrand Monk, "'Welcome to Crisis!': Notes for a Pictorial History of the Pictorial Histories of the Arab Israeli War of June 1967," *Grey Room* 7 (Spring 2002): 139, http://www.jstor.org/stable/1262596.
> 4. Monk, "'Welcome to Crisis!,'" 140.

When a title ending with a question mark or an exclamation mark would normally be followed by a period, however, the period is omitted; see 6.118.

Abrams, Marshall. "How Do Natural Selection and Random Drift Interact?" *Philosophy of Science* 74 (December 2007): 666–79. doi:10.1086/525612.

14.179 *Title of journal.* Titles of journals are italicized and capitalized headline-style. They are usually given in full—except for the omission of an initial *The*—in notes and bibliographies (e.g., *Journal of Business*). With foreign-language journals and magazines, an initial article should be retained (e.g., *Der Spiegel*). Occasionally an initialism, such as *PMLA*, is the official title and is never spelled out. In some disciplines, especially in science and medicine, journal titles are routinely abbreviated (e.g., *Plant Syst Evol*), unless they consist of only one word (e.g., *Science, Mind*); see 15.44. Chicago recommends giving titles in full unless a particular publisher or discipline requires otherwise.

14.180 *Journal volume, issue, and date.* Most journal citations include volume, issue number or month, and year. The volume number, set in roman, follows the title without intervening punctuation; arabic numerals are used even if the journal itself uses roman numerals. The issue number may be omitted if pagination is continuous throughout a volume or when a month or season precedes the year. Nonetheless, it is never wrong to include the issue number, and doing so can be a hedge against other errors. When the issue number is given, it follows the volume number, separated by a comma and preceded by *no*. The year, sometimes preceded by an exact date, a month, or a season, appears in parentheses after the volume number (or issue number, if given). Seasons, though not capitalized in running text (see 8.87), are capitalized in source citations. Months may be abbreviated or spelled in full (as here); seasons are best spelled out (see also 10.40). Neither month nor season is necessary when the issue number is given, though it is never incorrect to include it.

2. David Meban, "Temple Building, *Primus* Language, and the Proem to Virgil's Third *Georgic*," *Classical Philology* 103, no. 2 (2008): 153, doi:10.1086/591611.

18. Jeanette Kennett, "True and Proper Selves: Velleman on Love," *Ethics* 118 (January 2008): 215, doi:10.1086/523747.

23. Boyan Jovanovic and Peter L. Rousseau, "Specific Capital and Technological Variety," *Journal of Human Capital* 2 (Summer 2008): 135, doi:10.1086/590066.

Jovanovic, Boyan, and Peter L. Rousseau. "Specific Capital and Technological Variety." *Journal of Human Capital* 2 (Summer 2008): 129–52. doi:10.1086/590066.

Kennett, Jeanette. "True and Proper Selves: Velleman on Love." *Ethics* 118 (January 2008): 213–27. doi:10.1086/523747.

Meban, David. "Temple Building, *Primus* Language, and the Proem to Virgil's Third *Georgic*." *Classical Philology* 103, no. 2 (2008): 150–74. doi:10.1086/591611.

Where a span of months or seasons is given, use an en dash (e.g., September–December 2010); consecutive months are sometimes indicated by a slash (March/April).

1. Dean Amadon, "Ecology and the Evolution of Some Hawaiian Birds," *Evolution* 1 (March–June 1947): 65–66, http://www.jstor.org/stable/2405404.

14.181 *No volume number or date only.* When a journal uses issue numbers only, without volume numbers, a comma follows the journal title.

Beattie, J. M. "The Pattern of Crime in England, 1660–1800." *Past and Present*, no. 62 (1974): 47–95.

When only a date is available, it becomes an indispensable element and should therefore not be enclosed in parentheses; a comma follows the journal title and the date.

Saberhagen, Kelvin. "Lake Superior Beluga?" *Sturgeon Review*, Winter 1928, 21–45.

14.182   *Forthcoming articles.* If an article has been accepted for publication by a journal but has not yet appeared, *forthcoming* stands in place of the year and the page numbers. Any article not yet accepted should be treated as an unpublished manuscript (see 14.228).

> 4. Margaret M. Author, "Article Title," *Journal Name* 98 (forthcoming).

> Author, Margaret M. "Article Title." *Journal Name* 98 (forthcoming).

If an article is published by a journal electronically ahead of the official publication date, use the posted publication date. In such cases, information about pagination may not yet be available.

> Black, Steven. "Changing Epidemiology of Invasive Pneumococcal Disease: A Complicated Story." *Clinical Infectious Diseases* 47. Published electronically July 14, 2008. doi:10.1086/590002.

14.183   *Journal page references.* In citing a particular passage in a journal article, only the pages concerned are given. In references to the article as a whole (as in a bibliography), first and last pages are given.

> 4. Paul Thompson, "Democracy and Popular Power in Beijing," *Radical America* 22 (September–October 1988): 22.

> Gold, Ann Grodzins. "Grains of Truth: Shifting Hierarchies of Food and Grace in Three Rajasthani Tales." *History of Religions* 38, no. 2 (1998): 150–71.

Most electronic journals provide page numbers. Where this is not the case, another type of locator such as a subheading may become appropriate in a note. None, however, is required. See also 14.17.

> 15. Jamison, Shelly, "I(nternet) Do(mains): The New Rules of Selection," *Culture Critique* 3, no. 5 (2009), under "Park Avenue Revisited."

14.184   *Electronic journal articles—URL or DOI.* Many of the examples in this section include a URL or a DOI at the end of the citation. A DOI, if it is available, is preferable to a URL. If using a URL, use the address that appears in your browser's address bar when viewing the article (or the abstract) unless a shorter, more stable form of the URL is offered along with the electronic article. Note that a single DOI assigned to a journal article as a whole applies to that article in any medium, print or electronic. Nonetheless, unless their publisher or discipline requires otherwise, authors need only include an article's DOI to indicate that an electronic version was cited. (Because the DOI points to all available formats simultaneously, it is not necessary to specify *which* electronic format was cited—e.g., PDF or HTML.) See also 14.4–13.

> 4. Frank P. Whitney, "The Six-Year High School in Cleveland," *School Review* 37, no. 4 (1929): 268, http://www.jstor.org/stable/1078814.
> 5. María de la Luz Inclán, "From the ¡*Ya Basta!* to the *Caracoles*: Zapatista Mobilization under Transitional Conditions," *American Journal of Sociology* 113, no. 5 (2008): 1318, doi:10.1086/525508.

> Inclán, María de la Luz. "From the ¡*Ya Basta!* to the *Caracoles*: Zapatista Mobilization under Transitional Conditions." *American Journal of Sociology* 113, no. 5 (2008): 1316–50. doi:10.1086/525508.
> Whitney, Frank P. "The Six-Year High School in Cleveland." *School Review* 37, no. 4 (1929): 267–71. http://www.jstor.org/stable/1078814.

14.185 *Electronic journal articles—access dates.* Access dates are not required by Chicago in citations of formally published electronic sources, for the reasons discussed in 14.7. Some publishers and some disciplines, however, may require them. When they are included, they should immediately precede the DOI or URL, separated from the surrounding citation by commas in a note and periods in a bibliography entry. This departure from Chicago's earlier recommendation recognizes the increasing importance of uniform placement of URLs and DOIs in source citations.

> 1. Patrick G. P. Charles et al., "SMART-COP: A Tool for Predicting the Need for Intensive Respiratory or Vasopressor Support in Community-Acquired Pneumonia," *Clinical Infectious Diseases* 47 (August 1, 2008): 377, accessed July 17, 2008, doi:10.1086/589754.
> 3. Charles et al., "SMART-COP," 378–79.

> Charles, Patrick G. P., Rory Wolfe, Michael Whitby, Michael J. Fine, Andrew J. Fuller, Robert Stirling, Alistair A. Wright, et al. "SMART-COP: A Tool for Predicting the Need for Intensive Respiratory or Vasopressor Support in Community-Acquired Pneumonia." *Clinical Infectious Diseases* 47 (August 1, 2008): 375–84. Accessed July 17, 2008. doi:10.1086/589754.

For citing articles credited to more than ten authors, see 14.76.

14.186 *Article page numbers in relation to volume or issue numbers.* When page numbers immediately follow a volume number, separated only by a colon, no space follows the colon. But when parenthetical information intervenes, a space follows the colon. (This rule applies to other types of volumes as well; see, e.g., 14.121.)

Social Networks 14:213–29
Critical Inquiry 19 (Autumn): 164–85

When, as occasionally happens, the page number follows an issue number, a comma—not a colon—should be used.

Diogenes, no. 25, 84–117.

14.187 **Special issues.** A journal issue (occasionally a double issue) devoted to a single theme is known as a special issue. It carries the normal volume and issue number (or numbers if a double issue). Such an issue may have an editor and a title of its own. An article within the issue is cited as in the first example; a special issue as a whole may be cited as in the second example.

> 42. Sharon Sassler, "Learning to Be an 'American Lady'? Ethnic Variation in Daughters' Pursuits in the Early 1900s," in "Emergent and Reconfigured Forms of Family Life," ed. Lora Bex Lempert and Marjorie L. DeVault, special issue, *Gender and Society* 14, no. 1 (2000): 201–2, http://www.jstor.org/stable/190427.

> Good, Thomas L., ed. "Non-Subject-Matter Outcomes of Schooling." Special issue, *Elementary School Journal* 99, no. 5 (1999).

14.188 **Supplements.** A journal supplement, unlike a special issue (see 14.187), is numbered separately from the regular issues of the journal. Like a special issue, however, it may have a title and author or editor of its own.

> MacDonald, Glenn, and Michael S. Weisbach. "The Economics of Has-Beens." In "Papers in Honor of Sherwin Rosen," supplement, *Journal of Political Economy* 112, no. S1 (2004): S289–S310. doi:10.1086/380948.

14.189 **Articles published in installments.** Articles published in parts over two or more issues may be listed separately or in the same entry, depending on whether the part or the whole is cited.

> 68. George C. Brown, ed., "A Swedish Traveler in Early Wisconsin: The Observations of Fredrika Bremer," pt. 1, *Wisconsin Magazine of History* 61 (Summer 1978): 312.
> 69. Ibid., pt. 2, *Wisconsin Magazine of History* 62 (Autumn 1978): 50.

Brown, George C., ed. "A Swedish Traveler in Early Wisconsin: The Observations of Fredrika Bremer." Pts. 1 and 2. *Wisconsin Magazine of History* 61 (Summer 1978): 300–318; 62 (Autumn 1978): 41–56.

14.190 *Article appearing in two publications.* Chapters in books have sometimes begun their lives as journal articles, or vice versa. Revisions are often made along the way. The version actually consulted should be cited in a note or text citation, but annotation such as the following, if of specific interest to readers, may follow the citation. See also 14.49.

Previously published as "Article Title," *Journal Title* 20, no. 3 (2009): 345–62.

A slightly revised version appears in *Book Title*, ed. E. Editor (Place: Publisher, 2010), 15–30.

14.191 *Place where journal is published.* If a journal might be confused with another with a similar title, or if it might not be known to the users of a bibliography, add the name of the place or institution where it is published in parentheses after the journal title.

87. Diane-Dinh Kim Luu, "Diethylstilbestrol and Media Coverage of the 'Morning After' Pill," *Lost in Thought: Undergraduate Research Journal* (Indiana University South Bend) 2 (1999): 65–70.

Garrett, Marvin P. "Language and Design in *Pippa Passes*." *Victorian Poetry* (West Virginia University) 13, no. 1 (1975): 47–60.

14.192 *Translated or edited article.* A translated or edited article follows essentially the same style as a translated or edited book (see 14.87, 14.88).

1. Arthur Q. Author, "Article Title," trans. So-and-So, *Journal Title* . . .

Author, Arthur Q. "Article Title." Edited by So-and-So. *Journal Title* . . .

14.193 *Foreign-language article and journal titles.* Titles of foreign-language articles, like foreign book titles, are usually capitalized sentence-style (see 8.156) but according to the conventions of the particular language (see 14.107). German, for example, capitalizes common nouns in running text as well as in titles (see 11.42). Journal titles may either be treated the same way or, if an author has done so consistently, be capitalized headline-style. An initial definite article (*Le, Der,* etc.) should be retained, since it may govern the inflection of the following word. Months and the equivalents of such abbreviations as *no.* or *pt.* are usually given in English (but see 14.71).

> 22. Dinda L. Gorlée, "¡Eureka! La traducción como un descubrimiento pragmático," *Anuario filosófico* 29, no. 3 (1996): 1403.
> 23. Marcel Garaud, "Recherches sur les défrichements dans la Gâtine poitevine aux XIᵉ et XIIᵉ siècles," *Bulletin de la Société des antiquaires de l'Ouest*, 4th ser., 9 (1967): 11–27.

Note the capitalization of *Société* (the first word of an organization name) and *Ouest* (the West). Headline-style capitalization of the two journal titles would call for *Anuario Filosófico* and *Bulletin de la Société des Antiquaires de l'Ouest*.

14.194   **Translated article titles.** If an English translation is added to a foreign-language article title, it is enclosed in brackets, without quotation marks, and capitalized sentence-style. If a title is given only in English translation, however, the original language must be specified. See also 14.108, 14.110.

> 1. W. Kern, "Waar verzamelde Pigafetta zijn Maleise woorden?" [Where did Pigafetta collect his Malaysian words?], *Tijdschrift voor Indische taal-, land- en volkenkunde* 78 (1938): 271–73.

> Chu Ching and Long Zhi. "The Vicissitudes of the Giant Panda, *Ailuropoda melanoleuca* (David)." [In Chinese.] *Acta Zoologica Sinica* 29, no. 1 (1983): 93–104.

14.195   **New series for journal volumes.** New series in journal volumes are identified by *n.s.* (new series), *2nd ser.*, and so forth, as they are for books (see 14.132). Note the comma between the series identifier and the volume number.

> 23. "Letter of Jonathan Sewall," *Proceedings of the Massachusetts Historical Society*, 2nd ser., 10 (January 1896): 414.

> Moraes, G. M. "St. Francis Xavier, Apostolic Nuncio, 1542–52." *Journal of the Bombay Branch of the Royal Asiatic Society*, n.s., 26 (1950): 279–313.

14.196   **Short titles for articles.** In subsequent references to journal articles, the author's last name and the main title of the article (often shortened) are most commonly used. In the absence of a full bibliography, however, the journal title, volume number, and page number(s) may prove more helpful guides to the source. See also 14.177.

24. Pablo Cotler and Christopher Woodruff, "The Impact of Short-Term Credit on Microenterprises: Evidence from the *Fincomun-Bimbo* Program in Mexico," *Economic Development and Cultural Change* 56 (July 2008): 831, doi:10.1086/588169.
26. Cotler and Woodruff, "Short-Term Credit," 840.

or

26. Cotler and Woodruff, *Economic Development and Cultural Change* 56:840.

14.197 *Abstract.* An abstract is treated like a journal article, but the word *abstract* must be added.

Hoover, Susan E., Junichi Kawada, Wyndham Wilson, and Jeffrey I. Cohen. "Oropharyngeal Shedding of Epstein-Barr Virus in the Absence of Circulating B Cells." Abstract. *Journal of Infectious Diseases* 198 (August 1, 2008). doi:10.1086/589714.

14.198 *Electronic enhancements to journal articles.* Electronic-only enhancements to journal articles—including sound or video files and appendixes—can be cited in notes as follows:

3. "Ghost Dancing Music," Naraya no. 2, MP3 audio file, cited in Richard W. Stoffle et al., "Ghost Dancing the Grand Canyon," *Current Anthropology* 41, no. 1 (2000), doi:10.1086/300101.
11. "RNA/DNA Quantitation Methods," appendix A (online only), Daniel I. Bolnick and On Lee Lau, "Predictable Patterns of Disruptive Selection in Stickleback in Postglacial Lakes," *American Naturalist* 172 (July 2008), doi:10.1086/587805.

See also 14.274–80.

Magazines

14.199 *Citing magazines by date.* For the use of *magazine* as against *journal*, see 14.172. Many of the guidelines for citing journals apply to magazines also. Weekly or monthly (or bimonthly) magazines, even if numbered by volume and issue, are usually cited by date only. The date, being an essential element in the citation, is not enclosed in parentheses. While a specific page number may be cited in a note, the inclusive page numbers of an article may be omitted, since they are often widely separated by extraneous material. When page numbers are included, a comma rather than a colon separates them from the date of issue.

1. Beth Saulnier, "From Vine to Wine," *Cornell Alumni Magazine*, September/ October 2008, 48.

2. Jill Lepore, "Just the Facts, Ma'am: Fake Memoirs, Factual Fictions, and the History of History," *New Yorker*, March 24, 2008, 81.

See also 14.202 and the guidelines for newspapers (14.203–13).

14.200   *Online magazine articles.* For magazine articles consulted online, include a URL (or DOI, if available) at the end of a citation. See also 14.4–13, 14.184.

1. Wendy Cole and Janice Castro, "Scientology's Largesse in Russia," *Time*, April 13, 1992, http://www.time.com/time/magazine/article/0,9171,975290,00.html.

14.201   *Magazine article titles.* Titles of magazine articles are treated like titles of journal articles: they are capitalized headline-style, set in roman, and placed in quotation marks. See 14.176; see also 8.157.

1. Michael Frank, "La Concha Revival: San Juan's Tropical Modernist Gem Makes a Comeback," *Architectural Digest*, August 2009, 103–4.

14.202   *Magazine departments.* Titles of regular departments in a magazine are capitalized headline-style but not put in quotation marks.

2. Rebecca Mead, "Isn't It Romantic?," Talk of the Town (Ink), *New Yorker*, July 21, 2008, http://www.newyorker.com/talk/2008/07/21/080721ta_talk_mead.
3. Debra Klein, Focus on Travel, *Newsweek*, April 17, 2000.

Wallraff, Barbara. Word Fugitives. *Atlantic Monthly*, July/August 2008.

A department without a named author is best cited by the name of the magazine.

Gourmet. Kitchen Notebook. May 2000.

Newspapers

14.203   *Newspaper citations—basic elements.* The name of the author (if known) and the headline or column heading in a daily newspaper are cited much like the corresponding elements in magazines (see 14.199–202). The month (often abbreviated), day, and year are the indispensable elements. Because a newspaper's issue of any given day may include several editions, and items may be moved or eliminated in various editions, page numbers may usually be omitted (for an example of a page number in a citation, see 14.209). In a note or bibliographical entry, it may be useful to add "final edition," "Midwest edition," or some such identifier. If the paper is published in several sections, the section number or name may be given (e.g., sec. 1). To cite an article consulted online, include the URL; in some cases, it may be advisable to shorten a particularly unwieldy URL to end after the first single forward slash (i.e., the slash that follows a domain extension such as *.com*).

1. Editorial, *Philadelphia Inquirer*, July 30, 1990.

2. Mike Royko, "Next Time, Dan, Take Aim at Arnold," *Chicago Tribune*, September 23, 1992.

3. Christopher Lehmann-Haupt, "Robert Giroux, Editor, Publisher and Nurturer of Literary Giants, Is Dead at 94," *New York Times*, September 6, 2008, New York edition.

4. "Pushcarts Evolve to Trendy Kiosks," *Lake Forester* (Lake Forest, IL), March 23, 2000.

5. Julie Bosman, "Jets? Yes! Sharks? ¡Sí! in Bilingual 'West Side,'" *New York Times*, July 17, 2008, http://www.nytimes.com/2008/07/17/theater/17bway.html.

14.204 *Newspaper headlines.* Since headlines are often grammatical sentences, sentence-style capitalization is preferred in the headlines of many major newspapers. In documentation, however, Chicago recommends headline style for citing headlines in notes and bibliographies for the sake of consistency with other titles. See also 8.156, 8.157.

"Justices Limit Visiting Rights of Grandparents in Divided Case"

Headlines presented entirely in full capitals in the original are usually converted to upper- and lowercase in documentation (but see 7.48).

14.205 *Regular columns.* Many regular columns carry headlines as well as column titles. When such columns are cited, both may be used or, to save space, the column title alone.

5. Marguerite Fields, "Want to Be My Boyfriend? Please Define," Modern Love, *New York Times*, May 4, 2008, http://www.nytimes.com/2008/05/04/fashion/04 love.html.

or

5. Marguerite Fields, Modern Love, *New York Times*, May 4, 2008, http://www .nytimes.com/2008/05/04/fashion/04love.html.

14.206 *Citing in text rather than in a bibliography.* Newspapers are more commonly cited in notes or parenthetical references than in bibliographies. A list of works cited need not list newspaper items if these have been documented in the text. No corresponding entry in a bibliography would be needed for the following citation (nor would it be necessary in such a case to include information about edition or, for an article consulted online, a URL):

In an article discussing the end of Favre's second-straight postretirement season— this time with the Minnesota Vikings—Pat Borzi reminds us that when it comes to the aging quarterback's uncertain prospects for yet another season, "there is final, and there is Favre" (*New York Times*, January 25, 2010).

If, for some reason, a bibliography entry were included, it would appear as follows:

Borzi, Pat. "Retirement Discussion Begins Anew for Favre." *New York Times*, January 25, 2010. http://www.nytimes.com/2010/01/26/sports/football/26vikings .html?emc=eta1.

14.207 *Unsigned newspaper articles.* Unsigned newspaper articles or features are best dealt with in text or notes. But if a bibliography entry should be needed, the name of the newspaper stands in place of the author.

1. "In Texas, Ad Heats Up Race for Governor," *New York Times*, July 30, 2002.

New York Times. "In Texas, Ad Heats Up Race for Governor." July 30, 2002.

14.208 *Letters to the editor.* Published letters to the editor are treated generically, without headlines.

6. Brian Sheridan, letter to the editor, *Los Angeles Times*, September 7, 2008.

14.209 *Weekend supplements, magazines, and the like.* Articles from Sunday supplements or other special sections are treated in the same way as magazine articles—that is, cited by date. They are usually dealt with in notes or parenthetical references rather than in bibliographies. Citations of print editions may include a specific page reference (see 14.199).

45. David Frum, "The Vanishing Republican Voter," *New York Times Magazine*, September 7, 2008, New York edition, MM48.

14.210 *Names of newspapers.* An initial *The* is omitted (see 8.168). A city name, even if not part of the name of an American newspaper, should be added, italicized along with the official title. The name (usually abbreviated) of the state or, in the case of Canada, province may be added in parentheses if needed. Odd cases may call for special treatment.

Chicago Tribune
Hackensack (NJ) Record
Ottawa (IL) Daily Times
Saint Paul (Alberta or AB) Journal
but
Oregonian (Portland, OR)

For such well-known national papers as the *Wall Street Journal* or the *Christian Science Monitor*, no city name is added.

14.211 **Names of foreign newspapers.** Names of cities not part of the titles of foreign newspapers may be added in parentheses after the title, not italicized. An initial *The*, omitted in English-language papers, is retained in titles of foreign-language papers if the article is part of the name. Foreign newspaper names, like those of foreign journals, are often capitalized headline-style. When in doubt, however, use sentence style.

Frankfurter Zeitung   *Guardian* (Manchester)
La Crónica de Hoy (Mexico City)   *Le Monde*
Times (London)

14.212 **News services.** Names of news services, as opposed to newspapers, are capitalized but not italicized.

the Associated Press (AP)   United Press International (UPI)

> 1. Associated Press, "Afraid of Laundry? You Will Be after Reading This," *USA Today*, July 17, 2008, http://www.usatoday.com/news/topstories/2008-07-17 -861610133_x.htm.

14.213 **News releases.** A news release is treated like an article in a magazine (see 14.199–202), its title set in roman and placed in quotation marks.

> 6. National Transportation Safety Board, "NTSB Chairman Commends FAA on Major Advancement in Aviation Safety," news release, July 16, 2008, http://www .ntsb.gov/Pressrel/2008/080716.html.

Reviews

14.214 **Reviews—elements of the citation.** In citations of reviews, the elements are given in the following order:

1. Name of reviewer if the review is signed
2. Title of the review, if any (a headline should be included only if needed for locating the review)
3. The words *review of*, followed by the name of the work reviewed and its author (or composer, or director, or whomever) or sponsor (network, studio, label, etc.)
4. Location and date (in the case of a performance)
5. The listing of the periodical in which the review appeared

If a review is included in a bibliography, it is alphabetized by the name of the reviewer or, if unattributed, by the name of the periodical (see 14.217). See also 14.215.

14.215 *Book reviews.* Cite book reviews by author of the review and include book title and author(s) or editor(s). Follow applicable guidelines for citing periodicals.

> 1. Ben Ratliff, review of *The Mystery of Samba: Popular Music and National Identity in Brazil*, by Hermano Vianna, ed. and trans. John Charles Chasteen, *Lingua Franca* 9 (April 1999): B13–B14.
>
> 2. David Kamp, "Deconstructing Dinner," review of *The Omnivore's Dilemma: A Natural History of Four Meals*, by Michael Pollan, *New York Times*, April 23, 2006, Sunday Book Review, http://www.nytimes.com/2006/04/23/books/review/23kamp.html.

> Sorby, Angela. Review of *Songs of Ourselves: The Uses of Poetry in America*, by Joan Shelley Rubin. *American Historical Review* 113 (April 2008): 449–51. doi:10.1086/ahr.113.2.449.

14.216 *Reviews of plays, movies, television programs, concerts, and the like.* Reviews of plays, concerts, movies, and the like may include the name of a director in addition to any author, producer, sponsor, or performer, as applicable.

> 3. Ben Brantley, review of *Our Lady of Sligo*, by Sebastian Barry, directed by Max Stafford-Clark, Irish Repertory Theater, New York, *New York Times*, April 21, 2000, Weekend section.
>
> 4. Jon Pareles, review of *Men Strike Back* (VH1 television), *New York Times*, April 18, 2000, Living Arts section.
>
> 5. David Denby, review of *WALL-E*, Disney/Pixar, *New Yorker*, July 21, 2008, http://www.newyorker.com/arts/critics/cinema/2008/07/21/080721crci_cinema_denby.
>
> 6. Pareles, review of *Men Strike Back*.

Kozinn, Allan. Review of concert performance by Timothy Fain (violin) and Steven Beck (piano), 92nd Street Y, New York. *New York Times*, April 21, 2000, Weekend section.

14.217 *Unsigned reviews.* Unsigned reviews are treated similarly to unsigned articles (see 14.207). If such a review must appear in the bibliography, it is listed under the name of the periodical.

34. Unsigned review of *Geschichten der romanischen und germanischen Völker*, by Leopold von Ranke, *Ergänzungsblätter zur Allgemeinen Literatur-Zeitung*, February 1828, nos. 23–24.

Ergänzungsblätter zur Allgemeinen Literatur-Zeitung. Unsigned review of *Geschichten der romanischen und germanischen Völker*, by Leopold von Ranke. February 1828, nos. 23–24.

Interviews and Personal Communications

14.218 *Interviews and personal communications—order of attribution.* In whatever form interviews or personal communications exist—published, broadcast, preserved in audiovisual form, available online—the citation normally begins with the name of the person interviewed or the person from whom the communication was received. The interviewer or recipient, if mentioned, comes second.

14.219 *Unpublished interviews.* Unpublished interviews are best cited in text or in notes, though they occasionally appear in bibliographies. Citations should include the names of both the person interviewed and the interviewer; brief identifying information, if appropriate; the place or date of the interview (or both, if known); and, if a transcript or recording is available, where it may be found. Permission to quote may be needed; see chapter 4.

7. Andrew Macmillan (principal adviser, Investment Center Division, FAO), in discussion with the author, September 1998.

8. Benjamin Spock, interview by Milton J. E. Senn, November 20, 1974, interview 67A, transcript, Senn Oral History Collection, National Library of Medicine, Bethesda, MD.

9. Macmillan, discussion; Spock, interview.

14.220   *Unattributed interviews.* An interview with a person who prefers to remain anonymous or whose name the author does not wish to reveal may be cited in whatever form is appropriate in context. The absence of a name should be explained (e.g., "All interviews were conducted in confidentiality, and the names of interviewees are withheld by mutual agreement").

> 10. Interview with health care worker, March 23, 2010.

14.221   *Published or broadcast interviews.* An interview that has already been published or broadcast is treated like an article in a periodical or a chapter in a book. Interviews consulted online should include a URL or similar identifier and, for audiovisual materials, an indication of the medium (see 14.4–13). See also 14.277, 14.280.

> 117. "*Mil Máscaras*: An Interview with Pulitzer-Winner Junot Díaz (*The Brief Wondrous Life of Oscar Wao*)," by Matt Okie, *Identitytheory.com*, September 2, 2008, http://www.identitytheory.com/interviews/okie_diaz.php.
>
> 118. McGeorge Bundy, interview by Robert MacNeil, *MacNeil/Lehrer NewsHour*, PBS, February 7, 1990.
>
> 119. Darcey Steinke, interview by Sam Tanenhaus and Dwight Garner, *New York Times Book Review*, podcast audio, April 22, 2007, http://podcasts.nytimes.com/podcasts/2007/04/20/21bookupdate.mp3.

> Bellour, Raymond. "Alternation, Segmentation, Hypnosis: Interview with Raymond Bellour." By Janet Bergstrom. *Camera Obscura*, nos. 3–4 (Summer 1979): 89–94.

If an interview is included or excerpted in the form of a direct quotation within an article or chapter by the interviewer, the interviewer's name may come first.

> 120. Michael Fortun and Kim Fortun, "Making Space, Speaking Truth: The Institute for Policy Studies, 1963–1995" (includes an interview with Marcus Raskin and Richard Barnet), in *Corporate Futures*, ed. George E. Marcus, Late Editions 5 (Chicago: University of Chicago Press, 1998), 257.

14.222   *Personal communications.* References to conversations (whether face-to-face or by telephone) or to letters, e-mail or text messages, and the like received by the author are usually run in to the text or given in a note. They are rarely listed in a bibliography. For references to electronic mailing lists, see 14.223. See also 13.3.

In a telephone conversation with the author on January 6, 2009, lobbyist Pat Fenshaw admitted that . . .

2. Constance Conlon, e-mail message to author, April 17, 2000.

An e-mail address belonging to an individual should be omitted. Should it be needed in a specific context, it must be cited only with the permission of its owner. For breaking an e-mail address at the end of a line, see 7.42.

14.223 *Electronic mailing lists.* To cite material from an electronic mailing list, include the name of the list, the date of the individual posting, and a URL where the archive can be found. Additional information such as a file name or number may be appropriate. Citations of such material should generally be limited to text and notes.

17. John Powell to Grapevine mailing list, April 23, 1998, no. 83, http://www .electriceditors.net/grapevine/archives.php.
18. Edela Fontane to LLTI@listserv.dartmouth.edu, June 2, 2008, no. 8865a, Language Learning and Technology International Information Forum, http:// listserv.dartmouth.edu/scripts/wa.exe?A0=LLTI.

Unpublished and Informally Published Material

Theses, Dissertations, Papers, and the Like

14.224 *Theses and dissertations.* Titles of unpublished works appear in quotation marks—not in italics. This treatment extends to theses and dissertations, which are otherwise cited like books. The kind of thesis, the academic institution, and the date follow the title. Like the publication data of a book, these are enclosed in parentheses in a note but not in a bibliography. If the document was consulted online, include a URL or, for documents retrieved from a commercial database, give the name of the database and, in parentheses, any identification number supplied or recommended by the database. For dissertations issued on microfilm, see 14.120. For published abstracts of dissertations, see 14.197.

1. Ilya Vedrashko, "Advertising in Computer Games" (master's thesis, MIT, 2006), 59, http://cms.mit.edu/research/theses/IlyaVedrashko2006.pdf.
5. Vedrashko, "Advertising in Computer Games," 61–62.

Choi, Mihwa. "Contesting *Imaginaires* in Death Rituals during the Northern Song Dynasty." PhD diss., University of Chicago, 2008. ProQuest (AAT 3300426).

14.225   *Unpublished manuscripts.* Titles of unpublished manuscripts, like the titles of other unpublished works, appear in quotation marks. (For manuscripts under contract but not yet published, see 14.153.) Include the words *unpublished manuscript* and the date of the version consulted, if possible (for electronic files, a last-saved or last-modified date may be appropriate). End the citation with an indication of format(s).

1. Nora Bradburn, "Watch Crystals and the Mohs Scale" (unpublished manuscript, December 3, 2008), LaTeX and Excel files.

Cotter, Cory. "The Weakest Link: The Argument for On-Wrist Band Welding." Unpublished manuscript, last modified December 3, 2008. Microsoft Word file.

14.226   *Lectures, papers presented at meetings, and the like.* The sponsorship, location, and date of the meeting at which a speech was given or a paper presented follow the title. This information, like that following a thesis title, is put in parentheses in a note but not in a bibliography.

2. Stacy D'Erasmo, "The Craft and Career of Writing" (lecture, Northwestern University, Evanston, IL, April 26, 2000).

Teplin, Linda A., Gary M. McClelland, Karen M. Abram, and Jason J. Washburn. "Early Violent Death in Delinquent Youth: A Prospective Longitudinal Study." Paper presented at the Annual Meeting of the American Psychology-Law Society, La Jolla, CA, March 2005.

A paper included in the published proceedings of a meeting may be treated like a chapter in a book (see 14.125). If published in a journal, it is treated as an article (see 14.175–98).

14.227   *Poster papers.* Papers presented at poster sessions are treated like other unpublished papers.

Rohde, Hannah, Roger Levy, and Andrew Kehler. "Implicit Causality Biases Influence Relative Clause Attachment." Poster presented at the 21st CUNY Conference on Human Sentence Processing, Chapel Hill, NC, March 2008.

14.228   *Working papers and other unpublished works.* Most unpublished papers can be treated in much the same way as a dissertation or thesis (14.224) or a lecture, paper, or other presentation (14.226).

4. Deborah D. Lucki and Richard W. Pollay, "Content Analyses of Advertising: A Review of the Literature" (working paper, History of Advertising Archives, Faculty of Commerce, University of British Columbia, Vancouver, 1980).

Dyer, Lee, and Jeff Ericksen. "Complexity-Based Agile Enterprises: Putting Self-Organizing Emergence to Work." CAHRS Working Paper 08-01, School of Industrial and Labor Relations, Center for Advanced Human Resource Studies, Cornell University, Ithaca, NY, 1980. http://digitalcommons.ilr.cornell.edu /cahrswp/473.

In the second example above the term *working paper* is part of a formal series title, therefore capitalized (see 14.128–32). Unless the item is available online, it is sometimes useful to add *photocopy* or otherwise indicate the form in which an unpublished document may be consulted.

Alarcón, Salvador Florencio de. "Compendio de las noticias correspondientes a el real y minas San Francisco de Aziz de Río Chico . . . de 20 de octobre [1771]." Photocopy, Department of Geography, University of California, Berkeley.

14.229 Preprints. Not being subject to peer review, preprints are treated as unpublished material. See also 1.106.

Lein, Matthias. "Characterization of Agostic Interactions in Theory and Computation." Preprint, submitted July 10, 2008. http://xxx.lanl.gov/abs/0807.1751.

14.230 Patents. Patents are cited under the names of the creators and dated by the year of filing.

Iizuka, Masanori, and Hideki Tanaka. Cement admixture. US Patent 4,586,960, filed June 26, 1984, and issued May 6, 1986.

14.231 Private contracts, wills, and such. Private documents are occasionally cited in notes but rarely in bibliographies. More appropriately they are referred to in text (e.g., "Marcy T. Feldspar, in her will dated January 20, 1976, directed . . .") or in notes. Capitalization is usually a matter of editorial discretion.

4. Samuel Henshaw, will dated June 5, 1806, proved July 5, 1809, no. 46, box 70, Hampshire County Registry of Probate, Northampton, MA.

5. Agreement to teach in the Publishing Program of the Graham School, University of Chicago, signed by Jemma Granite, May 29, 2010.

Manuscript Collections

14.232   *Overview and additional resources.* The 1987 edition of the *Guide to the National Archives of the United States* offers the following advice: "The most convenient citation for archives is one similar to that used for personal papers and other historical manuscripts. Full identification of most unpublished material usually requires giving the title and date of the item, series title (if applicable), name of the collection, and name of the depository. Except for placing the cited item first [in a note], there is no general agreement on the sequence of the remaining elements in the citation. . . . Whatever sequence is adopted, however, should be used consistently throughout the same work" (761). This advice has been extended by the leaflet *Citing Records in the National Archives of the United States* (available at the National Archives and Records Administration website), which includes advice on citing textual and nontextual records, including electronic records. See also bibliog. 4.5. It should be noted that citations of collections consulted online (which remain a relative rarity given the cost of digitizing the miscellaneous, nonstandard items typical of most manuscript collections) will usually be the same as citations of physical collections, aside from the addition of a URL or DOI (see 14.4–13).

14.233   *Note forms versus bibliography entries.* In a note, the main element of a manuscript citation is usually a specific item (a letter, a memorandum, or whatever) and is thus cited first. In a bibliography, the main element is usually either the collection in which the specific item may be found, the author(s) of the items in the collection, or the depository for the collection. (Entries beginning with the name of the collection or the last name of the author—which sometimes overlap—tend to be easiest to locate in a bibliography.)

38. James Oglethorpe to the Trustees, 13 January 1733, Phillipps Collection of Egmont Manuscripts, 14200:13, University of Georgia Library.
39. Alvin Johnson, memorandum, 1937, file 36, Horace Kallen Papers, YIVO Institute for Jewish Research, New York.
40. Revere's Waste and Memoranda Book (vol. 1, 1761–83; vol. 2, 1783–97), Revere Family Papers, Massachusetts Historical Society, Boston.

Egmont Manuscripts. Phillipps Collection. University of Georgia Library.
Kallen, Horace. Papers. YIVO Institute for Jewish Research, New York.
Revere Family Papers. Massachusetts Historical Society, Boston.

Specific items are not included in a bibliography unless only one item from a collection is cited. For more examples, see 14.240, 14.241.

14.234 *Specific versus generic titles for manuscript collections.* In notes and bibliographies, quotation marks are used only for specific titles (e.g., "Canoeing through Northern Minnesota"), but not for generic names such as *report* or *minutes.* Generic names of this kind are capitalized if part of a formal heading actually appearing on the manuscript, lowercased if merely descriptive. Compare 14.240, example notes 46–49.

14.235 *Dates for manuscript collections.* Names of months may be spelled out or abbreviated, as long as done consistently (see 10.40). If there are many references to specific dates, as in a collection of letters or diaries, the day-month-year form (8 May 1945), used in some of the examples below, will reduce clutter. See also 6.45.

14.236 *Folios, page numbers, and such for manuscript collections.* Older manuscripts are usually numbered by signatures only or by folios (*fol., fols.*) rather than by page (see 14.161, 14.162). More recent ones usually carry page numbers; if needed, the abbreviations *p.* and *pp.* should be used to avoid ambiguity. Some manuscript collections have identifying series or file numbers, which may be included in a citation.

14.237 *"Papers" and "manuscripts."* In titles of manuscript collections, the terms *papers* and *manuscripts* are synonymous. Both are acceptable, as are the abbreviations *MS* and (pl.) *MSS.* If it is necessary to distinguish a typescript or computer printout from a handwritten document, the abbreviation *TS* may be used.

14.238 *Location of depositories.* The location (city and state) of such well-known depositories as major university libraries is rarely necessary (see examples in 14.240).

University of Chicago Library
Oberlin College Library

14.239 *Collections of letters and the like.* A note citation of a letter starts with the name of the letter writer, followed by *to*, followed by the name of the recipient. Given names may be omitted if the identities of sender and recipient are clear from the text. (Identifying material may be added if appropriate; see 14.219.) The word *letter* is usually omitted—that is, understood—but other forms of communication (telegram, memorandum) are specified. If such other forms occur frequently in the same collection, it may be helpful to specify letters also. For capitalization and the use of quotation marks, see 14.234. For date form, see 6.45, 9.32. See also 14.117, 14.222, 14.242.

14.240   *Examples of note forms for manuscript collections.*

> 40. George Creel to Colonel House, 25 September 1918, Edward M. House Papers, Yale University Library.
> 41. James Oglethorpe to the Trustees, 13 January 1733, Phillipps Collection of Egmont Manuscripts, 14200:13, University of Georgia Library (hereafter cited as Egmont MSS).
> 42. Burton to Merriam, telegram, 26 January 1923, Charles E. Merriam Papers, University of Chicago Library.
> 43. Minutes of the Committee for Improving the Condition of the Free Blacks, Pennsylvania Abolition Society, 1790–1803, Papers of the Pennsylvania Society for the Abolition of Slavery, Historical Society of Pennsylvania, Philadelphia (hereafter cited as Minutes, Pennsylvania Society).
> 44. Hiram Johnson to John Callan O'Laughlin, 13 and 16 July 1916, 28 November 1916, O'Laughlin Papers, Theodore Roosevelt Collection, Harvard College Library.
> 45. Memorandum by Alvin Johnson, 1937, file 36, Horace Kallen Papers, YIVO Institute for Jewish Research, New York.
> 46. Undated correspondence between French Strother and Edward Lowry, container 1-G/961 600, Herbert Hoover Presidential Library, West Branch, IA.
> 47. Memorandum, "Concerning a Court of Arbitration," n.d., Philander C. Knox Papers, Manuscripts Division, Library of Congress.
> 48. Joseph Purcell, "A Map of the Southern Indian District of North America" [ca. 1772], MS 228, Ayer Collection, Newberry Library, Chicago.
> 49. Louis Agassiz, report to the Committee of Overseers . . . [28 December 1859], Overseers Reports, Professional Series, vol. 2, Harvard University Archives.
> 50. Gilbert McMicken to Alexander Morris, 29 November 1881, Glasgow (Scotland), Document 1359, fol. 1r, Alexander Morris Papers, MG-12-84, Provincial Archives of Manitoba, Winnipeg.

The content of subsequent citations of other items in a cited manuscript collection (short forms) will vary according to the proximity of the earlier notes, the use of abbreviations, and other factors. Absolute consistency may occasionally be sacrificed to readers' convenience.

> 51. R. S. Baker to House, 1 November 1919, House Papers.
> 52. Thomas Causton to his wife, 12 March 1733, Egmont MSS, 14200:53.
> 53. Minutes, 15 April 1795, Pennsylvania Society.

14.241   *Examples of bibliography entries for manuscript collections.* The style of the first six examples below is appropriate if more than one item from a collection is cited in the text or notes. In the second and third examples, commas are added after the initials to avoid misreading. See also 14.233.

Egmont Manuscripts. Phillipps Collection. University of Georgia Library.

House, Edward M., Papers. Yale University Library.

Merriam, Charles E., Papers. University of Chicago Library.

Pennsylvania Society for the Abolition of Slavery. Papers. Historical Society of Pennsylvania, Philadelphia.

Strother, French, and Edward Lowry. Undated correspondence. Herbert Hoover Presidential Library, West Branch, IA.

Women's Organization for National Prohibition Reform. Papers. Alice Belin du Pont files, Pierre S. du Pont Papers. Eleutherian Mills Historical Library, Wilmington, DE.

If only one item from a collection has been mentioned in text or in a note and is considered important enough to include in a bibliography, the entry will begin with the item.

Dinkel, Joseph. Description of Louis Agassiz written at the request of Elizabeth Cary Agassiz. Agassiz Papers. Houghton Library, Harvard University.

14.242 *Letters and the like in private collections.* Letters, memoranda, and such that have not been archived may be cited like other unpublished material. Information on the depository is replaced by such wording as "in the author's possession" or "private collection," and the location is not mentioned.

Websites and Blogs

14.243 *Websites and blogs—overview.* For the purposes of this discussion, *website* refers to the collection of documents made available at a specific location on the World Wide Web by an individual or organization. (The term *web page*, on the other hand, is used to refer to any one of the "pages," or subdocuments, that can be viewed within a website.) Formal citations should normally be limited to the documents themselves—for example, the articles, books, and other published documents offered by the websites of university publishers and other formal organizations and discussed elsewhere in this chapter. A weblog—or blog—is a category of website that has evolved to include a few more or less standard components, including dated entries and dated comments. Citations of blog entries and comments are therefore similar to citations of articles in periodicals (see 14.246).

14.244 *Titles for websites and blogs.* Websites should be referred to in text and notes by specific title (if any), by the name of the sponsor or author, or by a descriptive phrase. Some sites refer to themselves by their domain name (the first part of a URL, following the double slash and ending in a domain-type indication such as *.com, .edu*, or *.org*); such monikers, which are not case sensitive, are often shortened and capitalized in a logical way (e.g., *www.nytimes.com* becomes *NYTimes.com*; *www.google.com* becomes *Google*). Titles of websites are generally set in roman without quotation marks and capitalized headline-style, but titles that are analogous to books or other types of publications may be styled accordingly. Titled sections or pages within a website should be placed in quotation marks. Specific titles of blogs—which are analogous to periodicals—should be set in italics; titles of blog entries (analogous to articles in a periodical) should be in quotation marks. For additional examples, see 8.186–87.

the website of the *New York Times*; the *New York Times* online; NYTimes.com
The Chicago Manual of Style Online; "Chicago Style Q&A"
Google; Google Maps; the "Google Maps Help Center"
The Becker-Posner Blog; "Should Dogs Get $8 Billion from the Helmsley Estate?," blog entry by Richard Posner, July 13, 2008

14.245   *Citations of website content.* For original content from online sources other than the types of formally published documents discussed elsewhere in this chapter, include as much of the following as can be determined: the title or a description of the page (see 14.244), the author of the content (if any), the owner or sponsor of the site, and a URL. Also include a publication date or date of revision or modification (see 14.8); if no such date can be determined, include an access date (see 14.7). Citations of site content are best relegated to notes; in works with no notes, they may be included in the bibliography. Some editorial discretion will be required.

14. "WD2000: Visual Basic Macro to Assign Clipboard Text to a String Variable," revision 1.3, Microsoft Help and Support, last modified November 23, 2006, http://support.microsoft.com/kb/212730.

15. "Google Privacy Policy," last modified October 14, 2005, accessed July 19, 2008, http://www.google.com/intl/en/privacypolicy.html.

16. "McDonald's Happy Meal Toy Safety Facts," McDonald's Corporation, accessed July 19, 2008, http://www.mcdonalds.com/corp/about/factsheets.html.

17. Barack Obama's Facebook page, accessed July 19, 2008, http://www.facebook.com/barackobama.

18. "Style Guide," *Wikipedia*, last modified July 18, 2008, http://en.wikipedia.org/wiki/Style_guide.

Microsoft Corporation. "WD2000: Visual Basic Macro to Assign Clipboard Text to a String Variable." Revision 1.3. Microsoft Help and Support. Last modified November 23, 2006. http://support.microsoft.com/kb/212730.

If a site ceases to exist before publication, or if the information cited is modified or deleted, such information should be included in the text or note.

As of July 18, 2008, Hefferman was claiming on her Facebook page that . . . (a claim that had disappeared from her page by September 1, 2008) . . .

4. "Biography," on Pete Townshend's official website, accessed December 15, 2001, http://www.petetownshend.co.uk/petet_bio.html (site discontinued).

14.246 *Citations of blog entries.* Citations of blog entries should include the author of the entry; the name of the entry, in quotation marks; the title or description of the blog (see 14.244); and a URL. Citations of a comment should start with the identity of the commenter and the date of the comment (if a time stamp appears with the comment), the words "comment on," and the citation information for the related entry. If the blog entry has been cited previously, use a shortened form; see 14.25. There is no need to add *pseud.* after an apparently fictitious name of a commenter; it may be assumed that the identity of any commenter may be an alias. If known, the identity can be given in the text or in the citation (in square brackets; see 14.82). Blogs that are part of a larger publication should also include the name of that publication. Add the word *blog* in parentheses after the name of the blog (unless the word *blog* is part of the name). Citations of blog entries are generally relegated to the notes; a frequently cited blog, however, may be included in the bibliography.

1. Mike Nizza, "Go Ahead, Annoy Away, an Australian Court Says," *The Lede* (blog), *New York Times*, July 15, 2008, http://thelede.blogs.nytimes.com/2008/07/15/.
2. SteveCO, comment on Nizza, "Go Ahead, Annoy Away."
16. Matthew Lasar, "FCC Chair Willing to Consecrate XM-Sirius Union," *Ars Technica* (blog), June 16, 2008, http://arstechnica.com/news.ars/post/20080616-fcc-chair-willing-to-consecrate-xm-sirius-union.html.
19. AC, July 1, 2008 (10:18 a.m.), comment on Rhian Ellis, "Squatters' Rights," *Ward Six* (blog), June 30, 2008, http://wardsix.blogspot.com/2008/06/squatters-rights.html.

Ellis, Rhian, J. Robert Lennon, and Ed Skoog. *Ward Six* (blog). http://wardsix.blogspot.com/.

Special Types of References

Dictionaries and Encyclopedias

14.247 *Dictionaries and encyclopedias.* Well-known reference books, such as major dictionaries and encyclopedias, are normally cited in notes rather than in bibliographies. The facts of publication are often omitted, but the edition (if not the first) must be specified. References to an alphabetically arranged work cite the item (not the volume or page number) preceded by *s.v.* (*sub verbo*, "under the word"; pl. *s.vv.*)

> 1. *Encyclopaedia Britannica*, 15th ed., s.v. "salvation."
> 2. *Oxford English Dictionary*, 2nd ed. (CD-ROM, version 3.0), s.v. "hoot(e)nanny, hootananny."
> 3. *Dictionary of American Biography*, s.v. "Wadsworth, Jeremiah."

Certain reference works, however, may appropriately be listed with their publication details. (For examples of how to cite individual entries by author, see 14.248.)

> 4. *The Times Style and Usage Guide*, comp. Tim Austin (London: Times Books, 2003), s.vv. "police ranks," "postal addresses."
> 5. *MLA Style Manual and Guide to Scholarly Publishing*, 3rd ed. (New York: Modern Language Association of America, 2008), 6.8.2.

> *Diccionario de historia de Venezuela*. 2nd ed. 4 vols. Caracas: Fundación Polar, 1997.
> Garner, Bryan A. *Garner's Modern American Usage*. New York: Oxford University Press, 2003.

14.248 *Dictionaries and encyclopedias online.* Online versions of encyclopedias should be cited like their printed corollaries. In addition, in the absence of a posted publication or revision date for the cited entry, supply an access date. If the article includes a recommended form for the URL, include it; otherwise, include a short form of the URL (as in the second example) from which interested readers may enter the search term. If a DOI for the article is available, use that instead. Well-known online reference works, such as major dictionaries and encyclopedias, are normally cited, like their printed counterparts, in notes rather than in bibliographies. The facts of publication are often omitted, but signed entries may include the name of the author. See also 14.5, 14.6.

1. *Encyclopaedia Britannica Online*, s.v. "Sibelius, Jean," accessed July 19, 2008, http://original.britannica.com/eb/article-9067596.

2. *Grove Music Online*, s.v. "Toscanini, Arturo," by David Cairns, accessed July 19, 2008, http://www.oxfordmusiconline.com/.

3. *Wikipedia*, s.v. "Stevie Nicks," last modified July 19, 2008, http://en.wikipedia.org/wiki/Stevie_Nicks.

4. *Merriam-Webster OnLine*, s.v. "mondegreen," accessed July 19, 2008, http://www.merriam-webster.com/dictionary/mondegreen.

For certain reference works—particularly those with substantial, authored entries—it may be appropriate to cite individual entries by author, much like contributions to a multiauthor book (see 14.112). Such citations may be included in a bibliography.

Baldwin, Olive, and Thelma Wilson. "Ann Catley (1745–1789)." In *Oxford Dictionary of National Biography*. Oxford University Press, 2004–. Accessed October 8, 2009. doi:10.1093/ref:odnb/4895.

Isaacson, Melissa. "Bulls." In *Encyclopedia of Chicago*, edited by Janice L. Reiff, Ann Durkin Keating, and James R. Grossman. Chicago Historical Society, 2005. http://www.encyclopedia.chicagohistory.org/pages/184.html.

Masolo, Dismas. "African Sage Philosophy." In *Stanford Encyclopedia of Philosophy*. Stanford University, 1997–. Article published February 14, 2006. http://plato.stanford.edu/entries/african-sage/.

Pamphlets and the Like

14.249 *Pamphlets, reports, and the like.* Pamphlets, corporate reports, brochures, and other freestanding publications are treated essentially as books. Data on author and publisher may not fit the normal pattern, but sufficient information should be given to identify the document. For special issues of journals, see 14.187. For access dates, see 14.7. For the use of ampersands in company names, see 10.23.

34. Hazel V. Clark, *Mesopotamia: Between Two Rivers* (Mesopotamia, OH: Trumbull County Historical Society, 1957).

35. *Lifestyles in Retirement*, Library Series (New York: TIAA-CREF, 1996).

36. Merrill Lynch & Co., *2008 Proxy Statement*, accessed April 9, 2009, http://www.ml.com/annualmeetingmaterials/2007/ar/pdfs/2008Proxy.pdf.

14.250 *Exhibition catalogs.* An exhibition catalog is often published as a book and is treated as such.

Mary Cassatt: Modern Woman. Edited by Judith A. Barter. Chicago: Art Institute of Chicago, in association with Harry N. Abrams, 1998. Published in conjunction with the exhibition of the same name, shown at the Boston Museum of Fine Arts, the National Gallery in Washington, DC, and the Art Institute of Chicago.

or, if space is tight,

Mary Cassatt: Modern Woman. Edited by Judith A. Barter. Chicago: Art Institute of Chicago, with Harry N. Abrams, 1998. Exhibition catalog.

A brochure—the kind often handed to visitors to an exhibition—may be treated similarly.

14.251   *Loose-leaf services.* Documentation of material obtained through loose-leaf services is handled like that of books.

> 13. Commerce Clearing House, *1990 Standard Federal Tax Reports* (Chicago: Commerce Clearing House, 1990), 20, 050.15.

Scriptural References

14.252   *Biblical references—additional resource.* Any scholarly writer or editor working extensively with biblical material should consult the latest edition of *The SBL Handbook of Style* (bibliog. 1.1), which offers excellent advice and numerous abbreviations.

14.253   *Bible chapter and verse.* References to the Jewish or Christian scriptures usually appear in text citations or notes rather than in bibliographies. Parenthetical or note references to the Bible should include book (in roman and usually abbreviated), chapter, and verse—never a page number. A colon is used between chapter and verse. Note that the traditional abbreviations use periods but the shorter forms do not. For guidance on when to abbreviate and when not to, see 10.46. For full forms and abbreviations, see 10.48, 10.49, 10.50.

Traditional abbreviations:

> 4. 1 Thess. 4:11, 5:2–5, 5:14.
> 5. Heb. 13:8, 13:12.
> 6. Gen. 25:19–36:43.

Shorter abbreviations:

7. 2 Sm 11:1–17, 11:26–27; 1 Chr 10:13–14.   8. Jo 5:9–12; Mt 26:2–5.

14.254   *Versions of the Bible.* Since books and numbering are not identical in different versions, it is essential to identify which version is being cited. For a work intended for general readers, the version should be spelled out, at least on first occurrence. For specialists, abbreviations may be used throughout. For abbreviations of versions, see 10.51.

>   6. 2 Kings 11:8 (New Revised Standard Version).
>   7. 1 Cor. 6:1–10 (NRSV).

14.255   *Other sacred works.* References to the sacred and revered works of other religious traditions may, according to context, be treated in a manner similar to those of biblical or classical works. Citations of transliterated texts should indicate the name of the version or translator. The Koran (or Qur'an) is set in roman, and citations of its sections use arabic numerals and colons (e.g., Koran 19:17–21). Such collective terms as the Vedas or the Upanishads are normally capitalized and set in roman, but particular parts are italicized (e.g., the *Rig-Veda* or the *Brihad-Aranyaka Upanishad*). For authoritative usage, consult *History of Religions,* an international journal for comparative historical studies (bibliog. 5).

Classical Greek and Latin References

14.256   *Where to cite classical references.* Classical primary source references are ordinarily given in text or notes. They are included in a bibliography only when the reference is to information or annotation supplied by a modern author (see 14.260, 14.265).

The eighty days of inactivity reported by Thucydides (8.44.4) for the Peloponnesian fleet at Rhodes, terminating before the end of Thucydides's winter (8.60.2–3), suggests . . .

14.257   *Identifying numbers in classical references.* The numbers identifying the various parts of classical works—books, sections, lines, and so on—remain the same in all editions, whether in the original language or in translation. (In poetry, line content may vary slightly from the original in some translations.) Arabic numerals are used. Where letters also are used, they are usually lowercased but may be capitalized if the source being cited uses capitals. Page numbers are omitted except in references to introductions, notes, and the like supplied by a modern editor or to specific translations. See also 14.259, 14.264.

> 1. Ovid, *Amores* 1.7.27.
> 2. Aristotle, *Metaphysics* 3.2.996b5–8; Plato, *Republic* 360e–361b.

14.258   *Abbreviations in classical references.* Abbreviations of authors' names as well as of works, collections, and so forth are used extensively in classical references. The most widely accepted standard for abbreviations is the list included in *The Oxford Classical Dictionary* (bibliog. 5). When abbreviations are used, these rather than *ibid.* should be used in succeeding references to the same work. (Abbreviations are best avoided when only two letters are omitted, and they must not be used when more than one writer could be meant—Hipponax or Hipparchus, Aristotle or Aristophanes.)

> 3. Thuc. 2.40.2–3.
> 4. Pindar, *Isthm.* 7.43–45.

14.259   *Punctuation in classical references.* In a departure from earlier recommendations, Chicago recommends placing a comma between the name of a classical author (abbreviated or not) and the title of a work. No punctuation intervenes, however, between title and identifying number (or between author and number when the author is standing in for the title). Numerical divisions are separated by periods with no space following each period. Commas are used between two or more references to the same source, semicolons between references to different sources, and en dashes between continuing numbers. If such abbreviations as *bk.* or *sec.* are needed for clarity, commas separate the different elements.

> 5. Aristophanes, *Frogs* 1019–30.
> 6. Cic., *Verr.* 1.3.21, 2.3.120; Caes., *B Gall.* 6.19; Tac., *Germ.* 10.2–3.
> 7. Hdt. 7.1.2.
> 8. Sappho, *Invocation to Aphrodite*, st. 1, lines 1–6.

14.260   *Citing specific editions of classical references.* Details of the edition used, along with translator (if any) and the facts of publication, should be either specified the first time a classical work is cited or given elsewhere in the scholarly apparatus. If several editions are used, the edition (or an abbreviation) should accompany each citation. Although many classicists will recognize a well-known edition merely from the last name of the editor or translator, a full citation, at least in the bibliography, should be furnished as a courtesy.

8. Epictetus, *Dissertationes*, ed. Heinrich Schenkl (Stuttgart: Teubner, 1916).

9. Herodotus, *The History*, trans. David Grene (Chicago: University of Chicago Press, 1987).

10. Solon (Edmonds's numbering) 36.20–27.

14.261 *Titles of classical works and collections.* Titles of works and published collections are italicized whether given in full or abbreviated (see 14.258). Latin and transliterated Greek titles are capitalized sentence-style (see 8.156, 11.3, 11.59).

11. Cato's uses of *pater familias* in *Agr.* (2.1, 2.7, 3.1, 3.2) are exclusively in reference to estate management. For the *diligens pater familias* in Columella, see *Rust.* 1.1.3, 1.2.1, 5.6.37, 9.1.6, 12.21.6.

12. *Scholia graeca in Homeri Odysseam*, ed. Wilhelm Dindorf (Oxford, 1855; repr. 1962).

13. *Patrologiae cursus completus, series graeca* (Paris: Migne, 1857–66).

14.262 *Superscripts in classical references.* In classical references, a superior figure is sometimes used immediately after the title of a work (or its abbreviation), and preceding any other punctuation, to indicate the number of the edition.

14. Stolz-Schmalz, *Lat. Gram.*[5] (rev. Leumann-Hoffmann; Munich, 1928), 390–91.

15. *Ausgewählte Komödien des T. M. Plautus*[2], vol. 2 (1883).

In former practice, the letters accompanying numerals in citations of classical works (see 14.257) sometimes appeared as superscripts (e.g., 3.2.996[b]5–8).

14.263 *Collections of inscriptions.* Arabic numerals are used in references to volumes in collections of inscriptions. Periods follow the volume and inscription numbers, and further subdivisions are treated as in other classical references.

16. *IG* 2[2].3274. [= *Inscriptiones graecae*, vol. 2, 2nd ed., inscription no. 3274]

17. *IG Rom.* 3.739.9–10. [*IG Rom.* = *Inscriptiones graecae ad res romanas pertinentes*]

18. *POxy.* 1485. [= *Oxyrhynchus papyri*, document no. 1485]

Some collections are cited only by the name of the editor. Since the editor's name here stands in place of a title, no comma is needed.

19. Dessau 6964.23–29. [= H. Dessau, ed., *Inscriptiones latinae selectae*]

14.264   *Fragments of classical texts.* Fragments of classical texts (some only recently discovered) are not uniformly numbered. They are published in collections, and the numbering is usually unique to a particular edition. Two numbers separated by a period usually indicate fragment and line. The editor's name, often abbreviated in subsequent references, must therefore follow the number.

20. Empedocles, frag. 115 Diels-Kranz.
21. Anacreon, frag. 2.10 Diehl.
22. Hesiod, frag. 239.1 Merkelbach and West.
23. Anacreon, frag. 5.2 D.
24. Hesiod, frag. 220 M.-W.

In citations of two or more editions of the same set of fragments, either parentheses or an equals sign may be used.

25. Pindar, frag. 133 Bergk (frag. 127 Bowra).
or
26. Pindar, frag. 133 Bergk = 127 Bowra.

14.265   *Modern editions of the classics.* When Greek, Latin, or medieval classics are cited by page number, the edition must be specified, and the normal rules for citing books are followed. See also 14.260.

35. Propertius, *Elegies*, ed. and trans. G. P. Goold, Loeb Classical Library 18 (Cambridge, MA: Harvard University Press, 1990), 45.

Aristotle. *Complete Works of Aristotle: The Revised Oxford Translation.* Edited by J. Barnes. 2 vols. Bollingen Series. Princeton, NJ: Princeton University Press, 1983.
Maimonides. *The Code of Maimonides, Book 5: The Book of Holiness.* Edited by Leon Nemoy. Translated by Louis I. Rabinowitz and Philip Grossman. New Haven, CT: Yale University Press, 1965.

14.266   *Medieval references.* The form for classical references may equally well be applied to medieval works.

27. Augustine, *De civitate Dei* 20.2.
28. Augustine, *The City of God*, trans. John Healey (New York: Dutton, 1931), 20.2.
29. *Beowulf*, lines 2401–7.

30. Abelard, *Epistle 17 to Heloïse* (Migne, *PL* 180.375c–378a).

31. *Sir Gawain and the Green Knight*, trans. Theodore Silverstein (Chicago: University of Chicago Press, 1974), pt. 3, p. 57.

Classic English Poems and Plays

14.267   *Citing editions of classic English poems and plays.* Classic English poems and plays can often be cited by book, canto, and stanza; stanza and line; act, scene, and line; or similar divisions. Publication facts can then be omitted. For frequently cited works—especially those of Shakespeare, where variations can occur in wording, line numbering, and even scene division—the edition is normally specified in the first note reference or in the bibliography. The edition must be mentioned if page numbers are cited (see 14.265).

1. Chaucer, "Wife of Bath's Prologue," *Canterbury Tales*, fragment 3, lines 105–14.

2. Spenser, *The Faerie Queene*, bk. 2, canto 8, st. 14.

3. Milton, *Paradise Lost*, bk. 1, lines 83–86.

4. *King Lear*, ed. David Bevington et al. (New York: Bantam Books, 2005), 3.2.49–60. References are to act, scene, and line.

Dryden, John. *Dramatic Essays*. Everyman's Library. New York: Dutton, 1912.

Shakespeare, William. *Hamlet*. Edited by Ann Thompson and Neil Taylor. Arden Shakespeare, 3rd ser. London: Thomson Learning, 2006.

14.268   *Short forms for citing classic English poems and plays.* A citation may be shortened by omitting *act*, *line*, and the like, as long as the system used has been explained. Arabic numerals are used, separated by periods. In immediately succeeding references, it is usually safer to repeat all the numbers. The author's name may be omitted if clear from the text. For citing sources in text, see 13.65, 14.54, 14.55.

5. Pope, *Rape of the Lock*, 3.28–29.

6. *Lear* (Bevington), 4.1.1–9, 4.1.18–24.

7. "Wife of Bath's Prologue," 115–16.

Musical Scores

14.269   *Published scores.* Published musical scores are treated in much the same way as books.

1. Giuseppe Verdi, *Il corsaro* (*melodramma tragico* in three acts), libretto by Francesco Maria Piave, ed. Elizabeth Hudson, 2 vols., *The Works of Giuseppe Verdi*, ser. 1, *Operas* (Chicago: University of Chicago Press; Milan: G. Ricordi, 1998).

Mozart, Wolfgang Amadeus. *Sonatas and Fantasies for the Piano*. Prepared from the autographs and earliest printed sources by Nathan Broder. Rev. ed. Bryn Mawr, PA: Theodore Presser, 1960.
Schubert, Franz. "Das Wandern (Wandering)," *Die schöne Müllerin (The Maid of the Mill)*. In *First Vocal Album* (for high voice). New York: G. Schirmer, 1895.

In the last example above, the words and titles are given in both German and English in the score itself. See also 14.108.

14.270   *Unpublished scores.* Unpublished scores are treated in the same way as other unpublished material in manuscript collections (see 14.232–42).

2. Ralph Shapey, "Partita for Violin and Thirteen Players," score, 1966, Special Collections, Joseph Regenstein Library, University of Chicago.

Databases

14.271   *Library and other commercial databases.* When citing items such as news or journal articles obtained through a third-party commercial database that archives and offers such material whether by subscription or otherwise, follow the recommendations in the sections on the applicable publication type. In addition, include a URL, but only if the database includes a recommended stable or persistent form with the document (as in the third example). Otherwise, include the name of the database and, in parentheses, any identification number provided with the source (as in the second and fourth examples). For items that do not include a publication or revision date, include an access date. For theses and dissertations, see 14.224.

2. Beth Daley, "A Tale of a Whale: Scientists, Museum Are Eager to Study, Display Rare Creature," *Boston Globe*, June 11, 2002, third edition, LexisNexis Academic.
3. *Encyclopedia of Animals*, s.v. "emperor penguin," accessed June 21, 2008, EBSCO Animals (9500100510).
4. William Maiben, "A Tombeau for John Lennon, 1940–1980," *Perspectives of New Music* 19, nos. 1/2 (Autumn 1980–Summer 1981): 533, http://www.jstor.org/stable/832614.

Howard, David H. "Hospital Quality and Selective Contracting: Evidence from Kidney Transplantation." *Forum for Health Economics and Policy* 11, no. 2 (2008). PubMed Central (PMC2600561).

14.272 *Scientific databases.* In the sciences especially, it has become customary to cite databases by listing, at a minimum, the name of the database, a descriptive phrase or record locator (such as a data marker or accession number) indicating the part of the database being cited or explaining the nature of the reference, an access date, and a URL. In bibliographies, list under the name of the database.

> 1. NASA/IPAC Extragalactic Database (object name IRAS F00400+4059; accessed October 6, 2009), http://nedwww.ipac.caltech.edu/.
> 2. GenBank (for RP11-322N14 BAC [accession number AC017046]; accessed October 6, 2009), http://www.ncbi.nlm.nih.gov/Genbank/.

GenBank (for RP11-322N14 BAC [accession number AC017046]; accessed October 6, 2009). http://www.ncbi.nlm.nih.gov/Genbank/.
NASA/IPAC Extragalactic Database (object name IRAS F00400+4059; accessed October 6, 2009). http://nedwww.ipac.caltech.edu/.

Citations Taken from Secondary Sources

14.273 *Citations taken from secondary sources.* To cite a source from a secondary source ("quoted in . . .") is generally to be discouraged, since authors are expected to have examined the works they cite. If an original source is unavailable, however, both the original and the secondary source must be listed.

> 1. Louis Zukofsky, "Sincerity and Objectification," *Poetry* 37 (February 1931): 269, quoted in Bonnie Costello, *Marianne Moore: Imaginary Possessions* (Cambridge, MA: Harvard University Press, 1981), 78.

Audiovisual Materials

14.274 *Audiovisual materials—elements to include.* Documentation of a recording usually includes some or all of the following pieces of information: the name of the composer, writer, performer, or other person primarily responsible for the content; the title, in italics or quotation marks, as applicable (see 8.192); the name of the recording company or publisher;

any identifying number of the recording; indication of medium (compact disc, audiocassette, audiovisual file, etc.); and the copyright date or date of production or performance. Recordings consulted online should include a URL or DOI (see 14.5, 14.6). Supplementary information, such as the number of discs in an album and the duration of the recording, as applicable, may also be given.

14.275   *Discographies.* Discographies are specialized bibliographies that list audiovisual materials such as audio recordings, video recordings, and multimedia packages. For advice on discographies, consult Suzanne E. Thorin and Carole Franklin Vidali, *The Acquisition and Cataloging of Music and Sound Recordings* (bibliog. 5). For an example, see figure 14.12.

Sound Recordings

14.276   *Musical recordings.* For the typographic treatment of musical compositions in running text, see 8.188–92. Those guidelines, however, do not necessarily apply to recordings when listed in a discography (see fig. 14.12), bibliography, or note. *Symphony* or *sonata*, for example, is capitalized when part of the title of a recording. If the conductor or performer is the focus of the recording or is more relevant to the discussion than the composer, either one may be listed first. For the date, include the date of the recording, the copyright date or published date included with the recording, or both. If a date cannot be determined from the recording (a common problem with some LPs and other older media), consult a library catalog or other resource; citations without a date are generally unacceptable. If no date can be found, use "n.d." (for *no date*).

1. *The Fireside Treasury of Folk Songs*, vol. 1, orchestra and chorus dir. Mitch Miller, Golden Record A198:17A–B, 1958, 33⅓ rpm.

2. New York Trumpet Ensemble, with Edward Carroll (trumpet) and Edward Brewer (organ), *Art of the Trumpet*, recorded at the Madeira Festival, June 1–2, 1981, Vox/Turnabout, PVT 7183, 1982, compact disc.

3. Richard Strauss, *Don Quixote*, with Emanuel Feuermann (violoncello) and the Philadelphia Orchestra, conducted by Eugene Ormandy, recorded February 24, 1940, Biddulph LAB 042, 1991, compact disc.

4. Billie Holiday, vocal performance of "I'm a Fool to Want You," by Joel Herron, Frank Sinatra, and Jack Wolf, recorded February 20, 1958, with Ray Ellis, on *Lady in Satin*, Columbia CL 1157, 33⅓ rpm.

Mozart, Wolfgang Amadeus. *Don Giovanni.* Orchestra and Chorus of the Royal Opera House, Covent Garden. Sir Colin Davis. With Ingvar Wixell, Luigi Roni,

ANNOTATED

DISCOGRAPHY

This brief discography primarily lists commercial records readily available in the United States which have selections that pertain to genres, styles, instruments, and ensemble types that I have discussed in the book.

Huayno Music of Peru, vol. 1 (1949–1989), Arhoolie (CD 320), edited with notes by John Cohen (1989). This recording includes reissues of Peruvian recordings of the type that I have called the "commercial wayno style" (or "urban-country" style) from the 1950s and 1960s in Lima. Selections 1 (Jilguero del Huascarán) and 3 (Pastorita Huaracina) are by particularly important "country music" stars from Ancash; selection 2 is by a Junín orquesta with harp, violin, saxes, and clarinets.

Kingdom of the Sun: Peru's Inca Heritage, Nonesuch (H-72029), recorded by David Lewiston (n.d.). This recording includes an excellent example of a sikumoreno ensemble (side 1, band 4) of the type heard in the city of Puno and in the Province of Chucuito, Puno. It also includes a wayno that I refer to in chapter 9, "Adios pueblo de Ayacucho" (side 1, band 1), played in Ayacuchano style, and waynos from other regions. Side 2, band 2 is a good example of a kena solo.

Music of Peru, Folkways (FE 4415), notes by Harry Tschopik, Jr. (1950 [1959]). The recordings on side 1, bands 1 and 3, and side 2, band 1, demonstrate the ensemble sound approximating early estudiantinas (especially side 1, band 3); the bass support provided by the guitars is particularly typical. Wayno (huayno) and marinera genres are included.

Música Andina del Perú, Patronato Popular y Porvenir Pro Música Clásica (write: Proyecto de Preservación de la Música Tradicional Andina, Pontificia Universidad Católica del Perú, Instituto Riva Agüero, Jr., Camaná 459-Lima 1, for this and other recordings from Junín, Cajamarca, and Arequipa), edited with notes by Raúl Romero (1987). This excellent survey of highland Peruvian music includes examples of charango music from Cusco (side 1, band 1); the unison pitu style from Cusco (side 3, band 8—this style is quite different from the sound of pitu ensembles in Conima); the music for the Puneño traje de luz dance, "La Diablada," performed by a brass band (side 3, band 9); chiriguano panpipe music from Huancané (side 3, band 10); and choquela (chokela) music from Puno (side 3, band 11), a tradition previously performed in Conima.

315

FIGURE 14.12. The first page of a discography. See 14.275.

Martina Arroyo, Stuart Burrows, Kiri Te Kanawa, et al. Recorded May 1973. Philips 422 541-2, 1991, 3 compact discs.

Pink Floyd. *Atom Heart Mother*. Capitol CDP 7 46381 2, 1990, compact disc. Originally released in 1970.

Rubinstein, Artur. *The Chopin Collection*. RCA Victor/BMG 60822-2-RG, 1991, 11 compact discs. Recorded 1946, 1958–67.

Weingartner, Felix von (conductor). *150 Jahre Wiener Philharmoniker.* Preiser
   Records, PR90113 (mono), 1992, compact disc. Recorded in 1936. Includes
   Beethoven's Symphony no. 3 in E-flat Major and Symphony no. 8 in F Major.

Recordings are usually listed in a separate discography (see fig. 14.12)
rather than in a bibliography. If included in a bibliography, they are best
grouped under an appropriate subhead (see 14.58).

14.277 *Recordings of literature, lectures, and such.* Recordings of drama, prose or
poetry readings, lectures, and the like are treated much the same as musical recordings. Facts of publication, where needed, follow the style for
print media. For electronic sources, include information about the medium; online sources should include a URL or similar identifier (see 14.4–
13). See also 14.280.

   1. Dylan Thomas, *Under Milk Wood,* performed by Dylan Thomas et al., Caed-
mon TC-2005, 1953, 33⅓ rpm, 2 LPs.
   2. Harry S. Truman, "First Speech to Congress," April 16, 1945, transcript and
Adobe Flash audio, 18:13, Miller Center of Public Affairs, University of Virginia,
http://millercenter.org/scripps/archive/speeches/detail/3339.
   3. Calvin Coolidge, "Equal Rights" (speech), copy of an undated 78 rpm disc, ca.
1920, Library of Congress, "American Leaders Speak: Recordings from World War I
and the 1920 Election, 1918–1920," RealAudio and WAV formats, http://memory
.loc.gov/ammem/nfhtml/nforSpeakers01.html.
   4. Eleanor Roosevelt, "Is America Facing World Leadership?," convocation
speech, Ball State Teacher's College, May 6, 1959, radio broadcast, Windows Media
Audio, 47:46, http://libx.bsu.edu/cdm4/item_viewer.php?CISOROOT=/ElRoos
&CISOPTR=0&CISOBOX=1&REC=2.

Auden, W. H. *Selected Poems.* Read by the author. Spoken Arts 7137, 1991. Audiocassette.
Schlosser, Eric. *Fast Food Nation: The Dark Side of the All-American Meal.* Read by
   Rick Adamson. New York: Random House Audible, 2004. Audiobook, 8 compact discs; 9 hrs.

Video Recordings

14.278 *Slides and filmstrips.* Citations of slides and filmstrips should indicate creator (if credited), title, publisher, date, and information about the medium.

1. Louis J. Mihalyi, *Landscapes of Zambia, Central Africa* (Santa Barbara, CA: Visual Education, 1975), 35 mm slides, 40 frames.

The Greek and Roman World. Chicago: Society for Visual Education, 1977. Filmstrip, 44 min.

14.279   *DVDs and videocassettes.* Citations of video recordings, like citations of sound recordings, will vary according to the nature of the material. Any facts relevant to identifying the item should be included. Indexed scenes are treated as chapters and cited by title or by number. Ancillary material, such as critical commentary, is cited by author and title. Note that in the *Monty Python* example, the citation is of material original to the 2001 edition, so the original release date of the film (1975) is omitted.

7. Michael Curtis and Gregory S. Malins, "The One with the Princess Leia Fantasy," *Friends*, season 3, episode 1, directed by Gail Mancuso, aired September 19, 1996 (Burbank, CA: Warner Home Video, 2003), DVD.
8. "Crop Duster Attack," *North by Northwest*, directed by Alfred Hitchcock (1959; Burbank, CA: Warner Home Video, 2000), DVD.

Cleese, John, Terry Gilliam, Eric Idle, Terry Jones, and Michael Palin. "Commentaries." Disc 2. *Monty Python and the Holy Grail*, special ed. DVD. Directed by Terry Gilliam and Terry Jones. Culver City, CA: Columbia Tristar Home Entertainment, 2001.
Handel, George Frideric. *Messiah*. Atlanta Symphony Orchestra and Chamber Chorus, Robert Shaw. Performed December 19, 1987. Ansonia Station, NY: Video Artists International, 1988. Videocassette (VHS), 141 min.

14.280   *Online multimedia.* Citations of online multimedia must thoroughly identify the material cited by incorporating the elements discussed and exemplified throughout this section; it is never enough simply to cite an electronic file name or URL, though this information should be included as well. If no date can be determined from the source, include the date the material was last accessed. (See also 14.4–13.) If the material is a recording of a speech or other performance, or if it is a digital version of a published source, include information about the original performance or source. Whether to list information about the original or the digitized copy first will depend on the information available and is usually up to the author. Include an indication of the source type (e.g., "video") and length. Note the idiosyncratic capitalization and spacing in the second example, preserved as an aid to identifying the source; this approach, if used at all, should be reserved for sources that have no ties to any publishing body (and any outright errors should be indicated in the text or note; see also 13.59). See also 14.277, 14.198. For an example of a podcast, see 14.221.

    1. A. E. Weed, *At the Foot of the Flatiron* (American Mutoscope and Biograph Co., 1903), 35 mm film, from Library of Congress, *The Life of a City: Early Films of New York, 1898–1906*, MPEG video, 2:19, http://lcweb2.loc.gov/ammem/papr/nyc home.html.
    2. "HOROWITZ AT CARNEGIE HALL 2-Chopin Nocturne in Fm Op.55," YouTube video, 5:53, from a performance televised by CBS on September 22, 1968, posted by "hubanj," January 9, 2009, http://www.youtube.com/watch?v =cDVBtuWkMS8.

Harwood, John. "The Pros and Cons of Biden." *New York Times* video, 2:00. August 23, 2008. http://video.on.nytimes.com/?fr_story=a425c9aca92f51bd19f 2a621fd93b5e266507191.
Pollan, Michael. "Michael Pollan Gives a Plant's-Eye View." Filmed March 2007. TED video, 17:31. Posted February 2008. http://www.ted.com/index.php/talks /michael_pollan_gives_a_plant_s_eye_view.html.

Legal and Public Documents

14.281   *Recommended stylebooks.* Citations in predominantly legal works generally follow one of two guides: (1) *The Bluebook: A Uniform System of Citation*, published by the Harvard Law Review Association and available online (with a subscription); or (2) the *ALWD Citation Manual: A Professional System of Citation*, prepared and published by the Association of Legal Writing Directors and Darby Dickerson (see bibliog. 1.1). For Canada, see 14.305. *The Bluebook* is the most widely used citation guide; its conventions predominate in law reviews. The *ALWD Citation Manual* differs in some elements and aims to be somewhat simpler. Chicago recommends using one of these systems for citing legal and public documents—including cases, constitutions, statutes, and other government documents— even in works with a predominantly nonlegal subject matter. This departure from Chicago's previous recommendations recognizes the ubiquity of these systems in legal publications, commercial databases, and government archives. Any editor working extensively with legal and public documents should have one of these manuals on hand. Most of the examples of legal-style citations in this section are based on *The Bluebook* (exceptions are made for secondary sources and certain unpublished government documents; see 14.303, 14.304, 14.308, 14.315).

14.282   *Legal and public documents online. The Bluebook* includes specific recommendations for citing electronic sources. In general, however, for citations to cases, constitutions and statutes, and other such materials, print sources are preferred. Sources consulted through commercial databases such as Westlaw or LexisNexis may also be cited; these are treated like print sources but with the addition of the database name and any identification number (or, in the case of constitutions and statutes, information about the currency of the database). For examples, see 14.288. *The Bluebook* also provides advice for citing Internet sources, including documents available from government archives outside the United States. In general, such citations should follow the format for printed sources with the addition of a URL. Access dates ("last visited" in *Bluebook* parlance) are recommended only for undated documents. This advice is similar to Chicago's recommendations (see 14.4–13). For examples, see 14.317. Authors who need to cite more than a few electronic sources in *Bluebook* style should consult that manual. For documents in a national archive, any citations to electronic versions should generally be limited to those made available by the archive itself or through a commercial database.

14.283   *Note form for legal-style citations.* Almost all legal works use notes for documentation and few use bibliographies. The examples in this section, based on the recommendations in *The Bluebook*, are accordingly given in note form only. Any work so cited need not be listed in a bibliography. Works using the author-date style (chapter 15) and citing only a handful of legal and public documents may limit those citations to the text, using citation sentences and clauses that include the same information as footnotes, as suggested in *The Bluebook*; those with more than a very few legal-style citations, however, may need to supplement the author-date system with footnotes or endnotes. See 15.54–55.

14.284   *Typefaces in legal-style citations.* In *Bluebook* style, italics are used for titles of articles and chapters (a major difference from nonlegal usage), uncommon words or phrases in languages other than English (but not such well-known terms as *de facto* or *habeas corpus*), certain introductory signals indicating a cross-reference (such as *See*), subsequent case history (such as *cert. denied*; see 14.290), and procedural phrases (such as *In re*). Italics are also used for case names mentioned in running text. All other material, including case names in citations (but see 14.288), is presented in roman. In formal *Bluebook* style, caps and small caps are used for the titles of books and their authors and for the names of periodicals and newspapers. The examples in this section use a simpler style advocated by some law reviews, substituting upper- and lowercase roman type for caps and small caps. It should be noted that the examples in this section are limited to legal and public documents. Though *Bluebook*-style citations to books, articles, and other types of secondary sources may be appropriate in works with predominantly legal subject matter, these are not covered here (but see 14.303).

14.285   *Page numbers and other locators in legal-style citations.* In *Bluebook* style, for most authorities the first page number is cited, following the name of the authority (usually abbreviated) and usually with no intervening punctuation; references to specific page numbers follow the first page number, separated by a comma. Some authorities are cited by section (§) or paragraph (¶) number; references to specific pages within such sections follow a comma and are preceded by *at*.

14.286   *Abbreviations in legal-style citations.* Most abbreviations in *The Bluebook* use periods or apostrophes. In citations (but not in running text), *Bluebook* style uses *2d* and *3d* rather than *2nd* and *3rd* and capitalizes abbreviations like *No.* and *Sess.* Works that otherwise follow Chicago style—which differs on some of these points (see, e.g., 10.4)—should, for legal citations, follow the style of the examples in this section, which illustrate *Bluebook* style. The following example cites a decision by the United States Court of Appeals for the Seventh Circuit, reported in volume 206 of the *Federal Reporter*, third series, beginning on page 752, with the citation specifically referring to footnote 1 on that page. For more abbreviations, consult *The Bluebook*.

  1. NLRB v. Somerville Constr. Co., 206 F.3d 752, 752 n.1 (7th Cir. 2000).

It should be noted that in running text, most terms should be spelled out—including terms such as *chapter, part, article, section, paragraph,* and so forth (but, in case names, not *v.* or common abbreviations such as *Co.* and *Inc.*). See also 8.79, 8.81.

14.287   *Short forms for legal-style citations.* The *Bluebook* allows certain short forms for subsequent citations to the same source. In general, it limits this use to those items that have been cited within the previous five notes. Short forms include case names reduced to the name of only one party (usually the plaintiff or the nongovernmental party); statutes and legislative documents identified only by name or document and section numbers; treaties identified only by name (or sometimes a short form thereof); and the use of *id.* (in italics). Cases are the most readily shortened forms; examples are included in the section that treats them (14.288–91). Works that cite only a few legal documents may be better off using the full form for each citation. See also 14.24–31.

Cases and Court Decisions

14.288 *Cases or court decisions—basic elements.* Case names, including the abbreviation *v.*, are set roman in notes; short forms in subsequent citations are italicized (as are case names mentioned in running text). Full citations include volume number (arabic), abbreviated name of the reporter, the ordinal series number of the reporter (if applicable), the abbreviated name of the court (if not specified by the reporter) and the date together in parentheses, and other relevant information (see 14.291). A single page number designates the opening page of a decision; an additional number designates an actual page cited. In a shortened citation, *at* is used to cite a particular page (example 18); absence of *at* implies reference to the decision as a whole (example 19). See also 14.287.

> 16. United States v. Christmas, 222 F.3d 141, 145 (4th Cir. 2000).
> 17. Profit Sharing Plan v. Mbank Dallas, N.A., 683 F. Supp. 592 (N.D. Tex. 1988).
> 18. *Christmas*, 222 F.3d at 145.
> 19. *Profit Sharing Plan*, 683 F. Supp. 592.

When a commercial electronic database is cited, include the docket number, name of the database, and any identifying date and number supplied by the database. References to page or screen numbers are preceded by an asterisk. Short forms may include only the database identifier. See also 14.282.

> 20. McNamee v. Dep't of the Treasury, No. 05-6151-CV, 2007 U.S. App. LEXIS 12016 (2d Cir. May 23, 2007).
> 21. Horn v. Pub. Water Supply Dist. No. 8, No. WD 63889, 2005 WL 119835 (Mo. Ct. App. Jan. 21, 2005).
> 22. *McNamee*, 2007 U.S. App. LEXIS 12016, at *5.
> 23. *Horn*, 2005 WL 119835, at *3.

14.289 *United States Supreme Court decisions.* All Supreme Court decisions are published in the *United States Supreme Court Reports* (abbreviated U.S.) and are preferably cited to that reporter. Cases not yet published therein may be cited to the *Supreme Court Reporter* (S. Ct.), which publishes decisions more quickly. Because the court's name is identified by the reporter, it is not repeated before the date.

24. AT&T Corp. v. Iowa Utils. Bd., 525 U.S. 366 (1999).

25. Brendlin v. California, 127 S. Ct. 2400 (2007).

26. AT&T, 525 U.S. at 366–67.

14.290 *Lower federal-court decisions.* Lower federal-court decisions are usually cited to the *Federal Reporter* (F.) or to the *Federal Supplement* (F. Supp.). If relevant, the Supreme Court's grant or denial of certiorari may be indicated.

27. United States v. Dennis, 183 F. 201 (2d Cir. 1950).

28. City of Las Vegas v. Walsh, 124 P.3d 203 (Nev. 2005), *cert. denied*, 547 U.S. 1071 (2006).

29. Eaton v. IBM Corp., 925 F. Supp. 487 (S.D. Tex. 1996).

30. *Dennis*, 183 F. at 202.

31. *Walsh*, 124 P.3d at 215.

14.291 *State- and local-court decisions.* Decisions of state and local courts are cited much like federal-court decisions. If both the official and the commercial reporters are cited, they are separated by a comma. If the court's name is identified unambiguously by the reporter, it is not repeated before the date. If a case was decided in a lower court, the abbreviated court name appears before the date. Note that a space is used after a two- or three-letter abbreviated reporter name—"Cal. 2d" (*California Reports*, second series)—but not after initialisms like "A." or "N.Y.S." in "A.2d" (*Atlantic Reporter*) or "N.Y.S.2d" (*New York Supplement*).

32. Williams v. Davis, 27 Cal. 2d 746 (1946).

33. *Id.* at 747.

34. Henningsen v. Bloomfield Motors, Inc., 32 N.J. 358, 161 A.2d 69 (1960).

35. Stambovsky v. Ackley, 572 N.Y.S.2d 672 (App. Div. 2007).

36. *Williams*, 27 Cal. 2d 746.

Constitutions

14.292 *Constitutions.* In citations to constitutions, the article and amendment numbers appear in roman numerals; other subdivision numbers are in arabic. (For nonlegal style see 9.29.) In *Bluebook* style the name of the constitution is capitalized; other abbreviations are lowercased.

37. U.S. Const. art. I, § 4, cl. 2.

38. U.S. Const. amend. XIV, § 2.

39. Ariz. Const. art. VII, § 5.

40. Ark. Const. of 1868, art. III, § 2 (superseded 1874).

Legislative and Executive Documents

14.293 *Legislative documents—abbreviations.* Abbreviations for United States leg-islative documents include "Cong." (Congress), "H." (House), "S." (Sen-ate), and other standard abbreviations for such terms as document, ses-sion, resolution, and so forth. Unless it is not clear from the context, "U.S." may be omitted. For lists of abbreviations and many examples, consult *The Bluebook*. See also 14.286.

14.294 *Laws and statutes.* Bills or joint resolutions that have been signed into law—"public laws," or statutes—are first published separately, as slip laws, and then collected in the annual bound volumes of the *United States Statutes at Large* (abbreviated in legal style as Stat.), where they are re-ferred to as session laws. Later they are incorporated into the *United States Code* (U.S.C.).

> 17. Homeland Security Act of 2002, Pub. L. No. 107-296, 116 Stat. 2135 (2002).
> 18. Homeland Security Act of 2002, 6 U.S.C. § 101 (2002).

14.295 *Bills and resolutions.* Congressional bills (proposed laws) and resolutions are published in pamphlet form (slip bills). In citations, bills or resolu-tions originating in the House of Representatives are abbreviated "H.R." or "H.R. Res.," and those originating in the Senate, "S." or "S. Res." The title of the bill (if there is one) is followed by the bill number, the con-gressional session, a section number (if relevant), and the year of publi-cation in parentheses. Authors wishing to cite a bill that has since been enacted should cite it as a statute (see 14.294).

> 16. Homeland Security Act of 2002, H.R. 5005, 107th Cong. (2002).

14.296 *Hearings.* Records of testimony given before congressional committees are usually published with titles, which should be cited in full and set in italics. The relevant committee should be listed as part of the title. Note that *Before*—which Chicago would normally lowercase in a title (see 8.157)—is capitalized according to *Bluebook* style, which capitalizes prep-ositions of more than four letters. Include the number of the Congress, the page number cited (if any), the date in parentheses, and the speaker's name, title, and affiliation in parentheses. Note that *The Bluebook* does not require a session number for citations to *House Reports* published as of the 60th Congress, where an odd-numbered year indicates a first session and an even year a second session.

> 11. *Homeland Security Act of 2002: Hearings on H.R. 5005, Day 3, Before the Select Comm. on Homeland Security*, 107th Cong. 203 (2002) (statement of David Walker, Comptroller General of the United States).

14.297   *Congressional reports and documents.* In *Bluebook* style, numbered reports and documents are cited by the number of Congress, which is joined to the document number by a hyphen. House and Senate reports are abbreviated "H.R. Rep." or "S. Rep."; documents are cited to "H.R. Doc." or "S. Doc." A specific page reference, if needed, is added following *at*. The year of the report or document is placed in parentheses. Additional information (e.g., to indicate a conference report) follows the year, in parentheses. If not mentioned in text, a title and author (if any) may be included in the citation.

> 8. Select Comm. on Homeland Security, Homeland Security Act of 2002, H.R. Rep. No. 107-609, pt. 1 (2002).
> 9. H.R. Rep. No. 106-661, at 9 (2000) (Conf. Rep.).
> 10. S. Doc. No. 77-148, at 2–5 (1941).

14.298   *Congressional debates since 1873.* Since 1873, congressional debates have been published by the government in the *Congressional Record*. Daily issues are bound in paper biweekly and in permanent volumes (divided into parts) yearly. Since material may be added, deleted, or modified when the final volumes are prepared, pagination will vary between the different editions. Whenever possible, citation should be made to the permanent volumes. Note that, following *Bluebook* style, italics are not used for the name of the publication. The page number (preceded by "H" or "S," for House or Senate, in the daily edition) is followed by the date, which is placed in parentheses. If the identity of a speaker is necessary, include it in parentheses.

> 16. 147 Cong. Rec. 19,000 (2001).
> 17. 148 Cong. Rec. S10,491 (daily ed. Oct. 16, 2002) (statement of Sen. Dodd).

14.299   *Records of congressional debates before 1873.* Until 1873, congressional debates were privately printed in *Annals of the Congress of the United States* (covering the years 1789–1824; also known by other names), *Register of Debates* (1824–37), and *Congressional Globe* (1833–73). In citing the date, refer to the year covered rather than the date of publication. Note that the *Globe* is normally cited by session, whereas the *Annals* and *Debates* are cited by volume number. As with citations to the *Congressional Record*, the titles are abbreviated and not italicized.

> 5. Cong. Globe, 39th Cong., 2d Sess. 39 (1866).
> 6. 42 Annals of Cong. 1697 (1824).
> 7. 3 Reg. Deb. 388 (1827).

14.300 *State laws and municipal ordinances.* The titles of state codes (compilations) for laws and municipal ordinances are set in roman type. A name is included in parentheses where necessary to indicate the version of a code cited. The date following a code (or the version of a code) indicates the year the volume was updated or supplemented to include the law being cited. Form of citation will vary by state. The date a specific law was passed may be included in parentheses at the end of the citation. For an exhaustive treatment of state-by-state variations, consult *The Bluebook*.

> 41. Ohio Rev. Code Ann. § 3566 (West 2000).
> 42. An Act Guaranteeing Governmental Independence, Ky. Rev. Stat. Ann. § 520.020 (LexisNexis 1985) (passed Jan. 3, 1974).

14.301 *Presidential documents.* Presidential proclamations, executive orders, vetoes, addresses, and the like are published in the *Weekly Compilation of Presidential Documents* (Weekly Comp. Pres. Doc.) and in the *Public Papers of the Presidents of the United States* (Pub. Papers). Proclamations and executive orders are also carried in the daily *Federal Register* (Fed. Reg.) and then published in title 3 of the *Code of Federal Regulations* (C.F.R.).

> 25. Proclamation No. 8214, 73 Fed. Reg. 1439 (Jan. 8, 2008).
> 26. Exec. Order No. 11,609, 3 C.F.R. 586 (1971–75).

Some executive orders and proclamations become part of the *United States Code* and are best so cited. For more examples, consult *The Bluebook*.

14.302 *Treaties.* The texts of treaties signed before 1950 are published in *United States Statutes at Large*; the unofficial citation is to the *Treaty Series* (T.S.) or the *Executive Agreement Series* (E.A.S.), each of which assigns a number to a treaty covered. Those signed in 1950 and later appear in *United States Treaties and Other International Agreements* (U.S.T., 1950–), or *Treaties and Other International Acts Series* (T.I.A.S., 1945–), which also assigns a number. Treaties involving more than two nations may be found in the *United Nations Treaty Series* (U.N.T.S., 1946–) or, from 1920 to 1946, in the *League of Nations Treaty Series* (L.N.T.S., 1920–46). These and other sources are listed in *The Bluebook*. Titles of treaties are set in roman and capitalized headline-style (recall that *The Bluebook* capitalizes prepositions of more than four letters). An exact date indicates the date of signing and is therefore preferable to a year alone, which may differ from the year the treaty was published in one of the works above. Page numbers are given where relevant.

> 34. Treaty Banning Nuclear Weapon Tests in the Atmosphere, in Outer Space and Under Water, U.S.-U.K.-U.S.S.R., Aug. 5, 1963, 14 U.S.T. 1313.
>
> 35. Convention Concerning Military Service, Den.-Italy, July 15, 1954, 250 T.I.A.S. 3516, at 45.

14.303 *Secondary sources and freestanding publications.* For the generalist citing legal and public documents that appear in secondary sources or as freestanding publications, *Bluebook* style should generally *not* be followed. Moreover, any source that is analogous to a secondary source—including not just books or articles but also pamphlets and other titled publications—can be cited by title and author (if any) rather than in an abbreviated form. The following examples are not meant to be exhaustive. Those who are required to follow *Bluebook* style should consult that manual, whose recommendations differ.

> 1. *Journals of the Continental Congress, 1774–1789*, ed. Worthington C. Ford et al. (Washington, DC, 1904–37), 15:1341.
>
> 2. *JCC* 25:863.
>
> 3. *House Miscellaneous Document no. 210, 53d Cong., 2d sess., in Compilation of the Messages and Papers of the Presidents, 1789–1897*, ed. J. D. Richardson (Washington, DC: Government Printing Office, 1907), 4:16.
>
> 4. *Public Papers of the Presidents of the United States: Herbert Hoover, 1929–1933*, 4 vols. (Washington, DC: Government Printing Office, 1974–77), 1:134.
>
> 5. *Median Gross Rent by Counties of the United States, 1970*, prepared by the Geography Division in cooperation with the Housing Division, Bureau of the Census (Washington, DC, 1975).
>
> 6. US Department of the Treasury, *Report of the Secretary of the Treasury Transmitting a Report from the Register of the Treasury of the Commerce and Navigation of the United States for the Year Ending the 30th of June, 1850*, 31st Cong., 2d sess., House Executive Document 8 (Washington, DC, 1850–51).
>
> 7. Ralph I. Straus, *Expanding Private Investment for Free World Economic Growth*, special report prepared at the request of the Department of State, April 1959, 12.
>
> 8. Illinois General Assembly, Law Revision Commission, *Report to the 80th General Assembly of the State of Illinois* (Chicago, 1977), 14–18.

Unlike most of the legal-style citations discussed elsewhere in this section, public documents published in secondary sources or as freestanding works may be suitable for inclusion in a bibliography.

> Continental Congress. *Journals of the Continental Congress, 1774–1789.* Edited by Worthington C. Ford et al. 34 vols. Washington, DC, 1904–37.

14.304 *Unpublished government documents.* For general guidelines and many examples that can be adapted to government documents, see 14.232–42. Most unpublished documents of the United States government are housed in the National Archives and Records Administration (NARA) in Washington, DC, or in one of its branches. All, including films, photographs, and sound recordings as well as written materials, are cited by record group (RG) number. A list of the record groups and their numbers is given in the *Guide to the National Archives of the United States*, augmented by the leaflet *Citing Records in the National Archives of the United States* (available at the National Archives website), which includes advice on citing its electronic records (see bibliog. 4.5). Names of specific documents are given in quotation marks.

> 40. Senate Committee on the Judiciary, "Lobbying," file 71A-F15, RG 46, National Archives.
>
> 41. National Archives Branch Depository, Suitland, MD, Records of the National Commission on Law Observance and Enforcement, RG 10.

Canada

14.305 *Canadian reference works.* The major reference work for citing Canadian public documents and legal cases in a Canadian context is the *Canadian Guide to Uniform Legal Citation*, edited and published (in English and French) by the Carswell/McGill Law Journal (see bibliog. 1.1). Also valuable are Douglass T. MacEllven, Michael J. McGuire, Neil A. Campbell, and John N. Davis, *Legal Research Handbook*, 5th edition (bibliog. 5); *Canadian Almanac and Directory* (bibliog. 4.4); and Gerald L. Gall, F. Pearl Eliadis, and France Allard, *The Canadian Legal System*, 5th edition (bibliog. 5). Authors citing more than a few Canadian authorities should consult one of these works. Additional resources may be found online through LexUM, a service provided through the University of Montreal. For citing the occasional example in a US context, *The Bluebook* (see 14.281) provides some recommendations and examples.

14.306   *Canadian legal cases.* The following examples illustrate *Bluebook* style. The basic elements are similar to those used in US law citations; the date is enclosed in square brackets, followed by the volume number if pertinent, the abbreviated name of the reporter, and the page number. Canadian Supreme Court cases since 1876 are cited to *Supreme Court Reports* (S.C.R.); cases after 1974 should include the volume number of the reporter. Federal court cases are cited to *Federal Courts Reports* (F.C., 1971–) or *Exchequer Court Reports* (Ex. C.R., 1875–1971). Cases not found in any of these sources are cited to *Dominion Law Reports* (D.L.R.). Add "Can." in parentheses if it is not clear from the context or the citation.

> 10. Robertson v. Thomson Corp., [2006] 2 S.C.R. 363 (Can.).
> 11. Boldy v. Royal Bank of Canada, [2008] F.C. 99.

14.307   *Canadian statutes.* Federal statutes appear in the *Revised Statutes of Canada* (R.S.C.), a consolidation that is published every fifteen or twenty years; in the interim they are cited as session laws in the annual *Statutes of Canada* (S.C.). Citation elements are similar to US statutes: the name of the act, the abbreviated name of the compilation, chapter number (in R.S.C., the chapter number includes the initial letter of the name of the act), section number if applicable, and publication date. Add "Can." in parentheses if it is not clear from the context or the citation.

> 12. Companies' Creditors Arrangement Act, R.S.C., ch. C-36, s. 5 (1985) (Can.).
> 13. Canada Elections Act, 2000 S.C., ch. 9.

14.308   *Unpublished Canadian government documents.* The Library and Archives Canada (LAC) houses the unpublished records of the federal government, both individually written and institutional, as well as historically significant documents from the private sector. The guide to the entire LAC collections is available online, as are the archives for each province and territory. For citing unpublished materials, see the guidelines and examples in 14.232–42.

United Kingdom

14.309   *UK reference works.* The catalogs of the National Archives (the official archive for England, Wales, and the central UK government), available online, extend to the documents of the former Public Record Office, the Historical Manuscripts Commission, the Office of Public Sector Information, and Her Majesty's Stationery Office (HMSO), among others. The UK

Parliament also makes its catalogs available online. Printed guides include the *Guide to the Contents of the Public Record Office*; Frank Rodgers, *A Guide to British Government Publications*; and John E. Pemberton, ed., *The Bibliographic Control of Official Publications* (all in bibliog. 4.5). For citing UK legal and public documents in a US context, *The Bluebook* (see 14.281) provides an overview.

14.310 *UK legal cases.* In *Bluebook* style, the basic elements in citations to UK legal cases are similar to those used in US law citations: the name of the case, in roman (cases involving the Crown use the abbreviation "R" for Rex or Regina); the date, which is enclosed in parentheses when the volumes of the reporter are numbered cumulatively, or in square brackets when the year is essential to locating the case (there is either no volume number or the volumes for each year are numbered anew, not cumulatively); the abbreviated name of the reporter; and the opening page of the decision. If the court is not apparent from the name of the reporter, or if the jurisdiction is not clear from context, include either or both, as necessary, in parentheses. Until recently, the courts of highest appeal in the United Kingdom (except for criminal cases in Scotland) had been the House of Lords (H.L.) and the Judicial Committee of the Privy Council (P.C.). In 2005, the Supreme Court of the United Kingdom was established. In 2009 it assumed the jurisdiction of the Appellate Committee of the House of Lords and the devolution jurisdiction of the Judicial Committee of the Privy Council. Most cases are cited to the applicable report in the *Law Reports*, among these the Appeal Cases (A.C.), Queen's (King's) Bench (Q.B., K.B.), Chancery (Ch.), Family (Fam.), and Probate (P.) reports. For other reports applicable to cases dating back to AD 1094, consult *The Bluebook*.

> 10. R v. Dudley and Stephens, (1884) 14 Q.B.D. 273 (D.C.).
> 11. Regal (Hastings) Ltd. v. Gulliver and Ors, [1967] 2 A.C. 134 (H.L.) (Eng.).

14.311 *UK parliamentary publications.* Parliamentary publications include all materials issued by both houses of Parliament, the House of Commons (H.C.) and the House of Lords (H.L.): journals of both houses (sometimes abbreviated *CJ* and *LJ*); votes and proceedings; debates; bills, reports, and papers; and statutes.

14.312 *UK statutes.* More often cited in notes than in bibliographies, the Acts of Parliament are identified by title (in roman), year (also include the regnal year for statutes enacted before 1963), and chapter number (c. for chapter; arabic numeral for national number, lowercase roman for local). Monarchs' names in regnal-year citations are abbreviated as follows: Car. (Charles), Edw., Eliz., Geo., Hen., Jac. (James), Phil. & M., Rich., Vict.,

Will., W. & M. The year precedes the name; the monarch's ordinal, if any, follows it (15 Geo. 6), both in arabic numerals. An ampersand is used between regnal years and between names of dual monarchs (1 & 2 W. & M.). *The Bluebook* advises including the jurisdiction if it is not clear from the context or the citation (example 8).

> 7. Act of Settlement, 1701, 12 & 13 Will. 3, c. 2.
> 8. Consolidated Fund Act, 1963, c. 1 (Eng.).
> 9. Manchester Corporation Act, 1967, c. xl.

The three chief compilations of statutory material for the United Kingdom are the following:

- *The Statutes of the Realm*. Statutes from 1235 through 1948, with the exception of the years 1642–60.
- *Acts and Ordinances of the Interregnum*, ed. C. H. Firth and R. S. Rait, 3 vols. (London, 1911). Statutes for the years 1642–60.
- *Public General Acts and Measures*, published annually since 1831 by HMSO.

An additional source is the UK Statute Law Database, which has been available to the public since 2006 and is published with authority of the British Crown; the Statute Law Database draws on *The Statutes of the Realm* and its official revisions.

14.313   *Publication of UK parliamentary debates.* Before 1909, debates from both houses were published together; since then they have been published in separate series.

> *Hansard Parliamentary Debates*, 1st series (1803–20)
> *Hansard Parliamentary Debates*, 2d series (1820–30)
> *Hansard Parliamentary Debates*, 3d series (1830–91)
> *Parliamentary Debates*, 4th series (1892–1908)
> *Parliamentary Debates*, Commons, 5th series (1909–80)
> *Parliamentary Debates*, Commons, 6th series (1980/81–)
> *Parliamentary Debates*, Lords, 5th series (1909–)

In *Bluebook* style, cite the volume number and series and include the year and column number. In the third example, H.C. stands for House of Commons. (In the first two examples, no such indication is necessary.)

> 1. 249 Parl. Deb. (3d ser.) (1879) 611–27.
> 2. 13 Parl. Deb. (4th ser.) (1893) 1273.
> 3. 407 Parl. Deb., H.C. (5th ser.) (1944–45) 425–46.

Although no longer the official name, *Hansard* (less often, *Hansard's*) is still sometimes used in citations to all series of parliamentary debates. Such usage is best avoided, however.

14.314 *UK command papers.* Command papers are so called because they originate outside Parliament and are ostensibly presented to Parliament "by command of Her [His] Majesty." The different abbreviations for "command" indicate the series and must not be altered. No *s* is added to the plural (Cmnd. 3834, 3835).

No. 1 to No. 4222 (1833–69)
C. 1 to C. 9550 (1870–99)
Cd. 1 to Cd. 9239 (1900–1918)
Cmd. 1 to Cmd. 9889 (1919–56)
Cmnd. 1–9927 (1956–86)
Cm. 1– (1986–)

Command papers may consist of a pamphlet or several volumes. If not clear from the context, the author of the report is included. Dates may include a month or just a year.

4. HM Treasury, The Basle Facility and the Sterling Area, 1968, Cmnd. 3787, at 15–16.

5. First Interim Report of the Committee on Currency and Foreign Exchanges after the War, 1918, Cd. 9182.

6. Review Body on Doctors' and Dentists' Remuneration, Thirteenth Report, 1983, Cmnd. 8878.

14.315 *Unpublished UK government documents.* For general guidelines and many examples, which can be adapted to government documents, see 14.232–42. The main depositories for unpublished government documents in the United Kingdom are the National Archives (NA) and the British Library (BL), both in London. Their catalogs are available online through the websites of the National Archives and the British Library. (The British Library is a division of the British Museum; before it was called the British Library, citations to documents housed therein used the abbreviation BM.) References usually include such classifications as Admiralty (Adm.), Chancery (C), Colonial Office (CO), Exchequer (E), Foreign Office (FO), or State Papers (SP) as well as the collection and volume numbers and, where relevant, the folio or page number(s). Among important collections in the British Library are the Cotton Manuscripts (with subdivisions named after Roman emperors, e.g., Cotton MSS, Caligula [Calig.]

D.VII), the Harleian Manuscripts, the Sloane Manuscripts, and the Additional Manuscripts (Add. or Addit.).

> 10. Patent Rolls, 3 Rich. 2, pt. 1, m. 12d (Calendar of Patent Rolls, 1377–1381, 470).
> 11. Hodgson to Halifax, 22 Feb. 1752, NA, CO 137:48.
> 12. Clarendon to Lumley, 16 Jan. 1869, NA, FO Belgium/133, no. 6.
> 13. [Henry Elsynge], "The moderne forme of the Parliaments of England," BL, Add. MSS 26645.
> 14. Minutes of the General Court, 17 Apr. 1733, 3:21, BL, Add. MSS 25545.
> 15. Letter of a Bristol Man, BL, Add. MSS 33029:152–55.

International Entities

14.316   *Intergovernmental bodies.* The Bluebook outlines the main reporters for international courts (such as the International Court of Justice), commissions, and tribunals. Also included are abbreviations for intergovernmental bodies such as the United Nations (and its principal organs), the European Union, and those devoted to specific areas such as human rights, trade, and health. The basic elements of citations to international law cases are similar to those used in US law citations (see 14.288–91); for examples, consult *The Bluebook*. (In addition to intergovernmental bodies, *The Bluebook* covers about three dozen foreign jurisdictions.) For treaties, see 14.302.

14.317   *International legal and public documents online.* The United Nations makes many of its documents available online (in English)—including those published by the General Assembly and the Security Council and dating back to the first General Assembly in 1946. *The Bluebook* provides guidance primarily for citing documents in the Official Records, but it considers the United Nations website an acceptable alternative. Many of the documents published by the United Nations and other intergovernmental bodies are issued in the form of reports. In general, list by the authorizing body (and the author or editor where appropriate), the topic or title of the paper, and the date. Series and publication numbers, place of publication, and a page reference may be included. Abbreviations may be used in notes and, to avoid duplication, in bibliographies (UN = United Nations, LoNP = League of Nation Papers, WTO = World Trade Organization, and so forth). Include a URL as the final element in the citation (see 14.4–13).

1. United Nations Security Council (SC), Resolution 7, "The Spanish Question," June 26, 1946, http://www.un.org/documents/sc/res/1946/scres46.htm.

2. SC, Resolution 1731, "The Situation in Liberia," ¶ 4(a), Dec. 20, 2006, http://www.un.org/Docs/sc/unsc_resolutions06.htm.

3. UN General Assembly, Resolution 45/1, "Admission of the Principality of Lichtenstein to Membership in the United Nations," Sept. 18, 1990, http://www.un.org/Depts/dhl/res/resa45.htm.

15 Documentation II: Author-Date References

Overview

15.1   *The scope of this chapter.* This chapter describes the second of Chicago's two systems of documentation, which uses parenthetical author-date references and a corresponding reference list. Because this system is similar in many respects to the notes and bibliography system discussed in chapter 14, much of the information from that chapter is not repeated here. For an introduction to source citations in general, including a discussion of systems other than the two recommended by Chicago, readers are encouraged to consult the overview in chapter 14 (14.1–13).

15.2   *Uniform treatment in author-date references and notes and bibliography.* In a departure from previous editions of this manual, Chicago now recommends a uniform treatment for the main elements of citation in both of its systems of documentation. In particular, the forms recommended in chapter 14 for authors' names (full names rather than initials) and titles of works (headline-style capitalization and use of quotation marks and italics) are now identical in the author-date system, as are recommendations regarding the use of abbreviations. Other differences remain unchanged—namely, the author-date system's use of parenthetical text citations rather than citations in notes and, in the bibliography (called a reference list), a different placement for the year of publication. For the use of notes with the author-date system, see 15.30.

15.3   *Notes and bibliography entries as models for author-date references.* Most of the examples in chapter 14 are readily adapted to the author-date style—in almost all cases by a different ordering or arrangement of elements. Most reference list entries are identical to entries in a bibliography except for the position of the year of publication, which in a reference list follows the author's name. Unlike bibliography entries (see 14.59), each entry in the reference list must correspond to a work cited in the text. Text citations differ from citations in notes by presenting only the author's last name and the year of publication, followed by a page number or other locator, if any. This chapter, by focusing on these and other differences, will allow readers to adapt any of the examples in chapter 14 to the author-date system.

15.4   *Considerations for electronic sources.* For a detailed discussion of URLs and DOIs, access dates and revision dates, and other considerations for citing electronic sources, see 14.4–13. For most electronic sources, Chicago recommends the addition of a URL or DOI following the full facts of publication. For examples in the author-date style, see 15.9, under *Journal Article*.

For more examples, see 14.167, 14.169, and throughout the discussions on periodicals (14.170–217) and elsewhere in chapter 14. Some citations will require an access date; for examples, see 14.245, 14.248, 15.51.

Author-Date References: Basic Format, with Examples and Variations

15.5   *The author-date system—overview.* The author-date system is used by many in the physical, natural, and social sciences and is recommended by Chicago for works in those areas. Sources are cited in the text, usually in parentheses, by the author's last (family) name, the publication date of the work cited, and a page number if needed. Full details appear in the reference list—usually titled "References" or "Works Cited"—in which the year of publication appears immediately after the author's name (see fig. 15.1). This arrangement makes it easy to follow a text citation to the corresponding full source in the reference list. (In electronic works, text entries may be hyperlinked to their corresponding reference list entries.)

Text citations:

As legal observers point out, much dispute resolution transpires outside the courtroom but in the "shadow of the law" (Mnookin and Kornhauser 1979). . . . Here we empirically demonstrate that workers' and regulatory agents' understandings of discrimination and legality emerge not only in the shadow of the law but also, as Albiston (2005) suggests, in the "shadow of organizations."

Reference list entries:

Albiston, Catherine R. 2005. "Bargaining in the Shadow of Social Institutions: Competing Discourses and Social Change in the Workplace Mobilization of Civil Rights." *Law and Society Review* 39 (1): 11–47.
Mnookin, Robert, and Lewis Kornhauser. 1979. "Bargaining in the Shadow of the Law: The Case of Divorce." *Yale Law Journal* 88 (5): 950–97.

For more examples of text citations and reference list entries, see 15.9. For a detailed discussion of reference lists, see 15.10–16 and 15.17–19. For text citations, see 15.20–30.

15.6   *Basic structure of a reference list entry.* In a reference list entry, the year of publication is the second element, following the author's name. Oth-

The good news, however, is that the intersection of pairwise stable networks in the SW model and Nash networks in the GM model can easily be characterized. It is exactly the set of strongly pairwise stable networks (see Cálvo-Armengol 2004). Therefore, unilateral stability, being a refinement of strong pairwise stability, can also be recast as a refinement of Nash equilibrium in the GM model (see Van de Rijt and Buskens 2008). By using unilateral stability, we can analyze stability in both models while considering only the SW model in the main text.

REFERENCES

Bala, Venkatesh, and Sanjeev Goyal. 2000. "A Noncooperative Model of Network Formation." *Econometrica* 68:1181–229.

Bian, Yanjie. 1994. *Work and Equality in Urban China.* Albany: State University of New York Press.

Blau, Peter M., and Joseph E. Schwartz. 1984. *Crosscutting Social Circles: Testing a Macro-structural Theory of Intergroup Relations.* Orlando, Fla.: Academic Press.

Breiger, Ronald L., Kathleen M. Carley, and Philippa E. Pattison. 2003. *Dynamic Social Network Modeling and Analysis: Workshop Summary and Papers.* Washington, D.C.: National Academies Press.

Burger, Martijn, and Vincent Buskens. 2008. *Social Context and Network Formation: An Experimental Study.* ISCORE paper no. 234. Utrecht University, Institute for the Study of Cooperative Relations.

Burt, Ronald S. 1992. *Structural Holes: The Social Structure of Competition.* Cambridge, Mass.: Harvard University Press.

———. 1997. "The Contingent Value of Social Capital." *Administrative Science Quarterly* 42:339–65.

———. 1998. "The Gender of Social Capital." *Rationality and Society* 10:5–46.

———. 2000. "The Network Structure of Social Capital." Pp. 345–423 in *Research in Organizational Behavior,* vol. 22, edited by Robert I. Sutton and Barry M. Staw. Greenwich, Conn.: Elsevier Science.

———. 2001. "Bridge Decay." *Social Networks* 24 (4): 333–63.

———. 2002. "The Social Capital of Structural Holes." Chap. 7 in *New Directions in Economic Sociology,* edited by Mauro F. Guillén, Randall Collins, Paula England, and Marshall Meyer. New York: Russell Sage.

———. 2004. "Structural Holes and Good Ideas." *American Journal of Sociology* 110: 349–99.

———. 2005. *Brokerage and Closure: An Introduction to Social Capital.* Oxford: Oxford University Press.

———. 2007. "Second-Hand Brokerage: Evidence on the Importance of Local Structure for Managers, Bankers, and Analysts." *Academy of Management Journal* 50:119–48.

Burt, Ronald S., Miguel Guilarte, Holly J. Raider, and Yuki Yasuda. 2002. "Competition, Contingency, and the External Structure of Markets." *Advances in Strategic Management* 19:167–217.

Burt, Ronald S., Robin M. Hogarth, and Claude Michaud. 2000. "The Social Capital of French and American Managers." *Organization Science* 11:123–47.

Burt, Ronald S., and Don Ronchi. 2007. "Teaching Executives How to See Social Capital: Results from a Field Experiment." *Social Science Research* 36:1156–83.

Buskens, Vincent. 2002. *Social Networks and Trust.* Boston: Kluwer.

Buskens, Vincent, and Chris Snijders. 2008. *Effects of Network Characteristics on*

FIGURE 15.1. Part of a reference list for a journal article in the social sciences. See 15.5, 15.6, 15.10–16.

erwise, a reference list entry is structured like an entry in a bibliography (see 14.16): the elements are separated by periods, and the first-listed author's name, according to which the entry is alphabetized in the reference list, is usually inverted (last name first). Titles are capitalized headline-style unless they are in a foreign language (see 8.157, 11.3); titles of larger works such as books and journals are italicized; and titles of smaller works such as journal articles are presented in roman and enclosed in quotation marks (see 8.161). Noun forms such as *editor, translator, volume,* and *edition* are abbreviated, but verb forms such as *edited by* and *translated by* are spelled out.

15.7 **Basic structure of an in-text citation.** In the author-date system, a citation in the text usually appears in parentheses and includes only the first two elements in a reference list—the author and the year of publication (hence the name of the system), with no intervening punctuation. In addition, a page number or other locator may be added, following a comma. Terms such as *editor* or *translator,* abbreviated in a reference list, are not included in a text citation.

15.8 **Page numbers and other locators.** In text citations, where reference is usually to a particular passage in a book or journal, only the page number(s) pertaining to that passage are given. In reference lists, no page numbers are given for books; for easier location of journal articles or chapters or other sections of a book, the beginning and ending page numbers of the entire article or chapter are given. Electronic sources do not always include page numbers (and some that do include them repaginate according to user-defined font sizes). For such works without fixed pagination, it may be appropriate in text to cite a chapter or paragraph number (if available), a section heading, or a descriptive phrase that follows the organizational divisions of the work. For examples, see 15.22. For citations of shorter electronic works presented as a single, searchable document, such locators may be unnecessary.

15.9 **Author-date references—examples and variations.** The examples that follow are intended to provide an overview of the author-date system, featuring books and journal articles as models. Each example includes a reference list entry and a corresponding text citation. For the sake of consistency, text citations are presented in parentheses, though they do not always appear that way in practice (see 15.27). For more examples, consult the sections dealing with specific types of works throughout this chapter.

For a book with a single author, invert the name in the reference list; in the text, include only the last name. Punctuate and capitalize as shown. To cite a specific passage, a page number or range is included in a text citation (separated from the year by a comma) but not in a reference list, unless the entry is for a chapter, in which case the page range on which the item appears is included (see "Chapter in an Edited Book," below; see also 9.58–63).

Pollan, Michael. 2006. *The Omnivore's Dilemma: A Natural History of Four Meals.* New York: Penguin.

(Pollan 2006, 99–100)

A book with an editor in place of an author includes the abbreviation *ed. (editor;* for more than one editor, use *eds.).* Note that the text citation does not include *ed.*

Greenberg, Joel, ed. 2008. *Of Prairie, Woods, and Water: Two Centuries of Chicago Nature Writing.* Chicago: University of Chicago Press.

(Greenberg 2008, 42)

For a book with two authors, only the first-listed name is inverted in the reference list.

Ward, Geoffrey C., and Ken Burns. 2007. *The War: An Intimate History, 1941–1945.* New York: Knopf.

(Ward and Burns 2007, 52)

For a book with three authors, adapt as follows:

Heatherton, Joyce, James Fitzgilroy, and Jackson Hsu. 2008. *Meteors and Mudslides: A Trip through . . .*

(Heatherton, Fitzgilroy, and Hsu 2008, 188–89)

For a book with four or more authors, include all the authors in the reference list entry (see also 14.76). Word order and punctuation are the same as for two or three authors. In the text, however, cite only the last name of the first-listed author, followed by *et al.* (see also 15.28).

(Barnes et al. 2008, 118–19)

BOOK WITH AUTHOR PLUS EDITOR OR TRANSLATOR

In the reference list, do not abbreviate *Edited by* or *Translated by*. See also 14.88.

García Márquez, Gabriel. 1988. *Love in the Time of Cholera*. Translated by Edith Grossman. London: Cape.

(García Márquez 1988, 242–55)

CHAPTER IN AN EDITED BOOK

In citations of a chapter or similar part of an edited book, include the chapter author; the chapter title, in quotation marks; and the editor. Precede the title of the book with *In*. Note the location of the page range for the chapter in the reference list entry. See also 14.111–17.

Gould, Glenn. 1984. "Streisand as Schwarzkopf." In *The Glenn Gould Reader*, edited by Tim Page, 308–11. New York: Vintage.

(Gould 1984, 310)

JOURNAL ARTICLE

Citations of journals include the volume and issue number and date of publication. The volume number follows the italicized journal title in roman and with no intervening punctuation. A specific page reference is included in the text; the page range for an article is included in the reference list, preceded by a colon. The issue number often appears in parentheses (as in the first pair of examples below). If a journal is paginated consecutively across a volume or if the month or season is included in the reference list entry, however, the issue number (or month or season) may be omitted (as in the second and third pairs of examples).

Blair, Walter. 1977. "Americanized Comic Braggarts." *Critical Inquiry* 4 (2): 331–49.

(Blair 1977, 331–32)

For citations of journals consulted online, Chicago recommends the inclusion of a DOI or a URL; the DOI is preferred to a URL (see 14.5, 14.6). Note that *DOI*, so capitalized when mentioned in running text, is lowercased and followed by a colon (with no space after) in source citations.

Novak, William J. 2008. "The Myth of the 'Weak' American State." *American Historical Review* 113:752–72. doi:10.1086/ahr.113.3.752.

(Novak 2008, 758)

When no DOI has been provided along with the article at the site where it is consulted (even if one has been assigned), include a URL. The URL in the following example—consulted through the online journals archive JSTOR—was listed along with the article as a more stable (and shorter) alternative to the URL that appeared in the browser's address bar:

Karmaus, Wilfried, and John F. Riebow. 2004. "Storage of Serum in Plastic and Glass Containers May Alter the Serum Concentration of Polychlorinated Biphenyls." *Environmental Health Perspectives* 112 (May): 643–47. http://www.jstor.org/stable/3435987.

(Karmaus and Riebow 2004, 645)

Reference Lists and Text Citations

Reference Lists

15.10 *Function and placement of reference lists.* In the author-date system, the reference list is the prime vehicle for documentation. The text citations (see 15.20–30) are merely pointers to the full list. A reference list, like other types of bibliographies (see 14.59), is normally placed at the end of a work, preceding the index, if there is one. In a multiauthor book, a textbook, or a journal article, each chapter or article may be followed by its own reference list, in which case the list is preceded by a subhead such as References or Literature Cited.

15.11 *Alphabetical arrangement of reference list entries.* A reference list is always arranged alphabetically (except in a numbered reference system; see 14.3) and should generally not be divided into sections. (Types of sources that are not readily adapted to author-date style are often better cited in notes;

see, for example, 15.54–55.) All sources are listed by the last names of the authors (or, if no author or editor is given, by the title or by a keyword readers are most likely to seek). Rules for alphabetizing an index (see 16.56–93) apply also to a reference list, with the modifications described in 14.61, 14.62, and 15.17–19. For an illustration, see figure 15.1.

15.12 *Authors' names in reference list entries.* In a reference list as in a bibliography, use the form of authors' names as they appear on the title page or at the head of an article or chapter, with the exceptions noted in 14.72–92; see also 14.175. This treatment brings Chicago's author-date system into conformity with the style recommended for notes and bibliographies in chapter 14. Some publications, especially in the natural sciences, use initials rather than full given names (see 15.43). Where this practice is followed, an exception should be made where two authors share the same initials and last name. For text citations, see 15.21.

15.13 *Titles in reference list entries.* Titles and subtitles of books and articles in reference lists should be treated according to the rules set forth in 8.154–95 (see also 11.3). This is also the treatment recommended for titles in chapter 14, bringing Chicago's author-date system into conformity with the style for notes and bibliographies. It is recognized, however, that some publications—particularly journals in the natural sciences—prefer sentence-style treatment for titles (see 8.156), tend not to use quotation marks or italics, and abbreviate journal titles (see 15.44).

15.14 *Placement of dates in reference list entries.* Because the text citations consist of the last name of the author or authors (or that of the editor or translator) and the year of publication, the year in the reference list appears directly after the name, not with the publication details. This arrangement facilitates easy lookup of reference list entries.

> Choi, Stephen J., and G. Mitu Gulati. 2008. "Bias in Judicial Citations: A Window into the Behavior of Judges?" *Journal of Legal Studies* 37 (January): 87–129. doi:10.1086/588263.
> Heinrich, Larissa. 2008. *The Afterlife of Images: Translating the Pathological Body between China and the West.* Durham, NC: Duke University Press.

15.15 *Abbreviations in reference list entries.* Chicago's primary recommendations for the use of abbreviations in reference lists are now identical to the recommendations for bibliographies outlined in chapter 14. Spell out such phrases as *edited by* or *translated by*, which are capitalized if following a period. On the other hand, noun forms such as *editor (ed.)*, and *transla-*

tor (*trans.*) are always abbreviated in reference lists, as are such standard bibliographical terms as *volume* (*vol.*), number (*no.*), and so forth. Abbreviations may be used with greater frequency as long as they are used consistently. For example, *University* may be abbreviated to *Univ.*, and months given with journal citations may be abbreviated (see 10.40). See also 15.43, 15.44.

15.16 *Single author versus several authors—reference list order.* As in a bibliography, a single-author entry precedes a multiauthor entry beginning with the same name. Only the first author's name is inverted. Successive entries by two or more authors in which only the first author's name is the same are alphabetized according to the coauthors' last names (regardless of how many coauthors there are).

> Edelman, Lauren B. 1992. "Legal Ambiguity and Symbolic Structures: Organizational Mediation of Civil Rights Law." *American Journal of Sociology* 97 (6): 1531–76.
> Edelman, Lauren B., Sally Riggs Fuller, and Iona Mara-Drita. 2001. "Diversity Rhetoric and the Managerialization of the Law." *American Journal of Sociology* 106 (6): 1589–641.
> Edelman, Lauren B., and S. M. Petterson. 1999. "Symbols and Substance in Organizational Response to Civil Rights Law." *Research in Social Stratification and Mobility* 17:107–35.
> Edelman, Lauren B., Christopher Uggen, and Howard S. Erlanger. 1999. "The Endogeneity of Legal Regulation: Grievance Procedures as Rational Myth." *American Journal of Sociology* 105 (2): 406–54.

The 3-Em Dash for Repeated Names in a Reference List

15.17 *Chronological order for repeated names in a reference list.* For successive entries by the same author(s), translator(s), editor(s), or compiler(s), a 3-em dash replaces the name(s) after the first appearance. The entries are arranged chronologically by year of publication in ascending order, *not* alphabetized by title (as in a bibliography; see 14.67). Undated works designated *n.d.* or *forthcoming* follow all dated works (see 15.41, 15.42). See also 14.63.

> Schuman, Howard, and Jacqueline Scott. 1987. "Problems in the Use of Survey Questions to Measure Public Opinion." *Science* 236:957–59.
> ———. 1989. "Generations and Collective Memories." *American Sociological Review* 54:359–81.

Note that the 3-em dash *cannot* stand in for the same two or more authors as in the previous entry if they appear in a different order. The following two entries are alphabetized as if they are by two different sets of authors:

Comaroff, Jean, and John Comaroff, eds. 1993. *Modernity and Its Malcontents: Ritual and Power in Postcolonial Africa*. Chicago: University of Chicago Press.
Comaroff, John, and Jean Comaroff. 1991–97. *Of Revelation and Revolution*. 2 vols. Chicago: University of Chicago Press.

15.18   *The 3-em dash with edited, translated, or compiled works.* The 3-em dash replaces the preceding name or names only, not an added *ed., trans., comp.,* or whatever. The chronological order is maintained, regardless of the added abbreviation.

Woodward, David. 1977. *The All-American Map: Wax Engraving and Its Influence on Cartography*. Chicago: University of Chicago Press.
———, ed. 1987. *Art and Cartography: Six Historical Essays*. Chicago: University of Chicago Press.
———. 1996. *Catalogue of Watermarks in Italian Printed Maps, ca. 1540–1600*. Chicago: University of Chicago Press.

Woodward is the author of the first and third items, editor of the second.

15.19   *Reference list entries with same author(s), same year.* Two or more works by the same author in the same year must be differentiated by the addition of *a*, *b*, and so forth (regardless of whether they were authored, edited, compiled, or translated), and are listed alphabetically by title. Text citations consist of author and year plus letter.

Fogel, Robert William. 2004a. *The Escape from Hunger and Premature Death, 1700–2100: Europe, America, and the Third World*. New York: Cambridge University Press.
———. 2004b. "Technophysio Evolution and the Measurement of Economic Growth." *Journal of Evolutionary Economics* 14 (2): 217–21. doi:10.1007/s00191-004-0188-x.

(Fogel 2004b, 218)
(Fogel 2004a, 45–46)

When works by the same two or more authors list their names in a different order, then *a*, *b*, and so forth cannot be used. See 15.17.

Text Citations

15.20 *Agreement of text citation and reference list entry.* For each author-date citation in the text, there must be a corresponding entry in the reference list under the same name and date. It is the author's responsibility to ensure such agreement as well as the accuracy of the reference (see 2.29). Among other things, specific page references to a journal article, when given in a text citation, must fall within the range of pages given for the article in the reference list entry. Manuscript editors can help authors by cross-checking text citations and reference lists and rectifying or querying any discrepancies or omissions (see 2.60).

15.21 *Text citations—basic form.* An author-date citation in running text or at the end of a block quotation consists of the last (family) name of the author, followed by the year of publication of the work in question. In this context, *author* may refer not only to one or more authors or an institution but also to one or more editors, translators, or compilers. No punctuation appears between author and date. Abbreviations such as *ed.* or *trans.* are omitted. See also 15.22.

Text citations:

(Woodward 1987)
(Schuman and Scott 1987)

References:

Schuman, Howard, and Jacqueline Scott. 1987. "Problems in the Use of Survey Questions to Measure Public Opinion." *Science* 236:957–59.
Woodward, David, ed. 1987. *Art and Cartography: Six Historical Essays*. Chicago: University of Chicago Press.

Where two or more works by different authors with the same last name are listed in a reference list, the text citation must include an initial (or two initials or a given name if necessary).

Text citations:

(C. Doershuk 2010)   (J. Doershuk 2009)

References:

Doershuk, Carl. 2010. . . .   Doershuk, John. 2009. . . .

15.22   *Page and volume numbers or other specific locators in text citations.* When a specific page, section, equation, or other division of the work is cited, it follows the date, preceded by a comma. When a volume as a whole is referred to, without a page number, *vol.* is used. For volume plus page, only a colon is needed. The *n* in the Fischer and Siple example below indicates "note" (see 14.164). The last example shows how one might cite a section of a work that contains no page or section numbers or other numerical signposts—the case for some electronic documents (see 15.8).

> (Piaget 1980, 74)
> (LaFree 2010, 413, 417–18)
> (Johnson 1979, sec. 24)
> (Fowler and Hoyle 1965, eq. 87)
> (García 1987, vol. 2)
> (García 1987, 2:345)
> (Barnes 1998, 2:354–55, 3:29)
> (Fischer and Siple 1990, 212n3)
> (Hellman 1998, under "The Battleground")

Some journals omit page numbers in citations of other journal articles except when citing a direct quotation.

15.23   *Additional material in text citations.* The parentheses that enclose a text citation may also include a comment, separated from the citation by a semicolon.

> (Mandolan 2009; *t*-tests are used here)

15.24   *Text citations in relation to surrounding text and punctuation.* Except at the end of block quotations (see 15.25), author-date citations are usually placed just before a mark of punctuation. See also 15.27.

Recent literature has examined long-run price drifts following initial public offerings (Ritter 1991; Loughran and Ritter 1995), stock splits (Ikenberry, Rankine, and Stice 1996), seasoned equity offerings (Loughran and Ritter 1995), and equity repurchases (Ikenberry, Lakonishok, and Vermaelen 1995).

Where the author's name appears in the text, it need not be repeated in the parenthetical citation. Note that the date should immediately follow the author's name, even if the name is used in the possessive. This slight departure from advice in earlier editions of the manual serves the logic and economy of the author-date style.

Fiorina et al. (2005) and Fischer and Hout (2006) reach more or less the same conclusions. In contrast, Abramowitz and Saunders (2005) suggest that the mass public is deeply divided between red states and blue states and between church-goers and secular voters.

Tufte's (2001) excellent book on chart design warns against a common error.

15.25 *Text citations in relation to direct quotations.* Although citation of a source normally follows a direct quotation, it may precede the quotation—especially if such a placement allows the date to appear with the author's name.

As Edward Tufte points out, "A graphical element may carry data information and also perform a design function usually left to non-data-ink" (2001, 139).
or
As Edward Tufte (2001, 139) points out, "A graphical element may carry data information and also perform a design function usually left to non-data-ink."

When the source of a block quotation is given in parentheses at the end of the quotation, the opening parenthesis appears *after* the final punctuation mark of the quoted material. No period either precedes or follows the closing parenthesis.

If you happen to be fishing, and you get a strike, and whatever it is starts off with the preliminaries of a vigorous fight; and by and by, looking down over the side through the glassy water, you see a rosy golden gleam, the mere specter of a fish, shining below in the clear depths; and when you look again a sort of glory of golden light flashes and dazzles as it circles nearer beneath and around and under the boat; . . . and you land a slim and graceful and impossibly beautiful three-foot goldfish, whose fierce and vivid yellow is touched around the edges with a violent red—when all these things happen to you, fortunate but bewildered fisherman, then you may know you have been fishing in the Galapagos Islands and have taken a Golden Grouper. (Pinchot 1930, 123)

See also 13.68–70.

15.26 *Several references to the same source.* When the same page (or page range) in the same source is cited more than once in one paragraph, the parenthetical citation can be placed after the last reference or at the end of the paragraph (but preceding the final period). When referring to different pages in the same source, however, include a full parenthetical citation at the first reference; subsequent citations need only include page numbers.

Complexion figures prominently in Morgan's descriptions. When Jasper compliments his mother's choice of car (a twelve-cylinder Mediterranean roadster with leather and wood-grained interior), "his cheeks blotch indignantly, painted by jealousy and rage" (Chaston 2000, 47). On the other hand, his mother's mask never changes, her "even-tanned good looks" (56), "burnished visage" (101), and "airbrushed confidence" (211) providing the foil to the drama in her midst.

15.27   *Syntactic considerations with text citations.* An author-date citation is a form of bibliographic shorthand that corresponds to a fully cited work; it does not refer to a person. Note how, in the examples in 15.24 and 15.25, the wording distinguishes between authors and works. A locution such as "in Smith 2009," though technically proper, is usually best avoided except as part of a parenthetical citation. Reword—for example, "Smith's (1999) study indicates that . . ." Note that square brackets should be used in parenthetical text references that require additional parentheses, as in the second example (see 6.99).

There are at least three works that satisfy the criteria outlined in Smith's (1999) study (see Rowen 2006; Bettelthorp 2004a; Choi 2008).

These processes have, in turn, affected the way many Latin Americans are treated in the United States (see, e.g., Haviland [2003, 767] on how US courts disregard the existence of indigenous languages and "reluctantly" make allowance only for Spanish in translation services).

15.28   *Text citations of works with more than three authors.* For more than three authors (or in some science publications, more than two), only the name of the first author is used, followed by *et al.* (and others). Note that *et al.* is not italicized in text citations.

(Schonen et al. 2009)
According to the data collected by Schonen et al. (2009), . . .

If a reference list includes another work of the same date that would also be abbreviated as "Schonen et al." but whose coauthors are different persons or listed in a different order, the text citations must distinguish between them. In such cases, the first two authors (or the first three) should be cited, followed by *et al.*

(Schonen, Baker, et al. 2009)   (Schonen, Brooks, et al. 2009)

Alternatively, a shortened title, enclosed in commas, may be added. In the following examples, *et al.* refers to different coauthors, so *a*, *b*, and so on cannot be used (see 15.19):

(Schonen et al., "Tilting at Windmills," 2009)
(Schonen et al., "Gasoline Farmers," 2009)

For treatment of multiple authors in a bibliography or reference list, see 14.76, 15.9.

15.29 *Multiple text references.* Two or more references in a single parenthetical citation are separated by semicolons. The order in which they are given may depend on what is being cited, and in what order, or it may reflect the relative importance of the items cited. If neither criterion applies, alphabetical or chronological order may be appropriate. Unless the order is prescribed by a particular journal style, the decision is the author's.

(Armstrong and Malacinski 1989; Beigl 1989; Pickett and White 1985)

Additional works by the same author(s) are cited by date only, separated by commas except where page numbers are required.

(Whittaker 1967, 1975; Wiens 1989a, 1989b)
(Wong 1999, 328; 2000, 475; García 1998, 67)

15.30 *Author-date system with notes.* Where footnotes or endnotes are used to supplement the author-date system, source citations within notes are treated in the same way as in text (see fig. 15.2).

10. James Wilson has noted that "no politician ever lost votes by denouncing the bureaucracy" (1989, 235). Yet little is actually ever done to bring major reforms to the system.

For the use of notes with legal-style citations, see 15.54. For more on footnotes and endnotes, see 14.19–55.

Author-Date References: Special Cases

15.31 *Items not necessarily covered in chapter 14.* The majority of examples in chapter 14 can be adapted to the author-date system with relative ease (see 15.3). This section focuses on special cases not necessarily covered there or for which a suitable author-date form may not be apparent.

> Turning to the econometric evidence, I present some estimates of changes in expected retirement ages drawn from the Bank of Italy panel of household-level data. The methodology adopted is a "difference-in-difference" estimator and draws heavily on the work of Attanasio and Brugiavini (1997) described above. In particular, the basic identifying assumption is that the 1992 reform is the only relevant change (as far as differential labor supply decisions are concerned), and I therefore exploit the reform to measure behavioral responses before and after the event. The first difference is the time difference, the second that between groups. Groups in the population are assumed to be exogenously determined, and, given the availability of panel data, I can control for individuals' characteristics throughout (Venti and Wise 1995). It is worth recalling at this stage that the Amato reform of 1992 has gradually postponed the normal retirement age but has not tackled the early retirement option, apart from restricting eligibility requirements in the public sector.[47]
>
> 47. The normal retirement age gradually moves from sixty to sixty-five for men. The early retirement option is available (Hoy 1996), but public-sector employees need thirty-five years of contributions to become eligible in place of the previous twenty years (fifteen for married women). In the public sector, normal retirement age has been sixty-five throughout.

FIGURE 15.2. A sample of text with both parenthetical text citations and a footnote. See 15.30.

Books

AUTHOR'S NAME

15.32   *Anonymous works—unknown authorship.* If the author or editor is unknown, the reference list entry should normally begin with the title. An initial article is ignored in alphabetizing. Text citations may refer to a short form of the title but must include the first word (other than an initial article). See also 14.79.

Stanze in lode della donna brutta. 1547. Florence.
A True and Sincere Declaration of the Purpose and Ends of the Plantation Begun in Virginia, of the Degrees Which It Hath Received, and Means by Which It Hath Been Advanced. 1610. London.

(*True and Sincere Declaration* 1610)
(*Stanze in lode della donna brutta* 1547) or (*Stanze* 1547)

15.33   *Anonymous works—known authorship.* As in notes and bibliographies (see 14.80), bracket a name in reference lists and text citations if the authorship is known or guessed at but was omitted on the title page.

[Cook, Ebenezer?]. 1730. *Sotweed Redivivus; or, The Planter's Looking-Glass*. By "E. C. Gent." Annapolis.

[Horsley, Samuel]. 1796. *On the Prosodies of the Greek and Latin Languages*. London.

([Horsley] 1796)   ([Cook?] 1730)

15.34   *Pseudonyms in author-date references.* For indicating pseudonyms in reference lists, see 14.81, 14.82, 14.83, 14.84. Text citations should refer to the first-listed name and will omit the indication *pseud.*

Centinel [pseud.]. 1981. Letters. In *The Complete Anti-Federalist*, edited by Herbert J. Storing. Chicago: University of Chicago Press.

Stendhal [Marie-Henri Beyle]. 1925. *The Charterhouse of Parma*. Translated by C. K. Scott-Moncrieff. New York: Boni and Liveright.

(Stendhal 1925)   (Centinel 1981)

See also 14.85, 14.86.

15.35   *Editor in place of author in text citations.* For works listed by editor(s) or compiler(s) or translator(s) in a reference list, abbreviations such as *ed.* or *eds., comp.* or *comps.*, or *trans.* following the name are omitted in text citations.

Silverstein, Theodore, trans. 1974. *Sir Gawain and the Green Knight*. Chicago: University of Chicago Press.

Soltes, Ori Z., ed. 1999. *Georgia: Art and Civilization through the Ages*. London: Philip Wilson.

(Silverstein 1974)   (Soltes 1999)

15.36   *Organization as author in author-date references.* If a publication issued by an organization, association, or corporation carries no personal author's name on the title page, the organization may be listed as author in the reference list, even if it is also given as publisher. To facilitate shorter parenthetical text citations, the organization may be listed under an abbreviation, in which case the entry must be alphabetized under that abbreviation (rather than the spelled-out name) in the reference list.

BSI (British Standards Institution). 1985. *Specification for Abbreviation of Title Words and Titles of Publications*. London: BSI.

ISO (International Organization for Standardization). 1997. *Information and Documentation—Bibliographic References*. Part 2, *Electronic Documents or Parts
Thereof*. ISO 690-2. New York: American National Standards Institute.

(BSI 1985)   (ISO 1997)

TITLE

15.37   *Cross-references to other titles in reference lists.* To avoid repeating information, individual contributions to an edited volume may include
cross-references to an entry for the volume as a whole. Note that cross-
references to other titles in the reference list take the form of text citations but without any parentheses.

Draper, Joan E. 1987. "Paris by the Lake: Sources of Burnham's Plan of Chicago."
In Zukowsky 1987, 107–19.
Harrington, Elaine. 1987. "International Influences on Henry Hobson Richard-
son's Glessner House." In Zukowsky 1987, 189–207.
Zukowsky, John, ed. 1987. *Chicago Architecture, 1872–1922: Birth of a Metropolis*. Mu-
nich: Prestel-Verlag in association with the Art Institute of Chicago.

This approach is best used only if more than a few individual contributions to the same volume are cited or if the volume itself is also cited in
the text. Otherwise, include full publication details in the entry for each
individual contribution. See also 14.112.

Draper, Joan E. 1987. "Paris by the Lake: Sources of Burnham's Plan of Chicago." In
Chicago Architecture, 1872–1922: Birth of a Metropolis, edited by John Zukowsky,
107–19. Munich: Prestel-Verlag in association with the Art Institute of Chicago.

EDITION, VOLUME, OR COLLECTION

15.38   *Reprint editions and modern editions—more than one date.* When citing a
reprint or modern edition in the author-date system, it is sometimes desirable to include the original date of publication. Whether or not any information about the original publication is included, the original date is
listed first, in parentheses. If the pagination of the original edition does
not match that of the reprint, indicate the edition cited.

Austen, Jane. (1813) 2003. *Pride and Prejudice*. London: T. Egerton. Reprint, New
York: Penguin Classics. Citations refer to the Penguin edition.

Darwin, Charles. (1859) 1964. *On the Origin of Species*. Facsimile of the first edition, with an introduction by Ernest Mayr. Cambridge, MA: Harvard University Press.

Maitland, Frederic W. (1898) 1998. *Roman Canon Law in the Church of England*. Reprint, Union, NJ: Lawbook Exchange.

The parentheses are rendered as square brackets in the in-text citation (see 6.99).

(Austen [1813] 2003)   (Darwin [1859] 1964)   (Maitland [1898] 1998)

For more than one work by the same author, the first date determines placement in the reference list (see 15.17).

Maitland, Frederic W. (1898) 1998. *Roman Canon Law in the Church of England*. Reprint, Union, NJ: Lawbook Exchange.

————. (1909) 1926. *Equity, Also the Forms of Action at Common Law: Two Courses of Lectures*. Edited by A. H. Chaytor and W. J. Whittaker. Reprint, Cambridge: Cambridge University Press.

When the original date is less important to the discussion, use the date of the modern source. The date of original publication may be included at the end of the reference list entry but need not be.

Trollope, Anthony. 1977. *The Claverings*. With a new introduction by Norman Donaldson. New York: Dover. First published 1866–67.

————. 1983. *He Knew He Was Right*. 2 vols. in one. New York: Dover. First published 1869.

(Trollope 1977)   (Trollope 1983)

15.39   *Multivolume works published over more than one year.* When an entire multivolume, multiyear work is cited, the range of dates is given. In a reference list, the date for an individual volume should be included in addition to the range for the work as a whole. If the work has not yet been completed, the date of the first volume is followed by an en dash (with no space between the en dash and the punctuation that follows). In text citations of volumes listed individually in the reference list, the volume number is *not* included with references to specific page numbers. See also 14.121–27. For en dashes with numbers, see 6.78, 6.79, 9.63.

Hayek, F. A. 1995. *Contra Keynes and Cambridge: Essays, Correspondence*. Vol. 9 of *The Collected Works of F. A. Hayek*. Chicago: University of Chicago Press, 1988–.

Tillich, Paul. 1951–63. *Systematic Theology*. 3 vols. Chicago: University of Chicago Press.

(Tillich 1951–63, 1:133)   (Hayek 1995, 124–25)

15.40   *Letters in published collections.* In the author-date system, letters in published collections should be cited by the date of the collection. The dates of individual correspondence should be woven into the text. The material in the examples to 14.117 could be cited as follows:

Adams, Henry. 1930. *Letters of Henry Adams, 1858–1891.* Edited by Worthington Chauncey Ford. Boston: Houghton Mifflin.
White, E. B. 1976. *Letters of E. B. White.* Edited by Dorothy Lobrano Guth. New York: Harper & Row.

In a letter to Charles Milnes Gaskell from London, March 30, 1868 (Adams 1930, 141), Adams wrote . . .

White (1976, 273) sent Ross an interoffice memo on May 2, 1946, pointing out that . . .

FACTS OF PUBLICATION

15.41   *"No date" in author-date references.* When the publication date of a printed work cannot be ascertained, the abbreviation *n.d.* takes the place of the year in the reference list entry and text citations. Though it follows a period in the reference list, *n.d.* remains lowercased to avoid conflation with the author's name; in text citations, it is preceded by a comma. A guessed-at date may be substituted (in brackets). See also 14.138, 15.51.

Nano, Jasmine L. [1750?] *Title of Work* . . .
———. n.d. *Title of Another Work* . . .

(Nano [1750?])   (Nano, n.d.)

15.42   *"Forthcoming" in author-date references.* Like *n.d.* (see 15.41), *forthcoming* can stand in place of the date in author-date references to books under contract with a publisher and already titled but for which the date of publication is not yet known. If page numbers are available, they should be given as needed. Books not under contract are treated as unpublished manuscripts (see 14.225). In text citations, *forthcoming* is preceded by a comma. See also 14.153.

Faraday, Carry. Forthcoming. "Protean Photography." In *Seven Trips beyond the Asteroid Belt*, edited by James Oring. Cape Canaveral, FL: Launch Press.

(Faraday, forthcoming)

Periodicals

15.43 *Publications preferring initials for authors' names.* The reference lists in some journals (especially in the natural sciences) always use initials instead of given names. When periods are used, space appears between them (Wells, H. G.); when periods are omitted, as in some journals' styles, no comma intervenes between last name and initials, and no space appears between the initials (Wells HG).

15.44 *Publications preferring abbreviations for journal titles.* In many publications in the sciences, journal titles are abbreviated (often with periods omitted) unless they consist of only one word. Standard abbreviations for scientific journals may be found in *BIOSIS Serial Sources* (bibliog. 5) and through PubMed, a service of the US National Library of Medicine (bibliog. 4.5), among other reference works. For a partial list of standard abbreviations of frequently used journal title words, see the latest edition of *Scientific Style and Format* or the *AMA Manual of Style* (bibliog. 1.1).

15.45 *Publications preferring sentence-style capitalization for titles.* Especially in the natural sciences, many publications that use a version of the author-date style prefer sentence-style capitalization for all titles (except, usually, the titles of journals, which are often abbreviated; see 15.44). In sentence style, only the first word in a title or a subtitle and any proper names are capitalized (see 8.156). In addition, works that prefer this style may eschew quotation marks for chapter or article titles (sometimes dispensing also with italics for book titles). Though Chicago now recommends headline style and the use of quotation marks or italics in both its systems of documentation, these forms can be readily adapted to other, sparer systems.

15.46 *Parentheses with issue number.* As discussed elsewhere (e.g., 15.9, under *Journal Article*; see also 14.180), the issue number may be omitted if pagination is continuous throughout a volume or when a month or season is included. When volume and issue number alone are used, the issue number is placed in parentheses. When only an issue number is used, it is not enclosed in parentheses.

Meyerovitch, Eva. 1959. "The Gnostic Manuscripts of Upper Egypt." *Diogenes*, no. 25, 84–117.

Morasse, Sébastien, Helga Guderley, and Julian J. Dodson. 2008. "Paternal Reproductive Strategy Influences Metabolic Capacities and Muscle Development of Atlantic Salmon (*Salmo salar* L.) Embryos." *Physiological and Biochemical Zoology* 81 (4): 402–13. doi:10.1086/589012.

15.47 *Newspapers and magazines in reference lists.* It is usually sufficient to cite newspaper and magazines articles entirely within the text—a strategy that is identical in form in both systems of citation. See 14.206. If, for some reason, a reference list entry is needed, the year of publication is separated from the month and day (if any).

Carey, Benedict. 2008. "For the Brain, Remembering Is Like Reliving." *New York Times*, September 4. http://www.nytimes.com/2008/09/05/science/05brain .html.

Kauffman, Stanley. 1989. Review of *A Dry White Season* (film), directed by Euzhan Palcy. *New Republic*, October 9, 24–25.

Unpublished and Informally Published Material

15.48 *Unpublished interviews and personal communications.* In a parenthetical citation, the terms *personal communication* (or *pers. comm.*), *unpublished data*, and the like may be used after the name(s) of the person(s) concerned, following a comma. Reference list entries are unneeded, though each person cited must be fully identified elsewhere in the text. Initials may be used for first names. The abbreviation *et al.* should be avoided in such citations.

(Julie Cantor, pers. comm.)

(A. P. Møller, unpublished data; C. R. Brown and M. B. Brown, unpublished data)

15.49 *Manuscript collections in the author-date style.* When citing manuscript collections in the author-date style, it is unnecessary to use *n.d.* (no date) in place of the date. Dates of individual items should be mentioned in the text, when applicable.

Egmont Manuscripts. Phillipps Collection. University of Georgia Library.

Kallen, Horace. Papers. YIVO Institute for Jewish Research, New York.

Oglethorpe wrote to the trustees on January 13, 1733 (Egmont Manuscripts), to say . . .

Alvin Johnson, in a memorandum prepared sometime in 1937 (Kallen Papers, file 36), observed that . . .

If only one item from a collection has been mentioned in the text, however, the entry may begin with the writer's name (if known). In such a case, the use of *n.d.* may become appropriate. See also 15.41.

Dinkel, Joseph. n.d. Description of Louis Agassiz written at the request of Elizabeth Cary Agassiz. Agassiz Papers. Houghton Library, Harvard University.

(Dinkel, n.d.)

15.50 *Patents or other documents cited by more than one date.* Cite patents and other documents that include more than one date as follows (note that the year of issue is repeated to avoid ambiguity):

Iizuka, Masanori, and Hideki Tanaka. 1986. Cement admixture. US Patent 4,586,960, filed June 26, 1984, and issued May 6, 1986.

15.51 *Access dates with website content.* To cite an undated online document in a reference list, use an access date rather than *n.d.* (no date). See also 14.7, 14.245, 15.41.

Evanston Public Library Board of Trustees. 2008. "Evanston Public Library Strategic Plan, 2000–2010: A Decade of Outreach." Evanston Public Library. Accessed July 19. http://www.epl.org/library/strategic-plan-00.html.

(Evanston Public Library 2008)

Citations Taken from Secondary Sources

15.52 *"Quoted in" in author-date references.* If an original source is unavailable, and "quoted in" must be resorted to, mention the original author and date in the text, and cite the secondary source in the reference list entry. The text citation would include the words "quoted in."

Costello, Bonnie. 1981. *Marianne Moore: Imaginary Possessions*. Cambridge, MA: Harvard University Press.

In Louis Zukofsky's "Sincerity and Objectification," from the February 1931 issue of *Poetry* magazine (quoted in Costello 1981) . . .

Audiovisual Materials

15.53 *Citing audiovisual materials in author-date format.* Chicago recommends a more comprehensive approach to dating audiovisual materials than in previous editions of the manual (see 14.274, 14.276). Though citations in the author-date system have therefore become somewhat easier to format, it is often more appropriate to list such materials in running text and group them in a separate section or discography; see 14.275. Older sources are more likely to have been consulted in the form of a digital copy; though authors should cite the format consulted, it is generally useful to give information about the original source, if available. Moreover, the date of the original recording should be privileged in the citation. Whom to list as "author" depends on the focus of the citation and is a matter of authorial discretion.

> Coolidge, Calvin. [1920?] "Equal Rights" (speech). Copy of 78 rpm disc in RealAudio and WAV formats from the Library of Congress, "American Leaders Speak: Recordings from World War I and the 1920 Election, 1918–1920." http://memory .loc.gov/ammem/nfhtml/nforSpeakers01.html.
>
> Holiday, Billie. 1958. "I'm a Fool to Want You" (vocal performance). By Joel Herron, Frank Sinatra, and Jack Wolf. Recorded February 20, with Ray Ellis. On *Lady in Satin*, Columbia CL 1157, 33⅓ rpm.
>
> Pink Floyd. 1970. *Atom Heart Mother*. Capitol CDP 7 46381 2, 1990, compact disc.
>
> Weingartner, Felix von (conductor). 1936. *150 Jahre Wiener Philharmoniker*. Preiser Records, PR90113 (mono), 1992, compact disc. Includes Beethoven's Symphony no. 3 in E-flat Major and Symphony no. 8 in F Major.

> (Coolidge [1920?])
> (Holiday 1958)
> (Pink Floyd 1970)
> (Weingartner 1936)

Legal and Public Documents

15.54 *Using notes for legal and public documents.* Almost all legal works use notes for documentation and few use bibliographies. Any work using the author-date style that needs to do more than mention the occasional source in the text should therefore use supplementary footnotes or endnotes; see 15.30. This advice does not extend to documents that are cited in secondary sources or as freestanding works (see 14.303), since these are readily adaptable to the author-date system (see 15.3). For a full discussion of legal and public documents, including examples, see 14.281–317.

15.55 *Citing legal and public documents in text.* Works with only a handful of citations to legal and public documents may be able to limit these to the text, using the forms detailed in 14.281–317. Note that in legal style, parentheses within parentheses are used (see also 6.95).

In *NLRB v. Somerville Constr. Co.* (206 F.3d 752 (7th Cir. 2000)), the court ruled that . . .

In the *Congressional Record* for that day (147 Cong. Rec. 19,000 (2001)), Senator Conrad Burns was reported as saying that . . .

In order to avoid such awkward constructions in the text, however, Chicago advises using notes for citations to legal and public documents whenever possible (see 14.283).

16 Indexes

Overview

16.1 *The back-of-the-book index as model.* This chapter offers basic guidelines for preparing and editing an index. Much of the advice—modeled on the requirements for a back-of-the-book index for a printed-and-bound scholarly monograph—applies also to indexes for journals and other types of works. General principles of indexing are covered, as are the specifics of Chicago's preferred style in matters of typography, alphabetizing, and the like.

16.2 *Why index?* In this age of search engines, the question "Why index?" is frequently asked. For a printed-and-bound book, the answers are clear. A good index gathers all the key terms and subjects (grouping many of the former under the conceptual and thematic umbrella of the latter), sorts them alphabetically, provides cross-references to and from related terms, and includes specific page numbers or other locators. This painstaking intellectual labor serves readers of any book-length text, whether it is published on paper or online. An index, a highly organized, detailed counterpart to a table of contents and other navigational aids, is also insurance—in searchable texts—against fruitless queries and unintended results.

16.3 *Who should index a work?* The ideal indexer sees the work as a whole, understands the emphasis of the various parts and their relation to the whole, and knows—or guesses—what readers of the particular work are likely to look for and what headings they will think of. The indexer should be widely read, scrupulous in handling detail, analytically minded, well acquainted with publishing practices, and capable of meeting almost impossible deadlines. Although authors know better than anyone else their subject matter and the audience to whom the work is addressed, not all can look at their work through the eyes of a potential reader. Nor do many authors have the technical skills, let alone the time, necessary to prepare a good index that meets the publisher's deadline. Some authors produce excellent indexes. Others would do better to enlist the aid of a professional indexer.

16.4 *The indexer and deadlines.* Most book indexes have to be made between the time page proofs are issued and the time they are returned to the typesetter—usually about four weeks. (For an illustration of how indexing fits into the overall publishing process for books, see 2.2.) An author preparing his or her own index will have to proofread as well as index the work in that short time span. Good indexing requires reflection; the indexer needs to stop frequently and decide whether the right choices have been made. A professional indexer, familiar with the publisher's requirements, may be better equipped for such reflection. For journals that publish a volume index (see 1.103), the indexer may have several months to prepare a preliminary index, adding entries as new issues of the journal arrive. The final issue in the volume is typically indexed from page proofs, however, and the indexer may have as little as a week to work on the last issue and prepare the final draft of the index.

16.5   *The role of software in indexing.* A concordance—or a complete list of terms (typically minus articles, prepositions, and other irrelevant elements), with page references—can be produced for any manuscript by any number of word-processing programs. Such concordances are mainly unhelpful; in fact, the assumption that an index rather than a concordance can be generated from an electronic document without significant human intervention is false. Most indexes for publications destined for print are produced from scratch, typically from paginated page proofs, either electronic or hard copy, generated by a page-layout program. Word processors are typically used in entering and editing terms and locators in a separate document and can provide rudimentary help in the process of sorting entries and managing cross-references. Dedicated word processors for indexers can automate many of the formatting and cross-referencing tasks particular to indexing and are a good investment especially for professional indexers (see 16.104). See also 16.7.

16.6   *Single versus multiple indexes.* A single, comprehensive index—one that includes concepts and names of persons and other subjects—is recommended for most works. Certain publications, however, such as journals and lengthy scientific works that cite numerous authors of other studies, may include an index of named authors (see 16.115) in addition to a subject index. An anthology may include an author-and-title index, and a collection of poetry or hymns may have an index of first lines as well as an index of titles. It is generally an advantage if two or more indexes appearing in one work are visually distinct from one another so that users know immediately where they are. In a biological work, for example, the headings in the index of names will all be in roman type and will begin with capital letters, and there will be no subentries, whereas most of the headings in the general subject index will begin lowercase and many subentries will appear; and if there is a taxonomic index, many headings will be in italics. Separate running heads should be used, indicating the title of each index (e.g., Index of Names, Index of Subjects).

16.7   *Embedded indexes.* An embedded index consists of key terms anchored with underlying codes to particular points in the text of an electronic publication. These terms can facilitate a reader's queries to a search engine in much the same way that a good subject index gathers keywords under subject headings to increase the chances that a reader will be led only to the relevant areas of a text. For example, a search for the word "because" in a properly coded online encyclopedia might lead to those passages that discuss the Beatles' *Abbey Road* song "Because" rather than to every instance of the omnipresent conjunction. The principles of selection for embedded indexes are similar to those for traditional back-of-the-book indexes. In fact, some publishers anchor traditional back-of-the-book indexes to the files that drive their print publications in order to facilitate hyperlinked and page-independent indexes for concurrent or future electronic editions.

16.8   *Resources for indexers.* For greatly expanded coverage of the present guidelines, along with alternative methods, consult the second edition of Nancy Mulvany's *Indexing Books* (bibliog. 2.5). Anyone likely to prepare a number of indexes should acquire that work. For further reference, see Hans H. Wellisch, *Indexing from A to Z*, and Linda K. Fetters, *Handbook of Indexing Techniques* (bibliog. 2.5).

Components of an Index

Main Headings, Subentries, and Locators

16.9   *Main headings for index entries.* The main heading of an index entry is normally a noun or noun phrase—the name of a person, a place, an object, or an abstraction. An adjective alone should almost never constitute a heading; it should rather be paired with a noun to form a noun phrase. A noun phrase is sometimes inverted to allow the keyword—the word a reader is most likely to look under—to appear first. The heading is typically followed by page (or paragraph) numbers (see 16.13) and sometimes a cross-reference (see 16.15–23). For capitalization, see 16.11.

agricultural collectivization, 143–46, 198
Aron, Raymond, 312–14
Bloomsbury group, 269
Brest-Litovsk, Treaty of, 61, 76, 85
Cold War, 396–437
Communist Party (American), 425
Communist Party (British), 268
imperialism, American, 393, 403
police, Soviet secret. *See* Soviet secret police
war communism, 90, 95, 125
World War I, 34–61
Yalta conference, 348, 398

16.10 *Index subentries.* An entry that requires more than five or six locators (page or paragraph numbers) is usually broken up into subentries to spare readers unnecessary excursions. A subentry, like an entry, consists of a heading (usually referred to as a subheading), page references, and, rarely, cross-references. Subheadings often form a grammatical relationship with the main heading, whereby heading and subheading combine into a single phrase, as in the first example below. Other subheadings form divisions or units within the larger category of the heading, as in the second example. Both kinds can be used within one index. See also 16.127. For sub-subentries, see 16.27, 16.28.

capitalism: and American pro-Sovietism, 273, 274; bourgeoisie as symbol of, 4, 13; as creation of society, 7; Khrushchev on burying, 480; student protests against, 491, 493

Native American peoples: Ahualucos, 140–41; Chichimecs, 67–68; Huastecs, 154; Toltecs, 128–36; Zapotecs, 168–72

16.11 *Initial lowercase letters in main headings.* The first word of a main heading is normally capitalized only if capitalized in text—a proper noun (as in the second example in 16.10), a genus name, the title of a work, and so on. Traditionally, all main headings in an index were capitalized. Chicago recommends this practice only where the subentries are so numerous that capitalized main headings make for easier navigation. Indexes in the sciences, however, should generally avoid initial capitals because the distinction between capitalized and lowercased terms in the text may be crucial.

16.12 *Initial lowercase letters in subheadings.* Subheadings are always lowercased unless, as in the second example in 16.10, the keyword is capitalized in text (a proper noun, a genus name, the title of a work, etc.).

16.13 *Locators in indexes.* In a printed work, locators are usually page numbers, though they can also be paragraph numbers (as in this manual), section numbers, or the like. When discussion of a subject continues for more than a page, paragraph, or section, the first and last numbers (inclusive numbers) are given: 34–36 (if pages), 10.36–41 (if paragraphs), and so on (see 16.14). The abbreviations *ff.* or *et seq.* should never be used in an index. Scattered references to a subject over several pages or sections are usually indicated by separate locators (34, 35, 36; *or* 8.18, 8.20, 8.21). Though the term *passim* has often been used to indicate scattered references over a number of not necessarily sequential pages or sections (e.g., 78–88 passim), individual locators are preferred. For use of the en dash, see 6.78.

16.14 *Inclusive numbers in indexes.* Publishers vary in their preferences for the form of inclusive numbers (also known as continuing numbers). Although the simplest and most foolproof system is to give the full form of numbers everywhere (e.g., 234–235), Chicago prefers its traditional system (presented below), which is efficient and unambiguous. The system is followed in all examples in this chapter. Whichever form is used in the text should be used in the index as well.

FIRST NUMBER	SECOND NUMBER	EXAMPLES
Less than 100	Use all digits	3–10
		71–72
		96–117
100 or multiples of 100	Use all digits	100–104
		1100–1113
101 through 109, 201 through 209, etc.	Use changed part only	101–8
		808–33
		1103–4
110 through 199, 210 through 299, etc.	Use two digits unless more are needed to include all changed parts	321–28
		498–532
		1087–89
		1496–500
		11564–615
		12991–3001

Roman numerals are always given in full—for example, xxv–xxviii, cvi–cix. For use of the en dash between numerals, see 6.78; see also 9.58, 9.59.

Cross-References

16.15 *Cross-references in indexes—general principles.* Cross-references are of two main kinds—*see* references and *see also* references. Both are treated differently according to whether they refer to a main heading or to a subheading. *See* and *see also* are set in italics (but see 16.22). Cross-references should be used with discretion; an overabundance, besides irritating the reader, may signal the need for consolidation of entries.

16.16 *"See" references and "double posting."* *See* references direct a reader from, for example, an informal term to a technical one, a pseudonym to a real name, an inverted term to a noninverted one. They are also used for variant spellings, synonyms, aliases, abbreviations, and so on. The choice of the term under which the full entry appears depends largely on where readers are most likely to look. *See* references should therefore be given only where the indexer believes many readers might otherwise miss the full entry. Further, the indexer and anyone editing an index must make certain that no *see* reference merely leads to another *see* reference (a "blind cross-reference"). If, on the other hand, the entry to which the *see* reference refers is about the same length as the *see* reference itself, it is often more useful to omit the *see* reference and simply give the page numbers under both headings. Such duplication (or "double posting") will save readers a trip.

FBI (Federal Bureau of Investigation),
    145–48
Federal Bureau of Investigation, 145–
    48
rather than
Federal Bureau of Investigation. *See*
    FBI

See also 16.46.

16.17   *"See" references following a main heading.* When a *see* reference follows a main heading, as it usually does, it is preceded by a period and *See* is capitalized. If two or more *see* references are needed, they are arranged in alphabetical order and separated by semicolons. They reflect the capitalization and word order of the main heading.

adolescence. *See* teenagers; youth
American Communist Party. *See* Communist Party (American)
baking soda. *See* sodium bicarbonate
Clemens, Samuel. *See* Twain, Mark
de Kooning, Willem. *See* Kooning, Willem de
Den Haag ('s Gravenhage). *See* Hague, The
Lunt, Mrs. Alfred. *See* Fontanne, Lynn
Mormons. *See* Latter-day Saints, Church of Jesus Christ of

Roman Catholic Church. *See* Catholicism
The Hague. *See* Hague, The
Turwyn. *See* Terouenne
universities. *See* Harvard University; Princeton University; University of Chicago
van Gogh, Vincent. *See* Gogh, Vincent van
Virgin Queen. *See* Elizabeth I

16.18   *"See" references following a subheading.* When a *see* reference follows a subheading, it is put in parentheses and *see* is lowercased.

statistical material, 16, 17, 89; coding
   of, for typesetter (*see* typesetting);
   proofreading, 183

This usage applies to both run-in and indented indexes, and to sub-subentries. See 16.27, 16.28.

16.19   *"See" references to a subheading.* Most *see* references are to a main entry, as in the examples in 16.17. When a cross-reference directs readers to a subentry under another main heading, *see under* may be used.

lace making. *See under* Bruges
Pride and Prejudice. See under Austen, Jane

An alternative, to be used when a *see under* reference might fail to direct readers to the right spot, is to drop the word *under* and add the wording of the subheading, following a colon. (Although a comma is sometimes used, a colon is preferred.) The wording of the cross-reference must correspond to that of the relevant subheading so that readers can find it quickly.

lace making. *See* Bruges: lace making
Pride and Prejudice. See Austen, Jane:
   Pride and Prejudice

16.20   *"See also" references.* *See also* references are placed at the end of an entry when *additional* information can be found in another entry. In run-in indexes, they follow a period; in indented indexes, they appear on a separate line (see 16.26). *See* is capitalized, and both words are in italics. If the cross-reference is to a subentry under another main heading, the words *see also under* may be used. If two or more *see also* references are needed, they are arranged in alphabetical order and separated by semicolons. As with *see* references, *see also* references must never lead to a *see* reference.

copyright, 95–100. *See also* permission to reprint; source notes
Maya: art of, 236–43; cities of, 178;
   present day, 267. *See also under* Yucatán

If *see also under* does not work in a particular context—for example, when one of the *see also* references is to a main entry and another to a subentry—the word *under* should be dropped and the wording of the subentry added after a colon.

> Maya: art of, 236–43; cities of, 178. *See*
>   *also* Mexican art; Yucatán: Maya

When a *see also* reference comes at the end of a subentry—a rare occurrence, and somewhat distracting—it is put in parentheses and *see* is lowercased.

> equality: as bourgeois ideal, 5–6, 7;
>   contractual quality, 13; in democra-
>   cy's definition, 24 (*see also* democ-
>   racy); League of the Rights of Man
>   debate on, 234–35

16.21   *Correspondence between cross-references and headings.* All cross-referenced headings (and subheadings, if used) should generally be cited in full, with capitalization, inversion, and punctuation exactly as in the heading referred to. But a long heading may occasionally be shortened if no confusion results. For example, in an index with frequent references to Beethoven, "*See also* Beethoven, Ludwig van" could be shortened to "*See also* Beethoven" if done consistently.

16.22   *Italics for "see," "see also," and so forth.* The words *see*, *see under*, and *see also* are normally italicized. But if what follows (e.g., a book title or a foreign word) is in italics, the words are preferably set in roman to distinguish them from the rest of the cross-reference. This is not necessary when they follow italics.

> Austen, Jane. See *Pride and Prejudice*
> *but*
> *Pride and Prejudice.* See Austen, Jane

16.23   *Generic cross-references.* Both *see* and *see also* references may include generic references; that is, they may refer to a type of heading rather than to several specific headings. The entire cross-reference is then set in italics.

> public buildings. *See names of individ-*
>   *ual buildings*
> sacred writings, 345–46, 390–401,
>   455–65. *See also specific titles*

When generic cross-references accompany specific cross-references, the former are placed last, even if out of alphabetic order. The conjunction *and* is normally used, following a semicolon (even if the generic cross-reference follows only one other cross-reference).

> dogs, 35–42. *See also* American Ken-
> nel Club; shelters; *and individual*
> *breed names*

Run-In versus Indented Indexes

16.24   *Flush-and-hang formatting for indexes.* Indexes are generally formatted in flush-and-hang (or hanging-indention) style. The first line of each entry, the main heading, is set flush left, and any following lines are indented. When there are subentries, a choice must be made between run-in and indented styles (see 16.25, 16.26). In print publications (and electronic works modeled on the printed page), indexes are usually set in multiple columns. In manuscripts, however, columns should not be used (see 16.131).

16.25   *Run-in style for indexes.* In run-in style, the subentries follow the main entry and one another without starting a new line. They are separated by semicolons. If the main heading is immediately followed by subentries, it is separated from them by a colon (see first example below). If it is immediately followed by locators, these are preceded by a comma and followed by a semicolon (see second example below). Further examples of run-in entries may be seen in 16.10, 16.20, 16.141.

> coordinate systems: Cartesian, 14; dis-
> tance within, 154–55; time dilation
> and, 108–14. *See also* inertial sys-
> tems; moving systems

> Sabba da Castiglione, Monsignor, 209,
> 337; on cosmetics, 190; on whether
> to marry, 210–11; on wives' proper
> behavior, 230–40, 350

Chicago and many other scholarly publishers generally prefer run-in style because it requires less space. It works best, however, when there is only one level of subentry (but see 16.27). For the examples above in indented style, see 16.26.

16.26   *Indented style for indexes.* In indented style (also known as stacked style), each subentry begins a new line and is indented (usually one em). No colon appears before the first subheading, and subentries are not separated by semicolons. Runover lines must therefore be further indented (usually two ems) to distinguish them clearly from subentries; whether runover lines belong to the main entry or to subentries, their indention should be the same. (Indention is always measured from the left margin, not from the first word in the line above.) *See also* cross-references belonging to the entry as a whole appear at the end of the list of subentries (as shown in the first example below). A *see* or *see also* reference belonging to a specific subentry is placed in parentheses at the end of the subentry, as in run-in indexes (see 16.18, 16.20). See also 16.23.

coordinate systems
   Cartesian, 14
   distance within, 154–55
   time dilation and, 108–14
   See also inertial systems; moving
     systems

Sabba da Castiglione, Monsignor,
   209, 337
   on cosmetics, 190
   on whether to marry, 210–11
   on wives' proper behavior, 230–
     40, 350

Indented style is usually preferred in scientific works and reference works (such as this manual). It is particularly useful where sub-subentries are required (see 16.28).

16.27   *Sub-subentries in run-in indexes.* If more than a handful of sub-subentries are needed in an index, the indented format rather than the run-in type should be chosen. A very few, however, can be accommodated in a run-in index or, better, avoided by repeating a keyword (see example A). If repetition will not work, subentries requiring sub-subentries can be indented, each starting a new line but preceded by an em dash flush with the margin; the sub-subentries are then run in (see example B). Em dashes are *not* used where only one level of subentry is needed.

Example A (run-in index: sub-subentries avoided)

Inuits: language, 18; pottery, 432–37;
   tradition of, in Alaska, 123; tradition of, in California, 127

Example B (run-in index: subentries requiring sub-subentries indented with em dash, sub-subentries run in)

Argos: cremation at, 302; and Danaos
   of Egypt, 108; Middle Helladic, 77;
   shaft graves at, 84
Arkadia, 4; Early Helladic, 26, 40; Mycenaean, 269, 306

armor and weapons
—attack weapons (general): Early
   Helladic and Cycladic, 33; Mycenaean, 225, 255, 258–60; from shaft
   graves, 89, 98–100; from tholos
   tombs, 128, 131, 133

—body armor: cuirass, 135–36, 147, 152, 244, 258, 260, 311; greaves, 135, 179, 260; helmets, 101, 135, 147, 221, 243, 258

—bow and arrow, 14, 99, 101, 166, 276
Asine: Early Helladic, 29, 36; Middle Helladic, 74; Mycenaean town and trade, 233, 258, 263; tombs at, 300

16.28 *Sub-subentries in indented indexes.* In an indented index, sub-subentries are best run in (see example A below). If, in a particular index, running them in makes the index hard to use, they have to be indented more deeply than the subentries (example B). When the first method is used, runover lines need not be indented more than the standard two ems, already a fairly deep indention. When the second is used, runover lines have to be indented three ems, which may result in some very short lines. See also 16.142, 16.143.

Example A (indented index: run-in sub-subentries)

nutritional analysis of bamboo, 72–81
  digestible energy, 94–96, 213–14, 222
  inorganic constituents: minerals, 81, 83–85, 89; silica (*see* silica levels in bamboo); total ash, 73, 79, 80, 91, 269, 270
  methods used, 72–73

organic constituents, 73–79, 269, 270; amino acids, 75–76, 86, 89; amino acids compared with other foods, 77; cellulose, 73, 78, 269, 270; crude protein, 73–75, 80, 89–91, 213, 269, 270; standard proximate analysis of, 78–80; vitamin C, 78, 79

Example B (indented index: sub-subentries indented)

nutritional analysis of bamboo, 72–81
  digestible energy, 94–96, 213–14, 222
  inorganic constituents
    minerals, 81, 83–85, 89
    silica (*see* silica levels in bamboo)
    total ash, 73, 79, 80, 91, 269, 270
  methods used, 72–73
  organic constituents, 73–79, 269, 270
    amino acids, 75–76, 86, 89
    amino acids compared with other foods, 77

cellulose, 73, 78, 269, 270
crude protein, 73–75, 80, 89–91, 213, 269, 270
standard proximate analysis of, 78–80
vitamin C, 78, 79

If sub-sub-subentries are required (which heaven forbid!), style B must be used, and they must be run in.

General Principles of Indexing

16.29   *Style and usage in the index relative to the work.* Each index is a tool for one particular work. By the time the index is prepared, the style used in the work has long been determined, and the index must reflect that style. If British spelling has been used throughout the text, it must be used in the index. Shakspere in the text calls for Shakspere in the index. Hernando Cortez should not be indexed as Cortés. Older geographical terms should not be altered to their present form (Constantinople to Istanbul, Siam to Thailand, etc.). The use of accents and other diacritical marks must be observed exactly as in the text (*Schönberg* not Schoenberg). Only in the rare instance in which readers might not find information sought should a cross-reference be given. Any terms italicized or enclosed in quotation marks in the text should be treated similarly in the index. If inclusive numbers are given in full in the text (see 16.14; see also 9.61), that style should be used in the index.

16.30   *Choosing indexing terms.* The wording for all headings should be concise and logical. As far as possible, terms should be chosen according to the author's usage. If, for example, the author of a philosophical work uses *essence* to mean *being*, the main entry should be under *essence*, possibly with a cross-reference from *being*. If the terms are used interchangeably, the indexer must choose one; in this case a cross-reference is imperative. An indexer relatively unfamiliar with the subject matter may find it useful to ask the author for a brief list of terms that must appear in the index, though such terms will usually suggest themselves as the indexer proceeds through the proofs. Common sense is the best guide. For journals, terms may have been established in advance, either by a predetermined list of keywords within the discipline or by previous journal indexes (see 1.104). See also 16.21.

16.31   *Terms that should not be indexed.* Although proper names are an important element in most indexes, there are times when they should be ignored. In a work on the history of the automobile in the United States, for example, an author might write, "After World War II small sports cars like the British MG, often owned by returning veterans, began to make their appearance in college towns like Northampton, Massachusetts, and Ann Arbor, Michigan." An indexer should resist the temptation to index these place-names; the two towns mentioned have nothing to do with the theme of the work. The MG sports car, on the other hand, should be indexed, given the subject of the work. Similarly, names or terms that occur in passing references and scene-setting elements that are not essential to the theme of a work need not be indexed. (An exception might be made if certain readers of a publication would be likely to look for their own names in the index. Occasional vanity entries are not forbidden.)

Indexing Proper Names and Variants

16.32 *Choosing between variant names.* When proper names appear in the text in more than one form, or in an incomplete form, the indexer must decide which form to use for the main entry and which for the cross-reference (if any) and occasionally must furnish identifying information not given in the text. Few indexes need to provide the kind of detail found in biographical or geographical dictionaries, though reference works of that kind will help in decision making.

16.33 *Indexing familiar forms of personal names.* The full form of personal names should be indexed as they have become widely known. (Any variant spelling preferred in the text, however, must likewise be preferred in the index; see 16.29.) Note that brackets are used in the following examples to distinguish Chicago's editorial glosses from parenthetical tags such as those in some of the examples in 16.34, 16.35, 16.36, 16.37, and 16.38, which would actually appear in a published index.

Cervantes, Miguel de [*not* Cervantes Saavedra, Miguel de]
Fisher, M. F. K. [*not* Fisher, Mary Frances Kennedy]
London, Jack [*not* London, John Griffith]
Poe, Edgar Allan [*not* Poe, E. A., *or* Poe, Edgar A.]

But in a work devoted to, say, M. F. K. Fisher or Cervantes, the full form of the name should appear in the index.

16.34 *Indexing pseudonyms.* Persons who have used pseudonyms or other professional names are usually listed under their real names. If the pseudonym has become a household word, however, it should be used as the main entry, with the real name in parentheses if it is relevant to the work; a cross-reference is seldom necessary.

Æ. *See* Russell, George William
Ouida. *See* Ramée, Marie Louise de la
Ramée, Marie Louise de la (pseud. Ouida)
Russell, George William (pseud. Æ)

but
Molière (Jean-Baptiste Poquelin)
Monroe, Marilyn (Norma Jean Baker)
Twain, Mark (Samuel Langhorne Clemens)
Voltaire (François-Marie Arouet)

16.35   *Indexing persons with the same name.* Persons with the same name should be distinguished by a middle initial (if either has one) or by a parenthetical tag.

Campbell, James   Field, David Dudley (lawyer)
Campbell, James B.   Pitt, William (the elder)
Field, David Dudley (clergyman)   Pitt, William (the younger)

In works that include many persons with the same last name (often a family name), parenthetical identifications are useful. For example, in *Two Lucky People*, by Milton Friedman and Rose D. Friedman (University of Chicago Press, 1998), the following identifications appear:

Friedman, David (son of MF and RDF)   Friedman, Milton (MF)
Friedman, Helen (sister of MF)   Friedman, Rose Director (RDF)
Friedman, Janet (daughter of MF and   Friedman, Sarah Ethel Landau
   RDF)   (mother of MF)

16.36   *Indexing married women's names.* A married woman who is known variously by her birth name or by her married name, depending on context, should be indexed by her birth name unless the married name is the more familiar. A married woman who uses both birth and married names together is usually indexed by her married name (unless the two names are hyphenated). Parenthetical clarifications or cross-references may be supplied as necessary.

Marinoff, Fania (Mrs. Carl Van Vechten)
Sutherland, Joan (Mrs. Richard Bonynge)
Van Vechten, Fania. *See* Marinoff, Fania
but
Besant, Annie (née Wood)
Browning, Elizabeth Barrett
Clinton, Hillary Rodham

16.37   *Indexing monarchs, popes, and the like.* Monarchs, popes, and others who are known by their official names, often including a roman numeral, should be indexed under the official name. Identifying tags may be omitted or expanded as appropriate in a particular work.

Anne, Queen   Benedict XVI (pope)   Elizabeth II (queen)

16.38   *Indexing princes, dukes, and other titled persons.* Princes and princesses are usually indexed under their given names. Dukes, earls, and the like are indexed under the title. A cross-reference may be needed where a title differs from a family name.

Charles, Prince of Wales   Shaftesbury, 7th Earl of (Anthony
Cooper, Anthony Ashley. *See* Shaftes-   Ashley Cooper)
   bury, 7th Earl of   William, Prince

Unless necessary for identification, the titles *Lord* and *Lady* are best omitted from an index, since their use with given names is far from simple. *Sir* and *Dame*, while easier to cope with, are also unnecessary in most indexes. Brackets are used here to denote Chicago's editorial glosses (see 16.33).

Churchill, Winston [*or* Churchill, Sir Winston]
Hess, Myra [*or* Hess, Dame Myra]
Thatcher, Margaret [even if referred to as Lady Thatcher in text]

But in a work dealing with the nobility, or a historical work such as *The Lisle Letters* (University of Chicago Press, 1981), from which the following examples are taken, titles may be an appropriate or needed element in index entries. The last two examples illustrate distinctions for which expert advice may be needed.

Arundell, Sir John   Whethill, Elizabeth (Muston), Lady
Audley, Thomas Lord   ["Lady Whethill" in text]
Grey, Lady Jane ["Lady Jane Grey" in
   text]

16.39   *Clerical titles in index entries.* Like titles of nobility, such abbreviations as *Rev.* or *Msgr.* should be used only when necessary for identification (see 16.38).

Cranmer, Thomas (archbishop of Canterbury)
Councell, George E. (rector of the Church of the Holy Spirit)
Jaki, Rev. Stanley S.
Manniere, Msgr. Charles L.

16.40   *Academic titles and degrees in index entries.* Academic titles such as *Prof.* and *Dr.*, used before a name, are not retained in indexing, nor are abbreviations of degrees such as *PhD* or *MD*.

16.41   *"Jr.," "Sr.," "III," and the like in index entries.* Abbreviations such as *Jr.* are retained in indexing but are placed after the given name and preceded by a comma.

King, Martin Luther, Jr.
Stevenson, Adlai E., III

16.42   *Indexing saints.* Saints are indexed under their given names unless another name is equally well or better known. Parenthetical identifications or cross-references (as well as discretion) may be needed. See also 16.75.

Aquinas. *See* Thomas Aquinas, Saint   Thomas, Saint (the apostle)
Borromeo, Saint Charles   Thomas Aquinas, Saint
Catherine of Siena, Saint
Chrysostom, Saint John

16.43   *Indexing persons whose full names are unknown.* Persons referred to in the work by first or last names only should be parenthetically identified if the full name is unavailable.

John (Smith's shipmate on *Stella*)
Thaxter (family physician)

16.44   *Indexing incomplete names or names alluded to in text.* Even if only an epithet or a shortened form of a name is used in the text, the index should give the full form.

TEXT	INDEX
the lake	Michigan, Lake
the bay	San Francisco Bay
the Village	Greenwich Village
the Great Emancipator	Lincoln, Abraham

16.45   *Indexing confusing names.* When the same name is used of more than one entity, identifying tags should be provided.

New York (city)   *or*   New York City
New York (state)   *or*   New York State

16.46 *Indexing abbreviations and acronyms.* Organizations that are widely known under their abbreviations should be indexed and alphabetized according to the abbreviations. Parenthetical glosses, cross-references, or both should be added if the abbreviations, however familiar to the indexer, may not be known to all readers of the particular work. Lesser-known organizations are better indexed under the full name, with a cross-reference from the abbreviation if it is used frequently in the work. See also 16.16.

EEC (European Economic Community)
MLA. *See* Modern Language Association
NATO

Indexing Titles of Publications and Other Works

16.47 *Typographic treatment for indexed titles of works.* Titles of newspapers, books, journals, stories, poems, artwork, musical compositions, and such should be treated typographically as they appear in text—whether italicized, set in roman and enclosed in quotation marks, or simply capitalized (see also 8.154–95).

16.48 *Indexing newspaper titles.* English-language newspapers should be indexed as they are generally known, whether or not the city of publication appears on the masthead. The name is italicized, as in text, and *The* is omitted. If necessary, a city of publication may be added in parentheses following the title.

Chicago Sun-Times	*New York Times*
Christian Science Monitor	*Times* (London)
Cleveland Plain Dealer	*Wall Street Journal*

For foreign-language newspapers, any article (*Le, Die,* etc.) normally follows the name, separated by a comma (but see 16.52). The city of publication may be added parenthetically, following the title.

Monde, Le (Paris)	*Prensa, La* (Buenos Aires)	*Süddeutsche Zeitung, Die*

16.49 *Indexing magazine and journal titles.* Magazines and journals are indexed in the same way as newspapers (see 16.48). *The* is omitted in English-language publications, but the article is included, following the name, in foreign ones (but see 16.52).

JAMA (*Journal of the American Medical Association*)
New England Journal of Medicine
Spiegel, Der
Time

16.50   *Indexing authored titles of works.* A published work, a musical composition, or a piece of art that merits its own main entry should also be indexed under the name of its creator, often as a subentry. The main heading is followed by the creator's name in parentheses (except in an index in which all titles cited have the same creator).

Look Homeward, Angel (Wolfe), 34–37
Wolfe, Thomas: childhood, 6–8; early
   literary influences on, 7–10; *Look
   Homeward, Angel*, 34–37; and Max-
   well Perkins, 30–41

Several works by a single creator are sometimes treated as subentries under a new main heading, following a main entry on the creator. This device is best employed when many works as well as many topics are listed. Separate main entries may also be included for the works.

Mozart, Wolfgang Amadeus, 49–51,
   55–56; early musical compositions
   of, 67–72, 74–80; to Italy with father, 85–92; Salzburg appointment,
   93–95; in Vienna, 98–105

Mozart, Wolfgang Amadeus, works of:
   La clemenza di Tito, 114; *Don Giovanni*, 115; *Idomeneo*, 105–6; *Jupiter
   Symphony*, 107; *The Magic Flute*, 111–
   13; *The Marriage of Figaro*, 109–12

16.51   *Indexing English-language titles beginning with an article.* In titles beginning with *A, An,* or *The,* the article is traditionally placed at the end of the title, following a comma, when the title forms a main heading. When such a title occurs as a subheading, it appears in its normal position in a run-in index, where inversion would be clumsy and unnecessary, but is inverted in an indented index for easier alphabetic scanning.

Professor and the Madman, The (Winchester), 209–11
Winchester, Simon: *Pacific Rising*,
   190–95; *The Professor and the Madman*, 209–11; *The River at the Center
   of the World*, 211–15

Winchester, Simon
   Pacific Rising, 190–95
   Professor and the Madman, The, 209–
      11
   River at the Center of the World, The,
      211–15

See also 16.56.

16.52   *Indexing foreign-language titles beginning with an article.* Since initial articles in foreign titles sometimes modify the following word, they are usually retained in an index. In publications intended for a general audience, especially those that mention only a few such titles, it is acceptable to list the titles in the index exactly as they appear in the text, without inversion and alphabetized according to the article.

> *Eine kleine Nachtmusik* (Mozart), 23
> *La bohème* (Puccini), 211

In a more specialized work, or any work intended for readers who are likely to be well versed in the languages of any foreign titles mentioned in the text, the titles may be inverted as they are in English (see 16.51). According to this practice, the articles follow the rest of the title in main headings but remain, as in English titles, in their normal position in run-in subheadings. In both positions, the articles are ignored in alphabetizing.

> *bohème, La* (Puccini), 211
> *clemenza de Tito, La* (Mozart), 22
> *kleine Nachtmusik, Eine* (Mozart), 23
> Mozart, Wolfgang Amadeus: *La clem-*
>   *enza de Tito*, 22; *Eine kleine Nacht-*
>   *musik*, 23
> *trovatore, Il* (Verdi), 323
> *but*
> "Un deux trois" (Luboff), 47 [alphabet-
>   ize under U]

An indexer unfamiliar with the language of a title should make sure that the article is indeed an article and not a number (see last example above). French *un* and *une*, for example, and German *ein* and *eine* can mean *one* as well as *a*.

16.53   *Indexing titles beginning with a preposition.* Unlike articles, prepositions beginning a title always remain in their original position and are never dropped, whether in English or foreign titles—nor are they ignored in alphabetizing.

> *For Whom the Bell Tolls*
> *Por quién doblan las campanas*

16.54   *Indexing titles ending with a question mark or exclamation point.* A question mark or exclamation point at the end of an indexed title should be followed by a comma wherever a comma is called for by the syntax of the heading. This slight departure from previous editions of the manual favors logic over aesthetic considerations. See also 16.94, 6.119.

> Carver, Raymond, 23–27, 101, 143–44;
>   "Are You a Doctor?," 25; *Will You*
>   *Please Be Quiet, Please?*, 25–27, 143.
>   *See also* Iowa Writers' Workshop

16.55   *Subtitles in index entries.* Subtitles of books or articles are omitted both in main headings and in subheadings unless essential for identification.

Alphabetizing

16.56   *Alphabetizing main headings—the basic rule.* To exploit the virtues of alphabetizing and thus ease the way for readers, the first word in a main heading should always determine the location of the entry. This principle occasionally entails inversion of the main heading. Thus, for example, *A Tale of Two Cities* is inverted as *Tale of Two Cities, A* and alphabetized under *T*, where readers would be inclined to look first. See also 16.9, 16.51, 16.52. For subentries, see 16.68–70.

16.57   *Computerized sorting.* Few computerized sorting options—and none of the standard options available with ordinary word processors—can perfectly conform to either system of alphabetization as described here. Some dedicated indexing programs, on the other hand, have been specially programmed to sort according to the letter-by-letter or word-by-word system in conformance with the detailed guidelines presented in this section. Those using a word processor to create their indexes will have to edit the finished product for the glitches and inconsistencies that invariably remain. See also 16.104, 16.67.

Letter by Letter or Word by Word?

16.58   *Two systems of alphabetizing—an overview.* The two principal modes of alphabetizing—or sorting—indexes are the *letter-by-letter* and the *word-by-word* systems. A choice between the two should be made before indexing begins, though occasionally an indexer will find, as indexing progresses, that a change from one to the other is appropriate. (Such a change would of course need to be applied to the entire index.) Dictionaries are arranged letter by letter, library catalogs word by word (though online catalogs can often be sorted by other criteria, such as format or availability). Chicago, most university presses, and many other publishers have traditionally preferred the letter-by-letter system but will normally not impose it on a well-prepared index that has been arranged word by word. In an index including many open compounds starting with the same word, the word-by-word system may be easier for users (the word-by-word system is customary in telephone directories). Both systems have their advantages and disadvantages, and few users are confused by either. Most people simply scan an alphabetic block of an index until they find what they are looking for. The indexer must understand both systems, however, and the following paragraphs offer guidelines for each. For a fuller discussion, consult Nancy Mulvany, *Indexing Books* (bibliog. 2.5).

16.59   *The letter-by-letter system.* In the letter-by-letter system, alphabetizing continues up to the first parenthesis or comma; it then starts again after the punctuation point. Spaces and all other punctuation marks are ignored. Both open and hyphenated compounds such as *New York* or *self-pity* are treated as single words. The order of precedence is one word, word followed by a parenthesis, word followed by a comma, then (ignoring spaces and other punctuation) word followed by a number, and word followed by letters. The index to this manual, in accordance with Chicago's traditional preference, is arranged letter by letter.

16.60   *The word-by-word system.* In the word-by-word system, alphabetizing continues only up to the end of the first word (counting hyphenated compounds as one word), using subsequent words only when additional headings begin with the same word. As in the letter-by-letter system, alphabetizing continues up to the first parenthesis or comma; it then starts again after the punctuation point. The order of precedence is one word, word followed by a parenthesis, word followed by a comma, word followed by a space, then (ignoring other punctuation) word followed by a number, and word followed by letters.

16.61   *The two systems compared.* In both systems a parenthesis or comma (in that order) interrupts the alphabetizing, and other punctuation marks (hyphens, slashes, quotation marks, periods, etc.) are ignored. The columns below illustrate the similarities and differences between the systems.

LETTER BY LETTER	WORD BY WORD
NEW (Neighbors Ever Watchful)	NEW (Neighbors Ever Watchful)
NEW (Now End War)	NEW (Now End War)
New, Arthur	New, Arthur
New, Zoe	New, Zoe
new-12 compound	New Deal
newborn	new economics
newcomer	New England
New Deal	new math
new economics	New Thorndale
newel	new town
New England	New Year's Day
"new-fangled notions"	new-12 compound
Newfoundland	newborn
newlyweds	newcomer
new math	newel
new/old continuum	"new-fangled notions"
news, lamentable	Newfoundland
News, Networks, and the Arts	newlyweds
newsboy	new/old continuum
news conference	news, lamentable
newsletter	*News, Networks, and the Arts*
News of the World (Queen)	news conference
news release	*News of the World* (Queen)
newt	news release
NEWT (Northern Estuary Wind Tunnel)	newsboy
New Thorndale	newsletter
new town	newt
New Year's Day	NEWT (Northern Estuary Wind Tunnel)

General Rules of Alphabetizing

16.62 *Alphabetizing items with the same name.* When a person, a place, and a thing have the same name, they are arranged in normal alphabetical order.

hoe, garden	London, England
Hoe, Robert	London, Jack

Common sense must be exercised. If Amy London and Carolyn Hoe were to appear in the same index as illustrated above, adjustments in the other entries would be needed.

garden hoe	London (England)
hoe. *See* garden hoe	London, Amy
Hoe, Carolyn	London, Jack
Hoe, Robert	

16.63 **Alphabetizing initials versus spelled-out names.** Initials used in place of a given name come before any spelled-out name beginning with the same letter.

Oppenheimer, J. Robert	Oppenheimer, K. T.
Oppenheimer, James N.	Oppenheimer, Katharine S.

16.64 **Alphabetizing abbreviations.** Acronyms, initialisms, and most abbreviations are alphabetized as they appear, not according to their spelled-out versions, and are interspersed alphabetically among entries. See also 16.46, 16.75.

faculty clubs	NATO
FBI	North Pole
Feely, John	NOW (National Organization for
LBJ. *See* Johnson, Lyndon B.	Women)

16.65 **Alphabetizing headings beginning with numerals.** Isolated entries beginning with numerals are alphabetized as though spelled out. (For numerals occurring in the middle of a heading, see 16.61, 16.66.)

1984 (Orwell) [*alphabetized as* nineteen eighty-four]	10 Downing Street [*alphabetized as* ten downing street]
125th Street [*alphabetized as* one hundred twenty-fifth street]	

If many numerals occur in an index, they may be listed together in numerical order at the beginning of the index, before the As.

16.66 **Alphabetizing similar headings containing numerals.** When two or more similar headings with numerals occur together, they are ordered numerically, regardless of how they would be spelled out.

Henry III	L7	section 9
Henry IV	L44	section 44
Henry V	L50	section 77

The *L* entries above would be placed at the beginning of the *L* section. See also 16.61.

16.67 *Alphabetizing accented letters.* Words beginning with or including accented letters are alphabetized as though they were unaccented. (Note that this rule is intended for English-language indexes that include some foreign words. The alphabetizing practices of other languages are not relevant in such instances.)

Ubeda	Schoenberg
Über den Gipfel	Schomberg
Ubina	Schönborn

This system, more than adequate for most English-language indexes, may need to be supplemented by more comprehensive systems for indexes that contain many terms in other languages. The Unicode Consortium has developed extensive specifications and recommendations for sorting (or collating) the characters used in many of the world's languages. For more information, refer to the latest version of the *Unicode Collation Algorithm*, published by the Unicode Consortium (bibliog. 5). See also 11.2.

Subentries

16.68 *Alphabetical order of subentries.* Introductory articles, prepositions, and conjunctions are disregarded in alphabetizing subentries (but see 16.53), whether the subentries are run in or indented. To preserve the alphabetic logic of the keywords, avoid substantive introductory words at the beginnings of subheadings (e.g., "*relations* with," "*views* on").

Churchill, Winston: as anti-Fascist,
    369; on Curzon line, 348, 379; and
    de Gaulle, 544n4

In indented style, where alphabetizing functions more visually, it may be better to dispense with such introductory words or to invert the headings, amplifying them as needed. The subheadings from the first example could be edited for an indented index as follows:

Churchill, Winston
    anti-Fascism of, 369
    Curzon line, views on, 348, 379
    de Gaulle, relations with, 544n4

16.69 *Numerical order of subentries.* Occasional subentries demand numerical order even if others in the same index (but not the same entry) are alphabetized.

> Daley, Richard J. (mayor): third term,
> 205; fourth term, 206–7
> flora, alpine: at 1,000-meter level, 46,
> 130–35; at 1,500-meter level, 146–
> 54; at 2,000-meter level, 49, 164–74

16.70 *Chronological order of subentries.* In a run-in index, the subentries for the subject of a biography may be arranged chronologically rather than alphabetically so as to provide a quick summary of the subject's career and to avoid, for example, a subheading "death of" near the beginning of the entry. This system should be used with caution, however, and only when the biographical and chronological logic is obvious from the subentries.

Personal Names

16.71 *Indexing names with particles.* In alphabetizing family names containing particles, the indexer must consider the individual's personal preference (if known) as well as traditional and national usages. *Merriam-Webster's Biographical Dictionary* (bibliog. 4.1) is an authoritative guide for well-known persons long deceased; library catalogs and encyclopedias are far broader in scope. Cross-references are often advisable (see 16.17). Note the wide variations in the following list of actual names arranged alphabetically as they might appear in an index. See also 8.5, 16.76, 16.84.

> Beauvoir, Simone de   Keere, Pieter van den
> Ben-Gurion, David   Kooning, Willem de
> Costa, Uriel da   La Fontaine, Jean de
> da Cunha, Euclides   Leonardo da Vinci
> D'Amato, Alfonse   Medici, Lorenzo de'
> de Gaulle, Charles   Van Rensselaer, Stephen
> di Leonardo, Micaela

Charles de Gaulle is a good example of the opportunity for occasional editorial discretion: *Webster's* and the Library of Congress, for example, list the French statesman under "Gaulle"; the entry in *American Heritage* is under "de Gaulle"—the usage normally preferred by Chicago.

16.72 *Indexing compound names.* Compound family names, with or without hyphens, are usually alphabetized according to the first element (but see 16.36). See also 8.6, 8.11, 16.83, 16.84.

Lloyd George, David	Sackville-West, Victoria
Mies van der Rohe, Ludwig	Teilhard de Chardin, Pierre

16.73 *Indexing names with "Mac" or "Mc."* Names beginning with *Mac* or *Mc* are alphabetized letter by letter, as they appear.

Macalister, Donald	Madison, James
MacAlister, Paul	McAllister, Ward
Macauley, Catharine	McAuley, Catherine
Macmillan, Harold	McMillan, Edwin M.

16.74 *Indexing names with "O'."* Names beginning with *O'* are alphabetized as if the apostrophe were missing.

Onassis, Aristotle
O'Neill, Eugene
Ongaro, Francesco dall'

16.75 *Indexing names with "Saint."* A family name in the form of a saint's name is alphabetized letter by letter as the name is spelled, whether *Saint, San, St.,* or however. A cross-reference may be useful if *Saint* and *St.* are far apart in an index. See also 16.42, 16.93.

Sainte-Beuve, Charles-Augustin	San Martin, José de
Saint-Gaudens, Augustus	St. Denis, Ruth
Saint-Saëns, Camille	St. Laurent, Louis Stephen

Foreign Personal Names

16.76 *Indexing Arabic names.* Modern Arabic names consisting of one or more given names followed by a surname present no problem.

Himsi, Ahmad Hamid
Sadat, Anwar

Arabic surnames prefixed by *al* or *el* (the) are alphabetized under the element following the particle; the article is treated like *de* in French names.

Hakim, Tawfiq al-
Jamal, Muhammad Hamid al-

Names beginning with *Abu*, *Abd*, and *Ibn*, elements as integral to the names as *Mc* or *Fitz*, are alphabetized under those elements.

Abu Zafar Nadvi, Syed
Ibn Saud, Abdul Aziz

Context and readership may suggest cross-references. For example, in an index to a work likely to have readers unfamiliar with Arabic names, a cross-reference may be useful (i.e., "al-Farabi. *See* Farabi, al-").

16.77 **Indexing Burmese names.** Burmese persons are usually known by a given name of one or more elements and should be indexed under the first element. If the name is preceded in text by a term of respect (*U*, *Daw*, etc.), that term either is omitted or follows in the index.

Aung San Suu Kyi [alphabetize under A]
Thant, U [alphabetize under T]

16.78 **Indexing Chinese names.** Chinese names should be indexed as spelled in the work, whether in the pinyin or the Wade-Giles system. Cross-references are needed only if alternative forms are used in the text. Since the family name precedes the given name in Chinese usage, names are not inverted in the index, and no comma is used.

Li Bai [pinyin; alphabetize under L]
Mao Tse-tung [Wade-Giles; alphabetize under M]

Persons of Chinese ancestry or origin who have adopted the Western practice of giving the family name last are indexed with inversion and a comma.

Kung, H. H.   Tsou, Tang

16.79 **Indexing Hungarian names.** In Hungarian practice the family name precedes the given name—for example, Bartók Béla, Molnár Ferenc. In English contexts, however, such names are usually inverted; in an index they are therefore reinverted, with a comma added.

Bartók, Béla   Molnár, Ferenc

Family names beginning with an initial should be indexed under the initial (see also 8.13).

É. Kiss, Katalin

16.80   *Indexing Indian names.* Modern Indian names generally appear with the family name last and are indexed accordingly. As with all names, the personal preference of the individual as well as usage should be observed.

Gandhi, Mohandas Karamchand
Krishna Menon, V. K.
Narayan, R. K.

16.81   *Indexing Indonesian names.* Usage varies. Some Indonesians (especially Javanese) use only a single, given name. Others use more than one name; even though the given name comes first, these are often indexed like Chinese names, with no inversion or punctuation (see third and fourth examples). Indonesians with Muslim names and certain others whose names may include a title or an honorific are indexed by the final element, with inversion. The indexer must therefore ascertain how a person's full name is referred to in text and which part of the name is used for a short reference.

Habibi, B. J.	Suharto
Hatta, Mohammed	Sukarno
Marzuki Darusman	Suryokusumo, Wiyono
Pramoedya Ananta Toer	

16.82   *Indexing Japanese names.* In Japanese usage the family name precedes the given name; names are therefore not inverted in the index, and no comma is used. If the name is westernized, as it often is by authors writing in English, the family name comes last. The indexer must therefore make certain which practice is followed in the text so that the family name always appears first in the index.

Tajima Yumiko [alphabetize under T]
Yoshida Shigeru [alphabetize under Y]
but
Kurosawa, Noriaki [referred to in text as Noriaki Kurosawa]

16.83   *Indexing Portuguese names.* The Portuguese, unlike the Spanish (see below), index surnames by the last element. This does not include the designations *Filho* (son), *Neto* (grandson), and *Júnior*, which always follow the second family name.

Câmara Júnior, José Mattoso   Silva Neto, Serafim da
Jucá Filho, Cândido   Vasconcellos, J. Leite de
Martins, Luciana de Lima

Where both Portuguese and Spanish names appear in the same context, cross-references may be necessary.

16.84   *Indexing Spanish names.* In Spain and in some Latin American countries a double family name is often used, of which the first element is the father's family name and the second the mother's birth name (*her* father's family name). The two names are sometimes joined by *y* (and). Such compound names are alphabetized under the first element. Cross-references will often be needed, especially if the person is generally known under the second element or if the indexer is uncertain where to place the main entry. *Webster's* is a good guide for persons listed there. Where many Spanish names appear, an indexer not conversant with Spanish or Latin American culture should seek help.

García Lorca, Federico
Lorca, Federico García. *See* García Lorca, Federico
Ortega y Gasset, José
Sánchez Mendoza, Juana

When the particle *de* appears in a Spanish name, the family name, under which the person is indexed, may be either the preceding or the following name (depending in part on how a person is known). If it is not clear from the text and the name is not in *Webster's* or otherwise widely known, a cross-reference will be needed.

Balboa, Vasco Núñez de
Esquivel de Sánchez, María
Fernández de Navarrete, Juan
Fernández de Oviedo, Gonzalo

Traditionally, a married woman replaced her mother's family name with her husband's (first) family name, sometimes preceded by *de*. Her name should be alphabetized, however, by the first family name (her father's).

Mendoza de Peña, María Carmen [woman's name after marriage]
Mendoza Salinas, María Carmen [woman's name before marriage]
Peña Montalvo, Juan Alberto [husband's name]

In telephone directories and elsewhere, some women appear under the husband's family name, but this is not a recommended bibliographic or indexing practice. Many modern women in Spanish-speaking countries no longer take the husband's family name. See also 8.11.

16.85   *Indexing Thai names.* Although family names are used in Thailand, Thais are normally known by their given names, which come first, as in English names. The name is often alphabetized under the first name, but practice varies. Seek expert help.

> Sarit Thanarat [*or* Thanarat, Sarit]
> Sivaraksa, Sulak [*or* Sulak Sivaraksa]
> Supachai Panitchpakdi

16.86   *Indexing Vietnamese names.* Vietnamese names consist of three elements, the family name being the first. Since Vietnamese persons are usually referred to by the last part of their given names (Premier Diem, General Giap), they are best indexed under that form.

> Diem, Ngo Dinh [*cross-reference under* Ngo Dinh Diem]
> Giap, Vo Nguyen [*cross-reference under* Vo Nguyen Giap]

16.87   *Indexing other Asian names.* Throughout Asia, many names derive from Arabic, Chinese, the European languages, and other languages, regardless of where the bearers of the names were born. In the Philippines, for example, names follow a Western order, giving precedence to the family name, though the names themselves may be derived from local languages. In some parts of Asia, titles denoting status form part of a name as it appears in written work and must be dealt with appropriately. When the standard reference works do not supply an answer, query the author.

Names of Organizations and Businesses

16.88   *Omission of article in indexed names of organizations.* In indexing organizations whose names begin with *the* (which would be lowercased in running text), the article is omitted.

> Sutherland Group
> University of Chicago

16.89   *Indexing personal names as corporate names.* When used as names of businesses or other organizations, full personal names are not inverted, and the corporate name is alphabetized under the first name or initials. An organization widely known by the family name, however, should be indexed under that name. In both instances, cross-references may be appropriate.

A. G. Edwards & Sons, Inc. [alphabetize under A]
Penney, J. C. *See* J. C. Penney Company, Inc.
Saphir, Kurt. *See* Kurt Saphir Pianos, Inc.
but
John G. Shedd Aquarium. *See* Shedd Aquarium

A personal name and the name of that person's company should be indexed separately.

Morgan, Junius S., 39, 42–44; J. S.
  Morgan & Company, 45–48
J. S. Morgan & Company, 45–48. *See*
  also Morgan, Junius S.

Names of Places

16.90 *Indexing names beginning with "Mount," "Lake," and such.* Proper names of mountains, lakes, and so forth that begin with a generic name are usually inverted and alphabetized under the nongeneric name.

Geneva, Lake
Japan, Sea of
McKinley, Mount

Names of cities or towns beginning with topographic elements, as well as islands known as "Isle of . . . ," are alphabetized under the first element.

Isle of Pines   Mount Vernon, NY
Isle of Wight   Valley Forge
Lake Geneva, WI

16.91 *Indexing names beginning with the definite article.* Aside from a very few cities such as The Hague (unless the Dutch form *Den Haag* is used; see 16.92) or The Dalles, where *The* is part of the formal name and thus capitalized, an initial *the* used informally with place-names is omitted in indexing. See also 8.44.

Bronx	Netherlands
Hague, The	Ozarks
Loop (Chicago's downtown)	Philippines

16.92 *Indexing names beginning with foreign definite articles.* Names of places beginning with *El, Le, La,* and such, whether in English- or non-English-speaking countries, are alphabetized according to the article.

Den Haag	La Mancha
El Dorado	Le Havre
El Paso	Les Baux-de-Provence
La Crosse	Los Alamos

16.93 *Indexing names of places beginning with "Saint."* Names of places beginning with *Saint, Sainte, St.,* or *Ste.* should be indexed as they appear in the text—that is, abbreviated only if abbreviated in text. Like personal names, they are alphabetized as they appear. Cross-references may be appropriate (e.g., "Saint. *See* St.," or vice versa). Note that French hyphenates place-names with *Saint. See also* 10.31, 11.29.

Saint-Cloud (in France)	Ste. Genevieve
Sainte-Foy	St. Louis
Saint-Luc	St. Vincent Island
St. Cloud (in Florida)	

Punctuating Indexes: A Summary

16.94 *Comma in index entries.* In both run-in and indented indexes, when a main heading is followed immediately by locators (usually page or paragraph numbers; see 16.13), a comma appears before the first locator. Commas appear between locators. Commas are also used when a heading is an inversion or when a main heading is qualified, without subentries. The second example illustrates three uses of the comma. For the role of commas in alphabetizing, see 16.61.

lighthouses, early history of, 40–42
Sabba da Castiglione, Monsignor, 209,
    337; on cosmetics, 190, 195, 198

16.95 *Colon in index entries.* In a run-in index, when a main heading is followed immediately by subentries, a colon appears before the first subheading.

In an indented index, no punctuation is used after the main heading. A colon is also used in a cross-reference to a subentry. See also 16.20.

Maya: art of, 236–43; cities of, 178. *See also* Yucatán: Maya

Maya
art of, 236–43
cities of, 178
See also Yucatán: Maya

16.96 *Semicolon in index entries.* When subentries or sub-subentries are run in, they are separated by semicolons. Cross-references, if more than one, are also separated by semicolons.

astronomy: Galileo's works on, 20–21, 22–23, 24; skills needed in, 548–49. *See also* Brahe, Tycho; comets; Flamsteed, John

16.97 *Period in index entries.* In a run-in index a period is used only before *See* (or *See under*) or *See also* (or *See also under*). In an indented index a period is used only before *See*. When a *see* or *see also* reference in parentheses follows a subheading or a subentry in either a run-in or an indented index, no period is used. No period follows the final word of any entry. For examples, see 16.17, 16.20, 16.19, 16.143.

16.98 *Parentheses in index headings.* Parentheses enclose identification or supplementary information. For the role of parentheses in alphabetizing, see 16.61.

Charles I (king of England)
Charles I (king of Portugal)
Of Human Bondage (Maugham)

16.99 *Em dash in index entries.* For use of the em dash in run-in indexes that require occasional sub-subentries, see example B in 16.27.

16.100 *En dash in index entries.* The en dash is used for page ranges and all other inclusive locators (e.g., "dogs, 135–42"). For abbreviating inclusive numbers in indexes, see 16.14. See also 6.78, the index to this manual, and examples throughout this chapter.

The Mechanics of Indexing

Before Indexing Begins: Tools and Decisions

16.101   *Schedule for indexing.* Anyone making an index for the first time should know that the task is intensive and time-consuming. An index for a three-hundred-page book could take as much as three weeks' work or more. See also 16.4.

16.102   *Indexing from page proofs.* For a printed work, the indexer must have in hand a clean and complete set of proofs before beginning to index. Some indexers prefer also to have a PDF version of the proofs so that they can search for specific terms (see 16.105). For a journal volume, the work may begin when the first issue to be indexed has been paginated, and it may continue for several months, until page proofs for the final issue in the volume have been generated. For an electronic work, unless the index is produced by coding the electronic files, a printout showing both content and locators may be required. See also 16.108, 16.117–25.

16.103   *Publisher's indexing preferences.* Before beginning work, the indexer should know the publisher's preferences in such matters as alphabetizing, run-in or indented style, inclusive numbers, handling of numeric headings, and the like (all matters dealt with in earlier sections of this chapter). For a journal volume index, the style is likely to be well established, and the indexer must follow that style. If the publisher requests an index of a particular length, the indexer should adjust the normal editing time accordingly. See also 16.131.

16.104   *Indexing tools.* The dedicated indexing programs used by many professional indexers automate such tasks as cross-referencing and the collation of entries and subentries and include special options for alphabetizing—for example, to exclude certain words or characters and to conform to either the letter-by-letter or word-by-word system (see 16.58). Such programs, however, tend to require more learning time than most authors can afford (see 16.4). Fortunately, an index can be prepared according to the guidelines in this chapter by simply entering terms and locators into a separate document using an ordinary word processor—though cross-references and alphabetizing, in particular, will need to be checked manually throughout the process (see 16.57; see also 16.5). For the latest information about tools for indexing, consult the website of the American Society for Indexing.

16.105   *Using the electronic files to index.* Publishers' policies vary as to whether they can agree to supply indexers with page proofs in electronic form. Some publishers may agree to provide a searchable PDF—which can be helpful in double-checking that additional instances of particular terms have not been overlooked. Some indexers may prefer also to highlight and refer to the PDF rather than a paper copy as they create the index. It should be noted, however, that an index cannot be automatically "generated" from a PDF and that there is no substitute for rereading the whole work. See also 16.5, 16.119.

16.106   *Formatting index entries.* Consult with the publisher up front to determine whether a run-in or indented index is required (see 16.24–28) and whether there are any other specific requirements. Format the manuscript accordingly, using a flush-and-hang style (see 16.24). See also 16.131.

16.107   *Indexing the old-fashioned way.* Before the advent of word processors (and their cutting-and-pasting and sorting functions), indexers used to handwrite or type preliminary entries and subentries on 3″ × 5″ index cards, then alphabetize and edit the cards, and finally type the index, while further refining it, on 8½″ × 11″ sheets. For details, consult Nancy Mulvany, *Indexing Books* (bibliog. 2.5), or the thirteenth or fourteenth edition of this manual (no longer in print but available in large libraries). The procedures described in the following sections can be adapted to the index-card method.

When to Begin

16.108   *Preliminary indexing work.* Although some planning can be done at the manuscript stage, most indexes are prepared as soon as a work is in final, paginated form, or "page proofs." It is crucial, in fact, that indexing not begin until pagination is final. For indexes in which the locators are paragraph or section numbers rather than page numbers, however, earlier iterations of the final or near-final manuscript can often be used to get a head start. Authors who are not preparing their own indexes may compile a list of important terms for the indexer, but doing much more is likely to cause duplication or backtracking.

What Parts of the Work to Index

16.109   *Indexing the text, front matter, and back matter.* The entire text of a book or journal article, including substantive content in notes (see 16.110), should be indexed. Much of the front matter, however, is not indexable—title page, dedication, epigraphs, lists of illustrations and tables, and acknowledgments. A preface, or a foreword by someone other than the author of the work, may be indexed if it concerns the subject of the work and not simply how the work came to be written. A true introduction, whether in the front matter or, more commonly, in the body of the work, is always indexed (for introduction versus preface, see 1.42). Book appendixes should be indexed if they contain information that supplements the text, but not if they merely reproduce documents that are discussed in the text (the full text of a treaty, for example, or a questionnaire). Appendixes to journal articles are indexed as part of the articles. Glossaries, bibliographies, and other such lists are usually not indexed.

16.110 *Indexing footnotes and endnotes.* Notes, whether footnotes or endnotes, should be indexed only if they continue or amplify discussion in the text (substantive notes). Notes that merely contain source citations documenting statements in the text (reference notes) need not be indexed.

16.111 *Endnote locators in index entries.* Endnotes in printed works are referred to by page, the letter *n* (for *note*), and—extremely important—the note number, with no internal space (334n14). If two or more consecutive notes are referred to, two *n*'s and an en dash are used (e.g., 334nn14–16). Nonconsecutive notes on the same page are treated separately (334n14, 334n16, 334n19). Occasionally, when reference to a note near the end of one chapter of a book is followed by reference to a note near the beginning of the next, nonchronological order will result (334n19, 334n2). To avoid the appearance of error, the chapter number may be added in parentheses after the lower note number.

cats, 334n19, 334n2 (chap. 9), 335n5

16.112 *Footnote locators in index entries.* Footnotes in a printed work are generally referred to in the same way as endnotes. When a footnote is the only one on the page, however, the note number (or symbol, if numbers are not used) may be omitted (156n). Note numbers should never be omitted when several notes appear on the same page. If there is indexable material in a text passage and in a related footnote, only the page number need be given. But if the text and the footnote materials are not connected, both text and note should be cited (156, 156n, 278, 278n30).

16.113 *Indexing notes spanning more than one printed page.* For endnotes or footnotes that continue onto another page, normally only the first page number is given. But if the reference is specifically to a part of a note that appears on the second page, the second page number should be used. Referring to a succession of notes, however, may require inclusive page numbers (e.g., 234–35nn19–23).

16.114 *Indexing parenthetical text citations.* Documentation given as parenthetical author-date citations in text is not normally indexed unless the citation documents an otherwise unattributed statement in the text (see 16.110). Any author discussed in text should be indexed. In some fields it is customary to index every author *named* in the text; check with the publisher on the degree of inclusiveness required. See also 16.115.

16.115 *Indexing authors' names for an author index.* Author indexes are more common in disciplines that use a variation of the author-date system (see chapter 15). Since most authors are cited in text by last name and date only, full names must be sought in the reference list. Occasional discrepancies between text and reference list, not caught in editing, have to be sorted out or queried, adding to the time it takes to create an author index. Is L. W. Dinero, cited on page 345, the same person as Lauren Dinero, discussed on page 456? If so, should she be indexed as Dinero, Lauren W.? (Answer: only if all or most authors are indexed with full first names—a situation that may be determined by the reference list.) Where a work by two or more authors is cited in text, the indexer must determine whether each author named requires a separate entry. Should Jones, Smith, and Black share one index entry, or should three entries appear? And what about Jones et al.? Chicago recommends the following procedure: Make separate entries for each author whose name appears in text. Do not index those unfortunates whose names are concealed under *et al.* in text.

TEXT CITATIONS	INDEX ENTRIES
(Jones, Smith, and Black 1999)	Black, M. X., 366
(Sánchez et al. 2001)	Cruz, M. M., 435
(Sánchez, Cruz, et al. 2002)	Jones, E. J., 366
	Sánchez, J. G., 435, 657
	Smith, R. A., 366

16.116 *Indexing illustrations, tables, charts, and such.* Illustrative matter may be indexed if it is of particular importance to the discussion, especially when such items are not listed in or after the table of contents. References to illustrations may be set in italics (or boldface, if preferred); a headnote should then be inserted at the beginning of the index (see 16.141 for an example). Such references usually follow in page order.

reptilian brain, 199, 201–3, 202, 341,
    477, 477–81

Alternatively, references to tables may be denoted by *t*, to figures by *f*, plates by *pl*, or whatever works (all set in roman, with no space following the page number). Add an appropriate headnote (e.g., "The letter *t* following a page number denotes a table"). If the number of an illustration is essential, it is safer to use *table*, *fig.*, and so on, with no comma following the page number.

authors and printers, 88 table 5, 89–
    90, 122–25, 122 fig. 7
titi monkeys, 69, 208t, 209t, 210f

Marking Proofs and Preparing Entries

16.117   *Beginning to highlight and enter terms.* After a perusal of the table of contents and the work as a whole, an indexer should begin highlighting terms to be used as main headings or subheadings. This is normally done by hand-marking a set of proofs. Inexperienced indexers are advised to mark the proofs—at least in the early stages—with the same kind of detail as is illustrated in figure 16.1. Most indexers prefer to mark one section (or chapter or journal issue) at a time and—using a word processor or dedicated indexing software (see 16.104)—to enter and alphabetize the marked terms in that section before going on to the next section. The notes belonging to the section, even if endnotes, should be checked and, if necessary, indexed at the same time (see 16.110). As the indexer becomes more skilled in marking the proofs, less underlining and fewer marginal notes may suffice.

16.118   *Deciding how many terms to mark.* The number of terms to mark on any one printed page obviously depends on the kind of work being indexed. As a very rough guide, an average of five references per text page in a book will yield a modest index (one-fiftieth the length of the text), whereas fifteen or more will yield a fairly long index (about one-twentieth the length of the text or more). If the publisher has budgeted for a strictly limited number of pages, the indexer should work accordingly. Remember that it is always easier to drop entries than to add them; err on the side of inclusiveness. See also 16.30, 16.31, 16.103, 16.109–16.

16.119   *How to mark index entries.* To visualize the method advocated here, suppose you are indexing a chapter from Wayne Booth's *For the Love of It*

those who find the hurting of others fun, no arguments against it can fully succeed, and the history of efforts to explain why "human nature" includes such impulses and what we might do to combat them could fill a library: books on the history of Satan and the Fall, on the cosmogonies of other cultures, on our genetic inheritance, including recently the structure of our brains, on sadism and why it is terrible or defensible. And so on. I'll just hope that here we can all agree that to hurt or harm for the fun of it is self-evidently not a loving choice.[1]

One embarrassing qualification: we amateurish amateurs do often inflict pain on others. We just don't do it on purpose.

Work and Play, _Work as Play_   : as play −56   : work as −56

To celebrate playing for the love of it risks downgrading the work we do that we love. In fact we amateurs are often tempted to talk snobbishly about those who cannot claim that what they do they do for the love of it. As <u>Bliss Perry</u> put the danger: "[T]he prejudice which the <u>amateur</u> feels toward the <u>professional</u>, the more or less veiled hostility between the man who does something for love which another man does for money, is one of those instinctive reactions—like the vague alarm of some wild creature in the woods—which give a hint of danger."

: loving one's

The words "professional" and "<u>work</u>" are almost as ambiguous as the word "<u>love</u>." Some work is fun, some gruesome. <u>Churchill</u> loved his work— but needed to escape it regularly. I hated most of the farm work I did as an adolescent, and escaped it as soon as possible. I hated having to dig ditches eight hours a day for twenty-five cents an hour. Yet working as teacher and a scholar, I have loved most of my duties—even the drudgery parts. A member of the <u>Chicago Symphony Orchestra</u> told me that he hates his work—his playing—and is eager for retirement. <u>Politicians</u> celebrate work as what will save welfare recipients from degradation; for them, to require people to work, even if they're underpaid and even if the job is awful, is a virtuous act.

Winston

: of one's work

: work celebrated by

Such a mishmash of implied definitions makes it impossible to place work in any simple opposition to play or pleasure. In <u>Homo Ludens</u> Huizinga occasionally writes as if the whole point of life were to have fun by _escaping_

Johan

---

1. A fine discussion of the dangers threatened by "doing things for the love of the doing" is given by <u>Roger Shattuck</u> in <u>Forbidden Knowledge</u>. Shattuck argues that the <u>art-for-art's-sake</u> movement, with its many echoes of <u>Pater</u>'s celebration of "burning" with a "hard, gemlike flame" and living for the "highest quality" of a given moment, risks moving us toward "worship of pure experience without restraint of any kind." The temptations of sadistic ecstasies lurk in the wings. As I shall insist again and again, to make sense out of a title like _For the Love of It_ requires careful distinction among diverse "loves," many of them potentially harmful.

Walter

FIGURE 16.1. Sample page of proof from Wayne Booth's _For the Love of It,_ marked up for indexing. See 16.117–25.

(University of Chicago Press, 1999), a consideration of work and play and work as play (see fig. 16.1). You have read through the chapter once and now have to go back and select headings and subheadings for indexing this particular section (of which only the first paragraphs are shown here). You decide that the whole section (pp. 54–56) will have to be indexed under both *work* and *play*, so you mark the section head as shown. (On the marked proofs, a colon separates a proposed principal heading from a proposed subheading.) Going down the page, you underline *Bliss Perry* (which will of course be inverted—Perry, Bliss—as a heading; similarly for the other personal names). You also underline *amateur* and *professional* (modifying them to the plural). In the second paragraph, you underline *work* and *love*, with proposed subheads, and *Churchill* (noting the first name in the margin). You decide to index *Chicago Symphony Orchestra*—which in another work might be tangential but here ties in with the book's major subtheme of musical performance and appreciation—and also mark *politicians*, with proposed subhead. You underline *Huizinga* (adding "Johan" in the margin) and the work *Homo Ludens*, which might also be a subheading under "Huizinga, Johan." In the note, you mark two names (supplying a first name for Pater), one title, and one additional term (see also 16.110).

16.120 *Planning index subentries.* For each term marked, you should make an effort to write in a modification—a word or phrase that narrows the application of the heading, hence a potential subentry. Although some such modifications may eventually be dropped, they should be kept on hand in case they are needed. Otherwise you may end up with some headings that are followed by nothing but a long string of numbers, which makes for an all but useless index entry. The modifications can be altered and added to as the indexing proceeds.

16.121 *Recording inclusive numbers for index terms.* If a text discussion extends over more than one page, section, or paragraph, both beginning and ending numbers—which will depend on what locator system is being used (see 16.13)—must be written in. See also 16.14.

16.122 *Typing and modifying index entries.* Most entries at this stage will include three elements: a heading, a modification (or provisional subentry), and a locator (page or paragraph number). While typing, you will probably modify some of the headings and add, delete, or alter subheadings and locators. After typing each entry, read it carefully against the page proofs— in particular, checking that the page numbers or other locators are correct. You are unlikely to have time to read your final index manuscript against the marked-up proofs, though you should certainly retain the proofs for reference until the work has been published. See also 16.106.

16.123 *Alphabetizing entries as part of the indexing process.* Many indexers alphabetize as they type; others let their software do it, intervening as necessary. By this time the indexer should have decided whether to use the letter-by-letter or the word-by-word system (see 16.58–61). If the system chosen proves unsatisfactory for the particular work as the index proceeds, a switch can be made if the publisher agrees. See also 16.57.

16.124 *Final check of indexed proofs.* After typing all the entries, read quickly through the marked-up proofs once again to see whether anything indexable has been omitted. You may find some unmarked items that seemed peripheral at the time but now, in the light of themes developed in later chapters, declare themselves to be significant. Or you may have missed major items. Now is the time to remedy all omissions.

16.125 *Noting errors during indexing.* Although not engaged to proofread, the indexer has to read carefully and usually finds a number of typographical errors and minor inconsistencies. If indexing a book (rather than a journal volume, most of which will already have been published), keep track of all such errors and send a list to the publisher (who will be very grateful) when, or before, submitting the index.

Editing and Refining the Entries

16.126 *Refining the terms for main headings.* The assembled entries must now be edited to a coherent whole. You have to make a final choice among synonymous or closely related terms—*agriculture, farming,* or *crop raising; clothing, costume,* or *dress; life, existence,* or *being*—and, if you think necessary, prepare suitable cross-references to reflect those choices. For journals, the terms may have been established in the indexes for previous volumes and should be retained.

16.127 *Main entries versus subentries.* You also have to decide whether certain items are best treated as main entries or as subentries under another heading. Where will readers look first? In a work dealing with schools of various kinds, such terms as *kindergarten, elementary school, middle school,* and *public school* should constitute separate entries; in a work in which those terms appear but are not the primary subject matter, they may better be treated as subentries under *school.* An index with relatively few main entries but masses of subentries is unhelpful as a search tool.

Furthermore, in an indented index an excessively long string of subentries may begin to look like a set of main entries, so that users lose their way alphabetically. Promote subentries to main entries and use the alphabet to its best advantage.

16.128   *When to furnish subentries.* Main headings unmodified by subentries should not be followed by more than five or six locators. If, for example, the draft index of a work on health care includes an entry like the first example below, it should be broken up into a number of subentries, such as those in the second example, to lead readers quickly to the information sought. The extra space needed is a small price to pay for their convenience.

hospitals, 17, 22, 23, 24, 25, 28, 29–31, 33, 35, 36, 38, 42, 91–92, 94, 95, 96, 98, 101, 111–14, 197
hospitals: administration of, 22, 96; and demand for patient services, 23, 91–92; efficiency of, 17, 29–31, 33, 111–14; finances of, 28, 33, 36, 38, 42, 95, 112; and length of patient stay, 35, 94, 98, 101, 197; quality control in, 22–25, 31

16.129   *How to phrase subheadings.* Subheadings should be as concise and informative as possible and begin with a keyword likely to be sought. *A, an,* and *the* are omitted whenever possible. Example A below, *not* to be emulated, shows poorly worded and rambling subheadings. Example B shows greatly improved subentries that conserve space. Example C adds subsubentries, making for quicker reference but requiring more space (see 16.27, 16.28). For arrangement of subentries, see 16.68–70.

Example A (*not* to be emulated)

house renovation
balancing heating system, 65
building permit required, 7
called "rehabbing," 8
correcting overloaded electrical circuits, 136
how wallboard is finished, 140–44
installing ready-made fireplace, 191–205
painting outside of house adds value, 11
plumbing permit required, 7
removing paint from doors and woodwork, 156–58
repairing dripping faucets, 99–100
replacing clogged water pipes, 125–28
replacing old wiring, 129–34
separate chimney required for fireplace, 192
straightening sagging joists, 40–42
termite damage to sills a problem, 25
three ways to deal with broken plaster, 160–62
violations of electrical code corrected, 135
what is involved in, 5

Example B (improvement with fairly inclusive subentries)

house renovation, 5, 8
   electrical repairs, 129–34, 135, 136
   fireplace, installing, 191–205
   heating system, balancing, 65
   legal requirements, 7, 135, 192

painting and decorating, 11, 156–58
plaster repair, 160–62
plumbing repairs, 99–100, 125–28
structural problems, 25, 40–42
wallboard, finishing, 140–44

Example C (improvement with sub-subentries)

house renovation, 5, 8
   electrical repairs: circuit overload, 136; code violations, 135; old wiring, 129–34
   heating system: balancing, 65; fireplace installation, 191–205
   legal requirements: electrical code, 135; permits, 7; separate chimney for fireplace, 192
   painting and decorating: painting exterior, 11; stripping woodwork, 156–58

plumbing repairs: clogged water pipes, 125–28; dripping faucets, 99–100
structural problems: sagging joists, 40–42; termite damage, 25
wall and ceiling repairs: broken plaster, 160–62; wallboard, finishing, 140–44

If it looks as though an index is going to require a great many sub-subentries, the indexer should check with the publisher before proceeding.

16.130 *Checking cross-references against edited index headings.* As a final or near-final step in editing the index, make sure that all cross-references match the edited headings. See also 16.15–23.

Submitting the Index

16.131 *Index submission format.* Having carefully proofread the draft and checked alphabetical order and all cross-references, punctuation, and capitalization to ensure consistency—and having produced an index of the required length, if one has been specified—you will now send the final draft to the publisher. If the publisher requires a printout, allow margins of at least one inch both left and right, and leave the text unjustified. Do not format the index in columns. Use hard returns only at the end of each entry and, for an indented-style index (see 16.26), at the end of each subentry. Use single line spacing, and apply hanging indents using your software's indention feature (see 16.24; see also 2.22). Do not impose end-of-line hyphenation (see 2.12). If there is more than one index, give each an appropriate title (Author Index, Subject Index, etc.) and save each in a separate file. To avert disaster, keep a copy of the final draft that you send to the publisher, as well as your marked-up proofs, until the work has been published. Send the publisher a list of any errors you have found (see 16.125).

Editing an Index Compiled by Someone Else

16.132   *What to do with a very bad index.* Editing a well-prepared index can be a pleasure. Little work should be needed. A poorly prepared one, however, presents serious problems. As an editor, you cannot remake a really bad index. If an index cannot be repaired, you have two choices: omit it or have a new one made by another indexer (at additional cost)—thereby delaying publication.

16.133   *Index-editing checklist.* Editing an index requires some or all of the following steps, not necessarily in the order given here. Note that it is not necessary to check every heading and every locator against the work—which would take forever—but it is necessary to read the index carefully and to refer to the page proofs (or final electronic version) from time to time.

1. Check headings—in both the main entries and subentries—for alphabetical order.
2. Check the spelling, capitalization, and font (i.e., italics or roman) of each heading, consulting the page proofs if in doubt.
3. Check punctuation—commas, colons, semicolons, en dashes, etc.—for proper style and consistency (see 16.94–100).
4. Check cross-references to make sure they go somewhere and that headings match (see 16.21). Make sure they are needed; if only a few locators are involved, substitute these for the *see* reference (see 16.16). Ensure that the placement of all cross-references within entries is consistent.
5. Add cross-references you believe are necessary.
6. Check to make sure there are no false locators such as "193–93" or "12102" (and figure out whether these may be the product of a typo) and make sure the locators to each main heading and subheading are in ascending order.
7. Check subentries for consistency of order, whether alphabetical or chronological. See 16.68–70.

8. If some entries seem overanalyzed (many subentries with only one locator or, worse, with the same locator), try to combine some of them if it can be done without sacrificing their usefulness. If subheadings are more elaborately worded than necessary, try to simplify them.

9. If awkward or unnecessary sub-subentries appear, correct them by adding appropriate repeated subentries or by adjusting punctuation (see 16.27, 16.28).

10. Look for long strings of unanalyzed locators and break them up, if possible, with subentries (see 16.10, 16.129).

11. Evaluate the accuracy of locators by a random check of five to ten entries. If more than one error shows up, consult the author or the indexer; every locator may have to be rechecked.

12. If the index needs trimming, delete any entries (and cross-references thereto) that you know from your work on the book are trivial, such as references to persons or places used only as examples of something. But be careful. You may offend someone or let yourself in for a lot of work. A handful of unnecessary entries, if they are very short, does not mar an otherwise good index.

16.134 *Instructions for typesetting the index.* At this stage the publisher will have prepared specifications for typesetting the index, and few further instructions are needed. To avoid problems, a brief note such as the following (for an indented index to a book) may be prefixed to the index manuscript after consulting the detailed specifications:

Set two columns, flush and hang, ragged right; indent subentries one em; indent runovers two ems; preserve en dashes between continuing numbers; leave one line space between alphabetical blocks. Set headnote across both columns. See publisher's design specifications for size and measure.

For an example of a headnote, see 16.141.

Typographical Considerations for Indexes

16.135 *Type size and column width for indexes.* In print works, indexes are usually set in smaller type than the body of the work, often two sizes smaller. That is, if the body copy is set in ten-on-twelve-point type, and the extracts, bibliography, and appendixes in nine-on-eleven, the index will probably be set in eight-on-ten. Indexes are usually set in two columns; with a type page twenty-seven picas wide, the index columns will each be thirteen picas, with a one-pica space between them. In large-format print works, however, the index may be set in three or even four columns.

16.136 *Ragged right-hand margin for indexes.* For very short lines, such as those in an index, justifying the text usually results in either gaping word spaces or excessive hyphenation, making for difficult reading. Chicago therefore sets all indexes without justification ("ragged right").

16.137 *Index indention.* All runover lines are indented, whether the subentries are run in or indented. In indexes with indented subentries (see 16.26), runover lines have to be indented more deeply than the subentries; all runovers, whether from a main entry or a subentry (or even a sub-subentry, should these too be indented), should be indented equally from the left margin. Thus, in an indented index the subentries may be indented one em, the sub-subentries two ems, and the runovers for all entries three ems. (For avoiding sub-subentries, see 16.27, 16.28.) All these matters, however, must be determined before type is set.

16.138 *Fixing bad breaks in indexes.* The final, typeset index should be checked for bad breaks. A line consisting of only one or two page numbers should not be left at the top of a column, for example. A single line at the end of an alphabetic section (followed by a blank line) should not head a column, nor should a single line at the beginning of an alphabetic section remain at the foot of a column. Blemishes like these are eliminated by rebreaking entries or transposing lines from one column to another, by adding to the white space between alphabetic sections, and sometimes by lengthening or shortening all columns on facing pages by one line.

16.139 *Adding "continued" lines in an index.* If an entry breaks at the foot of the last column on a right-hand page (a recto) and resumes at the top of the following left-hand page (a verso), the main heading should be repeated, followed by the word *continued* in parentheses, above the carried-over part of the index.

> ingestive behavior (*continued*)
>   network of causes underlying, 68;
>   physiology of, 69–70, 86–87; in
>   rat, 100; in starfish, 45, 52–62

In an indented index with indented sub-subentries it may be necessary to repeat a subentry if the subentry has been broken.

> house renovation (*continued*)
>   structural problems (*continued*)
>   termite damage, 25–27
>   warped overhangs, 46–49

16.140 *Making typographic distinctions in index entries.* A complicated index can sometimes be made easier to read by using different type styles or fonts. If, for example, names of writers need to be distinguished from names of literary characters, one or the other might be set in caps and small caps. Page references to illustrations might be in italic type (see 16.116) and references to the principal treatment of a subject in boldface. If devices of this kind are used, a headnote to the index must furnish a key (see 16.141, 16.143).

Examples of Indexes

16.141 *A run-in index with italicized references to figures and tables.* Run-in indexes are the most economical of the five formats exemplified in this section. Note the italic page references and the headnote explaining their use. Boldface could also be used for that purpose (see 16.143). For more examples and further discussion, see 16.25, 16.27, 16.94–100. See also 16.68, 16.140.

Page numbers in italics refer to figures and tables.

Abbot, George, 241–42
ABC, printing of, 164
abridgment: cases of, 246n161; as offense, 455–56, 607; of *Philosophical Transactions,* 579n83; restrictions on, 226, 227; works as, *302–3, 316,* 316–17
Abridgement (Croke), *302–3*
Abridgment (Rolle), *316,* 316–17
absolutism: absence of in England, 48; arbitrary government and, 251–52, 252n182; Cromwell and, 273–74; Hobbes and, 308; patronage and, 24; property and, 253, 255; royal authorship of laws and, 312, 317, 336n29; royal prerogative and, 251, 253–54
Académie Royale des Sciences (France), 436, 491n91, 510, 554

If occasional sub-subentries are required in a run-in index, you may resort to the style illustrated in 16.27, example B, using em dashes.

16.142 *An indented index with run-in sub-subentries.* For further examples and discussion, see 16.28. See also 16.68.

American black bear
    compared with giant panda: activity, 216–17; habitat, 211–12; home range, 219; litter size, 221; movement patterns of males, 124–26, 219

delayed implantation in, 191
reproductive flexibility of, 221
See also bears
amino acid content of bamboo, 75–
76, 86, 89; compared with other
foods, 77
artificial insemination, 179

Ascaris schroederi, 162
Asiatic black bear
constructing sleeping nests, 140
giant panda serologically close to,
228
See also bears

16.143 *An indented index with indented sub-subentries and highlighted definitions.* Note the deep indention for runover lines (see 16.137). A boldface page number indicates that the term is defined on that page (explained in a headnote at the beginning of the index). Italics could also be used for that purpose (see 16.141). For further discussion and examples, see 16.28. See also 16.68, 16.140.

Page numbers for definitions are in boldface.

brightness temperatures, 388, 582,
589, 602
bright rims, **7**, 16, 27–28 (*see also* nebular forms)
B stars, **3**, 7, 26–27, 647
bulbs (in nebulae). *See* nebular forms
cameras, electronic, 492, 499
carbon flash, 559
Cassiopeia A (3C461). *See* radio
sources; supernovae
catalogs
of bright nebulae, 74
of dark nebulae, 74, 120
Lundmark, 121

Lynds, 123
Schoenberg, 123
Herschel's (of nebulae), 119
of planetary nebulae, 484–85, 563
Perek-Kohoutek, 484, 563
Vorontsov-Velyaminov, 484
of reflection nebulae, 74
3C catalog of radio sources, revised,
630
central stars. *See* planetary nebulae
Cerenkov radiation, **668**, 709
chemical composition, 71. *See also*
abundances; *and names of indi-*
vidual elements

If occasional sub-sub-subentries are essential (they should be avoided if at all possible), they must be run in to the sub-subentries in the same way as sub-subentries are run in at 16.28, example A.

16.144 *An index of first lines.* Unless all the poems, hymns, or songs indexed have very short lines, indexes of this kind are often set full measure (rather than in multiple columns) for easier reading. Letter-by-letter alphabetizing is normally used. Note that lines beginning with *A, An,* or *The* are alphabetized under *A* or *T.*

After so long an absence, 295
A handful of red sand, from the hot clime, 108
An old man in a lodge within a park, 315
Beautiful valley! through whose verdant meads, 325
From this high portal, where upsprings, 630
O'er all the hill-tops, 617
Of Prometheus, how undaunted, 185
O hemlock tree! O hemlock tree! how faithful are thy branches, 614
There is no flock, however watched and tended, 107
The young Endymion sleeps Endymion's sleep, 316

16.145 *An index with authors, titles, and first lines combined.* To distinguish the elements, authors' names may be set in caps and small caps, titles of poems in italics, and first lines in roman type, sentence style, without quotation marks. If needed, a headnote to this effect could be furnished. Letter-by-letter alphabetizing should be used.

Cermak, it was, who entertained so great astonishment, 819
Certain she was that tigers fathered him, 724
CHESTERVILLE, NORA M., 212
Come, you whose loves are dead, 394
Coming Homeward Out of Spain, 73
Commemorate me before you leave me, Charlotte, 292
Complaint of a Lover Rebuked, 29
COMPTON, WILBER C., 96
Confound you, Marilyn, confound you, 459

In a general index, poem titles would be set in roman and enclosed in quotation marks, as in text or notes (see 8.179, 8.180).

Appendix A:
Production and Digital Technology

Overview

A.1   *Understanding the process.* This appendix, which is intended to give authors and editors an overview of the production process and the technologies involved, begins where the discussion of manuscript editing in chapter 2 ends. Production—of a book or a journal article, for publication in electronic or printed form—generally begins once an edited manuscript is considered final. Many of the details of what subsequently happens to the edited manuscript depend on the hardware and software that are used to turn it into a finished publication. Authors and editors do not necessarily need to understand production processes in all their detail, but anyone who works with designers, typesetters, information technology specialists, and other production personnel should have a basic understanding of what they do. For more detailed coverage of production processes, consult the sources listed in the bibliography, sections 2.6 and 2.7.

A.2   *Divisions of labor.* Though most of the physical aspects of producing a publication are now accomplished with software, publishing has become if anything more complex than it once was. And, whereas many of the traditional divisions of labor are still firmly in place, new tasks—particularly in information technology—have been added to the mix. Designers still create a typographic and visual format for a work that is appropriate for the content of that work in a particular medium. Production controllers continue to coordinate the efforts of in-house staff and vendors to ensure timely publication, within budget, and adherence to acceptable manufacturing and electronic publication standards. Meanwhile, editors and authors—once their main roles are done—continue to play a key role in reviewing a publication at various stages of production. But, increasingly, programmers and other IT specialists have come to play an important role, developing and maintaining systems for document conversion and typesetting as well as many other aspects of electronic publication. In fact, much of the discussion below—especially of electronic markup and other more technical aspects of production—assumes the indispensable role of IT specialists in the production process.

A.3   *Terminology.* Many design and production terms are derived from the technologies and processes used before the advent of computers. The word *leading*—synonymous with *line spacing*—once referred to actual strips of metal inserted between lines of type. The term *font* once referred to a specific size and cut (e.g., twelve-point italic) of a particular type family, or *typeface* (once literally the surface, or face, of a piece of type); now that type is rendered and scaled by software, the terms are often used interchangeably. Similarly, the terms *typesetting* and *composition* have become interchangeable, both referring to the process of arranging words and images on a screen more or less as they are intended to appear in published form. Even the term *markup*, which now often refers to the tags used in XML (extensible markup language) and other markup languages to describe the structure and label the components of an electronic document, has its antecedent in pencil markup on paper typescripts and proof. For definitions of these terms and others used throughout this discussion, see appendix B.

A.4   *Preparing for more than print.* If computers have become the primary tool in the production of virtually all published works, they have also increasingly come to play a role in how readers find, buy, read, and share publications. Publishers face a growing demand for electronic versions of the books and journals they produce—whether as web-based publications or in an e-book format or for full-text storage in searchable electronic archives. It is to the advantage of publishers, then, to tailor their production processes to allow for the delivery of any work in any format—electronic or printed—ideally from a single set of source files. XML—which, as an open standard for electronic markup, is available to any publisher—provides the most promising means to date for achieving such flexibility. Moreover, any manuscript that has been consistently marked up with one of the methods described in chapter 2 (see 2.78–80) can become part of an XML production workflow. This appendix assumes that even those who do not work with XML might benefit from an introduction to XML and a more general consideration of electronic markup languages.

A.5   *The journals publishing model.* The XML workflow outlined below grows in part out of the experience of publishers of scholarly journals, many of whom have had to respond to a demand for simultaneous print and electronic publication that dates to the 1990s. A journal, because it tends to maintain the same format from issue to issue, is particularly well suited to an XML workflow. Once implemented, the same sets of tags and the same procedures (some of which have been developed specifically for the scholarly publishing industry and enjoy broad support) can be reused and refined as necessary, leading to certain economies of scale. Book publishers can streamline their production processes to accommodate a similar, if less straightforward, approach, but the decision to adopt an XML workflow may ultimately be based on the demand for electronic book formats. On the other hand, publishers of web-based works such as the online edition of this manual can benefit from the fact that XML was initially designed to facilitate HTML presentations (see A.12). For a discussion of print technologies, which have changed little in recent years, see A.41–50.

Markup

General Principles

A.6   *What is markup?* Markup comprises the labels or annotations that are applied to a manuscript or other document in order to identify its structure and its components. There are four basic ways to apply markup, and these techniques are described in chapter 2 from the point of view of the manuscript editor. Briefly, they include markup by pencil on paper; generic markup in a word processor, which is similar to paper markup except that it is typed into the document (see 2.78); word-processing styles (see 2.79); and markup in a formal language such as XML (see 2.80). All of these share a fundamental purpose: to identify each element of a manuscript, from chapter numbers to chapter titles, subheads, paragraphs for running text and block quotations, emphasized text, entries in a bibliography, and so forth. Markup, in the most basic sense, allows a typesetter to interpret a manuscript and—design specifications in hand—format it for publication as an article, book, or other type of publication.

A.7   *Semantic and functional markup.* A formal markup language describes the structure of a document and identifies its components. This type of markup is sometimes referred to as *semantic* markup because it names the parts of a document rather than describing their appearance. To take one example, though the title *Origin of Species* might be distinguished from the surrounding text by italics, more meaningful markup would label it as a book title. Such markup would not only differentiate book titles from other types of italicized text (such as names of species or emphasized terms) but would allow them to be presented in something other than the customary italics if desired—for example, boldface or underscored. In fact, matters of presentation—the *appearance* of the text—are best defined in a separate document called a style sheet (see A.9). On the other hand, markup doesn't ultimately need to be associated with any typographic characteristic or other type of formatting. It can be purely functional. For example, the title *Origin of Species* might be tagged to include the keyword *evolution*—facilitating queries to search engines in an electronic publication (see 16.8). Moreover, some markup may have formatting or functionality associated with it in one medium but not another. For example, markup that determines hyperlinked text—graphically distinct and clickable in an electronic document—may not be evident on the printed page.

A.8 *Document type definitions.* The formal definition of a document's structure—among other things, the names of all of its elements and the rules that govern their markup—is encoded in a document type definition (DTD) or other schema. The process of creating a DTD is roughly analogous to the one that a designer follows to identify and design each element of a book. But DTDs—which take considerable time and expertise to develop—must also be programmed to define every possible relationship among the elements in order to establish rules about the document's structure. For example, a DTD may require that any element tagged as a "list" contain at least two "items," or that any "image" tag point to the name of a file in a specific directory. Marked-up documents can be analyzed with the help of parsing programs to make sure they conform to a specific DTD, allowing for the ready identification and correction of some kinds of tagging errors. Once developed, a DTD can be reused for similar documents of the same type—for example, book-length monographs or articles in a scholarly journal. Many organizations use industry-standard DTDs for publishing and archiving their articles or books. For example, certain journal publishers rely on the family of DTDs developed for the National Library of Medicine (which also includes a DTD for books).

A.9 *Style sheets.* While a DTD describes the structure of the tagged elements in a formally marked-up document, a style sheet provides the formatting specifications that define and automate their presentation—that is, how they look on the screen or on the page. (For a different meaning of style sheet, see 2.52.) A formally marked-up document published in more than one medium—for example, print and HTML—will need a different style sheet for each in order to specify typefaces, layouts, and other features appropriate to each medium. Meanwhile, the document itself— its markup plus text and any illustrations or other components—does not need to be altered for either presentation. This separation of content from presentation—though it is never perfect (see A.17)—is one of the primary benefits of an XML-based production workflow (see A.24). Style sheets are prepared (generally by IT specialists in collaboration with designers) in one of several programming languages, such as CSS (cascading style sheets), which can be used to describe how the components of an HTML document look and function in a particular browser or how the document prints on a laser printer. Another language, XSL (extensible style sheet language), not only defines presentation but also enables the conversion of XML documents to other formats, including HTML. Vendors of e-book formats generally have their own style sheets, and any style sheet may be reused or adapted for similar types of documents.

A.10   *Metadata.* Metadata—or data about data—is a part of any marked-up document. Publishers generally include certain types of bibliographic metadata—for example, creator, title, publication date, description, and keywords—some or all of which may be displayed within (or alongside) their publications. Such metadata is a lot like the information that once resided in a library's card-catalog system and can facilitate discovery by search engines. More specific categories of metadata may be appropriate depending on the publication. For example, file format descriptions, language(s) of publication, and security level (to specify who can access the content) may be encoded in a document as needed. With the help of software, metadata can be derived, or extracted, from the markup of a publication before, during, and after production for a variety of purposes. For example, metadata about a document's revision status can help track the versions of a document through the proofreading and testing stages. Other types of metadata—for example, the DOIs of journal articles in a reference list—can facilitate linking of source citations to information about the actual location of the texts to which they refer (see also 14.6). For more information on metadata, including information about best practices, consult the website of the Dublin Core Metadata Initiative, an organization responsible for developing standards related to electronic resource description.

XML

A.11   *What is XML?* XML (an abbreviation for extensible markup language) is a detailed specification for defining and marking up the logical structure of any type of document—in other words, it is a metalanguage that provides rules for naming and defining the parts of a document and their relationship to each other. It has been in development since the mid-1990s by various working groups of the World Wide Web Consortium (W3C). XML is an open standard, meaning it is available for free to the general public through the website of the W3C. As described in 2.80, XML markup requires that each element in a document, including the document as a whole, be enclosed between a pair of opening and closing tags. XML does not contain a standard set of tags; rather, it allows users to create unique tags customized for any type of document: chapters, journal articles, catalog entries, database records, and so forth. For examples of XML markup, see figures A.1 and A.2.

A.12   *SGML, HTML, XML—a brief history.* XML traces its origins to SGML, which stands for standard generalized markup language. SGML became an international standard in 1986, defined by the International Organization for Standardization as ISO 8879, after which it became the primary specification according to which many publishers marked up and maintained electronic versions of their documents. Such a standard was originally developed to ensure that governments and other organizations could maintain electronic archives that would be relatively impervious to changes in technology. Like XML, SGML is a metalanguage—in the case of SGML, a comprehensive set of rules not just for naming and defining the parts of a document but for developing other, related markup languages. One such language is HTML (hypertext markup language), which was introduced in the early 1990s as a set of presentation tags for preparing documents for web browsers. HTML tags (often in conjunction with a style sheet; see A.9) work much like typesetting codes for print publications, determining how a document will appear, not on the page, but on the screen. Soon after the introduction of HTML, XML was developed as a refinement of SGML that would make it easier to prepare documents for use on the web.

A.13   *Why XML?* As outlined in A.12, XML was initially developed as a simplified version of SGML that would facilitate conversion to HTML for publishing on the web. As electronic formats have proliferated, some publishers have found it advantageous to use XML as the basis of their publications in order to make them available for other purposes, such as electronic archives and various e-book formats. Like SGML but unlike HTML, XML can be adapted to describe any type of document and does not depend on any specific software or format. This flexibility can facilitate the presentation of content in ways that were not possible at initial publication—a potential hedge against changing technologies. To take an early example, HTML for tables did not exist in the early 1990s; tables on the web were presented only as static images rather than as text. Publishers who at that time were using SGML to tag such things as the arrangement of cells into rows and columns were prepared to regenerate full-text HTML tables in their web publications as this functionality became available in later versions of HTML (but see A.33). A similar phenomenon is taking place for mathematical expressions marked up in MathML (mathematical markup language, an application of XML) that cannot be displayed by all web browsers. See also A.34.

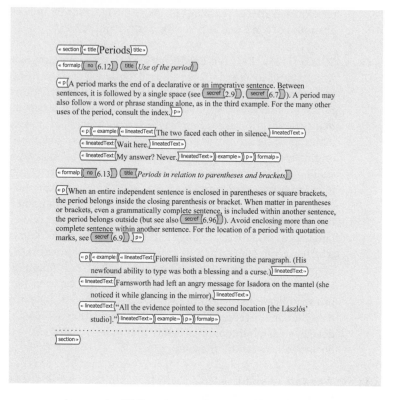

FIGURE A.1. An example of XML markup in a graphical interface, showing two numbered paragraphs from the section on periods in chapter 6 of this manual. Compare figure A.2.

A.14 *XML elements and attributes.* An XML document, simply stated, consists of elements and attributes. An *element* is really just a specific part of the document—in other words, any part that has been labeled with a pair of XML tags. Elements might include such items as document title, section headings, paragraphs, titles of works, terms marked for emphasis (and destined to be italicized or otherwise distinguished from the surrounding text), names of authors, and cross-references. An XML *attribute* is included inside the opening tag for an XML element and provides additional information about that element. For example, a document may include various lists, each tagged with a pair of "list" tags. These lists could be further distinguished from each other by attributes that identify the type of list—"ordered" versus "unordered," for example. An associated style sheet would recognize the attributes and format the two kinds of lists differently—for example, the "ordered list" as a list numbered with

```
<section id="ch06_s1_03">
<title>Periods</title>
<formalp id="ch06_sec012"><no>6.12</no><title>Use of the period</title>
<p>A period marks the end of a declarative or an imperative sentence. Between
sentences, it is followed by a single space (see <secref
rid="ch02_sec009">2.9</secref>, <secref rid="ch06_sec007">6.7</secref>). A period may
also follow a word or phrase standing alone, as in the third example. For the many
other uses of the period, consult the index.</p>
<p><example>
<lineatedText>The two faced each other in silence.</lineatedText>
<lineatedText>Wait here.</lineatedText>
<lineatedText>My answer? Never.</lineatedText>
</example></p>
</formalp>
<formalp id="ch06_sec013"><no>6.13</no><title>Periods in relation to parentheses and
brackets</title>
<p>When an entire independent sentence is enclosed in parentheses or square brackets,
the period belongs inside the closing parenthesis or bracket. When matter in
parentheses or brackets, even a grammatically complete sentence, is included within
another sentence, the period belongs outside (but see also <secref
rid="ch06_sec096">6.96</secref>). Avoid enclosing more than one complete sentence
within another sentence. For the location of a period with quotation marks, see <secref
rid="ch06_sec009">6.9</secref>.</p>
<p><example>
<lineatedText>Fiorelli insisted on rewriting the paragraph. (His newfound ability to
type was both a blessing and a curse.)</lineatedText>
<lineatedText>Farnsworth had left an angry message for Isadora on the mantel (she
noticed it while glancing in the mirror).</lineatedText>
<lineatedText>&#x201C;All the evidence pointed to the second location [the
L&#x00E1;szl&#x00F3;s&#x2019; studio].&#x201D;</lineatedText>
</example></p>
</formalp>
. . .
</section>
```

FIGURE A.2. Another view of figure A.1, showing the XML markup as plain text.

arabic numerals starting at 1 and the "unordered list" as a bulleted list (see also A.9). Another type of attribute might specify a URL for a textual element to facilitate the creation of a hyperlink.

A.15 **XML character references.** An XML character reference is a plain-text placeholder for a special character that may be unavailable in a particular software program or from a particular input device (e.g., a keyboard). Character references are set off from the surrounding text by an ampersand and a semicolon. By default, XML supports references defined by the Unicode standard. For example, a multiplication sign (defined by Unicode as U+00D7) can be represented in XML as the character reference × (the #x signals the hexadecimal Unicode code point). In a program that interprets the XML document, the character reference would display as a multiplication sign (×). Alternatively, character references can consist of names taken from other ISO standard character sets—for example, é or α (which resolve to é and α, respectively)—when these are specified in the DTD (see A.8). (Some special characters that may not display properly for all users may need to be rendered as images; see A.34.) For more on Unicode, see chapter 11 (esp. 11.2).

Design

A.16 *Mapping markup to design.* In the most basic sense, markup describes the structure and content of a work, whereas a design determines how it looks—either on the printed page or on a screen. Whatever method has been used to mark up an edited manuscript—generic codes (electronic or on paper), software-generated style tags, or XML—each element must correspond to a particular design specification. In some cases, editors work with designers to identify the design elements before a manuscript is submitted for production. For projects that are intended for publication in both print and on the web, two different designs with corresponding sets of design specifications will be necessary. If XML or other formal markup is used, the design specifications are usually encoded for production in electronic style sheets (see A.9). (The design of dust jackets, paperback covers, and packaging for electronic storage media—which requires some technical and marketing considerations beyond the scope of this appendix—is not covered here. For works covering these topics, see sections 2.6 and 2.7 of the bibliography.)

A.17 *Some limitations of style sheets.* Electronic style sheets, as described in A.9, provide a means of rendering a formally marked-up document according to a set of design specifications, but they cannot predict certain factors that might affect the published document's appearance, such as where line and page breaks will fall. When used to produce printed publications, style sheets are usually supplemented with a publisher's preferred set of rules for composition and page makeup (see fig. A.3). As with conventionally typeset print publications, these rules direct typesetters to make small adjustments in a page-layout program to fix such things as loose lines and uneven facing pages and to reposition images to fit the available space. Additional adjustments may be necessary to achieve precise alignment in tables or other textual environments with complex layouts (see A.33). Such tweaks made in the files for the printed publication will not be reflected either in the style sheets or in the tagged source files (see A.31–34) for any electronic version and may be difficult to achieve online without resorting to images. For most types of electronic publications, however, publishers have come to accept inevitable variations in spacing and other aspects of presentation that might depend on a particular browser or device and that cannot be controlled for in a style sheet.

A.18 *Determining length.* For printed books, publishers will often specify a target page count (usually for a specific, often standard, trim size—e.g., 6″ × 9″), taking into account the length of the manuscript. Designers must

House Style for Composition and Page Makeup
The University of Chicago Press, 1427 E. 60th Street, Chicago IL 60637

(Unless otherwise specified, these standing specifications apply.)

<u>TYPOGRAPHY</u>

1. **Vertical spacing** is specified as baseline to baseline.

2. **Letter spacing:** Text and smaller type are to be set at the standard character fit designed for the typeface unless specified otherwise.

3. **Word spacing:** Tight horizontal word space is the preference with no extra space after punctuation. Word space should average the width of a lowercase n, and be no tighter than the width of a lowercase i.

4. **Line breaks and hyphenation:**
   ‣ Standards call for a minimum of two characters at the end of the line, with a minimum of three carried down.
   ‣ No more than three consecutive end-of-line hyphens or punctuation (or a combination of hyphens and punctuation) are allowed.
   ‣ Up to eight hyphens are allowed per 35-to-40-line page.
   ‣ Hyphenated compound words should be broken only at the hyphen.
   ‣ The final word of a paragraph is allowed to hyphenate except that a minimum of four characters (not counting periods, commas, and quotation marks) is required on the final line.
   ‣ It is best not to have a hyphenated word as the last word on a page. However, it is allowable if the syllable or syllables leave little doubt as to the identity of the full word.
   ‣ It is preferable not to break proper names but allowable when difficult to avoid. Line breaks are allowed after a first name or middle initial; names using two initials will not break between the initials.
   ‣ More guidelines on word division are found in the CHICAGO MANUAL OF STYLE. Follow it for more detailed guidance.

5. **"Carding":** Adding extra space between lines or paragraphs to make facing pages align is not allowed.

6. **Density:** Type density must be consistent from page to page throughout the book, and patches and reruns must match the original type. Repros will be returned if there are variations in density.

7. **Ligatures:** Use for lowercase Roman and italic letter combinations such as ti, ff, fl, fi, and ffl, and other combinations (except ae, oe) when available in the font.

FIGURE A.3. Sample set of rules for composition and page makeup (*continues overleaf*).

figure out type sizes, spacing, and margins that will result in a book that comes close to this target. The traditional way to determine this is to start by getting a character count, or castoff, and dividing this count by the target number of characters per printed page. Since each category of text will likely be given its own set of type characteristics, the designer needs not just a total character count for the work but a count broken down by type of material (e.g., text, extracts, appendix, notes, and bibliography). Some designers will prefer instead to look at the entire manuscript in a page-layout program, where decisions about type sizes and layout can be

<u>PAGE MAKEUP</u>

1. **Type page depth:** The depth of the type page is measured from the base of the running head to the base of the last line of the standard text page. If there is no running head, the depth is measured from the base of the first line of text to the base of the running foot, or of the last line of the text if there is no running foot.

2. **Corner marks:** The compositor is to include corner marks left and right at the base of the running head position on all sink pages (i.e., front matter, part title, chapter openings, end matter).

3. **Chapter opening text:** The number of lines on chapter opening pages may be up to two lines short if necessary to avoid a bad page break. Keep chapter drop position.

4. **Subheads:**
   - The text page may be up to four lines short if there is no room for a subhead at the bottom of a page. The subhead begins at the top of the next page.
   - The minimum number of lines of text below a subhead at the bottom of a page is two.
   - If a subhead falls near the top of a page, the minimum number of lines of text above is two.

5. **Line minimums for breaking elements:**
   - A minimum of two text lines must appear above or below a separate text element such as an extract, poem, or list.
   - A minimum of two lines of a separate text element may fall at the top or bottom of a page.
   - The minimum number of lines of text that may appear on a page with an illustration or table is five.
   - The minimum number of lines on the last page of a chapter is five.
   - If a designated space-break in text falls between pages, the extra space will be left at the foot of the preceding page.

6. **Page length:** Facing text pages should be of equal depth and must align.

7. **Orphans and widows:** The first line of a paragraph (orphan) may fall at the foot of a page. The last line of a paragraph (widow) may not fall at the top of a page unless it is full measure.

8. **Variable vertical space:** The space above subheads should not vary unless specified otherwise. The space above and below a separate text element may be adjusted if necessary to avoid a widow or to make a text spread align. Space must be adjusted equally: 4 pts. maximum to be added above and 4 pts. below, or 2 pts. maximum to be subtracted above and 2 pts. below. The resulting text spreads must align so that the last lines on the spread adhere to the main text grid: either at normal depth, or exactly one line short or one line long.

FIGURE A.3. *(continued)*

made and the resulting page count determined at the same time. For the most accurate result, it is best to use the final, edited manuscript. Whatever method is used, it is important also to account for illustrations, tables, and other nontextual material. For journals, which have fixed designs and page allotments, the total number of articles must be adjusted to fill each issue. For electronic-only publications, length is less of a consideration from a production standpoint, though it is always an editorial and design consideration.

9. **Back matter:** In bibliographies and endnotes, facing pages may differ by one line if necessary to avoid a widow. Index columns on the same page or across a spread may differ in length by one line if necessary. There should be a minimum of five lines in each column on the last page of the index. Columns on the last page of an index may vary in length by one line or more if necessary, with the left column being longer. Widows are permitted at the top of columns in back matter and index provided the line is at least three-fourths full.

10. **Illustrations and tables:** Figures and tables are to be positioned as close to their text citation as possible, preferably after the citation but before the next major subhead; at the top of the type page if possible, or at the foot if necessary. When figures/tables of different depths occur on facing pages, place one at the top and the other at the bottom of their respective pages. Full-page broadside figures/tables should fit within the text measure and align with the top of the first line of text. No running head or folio should appear on a broadside page unless otherwise specified. Where more than one table/figure appears on a page with text, table-table-text or text-table-table is preferable to table-text-table.

11. **Footnotes/endnotes:** Long footnotes may be broken from one page to the next. Ideally, at least two lines of the footnote should appear on each page and the note should be broken in midsentence. A 5-pica ¼ pt. rule will be inserted above the continued portion of the footnote, with no extra space below.

   ▸ Short footnotes/endnotes (those running at most to 1 pica short of a half-line measure) may be double-columned when there are three or more in a row on one page. Doubling should be vertical:

1	3		1	2
2	4	not	3	4

   ▸ When three or more very short notes (e.g., "Ibid.") occur in succession on one page, tripling is permissible.

12. **Additional corrections:**
   ▸ Please mark type sections that have been rerun since the last stage of page proof. We assume that there have been no changes in type or line breaks within type blocks not so marked.
   ▸ All queries should be marked on proofs (not on manuscript) and, if possible, keyed to manuscript pages.

FIGURE A.3. *(continued)*

A.19   *Design specifications for printed works.* A complete design for a book or other work should include full type specifications and representative layouts for all the various categories of text. Common elements might include the front (or preliminary) matter; a chapter opening page; two or more facing pages showing primary textual elements such as running text, extracts, subheads, footnotes, illustrations, running heads, and folios; and the back (or end) matter (including, as relevant, the appendix, endnotes, glossary, bibliography, and index). See figure A.4 for an ex-

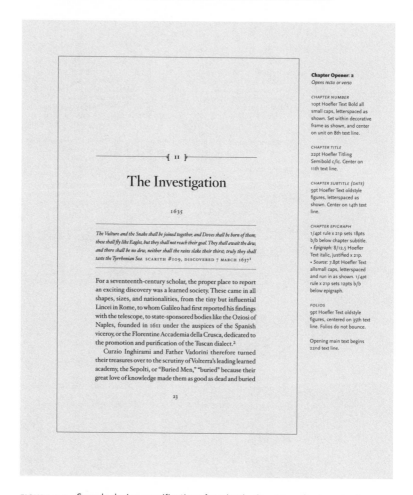

FIGURE A.4. Sample design specifications for a book, showing a chapter-opening page and a page for an index.

ample of a partial text design for a printed book showing marginal type specifications. Before typesetting, the final, edited manuscript is checked by the editor against the design specifications to make sure that each element has been properly accounted for. If an electronic style sheet will be used to encode these specifications for typesetting, it must also include every element in every possible context that might signal a design change (see also A.9).

A.20   *Design specifications for web-based works.* In addition to identifying every element of the work in every context—as for a print publication—the

INDEX HEAD
18pt Hoefler Titling
Semibold Italic. Center on
11th text line. Decorative rule
sets above head, as shown,
on 8th text line.

INDEX HEAD NOTE
1/4pt rule x 21p sets 4p11 b/r
below Index head. Text sets
7pt Hoefler Text, centered x
21p. A second 1/4pt rule x
21p sets 25pts below 1st rule.

INDEX TEXT
7.8/10.5 Hoefler Text x two
columns of 10p1.5 each; 9pt
alley in between. Set on 9pt
hanging indent; subentries
run in. Allow one line space
between alphabet breaks.

FOLIOS
9pt Hoefler Text oldstyle
figures, centered on 35th text
line. Folios do not bounce.

Opening index text begins
19th text line.

Index

Page numbers for illustrations are in italic.

academies, 23, 47–48, 71, 83, 86; Florentine, 47, 71, 83; Tuscan, 48–49, 83, 92
Accademia degli Oziosi, 23, 48
Accademia dei Lincei, 23, 48
Accademia dei Sepolti, 23–24, 82–84
Accademia della Crusca, 23, 31, 46, 68, 71, 83, 86, 99, 126
Acta Sanctorum, 118
Aesar, 18, 19, 89
Alexander VI, Pope (Rodrigo Borgia), 124, 125
Alexander VII, Pope, 119. *See also* Chigi, Fabio
Allacci, Leone, 53, 62, 72, 74–81, 83–85, 88–91, 93, 96, 101–3, 105, 109, 115, 130, 151; *Animadversiones*, 74–81, 83–85, 91, 93, 104, 109–11, 115, 128, 131, 134; *Apes Urbanae*, 73, 93

Allegory of Divine Wisdom (Sacchi), 49
alphabet: Etruscan, 110; Greek, 111; Latin, 111; scarith, 110, 128; Umbrian, 110
Ammirato, Scipione, the Elder, 120
Ammirato, Scipione, the Younger (Cristoforo Bianco), 120, 190n26
Annius of Viterbo (1438–1502), 33, 76, 80, 101, 102, 107, 115, 124–26, 129, 131–33, 135, 192n7
antiquarians, 42, 69, 85, 99, 103, 107, 125, 127–28, 130, 133, 138, 148
Apes Urbanae (Allacci), 73, 93
Arabic, 93, 94, 106, 107
archaeologists, 139. *See also* Bianchi Bandinelli, Ranuccio; Fiumi, Enrico; Phillips, Kyle
archaeology, 24, 43–44, 65, 123,

221

FIGURE A.4. *(continued)*

design for an electronic work must identify any additional elements required for the presentation, including such things as navigational elements, additional copyright statements, and help screens. Some of these elements, such as error messages and titles in browsers, will be generated by a particular web browser or other program, and the degree of control that a designer has over their appearance may be limited. In fact, designs for electronic works are not like those for print. Specifications for print assume fixed layouts and predictable results; those for electronic works must take into account the technical limitations of particular software programs and devices at the time of publication. Therefore, though the design for an electronic work might start with a set of specifications like those for print, some of the details may need to be adjusted closer to the publication date, during the proofreading and testing stages (see 2.133–36).

A.21   *Picas, points, and pixels.* For printed works, type sizes and line spacing are measured in points. The dimensions of the type page—the area occupied by the running head, the text proper, the footnotes (if any), and the page number (or folio)—are measured in picas. A pica is approximately one-sixth of an inch; there are twelve points in a pica. Type specifications for the screen may be given in the same dimensions used for print; alternatively, pixels may be specified for type sizes and line spacing. (A pixel is the smallest element making up an image on the screen; for a resolution of 72 pixels per inch measured horizontally or vertically, a pixel is equal to a point.) Another option is to specify type size and line spacing in relative terms—for example, as a percentage of a web browser's default size for a particular category of type. All of these dimensions have been incorporated into the language of electronic style sheets such as CSS (see A.9). See also appendix B (for these and other terms related to size and spacing) and figure A.4.

A.22   *Em spaces, en spaces, and so forth.* Sometimes designers will specify a particular space between two elements—for example, between single and double quotation marks, where a thin space may be called for (see 6.11). Such spaces are usually specified relative to the size of the type in question. Some of the more common specifications—including the em space, on which all of them are based—are as follows:

UNIT	DEFINITION	UNICODE NUMBER
em space	the width of a capital *M* in a given font at a given size	2003
en space	half the size of an em	2002
thick space	one-third of an em	2004
medium (or mid) space	one-fourth of an em	2005
thin space	a fifth (or sometimes a sixth) of an em	2009
hair space	thinner than a thin space	200A

All of these distinctions can be achieved for the printed page in page-layout or typesetting programs. They can also be specified in a limited way in electronic style sheets—for example, as an instruction to increase (or decrease) the spacing between all the letters or words in a particular type of paragraph. To date, however, though these spaces have been defined for Unicode, they are not available in many fonts, limiting their usefulness in electronic documents and publications. See also 11.2.

The Electronic Workflow

Introduction

A.23 *Converting marked-up manuscripts for production.* Many manuscripts are imported directly from word-processing software to a desktop publishing platform such as QuarkXPress or Adobe's InDesign or one of a number of typesetting systems used by commercial vendors of publishing services. Such conversions have typically involved replacing generic typesetting codes or word-processing styles with corresponding codes used by the typesetting system. Many of these same applications can now use XML tags in addition to their own systems of markup (though not without increasing the complexity of the workflow; see A.25, A.31). Manuscripts not tagged in XML are increasingly being converted to XML in order to take advantage of its downstream flexibility (e.g., for publishing a printed book on the web or in various e-book formats for which XML may be a requirement). See also A.27–30.

A.24 *Steps in an XML workflow.* Publishers who introduce XML into the process at an early stage can make it the basis of their entire production workflow. Such a workflow, which is determined by the principles of markup discussed in the previous sections, might be summarized very briefly as follows:

1. XML tags are added to a manuscript in conformance with a DTD (see A.8). This can be done before or after the manuscript editing stage (see A.27–30).
2. Meanwhile, any artwork is scanned and converted as necessary to the recommended file formats and resolutions for publication in print and electronic formats. XML tags that indicate the correct versions of each publication-ready file must be included in the manuscript. These are similar to generic figure-placement callouts in an edited manuscript (see 2.27).
3. The XML-tagged file—that is, the marked-up manuscript from step 1—can be converted to a variety of formats and, in conjunction with the artwork from step 2, typeset for print, on the one hand, and, on the other, used as the basis of one or more electronic formats. In each case, a particular style sheet determines what the presentation will look like (see A.9).

For an illustration of such a workflow, see figure A.5. For a broader outline of the publishing process—one that factors in editing and proofreading stages—see 2.2.

A.25 *Where does proofreading fit in?* In any workflow, the final output—whether print or electronic—needs to be proofread, as detailed in chapter 2 (see 2.97–136). For simultaneous print and electronic publication, there are a number of options for doing this. Especially for longer works, it can be expedient to proofread the work as it is typeset for print first. Corrections made during the proofreading process are incorporated into the XML file used for typesetting. Then, the corrected XML (including any index produced during the proofreading stage) can be converted to HTML, e-book formats, and any other electronic version using a range of style sheets and conversion programs. This saves the trouble of having to proofread print and electronic versions from scratch simultaneously, though the electronic versions still need to be carefully reviewed and tested (see 2.133–36). Alternatively, the print and electronic versions can be produced and proofread simultaneously, an option especially suited to shorter works such as journal articles.

A.26 *Cyclical workflow for web-based publications.* Like the traditional workflow followed for print publications before the advent of computerized typesetting, the electronic workflow described above, which focuses on print publications and electronic books and journals, is essentially linear. Web-based publications that require the development and implementation of functional and navigational features generally follow a different model— one that allows for technological design, engineering, testing, release, and maintenance of the website itself, apart from the content that will be presented on the site. Web-development workflows tend to be cyclical, allowing for the refinement of features to improve usability and to optimize the presentation. While a full discussion of this process is beyond the scope of this appendix, authors, editors, designers, and other publishing professionals who become involved in web-based projects should be prepared to adapt to the processes and requirements of that environment.

When Should XML Be Introduced into the Process?

A.27 *Who applies the markup?* To date, few editors and even fewer authors work directly with XML markup. Most of the coding that goes into such markup—not to mention the DTDs, style sheets, and converters that are used to implement it—requires an immersion in software and pro-

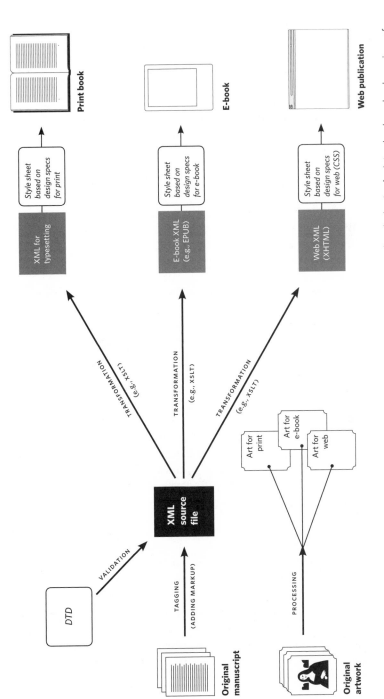

FIGURE A.5. A simplified XML workflow, in which an XML-tagged book manuscript is used as the basis of print, e-book, and web versions of the publication. Any artwork is processed and converted as appropriate and integrated into each version before publication.

gramming that is generally the arena of IT specialists. Thus, it usually falls to the publisher or one of its vendors to apply the XML. This can be done at various points in the production process, each with its benefits and costs, as discussed below. Meanwhile, IT specialists are also typically responsible for developing DTDs (or ensuring compliance with existing or standard DTDs), writing style sheets (or making modifications to existing style sheets), and coordinating the systems that allow a publisher to maintain an archive of the latest versions of the electronic files used to publish every version of every work in its inventory.

A.28 *Author's final manuscript converted to XML before editing.* There are advantages to introducing XML markup to a manuscript before it is edited. Manuscript editors are in many ways closest to the content; they are therefore in a good position to ensure the quality of the markup. A publisher may invest in XML tools that facilitate traditional and new editing tasks by allowing editors who have little knowledge of XML syntax to modify content and structure without invalidating the underlying code. Such an approach is especially suited to a journal publisher, where each article can be marked up in essentially the same manner and according to the same DTD and style sheet for each issue. Book publishers, on the other hand, might develop sets of templates that correspond to different types of books.

A.29 *Edited manuscript converted for typesetting.* Typesetters who have converted their internal processes to use XML will usually convert generic word-processing files to XML when they get them. Manuscript editors can help this along, using word-processor styles or generic tagging in a consistent manner even if they do not use XML. Some publishers further facilitate this process by providing editors with word-processing style templates that map to XML tags for a specific document type such as a book or journal article.

A.30 *XML added to files after typesetting.* There are two scenarios for adding XML to files after the typesetting of a print publication is completed: (1) the typesetter's electronic files are used to create the XML (for example, by deriving XML from a program such as QuarkXPress or Adobe's InDesign); or (2) XML is derived from PDF files—either those that are required to print the work or, in the case of older works for which there are no suitable electronic files, those that are obtained from scanning printed pages. Publishers who do this need to implement quality-assurance procedures (QA) to test the resulting XML, much as is done for any new electronic publication. See also 2.133–36.

Source Files

A.31   *XML source files.* XML source files comprise the XML text files and any electronic files for illustrations or audiovisual materials that, in conjunction with style sheets, converters, and an array of software programs, can be rendered in published form in a variety of media. As the basis of an electronic workflow, these files should accurately reflect the *content* of a published work, including any subsequent changes thereto. For example, if it is necessary to correct an error in the text of an HTML version of a journal article or a chapter in a book, it is not enough to make the correction in the HTML file; the correction must also be made in the corresponding XML source file to ensure that it will be reflected in any future versions of the work generated from that source. If extensive corrections are required, it may be better to make them in the source files and then reconvert them to HTML. Any changes to the way the content is presented, on the other hand, are usually made in a style sheet or, for some types of adjustments in printed works, with a page-layout or typesetting program (see A.9, A.17).

A.32   *Illustrations.* Electronic versions of files for such nontext items as illustrations or audiovisual materials may be needed in various sizes (thumbnails, medium resolution, high resolution, low bit rate, high bit rate, etc.) to allow for optimal presentation in various media. All of these versions should be derived either from high-resolution bitmapped graphics in a lossless format such as TIFF (e.g., for photographic images) or from vector-based graphics (e.g., for line art created in a program such as Adobe Illustrator). The richer the source, the higher the level of quality not only in print but on the screen, where image files are typically downsampled (i.e., prepared at a lower resolution) and compressed for faster downloading and rendering. Moreover, it should be noted that once information is discarded from a file (e.g., using a lossy compression format such as JPEG), it cannot be recovered. And, though resolution requirements for the screen are lower than those for print, the original, high-quality source files should always be retained, as they are more likely to meet requirements for republishing the work in alternative formats in the future. Many publishers provide authors with guidelines for preparing and submitting artwork; Chicago makes detailed guidelines available on its books and journals websites. See also 3.15.

A.33   *Tables.* Tables are generally marked up and included as part of the XML source files with the rest of the text. In online publications, the HTML tables derived from this markup are sometimes supplemented by image files or PDF versions of the same (often derived from pages typeset for print). Though not strictly necessary, this can be desirable because, to date, HTML table markup does not include layout options sufficient to achieve all of the typesetting niceties discussed in chapter 3, such as certain types of character alignment within a column. Meanwhile, the character data in the rough-hewn HTML tables derived from XML can be useful—for example, the data can be cut and pasted or otherwise exported into spreadsheets and other tools for efficient verification of results. It is important to keep track of each version of a table: any correction must not only be made in the XML source file but also reflected in any published version of the table.

A.34 *Mathematical expressions.* Although XML may be used to typeset math— tagged using MathML—complex, built-up mathematical expressions are not generally rendered for online publications directly from MathML or XML-based HTML. Though browser support for MathML continues to improve, math in web publications is typically presented using bit-mapped images, which can be derived from typeset pages when they are available. Otherwise, the images must be derived from math-editing tools in word-processing applications such as Microsoft Word or LaTeX (see 12.2). As with tables, it is important to make sure that the MathML in the source file reflects any changes or adjustments made to the embedded images.

Options for Presenting Content

A.35 *Print.* Print remains the preferred medium for many types of publications. From the standpoint of a typical publisher's electronic workflow, however, it has become one option among several. For a discussion of the technologies of printing, including considerations for paper selection and binding, see A.41–50.

A.36 *Web.* Two standards have emerged for presenting publications on the web: full-text web presentations and PDF (portable document format). Full-text presentations, usually in HTML (or XHTML; see A.37), are especially common for journals, particularly those in the scientific, technical, and medical fields (so-called STM publications), and for reference works. Such presentations, by taking advantage of all the textual and audiovisual functionality of modern browsers, are extremely flexible. On the other hand, they are costly, requiring a lot of maintenance to adapt to changing technologies and evolving standards. PDF, because it presents fixed layouts and typefaces that match the printed page, is easier to produce and maintain, especially as a supplement to print. In fact, printed publications generally must be submitted to the printer as PDF files, and optimizing these files for electronic publication is a relatively straightforward process (e.g., using a PDF-creation program such as Adobe Acrobat). Journals that publish on the web typically provide PDF versions of their articles accompanied either by full-text HTML versions or, to facilitate search engines and other services, by HTML metadata (sometimes accompanied by an abstract). See also A.10.

A.37   *Converting XML to HTML.* To create a full-text web presentation, the XML source files must be converted to HTML. As noted in A.12, HTML is a set of tags that function much like typesetting codes for web presentations. Usually in conjunction with CSS (see A.9), it tells a browser how to format and display content and facilitates linking. XML files are converted, or transformed, to HTML using scripts, often in XSLT (extensible stylesheet language transformations), a language that allows XML to be converted to a variety of formats. If you are reading this online, you are viewing XHTML (HTML defined as an application of XML) derived from XML source files for the purpose of web presentation.

A.38   *E-book formats.* Publishers have an increasing number of options for offering content in an e-book format. For works also published in print, PDF-based e-books are the most straightforward. More sophisticated e-book formats include International Digital Publishing Forum's EPUB, DAISY (digital accessible information system, a format for digital talking books), and such proprietary formats as Microsoft Reader (LIT) and Amazon Kindle (AZW). Conversion to each of these formats can be facilitated by XML-encoded source files (see A.31–34).

A.39   *Additional publishing options.* Book chapters, journal articles, and even smaller components of a complete publication can be presented and sold on their own, separately from the publication in which they originally appeared. This has always been true of print publications—for example, the University of Chicago Press offers an offprint of the indexing chapter that appears in this manual—but digital technology has greatly expanded the possibilities for such derivative works. For example, a medical publisher might group together all the articles that, according to their metadata, are about Tamiflu-resistant flu strains and sell them as a new publication. Such "virtual" publications can be assembled automatically from a publisher's source files or they can be curated by content experts—or some combination of the two strategies. Electronic content can also be sold in smaller pieces. Journal articles are often published one at a time, when they are ready—in advance of, or independently of, the print publication. This approach facilitates the way readers tend to find articles: thanks to search engines and citation-linking networks such as CrossRef, much of the traffic coming into journal sites goes directly to single articles.

A.40   *Digital rights management strategies.* Publishers who present their content in electronic form face challenges from those who might attempt to copy and redistribute electronic materials in violation of copyright law. To ensure that copyright holders and publishers are fairly compensated for their intellectual property, on the one hand, while providing content to readers in an easily accessible manner, on the other, publishers can employ a number of strategies. These strategies—which include technologies such as encrypted passwords, user-authentication schemes, and digital watermarks—are collectively referred to as digital rights management (DRM). Essentially, DRM can be seen as the intersection between copyright law, distribution models, and technology. Some of the legal aspects of electronic distribution and licensing are discussed in chapter 4 (see 4.56, 4.57, 4.60 [especially *Electronic rights* and *Rights for educational use*], 4.61, 4.62). The technological aspects of DRM will depend on the software used to implement it and on the medium of publication. For a detailed overview of these considerations and others, consult *The Columbia Guide to Digital Publishing* (bibliog. 2.7).

Print Technologies

A.41   *Electronic markup and print.* The principles of electronic markup occupy a central place in the production of publications intended for print. The advantages of applying XML before or during typesetting, as outlined above—even if a book or journal is initially intended only for print distribution—can be central to a goal of being prepared to republish the same content in electronic form or to make it available to electronic archives and search engines. The difference is that for print, the product is physical. Whereas the appearance of an electronic publication might vary depending on the device and software used to view it, a printed book or journal is a unique artifact with a permanent design. The physical aspects of the production of printed works—the details of which have changed little since the last edition of this manual—are the subject of this section.

A.42   *The role of PDF in the print process.* To date, most printed publications rely on PDF (portable document format) to display the final publication on-screen before it is sent to the printer. PDF presents fonts, images, layout, and pagination exactly as they will appear on the printed page. This makes it an essential tool in the proofing process. After a book or article is typeset, first proof is generated as PDF and supplied to authors, editors, and indexers either as a printout or for on-screen review. One or more rounds of revised proof can be offered in the same manner. Moreover, PDF tends to obviate the need to review printer's proof—what was once commonly referred to as bluelines—because the files used by the printer are typically the same as those generated by the typesetter. Nonetheless, the PDF files themselves must be print-ready. Among other things, it is important to check that the latest versions of files are present; that they are properly and consistently named; that any specialized fonts have been embedded or otherwise included; that any images have been provided as high-resolution files appropriate for printing; and that all specifications regarding paper, trim size, resolution, and so forth have been provided. See also 2.100–106.

A.43   *Preliminary presswork, or "prepress."* The prepress phase includes all the steps that a printer takes from the time it receives the final files (and any other materials, such as artwork, needed for printing) to the time the publication is put on press, or printed. These days, the final electronic files received by the printer that have been reviewed by the typesetter, designer, and others at the publisher need no further review. But for works in which the reproduction quality of the illustrations is critical, the printer may supply a high-quality proof that can be checked for contrast and quality and, if applicable, color.

A.44   *Paper selection.* Paper comes in varying weights, sizes, shades, coatings, and degrees of opacity and smoothness (i.e., finish). In consultation with the printer or a paper merchant, the publisher must determine which type of paper best suits a particular publication and which will print on and run through a given printing press most efficiently. Other considerations include cost, availability, and durability of the paper. Publications printed on acid-free paper have a longer life expectancy than those that are not, and they may carry a notice on the copyright page indicating their compliance with the durability standards of the American National Standards Institute (see 1.34). For environmental considerations, see A.46.

A.45   *Paper sizes.* Paper is manufactured to standard roll and sheet sizes. Because printing presses and bindery equipment are set up to accommodate these roll and sheet sizes with minimal waste of paper, publishers usually find it most economical to choose one of a handful of corresponding trim sizes for their books and journals—in the United States, these are 5½ × 8½ inches, 6⅛ × 9¼ inches, 7 × 10 inches, and 8½ × 11 inches. Publications requiring a nonstandard trim size will generally cost more. Note that the dimensions for the type page (that part of the page occupied by the text, the running head, and the folio, if any) must leave adequate margins for the given trim size and, if required, allow for illustrations to bleed.

A.46 *Paper and the environment.* Environmental issues have come to play a significant role in paper selection. Most works can be printed on recycled paper, generally a combination of virgin fiber and pre- and postconsumer wastepaper. Using papers certified by the Forest Stewardship Council (FSC) is another way to minimize environmental impacts. FSC is a nonprofit organization widely regarded as ensuring the best practices in forest management. Publishers who use recycled and FSC-certified papers not only contribute to the reduction of greenhouse gas emissions but also minimize the negative impact on endangered forests and forest-dependent communities. Also important are the bleaching methods used to make papers, which employ varying amounts of chlorine and chlorine derivatives, the use of which contributes to the formation of dioxins and other hazardous substances. Processed chlorine-free (PCF) papers are recycled papers that have been produced with no chlorine or derivatives beyond what may have been used originally to produce the recovered wastepaper. A totally chlorine-free (TCF) process can be used on virgin fibers. Elemental chlorine-free (ECF) and enhanced ECF papers are bleached using a chlorine derivative (chlorine dioxide) in order to minimize hazardous by-products but are less safe than TCF or PCF papers. Publishers wishing to learn more about the environmental impact of paper purchasing should seek the advice of the Forest Stewardship Council. Additional resources include the US-based Green Press Initiative and the Canadian-based Canopy.

A.47 *Offset printing.* The most common method for producing books is through offset printing, or offset lithography. This process involves the transfer of images (text, illustrations, and any other marks that will be distinct from the background color of the page) from metal plates to paper through an intermediate cylinder. The images are usually imposed directly onto the photosensitive plates using the typesetter's electronic files (referred to as computer-to-plate technology, or CTP) or, using an older process, by contact with film negatives (also typically generated from the typesetter's files). Ink is applied to each plate, and the inked images are offset onto the paper through the rubber-blanketed intermediate cylinder (see fig. A.6). The printing press itself may be either sheet-fed, using sheets

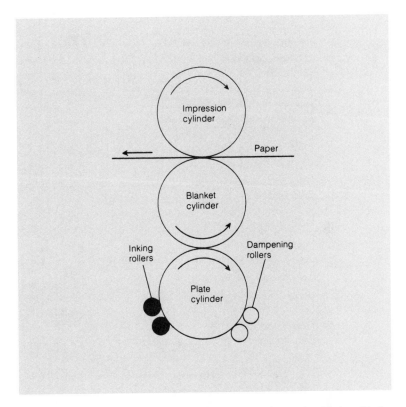

FIGURE A.6. Principle of offset printing. A plate is wrapped around and fastened to the plate cylinder. Water applied by the dampening rollers adheres only to the background area of the plate; ink applied by the inking rollers adheres only to the dry image of the type on the plate. As the plate cylinder revolves, it transfers the ink to the rubber blanket of the blanket cylinder, which in turn transfers (or offsets) it onto the paper, which is held in place by the impression cylinder.

of paper that have been precut, or web-fed, using rolls of paper that will be folded and trimmed at the end of the printing stage.

A.48   *Digital printing.* In digital printing, images are printed directly onto paper through ink jets or thermal transfer using either powder- or liquid-based toners. The quality of the reproduction is typically not as high as that achieved through the offset process (though the gap has closed), but digital printing makes it economically viable to print small quantities of a publication on demand (as few as one), preferably from archived electronic files, and can reduce the publisher's cost of warehousing unsold stock. Digital printing also makes it feasible to customize each copy.

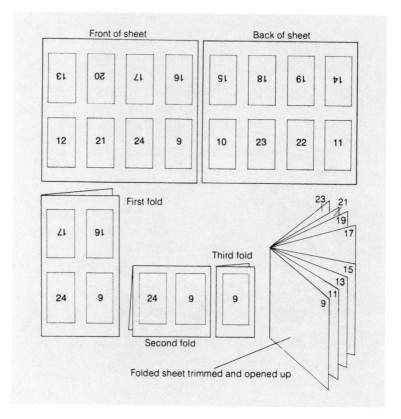

FIGURE A.7. A sheet consisting of sixteen printed pages. After being folded, the pages fall into proper numerical sequence.

Short-run digital copies of books can be bound either as hardcover or paperback editions.

A.49 *Folded and gathered sheets (F&Gs).* Before binding can begin, the press sheets, or printed sheets, that emerge from the printing press must be folded and trimmed. A press sheet has printed pages on both sides, and when it is folded in half, and then in half again—continuing until only one page is showing—all the pages fall into proper sequence in a process known as imposition (see fig. A.7). The folded sheet, called a signature, usually consists of thirty-two pages, but this number may vary depending on the bulk and flexibility of the paper and the size of the offset printing press. When all the signatures have been gathered in the proper order, they are referred to as folded and gathered sheets, or F&Gs. The F&Gs can then be bound in either hardcover or paperback format. (Pub-

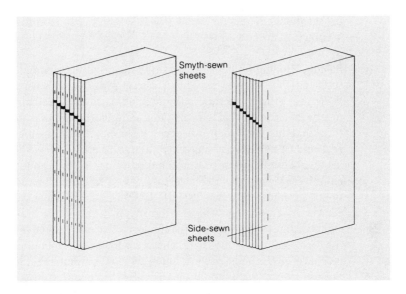

FIGURE A.8. Two methods of sewing used in binding. In Smyth sewing the sheets are stitched individually through the fold; in side sewing they are stitched from the side, close to the spine. The black rectangles printed on the folds in both methods help the binder recognize whether a signature is missing, duplicated, out of order, or upside down.

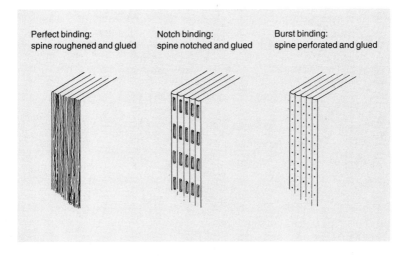

FIGURE A.9. Three methods of adhesive binding: perfect, notch, and burst binding.

lishers should, if possible, review the first set of F&Gs for completeness, accuracy, and proper order; see 2.104.)

A.50   *Binding.* Binding hardcover books typically requires sewing the signatures together, usually by either Smyth sewing or side sewing (see fig. A.8). An alternative method, adhesive binding, involves notching or fraying the folded edges and then applying adhesive to the signatures to hold them together. Smyth- or side-sewn books may have a sturdier binding and hold up better over time, but adhesive binding, which is faster and less costly, is often just as strong, thanks to improved polyurethane-based adhesives. Meanwhile, the hardcover case is fashioned by the application of cover material (such as cloth, synthetic fabric, leather, or paper) to boards. The case is then affixed to the body of the book through the application of glue to the endpapers, and a dust jacket may be wrapped around the case. Paperback books are almost always adhesive-bound through one of three methods: perfect, notch, or burst binding (see fig. A.9). In the perfect-binding method, about an eighth of an inch is mechanically roughened off the spine of the tightly gathered F&Gs, reducing them to a series of separate pages. The roughened spine is then coated with a flexible glue, and a paper cover is wrapped around the pages. In the other two methods, the spine is either scored by a series of notches (notch binding) or perforated (burst binding) and then force-fed with glue. Unlike perfect binding, these methods prevent the loss of part of the back margin and ensure that signatures remain intact, reducing the risk of pages coming loose. For paperbound books of higher quality, the signatures can be sewn and the covers (sometimes with flaps) then affixed, as with adhesive-bound books; this style of binding is known as flexibinding or limp binding. See also 1.66–71.

Appendix B: Glossary

This glossary focuses on key terms related to the typography, design, and production of both print and electronic works. Many of these terms are too specialized to be treated in the text of the manual; for terms not covered here that may be defined within the text, consult the index. For additional sources that treat publishing terminology, consult section 2 of the bibliography.

AA. An abbreviation for *author's alteration*. See also **alteration**.

adhesive binding. A method of binding that employs glue instead of stitching to hold the pages or signatures together and is widely used for journals and paperback books. Three types of adhesive binding are currently used: perfect binding, notch binding, and burst binding. Contrast **case binding**; **flexibinding**.

alteration. A change from the manuscript copy introduced in proof, as distinguished from a *correction* made to eliminate a typesetter's or printer's error. See also **AA**; **DA**; **EA**.

arabic numerals. The familiar digits used in arithmetical computation. In many type fonts arabic numerals are available in two forms: *lining*, or *aligning* (1 2 3 4 5 6 7 8 9 0), and *old style* (1 2 3 4 5 6 7 8 9 0), abbreviated OS and characterized by ascenders and descenders. Contrast **roman numerals**.

artwork. Illustrative material (photographs, drawings, maps, and so forth) intended for reproduction.

ascender. The portion of a lowercase letter that extends above the *x-height*, as in *b* and *d*. Contrast **descender**; see also **arabic numerals**.

ASCII file. See **plain-text file**.

back margin. The inner margin of a page; that is, the margin along the binding side of the page. See also **gutter**.

baseline. In type, an imaginary common line that all capital letters, x-heights, and lining arabic numerals rest on.

beta testing. The final checking of a computer application (such as a website) before it is released. Such testing is ideally carried out under normal operating conditions by users who are not directly involved in developing the application.

binding. (1) A covering for the pages of a publication, using such materials as leather, cloth, and paper. (2) The process by which such a covering is attached. See also **adhesive binding**; **case binding**; **flexibinding**.

bitmap. A digital representation of an image consisting of an array of pixels, in rows and columns, that can be saved to a file. Each pixel in the grid of the bitmap contains information about the color value of its position, which is used, for example, to display an image on a monitor or print it to a page. Compare *vector graphic*.

blanket. In offset printing, the resilient rubber covering of the blanket cylinder, which receives the ink impression from the plate cylinder and offsets it onto the paper.

blind embossing. See *embossing*.

blind folio. See *folio*.

blind stamping. See *stamping*.

block quotation. Quoted material set off typographically from the text (see 13.9). Also called *extract*. Contrast **run in**.

bluelines. An abbreviation for *blueline proof*; also called *blues* or (in Europe and Asia) *ozalids*. A type of photographic proof generated by a printing firm either from repro or from the typesetter's electronic files. See also **digital proof**.

boards. Stiffening material used in binding to form the foundation of the cover; formerly wood, now generally a paper product such as binder's board (the finest quality), pasted board (often used in case binding), or chipboard (low quality). Redboard is used for flexible bindings. The bare board is sheathed in one of a variety of cover materials.

body text. The running text of a work, as distinguished from the display text used for chapter openings, subheads, and so forth.

boldface. Type that has a darker and heavier appearance than standard type (as in the entries in this list of key terms).

broadside. Designed to be read or viewed normally when the publication is turned ninety degrees. In University of Chicago Press practice, the *left* side of a broadside table or illustration is at the *bottom* of the page. Because most publications are longer than they are wide, broadside images are usually landscape, but not all landscape images are broadside. See also **landscape**.

browser. See **web browser**.

bulk. The thickness of paper measured in number of pages per inch; also used loosely to indicate the thickness of a publication, excluding the cover.

burst binding. A type of adhesive binding in which the untrimmed spine is perforated and force-fed with glue.

caps. An abbreviation for *capital letters*. See also **small caps**.

case. A hard cover or binding made by a case-making machine or by hand and usually printed, stamped, or labeled before being glued to the gathered endpapers that are attached to the signatures. A case that is covered entirely by one type of material is a one-piece case; a case in which the spine is covered by one type of material and the front and back cover boards by another (often in a different color) is a three-piece case.

case binding. A method of encasing a book in a rigid cover, or *case*. The gathered signatures can be Smyth sewn or side sewn together or adhesive-bound; endpapers are glued to the first and last signatures; a hinge of heavy gauze (the *super*) is glued to the spine of the sewn signatures; and the case is secured to the book by being glued to the flaps of the super and to both endpapers. Contrast **adhesive binding**; **flexibinding**.

castoff. An estimate of the space, or number of printed pages, that a manuscript will occupy when typeset.

character. A letter, numeral, symbol, or mark of punctuation.

character count. An approximate measure of the length of a manuscript made by multiplying the number of characters and spaces in an average line by the number of lines in the manuscript. The "character count" feature of many word-processing programs can also provide such a total.

character encoding. A set of machine-readable numbers or other elements—or *code points*—that correspond to a set of alphanumeric characters and symbols such that they can be interpreted by a computer. See also **Unicode**.

character reference. A plain-text placeholder defined for a markup language such as SGML, HTML, or XML and used to refer to a special character that is unavailable in a particular character encoding or from a particular input device such as a keyboard. See also A.15.

clothbound. Bound with a rigid cover, usually cloth wrapped around boards. Contrast **paperback**.

CMYK. An abbreviation for the basic colors used in process color printing—cyan (C), magenta (M), and yellow (Y), plus black (K)—to approximate all the colors in the spectrum.

code. A generic marker that identifies a particular type of text throughout a manuscript. A code is usually associated with a set of formatting instructions specified by the designer and followed by the typesetter. See also **tag**.

colophon. A statement, usually at the back of a publication (as in this manual), about the materials, processes, and individuals or companies involved in its preparation, production, and manufacturing. The term is also used to refer to a publisher's logo as it often appears on the title page and spine of a book.

color printing. See **process color printing**.

color separation. (1) The analysis of color copy for reproduction in terms of the three process colors (plus black) to be used in printing; separation is achieved by shooting through filters or by electronic scanning. (2) A film negative or positive, or a digital file, so produced for preparation of the printing plate. See also **process color printing**.

comp. An abbreviation for *comprehensive layout*, as for a dust jacket, and also for *composition* or *compositor*.

compositor. See **typesetter**.

computer-to-plate (CTP) technology. A process in which print-ready electronic files are imposed directly onto offset printing plates, thus eliminating the need for an intermediate stage involving film.

contact proof. A photographic proof used to show the reproduction quality of an image. Also called *velox*.

continuous tone. An image, such as a photograph, with gradations of tone from dark to light, in contrast to an image formed of pure blacks and whites, such as a pen-and-ink drawing. See also **halftone**.

cover. The two hinged parts of a binding, front and back, and the center panel, or *spine*, that joins them; also the four surfaces making up the covers in this sense, when used to carry printed matter. See also **dust jacket**.

crop. To cut down an illustration, such as a photograph, to improve the appearance of the image by removing extraneous areas.

CSS. An abbreviation for *cascading style sheets*. A style sheet language used to define the presentation of a document marked up in HTML or another formal markup language.

cyan. A greenish blue, one of the three primary colors (plus black) used in process color printing. See also **CMYK**.

DA. An abbreviation for *designer's alteration*. See also **alteration**.

descender. The portion of a lowercase letter that extends below the x-height, as in *g* and *p*. Contrast **ascender**; see also **arabic numerals**.

die. See **stamping**.

digital printing. A type of printing in which the transfer of electronic images to paper is accomplished with ink-jet or laser printers. Contrast **offset printing**.

digital proof. A type of proof generated directly from electronic files and typically output on a laser printer. See also **bluelines**.

display type. Type used for title pages, chapter openings, subheads, and so on, usually distinguished from the type used for body text by a different, often larger font. See also **body text**.

DOI. An abbreviation for *Digital Object Identifier*, a unique alphanumeric string (e.g., 10.1086/597483) assigned to a publication or other unit of intellectual property. As a *digital identifier*, a DOI also provides a means of looking up the current location(s) of such an object on the Internet.

DRM. An abbreviation for *digital rights management*. Refers to a system designed to protect copyrighted electronic works from unauthorized use, copying, or distribution. See also A.40.

drop cap. An uppercase character set in a type size larger than the text and "dropped," or nested, into lines of text, usually as the first character in the opening paragraph of a chapter or other section of text.

drop folio. See **folio**.

DTD. An abbreviation for *document type definition*. In a markup language such as XML, a set of rules about the structure of a document that dictate the relationship among different tags and allowable text or elements within specified tags. Also called *schema*. See also **tag**.

dust jacket. Also called *jacket*. A protective wrapping, usually made of paper, for a clothbound book; its *flaps*, which fold around the front and back covers, usually carry promotional copy. See also **cover**.

EA. An abbreviation for *editor's alteration*. See also **alteration**.

ECF. An abbreviation for *elemental chlorine-free*. Refers to paper bleached with a chlorine derivative that releases hazardous substances, including dioxin, into the environment. Contrast **PCF**; **TCF**.

edition. (1) A publication in its original form, or any subsequent reissue of the publication in which its content is significantly revised. (2) More informally, a term used to refer to each format in which a publication appears (for example, a book published in both cloth and paperback bindings, or a journal published in both electronic and print forms). However, the designation *second edition* would not be applied to the secondary format, or to a second or subsequent *impression* of the publication, in the absence of significant content changes. See also 1.26; **impression**; **reprint**.

em. A unit of type measurement equal to the point size of the type in question; for example, a six-point em is six points wide. See also **point**.

embossing. Forming an image in relief (that is, a raised image) on a surface such as a case or a paper cover or dust jacket. If the process does not involve metallic leaf or ink, it is called *blind embossing*. See also **stamping**.

em dash. A short typographical rule measuring the width of an em. See also 6.82–89.

en. A unit of type measurement half the size of an em.

en dash. A short typographical rule measuring the width of an en. See also 6.78–81.

endpapers. Folded sheets pasted or, rarely, sewn to the first and last signatures of a book; the free leaves are then pasted to the inside of the front and back covers to secure the book within the covers. Sometimes endpapers feature printed text or illustrations. Also called *endsheets*.

EPS. An abbreviation for *encapsulated PostScript*. A type of file used to encode graphics so they can be embedded in a larger PostScript file.

extract. See **block quotation**.

F&Gs. See **folded and gathered sheets**.

figure. An illustration printed with the text (hence also called a *text figure*), as distinguished from a plate, which is printed separately. More generally, *figure* is used to refer to any illustration in a published work, including charts (but not tables).

file. A block of digital information with a unique name and location in a computer system or external storage medium (such as a disk) that can be accessed and manipulated by users of the system or by the system itself. Programs, documents, and images are all examples of data stored in files.

flaps. See **dust jacket**.

flexibinding. Also called *limp binding*. A method of binding in which the pages or signatures are sewn together and the lightweight cover (sometimes with flaps) is then affixed, as in adhesive binding. The result is a publication that is lighter and less bulky than a casebound book but sturdier and more flexible than an adhesive-bound paperback. Contrast **adhesive binding**; **case binding**.

flush. Even, as with typeset margins. Lines that are set *flush left* are aligned vertically along the left-hand margin; lines set *flush right* are aligned along the right-hand margin. Contrast **ragged right**.

flush-and-hang style. A copy-setting style in which the first line of each paragraph begins flush left and subsequent, or runover, lines are indented (as in this list of key terms). Also referred to as *hanging indention* or *hanging indent*.

folded and gathered sheets. Also called *F&Gs* or *sheets*. The collection of all printed signatures in a publication, folded into imposed page sequence and gathered for binding. See also **signature**.

folio. A page number, often placed at the outside of the running head at the top of the page. If it is placed consistently at the bottom of the page, the number is a *foot folio*; if it is placed at the bottom of the page on display pages only, it is a *drop folio*. A folio counted in numbering pages but not printed (as on the title page) is a *blind folio*; any folio printed is an *expressed folio*.

font. A complete assortment of a given size and style of type, usually including capitals, small capitals, and lowercase together with numerals, punctuation marks, ligatures, and the commonly used symbols and accents. The italic of a typeface is considered a part of the equipment of a font of type but is often spoken of as a separate font. Often used as a synonym for **typeface**.

foot folio. See **folio**.

four-color process. See **process color printing**.

FTP. An abbreviation for *file transfer protocol*. The protocol, or set of instructions and syntax, for moving files between computers on the Internet.

gallery. A section of illustrations grouped on consecutive pages rather than scattered throughout the text.

galley proof. Proof showing typeset material but without final pagination. The term, an anachronism, once referred to the long, narrow columns of type, or "galleys," prepared by a printer before pages were composed, by hand. See also **page proof**.

GIF. An abbreviation for *graphic interchange format*. A file format for compressing and storing bitmapped graphics that contain line art or text for viewing on-screen. See also **PNG**; compare **JPEG**.

gutter. The two inner margins (back margins) of facing pages of a book or journal.

hairline rule. A very thin rule—whose width is variously defined as one-quarter point, one-half point, or one-fifth of an em.

halftone. An image formed by breaking up a continuous-tone image, such as a photograph, into a pattern of dots of varying sizes. When printed, the dots, though clearly visible through a magnifying glass, merge to give an illusion of continuous tone to the naked eye.

halftone screen. A grid used in the halftone process to break an image up into dots. The fineness of the screen is denoted in terms of lines per inch, as in *a 133-line screen*.

hanging indention. See *flush-and-hang style*.

hard copy. A paper copy of text, artwork, or other material, as opposed to a copy that has been stored in digital form.

hardcover binding. See **case binding**.

head margin. The top margin of a page.

HTML. An abbreviation for *hypertext markup language*. A specific set of tags used to describe the structure of hypertext documents that make up most web pages. Web browsers interpret these tags to display text and graphics. HTML is an application of SGML.

HTTP. An abbreviation for *hypertext transfer protocol*. The protocol, or set of instructions and syntax, for retrieving files on the Internet and for enabling links between such files.

hypertext. The organization of digital information into associations connected by links. In a hypertext environment, objects such as text and images can contain links to other objects in the same file or in external files, which users can choose to follow. See also **HTML**; **HTTP**.

impression. (1) The inked image on the paper created during a single cycle of a press; the speed of a sheet-fed printing press is given in terms of impressions per hour. (2) A single printing of a publication; that is, all the copies printed at a given time. See also 1.26; *edition*; *reprint*.

indent. To set a line of type so that it begins or ends inside the normal margin. In *paragraph* indention the first line is indented from the left margin and the following lines are set full measure. In *hanging* indention (also referred to as *flush and hang*) the first line is set full measure and the following lines are indented. See also *flush-and-hang style*.

Internet. A global, public network of computers and computer networks that communicate using TCP/IP (transmission control protocol/Internet protocol).

italic. A slanted type style suggestive of cursive writing (*like this*). Contrast **roman**.

jacket. See **dust jacket**.

JPEG. An abbreviation for *Joint Photographic Experts Group*. A file format commonly used to compress and store bitmapped graphics that contain photographic and other continuous-tone images for viewing on-screen. Compare **GIF** and **PNG**.

justified. Spaced out to a specified measure, as with printed lines, so that left and right margins are aligned. Contrast **ragged right**.

kern. The part of a letter that extends beyond the edge of the type body and overlaps the adjacent character, as the *j* in *adjacent* or the T in *To*.

kerning. The selective adjustment of space between particular characters (called "letterspacing") to improve appearance or ease of reading.

landscape. Having a greater dimension in width than in length, as with an image or a document. Contrast **portrait**; see also **broadside**.

layout. A designer's plan of how the published material, including illustrative content, should appear.

leading. Also called *line spacing*. The visual space between lines of type, usually measured in points from baseline to baseline. This word, derived from the element *lead*, rhymes with "heading."

letterspacing. See **kerning**.

ligature. A single character formed by joining two characters, such as *œ*, *fi*, or *ff*. Older, more decorative forms (such as *ct*—a *c* joined to a *t* by a loop) are known as *quaint characters*.

line art. Copy for reproduction that contains only solid blacks and whites, such as a pen-and-ink drawing. Contrast **continuous tone**.

line spacing. See **leading**.

lining numbers. See under **arabic numerals**.

lowercase. The uncapitalized letters of a font. Contrast **uppercase**.

macro. A sequence of operations that is defined for reuse in a computer program. In word processing, a macro can be used to perform complex or repetitive tasks. Short for *macroinstruction*.

makeup. Arranging of type lines and illustrations into page form.

margin. The white space surrounding the printed area of a page, including the back, or gutter, margin; the head, or top, margin; the fore-edge, or outside, margin; and the tail, foot, or bottom, margin. Contrast **type page**.

markup. (1) A sequence of characters, often called *tags* or *codes*, that indicate the logical structure of a manuscript or provide instructions for formatting it. (2) The insertion of such tags in an electronic manuscript; also, traditionally, editing and coding a paper manuscript.

MathML. An application of XML for tagging mathematical expressions.

measure. The length of the line (usually in picas) in which type is set. *Full measure* refers to copy set the full width of the type page. *Narrow measure* refers to a block of copy (such as a long quotation) indented from one or both margins to distinguish it from surrounding full-measure copy, or to copy set in short lines for multicolumn makeup.

metadata. Data about data. The metadata for a given publication may include, among other things, copyright information, an ISBN or ISSN, a volume or issue number, and keywords—including the title and creator of the work and a description. Metadata is a component of markup languages such as SGML, HTML, and XML.

notch binding. A type of adhesive binding in which the untrimmed spine is notched and force-fed with glue.

OCR. An abbreviation for *optical character recognition*. A technology that converts images of text (as from a scan of a printed page) into character data that can be manipulated like any other digital text.

offprint. An article, chapter, or other excerpt from a larger work issued as a separate unit.

offset printing. Also called *offset lithography*. The most common type of printing used for books and journals. The pages to be printed are transferred either photographically or through computer-to-plate technology to a thin, flexible metal plate, curved to fit one of the revolving cylinders of a printing press. The image on this plate is then transferred to, or *offset* onto, the paper by means of a rubber blanket on another cylinder. Contrast **digital printing**.

old-style numbers. See under **arabic numerals**.

opacity. The measurement of transparency of paper. The higher a paper's opacity, the less tendency there is for text and images printed on one side of a sheet to show through to the other side.

orphan. The first line of a paragraph stranded at the bottom of a page or column. An orphan can be avoided by changes in wording or spacing to the text that precedes it. Contrast **widow**.

overlay. A hinged flap of paper or transparent plastic covering a piece of artwork. It may be there merely to protect the work (and sometimes includes instructions), or it may bear type or other artwork intended for reproduction along with what lies underneath.

page proof. Proof showing typeset material that has been paginated to reflect the placement of text, illustrations, and other design elements. Some publications may require one or more stages of *revised page proof* for checking corrections.

paperback. Bound with a cover stock rather than a cloth-and-board cover. Also called *paperbound*. Contrast **clothbound**.

pattern matching. In word processing, a search or search-and-replace operation that uses a formal syntax to find every instance of a specified string of text or "pattern" and, conditionally, replace it with a different string. In computer programming, such patterns are known as *regular expressions*.

PCF. An abbreviation for *process chlorine-free*. Refers to recycled papers bleached without using chlorine or chlorine derivatives beyond what may have been used originally to produce the recovered wastepaper. Contrast **ECF**; compare **TCF**.

PDF. An abbreviation for *portable document format*. An Adobe Systems file format—and now a formal, open standard (ISO 32000)—for stable, device-independent delivery of electronic documents. Preserving such elements as fonts, formatting, and pagination, PDF is used not only as the basis for many printed publications but also as a format for electronic publications, including many journal articles and e-books. See also **PostScript (PS)**.

PE. An abbreviation for *printer's error*. See also **printer's error (PE)**.

perfect binding. A type of adhesive binding that involves mechanically roughening off about an eighth of an inch from the spine of the folded and gathered sheets. This treatment produces a surface of intermingled fibers to which an adhesive is applied, and a cover (usually paper) is wrapped around the pages.

pica. A unit of type measurement equal to twelve points (approximately one-sixth of an inch).

pixel. See **resolution**.

plain-text file. An informal term for a file that contains data encoded using only letters, numerals, punctuation marks, spaces, returns, line breaks, and tabs with no additional formatting or special characters. Plain-text files are often referred to as ASCII files, although newer encoding schemes may be used, and other kinds of data (such as XML) can also be stored as plain-text files.

plate. (1) An image-bearing surface that, when inked, will produce one whole page or several pages of printed matter at a time. (2) A printed illustration, usually of high quality and produced on special paper, pasted or bound into a publication; when so printed, plates are numbered separately from other illustrations.

PNG. An abbreviation for *portable network graphic*. A file format for compressing and storing bitmapped graphics that contain line art or text for viewing on-screen. See also **GIF**; compare **JPEG**.

point. (1) The basic unit of type measurement—0.01384 (approximately one seventy-second) of an inch. (2) A unit used in measuring paper products employed in printing and binding—0.001 inches.

portable document format. See **PDF**.

portrait. Having a greater dimension in length than in width, as with an image or a document. Contrast **landscape**.

PostScript (PS). An Adobe Systems programming language used to describe pages (in terms of trim size, font, placement of graphics, and so forth) and to tell output devices how to render the data. Portable Document Format (PDF), a descendant of PostScript, is somewhat more flexible. See also **PDF**.

prepress. The processes undertaken by a printing firm between the receipt of the electronic files and any other materials from the publisher (or its typesetter) and the printing of the publication.

preprint. Part of a book or journal printed and distributed or posted online before publication for promotional purposes or, in time-sensitive fields such as science and medicine, to mitigate the delay of publication schedules. See also **offprint**.

press sheet. Also called *printed sheet* or *running sheet*. In offset printing, a large sheet of paper that emerges from the press with pages printed on both sides, each side printed from a single plate. The sheet must then be folded so that the pages fall into proper sequence. See also **signature**.

presswork. The actual printing of a publication, as distinguished from composition, which precedes it, and binding, which follows.

printer's error (PE). An error made by the typesetter (or *compositor*), as distinguished from an *alteration* made in proof by the author, editor, or designer.

process color printing. The halftone reproduction of full-color artwork or photographs using several plates (usually four), each printing a different color. Each plate is made with a halftone screen. *Process colors* are cyan, magenta, and yellow, plus black (CMYK). See also **halftone screen**.

proof. The printed copy made from electronic files, plates, negatives, or positives and used to examine and correct a work's text, illustrations, and design elements before final printing. A publication may involve several stages of proof; see **bluelines**; **contact proof**; **digital proof**; **galley proof**; **page proof**; **repro**.

protocol. A standard set of instructions and syntax that define the rules by which documents are shared between computers over a network. See also **FTP**; **HTTP**; **Internet**.

PS. See *PostScript (PS)*.

ragged right. Set with an uneven right-hand margin, as with printed lines. Contrast *justified*.

recto. The front side of a leaf; in a book or journal, a right-hand page. To *start recto* is to begin on a recto page, as a preface or an index normally does. Contrast **verso**.

redline. In word processing, a document in which changes (additions and deletions) are shown, or "tracked," by the application of text attributes such as strikethrough, underlining, boldface, or color. Often used as a verb: *to redline*. Also called *legal blackline*.

reprint. A publication in its second or subsequent printing, or *impression*. A reprint may include corrections or new material or both and may be published in a format different from the original printing (for example, as a paperback rather than a clothbound book). The extent of the changes usually determines whether the reprint is considered a new *edition* of the publication. See also **edition**; **impression**.

repro. An abbreviation for *reproduction copy*. A type of photographic proof generated by the typesetter that reflects the changes made in page proof. Many typesetters now provide final laser proof, generated from the electronic files, instead of repro.

resolution. (1) The number of pixels per unit of measure used to form an image. In the United States, image resolution is calculated per inch; the more pixels per inch, the higher the quality of the image. (2) The number of actual dots per unit of measure at which an image or page is output, usually by a printer or an image-setting device. In the United States, output resolution is usually expressed per inch; the more dots per inch, the higher the quality of the output.

roman. The primary type style (like this), as distinguished from italic (*like this*).

roman numerals. Numerals formed from traditional combinations of roman letters, either capitals (I, II, III, IV, etc.) or lowercase (i, ii, iii, iv, etc.). Contrast *arabic numerals*.

run in. (1) To merge a paragraph or line with the preceding one. (2) To set quoted matter continuously with text rather than setting it off as a block quotation.

running heads. Copy set at the top of printed pages, usually containing the title of the publication or chapter, chapter number, or other information. Such copy is sometimes placed at the bottom of the pages, in which case it is referred to as *running feet*.

runover. (1) The continuation of a heading, figure legend, or similar copy onto an additional line. (2) In flush-and-hang material, all lines after the first line of a particular item. (3) Text that is longer than intended, running onto another page, or reset material that is longer than the material it was meant to replace.

saddle stitching. Also called *saddle wiring*. A method of binding that involves inserting thread or staples through the folds of gathered sheets, as in pamphlets and magazines.

sans serif. A typeface with no serifs (like this). See also **serif**.

scale. To calculate (after cropping) the proportions and finish size of an illustration and the amount of reduction or enlargement needed to achieve this size.

scan. To produce a digital bitmap of an image (text or graphics) using a device that senses alternating patterns of light and dark and of color. The resolution and scaling percentage of the desired output should be considered before the image is scanned.

schema. See **DTD**.

screen. A halftone screen; also the dot pattern in the printed image produced by such a screen.

serif. A short, light line projecting from the top or bottom of a main stroke of a letter; originally, in handwritten letters, a beginning or finishing stroke of the pen. See also **sans serif**.

sewing. The process of stitching signatures together as part of binding. See also **side sewing**; **Smyth sewing**.

SGML. An abbreviation for *standard generalized markup language*, an international standard for constructing sets of tags. SGML is not a specific set of tags but a system for defining *vocabularies of tags* (the names of the tags and what they mean) and using them to encode documents. See also **tag**; **XML**.

sheet-fed press. A printing press using paper in sheet form. Contrast **web-fed press**.

sidehead. A subhead that (1) lies partly outside the margin of the text and is set on a line of its own; (2) lies wholly outside the text margin; or (3) begins a paragraph and is continuous with the text. A subhead of the third sort is sometimes called a *run-in sidehead*. See also **run in**.

side sewing. In binding, a method of sewing that involves stitching the signatures from the side, close to the spine, before attaching the case. Libraries typically rebind books in this manner. A side-sewn book is more durable than a Smyth-sewn book but will not open flat. See also **Smyth sewing**.

signature. A press sheet as folded, ready for binding. A signature is usually thirty-two pages but may be only sixteen, eight, or even four pages if the paper stock is very heavy, or sixty-four pages if the paper is thin enough to permit additional folding. The size of the press also affects the size of the signature. See also **folded and gathered sheets**; **press sheet**.

small caps. An abbreviation for *small capitals*. Capital letters set at the x-height of a font (LIKE THIS), usually for display.

Smyth sewing. A method of sewing that involves stitching the signatures individually through the fold before binding them. A Smyth-sewn book has the advantage of lying flat when open, unlike a side-sewn or perfect-bound book. See also **perfect binding**; **side sewing**.

spec. An abbreviation for *specification* (plural *specs* or *spex*)—as in *design specs*. See A.16–22.

spine. The "back" of a bound publication; that is, the center panel of the binding, hinged on each side to the two covers, front and back, and visible when the book or journal is shelved. Typically the title of the publication is printed on the spine. Also called the *backbone*.

spread. Two facing pages, a verso and a recto.

stamping. Imprinting the spine of a case and sometimes the front cover with hard metal dies. Stamping may involve ink, foil, or other coloring material; if it does not, it is called *blind stamping*. See also **embossing**.

stub. The left-hand column of a table. See 3.49–67.

style sheet. (1) A set of programming instructions that, in conjunction with a markup language such as XML or HTML, determine how a document is presented on a screen, on a printed page, or in another medium such as speech. (2) A record of terms kept by a manuscript editor to document particular usages for a specific manuscript (see 2.52). See also **CSS**.

subhead. A heading, or title, for a section within a chapter or an article. Subheads are usually set in type differing in some way from that of the text; for example, in boldface, all capitals, caps and small caps, or upper- and lowercase italic. See also **sidehead**.

subscript. A small numeral, letter, fraction, or symbol that prints partly below the baseline, usually in mathematical material or chemical formulas.

superscript. A small numeral, letter, fraction, or symbol that prints partly above the x-height, often in mathematical or tabular material or to indicate a footnote or endnote.

tag. (1) In SGML and languages derived from SGML, a generic marker used to specify and (when paired) delimit an element in the structure of a document. The process of adding tags to a manuscript is known as *tagging* or *markup*. (2) More informally, a synonym for *code*. See also **code**; **markup**; **SGML**; **XML**.

TCF. An abbreviation for *totally chlorine-free*. Refers to paper bleached without using chlorine or chlorine derivatives. Contrast **ECF**; compare **PCF**.

thin space. A very small space, defined as one-fifth (or sometimes one-sixth) of an em, added between characters. See A.22.

thumbnail. A miniature rendition of a page or an image. In electronic publications, a thumbnail is often used to indicate a link to a larger electronic object.

TIFF. An abbreviation for *tagged image file format*. A file format developed by Aldus and Microsoft and used to store bitmapped graphics, including scanned line art, halftones, and color images.

trim size. The dimensions, usually in inches, of a full page in a printed publication, including the margins.

typeface. A collection of fonts with common design or style characteristics. A typeface may include roman, italic, boldface, condensed, and other fonts. The various typefaces are designated by name: Baskerville, Caslon, and Times Roman, for example. See also **font**.

type page. The area of a typeset page occupied by the type image, from the running head to the last line of type on the page or the folio, whichever is lower, and from the inside margin to the outside margin, including any area occupied by sideheads.

typesetter. A person, firm, facility, or machine that prepares books, articles, or other documents for publication. The term, now somewhat of an anachronism, has its origins in the composing—or "setting"—of individual pieces of type, by hand, and binding them together to make individual pages. Also called *compositor*.

type styles. See **boldface**; **italic**; **roman**.

Unicode. A system of character encoding developed by the Unicode Consortium and incorporated into the ISO standard for universal multiple-octet coded characters (ISO/IEC 10646). See 11.2. See also **character encoding**.

unjustified. See **ragged right**.

uppercase. The capital letters of a font. Contrast **lowercase**.

URL. An abbreviation for *uniform resource locator*, or the address used to locate a document on the Internet (e.g., http://www.press.uchicago.edu/).

vector graphic. A digital representation of an image defined by shapes such as lines and curves rather than by pixels. Line art is typically created, edited, and scaled as a vector graphic. Contrast **bitmap**.

verso. The back side of a leaf; in a book or journal, a left-hand page. Contrast **recto**.

web browser. A computer program designed to access information on the Internet or on a local network. See also **HTML**; **web page**.

web-fed press. A printing press using paper in roll form. Contrast **sheet-fed press**.

web page. A virtual document delivered via the World Wide Web and viewed in a web browser.

website. A collection of closely related and hyperlinked web pages maintained by an individual or organization.

widow. A short, paragraph-ending line appearing at the top of a page. Widows should be avoided when possible by changes in wording or spacing that either remove the line or lengthen it. Contrast **orphan**.

wiki. A website designed to allow visitors to edit and contribute content.

World Wide Web. Also called *the web*. The Internet's most widely used information-retrieval service. The World Wide Web uses hypertext transfer protocol (HTTP) to allow users to request and retrieve documents (web pages and multimedia objects) from other computers on the Internet.

x-height. In type, a vertical dimension equal to the height of the lowercase letters (such as *x*) without ascenders or descenders.

XHTML. An application of XML for producing HTML that conforms to the rules established for a particular XML-based document. See also **HTML**.

XML. An abbreviation for *extensible markup language*. A subset of the SGML standard, used for structuring documents and data on the Internet. See also **SGML**.

XSL. An abbreviation for *extensible style sheet language*. A family of style sheet languages used to define the presentation of XML documents and their conversion, or transformation, into other formats such as HTML (using XSLT, extensible style sheet transformations).

Bibliography

The works listed here are a starting point for writers, editors, and others involved in publishing who would like more information about topics covered in this manual. The list includes all the works cited in the text as further resources along with other useful references. Although some make recommendations that diverge from those of this manual, they reflect the specific demands of different disciplines and the evolving traditions of writing, editing, and publishing. As with all reference sources, readers should carefully evaluate their suitability for a given purpose.

1 Works on Writing and Editing

1.1 STYLE

The ACS Style Guide: Effective Communication of Scientific Information. 3rd ed. Edited by Anne M. Coghill and Lorrin R. Garson. Washington, DC: American Chemical Society, 2006.

AIP Style Manual. 4th ed. New York: American Institute of Physics, 1990. Also available at http://www.aip.org/pubservs/style/4thed/toc.html.

ALWD Citation Manual: A Professional System of Citation. 3rd ed. Edited by the Association of Legal Writing Directors and Darby Dickerson. New York: Aspen, 2006.

AMA Manual of Style: A Guide for Authors and Editors. 10th ed. Edited by Cheryl Iverson. New York: Oxford University Press, 2007. Also available at http://www.ama manualofstyle.com/.

ASM Style Manual for Journals and Books. Washington, DC: American Society for Microbiology, 1991.

The Associated Press Stylebook and Briefing on Media Law. 44th ed. Edited by Darrell Christian, Sally Jacobsen, and David Minthorn. New York: Associated Press, 2009. Also available at http://www.apstylebook.com/.

The Bluebook: A Uniform System of Citation. 18th ed. Cambridge, MA: Harvard Law Review Association, 2005. Also available at http://www.legalbluebook.com/.

Canadian Guide to Uniform Legal Citation. 6th ed. In English and French. Toronto, ON: Carswell/McGill Law Journal, 2006.

Catholic News Service. CNS Stylebook on Religion: Reference Guide and Usage Manual. 3rd ed. Washington, DC: Catholic News Service, 2006.

The Complete Guide to Citing Government Information Resources: A Manual for Writers and Librarians. Rev. ed. Edited by Diane L. Garner and Diane H. Smith. Bethesda, MD: Congressional Information Service for the Government Documents Round Table, American Library Association, 1993.

CSE Manual. See Scientific Style and Format.

Editing Canadian English. 2nd ed. Prepared for the Editors' Association of Canada / Association canadienne des réviseurs by Catherine Cragg, Barbara Czarnecki, Iris Hossé Phillips, Katharine Vanderlinden, and Sheila Protti. Toronto, ON: Macfarlane Walter and Ross, 2000.

Garner, Bryan A. *The Elements of Legal Style*. 2nd ed. New York: Oxford University Press, 2002.

Holoman, D. Kern. *Writing about Music: A Style Sheet*. 2nd ed. Berkeley: University of California Press, 2008.

ISO (International Organization for Standardization). *Information and Documentation—Bibliographic References. Part 2, Electronic Documents or Parts Thereof*. ISO 690-2. New York: American National Standards Institute, 1997. Under revision.

Lipson, Charles. *Cite Right: A Quick Guide to Citation Styles—MLA, APA, Chicago, the Sciences, Professions, and More*. Chicago: University of Chicago Press, 2006.

MHRA Style Guide: A Handbook for Authors, Editors, and Writers of Theses. 2nd ed. London: Modern Humanities Research Association, 2008. Also available at http://www.mhra.org.uk/.

Microsoft Manual of Style for Technical Publications. 3rd ed. Redmond, WA: Microsoft Press, 2004.

MLA Style Manual and Guide to Scholarly Publishing. 3rd ed. New York: Modern Language Association of America, 2008.

The New York Public Library Writer's Guide to Style and Usage. New York: HarperCollins, 1994.

The New York Times Manual of Style and Usage. Rev. ed. Edited by Allan M. Siegal and William G. Connolly. New York: Three Rivers Press, 1999.

The Oxford Style Manual. Edited by Robert Ritter. New York: Oxford University Press, 2003. Combines *The Oxford Guide to Style* and *The Oxford Dictionary for Writers and Editors*.

Publication Manual of the American Psychological Association. 6th ed. Washington, DC: American Psychological Association, 2009.

Reporting on Religion 2: A Stylebook on Religion's Best Beat. Edited by Diane Connolly and Debra L. Mason. Westerville, OH: Religion Newswriters, 2007.

Sabin, William A. *The Gregg Reference Manual: A Manual of Style, Grammar, Usage, and Formatting*. 10th ed. Boston: McGraw-Hill, 2005. Also available online at http://www.gregg.com/.

The SBL Handbook of Style: For Ancient Near Eastern, Biblical, and Early Christian Studies. Edited by Patrick H. Alexander. Peabody, MA: Hendrickson, 1999. Also available at http://www.sbl-site.org/publications/publishingwithsbl.aspx.

Scientific Style and Format: The CSE Manual for Authors, Editors, and Publishers. 7th ed. Compiled by the Style Manual Committee of the Council of Science Editors. Reston, VA: Council of Science Editors in cooperation with the Rockefeller University Press, 2006.

Strunk, William, Jr., and E. B. White. *The Elements of Style*. 4th ed. Boston: Allyn and Bacon, 2000.

Style Manual for Political Science. Rev. ed. Washington, DC: American Political Science Association Committee on Publications, 2006.

The Times Style and Usage Guide. Rev. ed. Compiled by Tim Austin. London: Times Books, 2003.

Turabian, Kate L. *A Manual for Writers of Research Papers, Theses, and Dissertations: Chicago Style for Students and Researchers*. 7th ed. Revised by Wayne C. Booth, Gregory G. Colomb, Joseph M. Williams, and University of Chicago Press editorial staff. Chicago: University of Chicago Press, 2007.

———. *Student's Guide to Writing College Papers*. 4th ed. Revised by Gregory G. Colomb, Joseph M. Williams, and the University of Chicago Press editorial staff. Chicago: University of Chicago Press, 2010.

United States Government Printing Office Style Manual. 30th ed. Washington, DC: Government Printing Office, 2008. Also available at http://www.gpoaccess.gov/style manual/index.html.

The University of Chicago Manual of Legal Citation. 2nd ed. Edited by the *University of Chicago Law Review*. 2000. An updated version is available at http://lawreview .uchicago.edu/.

US Geological Survey. *Suggestions to Authors of the Reports of the United States Geological Survey*. 7th ed. Revised and edited by Wallace R. Hansen. Washington, DC: Government Printing Office, 1991. Also available at http://www.nwrc.usgs.gov /lib/lib_sta.htm.

Walker, Janice R., and Todd Taylor. *The Columbia Guide to Online Style*. 2nd ed. New York: Columbia University Press, 2006.

The Wall Street Journal Guide to Business Style and Usage. Edited by Paul R. Martin. London: Free Press, 2002.

Words into Type. 3rd ed. Based on studies by Marjorie E. Skillin, Robert M. Gay, and other authorities. Englewood Cliffs, NJ: Prentice Hall, 1974.

1.2 GRAMMAR AND USAGE

Aitchison, James. *Cassell Dictionary of English Grammar*. 2nd ed. London: Cassell, 2001.

Baron, Dennis. *Grammar and Gender*. New Haven: Yale University Press, 1986.

Bernstein, Theodore M. *The Careful Writer: A Modern Guide to English Usage*. New York: Atheneum, 1965.

———. *Miss Thistlebottom's Hobgoblins: The Careful Writer's Guide to the Taboos, Bugbears, and Outmoded Rules of English Usage*. New York: Farrar, Straus and Giroux, 1971.

Burchfield, Robert W. *Unlocking the English Language*. New York: Hill and Wang, 1991.

Copperud, Roy H. *American Usage and Style: The Consensus*. New York: Van Nostrand Reinhold, 1980.

Ebbitt, Wilma R., and David R. Ebbitt. *Index to English*. 8th ed. New York: Oxford University Press, 1990.

The Elements of Internet Style: The New Rules of Creating Valuable Content for Today's Readers. Rev. ed. of *E-What?* Alexandria, VA: EEI Press; New York: Allworth Press, 2007.

Follett, Wilson. *Modern American Usage: A Guide*. Revised by Erik Wensberg. New York: Hill and Wang, 1998.

Fowler, H. W. *A Dictionary of Modern English Usage*. 2nd ed. Revised and edited by Sir Ernest Gowers. Oxford: Oxford University Press, 1965. (See also *Fowler's Modern English Usage*.)

Fowler's Modern English Usage. 3rd ed. rev. Edited by R. W. Burchfield. New York: Oxford University Press, 2004.

Garner, Bryan A. *Garner's Modern American Usage*. New York: Oxford University Press, 2003.

Gordon, Karen Elizabeth. *The Deluxe Transitive Vampire: The Ultimate Handbook of Grammar for the Innocent, the Eager, and the Doomed*. New York: Pantheon, 1993.

———. *The New Well-Tempered Sentence: A Punctuation Handbook for the Innocent, the Eager, and the Doomed*. New York: Ticknor and Fields, 1993.

Gowers, Ernest. *The Complete Plain Words*. Edited by Sidney Greenbaum and Janet Whitcut. Boston: David R. Godine, 1988.

Greenbaum, Sydney. *Oxford English Grammar*. New York: Oxford University Press, 1996.

Hale, Constance. *Sin and Syntax: How to Craft Wickedly Effective Prose*. New York: Broadway Books, 1999.

Hale, Constance, and Jessie Scanlon, eds. *Wired Style: Principles of English Usage in the Digital Age*. Rev. ed. New York: Broadway Books, 1999.

Johnson, Edward D. *The Handbook of Good English*. New York: Pocket Books, 1991.

Maggio, Rosalie. *Talking about People: A Guide to Fair and Accurate Language*. Phoenix: Oryx Press, 1997.

Merriam-Webster's Dictionary of English Usage. Springfield, MA: Merriam-Webster, 1994.

O'Conner, Patricia T. *Woe Is I: The Grammarphobe's Guide to Better English in Plain English*. 3rd ed. New York: Riverhead Books, 2009.

The Oxford Dictionary of English Grammar. Edited by Sylvia Chalker and Edmund Weiner. New York: Oxford University Press, 1998.

Palmer, Frank. *Grammar*. 2nd ed. New York: Penguin, 1984.

Schwartz, Marilyn. *Guidelines for Bias-Free Writing*. Bloomington: Indiana University Press, 1995.

Trask, R. L. *Language: The Basics*. 2nd ed. New York: Routledge, 1999.

Trimble, John R. *Writing with Style: Conversations on the Art of Writing*. 2nd ed. Upper Saddle River, NJ: Prentice Hall, 2002.

Wallraff, Barbara. *Word Court: Wherein Verbal Virtue Is Rewarded, Crimes against the Language Are Punished, and Poetic Justice Is Done*. New York: Harcourt, 2000.

Walsh, Bill. *Lapsing into a Comma: A Curmudgeon's Guide to the Many Things That Can Go Wrong in Print—and How to Avoid Them*. Chicago: Contemporary Books, 2000.

Williams, Joseph M. *Style: Toward Clarity and Grace*. With two chapters coauthored by Gregory G. Colomb. Chicago: University of Chicago Press, 1995.

Zinsser, William. *On Writing Well: The Classic Guide to Writing Nonfiction*. 7th ed. New York: HarperCollins, 2006.

1.3 RESEARCH AND WRITING

Barzun, Jacques, and Henry F. Graff. *The Modern Researcher*. 6th ed. Belmont, CA: Thomson/Wadsworth, 2004.

Becker, Howard S. *Writing for Social Scientists: How to Start and Finish Your Thesis, Book, or Article*. 2nd ed. Chicago: University of Chicago Press, 2007.

Booth, Wayne C., Gregory G. Colomb, and Joseph M. Williams. *The Craft of Research*. 3rd ed. Chicago: University of Chicago Press, 2008.

Cook, Claire Kehrwald. *Line by Line: How to Improve Your Own Writing*. Boston: Houghton Mifflin, 1985.

Day, Robert A., and Barbara Gastel. *How to Write and Publish a Scientific Paper*. 6th ed. Westport, CT: Greenwood Press, 2006.

Germano, William. *From Dissertation to Book*. Chicago: University of Chicago Press, 2005.

Harman, Eleanor, Ian Montagnes, Siobhan McMenemy, and Chris Bucci, eds. *The Thesis and the Book: A Guide for First-Time Academic Authors*. 2nd ed. Toronto: University of Toronto Press, 2003.

Lanham, Richard A. *Revising Prose*. 5th ed. New York: Pearson Longman, 2007.

Lerner, Betsy. *The Forest for the Trees: An Editor's Advice to Writers*. New York: Riverhead Books, 2000.

Lipson, Charles. *How to Write a BA Thesis: A Practical Guide from Your First Ideas to Your Finished Paper*. Chicago: University of Chicago Press, 2005.

Luey, Beth, ed. *Revising Your Dissertation: Advice from Leading Editors*. Updated ed. Berkeley: University of California Press, 2007.

McMillan, Victoria E. *Writing Papers in the Biological Sciences*. 4th ed. Boston: Bedford/St. Martin's, 2006.

2 *Works on Publishing*

2.1 MANUSCRIPT EDITING AND PROOFREADING

Anderson, Laura. *McGraw-Hill's Proofreading Handbook*. 2nd ed. New York: McGraw-Hill, 2006.

Butcher, Judith, Caroline Drake, and Maureen Leach. *Butcher's Copy-Editing: The Cambridge Handbook for Editors, Copy-Editors, and Proofreaders*. 4th ed. New York: Cambridge University Press, 2006. Also available as an e-book.

Copyediting. Bimonthly newsletter published by McMurry, Inc. Also available at http://www.copyediting.com/.

Einsohn, Amy. *The Copyeditor's Handbook: A Guide for Book Publishing and Corporate Communications*. 2nd ed. Berkeley: University of California Press, 2006.

Judd, Karen. *Copyediting: A Practical Guide*. 3rd ed. Menlo Park, CA: Crisp Learning, 2001.

Lyon, Jack M. *Microsoft Word for Publishing Professionals*. West Valley City, UT: Editorium, 2008.

Norton, Scott. *Developmental Editing: A Handbook for Freelancers, Authors, and Publishers*. Chicago: University of Chicago Press, 2009.

Saller, Carol Fisher. *The Subversive Copy Editor: Advice from Chicago (or, How to Negotiate Good Relationships with Your Writers, Your Colleagues, and Yourself)*. Chicago: University of Chicago Press, 2009.

Smith, Peggy. *Mark My Words: Instruction and Practice in Proofreading*. 3rd ed. Alexandria, VA: EEI Press, 1997.

Stainton, Elsie Myers. *The Fine Art of Copyediting*. 2nd ed. New York: Columbia University Press, 2002.

Stoughton, Mary. *The Copyeditor's Guide to Substance and Style*. 3rd ed. Alexandria, VA: EEI Press, 2006.

2.2 ILLUSTRATIONS

Briscoe, Mary Helen. *Preparing Scientific Illustrations: A Guide to Better Posters, Presentations, and Publications*. 2nd ed. New York: Springer-Verlag, 1996.

CBE Scientific Illustration Committee. *Illustrating Science: Standards for Publication*. Bethesda, MD: Council of Biology Editors, 1988.

Monmonier, Mark. *Mapping It Out: Expository Cartography for the Humanities and Social Sciences*. Chicago: University of Chicago Press, 1993.

Ross, Ted. *The Art of Music Engraving and Processing: A Complete Manual, Reference, and Text Book on Preparing Music for Reproduction and Print*. Miami: Hansen Books, 1970.

Tufte, Edward R. *Envisioning Information*. Cheshire, CT: Graphics Press, 1990.

——. *The Visual Display of Quantitative Information*. 2nd ed. Cheshire, CT: Graphics Press, 2001.

——. *Visual Explanations: Images and Quantities, Evidence and Narrative*. Cheshire, CT: Graphics Press, 1997.

Zweifel, Frances W. *A Handbook of Biological Illustration*. 2nd ed. Chicago: University of Chicago Press, 1988.

2.3 RIGHTS AND PERMISSIONS

Bielstein, Susan M. *Permissions, a Survival Guide: Blunt Talk about Art as Intellectual Property*. Chicago: University of Chicago Press, 2006.

Fischer, Mark A., E. Gabriel Perle, and John Taylor Williams. *Perle and Williams on Publishing Law*. 3rd ed. Gaithersburg, MD: Aspen Law and Business, 1999.

Goldstein, Paul. *Goldstein on Copyright*. 3rd ed. New York: Aspen, 2005. Loose-leaf updates.

Kaufman, Roy S. *Publishing Forms and Contracts*. New York: Oxford University Press, 2008.

Kirsch, Jonathan. *Kirsch's Handbook of Publishing Law*. Los Angeles: Acrobat Books, 1996.

Nimmer, Melville. *Cases and Materials on Copyright and Other Aspects of Entertainment Litigation, Including Unfair Competition, Defamation, Privacy*. 7th ed. Newark, NJ: LexisNexis Matthew Bender, 2006.

———. *Nimmer on Copyright*. Rev. ed. 11 vols. Newark, NJ: LexisNexis Matthew Bender, 2005. Loose-leaf updates.

Nimmer, Melville, and Paul Edward Gellner, eds. *International Copyright Law and Practice*. Newark, NJ: LexisNexis Matthew Bender, 2004. Loose-leaf updates.

Patry, William F. *Copyright Law and Practice*. Washington, DC: Bureau of National Affairs, 1994. Annual supplements.

———. *The Fair Use Privilege in Copyright Law*. 2nd ed. Washington, DC: Bureau of National Affairs, 1995.

Strong, William S. *The Copyright Book: A Practical Guide*. 5th ed. Cambridge, MA: MIT Press, 1999.

2.4 MATHEMATICS

Clapham, Christopher, and James Nicholson. *Concise Dictionary of Mathematics*. 3rd ed. New York: Oxford University Press, 2005.

Higham, Nicholas J. *Handbook of Writing for the Mathematical Sciences*. 2nd ed. Philadelphia: Society for Industrial and Applied Mathematics, 1998.

The International System of Units (SI). 8th ed. Sèvres: Bureau International des Poids et Mesures, 2006. Also available at http://www.bipm.org/en/si/si_brochure/.

Knuth, Donald E. *The TeXbook*. Boston: Addison-Wesley, 2000.

Lamport, Leslie. *LaTeX: A Document Preparation System; User's Guide and Reference Manual*. 2nd ed. Reading, MA: Addison-Wesley, 1999.

A Manual for Authors of Mathematical Papers. 8th ed. Providence, RI: American Mathematical Society, 1990.

Mittelbach, Frank, and Michel Goossens. *The LaTeX Companion*. 2nd ed. Boston: Addison-Wesley, 2004.

Spivak, Michael. *The Joy of TeX: A Gourmet Guide to Typesetting with the AMS-TeXMacro Package*. 2nd ed. Providence, RI: American Mathematical Society, 1990.

Steenrod, Norman E., Paul R. Halmos, Menahem M. Schiffer, and Jean A. Dieudonné. *How to Write Mathematics*. Providence, RI: American Mathematical Society, 1981.

Swanson, Ellen. *Mathematics into Type*. Updated edition by Arlene O'Sean and Antoinette Schleyer. Providence, RI: American Mathematical Society, 1999.

Thompson, Ambler, and Barry N. Taylor. *Guide for the Use of the International System of Units (SI)*. Gaithersburg, MD: National Institute of Standards and Technology, 2008. Also available at http://physics.nist.gov/Pubs/SP811/.

2.5 INDEXING

Ament, Kurt. *Indexing: A Nuts-and-Bolts Guide for Technical Writers*. Norwich, NY: William Andrew, 2001.

Booth, Pat F. *Indexing: The Manual of Good Practice*. Munich: K. G. Saur, 2001.

Browne, Glenda, and Jon Jermey. *The Indexing Companion*. Melbourne: Cambridge University Press, 2007.

Fetters, Linda K. *Handbook of Indexing Techniques: A Guide for Beginning Indexers*. 3rd ed. Corpus Christi, TX: FimCo Books, 2001.

Mulvany, Nancy. *Indexing Books*. 2nd ed. Chicago: University of Chicago Press, 2005.

Wellisch, Hans H. *Indexing from A to Z*. 2nd ed. New York: H. W. Wilson, 1995.

2.6 DESIGN

Bringhurst, Robert. *The Elements of Typographic Style*. 3rd ed. Point Roberts, WA: Hartley and Marks, 2004.

Chappell, Warren, and Robert Bringhurst. *A Short History of the Printed Word*. 2nd ed. Point Roberts, WA: Hartley and Marks, 1999.

Dowding, Geoffrey. *Finer Points in the Spacing and Arrangement of Type*. Rev. ed. Point Roberts, WA: Hartley and Marks, 1995.

Gill, Eric. *An Essay on Typography*. Boston: David R. Godine, 1988.

Hendel, Richard. *On Book Design*. New Haven, CT: Yale University Press, 1998.

Hochuli, Jost, and Robin Kinross. *Designing Books: Practice and Theory*. Rev. ed. London: Hyphen Press, 2003.

Johnston, Edward. *Writing and Illuminating and Lettering*. 1946; repr., New York: Dover, 1995.

Lynch, Patrick J., and Sarah Horton. *Web Style Guide: Basic Design Principles for Creating Web Sites*. 3rd ed. New Haven, CT: Yale University Press, 2009.

McLean, Ruari. *The Thames and Hudson Manual of Typography*. New York: Thames and Hudson, 1992.

Tschichold, Jan. *The Form of the Book: Essays on the Morality of Good Design*. Point Roberts, WA: Hartley and Marks, 1995.

———. *The New Typography*. New ed. Berkeley: University of California Press, 2006.

Williamson, Hugh. *Methods of Book Design*. 3rd ed. New Haven, CT: Yale University Press, 1983.

2.7 PRODUCTION

Bann, David. *The All New Print Production Handbook*. New York: Watson-Guptill, 2007.

Beach, Mark, and Eric Kenly. *Getting It Printed*. 4th ed. Cincinnati: HOW Design Books, 2004.

The Bookman's Glossary. 6th ed. Edited by Jean Peters. New York: R. R. Bowker, 1983.

Burdett, Eric. *The Craft of Bookbinding*. Newton Abbot, UK: David and Charles, 1978.

The Columbia Guide to Digital Publishing. Edited by William E. Kasdorf. New York: Columbia University Press, 2003.

Dreyfus, John. *Into Print: Selected Writings on Printing History, Typography, and Book Production*. Boston: D. R. Godine, 1995.

Eckersley, Richard, Richard Angstadt, Charles M. Ellertson, Richard Hendel, Naomi B. Pascal, and Anita Walker Scott. *Glossary of Typesetting Terms*. Chicago: University of Chicago Press, 1994.

Extensible Markup Language (XML). 5th ed. Edited by Tim Bray, Jean Paoli, C. M. Sperberg-McQueen, Eve Maler, and François Yergeau. World Wide Web Consortium (W3C) recommendation, November 26, 2008. Available at http://www.w3 .org/TR/xml /.

Friedl, Jeffrey E. F. *Mastering Regular Expressions*. 3rd ed. Sebastopol, CA: O'Reilly, 2006.

Glaister, Geoffrey Ashall. *Encyclopedia of the Book*. 2nd ed. New Castle, DE: Oak Knoll Press, 2001.

Hackos, JoAnn, and Dawn Stevens. *Standards for Online Communication*. New York: John Wiley, 1997.

Kinross, Robin, Jaap van Triest, and Karel Martens, eds. *Karel Martens: Printed Matter*. 2nd ed. London: Hyphen Press, 2002.

Lee, Marshall. *Bookmaking: Editing, Design, Production*. 3rd ed. New York: Norton, 2004.

National Information Standards Organization. *Journal Article Versions (JAV): Recommendations of the NISO/ALPSP JAV Technical Working Group*. In partnership with the Association of Learned and Professional Society Publishers. April 2008. Available at http://www.niso.org/publications/rp/RP-8-2008.pdf.

Pocket Pal: A Graphic Arts Production Handbook. 19th ed. Memphis, TN: International Paper Company, 2003.

Rogondino, Michael, and Pat Rogondino. *Process Color Manual: 24,000 CMYK Combinations for Design, Prepress, and Printing*. San Francisco: Chronicle Books, 2000.

Romano, Frank J. *Pocket Guide to Digital Prepress*. Albany, NY: Delmar Thomson Learning, 1995.

Unicode Consortium. *The Unicode Standard*. Version 5.0. Edited by Julie D. Allen, Joe Becker, Richard Cook, Mark Davis, Michael Everson, Asmus Freytag, John H. Jenkins, et al. Upper Saddle River, NJ: Addison-Wesley, 2007. Available at http://www.unicode.org/.

XML. See *Extensible Markup Language*.

XML.com: XML from the Inside Out. O'Reilly Media. http://www.xml.com/.

2.8 THE PUBLISHING INDUSTRY

Derricourt, Robin. *An Author's Guide to Scholarly Publishing*. Princeton, NJ: Princeton University Press, 1996.

Germano, William. *Getting It Published: A Guide for Scholars and Anyone Else Serious about Serious Books*. 2nd ed. Chicago: University of Chicago Press, 2008.

Greco, Albert N. *The Book Publishing Industry*. 2nd ed. Mahwah, NJ: Lawrence Erlbaum, 2005.

ILMP (International Literary Market Place). Medford, NJ: Information Today. Published annually. Also available at http://www.literarymarketplace.com/lmp/us/index_us.asp.

Journal of Electronic Publishing. Published quarterly by the University of Michigan Library. http://www.journalofelectronicpublishing.org/.

Journal of Scholarly Publishing. Published quarterly by the University of Toronto Press. Also available at http://www.utpjournals.com/jsp/jsp.html.

LMP (Literary Market Place). Medford, NJ: Information Today. Published annually. Also available at http://www.literarymarketplace.com/lmp/us/index_us.asp.

Luey, Beth. *Handbook for Academic Authors*. 5th ed. New York: Cambridge University Press, 2009.

Rabiner, Susan, and Alfred Fortunato. *Thinking like Your Editor: How to Write Great Serious Nonfiction—and Get It Published*. New York: W. W. Norton, 2002.

Suzanne, Claudia. *This Business of Books: A Complete Overview of the Industry from Concept through Sales*. 4th ed. Tustin, CA: WC Publishing, 2003.

3 Dictionaries

3.1 ENGLISH DICTIONARIES

American Heritage Dictionary of the English Language. 4th ed. Boston: Houghton Mifflin, 2000.

Merriam-Webster's Collegiate Dictionary. 11th ed. Springfield, MA: Merriam-Webster, 2003. Also available at http://www.merriam-webster.com/.

New Oxford American Dictionary. 2nd ed. Edited by Erin McKean. New York: Oxford University Press, 2005. Also available at http://www.oxfordamericandictionary.com/.

Oxford English Dictionary. 2nd ed. 20 vols. Oxford: Oxford University Press, 1989. Also available at http://www.oed.com/.

Random House Webster's College Dictionary with CD-ROM. New York: Random House Reference, 2005.

Roget's II: The New Thesaurus. 3rd ed. Boston: Houghton Mifflin, 1995.

Roget's 21st Century Thesaurus in Dictionary Form. 3rd ed. Edited by Barbara Ann Kipfer. New York: Delta Trade Paperbacks, 2005.

Shorter Oxford English Dictionary. 6th ed. 2 vols. New York: Oxford University Press, 2007.

Webster's New World College Dictionary. 4th ed. Cleveland: Webster's New World, 2001.

Webster's Third New International Dictionary of the English Language, Unabridged. Springfield, MA: Merriam-Webster, 1993. Also available at http://www .merriam-webster.com/.

3.2 FOREIGN-LANGUAGE DICTIONARIES

ABC Chinese–English Comprehensive Dictionary. Edited by John DeFrancis. Honolulu: University of Hawaii Press, 2003.

Cassell's Italian Dictionary. Compiled by Piero Rebora, Francis M. Guercio, and Arthur L. Hayward. New York: John Wiley, 1994.

Kenkyūsha's New Japanese–English Dictionary. 5th ed. Tokyo: Kenkyūsha, 2003.

Larousse French–English, English–French Dictionary. New ed. Edited by Janice McNeillie. Paris: Larousse, 2007.

Minjung's Essence English–Korean Dictionary. 10th ed. Elizabeth, NJ: Hollym International Corp., 2008.

Oxford English–Arabic Dictionary of Current Usage. Edited by N. S. Doniach. Oxford: Clarendon Press, 1972.

Oxford German Dictionary: German–English, English–German. 3rd ed. Edited by Werner Scholze-Stubenrecht, J. B. Sykes, M. Clark, and O. Thyen. Oxford: Oxford University Press, 2008.

Oxford-Hachette French Dictionary. 4th ed. Edited by Marie-Hélène Corréard et al. Oxford: Oxford University Press, 2007.

Oxford Latin Dictionary. Combined ed. Edited by P. G. W. Glare. New York: Oxford University Press, 1982.

Oxford-Paravia Italian Dictionary. 2nd ed. Oxford: Oxford University Press, 2006.

Oxford Russian Dictionary. 4th ed. Edited by Marcus Wheeler, Boris Unbegaun, Paul Falla, and Della Thompson. Oxford: Oxford University Press, 2007.

Oxford Spanish Dictionary. 4th ed. Edited by Beatriz Galimberti Jarman and Roy Russell. Oxford: Oxford University Press, 2008.

The University of Chicago Spanish Dictionary. 5th ed. Edited by David Pharies. Chicago: University of Chicago Press, 2002.

4 General Reference Works

4.1 BIOGRAPHY

American Men and Women of Science. 25th ed. Edited by Katherine H. Nemeh. Farmington Hills, MI: Thomson/Gale, 2008.

American National Biography. New York: Oxford University Press, 2000–. Updated quarterly. http://www.anb.org/.

Burke's Peerage, Baronetage, and Knightage. 107th ed. Multiple vols. London: Burke's Peerage, 1826–.

Canadian Who's Who. Toronto: University of Toronto Press. Published annually, with semiannual supplements.

Concise Dictionary of National Biography: From Earliest Times to 1985. 3 vols. Oxford: Oxford University Press, 1992.

Dictionary of American Biography. 11 vols. New York: Scribner's, 1995. Supplements.

Dictionary of Canadian Biography. 14 vols. Toronto: University of Toronto Press, 1966–. Supplements.

Directory of American Scholars. 10th ed. 6 vols. Detroit: Gale Group, 2002.

International Who's Who. London: Europa. Published annually.

Marquis Who's Who on the Web. New Providence, NJ: Marquis Who's Who. Continually updated. http://www.marquiswhoswho.com/.

Merriam-Webster's Biographical Dictionary. Springfield, MA: Merriam-Webster, 1995.

Oxford Dictionary of National Biography. 60 vols. Prepared under various editors. New York: Oxford University Press, 1885–2004. Also available at http://www.oxforddnb.com/.

Who's Who: An Annual Biographical Dictionary. New York: St. Martin's Press. Published annually.

Who's Who in America. Chicago: A. N. Marquis. Published biennially. See also *Marquis Who's Who on the Web*.

4.2 GEOGRAPHY

Cambridge World Gazetteer: A Geographical Dictionary. Edited by David Munro. New York: Cambridge University Press, 1990.

Columbia Gazetteer of North America. Edited by Saul B. Cohen. New York: Columbia University Press, 2000.

Merriam-Webster's Geographical Dictionary. 3rd ed. Springfield, MA: Merriam-Webster, 1997.

Omni Gazetteer of the United States of America. Edited by Frank R. Abate. Detroit: Omnigraphics, 1991.

Oxford Atlas of the World. 16th ed. New York: Oxford University Press, 2009.

The Times Comprehensive Atlas of the World. 12th ed. London: Times Books, 2007.

The World Factbook. Washington, DC: Central Intelligence Agency. Continually updated. https://www.cia.gov/library/publications/the-world-factbook/.

4.3 ENCYCLOPEDIAS

Britannica Concise Encyclopaedia. Rev. ed. Chicago: Encyclopaedia Britannica, 2006.

Canadian Encyclopedia. 2000 ed. Toronto: McClelland and Stewart, 1999. Also available at http://www.thecanadianencyclopedia.com/.

Columbia Encyclopedia. 6th ed. New York: Columbia University Press, 2000.

Encyclopedia Americana. 30 vols. Danbury, CT: Scholastic Library, 2006.

The New Encyclopaedia Britannica. 15th ed. 32 vols. Chicago: Encyclopaedia Britannica, 2007. Also available at http://www.britannica.com/.

Wikipedia: The Free Encyclopedia. San Francisco: Wikimedia Foundation. http://en.wikipedia.org/.

4.4 ALMANACS AND YEARBOOKS

Canadian Almanac and Directory. Toronto: Grey House. Published annually.

Encyclopedia Britannica, Inc. *Time Almanac*. New York: Time Home Entertainment. Published annually.

The Europa World of Learning. London: Routledge. Published annually. Also available at http://www.worldoflearning.com/.

Europa World Year Book. London: Europa. Published annually. Also available at http://www.europaworld.com/pub/.

New York Times Almanac. New York: Penguin Group. Published annually.

The Statesman's Yearbook. Basingstoke: Palgrave Macmillan. Published annually. Also available at http://www.statesmansyearbook.com/public/.

Whitaker's Almanack. London: Stationery Office. Published annually.

World Almanac and Book of Facts. New York: World Almanac Books. Published annually.

4.5 GUIDES TO BOOKS, PERIODICALS, AND OTHER SOURCES

ABI/Inform Complete. Ann Arbor, MI: ProQuest Information and Learning. http://www.proquest.com/.

Anglo-American Cataloguing Rules. 2nd ed. Chicago: American Library Association; Ottawa: Canadian Library Association; London: Chartered Institute of Library and Information Professionals, 2002. Loose-leaf update, 2005.

Ashley, Lowell E. *Cataloging Musical Moving Image Material: A Guide to the Bibliographical Control of Videorecordings and Films of Musical Performances and Other Music-Related Moving Image Material*. Canton, MA: Music Library Association, 1996.

Australian Books in Print. Melbourne: D. W. Thorpe. Published annually.

Bibliographic Index. New York: H. W. Wilson. Published semiannually. Also available, as *Bibliographic Index Plus*, at http://www.hwwilson.com/databases/biblio.htm.

Book Review Digest. New York: H. W. Wilson. Published monthly, except for February and July, with annual cumulations. Also available, as *Book Review Digest Plus*, at http://www.hwwilson.com/databases/brdig.htm.

Book Review Index. Detroit: Gale Research Company. Published monthly, with quarterly and annual cumulation.

Books in Print. New York: R. R. Bowker. Published annually. Also available at http://www.booksinprint.com/.

Bowker's British Books in Print. New Providence, NJ: R. R. Bowker. Published annually. From 1988 to 2003 titled *Whitaker's Books in Print: The Reference Catalogue of Current Literature*; before 1988 titled *British Books in Print*.

Canadian Books in Print. Toronto: University of Toronto Press. Published annually.

Catalog of U.S. Government Publications. Washington, DC: GPO Access. http://catalog.gpo.gov/.

Dissertation Abstracts International. Ann Arbor, MI: University Microfilms International. Published monthly with annual cumulation.

Guide to Reference. 12th ed. Edited by Bob Kieft. Chicago: American Library Association, 2008. http://www.guidetoreference.org/.

Guide to the Contents of the Public Record Office. 3 vols. London: Her Majesty's Stationery Office, 1963–1968.

Guide to the National Archives of the United States. Washington, DC: Archives, 1987. Also available at http://www.archives.gov/.

Guide to U.S. Government Publications. Edited by Donna Batten. Formerly known as *Andriot*. Detroit: Gale Research Company. Updated annually.

Humanities Index. New York: H. W. Wilson. Published quarterly with annual cumulation. Also available at http://www.hwwilson.com/.

Index Islamicus. Leiden: Brill. Published quarterly with quinquennial cumulation. Also available at http://www.indexislamicus.com/.

Library of Congress Subject Headings. Washington, DC: Library of Congress Cataloging Distribution Service. Published annually. Also available at http://classweb.loc.gov/.

Livres disponibles [French books in print]. Paris: Cercle de la librairie, 1977–2004.

The New Walford Guide to Reference Resources. 9th ed. 3 vols. London: Facet, 2005–10.

New York Times Index. New York: New York Times Company. Annual cumulations.

PAIS International in Print. New York: Public Affairs Information Service. Published monthly, with every fourth issue being cumulative.

Pemberton, John E., ed. *The Bibliographic Control of Official Publications*. New York: Pergamon, 1982.

Periodical Title Abbreviations. 17th ed. Vol. 1, by abbreviation. Vol. 2, by title. Detroit: Thomson/Gale, 2007.

PubMed. Bethesda, MD: US National Library of Medicine. http://www.ncbi.nlm.nih.gov/pubmed/.

Reader's Guide to Periodical Literature. New York: H. W. Wilson. Published annually. Also available at http://www.hwwilson.com/.

Rodgers, Frank. *A Guide to British Government Publications*. New York: H. W. Wilson, 1980.

Schmeckebier, Laurence F., and Roy B. Eastin. *Government Publications and Their Use.* 2nd ed. Washington, DC: Brookings Institution, 1969.

Science Citation Index. Philadelphia: Institute for Scientific Information. Published bimonthly with annual cumulations. Also available at http://scientific .thomson.com/.

Social Science Index. New York: H. W. Wilson. Published quarterly with annual cumulation. Also available at http://www.hwwilson.com/.

UKOP: Catalogue of United Kingdom Official Publications. London: Chadwyck-Healey. Continually updated. http://www.ukop.co.uk/.

Ulrich's International Periodicals Directory. New York: R. R. Bowker. Published annually. Supplemented quarterly by *Ulrich's Update.* Also available at http://www .ulrichsweb.com/.

Verzeichnis Lieferbarer Bücher [German books in print]. Frankfurt am Main: Verlag der Buchhändler-Vereinigung. Published annually. Also available at http:// www.vlb.de/.

4.6 QUOTATIONS

Bartlett, John. *Bartlett's Familiar Quotations: A Collection of Passages, Phrases, and Proverbs Traced to Their Sources in Ancient and Modern Literature.* 17th ed. Edited by Justin Kaplan. Boston: Little, Brown, 2002.

Crystal, David, and Hilary Crystal. *Words on Words: Quotations about Language and Languages.* Chicago: University of Chicago Press, 2000.

The Oxford Dictionary of Quotations. 7th ed. Edited by Elizabeth Knowles. Oxford: Oxford University Press, 2009.

4.7 ABBREVIATIONS

Acronyms, Initialisms, and Abbreviations Dictionary: A Guide to Acronyms, Abbreviations, Contractions, Alphabetic Symbols, and Similar Condensed Appellations. 39th ed. 4 vols. Edited by Bohdan Romanenchuk. Detroit: Thomson/Gale, 2008.

Davis, Neil M. *Medical Abbreviations: 30,000 Conveniences at the Expense of Communication and Safety.* 14th ed. Warminster, PA: Neil M. Davis Associates, 2009.

Department of Defense Dictionary of Military and Associated Terms: Includes US Acronyms and Abbreviations and NATO Terms (English Only). Washington, DC: Joint Chiefs of Staff, 1998. Amended version available at http://www.dtic.mil /doctrine/dod_dictionary/.

Jablonski, Stanley. *Jablonski's Dictionary of Medical Acronyms and Abbreviations.* 6th ed. Philadelphia: Saunders, 2008.

Stahl, Dean, and Karen Kerchelich. *Abbreviations Dictionary.* 10th ed. Originated by Ralph De Sola. Boca Raton, FL: CRC Press, 2001.

Webster's Guide to Abbreviations. Springfield, MA: Merriam-Webster, 1985.

5 Miscellaneous Works Cited in Text

ALA-LC Romanization Tables: Transliteration Schemes for Non-Roman Scripts. Compiled and edited by Randall K. Barry. Washington, DC: Library of Congress, 1997. Also available at http://www.loc.gov/catdir/cpso/roman.html.

American Naturalist. Journal published monthly by the University of Chicago Press for the American Society of Naturalists. http://www.journals.uchicago.edu/toc/an/current.

Baker-Shenk, Charlotte, and Dennis Cokely. *American Sign Language: A Teacher's Resource Text on Grammar and Culture*. Washington, DC: Gallaudet University Press, 1991.

BIOSIS Serial Sources. Philadelphia: BIOSIS. Published annually through 2005. Current titles available at http://scientific.thomson.com/.

Daniels, Peter T., and William Bright, eds. *The World's Writing Systems*. New York: Oxford University Press, 1996.

Duden: Die deutsche Rechtschreibung. 24th ed. Vol. 1. Mannheim: Dudenverlag, 2006.

French Review. Journal published bimonthly by the American Association of Teachers of French.

Gall, Gerald L., F. Pearl Eliadis, and France Allard. *The Canadian Legal System*. 5th ed. Scarborough, ON: Carswell, 2004.

Grevisse, Maurice. *Le bon usage: Grammaire française*. 14th ed. Edited by André Goosse. Paris: Duculot, 2008.

History of Religions. Journal published quarterly by the University of Chicago Press. http://www.journals.uchicago.edu/toc/hr/current.

Horticulture. Magazine published ten times a year by F+W Publications.

HUGO Gene Nomenclature Database. http://www.genenames.org/.

International Code of Botanical Nomenclature (Vienna Code). Prepared and edited by John McNeill et al. Regnum vegetabile 146. Königstein, Germany: Koeltz, 2006. Also available at http://ibot.sav.sk/icbn/main.htm.

International Code of Zoological Nomenclature. 4th ed. London: International Trust for Zoological Nomenclature, 1999. Also available at http://www.iczn.org/iczn/index.jsp.

International Journal of Middle East Studies. Journal published quarterly by Cambridge University Press for the Middle East Studies Association of North America. Also available at http://www.jstor.org/journals/00207438.html.

MacEllven, Douglass T., Michael J. McGuire, Neil A. Campbell, and John N. Davis. *Legal Research Handbook*. 5th ed. Markham, ON: LexisNexis Butterworths, 2003.

Moliner, María. *Diccionario de uso del español*. 3rd ed. Madrid: Gredos, 2007.

Mouse Genome Database. Mouse Genome Informatics. http://www.informatics.jax.org/.

The New Grove Dictionary of Music and Musicians. 2nd ed. 29 vols. Edited by Stanley Sadie. New York: Grove, 2001. Also available at http://www.oxfordmusic online.com/.

The Oxford Classical Dictionary. 3rd ed. rev. Edited by Simon Hornblower and Anthony Spawforth. Oxford: Oxford University Press, 2003.

Physical Review Letters. Published semimonthly by the American Physical Society. http://prl.aps.org/.

PMLA. Journal published bimonthly by the Modern Language Association of America. http://www.mla.org/pmla.

Pullum, Geoffrey K., and William A. Ladusaw. *Phonetic Symbol Guide.* 2nd ed. Chicago: University of Chicago Press, 1996.

Raymond, Eric S. *The New Hacker's Dictionary.* 3rd ed. Cambridge, MA: MIT Press, 1996.

Real Academia Española. *Ortografía de la lengua española.* Madrid: Espasa, 1999. Also available at http://www.rae.es/.

Romanic Review. Journal published quarterly by the Columbia University Department of Romance Languages.

Thorin, Suzanne E., and Carole Franklin Vidali. *The Acquisition and Cataloging of Music and Sound Recordings: A Glossary.* Canton, MA: Music Library Association, 1984.

Unicode Collation Algorithm. By Mark Davis and Ken Whistler. Unicode Technical Standard no. 10. Unicode Consortium, 2008. http://www.unicode.org/reports /tr10/tr10-18.html.

USP Dictionary of USAN and International Drug Names. Rockville, MD: US Pharmacopeial Convention. Revised annually. Available at http://www.usp.org /products/dictionary/.

Valli, Clayton, Ceil Lucas, and Kristin J. Mulrooney. *Linguistics of American Sign Language: An Introduction.* 4th ed. Washington, DC: Gallaudet University Press, 2005.

Wertheim, Eric. *The Naval Institute Guide to Combat Fleets of the World: Their Ships, Aircraft, and Systems.* 15th ed. Annapolis, MD: Naval Institute Press, 2007.

Zurick, Timothy. *Army Dictionary and Desk Reference.* 3rd ed. Mechanicsburg, PA: Stackpole Books, 2004.

Index

References are to paragraph numbers except where specified as table, figure (fig.), or page number (p.). Page numbers in the online edition link directly to terms in the glossary (appendix B).

colophons (logos)
    on covers or jackets, 1.66–68
    definition, p. 893
    on title page, 1.18
colophons (publication details), defined,
    1.64, p. 893
color
    continuous tone vs. halftone images,
      3.3, 3.6, figs. 3.1–2, p. 894
    in editing paper-only manuscripts, 2.88
    in electronic journals, 1.100
    for ethnic groups, 8.39
    hyphenation guide on, 7.85
    illustrations in, 1.5, 2.34, 3.15
    for journal covers, 1.78
    for proofreading marks, 2.120
    of punctuation, in relation to surround-
      ing text, 6.3
color separation, defined, p. 893
columns
    avoiding multiple, 2.21
    in indexes, 1.63, 16.24, 16.135, 16.138
    in vertical lists, 6.124
    See also magazines; newspapers; tables
command papers (UK), 14.314
commas, 6.16–53
    with abbreviations: academic and pro-
      fessional designations, 10.4, 10.16,
      10.20–21; addresses, mailing, 6.46,
      10.28, 10.30; *e.g.* and *i.e.*, 5.220; *etc.*
      and *et al.*, 6.20; *Inc., Ltd.,* and such,
      6.48; *Jr., Sr.,* and such, 6.47
    with clauses: adverbial, 6.25, 6.55;
      dependent, 6.30–32; independent,
      6.28–29; relative, 6.22; restrictive
      and nonrestrictive, 5.21, 6.22–23,
      6.26
    in documentation: *and other stories* and
      such, 14.100; classical references,
      14.259; magazine dates and page
      numbers, 14.199; *or* with double
      titles, 14.99; page and issue num-
      bers, 14.186; titles of works, 6.17,
      14.99, 14.101; titles of works with
      question marks or exclamation
      points, 14.178
    em dashes instead of, 6.82, 6.86
    marking manuscript for, 2.90
    marking proofs for, 2.129
    other punctuation with: apostrophes,

commas (*continued*)
    6.115; brackets, 6.53; ellipsis points,
    13.52; exclamation points, 6.119;
    parentheses, 6.53, 6.96; ques-
    tion marks, 6.52, 6.119; quotation
    marks, 6.9, 6.50
    other uses: addresses, 6.46, 10.28,
    10.30; adverbial phrases, 6.36; *and
    if, that if,* and such, 6.32; appositives,
    5.21, 6.23; compound predicates,
    6.29; conjunctions joining indepen-
    dent clauses, 6.28; coordinate adjec-
    tives, 5.90, 6.33–34; dates, 5.82,
    6.17, 6.45; decimal places in non-US
    styles, 9.20; direct address, 6.38;
    editorial interpolations, 6.53; eli-
    sion indicated by, 6.49; homonyms,
    6.44; *however, therefore, indeed,* and
    such, 6.25; *including,* 6.27; indexes,
    16.25, 16.94; interjections, 5.208,
    6.37; introductory phrases, 6.35–36;
    main clause and, 6.31; maxims and
    proverbs, 6.51; *the more, the less,* and
    such, 6.42; "not" phrases, 6.40–41;
    numbers, 9.55, 9.62; pairs of com-
    mas, 6.17; parenthetical elements,
    6.24–27, 6.31, 6.43; participial
    phrases, 6.35; place-names, 6.46;
    preceding main clause, 6.30; ques-
    tions, 6.52; quotations, 6.50, 13.18;
    run-in list items separated by, 6.123;
    such as, 6.27; *that is, namely, for
    example,* and such, 6.43, 6.65; *which*
    vs. *that* and, 6.22
    pairs of, 6.17
    parentheses compared with, 6.92
    vs. semicolons, 6.19
    serial: argument for using, 6.18; *etc.*
    and *et al.* with, 6.20; omitted with
    ampersands, 6.21; semicolons
    instead of commas, 6.19
    when to omit, 6.119, 14.105
    See also punctuation
commercial terms and abbreviations, 10.72
common expressions. *See* figures of
    speech; maxims
common-law copyright, 4.2, 4.15, 4.19,
    4.22, 4.25
communications. *See* interviews and dis-
    cussions; personal communications

copyright (*continued*)
    of, 4.13–18; varieties of, 4.7–12;
        works made for hire, 4.9–12, 4.23
  benefits of registering, 4.49
  changes in, 1.24
  deposit requirements, 4.46
  digital rights management and, A.40
  dual system of, 4.19
  duration: jointly authored works, 4.22;
    lengthened in 1978, 4.20; for works
    created after 1977, 4.22–24; for
    works created before 1978, 4.19,
    4.25–29
  extensive paraphrasing under, 4.82
  of foreign works, 4.28–29, 4.33
  law relevant to, 4.2, 4.10, 4.19, 4.25
  material covered by, 4.3, 4.5
  for new editions, 4.27
  of online materials, 4.2, 14.9
  ownership of, 1.22, 4.6, 4.7–18, 4.30–31,
    4.41
  preregistration, 4.49
  of previously published materials, 2.43
  of public-domain works, 4.21
  publisher's responsibilities for, 4.31
  "reasonable effort" to correct mistakes,
    4.45
  registration of, 4.4, 4.47
  renewal of, 1.24, 4.19, 4.26, 4.30–32,
    4.40, 14.150
  subsidiary rights: author's electronic
    use of own works, 4.62; author's
    retention of, 4.18; basic rights vs.,
    4.17; categories of, 4.60; economic
    considerations, 4.61–62, 4.65;
    electronic-rights licensing, 4.61;
    Public Access Policy and, 4.64;
    university licenses, 4.63 (*see also*
    subsidiary rights)
  symbol for, 1.22, 4.40, 10.44
  termination of transfers under, 4.37
  works ineligible for, 4.11
  See also copyright notice; copyright
    page, contents of; credits and credit
    lines; fair-use doctrine; intellec-
    tual property rights; licenses for
    copyrighted works; permissions;
    publishing agreement
Copyright Act (and amendments), 1.19, 4.2,
    4.20, 4.88–90

Copyright Clearance Center (CCC), 1.74,
    1.97, 4.91
copyright lines, journals
  components of, 1.97
  for individual articles, 1.74, 1.97
  ISSN in, 1.97
  placement of, 1.78, 1.88
copyright management information, 4.15
copyright notice
  components, 1.22, 4.40–45, fig. 1.2
  different regimes of, 4.2, 4.39
  mistakes in, 4.45
  necessity for, 4.26
  in notes, unnumbered, 3.31, 14.49
  old rules, removed, 4.38
  placement of, 1.19, 4.42, figs. 1.1–4
  types of material: derivative works,
    4.44; electronic publications, 1.97;
    government-produced works, 4.43;
    journals, 1.74, 1.78, 1.88, 1.97, 4.42;
    photocopied material, 4.89–90
copyright page, contents of
  acknowledgments, 1.19, 1.30–31
  author's previous publications, 1.17
  biographical notes, 1.20
  changes and renewals, 1.24
  CIP data, 1.19, 1.33, fig. 1.1, figs. 1.3–4
  copyright dates of previous editions,
    1.23
  copyright notice, 1.22, 4.40
  country of printing, 1.19, 1.27
  credits, 1.30, 1.70, 3.29, 4.71
  editions, 1.23, 1.25–26, 14.118
  examples, figs. 1.1–4
  grant information, 1.31, 1.40
  impression, 1.23–25, 1.28
  ISBN, 1.32
  pagination omitted from, 1.6
  paper durability statement, 1.19, 1.34
  permissions, 1.30, 4.71
  proofreading of, 2.130
  publication date, 1.21–22, 1.25, 14.149
  publisher's address, 1.19, 1.21
  publishing history, 1.25
  running heads omitted from, 1.10
  translation information, 1.29, fig. 1.3
  See also copyright notice
corporations. *See* business and commerce;
    organizations
Council of Science Editors (CSE), 14.3

dates (*continued*)

> incomplete, 6.79
> months, 8.87, 9.32, 10.40, 14.180
> numbers for: decades, 9.34; eras, 9.35, 9.63; ISO all-numeral style, 9.37; month and day, 9.32; month-day-year and other forms, 6.45, 6.106, 9.36–37; year abbreviated, 9.31; year alone, 9.30
> periods: centuries, 8.70, 9.33–34; cultural, 8.73; decades, 9.34; descriptive designations, 8.71; eras, 9.35, 9.63, 10.39; geological, 8.134; numerical designations for, 8.70; traditional names for, 8.72
> in preface, 1.40
> punctuation: commas, 5.82, 6.17, 6.45, 14.199; en dashes, 6.78–79; hyphens, 9.37; slashes, 6.105–6
> in titles of works, 14.101
> uncertain, 6.66
> unspecified date of death, 6.79
> work period known (fl.), 10.43
> years: abbreviated (e.g., '76), 9.31; inclusive range of, 9.58, 9.63; incomplete range of, 6.79; placement in reference lists, 15.12; plurals of, 7.14; sentence beginning with, 9.5; slash with two-year spans, 6.105; uncertain, 6.66; unspecified date of death, 6.79; words vs. numerals for, 9.30; work period known (fl.), 10.43
> *See also* publication date; time

days of the week, 8.87, 10.41. *See also* dates

dead (foul) copy or proofs, 2.102, 2.107

deadlines

> indexing, 16.4, 16.101
> proofreading, 2.99
> publication schedule, 2.2, A.2, figs. 2.1–2

Deaf, deaf, 8.42

debates, documentation of

> governmental bodies, 8.61, 8.64
> UK parliamentary, 14.313
> US congressional, 14.298–99

decades, 9.34

decimal points

> in celestial coordinates, 10.64
> *dex (decimal exponent),* 9.12
> in double and multiple numeration, 1.55

decimal points (*continued*)

> with millions, billions, and so forth, 9.8, 9.25
> in monetary amounts, 9.21, 9.23–26
> number of places in, non-US style, 9.20
> in tables, alignment of, 3.70, 3.84, fig. 3.13, figs. 3.15–16, fig. 3.20
> in twenty-four-hour system, 9.40–41
> use of zero and, 9.19
> *See also* fractions

dedications

> format and placement of, 1.6, 1.35
> omitted in indexing, 16.109
> running heads omitted from page, 1.10

definite article. *See* articles (definite and indefinite)

definitions

> highlighted in index, 16.143
> mathematical, 12.56
> numbering of, 12.25
> punctuation of, 7.50
> *See also* dictionaries; glossaries

degrees (academic). *See* academic concerns: degrees and affiliations

degrees (measurement), abbreviations for, 10.52–53, 10.55. *See also* International System of Units (Système international d'unités, SI); measurement, US; metric system

deities, 8.90–91, 8.94. *See also* religions and religious concerns; religious works

deletions

> marking manuscript for, 2.91–92, 2.121, fig. 2.6
> stetting or reversal of, 2.127

departments

> administrative type, 8.62
> capitalization, 14.202
> in magazines, 8.175, 14.202
> *See also* academic concerns: institutions and departments

derivative works

> copyright issues and, 4.30, 4.44
> electronic works created with addition of hyperlinks, video data, and such, 4.60
> license to make, 4.33
> material copyrightable in, 4.5
> public-domain work in, 4.21
> publishing options for, A.39–40
> relicensing of, 4.30